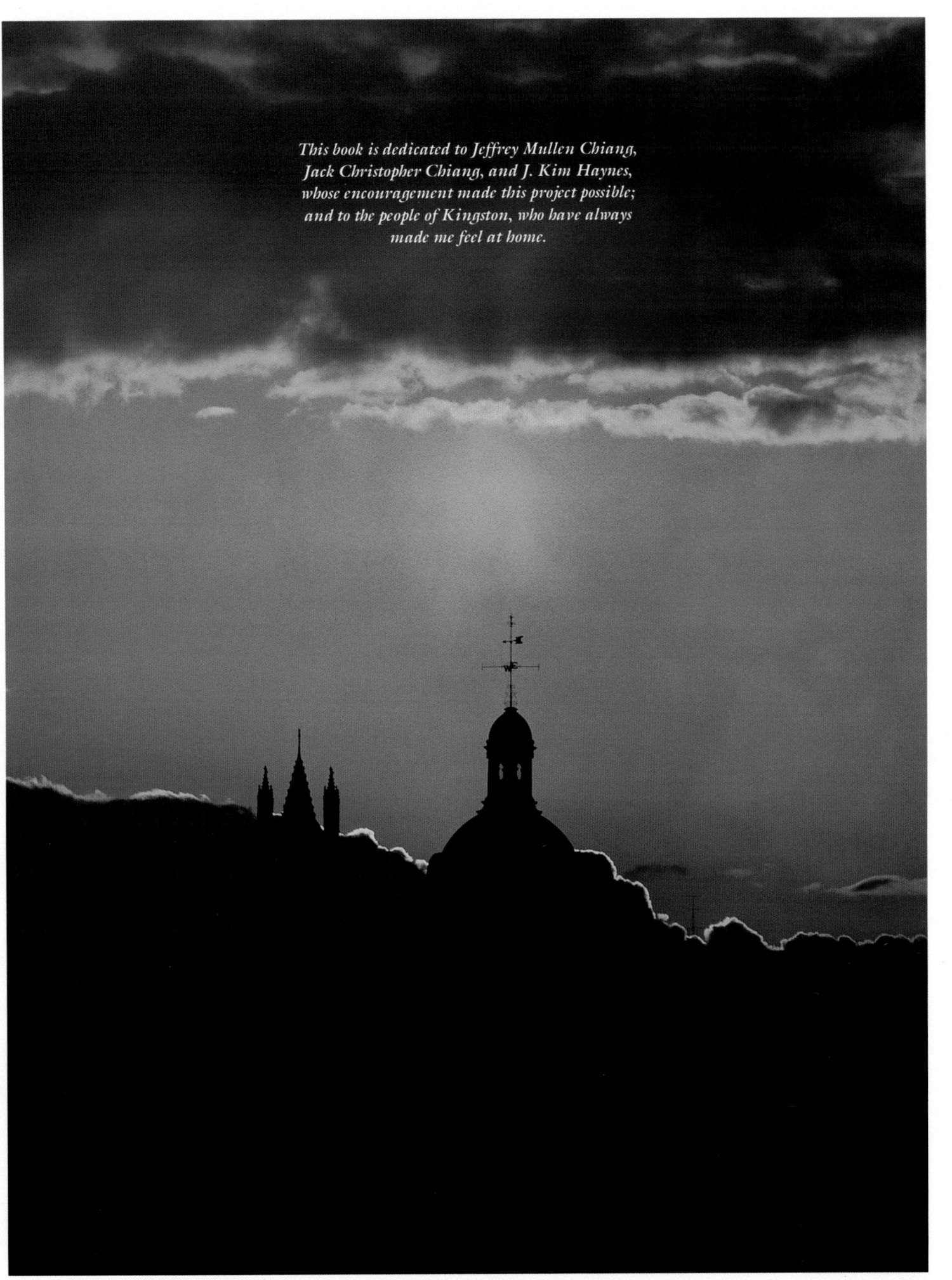

*This book is dedicated to Jeffrey Mullen Chiang,
Jack Christopher Chiang, and J. Kim Haynes,
whose encouragement made this project possible;
and to the people of Kingston, who have always
made me feel at home.*

KINGSTON PANORAMA
Situated at the confluence of
three bodies of water —
Lake Ontario (top), the
St. Lawrence River (left), and
the Cataraqui River (bottom)
— Kingston is a city defined
geographically, historically,
and culturally by nine miles of
waterfront.

*"Until I came to Kingston, I
always went away — often far
away — to be by the water. A
stretch of waterfront is what
people pay thousands of dollars
to vacation beside, yet for us, it
is always available. Walks
beside the water, a chance to
read with waves splashing
nearby, a glorious spot to jog —
it's a special place that draws
me time and time again"*
Harvey Schachter, Deputy
Editor, *The Whig-Standard*.

RIM-LIT SPIRES
Golden sunlight (previous
page) accents the spires of two
historic landmarks, St. Mary's
Cathedral (left) and Kingston
City Hall (center).

IMAGES OF
KINGSTON

Jack Chiang

PREFACE BY *Michael Davies*
INTRODUCTION BY *Neil Reynolds*
EDITED BY *Bob Hilderley*

Quarry Press

Canadian Cataloguing in Publication Data

Chiang, Jack
Images of Kingston
ISBN 0-919627-93-5

1. Kingston Region (Ont.) – History.
2. Kingston Region (Ont.) – History–Pictorial Works.
3. Kingston Region (Ont.) – Description and travel–Views.
I. Title.

FC3099.K5C44 1990
971.3'72   C90-090346-5
F1059.5.K46C44 1990

Design by Keith Abraham

Published by Quarry Press, Inc., P.O. Box 1061, Kingston, Ontario K7L 4Y5 and P.O. Box 348, Clayton, New York 13624.
Printed in Hong Kong by Everbest.

POINT FREDERICK FIREWORKS
Fireworks cascade over Point Frederick on the grounds of the Royal Military College of Canada as seen from Fort Henry across Navy Bay. From the founding of Fort Frontenac in 1673 through the building of Fort Henry in the 1830s and the establishment of the Royal Military College in 1874 to the creation of a Canadian Forces Base and National Defence College in this century, Kingston has been known as a "garrison" town. Point Frederick, the site of a former British naval station and dockyard, overlooks Kingston's outer harbor and guards the entrance to the inner harbor which leads via the Cataraqui River to the Rideau Canal.

Preface

There is always a geographical reason for the establishment of a city and Kingston is no exception. Located at the end of the Great Lakes and the confluence of the St. Lawrence and Cataraqui Rivers, Kingston was the western gate to North America in the late sixteenth century. As one of the oldest cities in Canada, Kingston boasts an extensive heritage.

As a fort founded in 1673, Kingston grew in influence until it reached national prominence as the first capital of the Province of Canada in 1841. Alas, its national role was shortlived due to its close proximity to the United States, a hostile neighbor at that time. The loss of capital status turned out to be a blessing in disguise. Kingston escaped forced growth and was left to gently increase over the decades. Two national universities, a community college, a medical school, and three teaching hospitals all give Kingston big city influence, but a regular farmers' market and easy access to cottage country give it small city accessibility and charm. Dominated by the harbor and graced by fine institutional buildings, Kingston has become a very pleasant place to reside.

Many books have been written on Kingston, its heritage and its famous citizens, but this is the first photographic essay of the King's Town. Jack Chiang has attempted to portray the flavor of Kingston. In my opinion he has succeeded admirably.

Michael Davies

Introduction

If journalism is literature on the run, as the English poet Matthew Arnold described it, news photography must be art at the speed of light. I do not mean this in a mere technical or mechanical sense, as a reference — for example — to shutter speed. I mean it as a measure of a photographer's mental and physical reflexes. After all, the difference between an ordinary picture and a photograph that ranks as a work of art is frequently a split-second. A great photographer anticipates particular split-seconds, works tenaciously to get close to them, waits patiently for them to occur, and captures them unaware.

In body, mind, and spirit, Jack Chiang personifies this speed-of-light standard. Physically, he bounds. Mentally, he dashes. Spiritually, he soars. He doesn't walk somewhere: he simply appears. He doesn't cogitate: he imagines and intuits. He doesn't recognize physical and mental limitations: he does impossible assignments all the time. He is part sprite, a terrestrial being who radiates solar energy (and warmth) wherever he goes. Or, rather, appears.

I have worked with Jack Chiang for 12 years. My professional admiration for him is matched only by my personal respect and affection for him. He is a great photographer; he is an amazing man. He exists in a state of perpetual motion, but never in a state of aimless motion. He is a man in a hurry because he has much to do. His austere self-discipline is legendary. The pictures he *makes* — for he never merely "takes" pictures — expose the man behind the maelstrom as a dedicated perfectionist.

These comments, however, don't begin to suggest the limits of Jack's concentration, dedication, courage, and enterprise. His pictures reveal as much about Jack as the taking of them does. For Jack's pictures, even his action pictures, reflect paradoxically a sense of peace and order, a special kind of quiet, an almost ethereal calm. His shutter stops the kinetic world at the very moments when everyday occurrences are preserved as aesthetic experiences. Jack's particular genius is his gift of extracting the extraordinary from the ordinary. All news photographers seek to freeze a moment of action to illustrate the action. Jack's photographs transcend the "freezing" of action; they extract art from action; and the art form is distinctly Oriental. Jack's photographs are, simply put, artistic meditations.

Jack Chiang was born in Canton in the first year of Mao Tse-tung's revolutionary China. Born into turbulence, he grew up in turbulence. His father, although uneducated, had been a prominent leader in his village near Canton in pre-Maoist times. He had been a landlord, too, and prosperous, at least in relative terms. The revolution was not gentle with landlords: Jack's family fled to Hong Kong, carrying with it three sacks of worthless currency. Jack's earliest memories are of a time in Hong Kong when everyone was a refugee, and everyone was poor. He remembers long lines of children, waiting to get free pencils donated by the United States of America, the distant land of dreams for hundreds of thousands of dispossessed people around the world.

Jack's father died when he was eight. His family — his mother, his two brothers, and his three sisters — was compelled to split up. For a few years, Jack lived with a family in Portuguese Macau; he returned to Hong Kong for his high school education. At this age, he spoke Cantonese, Taiwanese, and Mandarin, but not English. After high school, he went to Taiwan and enrolled in the National Taiwan University in Taipei to study languages and literature. He learned French and Japanese there but still spoke no English.

For many Chinese young people in the 1960s and 1970s, a scholarship to an American university meant a ticket to their wildest dream. In 1972, at 22, Jack won a scholarship to study at Marquette University in Milwaukee. He spoke little English. At Marquette, Jack simultaneously learned English, became a full-time student (in journalism!), and worked 20 hours a week as a research assistant to earn money. Beyond all of the mandatory work, he read and he read and he read. He was awake and working 20 hours a day. In his first two years in America, he took time out to see only one movie. (It was at Marquette that Jack took the only formal instruction in photography he has ever had. He took one course, and failed it.)

One of his brothers, meanwhile, had made it to Toronto, and, in 1974, Jack began to look for work in Ontario. As it turned out, it was a man of Polish descent, an immigrant who had never finished high school, who gave him his first chance. George Czerny, the managing editor of the Orillia *Packet and Times*, hired Jack as a reporter. (Mr. Czerny is now editor and publisher of the Collingwood *Enterprise-Bulletin*.) On small newspapers, however, reporters often work as photographers as well, and Jack began to teach himself what he needed to know. In 1978, Jack joined *The Whig-Standard* as a photographer. Only two years later, he became the picture editor of the newspaper.

In Kingston, Jack has taken thousands of pictures — of fires and accidents, of school children and politicians, of animals and of buildings, and of the people of Kingston. All of these are the pictures by which a newspaper transmits images of its everyday life to the community it serves. He has also taken all of the photographs published in this book, photographs that dramatically illustrate his extraordinary skill and enterprise.

Jack's purpose in making this book was to illuminate Kingston in a special way, of course, not to illuminate himself. He has nevertheless done both — to the credit of both. This book celebrates a magnificent city and confirms Kingston's good fortune in possessing Jack Chiang as a citizen. But good fortune is often the result of hard work. Jack's personal belief is that the harder he works, the luckier he gets. And the luckier we all get.

Neil Reynolds

MARKET SQUARE
First established in 1801, the Market Square behind City Hall is one of the oldest open-air farmers' markets in Ontario.

HISTORIC HOCKEY
The first hockey game in Canada was played between teams from Queen's University and Royal Military College in 1886 on the ice in front of City Hall. Since 1969 this match has been re-enacted annually as part of winter festivities.

TOWN CRIER
Kingston Town Crier Chris Whyman adds color to most civic events, bellowing proclamations. He is the North American champion of town criers.

**FRONTENAC COUNTY
COURT HOUSE**
Overlooking the serene
common of City Park, the
Frontenac County Court
House was built in 1858 on
property that had been
purchased for the site of the
parliament of the Province
of Canada. Kingston was the
capital of Canada from 1841
to 1844.

FORT HENRY

Fort Henry, originally constructed in the 1830s, was restored in the 1930s and officially designated as an historic site in 1938. The Fort attracts close to 200,000 visitors each year to tour the battlements, view the military memorabilia, and thrill to the firing of the cannons and rifles (previous page) by the Fort Henry Guard as these precision-trained summer students stage the traditional officers' parade and a ceremonial retreat.

"Of all the pictures I shot for this book the photo of the cannons and rifles firing simultaneously required the greatest effort. To capture this image I traveled to the Fort twenty times and shot untold rolls of film. For the image, the sky had to be dark; there had to be many spectators in the background; all the guardsmen had to fire off their rifles and cannons at the same time; and the camera, a Hasselblad, had to be triggered 1/20th of a second before the actual firing of the guns" Jack Chiang.

WATERFRONT AGLOW
"This photo (previous page) required 20 seconds of my time and cost 95¢ for film. A dramatic image of the waterfront presented itself to me as I stood at Royal Military College preparing to photograph a fireworks display in front of City Hall. Nature's light again proved to be more spectacular than human fireworks" Jack Chiang.

MARTELLO TOWER SWIMMERS
Hundreds of participants in the annual "K-Town" Triathlon swim past the Martello Tower set in Kingston harbor to protect City Hall. The waterfront boasts several other Martello towers (named after the eighteenth-century French architect of this style of fortification), including Murney Tower which is located in Macdonald Park and houses a museum open to the public.

NAVY BAY FLEET
During the war of 1812–14, Navy Bay (opposite) harbored the largest fleet of British vessels on Lake Ontario. Today the naval corvettes, schooners, and gunboats have been replaced by lasers, catamarans, and other pleasure craft.

INNER HARBOR SCULLERS
Kingston Rowing Club members work out on the waters of the Cataraqui River. The Club was founded in 1977 to encourage competitive and recreational rowing. These eight-oared crews cut figures in the twilight of dawn and dusk.

WATERSPORTS CAPITAL
Some people consider Kingston to be the fresh-water sailing capital of the world. The city hosted the 1976 Olympics sailing events and hosts an annual C.O.R.K. regatta. Other watersports — rowing, canoeing, steamboating, waterskiing, fishing, windsurfing — are also popular.

MOON-LIT CITY
"*This double-exposure photo shows the moon rising over the city. I'm always looking for ways to see Kingston in a special light*" Jack Chiang.

JUST BALANCE
The architectural balance of the County Court House (right) is a fit background for this traditional image of justice.

GOTHIC GRANDEUR
Kingston's "old stones" —
her grand private residences
and public institutions built
from local limestone in a
variety of architectural styles —
are the pride of the city.
Indeed, Kingston is often
called the "Limestone City."
This limestone castle (top) is
set on the corner of West
Street and Sydenham Street,
across from the Court House.

VICTORIAN ASYMMETRY
On the corner of West Street
and King Street across from
City Park stands this monu-
ment to Victorian sensibility.

"In Kingston, I like the feeling for history. I can't think of living in any other place. I'm interested in Kingston as a living museum. I found it exciting to live in a place where history is right in front of your eyes, if you care to look"
Margaret Angus.

GEORGIAN GRACE
"Summerhill" (top) was built for Archdeacon George Okill Stuart in the 1830s. This enormous residence was called "Okill's Folly" or "The Archdeacon's Castle." The building was purchased by Queen's University in 1853 and now serves as the Principal's residence.

HISTORIC HOTEL
The Prince George Hotel has been designated for restoration and preservation under the Ontario Heritage Act. The "PG" is one of the few nineteenth-century hotels still operating in the province.

SPIRES OF KINGSTON
The spire of St. Mary's
Cathedral and the crosses of
the Hotel Dieu Hospital
(far left) cut silhouettes against
the afternoon sun. The dome
of St. George's Cathedral
(near left) glows in the moon-
light. The steeple of St. Mary's
Cathedral (top) stretches into
the sky.

*"While I was waiting
for this afternoon cloud
formation to take shape above
the Cathedral, I realized I was
attracting a crowd, with
passing pedestrians and motor-
ists stopping to look skyward
with me"* Jack Chiang.

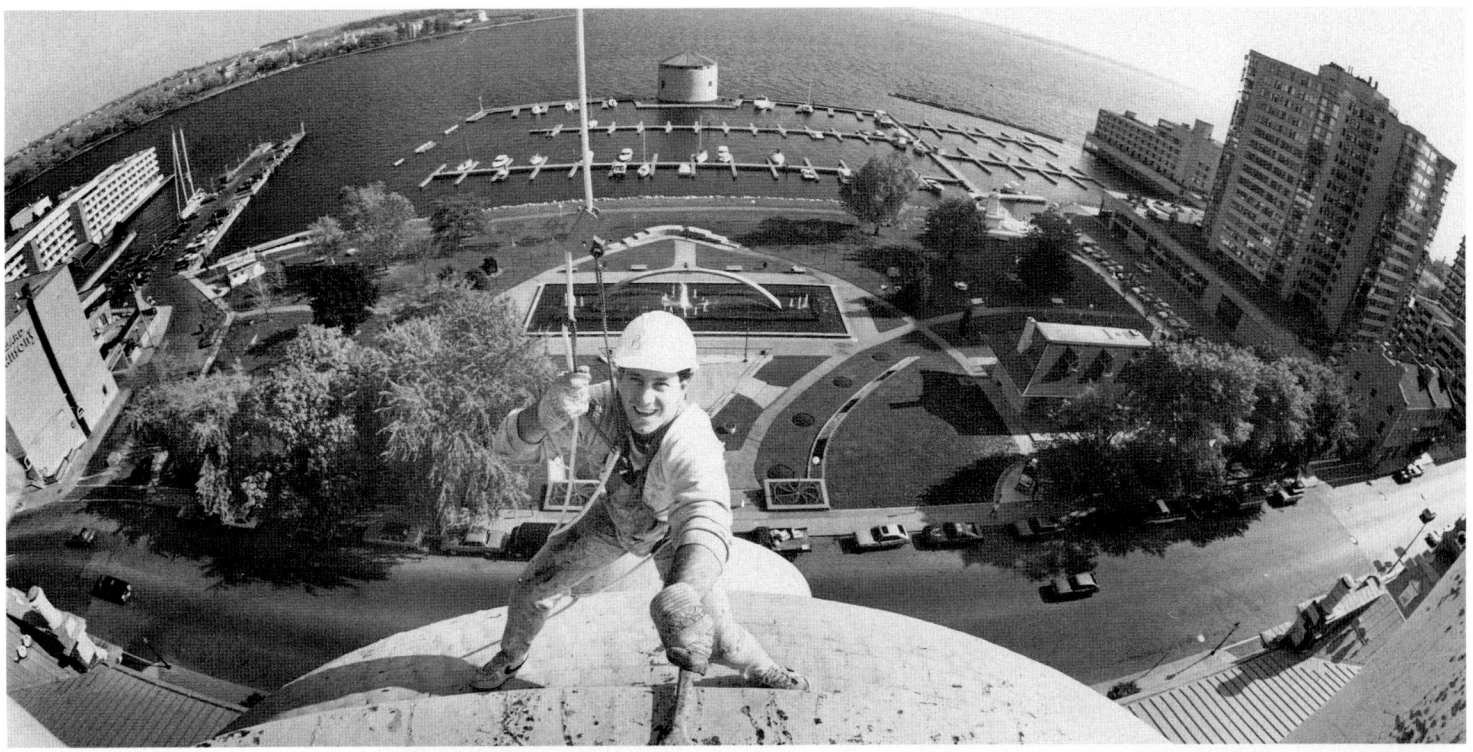

AERIAL VIEWS
Steeplejacks work on restoring St. Mary's Cathedral (opposite) and City Hall (top right), while students of Ecole Cathedrale point themselves out to a passing aerial photographer. The students were directed by teacher Sharon Mulligan.

FOLKLORE DANCERS
Dancers perform a Portuguese promenade (top) while others execute a Lithuanian light step (bottom) during the annual Kingston Folklore Festival, a multicultural extravaganza featuring good food and even better entertainment from more than 20 ethnic groups.

Leaping into the air (far right) during a Ukrainian dance is Jeffrey Garvin who has been entertaining at Folklore since the age of four.

CELLO SOLO
Matthew McFarlane appears as
a silhouette while rehearsing
for the annual Kiwanis Music
Festival.
TUNED OUT
Adrienne Babcock listens to
the music at the YMCA day
care center.

ORCHESTRA OF ONE
Jeffrey Coull has the stage to himself as he prepares for an orchestral performance at the Kiwanis Music Festival.
SOUR NOTE
Gregory Riddoch grimaces while he practices with Emma Banfield.

TAEKWONDO FORCE
Members of Fraser's Taekwondo, led by fourth-degree black belt instructor Don Fraser, strike this formation at Lake Ontario Park.
VELO DRIVE
Cyclists compete in an annual race around City Park sponsored by Kingston's Velo Club.

SKATING ESCAPADE
The "Kommotion" precision
skating team, winners of a
silver medal at an international
competition in Helsinki in
1990, poses in front of a
Martello tower.
   "*This picture was taken
during a frigid day in
December: I set up the camera,
marked a spot for each skater,
then they ran from the warmth
of waiting cars, posed for the
photo, and ran back*" Jack
Chiang.

LADY OF THE LAKE
Marathon swimmer Vicki Keith was the first person to complete a double-crossing of Lake Ontario and the first to swim across all five Great lakes during one summer.

"*To take this action photo of Vicki (left) I placed the camera in a glass aquarium and leaned out the back of the boat with a friend holding my heels. For a non-swimmer like me, this was no mean feat* " Jack Chiang.

PRISON REFLECTIONS
A colorful evening sky projects an image of Collins Bay and Frontenac Institutions across the waters of Little Cataraqui Creek. One of the eight major prisons in the Kingston region, Collins Bay is often mistaken by travelers as a Disneyland tourist attraction.

SOLITARY IMAGES
A lone archer (left) is dwarfed
by the expansive sky at Seeleys
Bay, north of Kingston.
A solitary jogger (top) runs
across the La Salle Causeway.
A blithe student skips through
the snow in City Park.

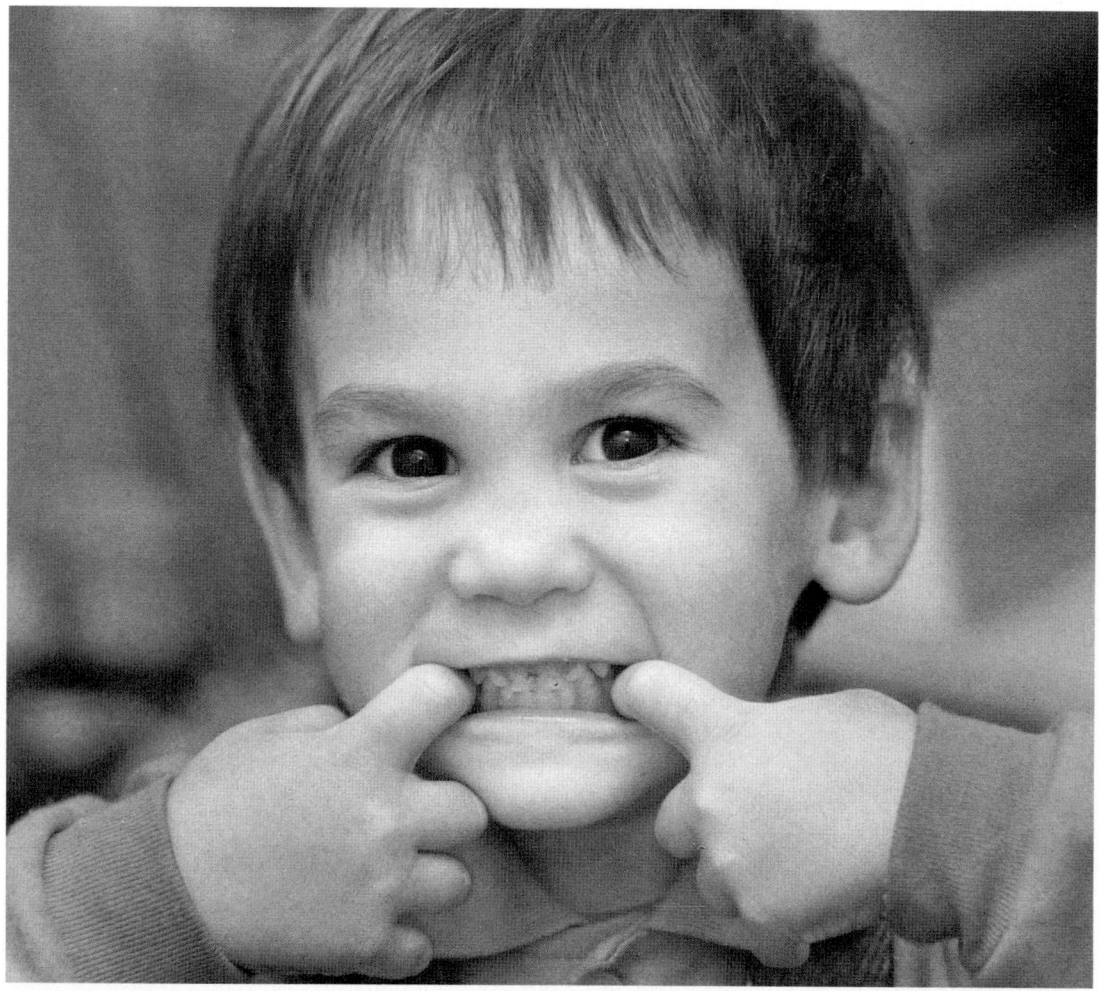

KINGSTON MILLS REFLECTIONS

Scenic Kingston Mills (previous page) is the site of the first lock station on the Rideau Canal for vessels traveling from Lake Ontario to the Ottawa River. Under the supervision of Colonel John By the canal was built between 1826 and 1832 at a cost of nearly £100,000 and over 500 lives.

SAY CHEESE!

"*The favorite subject of most photographers is a child's face, largely because most children are not self-conscious in front of a camera. I often caution my photographers at* The Whig-Standard *not to fill the paper with images of children*" Jack Chiang.

The tooth monster (top left) is not camera shy. Quinton Steacy of Holy Family School (bottom left) and Jamie Hazel of J.G. Simcoe Public School (near right) obviously enjoy the snowfall. Katrina McCann of Gananoque (far right) patiently waits her turn to skate at the local recreation center.

"What I like best about Kingston is the downtown area. You get old historic buildings that store owners have restored on the outside, yet at the same time have given a modern look on the inside"
Krista Lappan, St. Peter School.

THE ROYAL MILITARY COLLEGE OF CANADA

The Royal Military College (RMC) has gained a well-deserved international reputation for educating superior officers. RMC graduates have served Canada, the Commonwealth, NATO, and the United Nations with distinction in war and in peace.

Liberal Prime Minister Alexander Mackenzie spear-headed the founding of The College in the 1870s, after whom the stately Mackenzie Building (center with bell tower) was named.

GRADUATION DAY

Graduating cadets parade across the square for the last time (top), while a squirrel posing as a drill sergeant (below) inspects the troops.

RITES OF PASSAGE

The legendary RMC obstacle course tests the individual fortitude and forges the team spirit of first-year cadets. The first group of 18 cadets to enroll in 1876 are now proudly referred to as the "Old Eighteen." Today over 700 cadets are enrolled annually; most cadets study engineering. Tuition is free, so are books and uniforms, and each cadet receives a monthly allowance. After graduation cadets are contracted to serve as officers in the Canadian Forces for five years.

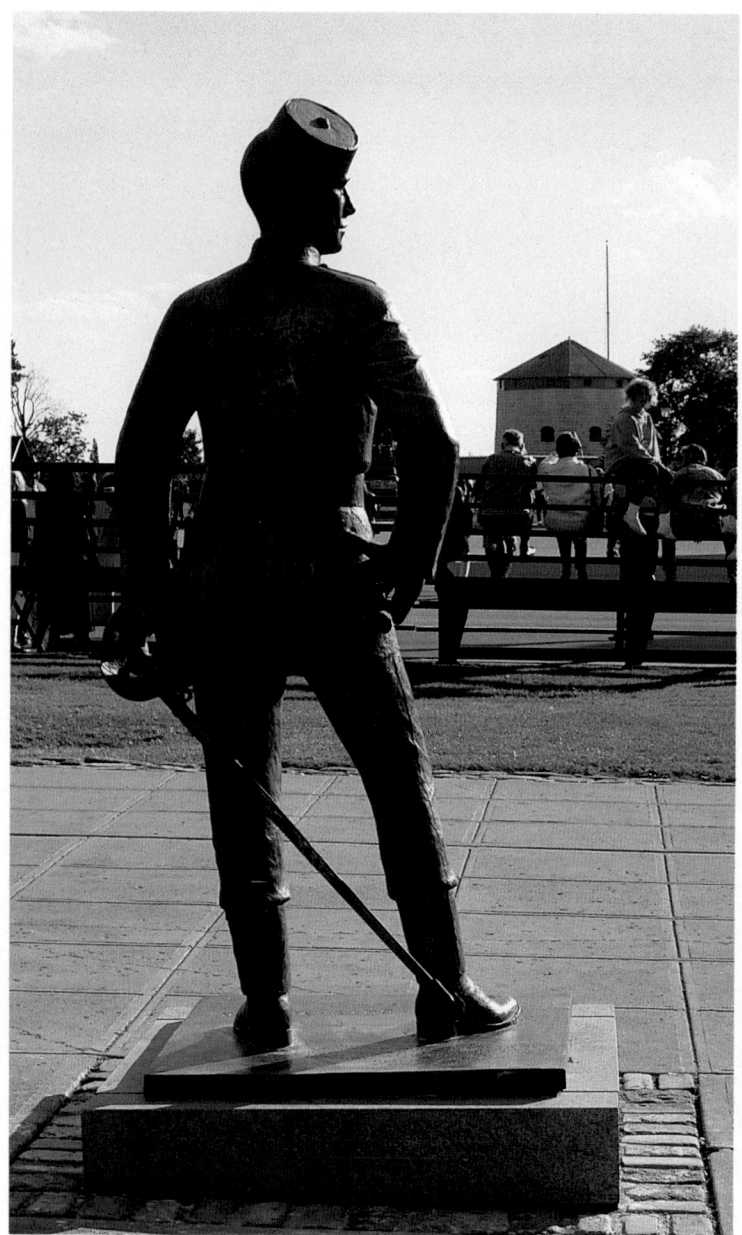

PATRIOTIC FORMATION
"To commemorate Canada Day, I asked RMC Commandant E.R. Murray (front and center) for his cooperation in creating this image. He assigned Drill Sgt.-Major Gino Moretti (bottom right) the task of drilling 285 cadets and senior staff into a maple leaf formation. I took the picture from the clock tower of the Mackenzie Building" Jack Chiang.

A bronze statue of a cadet (above) overlooks the parade square.

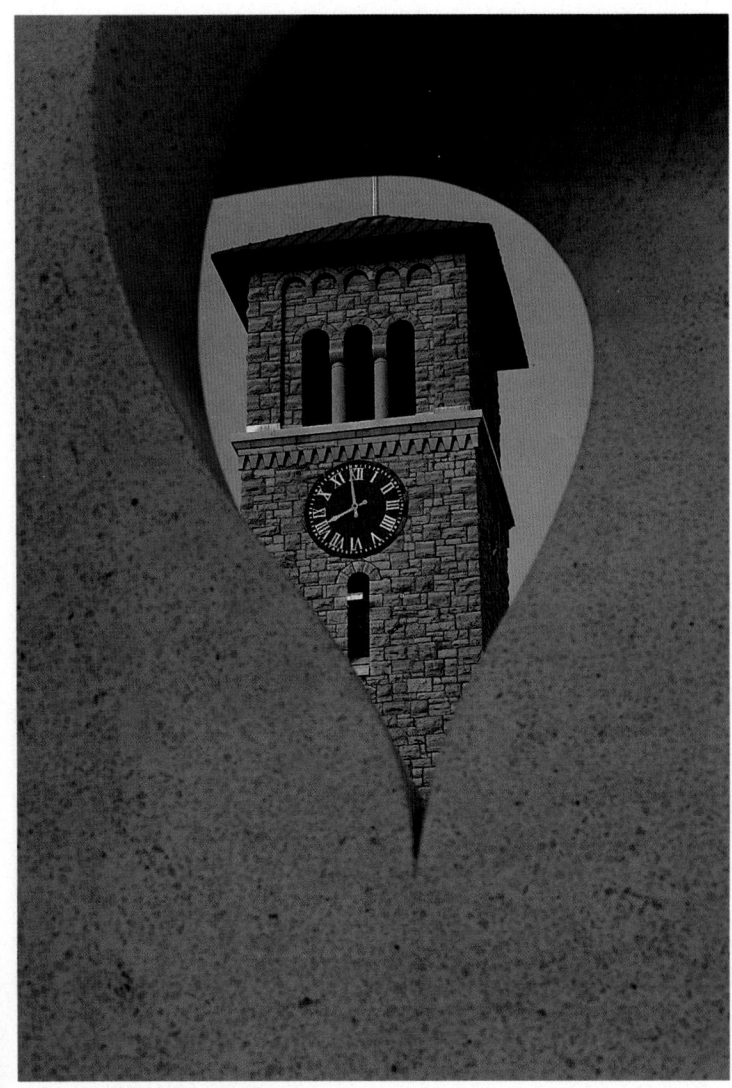

QUEEN'S UNIVERSITY
Pictured here (left and detail above) is the landmark tower of Grant Hall at the heart of Queen's University. The hall is named after George Munro Grant, principal of the university from 1877 to 1902, during which time he established Queen's as a renowned national educational institution. The royal charter founding Queen's University was issued in 1841 by Queen Victoria.

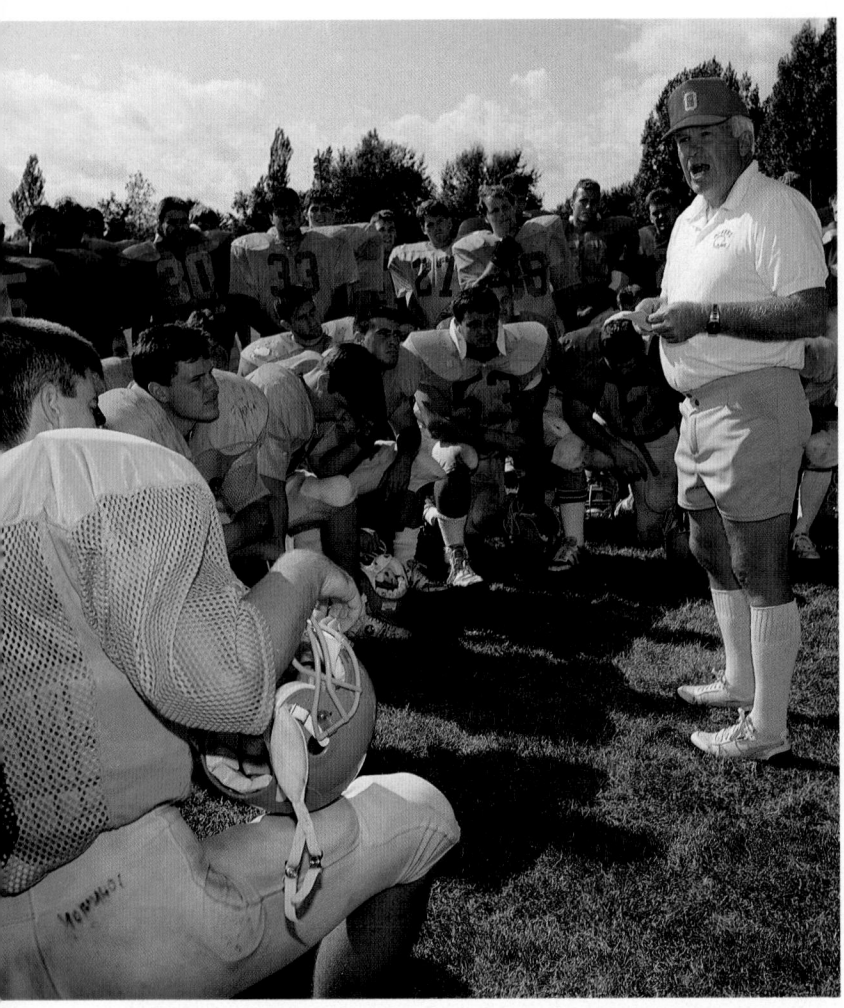

GOLDEN GAELS
Queen's football coach Doug Hargreaves (above) instructs members of the Golden Gaels during a practice at Richardson Stadium. Over 10,000 fans (right) cheer for the Gaels during a homecoming game.

Painted faces in the crowd are first-year students undergoing initiation. Nearly 16,000 students are enrolled annually in full- and part-time studies on the 160-acre campus. Founded as a denominational college of the Presbyterian Church, Queen's still offers programs in theology, though the university is now non-denominational, with many international students attending.

"*My eye seizes upon human formations and patterns of color, whether they emerge spontaneously as in the photograph of the red-gold-blue tricolors of Queen's fans above or whether they appear orchestrated as in the RMC maple leaf previously. Groups of people acting in concert fascinate me*" Jack Chiang.

COMMENCEMENT DAY
Queen's graduates with their families and friends gather outside Jock Harty Arena on Union Street. There are over 80,000 living graduates of Queen's and over 11,000 deceased. Alumni are resident in over 128 countries, with nearly 50 alumni branches in Canada and seven abroad. Queen's University alumni are famous for their ongoing contributions to campus life.

SUN SPOTS
The sun sets across the yard-arm of *The Pathfinder* (right), a tall ship from Toronto temporarily docked at La Salle Causeway, while the setting sun makes the city sparkle (opposite).

"*The old adage that no two sunsets are the same is true, believe me. I have gone to the same spot at Point Frederick day after day in search of sunsets with identical light but I have come away with a different picture every time*" Jack Chiang.

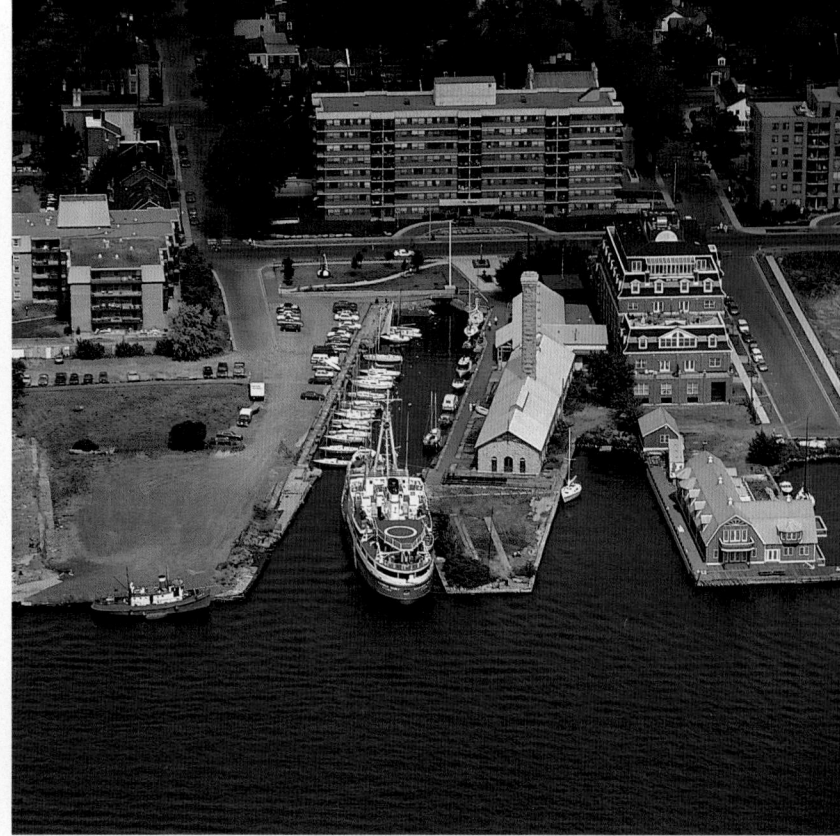

DOCKED DREAMS
Early morning fog engulfs
dry-docked boats at the
Kingston Yacht Club (left).
The Alexander Henry (above),
a 3,000-ton ice-breaker built
in 1958, is docked at the
Marine Museum of the Great
Lakes, where the ship now
serves as an exhibit and a novel
bed and breakfast.

DESERT ISLAND
Snake Island (opposite) offers
a picturesque image as seen
from the Kingston waterfront.
SHORE SPRAY
Waves pound the rocks near
Richardson Beach (above) on
the waterfront across from
Kingston General Hospital.

FOG BOUND
The Wolfe Islander III
appears lost in the early
morning mist as she ferries
passengers between Wolfe
Island and Kingston.

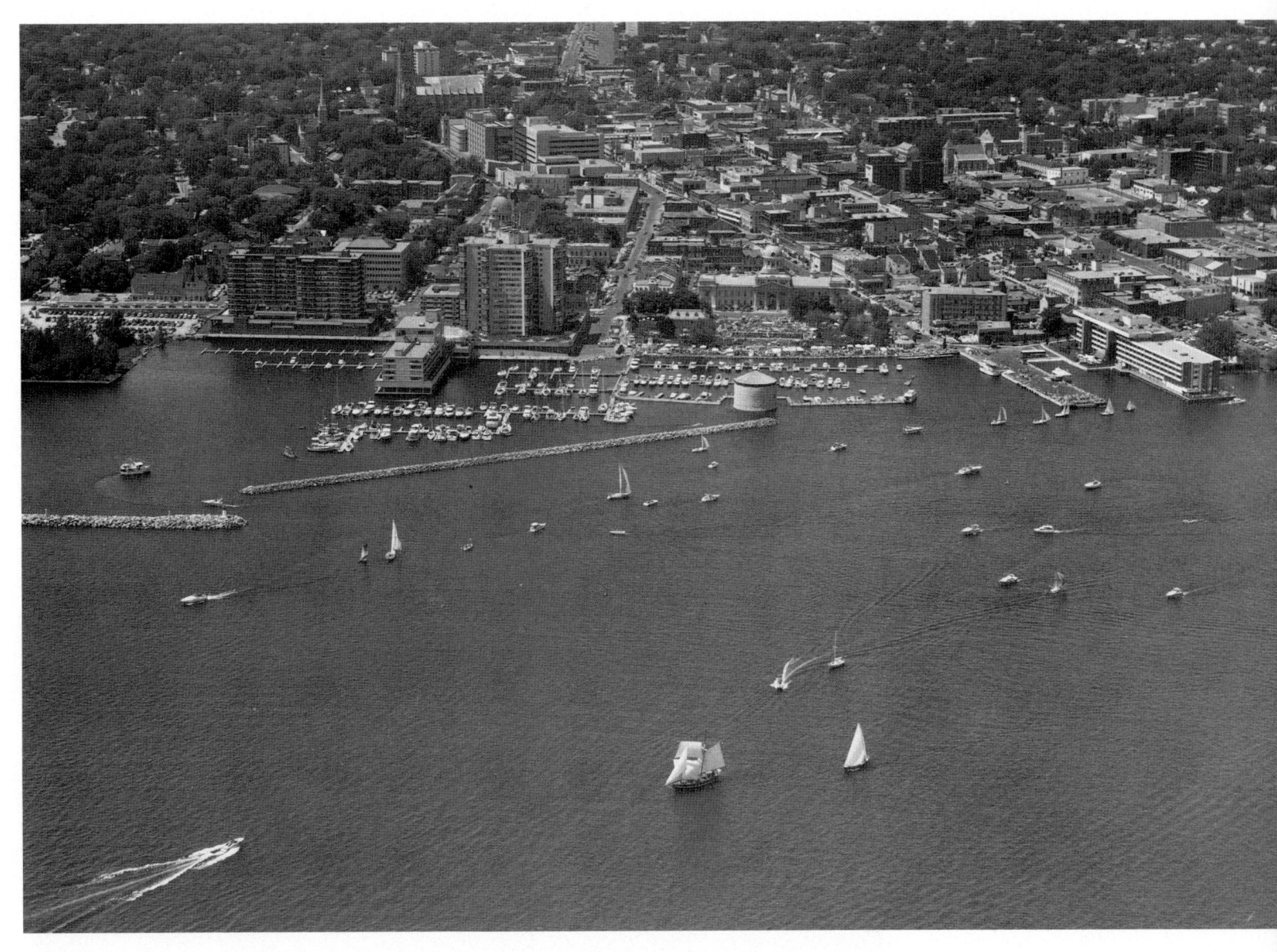

*"Throughout all four seasons, the very best view of Kingston's
historic and modern waterfront can be had by taking a
relaxing free ride on the upper deck of the Wolfe Islander III
ferry as it makes one of its 20-minute crossings between
Kingston and Wolfe Island"*
Nicholas Taggart, Sacred Heart School, Wolfe Island.

CANADA DAY

Dozens of sail and power-boats, including the *St. Lawrence II* in the foreground, parade past Confederation Park on Canada Day (previous). Students at Collins Bay Public School (above) are proud Canadians.

SCHOOL DAYS

Sitting with their backs straight and their hands folded are past and present directors of education from various school boards in the Kingston region. Beginning front left and moving clockwise around to the front right are J.B. Slack (*ex* Frontenac), Frank Kinsella (Leeds & Grenville), J.C. McLeod (*ex* Lennox & Addington), John Bates (Frontenac), Reg Shadbolt (*ex* Frontenac), Joe Mills (*ex* Prince Edward), Willis Boston (Lennox & Addington), and Greg Cosgrove (Separate School Board).

"I like Kingston because it is on the shore of Lake Ontario. It also has lots of limestone, so the Court House and City Hall look very, very old"
Brian Owens, Ecole Cathedrale.

SIR JOHN A. MACDONALD
A memorial statue of Sir John A. Macdonald (left), Canada's first prime minister and Kingston's most celebrated citizen, stands in City Park.

The staff of Bellevue House, a former residence of Sir John A. and now a national historic park, is ready to welcome visitors back to nineteenth-century Canada.

CATARAQUI TRANQUILLITY
Sir John A. Macdonald is
buried at Cataraqui Cemetery
on Sydenham Road with his
first wife Isabella.

Sir John A. not only strove
to create Canada, he left his
indelible mark on the nation's
character.

SIR JOHN A. MACDONALD
GRAVESITE

RESTORED 1982 BY CONTRIBUTIONS FROM:
ONTARIO HERITAGE FOUNDATION
MANUFACTURERS LIFE INSURANCE COMPANY
THE CITY OF KINGSTON
DOMINION OF CANADA GENERAL INSURANCE COMPANY
KINGSTON HISTORICAL SOCIETY
PRIVATE AND GROUP DONORS

C'EST GRÂCE À LA GÉNÉROSITÉ DE CES BIENFAITEURS
QUE CETTE RESTAURATION PUT ÊTRE EFFECTUÉE EN 1982

NORTHERN PERSPECTIVE
The north end of Kingston is featured in this aerial photo (opposite), with the Cataraqui River and Pittsburgh Township showing in the distance.

FRIENDSHIP
Two boys stroll along Richardson Beach, while a silhouetted couple stand placid on the shore.

CIVIC CHIEFS
Pictured here are (left to right) Ernestown Township Reeve Ian Wilson, Kingston Mayor Helen Cooper, and Kingston Township Reeve Isabel Turner. Pictured below is Pittsburgh Township Reeve Barry Gordon. The combined population of the four "Greater Kingston" municipalities numbers well over 116,000 people.

MEMBERS OF PARLIAMENT
During her 16 years as Member of Parliament for Kingston and the Islands, Flora MacDonald (above) proved to be a worthy heir to her political namesake in Kingston, Sir John A. Macdonald.

Peter Milliken (above left) now serves the riding in Ottawa. Pictured below at Queen's Park are MPP Ken Keyes (left) and Larry South (right), who represent Kingston and the Islands and Frontenac and Lennox, respectively.

"I like Kingston because of the Inner Harbor. I like the Inner Harbor area because of all the different boats and because you can see for miles"
Katie O'Brien, R.G. Sinclair Public School.

INNER HARBOR LIGHT
"Some pictures are meant to be. When I caught these images of the Inner Harbor, I was supposed to be dining with a friend. She cancelled the date, though I don't think she will ever understand why I'm glad she did so" Jack Chiang.

EXERCISES
Nadia Luciuk (top left) appears to take flight while performing at the Ukrainian pavilion during Folklore. Taekwondo expert Don Fraser (above center) is in the process of breaking with his hands 1,000 inch-thick boards to raise funds for the Muscular Dystrophy Association. Scrubs on skates (bottom left) enjoy a pick-up game beside the Ramada Inn. Duane Ramsay (top right) trains his sled dogs for a 75-mile marathon race. Pictured opposite are (left to right) Linda Galasso, Jocelyn Hession, and Nancy Lascelle working out at the Downtown Workout on Princess Street.

SAILORS' WARNING
Birds fly overhead as the sun sets on the Kingston Yacht Club (above).

KINGSTON GENERAL HOSPITAL
Founded in 1838, Kingston General Hospital (right) now employs almost 2,500 employees who receive an annual payroll of nearly $55 million. KGH is the third largest employer in the Kingston region after the Department of National Defence and Queen's University. The hospital is a well-respected research, teaching, and care-giving facility.

COMMUNITY LEADERS
Dennis Curtis (above) is spokesman for the federal prisons in the area, including the legendary Kingston Penitentiary (background). He is also an accomplished actor and auctioneer.

Irene Mooney (opposite) is often called the Watchdog of Kingston City Hall. She has attended more than 5,000 municipal meetings and ran for mayor in 1982, spending $28.00 on her campaign and winning 42% of the votes.

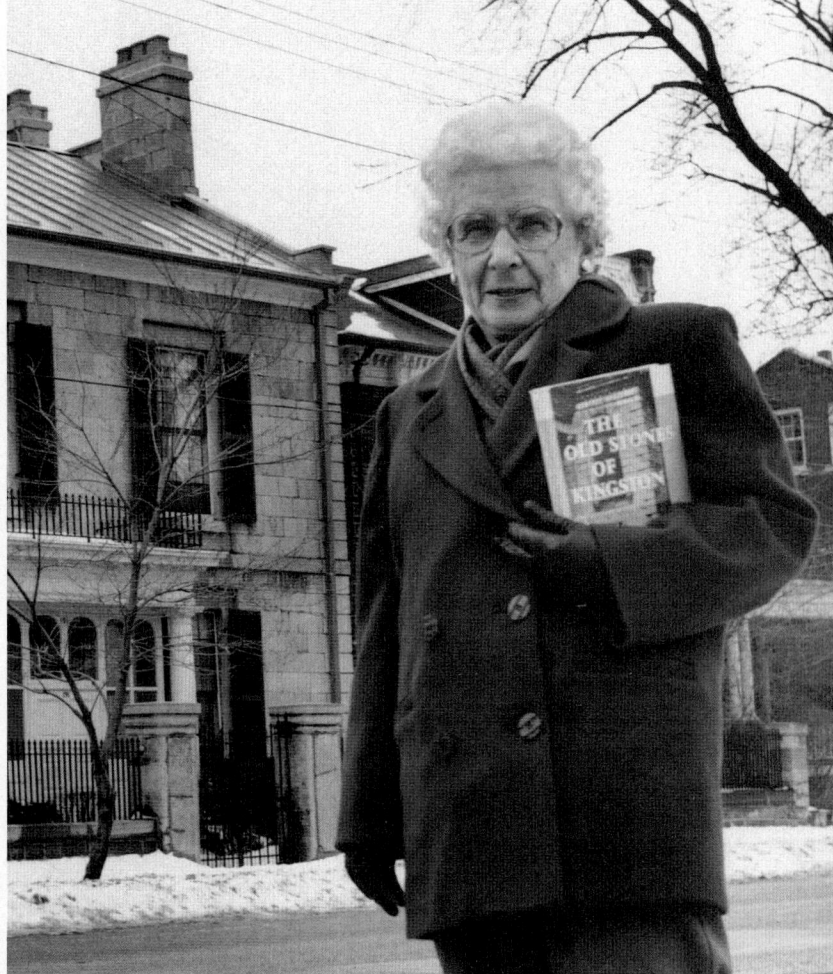

Margaret Angus (above) has
devoted much of her life to
the preservation of Kingston's
heritage. She poses here in
front of her home, the former
residence of prominent
Kingston politician Sir Richard
Cartwright, holding her very
popular book, *The Old Stones
of Kingston*.

   Diana Abramsky (opposite)
founded the Thyroid Foundation of Canada in 1980.
She keeps watch over the city,
regularly contributing letters
to the editor of the Kingston
Whig-Standard.

STREETS OF GOLD
Princess Street (top left) glitters in golden morning sun as does Queen Street (bottom left) in the afternoon glow. Clarence Street (opposite) quickens to the rising sun reflecting up from the harbor.

BIKERS AND BOXERS

BMX bikers (top left) challenge the track at Woodbine Park. North American marathon speed skating champion Bob Tysen (left) also competes in the Race Across America bicycle marathon. Mark Leduc (bottom left) is the light welterweight boxing champion of Canada.

Melanie Macdonald (right) from Wolfe Island is one of the top drag bike racers in North America. Ralph the dog (below right) may not be a national champion but he often does accompany his master Greg Webster on motorcycle trips to Toronto, Ottawa, and Montreal.

GOLD CUP
The Gold Cup speed boat race (opposite) attracts competitors and spectators from far and wide to Hayward Long Reach near Picton in Prince Edward County.

STACKS OF SKIERS
Members of the Collins Bay Water-Ski Club (left) perform in a pyramid formation. Pictured here (left to right from top) are Stacy Ungar, Marilyn Lane, Laura Nickerson, Kelly Bates, Sil Fernetich, Ted Lane, Paul Wyminga, and Tracy Curzon.

AT THE RACES
During a speed boat race on Sydenham Lake (left), one competitor makes quite a splash. He was not injured. "Pork Chop" and "Ham Bone" race down the back stretch at the Kingston Exhibition (top), while competitors in the annual demolition derby declare "no fault" (above).

FESTIVE SMILES
Two children (top left) dressed for Folklore at the Polish pavilion take a break. Corrie van der Zwan (top right) appears as a princess on Trousdale's General Store float during the annual Santa Claus Parade in Sydenham, just north of Kingston. Students of Central Public School (right) strut their stuff down Princess Street during a Hallowe'en celebration.

FESTIVE COLOR
Gita Raman dazzles the audience at the Indian pavilion during Folklore.

NUTCRACKER SUITE
Students of Polson Park Public School are in costume for a performance of *The Nutcracker*. The dancers pictured in the group photograph are (from left to right) Shenoah Crockett, Julie Ashe, Gavin McCarthy, Nancy Truong, and Stasia Landers. Ashley Spencer (above) and Rhandi Wiltshire (right) prepare for their moment in the spotlight.

" I spend a lot of time working with school children while shooting photographs for the Newspaper in Education weekly feature in The Whig-Standard. *I try to bring a child's sense of wonder into my art of photography "* Jack Chiang.

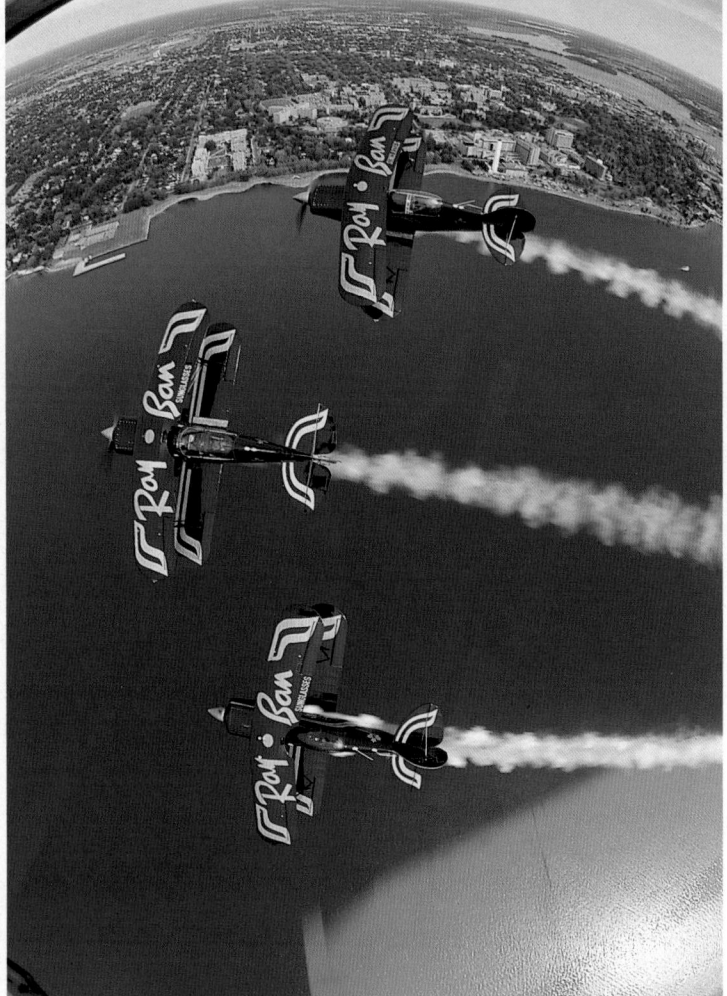

HEAVENLY HARMONY

"*To take this picture of the Ray Ban Gold aerobatic team with lead pilot Rod Ellis looming in the foreground, I kneeled backwards in the front cockpit and positioned the camera 20 inches away from Rod. I used a 35-mm camera fitted with a full-frame fisheye lens and taped an electronic flash to the back of my left hand. Three photo sessions lasting about 30 minutes were required before I was able to compose the picture as you see it* " Jack Chiang.

The Ray Ban Gold team includes (from left to right) George Kirbyson, Al Hauff, Bill Cowan, and Rod Ellis.

GYMNASTIC ROUTINES
Kingston Gymnastics Club
coach Monica Tracey leads
Alison Raymond (left)
through a routine. Tammy
Larin (above) flips heels over
head.

AIRBORNE CAMERA
"Kingston Flying Club instructor Jim Reside maneuvered a Cessna 172 plane into this position over the city while I triggered a wing-mounted camera by remote control. I asked Jim to remove the door from the plane so I could achieve this effect. It's fun to play at being a stunt photographer " Jack Chiang.

UP UP TOWN
This photograph depicts Princess Street stretching through the city. The red roof marks the site of Pizza Hut.

COLORFUL SAILS
The color of the sails on these passing vessels (opposite) is accentuated by the deep blue water of the St. Lawrence River east of Kingston.

MASKED FENCER
The protective mesh of the mask worn by this member of the Queen's University Fencing Club adds an element of mystery to the portrait.

MASK-MAKER
Artist Joan Belch poses for this portrait beside her sculpture called "Alice" and in front of her work called "Fans" — dozens of life-size images of fans watching a hockey game.

BATHED IN FOG
"Every time I drive along Bath Road leading into the city my eye is drawn to this solitary tree (previous page). I've tried to capture the spirit of this image many times on film, but nothing worked until one day the fog masked the background" Jack Chiang.

PORTRAIT OF COURAGE
Blind triathlete Ron Hackett (left) and Dr. Robert McCaldon enjoy training for the grueling triathlon event consisting of a 2-km swim, 55-km bike ride, and 15-km run.

WAR GAMES
Capt. Hugh Egener (left) and Capt. Neil Dukas of the Canadian Land Forces Command & Staff College, located at Fort Frontenac along with the National Defence College, rehearse maneuvers. The college trains experienced military staff to become experts in brigade and division command.

VIMY BAND
The Vimy Band of Canadian Forces Base (CFB) Kingston plays during a ceremony. The military complement of CFB Kingston centered at Vimy Barracks just east of Fort Henry includes the First Canadian Signal Regiment, HMCS *Cataraqui*, The Princess of Wales Own Regiment, and the Brockville Rifles.

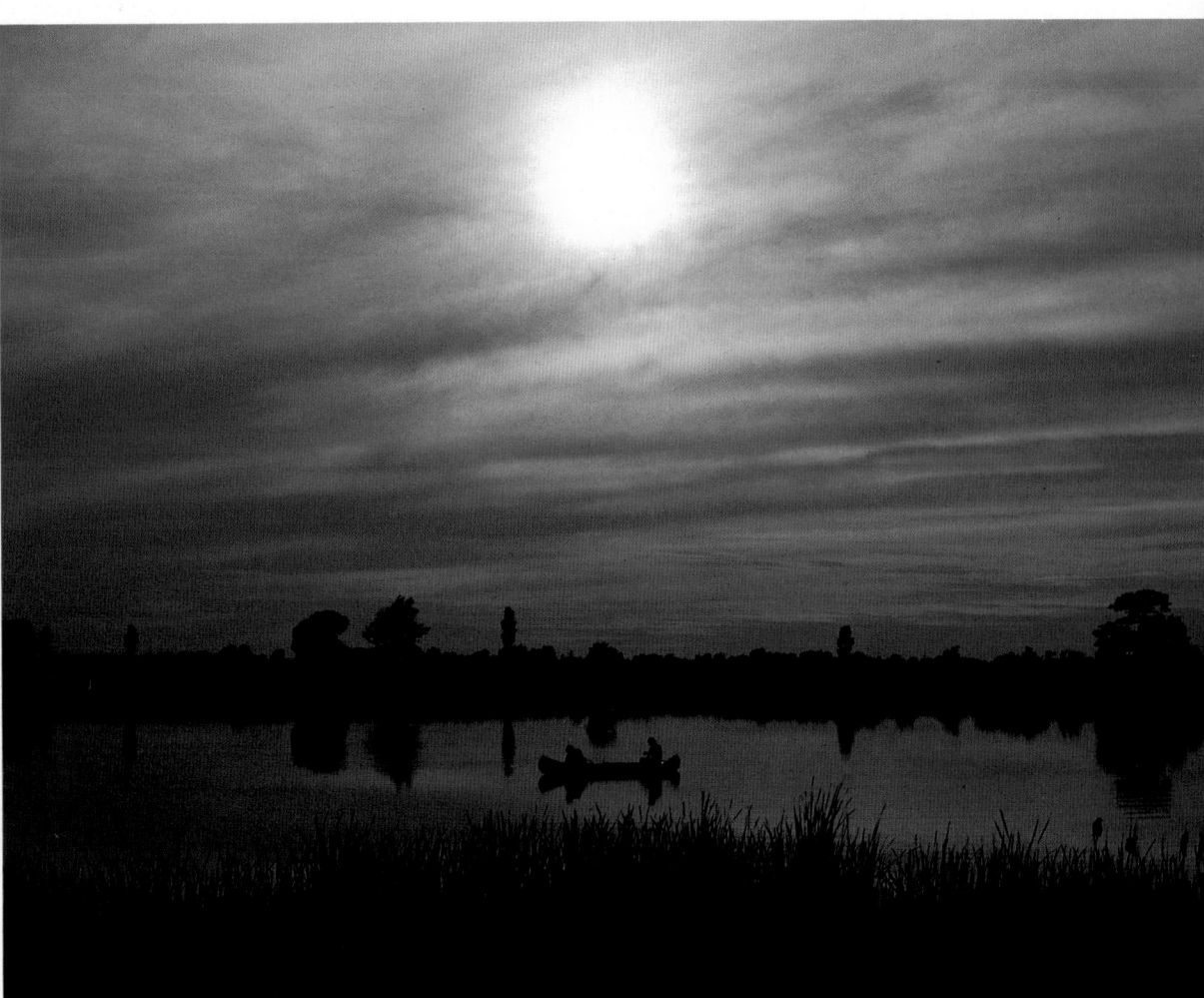

BATHED IN SUNLIGHT
While the glow of the afternoon sun casts a spell over Collins Bay Institution (left), two anglers try their luck just south on Little Cataraqui Creek near the Du Pont site on Lake Ontario.

THE FOUR TRUMPETEERS
These band members entertain during a Kingfest Tattoo in Richardson Stadium. Kingfest is an annual summer recreational and educational program for adults and children.

ONE-HORSE POWER
Matthew Lane has his water-skiing lesson "man-powered" by his father, Ted Lane.

LIP-SYNC SILHOUETTE
This rising star (far right) performs during a "lip-sync" contest at Lake Ontario Park, sponsored by CKLC Radio.

LOCOMOTION
A fog enshrouded VIA passenger train (left) pulls out of the Kingston station. From 1855 to 1969, Kingston was the site of a major train manufacturing firm, the Canadian Locomotive Works.

POOR CAMOUFLAGE
The Kingston region is an internationally renowned center for bird watching and ornithological study. This species (above) makes no effort to hide from the amateur birder.

CATS, QUACKS, AND TORIES
Jack Wright (top) won the
National Enquirer contest for
"Most Cats Under One
Roof." He shares his home
with over 400 cats.

Dick Cherry (bottom), a
former hockey player with the
Philadelphia Flyers and long-
time local school principal, has
won over 50 awards for his
duck decoy carving.

Loyal Tories (right) hide
behind placards to avoid the
rain while waiting for their
party leader Brian Mulroney to
arrive.

INDUSTRIAL PROSPECTS
The Kingston region is the site of many national and multinational industries, including Alcan Rolled Products and Kingston Spinners (above), Northern Telecom (near right), and Celanese Canada (far right). Shown here are Northern Telecom works manager Ken Mann and Celanese general managers Ron McNeely and George McGinn.

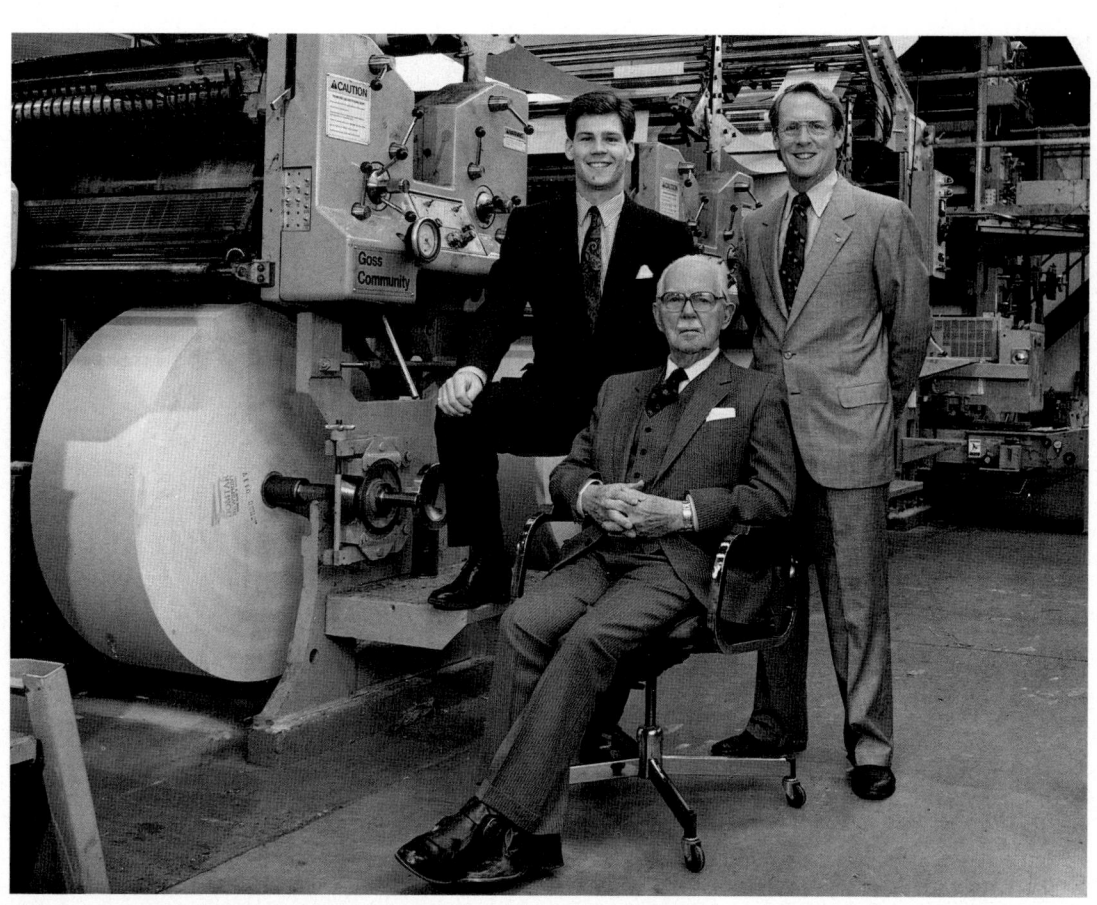

BUSINESS TRADITIONS

The Whig-Standard, founded in 1834 by Edward John Barker as the *British Whig*, is now owned by the Davies family and respected by the journalism community as one of the best daily newspapers in Canada. Pictured here are Arthur Davies (center), his son Michael (right), and his grandson Eric (left).

David Pattenden, President and Chief Executive Officer of the Urban Transportation Development Corporation/Lavalin Ltd., shows off the fleet of military vehicles manufactured at the Kingston plant. He previously taught at Queen's University and practiced law in Kingston.

"My favorite sight is when I look out of the City Hall
clock tower and see the lake and look at the boats go by
while I watch the people from higher ground"
Matt Birnell, Polson Park Public School.

Entrepreneur Rick Hession, long-time owner of five McDonald's restaurants in the Kingston area, left the franchise in 1990 to pursue other business interests.

Don Elliott, President of Empire Financial Group, poses in front of the historic Empire head office building on King Street. The company was founded in the nineteenth century and now employs over 700 people.

INDUSTRIAL ROMANTIC
"I've been told my vision of industry is strangely romantic. As a photographer, I try not to take things for granted, try not to accept the conventional images of the world found in the press and elsewhere. Industrial sites, such as the Du Pont research lab and manufacturing plant shown in these two photographs, often appeal to my vision" Jack Chiang.

COMMUNITY LEADERS
David Helwig, nationally
renowned novelist and poet,
and Nancy Helwig, manager
of Kingston's Grand Theatre,
play a vital role in the cultural
life of the city.

Kitt and Robin Chubb run
an aviary and hospital for
injured birds near Verona,
north of Kingston.

Neil Reynolds, editor of
The Whig-Standard, and
Donna Jacobs, co-ordinator of
the award-winning Newspaper
in Education section of *The
Whig*, relax in their home overlooking Collins Bay.

Gordon and Valerie Robertson of Theatre 5 ham it up for the camera. Their love for theatre and their support for the arts is infectious.

Janette Turner Hospital, author of such well-known novels as *The Ivory Swing* and *Charades*, poses under a sign which alludes to her birthplace, Australia.

SANDBANKS
Sandbanks Provincial Park in Prince Edward County south of Picton is a popular day-trip destination for Kingston travelers.

LAKE ONTARIO CEMENT
Overlooking the Picton harbor, the Lake Ontario Cement plant looms large on the shore, dwarfing the lake freighter in the foreground (opposite) and casting wonderful colors across the water.

SAILING PATTERNS
Two sailboats (far left) cast striking shadows on Lake Ontario.

FAST FOOD SERVICE
A sea gull picks up lunch at a "fly-thru" near Picton (top), while a chickadee takes a risk with a human vending machine (bottom) in the shape of the hand of Tibor Vaghy, a resident of Joyceville, north of Kingston.

FOUNTAIN OF HOPE
Participants in the annual
Terry Fox run to raise funds
for cancer research prepare
themselves in front of the
Napanee Town Hall.

RIBBONS OF GOLD
The setting sun gilds the
train tracks leading west from
Kingston to Napanee, while
vehicles on Highway 401
between these neighboring
towns acquire a golden lustre.
An average of 20,000 vehicles
travel on the 401 in this
region each day, though more
than 30,000 travel on Highway 33 (Bath Road at Days
Road). Passenger train service
has been curtailed in recent
years, though the tracks are
still heavily used for freight
trains.

MISS PIGGY
This strangely attired crossing guard (Irene Snider) escorts a kitten across the road in Amherstview. She was dressed up for Hallowe'en; the kitten was not going to school.

BEST FRIENDS
Jack Haynes and Fred the dog beat the heat. Fred's favorite flavor is vanilla.

SELF-RESTRAINT
Young Orissa Worth shows greater self-restraint than her canine counterpart on the leash.

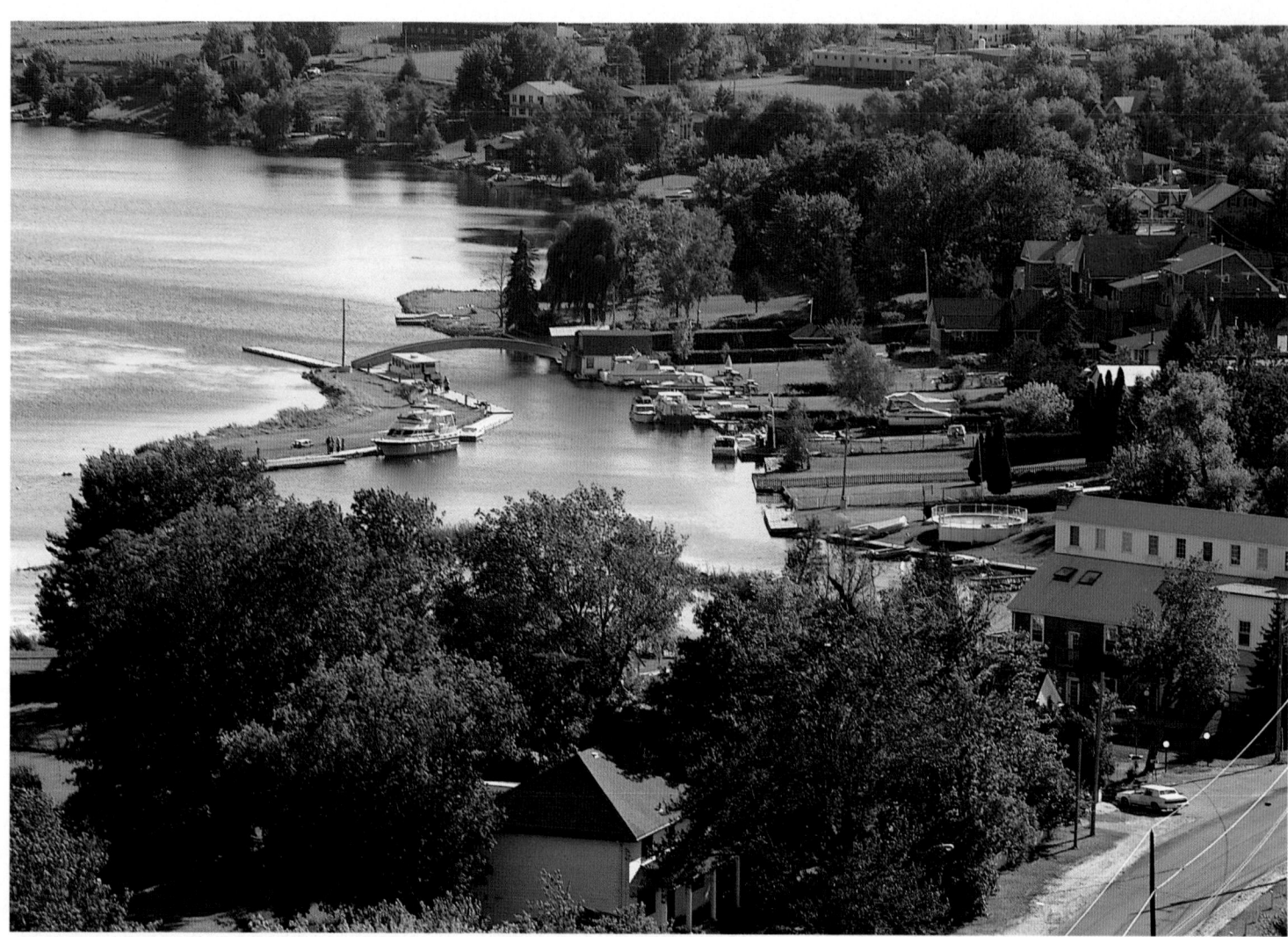

VIEW FROM FOLEY MOUNTAIN
Picturesque Westport is located on the shores of Big Rideau Lake and under the shadow of Foley Mountain. The village is a popular day-trip stop for travelers from Kingston and Ottawa.

PASTORAL SPLENDOR
A flock of sheep graze peacefully in a road-side pasture between Kingston and Gananoque.

COOL COW
"*I was driving down a road near Glenburnie when I spotted this cow in a barn. I took one picture (above) but realized that the image would be better if the cow's tail were visible, so I waited and waited for 50 minutes before the tail came into view*" Jack Chiang.

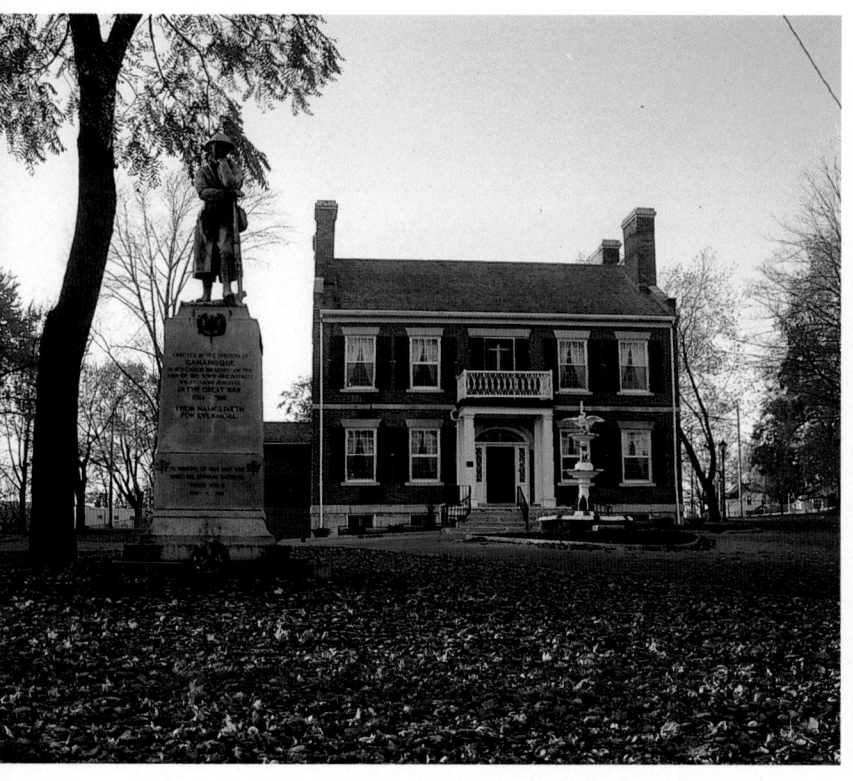

GANANOQUE
An unknown soldier on the war memorial in Gananoque guards the town hall, while a swan flaps its wings with joy after eating food tossed in the Gananoque River by tourists visiting the many attractions in this town known as the "Gateway to the Thousand Islands."

LEADER OF THE PACK
A sheep dog owned by
Amanda Milliken guards the
flock, while members of the
Frontenac Hunt Club follow
the crowd.

LOCKED UP
Pictured here are two pleasure boats being lifted at one of the 47 locking stations on the Rideau Canal between Kingston and Ottawa.

1000 ISLANDS

Spanning the St. Lawrence River from Ivy Lea (in Canada) to Hill Island (in the United States), this bridge was officially opened in 1938 by U.S. President Franklin D. Roosevelt and Canadian Prime Minister William Lyon Mackenzie King.

The islands in this chain vary in size from the 27-mile-long Wolfe Island to some that are not even big enough for one cottage. The most famous landmark in the Thousand Islands is Boldt Castle (right), the legacy of George Boldt who built this mansion for his wife; she died, however, before the castle was completed.

"The thing I like about Kingston is windsurfing. The reason why is that Lake Ontario has really big waves. In the summer, when the wind is strong, the waves get really big and are at least four feet tall"
Justin Salter, R.G. Sinclair Public School.

KEELING OVER
This sailor is obviously not upset even though his boat is overturned during the annual Canadian Olympic-Training Regatta, Kingston (C.O.R.K.), one of the largest sailing events in the world.

CROSS COUNTRY CLUB SKIING
The Cataraqui Golf and Country Club offer skiers a picturesque setting for their sport.

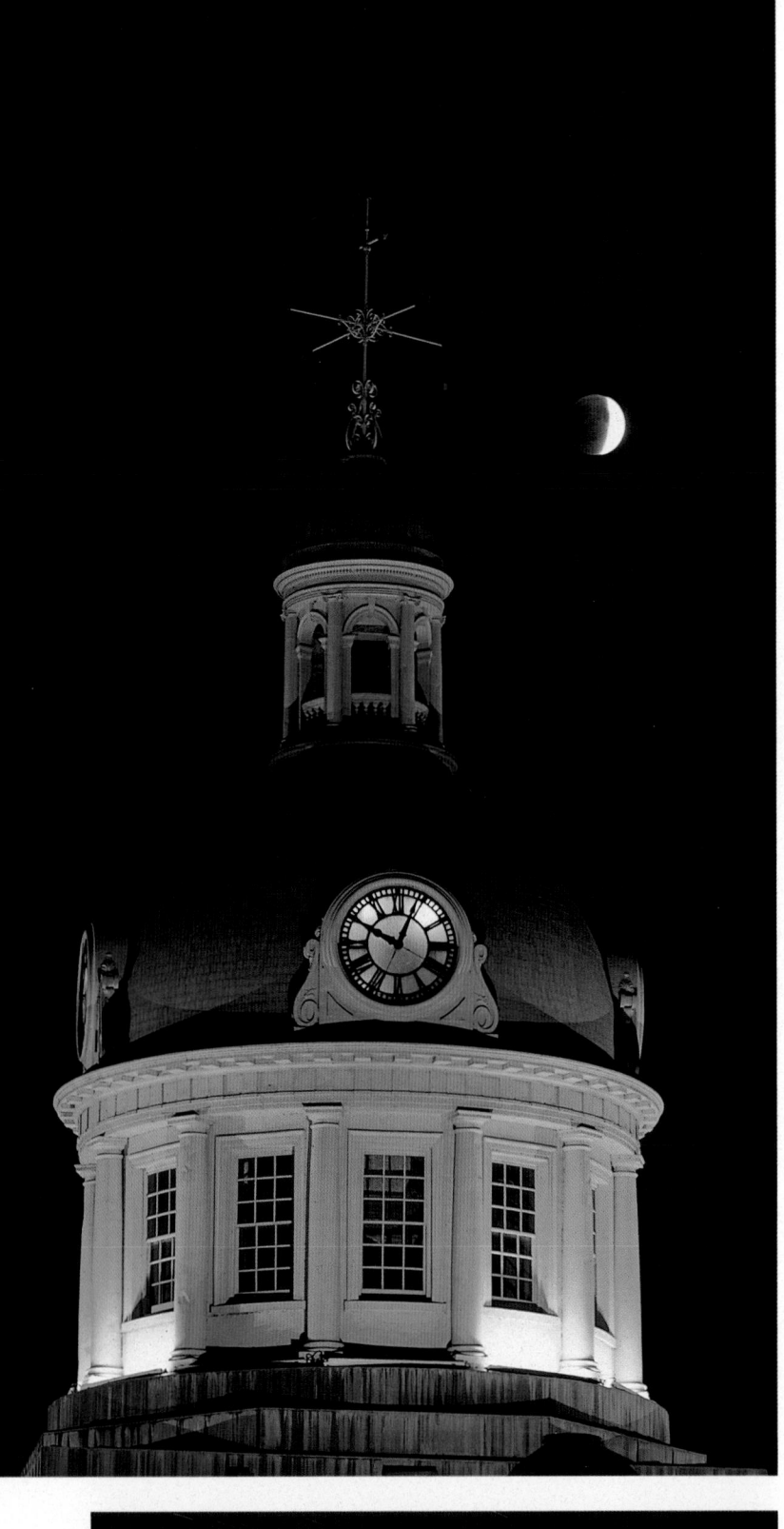

CITY HALL ECLIPSE
The moon eclipses over City Hall making for a striking image.

SHOOTING STARS
"*This picture of the stars streaking across the sky behind the Martello tower at Point Frederick was taken with the assistance of local astronomer Terence Dickinson (bottom). To take this picture, I went to the tower for five consecutive nights in September and each night I took two time-lapse exposures, lasting between two and four hours, using a 50-mm lens on a Hasselblad camera with lens aperture set at f5.6. On the third night I absent-mindedly locked my keys in the car, and this picture was taken while I was away in the guard-house at RMC calling a tow truck. I'm forever amazed at how much better a camera sees than the naked eye*" Jack Chiang.

Acknowledgements

Hundreds of people in the Kingston area helped produce this book and I'm indebted to them for their generosity. Before I started working on the book, I consulted Kingston Mayor Helen Cooper, Kingston Township Reeve Isabel Turner, Lyn Williams, Manager of the Visitor and Convention Bureau, Doug Ritchie, Manager of Kingston Downtown Business Improvement Association, and Rick Hession of Hession Foods Ltd.

My colleagues at *The Whig-Standard* often overwhelmed me with their enthusiasm for the book. Donna Jacobs tirelessly encouraged local school children to send in their comments about why they like Kingston. Therese Greenwood and Gary Lupton helped sort out some of the comments. Michael Lea, Ian MacAlpine, Lisa Lowry, Rob Cowperthwaite, and Neil Ward helped me take some of the pictures. Louise Doolan and Cynthia Howard, who keep a well-organized picture-and-negative file, made it possible for me to dig up some of the older pictures. Fred Madden, Norris McDonald, Bill Fitsell, Alan Capon, Gillian Sadinsky, Ann Lukits, Sheldon MacNeil, and Harvey Schachter all gave me many good ideas. And I am especially indebted to Michael Davies and Neil Reynolds, publisher and editor respectively of *The Whig-Standard*.

Others were generous with their time and advice: Doug and Joan Belch; Dr. Jim Beliveau; Sharon Mulligan; Vicki Keith; Gary Droppo; Sylvia Hamer of the Ontario Ministry of Transportation; Ken Cuthbertson and Tim Lougheed of Queen's University; John Armitage of the Kingston Rowing Club; Don Fraser and Karen Burnside of Fraser's Taekwondo; Debbie Kincaid, Sharon Suddergaard, and Heather Agnew of the Precision-Skating Club; Captain Neil Dukas of the Canadian Land Forces Command and Staff College; Dennis Curtis of Correctional Services Canada; and Roland Billings and Tony Earley of Alcan.

Many people from our local schools helped make this book a better one: Frontenac County Board of Education director John Bates helped gather all the directors of education for a group picture; Collins Bay Public School principal Allan Glenn, vice-principal Spencer Storms, teachers Debbie Jacobi, Diane Ross, and Wolfgang Piribauer helped arrange for the picture of their students; Polson Park Public School's Gary Smith, Cathy Lincoln, Therese Lavoie, and Betsy Cotton made it possible for me to include pictures of a school play, *The Nutcracker*; Tom Murphy of Archbishop O'Sullivan School, Paul Proderick of St. Peter School, and Bev Ralph of R.G. Sinclair School encouraged their students to submit their thoughts on Kingston.

Don Gillespie of Camera Kingston and Vern Napier of Vern Napier's Cameras gave me many discounts on films and photo supplies.

John Robertson and his staff at Fort Henry were generous with their help. I spent many hours there while trying to capture the simultaneous firing of their guns and cannons. Their co-operation made my job easier.

Half a dozen of the best pictures in this book were taken at the Royal Military College of Canada. I want to thank the Commandant, Commodore E. R. Murray, Lieutenant-Commander Gerald Stowe, and Master Drill-Sgt. Gino Moretti. Their speed and efficiency made me go back to RMC again and again.

Bob Hilderley, publisher and editor of this book, often amazed me with his knowledge of Kingston. He also spent many hours with designer Keith Abraham poring over the layout. It was a pleasure working with him. Jill Smith, Linda Bussière, and Kathryn Morris helped in the promotion and production of this book.

I am also grateful to J. Kim Haynes, who listened to many hours of my monologues and offered many useful suggestions, such as including more people in the book.

When I first came to Kingston 12 years ago, I intended to stay here for two years or less. The reason I'm still here today is because I like working for *The Whig-Standard*, which I believe is one of Canada's best newspapers. I also enjoy working with Michael Davies and Neil Reynolds because they have always treated me more like a family member than an employee.

Finally, I would like to thank someone whom I've never met, but his influence on this book is great. When I started out doing this book, I was an experienced photojournalist, but I wasn't good at landscape photography. During the first couple of months, I wasted a lot of time and money, but I wasn't getting the kind of photos I wanted. That changed when I happened to see Galen Rowell's book, *Mountain Light*. Many of the landscape pictures in this book are the result of what I learned from *Mountain Light*.

Jack Chiang

Look for this iPod icon throughout the text.

Icons connect textbook content to your iPod or other MP3 device.

Images courtesy of Apple.

Don't have an iPod? Content can be viewed on any computer! Visit the text website for directions.

Website includes:

- Lecture presentations
  - *Audio and video*
  - *Audio only*
  - *Video only*
- Demonstration problems[+]
- Interactive self quizzes*
- Accounting videos

+Available with some textbooks

Want to see iPod in action?

Visit **www.mhhe.com/ipod** to view a demonstration of our iPod® content.

McGraw-Hill's HOMEWORK MANAGER PLUS™ ■■ online

THE COMPLETE SOLUTION

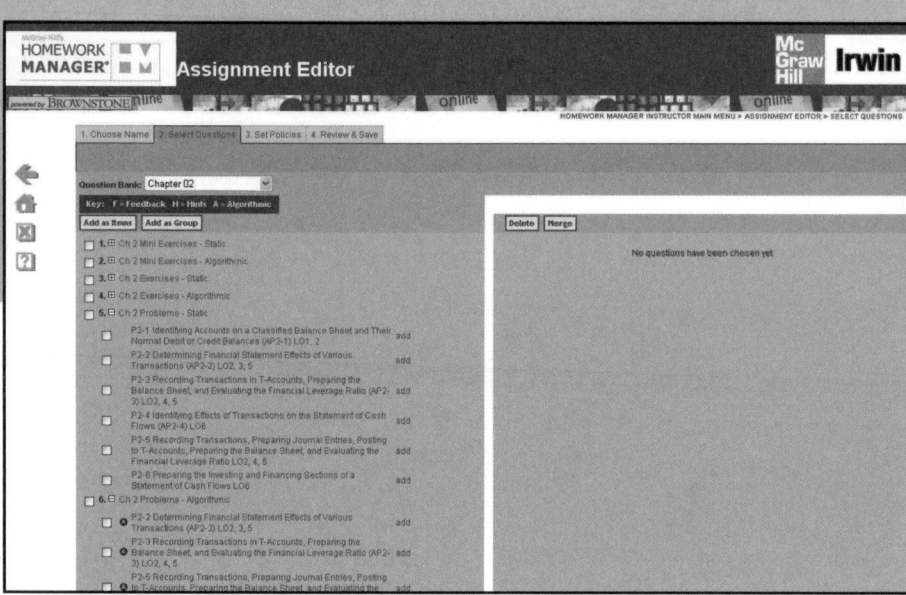

McGraw-Hill's
Homework Manager®

™ This online homework management solution contains this textbook's end-of-chapter material. Now you have the option to build assignments from static and algorithmic versions of the text problems and exercises or to build self-graded quizzes from the additional questions provided in the online test bank.

Features:

- Assigns book-specific problems/exercises to students
- Provides integrated test bank questions for quizzes and tests
- Automatically grades assignments and quizzes, storing results in one grade book
- Dispenses immediate feedback to students regarding their work

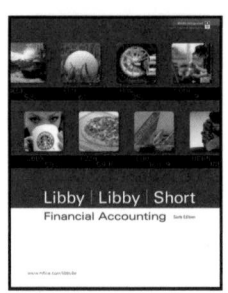

Libby / Libby / Short
Financial Accounting, 6/e
978-0-07-332483-8

1 TERM

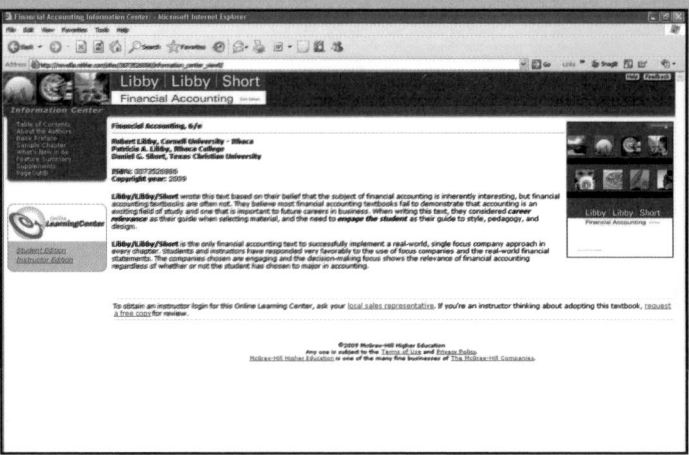

Interactive Online Version
of this Textbook

 In addition to the textbook, students can rely on this online version of the text for a convenient way to study. The interactive content is fully *integrated* with McGraw-Hill's Homework Manager® system to give students quick access to relevant content as they work through problems, exercises, and practice quizzes.

Features:
- Online version of the text *integrated* with McGraw-Hill's Homework Manager
- Students referred to appropriate sections of the online book as they complete an assignment or take a practice quiz
- Direct link to related material that corresponds with the learning objective within the text

McGraw-Hill's Homework Manager PLUS™ system combines the power of McGraw-Hill's Homework Manager® with the latest interactive learning technology to create a comprehensive, fully integrated online study package. Students working on assignments in McGraw-Hill's Homework Manager system can click a simple hotlink and instantly review the appropriate material in the Interactive Online Textbook.

By including McGraw-Hill's Homework Manager PLUS with your textbook adoption, you're giving your students a vital edge as they progress through the course and ensuring that the help they need is never more than a mouse click away. Contact your McGraw-Hill representative or visit the book's Web site to learn how to add McGraw-Hill's Homework Manager PLUS system to your adoption.

SIXTH EDITION

Financial Accounting

Robert Libby
Cornell University

Patricia A. Libby
Ithaca College

Daniel G. Short
Texas Christian University

 McGraw-Hill Irwin

Boston   Burr Ridge, IL   Dubuque, IA   New York   San Francisco   St. Louis
Bangkok   Bogotá   Caracas   Kuala Lumpur   Lisbon   London   Madrid   Mexico City
Milan   Montreal   New Delhi   Santiago   Seoul   Singapore   Sydney   Taipei   Toronto

To:
Jenni, Jon, Emma, and Sophia Drago
Herman and Doris Hargenrater
Laura Libby, Oscar, and Selma Libby
Bob and Mary Ann Short, Heather Short, and Maryrose Short

McGraw-Hill
Irwin

FINANCIAL ACCOUNTING

Published by McGraw-Hill/Irwin, a business unit of The McGraw-Hill Companies, Inc., 1221 Avenue of the
Americas, New York, NY, 10020. Copyright © 2009, 2007, 2004, 2001, 1998, 1996 by The McGraw-Hill
Companies, Inc. All rights reserved. No part of this publication may be reproduced or distributed in any form
or by any means, or stored in a database or retrieval system, without the prior written consent of The McGraw-Hill
Companies, Inc., including, but not limited to, in any network or other electronic storage or transmission, or
broadcast for distance learning.

Some ancillaries, including electronic and print components, may not be available to customers outside the United States.

This book is printed on acid-free paper.

2 3 4 5 6 7 8 9 0 DOW/DOW 0 9

ISBN 978-0-07-352688-1
MHID 0-07-352688-6

Vice President, Editor-in-Chief: *Brent Gordon*
Editorial director: *Stewart Mattson*
Senior sponsoring editor: *Alice Harra*
Senior developmental editor: *Kimberly D. Hooker*
Executive marketing manager: *Sankha Basu*
Manager of photo, design & publishing tools: *Mary Conzachi*
Senior production supervisor: *Debra R. Sylvester*
Interior and cover designer: *Cara Hawthorne*
Senior photo research coordinator: *Jeremy Cheshareck*
Photo researcher: *Editorial Image, LLC*
Lead media project manager: *Brian Nacik*
Typeface: *10.5/12 Times Roman*
Compositor: *Laserwords*
Printer: *R. R. Donnelley*
Starbucks image on cover: © Jürg Carstensen/dpa/Corbis
Southwest image on cover: © Justin Sullivan/Getty Images

Library of Congress Cataloging-in-Publication Data
Libby, Robert.
    Financial accounting / Robert Libby, Patricia Libby, Daniel Short.—6th ed.
      p. cm.
    Includes index.
    ISBN-13: 978-0-07-352688-1 (alk. paper)
    ISBN-10: 0-07-352688-6 (alk. paper)
    1. Accounting. 2. Corporations—Accounting. 3. Financial statements. I. Libby,
Patricia A. II. Short, Daniel G. III. Title.
HF5636.L53 2009
657—dc22

                                                    2008018247

www.mhhe.com

Robert Libby

Robert Libby is the David A. Thomas Professor of Accounting at Cornell University, where he teaches the introductory financial accounting course. He previously taught at the University of Illinois, Pennsylvania State University, the University of Texas at Austin, the University of Chicago, and the University of Michigan. He received his BS from Pennsylvania State University and his MAS and PhD from the University of Illinois. He is also a CPA.

Bob is a widely published author and researcher specializing in behavioral accounting. He was selected as the AAA Outstanding Educator in 2000, received the AAA Outstanding Service Award in 2006 and received the AAA Notable Contributions to the Literature Award in 1985 and 1996. He is the only person to have received all three of the Association's highest awards for teaching, service, and research. He has published numerous articles in *The Accounting Review; Journal of Accounting Research; Accounting, Organizations, and Society;* and other accounting journals. He has held a variety of offices including vice president in the American Accounting Association and is a member of the American Institute of CPAs and the editorial boards of *The Accounting Review; Accounting, Organizations and Society; Journal of Accounting Literature;* and *Journal of Behavioral Decision Making.*

Patricia A. Libby

Patricia Libby is associate professor of accounting at Ithaca College, where she teaches the undergraduate financial accounting course. She previously taught graduate and undergraduate financial accounting at Eastern Michigan University and the University of Texas. Before entering academe, she was an auditor with Price Waterhouse (now PricewaterhouseCoopers) and a financial administrator at the University of Chicago. She is also faculty advisor to Beta Alpha Psi, Ithaca College Accounting Association, and Ithaca College National Association of Black Accountants. She received her BS from Pennsylvania State University, her MBA from DePaul University, and her PhD from the University of Michigan. She is also a CPA.

Pat conducts research on using cases in the introductory course and other parts of the accounting curriculum. She has published articles in *The Accounting Review, Issues in Accounting Education,* and *The Michigan CPA.*

Daniel G. Short

Daniel Short is professor of accounting and former dean of the M.J. Neeley School of Business at Texas Christian University in Fort Worth, Texas. Before he joined TCU, he was dean at the Richard T. Farmer School of Business at Miami University and the College of Business at Kansas State University. Prior to that, he was associate dean at the University of Texas at Austin, where he taught the undergraduate and graduate financial accounting courses. He also taught at the University of Michigan and the University of Chicago. He received his undergraduate degree from Boston University and his MBA and PhD from the University of Michigan.

Dan has won numerous awards for his outstanding teaching abilities and has published articles in *The Wall Street Journal, The Accounting Review,* the *Journal of Accounting Research,* and other business journals. He has worked with a number of Fortune 500 companies, commercial banks, and investment banks to develop and teach executive education courses on the effective use of accounting information. Dan has also served on boards of directors in several industries, including manufacturing, commercial banking, and medical services. He is currently on the economic development committee of the Fort Worth Chamber of Commerce.

A trusted leader

Since it was first published, *Financial Accounting* has grown to be the market-leading financial accounting textbook on which both students and instructors rely. The award-winning author team of Bob Libby, Pat Libby, and Dan Short has made it a best-selling textbook by helping the instructor and student become partners in learning. The Libby/Libby/Short authors use a remarkable learning approach that keeps students engaged and involved in the material from the first day of class.

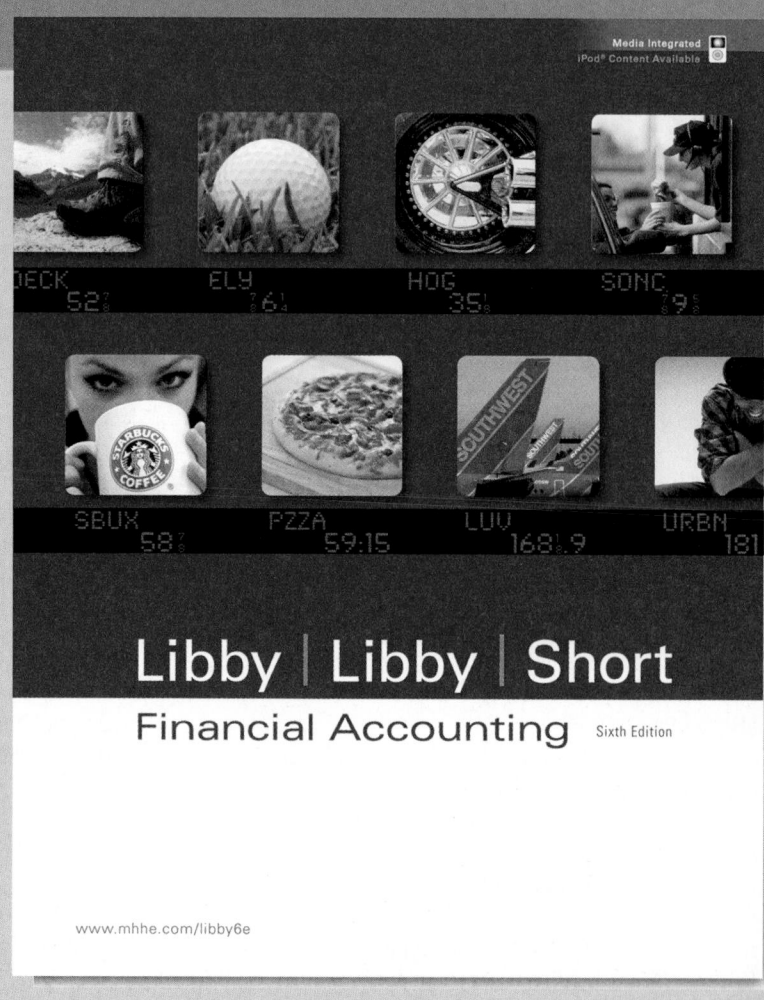

Financial Accounting's pioneering "focus company approach" involves students in the business decisions of real companies, demonstrating how financial accounting makes a difference in the success of a firm. That, combined with pedagogical features and technology assets that serve a variety of learning styles, makes *Financial Accounting* the textbook that both students and instructors agree is the <u>best of its kind on the market today.</u>

"*. . . It systematically guides readers through financial statements with focus companies and, at the same time, integrates the transaction analysis and journal entries in every chapter.*" Haihang He, California State University

for both students and instructors

Libby/Libby/Short's *Financial Accounting* maintains its leadership by focusing on three key attributes:

RELEVANCY—THE PIONEERING FOCUS COMPANY APPROACH:

The Libby/Libby/Short authors first introduced their focus company approach as the best method for helping students understand financial statements and real-world implications of financial accounting for future managers. **This approach shows that accounting is relevant and motivates students by explaining accounting in a real-world context.** Throughout each chapter, the material is focused around a familiar Real company, its decisions, and its financial statements. This provides the perfect setting for discussing the importance of accounting and how businesses use accounting information. Furthering its real-world applicability, the end-of-chapter cases tie directly to the American Eagle Outfitters Annual Report in Appendix B and the contrasting report from Urban Outfitters Form 10-K in Appendix C. This gives students valuable practice reading and interpreting real financial data. In addition, real-world excerpts expand on important chapter topics with insight into how real firms use financial accounting to their competitive advantage.

CLARITY—A BUILDING-BLOCK APPROACH TO TEACHING TRANSACTION ANALYSIS:

Most faculty agree that mastery of the accounting cycle is critical to success in financial accounting. And yet all other financial books introduce and develop transaction analysis in one chapter, bombarding a student early in the course with an overload of new concepts and terms. The authors believe that most faculty take more time with the accounting cycle, but other financial accounting textbooks don't. **By slowing down the introduction of transactions and giving students time to practice and gain mastery, this building-block approach leads to greater student success in their study of later topics in financial accounting such as adjusting entries.**

TECHNOLOGY—POWERFUL TOOLS FOR TEACHING AND STUDY:

Students have different learning styles and conflicting time commitments, so they want technology tools that help them study more efficiently and effectively. **McGraw-Hill's Homework Manager and Homework Manager Plus, iPod downloadable content, and ALEKS for Financial Accounting provide students with three powerful tools tied directly to** *Financial Accounting, 6e,* which will help them maximize their study time and make their learning experience more enjoyable. In addition, the Algorithmic Test Bank allows instructors to create an infinite number of algorithm-generated quizzes and test assignments and gives students an endless number of problems with which to practice.

Libby/Libby/Short's *Financial Accounting* is the proven choice for presenting financial accounting in a clear, relevant manner that keeps students engaged throughout your course. Read on for more insight into what has made this textbook such a success with faculty and students.

What's New in the 6th Edition?

One reason Libby/Libby/Short's *Financial Accounting* is a best-selling textbook is because instructors can trust the flexibility in key topical coverage, the simplified explanations of complex topics, and end-of-chapter material that relates directly to the chapter's text and engages the students with concepts and decision making using details from the chapter. Eighty percent of the end-of-chapter material throughout the sixth edition has been thoroughly revised with new companies and numerical data. Previous users will find familiar problem structures, making transition into this edition easier.

Chapter 1

- Shortened and simplified "Correcting Maxidrive's Statements" section.
- Updated material on Corporate Governance and IFRS.
- New demonstration case based on Apple Computer.
- Simplified cash flow self-study quiz.
- Substantial revision of end-of-chapter material: new numerical data for 75 percent of mini-exercises, exercises, and problems; three new alternate problems; and all new annual report cases.

Chapter 2

- New simplified Exhibit 2.1.
- Additional account title simplification in the balance sheet.
- Modified International Perspective to introduce IFRS.
- Updated Financial Analysis and Ethics features.
- Modified transaction analysis illustration to be clearer and more systematic.
- Revised Exhibits 2.4, 2.5, and 2.6 for improved clarity.
- Added explanation boxes for analytical tools (journal entries and T-accounts).
- Modified solutions to self-study quizzes to be consistent with presentation of journal entries and equation effects.

- Substantial revision of end-of-chapter material: multiple choice section now includes three computational questions, new numerical data for 60 percent of mini-exercises, exercises, and problems and all new annual report cases.

Chapter 3

- Updated International Perspective with another focus on IFRS.
- Continued simplification of the account titles in financial statements.
- New exhibit on revenue recognition with clearer explanation to follow exhibit.
- New exhibit on expense matching with clearer explanation to follow exhibit.
- Updated Question of Ethics feature.
- Clearer exhibit on the transaction analysis model.
- Clarified discussion on preparing the financial statements and their relationships.
- Substantial revision of end-of-chapter material: three computational questions added to the multiple choice section; new numerical data for 65 percent of mini-exercises, exercises, and problems; and all new annual report cases.

Chapter 4

- Reorganized discussion of the adjustment process.

- New visuals for adjusting entries.
- Clarified and simplified illustration of the adjustment process.
- Modified self-study quiz on adjusting entries.
- Substantial revision of end-of-chapter material: three computational questions added to the multiple choice section; new numerical data for 75 percent of mini-exercises, exercises, and problems; and all new annual report cases.

Chapter 5

- Updated focus and comparison companies.
- New graphic reflecting changes in accounting regulation.
- Updated coverage of the effects of accounting restatements and fraud on accountants, company management, and investors.
- Updated coverage of the importance of international accounting standards.
- New Financial Analysis feature on stock market reaction to earnings announcements.
- New exhibit illustrating information on reuters.com.
- New ROE Self-Study Quiz based on Apple Computer and HP.
- Updated Microsoft Demonstration Case.
- Updated discussion and illustration of nonrecurring items.

- Substantial revision of end-of-chapter material: three computational questions added to the multiple choice section; new numerical data for 60 percent of mini-exercises, exercises, and problems; and all new annual report cases.

Chapter 6

- Updated focus and comparison companies.
- Revised example of aging of accounts receivable.
- Updated coverage of electronic cash transactions.
- Substantial revision of end-of-chapter material: three computational questions added to the multiple choice section; new numerical data for 75 percent of mini-exercises, exercises, and problems; and all new annual report cases.

Chapter 7

- Updated focus and comparison companies.
- Modified inventory graphics illustrating cost flow assumptions.
- Substantial revision of end-of-chapter material: three computational questions added to the multiple choice section; new numerical data for 75 percent of mini-exercises, exercises, and problems; and all new annual report cases.

What's New?

Chapter 8

- New focus company— Southwest Airlines replaces Delta Airlines— and comparison companies.
- New International Perspective feature on IFRS.
- Updated financial disclosure examples.
- Substantial revision of end-of-chapter material: three computational questions added to the multiple choice section; new numerical data for 75 percent of mini-exercises, exercises, and problems; and all new annual report cases.

Chapter 9

- New comparison companies.
- Expanded discussion of lease liabilities.
- Updated focus company information.
- Addition of fractional year interest.
- Addition of demonstration case.
- Substantial revision of end-of-chapter material: three computational questions added to the multiple choice section; new numerical data for 80 percent of mini-exercises, exercises, and problems; and all new annual report cases.

Chapter 10

- Updated information for focus company.
- Inclusion of fractional year interest.
- Substantial revision of end-of-chapter material: three computational questions added to the multiple choice section; new numerical data for 75 percent of mini-exercises, exercises, and problems; and all new annual report cases.

Chapter 11

- New focus company— Sonic Drive-In Restaurant replaces Outback Steakhouse—and comparison companies.
- Elimination of actual statement of stockholders' equity due to increasing complexity of the statement.
- Elimination of discussion of restriction on retained earnings.
- Substantial revision of end-of-chapter material: three computational questions added to the multiple choice section; new numerical data for 75 percent of mini-exercises, exercises, and problems; and all new annual report cases.

Chapter 12

- New focus company— Washington Post Companies replaces Dow Jones—and comparison companies.
- New financial analysis feature on fair value for investments.
- Substantial revision of end-of-chapter material: three computational questions added to the multiple choice section; new numerical data for 75 percent of mini-exercises, exercises, and problems; and all new annual report cases.

Chapter 13

- Updated focus and comparison companies.
- Transfer of coverage of gains and losses on sale of property, plant and equipment from an end of chapter supplement to the chapter itself.
- Transfer of detailed discussion of preparation of the direct method operating activities section to end of chapter supplement.
- Addition of new exhibit at the end of the chapter summarizing the preparation process (indirect method).

- Substantial revision of end-of-chapter material: three computational questions added to the multiple choice section; new numerical data for 75 percent of mini-exercises, exercises, and problems; additional exercise, problem, and alternate problem involving preparation of complete cash flow statement; and all new annual report cases.

Chapter 14

- Revised financial analysis for Home Depot and Lowe's.
- Updated comparison companies and financial examples.
- Substantial revision of end-of-chapter material: three computational questions added to the multiple choice section; new numerical data for 75 percent of mini-exercises, exercises, and problems; and all new annual report cases.

A proven approach to

Faculty agree the accounting cycle is the most critical concept to learn and master for students studying financial accounting. The Libby/Libby/Short authors agree the accounting cycle is a critical concept. They believe students struggle with the accounting cycle when transaction analysis is covered in one chapter. If students are exposed to the accounting equation, journal entries, and T-accounts for both balance sheet and income statement accounts in a single chapter, many are left behind and are unable to grasp material in the next chapter which covers adjustments and financial statement preparation.

The market-leading Libby/Libby/Short approach covers transaction analysis over two chapters so that students have the time to master the material. In Chapter 2 of *Financial Accounting,* students are exposed to the accounting equation and transaction analysis for investing and financing transactions that only affect balance sheet accounts. This provides students with the opportunity to learn the basic structure and tools used in accounting in a simpler setting. In Chapter 3, students are exposed to more complex operating transactions that also affect income statement accounts. As a result of this slower building-block approach to transaction analysis, students are better prepared and ready to learn adjustments, financial statement preparation, and more advanced topics. After the students have developed an understanding of the complete accounting cycle and the resulting statements, Chapter 5 takes students through the corporate reporting and analysis process.

The graphic below shows a detailed comparison of the Libby/Libby/Short approach to the accounting cycle chapters compared to the approach taken by other market-leading financial accounting text books.

Accounting Cycle

Start Early	Compress Coverage	Extend Coverage (Libby/Libby/Short approach)
Overview of F/S & Users, B/S and I/S Transactions with Accounting Equation	Overview of F/S & Users	Overview of F/S & Users
	F/S, Ratios, & Conceptual Framework	B/S Transactions with Accounting Equation, Journal Entries & T-accounts
B/S and I/S Transactions with Journal Entries & T-accounts	B/S and I/S Transactions with Accounting Equation, Journal Entries & T-accounts	B/S and I/S Transactions with Accounting Equation, Journal Entries & T-accounts
Adjustments, Closing Entries, F/S Preparation	Adjustments, Closing Entries, F/S Preparation	Adjustments, Closing Entries, F/S Preparation

transaction analysis
and the accounting cycle

The Libby/Libby/Short approach is **better** because ... of the course.
transaction analysis, which is the foundation for ...
students more time to master

... overwhelmed.

- Students have more time to practice and fe... transactions in Chapter 2 before they
- Allows students to develop comfort with si... 3.
  move onto more complex transactions in ... ablishing and then operating a business
- It's intuitive and matches the sequence ... practice where it is needed.
- Builds on itself which allows more ti...

"Solid presentation of t-ac... *ts. Good that you use the same* ... *format so students can see the*
transactions in general j... *the transactions shown and that they*
transactions both ways.... *the Papa John's case."*
reflect what is occurri... *n University*
Phil Lewis, Eastern Mi...

"A fairly thorough ... erview of the adjusting and closing
processes ... Th... ook provides a nice linkage between the
closing process... the preparation of the financial statements."
Peter Woodlock ... ngstown State University

"The adjust ... entry process is clearly presented, which makes it
easier for ... students to grasp the concepts."
Rada Bro... University of California at Berkeley

"The u... of parenthesis in each journal entry is an excellent
appro... h... Very useful for engaging non-accounting majors."
Mich... Ulinski, Pace University

...ke the fact that when preparing adjusting entries that students
...ve to calculate.... It is important for students to have to think
...hrough this process—which doesn't occur when the amount is
provided."
Brian Nagel, Duquesne University

Inside the Textbook:

Financial Accounting, 6e, offers a host of pedagogical tools... implement the different ways you like to teach and the ways your students like to learn. Some offer i... plex subject; others highlight issues relevant to what your st... tion and tips that help you present a com-way, *Financial Accounting*'s pedagogical support will make a re... ead online or see on television. Either learning. ... ence in your course and in your students' learning.

Stock Market Reactions to Accounting Announcements

FINANCIAL ANALYSIS

Stock market analysts and investors use accounting information to make their investment decisions. Thus, the stock market, which is based on investors' expectations about a company's future performance, often reacts negatively when a company does not meet previously specified operating targets.

A net loss does not have to occur for a company to recognize that it is experiencing difficulty. Any unexpected variance in actual performance from the operating plan, such as lower than expected quarterly earnings or sales revenue needs to be explained. On November 2, 2006, Papa John's announced its third quarter results, reporting that comparable store sales in the last month of the quarter were down 0.6% at the company stores and down 2.2% at franchised stores. The October 2006 same-store sales decrease was the first negative monthly comparison in 22 months. On October 30, 2006, Papa John's stock had been selling at $37.79 per share. By November 3, 2006, the price dropped by $6.84 to $30.95 per share, an 18.1 percent decrease.*

...nancial Analysis

...e features tie important chapter
...ts to real-world decision-making
...vie.s. They also highlight alternative
and ...ts and add to the critical thinking
...on-making focus of the text.

Self-Study Quiz

Research shows that students learn best when they are actively engaged in the learning process. This active learning feature engages the student, provides interactivity, and promotes efficient learning. These quizzes ask students to pause at strategic points throughout each chapter to ensure they understand key points before moving ahead.

SELF-STUDY **QUIZ**

This self-study quiz allows you to practice a... counting. We recommend that you refer back ...he revenue principle under accrual ac-sented earlier as you answer each question. Our **revenue recognition criteria** pre-apply the principle. The following transactions a...his quiz now to make sure you can tivities of Papa John's (dollars in thousands). If re...s of typical monthly operating ac-dicate the title of the revenue account and the am...to be recognized in **January,** in-should refer to the Papa John's income statement pre...revenue to be recognized. You ... Exhibit 3.1 for account titles.

ACTIVITY	REVENUE ACCOUNT TITLE	AMOUNT OF REVENUE RECOGNIZED IN JANUARY
(a) In January, Papa John's company-owned restaurants sold food to customers for $32,000 cash.		

INTERNATIONAL PERSPECTIVE

The International Accounting Standards Board and Global Convergence of Accounting Standards

IFRS

Financial accounting standards and disclosure requirements are set by national regulatory agencies and standard-setting bodies. However, since 2002, there has been substantial movement to develop international financial reporting standards (IFRS) by the International Accounting Standards Board (IASB). The current status of these standards is as follows.

Example countries requiring use of IFRS (currently or by 2011):

- **European Union (United Kingdom, Germany, France, Netherlands, Belgium, Bulgaria, Poland, etc.)**
- **Australia and New Zealand**
- **India, Hong Kong, and South Korea**
- **Turkey**
- **Brazil and Chile**

REAL WORLD EXCERPT
Deloitte IAS Plus
Website

International Perspec...ve

These features **highlight the emergen...f global accounting standards (IFRS)** at... level appropriate for the introductory stud...

A Complete Learning System

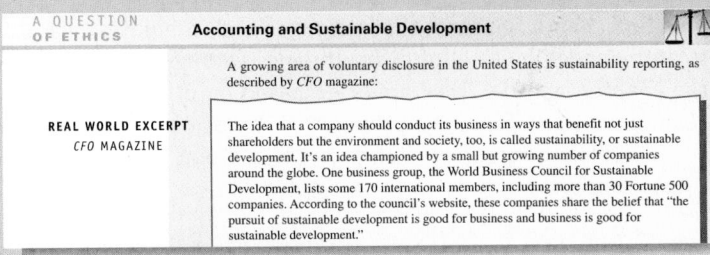

A Question of Ethics

These boxes appear throughout the text, **conveying the importance and consequences of acting responsibly in business practice.**

Key Ratio Analysis

Students will be better prepared to use financial information if they learn to evaluate elements of financial performance as they learn how to measure and report them. For this reason we include relevant key ratios in each chapter in Key Ratio Analysis sections. Each Key Ratio Analysis box presents ratio analysis for the focus company in the chapter as well as for comparative companies. Cautions are also provided to help students understand the limitations of certain ratios.

Focus on Cash Flows

The early and consistent coverage of cash flows encourages students to think more critically about the decisions they will face as managers and the impact those decisions will have on the company's cash flow. Each of the first 12 chapters includes a discussion and analysis of changes in the cash flow of the focus company and explores the decisions that caused those changes.

ALL JOURNAL ENTRIES TIED TO THE ACCOUNTING EQUATION

Journal entries marked with (A), (L), (SE), (R), (E), or (X, if a contra-account) and plus and minus signs in early chapters assist students in transaction analysis. In addition, following each journal entry is a summary of the effects of the transaction on the fundamental accounting equation.

Practice Is Key to Success

Each chapter is followed by an extensive set of end-of-chapter material that examines and integrates concepts presented in the chapter. Assignments are arranged by level of difficulty and learning objectives. To maintain the real-world emphasis of the chapter material, they are often based on other **real domestic and international companies,** and require analysis, conceptual thought, calculation, and written communication. Assignments suitable for individual or group written projects and oral presentations are included in the Cases and Projects section.

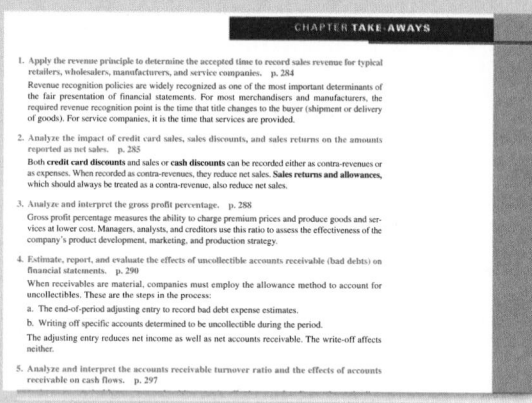

Chapter Take-Aways

Bulleted end-of-chapter summaries complement the learning objectives outlined at the beginning of the chapter.

Key Ratios

Summary of the key ratios presented in the chapter.

Finding Financial Information

Graphic that highlights the chapter's key concepts, numbers, and totals in an easy-to-review graphic; includes balance sheet, income statement, statement of cash flows, and note information.

Key Terms

Page referenced to the chapter text.

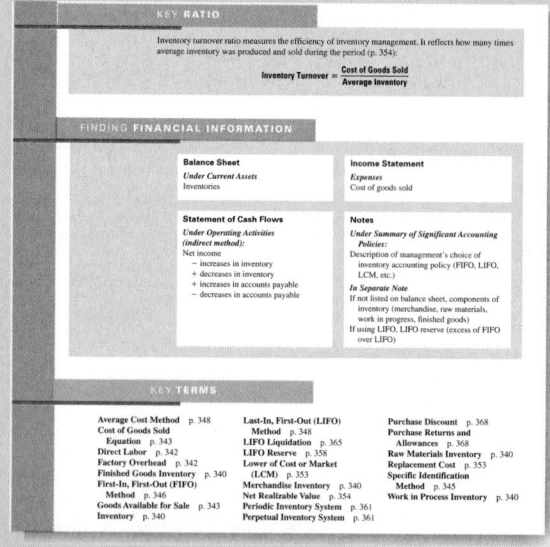

in Financial Accounting

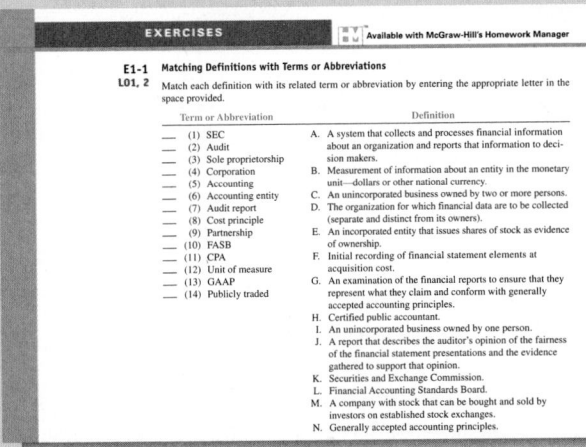

Questions
Multiple Choice
Mini-Exercises
Exercises

Problems

Cross-referenced in blue to the Alternative Problems.

Alternative Problems

Similar in level and content to the end of chapter problems.

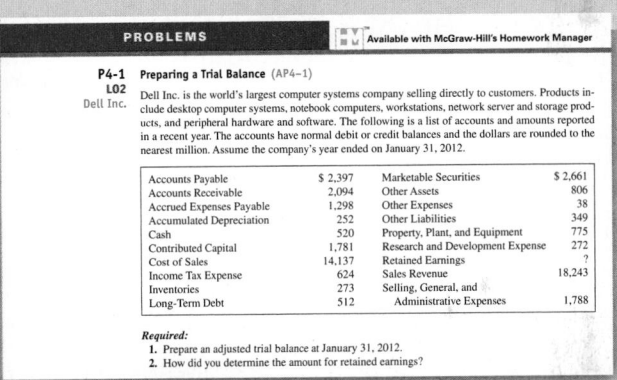

Cases and Projects

Includes Annual Report Cases, Financial Reporting and Analysis Cases, Critical Thinking Cases, and Financial Reporting and Analysis Team Projects

Beyond the Textbook:

Libby/Libby/Short's *Financial Accounting,* 6e, offers a **Digital Learning System** that goes beyond the textbook to give students the extra help they need while providing instructors with tools for teaching a stimulating and rewarding class. The following tools are tied directly to the textbook and help to maximize study time and make learning more enjoyable:

Photo Courtesy of Apple.®

iPod Downloadable Content

You are holding a *media-integrated textbook* that provides students with portable educational content—just right for those students who want to study when and where it's most convenient for them. *Financial Accounting,* 6e, gives students the option to download content for review and study to their Apple® iPods and most other MP3/MP4 devices. iPod icons appear throughout the text pointing students to chapter-specific quizzes, audio and video lecture presentation slides, and course-related videos.

Quick reference to iPod icons

Lectured slideshow–LP1-1
www.mhhe.com/libby6e

Lecture Presentations available for download to your **iPod, Zune, or MP3 device** (audio and visual depending on your device).

Video 2-1
www.mhhe.com/libby6e

Topical videos available for download to your **iPod, Zune, or MP3** (depending on your device).

Audio lecture–AP3-1
www.mhhe.com/libby6e

Audio lecture presentations available for download to your **iPod, Zune, or MP3** device (audio and visual depending on your device).

A Digital Learning System

ONLINE LEARNING CENTER
www.mhhe.com/libby6e

For instructors, *Financial Accounting*'s Online Learning Center includes the Instructor's Resource Manual, PowerPoint slides, Solutions Manual, and Excel Template solutions tied to the end-of-chapter material. There are also links to professional resources.

For students and instructors, the OLC includes American Eagle Outfitters annual report and Urban Outfitters Form 10-K linked to the text material, check figures, Web links, and McGraw-Hill's Homework Manager (see below). Instructors can pull all of this material as part of another online course management system.

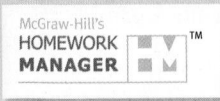

MCGRAW-HILL'S HOMEWORK MANAGER

ISBN 0073324825

McGraw-Hill's Homework Manager System is a Web-enhanced study tool that duplicates problem structures directly from the end-of-chapter material in *Financial Accounting,* 6e, using algorithms to provide a limitless supply of online self-graded practice for students, or assignments and tests with unique versions of every problem. Say goodbye to cheating in your classroom; say hello to the power and flexibility you've been waiting for in creating assignments.

McGraw-Hill's Homework Manager is also a useful grading tool. All assignments can be delivered over the Web and are graded automatically, with the results stored in your private gradebook. Detailed results let you see at a glance how each student does on an assignment or an individual problem—even to how many tries were required to solve it.

Learn more about McGraw-Hill's Homework Manager by referring to the front cover insert.

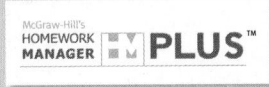

MCGRAW-HILL'S HOMEWORK MANAGER PLUS

ISBN 0073324833

McGraw-Hill's Homework Manager Plus gathers all of *Financial Accounting*'s online student resources under one convenient access point. Combining the power and flexibility of McGraw-Hill's Homework Manager with other proven technology tools, McGraw-Hill's Homework Manager Plus provides the best value available for the student eager to embrace the full benefits of online study and review.

In addition to McGraw-Hill's Homework Manager Plus, students may also access:

Interactive Online Version of the Textbook
In addition to the textbook, students can rely on this online version of the text for a convenient way to study. This interactive Web-based textbook contains hotlinks to key definitions and real company websites and is integrated with Homework Manager to give students quick access to relevant content as they work through problems, exercises, and practice quizzes.

Digital Learning System

ALEKS® ALEKS®

ALEKS (Assessment and LEarning in Knowledge Spaces) delivers precise, qualitative diagnostic assessments of students' knowledge, guides them in the selection of appropriate new study material, and records their progress toward mastery of curricular goals in a robust classroom management system.

ALEKS interacts with the student much as a skilled human tutor would, moving between explanation and practice as needed, correcting and analyzing errors, defining terms and changing topics on request. By sophisticated modeling of a student's knowledge state for a given subject, ALEKS can focus clearly on what the student is most ready to learn next. When students focus on exactly what they are ready to learn, they build confidence and a learning momentum that fuels success.

ALEKS Math Prep for Accounting provides coverage of the basic math skills needed to succeed in introductory financial accounting, while ALEKS for the Accounting Cycle provides a detailed, guided overview through every stage of the accounting cycle.

For more information, visit the ALEKS website at **www.business.aleks.com.**

CourseSmart

Learn Smart. Choose Smart.

CourseSmart is a new way for faculty to find and review eTextbooks. It's also a great option for students who are interested in accessing their course materials digitally and saving money.

CourseSmart offers thousands of the most commonly adopted textbooks across hundreds of courses from a wide variety of higher education publishers. It is the only place for faculty to review and compare the full text of a textbook online, providing immediate access without the environmental impact of requesting a print exam copy.

With the CourseSmart eTextbook, students can save up to 45 percent off the cost of a print book, reduce their impact on the environment, and access powerful Web tools for learning. CourseSmart is an online eTextbook, which means users access and view their textbook online when connected to the Internet. Students can also print sections of the book for maximum portability. CourseSmart eTextbooks are available in one standard online reader with full text search, notes and highlighting, and e-mail tools for sharing notes between classmates.

http://www.coursesmart.com

CONTENTS

Chapter One

Financial Statements and Business Decisions   2

Maxidrive Corporation   3
Understanding the Business   3
The Players   3
The Business Operations   4
The Accounting System   4
**The Four Basic Financial Statements:
An Overview   6**
The Balance Sheet   7

>   FINANCIAL ANALYSIS:
>   *Interpreting Assets, Liabilities, and Stockholders' Equity
>   on the Balance Sheet   9*
>
>   ■ Self-Study Quiz   10

The Income Statement   10

>   ■ Self-Study Quiz   12
>
>   FINANCIAL ANALYSIS:
>   *Analyzing the Income Statement: Beyond the
>   Bottom Line   13*

Statement of Retained Earnings   13

>   FINANCIAL ANALYSIS:
>   *Interpreting Retained Earnings   14*
>
>   ■ Self-Study Quiz   14

Statement of Cash Flows   14

>   FINANCIAL ANALYSIS:
>   *Interpreting the Cash Flow Statement   16*
>
>   ■ Self-Study Quiz   16

Relationships Among the Statements   17
Notes   17

>   FINANCIAL ANALYSIS:
>   *Management Uses of Financial Statements   18*

Summary of the Four Basic Financial Statements   18
**Responsibilities for the Accounting Communication
Process   18**
Generally Accepted Accounting Principles   19

>   INTERNATIONAL PERSPECTIVE:
>   *The International Accounting Standards Board and Global
>   Accounting Standards   20*

Management Responsibility and the Demand
for Auditing   21

>   FINANCIAL ANALYSIS:
>   *Using Financial Statements to Determine
>   Maxidrive's Value   22*

Ethics, Reputation, and Legal Liability   23
Epilogue   23

>   *DEMONSTRATION CASE   24*
>
>   CHAPTER SUPPLEMENT A: TYPES OF BUSINESS
>   ENTITIES   26
>
>   CHAPTER SUPPLEMENT B: EMPLOYMENT IN THE
>   ACCOUNTING PROFESSION TODAY   26
>
>   *Chapter Take-Aways   28*
>
>   *Finding Financial Information   28*
>
>   *Key Terms   29*
>
>   *Questions   29*
>
>   *Multiple-Choice Questions   30*
>
>   *Mini-Exercises   31*
>
>   *Exercises   32*
>
>   *Problems   37*
>
>   *Alternate Problems   40*
>
>   *Cases and Projects   41*
>
>>   *Annual Report Cases   41*
>>
>>   *Financial Reporting and Analysis Cases   42*
>>
>>   *Critical Thinking Cases   43*
>>
>>   *Financial Reporting and Analysis Team Project   44*

Chapter Two

Investing and Financing Decisions and the Balance Sheet   46

Papa John's International   47

Understanding the Business   48
Overview of Accounting Concepts   49
Concepts Emphasized in Chapter 2   49
Elements of the Balance Sheet   50

>   FINANCIAL ANALYSIS:
>   *Unrecorded But Valuable Assets   52*
>
>   A QUESTION OF ETHICS:
>   *Environmental Liabilities: The "Greening of GAAP"   52*

■ Self-Study Quiz   53

What Business Activities Cause Changes in Financial Statement Amounts?   53

Nature of Business Transactions   53

Accounts   54

INTERNATIONAL PERSPECTIVE:

Understanding Foreign Financial Statements   55

How Do Transactions Affect Accounts?   55

Principles of Transaction Analysis   55

Analyzing Papa John's Transactions   57

■ Self-Study Quiz   59

How Do Companies Keep Track of Account Balances?   60

The Direction of Transaction Effects   61

Analytical Tools   62

Transaction Analysis Illustrated   64

■ Self-Study Quiz   66

FINANCIAL ANALYSIS:

Inferring Business Activities from T-Accounts   68

How Is the Balance Sheet Prepared and Analyzed?   68

Classified Balance Sheet   68

KEY RATIO ANALYSIS:

Financial Leverage Ratio   70

■ Self-Study Quiz   72

FOCUS ON CASH FLOWS:

Investing and Financing Activities   72

■ Self-Study Quiz   73

DEMONSTRATION CASE   73

Chapter Take-Aways   77

Key Ratio   79

Finding Financial Information   79

Key Terms   79

Questions   80

Multiple-Choice Questions   80

Mini-Exercises   81

Exercises   84

Problems   91

Alternate Problems   94

Cases and Projects   96

Annual Report Cases   96

Financial Reporting and Analysis Cases   97

Critical Thinking Cases   100

Financial Reporting and Analysis Team Project   101

Chapter Three

Operating Decisions and the Income Statement   102

Papa John's International   103

Understanding the Business   104

How Do Business Activities Affect the Income Statement?   105

The Operating Cycle   105

Elements on the Income Statement   106

INTERNATIONAL PERSPECTIVE:

Differences in Accounts in Foreign Financial Statements   109

How Are Operating Activities Recognized and Measured?   110

Accrual Accounting   110

REAL WORLD EXCERPT:

2. Significant Accounting Policies   111

■ Self-Study Quiz   112

A QUESTION OF ETHICS:

Management's Incentives to Violate Accounting Rules   112

■ Self-Study Quiz   114

FINANCIAL ANALYSIS:

Stock Market Reactions to Accounting Announcements   115

The Expanded Transaction Analysis Model   116

Transaction Analysis Rules   116

Analyzing Papa John's Transactions   117

■ Self-Study Quiz   119

How Are Financial Statements Prepared and Analyzed?   122

Classified Income Statement   123

FINANCIAL ANALYSIS:

Reporting More Detailed Financial Information in the Notes   123

Statement of Retained Earnings   124

Classified Balance Sheet   124

FOCUS ON CASH FLOWS:

Operating Activities   125

KEY RATIO ANALYSIS:

Total Asset Turnover Ratio   126

DEMONSTRATION CASE

Chapter Take-Aways   133

Key Ratio   134

Finding Financial Information   134

Key Terms 135

Questions 135

Multiple-Choice Questions 136

Mini-Exercises 137

Exercises 140

Problems 149

Alternate Problems 153

Cases and Projects 156

   Annual Report Cases 156

   Financial Reporting and Analysis Cases 157

   Critical Thinking Cases 159

   Financial Reporting and Analysis Team Project 160

Chapter Four

Adjustments, Financial Statements, and the Quality of Earnings 162

Papa John's International   163

Understanding the Business   164

Adjusting Revenues and Expenses   165

Accounting Cycle   165

Purpose and Types of Adjustments   165

Adjustment Process   167

   ■ Self-Study Quiz   174

   A QUESTION OF ETHICS:

   Adjustments and Incentives   175

Preparing Financial Statements   175

Income Statement   177

Statement of Stockholders' Equity   179

Balance Sheet   179

   FOCUS ON CASH FLOWS:

   Disclosure   179

   FINANCIAL ANALYSIS:

   Cash Flows from Operations, Net Income, and the Quality of Earnings   181

   KEY RATIO ANALYSIS:

   Net Profit Margin   181

Closing the Books   182

End of the Accounting Cycle   182

Post-Closing Trial Balance   184

   FINANCIAL ANALYSIS:

   Accruals and Deferrals: Judging Earnings Quality   186

   DEMONSTRATION CASE   186

   Chapter Take-Aways   193

Key Ratio 194

Finding Financial Information 195

Key Terms 195

Questions 195

Multiple-Choice Questions 196

Mini-Exercises 197

Exercises 200

Problems 210

Alternate Problems 215

Cases and Projects 221

   Annual Report Cases 221

   Financial Reporting and Analysis Cases 222

   Critical Thinking Cases 226

   Financial Reporting and Analysis Team Project 228

Chapter Five

Communicating and Interpreting Accounting Information 230

Callaway Golf   231

Understanding the Business   232

Players in the Accounting Communication Process   233

Regulators (SEC, FASB, PCAOB, Stock Exchanges)   233

Managers (CEO, CFO, and Accounting Staff)   234

Board of Directors (Audit Committee)   235

Auditors   235

Information Intermediaries: Financial Analysts and Information Services   235

   FINANCIAL ANALYSIS:

   Information Services and Job Searches   237

Users: Institutional and Private Investors, Creditors, and Others   238

Guiding Principles for Communicating Useful Information   239

   INTERNATIONAL PERSPECTIVE:

   International Accounting Standards Board and Global Differences in Accounting Standards   239

   ■ Self-Study Quiz   240

The Disclosure Process   240

Press Releases   240

   FINANCIAL ANALYSIS:

   How Does the Stock Market React to Earnings Announcements?   241

Annual Reports   242

Quarterly Reports 242

SEC Reports—10-K, 10-Q, 8-K 243

A Closer Look at Financial Statement Formats and Notes 243

Classified Balance Sheet 243

Classified Income Statement 245

> **FINANCIAL ANALYSIS:**
>
> *Interpreting the Common-Size Income Statement 247*
>
> ■ Self-Study Quiz 247

Statement of Stockholders' Equity 248

Statement of Cash Flows 248

Notes to Financial Statements 248

> **FOCUS ON CASH FLOWS:**
>
> *Operating Activities (Indirect Method) 248*

> **FINANCIAL ANALYSIS:**
>
> *Alternative Accounting Methods and GAAP 250*

Voluntary Disclosures 252

> **A QUESTION OF ETHICS:**
>
> *Accounting and Sustainable Development 252*

Return on Equity Analysis: A Framework for Evaluating Company Performance 252

> **KEY RATIO ANALYSIS:**
>
> *Return on Equity 253*

ROE Profit Driver Analysis 253

Profit Drivers and Business Strategy 254

> ■ Self-Study Quiz 255

Epilogue 256

> ***DEMONSTRATION CASE 256***
>
> **CHAPTER SUPPLEMENT: NONRECURRING ITEMS 258**
>
> *Chapter Take-Aways 259*
>
> *Key Ratio 259*
>
> *Finding Financial Information 260*
>
> *Key Terms 260*
>
> *Questions 260*
>
> *Multiple-Choice Questions 261*
>
> *Mini-Exercises 262*
>
> *Exercises 263*
>
> *Problems 268*
>
> *Alternate Problems 274*
>
> *Cases and Projects 276*
>
>> *Annual Report Cases 276*
>>
>> *Financial Reporting and Analysis Cases 277*
>>
>> *Critical Thinking Cases 278*
>>
>> *Financial Reporting and Analysis Team Project 280*

Chapter Six

Reporting and Interpreting Sales Revenue, Receivables, and Cash 282

Deckers Outdoor Corporation 283

Understanding the Business 283

Accounting for Sales Revenue 284

Credit Card Sales to Consumers 285

Sales Discounts to Businesses 286

> **FINANCIAL ANALYSIS:**
>
> *To Take or Not to Take the Discount, That Is the Question 287*

Sales Returns and Allowances 287

Reporting Net Sales 288

> **KEY RATIO ANALYSIS:**
>
> *Gross Profit Percentage 288*
>
> ■ Self-Study Quiz 289

Measuring and Reporting Receivables 290

Classifying Receivables 290

Accounting for Bad Debts 290

Reporting Accounts Receivable and Bad Debts 292

Estimating Bad Debts 293

> ■ Self-Study Quiz 294

Control Over Accounts Receivable 296

> **KEY RATIO ANALYSIS:**
>
> *Receivables Turnover 297*

> **FOCUS ON CASH FLOWS:**
>
> *Accounts Receivable 298*
>
> ■ Self-Study Quiz 298

Reporting and Safeguarding Cash 299

Cash and Cash Equivalents Defined 299

Cash Management 300

Internal Control of Cash 300

> **A QUESTION OF ETHICS:**
>
> *Ethics and the Need for Internal Control 301*

Reconciliation of the Cash Accounts and the Bank Statements 301

> ■ Self-Study Quiz 305

Epilogue 305

> ***DEMONSTRATION CASE A 306***
>
> ***DEMONSTRATION CASE B 307***
>
> **CHAPTER SUPPLEMENT A: RECORDING DISCOUNTS AND RETURNS 308**
>
> **CHAPTER SUPPLEMENT B: APPLYING THE REVENUE PRINCIPLE IN SPECIAL CIRCUMSTANCES 309**
>
> *Chapter Take-Aways 309*

Key Ratios   310

Finding Financial Information   310

Key Terms   310

Questions   311

Multiple-Choice Questions   311

Mini-Exercises   312

Exercises   314

Problems   322

Alternate Problems   327

Cases and Projects   331

　Annual Report Cases   331

　Financial Reporting and Analysis Cases   332

　Critical Thinking Cases   332

　Financial Reporting and Analysis Team Project   334

Chapter Seven

Reporting and Interpreting Cost of Goods Sold and Inventory   336

Harley-Davidson, Inc.   337

Understanding the Business   337
Nature of Inventory and Cost of Goods Sold   340
Items Included in Inventory   340
Costs Included in Inventory Purchases   341

FINANCIAL ANALYSIS:
Applying the Materiality Constraint in Practice   341

Flow of Inventory Costs   341

FINANCIAL ANALYSIS:
Modern Manufacturing Techniques and Inventory Costs   343

Nature of Cost of Goods Sold   343

■ Self-Study Quiz   344

Inventory Costing Methods   345
Specific Identification Method   345
Cost Flow Assumptions   346
Financial Statement Effects of Inventory Methods   349
Managers' Choice of Inventory Methods   350

A QUESTION OF ETHICS:
LIFO and Conflicts between Managers' and Owners' Interests   351

■ Self-Study Quiz   352

Valuation at Lower of Cost or Market   353
Evaluating Inventory Management   354
Measuring Efficiency in Inventory Management   354

KEY RATIO ANALYSIS:
Inventory Turnover   354

Inventory and Cash Flows   355

FOCUS ON CASH FLOWS:
Inventory   356

■ Self-Study Quiz   357

Inventory Methods and Financial Statement Analysis   358

FINANCIAL ANALYSIS:
LIFO and Inventory Turnover Ratio   359

INTERNATIONAL PERSPECTIVE
LIFO and International Comparisons   360

■ Self-Study Quiz   360

Control of Inventory   361
Internal Control of Inventory   361
Perpetual and Periodic Inventory Systems   361
Errors in Measuring Ending Inventory   362

■ Self-Study Quiz   363

DEMONSTRATION CASE   364

CHAPTER SUPPLEMENT A: LIFO LIQUIDATIONS   365

FINANCIAL ANALYSIS:
Inventory Management and LIFO Liquidations   367

CHAPTER SUPPLEMENT B: ADDITIONAL ISSUES IN MEASURING PURCHASES   368

CHAPTER SUPPLEMENT C: COMPARISON OF PERPETUAL AND PERIODIC INVENTORY SYSTEMS   369

Chapter Take-Aways   370
Key Ratio   372
Finding Financial Information   372
Key Terms   372
Questions   372
Multiple-Choice Questions   373
Mini-Exercises   374
Exercises   376
Problems   383
Alternate Problems   389
Cases and Projects   392
　Annual Report Cases   392
　Financial Reporting and Analysis Cases   392
　Critical Thinking Cases   393
　Financial Reporting and Analysis Team Project   394

Chapter Eight

Reporting and Interpreting Property, Plant, and Equipment; Natural Resources; and Intangibles   396

Southwest Airlines   397

Understanding the Business   397
Acquisition and Maintenance of Plant and Equipment   399
Classifying Long-Lived Assets   399

KEY RATIO ANALYSIS:

Fixed Asset Turnover   400

Measuring and Recording Acquisition Cost   401

■ Self-Study Quiz   404

Repairs, Maintenance, and Additions   404

FINANCIAL ANALYSIS:

WorldCom: Hiding Billions in Expenses through Capitalization   405

■ Self-Study Quiz   406

Use, Impairment, and Disposal of Plant and Equipment   406

Depreciation Concepts   406

FINANCIAL ANALYSIS:

Book Value as an Approximation of Remaining Life   408

FINANCIAL ANALYSIS:

Differences in Estimated Lives within a Single Industry   408

Alternative Depreciation Methods   409

FINANCIAL ANALYSIS:

Impact of Alternative Depreciation Methods   413

■ Self-Study Quiz   414

FINANCIAL ANALYSIS:

Increased Profitability Due to an Accounting Adjustment? Reading the Notes   414

How Managers Choose   414

A QUESTION OF ETHICS:

Two Sets of Books   416

Measuring Asset Impairment   416

Disposal of Property, Plant, and Equipment   417

■ Self-Study Quiz   418

INTERNATIONAL PERSPECTIVE:

Measurement Basis for Property, Plant, and Equipment   419

Natural Resources and Intangible Assets   419

Acquisition and Depletion of Natural Resources   419

Acquisition and Amortization of Intangible Assets   420

INTERNATIONAL PERSPECTIVE:

Standards in Process   423

FOCUS ON CASH FLOWS:

Productive Assets and Depreciation   423

FINANCIAL ANALYSIS:

A Misinterpretation   425

DEMONSTRATION CASE   425

CHAPTER SUPPLEMENT A: CHANGES IN DEPRECIATION ESTIMATES   428

■ Self-Study Quiz   429

Chapter Take-Aways   429

Key Ratio   430

Finding Financial Information   431

Key Terms   431

Questions   431

Multiple-Choice Questions   432

Mini-Exercises   433

Exercises   435

Problems   442

Alternate Problems   448

Cases and Projects   452

Annual Report Cases   452

Financial Reporting and Analysis Cases   453

Critical Thinking Cases   454

Financial Reporting and Analysis Team Project   456

Chapter Nine

Reporting and Interpreting Liabilities   458

Starbucks   459

Understanding the Business   459

Liabilities Defined and Classified   461

KEY RATIO ANALYSIS:

Current Ratio   462

Current Liabilities   462

Accounts Payable   463

KEY RATIO ANALYSIS:

Accounts Payable Turnover   464

Accrued Liabilities   464

Notes Payable   467

Current Portion of Long-Term Debt   468

FINANCIAL ANALYSIS:

Refinanced Debt: Current or Noncurrent?   468

Deferred Revenues   469

Estimated Liabilities Reported on the Balance Sheet   469

Estimated Liabilities Reported in the Notes   469

Working Capital Management   471

FOCUS ON CASH FLOWS:

Working Capital and Cash Flows   471

■ Self-Study Quiz   473

Long-Term Liabilities   473

Long-Term Notes Payable and Bonds   473

INTERNATIONAL PERSPECTIVE:

Borrowing in Foreign Currencies   474

Lease Liabilities 474

Present Value Concepts 475

Present Value of a Single Amount 476

■ Self-Study Quiz 477

Present Values of an Annuity 477

A QUESTION OF ETHICS

Truth in Advertising 478

Accounting Applications of Present Values 479

DEMONSTRATION CASE 481

CHAPTER SUPPLEMENT A: INCOME TAXES AND RETIREMENT BENEFITS 482

CHAPTER SUPPLEMENT B: FEDERAL INCOME TAX CONCEPTS 484

CHAPTER SUPPLEMENT C: PRESENT VALUE COMPUTATIONS USING EXCEL 486

CHAPTER SUPPLEMENT D 487

Chapter Take-Aways 489

Key Ratio 490

Finding Financial Information 491

Key Terms 491

Questions 491

Multiple-Choice Questions 492

Mini-Exercises 493

Exercises 495

Problems 501

Alternate Problems 506

Cases and Projects 509

Annual Report Cases 509

Financial Reporting and Analysis Cases 509

Critical Thinking Cases 510

Financial Reporting and Analysis Team Project 510

■ Self-Study Quiz 525
■ Self-Study Quiz 527

FINANCIAL ANALYSIS:

Zero Coupon Bonds 527

Bonds Issued at a Premium 528

■ Self-Study Quiz 530
■ Self-Study Quiz 531

KEY RATIO ANALYSIS:

Debt-to-Equity 531

Early Retirement of Debt 532

■ Self-Study Quiz 533

FOCUS ON CASH FLOWS:

Bonds Payable 533

DEMONSTRATION CASE 535

CHAPTER SUPPLEMENT A: BOND CALCULATIONS USING EXCEL 536

Chapter Take-Aways 538

Key Ratios 538

Finding Financial Information 539

Key Terms 539

Questions 540

Multiple-Choice Questions 540

Mini-Exercises 541

Exercises 542

Problems 547

Alternate Problems 552

Cases and Projects 554

Annual Report Cases 554

Critical Thinking Cases 555

Financial Reporting and Analysis Team Project 555

Chapter Ten

Reporting and Interpreting Bonds 512

Harrah's Entertainment, Inc. 513

Understanding the Business 513

Characteristics of Bonds Payable 515

FINANCIAL ANALYSIS:

Bond Information from the Business Press 518

Reporting Bond Transactions 518

■ Self-Study Quiz 520

Bonds Issued at Par 520

■ Self-Study Quiz 521

KEY RATIO ANALYSIS:

Times Interest Earned 522

Bonds Issued at a Discount 523

Chapter Eleven

Reporting and Interpreting Owners' Equity 556

Sonic Drive-In 557

Understanding the Business 557

Ownership of a Corporation 559

Benefits of Stock Ownership 559

Authorized, Issued, and Outstanding Shares 560

KEY RATIO ANALYSIS:

Earnings per Share (EPS) 562

Common Stock Transactions 563

Initial Sale of Stock 563

Sale of Stock in Secondary Markets 564

Stock Issued for Employee Compensation 564

Repurchase of Stock   564

■ Self-Study Quiz   566

Dividends on Common Stock   566

KEY RATIO ANALYSIS:

Dividend Yield   566

FINANCIAL ANALYSIS:

Impact of Dividends on Stock Price   568

■ Self-Study Quiz   569

Stock Dividends and Stock Splits   569

Stock Dividends   569

Stock Splits   570

■ Self-Study Quiz   571

Preferred Stock   571

Dividends on Preferred Stock   572

FINANCIAL ANALYSIS:

Restrictions on the Payment of Dividends   573

FOCUS ON CASH FLOWS:

Financing Activities   573

DEMONSTRATION CASE   574

CHAPTER SUPPLEMENT A: ACCOUNTING FOR OWNERS' EQUITY FOR SOLE PROPRIETORSHIPS AND PARTNERSHIPS   576

Chapter Take-Aways   579

Key Ratios   580

Finding Financial Information   581

Key Terms   581

Questions   581

Multiple-Choice Questions   582

Mini-Exercises   583

Exercises   584

Problems   592

Alternate Problems   597

Cases and Projects   598

  Annual Report Cases   598

  Financial Reporting and Analysis Cases   599

  Critical Thinking Cases   600

  Financial Reporting and Analysis Team Project   600

Chapter Twelve

Reporting and Interpreting Investments in Other Corporations   602

The Washington Post Company   603

Understanding the Business   603

Types of Investments and Accounting Methods   605

Passive Investments in Debt and Equity Securities   605

Investments in Stock for Significant Influence   605

Investments in Stock for Control   605

Debt Held to Maturity: Amortized Cost Method   606

Bond Purchases   606

Interest Earned   607

Principal at Maturity   607

Passive Stock Investments: Market Value Method   607

Classifying Passive Stock Investments   608

Securities Available for Sale   609

Comparing Trading and Available-for-Sale Securities   612

FINANCIAL ANALYSIS:

Passive Investments and the Fair Value Option   614

■ Self-Study Quiz   614

Investments for Significant Influence: Equity Method   615

Recording Investments under the Equity Method   616

Reporting Investments under the Equity Method   618

A QUESTION OF ETHICS

Improper Influence   618

■ Self-Study Quiz   619

FINANCIAL ANALYSIS:

Transaction Structuring: Selecting Accounting Methods for Minority Investments   620

FOCUS ON CASH FLOWS:

Investments   620

Controlling Interests: Mergers and Acquisitions   621

What Are Consolidated Statements?   622

Recording a Merger   622

Reporting a Merger   623

KEY RATIO ANALYSIS:

Return on Assets (ROA)   625

■ Self-Study Quiz   626

DEMONSTRATION CASE A   627

DEMONSTRATION CASE B   627

DEMONSTRATION CASE C   628

DEMONSTRATION CASE D   629

CHAPTER SUPPLEMENT A: PREPARING CONSOLIDATED STATEMENTS   629

DEMONSTRATION CASE E   632

Chapter Take-Aways   633

Key Ratio   634

Finding Financial Information 634

Key Terms 635

Questions 635

Multiple-Choice Questions 635

Mini-Exercises 637

Exercises 638

Problems 642

Alternate Problems 646

Cases and Projects 648

   Annual Report Cases 648

   Financial Reporting and Analysis Cases 649

   Critical Thinking Cases 650

   Financial Reporting and Analysis Team Project 650

Chapter Thirteen

Statement of Cash Flows   652

Boston Beer Company   653

Understanding the Company   653
**Classifications of the Statement of
Cash Flows   655**

Cash Flows from Operating Activities   655

Cash Flows from Investing Activities   657

Cash Flows from Financing Activities   657

Net Increase (Decrease) in Cash   657

   ■ Self-Study Quiz   658

Relationships to the Balance Sheet and income
Statement   658

**Reporting and Interpreting Cash Flows from
Operating Activities   661**

Reporting Cash Flows from Operating Activities—Indirect
Method   661

   INTERNATIONAL PERSPECTIVE:

   Foreign Currency and the Cash Flow Statement 665

   ■ Self-Study Quiz   666

Interpreting Cash Flows from Operating Activities   666

   KEY RATIO ANALYSIS:

   Quality of Income Ratio 667

   A QUESTION OF ETHICS

   Fraud and Cash Flows from Operations 668

**Reporting and Interpreting Cash Flows from
Investing Activities   668**

Reporting Cash Flows from Investing Activities   668

Interpreting Cash Flows from Investing Activities   670

   KEY RATIO ANALYSIS:

   Capital Acquisitions Ratio 670

   FINANCIAL ANALYSIS:

   Free Cash Flow 671

**Reporting and Interpreting Cash Flows from
Financing Activities   671**

Reporting Cash Flows from Financing Activities   671

Interpreting Cash Flows from Financing Activities   673

   ■ Self-Study Quiz   674

**Completing the Statement and Additional
Disclosures   674**

Statement Structure   674

Noncash Investing and Financing Activities   674

Supplemental Cash Flow Information   675

Epilogue   675

   DEMONSTRATION CASE   676

   **CHAPTER SUPPLEMENT A: REPORTING CASH FLOWS
   FROM OPERATING ACTIVITIES—DIRECT METHOD   677**

   **CHAPTER SUPPLEMENT B: SPREADSHEET
   APPROACH—STATEMENT OF CASH FLOWS: INDIRECT
   METHOD   681**

   Chapter Take-Aways 683

   Key Ratios 685

   Finding Financial Information 685

   Key Terms 685

   Questions 685

   Multiple-Choice Questions 686

   Mini-Exercises 687

   Exercises 688

   Problems 697

   Alternate Problems 700

   Cases and Projects 702

      Annual Report Cases 702

      Financial Reporting and Analysis Cases 702

      Critical Thinking Cases 704

      Financial Reporting and Analysis Team Project 705

Chapter Fourteen

Analyzing Financial Statements   706

Home Depot   707

Understanding the Business   707
The Investment Decision   712
Understanding a Company's Strategy   713
Financial Statement Analysis   714
Ratio and Percentage Analysis   716

Component Percentages   716

Tests of Profitability   718

   ■ Self-Study Quiz   723

Tests of Liquidity   723

   ■ Self-Study Quiz   727

Tests of Solvency   727

Market Tests   729

■ Self-Study Quiz   730

Interpreting Ratios and Other Analytical
Considerations   730

Other Financial Information   731

A QUESTION OF ETHICS

Insider Information   732

Information in an Efficient Market   733

Chapter Take-Aways   733

Finding Financial Information   734

Key Terms   734

Questions   735

Multiple-Choice Questions   735

Mini-Exercises   736

Exercises   737

Problems   742

Alternate Problems   748

Cases and Projects   753

Annual Report Cases   753

Financial Reporting and Analysis Cases   753

Critical Thinking Cases   754

Financial Reporting and Analysis Team Project   754

Appendix A:

Present and Future Value Tables   A–1

Appendix B:

**American Eagle Outfitters 2006 Annual
Report   B–1**

Appendix C:

**Urban Outfitters, Inc. Form 10-K
Report   C–1**

Appendix D:

Industry Ratio Report   D–1

Glossary   G–1

Credits   CR–1

Index   I–1

Financial Accounting

Lectured slideshow–LP1-1
www.mhhe.com/libby6e

LEARNING OBJECTIVES

After studying this chapter, you should be able to:

1. Recognize the information conveyed in each of the four basic financial statements and the way that it is used by different decision makers (investors, creditors, and managers). p. 5

2. Identify the role of generally accepted accounting principles (GAAP) in determining the content of financial statements. p. 18

3. Distinguish the roles of managers and auditors in the accounting communication process. p. 21

4. Appreciate the importance of ethics, reputation, and legal liability in accounting. p. 23

FINANCIAL STATEMENTS AND BUSINESS DECISIONS

I n January, Exeter Investors purchased Maxidrive Corp., a fast-growing manufacturer of personal computer disk drives, for $33 million. The price Exeter paid was determined by considering the value of Maxidrive's assets, its debts to others, its ability to sell goods for more than the cost to produce them, and its ability to generate the cash necessary to pay its current bills. Much of this assessment was based on financial information that Maxidrive provided to Exeter in the form of financial statements. By July, Exeter had discovered a variety of problems in the company's operations and its financial statements. Maxidrive appeared to be worth only about half of what Exeter had paid for the company. Furthermore, Maxidrive did not have enough cash to pay its debt to American Bank. Exeter Investors filed a lawsuit against the previous owners and others responsible for Maxidrive's financial statements to recover its losses.

FOCUS COMPANY:

Maxidrive Corporation

VALUING AN ACQUISITION USING FINANCIAL STATEMENT INFORMATION*

UNDERSTANDING THE BUSINESS

The Players

Maxidrive was founded by two engineers who had formerly worked for General Data, then a manufacturer of large computers. Predicting the rise in demand for personal computers with a hard disk drive, they started a company to manufacture this component. The founders invested a major portion of their savings, becoming the sole owners of Maxidrive. As is common in new businesses, the founders also functioned as managers of the business (they were **owner-managers**).

The founders soon discovered that they needed additional money to develop the business. Based on the recommendation of a close friend, they asked American Bank for a loan. American Bank continued to lend to Maxidrive as the need arose, becoming its

The Maxidrive case is a realistic representation of an actual case of fraud. No names in the case are real. The actual fraud is discussed in the epilogue to the chapter.

largest lender, or **creditor.** Early last year, one of the founders of the business became gravely ill. This event, plus the stresses of operating in their highly competitive industry, led the founders to search for a buyer for their company. In January of this year, they struck a deal for the sale of the company to Exeter Investors, a small group of wealthy private **investors.** Both founders retired and a new manager was hired to run Maxidrive for the new owners. The new **manager** worked on behalf of Exeter Investors, but was not an owner of the company.

Whether investors are groups such as Exeter who recently bought all of Maxidrive Corp. or individuals who buy small percentages of large corporations, they make their purchases hoping to gain in two ways. They hope to receive a portion of what the company earns in the form of cash payments called **dividends** and eventually sell their share of the company at a higher price than they paid. As the Maxidrive case suggests, not all companies increase in value or have sufficient cash to pay dividends. Creditors lend money to a company for a specific length of time. They hope to gain by charging interest on the money they lend. As American Bank, Maxidrive's major creditor, has learned, some borrowers cannot repay their debts. When Maxidrive borrows additional money or pays back money to its lenders and receives additional funds or pays dividends to owners, these are called **financing activities.** When Maxidrive buys or sells items such as plant and equipment used in producing disk drives, these are called **investing activities.**

The Business Operations

To understand any company's financial statements, you must first understand its **operating activities.** As noted, Maxidrive designs and manufactures hard disk drives for personal computers. The major parts that go into the drive include the disks on which information is stored, the motors that spin the disks, the heads that read and write to the disks, and the computer chips that control the operations of the drive. Maxidrive purchases the disks and motors from other companies, called **suppliers.** It designs and manufactures the heads and chips and then assembles the drives. Maxidrive does not sell disk drives directly to the public. Instead, its **customers** are computer manufacturers such as Dell Inc. and Apple Inc. which install the drives in machines they sell to retailers such as Best Buy and to consumers. Thus, Maxidrive is a supplier to Dell and Apple.

The Accounting System

Like all businesses, Maxidrive has an **accounting** system that collects and processes financial information about an organization and reports that information to decision makers. Maxidrive's managers (often called **internal decision makers**) and parties outside the firm such as Exeter Investors and American Bank (often called **external decision makers**) use the reports produced by this system. Exhibit 1.1 outlines the two parts of the accounting system. Internal managers typically require continuous, detailed information because they must plan and manage the day-to-day operations of the organization. Developing accounting information for internal decision makers, called **managerial** or **management accounting**, is the subject of a separate accounting course. The focus of this text is accounting for external decision makers, called **financial accounting,** and the four basic financial statements and related disclosures that are the output of that system.

We begin with a brief but comprehensive overview of the information reported in four basic financial statements and the people and organizations involved in their

ACCOUNTING is a system that collects and processes (analyzes, measures, and records) financial information about an organization and reports that information to decision makers.

EXHIBIT 1.1

The Accounting System
and Decision Makers

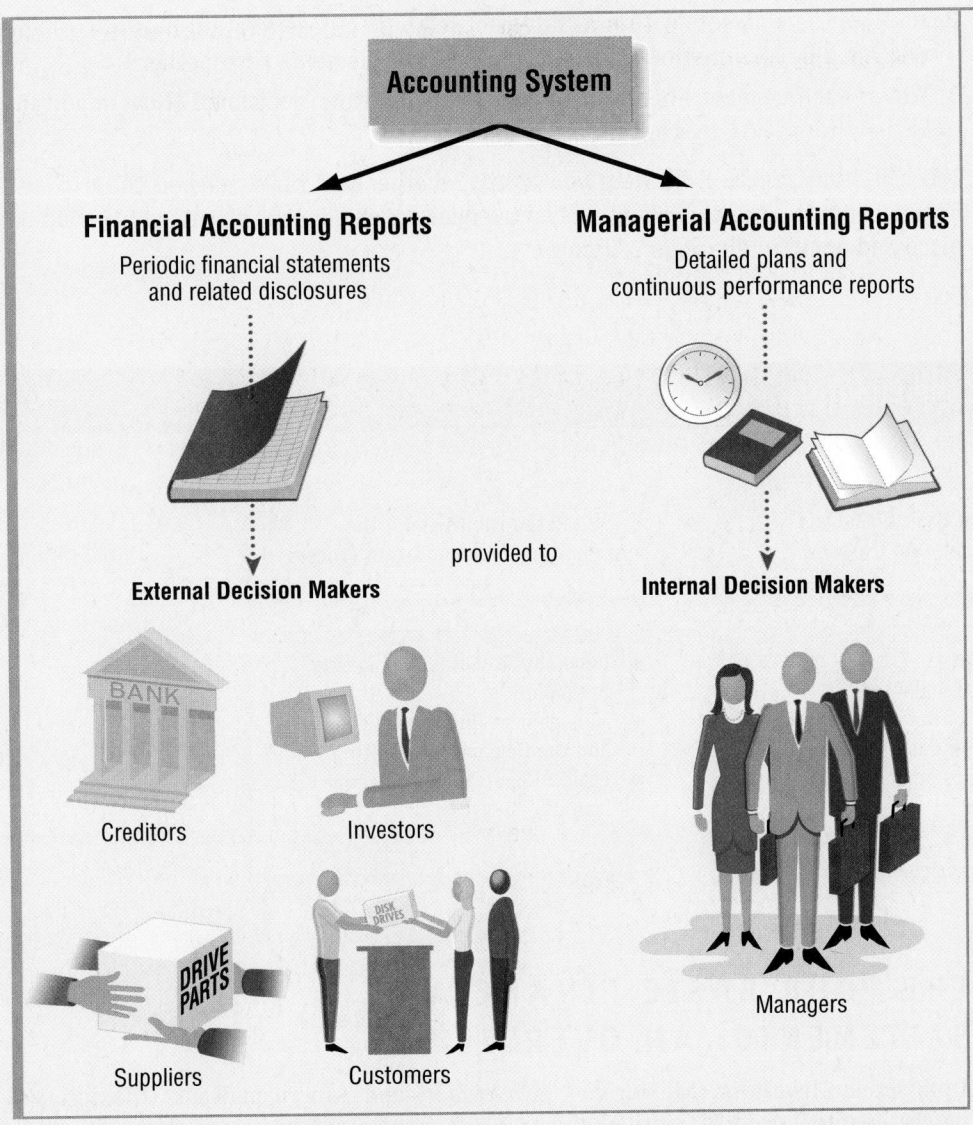

preparation and use. This overview provides you a context in which you can learn the more detailed material presented in the following chapters. In particular, we focus on how two primary users of the statements, investors (owners) and creditors (lenders), relied on each of Maxidrive's four basic financial statements in their ill-fated decisions to buy and lend money to Maxidrive. Then we discuss the ethical and legal responsibilities of various parties for those errors.

To understand the way in which Exeter Investors used Maxidrive's financial statements in its decision and the way it was misled, we must first understand what specific information is presented in the four basic financial statements for a company such as Maxidrive. **Rather than trying to memorize the definitions of every term used in this chapter, try to focus your attention on learning the general structure and content of the statements. Specifically:**

1. What categories of items (often called **elements**) are reported on each of the four statements? (What type of information does a statement convey, and where can you find it?)

Learning Objective 1

Recognize the information conveyed in each of the four basic financial statements and the way that it is used by different decision makers (investors, creditors, and managers).

Video 1-1
www.mhhe.com/libby6e

2. How are the elements within a statement related? (These relationships are usually described by an equation that tells you how the elements fit together.)

3. Why is each element important to owners' or creditors' decisions? (How important is the information to decision makers?)

The self-study quizzes will help you assess whether you have reached these goals. Remember that since this chapter is an overview, each concept discussed here will be discussed again in Chapters 2 through 5.

ORGANIZATION of the Chapter

The Four Basic Financials Statements: An Overview	Responsibilities for the Accounting Communication Process
■ Balance Sheet ■ Income Statement ■ Statement of Retained Earnings ■ Statement of Cash Flows ■ Relationships among the Statements ■ Notes	■ Generally Accepted Accounting Principles ■ Management Responsibility and the Demand for Auditing ■ Ethics, Reputation, and Legal Liability

THE FOUR BASIC FINANCIAL STATEMENTS: AN OVERVIEW

Both Exeter Investors (Maxidrive's new owner) and American Bank (Maxidrive's largest creditor) used Maxidrive's financial statements to learn more about the company before making their purchase and lending decisions. In doing so, Exeter and American Bank assumed that the statements accurately represented Maxidrive's financial condition. As they soon learned, and now have claimed in their lawsuits, the statements were in error.

1. On its **balance sheet,** Maxidrive overstated the economic resources it owned and understated its debts to others.

2. On its **income statement,** Maxidrive overstated its ability to sell goods for more than the cost to produce and sell them.

3. On its **statement of retained earnings,** Maxidrive overstated the amount of income it reinvested in the company for future growth.

4. On its **statement of cash flows,** Maxidrive overstated its ability to generate from sales of disk drives the cash necessary to meet its current debts.

These four financial statements are the basic statements normally prepared by profit-making organizations for use by investors, creditors, and other external decision makers.

The four basic statements summarize the financial activities of the business. They can be prepared at any point in time (such as the end of the year, quarter, or month) and can apply to any time span (such as one year, one quarter, or one month). Like most companies, Maxidrive prepares financial statements for investors and creditors at the end of each quarter (known as **quarterly reports**) and at the end of the year (known as **annual reports**).

The Balance Sheet

The purpose of the balance sheet is to report the financial position (amount of assets, liabilities, and stockholders' equity) of an accounting entity at a particular point in time. We can learn a great deal about what the balance sheet reports just by reading the statement from the top. The balance sheet of Maxidrive Corp., presented by its former owners to Exeter Investors, is shown in Exhibit 1.2.

A BALANCE SHEET (Statement of Financial Position) reports the amount of assets, liabilities, and stockholders' equity of an accounting entity at a point in time.

Structure

Notice that the **heading** specifically identifies four significant items related to the statement:

1. **Name of the entity,** Maxidrive Corp.
2. **Title of the statement,** Balance Sheet.
3. **Specific date of the statement,** At December 31, 2009.
4. **Unit of measure** (in thousands of dollars).

The organization for which financial data are to be collected, called an accounting entity, must be precisely defined. On the balance sheet, the business entity itself, not the business owners, is viewed as owning the resources it uses and as owing its debts. The heading of each statement indicates the time dimension of the report. The balance

An ACCOUNTING ENTITY is the organization for which financial data are to be collected.

MAXIDRIVE CORP. Balance Sheet At December 31, 2009 (in thousands of dollars)		
Assets		
Cash	$ 4,895	the amount of cash in the company's bank accounts
Accounts receivable	5,714	amounts owed by customers from prior sales
Inventories	8,517	parts and completed but unsold disk drives
Plant and equipment	7,154	factories and production machinery
Land	981	land on which the factories are built
Total assets	$27,261	
Liabilities		
Accounts payable	$ 7,156	amounts owed to suppliers for prior purchases
Notes payable	9,000	amounts owed on written debt contracts
Total liabilities	16,156	
Stockholders' Equity		
Contributed capital	2,000	amounts invested in the business by stockholders
Retained earnings	9,105	past earnings not distributed to stockholders
Total stockholders' equity	11,105	
Total liabilities and stockholders' equity	$27,261	

name of the entity
title of the statement
specific date of the statement
unit of measure

EXHIBIT 1.2

Balance Sheet

The notes are an integral part of these financial statements.

sheet is like a financial snapshot indicating the entity's financial position at a specific point in time—in this case, December 31, 2009—which is stated clearly on the balance sheet. Financial reports are normally denominated in the currency of the country in which they are located. U.S. companies report in U.S. dollars, Canadian companies in Canadian dollars, and Mexican companies in Mexican pesos. Medium-sized companies such as Maxidrive often report in thousands of dollars; that is, they round the last three digits to the nearest thousand. The listing of Cash $4,895 on Maxidrive's balance sheet actually means $4,895,000.

Maxidrive's balance sheet first lists the company's assets. Assets are economic resources owned by the entity. It next lists its liabilities and stockholders' equity. They are the sources of financing or claims against the company's economic resources. Financing provided by creditors creates a liability. Financing provided by owners creates owners' equity. Since Maxidrive is a corporation, its owners' equity is designated as stockholders' equity.[1] Since each asset must have a source of financing, a company's assets must, by definition, equal the combined total of its liabilities and stockholders' equity. This **basic accounting equation,** often called the balance sheet equation**,** is written:

BASIC ACCOUNTING EQUATION (balance sheet equation): Assets = Liabilities + Stockholders' Equity.

Assets   =   **Liabilities + Stockholders' Equity**
Economic resources   Sources of financing for the economic resources
(e.g., cash, inventory)   Liabilities: From creditors
Stockholders' Equity: From stockholders

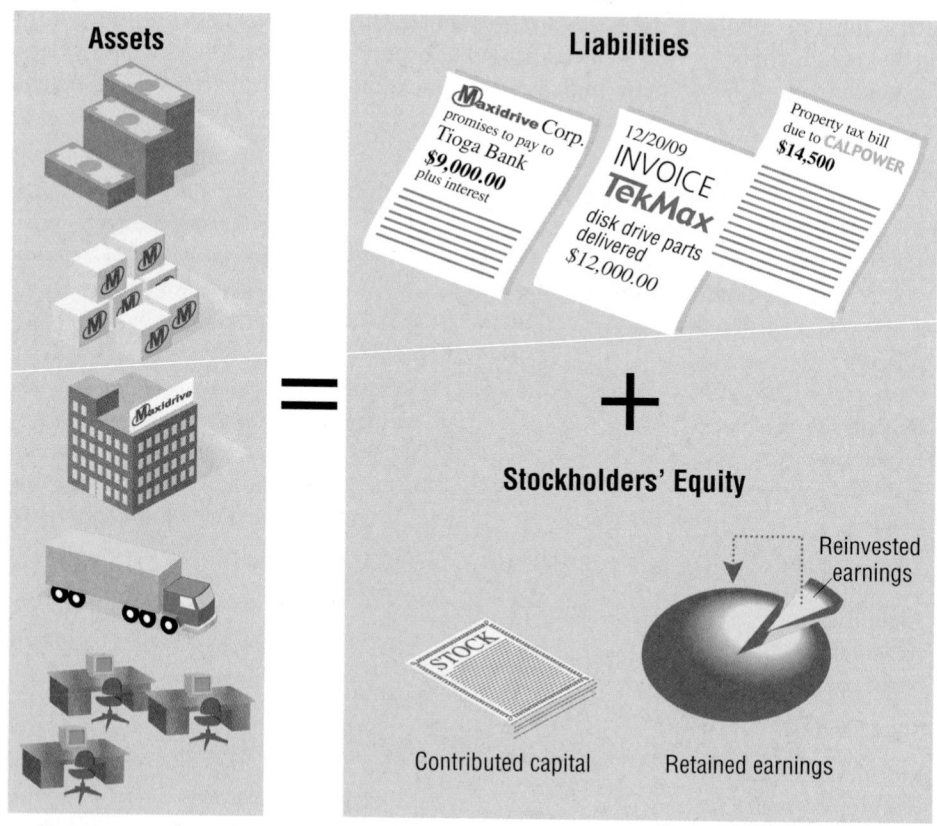

---

[1]A corporation is a business that is incorporated under the laws of a particular state. The owners are called **stockholders** or **shareholders.** Ownership is represented by shares of capital stock that usually can be bought and sold freely. The corporation operates as a separate legal entity, separate and apart from its owners. The stockholders enjoy limited liability; they are liable for the debts of the corporation only to the extent of their investments. Chapter Supplement A discusses forms of ownership in more detail.

The basic accounting equation shows what we mean when we refer to a company's **financial position:** the economic resources that the company owns and the sources of financing for those resources.

Elements

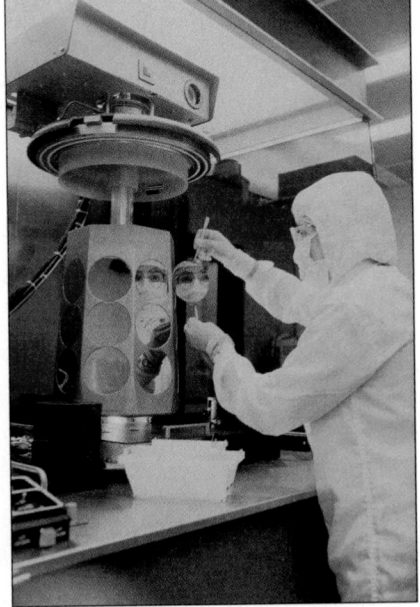

Assets are the economic resources owned by the company. Maxidrive lists five items under the category Assets. The exact items listed as assets on a company's balance sheet depend on the nature of its operations. But these are common names used by many companies. The five items listed by Maxidrive are the economic resources needed to manufacture and sell disk drives to companies such as Dell. Each of these economic resources is expected to provide future benefits to the firm. To prepare to manufacture the drives, Maxidrive first needed cash to purchase land on which to build factories and install production machinery (plant and equipment). Maxidrive then began purchasing parts and producing disk drives, which led to the balance assigned to inventories. When Maxidrive sells its disk drives to Dell and others, it sells them on credit and receives promises to pay called accounts receivable, which are collected in cash later.

Every asset on the balance sheet is initially measured at the total cost incurred to acquire it. For example, the balance sheet for Maxidrive reports Land, $981; this is the amount paid (in thousands) for the land when it was acquired. Balance sheets do not generally show the amounts for which the assets could currently be sold.

Liabilities are the company's debts or obligations. Under the category Liabilities, Maxidrive lists two items. The accounts payable arise from the purchase of goods or services from suppliers on credit without a formal written contract (or a note). The notes payable result from cash borrowings based on a formal written debt contract with lending institutions such as banks.

Stockholders' equity indicates the amount of financing provided by owners of the business and earnings. The investment of cash and other assets in the business by the owners is called contributed capital. The amount of earnings (profits) reinvested in the business (and thus not distributed to stockholders in the form of dividends) is called retained earnings.

In Exhibit 1.2, the Stockholders' Equity section reports two items. The two founding stockholders' investment of $2,000,000 is reported as contributed capital. Maxidrive's total earnings (or losses incurred) less all dividends paid to the stockholders since formation of the corporation equaled $9,105,000 and is reported as retained earnings. Total stockholders' equity is the sum of the contributed capital plus the retained earnings.

Interpreting Assets, Liabilities, and Stockholders' Equity on the Balance Sheet

FINANCIAL ANALYSIS

Assessment of Maxidrive's assets was important to its creditor, American Bank, and its prospective investor, Exeter, because assets provide a basis for judging whether the company has sufficient resources available to operate. Assets were also important because they could be sold for cash in the event that Maxidrive went out of business.

Exeter Investors was interested in Maxidrive's debts because of its concern about whether the company has sufficient sources of cash to pay its debts. Maxidrive's debts were also relevant to American Bank's decision to lend money to the company because existing creditors share American Bank's claim against Maxidrive's assets. If a business does not pay its creditors, the creditors may force the sale of assets sufficient to meet their claims. The sale of assets often fails to cover all of a company's debts, and some creditors may take a loss.

continued

Maxidrive's stockholders' equity or net worth is important to American Bank because creditors' claims legally come before those of owners. If Maxidrive goes out of business and its assets are sold, the proceeds of that sale must be used to pay back creditors such as American Bank before the owners receive any money. Thus, creditors consider stockholders' equity a protective "cushion."

SELF-STUDY QUIZ

1. Maxidrive's **assets** are listed in one section and **liabilities** and **stockholders' equity** in another. Notice that the two sections balance in conformity with the basic accounting equation. In the following chapters, you will learn that the basic accounting equation is the basic building block for the entire accounting process. Your task here is to verify that the assets of $27,261,000 is correct using the numbers for liabilities and stockholders' equity presented in Exhibit 1.2. Recall the basic accounting equation:

$$\textbf{Assets} = \textbf{Liabilities} + \textbf{Stockholders' Equity}$$

2. Learning which items belong in each of the balance sheet categories is an important first step in understanding their meaning. Without referring to Exhibit 1.2, mark each balance sheet item in the following list as an asset (A), liability (L), or stockholders' equity (SE).

_____ Accounts payable   _____ Inventories

_____ Accounts receivable   _____ Land

_____ Cash   _____ Notes payable

_____ Contributed capital   _____ Retained earnings

_____ Buildings and equipment

After you have completed your answers, check them with the solutions at the bottom of the page.

The INCOME STATEMENT (Statement of Income, Statement of Earnings, Statement of Operations) reports the revenues less the expenses of the accounting period.

Income Statement

Revenues
– Expenses

Net Income

The Income Statement

Structure

The **income statement** (statement of income, statement of earnings, or statement of operations) reports the accountant's primary measure of performance of a business, revenues less expenses during the accounting period. While the term profit is used widely for this measure of performance, accountants prefer to use the technical terms **net income** or net earnings. Maxidrive's net income measures its success in selling disk drives for more than the cost to generate those sales.

A quick reading of Maxidrive's income statement (Exhibit 1.3) indicates a great deal about its purpose and content. The heading identifies the name of the entity, the title of the report, and the unit of measure used in the statement. Unlike the balance sheet, however, which reports as of a certain date, the income statement reports for a specified period of time (for the year ended December 31, 2009). The time period covered by the financial statements (one year in this case) is called an

Self-Study Quiz
Solutions

1. Assets ($27,261,000) = Liabilities ($16,156,000) + Stockholders' Equity ($11,105,000).

2. L, A, A, SE, A, A, A, L, SE (reading down the columns).

Revenues   **−**   **Expenses**   **=**   **Net Income**

accounting period. Notice that Maxidrive's income statement has three major captions, revenues, expenses, and net income. The income statement equation that describes their relationship is

The ACCOUNTING PERIOD is the time period covered by the financial statements.

$$\text{Revenues} - \text{Expenses} = \text{Net Income}$$

Elements

Companies earn **revenues** from the sale of goods or services to customers (in Maxidrive's case, from the sale of disk drives). Revenues normally are reported for goods or services that have been sold to a customer **whether or not they have yet been paid for.** Retail stores such as Wal-Mart and McDonald's often receive cash at the time of sale. However, when Maxidrive sells its disk drives to Dell and Apple, it receives a promise of future payment called an account receivable, which later is collected in cash. In either case, the business recognizes total sales (cash and credit) as revenue for the period. Various terms are used in income statements to describe different sources of revenue (e.g., provision of services, sale of goods, rental of property). Maxidrive lists only one, sales revenue, in its income statement.

MAXIDRIVE CORP.		name of the entity
Income Statement		title of the statement
For the Year Ended December 31, 2009		accounting period
(in thousands of dollars)		unit of measure
Revenues		
Sales revenue	$37,436	cash and promises received from sale of disk drives
Total revenues	37,436	
Expenses		
Cost of goods sold expense	26,980	cost to produce disk drives sold
Selling, general, and administrative expense	3,624	operating expenses not directly related to production
Research and development expense	1,982	expenses incurred to develop new products
Interest expense	450	cost of using borrowed funds
Total expenses	33,036	
Pretax income	4,400	
Income tax expense	1,100	income taxes on period's pretax income ($4,400 × 25%)
Net income	$ 3,300	

EXHIBIT 1.3

Income Statement

The notes are an integral part of these financial statements.

Expenses represent the dollar amount of resources the entity used to earn revenues during the period. Expenses reported in one accounting period may actually be paid for in another accounting period. Some expenses require the payment of cash immediately while some require payment at a later date. Some may also require the use of another resource, such as an inventory item, which may have been paid for in a prior period. Maxidrive lists five types of expenses on its income statement, which are described in Exhibit 1.3. These expenses include income tax expense, which, as a corporation, Maxidrive must pay on pretax income.[2]

Net income or net earnings (often called "the bottom line") is the excess of total revenues over total expenses. If total expenses exceed total revenues, a net loss is reported.[3] We noted earlier that revenues are not necessarily the same as collections from customers and expenses are not necessarily the same as payments to suppliers. As a result, net income normally **does not equal** the net cash generated by operations. This latter amount is reported on the cash flow statement discussed later in this chapter.

SELF-STUDY QUIZ

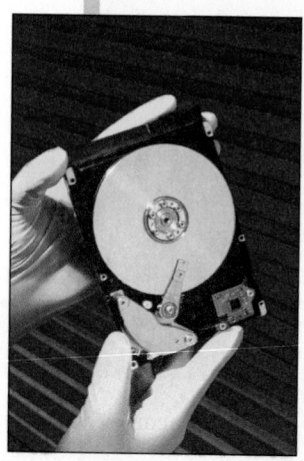

1. Learning which items belong in each of the income statement categories is an important first step in understanding their meaning. Without referring to Exhibit 1.3, mark each income statement item in the following list as a revenue (R) or an expense (E).

   _____ Cost of goods sold   _____ Sales

   _____ Income tax   _____ Selling, general, and administrative

2. During the period 2009, Maxidrive delivered disk drives for which customers paid or promised to pay amounts totaling $37,436,000. During the same period, it collected $33,563,000 in cash from its customers. Without referring to Exhibit 1.3, indicate which of these two amounts will be shown on Maxidrive's income statement as **sales revenue** for 2009. Why did you select your answer?

3. During the period 2009, Maxidrive **produced** disk drives with a total cost of production of $27,130,000. During the same period, it **delivered** to customers disk drives that had cost a total of $26,980,000 to produce. Without referring to Exhibit 1.3, indicate which of the two numbers will be shown on Maxidrive's income statement as **cost of goods sold expense** for 2009. Why did you select your answer?

After you have completed your answers, check them with the solutions at the bottom of the page.

---

[2]This example uses a 25 percent rate. Federal tax rates for corporations actually ranged from 15 percent to 35 percent at the time this book was written. State and local governments may levy additional taxes on corporate income, resulting in a higher total income tax rate.

[3]Net losses are normally noted by parentheses around the income figure.

Self-Study Quiz Solutions

1. E, E, R, E (reading down the columns).

2. Sales revenue in the amount of $37,436,000 is recognized. Sales revenue is normally reported on the income statement when goods or services have been delivered to customers who have either paid or promised to pay for them in the future.

3. Cost of goods sold expense is $26,980,000. Expenses are the dollar amount of resources used up to earn revenues during the period. Only those disk drives that have been delivered to customers have been used up. Those disk drives that are still on hand are part of the asset inventory.

Analyzing the Income Statement: Beyond the Bottom Line

Investors such as Exeter and creditors such as American Bank closely monitor a firm's net income because it indicates the firm's ability to sell goods and services for more than they cost to produce and deliver. Investors buy stock when they believe that future earnings will improve and lead to a higher stock price. Lenders also rely on future earnings to provide the resources to repay loans. The details of the statement also are important. For example, Maxidrive had to sell more than $37 million worth of disk drives to make just over $3 million. If a competitor were to lower prices just 10 percent, forcing Maxidrive to do the same, its net income could easily turn into a net loss. These factors and others help investors and creditors estimate the company's future earnings.

Statement of Retained Earnings

Structure

Maxidrive prepares a separate **statement of retained earnings,** shown in Exhibit 1.4. The heading identifies the name of the entity, the title of the report, and the unit of measure used in the statement. Like the income statement, the statement of retained earnings covers a specified period of time (the accounting period), which in this case is one year. The statement reports the way that net income and the distribution of dividends affected the company's financial position during the accounting period.[4] Net income earned during the year increases the balance of retained earnings, showing the relationship of the income statement to the balance sheet. The declaration of dividends to the stockholders decreases retained earnings.[5]

The retained earnings equation that describes these relationships is

Beginning Retained Earnings + Net Income − Dividends = Ending Retained Earnings

Elements

The statement begins with Maxidrive's **beginning-of-the-year retained earnings.** The current year's **net income** reported on the income statement is added and the current year's **dividends** are subtracted from this amount. During 2009, Maxidrive earned

The STATEMENT OF RETAINED EARNINGS reports the way that net income and the distribution of dividends affected the financial position of the company during the accounting period.

MAXIDRIVE CORP. Statement of Retained Earnings For the Year Ended December 31, 2009 (in thousands of dollars)		
Retained earnings, January 1, 2009		$6,805
Net income for 2009		3,300
Dividends for 2009		(1,000)
Retained earnings, December 31, 2009		$9,105

name of the entity
title of the statement
accounting period
unit of measure

last period's ending retained earnings
net income reported on the income statement
dividends declared during the period

ending retained earnings on the balance sheet

EXHIBIT 1.4

Statement of Retained Earnings

The notes are an integral part of these financial statements.

[4]Other corporations report these changes at the end of the income statement or in a more general statement of stockholders' equity, which we discuss in Chapter 4.

[5]Net losses are subtracted.

$3,300,000, as shown on the income statement (Exhibit 1.3). This amount was added to the beginning-of-the-year retained earnings. Also, during 2009, Maxidrive declared and paid a total of $1,000,000 in dividends to its two original stockholders. This amount was subtracted in computing **end-of-the-year retained earnings** on the balance sheet. Note that retained earnings increased by the portion of income reinvested in the business ($3,300,000 − $1,000,000 = $2,300,000). The ending retained earnings amount of $9,105,000 is the same as that reported in Exhibit 1.2 on Maxidrive's balance sheet. Thus, the retained earnings statement indicates the relationship of the income statement to the balance sheet.

FINANCIAL ANALYSIS

Interpreting Retained Earnings

Reinvestment of earnings, or retained earnings, is an important source of financing for Maxidrive, representing more than one-third of its financing. Creditors such as American Bank closely monitor a firm's retained earnings statement because the firm's policy on dividend payments to the stockholders affects its ability to repay its debts. Every dollar Maxidrive pays to stockholders as a dividend is not available for use in paying back its debt to American Bank. Investors examine retained earnings to determine whether the company is reinvesting a sufficient portion of earnings to support future growth.

SELF-STUDY **QUIZ**

Maxidrive's statement of retained earnings reports the way that net income and the distribution of dividends affected the financial position of the company during the accounting period. In a prior period, Maxidrive's financial statements reported the following amounts: beginning retained earnings $5,510, total assets $20,450, dividends $900, cost of goods sold expense $19,475, net income $1,780. Without referring to Exhibit 1.4, compute ending retained earnings.

After you have completed your answer, check it with the solution at the bottom of the page.

Statement of Cash Flows

Structure

The STATEMENT OF CASH FLOWS (Cash Flow Statement) reports inflows and outflows of cash during the accounting period in the categories of operating, investing, and financing.

Maxidrive's statement of cash flows is presented in Exhibit 1.5. The **statement of cash flows** (cash flow statement) divides Maxidrive's cash inflows and outflows (receipts and payments) into the three primary categories of cash flows in a typical business: cash flows from operating, investing, and financing activities. The heading identifies the name of the entity, the title of the report, and the unit of measure used in the statement. Like the income statement, the cash flow statement covers a specified period of time (the accounting period), which in this case is one year.

As discussed earlier in this chapter, reported revenues do not always equal cash collected from customers because some sales may be on credit. Also, expenses reported on the income statement may not be equal to the cash paid out during the period because expenses may be incurred in one period and paid for in another. Because the

---

Self-Study Quiz
Solution

Beginning Retained Earnings ($5,510) + Net Income ($1,780) − Dividends ($900) = Ending Retained Earnings ($6,390).

income statement does not provide information concerning cash flows, accountants prepare the statement of cash flows to report inflows and outflows of cash. The cash flow statement equation describes the causes of the change in cash reported on the balance sheet from the end of last period to the end of the current period:

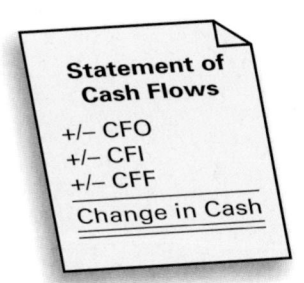

+/ − Cash Flows from Operating Activities (CFO)

+/ − Cash Flows from Investing Activities (CFI)

+/ − Cash Flows from Financing Activities (CFF)

Change in Cash

Note that each of the three cash flow sources can be positive or negative.

Elements

Cash flows from operating activities are cash flows that are directly related to earning income. For example, when Dell, Apple, and other customers pay Maxidrive for the disk drives it has delivered to them, it lists the amounts collected as cash collected from customers. When Maxidrive pays salaries to its employees in research and development or pays bills received from its parts suppliers, it includes the amounts in cash paid to suppliers and employees.[6]

Cash flows from investing activities include cash flows related to the acquisition or sale of the company's productive assets. This year, Maxidrive had only one cash

MAXIDRIVE CORP.		*name of the entity*
Statement of Cash Flows		*title of the statement*
For the Year Ended December 31, 2009		*accounting period*
(in thousands of dollars)		*unit of measure*
Cash flows from operating activities		*directly related to earning income*
Cash collected from customers	$33,563	
Cash paid to suppliers and employees	(30,854)	
Cash paid for interest	(450)	
Cash paid for taxes	(1,190)	
Net cash flow from operating activities	1,069	
Cash flows from investing activities		*purchase/sale of productive assets*
Cash paid to purchase manufacturing equipment	(1,625)	
Net cash flow from investing activities	(1,625)	
Cash flows from financing activities		*from investors and creditors*
Cash received from bank loan	1,400	
Cash paid for dividends	(1,000)	
Net cash flow from financing activities	400	
Net decrease in cash during the year	(156)	*change in cash during the period ($1,069 − 1,625 + 400)*
Cash at beginning of year	5,051	*last period's ending cash balance*
Cash at end of year	$ 4,895	*ending cash on the balance sheet*

EXHIBIT 1.5

Statement of Cash Flows

The notes are an integral part of these financial statements.

---

[6]Alternative ways to present cash flows from operations are discussed in Chapter 5.

outflow from investing activities, the purchase of additional manufacturing equipment to meet growing demand for its products. **Cash flows from financing activities** are directly related to the financing of the enterprise itself. They involve the receipt or payment of money to investors and creditors (except for suppliers). This year, Maxidrive borrowed an additional $1,400,000 from the bank to purchase most of the new manufacturing equipment. It also paid out $1,000,000 in dividends to the founding stockholders.

FINANCIAL ANALYSIS

Interpreting the Cash Flow Statement

Many analysts believe that the statement of cash flows is particularly useful in predicting future cash flows that may be available for payment of debt to creditors and dividends to investors. Bankers often consider the Operating Activities section to be most important because it indicates the company's ability to generate cash from sales to meet its current cash needs. Any amount left over can be used to pay back the bank debt or expand the company. Stockholders will invest in a company only if they believe that it will eventually generate more cash from operations than it uses so that cash will become available to pay dividends and expand.

SELF-STUDY QUIZ

1. During the period 2009, Maxidrive delivered disk drives to customers who paid or promised to pay a total of $37,436,000. During the same period, it collected $33,563,000 in cash from customers. Without referring to Exhibit 1.5, indicate which of the two amounts will be shown on Maxidrive's cash flow statement for 2009.

2. Your task here is to verify that Maxidrive's cash balance decreased by $156 during the year using the totals for cash flows from operating, investing, and financing activities presented in Exhibit 1.5. Recall the cash flow statement equation:

> +/− **Cash Flows from Operating Activities (CFO)**
> +/− **Cash Flows from Investing Activities (CFI)**
> +/− **Cash Flows from Financing Activities (CFF)**
> ―――――――――――――――――――――――――――――――
> **Change in Cash**

After you have completed your answers, check them with the solutions at the bottom of the page.

Self-Study Quiz
Solutions

1. The firm recognizes $33,563,000 on the cash flow statement because this number represents the actual cash collected from customers related to current and prior years' sales.

2.

+/− Cash Flows from Operating Activities (CFO)	$1,069
+/− Cash Flows from Investing Activities (CFI)	−1,625
+/− Cash Flows from Financing Activities (CFF)	+ 400
Change in Cash	$ (156)

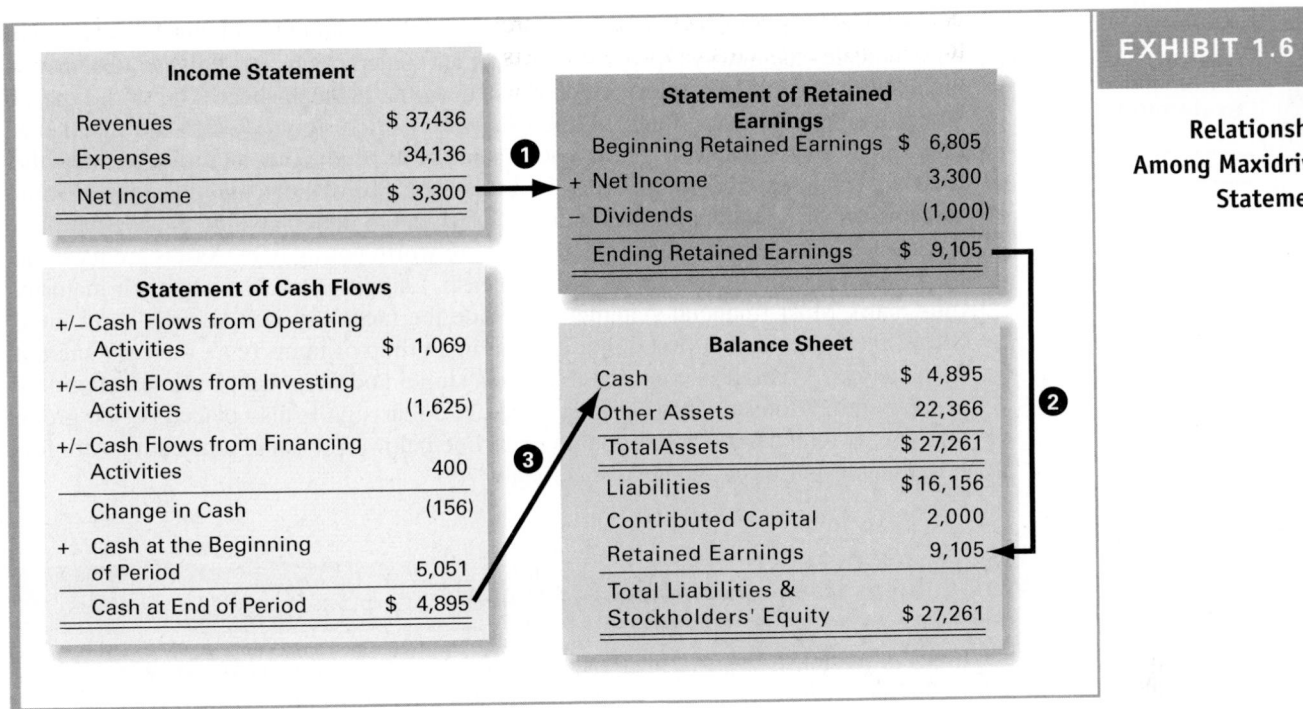

EXHIBIT 1.6

Relationships Among Maxidrive's Statements

Relationships Among the Statements

Our discussion of the four basic financial statements focused on what elements are reported in each statement, how the elements are related by the equation for each statement, and how the elements are important to the decisions of investors, creditors, and others. We have also discovered how the statements, all of which are outputs from the same system, are related to one another. In particular, we learned:

1. Net income from the income statement results in an increase in ending retained earnings on the statement of retained earnings.

2. Ending retained earnings from the statement of retained earnings is one of the two components of stockholders' equity on the balance sheet.

3. The change in cash on the cash flow statement added to the beginning-of-the-year balance in cash equals the end-of-year balance in cash on the balance sheet.

Thus, we can think of the income statement as explaining, through the statement of retained earnings, how the operations of the company improved or harmed the financial position of the company during the year. The cash flow statement explains how the operating, investing, and financing activities of the company affected the cash balance on the balance sheet during the year. These relationships are illustrated in Exhibit 1.6 for Maxidrive's financial statements.

Notes

At the bottom of each of Maxidrive's four basic financial statements is this statement: **"The notes are an integral part of these financial statements."** This is the accounting equivalent of the Surgeon General's warning on a package of cigarettes. It warns users that failure to read the **notes** (or footnotes) to the financial statements will result in an incomplete picture of the company's financial health. Notes provide supplemental information about the financial condition of a company without which the financial statements cannot be fully understood.

There are three basic types of notes. The first type provides descriptions of the accounting rules applied in the company's statements. The second presents additional

NOTES (footnotes) provide supplemental information about the financial condition of a company without which the financial statements cannot be fully understood.

detail about a line on the financial statements. For example, Maxidrive's inventory note indicates the amount of parts, drives under construction, and finished disk drives included in the total inventory amount listed on the balance sheet. The third type of note provides additional financial disclosures about items not listed on the statements themselves. For example, Maxidrive leases one of its production facilities; terms of the lease are disclosed in a note. Throughout this book, we will discuss many note disclosures because understanding their content is critical to understanding the company.

A few additional formatting conventions are worth noting here. Assets are listed on the balance sheet by ease of conversion to cash. Liabilities are listed by their maturity (due date). Most financial statements include the monetary unit sign (in the United States, the $) beside the first dollar amount in a group of items (e.g., the cash amount in the assets). Also, it is common to place a single underline below the last item in a group before a total or subtotal (e.g., land). A dollar sign is also placed beside group totals (e.g., total assets) and a double underline below. The same conventions are followed in all four basic financial statements.

FINANCIAL
ANALYSIS
Management Uses of Financial Statements

In our discussion of financial analysis thus far, we have focused on the perspectives of investors and creditors. Managers within the firm also make direct use of financial statements. For example, Maxidrive's **marketing managers** and **credit managers** use customers' financial statements to decide whether to extend credit for purchases of disk drives. Maxidrive's **purchasing managers** analyze parts suppliers' financial statements to see whether the suppliers have the resources to meet Maxidrive's demand and invest in the development of new parts. Both the **employees' union** and Maxidrive's **human resource managers** use Maxidrive's financial statements as a basis for contract negotiations over pay rates. The net income figure even serves as a basis for calculating **employee bonuses.** Regardless of the functional area of management in which you are employed, you will use financial statement data. You also will be evaluated based on the impact of your decisions on your company's financial statement data.

Summary of the Four Basic Financial Statements

We have learned a great deal about the content of the four basic statements. Exhibit 1.7 summarizes this information. Take a few minutes to review the information in the exhibit before you move on to the next section of the chapter.

RESPONSIBILITIES FOR THE ACCOUNTING COMMUNICATION PROCESS

Learning Objective 2

Identify the role of generally accepted accounting principles (GAAP) in determining the content of financial statements.

For the decision makers at Exeter to use the information in Maxidrive's financial statements effectively, they had to understand what information each of the statements conveyed. Yet the fraud perpetrated by Maxidrive employees suggests that this understanding is not sufficient. Exeter clearly needed to know that the numbers in the statements represented what they claimed. Numbers that do not represent what they claim to are meaningless. For example, if the balance sheet lists $2,000,000 for a factory that does not exist, that part of the statement does not convey useful information.

Decision makers also need to understand the **measurement rules** applied in computing the numbers on the statements. A swim coach would never try to evaluate a swimmer's time in the 100 freestyle without first asking if the time was for a race in

Audio lecture–AP1-1
www.mhhe.com/libby6e

Financial Statement	Purpose	Structure	Examples of Content
Balance Sheet (Statement of Financial Position)	Reports the financial position (economic resources and sources of financing) of an accounting entity *at a point in time.*	BALANCE SHEET Assets = Liabilities + Stockholders' Equity	Cash, accounts receivable, plant and equipment, notes payable, contributed capital
Income Statement (Statement of Income, Statement of Earnings, Statement of Operations)	Reports the accountant's primary measure of economic performance *during the accounting period.*	**Income Statement** Revenues − Expenses Net Income	Sales revenue, cost of goods sold, selling expense, interest expense
Statement of Retained Earnings	Reports the way that net income and the distribution of dividends affected the financial position of the company *during the accounting period.*	**Statement of Retained Earnings** Beginning RE + Net Income − Dividends Ending RE	Net income is taken from the income statement; Dividends are distributions to stockholders
Statement of Cash Flows (Cash Flow Statement)	Reports inflows (receipts) and outflows (payments) of cash *during the accounting period* in the categories operating, investing, and financing.	**Statement of Cash Flows** +/− CFO +/− CFI +/− CFF Change in Cash	Cash collected from customers, cash paid to suppliers, cash paid to purchase equipment, cash borrowed from banks

EXHIBIT 1.7

Summary of Four Basic Financial Statements

meters or in yards. Likewise, a decision maker should never attempt to use accounting information without first understanding the measurement rules that were used to develop the information. These measurement rules are called **generally accepted accounting principles,** or GAAP.

Generally Accepted Accounting Principles

How Are Generally Accepted Accounting Principles Determined?

The accounting system in use today has a long history. Its foundations are normally traced back to the works of an Italian monk and mathematician, Fr. Luca Pacioli, published in 1494. However, prior to 1933, each company's management largely determined its financial reporting practices. Thus, little uniformity in practice existed among companies.

Following the dramatic stock market decline of 1929, the Securities Act of 1933 and the Securities Exchange Act of 1934 were passed into law by the U.S. Congress. These acts created the **Securities and Exchange Commission** (SEC) and gave it broad powers to determine the measurement rules for financial statements that companies issuing

GENERALLY ACCEPTED ACCOUNTING PRINCIPLES (GAAP) are the measurement rules used to develop the information in financial statements.

The SECURITIES AND EXCHANGE COMMISSION (SEC) is the U.S. government agency that determines the financial statements that public companies must provide to stockholders and the measurement rules that they must use in producing those statements.

The FINANCIAL ACCOUNTING STANDARDS BOARD (FASB) is the private sector body given the primary responsibility to work out the detailed rules that become generally accepted accounting principles.

stock to the public (publicly traded companies) must provide to stockholders.[7] The SEC has worked with organizations of professional accountants to establish groups that are given the primary responsibilities to work out the detailed rules that become generally accepted accounting principles. Today, the Financial Accounting Standards Board (FASB) has this responsibility. The Board has five full-time voting members and a permanent staff who consider the appropriate financial reporting responses to ever-changing business practices. As of the date of publication of this book, the official pronouncements of the FASB (**Financial Accounting Standards**) and its predecessors totaled more than 5,000 pages of very fine print. Such detail is made necessary by the enormous diversity and complexity of current business practices.

Most managers do not need to learn all the details included in these standards. Our approach is to focus on those details that have the greatest impact on the numbers presented in financial statements and are appropriate for an introductory course.

Why Is GAAP Important to Managers and External Users?

Generally accepted accounting principles (GAAP) are of great interest to the companies that must prepare financial statements, their auditors, and the readers of the statements. Companies and their managers and owners are most directly affected by the information presented in financial statements. Companies incur the cost of preparing the statements and bear the major economic consequences of their publication, which include, among others,

1. Effects on the selling price of a company's stock.

2. Effects on the amount of bonuses received by management and employees.

3. Loss of competitive information to other companies.

Recall that the amount that Exeter was willing to pay to purchase Maxidrive was determined in part by net income computed under GAAP. This presents the possibility that changes in GAAP can affect the price buyers are willing to pay for companies. Employees who receive part of their pay based on reaching stated targets for net income are directly concerned with any changes in how net income is computed under GAAP. Managers and owners also often are concerned that publishing certain information in financial statements will give away trade secrets to other companies that compete with them. As a consequence of these and other concerns, changes in GAAP are actively debated, political lobbying often takes place, and final rules are a compromise among the wishes of interested parties.

INTERNATIONAL PERSPECTIVE

The International Accounting Standards Board and Global Convergence of Accounting Standards

IFRS

Financial accounting standards and disclosure requirements are set by national regulatory agencies and standard-setting bodies. However, since 2002, there has been substantial movement to develop international financial reporting standards (IFRS) by the International Accounting Standards Board (IASB). The current status of these standards is as follows.

REAL WORLD EXCERPT
Deloitte IAS Plus Website

Example countries requiring use of IFRS (currently or by 2011):

- **European Union (United Kingdom, Germany, France, Netherlands, Belgium, Bulgaria, Poland, etc.)**
- **Australia and New Zealand**
- **India, Hong Kong, and South Korea**

---

[7]Contrary to popular belief, these rules are different from those that companies follow when filing their income tax returns. We discuss these differences further in later chapters.

- **Turkey**
- **Brazil and Chile**
- **Canada**
- **China**

In the U.S., the Securities and Exchange Commission allows foreign companies whose stock is traded in the U.S. to use IFRS and is considering allowing the same for domestic companies in the future.

SOURCE: Deloitte IAS PLUS website

Management Responsibility and the Demand for Auditing

Exeter's owners and managers were well aware of the details of U.S. GAAP, but they were still misled. Although the measurement rules that Maxidrive had used to produce its financial statements were consistent with GAAP, the underlying figures were fictitious. Who was responsible for the accuracy of the numbers in Maxidrive's financial statements?

Primary responsibility for the information in the financial statements lies with management, represented by the highest officer of the company and the highest financial officer. Companies take three important steps to assure investors that the company's records are accurate: (1) they maintain a system of controls over both the records and the assets of the company, (2) they hire outside independent auditors to verify the fairness of the financial statements, and (3) they form a committee of the board of directors to oversee the integrity of these other two safeguards. These responsibilities are often reiterated in a formal **report of management** or **management certification** in the annual report. These three safeguards and a management certification are required for companies with publicly traded stock. These safeguards failed in Maxidrive's case. Managers of companies that prepare fraudulent financial statements are subject to criminal and civil penalties.

Learning Objective 3
Distinguish the roles of managers and auditors in the accounting communication process.

Three steps to ensure the accuracy of records:

System of Controls   External Auditors   Board of Directors

The role of the independent auditor is described in more detail in the **audit report** in Exhibit 1.8 (report of independent accountants or independent registered public accounting firm)**.** The audit report describes the auditor's opinion of the fairness of the financial statements and the evidence gathered to support that opinion. An accountant may be licensed as a **certified public accountant,** or **CPA,** only on completion of requirements specified by each state. Only a licensed CPA can issue an audit report. In this role, accountants are known as **independent CPAs** (or **independent accountants**) because they have certain responsibilities that extend to the general public as well as to the specific business that pays for this service.

An **audit** involves the examination of the financial reports (prepared by the management of the entity) to ensure that they represent what they claim to and conform with generally accepted accounting principles (GAAP). In performing an audit, the

An AUDIT is an examination of the financial reports to ensure that they represent what they claim and conform with GAAP.

EXHIBIT 1.8

Report of Independent Accountants

> ### Report of Independent Accountants to the Stockholders and Board of Directors of Maxidrive Corp.
>
> We have audited the accompanying balance sheet of Maxidrive Corp. as of December 31, 2009, and the related statements of income, retained earnings, and cash flows for the period ended December 31, 2009. These financial statements are the responsibility of the Company's management. Our responsibility is to express an opinion on these financial statements based on our audits.
>
> We conducted our audits in accordance with generally accepted auditing standards in the United States of America. Those standards require that we plan and perform the audit to obtain reasonable assurance about whether the financial statements are free of material misstatement. An audit includes examining, on a test basis, evidence supporting the amounts and disclosures in the financial statements. An audit also includes assessing the accounting principles used and significant estimates made by management, as well as evaluating the overall financial statement presentation. We believe that our audits provide a reasonable basis for our opinion.
>
> In our opinion, the financial statements referred to above present fairly, in all material respects, the financial position of Maxidrive Corp. at December 31, 2009, and the results of its operations and its cash flows for the year ended December 31, 2009, in conformity with generally accepted accounting principles in the United States of America.
>
> *Smith and Walker, CPAs*
>
> Smith and Walker, CPAs
> February 26, 2010

The PUBLIC COMPANY ACCOUNTING OVERSIGHT BOARD (PCAOB) is the private sector body given the primary responsibility to issue detailed auditing standards.

independent CPA examines the underlying transactions and the accounting methods used to account for these transactions. Because of the enormous number of transactions involving a major enterprise such as Apple, the CPA does not examine each of these transactions. Rather, professional approaches are used to ascertain beyond reasonable doubt that transactions were measured and reported properly. The **Public Company Accounting Oversight Board** (PCAOB), in consultation with the SEC, sets standards for these tests for the audits of public companies.

FINANCIAL ANALYSIS

Using Financial Statements to Determine Maxidrive's Value

Maxidrive's current and prior years' income statements played a particularly important part in the price Exeter was willing to pay for Maxidrive Corp. Prior years' income statements (which were not presented here) indicated that the company had earned income every year since its founding except for the first year. Furthermore, both sales revenue and net income had risen every year. One method for estimating the value of a company that relies on net income and growth in net income is the **price/earnings ratio** (P/E ratio, or P/E multiple). The P/E ratio measures how many times current year's earnings investors are willing to pay for a company's stock. A higher P/E ratio means that investors have more confidence in the company's ability to produce higher profits in future years. A first approximation of Exeter's overpayment, and the amount they would hope to recover from the perpetrators of the fraud would be:

$$\text{Income Overstatement} \times \text{P/E Ratio} = \text{Overpayment}$$

If income was overstated by $1,650,000 and Maxidrive's P/E ratio was 10, Exeter would have overpaid $16.5 million for the purchase of Maxidrive. The role of net income in determining the value of a company will be discussed in more detail in your corporate finance course and more advanced courses in financial statement analysis.

Ethics, Reputation, and Legal Liability

If financial statements are to be of any value to decision makers, users must have confidence in the fairness of the information they present. Users will have greater confidence in the information if they know that the people who audited the statements were required to meet professional standards of ethics and competence.

The American Institute of Certified Public Accountants (AICPA) requires all of its members to adhere to a professional code of ethics and professional auditing standards, and auditors of public companies must register with and comply with standards set by the PCAOB. Failure to comply with the rules of conduct can result in serious professional penalties. CPAs' reputations for honesty and competence are their most important assets. The potential economic effects of damage to reputation, malpractice liability, and potential fines provide even stronger incentives to abide by professional standards.

In case of malpractice, the independent CPA may be held liable for losses suffered by those who relied on the statements the CPA examined. As a result of the fraud, Maxidrive filed for bankruptcy and will likely be sold in an attempt to pay off creditors. In a civil lawsuit, Exeter Investors and American Bank claimed losses of $16.5 million and $9 million, respectively, charging that the officers of Maxidrive had "perpetrated a massive fraud" and the auditors had "overlooked the errors" in the audit. Exeter and American Bank also have asked for punitive damages for gross negligence. In addition, the president and the chief financial officer of Maxidrive were convicted by a federal jury on three counts of criminal securities fraud for which they were fined and imprisoned.

EPILOGUE

Although financial statement fraud is a fairly rare event, the misrepresentations in Maxidrive's statements aptly illustrate the importance of fairly presented financial statements to investors and creditors. They also indicate the crucial importance of the public accounting profession in ensuring the integrity of the financial reporting system. The recent Enron and WorldCom debacles have brought the importance of these issues to the attention of the general public.

As noted at the beginning of this chapter, Maxidrive is not a real company but is based on a real company that perpetrated a similar fraud. (The focus companies and contrasting examples in the remaining chapters are *real* companies.) Maxidrive is loosely based on the infamous fraud at MiniScribe, a real disk drive manufacturer. The size of the real fraud, however, was more than 10 times as great as that in the fictional case, as were the losses incurred and the damages claimed in the lawsuits that followed. (Many of the numbers in Maxidrive's financial statements are simply one-tenth the amounts presented in MiniScribe's fraudulent statements.) The nature of the fraud also was quite similar. At MiniScribe, sales revenue was overstated by transferring nonexistent inventory between two facilities and creating phony documents to make it look as though the inventory was transferred to customers. MiniScribe even packaged bricks as finished products, shipped them to distributors, and counted them as sold. Cost of goods sold was understated by activities such as counting scrap parts and damaged drives as usable inventory. MiniScribe managers even broke into the auditors' locked trunks to change numbers on their audit papers.

As a consequence, MiniScribe reported net income of $31 million, which was subsequently shown to be $9 million. MiniScribe's investors and creditors filed lawsuits claiming more than $1 billion in damages. Actual damages in the hundreds of millions were paid. Both the chairman and the chief financial officer of MiniScribe were convicted of federal securities and wire fraud charges and sentenced to jail. Although most managers and owners act in an honest and responsible fashion, this incident, and the much larger frauds at Enron and WorldCom, are stark reminders of the economic consequences of lack of fair presentation in financial reports. Both companies were forced into bankruptcy when their fraudulent financial reporting practices were brought to light. Penalties against their audit firm, Arthur Andersen, also led to its bankruptcy and dissolution. A sampling of firms that have recently been involved in financial statement misrepresentations follows:

Enron	Parmalat
WorldCom	Nortel
Adelphia	Goodyear
Global Crossing	Cardinal Health
Computer Associates	Homestore.com
Tyco	Dynegy
HealthSouth	Fannie Mae
McKesson	Freddie Mac
Xerox	Qwest Communications
Rite-Aid	Gerber Scientific
Aurora Foods	Stanley Works
Halliburton	AIG

DEMONSTRATION CASE

Apple Inc.

At the end of most chapters, one or more demonstration cases are presented. These cases provide an overview of the primary issues discussed in the chapter. Each demonstration case is followed by a recommended solution. You should read the case carefully and then prepare your own solution before you study the recommended solution. This self-evaluation is highly recommended. The introductory case presented here reviews the elements reported on the income statement and balance sheet and how the elements within the statements are related.

Apple's iPods, iPhones, and iTunes stores have become the center of the digital lifestyle for professionals and consumers alike. Extensive iPod content is even available for this textbook. The ease-of-use, seamless integration, and innovative design of Apple's products have produced record profits and stock price for Apple's shareholders. Following is a list of the financial statement items and amounts adapted from a recent Apple income statement and balance sheet. The numbers are presented in millions of dollars for the year ended September 30, 2006.

Accounts payable	$ 6,471	Research and development expenses	712
Accounts receivable	1,252		
Cash	10,110	Retained earnings	5,629
Contributed capital	4,355	Sales revenues	19,315
Cost of Sales	13,717	Selling, general, and administrative expenses	2,433
Income tax expense	829		
Inventories	270	Total assets	17,205
Net income	1,989	Total expenses	16,862
Notes payable	750	Total liabilities	7,221
Other assets	4,292	Total liabilities and stockholders' equity	17,205
Other revenues	365		
Pretax income	2,818	Total revenues	19,680
Property and equipment	1,281	Total stockholders' equity	9,984

Required:

1. Prepare a balance sheet and an income statement for the year following the formats in Exhibits 1.2 and 1.3.

2. Specify what information these two statements provide.

3. Indicate the other two statements that would be included in its annual report.

4. Securities regulations require that Apple's statements be subject to an independent audit. Suggest why Apple might voluntarily subject its statements to an independent audit if there were no such requirement.

SUGGESTED SOLUTION

1.

APPLE INC. Balance Sheet At September 30, 2006 (in millions of dollars)	
Assets	
Cash	$10,110
Accounts receivable	1,252
Inventories	270
Property and equipment	1,281
Other assets	4,292
Total assets	$17,205
Liabilities	
Accounts payable	$ 6,471
Notes payable	750
Total liabilities	7,221
Stockholders' Equity	
Contributed capital	4,355
Retained earnings	5,629
Total stockholders' equity	9,984
Total liabilities and stockholders' equity	$17,205

APPLE INC. Income Statement For the Year Ended September 30, 2006 (in millions of dollars)	
Revenues	
Sales revenues	$19,315
Other revenues	365
Total revenues	19,680
Expenses	
Cost of sales	13,717
Selling, general, and administrative expenses	2,433
Research and development expenses	712
Total expenses	16,862
Pretax income	2,818
Income tax expense	829
Net income	$ 1,989

2. The balance sheet reports the amount of assets, liabilities, and stockholders' equity of an accounting entity at a point in time. The income statement reports the accountant's primary measure of performance of a business, revenues less expenses, during the accounting period.

3. Apple would also present a statement of retained earnings and a statement of cash flows.

4. Users will have greater confidence in the accuracy of financial statement information if they know that the people who audited the statements were required to meet professional standards of ethics and competence.

Chapter Supplement A

Types of Business Entities

This textbook emphasizes **accounting for profit-making business entities.** The three main types of business entities are sole proprietorship, partnership, and corporation. A **sole proprietorship** is an unincorporated business owned by one person; it usually is small in size and is common in the service, retailing, and farming industries. Often the owner is the manager. Legally, the business and the owner are not separate entities. Accounting views the business as a separate entity, however, that must be accounted for separately from its owner.

A **partnership** is an unincorporated business owned by two or more persons known as **partners.** The agreements between the owners are specified in a partnership contract. This contract deals with matters such as division of income each reporting period and distribution of resources of the business on termination of its operations. A partnership is not legally separate from its owners. Legally, each partner in a general partnership is responsible for the debts of the business (each general partner has **unlimited liability**). The partnership, however, is a separate business entity to be accounted for separately from its several owners.

A **corporation** is a business incorporated under the laws of a particular state. The owners are called **stockholders** or **shareholders.** Ownership is represented by shares of capital stock that usually can be bought and sold freely. When the organizers file an approved application for incorporation, the state issues a charter. This charter gives the corporation the right to operate as a separate legal entity, separate and apart from its owners. The stockholders enjoy **limited liability.** Stockholders are liable for the corporation's debts only to the extent of their investments. The corporate charter specifies the types and amounts of capital stock that can be issued. Most states require a minimum of two or three stockholders and a minimum amount of resources to be contributed at the time of organization. The stockholders elect a governing board of directors, which in turn employs managers and exercises general supervision of the corporation. Accounting also views the corporation as a separate business entity that must be accounted for separately from its owners.

In terms of economic importance, the corporation is the dominant form of business organization in the United States. This dominance is caused by the many advantages of the corporate form: (1) limited liability for the stockholders, (2) continuity of life, (3) ease in transferring ownership (stock), and (4) opportunities to raise large amounts of money by selling shares to a large number of people. The primary disadvantage of a corporation is that its income may be subject to double taxation (it is taxed when it is earned and again when it is distributed to stockholders as dividends). In this textbook, we emphasize the corporate form of business. Nevertheless, the accounting concepts and procedures that we discuss also apply to other types of businesses.

Chapter Supplement B

Employment in the Accounting Profession Today

Since 1900, accounting has attained the stature of professions such as law, medicine, engineering, and architecture. As with all recognized professions, accounting is subject to professional competence requirements, is dedicated to service to the public, requires a high level of academic study, and rests on a common body of knowledge. An accountant may be licensed as a certified public accountant, or CPA. This designation is granted only on completion of requirements specified by the state that issues the license. Although CPA requirements vary among states, they include a college degree with a specified number of accounting courses, good character, one to five years of professional experience, and successful completion of a professional examination. The CPA examination is prepared by the American Institute of Certified Public Accountants.

Accountants (including CPAs) commonly are engaged in professional practice or are employed by businesses, government entities, nonprofit organizations, and so on. Accountants employed in these activities may take and pass a professional examination to become a certified management accountant, or CMA (the CMA examination is administered by the Institute of Management Accountants) or a certified internal auditor, or CIA (the CIA examination is administered by the Institute of Internal Auditors).

Practice of Public Accounting

Although an individual may practice public accounting, usually two or more individuals organize an accounting firm in the form of a partnership (in many cases, a limited liability partnership, or LLP). Accounting firms vary in size from a one-person office, to regional firms, to the Big Four firms (Deloitte & Touche, Ernst & Young, KPMG, and PricewaterhouseCoopers), which have hundreds of offices located worldwide. Accounting firms usually render three types of services: audit or assurance services, management consulting services, and tax services.

Audit or Assurance Services

Audit or assurance services are independent professional services that improve the quality of information, or its context, for decision makers. The most important assurance service performed by the CPA in public practice is financial statement auditing. The purpose of an audit is to lend credibility to the financial reports, that is, to ensure that they fairly represent what they claim. An audit involves an examination of the financial reports (prepared by the management of the entity) to ensure that they conform with GAAP. Other areas of assurance services include electronic commerce integrity and security and information systems reliability.

Management Consulting Services

Many independent CPA firms offer management consulting services. These services usually are accounting based and encompass such activities as the design and installation of accounting, data processing, and profit-planning and control (budget) systems; financial advice; forecasting; inventory controls; cost-effectiveness studies; and operational analysis. To maintain their independence, CPAs are prohibited from performing certain consulting services for the public companies that they audit.

Tax Services

CPAs in public practice usually provide income tax services to their clients. These services include both tax planning as a part of the decision-making process and the determination of the income tax liability (reported on the annual income tax return). Because of the increasing complexity of state and federal tax laws, a high level of competence is required, which CPAs specializing in taxation can provide. The CPA's involvement in tax planning often is quite significant. Most major business decisions have significant tax impacts; in fact, tax-planning considerations often govern certain business decisions.

Employment by Organizations

Many accountants, including CPAs, CMAs, and CIAs, are employed by profit-making and nonprofit organizations. An organization, depending on its size and complexity, may employ from a few to hundreds of accountants. In a business enterprise, the chief financial officer (usually a vice president or controller) is a member of the management team. This responsibility usually entails a wide range of management, financial, and accounting duties.

In a business entity, accountants typically are engaged in a wide variety of activities, such as general management, general accounting, cost accounting, profit planning and control (budgeting), internal auditing, and computerized data processing. A primary function of the accountants in organizations is to provide data that are useful for internal managerial decision making and for controlling operations. The functions of external reporting, tax planning, control of assets, and a host of related responsibilities normally are also performed by accountants in industry.

Employment in the Public and Not-for-Profit Sector

The vast and complex operations of governmental units, from the local to the international level, create a need for accountants. The same holds true for other not-for-profit organizations such as hospitals and universities. Accountants employed in the public and not-for-profit sector perform functions similar to those performed by their counterparts in private organizations. The Government Accountability Office (GAO) and the regulatory agencies, such as the SEC and Federal Communications Commission (FCC), also use the services of accountants in carrying out their regulatory duties.

CHAPTER **TAKE-AWAYS**

1. **Recognize the information conveyed in each of the four basic financial statements and the way that it is used by different decision makers (investors, creditors, and managers).** p. 5

   The **balance sheet** is a statement of financial position that reports dollar amounts for the assets, liabilities, and stockholders' equity at a specific point in time.

   The **income statement** is a statement of operations that reports revenues, expenses, and net income for a stated period of time.

   The **statement of retained earnings** explains changes to the retained earnings balance that occurred during the reporting period.

   The **statement of cash flows** reports inflows and outflows of cash for a stated period of time.

   The statements are used by investors and creditors to evaluate different aspects of the firm's financial position and performance.

2. **Identify the role of generally accepted accounting principles (GAAP) in determining the content of financial statements.** p. 18

   GAAP are the measurement rules used to develop the information in financial statements. Knowledge of GAAP is necessary for accurate interpretation of the numbers in financial statements.

3. **Distinguish the roles of managers and auditors in the accounting communication process.** p. 21

   Management has primary responsibility for the accuracy of a company's financial information. Auditors are responsible for expressing an opinion on the fairness of the financial statement presentations based on their examination of the reports and records of the company.

4. **Appreciate the importance of ethics, reputation, and legal liability in accounting.** p. 23

   Users will have confidence in the accuracy of financial statement numbers only if the people associated with their preparation and audit have reputations for ethical behavior and competence. Management and auditors can also be held legally liable for fraudulent financial statements and malpractice.

In this chapter, we studied the basic financial statements that communicate financial information to external users. Chapters 2, 3, and 4 provide a more detailed look at financial statements and examine how to translate data about business transactions into these statements. Learning how to translate back and forth between business transactions and financial statements is the key to using financial statements in planning and decision making. Chapter 2 begins our discussion of the way that the accounting function collects data about business transactions and processes the data to provide periodic financial statements, with emphasis on the balance sheet. To accomplish this purpose, Chapter 2 discusses key accounting concepts, the accounting model, transaction analysis, and analytical tools. We examine typical business activities of an actual service-oriented company to demonstrate the concepts in Chapters 2, 3, and 4.

FINDING **FINANCIAL INFORMATION**

Balance Sheet

Assets = Liabilities + Stockholders' Equity

Income Statement

   Revenues
− Expenses
   Net Income

Statement of Retained Earnings

   Retained Earnings, beginning of the period
+ Net Income
− Dividends
   Retained Earnings, end of the period

Statement of Cash Flows

+/− Cash Flow from Operating Activities
+/− Cash Flow from Investing Activities
+/− Cash Flow from Financing Activities
   Net Change in Cash

Accounting p. 4
Accounting Entity p. 7
Accounting Period p. 11
Audit p. 21
Balance Sheet (Statement of
   Financial Position) p. 7
Basic Accounting Equation
   (Balance Sheet Equation) p. 8

**Financial Accounting Standards
   Board (FASB)** p. 20
**Generally Accepted Accounting
   Principles (GAAP)** p. 19
Income Statement (Statement of
   Income, Statement of Earnings, or
   Statement of Operations) p. 10
Notes (Footnotes) p. 17

**Public Company Accounting
   Oversight Board (PCAOB)** p. 22
**Securities and Exchange
   Commission (SEC)** p. 19
Statement of Cash Flows p. 14
Statement of Retained Earnings
   p. 13

QUESTIONS

1. Define **accounting.**
2. Briefly distinguish financial accounting from managerial accounting.
3. The accounting process generates financial reports for both internal and external users. Identify some of the groups of users.
4. Briefly distinguish investors from creditors.
5. What is an accounting entity? Why is a business treated as a separate entity for accounting purposes?
6. Complete the following:

Name of Statement	Alternative Title
a. Income statement	a. _____
b. Balance sheet	b. _____
c. Audit report	c. _____

7. What information should be included in the heading of each of the four primary financial statements?
8. What are the purposes of (a) the income statement, (b) the balance sheet, (c) the statement of cash flows, and (d) the statement of retained earnings?
9. Explain why the income statement and the statement of cash flows are dated "For the Year Ended December 31, 2008," whereas the balance sheet is dated "At December 31, 2008."
10. Briefly explain the importance of assets and liabilities to the decisions of investors and creditors.
11. Briefly define **net income** and **net loss.**
12. Explain the accounting equation for the income statement. What are the three major items reported on the income statement?
13. Explain the accounting equation for the balance sheet. Define the three major components reported on the balance sheet.
14. Explain the accounting equation for the statement of cash flows. Explain the three major components reported on the statement.
15. Explain the accounting equation for the statement of retained earnings. Explain the four major items reported on the statement of retained earnings.
16. Financial statements discussed in this chapter are aimed at **external** users. Briefly explain how a company's **internal** managers in different functional areas (e.g., marketing, purchasing, human resources) might use financial statement information from their own and other companies.
17. Briefly describe the way that accounting measurement rules (generally accepted accounting principles) are determined in the United States.
18. Briefly explain the responsibility of company management and the independent auditors in the accounting communication process.
19. (Supplement A) Briefly differentiate between a sole proprietorship, a partnership, and a corporation.
20. (Supplement B) List and briefly explain the three primary services that CPAs in public practice provide.

MULTIPLE-CHOICE QUESTIONS

1. Which of the following is **not** one of the four basic financial statements?
   a. Balance sheet
   b. Audit report
   c. Income statement
   d. Statement of cash flows

2. As stated in the audit report, or **Report of Independent Accountants,** the primary responsibility for a company's financial statements lies with
   a. The owners of the company.
   b. Independent financial analysts.
   c. The auditors.
   d. The company's management.

3. Which of the following is true?
   a. FASB creates SEC.
   b. GAAP creates FASB.
   c. SEC creates AICPA.
   d. FASB creates GAAP.

4. Which of the following regarding retained earnings is false?
   a. Retained earnings is increased by net income and decreased by a net loss.
   b. Retained earnings is a component of stockholders' equity on the balance sheet.
   c. Retained earnings is an asset on the balance sheet.
   d. Retained earnings represents earnings not distributed to stockholders in the form of dividends.

5. Which of the following is **not** one of the four items required to be shown in the heading of a financial statement?
   a. The financial statement preparer's name.
   b. The title of the financial statement.
   c. The unit of measure in the financial statement.
   d. The name of the business entity.

6. How many of the following statements regarding the statement of cash flows is true?
   - The statement of cash flows separates cash inflows and outflows into three major categories: operations, investing, and financing.
   - The ending cash balance shown on the statement of cash flows must agree with the amount shown on the balance sheet for the same fiscal period.
   - The total increase or decrease in cash shown on the statement of cash flows must agree with the "bottom line" (net income or net loss) reported on the income statement.
   a. None
   b. One
   c. Two
   d. Three

7. Which of the following is **not** a typical note included in an annual report?
   a. A note describing the auditor's opinion of the management's past and future financial planning for the business.
   b. A note providing more detail about a specific item shown in the financial statements.
   c. A note describing the accounting rules applied in the financial statements.
   d. A note describing financial disclosures about items not appearing in the financial statements.

8. Which of the following is true regarding the income statement?
   a. The income statement is sometimes called the **statement of operations.**
   b. The income statement reports revenues, expenses, and liabilities.
   c. The income statement reports only revenue for which cash was received at the point of sale.
   d. The income statement reports the financial position of a business at a particular point in time.

9. Which of the following is false regarding the balance sheet?
   a. The accounts shown on a balance sheet represent the basic accounting equation for a particular business entity.
   b. The retained earnings balance shown on the balance sheet must agree with the ending retained earnings balance shown on the statement of retained earnings.
   c. The balance sheet reports the changes in specific account balances over a period of time.
   d. The balance sheet reports the amount of assets, liabilities, and stockholders' equity of an accounting entity at a point in time.

10. Which of the following regarding GAAP is true?
    a. U.S. GAAP is the body of accounting knowledge followed by all countries in the world.
    b. Changes in GAAP can affect the interests of managers and stockholders.
    c. GAAP is the abbreviation for generally accepted auditing procedures.
    d. Changes to GAAP must be approved by the Senate Finance Committee.

To practice with more multiple-choice questions, go to the text website www.mhhe.com/libby6e.

HM™ **Available with McGraw-Hill's Homework Manager**

Matching Elements with Financial Statements

M1-1
LO1

Match each element with its financial statement by entering the appropriate letter in the space provided.

Element	Financial Statement
___ (1) Expenses	A. Balance sheet
___ (2) Cash flow from investing activities	B. Income statement
___ (3) Assets	C. Statement of retained earnings
___ (4) Dividends	D. Statement of cash flows
___ (5) Revenues	
___ (6) Cash flow from operating activities	
___ (7) Liabilities	
___ (8) Cash flow from financing activities	

Matching Financial Statement Items to Financial Statement Categories

M1-2
LO1

Mark each item in the following list as an asset (A), liability (L), or stockholders' equity (SE) that would appear on the balance sheet or a revenue (R) or expense (E) that would appear on the income statement.

___ (1) Retained earnings	___ (6) Inventories
___ (2) Accounts receivable	___ (7) Interest expense
___ (3) Sales revenue	___ (8) Accounts payable
___ (4) Property, plant, and equipment	___ (9) Land
___ (5) Cost of goods sold expense	

Identifying Important Accounting Abbreviations

M1-3
LO2, 3

The following is a list of important abbreviations used in the chapter. These abbreviations also are used widely in business. For each abbreviation, give the full designation. The first one is an example.

Abbreviation	Full Designation
(1) CPA	Certified Public Accountant
(2) GAAP	_____
(3) CMA	_____
(4) AICPA	_____
(5) SEC	_____
(6) FASB	_____

EXERCISES

E1-1
L01, 2

Matching Definitions with Terms or Abbreviations

Match each definition with its related term or abbreviation by entering the appropriate letter in the space provided.

Term or Abbreviation	Definition
___ (1) SEC	A. A system that collects and processes financial information about an organization and reports that information to decision makers.
___ (2) Audit	
___ (3) Sole proprietorship	
___ (4) Corporation	B. Measurement of information about an entity in the monetary unit—dollars or other national currency.
___ (5) Accounting	
___ (6) Accounting entity	C. An unincorporated business owned by two or more persons.
___ (7) Audit report	D. The organization for which financial data are to be collected (separate and distinct from its owners).
___ (8) Cost principle	
___ (9) Partnership	E. An incorporated entity that issues shares of stock as evidence of ownership.
___ (10) FASB	
___ (11) CPA	F. Initial recording of financial statement elements at acquisition cost.
___ (12) Unit of measure	
___ (13) GAAP	G. An examination of the financial reports to ensure that they represent what they claim and conform with generally accepted accounting principles.
___ (14) Publicly traded	
	H. Certified public accountant.
	I. An unincorporated business owned by one person.
	J. A report that describes the auditor's opinion of the fairness of the financial statement presentations and the evidence gathered to support that opinion.
	K. Securities and Exchange Commission.
	L. Financial Accounting Standards Board.
	M. A company with stock that can be bought and sold by investors on established stock exchanges.
	N. Generally accepted accounting principles.

E1-2
L01

Matching Financial Statement Items to Financial Statement Categories

According to its annual report, "P&G's more than 250 brands include Pampers, Tide, Ariel, Always, Whisper, Pantene, Bounty, Pringles, Folgers, Charmin, Downy, Lenor, Iams, Olay, Crest, Vicks and Actonel." The following are items taken from its recent balance sheet and income statement. Note that different companies use slightly different titles for the same item. Mark each item in the following list as an asset (A), liability (L), or stockholders' equity (SE) that would appear on the balance sheet or a revenue (R) or expense (E) that would appear on the income statement.

___ (1) Accounts receivable		___ (9) Income taxes	
___ (2) Cash and cash equivalents		___ (10) Accounts payable	
___ (3) Net sales		___ (11) Land	
___ (4) Notes payable		___ (12) Property, plant, and equipment	
___ (5) Taxes payable		___ (13) Long-term debt	
___ (6) Retained earnings		___ (14) Inventories	
___ (7) Cost of products sold		___ (15) Interest expense	
___ (8) Marketing, administrative, and other operating expenses			

E1-3
L01

Matching Financial Statement Items to Financial Statement Categories

Tootsie Roll Industries is engaged in the manufacture and sale of candy. Major products include Tootsie Roll, Tootsie Roll Pops, Tootsie Pop Drops, Tootsie Flavor Rolls, Charms, and Blow-Pop lollipops. The following items were listed on Tootsie Roll's recent income statement and balance sheet. Mark each item from the balance sheet as an asset (A), liability (L), or shareholders' equity (SE) and each item from the income statement as a revenue (R) or expense (E).

_____ (1) Notes payable to banks
_____ (2) General and administrative
_____ (3) Accounts payable
_____ (4) Dividends payable
_____ (5) Retained earnings
_____ (6) Cash and cash equivalents
_____ (7) Accounts receivable
_____ (8) Provision for income taxes*
_____ (9) Cost of goods sold

_____ (10) Machinery and equipment
_____ (11) Net sales
_____ (12) Inventories
_____ (13) Marketing, selling, and advertising
_____ (14) Buildings
_____ (15) Land
_____ (16) Income taxes payable
_____ (17) Distribution and warehousing costs
_____ (18) Investments (in other companies)

Preparing a Balance Sheet

E1-4
LO1
Honda Motor Co.

Honda Motor Corporation of Japan is a leading international manufacturer of automobiles, motorcycles, all-terrain vehicles, and personal watercraft. As a Japanese company, it follows Japanese GAAP and reports its financial statements in billions of yen (the sign for yen is ¥). Its recent balance sheet contained the following items (in billions). Prepare a balance sheet as of March 31, 2007, solving for the missing amount. (**Hint:** Exhibit 1.2 in the chapter provides a good model for completing this exercise.)

Cash and cash equivalents	¥ 946
Contributed capital	123
Accounts payable and other current liabilities	4,288
Inventories	1,183
Investments	742
Long-term debt	1,906
Net property, plant, and equipment	2,079
Other assets	4,606
Other liabilities	1,238
Retained earnings	4,482
Total assets	12,037
Total liabilities and stockholders' equity	?
Trade accounts, notes, and other receivables	2,481

Completing a Balance Sheet and Inferring Net Income

E1-5
LO1

Terry Lloyd and Joan Lopez organized Read More Store as a corporation; each contributed $75,000 cash to start the business and received 4,000 shares of common stock. The store completed its first year of operations on December 31, 2010. On that date, the following financial items for the year were determined: December 31, 2010, cash on hand and in the bank, $73,350; December 31, 2010, amounts due from customers from sales of books, $39,000; unused portion of store and office equipment, $72,000; December 31, 2010, amounts owed to publishers for books purchased, $12,000; one-year note payable to a local bank for $3,000. No dividends were declared or paid to the stockholders during the year.

Required:
1. Complete the following balance sheet as of the end of 2010.
2. What was the amount of net income for the year? (**Hint:** Use the retained earnings equation [Beginning Retained Earnings + Net Income − Dividends = Ending Retained Earnings] to solve for net income.)

_____
_____
_____

(continued on next page)

---

*In the United States, "provision for income taxes" is most often used as a synonym for "income tax expense."

Assets		Liabilities	
Cash	$ ___	Accounts payable	$ ___
Accounts receivable	___	Note payable	___
Store and office equipment	___	Interest payable	120
		Total liabilities	$ ___
		Stockholders' Equity	
		Contributed capital	$ ___
		Retained earnings	19,230
		Total stockholders' equity	___
Total assets	$ ___	Total liabilities and stockholders' equity	$ ___

E1-6   Analyzing Revenues and Expenses and Preparing an Income Statement
L01

Assume that you are the owner of The University Shop, which specializes in items that interest students. At the end of January 2010, you find (for January only) this information:

a. Sales, per the cash register tapes, of $110,000, plus one sale on credit (a special situation) of $3,000.

b. With the help of a friend (who majored in accounting), you determined that all of the goods sold during January had cost $40,000 to purchase.

c. During the month, according to the checkbook, you paid $37,000 for salaries, rent, supplies, advertising, and other expenses; however, you have not yet paid the $900 monthly utilities for January on the store and fixtures.

Required:

On the basis of the data given (disregard income taxes), what was the amount of net income for January? Show computations. (**Hint:** A convenient form to use has the following major side captions: Revenue from Sales, Expenses, and the difference—Net Income.)

E1-7   Preparing an Income Statement and Inferring Missing Values
L01

Walgreen Co. is the nation's leading drugstore chain. Its recent quarterly income statement contained the following items (in millions). Solve for the missing amounts and prepare an income statement for the quarter ended May 31, 2007. (**Hint:** First order the items as they would appear on the income statement and then solve for the missing values. Exhibit 1.3 in the chapter provides a good model for completing this exercise.)

Cost of sales	$9,821
Provision for income taxes*	305
Interest revenue	11
Net earnings	?
Net sales	13,698
Pretax income	?
Selling, occupancy and administration expense	3,022
Total expenses	?
Total revenues	?

E1-8   Analyzing Revenues and Expenses and Completing an Income Statement
L01

Home Realty, Incorporated, has been operating for three years and is owned by three investors. J. Doe owns 60 percent of the total outstanding stock of 9,000 shares and is the managing executive in charge. On December 31, 2012, the following financial items for the entire year were determined: commissions earned and collected in cash, $150,900, plus $16,800 uncollected; rental service fees earned and collected, $20,000; salaries expense paid, $62,740; commissions expense paid, $35,330; payroll taxes paid, $2,500; rent paid, $2,475 (not including December rent yet to be paid); utilities

---

*In the United States, "provision for income taxes" is a common synonym for "income tax expense."

expense paid, $1,600; promotion and advertising paid, $7,750; income taxes paid, $19,400; and miscellaneous expenses paid, $500. There were no other unpaid expenses at December 31. Also during the year, the company paid the owners "out-of-profit" cash dividends amounting to $12,000. Complete the following income statement:

Revenues	
Commissions earned	$ _____
Rental service fees	_____
Total revenues	$ _____
Expenses	
Salaries expense	_____
Commission expense	_____
Payroll tax expense	_____
Rent expense	_____
Utilities expense	_____
Promotion and advertising expense	_____
Miscellaneous expenses	_____
Total expenses (excluding income taxes)	_____
Pretax income	_____
Income tax expense	_____
Net income	$55,180

Inferring Values Using the Income Statement and Balance Sheet Equations

E1-9
LO1

Review the chapter explanations of the income statement and the balance sheet equations. Apply these equations in each independent case to compute the two missing amounts for each case. Assume that it is the end of 2010, the first full year of operations for the company. (**Hint:** Organize the listed items as they are presented in the balance sheet and income statement equations and then compute the missing amounts.)

Independent Cases	Total Revenues	Total Expenses	Net Income (Loss)	Total Assets	Total Liabilities	Stockholders' Equity
A	$94,700	$76,940	$	$140,200	$66,000	$
B		84,240	14,740	107,880		79,010
C	69,260	76,430		97,850	69,850	
D	58,680		19,770		17,890	78,680
E	84,840	78,720			20,520	79,580

Inferring Values Using the Income Statement and Balance Sheet Equations

E1-10
LO1

Review the chapter explanations of the income statement and the balance sheet equations. Apply these equations in each independent case to compute the two missing amounts for each case. Assume that it is the end of 2011, the first full year of operations for the company. (**Hint:** Organize the listed items as they are presented in the balance sheet and income statement equations and then compute the missing amounts.)

Independent Cases	Total Revenues	Total Expenses	Net Income (Loss)	Total Assets	Total Liabilities	Stockholders' Equity
A	$231,820	$186,700	$	$294,300	$75,000	$
B		175,780	19,920	590,000		348,400
C	72,990	91,890		258,200	200,760	
D	36,590		13,840		189,675	97,525
E	224,130	210,630			173,850	471,240

E1-11   **Preparing an Income Statement and Balance Sheet**

LO1   Clay Corporation was organized by five individuals on January 1, 2011. At the end of January 2011, the following monthly financial data are available:

Total revenues	$299,000
Total expenses (excluding income taxes)	184,000
Income tax expense (all unpaid as of January 31)	34,500
Cash balance, January 31, 2011	70,150
Receivables from customers (all considered collectible)	34,500
Merchandise inventory (by inventory count at cost)	96,600
Payables to suppliers for merchandise purchased from them	
(will be paid during February 2011)	26,450
Contributed capital (2,600 shares)	59,800

No dividends were declared or paid during 2011.

Required:

Complete the following two statements:

CLAY CORPORATION
Income Statement
For the Month of January 2011

Total revenues	$ _____
Less: Total expenses (excluding income tax)	_____
Pretax income	_____
Less: Income tax expense	_____
Net income	$ _____

CLAY CORPORATION
Balance Sheet
At January 31, 2011

Assets	
Cash	$ _____
Receivables from customers	_____
Merchandise inventory	_____
Total assets	$ _____
Liabilities	
Payables to suppliers	$ _____
Income taxes payable	_____
Total liabilities	_____
Stockholders' Equity	
Contributed capital	
Retained earnings	_____
Total stockholders' equity	_____
Total liabilities and stockholders' equity	$ _____

Preparing a Statement of Retained Earnings

E1-12
LO1

Stone Culture Corporation was organized on January 1, 2009. For its first two years of operations, it reported the following:

Net income for 2009	$34,000
Net income for 2010	42,000
Dividends for 2009	14,200
Dividends for 2010	18,700
Total assets at the end of 2009	130,000
Total assets at the end of 2010	250,000

Required:
On the basis of the data given, prepare a statement of retained earnings for 2010. Show computations.

Focus on Cash Flows: Matching Cash Flow Statement Items to Categories

E1-13
LO1

The following items were taken from a recent cash flow statement. Note that different companies use slightly different titles for the same item. Without referring to Exhibit 1.5, mark each item in the list as a cash flow from operating activities (O), investing activities (I), or financing activities (F). Also place parentheses around the letter only if it is a cash outflow.
_____ (1) Purchases of property, plant, and equipment
_____ (2) Cash received from customers
_____ (3) Cash paid for dividends to stockholders
_____ (4) Cash paid to suppliers
_____ (5) Income taxes paid
_____ (6) Cash paid to employees
_____ (7) Cash proceeds received from sale of investment in another company
_____ (8) Repayment of borrowings

Preparing a Statement of Cash Flows

E1-14
LO1

NITSU Manufacturing Corporation is preparing the annual financial statements for the stockholders. A statement of cash flows must be prepared. The following data on cash flows were developed for the entire year ended December 31, 2011: cash collections from sales, $280,000; cash expended for operating expenses, $175,000; sale of unissued NITSU stock for cash, $30,000; cash dividends declared and paid to stockholders during the year, $18,000; and payments on long-term notes payable, $80,000. During the year, a tract of land held as an investment was sold for $10,000 cash (which was the same price that NITSU had paid for the land in 2010), and $48,000 cash was expended for two new machines. The machines were used in the factory. The beginning-of-the-year cash balance was $63,000.

Required:
Prepare the statement of cash flows for 2011. Follow the format illustrated in the chapter.

 Available with McGraw-Hill's Homework Manager

PROBLEMS

Preparing an Income Statement, Statement of Retained Earnings, and Balance Sheet (AP1–1)

P1-1
LO1

e**X**cel
www.mhhe.com/libby6e

Assume that you are the president of Propane Company. At the end of the first year (December 31, 2009) of operations, the following financial data for the company are available:

Cash	$22,500
Receivables from customers (all considered collectible)	10,800
Inventory of merchandise (based on physical count and priced at cost)	81,000
Equipment owned, at cost less used portion	40,700
Accounts payable owed to suppliers	46,140
Salary payable for 2009 (on December 31, 2009, this was owed to an employee who was away because of an emergency; will return around January 10, 2010, at which time the payment will be made)	1,800

Total sales revenue	126,000
Expenses, including the cost of the merchandise sold (excluding income taxes)	80,200
Income taxes expense at 30% × pretax income; all paid during 2009	?
Contributed capital, 7,000 shares outstanding	87,000
Dividends declared and paid during 2009	12,000

Required (show computations):

Using the financial statement exhibits in the chapter as models:

1. Prepare a summarized income statement for the year 2009.
2. Prepare a statement of retained earnings for the year 2009.
3. Prepare a balance sheet at December 31, 2009.

P1-2
LO1

eXcel

www.mhhe.com/libby6e

P1-2 Analyzing a Student's Business and Preparing an Income Statement (AP1–2)

During the summer between her junior and senior years, Susan Irwin needed to earn sufficient money for the coming academic year. Unable to obtain a job with a reasonable salary, she decided to try the lawn care business for three months. After a survey of the market potential, Susan bought a used pickup truck on June 1 for $1,500. On each door she painted "Susan's Lawn Service, Phone 471-4487." She also spent $900 for mowers, trimmers, and tools. To acquire these items, she borrowed $2,500 cash by signing a note payable promising to pay the $2,500 plus interest of $65 at the end of the three months (ending August 31).

At the end of the summer, Susan realized that she had done a lot of work, and her bank account looked good. This fact prompted her to become concerned about how much profit the business had earned.

A review of the check stubs showed the following: Bank deposits of collections from customers totaled $12,300. The following checks had been written: gas, oil, and lubrication, $940; pickup repairs, $250; mower repair, $110; miscellaneous supplies used, $80; helpers, $4,200; payroll taxes, $190; payment for assistance in preparing payroll tax forms, $25; insurance, $125; telephone, $110; and $2,565 to pay off the note including interest (on August 31). A notebook kept in the pickup, plus some unpaid bills, reflected that customers still owed her $700 for lawn services rendered and that she owed $180 for gas and oil (credit card charges). She estimated that the cost for use of the truck and the other equipment (called **depreciation**) for three months amounted to $600.

Required:

1. Prepare a quarterly income statement for Susan's Lawn Service for the months June, July, and August 2011. Use the following main captions: Revenues from Services, Expenses, and Net Income. Because this is a sole proprietorship, the company will not be subject to income tax.
2. Do you see a need for one or more additional financial reports for this company for 2011 and thereafter? Explain.

P1-3
LO1

Comparing Income with Cash Flow (A Challenging Problem) (AP1–3)

Ace Trucking Company was organized on January 1, 2010. At the end of the first quarter (three months) of operations, the owner prepared a summary of its activities as shown in the first row of the following tabulation:

Summary of Transactions	Computation of	
	Income	Cash
a. Services performed for customers, $66,000, of which $11,000 remained uncollected at the end of the quarter.	+$66,000	+$55,000
b. Cash borrowed from the local bank, $35,000 (one-year note).		
c. Small service truck purchased at the end of the quarter to be used in the business for two years starting the next quarter: cost, $9,500 cash.		
d. Wages earned by employees, $23,000, of which one-half remained unpaid at the end of the quarter.		

e. Service supplies purchased for use in the business, $3,800 cash, of which $900 were unused (still on hand) at the end of the quarter.		
f. Other operating expenses, $39,000, of which $6,500 remained unpaid at the end of the quarter.	_____	_____

Based only on these transactions, compute the following for the quarter:
   Income (or loss)
   Cash inflow (or outflow)
	═══════	═══════

Required:
1. For each of the six transactions given in this tabulation, enter what you consider the correct amounts. Enter a zero when appropriate. The first transaction is illustrated.
2. For each transaction, explain the basis for your dollar responses.

Evaluating Data to Support a Loan Application (A Challenging Problem)

P1-4
LO1

On January 1, 2009, three individuals organized West Company as a corporation. Each individual invested $10,000 cash in the business. On December 31, 2009, they prepared a list of resources owned (assets) and a list of the debts (liabilities) to support a company loan request for $70,000 submitted to a local bank. None of the three investors had studied accounting. The two lists prepared were as follows:

Company resources	
Cash	$ 12,000
Service supplies inventory (on hand)	7,000
Service trucks (four practically new)	68,000
Personal residences of organizers (three houses)	190,000
Service equipment used in the business (practically new)	30,000
Bills due from customers (for services already completed)	15,000
Total	$322,000

Company obligations	
Unpaid wages to employees	$19,000
Unpaid taxes	8,000
Owed to suppliers	10,000
Owed on service trucks and equipment (to a finance company)	50,000
Loan from organizer	10,000
Total	$ 97,000

Required:
Prepare a short memo indicating:
1. Which of these items do not belong on the balance sheet? (Bear in mind that the company is considered to be separate from the owners.)
2. What additional questions would you raise about the measurement of items on the list? Explain the basis for each question.
3. If you were advising the local bank on its loan decision, which amounts on the list would create special concerns? Explain the basis for each concern and include any recommendations that you have.
4. In view of your responses to (1) and (2), what do you think the amount of stockholders' equity (i.e., assets minus liabilities) of the company would be? Show your computations.

ALTERNATE PROBLEMS

AP1-1   **Preparing an Income Statement, Statement of Retained Earnings, and Balance Sheet**
L01   (P1–1)

Assume that you are the president of Arkur Corporation. At the end of the first year (June 30, 2010) of operations, the following financial data for the company are available:

Cash	$13,150
Receivables from customers (all considered collectible)	9,500
Inventory of merchandise (based on physical count and priced at cost)	27,000
Equipment owned, at cost less used portion	66,000
Accounts payable owed to suppliers	31,500
Salary payable for 2010 (on June 30, 2010, this was owed to an employee who was away because of an emergency; will return around July 7, 2010, at which time the payment will be made)	1,500
Total sales revenue	100,000
Expenses, including the cost of the merchandise sold (excluding income taxes)	70,500
Income taxes expense at 30% × pretax income; all paid during 2010	?
Contributed capital, 5,000 shares outstanding	62,000
No dividends were declared or paid during 2010.	

Required (show computations):
Using the financial statement exhibits in the chapter as models:
1. Prepare a summarized income statement for the year ended June 30, 2010.
2. Prepare a statement of retained earnings for the year ended June 30, 2010.
3. Prepare a balance sheet at June 30, 2010.

AP1-2   **Analyzing a Student's Business and Preparing an Income Statement** (P1–2)
L01

Upon graduation from high school, John Abel immediately accepted a job as an electrician's assistant for a large local electrical repair company. After three years of hard work, John received an electrician's license and decided to start his own business. He had saved $12,000, which he invested in the business. First, he transferred this amount from his savings account to a business bank account for Abel Electric Repair Company, Incorporated. His lawyer had advised him to start as a corporation. He then purchased a used panel truck for $9,000 cash and secondhand tools for $1,500; rented space in a small building; inserted an ad in the local paper; and opened the doors on October 1, 2009. Immediately, John was very busy; after one month, he employed an assistant.

Although John knew practically nothing about the financial side of the business, he realized that a number of reports were required and that costs and collections had to be controlled carefully. At the end of the year, prompted in part by concern about his income tax situation (previously he had to report only salary), John recognized the need for financial statements. His wife Jane developed some financial statements for the business. On December 31, 2009, with the help of a friend, she gathered the following data for the three months just ended. Bank account deposits of collections for electric repair services totaled $32,000. The following checks had been written: electrician's assistant, $8,500; payroll taxes, $175; supplies purchased and used on jobs, $9,500; oil, gas, and maintenance on truck, $1,200; insurance, $700; rent, $500; utilities and telephone, $825; and miscellaneous expenses (including advertising), $600. Also, uncollected bills to customers for electric repair services amounted to $3,000. The $200 rent for December had not been paid. John estimated the cost of using the truck and tools (depreciation) during the three months to be $1,200. Income taxes for the three-month period were $3,480.

Required:
1. Prepare a quarterly income statement for Abel Electric Repair for the three months October through December 2009. Use the following main captions: Revenues from Services, Expenses, Pretax Income, and Net Income.
2. Do you think that John may need one or more additional financial reports for 2009 and thereafter? Explain.

AP1-3 Comparing Income with Cash Flow (A Challenging Problem)(P1–3)

Bocarex Poultry Company was organized on January 1, 2010. At the end of the first quarter (three months) of operations, the owner prepared a summary of its activities as shown in the first row of the following tabulation:

Summary of Transactions	Computation of Income	Computation of Cash
a. Services performed for customers, $75,000, of which $15,000 remained uncollected at the end of the quarter.	+$75,000	+$60,000
b. Cash borrowed from the local bank, $30,000 (one-year note).		
c. Small service truck purchased at the end of the quarter to be used in the business for two years starting the next quarter: cost, $8,000 cash.		
d. Wages earned by employees, $36,000, of which one-sixth remained unpaid at the end of the quarter.		
e. Service supplies purchased for use in the business, $4,000 cash, of which $1,000 were unused (still on hand) at the end of the quarter.		
f. Other operating expenses, $27,000, of which one-half remained unpaid at the end of the quarter.	_____	_____
Based only on these transactions, compute the following for the quarter: Income (or loss) Cash inflow (or outflow)	=====	=====

Required:
1. For each of the six transactions given in this tabulation, enter what you consider the correct amounts. Enter a zero when appropriate. The first transaction is illustrated.
2. For each transaction, explain the basis for your dollar responses.

CASES **AND PROJECTS**

ANNUAL REPORT CASES

Finding Financial Information

Refer to the financial statements of American Eagle Outfitters in Appendix B at the end of this book.

AMERICAN EAGLE OUTFITTERS

Required:
Skim the annual report. Look at the income statement, balance sheet, and cash flow statement closely and attempt to infer what kinds of information they report. Then answer the following questions based on the report.
1. What types of products does it sell?
2. On what date does American Eagle Outfitters' most recent reporting year end?
3. For how many years does it present complete
   a. Balance sheets?
   b. Income statements?
   c. Cash flow statements?
4. Are its financial statements audited by independent CPAs? How do you know?
5. Did its total assets increase or decrease over the last year?
6. How much inventory (in dollars) did the company have as of February 3, 2007 (accountants would call this the ending balance)?

7. Write out the basic accounting (balance sheet) equation and provide the values in dollars reported by the company as of February 3, 2007.

CP1-2
LO1, 3
Urban Outfitters

CP1-2 Finding Financial Information

Refer to the financial statements of Urban Outfitters in Appendix C at the end of this book.

Required:
1. What is the amount of net income for the most recent year?
2. What amount of revenue was earned in the most recent year?
3. How much inventory (in dollars) does the company have as of January 31, 2007?
4. By what amount did cash and cash equivalents* change during the most recent year?
5. Who is the auditor for the company?

CP1-3
LO1
AMERICAN EAGLE OUTFITTERS

Urban Outfitters

www.mhhe.com/libby6e

CP1-3 Comparing Companies Within an Industry

Refer to the financial statements of American Eagle Outfitters in Appendix B and Urban Outfitters in Appendix C.

Required:
1. Total assets is a common measure of the size of a company. Which company had the higher total assets at the end of the most recent year? **(Note: some companies will label a year that has a January year end as having a fiscal year end dated one year earlier. For example, a January 2007 year-end may be labeled as Fiscal 2006 since the year actually has more months that fall in the 2006 calendar year than in the 2007 calendar year.)**
2. Net sales is also a common measure of the size of a company. Which company had the higher net sales for the most recent year?
3. Growth during a period is calculated as:

$$\frac{\text{Ending amount} - \text{Beginning amount}}{\text{Beginning amount}} \times 100 = \text{Growth rate}$$

Which company had the highest growth in total assets during the most recent year? Which company had the highest growth in net sales during the most recent year?

FINANCIAL REPORTING AND ANALYSIS CASES

CP1-4
LO1

Using Financial Reports: Identifying and Correcting Deficiencies in an Income Statement and Balance Sheet

Performance Corporation was organized on January 1, 2009. At the end of 2009, the company had not yet employed an accountant; however, an employee who was "good with numbers" prepared the following statements at that date:

PERFORMANCE CORPORATION
December 31, 2009

Income from sales of merchandise	$175,000
Total amount paid for goods sold during 2006	(90,000)
Selling costs	(25,000)
Depreciation (on service vehicles used)	(10,000)
Income from services rendered	52,000
Salaries and wages paid	(62,000)

---

*Cash equivalents are short-term investments readily convertible to cash whose value is unlikely to change.

PERFORMANCE CORPORATION
December 31, 2009

Resources	
Cash	$ 32,000
Merchandise inventory (held for resale)	42,000
Service vehicles	50,000
Retained earnings (profit earned in 2009)	30,000
Grand total	$154,000
Debts	
Payables to suppliers	$ 22,000
Note owed to bank	25,000
Due from customers	13,000
Total	$ 60,000

Supplies on hand (to be used in rendering services)	$15,000	
Accumulated depreciation* (on service vehicles)	10,000	
Contributed capital, 6,500 shares	65,000	
Total		90,000
Grand total		$150,000

Required:
1. List all deficiencies that you can identify in these statements. Give a brief explanation of each one.
2. Prepare a proper income statement (correct net income is $30,000 and income tax expense is $10,000) and balance sheet (correct total assets are $142,000).

CRITICAL THINKING CASES

Making Decisions as an Owner: Deciding about a Proposed Audit

CP1-5
LO3

You are one of three partners who own and operate Mary's Maid Service. The company has been operating for seven years. One of the other partners has always prepared the company's annual financial statements. Recently you proposed that the statements be audited each year because it would benefit the partners and preclude possible disagreements about the division of profits. The partner who prepares the statements proposed that his Uncle Ray, who has a lot of financial experience, can do the job and at little cost. Your other partner remained silent.

Required:
1. What position would you take on the proposal? Justify your response.
2. What would you strongly recommend? Give the basis for your recommendation.

Evaluating an Ethical Dilemma: Ethics and Auditor Responsibilities

CP1-6
LO3, 4

A key factor that an auditor provides is independence. The **AICPA Code of Professional Conduct** states that "a member in public practice should be independent in fact and appearance when providing auditing and other attestation services."

Required:
Do you consider the following circumstances to suggest a lack of independence? Justify your position. (Use your imagination. Specific answers are not provided in the chapter.)
1. Jack Jones is a partner with a large audit firm and is assigned to the Ford audit. Jack owns 10 shares of Ford.
2. Jane Winkler has invested in a mutual fund company that owns 500,000 shares of Sears stock. She is the auditor of Sears.

*Accumulated depreciation represents the used portion of the asset and should be subtracted from the assets balance.

3. Bob Franklin is a clerk/typist who works on the audit of AT&T. He has just inherited 50,000 shares of AT&T stock. (Bob enjoys his work and plans to continue despite his new wealth.)
4. Nancy Sodoma worked on weekends as the controller for a small business that a friend started. Nancy quit the job in midyear and now has no association with the company. She works full-time for a large CPA firm and has been assigned to do the audit of her friend's business.
5. Mark Jacobs borrowed $100,000 for a home mortgage from First City National Bank. The mortgage was granted on normal credit terms. Mark is the partner in charge of the First City audit.

FINANCIAL REPORTING AND ANALYSIS TEAM PROJECT

CP1-7
LO3, 4

Team Project: Examining an Annual Report

As a team, select an industry to analyze. *Reuters* provides lists of industries and their makeup at **www.reuters.com/finance/industries**. Each team member should acquire the annual report or 10-K for one publicly traded company in the industry, with each member selecting a different company. (Library files, the SEC EDGAR service at **www.sec.gov**, or the company itself are good sources.)

Required:

On an individual basis, each team member should write a short report answering the following questions about the selected company. Discuss any patterns across the companies that you as a team observe. Then, as a team, write a short report comparing and contrasting your companies.

1. What types of products or services does it sell?
2. On what day of the year does its fiscal year end?
3. For how many years does it present complete
   a. Balance sheets?
   b. Income statements?
   c. Cash flow statements?
4. Are its financial statements audited by independent CPAs? If so, by whom?
5. Did its total assets increase or decrease over last year? By what percentage? [Percentage change is calculated as (current year − last year) ÷ last year. Show supporting computations.]
6. Did its net income increase or decrease over last year? By what percentage?

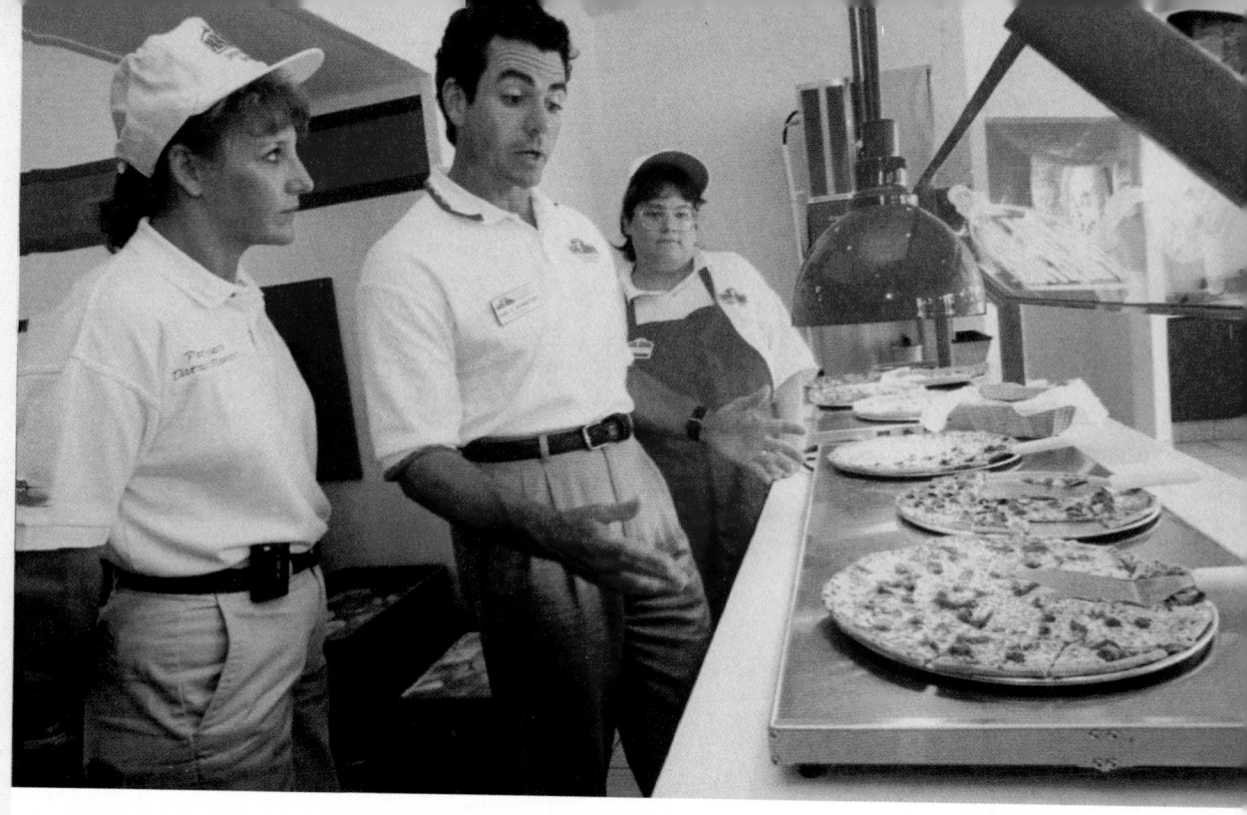

LEARNING OBJECTIVES

After studying this chapter, you should be able to:

1. Define the objective of financial reporting, the elements of the balance sheet, and the related key accounting assumptions and principles. p. 49

2. Identify what constitutes a business transaction and recognize common balance sheet account titles used in business. p. 53

3. Apply transaction analysis to simple business transactions in terms of the accounting model: Assets = Liabilities + Stockholders' Equity. p. 55

4. Determine the impact of business transactions on the balance sheet using two basic tools, journal entries and T-accounts. p. 60

5. Prepare a simple classified balance sheet and analyze the company using the financial leverage ratio. p. 68

6. Identify investing and financing transactions and demonstrate how they are reported on the statement of cash flows. p. 72

Lectured slideshow–LP2-1
www.mhhe.com/libby6e

INVESTING AND FINANCING DECISIONS AND THE BALANCE SHEET

FOCUS COMPANY:

Papa John's International

EXPANSION STRATEGY IN THE "PIZZA WARS"

www.papajohns.com

I n the pizza segment of the highly competitive restaurant business, Papa John's continues to fight the battle to become the No. 1 pizza brand in the world, taking on industry leader Pizza Hut as its primary target. In 2000, through aggressive expansion, Papa John's moved ahead of Little Caesar's to rank third in sales behind giants Pizza Hut and Domino's.

With more than 3,000 restaurants in the United States and abroad, the company has grown tremendously since its beginnings in 1983 when John Schnatter, founder and chief executive officer, knocked down closet walls at a bar he was tending to install a pizza oven. Ten years later, Papa John's became a public company with stock trading on the NASDAQ exchange (under the symbol PZZA). The company's balance sheet at the end of 2006 compared to the end of 1994 (in thousands of dollars*) highlight its growth:

	Assets	=	Liabilities	+	Stockholders' Equity
End of 2006	$379,639		$233,471		$146,168
End of 1994	76,173		13,564		62,609
Change	+$303,466		+$219,907		+$ 83,559

In recent years, competition has stiffened not only from traditional pizza chains but also from niche dwellers—take-and-bake pizza chains, frozen pizza companies,

*These totals are rounded amounts from the actual financial statements for the respective years. Amounts used in illustrations throughout Chapters 2, 3, and 4 are realistic estimates of actual monthly amounts.

carry-out initiatives from restaurants such as Applebee's and Chili's, and restaurants meeting the shift in consumer interests to low-carb menu options. While addressing the competition and meeting changing consumer interests, Papa John's continues to expand, with plans to add approximately 260 new restaurants in 2007 in the United States and abroad. The Pizza Wars continue.

UNDERSTANDING THE BUSINESS

Pizza is a global commodity, generating more than $32 billion in sales annually.[1] While the business depends heavily on human capital, companies can compete through product quality and marketing. Papa John's strategy is to offer "Better Ingredients. Better Pizza." To do so requires an almost fanatical focus on testing ingredients and checking product quality, right down to the size of the black olives and the fat content of the mozzarella and meat. The company keeps operations simple, sticking to a focused menu of pizza, bread sticks, cheese sticks, chicken strips, and soft drinks for pickup or delivery. To control quality and increase efficiency, the company builds regional commissaries (called quality control centers) that make the dough and sell it to the stores. The commissaries plus new company-owned stores and the sale of franchises[2] explain most of the change in Papa John's assets and liabilities from year to year.

To understand how the results of Papa John's growth strategy are communicated in the balance sheet, we must answer the following questions:

- What business activities cause changes in the balance sheet amounts from one period to the next?
- How do specific business activities affect each of the balance sheet amounts?
- How do companies keep track of the balance sheet amounts?

Once we have answered these questions, we will be able to perform two key analytical tasks:

1. Analyze and predict the effects of business decisions on a company's financial statements.
2. Use the financial statements of other companies to identify and evaluate the activities managers engaged in during a past period. This is a key task in **financial statement analysis**.

In this chapter, we focus on some typical asset acquisition activities (often called **investing activities**), along with related **financing activities**, such as borrowing funds from creditors or selling stock to investors to acquire the assets. We examine only those activities that affect balance sheet amounts. Operating activities that affect both the income statement and the balance sheet are covered in Chapters 3 and 4. To begin, let's return to the basic concepts introduced in Chapter 1.

---

[1]http://www.pmq.com/mag/20061112/article.php?story=pizzapower2006
[2]Franchises are contracts in which a franchisor (such as Papa John's International) provides rights to franchisees (in this case, local restaurant operators) to sell or distribute a specific line of products or provide a particular service. In return, franchisees usually pay an initial fee to obtain the franchise, along with annual payments for ongoing services such as accounting, advertising, and training. Approximately 80 percent of Papa John's restaurants worldwide are franchises.

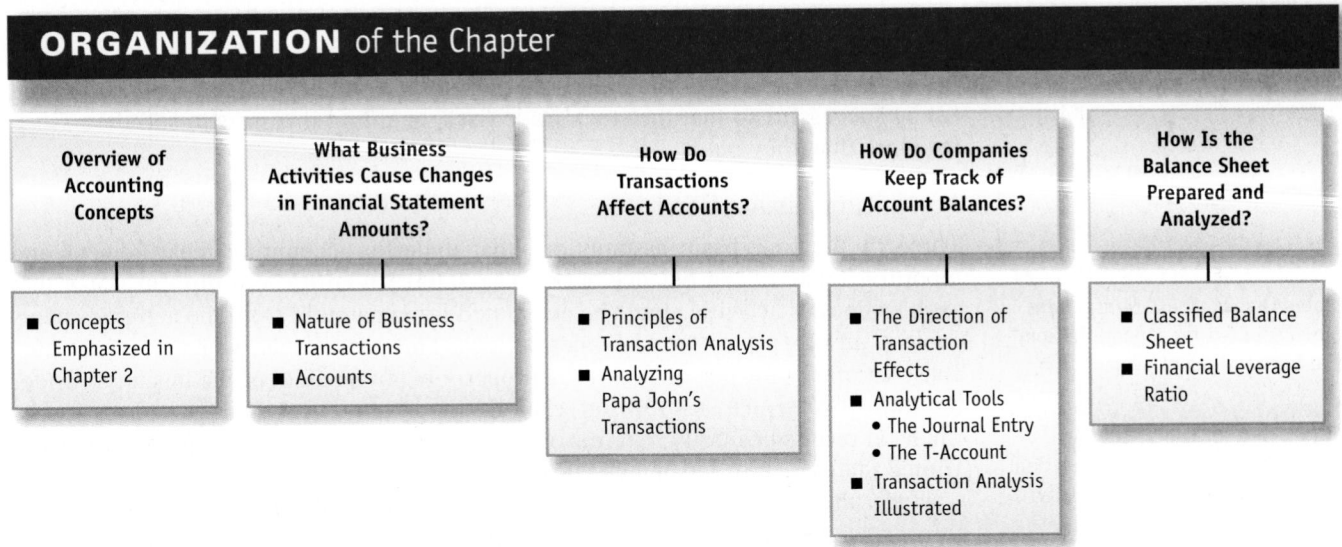

ORGANIZATION of the Chapter

Overview of Accounting Concepts	What Business Activities Cause Changes in Financial Statement Amounts?	How Do Transactions Affect Accounts?	How Do Companies Keep Track of Account Balances?	How Is the Balance Sheet Prepared and Analyzed?
■ Concepts Emphasized in Chapter 2	■ Nature of Business Transactions ■ Accounts	■ Principles of Transaction Analysis ■ Analyzing Papa John's Transactions	■ The Direction of Transaction Effects ■ Analytical Tools • The Journal Entry • The T-Account ■ Transaction Analysis Illustrated	■ Classified Balance Sheet ■ Financial Leverage Ratio

OVERVIEW OF ACCOUNTING CONCEPTS

The key accounting terms and concepts defined in Chapter 1 are part of a theoretical framework developed over many years and synthesized by the Financial Accounting Standards Board (FASB). This conceptual framework is presented in Exhibit 2.1 as an overview of the key concepts that will be discussed in each of the next four chapters. An understanding of these accounting concepts will be helpful as you study. That's because learning and remembering **how** the accounting process works is much easier if you know **why** it works a certain way. A clear understanding of these concepts will also help you in future chapters as we examine more complex business activities.

Learning Objective 1
Define the objective of financial reporting, the elements of the balance sheet, and the related key accounting assumptions and principles.

Concepts Emphasized in Chapter 2

Objective of Financial Reporting

The **primary objective of external financial reporting** is to provide useful economic information about a business to help external parties, primarily investors and creditors, make sound financial decisions. The users of accounting information are identified as **decision makers.** These decision makers include average investors, creditors, and experts who provide financial advice. They are all expected to have a reasonable understanding of accounting concepts and procedures (this may be one of the reasons you are studying accounting). Of course, as we discussed in Chapter 1, many other groups, such as suppliers and customers, also use external financial statements.

Users usually are interested in information to assist them in **projecting a business's future cash inflows and outflows.** For example, creditors and potential

The PRIMARY OBJECTIVE OF EXTERNAL FINANCIAL REPORTING is to provide useful economic information about a business to help external parties make sound financial decisions.

Objective of External Financial Reporting:
 To provide useful economic information to external users for decision making
 Useful information is:
 • Relevant, Reliable, Comparable, and Consistent
Elements to be Measured and Reported:
 • **Assets, Liabilities, Stockholders' Equity,** Revenues, Expenses, Gains, and Losses
Concepts for Measuring and Reporting Information:
 • **Assumptions: Separate-Entity, Unit-of-Measure, Continuity,** Time Period
 • **Principles: Historical Cost,** Revenue Recognition, Matching, Full Disclosure
 • **Exceptions:** Cost-benefit, Materiality, Conservatism, Industry Practices

EXHIBIT 2.1

Financial Accounting and Reporting—Conceptual Framework

Concepts in red are discussed in Chapters 1 and 2. Those in black will be discussed in Chapters 3, 4, and 5.

creditors need to assess an entity's ability to (1) pay interest on a loan over time and also (2) pay back the principal on the loan when it is due. Investors and potential investors want to assess the entity's ability to (1) pay dividends in the future and (2) be successful so that the stock price rises, enabling investors to sell their stock for more than they paid.

Accounting Assumptions

SEPARATE-ENTITY ASSUMPTION states that business transactions are accounted for separately from the transactions of owners.

Three of the four basic assumptions that underlie accounting measurement and reporting relate to the balance sheet. The **separate-entity assumption** states that each business's activities must be accounted for separately from the activities of its owners, all other persons, and other entities. This means that, when an owner purchases property for personal use, the property is not an asset of the business. Under the **unit-of-measure assumption,** each business entity accounts for and reports its financial results primarily in terms of the national monetary unit (e.g., dollars in the United States, yen in Japan, and euros in Germany).

UNIT-OF-MEASURE ASSUMPTION states that accounting information should be measured and reported in the national monetary unit.

Under the **continuity assumption** (sometimes called the **going-concern assumption**), a business normally is assumed to continue operating long enough to meet its contractual commitments and plans. If a company was not expected to continue, for example, due to the likelihood of bankruptcy, then its assets and liabilities should be valued and reported on the balance sheet as if the company were to be liquidated (that is, discontinued, with all of its assets sold and all debts paid). In future chapters, unless otherwise indicated, we assume that businesses meet the continuity assumption. The fourth assumption, the time period assumption, provides guidance on measuring revenues and expenses that we will introduce in Chapter 3.

CONTINUITY (or going-concern) **ASSUMPTION** states that businesses are assumed to continue to operate into the foreseeable future.

Elements of the Balance Sheet

Assets, liabilities, and shareholders' equity are the elements of a corporation's balance sheet, as we learned in Chapter 1. Let's examine their definitions in more detail.

Assets are economic resources with probable future benefits owned or controlled by an entity as a result of past transactions. In other words, they are the acquired resources the entity can use to operate in the future. To be reported, assets must have a measurable, verifiable value, usually based on the purchased amount. However, so as not to mislead users, managers use judgment (and past experience) to determine an acquired asset's most likely future benefit. For example, a company may have a list of customers who owe $10,000. History suggests, however, that only $9,800 is likely to be collected. The lower, more probable, and more conservative figure is reported to users for purposes of projecting future cash flows. In future chapters, we discuss the estimation process to determine the amount to report.

ASSETS are economic resources with probable future benefits owned by the entity as a result of past transactions.

The **HISTORICAL COST PRINCIPLE** (or cost principle) requires assets to be recorded at historical cost that, on the date of the transaction, is cash paid plus the current dollar value of all noncash considerations also given in the exchange.

Under the **historical cost principle,** cost is measured on the date of the transaction as the cash paid plus the dollar value of all noncash considerations (any assets, privileges, or rights) also given in the exchange. For example, if you trade your computer plus cash for a new car, the cost of the new car is equal to the cash paid plus the market

$15,000 Cash paid   + $2,000 Market value of computer   = $17,000 Historical cost of new car

EXHIBIT 2.2

Papa John's
Balance Sheet

PAPA JOHN'S INTERNATIONAL, INC. AND SUBSIDIARIES
Consolidated Balance Sheet
December 31, 2006
(dollars in thousands)

the last Sunday in December of each year

Assets		
Current Assets		
Cash	$ 13,000	
Accounts receivable	23,000	*payments due from franchisees and others on account*
Supplies	27,000	*food, beverages, and paper supplies on hand*
Prepaid expenses	8,000	*rent and insurance paid in advance*
Other current assets	14,000	*a summary of several current assets with smaller balances*
Total current assets	85,000	
Investments	1,000	*another company's stocks and bonds purchased with excess cash*
Property and equipment (net of accumulated depreciation of $189,000)	198,000	*the remaining cost of long-lived assets to be used in future operations (original cost minus the estimated portion of cost already used in the past)*
Notes receivable	12,000	*long-term amounts due from franchisees*
Intangibles	67,000	*patents, trademarks, and goodwill*
Other assets	17,000	*a summary of several long-term assets with smaller balances*
Total assets	$380,000	
Liabilities and Stockholders' Equity		
Current Liabilities		
Accounts payable	$ 29,000	*payments due to suppliers*
Accrued expenses payable	73,000	*a summary of payroll, rent, and other obligations*
Total current liabilities	102,000	
Unearned franchise fees	7,000	*amounts paid by franchisees for services they will receive*
Notes payable	96,000	*loans from creditors*
Other long-term liabilities	27,000	
Stockholders' Equity*		
Contributed capital	64,000	
Retained earnings	84,000	
Total stockholders' equity	148,000	
Total liabilities and stockholders' equity	$380,000	

*Contributed capital and retained earnings totals have been simplified. The company has repurchased shares of its stock from investors, a concept discussed in Chapter 11.

value of the computer. Thus, in most cases, cost is relatively easy to determine and can be verified. A disadvantage of this approach is that, subsequent to the date of acquisition, the continued reporting of historical cost on the balance sheet does not reflect any changes in market value, usually because market value is a less verifiable and objective measure. The conceptual framework also contains exceptions to this rule to allow for variations in practice while continuing to provide relevant and reliable information to users. These will be discussed in later chapters.

As shown in Papa John's balance sheet presented in Exhibit 2.2, most companies list assets **in order of liquidity,** or how soon an asset is expected to be turned into cash or used. Notice that several of Papa John's assets are categorized as **current assets.**

CURRENT ASSETS are assets that will be used or turned into cash within one year. Inventory is always considered a current asset regardless of the time needed to produce and sell it.

Current assets are those resources that Papa John's will use or turn into cash within one year (the next 12 months). Note that inventory is always considered a current asset, regardless of how long it takes to produce and sell the inventory. As indicated in Exhibit 2.2, Papa John's current assets include Cash, Accounts Receivable, Supplies, Prepaid Expenses, and Other Current Assets.

All other assets are considered long term. That is, they are to be used or turned into cash beyond the coming year. For Papa John's, that includes Long-Term Investments, Property and Equipment (net of amounts used in the past), Long-Term Notes Receivable, Intangibles, and Other Assets. Papa John's balance sheet includes assets of its company-owned restaurants only, about 20 percent of all Papa John's restaurants. The assets of the remaining 80 percent belong to franchisees and are appropriately reported in their own financial statements.

FINANCIAL ANALYSIS
Unrecorded But Valuable Assets

Many very valuable intangible assets, such as trademarks, patents, and copyrights that are developed inside a company (not purchased) are not reported on the balance sheet. For example, General Electric's balance sheet reveals no listing for the GE trademark because it was developed internally over time through research, development, and advertising (it was not purchased). Likewise, the Coca-Cola Company does not report any asset for its patented Coke formulae, although it does report more than $2 billion in various trademarks that it has purchased.

LIABILITIES are probable debts or obligations of the entity that result from past transactions, which will be paid with assets or services.

Liabilities are probable debts or obligations (claims to a company's resources) that result from an entity's past transactions and will be paid for with assets or services. Those entities that a company owes money to are called **creditors.** Creditors usually receive payment of the amounts owed and sometimes interest on those amounts. Papa John's balance sheet includes five liabilities: Accounts Payable, Accrued Expenses Payable, Unearned Franchise Fees, Long-Term Notes Payable, and Other Long-Term Liabilities. These and other liabilities will be discussed in subsequent chapters.

Just as assets are reported in order of liquidity, liabilities are usually listed on the balance sheet **in order of maturity** (how soon an obligation is to be paid). Those liabilities that Papa John's will need to pay or settle within the coming year (with cash, services, or other current assets) are classified as **current liabilities.** Distinguishing current assets and current liabilities assists external users of the financial statements in assessing the amounts and timing of future cash flows. Most corporations report current assets and liabilities separately, even though classifying them as such is not required.

CURRENT LIABILITIES are obligations that will be settled by providing cash, goods, or services within the coming year.

A QUESTION OF ETHICS
Environmental Liabilities: The "Greening of GAAP"

For many years, companies have faced a growing pressure to estimate and disclose environmental liabilities, such as the cleanup of hazardous waste sites. Effective in 2005, companies must record and report a reasonable estimate of any future environmental liabilities associated with an asset, if a reasonable amount can be projected. The obligations include estimated expenses for environmental cleanup and any demolition, disposal, or recycling of the asset in the future. Although some guidance is provided by the new rules, the issue of determining a reasonable estimate, however, remains.

Stockholders' equity (also called owners' equity or shareholders' equity) is the financing provided by the owners and by business operations. Owner-provided cash (and sometimes other assets) is referred to as contributed capital. Owners invest in the business and receive shares of stock as evidence of ownership. The largest investor in Papa John's International, Inc., is John Schnatter, founder and CEO, who owns approximately 17 percent of the stock. FMR Corporation of Boston owns another 9 percent of the stock; corporate employees, directors, and the general public own the rest.

Owners invest (or buy stock) in a company in the hope of receiving two types of cash flows: **dividends,** which are a distribution of a company's earnings (a return on the shareholders' investment), and gains from selling the stock for more than they paid (known as **capital gains**). Earnings that are not distributed to the owners but instead are reinvested in the business by management are called retained earnings.[3] A look at Papa John's balance sheet (Exhibit 2.2) indicates that its growth has been financed by substantial reinvestment of earnings. Nearly 57 percent of Papa John's stockholders' equity is retained earnings ($84 million Retained Earnings ÷ $148 million total stockholders' equity).

Before continuing, complete the following Self-Study Quiz to categorize accounts on the balance sheet.

> STOCKHOLDERS' EQUITY (also called owners' equity or shareholders' equity) is the financing provided by the owners and business operations.
>
> CONTRIBUTED CAPITAL results from owners providing cash (and sometimes other assets) to the business.
>
> RETAINED EARNINGS refers to the cumulative earnings of a company that are not distributed to the owners and are reinvested in the business.

SELF-STUDY **QUIZ**

The following is a list of items from a recent Wendy's International, Inc., balance sheet. Indicate on the line provided whether each of the following is categorized on the balance sheet as a current asset (CA), noncurrent asset (NCA), current liability (CL), noncurrent liability (NCL), or stockholders' equity (SE).

_____ Accrued Expenses Payable   _____ Retained Earnings

_____ Property and Equipment   _____ Inventories

_____ Accounts Receivable   _____ Notes Receivable (due in five years)

_____ Long-Term Debt   _____ Accounts Payable

After you have completed your answers, check them with the solutions at the bottom of the page.

Now that we have reviewed the basic elements of the balance sheet, let's see what economic activities cause changes in the amounts reported on this financial statement.

WHAT BUSINESS ACTIVITIES CAUSE CHANGES IN FINANCIAL STATEMENT AMOUNTS?

Nature of Business Transactions

Accounting focuses on certain events that have an economic impact on the entity. Those events that are recorded as part of the accounting process are called transactions. The first step in translating the results of business events to financial statement numbers is determining which events to include. As the definitions of assets and liabilities indicate, only economic resources and debts **resulting from past transactions** are recorded on the balance sheet. Transactions include two types of events:

1. External events: These are **exchanges** of assets, goods, or services by one party for assets, services, or promises to pay (liabilities) by one or more other parties. Examples

> **Learning Objective 2**
> Identify what constitutes a business transaction and recognize common balance sheet account titles used in business.
>
> A TRANSACTION is (1) an exchange of assets or services for assets, services, or promises to pay between a business and one or more external parties to a business or (2) a measurable internal event such as the use of assets in operations.

---

[3]Retained earnings can increase only from profitable operations. Retained earnings decrease when a firm has a loss. Also, as we discuss in Chapter 3, a company's annual income from operations is usually not equal to the net cash flows for the year.

Column 1: CL; NCA; CA; NCL. Column 2: SE; CA; NCA; CL.   Self-Study Quiz Solutions include the purchase of a machine from a supplier, sale of merchandise to customers, borrowing cash from a bank, and investment of cash in the business by the owners.

2. **Internal events:** These include certain events that are not exchanges between the business and other parties but nevertheless have a direct and measurable effect on the entity. Examples include using up insurance paid in advance and using buildings and equipment over several years.

Throughout this textbook, the word *transaction* is used in the broad sense to include both types of events.

Some important events that have a future economic impact on a company, however, are **not** reflected in the financial statements. In most cases, signing a contract is not considered to be a transaction because it involves **only the exchange of promises,** not of assets such as cash, goods, services, or property. For example, assume that Papa John's signs an employment contract with a new regional manager. From an accounting perspective, no transaction has occurred because no exchange of assets, goods, or services has been made. Each party to the contract has exchanged promises—the manager agrees to work; Papa John's agrees to pay the manager for work rendered. For each day the new manager works, however, the exchange of services for pay results in a transaction that Papa John's must record. Because of their importance, long-term employment contracts, leases, and other commitments may need to be disclosed in notes to the financial statements.

Accounts

An ACCOUNT is a standardized format that organizations use to accumulate the dollar effect of transactions on each financial statement item.

To accumulate the dollar effect of transactions on each financial statement item, organizations use a standardized format called an **account.** The resulting balances are kept separate for financial statement purposes. To facilitate the recording of transactions, each company establishes a **chart of accounts,** a list of all account titles and their unique numbers. The accounts are usually organized by financial statement element, with asset accounts listed first, followed by liability, stockholders' equity, revenue, and expense accounts in that order. Exhibit 2.3 lists various account titles that are quite common and are used by most companies. When you are completing assignments and are unsure of an account title, refer to this listing for help.

Notice that

- Accounts with "receivable" in the title are always assets; they represent amounts owed by (receivable from) customers and others to the business.

- Accounts with "payable" in the title are always liabilities and represent amounts owed by the company to be paid to others in the future.

EXHIBIT 2.3	Assets	Liabilities	Stockholders' Equity	Revenues	Expenses
Typical Account Titles	Cash Short-Term Investments Accounts Receivable Notes Receivable Inventory (to be sold) Supplies Prepaid Expenses Long-Term Investments Equipment Buildings Land Intangibles	Accounts Payable Accrued Expenses Payable Notes Payable Taxes Payable Unearned Revenue Bonds Payable	Contributed Capital Retained Earnings	Sales Revenue Fee Revenue Interest Revenue Rent Revenue Service Revenue	Cost of Goods Sold Wages Expense Rent Expense Interest Expense Depreciation Expense Advertising Expense Insurance Expense Repair Expense Income Tax Expense

- The account Prepaid Expenses is an asset since it represents amounts paid to others for future benefits, such as future insurance coverage or rental of property.
- Accounts with "unearned" in the title are always liabilities representing amounts paid in the past to the company by others expecting future goods or services from the company.

Every company has a variation on this chart of accounts, depending on the nature of its business activities. For example, a small lawn care service may have an asset account Lawn Mowing Equipment, but a large corporation such as General Motors is unlikely to report such an account. These differences in accounts will become more apparent as we examine the balance sheets of various companies. Because each company has its own chart of accounts, you should **not** try to memorize a typical chart of accounts. In homework problems, you will either be given the account names or be expected to select appropriate names, similar to the ones in the preceding lists. Once you select a name for an account, you must use the exact name in all transactions affecting that account.

The accounts you see in the financial statements of most large corporations are actually summations (or aggregations) of a number of specific accounts. For example, Papa John's keeps separate accounts for paper supplies, food supplies, and beverage supplies, but combines them under **Supplies** on the balance sheet. Equipment, buildings, and land are also combined into an account called **Property and Equipment.** Since our aim is to understand financial statements of actual entities, we will focus on aggregated accounts.

Understanding Foreign Financial Statements

The advent of International Financial Reporting Standards (IFRS), which are rules similar to U.S. GAAP, have made it easier to read foreign companies' financial statements. GlaxoSmithKline, the pharmaceutical giant in the United Kingdom, prepares its statements in English under IFRS as adopted by the European Union. However, there are still some differences in the structure of the statements and account titles which may cause confusion. For example, noncurrent assets are placed before current assets on the balance sheet. The key to avoiding confusion is to be sure to **pay attention to the subheadings** in the statement. They also use the term "provision" in place of "liability" in some account titles. The key to avoiding confusion here is again to **pay attention to the subheadings**. Any account under the heading "liabilities" must be a liability.

HOW DO TRANSACTIONS AFFECT ACCOUNTS?

Managers' business decisions often result in transactions that affect the financial statements. For example, the decisions to expand the number of stores, advertise a new product, change an employee benefit package, and invest excess cash would all affect the financial statements. Sometimes these decisions have unintended consequences as well. The decision to purchase additional inventory for cash in anticipation of a major sales initiative, for example, will increase inventory and decrease cash. But if there is no demand for the additional inventory, the lower cash balance will also reduce the company's ability to pay its other obligations.

Because business decisions often involve an element of risk, managers should understand exactly how transactions impact the financial statements. The process for determining the effects of transactions is called **transaction analysis.**

Principles of Transaction Analysis

Transaction analysis is the process of studying a transaction to determine its economic effect on the entity in terms of the accounting equation (also known as the **fundamental accounting model**). We outline the process in this section of the

Learning Objective 3
Apply transaction analysis to simple business transactions in terms of the accounting model: Assets = Liabilities + Stockholders' Equity.

TRANSACTION ANALYSIS is the process of studying a transaction to determine its economic effect on the business in terms of the accounting equation.

Video 2-1
www.mhhe.com/libby6e

chapter and create a visual tool representing the process (the transaction analysis model). The basic accounting equation and two principles are the foundation for this model. Recall from Chapter 1 that the basic accounting equation for a business that is organized as a corporation is as follows:

$$\text{Assets (A)} = \text{Liabilities (L)} + \text{Stockholders' Equity (SE)}$$

The two principles underlying the transaction analysis process follow:

- Every transaction affects at least two accounts; correctly identifying those accounts and the direction of the effect (whether an increase or a decrease) is critical.
- The accounting equation must remain in balance after each transaction.

Success in performing transaction analysis depends on a clear understanding of these principles. Study the following material well.

Dual Effects

The idea that every transaction has **at least two effects** on the basic accounting equation is known as the **dual effects** concept.[4] Most transactions with external parties involve an **exchange** by which the business entity both receives something and gives up something in return. For example, suppose Papa John's purchased some paper napkins for cash. In this exchange, Papa John's would receive supplies (an increase in an asset) and in return would give up cash (a decrease in an asset).

Transaction	Papa John's Received	Papa John's Gave
Purchased paper napkins for cash	Supplies (increased)	Cash (decreased)

In analyzing this transaction, we determined that the accounts affected were Supplies and Cash. As we discussed in Chapter 1, however, most supplies are purchased on credit (that is, money is owed to suppliers). In that case, Papa John's would engage in *two* transactions:

(1) The purchase of an asset on credit — In the first transaction, Papa John's would receive Supplies (an increase in an asset) and would give in return a promise to pay later called **Accounts Payable** (an increase in a liability).

(2) The eventual payment — In the second transaction, Papa John's would eliminate or receive back its promise to pay (a decrease in the Accounts Payable liability) and would give up Cash (a decrease in an asset).

---

[4]From this concept, accountants have developed what is known as the *double-entry system* of recordkeeping.

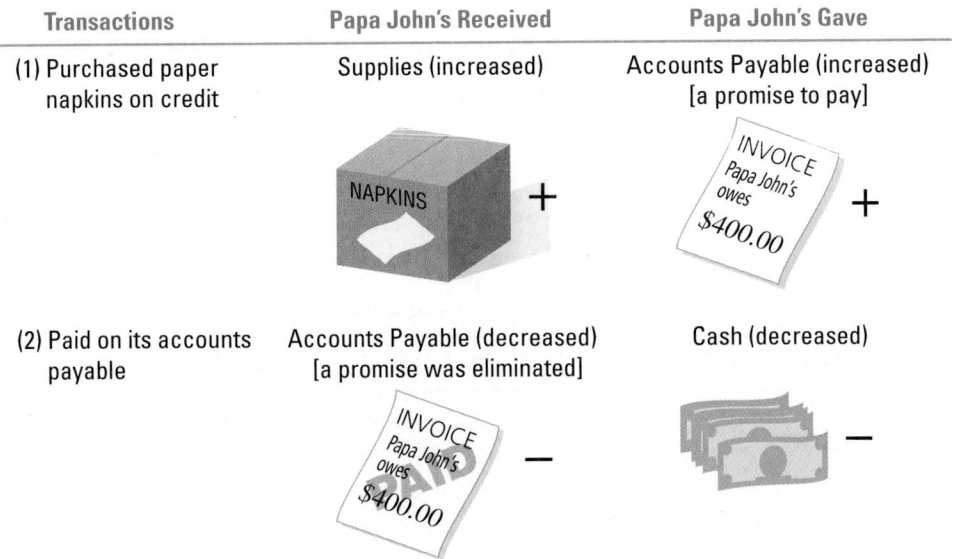

Transactions	Papa John's Received	Papa John's Gave
(1) Purchased paper napkins on credit	Supplies (increased)	Accounts Payable (increased) [a promise to pay]
(2) Paid on its accounts payable	Accounts Payable (decreased) [a promise was eliminated]	Cash (decreased)

As noted earlier, not all important business activities result in a transaction that affects the financial statements. Most importantly, signing a contract involving **the exchange of two promises to perform does not result in an accounting transaction** that is recorded. For example, if **Papa John's** sent an order for more napkins to its paper supplier and the supplier accepted the order but did not fill it immediately, no transaction took place. As soon as the goods are shipped to Papa John's, however, the supplier has given up its inventory in exchange for a promise from Papa John's to pay for the items in the near future, and Papa John's has exchanged its promise to pay for the supplies it receives. Because a **promise** has been exchanged for **goods,** a transaction has taken place. Both Papa John's and the supplier's statements will be affected.

Balancing the Accounting Equation

The accounting equation must remain in balance after each transaction. That is, total assets (resources) must equal total liabilities and stockholders' equity (claims to resources). If all correct accounts have been identified and the appropriate direction of the effect on each account has been determined, the equation should remain in balance. A systematic transaction analysis includes the following steps, in this order:

Step 1: Identify and classify accounts and effects
- **Identify the accounts (by title) affected,** making sure that at least two accounts change. Ask yourself: What is received and what is given?
- **Classify them by type of account.** Was each account an asset (A), a liability (L), or a stockholders' equity (SE)?
- **Determine the direction of the effect.** Did the account increase [+] or decrease [−]?

Step 2: Verify accounting equation is in balance
- **Verify that the accounting equation (A = L + SE) remains in balance.**

Analyzing Papa John's Transactions

To illustrate the use of the transaction analysis process, let's consider some typical transactions of Papa John's that are also common to most businesses. Remember that this chapter presents transactions that affect only the balance sheet accounts. Assume that Papa John's engages in the following events during January 2007, the month following the balance sheet in Exhibit 2.2. Account titles are from that balance sheet, and remember that, for simplicity, all amounts are in **thousands of dollars:**

(a) Papa John's issues $2,000 of additional common stock, receiving cash from investors.

Step 1: Identify and classify accounts and effects.
Received: Cash (+A) $2,000.   **Given:** Additional stock certificates, Contributed Capital (+SE) $2,000

Step 2: Is the accounting equation in balance?
Yes. The left side increased by $2,000 and the right side increased by $2,000.

	Assets	=	Liabilities	+	Stockholders' Equity
	Cash				Contributed Capital
(a)	+2,000	=			+2,000

(b) Papa John's borrows $6,000 from its local bank, signing a note to be paid in three years.

Step 1: Identify and classify accounts and effects.
Received: Cash (+A) $6,000.   **Given:** Written promise to bank, Notes Payable (+L) $6,000

Step 2: Is the accounting equation in balance?
Yes. The left side increased by $6,000 and the right side increased by $6,000.

	Assets	=	Liabilities	+	Stockholders' Equity
	Cash		Notes Payable		Contributed Capital
(a)	+2,000	=			+2,000
(b)	+6,000	=	+6,000		

Events (a) and (b) are **financing** transactions. Companies that need cash for **investing** purposes (to buy or build additional facilities) often seek funds by selling stock to investors as in event (a) or by borrowing from creditors as in event (b).

(c) Papa John's purchases $10,000 of new ovens, counters, refrigerators, and other equipment, paying $2,000 in cash and signing a two-year note payable to the equipment manufacturer for the rest.

Step 1: Identify and classify accounts and effects.
Received: Property and Equipment (+A) $10,000.   **Given:** (1) Cash (−A) $2,000
                                                              (2) Notes Payable (+L) $8,000

Step 2: Is the accounting equation in balance?
Yes. The left side increased by $8,000 and the right side increased by $8,000.

	Assets		=	Liabilities	+	Stockholders' Equity
	Cash	Property and Equipment		Notes Payable		Contributed Capital
(a)	+2,000		=			+2,000
(b)	+6,000		=	+6,000		
(c)	−2,000	+10,000	=	+8,000		

Notice that more than two accounts were affected by transaction (*c*). The effects of events (*a*), (*b*), and (*c*) are listed in the chart after the Self-Study Quiz. Space is left on the chart for your analysis of events (*d*), (*e*), and (*f*).

SELF-STUDY **QUIZ**

Practice is the most effective way to develop your transaction analysis skills. Review the analysis in events (*a*) through (*c*) and complete the analysis of events (*d*) through (*f*) in the chart following the three transactions. Repeat the steps until they become a natural part of your thought process. After you have completed the chart, check your answers with the solutions at the bottom of the following page.

(*d*) **Papa John's lends $3,000 cash to new franchisees who sign notes agreeing to repay the loans in five years.**

Step 1: Identify and classify accounts and effects.
Received: Notes Receivable (+A) $3,000.   **Given:** _____

Step 2: Is the accounting equation in balance?
Yes. The equation stays in balance because assets increase and decrease by the same amount $3,000.

Include these effects on the chart on page 60.

(*e*) **Papa John's purchases the stock of other companies as a long-term investment, paying $1,000 in cash.**

Step 1: Identify and classify accounts and effects.
Received: Investments (+A) $1,000.   **Given:** Cash (−A) $1,000

Step 2: Is the accounting equation in balance?
Yes or No?_____   Why? _____

Include these effects on the chart on page 60.

(*f*) **Papa John's board of directors declares that the Company will pay $3,000 in cash dividends to shareholders next month.[5]**

Retained Earnings represent the profits available to shareholders. When a company's board of directors declares a cash dividend, Retained Earnings is reduced. Thus, the company receives a reduction in the profits it has available to distribute to shareholders. On the other hand, until the dividends are paid, the company gives shareholders a promise to pay the dividends called Dividends Payable.

Step 1: Identify and classify accounts and effects.
Received: Retained Earnings (−SE) $3,000.   **Given:** _____

Step 2: Is the accounting equation in balance?
Yes or No?_____   Why? _____

Include these effects on the chart on page 60.

---

[5]At the time this chapter is being written, Papa John's has not declared dividends; this transaction, as well as later similar ones, is included for purposes of illustration only.

Self-Study Quiz
Solutions

(*d*) Given: Cash (−A) $3,000.

(*e*) Yes. The equation remains the same because assets increase and decrease by the same amount $1,000.

(*f*) Given: Dividends Payable (+L) $3,000.

   Yes, there is a $3,000 increase and a $3,000 decrease on the right side of the equation.

	Cash	Notes Receivable	Property and Equipment	Investments	=	Dividents Payable	Notes Payable	+	Contributed Capital	Retained Earnings
					Assets = **Liabilities** + **Stockholders' Equity**					
(a)	+2,000				=				+2,000	
(b)	+6,000				=		+6,000			
(c)	−2,000		+10,000		=		+8,000			
(d)	___	___			=	No change				
(e)	___			___	=	No change				
(f)				No change	=	___				___
Totals	**+2,000**	**+3,000**	**+10,000**	**+1,000**	=	**+3,000**	**+14,000**		**+2000**	**−3,000**

+16,000 = +16,000

After you have completed your answers, check them with the solutions at the bottom of the page.

HOW DO COMPANIES KEEP TRACK OF ACCOUNT BALANCES?

Learning Objective 4
Determine the impact of business transactions on the balance sheet using two basic tools, journal entries and T-accounts.

For most organizations, recording transaction effects and keeping track of account balances in the manner just presented is impractical. To handle the multitude of daily transactions that businesses generate, companies establish accounting systems, usually computerized, that follow a cycle. The accounting cycle, illustrated in Exhibit 2.4,

EXHIBIT 2.4

The Accounting Cycle

Start of new period

During the Period
(Chapters 2 and 3)
- **Analyze** transactions
- **Record** journal entries in the general journal
- **Post** amounts to the general ledger

At the End of the Period
(Chapter 4)
- **Adjust** revenues and expenses and related balance sheet accounts (record in journal and post to ledger)
- **Prepare** a complete set of financial statements and disseminate it to users
- **Close** revenues, gains, expenses, and losses to Retained Earnings (record in journal and post to ledger)

Self-Study Quiz
Solutions

	Cash	Notes Receivable	Property and Equipment	Investments	=	Dividents Payable	Notes Payable	+	Contributed Capital	Retained Earnings
					Assets / **Liabilities** / **Stockholders' Equity**					
(d)	−3,000	+3,000			= No change					
(e)	−1,000			+1,000	= No change					
(f)				No change	=	+3,000				−3,000

If your answers did not agree with ours, we recommend that you go back to each event to make sure you have completed each of the steps of transaction analysis.

highlights the primary activities performed during the accounting period to analyze, record, and post transactions. In Chapters 2 and 3, we will illustrate these activities **during the period.** In Chapter 4, we will complete the accounting cycle by discussing and illustrating activities at the end of the period to adjust the records, prepare financial statements, and close the accounting records.

Audio lecture–LP2-1
www.mhhe.com/libby6e

During the accounting period, transactions that result in exchanges between the company and other external parties are analyzed and recorded in the **general journal** in chronological order, and the related accounts are updated in the **general ledger.** These formal records are based on two very important tools used by accountants: journal entries and T-accounts. From the standpoint of accounting systems design, these analytical tools are a more efficient way to reflect the effects of transactions, determine account balances, and prepare financial statements. As future business managers, you should develop your understanding and use of these tools in financial analysis. For those studying accounting, this knowledge is the foundation for an understanding of the accounting system and future accounting coursework. After we explain how to perform transaction analysis using these tools, we illustrate their use in financial analysis.

The Direction of Transaction Effects

As we saw earlier, transactions increase and decrease assets, liabilities, and stockholders' equity. To reflect these effects efficiently, we need to structure the transaction analysis model in a manner that shows the **direction** of the effects. As shown in Exhibit 2.5, the critical structural factor is the following:

■ **The increase symbol + is located on the left side of the T for accounts on the left side of the accounting equation (assets) and on the right side of the T for accounts on the right side of the equation (liabilities and stockholders' equity).**

Also notice that:

■ The term **debit** (dr for short) is always written on the left side of an account.

■ The term **credit** (cr for short) is written on the right side of each account.

From this transaction analysis model, we can observe the following:

■ Asset accounts increase on the left (debit) side; they have debit balances. It would be highly unusual for an asset account, such as Inventory, to have a negative (credit) balance.

■ Liability and stockholders' equity accounts increase on the right (credit) side, creating credit balances.

To remember which accounts debits increase and which accounts credits increase, recall that a debit (left) increases asset accounts because assets are on the left side of the accounting equation (A = L + SE). Similarly, a credit (right) increases liability and stockholders' equity accounts because they are on the right side of the accounting equation.

DEBIT (dr) is on the left side of an account.

CREDIT (cr) is on the right side of an account.

ASSETS (many accounts)		=	LIABILITIES (many accounts)		+	STOCKHOLDERS' EQUITY (two accounts)					EXHIBIT 2.5
						Contributed Capital		**Retained Earnings**			
+ debit	− credit		− debit	+ credit		− debit	+ credit	− debit	+ credit		**Transaction Analysis Model**
							Investments by owners	Dividends declared	Net income of business		

In summary:

Assets	=	Liabilities	+	Stockholders' Equity
↑ with Debits		↑ with Credits		↑ with Credits
Accounts have debit balances		Accounts have credit balances		Accounts have credit balances

In Chapter 3, we will add revenue and expense account effects. Until then, as you are learning to perform transaction analysis, **you should refer to the transaction analysis model in Exhibit 2.5 often until you can construct it on your own without assistance.**

Many students have trouble with accounting because they forget that the term **debit** is simply the left side of an account and the term **credit** is simply the right side of an account. Perhaps someone once told you that you were a credit to your school or your family. As a result, you may think that credits are good and debits are bad. Such is not the case. Just remember that **debit is on the left** and **credit is on the right.**

If you have identified the correct accounts and effects through transaction analysis, the accounting equation will remain in balance. Moreover, **the total dollar value of all debits will equal the total dollar value of all credits** in a transaction. For an extra measure of assurance, add this equality check (Debits = Credits) to the transaction analysis process.

Analytical Tools

The Journal Entry

In a bookkeeping system, transactions are recorded in chronological order in a **general journal** (or simply journal). (See Appendix E at **www.mhhe.com/libby6e** for an illustration of formal recordkeeping procedures.) After analyzing the business documents that describe a transaction, the bookkeeper enters the effects on the accounts in the journal using debits and credits. The **journal entry,** then, is an accounting method for expressing the effects of a transaction on accounts. It is written in a debits-equal-credits format. The journal entry for event (*c*) in the Papa John's illustration is as follows:

A JOURNAL ENTRY is an accounting method for expressing the effects of a transaction on accounts in a debits-equal-credits format.

Notice the following:

■ It is useful to include a date or some form of reference for each transaction. The debited accounts are written first (on top) with the amounts on the left side of the two columns. The credited accounts are written below the debits and are usually indented in manual records; the credited amounts are written in the right column. The order of the debited accounts or credited accounts does not matter, as long as the debits are on top and the credits are on the bottom and indented to the right.

■ Total debits ($10,000) equal total credits ($2,000 + $8,000).

■ Three accounts are affected by this transaction. Any journal entry that affects more than two accounts is called a **compound entry.** Although this is the only transaction in the Papa John's illustration that affects more than two accounts, many transactions in subsequent chapters require a compound journal entry.

While you are learning to perform transaction analysis, use the symbols A, L, and SE next to each account title, as in the preceding journal entry. Specifically identifying accounts as assets (A), liabilities (L), or stockholders' equity (SE) clarifies the transaction analysis and makes journal entries easier to write. For example, if Cash is to be increased, we write Cash (+A). Throughout subsequent chapters, we include the direction of the effect along with the symbol to help you understand the effects of each transaction on the financial statements. In the transaction (c) above, we can see that assets are affected by +$8,000 (increase of $10,000 in Property and Equipment and decrease of $2,000 in Cash) and liabilities are affected by +$8,000. The accounting equation A = L + SE remains in balance.

Many students try to memorize journal entries without understanding or using the transaction analysis model. As more detailed transactions are presented in subsequent chapters, the task becomes increasingly more difficult. In the long run, **memorizing, understanding, and using the transaction analysis model** presented here will save you time and prevent confusion.

The T-Account

By themselves, journal entries do not provide the balances in accounts. After the journal entries have been recorded, the bookkeeper posts (transfers) the dollar amounts to each account affected by the transaction to determine the new account balances. (In most computerized accounting systems, this happens automatically.)

As a group, the accounts are called a **general ledger.** In the manual accounting system used by some small organizations, the ledger is often a three-ring binder with a separate page for each account. In a computerized system, accounts are stored on a disk. See Exhibit 2.6 on page 64 for an illustration of a journal page and the related ledger pages. Note that the cash effects from the journal entries have been posted to the Cash ledger page.

One very useful tool for summarizing the transaction effects and determining the balances for individual accounts is a T-account, a simplified representation of a ledger account. Exhibit 2.7 on page 65 shows the T-accounts for Papa John's Cash and Notes Payable accounts based on Events (a) through (c). Notice that, for Cash, which is classified as an asset, increases are shown on the left and decreases on the right side of the T-account. For Notes Payable, however, increases are shown on the right and decreases on the left since Notes Payable is a liability. Many small businesses still use handwritten or manually maintained accounts in this T-account format. Computerized systems retain the concept but not the format of the T-account.

In Exhibit 2.7 on page 65, notice that the ending balance is indicated on the positive side with a double underline. To find the account balances, we can express the T-accounts as equations:

The T-ACCOUNT is a tool for summarizing transaction effects for each account, determining balances, and drawing inferences about a company's activities.

	Cash	Notes Payable
Beginning balance	$ 13,000	$ 96,000
+ " + " side	+ 8,000	+ 14,000
− " − " side	− 2,000	− 0
Ending balance	$ 19,000	$ 110,000

EXHIBIT 2.6

Posting Transaction Effects from the Journal to the Ledger

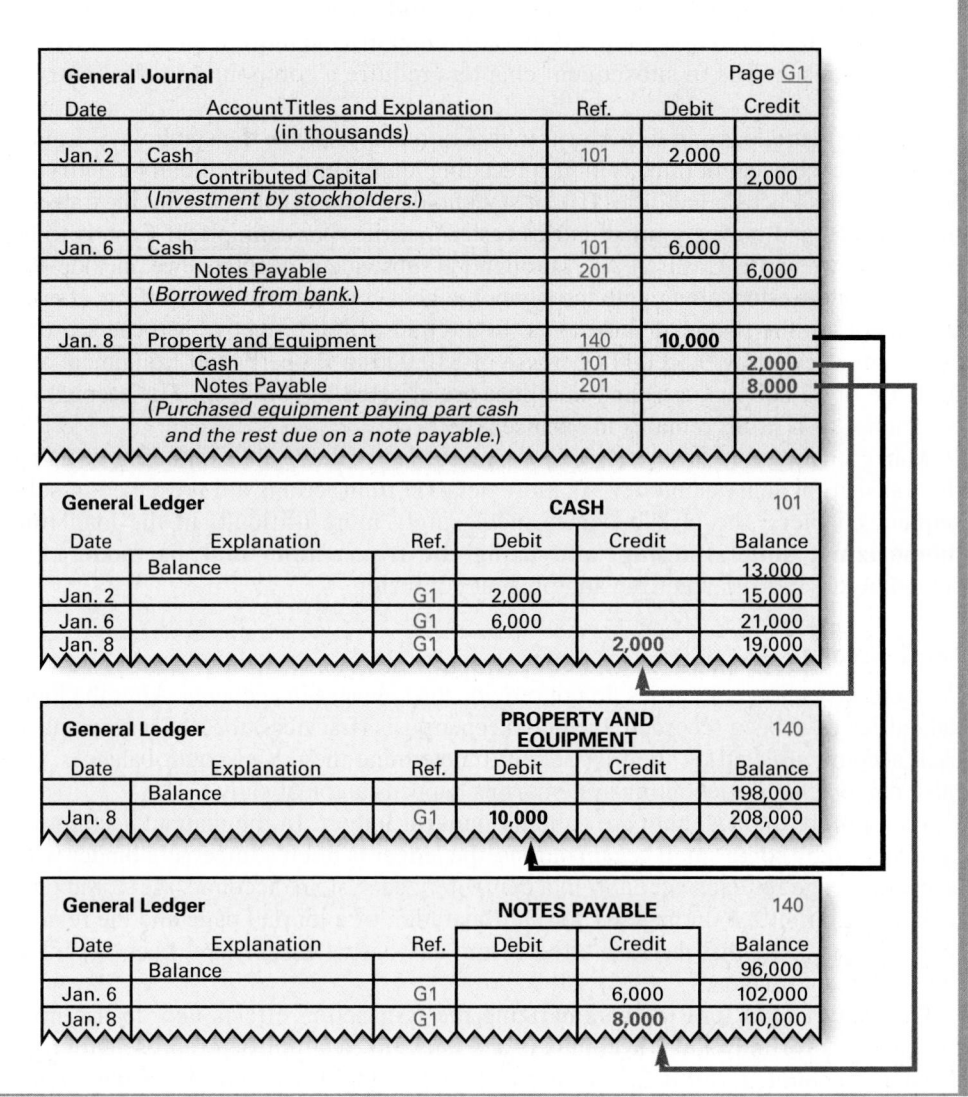

A word on terminology: The words **debit** and **credit** may be used as verbs, nouns, and adjectives. For example, we can say that Papa John's Cash account was debited (verb) when stock was issued to investors, meaning that the amount was entered on the left side of the T-account. Or we can say that a credit (noun) was entered on the right side of an account. Notes Payable may be described as a credit account (adjective). These terms will be used instead of **left** and **right** throughout the rest of this textbook. The next section illustrates the steps to follow in analyzing the effects of transactions, recording the effects in journal entries, and determining account balances using T-accounts.

Transaction Analysis Illustrated

In this section, we will use the monthly transactions for Papa John's that were presented earlier to demonstrate transaction analysis and the use of journal entries and T-accounts. We analyze each transaction, checking to make sure that the accounting equation remains in balance and that debits equal credits. In the T-accounts, located together at the end of the illustration, the amounts from Papa John's December 31,

EXHIBIT 2.7

T-Accounts Illustrated

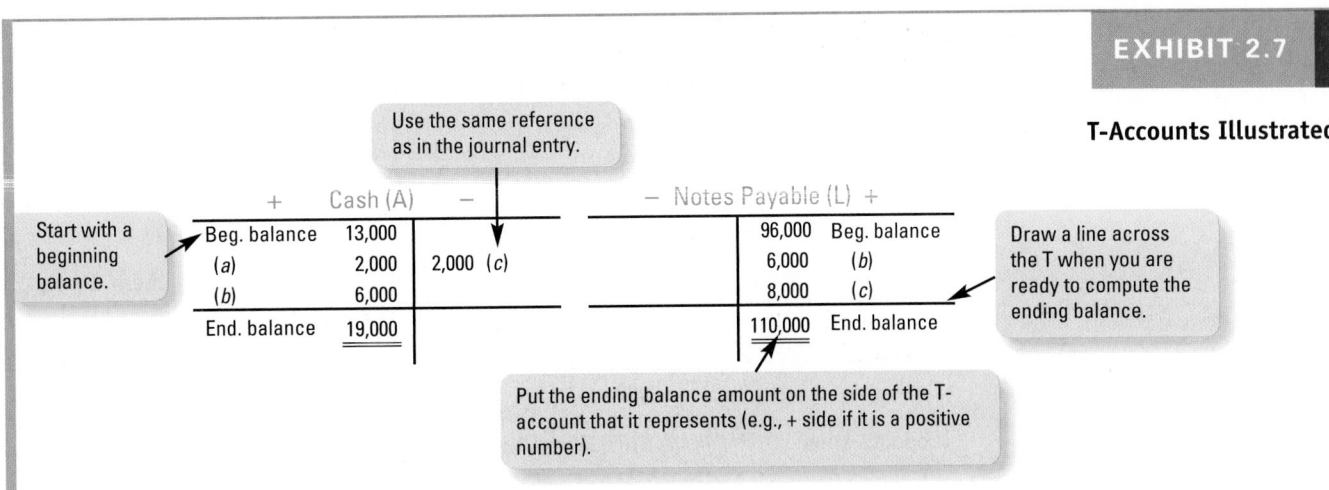

2006 balance sheet have been inserted as the beginning balances. After reviewing or preparing each journal entry, trace the effects to the appropriate T-accounts using the transaction letters (*a*) to (*f*) as a reference. The first transaction has been highlighted for you.

Study this illustration carefully, including the explanations of transaction analysis. Careful study is **essential** to an understanding of (1) the accounting model, (2) transaction analysis, (3) the dual effects of each transaction, and (4) the dual-balancing system. The most effective way to learn these critical concepts, which are basic to material throughout the rest of the text, is to practice, practice, practice.

(*a*) Papa John's issues $2,000 of additional common stock, receiving cash from investors.

| (*a*) Cash (+A) .... | 2,000 | |
| Contributed Capital (+SE) .... | | 2,000 |

Assets	=	Liabilities	+	Stockholders' Equity	
Cash	+2,000			Contributed Capital	+2,000

Equality checks: (1) Debits $2,000 = Credits $2,000; (2) the accounting equation is in balance.

These effects have been posted to the appropriate T-accounts at the end of the illustration. To post the amounts, transfer or copy the debit or credit amount on each line to the appropriate T-account. For example, the $2,000 debit is listed in the debit (increase) column of the Cash T-account.

(*b*) Papa John's borrows $6,000 from its local bank, signing a note to be paid in three years.

| (*b*) Cash (+A) .... | 6,000 | |
| Notes Payable (+L) .... | | 6,000 |

Assets	=	Liabilities	+	Stockholders' Equity
Cash	+6,000	Notes Payable	+6,000	

Equality checks: (1) Debits $6,000 = Credits $6,000; (2) the accounting equation is in balance.

(*c*) **Papa John's purchases $10,000 of new ovens, counters, refrigerators, and other equipment, paying $2,000 in cash and signing a two-year note payable to the equipment manufacturer for the rest.**

(c) Property and Equipment (+A)	10,000	
Cash (−A)		2,000
Notes Payable (+L)		8,000

Assets		=	Liabilities		+	Stockholders' Equity
Property and Equipment	+10,000		Notes Payable	+8,000		
Cash	− 2,000					

Equality checks: (1) Debits $10,000 = Credits $10,000; (2) the accounting equation is in balance.

SELF-STUDY QUIZ

For events (*d*), (*e*), and (*f*), fill in the missing information indicated; then post the entries to the T-accounts.

(*d*) **Papa John's lends $3,000 cash to new franchisees who sign notes agreeing to repay the loans in five years.** Write the journal entry, post it to the T-accounts, and complete the equality checks.

(d) _____ ( )	_____
_____ ( )	_____

Assets		=	Liabilities	+	Stockholders' Equity
Cash	−3,000				
Notes Receivable	+3,000				

Equality checks: (1) Debits $ _____ = Credits $ _____; (2) the accounting equation is in balance.

(*e*) **Papa John's purchases the stock of other companies as a long-term investment, paying $1,000 in cash.** Complete the effects on the accounting equation by indicating the accounts, amounts, and direction of the effect. Then, post the entry to the T-accounts.

(e) Investments (+A)	1,000	
Cash (−A)		1,000

Assets		=	Liabilities	+	Stockholders' Equity
_____	_____				
_____	_____				

Equality checks: (1) Debits $1,000 = Credits $1,000; (2) Is the accounting equation in balance? ____

(*f*) **Papa John's board of directors declares that the Company will pay $3,000 in cash dividends to shareholders next month.** When a company's board of directors declares a cash dividend, a legal obligation is created. Write the journal entry, post it to the T-accounts, and complete the effects on the accounting equation.

| _____ (   ) .... | 3,000 |
| _____ (   ) .... | 3,000 |

Assets	=	Liabilities	+	Stockholders' Equity
		+3,000		−3,000

Equality checks: (1) Debits $3,000 = Credits $3,000; (2) the accounting equation is in balance.

After you have completed your answers, check them with the solutions at the bottom of the page.

Following are the T-accounts that **changed** during the period because of these transactions. The beginning balances are the amounts from the December 31, 2006, Papa John's balance sheet. The balances of all other accounts remained the same.

+ Cash (A) −		
12/31/06 bal. 13,000		
(a) 2,000	2,000	(c)
(b) 6,000	___	(d)
		(e)
1/31/07 bal. 15,000		

+ Investments (A) −	
12/31/06 bal. 1,000	
(e) ___	
1/31/07 bal. 2,000	

+ Property and Equipment, Net (A) −	
12/31/06 bal. 198,000	
(c) 10,000	
1/31/07 bal. 208,000	

+ Notes Receivable (A) −	
12/31/06 bal. 12,000	
(d) ___	
1/31/07 bal. 15,000	

− Notes Payable (L) +	
	96,000 12/31/06 bal.
	6,000 (b)
	8,000 (c)
	110,000 1/31/07 bal.

− Dividends Payable (L) +	
	0 12/31/06 bal.
___	(f)
3,000	1/31/07 bal.

− Contributed Capital (SE) +	
	64,000 12/31/06 bal.
	2,000 (a)
	66,000 1/31/07 bal.

− Retained Earnings (SE) +	
	84,000 12/31/06 bal.
(f) ___	
	81,000 1/31/07 bal.

Self-Study Quiz
Solutions

(d) Journal entry:

| Notes Receivable (+A) .... | 3,000 | |
| Cash (−A) .... | | 3,000 |

Debits $3,000 = Credits $3,000

(e) Effect on the accounting equation:

Assets	=	Liabilities	+	Stockholders' Equity
Cash −1,000				
Investments +1,000				

Yes, the accounting equation is in balance.

(f) Journal entry:

| Retained Earnings (−SE) .... | 3,000 | |
| Dividends Payable (+L) .... | | 3,000 |

Effect on the accounting equation:

Assets	=	Liabilities	+	Stockholders' Equity
		Dividends Payable +3,000		Retained Earnings −3,000

You can verify that you posted the entries properly by adding the increase side and subtracting the decrease side of each T-account and comparing your answer with the ending balance for each T-account.

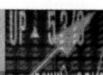

FINANCIAL ANALYSIS

Inferring Business Activities from T-accounts

T-accounts are useful primarily for instructional and analytical purposes. In many cases, we will use T-accounts to determine what transactions a company engaged in during a period. For example, the primary transactions affecting Accounts Payable for a period are purchases of assets on account and cash payments to suppliers. If we know the beginning and ending balances of Accounts Payable and all the amounts that were purchased on credit during a period, we can determine the amount of cash paid. A T-account analysis would include the following:

− Accounts Payable (L) +		
	600	Beg. bal.
Cash payments to suppliers ?	1,500	Purchases on account
	300	End. bal.

Solution:

Beginning Balance	+	Purchases on Account	−	Cash Payments to Suppliers	=	Ending Balance
$600	+	$1,500	−	?	=	$ 300
		$2,100	−	?	=	$ 300
				?	=	$1,800

Learning Objective 5
Prepare a simple classified balance sheet and analyze the company using the financial leverage ratio.

HOW IS THE BALANCE SHEET PREPARED AND ANALYZED?

As discussed in Chapter 1, a balance sheet is one of the financial statements that will be communicated to users, especially those external to the business. It is possible to prepare a balance sheet at any point in time using the balances in the accounts.

Classified Balance Sheet

The balance sheet in Exhibit 2.8 was prepared using the new balances shown in the T-accounts in the preceding Papa John's illustration (the shaded lines in the exhibit). As such, it needs a good heading (name of the company, title of the statement, date, and if the dollars are in thousands or millions). Notice in Exhibit 2.8 several additional features:

- The assets and liabilities are classified into two categories—current and noncurrent. Current assets are those to be used or turned into cash within the upcoming year, whereas noncurrent assets are those that will last longer than one year. Current liabilities are those obligations to be paid or settled within the next 12 months with current assets.

- Dollar signs are indicated at the top and bottom of the asset section and top and bottom of the liabilities and shareholders' equity section.

- The statement includes comparative data. That is, it compares the account balances at January 31, 2007, with those at December 31, 2006. When multiple periods are presented, the most recent balance sheet amounts are usually listed on the left.

At the beginning of the chapter, we presented the changes in Papa John's balance sheets from the years 1994 to 2006. We questioned what made the accounts change

EXHIBIT 2.8

Papa John's Balance Sheet

PAPA JOHN'S INTERNATIONAL, INC. AND SUBSIDIARIES
Consolidated Balance Sheets
(dollars in thousands)

	January 31, 2007	December 31, 2006
Assets		
Current Assets		
Cash	$ 15,000	$ 13,000
Accounts receivable	23,000	23,000
Supplies	27,000	27,000
Prepaid expenses	8,000	8,000
Other current assets	14,000	14,000
Total current assets	87,000	85,000
Investments	2,000	1,000
Property and equipment (net of accumulated depreciation of $189,000)	208,000	198,000
Notes receivable	15,000	12,000
Intangibles	67,000	67,000
Other assets	17,000	17,000
Total assets	$396,000	$380,000
Liabilities and Stockholders' Equity		
Current Liabilities		
Accounts payable	$ 29,000	$ 29,000
Dividends payable	3,000	0
Accrued expenses payable	73,000	73,000
Total current liabilities	105,000	102,000
Unearned franchise fees	7,000	7,000
Notes payable	110,000	96,000
Other long-term liabilities	27,000	27,000
Stockholders' Equity		
Contributed capital	66,000	64,000
Retained earnings	81,000	84,000
Total stockholders' equity	147,000	148,000
Total liabilities and stockholders' equity	$396,000	$380,000

Total Liabilities = $249,000 on January 31, 2007 and $232,000 on December 31, 2006

and what the process was for reflecting the changes. Now we can see that the accounts have changed again in one month due to the transactions illustrated in this chapter:

	Assets	=	Liabilities	+	Stockholders' Equity
End of January 2007	$396,000		$249,000		$147,000
End of 2006	380,000		232,000		148,000
Change	+ $ 16,000		+ $ 17,000		− $ 1,000

KEY RATIO
ANALYSIS

Financial Leverage Ratio

Users of financial information compute a number of ratios in analyzing a company's past performance and financial condition as input in predicting its future potential. How ratios change over time and how they compare to the ratios of the company's competitors or industry averages provide valuable information about a company's strategies for its operating, investing, and financing activities.

We introduce here the first of many ratios that will be presented throughout the rest of this textbook, with a final summary of ratio analysis in Chapter 14. In Chapters 2, 3, and 4, we present three ratios that provide information about management's effectiveness at managing debt and equity financing (financial leverage ratio), utilizing assets (total asset turnover ratio), and controlling revenues and costs (net profit margin), all for the purpose of enhancing returns to shareholders. In Chapter 5, we discuss the powerful effects of combining these three general ratios. The remaining chapters discuss the specific ratios affecting each of the general ratios for a more precise assessment of a company's strategies, strengths, and areas for concern.

As we discussed earlier in the chapter, companies raise large amounts of money to acquire additional assets by issuing stock to investors and borrowing funds from creditors. These additional assets are used to generate more income. However, since debt must be repaid, taking on increasing amounts of liabilities carries increased risk. The financial leverage ratio provides one measure for analysts to examine this financing and investing strategy.

▸ ANALYTICAL QUESTION

How is management using debt to increase the amount of assets the company employs to earn income for stockholders?

% RATIO AND COMPARISONS

$$\text{Financial Leverage Ratio} = \frac{\text{Average Total Assets}}{\text{Average Stockholders' Equity}}$$

"Average" is a simple average computed by adding together the beginning and ending balance of assets or stockholders' equity, then dividing by two. Averaging of the balance sheet amounts is done to capture the midpoint of activities during the period. In a formula format, the computation is:

$$(\text{Beginning balance} + \text{Ending balance}) / 2$$

The 2006 ratio for Papa John's is (dollars are in thousands):

	2005 Balance		2006 Balance	
	($351,000	+	$380,000)/2	= 2.37
	($161,000	+	$148,000)/2	

Comparisons over Time
Papa John's International, Inc.

2004	2005	2006
2.42	2.42	2.37

Comparisons with Competitors

California Pizza Kitchen, Inc.	Pizza Inn, Inc.
2006	2006
1.44	3.73

California Pizza Kitchen, Inc., focuses on offering premium pizza and other related menu items, operates over 210 casual dining restaurants (86 percent company-owned) located in 29 states and seven foreign countries. *Pizza Inn, Inc.,* has over 360 restaurants, mostly franchised, in 18 states, primarily in the southern half of the United States and nine foreign countries.

Determining the Competition
You cannot always compare the closest competitors. Pizza Hut and Domino's, noted as primary competitors for Papa John's, are not used in this analysis for the following reasons:
- *Pizza Hut is owned by Yum! Brands that also owns KFC and Taco Bell. Separate financial information for Pizza Hut is not publicly available.*
- *Until 2004, Domino's was involved in a change in ownership in previous years, causing a negative amount in stockholders' equity. The results would be unusual and, therefore, not useful as a basis for comparison.*

💡 INTERPRETATIONS

In General   The financial leverage ratio measures the relationship between total assets and the stockholders' equity that finances the assets. As noted, companies finance their assets with stockholders' equity and debt. The higher the proportion of assets financed by debt, the higher the financial leverage ratio. Conversely, the higher the proportion of assets financed with stockholders' equity, the lower the ratio. A ratio of 1.00 indicates the company has no liabilities. A ratio of 2.00 means the company uses debt and equity financing equally to acquire assets. A ratio above 2.00 suggests a heavier reliance on debt than equity. Let's illustrate this:

Selected Focus Companies' Financial Leverage Ratios

Harrah's	3.65
Harley-Davidson	1.85
Home Depot	1.86

	Assets	=	Liabilities	+	Stockholders' Equity	
If a company has no debt,	10		0		10	then the ratio = 1.00
If a company adds equal debt,	20		10		10	then the ratio = 2.00

In this case, twice as many assets are now available to generate profits for shareholders.

	Assets		Liabilities		Stockholders' Equity	
If a company adds more debt,	30		20		10	then the ratio = 3.00

In this case, even more profits can be generated with the additional assets, but the company has twice as much debt as stockholders' equity, and creditors will charge higher interest rates as a company's debt burden increases. The company is seen as riskier.

Increasing debt (and the leverage ratio) increases the amount of assets the company may acquire and use to earn income for stockholders, which increases the chances of earning higher income. However, it also increases **risk.** Debt financing is riskier than financing with stockholders' equity because the interest payments on debt must be made every period (they are legal obligations), whereas dividends on stock can be postponed. An increasing ratio over time signals more reliance on debt financing and more risk.

Creditors and security analysts use this ratio to assess a company's risk level, while managers use the ratio in deciding whether to expand by adding debt. As long as the interest on borrowing is less than the additional earnings generated, utilizing debt will enhance the stockholders' earnings.

Focus Company Analysis   Papa John's financial leverage decreased slightly in 2006. In 2006, the ratio indicates that Papa John's had $2.37 in assets per $1.00 in stockholders' equity and $1.37 in liabilities. The company financed its assets nearly one-and-one-half times more with debt than with stockholders' equity—a riskier strategy. In fact, since December 1999, Papa John's has undertaken a major effort to repurchase its issued stock from shareholders. The money to buy back the shares is financed primarily by borrowing. This results in decreasing stockholders' equity while increasing liabilities without increasing assets.

When compared against two other pizza restaurants, Papa John's 2006 financial leverage ratio is in the middle. The two competitors listed are eat-in restaurants that must invest more in facilities than Papa John's, which primarily rents space instead of constructing buildings. However, Papa John's share repurchase program causes its ratio to exceed that of California Pizza Kitchen. Reuters reports that the restaurant industry has an average leverage ratio of 1.72 (approximately two-thirds as much debt as equity financing). This suggests that Papa John's at 2.37 is following a riskier (more aggressive) financing strategy than other companies in the restaurant industry.

A Few Cautions   A financial leverage ratio near 1.00 indicates a company that is choosing not to utilize debt to expand. This suggests that the company has lower risk but is not enhancing the return to stockholders. When comparing competitors, the ratio may be influenced by differences in business strategies, such as whether the company rents or buys facilities.

SELF-STUDY QUIZ

Wendy's International, Inc., reported the following balances on its recent balance sheets (in thousands):

	Assets	Liabilities	Stockholders' Equity
Beginning of year	$3,440,318	$1,381,729	$2,058,589
End of year	$2,060,347	$1,048,670	$1,011,677

Compute Wendy's financial leverage ratio. What does this ratio suggest about Wendy's level of financial risk and financing strategy?

After you have completed your answers, check them with the solutions at the bottom of the page.

FOCUS ON CASH FLOWS

Investing and Financing Activities

Learning Objective 6

Identify investing and financing transactions and demonstrate how they are reported on the statement of cash flows.

Recall from Chapter 1 that companies report cash inflows and outflows over a period in their statement of cash flows. This statement divides all transactions that affect cash into three categories: operating, investing, and financing activities. Operating activities are covered in Chapter 3. Investing activities include buying and selling noncurrent assets and investments; financing activities include borrowing and repaying debt including short-term bank loans, issuing and repurchasing stock, and paying dividends. When cash is involved, these activities are reported on the statement of cash flows. (When cash is not included in the transaction, such as when a building is acquired with a long-term mortgage note payable, there is no cash effect to include on the statement of cash flows. You must see cash in the transaction for it to affect the statement of cash flows.) In general, the effects of such activities are as follows:

Effect on Cash Flows

Operating activities
  (No transactions in this chapter were operating activities.)
Investing activities

Purchasing long-term assets and investments for cash	−
Selling long-term assets and investments for cash	+
Lending cash to others	−
Receiving principal payments on loans made to others	+

Financing activities

Borrowing cash from banks	+
Repaying the principal on borrowings from banks	−
Issuing stock for cash	+
Repurchasing stock with cash	−
Paying cash dividends	−

Focus Company Analysis Exhibit 2.9 shows a statement of cash flows for Papa John's based on the activities listed in this chapter. It reports the sources and uses of cash that created the $2,000 increase in cash (from $13,000 to $15,000) in January 2007. Remember that only transactions that affect cash are reported on the cash flow statement.

The pattern of cash flows shown in Exhibit 2.9 (net cash outflows for investing activities and net cash inflows from financing activities) is typical of Papa John's past several annual statements of cash flows. Companies seeking to expand usually report cash outflows for investing activities.

Self-Study Quiz
Solutions

($3,440,318 + $2,060,347)/2 ÷ ($2,058,589 + $1,011,677)/2 = 1.79, so Wendy's is following a slightly riskier financing strategy than other companies in the industry. This ratio is higher than the industry average but lower than Papa John's.

PAPA JOHN'S INTERNATIONAL, INC.	
Consolidated Statement of Cash Flows	
For the month ended January 31, 2007	
(in thousands)	
Operating activities	
(None in this chapter.)	
Investing activities	
Purchased property and equipment (c)	$ (2,000)
Purchased investments (e)	(1,000)
Lent funds to franchisees (d)	(3,000)
Net cash used in investing activities	**(6,000)**
Financing activities	
Issued common stock (a)	2,000
Borrowed from banks (b)	6,000
Net cash provided by financing activities	**8,000**
Net increase in cash	**2,000**
Cash at beginning of month	13,000
Cash at end of month	**$15,000**

Agrees with the amount on the balance sheet.

EXHIBIT 2.9

Papa John's Statement of Cash Flows

Items are referenced to events (a) through (f) illustrated in this chapter.

SELF-STUDY QUIZ

Lance, Inc., manufactures and sells snack products. Indicate whether these transactions from a recent annual statement of cash flows were investing (I) or financing (F) activities and the direction of their effects on cash (+ for increases cash; − for decreases cash):

Lance, Inc.

TRANSACTIONS	TYPE OF ACTIVITY (I OR F)	EFFECT ON CASH FLOWS (+ OR −)
1. Paid dividends.		
2. Sold property.		
3. Repaid debt.		
4. Purchased property and equipment.		
5. Issued common stock.		

After you have completed the schedule, check it with the solutions at the bottom of the page.

DEMONSTRATION CASE

On April 1, 2009, three ambitious college students started Terrific Lawn Maintenance Corporation. A summary of transactions completed through April 30, 2009, for Terrific Lawn Maintenance Corporation follows:

a. Issued 500 shares of stock (1,500 shares in total) to each of the three investors in exchange for $9,000 cash.

b. Acquired rakes and other hand tools (equipment) with a list price of $690 for $600; paid the hardware store $200 cash and signed a three-month note for the balance.

1. F −   2. I +   3. F −   4. I −   5. F +

c. Ordered three lawn mowers and two edgers from XYZ Lawn Supply, Inc., for $4,000.

d. Purchased four acres of land for the future site of a storage garage; paid cash, $5,000.

e. Received the mowers and edgers that had been ordered, signing a note to pay XYZ Lawn Supply in full in 30 days.

f. Sold for $1,250 one acre of land to the city for a park. Accepted a note from the city for payment by the end of the month.

g. One of the owners borrowed $3,000 from a local bank for personal use.

Required:

1. Set up T-accounts for Cash, Notes Receivable (from the city), Equipment (hand tools and mowing equipment), Land, Notes Payable (to equipment supply companies), and Contributed Capital. Beginning balances are $0; indicate these beginning balances in the T-accounts. Analyze each transaction using the process outlined in the chapter. Prepare journal entries in chronological order. Enter the effects of the transactions in the appropriate T-accounts; identify each amount with its letter in the preceding list.

2. Use the amounts in the T-accounts developed in requirement (1) to prepare a classified balance sheet for Terrific Lawn Maintenance Corporation at April 30, 2009. Show the account balances for all assets, liabilities, and stockholders' equity. Use the following transaction analysis model.

ASSETS (many accounts)	=	LIABILITIES (many accounts)	+	STOCKHOLDERS' EQUITY (two accounts)			
+ debit	− credit	− debit	+ credit	Contributed Capital		Retained Earnings	
				− debit	+ credit	− debit	+ credit
					Investments by owners	Dividends declared	Net income of business

3. Prepare the investing and financing sections of the statement of cash flows. Check your answers with the solution in the following section.

SUGGESTED SOLUTION

1. Transaction analysis, journal entries, and T-accounts:

(a) Cash (+A) 9,000
        Contributed Capital (+SE) 9,000

Assets		=	Liabilities	+	Stockholders' Equity	
Cash	+9,000				Contributed Capital	+9,000

Equality checks: (1) Debits $9,000 = Credits $9,000; (2) the accounting equation is in balance.

(b) Equipment (+A) 600
        Cash (−A) 200
        Notes Payable (+L) 400

Assets		=	Liabilities		+	Stockholders' Equity
Equipment*	+600		Notes Payable	+400		
Cash	−200					

*The historical cost principle states that assets should be recorded at the amount paid on the date of the transaction, or $600, rather than at the $690 list price.

Equality checks: (1) Debits $600 = Credits $600; (2) the accounting equation is in balance.

(c) This is not an accounting transaction; no exchange has taken place. No accounts are affected.

(d) Land (+A) 5,000
       Cash (−A)   5,000

Assets		=	Liabilities	+	Stockholders' Equity
Land	+5,000				
Cash	−5,000				

Equality checks: (1) Debits $5,000 = Credits $5,000; (2) the accounting equation is in balance.

(e) Equipment (+A) 4,000
       Notes Payable (+L)   4,000

Assets		=	Liabilities		+	Stockholders' Equity
Equipment	+4,000		Notes Payable	+4,000		

Equality checks: (1) Debits $4,000 = Credits $4,000; (2) the accounting equation is in balance.

(f) Notes Receivable (+A) 1,250
       Land (−A)   1,250

Assets		=	Liabilities	+	Stockholders' Equity
Notes Receivable	+1,250				
Land*	−1,250				

*One acre of land cost the company $1,250 when it was purchased ($5,000 total cost ÷ 4 acres). When an asset is sold, the account is reduced by the asset's historical cost.

Equality checks: (1) Debits $1,250 = Credits $1,250; (2) the accounting equation is in balance.

(g) There is no transaction for the company. The separate-entity assumption states that transactions of the owners are separate from transactions of the business.

+ (dr)	Cash (A)		(cr) −
4/1/09 bal.	0		
(a)	9,000	200	(b)
		5,000	(d)
4/30/09 bal.	3,800		

+ (dr)	Notes Receivable (A)	(cr) −
4/1/09 bal.	0	
(f)	1,250	
4/30/09 bal.	1,250	

+ (dr)	Equipment (A)		(cr) −
4/1/09 bal.	0		
(b)	600		
(e)	4,000		
4/30/09 bal.	4,600		

+ (dr)	Land (A)		(cr) −
4/1/09 bal.	0	1,250	(f)
(d)	5,000		
4/30/09 bal.	3,750		

− (dr)	Notes Payable (L)	(cr) +
	0	4/1/09 bal.
	400	(b)
	4,000	(e)
	4,400	4/30/09 bal.

− (dr)	Contributed Capital (SE)	(cr) +
	0	4/1/09 bal.
	9,000	(a)
	9,000	4/30/09 bal.

2. Balance sheet:

TERRIFIC LAWN MAINTENANCE CORPORATION
Balance Sheet
At April 30, 2009

Assets		Liabilities	
Current Assets		*Current Liabilities*	
Cash	$ 3,800	Notes payable	$ 4,400
Notes receivable	1,250		
Total current assets	5,050		
Equipment	4,600	**Stockholders' Equity**	
Land	3,750	Contributed capital	9,000
Total assets	$13,400	Total liabilities and stockholders' equity	$13,400

Notice that the balance sheets presented earlier in the text listed assets on the top and liabilities and stockholders' equity on the bottom. It is also acceptable practice to prepare a balance sheet with assets on the left side and liabilities and stockholders' equity on the right side, as in the preceding example.

3. Investing and financing effects of the statement of cash flows:

TERRIFIC LAWN MAINTENANCE CORPORATION
Statement of Cash Flows
For the Month Ended April 30, 2009

Operating activities		
(none in this case)		
Investing activities		
Purchased land	$(5,000)	Transaction (*d*)
Purchased equipment	(200)	Transaction (*b*)
Net cash used in investing activities	**(5,200)**	
Financing activities		
Issued common stock	9,000	Transaction (*a*)
Net cash provided by financing activities	**9,000**	
Change in cash	3,800	
Beginning cash balance	0	
Ending cash balance	$ 3,800	

1. **Define the objective of financial reporting, the elements of the balance sheet, and the related key accounting assumptions and principles.**   p. 49

   - The primary objective of external financial reporting is to provide useful economic information about a business to help external parties, primarily investors and creditors, make sound financial decisions.
   - Elements of the balance sheet:
     a. Assets—probable future economic benefits owned by the entity as a result of past transactions.
     b. Liabilities—probable debts or obligations acquired by the entity as a result of past transactions, to be paid with assets or services.
     c. Stockholders' equity—the financing provided by the owners and by business operations.
   - Key accounting assumptions and principles:
     a. Separate-entity assumption—transactions of the business are accounted for separately from transactions of the owner.
     b. Unit-of-measure assumption—financial information is reported in the national monetary unit.
     c. Continuity (going-concern) assumption—a business is expected to continue to operate into the foreseeable future.
     d. Historical cost principle—financial statement elements should be recorded at the cash-equivalent cost on the date of the transaction.

2. **Identify what constitutes a business transaction and recognize common balance sheet account titles used in business.**   p. 53

   A transaction includes:
   - An exchange between a business and one or more external parties to a business.

   or

   - A measurable internal event, such as adjustments for the use of assets in operations.

   An account is a standardized format that organizations use to accumulate the dollar effects of transactions related to each financial statement item. Typical balance sheet account titles include the following:
   - *Assets:* Cash, Accounts Receivable, Inventory, Prepaid Expenses, and Buildings and Equipment.
   - *Liabilities:* Accounts Payable, Notes Payable, Accrued Expenses Payable, Unearned Revenues, and Taxes Payable.
   - *Stockholders' Equity:* Contributed Capital and Retained Earnings.

3. **Apply transaction analysis to simple business transactions in terms of the accounting model: Assets = Liabilities + Stockholders' Equity.**   p. 55

   To determine the economic effect of a transaction on an entity in terms of the accounting equation, each transaction must be analyzed to determine the accounts (at least two) that are affected. In an exchange, the company receives something and gives up something. If the accounts, direction of the effects, and amounts are correctly analyzed, the accounting equation must stay in balance. The transaction analysis model is

ASSETS (many accounts)	=	LIABILITIES (many accounts)	+	STOCKHOLDERS' EQUITY (two accounts)			
+ debit | − credit		− debit | + credit		**Contributed Capital**		**Retained Earnings**	
				− debit	+ credit	− debit	+ credit
					Investments by owners	Dividends declared	Net income of business

4. **Determine the impact of business transactions on the balance sheet using two basic tools, journal entries and T-accounts.**   p. 60

   • Journal entries express the effects of a transaction on accounts in a debits-equal-credits format. The accounts and amounts to be debited are listed first. Then the accounts and amounts to be credited are listed below the debits and indented, resulting in debits on the left and credits on the right.

		Debit	Credit
(date or reference)	Property and Equipment (+A)	10,000	
	Cash (−A)		2,000
	Notes Payable (+L)		8,000

   • T-accounts summarize the transaction effects for each account. These tools can be used to determine balances and draw inferences about a company's activities.

+ (dr)	Assets	(cr) −	− (dr) Liabilities and Stockholders' Equity (cr) +	
Beginning balance Increases		Decreases	Decreases	Beginning balance Increases
Ending Balance				Ending Balance

5. **Prepare a simple classified balance sheet and analyze the company using the financial leverage ratio.**   p. 68

   Classified balance sheets are structured with

   • Assets categorized as current assets (those to be used or turned into cash within the year, with inventory always considered a current asset) and noncurrent assets, such as long-term investments, property and equipment, and intangible assets.

   • Liabilities categorized as current liabilities (those that will be paid with current assets) and long-term liabilities.

   • Stockholders' equity accounts are listed as Contributed Capital first followed by Retained Earnings.

   The financial leverage ratio (Average Total Assets ÷ Average Stockholders' Equity) measures the relationship between total assets and the stockholders' capital that finances the assets. The higher the ratio, the more debt is used to finance the assets. As the ratio (and thus debt) increases, risk increases.

6. **Identify investing and financing transactions and demonstrate how they are reported on the statement of cash flows.**   p. 72

   A statement of cash flows reports the sources and uses of cash for the period by the type of activity that generated the cash flow: operating, investing, and financing. Investing activities are purchasing and selling long-term assets and making loans and receiving principal repayments from others. Financing activities are borrowing and repaying to banks the principal on loans, issuing and repurchasing stock, and paying dividends.

   In this chapter, we discussed the fundamental accounting model and transaction analysis. Journal entries and T-accounts were used to record the results of transaction analysis for investing and financing decisions that affect balance sheet accounts. In Chapter 3, we continue our detailed look at the financial statements, in particular the income statement. The purpose of Chapter 3 is to build on your knowledge by discussing the measurement of revenues and expenses and illustrating the transaction analysis of operating decisions.

Financial leverage ratio measures the relationship between total assets and the stockholders' capital that finances them. The higher the ratio, the more debt is assumed by the company to finance assets. It is computed as follows (p. 70):

$$\text{Financial Leverage Ratio} = \frac{\text{Average Total Assets}}{\text{Average Stockholders' Equity}}$$

"Average" is (Beginning balance + Ending balance) ÷ 2

FINDING **FINANCIAL INFORMATION**

Balance Sheet

Current Assets
Cash
Accounts and notes
  receivable
Inventory
Prepaid expenses

Noncurrent Assets
Long-term investments
Property and equipment
Intangibles

Current Liabilities
Accounts payable
Notes payable
Accrued expenses payable
Unearned revenue

Noncurrent Liabilities
Long-term debt

Stockholders' Equity
Contributed capital
Retained earnings

Income Statement
To be presented in Chapter 3

Statement of Cash Flows

Under Operating Activities
To be presented in Chapter 3

Under Investing Activities
+ Sales of noncurrent assets for cash
− Purchases of noncurrent assets for cash
− Loans to others
+ Receipt of loan principal payments from others

Under Financing Activities
+ Borrowing from banks
− Repayment of loan principal to banks
+ Issuance of stock
− Repurchasing stock

Notes
*To be discussed in future
  chapters*

KEY **TERMS**

Account p. 54
Assets p. 50
Continuity (Going-Concern)
  Assumption p. 50
Contributed Capital p. 53
Credit p. 61
Current Assets p. 51
Current Liabilities p. 52

Debit p. 61
Historical Cost Principle p. 50
Journal Entry p. 62
Liabilities p. 52
Primary Objective of External
  Financial Reporting p. 49
Retained Earnings p. 53
Separate-Entity Assumption p. 50

Stockholders' Equity (Owners' or
  Shareholders' Equity) p. 53
T-account p. 63
Transaction p. 53
Transaction Analysis p. 55
Unit-of-Measure Assumption
  p. 50

QUESTIONS

1. What is the primary objective of financial reporting for external users?
2. Define the following:
   a. Asset
   b. Current asset
   c. Liability
   d. Current liability
   e. Contributed capital
   f. Retained earnings
3. Explain what the following accounting terms mean:
   a. Separate-entity assumption
   b. Unit-of-measure assumption
   c. Continuity assumption
   d. Historical cost principle
4. Why are accounting assumptions necessary?
5. For accounting purposes, what is an account? Explain why accounts are used in an accounting system.
6. What is the fundamental accounting model?
7. Define a business transaction in the broad sense and give an example of two different kinds of transactions.
8. Explain what *debit* and *credit* mean.
9. Briefly explain what is meant by *transaction analysis*. What are the two steps in transaction analysis?
10. What two accounting equalities must be maintained in transaction analysis?
11. What is a journal entry?
12. What is a T-account? What is its purpose?
13. How is the financial leverage ratio computed and interpreted?
14. What transactions are classified as investing activities in a statement of cash flows? What transactions are classified as financing activities?

MULTIPLE-CHOICE QUESTIONS

1. If a publicly traded company is trying to maximize its perceived value to decision makers external to the corporation, the company is most likely to understate which of the following on its balance sheet?
   a. Assets
   b. Liabilities
   c. Retained Earnings
   d. Contributed Capital
2. Which of the following is not an asset?
   a. Investments
   b. Land
   c. Prepaid Expense
   d. Contributed Capital
3. Total liabilities on a balance sheet at the end of the year are $40,000, retained earnings at the end of the year are $30,000, net income for the year is $10,000, and contributed capital is $25,000. What amount of total assets would be reported on the balance sheet at the end of the year?
   a. $50,000
   b. $65,000
   c. $70,000
   d. $95,000
4. The dual effects concept can best be described as follows:
   a. When one records a transaction in the accounting system, at least two effects on the basic accounting equation will result.
   b. When an exchange takes place between two parties, both parties must record the transaction.
   c. When a transaction is recorded, both the balance sheet and the income statement must be impacted.
   d. When a transaction is recorded, one account will always increase and one account will always decrease.
5. The T-account is a tool commonly used for analyzing which of the following?
   a. Increases and decreases to a single account in the accounting system.
   b. Debits and credits to a single account in the accounting system.
   c. Changes in specific account balances over a time period.
   d. All of the above describe how T-accounts are used by accountants.

6. Which of the following describes how assets are listed on the balance sheet?
   a. In alphabetical order
   b. In order of magnitude, lowest value to highest value
   c. From most liquid to least liquid
   d. From least liquid to most liquid

7. The Cash T-account has a beginning balance of $12,000. During the year, $78,000 was debited and $85,000 was credited to the account. What is the ending balance of Cash?
   a. $ 5,000
   b. $19,000
   c. $ 7,000
   d. Cannot determine the ending balance from the information given.

8. How many of the following statements are true regarding the balance sheet?
   ■ One cannot determine the true fair market value of a company by reviewing its balance sheet.
   ■ Certain internally generated assets, such as a trademark, are not reported on a company's balance sheet.
   ■ A balance sheet shows only the ending balances, in a summarized format, of all balance sheet accounts in the accounting system as of a particular date.
   a. None   c. Two
   b. One   d. Three

9. At the end of a recent year, Apple Inc. reported an average total assets amount of $21,276 million, average total liabilities of $9,018 million, and average stockholders' equity of $12,258 million. What is its financial leverage ratio and what does it suggest about the company?
   a. The ratio of .74 suggests that Apple finances its assets primarily with debt.
   b. The ratio of 1.74 suggests that Apple finances its assets primarily with stockholders' equity.
   c. The ratio of .74 suggests that Apple finances its assets primarily with stockholders' equity.
   d. The ratio of 1.74 suggests that Apple finances its assets primarily with debt.

10. Which of the following is *not* a financing activity on the statement of cash flows?
   a. When the company lends money.
   b. When the company borrows money.
   c. When the company pays dividends.
   d. When the company issues stock to shareholders.

For more practice with multiple choice questions, go to the text website at www.mhhe.com/ libby6e.

 Available with McGraw-Hill's Homework Manager

MINI-**EXERCISES**

Matching Definitions with Terms

Match each definition with its related term by entering the appropriate letter in the space provided. There should be only one definition per term (that is, there are more definitions than terms).

M2-1
LO1, 4

Term	Definition
___ (1) Separate-entity assumption	A. = Liabilities + Stockholders' Equity.
___ (2) Historical cost principle	B. Reports assets, liabilities, and stockholders' equity.
___ (3) Credits	C. Accounts for a business separate from its owners.
___ (4) Assets	D. Increase assets; decrease liabilities and stockholders' equity.
___ (5) Account	E. An exchange between an entity and other parties.
	F. The concept that businesses will operate into the foreseeable future.
	G. Decrease assets; increase liabilities and stockholders' equity.
	H. The concept that assets should be recorded at amount paid on the date of the transaction.
	I. A standardized format used to accumulate data about each item reported on financial statements.

M2-2
LO1, 2, 3, 4

Matching Definitions with Terms

Match each definition with its related term by entering the appropriate letter in the space provided. There should be only one definition per term (that is, there are more definitions than terms).

Term	Definition
___ (1) Journal entry	A. Accounting model.
___ (2) A = L + SE, and	B. Four periodic financial statements.
Debits = Credits	C. The two equalities in accounting that aid in providing accuracy.
___ (3) Assets = Liabilities +	D. The results of transaction analysis in accounting format.
Stockholders' Equity	E. The account that is debited when money is borrowed from a bank.
___ (4) Liabilities	F. Probable future economic benefits owned by an entity.
___ (5) Income statement, balance sheet, statement of retained earnings, and statement of cash flows	G. Cumulative earnings of a company that are not distributed to the owners.
	H. Every transaction has at least two effects.
	I. Probable debts or obligations to be paid with assets or services.

M2-3
LO2

Identifying Events as Accounting Transactions

For each of the following events, which result in an exchange transaction for Dittman Company (Y for yes and N for no)?

___ (1)   Dittman purchased a machine that it paid for by signing a note payable.
___ (2)   Six investors in Dittman Company sold their stock to another investor.
___ (3)   The company lent $150,000 to a member of the board of directors.
___ (4)   Dittman Company ordered supplies from Staples to be delivered next week.
___ (5)   The founding owner, Megan Dittman, purchased additional stock in another company.
___ (6)   The company borrowed $1,000,000 from a local bank.

M2-4
LO2

Classifying Accounts on a Balance Sheet

The following are several of the accounts of Gomez-Sanchez Company:

___ (1) Accounts Payable	___ (9) Long-Term Investments
___ (2) Accounts Receivable	___ (10) Notes Payable (due in three years)
___ (3) Buildings	___ (11) Notes Receivable (due in six months)
___ (4) Cash	___ (12) Prepaid Rent
___ (5) Contributed Capital	___ (13) Retained Earnings
___ (6) Land	___ (14) Supplies
___ (7) Merchandise Inventory	___ (15) Utilities Payable
___ (8) Income Taxes Payable	___ (16) Wages Payable

In the space provided, classify each as it would be reported on a balance sheet. Use:

CA for current asset   CL for current liability   SE for stockholders' equity
NCA for noncurrent asset   NCL for noncurrent liability

M2-5
LO3

Determining Financial Statement Effects of Several Transactions

For each of the following transactions of Bandera Inc. for the month of January 2011, indicate the accounts, amounts, and direction of the effects on the accounting equation. A sample is provided.
a. (Sample) Borrowed $20,000 from a local bank.
b. Lent $7,000 to an affiliate; accepted a note due in one year.
c. Sold additional stock to investors for $1,000 cash.

d. Purchased $15,000 of equipment, paying $6,000 cash and the rest on a note due in one year.

e. Declared and paid $2,000 in dividends to stockholders.

Assets	=	Liabilities	+	Stockholders' Equity
a. Sample: Cash +20,000		Notes Payable +20,000		

Identifying Increase and Decrease Effects on Balance Sheet Elements

M2-6
LO4

Complete the following table by entering either the word *increases* or *decreases* in each column.

	Debit	Credit
Assets	_____	_____
Liabilities	_____	_____
Stockholders' equity	_____	_____

Identifying Debit and Credit Effects on Balance Sheet Elements

M2-7
LO4

Complete the following table by entering either the word *debit* or *credit* in each column.

	Increase	Decrease
Assets	_____	_____
Liabilities	_____	_____
Stockholders' equity	_____	_____

Recording Simple Transactions

M2-8
LO4

For each transaction in M2–5 (including the sample), write the journal entry in the proper form.

Completing T-Accounts

M2-9
LO4

For each transaction in M2–5 (including the sample), post the effects to the appropriate T-accounts and determine ending account balances. Beginning balances are provided.

Cash			Notes Receivable			Equipment	
Beg. bal. 800			Beg. bal. 900			Beg. bal. 15,000	

Notes Payable			Contributed Capital			Retained Earnings	
	Beg. bal. 2,700			Beg. bal. 5,000			Beg. bal. 9,000

Preparing a Simple Classified Balance Sheet

M2-10
LO5

Starting with the beginning balances in M2-9 and given the transactions in M2–5 (including the sample), prepare a balance sheet for Bandera Inc. as of January 31, 2011, classified into current and non-current assets and liabilities.

Computing and Interpreting the Financial Leverage Ratio

M2-11
LO5

Calculate the financial leverage ratio for Sal's Pizza Company based on the following data:

	Assets	Liabilities	Stockholders' Equity
End of 2005	$240,000	$100,000	$140,000
End of 2006	$280,000	$120,000	$160,000

What does the result suggest about the company? What can you say about Sal's Pizza Company's ratio when compared to Papa John's 2006 ratio?

M2-12
LO6

Identifying Transactions as Investing or Financing Activities on the Statement of Cash Flows

For the transactions in M2–5, identify each as an investing (I) activity or financing (F) activity on the statement of cash flows.

EXERCISES

Available with McGraw-Hill's Homework Manager

E2-1
LO1, 2, 3, 4

Matching Definitions with Terms

Match each definition with its related term by entering the appropriate letter in the space provided. There should be only one definition per term (that is, there are more definitions than terms).

Term	Definition
___ (1) Transaction	A. Economic resources to be used or turned into cash within one year.
___ (2) Continuity assumption	B. Reports assets, liabilities, and stockholders' equity.
___ (3) Balance sheet	C. Accounts for a business separate from its owners.
___ (4) Liabilities	D. Increase assets; decrease liabilities and stockholders' equity.
___ (5) Assets = Liabilities + Stockholders' Equity	E. An exchange between an entity and other parties.
___ (6) Historical cost principle	F. The concept that businesses will operate into the foreseeable future.
___ (7) Note payable	G. Decrease assets; increase liabilities and stockholders' equity.
___ (8) Dual effects	H. The concept that assets should be recorded at amount paid on exchange date.
___ (9) Retained earnings	I. A standardized format used to accumulate data about each item reported on financial statements.
___ (10) Debits	J. Amounts owed from customers.
___ (11) Separate-entity assumption	K. The accounting model.
___ (12) Current assets	L. The two equalities in accounting that aid in providing accuracy.
___ (13) Accounts receivable	M. The account that is credited when money is borrowed from a bank.
___ (14) Unit-of-measure assumption	N. Cumulative earnings of a company that are not distributed to the owners.
___ (15) Account	O. Every transaction has at least two effects.
	P. Probable debts or obligations to be paid with assets or services.
	Q. The concept that states that accounting information should be measured and reported in the national monetary unit.
	R. Financing provided by owners and by business operations.

E2-2
LO2

Identifying Account Titles

The following are independent situations.

a. A company orders and receives 10 personal computers for office use for which it signs a note promising to pay $25,000 within three months.
b. A company purchases for $21,000 cash a new delivery truck that has a list, or sticker, price of $24,000.
c. A women's clothing retailer orders 30 new display stands for $300 each for future delivery.
d. A new company is formed and sells 100 shares of stock for $12 per share to investors.

e. A manufacturing company signs a contract for the construction of a new warehouse for $500,000. At the signing, the company writes a check for $50,000 to the construction company as the initial payment for the construction (receiving construction in progress). Answer from the standpoint of the manufacturing company.

f. A publishing firm purchases for $40,000 cash the copyright (an intangible asset) to a manuscript for an introductory accounting text.

g. A manufacturing firm pays stockholders a $100,000 cash dividend.

h. A company purchases 100 shares of Apple Inc. common stock for $5,000 cash.

i. A company purchases a piece of land for $50,000 cash. An appraiser for the buyer valued the land at $52,500.

j. A manufacturing company acquires the patent (an intangible asset) on a new digital satellite system for television reception, paying $500,000 cash and signing a $400,000 note payable due in one year.

k. A local company is a sole proprietorship (one owner); its owner buys a car for $10,000 for personal use. Answer from the company's point of view.

l. A company borrows $1,000 from a local bank and signs a six-month note for the loan.

m. A company pays $1,500 principal on its note payable (ignore interest).

Required:
1. Indicate the appropriate account titles, if any, affected in each of the preceding events. Consider what is received and what is given.
2. At what amount would you record the truck in (b)? The land in (i)? What measurement principle are you applying?
3. For (c), what accounting concept did you apply? For (k), what accounting concept did you apply?

Classifying Accounts and Their Usual Balances

As described in a recent annual report, Polaroid Corporation designs, manufactures, and markets worldwide a variety of products primarily in instant image-recording fields, including instant photographic cameras and films, electronic imaging recording devices, conventional films, and light-polarizing filters and lenses. The following are accounts from a recent balance sheet for Polaroid.

E2-3
LO2, 4
Polaroid.

(1) Land
(2) Retained Earnings
(3) Taxes Payable
(4) Prepaid Expenses
(5) Contributed Capital
(6) Long-Term Investments
(7) Machinery and Equipment
(8) Accounts Payable
(9) Short-Term Investments
(10) Notes Payable (due in 3 years)

Required:
For each account, indicate whether the account is classified as a current asset (CA), noncurrent asset (NCA), current liability (CL), noncurrent liability (NCL), or stockholders' equity (SE), and whether the account usually has a debit or credit balance.

Determining Financial Statement Effects of Several Transactions

The following events occurred for Perkins Company:
a. Received investment of $24,000 cash by organizers and distributed stock to them.
b. Purchased $8,000 of equipment, paying $1,000 in cash and signing a note for the rest.
c. Loaned $500 to an employee who signed a note.
d. Borrowed $7,000 cash from a bank.
e. Purchased $15,000 of land; paid $4,000 in cash and signed a mortgage note for the balance.

E2-4
LO3

Required:
For each of the events (a) through (e), perform transaction analysis and indicate the account, amount, and direction of the effect (+ for increase and − for decrease) on the accounting equation. Check that the accounting equation remains in balance after each transaction. Use the following headings:

Event	Assets	=	Liabilities	+	Stockholders' Equity

E2-5

L03

Nike, Inc.

Determining Financial Statement Effects of Several Transactions

Nike, Inc., with headquarters in Beaverton, Oregon, is one of the world's leading manufacturers of athletic shoes and sports apparel. The following activities occurred during a recent year. The amounts are rounded to millions of dollars.

a. Purchased additional buildings for $182 and equipment for $21.9; paid $48.1 in cash and signed a long-term note for the rest.
b. Issued $253.6 in additional stock for cash.
c. Declared $179.2 in dividends to be paid in the following year.
d. Purchased additional short-term investments for $400.8 cash.
e. Several Nike investors sold their own stock to other investors on the stock exchange for $36.
f. Sold $1.4 in short-term investments in other companies for $1.4 cash.

Required:

1. For each of these events, perform transaction analysis and indicate the account, amount, and direction of the effect on the accounting equation. Check that the accounting equation remains in balance after each transaction. Use the following headings:

Event	Assets	=	Liabilities	+	Stockholders' Equity

2. Explain your response to event (e).

E2-6

L04

Recording Investing and Financing Activities

Refer to E2–4.

Required:

For each of the events in E2–4, prepare journal entries, checking that debits equal credits.

E2-7

L04

Nike, Inc.

Recording Investing and Financing Activities

Refer to E2–5.

Required:

1. For each of the events in E2–5, prepare journal entries, checking that debits equal credits.
2. Explain your response to event (e).

E2-8

L04

Analyzing the Effects of Transactions in T-Accounts

Grady Service Company, Inc., was organized by Chris Grady and five other investors. The following activities occurred during the year:

a. Received $63,000 cash from the investors; each was issued 1,400 shares of capital stock.
b. Signed an agreement with a cleaning service to pay it $120 per week for cleaning the corporate offices.
c. Received an additional contribution from investors who provided $4,000 in cash and land valued at $13,000 in exchange for stock in the company.
d. Purchased equipment for use in the business at a cost of $16,000; one-fourth was paid in cash and the company signed a note for the balance (due in six months).
e. Lent $2,200 to one of the investors who signed a note due in six months.
f. Chris Grady borrowed $10,000 for personal use from a local bank, signing a one-year note.

Required:

1. Create T-accounts for the following accounts: Cash, Note Receivable, Equipment, Land, Note Payable, and Contributed Capital. Beginning balances are zero. For each of the preceding transactions, record the effects of the transaction in the appropriate T-accounts. Include good referencing and totals for each T-account.
2. Using the balances in the T-accounts, fill in the following amounts for the accounting equation:

   Assets $_____ = Liabilities $_____ + Stockholders' Equity $_____

3. Explain your response to events (b) and (f).

Inferring Investing and Financing Transactions and Preparing a Balance Sheet

During its first week of operations ending January 7, 2011, Cirba Sports Inc. completed six transactions with the dollar effects indicated in the following schedule:

E2-9
L04, 5

	DOLLAR EFFECT OF EACH OF THE SIX TRANSACTIONS						Ending
Accounts	1	2	3	4	5	6	Balance
Cash	$16,000	$70,000	$(5,000)	$(4,000)	$(9,000)		
Note receivable (short-term)				4,000			
Store fixtures					9,000		
Land			16,000			$4,000	
Note payable (due in three months)		70,000	11,000			4,000	
Contributed capital	16,000						

Required:
1. Write a brief explanation of each transaction. Explain any assumptions that you made.
2. Compute the ending balance in each account and prepare a classified balance sheet for Cirba Sports Inc. on January 7, 2011.

Inferring Investing and Financing Transactions and Preparing a Balance Sheet

During its first month of operations, March 2010, Clifford's Cleaning, Inc., completed six transactions with the dollar effects indicated in the following schedule:

E2-10
L04, 5

	DOLLAR EFFECT OF EACH OF THE SIX TRANSACTIONS						Ending
Accounts	1	2	3	4	5	6	Balance
Cash	$60,000	$(4,000)	$(4,000)	$(7,000)	$2,000		
Investments (short-term)				7,000	(2,000)		
Note receivable (due in six months)			4,000				
Computer equipment						$4,000	
Delivery truck		30,000					
Note payable (due in ten years)		26,000					
Contributed capital	60,000					4,000	

Required:
1. Write a brief explanation of transactions 1 through 6. Explain any assumptions that you made.
2. Compute the ending balance in each account and prepare a classified balance sheet for Clifford's Cleaning, Inc., at the end of March 2010.

Recording Journal Entries

Franklin Corporation was organized on May 1, 2011. The following events occurred during the first month.

E2-11
L04

a. Received $60,000 cash from the five investors who organized Franklin Corporation.
b. Borrowed $10,000 cash and signed a note due in two years.
c. Ordered store fixtures costing $20,000.
d. Purchased $12,000 in equipment, paying $1,500 in cash and signing a six-month note for the balance.
e. Received and paid for the store fixtures ordered in (c).
f. Lent $1,000 to an employee who signed a note to repay the loan in three months.

Required:
Prepare journal entries for each transaction. (Remember that debits go on top and credits go on the bottom, indented.) Be sure to use good referencing and categorize each account as an asset (A), liability (L), or stockholders' equity (SE). If a transaction does not require a journal entry, explain the reason.

E2-12
L04

Recording Journal Entries

BMW Group, headquartered in Munich, Germany, manufactures several automotive brands including BMW, MINI, and Rolls-Royce. Financial information is reported in the euro (€) monetary unit using International Financial Reporting Standards as applicable to the European Union. The following transactions were adapted from the annual report of the BMW Group; amounts are in millions of euros.

  a. Declared € 532 in dividends to be paid next month.
  b. Ordered € 12,890 in equipment.
  c. Paid € 419 in dividends declared in prior months.
  d. Borrowed € 3,956 in cash from banks.
  e. Sold equipment at its cost of € 2,677 for cash.
  f. Received the equipment ordered in event (*b*), paying € 9,870 in cash and signing a note for the balance.
  g. Purchased investments for € 2,654 cash.

  Required:
  Prepare journal entries for each transaction. Be sure to use good referencing and categorize each account as an asset (A), liability (L), or stockholders' equity (SE). If a transaction does not require a journal entry, explain the reason.

E2-13
L04, 5

Analyzing the Effects of Transactions Using T-Accounts and Interpreting the Financial Leverage Ratio as a Manager of the Company

Massimo Company has been operating for one year (2010). You are a member of the management team investigating expansion ideas that will require borrowing funds from banks. At the start of 2011, Massimo's T-account balances were as follows:

Assets:

Cash		Short-Term Investments		Property and Equipment	
3,000		2,000		2,500	

Liabilities:

Short-Term Notes Payable		Long-Term Notes Payable	
	200		300

Stockholders' Equity:

Contributed Capital		Retained Earnings	
	5,000		2,000

  Required:
  1. Using the data from these T-accounts, determine the amounts for the following on January 1, 2011:

  Assets $_____ = Liabilities $_____ + Stockholders' Equity $_____

  2. Enter the following 2011 transactions in the T-accounts:
  a. Borrowed $2,000 from a local bank, signing a note due in three years.
  b. Sold $1,000 of the investments for $1,000 cash.
  c. Sold one-half of the property and equipment for $1,250 in cash.
  d. Paid $300 cash dividends to stockholders.
  3. Compute ending balances in the T-accounts to determine amounts for the following on December 31, 2011:

  Assets $_____ = Liabilities $_____ + Stockholders' Equity $_____

  4. Calculate the financial leverage ratio at December 31, 2011. If the industry average for the financial leverage ratio is 2.00, what does your computation suggest to you about Massimo Company? Would you support expansion by borrowing? Why or why not?

E2-14 Preparing a Balance Sheet

Refer to E2–13.

Required:
From the ending balances in the T-accounts in E2–13, prepare a classified balance sheet at December 31, 2011, in good form.

E2-14
LO5

Analyzing the Effects of Transactions Using T-Accounts, Preparing a Balance Sheet, and Evaluating the Financial Leverage Ratio over Time as a Bank Loan Officer

E2-15
LO4, 5

Chu Delivery Company, Inc., was organized in 2010. The following transactions occurred during year 2010:

a. Received $40,000 cash from organizers in exchange for stock in the new company.
b. Purchased land for $12,000, signing a one-year note (ignore interest).
c. Bought two used delivery trucks for operating purposes at the start of the year at a cost of $10,000 each; paid $4,000 cash and signed a note due in three years for the rest (ignore interest).
d. Sold one-fourth of the land for $3,000 to Pablo Moving, which signed a six-month note.
e. Paid $1,000 cash to a truck repair shop for a new motor for one of the trucks. (*Hint:* Increase the account you used to record the purchase of the trucks since the productive life of the truck has been improved.)
f. Stockholder Jingbi Chu paid $27,600 cash for a vacant lot (land) for her personal use.

Required:
1. Set up appropriate T-accounts with beginning balances of zero for Cash, Short-Term Note Receivable, Land, Equipment, Short-Term Notes Payable, Long-Term Notes Payable, and Contributed Capital. Using the T-accounts, record the effects of these transactions by Chu Delivery Company.
2. Prepare a classified balance sheet for Chu Delivery Company at December 31, 2010.
3. At the end of the next two years, Chu Delivery Company reported the following amounts on its balance sheets:

	December 31, 2011	December 31, 2012
Assets	$90,000	$120,000
Liabilities	40,000	60,000
Stockholders' Equity	50,000	60,000

Compute the company's financial leverage ratio for 2011 and 2012. What is the trend and what does this suggest about the company?
4. At the beginning of year 2013, Chu Delivery Company applied to your bank for a $100,000 loan to expand the business. The vice president of the bank asked you to review the information and make a recommendation on lending the funds based solely on the results of the financial leverage ratio. What recommendation would you make to the bank's vice president about lending the money to Chu Delivery Company?

Explaining the Effects of Transactions on Balance Sheet Accounts Using T-Accounts

E2-16
LO4

Staub and Gever Furniture Repair Service, a company with two stockholders, began operations on June 1, 2011. The following T-accounts indicate the activities for the month of June.

Cash (A)			
6/1/11	0		
a.	17,000	b.	10,000
d.	800	c.	1,500

Notes Receivable (A)		
6/1/11	0	
c.	1,500	

Tools and Equipment (A)			
6/1/11	0		
a.	3,000	d.	800

Building (A)	
6/1/11	0
b.	50,000

Notes Payable (L)		
	6/1/11	0
	b.	40,000

Contributed Capital (SE)		
	6/1/11	0
	a.	20,000

Required:

Explain events (*a*) through (*d*) that resulted in the entries in the T-accounts. That is, for each account, what transactions made it increase and/or decrease?

E2-17   Inferring Typical Investing and Financing Activities in Accounts
LO4

The following T-accounts indicate the effects of normal business transactions:

Equipment				Notes Receivable				Notes Payable		
1/1	500			1/1	150					100	1/1
	250	?			?	225			?	170	
12/31	50			12/31	150					160	12/31

Required:

1. Describe the typical investing and financing transactions that affect each T-account. That is, what economic events occur to make each of these accounts increase and decrease?
2. For each T-account, compute the missing amounts.

E2-18   Identifying Investing and Financing Activities Affecting Cash Flows
LO6

Foot Locker, Inc.

Foot Locker, Inc., (formally Woolworth Corporation) is a large global retailer of athletic footwear and apparel selling directly to customers and through the Internet, including the Foot Locker family of stores, Champs Sports, and Eastbay. The following are several of Foot Locker's investing and financing activities as reflected in a recent annual statement of cash flows.

a. Reduction of long-term debt.
b. Sale of land.
c. Issuance of common stock.
d. Capital expenditures (for property, plant, and equipment).
e. Issuance of short-term debt.

Required:

For each of these, indicate whether the activity is investing (I) or financing (F) and the direction of the effect on cash flows (+ for increases cash; − for decreases cash).

E2-19   Preparing the Investing and Financing Sections of the Statement of Cash Flows
LO6

Hilton Hotels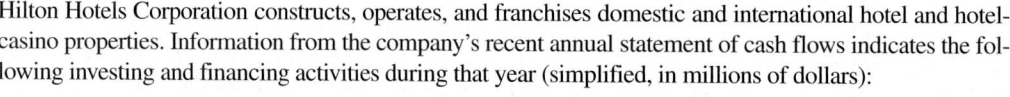

Hilton Hotels Corporation constructs, operates, and franchises domestic and international hotel and hotel-casino properties. Information from the company's recent annual statement of cash flows indicates the following investing and financing activities during that year (simplified, in millions of dollars):

Additional borrowing from banks	$992
Purchase of investments	139
Sale of property (assume sold at cost)	230
Issuance of stock	6
Purchase and renovation of properties	370
Payment of debt principal	24
Receipt of principal payment on a note receivable	125

Required:

Prepare the investing and financing sections of the statement of cash flows for Hilton Hotels. Assume that year-end is December 31, 2011.

E2-20   Finding Financial Information as a Potential Investor
LO2, 5, 6

You are considering investing the cash you inherited from your grandfather in various stocks. You have received the annual reports of several major companies.

Required:

For each of the following, indicate where you would locate the information in an annual report. The information may be in more than one location.

1. Total current assets.
2. Amount of debt principal repaid during the year.
3. Summary of significant accounting policies.
4. Cash received from sales of noncurrent assets.
5. Amount of dividends paid during the year.
6. Short-term obligations.
7. Date of the statement of financial position.

Available with McGraw-Hill's Homework Manager

PROBLEMS

Identifying Accounts on a Classified Balance Sheet and Their Normal Debit or Credit Balances (AP2–1)

Exxon Mobil Corporation explores, produces, refines, markets, and supplies crude oil, natural gas, and petroleum products in the United States and around the world. The following are accounts from a recent balance sheet of Exxon Mobil Corporation:

P2-1
LO1, 2
Exxon Mobil Corporation

	Balance Sheet Classification	Debit or Credit Balance
(1) Retained Earnings	_____	_____
(2) Note and Loans Payable (short-term)	_____	_____
(3) Materials and Supplies	_____	_____
(4) Long-Term Debt	_____	_____
(5) Prepaid Taxes and Expenses	_____	_____
(6) Patents (an intangible asset)	_____	_____
(7) Income Taxes Payable	_____	_____
(8) Contributed Capital	_____	_____
(9) Property, Plant, and Equipment	_____	_____
(10) Notes and Accounts Receivable (short-term)	_____	_____
(11) Cash and Cash Equivalents	_____	_____
(12) Accounts Payable	_____	_____
(13) Investments (long-term)	_____	_____
(14) Crude Oil Products and Merchandise	_____	_____

Required:

For each account, indicate how it normally should be categorized on a classified balance sheet. Use CA for current asset, NCA for noncurrent asset, CL for current liability, NCL for noncurrent liability, and SE for stockholders' equity. Also indicate whether the account normally has a debit or credit balance.

Determining Financial Statement Effects of Various Transactions (AP2–2)

Cornell Home Healthcare Services was organized on January 1, 2009, by four friends. Each organizer invested $10,000 in the company and, in turn, was issued 8,000 shares of stock. To date, they are the only stockholders. At the end of 2010, the accounting records reflected total assets of $700,000 ($50,000 cash; $500,000 land; $50,000 equipment; and $100,000 buildings), total liabilities of $200,000 (notes payable), and stockholders' equity of $500,000 ($100,000 contributed capital; $400,000 retained earnings). During the current year, 2011, the following summarized events occurred:

P2-2
LO2, 3, 5
eXcel
www.mhhe.com/libby6e

a. Sold 9,000 additional shares of stock to the original organizers for a total of $90,000 cash.
b. Purchased a building for $60,000, equipment for $15,000, and four acres of land for $14,000; paid $9,000 in cash and signed a note for the balance (due in 15 years). (*Hint:* Five different accounts are affected.)
c. Purchased short-term investments for $18,000 cash.
d. One stockholder reported to the company that 300 shares of his Cornell stock had been sold and transferred to another stockholder for $3,000 cash.

e.   Lent one of the shareholders $5,000 for moving costs, receiving a signed six-month note from the shareholder.

f.   Sold one acre of land acquired in (b) for $3,500 cash to another company.

Required:

1. Was Cornell Home Healthcare Services organized as a sole proprietorship, a partnership, or a corporation? Explain the basis for your answer.

2. During 2011, the records of the company were inadequate. You were asked to prepare the summary of the preceding transactions. To develop a quick assessment of their economic effects on Cornell Home Healthcare Services, you have decided to complete the tabulation that follows and to use plus (+) for increases and minus (−) for decreases for each account. The first event is used as an example.

	ASSETS						=	LIABILITIES	+	STOCKHOLDERS' EQUITY	
Cash	Short-Term Investments	Notes Receivable	Land	Building	Equipment			Notes Payable		Contributed Capital	Retained Earnings
Beg. 50,000			500,000	100,000	50,000		=	200,000		100,000	400,000
(a) +90,000							=			+ 90,000	

3. Did you include the transaction between the two stockholders—event (d)—in the tabulation? Why?

4. Based only on the completed tabulation, provide the following amounts (show computations):

   a.   Total assets at the end of the month.

   b.   Total liabilities at the end of the month.

   c.   Total stockholders' equity at the end of the month.

   d.   Cash balance at the end of the month.

   e.   Total current assets at the end of the month.

5. Compute the financial leverage ratio for 2011. What does this suggest about the company?

P2-3
LO2, 4, 5

Recording Transactions in T-Accounts, Preparing the Balance Sheet, and Evaluating the Financial Leverage Ratio (AP2–3)

www.mhhe.com/libby6e

Injection Plastics Company has been operating for three years. At December 31, 2010, the accounting records reflected the following:

Cash	$ 21,000	Intangibles	$ 3,000
Investments (short-term)	2,000	Accounts payable	15,000
Accounts receivable	3,000	Accrued liabilities payable	2,000
Inventory	24,000	Notes payable (short-term)	7,000
Notes receivable (long-term)	1,000	Long-term notes payable	48,000
Equipment	48,000	Contributed capital	90,000
Factory building	90,000	Retained earnings	30,000

During the year 2011, the company had the following summarized activities:

a.   Lent $7,000 to a supplier who signed a two-year note.

b.   Purchased equipment that cost $18,000; paid $6,000 cash and signed a one-year note for the balance.

c.   Issued an additional 2,000 shares of capital stock for $12,000 cash.

d.   Borrowed $12,000 cash from a local bank, payable in three months.

e.   Purchased short-term investments for $9,000 cash.

f.   Hired a new president at the end of the year. The contract was for $85,000 per year plus options to purchase company stock at a set price based on company performance.

g.   Purchased a patent (an intangible asset) for $3,000 cash.

h.   Returned defective equipment to the manufacturer, receiving a cash refund of $1,000.

i.   Built an addition to the factory for $25,000; paid $9,000 in cash and signed a three-year note for the balance.

Required:

1. Create T-accounts for each of the accounts on the balance sheet and enter the balances at the end of 2010 as beginning balances for 2011.

2. Record each of the events for 2011 in T-accounts (including referencing) and determine the ending balances.
3. Explain your response to event (*f*).
4. Prepare a classified balance sheet at December 31, 2011.
5. Compute the financial leverage ratio for 2011. What does this suggest about Injection Plastics?

Identifying Effects of Transactions on the Statement of Cash Flows (AP2–4)

Refer to P2–3.

Required:
Using the events (*a*) through (*i*) in P2–3, indicate whether each is an investing (I) or financing (F) activity for the year and the direction of the effect on cash flows (+ for increase and − for decrease). If there is no effect on cash flows, write NE.

P2-4
LO6

Recording Transactions, Preparing Journal Entries, Posting to T-Accounts, Preparing the Balance Sheet, and Evaluating the Financial Leverage Ratio

Dell Inc., headquartered in Austin, Texas, is the global leader in selling computer products and services. The following is Dell's (simplified) balance sheet from a recent year.

P2-5
LO2, 4, 5

www.mhhe.com/libby6e

DELL INC. Balance Sheet at February 3, 2006 (dollars in millions)	
Assets	
Current assets	
Cash	$ 7,042
Short-term investments	2,016
Receivables and other assets	5,452
Inventories	576
Other	2,620
	17,706
Noncurrent assets	
Property, plant, and equipment	2,005
Long-term investments	2,691
Other noncurrent assets	707
Total assets	**$23,109**
Liabilities and Stockholders' Equity	
Current liabilities	
Accounts payable	$ 9,840
Other short-term obligations	6,087
	15,927
Long-term liabilities	**3,053**
Stockholders' equity	
Contributed capital	284
Retained earnings	3,845
Total stockholders' equity and liabilities	**$23,109**

Assume that the following transactions (in millions of dollars) occurred during the remainder of 2006 (ending on January 28, 2007):

a. Issued additional shares of stock for $200 in cash.
b. Borrowed $30 from banks due in two years.

c. Purchased additional investments for $13,000 cash; one-fifth were long term and the rest were short term.

d. Purchased property, plant, and equipment; paid $875 in cash and $1,410 with additional long-term bank loans.

e. Lent $250 to affiliates, who signed a six-month note.

f. Sold short-term investments costing $10,000 for $10,000 cash.

g. Dell does not actually pay dividends; it reinvests its earnings into the company for growth purposes. Assume instead for this problem that Dell declared and paid $52 in dividends during 2006.

Required:

1. Prepare a journal entry for each transaction.

2. Create T-accounts for each balance sheet account and include the February 3, 2006, balances. Post each journal entry to the appropriate T-accounts.

3. Prepare a balance sheet from the T-account ending balances for Dell at January 28, 2007, based on these transactions.

4. Compute Dell's financial leverage ratio for 2006 (year ending on January 28, 2007). What does this suggest about the company?

P2-6 **Preparing the Investing and Financing Sections of a Statement of Cash Flows**

LO6 Refer to P2–5.

Required:

Based on the activities for the year ended January 28, 2007, prepare the investing and financing sections of a statement of cash flows.

ALTERNATE PROBLEMS

AP2-1 **Identifying Accounts on a Classified Balance Sheet and Their Normal Debit or Credit**
LO1, 2, 4 **Balances** (P2–1)

According to a recent Form 10-K report of Mattel, Inc., the company "designs, manufactures, and markets a broad variety of toy products worldwide." Mattel's brands include Barbie®, Hot Wheels®, Fisher-Price toys, and American Girl brand dolls and accessories. The following are several of the accounts from a recent balance sheet:

	Balance Sheet Classification	Debit or Credit Balance
(1) Accounts Receivable	_____	_____
(2) Prepaid Expenses	_____	_____
(3) Inventories	_____	_____
(4) Long-Term Debt	_____	_____
(5) Cash and Cash Equivalents	_____	_____
(6) Accounts Payable	_____	_____
(7) Income Taxes Payable	_____	_____
(8) Contributed Capital	_____	_____
(9) Property, Plant, and Equipment	_____	_____
(10) Retained Earnings	_____	_____
(11) Short-Term Borrowings	_____	_____
(12) Accrued Liabilities	_____	_____
(13) Goodwill (an intangible asset)	_____	_____

Required:

Indicate how each account normally should be categorized on a classified balance sheet. Use CA for current asset, NCA for noncurrent asset, CL for current liability, NCL for noncurrent liability, and SE for stockholders' equity. Also indicate whether the account normally has a debit or credit balance.

Determining Financial Statement Effects of Various Transactions (P2–2)

AP2-2
LO2, 3, 5

Kalman Incorporated is a small manufacturing company that makes model trains to sell to toy stores. It has a small service department that repairs customers' trains for a fee. The company has been in business for five years. At December 31, 2010 (the company's fiscal year-end), the accounting records reflected total assets of $500,000 (cash, $120,000; buildings, $310,000; equipment, $70,000), total liabilities of $200,000 (short-term notes payable, $140,000; long-term notes payable, $60,000), and total stockholders' equity of $300,000 (contributed capital, $220,000; retained earnings, $80,000). During the current year, 2011, the following summarized events occurred:

a. Purchased equipment for $30,000, paying $3,000 in cash and signing a note due in six months for the balance.
b. Issued an additional 10,000 shares of capital stock for $100,000 cash.
c. Borrowed $120,000 cash from the bank and signed a 10-year note.
d. Purchased a delivery truck (equipment) for $10,000; paid $5,000 cash and signed a short-term note payable for the remainder.
e. Built an addition on the factory for $200,000 and paid cash to the contractor.
f. Purchased $85,000 in long-term investments.
g. Returned a $3,000 piece of equipment purchased in (a) because it proved to be defective; received a reduction of its short-term note payable.
h. Lent $2,000 cash to the company president, Adam Kalman, who signed a note with terms showing the principal plus interest due in one year.
i. A stockholder sold $5,000 of his capital stock in Kalman Incorporated to his neighbor.

Required:
1. Was Kalman Incorporated organized as a sole proprietorship, a partnership, or a corporation? Explain the basis for your answer.
2. During 2011, the records of the company were inadequate. You were asked to prepare the summary of the preceding transactions. To develop a quick assessment of their economic effects on Kalman Incorporated, you have decided to complete the tabulation that follows and to use plus (+) for increases and minus (−) for decreases for each account. The first transaction is used as an example.

	ASSETS					=	LIABILITIES		+	STOCKHOLDERS' EQUITY	
	Cash	Notes Receivable	Long-Term Investments	Equipment	Building		Short-Term Notes Payable	Long-Term Notes Payable		Contributed Capital	Retained Earnings
Beg.	120,000			70,000	310,000	=	140,000	60,000		220,000	80,000
(a)	−3,000			+30,000		=	+27,000				

3. Did you include event (i) in the tabulation? Why?
4. Based on beginning balances plus the completed tabulation, provide the following amounts (show computations):
    a. Total assets at the end of the year.
    b. Total liabilities at the end of the year.
    c. Total stockholders' equity at the end of the year.
    d. Cash balance at the end of the year.
    e. Total current assets at the end of the year.
5. Compute the financial leverage ratio for 2011. What does this suggest about the company?

Recording Transactions in T-Accounts, Preparing the Balance Sheet, and Evaluating the Financial Leverage Ratio (P2–3)

AP2-3
LO2, 4, 5
Ethan Allen
Interiors, Inc.

Ethan Allen Interiors, Inc., is a leading manufacturer and retailer of home furnishings in the United States and abroad. The following is adapted from Ethan Allen's June 30, 2007, annual financial report. Dollars are in thousands.

Cash and cash equivalents	$ 147,879	Other assets	$ 5,484
Short-term investments	0	Accounts payable	78,722
Accounts receivable	14,602	Accrued expenses payable	68,677

Inventories	181,884	Long-term debt (includes the	
Prepaid expenses and		current portion of $40)	202,908
other current assets	38,064	Other long-term liabilities	42,649
Property, plant, and equipment	322,185	Contributed capital	79,374
Intangibles	92,500	Retained earnings	330,268

Assume that the following events occurred in the first quarter ended September 30, 2007:

a. Issued additional shares of stock for $1,020 in cash.
b. Purchased $3,400 in additional intangibles for cash.
c. Sold equipment at its cost for $4,020 cash.
d. Ordered $43,500 in wood and other raw materials for the manufacturing plants.
e. Purchased property, plant, and equipment; paid $1,830 in cash and signed additional long-term notes for $9,400.
f. Sold at cost other assets for $310 cash.
g. Purchased $2,980 in short-term investments for cash.
h. Declared and paid $300 in dividends.

Required:
1. Create T-accounts for each of the accounts on the balance sheet; enter the balances at June 30, 2007.
2. Record each of the transactions for the first quarter ended September 30, 2007, in the T-accounts (including referencing) and determine the ending balances.
3. Explain your response to event (*d*).
4. Prepare a classified balance sheet at September 30, 2007.
5. Compute the financial leverage ratio for the quarter ended September 30, 2007. What does this suggest about Ethan Allen Interiors, Inc.?

AP2-4
LO6
Ethan Allen
Interiors, Inc.

Identifying Effects of Transactions on the Statement of Cash Flows (P2–4)

Refer to AP2–3.

Required:
Using the events (*a*) through (*h*) in AP2–3, indicate whether each transaction is an investing (I) or financing (F) activity for the quarter and the direction of the effect on cash flows (+ for increase and − for decrease). If there is no effect on cash flows, write NE.

CASES **AND PROJECTS**

Annual Report Cases

CP2-1
LO1, 2, 5, 6
AMERICAN EAGLE
OUTFITTERS

Finding Financial Information

Refer to the financial statements of American Eagle Outfitters in Appendix B at the end of this book.

Required:
1. Is the company a corporation, a partnership, or a sole proprietorship? How do you know?
2. The company shows on the balance sheet that inventories are worth $263,644,000. Does this amount represent the expected selling price? Why or why not?
3. List the types of current obligations this company has. You need not provide the amounts.
4. Compute the company's financial leverage ratio and explain its meaning.
5. How much cash did the company spend on purchasing property and equipment each year (capital expenditures)? Where did you find the information?

Finding Financial Information

Refer to the financial statements of Urban Outfitters in Appendix C at the end of this book.

CP2-2
LO1, 2, 5, 6
Urban Outfitters

Required:

1. Use the company's balance sheet to determine the amounts in the accounting equation (A = L + SE) as of January 31, 2007.
2. If the company were liquidated at the end of the current year (January 31, 2007), are the share-holders guaranteed to receive $675,283,000?
3. What are the company's noncurrent liabilities?
4. What is the company's financial leverage ratio?
5. Did the company have a cash inflow or outflow from investing activities? Of how much?

Comparing Companies within an Industry

Refer to the financial statements of American Eagle Outfitters in Appendix B, Urban Outfitters given in Appendix C, and the Ratio Report in Appendix D at the end of this book.

CP2-3
LO2, 5, 6

AMERICAN EAGLE
OUTFITTERS

vs. Urban Outfitters

www.mhhe.com/libby6e

Required:

1. Compare the financial leverage ratio for both companies to the industry average from the Ratio Report. Are these two companies financing assets with debt more or less than the industry average? How is the financial leverage ratio influenced by these companies' choice to rent space instead of buying it?
2. In the most recent year, how much cash, if any, was spent buying back (repurchasing) the company's own common stock?
3. How much, if any, did each company pay in dividends for the most recent year?
4. What account title or titles does each company use to report any land, buildings, and equipment it may have?

Financial Reporting and Analysis Cases

Broadening Financial Research Skills: Locating Financial Information on the SEC's Database

CP2-4
LO2, 5, 6

The Securities and Exchange Commission (SEC) regulates companies that issue stock on the stock market. It receives financial reports from public companies electronically under a system called EDGAR (Electronic Data Gathering and Retrieval Service). Using the Internet, anyone may search the database for the reports that have been filed.

Using your Web browser, access the EDGAR database at www.sec.gov. To search the database, click on "Search for Company Filings," click on "Companies and Other Filers," type in "Papa Johns," and then click on "Find Companies."

Required:

To look at SEC filings, type in "10-Q" in the space indicating "Form Type" and click on "Retrieve Selected Filings." Skim down the left side until you locate the Form 10-Q (quarterly report) dated August 7, 2007. Click on the html for that report, click on 10-Q, and skim to the Table of Contents to Item 1.

1. Click on "Condensed Consolidated Balance Sheets."
   a. What was the amount of Papa John's total assets for the most recent period reported?
   b. Did long-term debt increase or decrease during the period?
   c. Compute the financial leverage ratio. How does it compare to the ratio indicated for Papa John's in the chapter? What does this suggest about the company?
2. Click on "Consolidated Statements of Cash Flows."
   a. What amount did Papa John's spend on property and equipment for the period?
   b. What was the total amount of cash flows from financing activities?

CP2-5   **Interpreting the Financial Press**

BusinessWeek

The December 22, 2003, edition of *BusinessWeek* magazine includes the article "Is Wilbur Ross Crazy?" You can access the article on the Libby/Libby/Short website at **www.mhhe.com/libby6e.**

Required:

Read the article and then answer the following questions:

1. What is *distressed investing* according to the article?
2. Mr. Ross usually becomes a bondholder but often swaps the debt for equity. Why is this riskier?
3. According to the article, what makes Mr. Ross successful (i.e., what is his approach and attitude toward investing)?

CP2-6   **Using Financial Reports: Evaluating the Reliability of a Balance Sheet**
LO1

Frances Sabatier asked a local bank for a $50,000 loan to expand her small company. The bank asked Frances to submit a financial statement of the business to supplement the loan application. Frances prepared the following balance sheet.

FS COMPANY
Balance Sheet
June 30, 2012

Assets

Cash and investments	$ 9,000
Inventory	30,000
Equipment	46,000
Personal residence (monthly payments, $2,800)	300,000
Remaining assets	20,000
Total assets	**$405,000**

Liabilities

Short-term debt to suppliers	$ 62,000
Long-term debt on equipment	38,000
Total debt	100,000
Stockholders' Equity	305,000
Total liabilities and stockholders' equity	**$405,000**

Required:

The balance sheet has several flaws. However, there is at least one major deficiency. Identify it and explain its significance.

CP2-7   **Using Financial Reports: Analyzing the Balance Sheet**
LO2, 4, 5

Gateway, Inc.   Recent balance sheets of Gateway, Inc., producer and marketer of a broad range of personal computers, consumer electronic products, and related tools and services, are provided.

Required:

1. Is Gateway a corporation, sole proprietorship, or partnership? Explain the basis of your answer.
2. Use the company's balance sheet to determine the amounts in the accounting equation (A = L + SE) for 2006.
3. Calculate the company's financial leverage ratio for 2006. Interpret the ratio that you calculated. What other information would make your interpretation more useful?
4. Give the journal entry the company will make in 2007 when it pays its 2006 accrued liabilities.
5. Does the company appear to have been profitable over its years in business? On what account are you basing your answer? Assuming no dividends were paid, how much was net income (or net loss) in 2006? If it is impossible to determine without an income statement, state so.

GATEWAY INC.
Consolidated Balance Sheets
December 31, 2006 and 2005
(dollars in millions)

	2006	2005
Assets		
Current assets		
Cash and cash equivalents	$ 346	$ 422
Marketable securities (investments)	71	163
Accounts receivable	522	559
Inventory	97	219
Other	216	211
Total current assets	1,252	1,574
Property, plant and equipment, net	111	83
Intangibles	267	245
Other assets	26	19
	$1,656	$1,921
Liabilities and Stockholders' Equity		
Current liabilities		
Accounts payable	$ 613	$ 762
Accrued liabilities	159	178
Accrued royalties	55	68
Other current liabilities	192	297
Total current liabilities	1,019	1,305
Other long-term obligations	366	361
Total liabilities	1,385	1,666
Stockholders' equity		
Contributed capital	974	972
Retained earnings (accumulated deficit)	(703)	(717)
Total stockholders' equity	271	255
	$1,656	$1,921

Using Financial Reports: Preparing a Classified Balance Sheet and Analyzing the Financial Leverage Ratio

CP2-8
LO5

The following accounts, in alphabetical order, are adapted from a recent McDonald's Corporation's balance sheet (amounts are in millions of dollars):

	Current Year	Prior Year		Current Year	Prior Year
Accounts and Notes Receivable	$ 609.4	$483.5	Long-Term Debt	$ 6,188.6	$ 4,834.1
			Notes Payable (short-term)	686.8	1,293.8
Accounts Payable	621.3	650.6	Notes Receivable due		
Accrued Liabilities	783.3	503.5	after One Year	67.9	67.0
Cash and Equivalents	299.2	341.4	Other Long-Term Liabilities	1,574.5	1,491.0
Contributed Capital	1,065.3	787.8	Other Noncurrent Assets	538.3	608.5
Current Maturities of			Prepaid Expenses and		
Long-Term Debt	168.0	335.6	Other Current Assets	323.5	246.9
Intangible Assets	973.1	827.5	Property and Equipment,		
Inventories	77.3	70.5	Net	16,041.6	14,961.4
Investments in and Advances			Retained Earnings	8,458.9	8,144.1
to Affiliates (long-term)	854.1	634.8	Taxes Payable	237.7	201.0

www.mhhe.com/libby6e

Required:

1. Construct a classified balance sheet (with two years reported) for McDonald's Corporation in good form (assume that the current year ends on December 31, 2011).
2. Compute the company's financial leverage ratio for the current year.
3. In comparison to the ratio for the companies in the restaurant industry (as indicated in the chapter for Papa John's and others), how do you interpret this ratio for McDonald's?

Critical Thinking Cases

CP2–9

LO1, 5

Making a Decision as a Financial Analyst: Preparing and Analyzing a Balance Sheet

Your best friend from home writes you a letter about an investment opportunity that has come her way. A company is raising money by issuing shares of stock and wants her to invest $20,000 (her recent inheritance from her great-aunt's estate). Your friend has never invested in a company before and, knowing that you are a financial analyst, asks that you look over the balance sheet and send her some advice. An **unaudited** balance sheet, in only moderately good form, is enclosed with the letter:

DEWEY, CHEETUM, AND HOWE, INC.
Balance Sheet
For the Year Ending December 31, 2012

Accounts receivable	$ 8,000
Cash	1,000
Inventory	8,000
Furniture and fixtures	52,000
Delivery truck	12,000
Buildings (estimated market value)	98,000
Total assets	**$179,000**
Accounts payable	$ 16,000
Payroll taxes payable	13,000
Notes payable (due in three years)	15,000
Mortgage payable	50,000
Total liabilities	**$ 94,000**
Contributed capital	$ 80,000
Retained earnings	5,000
Total stockholders' equity	**$ 85,000**

There is only one footnote, and it states that the building was purchased for $65,000, has been depreciated by $5,000 on the books, and still carries a mortgage (shown in the liability section). The footnote also states that, in the opinion of the company president, the building is "easily worth $98,000."

Required:

1. Draft a new balance sheet for your friend, correcting any errors you note. (If any of the account balances need to be corrected, you may need to adjust the retained earnings balance correspondingly.) If there are no errors or omissions, so state.
2. Write a letter to your friend explaining the changes you made to the balance sheet, if any, and offer your comments on the company's apparent financial condition based only on this information. Suggest other information your friend might want to review before coming to a final decision on whether to invest.

Evaluating an Ethical Dilemma: Analyzing Management Incentives

In July 2004, the U.S. government filed civil and criminal charges against four former executives of Netherlands-based Ahold's subsidiary U.S. Foodservice Inc., an operator of supermarkets such as Bi-Lo and Giant food stores. Two of the four executives have pleaded guilty, and the other two were indicted. The alleged widespread fraud included recording completely fictitious revenues for false promotions and persuading vendors to confirm to auditors the false promotional payments. U.S. Attorney David Kelley suggested the fraud was motivated by the greed of the executives to reap fat bonuses if the company met certain financial goals. The auditors were unable to catch the fraud.

Required:
1. Describe the parties who were harmed or helped by this fraud.
2. Explain how greed may have contributed to the fraud.
3. Why do you think the independent auditors failed to catch the fraud?

CP2-10
LO5
U.S. Foodservice, Inc.

Financial Reporting and Analysis Team Project

Team Project: Analysis of Balance Sheets and Ratios

As a team, select an industry to analyze. Reuters provides lists of industries and their makeup at www.reuters.com/finance/industries. Each team member should acquire the annual report or 10-K for one publicly traded company in the industry, with each member selecting a different company. (Library files, the SEC EDGAR service at www.sec.gov, or the company itself are good sources.)

CP2-11
LO2, 5, 6

Required:
On an individual basis, each team member should write a short report answering the following questions about the selected company. Discuss any patterns across the companies that you as a team observe. Then, as a team, write a short report comparing and contrasting your companies.
1. For the most recent year, what are the top three asset accounts by size? What percentage is each of total assets? [Calculated as Asset A ÷ Total Assets]
2. What are the major investing and financing activities (by dollar size) for the most recent year? [Look at the Statement of Cash Flows.]
3. Ratio Analysis:
   a. What does the financial leverage ratio measure in general?
   b. Compute the financial leverage ratio for each of the last three years. [You may find prior years' information in the section of the annual report or 10-K called "Selected Financial Information," or you may search for prior years' annual reports.]
   c. What do your results suggest about the company?
   d. If available, find the industry ratio for the most recent year, compare it to your results, and discuss why you believe your company differs or is similar to the industry ratio.

LEARNING OBJECTIVES

After studying this chapter, you should be able to:

1. Describe a typical business operating cycle and explain the necessity for the time period assumption. p. 105

2. Explain how business activities affect the elements of the income statement. p. 106

3. Explain the accrual basis of accounting and apply the revenue and matching principles to measure income. p. 110

4. Apply transaction analysis to examine and record the effects of operating activities on the financial statements. p. 116

5. Prepare financial statements. p. 122

6. Compute and interpret the total asset turnover ratio. p. 126

Lectured slideshow–LP3-1
www.mhhe.com/libby6e

OPERATING DECISIONS AND THE INCOME STATEMENT

3

Papa John's and Pizza Hut follow different operating strategies:

- Number-one Pizza Hut regularly creates new pizza varieties (such as the Big New Yorker, the Twisted Crust, the Stuffed Crust pizza you can eat backwards, the "P'Zone" calzone, and the "4forAll" with four individually topped pizzas in one) to attract customers to its eat-in, take-out, and delivery services. The company releases a new variety, advertises like crazy, waits for the customers to rush in, and hopes they will return.

- Papa John's focuses on producing a limited variety of pizzas for pick up or delivery. The company believes it can build strong customer loyalty and repeat business by advertising the simple slogan "Better Ingredients. Better Pizza."

Despite these different strategies, Papa John's, ranked number three through aggressive expansion, aims to become the number-one pizza brand in the world by building the strongest brand loyalty. Papa John's believes this requires extensive local marketing efforts supplemented with radio and television advertising. In 2006, for instance, Papa John's aired seven national television campaigns to compete against its rivals. To reach new markets, the company continues to expand its company-owned and franchising operations. Adding new restaurants increases efficiencies in the operation of its quality control centers by taking advantage of volume purchasing of food and supplies, thus lowering operating costs. At the same time, Papa John's spends additional resources in developing and motivating its team members, including hefty raises to restaurant managers.

However, one of the most significant effects on a pizza restaurant's financial performance for a period is the cost of cheese. When cheese prices are low, the pizza chains compete by offering low-price deals. When cheese prices are high, they use other gimmicks. In 2006, for example, Papa John's became the first pizza chain to offer 24/7 online ordering for all its restaurants. Papa John's decided to provide this convenience to its consumers after the company's online orders grew by 50 percent from the year before (2005).

UNDERSTANDING THE BUSINESS

To become the number-one pizza brand globally, Papa John's executives develop strategies, plans, and measurable indicators of progress toward their goals. For example, their growth plan in 2006 was to add 260 new restaurants and continue to tell customers about their fresh dough, tomato sauce, and high-quality cheese in various promotional advertising programs. In developing their growth strategies, companies such as Papa John's plan their companywide operations in terms of the elements of the income statement (specific revenues and expenses).

Financial analysts develop their own set of expectations about Papa John's future performance. Its published income statement provides the primary basis for comparing analysts' projections to the actual results of operations. We will discuss these comparisons and the stock market's reactions to Papa John's results throughout this chapter as we learn about income recognition and measurement. To understand how business plans and the results of operations are reflected on the income statement, we need to answer the following questions:

1. How do business activities affect the income statement?

2. How are business activities measured?

3. How are business activities reported on the income statement?

In this chapter we focus on Papa John's operating activities that involve the sale of food to the public and the sale of ingredients and services to franchisees. The results of these activities are reported on the income statement.

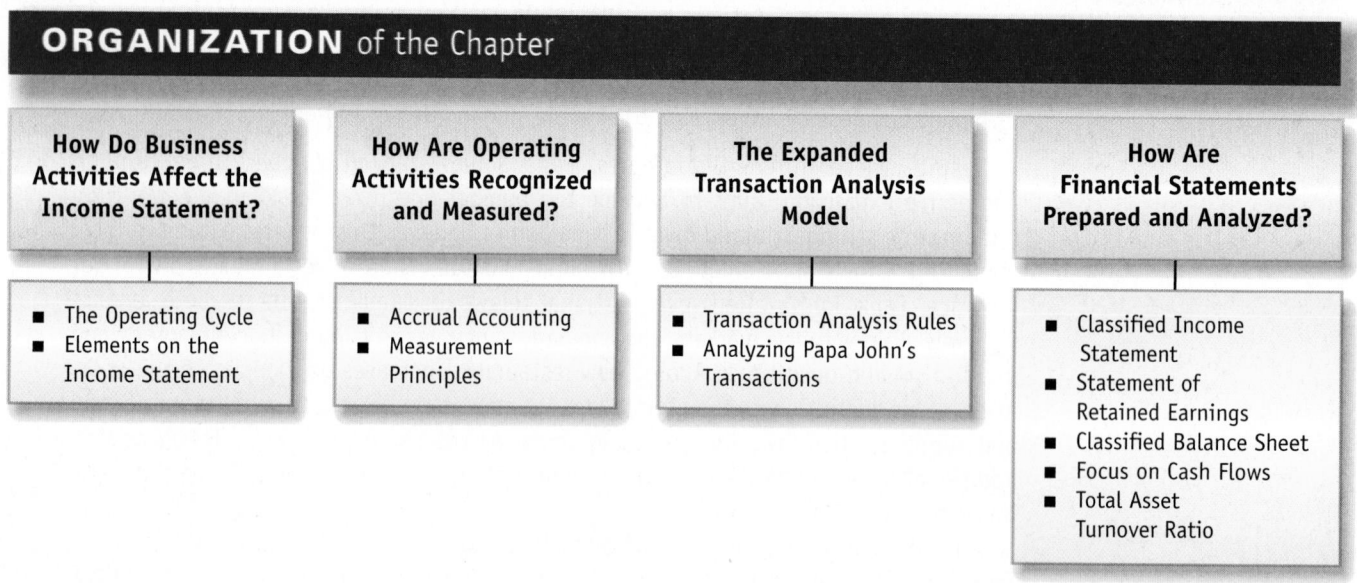

ORGANIZATION of the Chapter

How Do Business Activities Affect the Income Statement?	How Are Operating Activities Recognized and Measured?	The Expanded Transaction Analysis Model	How Are Financial Statements Prepared and Analyzed?
■ The Operating Cycle ■ Elements on the Income Statement	■ Accrual Accounting ■ Measurement Principles	■ Transaction Analysis Rules ■ Analyzing Papa John's Transactions	■ Classified Income Statement ■ Statement of Retained Earnings ■ Classified Balance Sheet ■ Focus on Cash Flows ■ Total Asset Turnover Ratio

HOW DO BUSINESS ACTIVITIES AFFECT THE INCOME STATEMENT?

The Operating Cycle

The long-term objective for any business is to **turn cash into more cash.** If a company is to stay in business, this excess cash must be generated from operations (that is, from the activities for which the business was established), not from borrowing money or selling long-lived assets.

Companies (1) acquire inventory and the services of employees and (2) sell inventory or services to customers. The operating (or cash-to-cash) cycle begins when a company receives goods to sell (or, in the case of a service company, has employees work) and ends when customers pay cash to the company. The length of time for completion of the operating cycle depends on the nature of the business.

Learning Objective 1
Describe a typical business operating cycle and explain the necessity for the time period assumption.

The OPERATING (CASH-TO-CASH) CYCLE is the time it takes for a company to pay cash to suppliers, sell goods and services to customers, and collect cash from customers.

Audio lecture–AP3-1
www.mhhe.com/libby6e

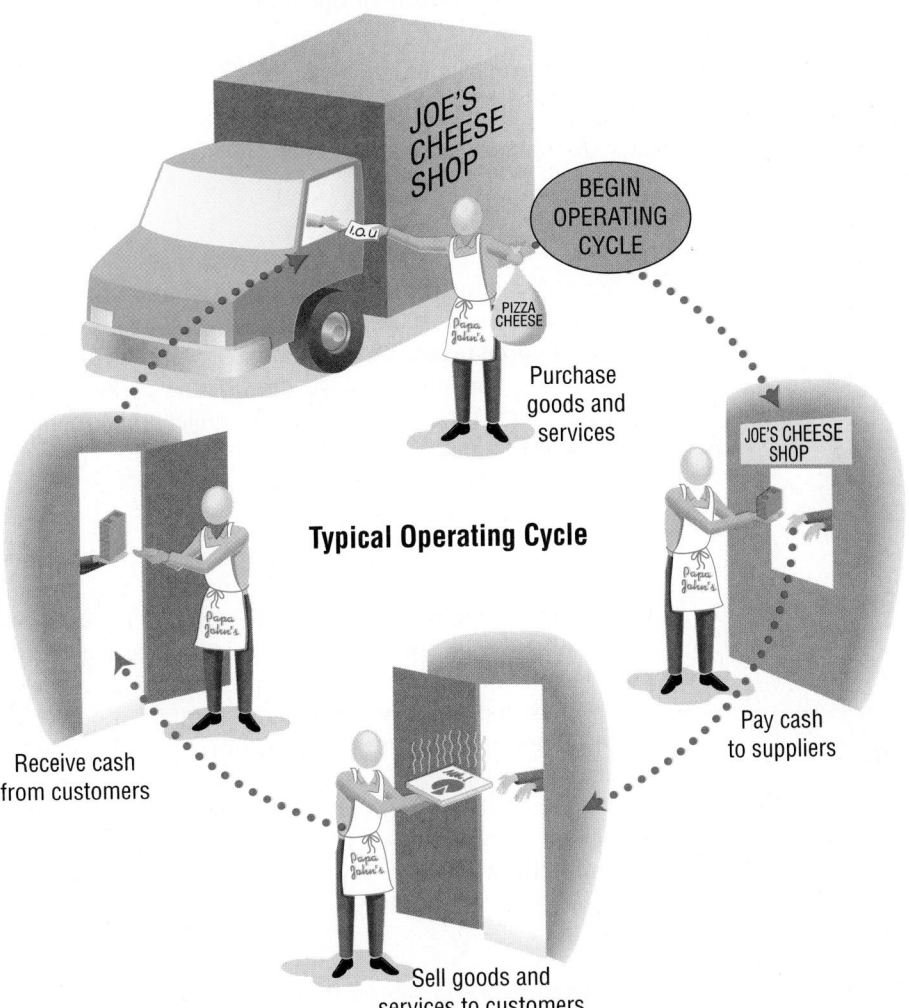

Typical Operating Cycle

BEGIN OPERATING CYCLE

Purchase goods and services

Pay cash to suppliers

Sell goods and services to customers

Receive cash from customers

The operating cycle for Papa John's is relatively short. It spends cash to purchase ingredients, makes pizzas, and sells them to customers for cash. In some companies, inventory is paid for well before it is sold. Toys R Us, for example, builds its inventory for months preceding the year-end holiday season. It borrows funds from banks to pay for the inventory and repays the loans with interest when it receives cash from customers. In other companies, cash is received from customers well after a sale takes place. For example, car dealerships often sell cars over time with monthly payments from customers due over several years. Shortening the operating cycle by creating incentives that encourage customers to buy sooner and/or pay faster improves a company's cash flows.

Managers know that reducing the time needed to turn cash into more cash (that is, shortening the operating cycle) means higher profit and faster growth. With the excess cash, managers may purchase additional inventory or other assets for growth, repay debt, or distribute it to owners as dividends.

Until a company ceases its activities, the operating cycle is repeated continuously. However, decision makers require information periodically about the company's financial condition and performance. To measure income for a specific period of time, accountants follow the **time period assumption,** which assumes that the long life of a company can be reported in shorter time periods, such as months, quarters, and years.[1] Two types of issues arise in reporting periodic income to users:

1. Recognition issues: **When** should the effects of operating activities be recognized (recorded)?

2. Measurement issues: **What amounts** should be recognized?

Before we examine the rules accountants follow in resolving these issues, however, let's examine the elements of financial statements that are affected by operating activities.

Elements on the Income Statement

Exhibit 3.1 shows a recent income statement for Papa John's, simplified for purposes of this chapter.[2] It has multiple subtotals, such as **operating income** and **income before income taxes.** This format is known as **multiple step** and is very common.[3] As we discuss the elements of the income statement, also refer to the conceptual framework outlined in Exhibit 2.1.

Operating Revenues

Revenues are defined as increases in assets or settlements of liabilities from **ongoing operations** of the business. Operating revenues result from the sale of goods or services. When Papa John's sells pizza to consumers or supplies to franchisees, it has earned revenue. When revenue is earned, assets, usually Cash or Accounts Receivables, often increase. Sometimes if a customer pays for goods or services in advance, a liability account, usually Unearned (or Deferred) Revenue, is created. At this point, no revenue has been earned. There is simply a receipt of cash in exchange for a promise to provide a good or service in the

The TIME PERIOD ASSUMPTION indicates that the long life of a company can be reported in shorter time periods.

Learning Objective 2
Explain how business activities affect the elements of the income statement.

REVENUES are increases in assets or settlements of liabilities from ongoing operations.

Revenues earned

---

[1]In addition to the audited annual statements, most businesses prepare quarterly financial statements (also known as **interim reports** covering a three-month period) for external users. The Securities and Exchange Commission requires public companies to do so.

[2]For simplification, dollar amounts have been rounded and several accounts in the original statement have been combined with other accounts and/or shown in a different section of the statement in the exhibit. In addition, only one year's income statement is presented. Publicly traded companies such as Papa John's are actually required to present income information for three years to help users assess trends over time.

[3]Another common format, **single step,** reorganizes all accounts on the multiple-step format. All revenues and gains are listed together and all expenses and losses except taxes are listed together. The two subtotals are then subtracted to arrive at income before income taxes, the same subtotal as on the multiple-step statement.

future. When the company provides the promised goods or services to the customer, the revenue is recognized and the liability settled.

Like most companies, Papa John's generates revenues from a variety of sources. Exhibit 3.1 shows operating revenues from two primary sources:

- **Restaurant Sales Revenue.** Approximately 20 percent of Papa John's stores are owned by the company, while 80 percent are owned by others through franchise agreements. Included in Restaurant Sales Revenue, the largest revenue account, are the sales of pizza ingredients and supplies to all of the chain's restaurants including the franchised stores and sales of pizzas in company-owned stores. Pizza sales for the franchised restaurants are reported in each of the franchisees' financial statements, not Papa John's.

- **Franchise Fee Revenue.** Approximately 11 percent of all Papa John's revenues in 2006 came from selling franchises. Franchisees pay initial fees of at least $25,000 for the right to open and operate a number of restaurants in a specific geographic area. Papa John's records these fees as a liability (Unearned Franchise Fees) until it provides management training, site selection, restaurant design, and other promised services. As part of the franchise agreement, franchisees also pay Papa John's a fixed percentage (between 4 and 5 percent) of their store sales as franchise royalties. Both the initial fees and annual royalty payments are reported on Papa John's income statement as Franchise Fee Revenue.

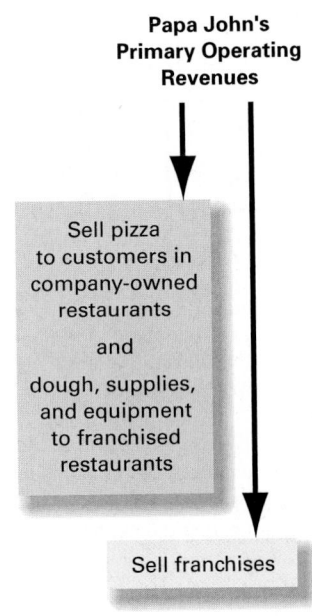

Papa John's Primary Operating Revenues

Sell pizza to customers in company-owned restaurants

and

dough, supplies, and equipment to franchised restaurants

Sell franchises

EXHIBIT 3.1

Income Statement

PAPA JOHN'S INTERNATIONAL, INC. AND SUBSIDIARIES
Consolidated Statement of Income
For the Year Ended December 31, 2006
(dollars in thousands)

Operating Revenues	
Restaurant sales revenue	$ 884,000
Franchise fee revenue	117,000
Total revenues	1,001,000
Operating Expenses	
Cost of sales	425,000
Salaries expense	164,000
Rent expense	27,000
Advertising expense	41,000
General and administrative expenses	103,000
Depreciation expense	27,000
Other operating expenses	116,000
Total expenses	903,000
Operating Income	98,000
Other Items	
Investment income	1,000
Interest expense	(3,000)
Income before Income Taxes	96,000
Income tax expense	33,000
Net Income	**$ 63,000**
Earnings per Share	$ 1.96

Operating activities (central focus of business)

Includes insurance, repairs, utilities, and fuel expenses

Subtotal of operating revenues minus operating expenses

Peripheral activities (not the main focus of the business)

Subtotal of all revenues minus all expenses except taxes

= *Net income/Average number of shares outstanding*
$63,000,000/32,100,000 shares (from Papa John's annual report)

EXPENSES are decreases in assets or increases in liabilities from ongoing operations incurred to generate revenues during the period.

Expenses incurred to generate revenues

Papa John's Primary Operating Expenses

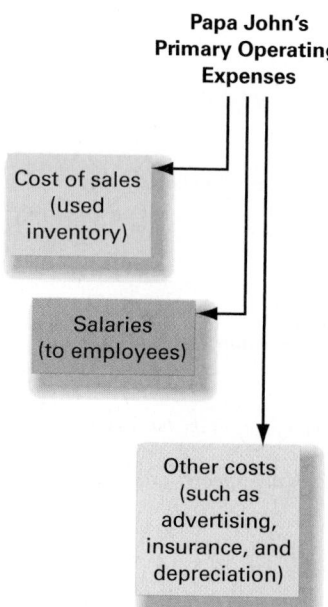

Operating Expenses

Some students confuse the terms **expenditures** and **expenses**. An expenditure is any outflow of cash for any purpose, whether to buy equipment, pay off a bank loan, or pay employees their wages. An expense is more narrowly defined.

■ When an asset, such as equipment or supplies, is **used to generate revenues during a period,** all or a portion of the asset's cost is recorded as an expense.

■ When an amount is **incurred to generate revenues during a period,** such as using electricity, whether already paid or to be paid in the future, an expense results.

Therefore, **not all expenditures are expenses,** and **expenses are necessary to generate revenues.** Expenses are decreases in assets or increases in liabilities from **ongoing operations** incurred to generate revenues during the period.

Papa John's pays employees to make and serve food, uses electricity to operate equipment and light its facilities, advertises its pizza, and uses food and paper supplies. Without incurring these expenses, Papa John's could not generate revenues. Although some of the expenses may result from expenditures of cash at the time they are incurred, some expenses may be incurred after cash has been paid and others may be incurred before cash is paid. When an expense is incurred, assets such as Supplies decrease (are used up) **or** liabilities such as Salaries Payable or Utilities Payable increase.

The following are Papa John's primary operating expenses:

■ **Cost of Sales.** In Papa John's restaurant operations, any ingredients or supplies that are used to produce meals are expensed as they are used. In addition, any ingredients and supplies that are sold to restaurants are expensed as they are provided to the restaurants. In companies with a manufacturing or merchandising focus, Cost of Sales (also called Cost of Goods Sold) is usually the most significant expense.

■ **Salaries Expense.** When employees work and generate pizza sales for Papa John's, the company incurs an expense, although salaries will be paid later. Salaries Expense of $164,000,000 is Papa John's second largest expense. In purely service-oriented companies in which no products are produced or sold, the cost of using employees to generate revenues is usually the largest expense.

■ **All other operating expenses.** The remaining large expenses include Rent Expense, Advertising Expense, General and Administrative Expenses (for insurance, executive salaries, and rental of headquarters facilities), and Depreciation Expense reflecting the use of a part of long-lived assets such as buildings and equipment.

Other Items

Subtracting operating revenues from operating expenses gives Operating Income—a measure of the profit from central ongoing operations. Not all activities affecting an income statement are, however, central to ongoing operations. Any revenues, expenses, gains, or losses that result from these other activities are not included as part of operating income, but are instead categorized as Other Items. For example, using excess cash to purchase stocks in other companies is an investing activity for Papa John's, not a central operation. However, any interest or dividends earned on the investment are called **Investment Income** (or **Investment Revenue**). Likewise, borrowing money is a financing activity. However, the cost of using that money is called **Interest Expense.** Except for financial institutions, incurring interest expense or earning investment income are **not** the central operations of most businesses including Papa John's. We say these are peripheral (normal but not central) transactions.

In similar fashion, companies sell property, plant, and equipment from time to time to maintain modern facilities. Selling land for more than the original purchase price does not result in earning revenue because the transaction is not the central operating focus for the business. Gains (with an account called Gain on Sale of Assets) result in an increase in assets or decrease in liabilities from a peripheral transaction. Losses are decreases in assets or increases in liabilities from peripheral transactions. If land with a recorded cost of $2,800 is sold for $2,500, Papa John's would recognize a loss of $300 on the sale. Papa John's did not report any gains or losses in its 2006 income statement.

GAINS are increases in assets or decreases in liabilities from peripheral transactions.

LOSSES are decreases in assets or increases in liabilities from peripheral transactions.

Income Tax Expense

Adding and subtracting other items to operating income gives a subtotal of income before income taxes (or pretax income). Income Tax Expense is the last expense listed on the income statement before determining net income. All profit-making corporations are required to compute income taxes owed to federal, state, and foreign governments. Income tax expense is calculated as a percentage of pretax income determined by applying the tax rates of the federal, state, local, and foreign taxing authorities. Papa John's effective tax rate in 2006 was 34 percent (income tax expense, $33 million, divided by income before income taxes, $96 million). This indicates that for every dollar of income before taxes that Papa John's made in 2006, the company paid $0.34 to taxing authorities.

Earnings per Share

Corporations are required to disclose earnings per share on the income statement or in the notes to the financial statements. This ratio is widely used in evaluating the operating performance and profitability of a company. To compute earnings per share, net income is divided by the average number of shares of stock outstanding.[4] We used the actual number computed by Papa John's. For 2006, Papa John's reported $1.96 in earnings for each share of stock owned by investors.

Differences in Accounts in Foreign Financial Statements

INTERNATIONAL PERSPECTIVE

GlaxoSmithKline
Unilever Group
BMW Group

IFRS

As mentioned in Chapters 1 and 2, foreign countries establish their own accounting and reporting rules with many adopting International Financial Reporting Standards (IFRS). The result is that foreign companies often use different account titles from U.S. companies. For example, GlaxoSmithKline (a U.K. pharmaceutical company) and Unilever (a U.K. and Netherlands-based company supplying food, home, and personal care products such as Hellman's mayonnaise, Dove soap, and Popsicle treats) use the term *turnover* to refer to sales revenue. They also use *finance income* for income from investments and *finance cost* for interest expense. BMW Group, on the other hand, reports *revenues* and uses *financial result* for the difference between income from investments and interest expense. All three companies follow IFRS.

A recent report indicates that "Research by the world's six largest accountancy firms shows that an overwhelming majority of countries—more than 90 percent of a total 59 countries surveyed—intend to converge with International Financial Reporting Standards (IFRS)."* As this text is being written, the Securities and Exchange Commission is conducting discussions on how adopting IFRS in the United States would impact U.S. companies and the significant costs that will be incurred in any transition to more globally uniform accounting standards.†

*http://www.deloitte.com/dtt/section_node/0,1042,sid%253D49563,00.html
†http://www.sec.gov/spotlight/ifrsroadmap/ifrsround121707-transcript.pdf

---

[4]The calculation of the ratio is actually much more complex and beyond the scope of this course.

Learning Objective 3
Explain the accrual basis of accounting and apply the revenue and matching principles to measure income.

CASH BASIS ACCOUNTING records revenues when cash is received and expenses when cash is paid.

CASH BASIS
Income Measurement
    Revenues (= cash receipts)
− Expenses (= cash payments)

    Net Income (cash basis)

ACCRUAL BASIS ACCOUNTING records revenues when earned and expenses when incurred, regardless of the timing of cash receipts or payments.

ACCRUAL BASIS
Income Measurement
    Revenues (= when earned)
− Expenses (= when incurred)

    Net Income (accrual basis)

The REVENUE PRINCIPLE states that revenues are recognized when (1) goods or services are delivered, (2) there is persuasive evidence of an arrangement for customer payment, (3) the price is fixed or determinable, and (4) collection is reasonably assured.

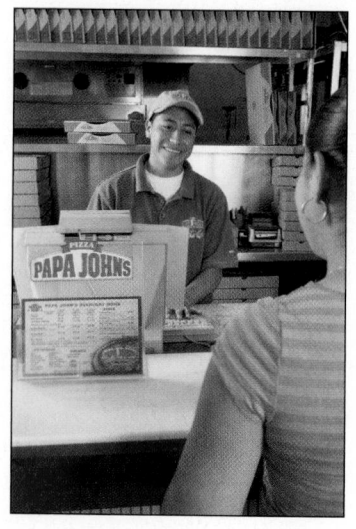

HOW ARE OPERATING ACTIVITIES RECOGNIZED AND MEASURED?

You probably determine your personal financial position by the cash balance in your bank account. Your financial performance is measured as the difference between your cash balance at the beginning of the period and the cash balance at the end of the period (that is, whether you end up with more or less cash). If you have a higher cash balance, cash receipts exceeded cash disbursements for the period. Many local retailers, medical offices, and other small businesses use **cash basis accounting** in which revenues are recorded when cash is received, and expenses are recorded when cash is paid, regardless of when the revenues were earned or the expenses incurred. This basis is often quite adequate for organizations that do not need to report to external users.

Accrual Accounting

Financial statements created under cash basis accounting normally postpone or accelerate recognition of revenues and expenses long before or after goods and services are produced and delivered (when cash is received or paid). They also do not necessarily reflect all assets or liabilities of a company on a particular date. For these reasons, cash basis financial statements are not very useful to external decision makers. Therefore, generally accepted accounting principles require **accrual basis accounting** for financial reporting purposes.

In accrual basis accounting, revenues and expenses are recognized when the transaction that causes them occurs, not necessarily when cash is received or paid. That is, **revenues are recognized when they are earned and expenses when they are incurred.** The two basic accounting principles that determine when revenues and expenses are recorded under accrual basis accounting are the **revenue principle** and the **matching principle.**

Revenue Principle

Under the **revenue principle,** four criteria or conditions must normally be met for revenue to be recognized. If **any** of the following criteria is **not** met, revenue normally is **not** recognized and cannot be recorded.

1. **Delivery has occurred or services have been rendered.** The company has performed or substantially performed the acts promised to the customer by providing goods or services.
2. **There is persuasive evidence of an arrangement for customer payment.** In exchange for the company's performance, the customer has provided cash or a promise to pay cash (a receivable).
3. **The price is fixed or determinable.** There are no uncertainties as to the amount to be collected.
4. **Collection is reasonably assured.** For cash sales, collection is not an issue since it is received on the date of the exchange. For sales on credit, the company reviews the customer's ability to pay. If the customer is considered creditworthy, collecting cash from the customer is reasonably likely.

These conditions normally occur when the title, risks, and rewards of ownership have transferred to the customers. For most businesses, these conditions are met at the point of delivery of goods or services, **regardless of when cash is received.**

Although businesses expect to receive cash in exchange for their goods and services at the time of delivery, the timing of cash receipts from customers does not dictate when businesses report revenues. Instead, the key to determining when to report revenue is whether the business has done what it promised to do. Thus, cash can be received (1) in the **same** period as, (2) in a period **before** the goods or services, or (3) in a period **after** the goods or services are delivered (see Exhibit 3.2). Let's see how to handle each of these cases.

EXHIBIT 3.2

Recording Revenues versus Cash Receipts

1. **Cash is received *in the same period* as the goods or services are delivered.** This is the most common timing for Papa John's, because most customers pay cash within a few minutes of receiving their pizza. Papa John's delivers the pizza to the customer as ordered, earning revenue in the process. In exchange, Papa John's receives cash from the customer. This is the typical timing of cash receipts and revenue recognition in the fast-food and restaurant industry.

2. **Cash is received *before* the goods or services are delivered.** Papa John's also sells franchises from which the company receives cash from new franchisees **before** providing start-up services to them. Thus, criteria 2, 3, and 4 are met. Until the company provides the services, it records no revenue. It records monies received from franchisees in the liability account Unearned Franchise Fees. This unearned (deferred) revenue account represents the amount of goods or services owed to the franchisees. Later, when Papa John's provides the services (criterion 1), it earns and records the revenue and reduces the liability account.

3. **Cash is received *after* the goods or services are delivered.** To boost business, Papa John's may also deliver pizza on account to some customers. That is, the restaurant delivers pizza when it is ordered and then bills the customer at the end of the month. When a business sells goods or services on account, the revenue is earned when the goods or services are delivered. For Papa John's, revenue is earned when the pizza is delivered, even though cash has not yet been received. At that time Papa John's will record both Restaurant Sales Revenue and the asset Accounts Receivable, representing the customer's promise to pay in the future for past pizza deliveries. When the customer pays its monthly bill, Papa John's will increase its Cash account and decrease Accounts Receivable.

Companies usually disclose their revenue recognition practices in a note to the financial statements. The following excerpt from Papa John's note describes how it recognizes its two forms of franchise-related revenue and pizza sales revenue at its restaurants:

Audio lecture–AP3-2
www.mhhe.com/libby6e

2. SIGNIFICANT ACCOUNTING POLICIES

Revenue Recognition

Franchise fees are recognized when a franchised restaurant begins operations, at which time we have performed our obligations related to such fees. Fees received pursuant to development agreements which grant the right to develop franchised restaurants in future periods in specific geographic areas are deferred and recognized on a pro rata basis as the franchised restaurants subject to the development agreements begin operations. Both franchise and development fees are nonrefundable. Retail sales from Company-owned restaurants and franchise royalties, which are based on a percentage of franchised restaurants' sales, are recognized as revenue when the products are delivered to or carried out by customers.

REAL WORLD EXCERPT

ANNUAL REPORT

SELF-STUDY **QUIZ**

This self-study quiz allows you to practice applying the revenue principle under accrual accounting. We recommend that you refer back to the four **revenue recognition criteria** presented earlier as you answer each question. Complete this quiz now to make sure you can apply the principle. The following transactions are samples of typical monthly operating activities of Papa John's (dollars in thousands). If revenue is to be recognized in **January,** indicate the title of the revenue account and the amount of revenue to be recognized. You should refer to the Papa John's income statement presented in Exhibit 3.1 for account titles.

ACTIVITY	REVENUE ACCOUNT TITLE	AMOUNT OF REVENUE RECOGNIZED IN JANUARY
(a) In January, Papa John's company-owned restaurants sold food to customers for $32,000 cash.		
(b) In January, Papa John's sold new franchises for $625 cash, providing $400 in services to these new franchisees during January; the remainder of services will be provided over the next three months.		
(c) In January, franchisees paid Papa John's $2,750 in cash for royalties based on the franchisees' weekly sales; $750 related to December sales and the rest to January sales.		
(d) In January, Papa John's commissaries sold sauce and dough to restaurants for $30,000 of which $20,000 was in cash and the rest was on account.		
(e) In January, franchisees paid $1,200 on account to Papa John's from December purchases of dough and sauce.		

After you have completed your answers, check them with the solutions at the bottom of the page.

Management's Incentives to Violate Accounting Rules

Investors in the stock market base their decisions on their expectations of a company's future earnings. When companies announce quarterly and annual earnings information, investors evaluate how well the companies have met expectations and adjust their investing decisions

Self-Study Quiz
Solutions

	Revenue Account Title	Amount of Revenue Recognized in January
(a)	Restaurant Sales Revenue	$32,000
(b)	Franchise Fee Revenue	$400
(c)	Franchise Fee Revenue	$2,000
(d)	Restaurant Sales Revenue	$30,000
(e)	No revenue earned in January.	—

accordingly. Companies that fail to meet expectations often experience a decline in stock price. Thus, managers are motivated to produce earnings results that meet or exceed investors' expectations to bolster stock prices. Greed may lead some managers to make unethical accounting and reporting decisions, often involving falsifying revenues and expenses. While this sometimes fools people for a short time, it rarely works in the long run and often leads to very bad consequences.

Fraud is a criminal offense for which managers may be sentenced to jail. A few cases involving faulty revenue and expense accounting are shown below. Just imagine what it must have been like to be 65-year-old Bernie Ebbers or 21-year-old Barry Minkow, both sentenced to 25 years in prison for accounting fraud.

The CEO	The Fraud	Conviction/Plea	The Outcome
Bernie Ebbers, 65 WorldCom	Recorded operating expenses as if they were assets; resulted in the largest fraud in U.S. history.	Convicted July 2005.	Sentenced to 25 years.
Sanjay Kumar, 44 Computer Associates	Recorded sales in the wrong accounting period.	Pleaded guilty, April 2006.	Sentenced to 12 years.
Martin Grass, 49 Rite Aid Corporation	Recorded rebates from drug companies before they were earned.	Pleaded guilty, June 2003.	Sentenced to 8 years.
Barry Minkow, 21 ZZZZ Best	Made up customers and sales to show profits when, in reality, the company was a sham.	Convicted, December 1988.	Sentenced to 25 years.

Many others are affected by fraud. Stockholders lose stock value, employees may lose their jobs (and pension funds, as in the case of Enron), and customers and suppliers may become wary of dealing with a company operating under the cloud of fraud. As a manager, you may face an ethical dilemma in the workplace. The ethical decision is the one you will be proud of 20 years later.

The Matching Principle

The **matching principle** requires that costs incurred to generate revenues be recognized in the same period—a matching of costs with benefits. For example, when Papa John's restaurants provide food service to customers, revenue is earned. The costs of generating the revenue include expenses incurred such as these:

The MATCHING PRINCIPLE requires that expenses be recorded when incurred in earning revenue.

- Wages to employees who worked **during the period** (Wages Expense)
- Utilities for the electricity used **during the period** (Utilities Expense)
- Food and paper products used **during the period** (Cost of Sales)
- Facilities rental **during the period** (Rent Expense)
- The use of ovens and other equipment **during the period** (Depreciation Expense)

As with revenues and cash receipts, expenses are recorded as incurred, **regardless of when cash is paid.** Cash may be paid (1) **before,** (2) **during,** or (3) **after** an expense is incurred (see Exhibit 3.3). An entry will be made on the date the expense is incurred and another on the date the cash is paid, if at different times. Let's see how to handle each of these cases related to the matching principle.

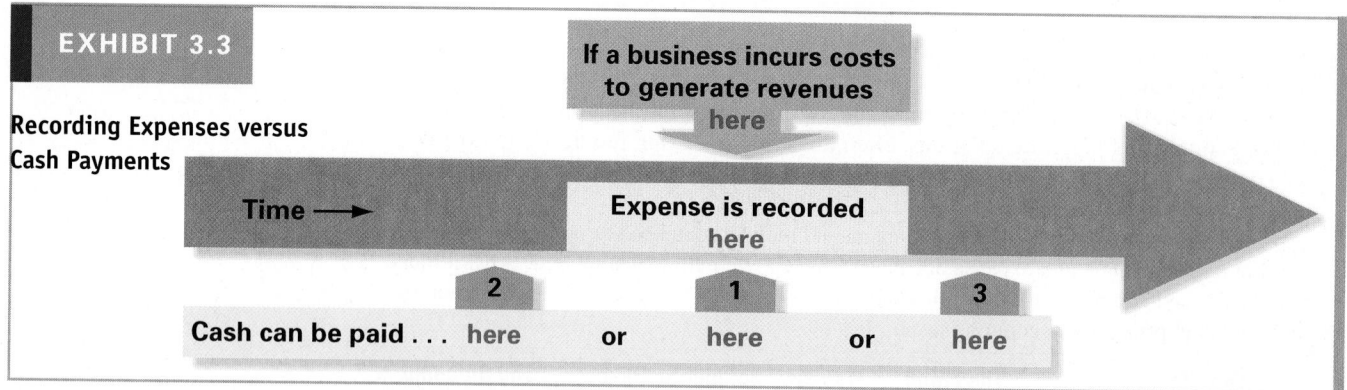

EXHIBIT 3.3

Recording Expenses versus
Cash Payments

1. **Cash is paid *in the same period* as the expense is incurred to generate revenue.** Expenses are sometimes incurred and paid for in the period that they arise. For example, Papa John's might spend $500 cash on December 8 for advertising the opening of a new restaurant on that day. This cost would be recorded as Advertising Expense on December 8 and would be reported in the current year's income statement because the advertising was used to generate revenue in the current accounting period.

2. **Cash is paid *before* the expense is incurred to generate revenue.** It is common for businesses to pay for something that provides benefits only in future periods. For example, Papa John's could buy paper plates in December, but not use them until January. Given the matching principle, the expense from using these supplies should be reported in January (next year) when the supplies are used to earn revenue, not in December when purchased. In December, the supplies represent an asset (called Supplies) because they will benefit future period. When they are used in January, Supplies Expense will be reported on the next year's income statement and the asset Supplies will decrease. Similar situations arise when a company prepays rent or insurance.

3. **Cash is paid *after* the cost is incurred to generate revenue.** Although rent and supplies are typically purchased before they are used, many costs are paid after goods or services have been received and used. For example, Papa John's restaurants uses electricity to heat the ovens and light the restaurant in December (the current accounting period), but does not pay for its December electricity usage until next month (the next accounting period). Because the cost of the electricity relates to revenues earned in December, it represents an expense (Utilities Expense) that will be reported on this year's income statement. Because the cost has not yet been paid at the end of the month, Papa John's also has incurred a liability called Accounts Payable. Similar situations arise when employees work in the current period but are not paid their salaries or wages until the following period.

SELF-STUDY QUIZ

This self-study quiz allows you to practice applying the **matching principle** under accrual accounting. Complete this quiz now to make sure you can apply this principle. The following transactions are samples of typical monthly operating activities of Papa John's (dollars in thousands). If expense is to be recognized in **January,** indicate the title of the expense account and the amount of the expense to be recognized. You should refer to the Papa John's income statement presented in Exhibit 3.1 for account titles. Note that Papa John's reports General and Administrative Expenses that is a summary of Insurance Expense, Repairs Expense, Utilities Expense, and Fuel Expense. Use these more descriptive account titles in your responses.

ACTIVITY	EXPENSE ACCOUNT TITLE	AMOUNT OF EXPENSE RECOGNIZED IN JANUARY
(a) At the beginning of January, Papa John's restaurants paid $3,000 in rent for the months of January, February, and March.		
(b) In January, Papa John's paid suppliers $10,000 on account for supplies received in December.		
(c) In January, the food and paper products inventory used in selling pizza products to customers was $9,500.		
(d) In late January, Papa John's received a $400 utility bill for electricity used in January. The bill will be paid in February.		

After you have completed your answers, check them with the solutions at the bottom of the page.

Stock Market Reactions to Accounting Announcements

Stock market analysts and investors use accounting information to make their investment decisions. Thus, the stock market, which is based on investors' expectations about a company's future performance, often reacts negatively when a company does not meet previously specified operating targets.

A net loss does not have to occur for a company to recognize that it is experiencing difficulty. Any unexpected variance in actual performance from the operating plan, such as lower than expected quarterly earnings or sales revenue needs to be explained. On November 2, 2006, Papa John's announced its third quarter results, reporting that comparable store sales in the last month of the quarter were down 0.6% at the company stores and down 2.2% at franchised stores. The October 2006 same-store sales decrease was the first negative monthly comparison in 22 months. On October 30, 2006, Papa John's stock (stock symbol PZZA) had been selling at $37.79 per share. By November 3, 2006, the price dropped by $6.84 to $30.95 per share, an 18.1 percent decrease.*

Self-Study Quiz
Solutions

Expense Account Title	Amount of Expense Recognized in January
(a) Rent Expense	$1,000 ($3,000 ÷ 3 months)
(b) No expense in January	Supplies will be expensed when used.
(c) Cost of Sales	$9,500
(d) Utilities Expense (General and Administrative Expenses)	$400

This is a clear example of how external users reacted to the information. Accounting information has a pervasive effect on all forms of corporate decision making, as well as on the economic decisions that investors and creditors make.

Source: B. Stouffer and Y. Gulmi, "PZZA: Was It Something We Said?" BB&T Capital Markets, November 6, 2006.

*Bigcharts.com

Learning Objective 4

Apply transaction analysis to examine and record the effects of operating activities on the financial statements.

Video 3-1
www.mhhe.com/libby6e

Revenues
• Increase net income and Stockholders' Equity
• ↑ with Credits
• Accounts have credit balances

Expenses
• Decrease net income and Stockholders' Equity
• ↑ with Debits
• Accounts have debit balances

THE EXPANDED TRANSACTION ANALYSIS MODEL

We discussed the variety of business activities affecting the income statement and how they are measured. Now we need to determine how these business activities are recorded in the accounting system and reflected in the financial statements. Chapter 2 covered investing and financing activities that affect assets, liabilities, and contributed capital. We now expand the transaction analysis model presented in that chapter to include operating activities.

Transaction Analysis Rules

The complete transaction model presented in Exhibit 3.4 includes **all five elements:** assets, liabilities, stockholders' equity, revenues, and expenses. Recall that the Retained Earnings account is the accumulation of all past revenues and expenses minus any income distributed to stockholders as dividends (that is, earnings not retained in the business).[5] When net income is positive, Retained Earnings increase; a net loss decreases Retained Earnings.

Before illustrating the use of the expanded transaction analysis model, we want to emphasize the following:

- Revenues increase stockholders' equity through Retained Earnings and therefore have **credit** balances.

- Expenses decrease net income, thus decreasing Retained Earnings and stockholders' equity. Therefore, they have **debit** balances (opposite of the balance in Retained Earnings). That is, to increase an expense, you debit it, which decreases net income and Retained Earnings. You are adding to the expenses when you debit the account.

- When revenues exceed expenses, the company reports net income, increasing Retained Earnings and stockholders' equity. However, when expenses exceed revenues, a net loss results that decreases Retained Earnings and thus stockholders' equity.

When constructing and using the transactions analysis model, as we saw in Chapter 2:

- All accounts can increase or decrease, although revenues and expenses tend to increase throughout a period. For accounts on the left side of the accounting equation, the increase symbol + is written on the left side of the T-account. For accounts on the right side of the accounting equation, the increase symbol + is written on the right side of the T-account.

- Debits (dr) are written on the left side of each T-account and credits (cr) are written on the right.

- Every transaction affects at least two accounts.

---

[5]Instead of reducing Retained Earnings directly when dividends are declared, companies may use the account Dividends Declared, which has a debit balance.

| ASSETS = | LIABILITIES + | STOCKHOLDERS' EQUITY (two accounts) | | | EXHIBIT 3.4 |

Expanded Transaction Analysis Model

In analyzing transactions, since revenues are defined as inflows of net assets, then by definition, recording a revenue results in either increasing an asset or decreasing a liability. In like manner, when recording an expense, an asset is decreased or a liability is increased.

You should refer to the expanded transaction analysis model until you can construct it on your own without assistance. Study Exhibit 3.4 carefully to make sure you understand the impact of operating activities on both the balance sheet and income statement.

Step 1: Identify and Classify Accounts and Effects

- **Identify the accounts (by title) affected,** making sure that at least two accounts change. Ask yourself: What is received (and earned) or what is given (and incurred)?
- **Classify them by type of account.** Was each account an asset (A), a liability (L), stockholders' equity (SE), a revenue (R), or an expense (E)?
- **Determine the direction of the effect.** Did the account increase [+] or decrease [−]?

Step 2: Verify Entries and Accounting Equation Balance

- **Verify that debits = credits.**
- **Verify that the accounting equation (A = L + SE) remains in balance.**

Analyzing Papa John's Transactions

Now we build on the Papa John's balance sheet presented at the end of Chapter 2. It included only investing and financing transactions occurring during the accounting cycle. We analyze, record, and post to the T-accounts the effects of this chapter's operating activities that also occurred during the accounting cycle (the month of January). In Chapter 4, we complete the accounting cycle with the activities at the end of the period (on January 31). All amounts are in thousands of dollars and the effects are posted to the appropriate T-accounts at the end of the illustration.

(*a*) Papa John's restaurants sold pizza to customers for $36,000 cash and $30,000 in supplies to restaurants, receiving $21,000 cash with the rest due on account.

Cash (+A) [$36,000 + $21,000]	57,000	
Accounts Receivable (+A)	9,000	
Restaurant Sales Revenue (+R, +SE)		66,000

Journal entry

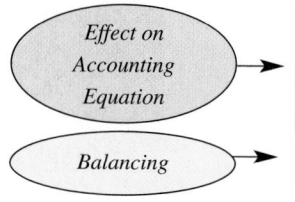

Assets		=	Liabilities	+	Stockholders' Equity	
Cash	+57,000				Restaurant Sales	
Accounts Receivable	+ 9,000				Revenue (+R)	+66,000

Equality checks: (1) Debits $66,000 = Credits $66,000; (2) the accounting equation is in balance.

(b) The cost of the dough, sauce, cheese, and other supplies for the restaurant sales in (a) was $30,000.

Cost of Sales (+E, −SE) 30,000
    Supplies (−A) 30,000

Assets		=	Liabilities	+	Stockholders' Equity	
Supplies	−30,000				Cost of Sales (+E)	−30,000

Equality checks: (1) Debits $30,000 = Credits $30,000; (2) the accounting equation is in balance.

(c) Papa John's sold new franchises for $400 cash, earning $100 immediately by performing services for franchisees; the rest will be earned over the next several months.

Cash (+A) 400
    Franchise Fee Revenue (+R, +SE) 100
    Unearned Franchise Fees (+L) 300

Assets		=	Liabilities		+	Stockholders' Equity	
Cash	+400		Unearned Franchise Fees	+300		Franchise Fee Revenue (+R)	+100

Equality checks: (1) Debits $400 = Credits $400; (2) the accounting equation is in balance.

(d) In January, Papa John's paid $7,000 for utilities, repairs, and fuel for delivery vehicles, all considered general and administrative expenses incurred during the month.

General and Administrative Expenses (+E, −SE) 7,000
    Cash (−A) 7,000

Assets		=	Liabilities	+	Stockholders' Equity	
Cash	−7,000				General and Administrative Expenses (+E)	−7,000

Equality checks: (1) Debits $7,000 = Credits $7,000; (2) the accounting equation is in balance.

(e) Papa John's commissaries ordered and received $29,000 in supplies, paying $9,000 in cash and owing the rest on account to suppliers.

Supplies (+A) 29,000
    Cash (−A) 9,000
    Accounts Payable (+L) 20,000

Assets		=	Liabilities		+	Stockholders' Equity
Cash	− 9,000		Accounts Payable	+20,000		
Supplies	+29,000					

Equality checks: (1) Debits $29,000 = Credits $29,000; (2) the accounting equation is in balance.

(f) Papa John's paid $14,000 cash to employees for their work in January.

Salaries Expense (+E, −SE) 14,000
    Cash (−A) 14,000

Assets	=	Liabilities	+	Stockholders' Equity	
Cash −14,000				Salaries Expense (+E)	−14,000

Equality checks: (1) Debits $14,000 = Credits $14,000; (2) the accounting equation is in balance.

(g) At the beginning of January, Papa John's paid the following, all of which are considered prepaid expenses when paid (any adjustments will be made in Chapter 4):

- **$2,000 for insurance (covering the next four months beginning January 1),**
- **$6,000 for renting space in shopping centers (over the next three months beginning January 1), and**
- **$1,000 for advertising (to be run in February).**

Prepaid Expenses (+A)	9,000
Cash (−A)	9,000

Assets	=	Liabilities	+	Stockholders' Equity
Cash −9,000				
Prepaid Expenses +9,000				

Equality checks: (1) Debits $9,000 = Credits $9,000; (2) the accounting equation is in balance.

(h) Papa John's sold land with an historical cost of $1,000 for $4,000 cash.[6]

Cash (+A)	4,000
Property and Equipment (−A)	1,000
Gain on Sale of Land (+R, +SE)	3,000

Assets	=	Liabilities	+	Stockholders' Equity
Property and Equipment −1,000				Gain on Sale of Land (+R) +3,000
Cash +4,000				

Equality checks: (1) Debits $4,000 = Credits $4,000; (2) the accounting equation is in balance.

The self-study quiz box

SELF-STUDY QUIZ

For transactions (*i*) through (*k*), fill in the missing information. Be sure to transfer (post) the effects of the journal entries to the T-accounts at the end of the illustration (in Exhibit 3.5).

(i) Papa John's received $3,500 in franchisee fees based on their weekly sales; $800 of the amount was due from franchisees' sales recorded as accounts receivable in December and the rest is from January sales.

Write the journal entry; post the effects to the T-accounts.

Assets	=	Liabilities	+	Stockholders' Equity	
Cash +3,500				Franchise Fee Revenue (+R)	+2,700
Accounts receivable − 800					

Equality checks: (1) Debits $3,500 = Credits $3,500; (2) the accounting equation is in balance.

---

[6]This is an example of a peripheral activity; it will be covered in more depth in Chapter 8.

(j) Papa John's paid $10,000 on accounts owed to suppliers.

Write the journal entry; post the effects to the T-accounts.

Show the effects on the accounting equation.

Assets	=	Liabilities	+	Stockholders' Equity

Equality checks: (1) Debits $10,000 = Credits $10,000; (2) the accounting equation is in balance.

(k) Papa John's received $13,000 in cash: $1,000 in interest earned on investments and $12,000 in payments made by franchisees on their accounts.

Cash (+A)	13,000	
Investment Income (+R, +SE)		1,000
Accounts Receivable (−A)		12,000

Assets	=	Liabilities	+	Stockholders' Equity

Show the effects on the accounting equation.

Verify equalities.

Equality checks: (1) Debits $_____ = Credits $_____; (2) Is the accounting equation in balance? _____

After you have completed your answers, check them with the solution at the bottom of the page.

Exhibit 3.5 shows the T-accounts that changed during the period because of transactions (*a*) through (*k*). The balances of all other accounts remained the same. Note that the amounts from Papa John's balance sheet at the end of Chapter 2 have been included as the beginning balances in Exhibit 3.5 for assets, liabilities, and stockholders' equity accounts. On the other hand, income statement accounts have a zero beginning balance so that revenue and expense activities can accumulate over the period.

You can verify that you posted the entries for transactions (*i*) through (*k*) properly by adding the increase side and subtracting the decrease side and then comparing your answer to the ending balance in each of the T-accounts.

Self-Study Quiz Solutions

(*i*) Cash (+A)	3,500	
Accounts Receivable (−A)		800
Franchise Fee Revenue (+R, +SE)		2,700
(*j*) Accounts Payable (−L)	10,000	
Cash (−A)		10,000

Assets	=	Liabilities	+	Stockholders' Equity
Cash −10,000		Accounts Payable −10,000		

(*k*)	Assets	=	Liabilities	+	Stockholders' Equity
	Cash +13,000				Investment Revenue (+R) +1,000
	Account Receivable −12,000				

Equality checks: (1) Debits $13,000 = Credits $13,000; (2) Is the accounting equation in balance? Yes

Balance Sheet Accounts (beginning balances are taken from Exhibit 2.8)

EXHIBIT 3.5

T-Accounts

+	Cash (A)		−
Bal.	15,000		
(a)	57,000	7,000	(d)
(c)	400	9,000	(e)
(h)	4,000	14,000	(f)
(i)	____	9,000	(g)
(k)	13,000	____	(j)
Bal.	43,900		

+	Accounts Receivable (A)		−
Bal.	23,000		
(a)	9,000	____	(i)
		12,000	(k)
Bal.	19,200		

+	Supplies (A)		−
Bal.	27,000		
(e)	29,000	30,000	(b)
Bal.	26,000		

+	Prepaid Expenses (A)	−
Bal.	8,000	
(g)	9,000	
Bal.	17,000	

+	Property and Equipment (A)		−
Bal.	208,000		
		1,000	(h)
Bal.	207,000		

−	Unearned Franchise Fees (L)		+
		7,000	Bal.
		300	(c)
		7,300	Bal.

−	Accounts Payable (L)		+
		29,000	Bal.
		20,000	(e)
(j)	____		
		39,000	Bal.

Income Statement Accounts (beginning balances start at zero)

−	Restaurant Sales Revenue (R)		+
		0	Bal.
		66,000	(a)
		66,000	Bal.

−	Franchise Fee Revenue (R)		+
		0	Bal.
		100	(c)
		____	(i)
		2,800	Bal.

−	Gain on Sale of Land (R)		+
		0	Bal.
		3,000	(h)
		3,000	Bal.

−	Investment Income (R)		+
		0	Bal.
		1,000	(k)
		1,000	Bal.

+	Cost of Sales (E)	−
Bal.	0	
(b)	30,000	
Bal.	30,000	

+	Salaries Expenses (E)	−
Bal.	0	
(f)	14,000	
Bal.	14,000	

+	General and Administrative Expenses (E)	−
Bal.	0	
(d)	7,000	
Bal.	7,000	

Learning Objective 5
Prepare financial statements.

HOW ARE FINANCIAL STATEMENTS PREPARED AND ANALYZED?

Based on the January transactions that have just been posted in the T-accounts, we can now prepare financial statements reflecting the operating activities for January. Recall from prior chapters what the four statements are and how they relate to each other.

Statement	Formula
Income statement	Revenues − Expenses = Net Income
Statement of retained earnings	Beginning Retained Earnings + Net Income − Dividends Declared = Ending Retained Earnings
Balance sheet	Assets = Liabilities + Stockholders' Equity (Contributed Capital and Retained Earnings) (includes Cash)
Statement of cash flows	Change in Cash = Cash Provided by or Used in Operating Activities + Cash Provided by or Used in Investing Activities + Cash Provided by or Used in Financing Activities

Because net income on the income statement is a component of Retained Earnings on the balance sheet, it is necessary to compute net income first. The statement of retained earnings (or a column for Retained Earnings in the statement of stockholders' equity) provides the connection to the balance sheet. Finally, the sources and uses of cash are reported on the statement of cash flows, and the ending balance for Cash on the statement equals the Cash balance on the balance sheet.

It is important to note that the statements we are about to present for Papa John's at the end of January do not at this point reflect all revenues earned or expenses incurred in January. For example:

■ The account Prepaid Expenses includes rent and insurance covering January and future months, but the expenses are not yet recorded for the amounts used in January. This is true of the equipment used during the month as well. Until adjusted, assets are overstated and expenses are understated.

■ We have not calculated income taxes for the amount incurred in January and owed within the next quarter. Thus, both liabilities and expenses are understated.

■ Unearned Franchise Fees (a liability account) is not updated for any amount of Franchise Fee Revenue earned in January. In this case, the liability is overstated and revenues are understated.

Chapter 4 will describe the adjustment process to update the accounting records. After the adjustments are recorded, the amount of tax expense will be determined and the statements will reflect generally accepted accounting principles following accrual basis accounting. Until then, here are the unadjusted financial statements for Papa John's at the end of January.

Classified Income Statement

PAPA JOHN'S INTERNATIONAL, INC. AND SUBSIDIARIES
Consolidated Statement of Income
For the Month Ended January 31, 2007
(dollars in thousands)

Operating Revenues	
Restaurant sales revenue	$66,000
Franchise fee revenue	2,800
Total revenues	68,800
Operating Expenses	
Cost of sales	30,000
Salaries expense	14,000
General and administrative expenses	7,000
Supplies expense	0
Rent expense	0
Insurance expense	0
Utilities expense	0
Depreciation expense	0
Interest expense	0
Other operating expenses	0
Total expenses	51,000
Operating Income	17,800
Other Items	
Investment income	1,000
Interest expense	(0)
Gain on sale of land	3,000
Income before Income Taxes	21,800
Income tax expense	0
Net Income	**$21,800**
Earnings per Share (for the month)	$0.68

(approximately 32,100,000 shares from Papa John's annual report)

In our illustration for Papa John's, the company earned positive net income of $21,800,000 in January, nearly 32% of operating revenues ($21,800,000 net income ÷ $68,800,000 total revenues) before adjustments.

Reporting More Detailed Financial Information in the Notes

FINANCIAL ANALYSIS

Many companies, especially very large ones, operate in more than one geographic area. These companies are often called **multinationals.** A consolidated income statement that is based on aggregated data may not prove useful to investors seeking to assess possible risks and returns from companies operating in foreign markets. The same may be true if a company operates more than a single business. Therefore, many companies provide additional information about geographic and business segments in notes to the financial statements. An excerpt from Papa John's 2006 annual report provides information on its geographic segments:

NOTES TO CONSOLIDATED FINANCIAL STATEMENTS

22. Segment Information

We have defined five reportable segments: domestic restaurants, domestic commissaries, domestic franchising, international operations, and variable interest entities. . . .

(dollars in thousands)	2006	2005	2004
Revenues from external customers:			
Domestic restaurants	$447,938	$434,525	$412,676
Domestic commissaries	413,075	398,372	376,642
Domestic franchising	58,971	55,315	52,767
International	23,209	18,389	15,757
Variable Interest Entities	7,859	11,713	14,387
All others	50,505	50,474	53,117
Total revenues from external customers	$1,001,557	$968,788	$925,346

Statement of Retained Earnings

The statement of retained earnings ties the information on Papa John's income statement to the balance sheet. Any transactions affecting Retained Earnings, such as generating net income and declaring dividends, are summarized in this statement.

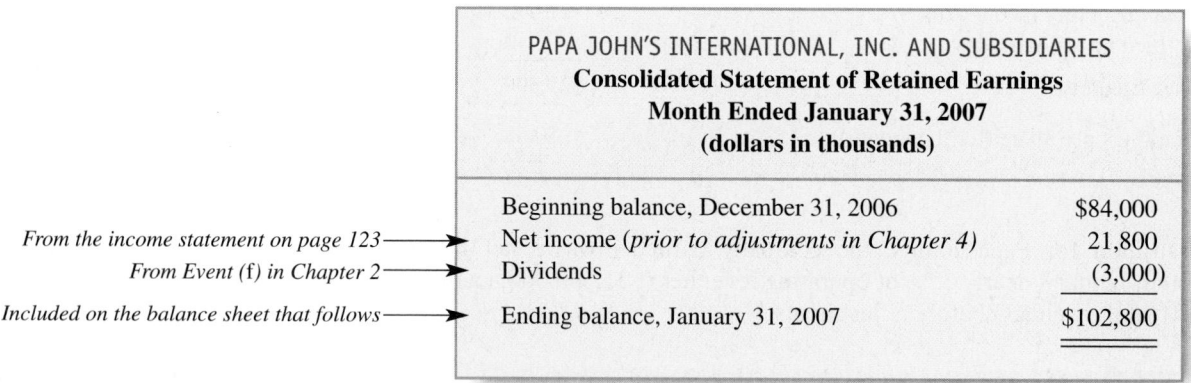

PAPA JOHN'S INTERNATIONAL, INC. AND SUBSIDIARIES
Consolidated Statement of Retained Earnings
Month Ended January 31, 2007
(dollars in thousands)

Beginning balance, December 31, 2006	$84,000
Net income (*prior to adjustments in Chapter 4*)	21,800
Dividends	(3,000)
Ending balance, January 31, 2007	$102,800

From the income statement on page 123
From Event (f) in Chapter 2
Included on the balance sheet that follows

Classified Balance Sheet

Finally, we can revise the balance sheet from Chapter 2 to reflect the effects of the operating activities discussed in this chapter. Accounts that were not affected by operating activities retain the same balances as in Exhibit 2.8, except for Retained Earnings. The ending balance in the statement of retained earnings $102,800,000 flows into the Stockholders' Equity section of the balance sheet. Accounts that were affected by this chapter's operating activities reflect the revised balances from the T-accounts in Exhibit 3.5. We explore the relationships among the financial statements further in the next chapter.

PAPA JOHN'S INTERNATIONAL, INC. AND SUBSIDIARIES
Consolidated Balance Sheet
January 31, 2007
(dollars in thousands)

Assets
Current Assets

Cash	$ 43,900
Accounts receivable	19,200
Supplies	26,000
Prepaid expenses	17,000
Other current assets	14,000
Total current assets	120,100
Investments	2,000
Property and equipment (net of accumulated depreciation of $189,000)	207,000
Notes receivable	15,000
Intangibles	67,000
Other assets	17,000
Total assets	**$428,100**

Liabilities and Stockholders' Equity
Current Liabilities

Accounts payable	$ 39,000
Dividends payable	3,000
Accrued expenses payable	73,000
Total current liabilities	115,000
Unearned franchise fees	7,300
Notes payable	110,000
Other long-term liabilities	27,000

Stockholders' Equity

Contributed capital	66,000
Retained earnings	102,800
Total stockholders' equity	168,800
Total liabilities and stockholders' equity	**$428,100**

From the Statement of Retained Earnings (pointing to Retained earnings 102,800)

Operating Activities

Chapter 2 presented a partial statement of cash flows for Papa John's—only its investing and financing activities. Recall that investing activities relate primarily to transactions affecting long-term assets; financing activities are those from bank borrowings, stock issuances, and dividend payments to stockholders.

In this chapter, we focus on cash flows from operating activities. This section of the statement of cash flows reports **cash from** operating sources, primarily customers, and **cash to** suppliers and others involved in operations. The accounts most often associated with operating activities are current assets, such as Accounts Receivable, Inventories, and Prepaid Expenses, and current liabilities, such as Accounts Payable, Wages Payable, and Unearned Revenue.

We present the Cash Flows from Operating Activities section of the statement of cash flows using the **direct method**—cash receipts and cash disbursements. However, most companies report cash from operations using the **indirect method** that will be discussed in later chapters.

		Effect on Cash Flows
Operating activities		
Cash received:	Customers	+
	Interest and dividends on investments	+
Cash paid:	Suppliers	−
	Employees	−
	Interest on debt obligations	−
	Income taxes	−
Investing activities (see Chapter 2)		
Financing activities (see Chapter 2)		

When a transaction affects cash, it is included on the statement of cash flows. When a transaction does not affect cash, such as acquiring a building with a long-term mortgage note payable or selling goods on account to customers, there is no cash effect to include on the statement. **If you see Cash in a transaction, it will be reflected on the statement of cash flows.** Therefore, when preparing the Cash Flows from Operating Activities section of the statement of cash flows using the direct method, the easiest way is to look at the activities in the Cash T-account.

		+ Cash (A) −			
	Bal.	15,000			
From customers	(a)	57,000	7,000	(d)	To suppliers
From franchisees	(c)	400	9,000	(e)	To suppliers
Investing activity	(h)	4,000	14,000	(f)	To employees
From franchisees	(i)	3,500	9,000	(g)	To suppliers
$12,000 from franchisees; $1,000 from investments	(k)	13,000	10,000	(j)	To suppliers
	Bal.	43,900			

KEY RATIO ANALYSIS

Total Asset Turnover Ratio

Learning Objective 6
Compute and interpret the total asset turnover ratio.

In Chapter 2, we discussed the financial leverage ratio, a tool to evaluate management's use of debt to improve earnings. We now introduce a ratio to assess managers' use of all of the company's assets to improve earnings. As we will see in other chapters, similar analysis on the use of each specific type of asset provides additional information for decision makers.

? ANALYTICAL QUESTION
How effective is management in generating sales from assets (resources)?

% RATIO AND COMPARISONS

$$\text{Total Asset Turnover Ratio} = \frac{\text{Sales (or Operating) Revenues}}{\text{Average Total Assets}}$$

The 2006 ratio for Papa John's is (dollars in thousands):

$$\frac{\$1,001,000}{(\$351,000 + \$380,000)/2} = 2.74$$

COMPARISONS OVER TIME			COMPARISONS WITH COMPETITORS	
Papa John's			**Domino's Inc.**	**Yum! Brands***
2004	**2005**	**2006**	**2006**	**2006**
2.56	2.67	2.74	3.42	1.59

*Yum! Brands is the parent company of Pizza Hut, KFC, Taco Bell, and others.

💡 INTERPRETATIONS

In General The total asset turnover ratio measures the sales generated per dollar of assets. A high asset turnover ratio signifies efficient management of assets; a low asset turnover ratio signifies less efficient management. A company's products and business strategy contribute significantly to its asset turnover ratio. However, when competitors are similar, management's ability to control the firm's assets is vital in determining its success. Stronger financial performance improves the asset turnover ratio.

Creditors and security analysts use this ratio to assess a company's effectiveness at controlling both current and noncurrent assets. In a well-run business, creditors expect the ratio to fluctuate due to seasonal upswings and downturns. For example, as inventory is built up prior to a heavy sales season, companies need to borrow funds. The asset turnover ratio declines with this increase in assets. Eventually, the season's high sales provide the cash needed to repay the loans. The asset turnover ratio then rises with the increased sales.

Focus Company Analysis Papa John's asset turnover ratio has increased slightly since 2004, suggesting an increase in management effectiveness in using assets to generate sales. In fact, Papa John's reported that as the number of stores in a geographic area increased, regional commissaries showed higher sales, allowing management to use the commissary assets more efficiently.

Compared to its main competitors, Papa John's 2006 total asset turnover ratio falls in the middle. The difference in ratios is due in part to differences in operating strategy: Pizza Hut (plus KFC and Taco Bell) operate primarily eat-in restaurants, so they must invest more in their facilities (that is, they are more asset intensive). Domino's, the leading pizza delivery company, operates primarily from rented facilities (that is, it is less asset intensive).

A Few Cautions While the total asset turnover ratio may decrease due to seasonal fluctuations, a declining ratio may also be caused by changes in corporate policies leading to a rising level of assets. Examples include relaxing credit policies for new customers or reducing collection efforts in accounts receivable. A detailed analysis of the changes in the key components of assets is needed to determine the causes of a change in the asset turnover ratio and thus management's decisions.

Selected Focus Companies' Total Asset Turnover Ratios for 2006

Southwest Airlines 0.36

Harley-Davidson 1.08

Boston Beer 1.85

DEMONSTRATION CASE

This case is a continuation of the Terrific Lawn Maintenance Corporation case introduced in Chapter 2. The company was established and supplies, property, and equipment were purchased. Terrific Lawn is ready for business. The balance sheet at April 30, 2009, based on investing and financing activities (from Chapter 2) is as follows:

TERRIFIC LAWN MAINTENANCE CORPORATION
Balance Sheet
At April 30, 2009

Assets		Liabilities	
Current Assets		Current Liability	
Cash	$ 3,800	Notes payable	$ 4,400
Notes receivable	1,250		
Total current assets	5,050		
Equipment	4,600	**Stockholders' Equity**	
Land	3,750	Contributed capital	9,000
Total assets	$13,400	Total liabilities and stockholders' equity	$13,400

The additional following activities occurred during April 2009:

a. Purchased and used gasoline for mowers and edgers, paying $90 in cash at a local gas station.

b. In early April, received from the city $1,600 cash in advance for lawn maintenance service for April through July ($400 each month). The entire amount was recorded as Unearned Revenue.

c. In early April, purchased $300 of insurance covering six months, April through September. The entire payment was recorded as Prepaid Expenses.

d. Mowed lawns for residential customers who are billed every two weeks. A total of $5,200 of service was billed in April.

e. Residential customers paid $3,500 on their accounts.

f. Paid wages every two weeks. Total cash paid in April was $3,900.

g. Received a bill for $320 from the local gas station for additional gasoline purchased on account and used in April.

h. Paid $700 principal and $40 interest on notes owed to XYZ Lawn Supply and the hardware store.

i. Paid $100 on accounts payable.

j. Collected $1,250 principal and $12 interest on the note owed by the city to Terrific Lawn Maintenance Corporation.

Required:

1. a. On a separate sheet of paper, set up T-accounts for Cash, Accounts Receivable, Notes Receivable, Prepaid Expenses, Equipment, Land, Accounts Payable, Unearned Revenue (same as deferred revenue), Notes Payable, Contributed Capital, Retained Earnings, Mowing Revenue, Interest Revenue, Wages Expense, Fuel Expense, and Interest Expense. Beginning balances for the balance sheet accounts should be taken from the preceding balance sheet. Beginning balances for the operating accounts are $0. Indicate these balances on the T-accounts.

   b. Analyze each transaction referring to the expanded transaction analysis model presented in this chapter.

   c. On a separate sheet of paper, prepare journal entries in chronological order and indicate their effects on the accounting model (Assets = Liabilities + Stockholders' Equity). Include the equality checks: (1) Debits = Credits and (2) the accounting equation is in balance.

d. Enter the effects of each transaction in the appropriate T-accounts. Identify each amount with its letter in the preceding list of activities.

e. Compute balances in each of the T-accounts.

2. Use the amounts in the T-accounts to prepare a full set of financial statements—income statement, statement of retained earnings, balance sheet, and statement of cash flows—for Terrific Lawn Maintenance Corporation at April 30, 2009. Refer to the cash flow statement presented in Chapter 2 for the investing and financing activities. (Adjustments to accounts will be presented in Chapter 4.)

Now check your answers with the following suggested solution.

SUGGESTED SOLUTION

1. Transaction analysis, journal entries, and T-accounts:

(*a*) Fuel Expense (+E, −SE)	90	
Cash (−A)		90

Assets	=	Liabilities	+	Stockholders' Equity	
Cash	−90			Fuel Expense (+E)	−90

Equality checks: (1) Debits $90 = Credits $90; (2) the accounting equation is in balance.

(*b*) Cash (+A)	1,600	
Unearned Revenue (+L)		1,600

Assets	=	Liabilities	+	Stockholders' Equity
Cash	+1,600	Unearned Revenue +1,600		

Equality checks: (1) Debits $1,600 = Credits $1,600; (2) the accounting equation is in balance.

(*c*) Prepaid Expenses (+A)	300	
Cash (−A)		300

Assets	=	Liabilities	+	Stockholders' Equity
Cash	−300			
Prepaid Expenses	+300			

Equality checks: (1) Debits $300 = Credits $300; (2) the accounting equation is in balance.

(*d*) Accounts Receivable (+A)	5,200	
Mowing Revenue (+R, +SE)		5,200

Assets	=	Liabilities	+	Stockholders' Equity
Accounts Receivable +5,200				Mowing Revenue (+R) + 5,200

Equality checks: (1) Debits $5,200 = Credits $5,200; (2) the accounting equation is in balance.

(*e*) Cash (+A)	3,500	
Accounts Receivable (−A)		3,500

Assets	=	Liabilities	+	Stockholders' Equity
Accounts Receivable −3,500				
Cash +3,500				

Equality checks: (1) Debits $3,500 = Credits $3,500; (2) the accounting equation is in balance.

(f)	Wages Expense (+E, −SE)	3,900	
	Cash (−A)		3,900

Assets	=	Liabilities	+	Stockholders' Equity
Cash −3,900				Wages Expense (+E) −3,900

Equality checks: (1) Debits $3,900 = Credits $3,900; (2) the accounting equation is in balance.

(g)	Fuel Expense (+E, −SE)	320	
	Accounts Payable (+L)		320

Assets	=	Liabilities	+	Stockholders' Equity
		Accounts Payable +320		Fuel Expense (+E) −320

Equality checks: (1) Debits $320 = Credits $320; (2) the accounting equation is in balance.

(h)	Interest Expense (+E, −SE)	40	
	Notes Payable (−L)	700	
	Cash (−A)		740

Assets	=	Liabilities	+	Stockholders' Equity
Cash −740		Notes Payable −700		Interest Expense (+E) −40

Equality checks: (1) Debits $740 = Credits $740; (2) the accounting equation is in balance.

(i)	Accounts Payable (−L)	100	
	Cash (−A)		100

Assets	=	Liabilities	+	Stockholders' Equity
Cash −100		Accounts Payable − 100		

Equality checks: (1) Debits $100 = Credits $100; (2) the accounting equation is in balance.

(j)	Cash (+A)	1,262	
	Notes Receivable (−A)		1,250
	Interest Revenue (+R, +SE)		12

Assets	=	Liabilities	+	Stockholders' Equity
Cash +1,262				Interest Revenue (+R) +12
Notes Receivable − 1,250				

Equality checks: (1) Debits $1,262 = Credits $1,262; (2) the accounting equation is in balance.

T-Accounts:

Assets

+	Cash		−
Beg.	3,800		
(b)	1,600	90	(a)
(e)	3,500	300	(c)
(j)	1,262	3,900	(f)
		740	(h)
		100	(i)
Bal.	5,032		

+	Accounts Receivable		−
Beg.	0		
(d)	5,200	3,500	(e)
Bal.	1,700		

+	Notes Receivable		−
Beg.	1,250	1,250	(j)
Bal.	0		

+	Prepaid Expenses		−
Beg.	0		
(c)	300		
Bal.	300		

+	Land		−
Beg.	3,750		
Bal.	3,750		

+	Equipment		−
Beg.	4,600		
Bal.	4,600		

Liabilities

−	Accounts Payable		+
		0	Beg.
(i)	100	320	(g)
		220	Bal.

−	Notes Payable		+
		4,400	Beg.
(h)	700		
		3,700	Bal.

−	Unearned Revenue		+
		0	Beg.
		1,600	(b)
		1,600	Bal.

Stockholders' Equity

−	Contributed Capital		+
		9,000	Beg.
		9,000	Bal.

−	Retained Earnings		+
		0	Beg.
		0	Bal.

Revenues

−	Mowing Revenue		+
		0	Beg.
		5,200	(d)
		5,200	Bal.

−	Interest Revenue		+
		0	Beg.
		12	(j)
		12	Bal.

Expenses

+	Wages Expense		−
Beg.	0		
(f)	3,900		
Bal.	3,900		

+	Fuel Expense		−
Beg.	0		
(a)	90		
(g)	320		
Bal.	410		

+	Interest Expense		−
Beg.	0		
(h)	40		
Bal.	40		

2. Financial statements:

TERRIFIC LAWN MAINTENANCE CORPORATION
Income Statement
For the Month Ended April 30, 2009

Operating Revenues		
Mowing revenue		$5,200
Operating Expenses		
Fuel expense	410	
Wages expense	3,900	
		4,310
Operating income		890
Other items		
Interest revenue		12
Interest expense		(40)
Pretax income		862
Income tax expense		0
Net Income		**$ 862**
Earnings per share for the month		$ .57

— ($862 net income divided by 1,500 shares outstanding)

TERRIFIC LAWN MAINTENANCE CORPORATION
Statement of Retained Earnings
For the Month Ended April 30, 2009

Balance, April 1, 2009	$ 0
Net income	862
Dividends declared	(0)
Balance, April 30, 2009	$862

TERRIFIC LAWN MAINTENANCE CORPORATION
Statement of Cash Flows
For the Month Ended April 30, 2009

Cash Flows from Operating Activities		
Cash received:	Customers (b, e)	$5,100
	Interest on notes receivable (j)	12
Cash paid:	Suppliers (a, c, i)	(490)
	Employees (f)	(3,900)
	Interest on notes payable (h)	(40)
Cash flows provided by operations		**682**
Cash Flows from Investing Activities		
Purchased land		(5,000)
Purchased equipment		(200)
Received principal payment on note receivable (j)		1,250
Cash flows used in investing activities		**(3,950)**
Cash Flows from Financing Activities		
Issued common stock		9,000
Payments on principal of notes payable (h)		(700)
Cash flows provided by financing activities		**8,300**
Change in cash		5,032
Beginning cash balance		0
Ending cash balance		**$5,032**

TERRIFIC LAWN MAINTENANCE CORPORATION
Balance Sheet
April 30, 2009

Assets			Liabilities		
Current Assets			Current Liabilities		
Cash	$ 5,032		Accounts payable	$ 220	
Accounts receivable	1,700		Notes payable	3,700	
Prepaid expenses	300		Unearned revenue	1,600	
			Total current liabilities	5,520	
Total current assets	7,032		**Stockholders' Equity**		
Equipment	4,600		Contributed capital	9,000	
Land	3,750		Retained earnings	862	
			Total liabilities and		
Total assets	**$15,382**		**stockholders' equity**	**$15,382**	

CHAPTER **TAKE-AWAYS**

1. Describe a typical business operating cycle and explain the necessity for the time period assumption.   p. 105

- The operating cycle, or cash-to-cash cycle, is the time needed to purchase goods or services from suppliers, sell the goods or services to customers, and collect cash from customers.

- Time period assumption—to measure and report financial information periodically, we assume the long life of a company can be cut into shorter periods.

2. Explain how business activities affect the elements of the income statement.   p. 106

- Elements on the income statement:
  a. Revenues—increases in assets or settlements of liabilities from ongoing operations.
  b. Expenses—decreases in assets or increases in liabilities from ongoing operations.
  c. Gains—increases in assets or settlements of liabilities from peripheral activities.
  d. Losses—decreases in assets or increases in liabilities from peripheral activities.

3. Explain the accrual basis of accounting and apply the revenue and matching principles to measure income.   p. 110

In accrual basis accounting, revenues are recognized when earned and expenses are recognized when incurred.

- Revenue principle—recognize revenues when (1) delivery has occurred, (2) there is persuasive evidence of an arrangement for customer payment, (3) the price is fixed or determinable, and (4) collection is reasonably assured.

- Matching principle—recognize expenses when they are incurred in generating revenue.

4. Apply transaction analysis to examine and record the effects of operating activities on the financial statements.   p. 116

The expanded transaction analysis model includes revenues and expenses:

5. Prepare financial statements.   p. 122

Until the accounts have been updated to include all revenues earned and expenses incurred in the period (due to a difference in the time when cash is received or paid), the financial statements are unadjusted:

- Classified income statement—net income is needed to determine ending Retained Earnings; classifications include Operating Revenues, Operating Expenses (to determine Operating Income), Other Items (to determine Pretax Income), Income Tax Expense, Net Income, and Earnings per Share.

- Statement of retained earnings—connects income statement to balance sheet.

- Classified balance sheet—classified into current and noncurrent assets, current and noncurrent liabilities, and stockholders' equity.

- Statement of cash flows.

6. Compute and interpret the total asset turnover ratio. p. 126

The total asset turnover ratio (Sales ÷ Average Total Assets) measures the sales generated per dollar of assets. The higher the ratio, the more efficient the company is at managing assets.

In this chapter, we discussed the operating cycle and accounting concepts relevant to income determination: the time period assumption, definitions of the income statement elements (revenues, expenses, gains, and losses), the revenue principle, and the matching principle. The accounting principles are defined in accordance with the accrual basis of accounting, which requires revenues to be recorded when earned and expenses to be recorded when incurred in the process of generating revenues. We expanded the transaction analysis model introduced in Chapter 2 by adding revenues and expenses and prepared unadjusted financial statements. In Chapter 4, we discuss the activities that occur at the end of the accounting period: the adjustment process, the preparation of adjusted financial statements, and the closing process.

KEY **RATIO**

Total asset turnover ratio measures the sales generated per dollar of assets. A high ratio suggests that a company is managing its assets (the resources used to generate revenues) efficiently. The ratio is computed as follows (p. 126):

$$\text{Total Asset Turnover Ratio} = \frac{\text{Sales (or Operating) Revenues}}{\text{Average Total Assets}}$$

"Average" is (Beginning balance + Ending balance) ÷ 2.

FINDING **FINANCIAL INFORMATION**

Balance Sheet

Current Assets
Cash
Accounts and notes receivable
Inventory
Prepaid expenses

Noncurrent Assets
Long-term investments
Property and equipment
Intangibles

Current Liabilities
Accounts payable
Notes payable
Accrued liabilities payable

Noncurrent Liabilities
Long-term debt

Stockholders' Equity
Contributed capital
Retained earnings

Income Statement

Revenues (operating)
Sales (from various operating activities)

Expenses (operating)
Cost of sales (used inventory)
Rent, wages, depreciation, insurance, etc.

Operating Income
Other Items
Interest expense
Investment income
Gains on sale of assets
Losses on sale of assets

Pretax Income
Income tax expense

Net Income
Earnings per share

Statement of Cash Flows

Under Operating Activities
+ Cash from customers
+ Cash from interest and dividends
− Cash to suppliers
− Cash to employees
− Interest paid
− Income taxes paid

Notes

Under Summary of Significant Accounting Policies
Description of the company's revenue recognition policy.

KEY TERMS

Accrual Basis Accounting   p. 110
Cash Basis Accounting   p. 110
Expenses   p. 108
Gains   p. 109

Losses   p. 109
Matching Principle   p. 113
Operating (Cash-to-Cash)
Cycle   p. 105

Revenues   p. 106
Revenue Principle   p. 110
Time Period Assumption   p. 106

QUESTIONS

1. Describe a typical business operating cycle.
2. Explain what the time period assumption means.
3. Write the income statement equation and define each element.
4. Explain the difference between
   a. Revenues and gains
   b. Expenses and losses.
5. Define **accrual accounting** and contrast it with cash basis accounting.
6. What four criteria must normally be met for revenue to be recognized under accrual basis accounting?
7. Explain the matching principle.
8. Explain why stockholders' equity is increased by revenues and decreased by expenses.
9. Explain why revenues are recorded as credits and expenses as debits.
10. Complete the following matrix by entering either **debit** or **credit** in each cell:

Item	Increase	Decrease
Revenues		
Losses		
Gains		
Expenses		

11. Complete the following matrix by entering either **increase** or **decrease** in each cell:

Item	Debit	Credit
Revenues		
Losses		
Gains		
Expenses		

12. Identify whether the following transactions affect cash flow from operating, investing, or financing activities, and indicate the effect of each on cash (+ for increase and − for decrease). If there is no cash flow effect, write "None."

Transaction	Operating, Investing, or Financing Effect on Cash	Direction of the Effect on Cash
Cash paid to suppliers		
Sale of goods on account		
Cash received from customers		
Purchase of investments		
Cash paid for interest		
Issuance of stock for cash		

13. State the equation for the asset turnover ratio and explain how it is interpreted.

MULTIPLE-CHOICE QUESTIONS

1. Which of the following is not a specific account in a company's chart of accounts?
   a. Gains
   b. Net Income
   c. Revenue
   d. Unearned Revenue

2. Which of the following is **not** one of the four criteria that normally must be met for revenue to be recognized according to the revenue principle for accrual basis accounting?
   a. The price is determinable.
   b. Services have been performed.
   c. Cash has been collected.
   d. Evidence of an arrangement exists.

3. The matching principle controls
   a. Where on the income statement expenses should be presented.
   b. How costs are allocated between Cost of Sales (sometimes called **Cost of Goods Sold**) and general and administrative expenses.
   c. The ordering of current assets and current liabilities on the balance sheet.
   d. When costs are recognized as expenses on the income statement.

4. When expenses exceed revenues in a given period,
   a. Retained earnings are not impacted.
   b. Retained earnings are increased.
   c. Retained earnings are decreased.
   d. One cannot determine the impact on retained earnings without additional information.

5. On January 1, 2010, Anson Company started the year with a $250,000 credit balance in Retained Earnings and $300,000 balance in Contributed Capital. During 2010, the company earned net income of $50,000, declared a dividend of $15,000 and issued more stock for $12,500. What is total stockholders' equity on December 31, 2010?
   a. $597,500.
   b. $585,000.
   c. $692,500.
   d. None of the above.

6. During 2009, CliffCo Inc., incurred operating expenses of $200,000 of which $150,000 was paid in cash; the balance will be paid in January 2010. Transaction analysis of operating expenses for 2009 should reflect only the following:
   a. Decrease stockholders' equity, $150,000; decrease assets, $150,000.
   b. Decrease assets, $200,000; decrease stockholders' equity, $200,000.
   c. Decrease assets, $200,000; increase liabilities, $50,000; decrease stockholders' equity, $150,000.
   d. Decrease stockholders' equity, $200,000; decrease assets, $150,000; increase liabilities, $50,000.
   e. None of the above is correct.

7. Which of the following is the entry to be recorded by a law firm when it receives a $2,000 retainer from a new client at the initial client meeting?
   a. Debit to Accounts Receivable, $2000; credit to Legal Fees Revenue, $2,000.
   b. Debit to Unearned Revenue, $2,000; credit to Legal Fees Revenue, $2,000.
   c. Debit to Cash, $2,000; credit to Unearned Revenue, $2,000.
   d. Debit to Unearned Revenue, $2,000; credit to Cash, $2,000.
   e. Debit to Cash, $2,000; credit to Legal Fees Revenue, $2,000.

8. You have observed that the asset turnover ratio for a retail chain has increased steadily over the last three years. The **most** likely explanation is which of the following?
   a. A successful advertising campaign increased sales companywide, but no new store locations were added over the last three years.
   b. Salaries for upper management as a percentage of total expenses have decreased over the last three years.
   c. New stores were added throughout the last three years, and sales increased as a result of the additional new locations.
   d. The company began construction of a new, larger main office location three years ago that was put into use at the end of the second year.

9. Cash payments for salaries are reported in what section of the Statement of Cash Flows?
   a. Financing.
   b. Operating.
   c. Investing.
   d. None of the above.

10. This period a company collects $100 cash on an account receivable from a customer for a sale last period. How would the receipt of cash impact the following two financial statements this period?

Income Statement	Statement of Cash Flows
a. Revenue + $100	Inflow from investing
b. No impact	Inflow from financing
c. Revenue − $100	Inflow from operations
d. No impact	Inflow from operations

For more practice on multiple choice questions, go to the text website at www.mhhe.com/libby6e.

 Available with McGraw-Hill's Homework Manager

MINI-**EXERCISES**

Matching Definitions with Terms

Match each definition with its related term by entering the appropriate letter in the space provided. There should be only one definition per term (that is, there are more definitions than terms).

M3-1
L01, 2, 3

Term	Definition
___ (1) Losses	A. Decreases in assets or increases in liabilities from ongoing operations.
___ (2) Matching principle	
___ (3) Revenues	B. Record revenues when earned and measurable (delivery of goods or services has been performed, there is persuasive evidence of an arrangement, the price is fixed or determinable, and collection is reasonably assured).
___ (4) Time period assumption	
___ (5) Operating cycle	
	C. Report the long life of a company in shorter time periods.
	D. Record expenses when incurred in earning revenue.
	E. The time it takes to purchase goods or services from suppliers, sell goods or services to customers, and collect cash from customers.
	F. Decreases in assets or increases in liabilities from peripheral transactions.
	G. Increases in assets or decreases in liabilities from ongoing operations.

Reporting Cash Basis versus Accrual Basis Income

M3-2
L03

Morrison Music Company had the following transactions in March:
a. Sold instruments to customers for $12,000; received $7,000 in cash and the rest on account. The cost of the instruments was $8,000.
b. Purchased $3,000 of new instruments inventory; paid $1,000 in cash and owed the rest on account.
c. Paid $500 in wages for the month.
d. Received a $200 bill for March utilities that will be paid in April.
e. Received $3,000 from customers as deposits on orders of new instruments to be sold to the customers in April.

Complete the following statements:

Cash Basis Income Statement	Accrual Basis Income Statement
Revenues	Revenues
Cash sales	Sales to customers
Customer deposits	
Expenses	Expenses
Inventory purchases	Cost of sales
Wages paid	Wages expense
	Utilities expense
Net income _____	Net income _____

M3-3   Identifying Revenues

LO2, 3

The following transactions are July 2011 activities of Bob's Bowling, Inc., which operates several bowling centers (for games and equipment sales). If revenue is to be recognized in **July**, indicate the revenue account title and amount. If revenue is not to be recognized in July, explain why.

Activity	Revenue Account Title and Amount
a. Bob's collected $11,000 from customers for games played in July.	
b. Bob's sold bowling equipment inventory for $6,000; received $4,000 in cash and the rest on account. [The cost of goods sold (expense) related to these sales is in M3-4e.]	
c. Bob's received $1,500 from customers on account who purchased merchandise in June.	
d. The men's and ladies' bowling leagues gave Bob's a deposit of $1,600 for the upcoming fall season.	

M3-4   Identifying Expenses

LO2, 3

The following transactions are July 2011 activities of Bob's Bowling, Inc., which operates several bowling centers (for games and equipment sales). If expense is to be recognized in **July**, indicate the expense account title and amount. If expense is not to be recognized in July, explain why.

Activity	Expense Account Title and Amount
e. Bob's sold bowling merchandise costing $2,190.	
f. Bob's paid $1,800 on the electricity bill for June (recorded as expense in June).	
g. Bob's paid $3,800 to employees for work in July.	
h. Bob's purchased $1,800 in insurance for coverage from July 1 to October 1.	
i. Bob's paid $1,200 to plumbers for repairing a broken pipe in the restrooms.	
j. Bob's received the July electricity bill for $2,300 to be paid in August.	

M3-5   Recording Revenues

LO4

For each of the transactions in M3–3, write the journal entry in good form.

M3-6   Recording Expenses

LO4

For each of the transactions in M3–4, write the journal entry in good form.

M3-7   Determining the Financial Statement Effects of Operating Activities Involving Revenues

LO4

The following transactions are July 2011 activities of Bob's Bowling, Inc., which operates several bowling centers (for games and equipment sales). For each of the following transactions, complete the tabulation, indicating the amount and effect (+ for increase and − for decrease) of each transaction. (Remember that A = L + SE, R − E = NI, and NI affects SE through Retained Earnings.) Write NE if there is no effect. The first transaction is provided as an example.

Transaction	BALANCE SHEET			INCOME STATEMENT		
	Assets	Liabil-ities	Stock-holders' Equity	Revenues	Expenses	Net Income
a. Bob's collected $11,000 from cus-tomers for games played in July.	+11,000	NE	+11,000	+11,000	NE	+11,000
b. Bob's sold $6,000 in bowling equip-ment inventory; received $4,000 in cash and the rest on account. (The cost of goods sold (expense) related to these sales is in M3-8e.)						
c. Bob's received $1,500 from cus-tomers on account who purchased merchandise in June.						
d. The men's and ladies' bowling leagues gave Bob's a deposit of $1,600 for the upcoming fall season.						

Determining the Financial Statement Effects of Operating Activities Involving Expenses

M3-8
LO4

The following transactions are July 2011 activities of Bob's Bowling, Inc., which operates several bowling centers (for games and equipment sales). For each of the following transactions, complete the tabulation, indicating the amount and effect (+ for increase and − for decrease) of each transaction. (Remember that A = L + SE, R − E = NI, and NI affects SE through Retained Earnings.) Write NE if there is no effect. The first transaction is provided as an example.

Transaction	BALANCE SHEET			INCOME STATEMENT		
	Assets	Liabil-ities	Stock-holders' Equity	Revenues	Expenses	Net Income
e. Bob's sold bowling merchandise costing $2,190.	−2,190	NE	−2,190	NE	+2,190	−2,190
f. Bob's paid $1,800 on the electricity bill for June (recorded as expense in June).						
g. Bob's paid $3,800 to employees for work in July.						
h. Bob's purchased $1,800 in insurance for coverage from July 1 to October 1.						
i. Bob's paid $1,200 to plumbers for repairing a broken pipe in the rest-rooms.						
j. Bob's received the July electricity bill for $2,300 to be paid in August.						

Preparing a Simple Income Statement

M3-9
LO5

Given the transactions in M3–7 and M3–8 (including the examples), prepare an income statement for Bob's Bowling, Inc., for the month of July 2011.

M3-10
L05

Preparing the Operating Activities Section of a Statement of Cash Flows

Given the transactions in M3–7 and M3–8 (including the examples), prepare the Operating Activities section of the statement of cash flows for Bob's Bowling, Inc., for the month of July 2011.

M3-11
L06

Computing and Explaining the Total Asset Turnover Ratio

The following data are from annual reports of Jill's Jewelry Company:

	2012	2011	2010
Total assets	$ 60,000	$ 53,000	$ 41,000
Total liabilities	14,000	11,000	6,000
Total stockholders' equity	46,000	42,000	35,000
Sales revenue	156,000	147,000	130,000
Net income	51,000	40,000	25,000

Compute Jill's total asset turnover ratio for 2012 and 2011. What do these results suggest to you about Jill's Jewelry Company?

EXERCISES

Available with McGraw-Hill's Homework Manager

E3-1
L01, 2, 3

Matching Definitions with Terms

Match each definition with its related term by entering the appropriate letter in the space provided. There should be only one definition per term (that is, there are more definitions than terms).

Term	Definition
_____ (1) Expenses	A. Report the long life of a company in shorter periods.
_____ (2) Gains	B. Record expenses when incurred in earning revenue.
_____ (3) Revenue principle	C. The time it takes to purchase goods or services from suppliers, sell goods or services to customers, and collect cash from customers.
_____ (4) Cash basis accounting	
_____ (5) Unearned revenue	
_____ (6) Operating cycle	D. A liability account used to record cash received before revenues have been earned.
_____ (7) Accrual basis accounting	E. Increases in assets or decreases in liabilities from peripheral transactions.
_____ (8) Prepaid expenses	
_____ (9) Revenues − Expenses = Net Income	F. Decreases in assets or increases in liabilities from ongoing operations.
_____ (10) Ending Retained Earnings = Beginning Retained Earnings + Net Income − Dividends Declared	G. Record revenues when earned and measurable (delivery of goods or services has occurred, there is persuasive evidence of an arrangement for customer payment, the price is fixed or determinable, and collection is reasonably assured).
	H. Decreases in assets or increases in liabilities from peripheral transactions.
	I. Record revenues when received and expenses when paid.
	J. The income statement equation.
	K. An asset account used to record cash paid before expenses have been incurred.
	L. The retained earnings equation.
	M. Record revenues when earned and expenses when incurred.

E3-2
L03

Reporting Cash Basis versus Accrual Basis Income

Ru's Sports, Inc., sells sports equipment to customers. Its fiscal year ends on December 31. The following transactions occurred in 2011:

a. Paid employees $54,200 in wages for the year; an additional $4,800 for 2011 wages will be paid in January 2012.

b. Purchased $334,000 of new sports equipment inventory; paid $90,000 in cash and owed the rest on account.

c. Sold sports equipment to customers for $410,000; received $340,000 in cash and the rest on account. The cost of the equipment was $287,000.

d. Paid $7,200 cash for utilities for the year.

e. Received $21,000 from customers as deposits on orders of new winter sports equipment to be sold to the customers in January 2012.

f. Received a $680 bill for December 2011 utilities that will be paid in January 2012.

Required:

1. Complete the following statements:

Cash Basis Income Statement		Accrual Basis Income Statement	
Revenues		Revenues	
Cash sales		Sales to customers	
Customer deposits			
Expenses		Expenses	
Inventory purchases		Cost of sales	
Wages paid		Wages expense	
Utilities paid	_____	Utilities expense	_____
Net income	======	Net income	======

2. Which basis of accounting (cash or accrual) provides more useful information to investors, creditors, and other users? Why?

Identifying Revenues

E3-3
LO2, 3

Revenues are normally recognized when the delivery of goods or services has occurred, there is persuasive evidence of an arrangement for customer payment, the price is fixed or determinable, and collection is reasonably assured. The amount recorded is the cash-equivalent sales price. The following transactions occurred in **September** 2012:

a. A customer orders and receives 10 personal computers from Dell; the customer promises to pay $18,400 within three months. Answer from Dell's standpoint.

b. Fucillo Hyundai, Inc., sells a truck with a list, or "sticker," price of $20,050 for $18,050 cash.

c. Bon-Ton Department Store orders 1,000 men's shirts from Arrow Shirt Company for $15 each for future delivery. The terms require payment in full within 30 days of delivery. Answer from Arrow's standpoint.

d. Arrow Shirt Company completes production of the shirts described in (c) and delivers the order. Answer from Arrow's standpoint.

e. Arrow receives payment from Bon-Ton for the order described in (c). Answer from Arrow's standpoint.

f. A customer purchases a ticket from American Airlines for $410 cash to travel the following January. Answer from American Airlines' standpoint.

g. General Motors issues $20 million in new common stock.

h. Penn State University receives $18,300,000 cash for 80,000 five-game season football tickets.

i. Penn State plays the first football game referred to in (h).

j. Precision Construction Company signs a contract with a customer for the construction of a new $500,000 warehouse. At the signing, Precision receives a check for $50,000 as a deposit on the future construction. Answer from Precision's standpoint.

k. On September 1, 2012, a bank lends $1,200 to a company; the note principal and $144 ($1,200 × 12 percent) annual interest are due in one year. Answer from the bank's standpoint.

l. A popular ski magazine company receives a total of $1,980 today from subscribers. The subscriptions begin in the next fiscal year. Answer from the magazine company's standpoint.

m. Sears, a retail store, sells a $100 lamp to a customer who charges the sale on his store credit card. Answer from Sears' standpoint.

Required:

For each of the transactions, if revenue is to be recognized in September, indicate the revenue account title and amount. If revenue is not to be recognized in September, explain why.

E3-4 Identifying Expenses

L02, 3

Revenues are normally recognized when goods or services have been provided and payment or promise of payment has been received. Expense recognition is guided by an attempt to match the costs associated with the generation of those revenues to the same time period. The following transactions occurred in **January** 2012:

a. Dell pays its computer service technicians $79,500 in salaries for the two weeks ended January 7. Answer from Dell's standpoint.

b. At the beginning of January, Turner Construction Company pays $4,410 in worker's compensation insurance for the first three months of the year.

c. McGraw-Hill Publishing Company uses $754 worth of electricity and natural gas in its headquarters building for which it has not yet been billed.

d. Arrow Shirt Company completes production of 500 men's shirts ordered by Bon-Ton's Department Store at a cost of $10 each and delivers the order. Answer from Arrow's standpoint.

e. The campus bookstore receives 500 accounting texts at a cost of $43 each. The terms indicate that payment is due within 30 days of delivery.

f. During the last week of January, the campus bookstore sold 450 accounting texts received in (e) at a sales price of $92 each.

g. Fucillo Hyundai, Inc., pays its salespersons $3,200 in commissions related to December automobile sales. Answer from Fucillo's standpoint.

h. On January 31, Fucillo Hyundai, Inc., determines that it will pay its salespersons $4,470 in commissions related to January sales. The payment will be made in early February. Answer from Fucillo's standpoint.

i. A new grill is purchased and installed at a Wendy's restaurant at the end of the day on January 31; a $8,750 cash payment is made on that day.

j. The University of Florida orders 60,000 season football tickets from its printer and pays $5,410 in advance for the custom printing. The first game will be played in September. Answer from the university's standpoint.

k. Carousel Mall had janitorial supplies costing $4,000 in storage. An additional $2,600 worth of supplies was purchased during January. At the end of January, $410 worth of janitorial supplies remained in storage.

l. An Iowa State University employee works eight hours, at $13 per hour, on January 31; however, payday is not until February 3. Answer from the university's point of view.

m. Wang Company paid $3,600 for a fire insurance policy on January 1. The policy covers 12 months beginning on January 1. Answer from Wang's point of view.

n. Darrius Incorporated has its delivery van repaired in January for $300 and charges the amount on account.

o. Haas Company, a farm equipment company, receives its phone bill at the end of January for $202 for January calls. The bill has not been paid to date.

p. Martin Company receives and pays in January a $1,285 invoice (bill) from a consulting firm for services received in January.

q. Parillo's Taxi Company pays a $595 invoice from a consulting firm for services received and recorded in December.

Required:

For each of the transactions, if an expense is to be recognized in January, indicate the expense account title and the amount. If an expense is not to be recognized in January, indicate why.

E3-5 Determining Financial Statement Effects of Various Transactions

L04

The following transactions occurred during a recent year:

a. Issued stock to organizers for cash (example).
b. Purchased equipment on credit.
c. Borrowed cash from local bank.
d. Earned revenue, collected cash.
e. Incurred expenses, on credit.
f. Earned revenue, on credit.
g. Paid cash on account.

h. Incurred expenses; paid cash.

i. Earned revenue; collected three-fourths in cash, balance on credit.

j. Declared and paid cash dividends.

k. Collected cash from customers on account.

l. Experienced theft (a loss) of $100 cash.

m. Incurred expenses; paid four-fifths in cash, balance on credit.

n. Paid income tax expense for the period.

Required:

For each of the transactions, complete the tabulation, indicating the effect (+ for increase and − for decrease) of each transaction. (Remember that A = L + SE, R − E = NI, and NI affects SE through Retained Earnings.) Write NE if there is no effect. The first transaction is provided as an example.

Transaction	BALANCE SHEET			INCOME STATEMENT		
	Assets	Liabilities	Stockholders' Equity	Revenues	Expenses	Net Income
(a) (example)	+	NE	+	NE	NE	NE

Determining Financial Statement Effects of Various Transactions

E3-6
LO4
Wolverine World Wide, Inc.

Wolverine World Wide, Inc., manufactures military, work, sport, and casual footwear and leather accessories under a variety of brand names, such as Hush Puppies, Wolverine, and Bates, to a global market. The following transactions occurred during a recent year. Dollars are in thousands.

a. Issued common stock to investors for $13,752 cash (example).

b. Purchased $723,261 of additional inventory on account.

c. Borrowed $61,685 on long-term notes.

d. Sold $1,141,887 of products to customers on account; cost of the products sold was $700,349.

e. Paid cash dividends of $16,079.

f. Purchased for cash $17,067 in additional property, plant, and equipment.

g. Incurred $318,240 in selling expenses, paying three-fourths in cash and owing the rest on account.

h. Earned $3,170 interest on investments, receiving 90 percent in cash.

i. Incurred $2,973 in interest expense to be paid at the beginning of next year.

Required:

For each of the transactions, complete the tabulation, indicating the effect (+ for increase and − for decrease) of each transaction. (Remember that A = L + SE, R − E = NI, and NI affects SE through Retained Earnings.) Write NE if there is no effect. The first transaction is provided as an example.

Transaction	BALANCE SHEET			INCOME STATEMENT		
	Assets	Liabilities	Stockholders' Equity	Revenues	Expenses	Net Income
(a) (example)	+13,752	NE	+13,752	NE	NE	NE

Recording Journal Entries

E3-7
LO4
Sysco

Sysco, formed in 1969, is North America's largest marketer and distributor of food service products, serving approximately 400,000 restaurants, hotels, schools, hospitals, and other institutions. The following summarized transactions are typical of those that occurred in a recent year (dollars are in thousands).

a. Borrowed $185,000 from a bank, signing a short-term note.

b. Provided $29,335 in service to customers during the year, with $21,300 on account and the rest received in cash.

c. Purchased plant and equipment for $530,000 in cash.

d. Purchased $23,836 inventory on account.

e. Paid payroll, $3,102 during the year.

f. Received $21,120 on account paid by customers.

g. Purchased and used fuel of $730,000 in delivery vehicles during the year (paid for in cash).

h. Declared and paid $310,000 in dividends for the year.

i. Paid $4,035 cash on accounts payable.

j. Incurred $61,000 in utility usage during the year; paid $53,000 in cash and owed the rest on account.

Required:

For each of the transactions, prepare journal entries. Determine whether the accounting equation remains in balance and debits equal credits after each entry.

E3-8   Recording Journal Entries

LO4

Vail Resorts, Inc.

Vail Resorts, Inc., owns and operates five premier year-round ski resort properties (Vail Mountain, Beaver Creek Resort, Breckenridge Mountain, and Keystone Resort, all located in the Colorado Rocky Mountains, and Heavenly Valley Mountain Resort, located in the Lake Tahoe area of California/Nevada). The company also owns a collection of luxury hotels, resorts, and lodging properties. The company sells lift tickets, ski lessons, and ski equipment. The following hypothetical December transactions are typical of those that occur at the resorts.

a. Borrowed $2,500,000 from the bank on December 1, signing a note payable due in six months.

b. Purchased a new snowplow for $90,000 cash on December 31.

c. Purchased ski equipment inventory for $40,000 on account to sell in the ski shops.

d. Incurred $62,000 in routine maintenance expenses for the chairlifts; paid cash.

e. Sold $372,000 of January through March season passes and received cash.

f. Sold daily lift passes in December for a total of $270,000 in cash.

g. Sold a pair of skis from a ski shop to a customer for $750 on account. (The cost of the skis was $450.)

h. Received a $3,200 deposit on a townhouse to be rented for five days in January.

i. Paid half the charges incurred on account in (c).

j. Received $200 on account from the customer in (g).

k. Paid $258,000 in wages to employees for the month of December.

Required:

1. Prepare journal entries for each transaction. (Remember to check that debits equal credits and that the accounting equation is in balance after each transaction.)

2. Assume that Vail Resorts had a $1,200 balance in Accounts Receivable at the beginning of December. Determine the ending balance in the Accounts Receivable account at the end of December based on transactions (a) through (k). Show your work in T-account format.

E3-9   Recording Journal Entries

LO4

Rowland & Sons Air Transport Service, Inc., has been in operation for three years. The following transactions occurred in February:

February 1	Paid $225 for rent of hangar space in February.
February 2	Purchased fuel costing $490 on account for the next flight to Dallas.
February 4	Received customer payment of $820 to ship several items to Philadelphia next month.
February 7	Flew cargo from Denver to Dallas; the customer paid $910 for the air transport.
February 10	Paid pilot $1,300 in wages for flying in January.
February 14	Paid $75 for an advertisement in the local paper to run on February 19.
February 18	Flew cargo for two customers from Dallas to Albuquerque for $1,800; one customer paid $600 cash and the other asked to be billed.
February 25	Purchased on account $1,550 in spare parts for the planes.
February 27	Declared a $250 cash dividend to be paid in March.

Required:

Prepare journal entries for each transaction. Be sure to categorize each account as an asset (A), liability (L), stockholders' equity (SE), revenue (R), or expense (E).

Analyzing the Effects of Transactions in T-Accounts and Computing Cash Basis versus Accrual Basis Net Income

E3-10
LO3, 4

Eddy's Piano Rebuilding Company has been operating for one year (2010). At the start of 2011, its income statement accounts had zero balances and its balance sheet account balances were as follows:

Cash	$ 7,200	Unearned fee revenue (deposits)	$ 3,840
Accounts receivable	30,000	Note payable (long-term)	48,000
Supplies	1,440	Contributed capital	9,600
Equipment	9,600	Retained earnings	10,800
Land	7,200	Building	26,400
Accounts payable	9,600		

Required:

1. Create T-accounts for the balance sheet accounts and for these additional accounts: Rebuilding Fees Revenue, Rent Revenue, Wages Expense, and Utilities Expense. Enter the beginning balances.

2. Enter the following January 2011 transactions in the T-accounts, using the letter of each transaction as the reference:
   a. Received a $600 deposit from a customer who wanted her piano rebuilt.
   b. Rented a part of the building to a bicycle repair shop; received $360 for rent in January.
   c. Rebuilt and delivered five pianos in January to customers who paid $17,400 in cash.
   d. Received $7,200 from customers as payment on their accounts.
   e. Received an electric and gas utility bill for $420 to be paid in February.
   f. Ordered $960 in supplies.
   g. Paid $2,040 on account in January.
   h. Received from the home of Ms. Eddy, the major shareholder, a $720 tool (equipment) to use in the business.
   i. Paid $12,000 in wages to employees who worked in January.
   j. Declared and paid a $3,600 dividend.
   k. Received and paid cash for the supplies in (*f*).

3. Using the data from the T-accounts, amounts for the following on January 31, 2011, were

   Revenues $_____ − Expenses $_____ = Net Income $_____
   Assets $_____ = Liabilities $_____ + Stockholders' Equity $_____

4. What is net income if Eddy's used the cash basis of accounting? Why does this differ from accrual basis net income (in requirement 3)?

Preparing an Income Statement, Statement of Retained Earnings, and Classified Balance Sheet

E3-11
LO5

Refer to E3–10.

Required:

Use the ending balances in the T-accounts in E3–10 to prepare the following:

1. An income statement for January 2011 in good form (ignore income taxes).
2. A statement of retained earnings for January 2011.
3. A classified balance sheet as of January 31, 2011, in good form.

Preparing a Statement of Cash Flows

E3-12
LO5

Refer to E3–10.

Required:

Use the transactions in E3–10 to prepare a statement of cash flows in good form.

E3-13   **Analyzing the Effects of Transactions in T-Accounts**

L04

Wendy Fonder and Susan Engelkemeyer had been operating a catering business, Traveling Gourmet, for several years. In March 2011, the partners were planning to expand by opening a retail sales shop and decided to form the business as a corporation called Traveling Gourmet, Inc. The following transactions occurred in March 2011:

a. Received $20,000 cash from each of the two shareholders to form the corporation, in addition to $2,000 in accounts receivable, $5,300 in equipment, a van (equipment) appraised at a fair market value of $13,000, and $1,200 in supplies.

b. Purchased a vacant store for sale in a good location for $160,000, making a $20,000 cash down payment and signing a 10-year mortgage from a local bank for the rest.

c. Borrowed $75,000 from the local bank on a 10 percent, one-year note.

d. Purchased and used food and paper supplies costing $8,830 in March; paid cash.

e. Made and sold food at the retail store for $10,900 cash.

f. Catered four parties in March for $3,200; $1,500 was billed, and the rest was received in cash.

g. Received a $320 telephone bill for March to be paid in April.

h. Paid $63 in gas for the van in March.

i. Paid $5,080 in wages to employees who worked in March.

j. Paid a $300 dividend from the corporation to each owner.

k. Purchased $35,000 of equipment (refrigerated display cases, cabinets, tables, and chairs) and renovated and decorated the new store for $20,000 (added to the cost of the building); paid cash.

Required:

1. Set up appropriate T-accounts for Cash, Accounts Receivable, Supplies, Equipment, Building, Accounts Payable, Note Payable, Mortgage Payable, Contributed Capital, Retained Earnings, Food Sales Revenue, Catering Sales Revenue, Cost of Food and Paper Products, Utilities Expense, Wages Expense, and Fuel Expense.

2. Record in the T-accounts the effects of each transaction for Traveling Gourmet, Inc., in March. Identify the amounts with the letters starting with (*a*). Compute ending balances.

E3-14   **Preparing an Income Statement, Statement of Retained Earnings, and Classified Balance**
L05   **Sheet**

Refer to E3–13.

Required:

Use the balances in the completed T-accounts in E3–13 to respond to the following:
1. Prepare an income statement in good form for the month of March 2011.
2. Prepare a statement of retained earnings for the month of March 2011.
3. Prepare a classified balance sheet in good form as of March 2011.
4. What do you think about the success of this company based on the results of the first month of operation?

E3-15   **Preparing a Statement of Cash Flows**
L05   Refer to E3–13.

Required:

Use the transactions in E3–13 to prepare a statement of cash flows in good form.

E3-16   **Inferring Operating Transactions and Preparing an Income Statement and Balance Sheet**
L02, 3, 4, 5

Katie's Kite Company (a corporation) sells and repairs kites from manufacturers around the world. Its stores are located in rented space in malls and shopping centers. During its first month of operations ended April 30, 2010, Katie's Kite Company completed eight transactions with the dollar effects indicated in the following schedule:

Accounts	DOLLAR EFFECT OF EACH OF THE EIGHT TRANSACTIONS								Ending Balance
	(a)	(b)	(c)	(d)	(e)	(f)	(g)	(h)	
Cash	$62,000	$(12,400)	$(6,200)	$ 8,680	$(2,480)	$(1,240)		$3,720	
Accounts Receivable				3,720					
Inventory			24,800	(3,720)					
Prepaid Expenses					1,860				
Store Fixtures		12,400							
Accounts Payable			18,600				$1,480		
Unearned Revenue								2,480	
Contributed Capital	62,000								
Sales Revenue				12,400				1,240	
Cost of Sales				3,720					
Wages Expense						1,240			
Rent Expense					620				
Utilities Expense							1,480		

Required:

1. Write a brief explanation of transactions (a) through (h). Include any assumptions that you made.
2. Compute the ending balance in each account and prepare an income statement and a classified balance sheet for Katie's Kite Company on April 30, 2010.

Analyzing the Effects of Transactions Using T-Accounts and Interpreting the Total Asset Turnover Ratio as a Financial Analyst

E3-17
LO4, 6

DeVita Company, which has been operating for three years, provides marketing consulting services worldwide for dot-com companies. You are a financial analyst assigned to report on the DeVita management team's effectiveness at managing its assets efficiently. At the start of 2012 (its fourth year), DeVita's T-account balances were as follows. Dollars are in thousands.

Assets

Cash		Accounts Receivable		Long-Term Investments	
3,200		8,000		6,400	

Liabilities

Accounts Payable		Unearned Revenue		Long-Term Notes Payable	
	2,400		5,600		1,600

Stockholders' Equity

Contributed Capital		Retained Earnings	
	4,800		3,200

Revenues

Consulting Fee Revenue		Investment Income	

Expenses

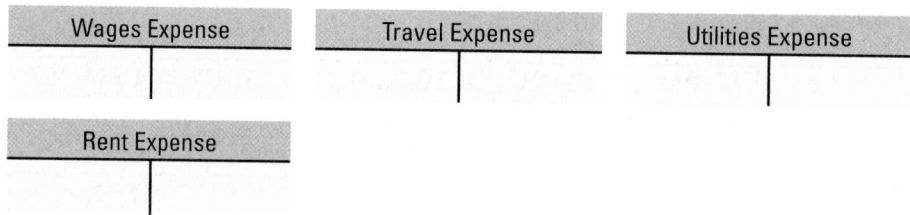

Required:

1. Using the data from these T-accounts, amounts for the following on January 1, 2012, were

    Assets $_____$ = Liabilities $ _____$ + Stockholders' Equity $_____$.

2. Enter the following 2012 transactions in the T-accounts:

    a. Received $5,600 cash from clients on account.

    b. Provided $56,000 in services to clients who paid $48,000 in cash and owed the rest on account.

    c. Received $400 in cash as income on investments.

    d. Paid $16,000 in wages, $16,000 in travel, $9,600 rent, and $1,600 on accounts payable.

    e. Received a utility bill for $800 for 2012 services.

    f. Paid $480 in dividends to stockholders.

    g. Received $1,600 in cash from clients in advance of services DeVita will provide next year.

3. Compute ending balances in the T-accounts to determine amounts for the following on December 31, 2012:

    Revenues $_____$ − Expenses $_____$ = Net Income $_____$.

    Assets $_____$ = Liabilities $ _____$ + Stockholders' Equity $_____$.

4. Calculate the total asset turnover ratio for 2012. If the company had an asset turnover ratio in 2011 of 2.00 and in 2010 of 1.80, what does your computation suggest to you about DeVita Company? What would you say in your report?

E3-18
LO4
The New York Times Company

Inferring Transactions and Computing Effects Using T-Accounts

A recent annual report of The New York Times Company, a diversified media company that currently includes newspapers (including *The New York Times*), Internet businesses, and television and radio stations, included the following accounts. Dollars are in millions:

Accounts Receivable				Prepaid Expenses				Unearned Subscriptions		
1/1	440			1/1	70				82	1/1
	3,143	?			378	?		?	147	
12/31	403			12/31	243				83	12/31

Required:

1. For each T-account, describe the typical transactions that affect each account (that is, the economic events that occur to make these accounts increase and decrease).

2. For each T-account, compute the missing amounts.

E3-19   **Finding Financial Information as an Investor**

You are evaluating your current portfolio of investments to determine those that are not performing to your expectations. You have all of the companies' most recent annual reports.

Required:

For each of the following, indicate where you would locate the information in an annual report. (**Hint:** The information may be in more than one location.)

1. Description of a company's primary business(es).

2. Income taxes paid.

3. Accounts receivable.

4. Cash flow from operating activities.
5. Description of a company's revenue recognition policy.
6. The inventory sold during the year.
7. The data needed to compute the total asset turnover ratio.

Available with McGraw-Hill's Homework Manager

PROBLEMS

Recording Nonquantitative Journal Entries (AP3–1)

P3-1
LO4

The following list includes a series of accounts for Sanjeev Corporation that has been operating for three years. These accounts are listed and numbered for identification. Following the accounts is a series of transactions. For each transaction, indicate the account(s) that should be debited and credited by entering the appropriate account number(s) to the right of each transaction. If no journal entry is needed, write **none** after the transaction. The first transaction is used as an example.

Account No.	Account Title	Account No.	Account Title
1	Cash	9	Wages Payable
2	Accounts Receivable	10	Income Taxes Payable
3	Supplies on Hand	11	Contributed Capital
4	Prepaid Expenses	12	Retained Earnings
5	Equipment	13	Service Revenue
6	Patents	14	Operating Expenses (wages, supplies)
7	Accounts Payable	15	Income Tax Expense
8	Note Payable	16	Interest Expense

Transactions	Debit	Credit
a. Example: Purchased equipment for use in the business; paid one-third cash and signed a note payable for the balance.	5	1, 8
b. Paid cash for salaries and wages earned by employees this period.	___	___
c. Collected cash on accounts receivable for services performed last period.	___	___
d. Purchased a patent (an intangible asset); paid cash.	___	___
e. Performed services this period on credit.	___	___
f. Paid cash on accounts payable for expenses incurred last period.	___	___
g. Issued stock to new investors.	___	___
h. Paid operating expenses incurred this period.	___	___
i. Incurred operating expenses this period to be paid next period.	___	___
j. Purchased supplies to be used later; paid cash.	___	___
k. Collected cash for services performed this period.	___	___
l. Used some of the supplies on hand for operations.	___	___
m. Paid three-fourths of the income tax expense for the year; the balance will be paid next year.	___	___
n. Made a payment on the equipment note in (a); the payment was part principal and part interest expense.	___	___
o. On the last day of the current period, paid cash for an insurance policy covering the next two years.	___	___

Recording Journal Entries (AP3–2)

P3-2
LO4

Chris Chudkosky organized a new company, CollegeCaps, Inc. The company operates a small store in an area mall and specializes in baseball-type caps with logos printed on them. Chris, who is never without a cap, believes that his target market is college and high school students. You have been hired to record the transactions occurring in the first two weeks of operations.

a. Issued 1,000 shares of stock to investors for cash at $30 per share.
b. Borrowed $50,000 from the bank to provide additional funding to begin operations; the note is due in two years.
c. Paid $1,200 for the current month's rent and another $1,200 for next month's rent.

 d. Paid $2,400 for a one-year fire insurance policy (recorded as a prepaid expense).
 e. Purchased furniture and fixtures for the store for $15,000 on account. The amount is due within 30 days.
 f. Purchased The University of Texas, Texas Christian University, Texas A&M, and Michigan State University baseball caps as inventory to sell in the store for $1,800 cash.
 g. Placed advertisements in local college newspapers for a total of $250 cash.
 h. Sold caps totaling $400, half of which was charged on account. The cost of the caps sold was $150.
 i. Made full payment for the furniture and fixtures purchased on account in (e).
 j. Received $50 from a customer on account.

Required:

For each of the transactions, prepare journal entries. Be sure to categorize each account as an asset (A), liability (L), stockholders' equity (SE), revenue (R), or expense (E). Note that transaction (h) will require two entries, one for revenue and one for the related expense.

P3-3 **Determining Financial Statement Effects of Various Transactions and Identifying Cash**
LO4 **Flow Effects** (AP3-3)

According to its annual report, Wendy's International serves "the best hamburgers in the business" and other fresh food including salads, chicken sandwiches, and baked potatoes in more than 6,600 restaurants worldwide. The company operates its own restaurants and sells franchises to others. The following activities were inferred from a recent annual report.

 a. Purchased food and paper products; paid part in cash and the rest on account.
 b. Purchased additional investments.
 c. Paid cash dividends.
 d. Served food to customers for cash.
 e. Used food and paper products.
 f. Incurred restaurant operating costs in company-owned facilities; paid part in cash and the rest on account.
 g. Sold franchises, receiving part in cash and the rest in notes due from franchisees.
 h. Paid interest on debt incurred and due during the period.

Required:

1. For each of the transactions, complete the tabulation, indicating the effect (+ for increase and − for decrease) of each transaction. (Remember that A = L + SE, R − E = NI, and NI affects SE through Retained Earnings.) Write NE if there is no effect. The first transaction is provided as an example.

	BALANCE SHEET			INCOME STATEMENT		
Transaction	Assets	Liabilities	Stockholders' Equity	Revenues	Expenses	Net Income
(a) (example)	+/−	+	NE	NE	NE	NE

2. Where, if at all, would each transaction be reported on the statement of cash flows? Use O for operating activities, I for investing activities, F for financing activities, and NE if the transaction would not be included on the statement.

P3-4 **Analyzing the Effects of Transactions Using T-Accounts, Preparing Financial Statements,**
LO4, 5, 6 **and Evaluating the Total Asset Turnover Ratio as a Manager** (AP3-4)

Syrena Shirley, a connoisseur of fine chocolate, opened Syrena's Sweets in Collegetown on February 1, 2011. The shop specializes in a selection of gourmet chocolate candies and a line of gourmet ice cream. You have been hired as manager. Your duties include maintaining the store's financial records. The following transactions occurred in February 2011, the first month of operations.

eXcel

 a. Received four shareholders' contributions totaling $17,600 cash to form the corporation; issued stock.
 b. Paid three months' rent for the store at $880 per month (recorded as prepaid expenses).
 c. Purchased supplies for $330 cash.
 d. Purchased and received candy for $5,500 on account, due in 60 days.
 e. Negotiated and signed a two-year $11,000 loan at the bank.

f. Used the money from (e) to purchase a computer for $2,750 (for recordkeeping and inventory tracking) and the balance for furniture and fixtures for the store.

g. Placed a grand opening advertisement in the local paper for $500 cash.

h. Made sales on Valentine's Day totaling $2,000; $1,675 was in cash and the rest on accounts receivable. The cost of the candy sold was $1,100.

i. Made a $550 payment on accounts payable.

j. Incurred and paid employee wages of $450.

k. Collected accounts receivable of $55 from customers.

l. Made a repair to one of the display cases for $130 cash.

m. Made cash sales of $2,200 during the rest of the month. The cost of the candy sold was $1,210.

Required:

1. Set up appropriate T-accounts for Cash, Accounts Receivable, Supplies, Merchandise Inventory, Prepaid Expenses, Equipment, Furniture and Fixtures, Accounts Payable, Notes Payable, Contributed Capital, Sales Revenue, Cost of Goods Sold (expense), Advertising Expense, Wage Expense, and Repair Expense. All accounts begin with zero balances.

2. Record in the T-accounts the effects of each transaction for Syrena's Sweets in February, referencing each transaction in the accounts with the transaction letter. Show the ending balances in the T-accounts. Note that transactions (h) and (m) require two types of entries, one for revenue recognition and one for the expense.

3. Prepare financial statements at the end of the month ended February 28, 2011 (income statement, statement of retained earnings, and balance sheet).

4. Write a short memo to Syrena offering your opinion on the results of operations during the first month of business.

5. After three years in business, you are being evaluated for a promotion. One measure is how efficiently you managed the assets of the business. The following data are available:

	2013*	2012	2011
Total assets	$88,000	$49,500	$38,500
Total liabilities	49,500	22,000	16,500
Total stockholders' equity	38,500	27,500	22,000
Total sales	93,500	82,500	55,000
Net income	22,000	11,000	4,400

*At the end of 2013, Syrena decided to open a second store, requiring loans and inventory purchases prior to the opening in early 2014.

Required:
Compute the total asset turnover ratio for 2012 and 2013 and evaluate the results. Do you think you should be promoted? Why?

Preparing a Statement of Cash Flows (AP3–5)

Refer to P3–4.

Required:
For the transactions listed in P3–4, prepare a statement of cash flows for the month.

Analyzing the Effects of Transactions Using T-Accounts, Preparing Financial Statements, and Evaluating the Total Asset Turnover Ratio (AP3–6)

Following are several account balances (in millions of dollars) from a recent FedEx annual report, followed by several typical transactions. Assume that the following are account balances on June 30, 2009:

Account	Balance	Account	Balance
Flight and ground equipment	$3,476	Contributed capital	$ 702
Retained earnings	970	Receivables	923
Accounts payable	554	Other assets	1,011
Prepaid expenses	64	Cash	155
Accrued expenses payable	761	Spare parts, supplies, and fuel	164
Long-term notes payable	2,016	Other noncurrent liabilities	790

P3-5
LO5

www.mhhe.com/
libby6e

P3-6
LO4, 5, 6
FedEx

www.mhhe.com/libby6e

These accounts are not necessarily in good order and have normal debit or credit balances. The following transactions (in millions of dollars) occurred the next year ending June 30, 2010:

a. Provided delivery service to customers, receiving $7,200 in accounts receivable and $600 in cash.
b. Purchased new equipment costing $816; signed a long-term note.
c. Paid $744 cash to rent equipment and aircraft, with $648 for rental this year and the rest for rent next year.
d. Spent $396 cash to maintain and repair facilities and equipment during the year.
e. Collected $6,524 from customers on account.
f. Borrowed $900 by signing a long-term note.
g. Issued additional stock for $240.
h. Paid employees $3,804 during the year.
i. Purchased for cash and used $492 in fuel for the aircraft and equipment during the year.
j. Paid $384 on accounts payable.
k. Ordered $72 in spare parts and supplies.

Required:

1. Prepare T-accounts for June 30, 2009, from the preceding list; enter the respective beginning balances. You will need additional T-accounts for income statement accounts; enter zero balances.
2. For each transaction, record the 2010 effects in the T-accounts. Label each using the letter of the transaction. Compute ending balances.
3. Prepare an income statement, statement of retained earnings, balance sheet, and statement of cash flows in good form for June 30, 2010.
4. Compute the company's total asset turnover ratio for the year ended June 30, 2010. What does it suggest to you about FedEx?

P3-7   Recording Journal Entries and Identifying Cash Flow Effects

L04

Cedar Fair

www.mhhe.com/libby6e

Cedar Fair, L. P. (Limited Partnership) is one of the largest regional amusement park operators in the world, owning 12 amusement parks, five outdoor water parks, one indoor water park, and six hotels. The parks include Cedar Point in Ohio, Valleyfair near Minneapolis/St. Paul, Dorney Park and Wildwater Kingdom near Allentown, Pennsylvania, Worlds of Fun/Oceans of Fun in Kansas City, Great America in Santa Clara, California, and Canada's Wonderland near Toronto, Canada, among others. The following are summarized transactions similar to those that occurred in a recent year (assume 2011). Dollars are in thousands:

a. Guests at the parks paid $459,475 cash in admissions.
b. The primary operating expenses (such as employee wages, utilities, repairs and maintenance, and depreciation on the rides, buildings, and equipment) for the year were $430,967 with $402,200 paid in cash and the rest on account.
c. Interest paid on long-term debt was $88,294.
d. The parks sell food and merchandise and operate games. The cash received during the year for these combined activities was $306,914. The cost of merchandise sold during the year was $80,202.
e. Cedar Fair purchased and built additional buildings, rides, and equipment during the year, paying $1,312,919 in cash.
f. Guests may stay in the parks at accommodations owned by the company. During the year, accommodations revenue was $65,000; $62,910 was paid by the guests in cash and the rest was owed on account.
g. Cedar Fair paid $64,962 principal on notes payable.
h. The company purchased $146,100 in food and merchandise inventory for the year, paying $118,000 in cash and owing the rest on account.
i. The selling, general, and administrative expenses such as the president's salary and advertising for the parks, classified as operating expenses, for the year were $100,724; $95,500 was paid in cash, and the rest was owed on account.
j. Cedar Fair paid $29,600 on accounts payable during the year.

Required:

1. For each of these transactions, record journal entries. Use the letter of each transaction as its reference. Note that transaction (d) will require two entries, one for revenue recognition and one for the related expense.

2. Use the following chart to identify whether each transaction results in a cash flow effect from operating (O), investing (I), or financing (F) activities, and indicate the direction and amount of the effect on cash (+ for increase and − for decrease). If there is no cash flow effect, write **none.** The first transaction is provided as an example.

Transaction	Operating, Investing, or Financing Effect	Direction and Amount of the Effect (in thousands)
(a)	O	+459,475

ALTERNATE PROBLEMS

Recording Nonquantitative Journal Entries (P3–1)

AP3-1
LO4

The following is a series of accounts for Kruger & Laurenzo, Incorporated, that has been operating for two years. The accounts are listed and numbered for identification. Following the accounts is a series of transactions. For each transaction, indicate the account(s) that should be debited and credited by entering the appropriate account number(s) to the right of each transaction. If no journal entry is needed, write **none** after the transaction. The first transaction is given as an example.

Account No.	Account Title	Account No.	Account Title
1	Cash	9	Wages Payable
2	Accounts Receivable	10	Income Taxes Payable
3	Supplies	11	Contributed Capital
4	Prepaid Expenses	12	Retained Earnings
5	Buildings	13	Service Revenue
6	Land	14	Other Expenses (wages, supplies, interest)
7	Accounts Payable	15	Income Tax Expense
8	Mortgage Payable		

Transactions	Debit	Credit
a. *Example:* Issued stock to new investors.	1	11
b. Purchased on credit but did not use supplies this period.		
c. Performed services for customers this period on credit.		
d. Prepaid a fire insurance policy this period to cover the next 12 months.		
e. Purchased a building this period by making a 20 percent cash down payment and signing a mortgage loan for the balance.		
f. Collected cash this year for services rendered and recorded in the prior year.		
g. Collected cash for services rendered this period.		
h. Paid cash this period for wages earned and recorded last period.		
i. Paid cash for operating expenses charged on accounts payable in the prior period.		
j. Paid cash for operating expenses incurred in the current period.		
k. Incurred and recorded operating expenses on credit to be paid next period.		
l. This period a shareholder sold some shares of her stock to another person for an amount above the original issuance price.		
m. Used supplies on hand to clean the offices.		
n. Recorded income taxes for this period to be paid at the beginning of the next period.		
o. Declared and paid a cash dividend this period.		
p. Made a payment on the building, which was part principal repayment and part interest.		

Recording Journal Entries (P3–2)

AP3-2
LO4

James Evans is the president of ServicePro, Inc., a company that provides temporary employees for not-for-profit companies. ServicePro has been operating for five years; its revenues are increasing with each passing year. You have been hired to help James analyze the following transactions for the first two weeks of April:

a. Billed the local United Way office $23,500 for temporary services provided.
b. Paid $3,005 for supplies purchased and recorded on account last period.
c. Placed an advertisement in the local paper for $1,400 cash.
d. Purchased a new computer for the office costing $3,800 cash.
e. Purchased office supplies for $2,600 on account.
f. Paid employee wages of $11,900. Of this amount, $3,800 had been earned and recorded in the Wages Payable account in the prior period.
g. Issued 3,000 additional shares of capital stock for cash at $40 per share in anticipation of building a new office.
h. Received $8,000 on account from the local United Way office from the services provided in (a).
i. Billed Family & Children's Service $14,500 for services rendered.
j. Purchased land as the site of a future office for $10,000. Paid $3,000 cash down and signed a note payable for the balance.
k. Received the April telephone bill for $1,950 to be paid next month.

Required:
For each of the transactions, prepare journal entries. Be sure to categorize each account as an asset (A), liability (L), stockholders' equity (SE), revenue (R), or expense (E).

AP3-3
LO4
Big Dog Holdings, Inc.

Determining Financial Statement Effects of Various Transactions and Identifying Cash Flow Effects (P3–3)

Big Dog Holdings, Inc., is the parent company of Big Dog USA, a company that develops, markets, and retails a collection of consumer products centered around the signature BIG DOGS® name, logo, and "Big Dog" characters. The following activities were inferred from a recent annual report.

a. *Example:* Incurred expenses, paid part cash and part on credit.
b. Sold merchandise to customers on account. (**Hint:** Indicate the effects for the sale; then reduce inventory for the amount sold—two transactions.)
c. Sold investments for cash for more than their cost.
d. Collected cash on account.
e. Used supplies.
f. Repaid long-term debt principal.
g. Paid interest on long-term debt.
h. Purchased equipment; paid part cash and part on credit.
i. Paid cash on account.
j. Issued additional stock.
k. Paid rent to discount mall owners.
l. Received dividends and interest on investments.

Required:
1. For each of the transactions, complete the tabulation, indicating the effect (+ for increase and − for decrease) of each transaction. (Remember that A = L + SE, R − E = NI, and NI affects SE through Retained Earnings.) Write NE if there is no effect. The first transaction is provided as an example.

	BALANCE SHEET			INCOME STATEMENT		
Transaction	Assets	Liabilities	Stockholders' Equity	Revenues	Expenses	Net Income
(a) (example)	−	+	−	NE	+	−

2. For each transaction, indicate where, if at all, it would be reported on the statement of cash flows. Use O for operating activities, I for investing activities, F for financing activities, and NE if the transaction would not be included on the statement.

Analyzing the Effects of Transactions Using T-Accounts, Preparing Financial Statements, and Evaluating the Total Asset Turnover Ratio as a Manager (P3–4)

AP3-4
LO4, 5, 6

Spicewood Stables, Inc., was established in Austin, Texas, on April 1, 2010. The company provides stables, care for animals, and grounds for riding and showing horses. You have been hired as the new assistant controller. The following transactions for April 2010 are provided for your review.

a. Received contributions from five investors of $60,000 in cash ($12,000 each), a barn valued at $100,000, land valued at $90,000, and supplies valued at $12,000. Each investor received 3,000 shares of stock.

b. Built a small barn for $62,000. The company paid half the amount in cash on April 1, 2010, and signed a three-year note payable for the balance.

c. Provided $35,260 in animal care services for customers, all on credit.

d. Rented stables to customers who cared for their own animals; received cash of $13,200.

e. Received from a customer $2,400 to board her horse in May, June, and July (record as unearned revenue).

f. Purchased hay and feed supplies on account for $3,210 to be used in the summer.

g. Paid $1,240 in cash for water utilities incurred in the month.

h. Paid $2,700 on accounts payable for previous purchases.

i. Received $10,000 from customers on accounts receivable.

j. Paid $6,000 in wages to employees who worked during the month.

k. At the end of the month, purchased a two-year insurance policy for $3,600.

l. Received an electric utility bill for $1,800 for usage in April; the bill will be paid next month.

m. Paid $100 cash dividend to each of the investors at the end of the month.

Required:

1. Set up appropriate T-accounts. All accounts begin with zero balances.

2. Record in the T-accounts the effects of each transaction for Spicewood Stables in April, referencing each transaction in the accounts with the transaction letter. Show the ending balances in the T-accounts.

3. Prepare financial statements at the end of April (income statement, statement of retained earnings, and balance sheet).

4. Write a short memo to the five owners offering your opinion on the results of operations during the first month of business.

5. After three years in business, you are being evaluated for a promotion to chief financial officer. One measure is how efficiently you managed the assets of the business. The following annual data are available:

	2012*	2011	2010
Total assets	$480,000	$320,000	$300,000
Total liabilities	125,000	28,000	30,000
Total stockholders' equity	355,000	292,000	270,000
Total revenues	450,000	400,000	360,000
Net income	50,000	30,000	(10,000)

*At the end of 2012, Spicewood Stables decided to build an indoor riding arena for giving lessons year-round. The company borrowed construction funds from a local bank in 2012, and the arena was opened in early 2013.

Compute the total asset turnover ratio for 2011 and 2012 and evaluate the results. Do you think you should be promoted? Why?

Preparing a Statement of Cash Flows (P3–5)

Refer to AP3–4.

AP3-5
LO5

Required:
For the transactions listed in AP3–4, prepare a statement of cash flows for the month.

AP3-6

LO4, 5, 6

Exxon Mobil Corporation

Analyzing the Effects of Transactions Using T-Accounts, Preparing Financial Statements, and Evaluating the Total Asset Turnover Ratio (P3–6)

The following are the summary account balances from a recent balance sheet of Exxon Mobil Corporation. The accounts have normal debit or credit balances, but they are not necessarily listed in good order. The amounts are shown in millions of dollars. Assume the year-end is December 31, 2010.

Cash	$ 1,157	Marketable securities	
Notes payable (long-term)	3,858	(short-term investments)	$ 618
Accounts receivable	8,073	Accounts payable	13,391
Inventories	5,541	Income tax payable	2,244
Other debt	30,954	Prepaid expenses	1,071
Property and equipment, net	63,425	Investments	5,394
Shareholders' equity*	37,415	Intangibles, net	2,583

* This account is a combination of Contributed Capital and Retained Earnings.

The following is a list of hypothetical transactions for January 2011.

a. Purchased on account $150,000,000 of new equipment.
b. Received $500,000,000 on accounts receivable.
c. Received and paid $1,000,000 for utility bills.
d. Earned $5,000,000 in sales on account with customers; cost of sales was $1,000,000.
e. Paid employees $1,000,000 for wages earned during the month.
f. Paid half of the income taxes payable.
g. Purchased $23,000,000 in supplies on account (include in Inventories).
h. Prepaid $12,000,000 to rent a warehouse next month.
i. Paid $10,000,000 of other debt and $1,000,000 in interest on the debt.
j. Purchased a patent (an intangible asset) for $8,000,000 cash.

Required:

1. Prepare T-accounts for December 31, 2010, from the preceding list; enter the beginning balances. You will need additional T-accounts for income statement accounts; enter zero balances.
2. For each transaction, record the effects in the T-accounts. Label each using the letter of the transaction. Compute ending balances. (**Note:** Record two transactions in (*d*), one for revenue recognition and one for the expense.)
3. Prepare an income statement, statement of stockholders' equity (since contributed capital and retained earnings are not separately reported), balance sheet, and statement of cash flows in good form.
4. Compute the company's total asset turnover ratio for the month ended January 31, 2011. What does it suggest to you about Exxon Mobil?

CASES **AND PROJECTS**

Annual Report Cases

CP3-1

LO2, 4, 6

AMERICAN EAGLE OUTFITTERS

Finding Financial Information

Refer to the financial statements of American Eagle Outfitters in Appendix B at the end of the book.

Required:

1. State the amount of the largest expense on the income statement for the year ended February 3, 2007, and describe the transaction represented by the expense.
2. Assuming that all net sales are on credit, how much cash did American Eagle Outfitters collect from customers?* (**Hint:** Use a T-account of accounts receivable to infer collection.)

**Note that most retailers settle sales in cash at the register and would not have accounts receivable related to sales unless they had layaway or private credit. For American Eagle, the accounts receivable on the balance sheet primarily relates to amounts owed from landlords for their construction allowances for building new American Eagle stores in malls.

3. A shareholder has complained that "more dividends should be paid because the company had net earnings of $387.4 million. Since this amount is all cash, more of it should go to the owners." Explain why the shareholder's assumption that earnings equal net cash inflow is valid. If you believe that the assumption is not valid, state so and support your position concisely.

4. Describe and contrast the purpose of an income statement versus a balance sheet.

5. Compute the company's total asset turnover for the year ended February 3, 2007. Explain its meaning.

Finding Financial Information

Refer to the financial statements of Urban Outfitters in Appendix C at the end of the book.

Required:

1. What is the company's revenue recognition policy? (**Hint:** Look in notes to the financial statements.)

2. Assuming that $50 million of cost of sales was due to noninventory purchase expenses (occupancy and warehousing costs), how much inventory did the company buy during the year? (**Hint:** Use a T-account of inventory to infer how much was purchased.)

3. Calculate general, administrative, and selling expenses as a percent of sales for the years ended January 31, 2007, and January 31, 2006. By what percent did it increase or decrease from fiscal year 2005 to 2006? (**Hint:** Percentage Change = [Current Year Amount − Prior Year Amount]/Prior Year.)

4. Compute the company's total asset turnover for the year ended January 31, 2007, and explain its meaning.

Comparing Companies within an Industry

Refer to the financial statements of American Eagle Outfitters in Appendix B, Urban Outfitters in Appendix C, and the Industry Ratio Report given in Appendix D at the end of this book.

Required:

1. What title does each company call its income statement? Explain what "Consolidated" means.

2. Which company had higher net income for the fiscal year?

3. Compute the total asset turnover ratio for both companies for the year. Which company is utilizing assets more effectively to generate sales? Why do you think that?

4. Compare the total asset turnover ratio for both companies to the industry average. On average, are these two companies utilizing assets to generate sales better or worse than their competitors?

5. How much cash was provided by operating activities for the year by each company? What was the percentage change in operating cash flows (1) from 2005 to 2006 and (2) from 2004 to 2005? (**Hint:** [Current Year Amount − Prior Year Amount]/Prior Year Amount.)

Financial Reporting and Analysis Cases

Comparing a Company over Time

Refer to the annual report for American Eagle Outfitters in Appendix C.

Required:

1. The annual report or 10-K report for American Eagle Outfitters provides selected financial data for the last five years. Compute the total asset turnover ratio for each of the most recent four years. (**Hint:** See Item 6 from the 10-K, which is disclosed within the annual report for the data. **Note:** Some companies will label a year that has a January year-end as having a fiscal year-end dated one year earlier. For example, a January 2005 year-end may be labeled as Fiscal 2004 since the year actually has more months that fall in the 2004 calendar year than in the 2005 calendar year.)

2. In Chapter 2, we discussed the financial leverage ratio. Compute this ratio for the most recent four years.

3. What do your results from the trends in the two ratios suggest to you about American Eagle Outfitters?

CP3-2
LO2, 4, 6
Urban Outfitters

CP3-3
LO2, 4, 6
AMERICAN EAGLE
OUTFITTERS

Urban Outfitters

www.mhhe.com/libby6e

CP3-4
LO6
AMERICAN EAGLE
OUTFITTERS

CP3-5

L03

Interpreting the Financial Press

The October 4, 2004, edition of *BusinessWeek* presented an article titled "Fuzzy Numbers" on issues related to accrual accounting and its weaknesses that have led some corporate executives to manipulate estimates in their favor, sometimes fraudulently. You can access the article on the Libby/Libby/Short website at **www.mhhe.com/libby6e**.

Required:

Read the article and then answer the following questions:
1. What is accrual accounting?
2. What does the article's title "Fuzzy Numbers" mean?
3. What does the article suggest about the reforms adopted by Congress and the SEC?

CP3-6

L04, 5

Using Financial Reports: Analyzing Changes in Accounts and Preparing Financial Statements

Lippitt Painting Service Company was organized on January 20, 2011, by three individuals, each receiving 5,000 shares of stock from the new company. The following is a schedule of the **cumulative** account balances immediately after each of the first 10 transactions ending on January 31, 2011.

Accounts	CUMULATIVE BALANCES									
	(a)	(b)	(c)	(d)	(e)	(f)	(g)	(h)	(i)	(j)
Cash	$75,000	$70,000	$85,000	$71,000	$61,000	$61,000	$57,000	$46,000	$41,000	$57,000
Accounts Receivable			12,000	12,000	12,000	26,000	26,000	26,000	26,000	10,000
Office Fixtures		20,000	20,000	20,000	20,000	20,000	20,000	20,000	20,000	20,000
Land				18,000	18,000	18,000	18,000	18,000	18,000	18,000
Accounts Payable					3,000	3,000	3,000	10,000	5,000	5,000
Note Payable (long-term)		15,000	15,000	19,000	19,000	19,000	19,000	19,000	19,000	19,000
Contributed Capital	75,000	75,000	75,000	75,000	75,000	75,000	75,000	75,000	75,000	75,000
Retained Earnings							(4,000)	(4,000)	(4,000)	(4,000)
Paint Revenue			27,000	27,000	27,000	41,000	41,000	41,000	41,000	41,000
Supplies Expense					5,000	5,000	5,000	8,000	8,000	8,000
Wages Expense					8,000	8,000	8,000	23,000	23,000	23,000

Required:
1. Analyze the changes in this schedule for each transaction; then explain the transaction. Transactions (*a*) and (*b*) are examples:
   a. Cash increased $75,000, and Contributed Capital (stockholders' equity) increased $75,000. Therefore, transaction (*a*) was an issuance of the capital stock of the corporation for $75,000 cash.
   b. Cash decreased $5,000, office fixtures (an asset) increased $20,000, and note payable (a liability) increased $15,000. Therefore, transaction (*b*) was a purchase of office fixtures that cost $20,000. Payment was made as follows: cash, $5,000; note payable, $15,000.
2. Based only on the preceding schedule after transaction (*j*), prepare an income statement, a statement of retained earnings, and a balance sheet.
3. For each of the transactions, indicate the type of effect on cash flows (O for operating, I for investing, or F for financing) and the direction (+ for increase and − for decrease) and amount of the effect. If there is no effect, write none. The first transaction is provided as an example.

Transaction	Operating, Investing, or Financing Effect	Direction and Amount of the Effect
(*a*)	F	+75,000

Critical Thinking Cases

Making a Decision as a Bank Loan Officer: Analyzing and Restating Financial Statements That Have Major Deficiencies (A Challenging Case)

CP3-7
LO3, 4, 5

Julio Estela started and operated a small boat repair service company during 2012. He is interested in obtaining a $100,000 loan from your bank to build a dry dock to store boats for customers in the winter months. At the end of the year, he prepared the following statements based on information stored in a large filing cabinet:

ESTELA COMPANY
Profit for 2012

Service fees collected during 2012		$ 55,000
Cash dividends received		10,000
Total		65,000
Expense for operations paid during 2012	$ 22,000	
Cash stolen	500	
New tools purchased during 2012 (cash paid)	1,000	
Supplies purchased for use on service jobs (cash paid)	3,200	
Total		26,700
Profit		$ 38,300

Assets Owned at the End of 2012

Cash in checking account	$ 29,300
Building (at current market value)	32,000
Tools and equipment	18,000
Land (at current market value)	30,000
Stock in ABC Industrial	130,000
Total	$239,300

The following is a summary of completed transactions:
- (a) Received the following contributions (at fair market value) to the business from the owner when it was started in exchange for 1,000 shares of stock in the new company:

Building	$21,000	Land	$20,000
Tools and equipment	17,000	Cash	1,000

- (b) Earned service fees during 2012 of $87,000; of the cash collected, $20,000 was for deposits from customers on work to be done by Julio in the next year.
- (c) Received the cash dividends on shares of ABC Industrial stock purchased by Julio Estela six years earlier (not owned by the company).
- (d) Incurred expenses during 2012 of $61,000.
- (e) Determined amount of supplies on hand (unused) at the end of 2012 as $700.

Required:
1. Did Julio prepare the income statement on a cash basis or an accrual basis? Explain how you can tell. Which basis should be used? Explain why.
2. Reconstruct the correct entries under accrual accounting principles and post the effects to T-accounts.
3. Prepare an accrual-based income statement, balance sheet, and statement of cash flows. Explain (using footnotes) the reason for each change that you make to the income statement.
4. What additional information would assist you in formulating your decision regarding the loan to Julio?
5. Based on the revised statements and additional information needed, write a letter to Julio explaining your decision at this time regarding the loan.

CP3-8 Evaluating an Ethical Dilemma

L03

Mike Lynch is the manager of an upstate New York regional office for an insurance company. As the regional manager, his compensation package comprises a base salary, commissions, and a bonus when the region sells new policies in excess of its quota. Mike has been under enormous pressure lately, stemming largely from two factors. First, he is experiencing a mounting personal debt due to a family member's illness. Second, compounding his worries, the region's sales of new policies have dipped below the normal quota for the first time in years.

You have been working for Mike for two years, and like everyone else in the office, you consider yourself lucky to work for such a supportive boss. You also feel great sympathy for his personal problems over the last few months. In your position as accountant for the regional office, you are only too aware of the drop in new policy sales and the impact this will have on the manager's bonus. While you are working late at year-end, Mike stops by your office.

Mike asks you to change the manner in which you have accounted for a new property insurance policy for a large local business. A substantial check for the premium came in the mail on December 31, the last day of the reporting year. The premium covers a period beginning on January 5. You deposited the check and correctly debited cash and credited an **unearned revenue** account. Mike says, "Hey, we have the money this year, so why not count the revenue this year? I never did understand why you accountants are so picky about these things anyway. I'd like you to change the way you have recorded the transaction. I want you to credit a *revenue* account. And anyway, I've done favors for you in the past, and I am asking for such a small thing in return." With that, he leaves for the day.

Required:
1. How should you handle this situation?
2. What are the ethical implications of Mike's request?
3. Who are the parties who would be helped or harmed if you complied with the request?
4. If you fail to comply with his request, how will you explain your position to him in the morning?

Financial Reporting and Analysis Team Project

CP3-9 Team Project: Analysis of Income Statements and Ratios

L02, 3, 6

As a team, select an industry to analyze. Reuters provides lists of industries and their makeup at **www.reuters.com/finance/industries**. Each team member should acquire the annual report or 10-K for one publicly traded company in the industry, with each member selecting a different company. (Library files, the SEC EDGAR service at **www.sec.gov**, or the company itself are good sources.)

Required:
1. On an individual basis, each team member should write a short report answering the following questions about the selected company. Discuss any patterns across the companies that you as a team observe. Then, as a team, write a short report comparing and contrasting your companies.
    1. For the most recent year, what is/are the major revenue account/s? What percentage is each to total operating revenues? [Calculated as Revenue A ÷ Total revenues.]
    2. For the most recent year, what is/are the major expense account/s? What percentage is each to total operating expenses? [Calculated as Expense A ÷ Total expenses.]
    3. Ratio Analysis:
        a. What does the total asset turnover ratio measure in general?
        b. Compute the ratio for the last three years.
        c. What do your results suggest about the company?
        d. If available, find the industry ratio for the most recent year, compare it to your results, and discuss why you believe your company differs or is similar to the industry ratio.
    4. Describe the company's revenue recognition policy, if reported. [Usually in the Significant Accounting Policies footnote.]
    5. The ratio of Cash from Operating Activities divided by Net Income measures how liberal (that is, speeding up revenue recognition or delaying expense recognition) or conservative (that is, taking care not to record revenues too early or expenses too late) a management is in choosing among various revenue and expense recognition policies. A ratio above 1.0 suggests more conservative policies and below 1.0, more liberal policies. Compute the ratio for each of the last three years. What do your results suggest about the company's choice in accounting policies?

LEARNING OBJECTIVES

After studying this chapter, you should be able to:

1. Explain the purpose of adjustments and analyze the adjustments necessary at the end of the period to update balance sheet and income statement accounts. p. 165

2. Explain the purpose of a trial balance. p. 167

3. Present an income statement with earnings per share, statement of stockholders' equity, balance sheet, and supplemental cash flow information. p. 175

4. Compute and interpret the net profit margin. p. 181

5. Explain the closing process. p. 182

Lectured slideshow–LP4-1
www.mhhe.com/libby6e

ADJUSTMENTS, FINANCIAL STATEMENTS, AND THE QUALITY OF EARNINGS

4

FOCUS COMPANY:

Papa John's International

ESTIMATING REVENUES AND EXPENSES

AT YEAR END

www.papajohns.com

The end of the accounting period is a very busy time for Papa John's. Although the last day of the fiscal year for Papa John's falls on the last Sunday of December each year, the financial statements are not distributed to users until management and the external auditors (independent CPAs) make many critical evaluations.

■ Management must ensure that the correct amounts are reported on the balance sheet and income statement. This often requires estimations, assumptions, and judgments about the timing of revenue and expense recognition and values for assets and liabilities.

■ The auditors have to (1) assess the strength of the controls established by management to safeguard the company's assets and ensure the accuracy of the financial records, and (2) evaluate the appropriateness of estimates and accounting principles used by management in determining revenues and expenses.

Managers of most companies understand the need to present financial information fairly so as not to mislead users. However, since end-of-period adjustments are the most complex portion of the annual recordkeeping process, they are prone to error. External auditors examine the company's records on a test, or sample, basis. To maximize the chance of detecting any errors significant enough to affect users' decisions, CPAs allocate more of their testing to transactions most likely to be in error.

Several accounting research studies have documented the most error-prone transactions for medium-size manufacturing companies. End-of-period adjustment errors such as failure to provide adequate product warranty liability, failure to include items that should be expensed, and end-of-period transactions recorded in the wrong period (called **cut-off errors**) are in the top category and thus receive a great deal of attention from the auditors.

For 2006, Papa John's year-end estimation and auditing process took until February 26, 2007, the date on which the auditor Ernst & Young LLP completed the audit work and signed its audit opinion. At that point, the financial statements were made available to the public.

UNDERSTANDING THE BUSINESS

Managers are responsible for preparing financial statements that are useful to investors, creditors, and others. Financial information is most useful for analyzing the past and predicting the future when it is considered by users to be of **high quality.** High-quality information should be relevant (that is, important in the analysis and available in a timely manner) and reliable (that is, verifiable and unbiased in portraying economic reality).

Users expect revenues and expenses to be reported in the proper period based on the revenue and matching principles discussed in Chapter 3. Revenues are to be recorded when earned, and expenses are to be recorded when incurred regardless of when cash receipts or payments occur. Many operating activities take place over a period of time or over several periods, such as using insurance that has been prepaid or owing wages to employees for past work. Because recording these and similar activities daily is often very costly, most companies wait until the end of the period to make **adjustments** to record related revenues and expenses in the correct period. These entries update the records and are the focus of this chapter.

Analysts assess the quality of financial information by determining how **conservative** the managers' estimates and judgments are. Choices that managers make that do not overstate assets and revenues or understate liabilities and expenses are considered more conservative. By applying conservative estimates and judgments, the resulting financial information is of higher quality for use by analysts. The information should not mislead the users into expecting the company to have a stronger financial position or higher earnings potential than exists. The effects of management's choices among alternative accounting methods and the use of estimates are presented throughout the rest of the text.

In this chapter, we emphasize the use of the same analytical tools illustrated in Chapters 2 and 3 (T-accounts and journal entries) to understand how the necessary adjustments are analyzed and recorded at the end of the accounting period. Then we prepare financial statements using adjusted accounts. Finally, we illustrate how to prepare the accounting records for the next period by performing a process called closing the books.

ORGANIZATION of the Chapter

Adjusting Revenues and Expenses

- Accounting Cycle
- Purpose and Types of Adjustments
- Adjustment Process
  - Unadjusted Trial Balance
  - Unearned Revenues
  - Accrued Revenues
  - Prepaid Expenses
  - Accrued Expenses

Preparing Financial Statements

- Income Statement
- Statement of Stockholders' Equity
- Balance Sheet
- Supplemental Cash Flows Information
- Net Profit Margin Ratio

Closing the Books

- End of the Accounting Cycle
- Post-Closing Trial Balance

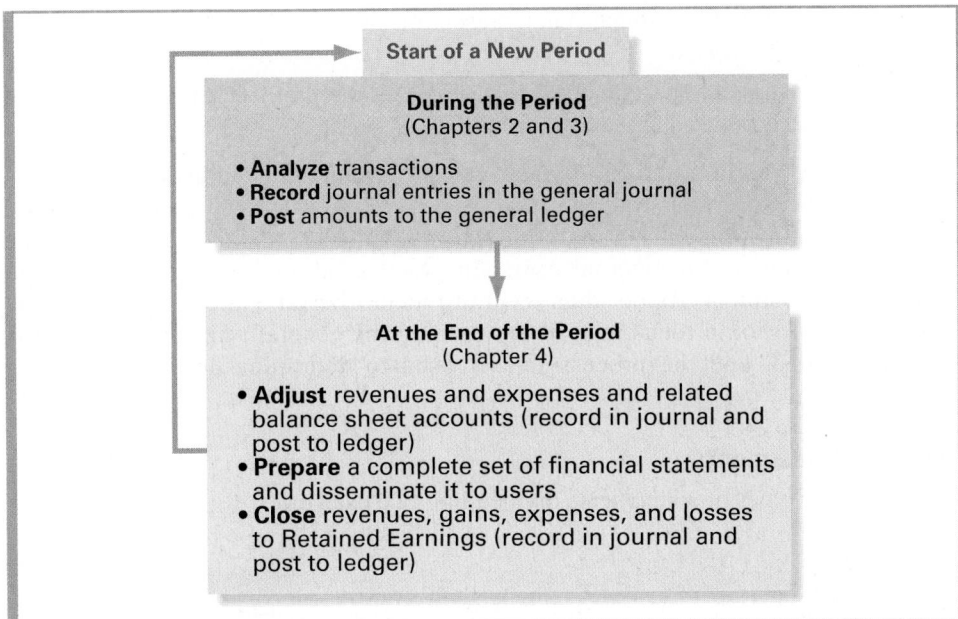

EXHIBIT 4.1

The Accounting Cycle

ADJUSTING REVENUES AND EXPENSES

Accounting Cycle

Exhibit 4.1 presents the basic steps in the **accounting cycle.** As initially discussed in Chapter 2, the accounting cycle is the process followed by entities to analyze and record transactions, adjust the records at the end of the period, prepare financial statements, and prepare the records for the next cycle. **During** the accounting period, transactions that result in exchanges between the company and other external parties are analyzed and recorded in the general journal in chronological order (journal entries), and the related accounts are updated in the general ledger (T-accounts), similar to our Papa John's illustrations in Chapters 2 and 3. In this chapter, we examine the **end-of-period** steps that focus primarily on adjustments to record revenues and expenses in the proper period and to update the balance sheet accounts for reporting purposes.

The ACCOUNTING CYCLE is the process followed by entities to analyze and record transactions, adjust the records at the end of the period, prepare financial statements, and prepare the records for the next cycle.

Purpose and Types of Adjustments

Purpose of Adjustments

Accounting systems are designed to record most recurring daily transactions, particularly those involving cash. As cash is received or paid, it is recorded in the accounting system. In general, this focus on cash works well, especially when cash receipts and payments occur in the same period as the activities that produce revenues and expenses. However, cash is not always received in the period in which the company earns revenue; likewise, cash is not always paid in the period in which the company incurs an expense.

How does the accounting system record revenues and expenses when one transaction is needed to record a cash receipt or payment and another transaction is needed to record revenue when it is earned or an expense when it is incurred? The solution to the problem created by such differences in timing is to record **adjusting entries** at the end of every accounting period, so that

■ Revenues are recorded when they are earned (the **revenue principle**).

■ Expenses are recorded when they are incurred to generate revenue (the **matching principle**).

Learning Objective 1

Explain the purpose of adjustments and analyze the adjustments necessary at the end of the period to update balance sheet and income statement accounts.

ADJUSTING ENTRIES are entries necessary at the end of the accounting period to measure all revenues and expenses of that period.

- **Assets** are reported at amounts that represent the probable future benefits remaining at the end of the period.

- **Liabilities** are reported at amounts that represent the probable future sacrifices of assets or services owed at the end of the period.

Companies wait until the **end of the accounting period** to adjust their accounts in this way because adjusting the records daily would be very costly and time-consuming. Adjusting entries are required every time a company wants to prepare financial statements for external users. In practice, almost every account could require an adjustment. Rather than trying to memorize an endless list of specific examples, you should focus instead on learning the general types of adjustments that are needed, and the process that is used to determine how to adjust the accounts.

Types of Adjustments

There are four types of adjustments divided into two categories:

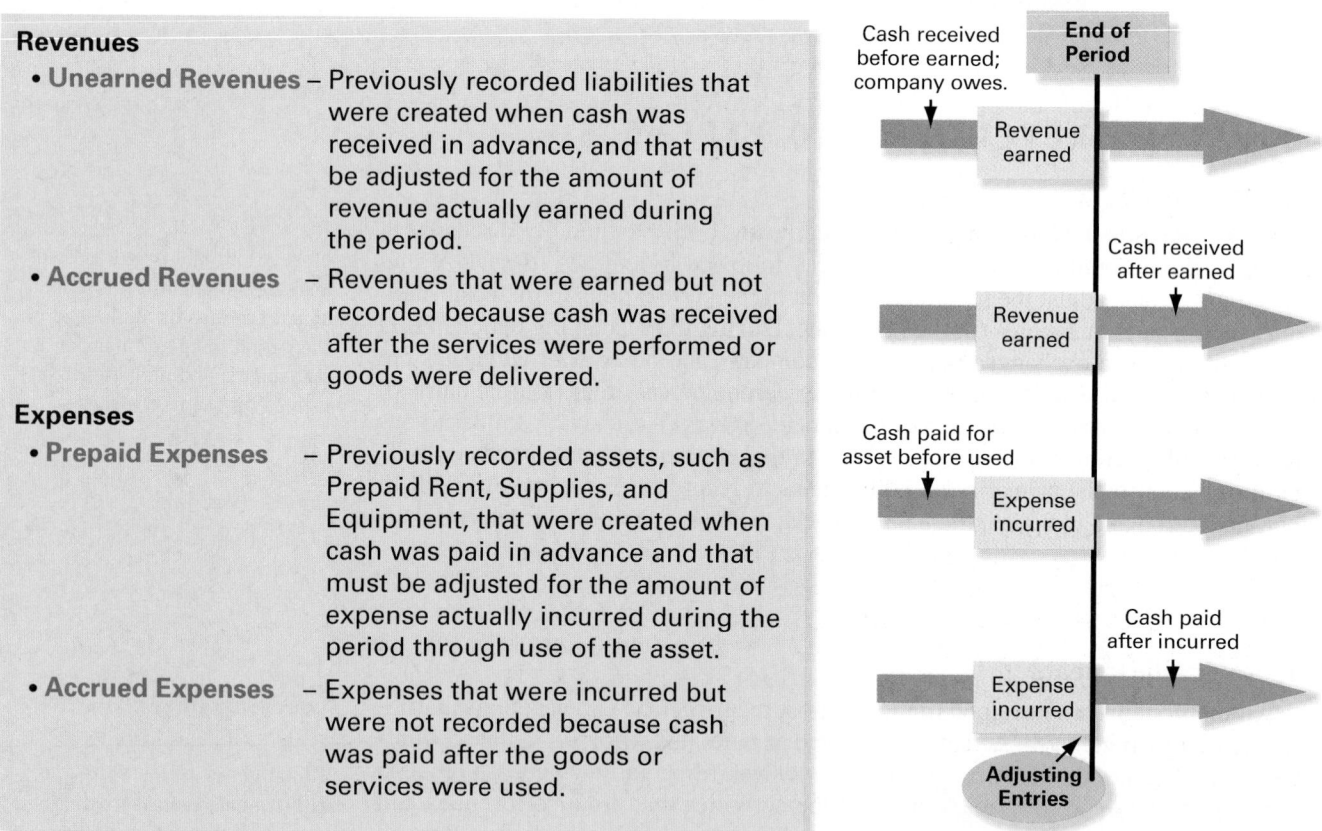

Revenues

- **Unearned Revenues** – Previously recorded liabilities that were created when cash was received in advance, and that must be adjusted for the amount of revenue actually earned during the period.

- **Accrued Revenues** – Revenues that were earned but not recorded because cash was received after the services were performed or goods were delivered.

Expenses

- **Prepaid Expenses** – Previously recorded assets, such as Prepaid Rent, Supplies, and Equipment, that were created when cash was paid in advance and that must be adjusted for the amount of expense actually incurred during the period through use of the asset.

- **Accrued Expenses** – Expenses that were incurred but were not recorded because cash was paid after the goods or services were used.

Each of these types of adjustments involves two entries:

1. One for the cash receipt or payment.

2. One for recording the revenue or expense in the proper period (through the adjusting entry).

We will illustrate the process involved in analyzing and adjusting the accounts by reviewing all the adjustments needed for Papa John's before preparing January's financial statements based on adjusted balances.

Adjustment Process

In analyzing adjustments at the end of the period, there are three steps:

Step 1: **Identify the type of adjustment.** Unearned Revenue and Prepaid Expense accounts exist at the end of the period, but are overstated. On the other hand, revenues and expenses that have accrued but have not been recorded are understated.

Step 2: **Determine the amount** of revenue that has been earned or expense that has been incurred during the period. Sometimes the amount is known, sometimes it is calculated, and sometimes it must be estimated. This will be the amount needed in the adjusting entry for the revenue or expense account.

Step 3: **Record the adjusting journal entry** and post it to the appropriate accounts. For Unearned Revenue or Prepaid Expense accounts, the other half of the adjusting journal entry will be the Unearned Revenue or Prepaid Expense account to reduce it to its remaining balance. For Accrued Revenues, the other half of the entry is to a receivable account; for Accrued Expenses, the other half of the entry is to a payable account.

So what are the adjustments needed for Papa John's at the end of January? We start by preparing and reviewing the unadjusted trial balance.

Unadjusted Trial Balance

Before adjusting the accounting records, managers normally review an unadjusted trial balance produced either manually or, more often, generated by computerized software. A **trial balance** is a list of individual accounts in one column, usually in financial statement order, with their ending debit or credit balances in the next two columns. Debit balances are indicated in the left column and credit balances are indicated in the right column. Then the two columns are totaled to provide a check on the equality of the debits and credits. Errors in a computer-generated trial balance may still exist even though debits equal credits when wrong accounts and/or amounts are used in the journal entries.[1] Once equality is established, the accounts on the trial balance can be reviewed to determine if there are any adjustments that need to be recorded.

Papa John's unadjusted trial is presented in Exhibit 4.2. It is based on the T-accounts balances from the illustration in Chapter 3 (Exhibit 3.5) plus other accounts that may be needed but currently have zero balances. Before illustrating the adjustment process, notice that the Property and Equipment account is stated at original cost of $396,000 in the trial balance but was stated at $207,000 (original cost minus the portion allocated to past operations) in previous chapters. Unlike supplies that are purchased and then used over a relatively short period, buildings and equipment represent prepaid expenses that will be used over many years. Building and equipment accounts increase when the assets are **acquired** and decrease when they are **sold.** However, these assets are also **used** over time to generate revenue. Thus, a part of their cost should be expensed in the same period (the matching principle). Accountants say that buildings and equipment **depreciate** over time as they are used. In accounting, **depreciation is an allocation of an asset's cost over its estimated useful life to the company.**

To keep track of the asset's historical cost, the amount that has been used is not subtracted directly from the asset account. Instead, it is accumulated in a new kind of account

Learning Objective 2
Explain the purpose of a trial balance.

A TRIAL BALANCE is a list of all accounts with their balances to provide a check on the equality of the debits and credits.

---

[1]Errors in a manually created trial balance also may occur in a manual recordkeeping system when wrong accounts and/or amounts are posted from correct journal entries. If the two columns are not equal, errors have occurred in one or more of the following:

- In preparing journal entries when debits do not equal credits.
- In posting the correct dollar effects of transactions from the journal entry to the ledger.
- In computing ending balances in accounts.
- In copying ending balances in the ledger to the trial balance.

These errors can be traced and should be corrected before adjusting the records.

EXHIBIT 4.2

**Unadjusted Trial Balance for
Papa John's International**

PAPA JOHN'S INTERNATIONAL, INC.
Trial Balance
At January 31, 2007

(dollars in thousands)	Unadjusted Trial Balance	
	Debit	Credit
Assets		
Cash	43,900	
Accounts receivable	19,200	
Interest receivable	0	
Supplies	26,000	
Prepaid expenses	17,000	
Other current assets	14,000	
Investments (long-term)	2,000	
Property and equipment	396,000	
Accumulated depreciation		189,000
Notes receivable (long-term)	15,000	
Intangibles	67,000	
Other assets	17,000	
Liabilities		
Accounts payable		39,000
Dividends payable		3,000
Accrued expenses payable		73,000
Income tax payable		0
Unearned franchise fees		7,300
Notes payable (long-term)		110,000
Other long-term liabilities		27,000
Stockholders' Equity		
Contributed capital		66,000
Retained earnings		81,000
Revenues and Gains		
Restaurant sales revenue		66,000
Franchise fee revenue		2,800
Investment income		1,000
Gain on sale of land		3,000
Expenses and Losses		
Cost of sales	30,000	
Salaries expense	14,000	
General and administrative expenses	7,000	
Supplies expense	0	
Rent expense	0	
Insurance expense	0	
Utilities expense	0	
Depreciation expense	0	
Interest expense	0	
Income tax expense	0	
Total	$668,100	$668,100

Accrued Revenue ⇨ Amount earned from franchisees but not yet recorded

Accrued Revenue ⇨ Amount of investment income earned but not yet recorded

Prepaid Expense ⇨ Determine amount of supplies used during period

Prepaid Expense ⇨ Determine amount of rent and insurance used during period

Represents the historical cost of property and equipment.

Prepaid Expense ⇨ Determine amount of equipment used during period

Represents the total amount of the cost of property and equipment used in the past

For reporting purposes:
Property and Equipment (cost) $396,000
−Accumulated Depreciation $189,000
Net book value $207,000

Accrued Expense ⇨ Amount of wages, utilities, and interest incurred

Accrued Expense ⇨ Amount of income tax expense incurred during period

Unearned Revenue ⇨ Determine amount earned from franchisees during period

Represents the beginning balance of retained earnings minus dividends declared during the month ($84,000 − $3,000).

Revenue from selling pizza and ingredients plus equipment to franchisees

Revenue from selling franchises during the period

Revenue on investments earned during the period

Expense for wages incurred during the period

Summary expense for many operating expenses

Expense for supplies used during period

Expense for rent used during period

Expense for insurance used during period

Expense for utilities used during period

Expense for property and equipment used during period

Expense for interest incurred on debt during period

Expense for income taxes incurred during period

Debits = Credits

called a **contra-account.** Contra-accounts are accounts that are **directly related to another account, but with an opposite balance.** For Property and Equipment, the contra-account is called **Accumulated Depreciation.** This is the first of several contra-accounts you will learn throughout the text. We will designate contra-accounts with an X in front of the type of account to which it is related (e.g., Accumulated Depreciation [XA]).

Since assets have debit balances, Accumulated Depreciation has a credit balance. On the balance sheet, the amount that is reported for Property and Equipment is its **net book value** (also called the book value or carrying value), which equals the ending balance in the Property and Equipment account minus the ending balance in the Accumulated Depreciation account.

A CONTRA-ACCOUNT is an account that is an offset to, or reduction of, the primary account.

NET BOOK VALUE (BOOK VALUE, CARRYING VALUE) of an asset is the difference between its acquisition cost and accumulated depreciation, its related contra-account.

+ Property and Equipment (A) −			− Accumulated Depreciation (XA) +	
Beginning bal. Buy	Sell			Beginning bal. Used
Ending bal.		−		Ending bal.

= **Net book value**

↑
Amount reported on the balance sheet

For Papa John's, Accumulated Depreciation has a credit balance of $189,000.

On the balance sheet:	
Property and equipment (net of accumulated depreciation of $189,000)	$207,000

Depreciation is discussed in much greater detail in Chapter 8. Now let's illustrate the adjustment process for Papa John's at the end of January.

Step 1: **Identify type of adjustment:** From a review of the unadjusted trial balance in Exhibit 4.2, we identify several accounts to adjust:

- One unearned revenue—Unearned Franchise Fees
- Two accrued revenues—Accounts Receivable and Interest Receivable
- Three prepaid expenses—Supplies, Prepaid Expenses related to rent and insurance, and Property and Equipment used during the period
- Two accrued expenses—Accrued Expenses Payable for wages, utilities, and interest and Income Tax Payable

Unearned Revenues

When a customer pays for goods or services before the company delivers them, the company records the amount of cash received in an **Unearned (or Deferred) Revenue** account. This unearned revenue is a liability representing the company's promise to perform or deliver the goods or services in the future. Recognition of (recording) the revenue is postponed (deferred) until the company meets its obligation.

UNEARNED (OR DEFERRED) REVENUES are previously recorded liabilities that need to be adjusted at the end of the accounting period to reflect the amount of revenue earned.

(AJE 1) **Unearned Franchise Fees** During January, Papa John's performed $1,100 in services for franchisees who had previously paid fees. When cash was received, Papa John's recorded the money into Unearned Franchise Fees, a liability, to recognize the business's obligation to provide future services to franchisees.

Step 2: **Determine the amount:** Sometimes a computation is needed to determine the amount of revenue earned. In this case, the amount is given as $1,100. That means that the $7,300 in the liability account at the end of January is overstated by $1,100 and Franchise Fee Revenue is understated by $1,100.

Step 3: **Record the adjusting journal entry (AJE):** An adjusting entry is necessary to reduce the Unearned Franchise Fees account by $1,100 and increase the Franchise Fee Revenue account by $1,100.

AJE 1

Unearned Franchise Fees (−L) 1,100
    Franchise Fee Revenue (+R, +SE) 1,100

Assets	=	Liabilities	+	Stockholders' Equity
		Unearned Franchise Fees −1,100		Franchise Fee Revenue (+R) +1,100

Equality checks: (1) Debits $1,100 = Credits $1,100; (2) the accounting equation is in balance.

Additional examples of unearned revenues include magazine subscriptions; season tickets to sporting events, plays, and concerts; airplane tickets sold in advance; and rent paid in advance by renters. Each of these requires an adjusting entry at the end of the accounting period to report the amount of revenue earned during the period.

Accrued Revenues

Sometimes companies perform services or provide goods (that is, earn revenue) before customers pay. Because the cash that is owed for these goods and services has not yet been received, the revenue that was earned has not been recorded. Revenues that have been earned but have not yet been recorded at the end of the accounting period are called **accrued revenues**.

ACCRUED REVENUES are previously unrecorded revenues that need to be adjusted at the end of the accounting period to reflect the amount earned and the related receivable account.

(AJE 2)   **Accounts Receivable**   Papa John's franchisees reported that they will pay Papa John's in February $830 in royalties for sales the franchisees made in the last week of January.

Step 2:   **Amount:** The amount is given as $830. Since no entry has yet been made, Franchise Fee Revenue and Accounts Receivable are both understated by $830.

Step 3:   **AJE:** An adjusting entry is necessary to increase Franchise Fee Revenue and Accounts Receivable by $830. This will recognize revenue in the current period.

AJE 2

Accounts Receivable (+A) 830
    Franchise Fee Revenue (+R, +SE) 830

Assets	=	Liabilities	+	Stockholders' Equity
Accounts Receivable +830				Franchise Fee Revenue (+R) +830

Equality checks: (1) Debits $830 = Credits $830; (2) the accounting equation is in balance.

(AJE 3)   **Interest Receivable**   Papa John's loaned $14,000 to franchisees in the past at 6 percent interest per year with interest to be paid at the end of each year. There are two components when lending money: **principal** and **interest.** Notes Receivable was recorded properly when the money was loaned. However, interest revenue is earned over time as the money is used by the franchisees.

Step 2:   **Amount:** It is important to note that **the interest rate is always given as an annual percentage.** To compute interest revenue for less than a full year, the number of months needed in the calculation is divided by 12. The formula to compute interest is:

Principal	×	Rate per year	×	Number of Months (since last computation)/12		Interest for the period
$14,000	×	.06	×	1/12	=	$70

The $70 interest earned on the loan has not yet been recorded. Therefore, revenues are understated as is the related Interest Receivable.

Step 3:   AJE: An adjusting entry is necessary to increase Investment Income and Interest Receivable by $70. This will recognize one month of interest revenue in January.

AJE 3

Interest Receivable (+A)	70	
Investment Income (+R, +SE)		70

Assets	=	Liabilities	+	Stockholders' Equity	
Interest Receivable	+70			Investment Income (+R)	+70

Equality checks: (1) Debits $70 = Credits $70; (2) the accounting equation is in balance.

Prepaid Expenses

Assets represent resources with probable future benefits to the company. Many assets are **prepaid expenses** that are used over time to generate revenues, including supplies, buildings, equipment, prepaid insurance, and prepaid rent. At the end of every period, an adjustment must be made to record the amount of the asset that was used during the period.

(AJE 4) **Supplies** Supplies include food and paper products. At the end of the month, Papa John's counted $22,000 in supplies on hand, but the Supplies account indicated a balance of $26,000 (from Exhibit 4.2). The difference is the supplies used during the month.

Step 2:   Amount: The easiest way to determine the dollar amount of supplies used is to add the dollar amount of supplies available at the beginning of the period plus any purchases made during the period, and then subtract the dollar amount of supplies remaining on hand at the end of the period.

> **Computation of Supplies Expense:**
>   Beginning balance of supplies
> \+ Supply purchases during period
> − Ending amount of supplies on hand
>   Supplies used during the period

The balance on Papa John's trial balance is $26,000 (includes purchases). With a count of supplies on hand of $22,000, the amount of supplies used during the period is $4,000.

Step 3:   AJE: An adjusting entry is necessary to record the use of $4,000 of supplies during January. Supplies will decrease to the amount on hand and Supplies Expense will increase, recognizing expense in the current period.

AJE 4

Supplies Expense (+E, −SE)	4,000	
Supplies (−A)		4,000

Assets	=	Liabilities	+	Stockholders' Equity	
Supplies	−4,000			Supplies Expense (+E)	−4,000

Equality checks: (1) Debits $4,000 = Credits $4,000; (2) the accounting equation is in balance.

(AJE 5) **Prepaid Rent and Insurance** Prepaid Expenses includes $2,000 paid on January 1 for insurance coverage for four months (January through April) and $6,000 paid on January 1 for rental of space at shopping centers over three months (January through March).

Step 2:   Amount: One month has expired for each of the prepaid amounts:

   1. Insurance—$2,000 × 1/4 = $500 per month

   2. Rent—$6,000 × 1/3 = $2,000 per month.

PREPAID EXPENSES are previously acquired assets that need to be adjusted at the end of the accounting period to reflect the amount of expense incurred in using the asset to generate revenue.

Until the $500 January insurance coverage and the $2,000 rent for January are recorded as expenses in January, Prepaid Expenses remains overstated and expenses are understated.

Step 3: **AJE:** An adjusting entry is necessary to reduce Prepaid Expenses by $2,500 and increase Insurance Expense by $500 and Rent Expense by $2,000.

AJE 5

Insurance Expense (+E, −SE)	500	
Rent Expense (+E, −SE)	2,000	
Prepaid Expenses (−A)		2,500

Assets	=	Liabilities	+	Stockholders' Equity	
Prepaid Expenses −2,500				Insurance Expense (+E) − 500	
				Rent Expense (+E) −2,000	

Equality checks: (1) Debits $2,500 = Credits $2,500; (2) the accounting equation is in balance.

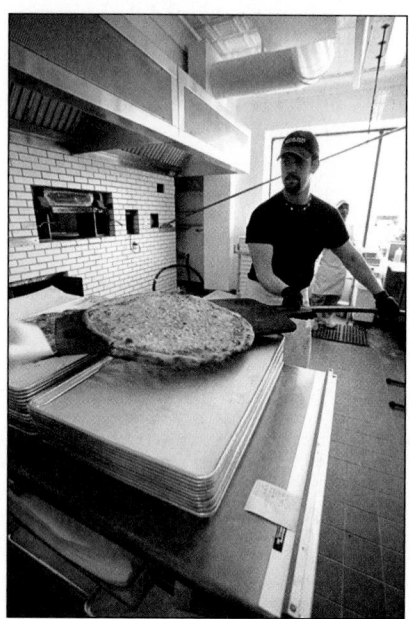

(AJE 6) Property and Equipment As previously discussed, a contra-account, Accumulated Depreciation, is used to accumulate the amount of the historical cost allocated to prior periods. It is directly related to the Property and Equipment account but has the opposite balance (a credit balance). Papa John's estimates depreciation to be $30,000 per year.

Step 2: **Amount:** The property and equipment has only been used to generate revenues for January. Thus, we need to calculate only one month of Depreciation Expense:

$$\$30,000 \text{ per year} \times 1/12 = \$2,500 \text{ for one month}$$

The net book value (cost − accumulated depreciation) of Papa John's property and equipment will be overstated until January's depreciation is recorded in the adjusting entry. Likewise, expenses will be understated.

Step 3: **AJE:** An adjusting entry is necessary to recognize the use of $2,500 of the cost of long-lived assets to generate revenues during the period.

AJE 6

Depreciation Expense (+E, −SE)	2,500	
Accumulated Depreciation (+XA, −A)		2,500

Assets	=	Liabilities	+	Stockholders' Equity
Accumulated Depreciation (+XA) −2,500				Depreciation Expense (+E) −2,500

Equality checks: (1) Debits $2,500 = Credits $2,500; (2) the accounting equation is in balance.

Accrued Expenses

Numerous expenses are incurred in the current period without being paid for until the next period. Common examples include Wages Expense for the wages owed to employees, Utilities Expense for the water, gas, and electricity used during the period, and the Interest Expense incurred on debt. These expenses accumulate (accrue) over time but are not recognized until the end of the period in an adjusting entry to record the **accrued expenses.**

ACCRUED EXPENSES are previously unrecorded expenses that need to be adjusted at the end of the accounting period to reflect the amount incurred and the related payable account.

(AJE 7) Accrued Expenses Payable (Salaries, Utilities, and Interest) Papa John's owed (1) its employees salaries for working four days at the end of January at $500 per day, (2) $600 for utilities used in January, and (3) interest on its long-term notes payable borrowed at a 6 percent annual rate.

Step 2:   **Amount:** Each of these is an expense in January:

1. Salaries—$500 per day $\times$ 4 days = $2,000
2. Utilities—Amount is given at $600
3. Interest on debt—Like interest earned, interest incurred is computed using the same formula:

Principal	$\times$	Rate per year	$\times$	Number of Months (since last computation)/12		Interest for the period
$110,000	$\times$	.06	$\times$	1/12	=	$550

Until the $2,000 in salaries, $600 in utilities, and $550 in interest are recorded as expenses in January, expenses on the income statement and liabilities on the balance sheet are understated.

Step 3:   **AJE:** An adjusting entry is necessary to increase Salaries Expense by $2,000, Utilities Expense by $600, Interest Expense by $550, and the related Accrued Expenses Payable by $3,150. Note that, alternatively, each of the expenses could have been recorded into a separate liability—Salaries Payable, Utilities Payable, and Interest Payable—instead of combined into one liability.

AJE 7

Salaries Expense (+E, −SE)	2,000	
Utilities Expense (+E, −SE).....................................	600	
Interest Expense (+E, −SE).....................................	550	
Accrued Expenses Payable (+L)		3,150

Assets	=	Liabilities	+	Stockholders' Equity	
		Accrued Expenses Payable +3,150		Salaries Expense (+E)	−2,000
				Utilities Expense (+E)	− 600
				Interest Expense (+E)	− 550

Equality checks: (1) Debits $3,150 = Credits $3,150; (2) the accounting equation is in balance.

(AJE 8)   **Income Taxes Payable**   The final adjusting journal entry is to record the accrual of income taxes that will be paid in the next quarter. This requires computing adjusted pretax income (that is, balances from the unadjusted trial balance plus the effects of all of the other adjustments):

	Revenues and Gains	Expenses and Losses	
Unadjusted totals	$72,800	$51,000	From Exhibit 4.2
AJE 1	1,100		
AJE 2	830		
AJE 3	70		
AJE 4		4,000	
AJE 5		2,500	
AJE 6		2,500	
AJE 7		3,150	
	$74,800 −	$63,150 =	**$11,650 Pretax income**

Papa John's average income tax rate is 34 percent.

Step 2:   **Amount:** $11,650 pretax income $\times$ .34 = $3,961 January income tax expense.

Until the $3,961 in income taxes is recorded as an expense in January, expenses on the income statement and liabilities on the balance sheet are understated.

Step 3:   **AJE:** An adjusting entry is necessary to increase Income Tax Expense and Income Tax Payable by $3,961.

AJE 8

Income Tax Expense (+E, −SE)			3,961	
Income Tax Payable (+L)				3,961

Assets	=	Liabilities	+	Stockholders' Equity
		Income Tax Payable +3,961		Income Tax Expense (+E) −3,961

Equality checks: (1) Debits $3,961 = Credits $3,961; (2) the accounting equation is in balance.

In all of the adjustments we completed, you may have noticed that Cash was never adjusted. The cash has already been received or paid by the end of the period or will be received or paid after the end of the period. Adjustments are required to record revenues and expenses in the proper period because the cash part of the transaction is at a different point in time. Now it's your turn to practice the adjustment process.

SELF-STUDY QUIZ

Florida Flippers, a scuba diving and instruction business, completed its first year of operations on December 31, 2010. Follow the three-step process (identify adjustment type, determine the amount, and record the entry) for each of the following adjustments.

AJE 1: Florida Flippers received $6,000 from customers on November 15, 2010, for diving trips to the Bahamas in December and January. The $6,000 was recorded in Unearned Revenue on that date. By the end of December, one-third of the diving trips had been completed.

AJE 2: On December 31, 2010, Florida Flippers provided advanced diving instruction to ten customers who will pay the business $800 in January. No entry was made when the instruction was provided.

AJE 3: On September 1, 2010, Florida Flippers paid $24,000 for insurance for the twelve months beginning on September 1. The amount was recorded as Prepaid Insurance on September 1.

AJE 4: On March 1, 2010, Florida Flippers borrowed $300,000 at 12 percent. Interest is payable each March 1 for three years.

	TYPE OF ADJUSTMENT	DETERMINATION OF AMOUNT OF ADJUSTMENT	ADJUSTING JOURNAL ENTRY ACCOUNTS	DEBIT	CREDIT
AJE 1					
AJE 2					
AJE 3					
AJE 4					

After you are done, check your answers with the solutions at the bottom of the page.

Self-Study Quiz Solutions

	TYPE	AMOUNT	ADJUSTING JOURNAL ENTRY ACCOUNTS	DEBIT	CREDIT
AJE 1	Unearned Revenue	$6,000 × 1/3 = $2,000 earned	Unearned Revenue (−L) Trip Revenue (+R, +SE)	2,000	2,000
AJE 2	Accrued Revenue	$800 earned (given)	Accounts Receivable (+A) Instruction Revenue (+R, +SE)	800	800
AJE 3	Prepaid Expense	$24,000 × 1/12 = $2,000 per month $2,000 × 4 months = $8,000 used	Insurance Expense (+E, −SE) Prepaid Insurance (−A)	8,000	8,000
AJE 4	Accrued Expense	$300,000 × .12 × 10/12 = $30,000 incurred and owed	Interest Expense (+E, −SE) Interest Payable (+L)	30,000	30,000

Adjustments and Incentives

Owners and managers of companies are most directly affected by the information presented in financial statements. If the financial performance and condition of the company appear strong, the company's stock price rises. Shareholders usually receive dividends and increase their investment value. Managers often receive bonuses based on the strength of a company's financial performance, and many in top management are compensated with options to buy their company's stock at prices below market.* The higher the market value, the more compensation they earn. When actual performance lags behind expectations, managers and owners may be tempted to manipulate accruals and deferrals to make up part of the difference. For example, managers may record cash received in advance of being earned as revenue in the current period or may fail to accrue certain expenses at year-end.

Evidence from studies of large samples of companies indicates that some managers do engage in such behavior. This research is borne out by enforcement actions of the Securities and Exchange Commission against companies and sometimes against their auditors. In January 2003, an SEC study reported that, in a five-year period, there were 227 enforcement investigations. Of these, "126 involved improper revenue recognition and 101 involved improper expense recognition. . . . Of the 227 enforcement matters during the Study period, 157 resulted in charges against at least one senior manager. . . . Furthermore, the Study found that 57 enforcement matters resulted in charges for auditing violations. . . ." (p. 47).†

In many of these cases, the firms involved, their managers, and their auditors are penalized for such actions. Furthermore, owners suffer because news of an SEC investigation negatively affects the company's stock price.

*M. Nelson, J. Elliott, and R. Tarpley, "How Are Earnings Managed? Examples from Auditors," *Accounting Horizons,* Supplement 2003, pp. 17–35.
†These statistics are reported in the Securities and Exchange Commission's study, "Report Pursuant to Section 704 of the Sarbanes-Oxley Act of 2002," January 27, 2003.

PREPARING FINANCIAL STATEMENTS

Before we prepare a complete set of financial statements, let's update the trial balance to reflect the adjustments and provide us with adjusted balances for the statements.[2] In Exhibit 4.3, four new columns are added. Two are used to reflect the adjustments to each of the accounts. The other two are the updated balances, determined by adding (or subtracting) across each row. Again, we note that the total debits equal the total credits in each of the columns. It is from these adjusted balances that we will prepare an income statement, statement of stockholders' equity (that includes a column for Retained Earnings), and a balance sheet, with supplemental cash flow information to accompany the statement of cash flows.

Learning Objective 3
Present an income statement with earnings per share, statement of stockholders' equity, balance sheet, and supplemental cash flow information.

[2]For a discussion and illustration of the use of a worksheet for end-of-period adjustments, refer to Appendix E located on the website at **www.mhhe.com/libby6e.**

EXHIBIT 4.3

Adjusted Trial Balance for Papa John's International

PAPA JOHN'S INTERNATIONAL, INC.
Trial Balance at January 31, 2007 (dollars in thousands)

17,000 − 2,500 =

To compute adjusted balances, add or subtract across each row: unadjusted balance +/− adjustment(s).

2,800 + 1,100 + 830 =

		Unadjusted Trial Balance		Adjustments		Adjusted Trial Balance	
		Debit	**Credit**	**Debit**	**Credit**	**Debit**	**Credit**
Assets	Cash	43,900				43,900	
	Accounts receivable	19,200		AJE 2 830		20,030	
	Interest receivable	0		AJE 3 70		70	
	Supplies	26,000			AJE 4 4,000	22,000	
	Prepaid expenses	17,000			AJE 5 2,500	14,500	
	Other current assets	14,000				14,000	
	Investments (long-term)	2,000				2,000	
	Property and equipment	396,000				396,000	
	Accumulated depreciation		189,000		AJE 6 2,500		191,500
	Notes receivable (long-term)	15,000				15,000	
	Intangibles	67,000				67,000	
	Other assets	17,000				17,000	
Liabilities	Accounts payable		39,000				39,000
	Dividends payable		3,000				3,000
	Accrued expenses payable		73,000		AJE 7 3,150		76,150
	Income tax payable		0		AJE 8 3,961		3,961
	Unearned franchise fees		7,300	AJE 1 1,100			6,200
	Notes payable (long-term)		110,000				110,000
	Other long-term liabilities		27,000				27,000
Stockholders' Equity	Contributed capital		66,000				66,000
	Retained earnings		81,000				81,000
Revenues and Gains	Restaurant sales revenue		66,000				66,000
	Franchise fee revenue		2,800		AJE 1 1,100 AJE 2 830		4,730
	Investment income		1,000		AJE 3 70		1,070
	Gain on sale of land		3,000				3,000
Expenses and Losses	Cost of sales	30,000				30,000	
	Salaries expense	14,000		AJE 7 2,000		16,000	
	General and administrative expenses	7,000				7,000	
	Supplies expense	0		AJE 4 4,000		4,000	
	Rent expense	0		AJE 5 2,000		2,000	
	Insurance expense	0		AJE 5 500		500	
	Utilities expense	0		AJE 7 600		600	
	Depreciation expense	0		AJE 6 2,500		2,500	
	Interest expense	0		AJE 7 550		550	
	Income tax expense	0		AJE 8 3,961		3,961	
	Total	$668,100	$668,100	$18,111	$18,111	$678,611	$678,611

Effects of the adjusting entries

EXHIBIT 4.4

Relationships of the Financial Statements Using the Transaction Analysis Model

As you learned in Chapter 1, the financial statements are interrelated—that is, the numbers from one statement flow into the next statement. Exhibit 4.4 illustrates the interconnections among the statements using the fundamental accounting equation. Starting on the bottom right, notice that

- Revenues minus expenses yields net income on the **Income Statement.**
- Net income (or net loss) and dividends to stockholders affect Retained Earnings and any additional issuances of stock during the period affect the balance in Contributed Capital, both on the **Statement of Stockholders' Equity.**
- The Stockholders' Equity is a component of the **Balance Sheet.**

Thus, if a number on the income statement changes or is in error, it will impact the other statements.

Exhibit 4.4 also includes special labels for the accounts. Balance sheet accounts are considered **permanent,** indicating that they retain their balances from the end of one period to the beginning of the next. Revenue, expense, gain, and loss accounts are **temporary** accounts because their balances accumulate for a period, but start with a zero balance at the beginning of the next period. These labels will be discussed in the section on closing the books following the presentation of Papa John's classified financial statements.

Another way of presenting the relationships among the statements follows. If a number on the income statement changes, it will impact the other statements.

Income Statement

The income statement is prepared first because net income is a component of Retained Earnings. The January income statement for Papa John's based on transactions in Chapters 2 and 3 and adjustments in Chapter 4 follows.

PAPA JOHN'S INTERNATIONAL, INC. AND SUBSIDIARIES
Consolidated Statement of Income
For the Month Ended January 31, 2007
(dollars in thousands)

Operating Revenues	
Restaurant sales revenue	$66,000
Franchise fee revenue	4,730
Total revenues	70,730
Operating Expenses	
Cost of sales	30,000
Salaries expense	16,000
General and administrative expenses	7,000
Supplies expense	4,000
Rent expense	2,000
Insurance expense	500
Utilities expense	600
Depreciation expense	2,500
Total expenses	62,600
Operating income	8,130
Other Items	
Investment income	1,070
Interest expense	(550)
Gain on sale of land	3,000
Income before income taxes	11,650
Income tax expense	3,961
Net income	$ 7,689
For the month → Earnings per share	$ .23

You will note that the earnings per share (EPS) ratio is reported on the income statement. It is widely used in evaluating the operating performance and profitability of a company, and it is the only ratio required to be disclosed on the statement or in the notes to the statements. The actual computation of the ratio is quite complex and appropriate for more advanced accounting courses. We simplify the earnings per share computation as:

$$\text{Earnings per Share} = \frac{\text{Net Income*}}{\text{Average Number of Shares of Common Stock Outstanding during the Period}}$$

The denominator is the average number of shares outstanding (number at the beginning of the period plus the number at the end of the period, divided by two). For Papa John's, we use the information in its 2006 annual report for the denominator —32,953,000 average number of shares of stock outstanding.

$7,689,000 Net Income/32,953,000 Shares = $.23 earnings per share for the month

---

*If there are preferred dividends (discussed in Chapter 11), the amount is subtracted from net income in the numerator.

Statement of Stockholders' Equity

The final total from the income statement, net income, is carried forward to the Retained Earnings column of the statement of stockholders' equity. To this, the additional elements of the statement are added. Dividends declared and an additional stock issuance (from prior chapters) are also included in the statement:

PAPA JOHN'S INTERNATIONAL, INC. AND SUBSIDIARIES
Consolidated Statement of Stockholders' Equity
For the Month Ended January 31, 2007
(dollars in thousands)

	Contributed Capital	Retained Earnings	Stockholders' Equity
Beginning balance	$64,000	$84,000	$148,000
Stock issuance	2,000		2,000
Net income		7,689	7,689 ← *From the income statement*
Dividends		(3,000)	(3,000)
Ending balance	$66,000	$88,689	$154,689

Disclosure

As presented in the previous chapters, the statement of cash flows explains the difference between the ending and beginning balances in the Cash account on the balance sheet (on page 180) during the accounting period. Put simply, the cash flow statement is a categorized list of all transactions of the period that affected the Cash account. The three categories are operating, investing, and financing activities. Since no adjustments made in this chapter affected cash, the statement of cash flows presented for Papa John's has not changed.

For complete disclosure, however, companies are required to provide supplemental information on the statement itself or in the notes to the statements:

1. Interest **paid.**

2. Income taxes **paid.**

3. A schedule of significant noncash investing and financing transactions.

Noncash investing and financing transactions include, for example, land acquired through the exchange of stock and acquisition of a building by signing a long-term mortgage payable. Below is the disclosure presented at the bottom of the statement of cash flows of Whole Foods, Inc., the world's leading natural and organic foods supermarket, headquartered in Austin, Texas.

For the fiscal year ended	Sept. 30, 2007	Sept. 24, 2006	Sept. 25, 2005
(in thousands)			
Supplemental disclosures of cash flow information:			
Interest paid	$ 4,561	$ 607	$ 1,063
Federal and state income taxes paid	$152,626	$ 70,220	$ 74,706
Non-cash transactions:			
. . .			
Conversion of convertible (*debt*) into common stock	$ 5,686	$ 4,922	$147,794

REAL WORLD EXCERPT

WHOLE FOODS
MARKET

ANNUAL REPORT

Balance Sheet

The ending balances for Contributed Capital and Retained Earnings from the statement of stockholders' equity are included on the balance sheet. You will notice that the contra-asset account, Accumulated Depreciation, has been subtracted from the Property and Equipment account to reflect net book value (or carrying value) at month-end for balance sheet purposes. Also recall that assets are listed in order of liquidity, and liabilities are listed in order of due dates. Current assets are those used or turned into cash within one year (as well as inventory). Current liabilities are obligations to be paid with current assets within one year.

PAPA JOHN'S INTERNATIONAL, INC. AND SUBSIDIARIES
Consolidated Balance Sheet
January 31, 2007
(dollars in thousands)

Assets	
Current Assets	
Cash	$43,900
Accounts receivable	20,030
Interest receivable	70
Supplies	22,000
Prepaid expenses	14,500
Other current assets	14,000
Total current assets	114,500
Investments	2,000
Property and equipment (net of accumulated depreciation of $191,500)	204,500
Notes receivable	15,000
Intangibles	67,000
Other assets	17,000
Total assets	**$420,000**
Liabilities and Stockholders' Equity	
Current Liabilities	
Accounts payable	$39,000
Dividends payable	3,000
Accrued expenses payable	76,150
Income taxes payable	3,961
Total current liabilities	122,111
Unearned franchise fees	6,200
Notes payable	110,000
Other long-term liabilities	27,000
Total liabilities	265,311
Stockholders' Equity	
Contributed capital	66,000
Retained earnings	88,689
Total stockholders' equity	154,689
Total liabilities and stockholders' equity	**$420,000**

From the Statement of Stockholders' Equity ⟶

Cash Flows From Operations, Net Income, and the Quality Of Earnings

Many standard financial analysis texts warn analysts to look for unusual deferrals and accruals when they attempt to predict future periods' earnings. They often suggest that wide disparities between net income and cash flow from operations are a useful warning sign. For example, Wild et al. suggest that

> Cash flows are often less subject to distortion than is net income. Accounting accruals determining net income rely on estimates, deferrals, allocations, and valuations. These considerations typically admit more subjectivity than factors determining cash flows. For this reason we often relate cash flows from operations to net income in assessing its quality. **Certain users consider earnings of higher quality when the ratio of cash flows from operations divided by net income is greater.** This derives from a concern with revenue recognition or expense accrual criteria yielding high net income but low cash flows. (emphasis added)*

The cash flows from operations to net income ratio is illustrated and discussed in more depth in Chapter 13.

*J. Wild, K. Subramanyan, and R. Halsey, *Financial Statement Analysis* (New York, McGraw-Hill/Irwin, 2004), p. 394.

Net Profit Margin

In Chapter 2, we introduced the financial leverage ratio to examine managers' use of debt as a tool to increase resources that would generate more profit for the shareholders. In Chapter 3, we introduced the total asset turnover ratio to examine managers' effectiveness at utilizing assets efficiently to generate more revenues for the shareholders. Now let's examine the third ratio, net profit margin, to examine managers' effectiveness at controlling revenues and expenses to generate more profit for the shareholders. These three ratios are the primary components of Return on Equity to shareholders to be discussed in Chapter 5.

Learning Objective 4
Compute and interpret the net profit margin.

⁇ ANALYTICAL QUESTION
How effective is management in generating profit on every dollar of sales?

% RATIO AND COMPARISONS

$$\text{Net Profit Margin} = \frac{\text{Net Income}}{\text{Net Sales (or Operating Revenues)}*}$$

The 2006 ratio for Papa John's using actual reported amounts is (dollars in thousands):

$$\frac{\$63,375,000}{\$1,001,557,000} = .0633\ (6.33\%)$$

COMPARISONS OVER TIME			COMPARISONS WITH COMPETITORS	
Papa John's			Domino's Inc.	Yum! Brands, Inc.†
2004	2005	2006	2006	2006
2.51%	4.75%	6.33%	7.39%	8.62%

💡 INTERPRETATIONS
In General Net profit margin measures how much of every sales dollar generated during the period is profit. A rising net profit margin signals more efficient management of sales and expenses. Differences among industries result from the nature of the products

Selected Focus Companies' Net Profit Margin Ratios for 2006

Washington Post   8.3%

Harley-Davidson   18.0%

Wal-Mart Stores   3.3%

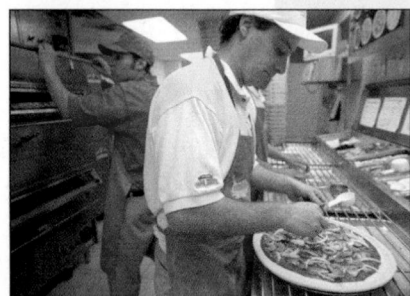

or services provided and the intensity of competition. Differences among competitors in the same industry reflect how each company responds to changes in competition (and demand for the product or service) and changes in managing sales volume, sales price, and costs. Financial analysts expect well-run businesses to maintain or improve their net profit margin over time.

Focus Company Analysis Papa John's net profit margin increased in 2005 and 2006, suggesting that the company is doing a better job of controlling sales and costs. Operating revenues steadily improved over the period, while salaries, advertising, and other expenses rose more slowly, leading to higher net income.

Domino's is Papa John's main competitor in the delivery segment of the pizza business. Domino's has an almost 17 percent higher net profit margin at 7.39%. This may suggest increased efficiency in commissary activities by Domino's. Similarly, Yum! Brands has an 8.62 percent net profit margin, more than one-third greater than that of Papa John's. Yum! Brands operates dine-in, take-out, and delivery restaurants that rely more heavily on facilities. Differences in business strategies explain some of the variation in the ratio analysis.

A Few Cautions The decisions that management makes to maintain the company's net profit margin in the current period may have negative long-run implications. Analysts should perform additional analysis of the ratio to identify trends in each component of revenues and expenses. This involves dividing each line on the income statement by net sales. Statements presented with these percentages are called **common-sized income statements.** Changes in the percentages of the individual components of net income provide information on shifts in management's strategies.

*Net sales is sales revenue less any returns from customers and other reductions. For companies in the service industry, total operating revenues is equivalent to net sales.

†Yum! Brands is the parent company of Pizza Hut, KFC, A&W, Long John Silver's and Taco Bell.

CLOSING THE BOOKS

End of the Accounting Cycle

Learning Objective 5
Explain the closing process.

PERMANENT (REAL) ACCOUNTS are the balance sheet accounts that carry their ending balances into the next accounting period.

TEMPORARY (NOMINAL) ACCOUNTS are income statement accounts that are closed to Retained Earnings at the end of the accounting period.

A CLOSING ENTRY transfers balances in temporary accounts to Retained Earnings and establishes zero balances in temporary accounts.

The ending balance in each of the asset, liability, and stockholders' equity accounts becomes the beginning account balance for the next period. These accounts, called **permanent (real) accounts** (shown in Exhibit 4.4), are not reduced to a zero balance at the end of the accounting period. For example, the ending Cash balance of the prior accounting period is the beginning Cash balance of the next accounting period. The only time a permanent account has a zero balance is when the item it represents is no longer owned or owed.

On the other hand, revenue, expense, gain, and loss accounts are used to accumulate data for the **current accounting period only;** they are called **temporary (nominal) accounts** (see Exhibit 4.4). The final step in the accounting cycle, closing the books, is done to prepare income statement accounts for the next accounting cycle. Therefore, at the end of each period, the balances in the temporary accounts are transferred, or **closed,** to the Retained Earnings account by recording a closing entry.

The **closing entry** has two purposes:

1. To transfer net income or loss to Retained Earnings.[3]

2. To establish a zero balance in each of the temporary accounts to start the accumulation in the next accounting period.

---

[3]Companies may close income statement accounts to a special temporary summary account, called **Income Summary,** which is then closed to Retained Earnings.

In this way, the income statement accounts are again ready for their temporary accumulation function for the next period. The closing entry is dated the last day of the accounting period, entered in the usual debits-equal-credits format (in the journal), and immediately posted to the ledger (or T-accounts). **Temporary accounts with debit balances are credited and accounts with credit balances are debited.** The net amount, equal to net income, affects Retained Earnings.

To illustrate the process, we create an example using just a few accounts. The journal entry amounts are taken from the pre-closing balances in the T-accounts:

Audio lecture–AP4-2
Video 4-2
www.mhhe.com/libby6e

Revenues have credit balances. Close them with debits. {

Sales Revenue (−R)	100	
Gain on Sale of Assets (−R)	30	
Wages Expense (−E)		40
Loss on Sale of Assets (−E)		10
Retained Earnings (+SE)		80

} *Expenses have debit balances. Close them with credits.*

= Net income

Wages Expense			
Bal.	40	40	CE
Closed	0		

Retained Earnings		
	6,000	Bal.
	80	CE
	6,080	Bal.

Sales Revenue			
CE	100	100	Bal.
		0	Closed

Loss on Sale of Assets			
Bal.	10	10	CE
Closed	0		

130 revenues − 50 expenses = 80
Net income

Gain on Sale of Assets			
CE	30	30	Bal.
		0	Closed

We will now prepare the closing entry for Papa John's at January 31, 2007, although companies close their records only at the end of the fiscal year.[4] These amounts are taken from the adjusted trial balance in Exhibit 4.3.

Restaurant Sales Revenue (−R).............................	66,000	
Franchise Fee Revenue (−R)	4,730	
Investment Income (−R)	1,070	
Gain on Sale of Land (−R)................................	3,000	
Cost of Sales (−E)		30,000
Salaries Expense (−E).................................		16,000
General and Administrative Expenses (−E)...................		7,000
Supplies Expense (−E)		4,000
Rent Expense (−E).....................................		2,000
Insurance Expense (−E)................................		500
Utilities Expense (−E)		600
Depreciation Expense (−E)		2,500
Interest Expense (−E)		550
Income Tax Expense (−E)...............................		3,961
Retained Earnings (+SE)		7,689

---

[4]Most companies use computerized accounting software to record journal entries, produce trial balances and financial statements, and close the books.

SELF-STUDY **QUIZ**

The following is an adjusted trial balance from a recent year for Toys "R" Us. Dollars are in millions. Record the journal entry at the end of the accounting cycle to close the books.

	DEBIT	CREDIT
Cash	2,003	
Accounts receivable	146	
Buildings	6,719	
Accumulated depreciation		1,984
Other assets	3,334	
Accounts payable		991
Notes payable		2,349
Other liabilities		2,656
Contributed capital		437
Retained earnings		3,698
Sales revenue		11,565
Interest income		15
Gain on sale of business		3
Cost of sales	7,849	
Selling, general, and administrative expenses	3,022	
Depreciation expense	348	
Other operating expenses	85	
Interest expense	142	
Income tax expense	50	
Totals	**23,698**	**23,698**

Closing entry:

After you are done, check your answers with the solutions at the bottom of the page.

Post-Closing Trial Balance

A POST-CLOSING TRIAL BALANCE should be prepared as the last step of the accounting cycle to check that debits equal credits and all temporary accounts have been closed.

After the closing process is complete, all income statement accounts have a zero balance. These accounts are then ready for recording revenues and expenses in the new accounting period. The ending balance in Retained Earnings now is up-to-date (matches the amount on the balance sheet) and is carried forward as the beginning balance for the next period. As the last step of the accounting information processing cycle, a **post-closing trial balance** (Exhibit 4.5) should be prepared as a check that debits still equal credits and that all temporary accounts have been closed.

Self-Study Quiz
Solutions

	Debit	Credit
Sales revenue (−R)	11,565	
Interest income (−R)	15	
Gain on sale of business (−R)	3	
Cost of sales (−E)		7,849
Selling, general, and administrative expenses (−E)		3,022
Depreciation expense (−E)		348
Other operating expenses (−E)		85
Interest expense (−E)		142
Income tax expense (−E)		50
Retained earnings (+SE)		87

EXHIBIT 4.5

Post-Closing Trial Balance for
Papa John's International

PAPA JOHN'S INTERNATIONAL, INC.
Trial Balance
At January 31, 2007 (dollars in thousands)

	Adjusted Trial Balance		Post-Closing Trial Balance	
	Debit	Credit	Debit	Credit
Cash	43,900		43,900	
Accounts receivable	20,030		20,030	
Interest receivable	70		70	
Supplies	22,000		22,000	
Prepaid expenses	14,500		14,500	
Other current assets	14,000		14,000	
Investments (long-term)	2,000		2,000	
Property and equipment	396,000		396,000	
Accumulated depreciation		191,500		191,500
Notes receivable (long-term)	15,000		15,000	
Intangibles	67,000		67,000	
Other assets	17,000		17,000	
Accounts payable		39,000		39,000
Dividends payable		3,000		3,000
Accrued expenses payable		76,150		76,150
Income tax payable		3,961		3,961
Unearned franchise fees		6,200		6,200
Notes payable (long-term)		110,000		110,000
Other long-term liabilities		27,000		27,000
Contributed capital		66,000		66,000
Retained earnings		81,000		88,689
Restaurant sales revenue		66,000		0
Franchise fees revenue		4,730		0
Investment income		1,070		0
Gain on sale of land		3,000		0
Cost of sales	30,000		0	
Salaries expense	16,000		0	
General and administrative expenses	7,000		0	
Supplies expense	4,000		0	
Rent expense	2,000		0	
Insurance expense	500		0	
Utilities expense	600		0	
Depreciation expense	2,500		0	
Interest expense	550		0	
Income tax expense	3,961		0	
Total	$678,611	$678,611	$611,500	$611,500

Assets / *Liabilities* / *Stockholders' Equity* / *Revenues and Gains* / *Expenses and Losses*

Net income of $7,689 is closed to Retained Earnings: $81,000 + $7,689 = $88,689

FINANCIAL ANALYSIS

Accruals and Deferrals: Judging Earnings Quality

Most of the adjustments discussed in this chapter, such as the allocation of prepaid insurance or the determination of accrued interest expense, involve direct calculations and require little judgment on the part of the company's management. In later chapters, we discuss many other adjustments that involve difficult and complex estimates about the future. These include, for example, estimates of customers' ability to make payments to the company for purchases on account, the useful lives of new machines, and future amounts that a company may owe on warranties of products sold in the past. Each of these estimates and many others can have significant effects on the stream of net earnings that companies report over time.

When attempting to value firms based on their balance sheet and income statement data, analysts also evaluate the estimates that form the basis for the adjustments. Those firms that make relatively pessimistic estimates that reduce current income are judged to follow **conservative** financial reporting strategies, and experienced analysts give these reports more credence. The earnings numbers reported by these companies are often said to be of **higher quality** because they are influenced less by management's natural optimism. Firms that consistently make optimistic estimates that result in reporting higher net income, however, are judged to be **aggressive.** Analysts judge these companies' operating performance to be of **lower quality.**

DEMONSTRATION CASE

We take our final look at the accounting activities of Terrific Lawn Maintenance Corporation by illustrating the activities at the end of the accounting cycle: the adjustment process, financial statement preparation, and the closing process. No adjustments had been made to the accounts to reflect all revenues earned and expenses incurred in April. The trial balance for Terrific Lawn on April 30, 2009, based on the unadjusted balances in Chapter 3, is as follows:

TERRIFIC LAWN MAINTENANCE CORPORATION **Unadjusted Trial Balance** **At April 30, 2009**		
	Debit	**Credit**
Cash	5,032	
Accounts receivable	1,700	
Notes receivable	0	
Prepaid expenses	300	
Land	3,750	
Equipment	4,600	
Accumulated depreciation		0
Accounts payable		220
Wages payable		0
Utilities payable		0
Notes payable		3,700
Interest payable		0
Income tax payable		0
Unearned revenues		1,600
Contributed capital		9,000
		continued

Retained earnings		0
Mowing revenue		5,200
Interest revenue		12
Wages expense	3,900	
Fuel expense	410	
Insurance expense	0	
Utilities expense	0	
Depreciation expense	0	
Interest expense	40	
Income tax expense	0	
Total	$19,732	$19,732

Additional Information follows:

a. One-fourth of the $1,600 cash received from the city at the beginning of April for future mowing service has been earned in April. The $1,600 in Unearned Revenues represents four months of service (April through July).

b. Insurance costing $300 providing coverage for six months (April through September) paid by Terrific Lawn at the beginning of April has been partially used in April.

c. Mowers, edgers, rakes, and hand tools (equipment) have been used in April to generate revenues. The company estimates $300 in depreciation each year.

d. Wages have been paid through April 28. Employees worked the last two days of April and will be paid in May. Wages accrue at $200 per day.

e. An extra telephone line was installed in April at an estimated cost of $52, including hookup and usage charges. The bill will be received and paid in May.

f. Interest accrues on the outstanding notes payable at an annual rate of 12 percent. The $3,700 in principal has been outstanding all month.

g. The estimated income tax rate for Terrific Lawn is 35 percent.

Required:

1. Using the three-step process outlined in this chapter, (1) identify the type of adjustment related to each transaction, (2) determine the amount for the adjustment, and (3) record the adjusting journal entries for April.

2. Prepare an adjusted trial balance.

3. Prepare an income statement, statement of stockholders' equity, and balance sheet from the amounts in the adjusted trial balance. Include earnings per share on the income statement. The company issued 1,500 shares.

4. Prepare the closing entry for April 30, 2009.

5. Compute the company's net profit margin for the month.

Now you can check your answers with the following solution to these requirements.

SUGGESTED SOLUTION

1. *a.* **Step 1: Identify type of adjustment.**   Unearned Revenue requires an unearned revenue adjustment.

Step 2: Determine the amount. $1,600 × 1/4 = $400 earned

Step 3: Record the adjusting entry.   The Unearned Revenues account is currently overstated by $400 and Mowing Revenue is understated.

AJE a

| Unearned Revenues (−L) .... | 400 | |
| Mowing Revenue (+R, +SE) .... | | 400 |

Assets	=	Liabilities	+	Stockholders' Equity
		Unearned Revenues −400		Mowing Revenue (+R) +400

Equality checks: (1) Debits $400 = Credits $400; (2) the accounting equation is in balance.

b. **Step 1: Identify type of adjustment.**   Prepaid Expenses requires a prepaid expense adjustment.

Step 2: Determine the amount. $300 × 1/6 = $50 insurance used in April

Step 3: Record the adjusting entry.   The Prepaid Expenses account is currently overstated by $50 and Insurance Expense is understated.

AJE b

| Insurance Expense (+E, −SE) .... | 50 | |
| Prepaid Expenses (−A) .... | | 50 |

Assets	=	Liabilities	+	Stockholders' Equity
Prepaid Expenses−50				Insurance Expense (+E) −50

Equality checks: (1) Debits $50 = Credits $50; (2) the accounting equation is in balance.

c. **Step 1: Identify type of adjustment.**   Equipment represents a prepaid expense that requires an adjustment for the amount used during the period.

Step 2: Determine the amount. $300 × 1/12 = $25 depreciation on equipment in April

Step 3: Record the adjusting entry.   Depreciation Expense is understated by $25 while the net book value of Equipment is overstated.

AJE c

| Depreciation Expense (+E, −SE)........................ | 25 | |
| Accumulated Depreciation (+XA, −A) .... | | 25 |

Assets	=	Liabilities	+	Stockholders' Equity
Accumulated Depreciation (+XA) −25				Depreciation Expense (+E) −25

Equality checks: (1) Debits $25 = Credits $25; (2) the accounting equation is in balance.

d. **Step 1: Identify type of adjustment.**   Unrecorded wages requires an accrued expense adjustment.

Step 2: Determine the amount. $200 per day × 2 days = $400 incurred

Step 3: Record the adjusting entry.   Wages Expense and Wages Payable are currently understated by $400.

AJE d

| Wages Expense (+E, −SE) .... | 400 | |
| Wages Payable (+L) .... | | 400 |

Assets	=	Liabilities	+	Stockholders' Equity
		Wages Payable +400		Wages Expense (+E) −400

Equality checks: (1) Debits $400 = Credits $400; (2) the accounting equation is in balance.

e. **Step 1: Identify type of adjustment.**   Unrecorded utilities used during the month requires an accrued expense adjustment.

Step 2: Determine the amount. $52 estimated expense incurred (given)

Step 3: Record the adjusting entry.   Utilities Expense and Utilities Payable are currently understated by $52.

AJE e

| Utilities Expense (+E, −SE)................................... | 52 | |
| Utilities Payable (+L)....................................... | | 52 |

Assets	=	Liabilities	+	Stockholders' Equity
		Utilities Payable +52		Utilities Expense (+E) −52

Equality checks: (1) Debits $52 = Credits $52; (2) the accounting equation is in balance.

f. **Step 1: Identify type of adjustment.**   Unrecorded interest expense for the month requires an accrued expense adjustment.

Step 2: Determine the amount. $3,700 principal × .12 rate × 1/12 = $37 interest

Step 3: Record the adjusting entry.   Interest Expense and Interest Payable are currently understated by $37.

AJE f

Interest Expense (+E, −SE)...............................	37	
Interest Payable (+L).................................		37

Assets	=	Liabilities	+	Stockholders' Equity	
		Interest Payable +37		Interest Expense (+E)	−37

Equality checks: (1) Debits $37 = Credits $37; (2) the accounting equation is in balance.

g. **Step 1: Identify type of adjustment.** Unrecorded income tax expense for the month requires an accrued expense adjustment.

Step 2: Determine the amount.

Computation of pretax income:

	Revenues	Expenses	
Unadjusted totals	$5,212	$4,350	From trial balance
a	400		
b		50	
c		25	
d		400	
e		52	
f		37	
Adjusted amounts	$5,612	$4,914	= $698 pretax income

$698 pretax income × .35 rate = $244 tax (rounded)

Step 3: Record the adjusting entry. Income Tax Expense and Income Tax Payable are currently understated by $244.

AJE g

Income Tax Expense (+E, −SE)	244	
Income Tax Payable (+L)		244

Assets	=	Liabilities	+	Stockholders' Equity	
		Income Tax Payable + 244		Income Tax Expense (+E)	− 244

Equality checks: (1) Debits $244 = Credits $244; (2) the accounting equation is in balance.

2. Adjusted trial balance:

	Unadjusted Trial Balance		Adjustments		Adjusted Trial Balance	
	Debit	**Credit**	**Debit**	**Credit**	**Debit**	**Credit**
Cash	5,032				5,032	
Accounts receivable	1,700				1,700	
Notes receivable	0				0	
Prepaid expenses	300			(b) 50	250	
Land	3,750				3,750	
Equipment	4,600				4,600	
Accumulated depreciation		0		(c) 25		25
Accounts payable		220				220
Wages payable		0		(d) 400		400
Utilities payable		0		(e) 52		52
Notes payable		3,700				3,700
Interest payable		0		(f) 37		37
Income tax payable		0		(g) 244		244
Unearned revenues		1,600	(a) 400			1,200
Contributed capital		9,000				9,000
Retained earnings		0				0
Mowing revenue		5,200		(a) 400		5,600
Interest revenue		12				12
Wages expense	3,900		(d) 400		4,300	
Fuel expense	410				410	
Insurance expense	0		(b) 50		50	
Utilities expense	0		(e) 52		52	
Depreciation expense	0		(c) 25		25	
Interest expense	40		(f) 37		77	
Income tax expense	0		(g) 244		244	
Total	$19,732	$19,732	$1,208	$1,208	$20,490	$20,490

TERRIFIC LAWN MAINTENANCE CORPORATION
Adjusted Trial Balance
At April 30, 2009

3. Financial statements

TERRIFIC LAWN MAINTENANCE CORPORATION
Income Statement
For the Month Ended April 30, 2009

Operating Revenues	
Mowing revenue	$5,600
Operating Expenses	
Fuel expense	410
Wages expense	4,300
Insurance expense	50
Utilities expense	52
Depreciation expense	25
	4,837
Operating income	763
Other items	
Interest revenue	12
Interest expense	(77)
Pretax income	698
Income tax expense	244
Net Income	$ 454
Earnings per share ($454 ÷ 1,500 shares)	$.30

TERRIFIC LAWN MAINTENANCE CORPORATION
Statement of Stockholders' Equity
For the Month Ended April 30, 2009

	Contributed Capital	Retained Earnings	Total
Balance, April 1, 2009	$ 0	$ 0	$ 0
Stock issuance	9,000		9,000
Net income		454	454
Dividends		0	0
Balance, April 30, 2009	$9,000	$454	$9,454

TERRIFIC LAWN MAINTENANCE CORPORATION
Balance Sheet
April 30, 2009

Assets		**Liabilities**	
Current Assets		Current Liabilities	
Cash	$ 5,032	Accounts payable	$ 220
Accounts receivable	1,700	Wages payable	400
Prepaid expenses	250	Utilities payable	52
Total current assets	6,982	Interest payable	37
		Notes payable	3,700
		Income taxes payable	244
		Unearned revenues	1,200
		Total current liabilities	5,853
Equipment (net of $25			
accumulated depreciation)	4,575		
Land	3,750	**Stockholders' Equity**	
		Contributed capital	9,000
		Retained earnings	454
		Total liabilities and	
Total assets	**$15,307**	**stockholders' equity**	**$15,307**

4. Closing entry:

Mowing revenue (−R)	5,600	
Interest revenue (−R)	12	
Wages expense (−E)		4,300
Fuel expense (−E)		410
Insurance expense (−E)		50
Utilities expense (−E)		52
Depreciation expense (−E)		25
Interest expense (−E)		77
Income tax expense (−E)		244
Retained earnings (+SE)		454

5. Net Profit Margin for April:

$$\frac{\textbf{Net Income}}{\textbf{Net Sales}} = \$454 \div \$5,600 = 8.1\% \text{ for the month of April.}$$

CHAPTER **TAKE-AWAYS**

1. **Explain the purpose of adjustments and analyze the adjustments necessary at the end of the period to update balance sheet and income statement accounts. p. 165**

   - Adjusting entries are necessary at the end of the accounting period to measure income properly, correct errors, and provide for adequate valuation of balance sheet accounts. The analysis involves

     Step 1: Identify the types of adjustments:

       - Unearned revenues—previously recorded liabilities created when cash was received in advance that must be adjusted for the amount of revenue earned during the period
       - Accrued revenues—revenues that were earned during the period but were not yet recorded (cash will be received in the future)
       - Prepaid expenses—previously recorded assets (Prepaid Rent, Supplies, and Equipment) that must be adjusted for the amount of expense incurred during the period
       - Accrued expenses—expenses that were incurred during the period but were not yet recorded (cash will be paid in the future)

     Step 2: Determine the amount of the earned revenue or incurred expense.

     Step 3: Record the adjusting entry needed to obtain the appropriate ending balances in the accounts and post the effects to the respective T-accounts.

   - Recording adjusting entries has no effect on the Cash account.

2. **Explain the purpose of a trial balance. p. 167**

   A trial balance is a list of all accounts with their debit or credit balances indicated in the appropriate column to provide a check on the equality of the debits and credits. The trial balance may be

   - Unadjusted—before adjustments are made.
   - Adjusted—after adjustments are made.
   - Post-closing—after revenues and expenses are closed to Retained Earnings.

3. **Present an income statement with earnings per share, statement of stockholders' equity, balance sheet, and supplemental cash flow information. p. 175**

   Adjusted account balances are used in preparing the following financial statements:

   - Income Statement: Revenues − Expenses = Net Income (including earnings per share computed as net income divided by the average number of shares of common stock outstanding during the period).

- Statement of Stockholders' Equity: (Beginning Contributed Capital + stock issuances − stock repurchases) + (Beginning Retained Earnings + net income − dividends) = Ending Total Stockholders' Equity.
- Balance Sheet: Assets = Liabilities + Stockholders' Equity.
- Supplemental cash flow information: Interest paid, income taxes paid, and significant noncash transactions.

4. **Compute and interpret the net profit margin.   p. 181**

Net profit margin (Net Income ÷ Net Sales) measures how much of every dollar of sales generated during the period is profit. A rising net profit margin signals more efficient management of sales and expenses.

5. **Explain the closing process.   p. 182**

Temporary accounts (revenues, expenses, gains, and losses) are closed to a zero balance at the end of the accounting period to allow for the accumulation of income items in the following period. To close these accounts, debit each revenue and gain account, credit each expense and loss account, and record the difference (equal to net income) to Retained Earnings.

Closing Entry:		
Each revenue	xx	
Each gain	xx	
Each expense		xx
Each loss		xx
Retained earnings		xx
(assumes net income is positive)		

This chapter discussed the important steps in the accounting process that take place at year-end. These include the adjustment process, the preparation of the basic financial statements, and the closing process that prepares the records for the next accounting period. This end to the internal portions of the accounting process, however, is just the beginning of the process of communicating accounting information to external users.

In the next chapter we take a closer look at more sophisticated financial statements and related disclosures. We also examine the process by which financial information is disseminated to professional analysts, investors, the Securities and Exchange Commission, and the public, and the role each plays in analyzing and interpreting the information. These discussions will help you consolidate much of what you have learned about the financial reporting process from previous chapters. It will also preview many of the important issues we address later in the book.

KEY **RATIO**

Net profit margin measures how much of every sales dollar generated during the period is profit. A high or rising ratio suggests that the company is managing its sales and expenses efficiently. It is computed as follows (p. 181):

$$\text{Net Profit Margin} = \frac{\text{Net Income}}{\text{Net Sales (or Operating Revenues)}}$$

FINDING **FINANCIAL INFORMATION**

Balance Sheet

Current Assets

Accrued revenues include:
   Interest receivable
   Rent receivable
Prepaid expenses include:
   Supplies
   Prepaid insurance
      expense

Noncurrent Assets

Prepaid expenses include:
   Property and equipment
   Intangibles

Current Liabilities

Accrued expenses include:
   Interest payable
   Wages payable
   Utilities payable
   Income tax payable
Unearned revenues include:
   Unearned ticket revenue

Income Statement

Revenues
   Increased by adjusting entries

Expenses
   Increased by adjusting entries

Pretax Income
   Income tax expense

Net Income

Notes

In Various Notes **(if not on the balance
   sheet)**
Details of accrued expenses payable
Interest paid, income taxes paid,
   significant noncash transactions
   (if not reported on the statement of
   cash flows)

Statement of Cash Flows

Adjusting Entries Do Not Affect Cash
Supplemental disclosure:
   Interest paid
   Income taxes paid
   Significant noncash transactions

KEY **TERMS**

Accounting Cycle   p. 165
Accrued Expenses   p. 172
Accrued Revenues   p. 170
Adjusting Entries   p. 165
Closing Entry   p. 182
Contra-Account   p. 168

**Net Book Value (Book Value,
   Carrying Value)**   p. 168
**Permanent (Real)
   Accounts**   p. 182
Post-Closing Trial Balance   p. 184
Prepaid Expenses   p. 171

**Temporary (Nominal)
   Accounts**   p. 182
Trial Balance   p. 167
**Unearned (Deferred)
   Revenues**   p. 168

QUESTIONS

1. What is the purpose of recording adjusting entries?
2. What is a trial balance? What is its purpose?
3. List the four types of adjusting entries, and give an example of each type.
4. What is a contra-asset? Give an example of one.
5. Explain how the financial statements relate to each other.
6. What is the equation for each of the following statements: (a) income statement, (b) balance
    sheet, (c) statement of cash flows, and (d) statement of stockholders' equity?

7. Explain the effect of adjusting entries on cash.
8. How is earnings per share computed and interpreted?
9. How is net profit margin computed and interpreted?
10. Contrast an unadjusted trial balance with an adjusted trial balance. What is the purpose of each?
11. What is the purpose of closing entries?
12. Differentiate among (a) permanent, (b) temporary, (c) real, and (d) nominal accounts.
13. Why are the income statement accounts closed but the balance sheet accounts are not?
14. What is a post-closing trial balance? Is it a useful part of the accounting information processing cycle? Explain.

MULTIPLE-CHOICE QUESTIONS

1. Which of the following accounts would not appear in a closing entry?
   a. Interest Income
   b. Accumulated Depreciation
   c. Retained Earnings
   d. Salary Expense
2. Which account is least likely to appear in an adjusting journal entry?
   a. Cash
   b. Interest Receivable
   c. Property Tax Expense
   d. Salaries Payable
3. On October 1, 2009, the $6,000 premium on a one-year insurance policy for the building was paid and recorded as Prepaid Insurance. At the end of 2009 (end of the accounting period), what adjusting entry is needed?

a.	Insurance Expense (+E)	4,500	
	Prepaid Insurance (−A)		4,500
b.	Prepaid Insurance (+A)	1,500	
	Insurance Expense (−E)		1,500
c.	Insurance Expense (+E)	1,500	
	Prepaid Insurance (−A)		1,500
d.	Prepaid Insurance (+A)	4,500	
	Insurance Expense (−E)		4,500

4. On March 1, 2010, Oakcrest Company signed a three-year $100,000 note payable with 9 percent interest. Interest is due on March 1 of each year beginning in 2011. What amount of interest expense should be reported on the income statement for the year ended December 31, 2010?
   a. $9,000
   b. $7,500
   c. $6,750
   d. $2,500
5. Failure to make an adjusting entry to recognize accrued salaries payable would cause which of the following?
   a. An overstatement of assets and stockholders' equity
   b. An overstatement of assets and liabilities
   c. An understatement of expenses, liabilities, and stockholders' equity
   d. An understatement of expenses and liabilities and an overstatement of stockholders' equity
6. An adjusted trial balance
   a. Shows the ending account balances in a "debit" and "credit" format before posting the adjusting journal entries.
   b. Is prepared after closing entries have been posted.
   c. Is a tool used by financial analysts to review the performance of publicly traded companies.
   d. Shows the ending account balances resulting from the adjusting journal entries in a "debit" and "credit" format.

7. JJ Company owns a building. Which of the following statements regarding depreciation as used by accountants is *false?*
   a. As the value of the building decreases over time, it "depreciates."
   b. Depreciation is an estimated expense to be recorded over the building's estimated useful life.
   c. As depreciation is recorded, stockholders' equity is reduced.
   d. As depreciation is recorded, the net book value of the asset is reduced.

8. At the beginning of 2010, Donna Company had $1,000 of supplies on hand. During 2010, the company purchased supplies amounting to $6,200 (paid for in cash and debited to Supplies). At December 31, 2010, a count of supplies reflected $1,600. The adjusting entry Donna Company will record on December 31, 2010, to adjust the Supplies account would include a
   a. Credit to Supplies Expense for $5,600.
   b. Credit to Supplies for $1,600.
   c. Debit to Supplies for $1,600.
   d. Debit to Supplies Expense for $5,600.

9. What ratio is required by GAAP to be reported on the financial statements or in the notes to the statements?
   a. Return on equity ratio.
   b. Net profit margin ratio.
   c. Current ratio.
   d. Earnings per share ratio.

10. If a company is successful in reducing selling and administrative costs while maintaining sales volume and the sales price of its product, what is the effect on the net profit margin ratio?
   a. The ratio will not change.
   b. The ratio will increase.
   c. The ratio will decrease.
   d. Either (a) or (c).

For more practice with multiple choice questions, go to the text website at www.mhhe.com/libby6e

Available with McGraw-Hill's Homework Manager

MINI-**EXERCISES**

Preparing a Trial Balance

M4-1
LO2

Puglisi Company has the following adjusted accounts and balances at year-end (June 30, 2010):

Accounts Payable	$200	Interest Expense	$ 70
Accounts Receivable	370	Interest Income	60
Accrued Expenses Payable	160	Inventories	660
Accumulated Depreciation	250	Land	300
Buildings and Equipment	1,400	Long-Term Debt	1,360
Cash	150	Prepaid Expenses	30
Contributed Capital	400	Salaries Expense	640
Cost of Sales	880	Sales Revenue	2,500
Depreciation Expense	150	Rent Expense	460
Income Taxes Expense	110	Retained Earnings	150
Income Taxes Payable	50	Unearned Fees	90

Prepare an adjusted trial balance in good form for the Puglisi Company at June 30, 2010.

Matching Definitions with Terms

M4-2
LO1

Match each definition with its related term by entering the appropriate letter in the space provided.

Definition	Term
____ (1) An expense incurred; not yet paid or recorded.	A. Accrued expense
____ (2) Rent revenue collected; not yet earned.	B. Prepaid expense
____ (3) Property taxes incurred; not yet paid.	C. Accrued revenue
____ (4) Rent not yet collected; already earned.	D. Unearned revenue
____ (5) A revenue not yet earned; collected in advance.	
____ (6) Office supplies on hand to be used next accounting period.	
____ (7) An expense not yet incurred; paid in advance.	
____ (8) A revenue earned; not yet collected.	

M4-3
LO1

Matching Definitions with Terms

Match each definition with its related term by entering the appropriate letter in the space provided.

Definition	Term
____ (1) At year-end, service revenue of $1,000 was collected in cash but was not yet earned.	A. Accrued expense
	B. Prepaid expense
____ (2) Interest of $550 on a note receivable was earned at year-end, although collection of the interest is not due until the following year.	C. Accrued revenue
	D. Unearned revenue
____ (3) Office supplies were purchased during the year for $700, and $100 of them remained on hand (unused) at year-end.	
____ (4) At year-end, wages payable of $5,600 had not been recorded or paid.	

M4-4
LO1

Recording Adjusting Entries (Deferred Accounts)

Using the three-step process illustrated in the chapter, (1) identify the type of adjustment that is required for each of the following transactions (a) through (c) for Morgan Marketing Company, (2) determine the amount of the adjustment, and (3) record the adjusting entry necessary at year-end December, 31, 2011.

a. Collected $1,000 rent for the period December 1, 2011, to April 1, 2012, which was credited to Unearned Rent Revenue on December 1, 2011.
b. Paid $3,800 for a two-year insurance premium on July 1, 2011; debited Prepaid Insurance for that amount.
c. Purchased a machine for $32,000 cash on January 1, 2008. The company estimates annual depreciation at $3,000.

M4-5
LO1

Determining Financial Statement Effects of Adjusting Entries (Deferred Accounts)

For each of the transactions in M4–4, indicate the amounts and direction of effects of the adjusting entry on the elements of the balance sheet and income statement. Using the following format, indicate + for increase, − for decrease, and NE for no effect.

	BALANCE SHEET			INCOME STATEMENT		
Transaction	Assets	Liabilities	Stockholders' Equity	Revenues	Expenses	Net Income
a.						
b.						
c.						

M4-6
LO1

Recording Adjusting Entries (Accrued Accounts)

Using the three-step process illustrated in the chapter, (1) identify the type of adjustment that is required for each of the following transactions (a) through (c) for Morgan Marketing Company, (2) determine the amount of the adjustment, and (3) record the adjusting entry necessary at year-end December 31, 2011.

a. Estimated electricity usage at $360 for December to be paid in January 2012.

b. Owed wages to 10 employees who each worked four days at $150 per day at the end of December. The company will pay employees at the end of the first week of January 2012.

c. On September 1, 2011, loaned $5,000 to an officer who will repay the loan principal and interest in one year at an annual interest rate of 14 percent.

Determining Financial Statement Effects of Adjusting Entries (Accrued Accounts)

M4-7
L01

For each of the transactions in M4–6, indicate the amounts and direction of effects of the adjusting entry on the elements of the balance sheet and income statement. Using the following format, indicate + for increase, − for decrease, and NE for no effect.

	BALANCE SHEET			INCOME STATEMENT		
Transaction	Assets	Liabilities	Stockholders' Equity	Revenues	Expenses	Net Income
a.						
b.						
c.						

Reporting an Income Statement with Earnings per Share

M4-8
L03

Morgan Marketing Company has the following adjusted trial balance at December 31, 2011. No dividends were declared. However, 500 shares issued at the end of the year for $3,000 are included below:

	Debit	Credit
Cash	$ 1,500	
Accounts receivable	2,000	
Interest receivable	100	
Prepaid insurance	1,600	
Notes receivable (long-term)	2,800	
Equipment	15,000	
Accumulated depreciation		$ 3,000
Accounts payable		2,400
Accrued expenses payable		3,920
Income taxes payable		2,700
Unearned rent revenue		500
Contributed capital (800 shares)		3,700
Retained earnings		2,000
Sales revenue		37,450
Interest revenue		100
Rent revenue		750
Wages expense	19,000	
Depreciation expense	1,800	
Utilities expense	320	
Insurance expense	700	
Rent expense	9,000	
Income tax expense	2,700	
Total	$56,520	$56,520

Prepare a classified income statement in good form for 2010. Include earnings per share.

Reporting a Statement of Stockholders' Equity

M4-9
L03

Refer to M4–8. Prepare a statement of stockholders' equity in good form for 2011.

M4-10
LO3

Reporting a Balance Sheet and Explaining the Effects of Adjustments on the Statement of Cash Flows

Refer to M4–8.
1. Prepare a classified balance sheet in good form at December 31, 2011.
2. Explain how the adjustments in M4–4 and M4–6 affected the operating, investing, and financing activities on the statement of cash flows.

M4-11
LO4

Analyzing Net Profit Margin

Compute net income based on the trial balance in M4–8. Then compute Morgan Marketing Company's net profit margin for 2011.

M4-12
LO5

Recording Closing Entries

Refer to the adjusted trial balance in M4–8. Prepare the closing entry on December 31, 2011.

EXERCISES

 Available with McGraw-Hill's Homework Manager

E4-1
LO2

Preparing a Trial Balance

Darrius Consultants, Inc., provides marketing research for clients in the retail industry. The company had the following unadjusted balances at September 30, 2010:

Accumulated Depreciation		Accrued Expenses Payable	
	18,100		25,650

Cash		General and Administrative Expenses		Supplies	
163,000		320,050		12,200	

Wages and Benefits Expense		Prepaid Expenses		Interest Expense	
1,590,000		10,200		17,200	

Accounts Receivable		Consulting Fees Revenue		Retained Earnings	
225,400			2,564,200		?

Income Taxes Payable		Travel Expense		Building and Equipment	
	2,030	23,990		323,040	

Utilities Expense		Gain on Sale of Land		Unearned Consulting Fees	
25,230			5,000		32,500

Investment Income		Accounts Payable		Land	
	10,800		86,830	60,000	

Other Operating Expenses		Contributed Capital		Professional Development Expense	
188,000			223,370	18,600	

Notes Payable		Rent Expense (on leased computers)		Investments	
	160,000	152,080		145,000	

Required:
Prepare in good form an unadjusted trial balance for Darrius Consultants, Inc., at September 30, 2010.

Identifying Adjusting Entries from Unadjusted Trial Balance

In its annual report, Hewlett-Packard Company states, "We are a leading global provider of products, technologies, solutions and services to consumers and businesses. Our offerings span information technology ('IT') infrastructure, personal computing and other access devices, global services and imaging and printing. Our products and services are available worldwide." Following is a trial balance listing accounts that Hewlett-Packard uses. Assume that the balances are unadjusted at the end of a recent fiscal year ended October 31.

E4-2
LO1, 2, 5
Hewlett-Packard
Company

HEWLETT-PACKARD COMPANY
Unadjusted Trial Balance
(dollars in millions)

	Debit	Credit
Cash	$ 14,200	
Short-term investments	400	
Accounts receivable	11,900	
Inventory	6,000	
Other current assets	8,500	
Property, plant, and equipment	13,300	
Accumulated depreciation		$ 6,800
Other assets	27,200	
Short-term note payable		1,000
Accounts payable		9,300
Accrued liabilities		11,000
Deferred revenue		3,700
Income tax payable		1,600
Long-term debt		6,500
Other liabilities		3,800
Contributed capital		24,600
Retained earnings		10,700
Product revenue		58,900
Service revenue		13,700
Interest revenue		500
Cost of products	43,700	
Cost of services	10,000	
Interest expense	200	
Research and development expense	3,700	
Selling, general, and administrative expense	11,000	
Other expenses	1,600	
Loss on investments	100	
Income tax expense	300	
Total	$152,100	$152,100

Required:
1. Based on the information in the unadjusted trial balance, list types of adjustments on the balance sheet that may need to be adjusted at October 31 and the related income statement account for each (no computations are necessary). You may need to make assumptions.
2. Which accounts should be closed at the end of the year? Why?

E4-3

L01

Recording Adjusting Entries

Gonzalez Company completed its first year of operations on December 31, 2010. All of the 2010 entries have been recorded except for the following:

a. At year-end, employees earned wages of $6,000, which will be paid on the next payroll date, January 6, 2011.

b. At year-end, the company had earned interest revenue of $3,000. The cash will be collected March 1, 2011.

Required:

1. What is the annual reporting period for this company?
2. Identify whether each transaction results in adjusting a deferred or an accrued account. Using the process illustrated in the chapter, give the required adjusting entry for transactions (*a*) and (*b*). Include appropriate dates and write a brief explanation of each entry.
3. Why are these adjustments made?

E4-4

L01, 3

Recording Adjusting Entries and Reporting Balances in Financial Statements

Latta Company is making adjusting entries for the year ended December 31, 2011. In developing information for the adjusting entries, the accountant learned the following:

a. A two-year insurance premium of $3,600 was paid on September 1, 2011, for coverage beginning on that date.

b. At December 31, 2011, the following data relating to Shipping Supplies were obtained from the records and supporting documents.

Shipping supplies on hand, January 1, 2011	$ 9,000
Purchases of shipping supplies during 2011	60,000
Shipping supplies on hand, counted on December 31, 2011	20,000

Required:

1. Using the process illustrated in the chapter, record the adjusting entry for insurance at December 31, 2011, assuming that the premium was paid on September 1, 2011, and the bookkeeper debited the full amount to Prepaid Insurance.
2. Using the process illustrated in the chapter, record the adjusting entry for supplies at December 31, 2011, assuming that the purchases of shipping supplies were debited in full to Shipping Supplies.
3. What amount should be reported on the 2011 income statement for Insurance Expense? For Shipping Supplies Expense?
4. What amount should be reported on the December 31, 2011, balance sheet for Prepaid Insurance? For Shipping Supplies?

E4-5

L02

Determining Financial Statement Effects of Adjusting Entries

Refer to E4–3 and E4–4.

Required:

For each of the transactions in E4–3 and E4–4, indicate the amount and direction of effects of the adjusting entry on the elements of the balance sheet and income statement. Using the following format, indicate + for increase, − for decrease, and NE for no effect.

	BALANCE SHEET			INCOME STATEMENT		
Transaction	Assets	Liabilities	Stockholders' Equity	Revenues	Expenses	Net Income
E4–3 (*a*)						
E4–3 (*b*)						
E4–4 (*a*)						
E4–4 (*b*)						

Recording Seven Typical Adjusting Entries

Heald's Variety Store is completing the accounting process for the year just ended, December 31, 2011. The transactions during 2011 have been journalized and posted. The following data with respect to adjusting entries are available:

a. Office supplies on hand at January 1, 2011, totaled $350. Office supplies purchased and debited to Office Supplies during the year amounted to $500. The year-end count showed $275 of supplies on hand.

b. Wages earned by employees during December 2011, unpaid and unrecorded at December 31, 2011, amounted to $2,200. The last payroll was December 28; the next payroll will be January 6, 2012.

c. Three-fourths of the basement of the store is rented for $1,600 per month to another merchant, M. Dittman Inc. Dittman sells compatible, but not competitive, merchandise. On November 1, 2011, the store collected six months' rent in the amount of $9,600 in advance from Dittman; it was credited in full to Unearned Rent Revenue when collected.

d. The remaining basement space is rented to Kathy's Specialty Shop for $480 per month, payable monthly. On December 31, 2011, the rent for November and December 2011 had not been collected or recorded. Collection is expected January 10, 2012.

e. The store used delivery equipment that cost $30,500; $6,100 was the estimated depreciation for 2011.

f. On July 1, 2011, a two-year insurance premium amounting to $2,200 was paid in cash and debited in full to Prepaid Insurance. Coverage began on July 1, 2011.

g. Heald's operates a repair shop to meet its own needs. The shop also does repairs for M. Dittman. At the end of December 31, 2011, Dittman had not paid $800 for completed repairs. This amount has not yet been recorded as Repair Shop Revenue. Collection is expected during January 2012.

Required:
1. Identify each of these transactions as an unearned revenue, prepaid expense, accrued revenue, or accrued expense.
2. Record the adjusting entry that should be recorded for Heald's at December 31, 2011.

E4-6
L01

Recording Seven Typical Adjusting Entries

Johnson's Boat Yard, Inc., is completing the accounting process for the year just ended, November 30, 2010. The transactions during 2010 have been journalized and posted. The following data with respect to adjusting entries are available:

a. Johnson's winterized (cleaned and covered) three boats for customers at the end of November, but did not record the service for $2,100.

b. The Carter family paid Johnson's $3,000 on November 1, 2010, to store their sailboat for the winter until May 1, 2011. Johnson's credited the full amount to Unearned Storage Revenue on November 1.

c. Wages earned by employees during November 2010, unpaid and unrecorded at November 30, 2010, amounted to $2,800. The next payroll date will be December 5, 2010.

d. On October 1, 2010, Johnson's paid $1,200 to the local newspaper for an advertisement to run every Thursday for 12 weeks. All ads have been run except for three Thursdays in December to complete the 12-week contract.

e. Johnson's used boat-lifting equipment that cost $200,000; $20,000 was the estimated depreciation for 2010.

f. Boat repair supplies on hand at December 1, 2009, totaled $15,500. Repair supplies purchased and debited to Supplies during the year amounted to $46,000. The year-end count showed $12,400 of the supplies on hand.

g. Johnson's borrowed $150,000 at a 12 percent annual interest rate on April 1, 2010, to expand its boat storage facility. The loan requires Johnson's to pay the interest quarterly until the note is repaid in three years. Johnson's paid quarterly interest on July 1 and October 1.

Required:
1. Identify each of these transactions as an unearned revenue, prepaid expense, accrued revenue, or accrued expense.
2. Record the adjusting entry that should be recorded for Johnson's at November 30, 2010.

E4-7
L01

E4-8   **Determining Financial Statement Effects of Seven Typical Adjusting Entries**

L01   Refer to E4–6.

Required:

For each of the transactions in E4–6, indicate the amount and direction of effects of the adjusting entry on the elements of the balance sheet and income statement. Using the following format, indicate + for increase, − for decrease, and NE for no effect.

	BALANCE SHEET			INCOME STATEMENT		
Transaction	Assets	Liabilities	Stockholders' Equity	Revenues	Expenses	Net Income
a.						
b.						
c.						
etc.						

E4-9   **Determining Financial Statement Effects of Seven Typical Adjusting Entries**

L01   Refer to E4–7.

Required:

For each of the transactions in E4–7, indicate the amount and direction of effects of the adjusting entry on the elements of the balance sheet and income statement. Using the following format, indicate + for increase, − for decrease, and NE for no effect.

	BALANCE SHEET			INCOME STATEMENT		
Transaction	Assets	Liabilities	Stockholders' Equity	Revenues	Expenses	Net Income
a.						
b.						
c.						
etc.						

E4-10   **Recording Transactions Including Adjusting and Closing Entries (Nonquantitative)**

L01, 5   The following accounts are used by Britt's Knits, Inc.

Codes	Accounts	Codes	Accounts
A	Cash	J	Contributed Capital
B	Office Supplies	K	Retained Earnings
C	Accounts Receivable	L	Service Revenue
D	Office Equipment	M	Interest Revenue
E	Accumulated Depreciation	N	Wage Expense
F	Note Payable	O	Depreciation Expense
G	Wages Payable	P	Interest Expense
H	Interest Payable	Q	Supplies Expense
I	Unearned Service Revenue	R	None of the above

Required:

For each of the following nine independent situations, give the journal entry by entering the appropriate code(s) and amount(s).

Independent Situations	DEBIT		CREDIT	
	Code	Amount	Code	Amount
a. Accrued wages, unrecorded and unpaid at year-end, $400 (example).	N	400	G	400
b. Service revenue collected in advance, $800.				
c. Dividends declared and paid during the year, $900.				
d. Depreciation expense for the year, $1,000.				
e. Service revenue earned but not yet collected at year-end, $600.				
f. Office supplies on hand during the year, $400; supplies on hand at year-end, $150.				
g. At year-end, interest on note payable not yet recorded or paid, $220.				
h. Balance at year-end in Service Revenue account, $62,000. Give the closing entry at year-end.				
i. Balance at year-end in Interest Expense account, $420. Give the closing entry at year-end.				

Determining Financial Statement Effects of Three Adjusting Entries

E4-11
LO2

DuPage Company started operations on January 1, 2010. It is now December 31, 2010, the end of the annual accounting period. The part-time bookkeeper needs your help to analyze the following three transactions:

a. On January 1, 2010, the company purchased a special machine for cash at a cost of $12,000. The machine's cost is estimated to depreciate at $1,200 per year.
b. During 2010, the company purchased office supplies that cost $1,400. At the end of 2010, office supplies of $400 remained on hand.
c. On July 1, 2010, the company paid cash of $400 for a two-year premium on an insurance policy on the machine; coverage begins on July 1, 2010.

Required:
Complete the following schedule with the amounts that should be reported for 2010:

Selected Balance Sheet Amounts at December 31, 2010	Amount to Be Reported
Assets	
Equipment	$_____
Accumulated depreciation	_____
Carrying value of equipment	_____
Office supplies	_____
Prepaid insurance	_____

Selected Income Statement Amounts for the Year Ended December 31, 2010	
Expenses	
Depreciation expense	$_____
Office supplies expense	_____
Insurance expense	_____

Determining Financial Statement Effects of Adjustments for Interest on Two Notes

E4-12
LO1

Note 1: On April 1, 2011, Seaquist Corporation received a $20,000, 10 percent note from a customer in settlement of a $20,000 open account receivable. According to the terms, the principal of the note and interest are payable at the end of 12 months. The annual accounting period for Seaquist ends on December 31, 2011.

Note 2: On August 1, 2011, to meet a cash shortage, Seaquist Corporation obtained a $20,000, 12 percent loan from a local bank. The principal of the note and interest expense are payable at the end of six months.

Required:

For the relevant transaction dates of each note, indicate the amounts and direction of effects on the elements of the balance sheet and income statement. Using the following format, indicate + for increase, − for decrease, and NE for no effect. (**Reminder:** Assets = Liabilities + Stockholders' Equity; Revenues − Expenses = Net Income; and Net Income accounts are closed to Retained Earnings, a part of Stockholders' Equity.)

	BALANCE SHEET			INCOME STATEMENT		
Date	Assets	Liabilities	Stockholders' Equity	Revenues	Expenses	Net Income
Note 1 April 1, 2011						
December 31, 2011						
March 31, 2012						
Note 2 August 1, 2011						
December 31, 2011						
January 31, 2012						

E4-13
LO1
Deere & Company

Inferring Transactions

Deere & Company is the world's leading producer of agricultural equipment; a leading supplier of a broad range of industrial equipment for construction, forestry, and public works; a producer and marketer of a broad line of lawn and grounds care equipment; and a provider of credit, managed health care plans, and insurance products for businesses and the general public. The following information is from a recent annual report (in millions of dollars):

Income Taxes Payable		
(a) ?	Beg. bal. 71 (b) 332	
	End. bal. 80	

Dividends Payable		
(c) ?	Beg. bal. 43 (d) 176	
	End. bal. 48	

Interest Payable		
(e) 297	Beg. bal. 45 (f) ?	
	End. bal. 51	

Required:
1. Identify the nature of each of the transactions (a) through (f). Specifically, what activities cause the accounts to increase and decrease?
2. For transactions (a), (c), and (f), compute the amount.

E4-14
LO1

Analyzing the Effects of Errors on Financial Statement Items

Goldberg & Broverman, Inc., publishers of movie and song trivia books, made the following errors in adjusting the accounts at year-end (December 31):

a. Did not record $15,000 depreciation on the equipment costing $115,000.
b. Failed to adjust the Unearned Fee Revenue account to reflect that $1,500 was earned by the end of the year.
c. Recorded a full year of accrued interest expense on a $19,000, 9 percent note payable that has been outstanding only since November 1.
d. Failed to adjust Prepaid Insurance to reflect that $650 of insurance coverage has been used.
e. Did not accrue $1,400 owed to the company by another company renting part of the building as a storage facility.

Required:

1. For each error, prepare the adjusting journal entry (a) that was made, if any, and (b) that should have been made at year-end.
2. Using the following headings, indicate the effect of each error and the amount of the effect (that is, the difference between the entry that was or was not made and the entry that should have been made). Use O if the effect overstates the item, U if the effect understates the item, and NE if there is no effect. (**Reminder:** Assets = Liabilities + Stockholders' Equity; Revenues − Expenses = Net Income; and Net Income accounts are closed to Retained Earnings, a part of Stockholders' Equity.)

	BALANCE SHEET			INCOME STATEMENT		
Transaction	Assets	Liabilities	Stockholders' Equity	Revenues	Expenses	Net Income
a.						
b.						
c.						
etc.						

Analyzing the Effects of Adjusting Entries on the Income Statement and Balance Sheet

E4-15
LO1, 3

On December 31, 2011, Quinlan-Cohen Company prepared an income statement and balance sheet and failed to take into account four adjusting entries. The income statement, prepared on this incorrect basis, reflected pretax income of $60,000. The balance sheet (before the effect of income taxes) reflected total assets, $180,000; total liabilities, $80,000; and stockholders' equity, $100,000. The data for the four adjusting entries follow:

a. Depreciation of $16,000 for the year on equipment that cost $170,000 was not recorded.
b. Wages amounting to $34,000 for the last three days of December 2011 were not paid and not recorded (the next payroll will be on January 10, 2012).
c. Rent revenue of $9,600 was collected on December 1, 2011, for office space for the period December 1, 2011, to February 28, 2012. The $9,600 was credited in full to Unearned Rent Revenue when collected.
d. Income taxes were not recorded. The income tax rate for the company is 30 percent.

Required:
Complete the following tabulation to correct the financial statements for the effects of the four errors (indicate deductions with parentheses):

Items	Net Income	Total Assets	Total Liabilities	Stockholders' Equity
Balances reported	$60,000	$180,000	$80,000	$100,000
Additional adjustments:				
a. Depreciation	‒‒‒‒‒	‒‒‒‒‒	‒‒‒‒‒	‒‒‒‒‒
b. Wages	‒‒‒‒‒	‒‒‒‒‒	‒‒‒‒‒	‒‒‒‒‒
c. Rent revenue	‒‒‒‒‒	‒‒‒‒‒	‒‒‒‒‒	‒‒‒‒‒
Adjusted balances	‒‒‒‒‒	‒‒‒‒‒	‒‒‒‒‒	‒‒‒‒‒
d. Income taxes	‒‒‒‒‒	‒‒‒‒‒	‒‒‒‒‒	‒‒‒‒‒
Correct balances	‒‒‒‒‒	‒‒‒‒‒	‒‒‒‒‒	‒‒‒‒‒

Recording the Effects of Adjusting Entries and Reporting a Corrected Income Statement and Balance Sheet

E4-16
LO1, 3

On December 31, 2010, the bookkeeper for Joseph Company prepared the following income statement and balance sheet summarized here but neglected to consider three adjusting entries.

	As Prepared	Effects of Adjusting Entries	Corrected Amounts
Income Statement			
Revenues	$98,000	_____	_____
Expenses	(72,000)	_____	_____
Income tax expense	_____	_____	_____
Net income	$26,000		_____
Balance Sheet			
Assets			
Cash	$20,000	_____	_____
Accounts receivable	22,000	_____	_____
Rent receivable		_____	_____
Equipment	50,000	_____	_____
Accumulated depreciation	(10,000)	_____	_____
	$82,000		_____
Liabilities			
Accounts payable	$10,000	_____	_____
Income taxes payable		_____	_____
Stockholders' Equity			
Contributed capital	40,000	_____	_____
Retained earnings	32,000	_____	_____
	$82,000		_____

Data on the three adjusting entries follow:

a. Depreciation of $4,500 on the equipment for 2010 was not recorded.
b. Rent revenue of $1,500 earned for December 2010 was neither collected nor recorded.
c. Income tax expense of $5,100 for 2010 was neither paid nor recorded.

Required:
1. Prepare the three adjusting entries that were omitted. Use the account titles shown in the income statement and balance sheet data.
2. Complete the two columns to the right in the preceding tabulation to show the correct amounts on the income statement and balance sheet.

E4-17
LO1, 3, 4

Reporting a Correct Income Statement with Earnings per Share to Include the Effects of Adjusting Entries and Evaluating the Net Profit Margin as an Auditor

Derek, Inc., a party rental business, completed its first year of operations on December 31, 2011. Because this is the end of the annual accounting period, the company bookkeeper prepared the following tentative income statement:

Income Statement, 2011	
Rental revenue	$109,000
Expenses	
Salaries and wages expense	26,500
Maintenance expense	12,000
Rent expense	8,800
Utilities expense	4,300
Gas and oil expense	3,000
Miscellaneous expenses (items not listed elsewhere)	1,000
Total expenses	55,600
Income	$ 53,400

You are an independent CPA hired by the company to audit the company's accounting systems and review the financial statements. In your audit, you developed additional data as follows:

a. Wages for the last three days of December amounting to $560 were not recorded or paid.
b. Derek estimated telephone usage at $440 for December 2011, but nothing has been recorded or paid.
c. Depreciation on rental autos, amounting to $24,000 for 2011, was not recorded.
d. Interest on a $15,000, one-year, 8 percent note payable dated October 1, 2011, was not recorded. The 8 percent interest is payable on the maturity date of the note.
e. The Unearned Rental Revenue account includes $4,100 of revenue to be earned in January 2012.
f. Maintenance expense excludes $1,100 that is the cost of maintenance supplies used during 2011.
g. The income tax expense is $5,800. Payment of income tax will be made in 2012.

Required:
1. What adjusting entry for each item (*a*) through (*g*) do you recommend Derek should record at December 31, 2011? If none is required, explain why.
2. Prepare a corrected income statement for 2011 in good form, including earnings per share, assuming that 8,000 shares of stock are outstanding all year. Show computations.
3. Compute the net profit margin based on the corrected information. What does this ratio suggest? If the average net profit margin for the industry is 18 percent, what might you infer about Derek?

Recording Four Adjusting Entries and Completing the Trial Balance Worksheet

E4-18
L01, 2

Seneca Company prepared the following trial balance at the end of its first year of operations ending December 31, 2010. To simplify the case, the amounts given are in thousands of dollars.

Account Titles	UNADJUSTED Debit	UNADJUSTED Credit	ADJUSTMENTS Debit	ADJUSTMENTS Credit	ADJUSTED Debit	ADJUSTED Credit
Cash	38					
Accounts receivable	9					
Prepaid insurance	6					
Machinery	80					
Accumulated depreciation						
Accounts payable		9				
Wages payable						
Income taxes payable						
Contributed capital (4,000 shares)		76				
Retained earnings	4					
Revenues (not detailed)		84				
Expenses (not detailed)	32					
Totals	169	169				

Other data not yet recorded at December 31, 2010:

a. Insurance expired during 2010, $5.
b. Depreciation expense for 2010, $7.
c. Wages payable, $5.
d. Income tax expense, $9.

Required:
1. Prepare the adjusting entries for 2010.
2. Complete the trial balance Adjustments and Adjusted columns.

Reporting an Income Statement, Statement of Stockholders' Equity, and Balance Sheet

E4-19
L03

Refer to E4–18.

Required:

Using the adjusted balances in E4–18, prepare an income statement, statement of stockholders' equity, and balance sheet for 2010.

E4-20   **Recording Closing Entries and Preparing a Post-Closing Trial Balance**

L05   Refer to E4–18.

Required:

1. What is the purpose of "closing the books" at the end of the accounting period?
2. Using the adjusted balances in E4–18, give the closing entry for 2010.
3. Prepare a post-closing trial balance for 2010.

PROBLEMS

  Available with McGraw-Hill's Homework Manager

P4-1   **Preparing a Trial Balance** (AP4–1)

L02

Dell Inc. is the world's largest computer systems company selling directly to customers. Products include desktop computer systems, notebook computers, workstations, network server and storage products, and peripheral hardware and software. The following is a list of accounts and amounts reported in a recent year. The accounts have normal debit or credit balances and the dollars are rounded to the nearest million. Assume the company's year ended on January 31, 2012.

Accounts Payable	$ 2,397	Marketable Securities	$ 2,661
Accounts Receivable	2,094	Other Assets	806
Accrued Expenses Payable	1,298	Other Expenses	38
Accumulated Depreciation	252	Other Liabilities	349
Cash	520	Property, Plant, and Equipment	775
Contributed Capital	1,781	Research and Development Expense	272
Cost of Sales	14,137	Retained Earnings	?
Income Tax Expense	624	Sales Revenue	18,243
Inventories	273	Selling, General, and	
Long-Term Debt	512	Administrative Expenses	1,788

Required:

1. Prepare an adjusted trial balance at January 31, 2012.
2. How did you determine the amount for retained earnings?

P4-2   **Recording Adjusting Entries** (AP4–2)

L01

Burress Company's annual accounting year ends on December 31. It is December 31, 2011, and all of the 2011 entries except the following adjusting entries have been made:

a. On September 1, 2011, Burress collected six months' rent of $7,200 on storage space. At that date, Burress debited Cash and credited Unearned Rent Revenue for $7,200.

b. At December 31, 2011, wages earned by employees totaled $14,000. The employees will be paid on the next payroll date, January 15, 2012.

c. The company earned service revenue of $3,000 on a special job that was completed December 29, 2011. Collection will be made during January 2012. No entry has been recorded.

d. On October 1, 2011, the company borrowed $18,000 from a local bank and signed a 12 percent note for that amount. The principal and interest are payable on the maturity date, September 30, 2012.

e. On November 1, 2011, Burress paid a one-year premium for property insurance, $7,000, for coverage starting on that date. Cash was credited and Prepaid Insurance was debited for this amount.

f. Depreciation of $2,000 must be recognized on a service truck purchased on July 1, 2011, at a cost of $15,000.

g. Cash of $3,000 was collected on November 1, 2011, for services to be rendered evenly over the next year beginning on November 1. Unearned Service Revenue was credited when the cash was received.

h. On December 31, 2011, the company estimated it owed $500 for 2011 property taxes on land. The tax will be paid when the bill is received in January 2012.

Required:
1. Indicate whether each transaction relates to an unearned revenue, prepaid expense, accrued revenue, or accrued expense.
2. Give the adjusting entry required for each transaction at December 31, 2011.

Recording Adjusting Entries (AP4–3)

P4-3
LO1

Totka Towing Company is at the end of its accounting year, December 31, 2011. The following data that must be considered were developed from the company's records and related documents:

a. On July 1, 2011, a three-year insurance premium on equipment in the amount of $1,200 was paid and debited in full to Prepaid Insurance on that date. Coverage began on July 1.

b. During 2011, office supplies amounting to $1,000 were purchased for cash and debited in full to Supplies. At the end of 2010, the count of supplies remaining on hand was $400. The inventory of supplies counted on hand at December 31, 2011, was $400.

c. On December 31, 2011, HH's Garage completed repairs on one of the company's trucks at a cost of $800; the amount is not yet recorded and by agreement will be paid during January 2012.

d. On December 31, 2011, property taxes on land owned during 2011 were estimated at $1,500. The taxes have not been recorded, and will be paid in 2012 when billed.

e. On December 31, 2011, the company completed a contract for an out-of-state company for $6,000 payable by the customer within 30 days. No cash has been collected, and no journal entry has been made for this transaction.

f. On January 1, 2011, the company purchased a new hauling van at a cash cost of $24,600. Depreciation estimated at $1,000 for the year has not been recorded for 2011.

g. On October 1, 2011, the company borrowed $11,000 from the local bank on a one-year, 14 percent note payable. The principal plus interest is payable at the end of 12 months.

h. The income before any of the adjustments or income taxes was $30,000. The company's federal income tax rate is 30 percent. (**Hint:** Compute adjusted income based on (a) through (g) to determine income tax expense.)

Required:
1. Indicate whether each transaction relates to an unearned revenue, prepaid expense, accrued revenue, or accrued expense.
2. Give the adjusting entry required for each transaction at December 31, 2011.

Determining Financial Statement Effects of Adjusting Entries (AP4–4)

P4-4
LO1
e**X**cel

Refer to P4–2.

www.mhhe.com/libby6e

Required:
1. Indicate whether each transaction relates to an unearned revenue, prepaid expense, accrued revenue, or accrued expense.
2. Using the following headings, indicate the effect of each adjusting entry and the amount of the effect. Use + for increase, − for decrease, and NE for no effect. (**Reminder:** Assets = Liabilities + Stockholders' Equity; Revenues − Expenses = Net Income; and Net Income accounts are closed to Retained Earnings, a part of Stockholders' Equity.)

	BALANCE SHEET			INCOME STATEMENT		
Transaction	Assets	Liabilities	Stockholders' Equity	Revenues	Expenses	Net Income
a.						
b.						
c.						
etc.						

P4-5
LO1

eXcel
www.mhhe.com/libby6e

Determining Financial Statement Effects of Adjusting Entries (AP4–5)

Refer to P4–3.

Required:

1. Indicate whether each transaction relates to an unearned revenue, prepaid expense, accrued revenue, or accrued expense.
2. Using the following headings, indicate the effect of each adjusting entry and the amount of each. Use + for increase, − for decrease, and NE for no effect. (**Reminder:** Assets = Liabilities + Stockholders' Equity; Revenues − Expenses = Net Income; and Net Income accounts are closed to Retained Earnings, a part of Stockholders' Equity.)

	BALANCE SHEET			INCOME STATEMENT		
Transaction	Assets	Liabilities	Stockholders' Equity	Revenues	Expenses	Net Income
a.						
b.						
c.						
etc.						

P4-6
LO1, 3

Computing Amounts on Financial Statements and Finding Financial Information

The following information was provided by the records of Collegetown Apartments (a corporation) at the end of the annual fiscal period, December 31, 2010:

Rent
a. Rent revenue collected in cash during 2010 for occupancy in 2010, $512,000
b. Rent revenue earned for occupancy in December 2010; not collected until 2011, $16,000
c. In December 2010, collected rent revenue in advance for January 2011, $12,000

Salaries
d. Cash payment in January 2010 to employees for work in December 2009 (accrued in 2009), $4,000
e. Salaries incurred and paid during 2010, $62,000
f. Salaries earned by employees during December 2010 that will be paid in January 2011, $3,000
g. Cash advances to employees in December 2010 for salaries that will be earned in January 2011, $1,500

Supplies
h. Maintenance supplies on January 1, 2010 (balance on hand), $3,000
i. Maintenance supplies purchased for cash during 2010, $8,000
j. Maintenance supplies counted on December 31, 2010, $1,700

Required:
For each of the following accounts, compute the balance to be reported in 2010, the statement the account will be reported on, and the effect (direction and amount) on cash flows (+ for increases cash and − for decreases cash). (**Hint:** Create T-accounts to determine balances.)

Account	2010 Balance	Financial Statement	Effect on Cash Flows
1. Rent revenue			
2. Salary expense			
3. Maintenance supplies expense			
4. Rent receivable			
5. Receivables from employees			
6. Maintenance supplies			
7. Unearned rent revenue			
8. Salaries payable			

Inferring Year-End Adjustments, Computing Earnings per Share and Net Profit Margin, and Recording Closing Entries (AP4–6)

P4-7
LO1, 2, 4, 5

Wagonblatt Company is completing the information processing cycle at its fiscal year-end, December 31, 2010. Following are the correct balances at December 31, 2010, for the accounts both before and after the adjusting entries for 2010.

Trial Balance, December 31, 2010						
	Before Adjusting Entries		Adjustments		After Adjusting Entries	
Items	Debit	Credit	Debit	Credit	Debit	Credit
a. Cash	$ 12,600				$ 12,600	
b. Accounts receivable					560	
c. Prepaid insurance	840				560	
d. Equipment	168,280				168,280	
e. Accumulated depreciation, equipment		$ 44,100				$ 56,000
f. Income taxes payable						6,580
g. Contributed capital		112,000				112,000
h. Retained earnings, January 1, 2010		19,600				19,600
i. Service revenue		64,400				64,960
j. Salary expense	58,380				58,380	
k. Depreciation expense					11,900	
l. Insurance expense					280	
m. Income tax expense					6,580	
	$240,100	$240,100			$259,140	$259,140

Required:
1. Compare the amounts in the columns before and after the adjusting entries to reconstruct the adjusting entries made in 2010. Provide an explanation of each.
2. Compute the amount of income assuming that it is based on the amounts (*a*) before adjusting entries and (*b*) after adjusting entries. Which income amount is correct? Explain why.
3. Compute earnings per share, assuming that 3,000 shares of stock are outstanding all year.
4. Compute the net profit margin. What does this suggest to you about the company?
5. Record the closing entry at December 31, 2010.
6. Prepare a post-closing trial balance at December 31, 2010.

Recording Adjusting and Closing Entries and Preparing a Balance Sheet and Income Statement Including Earnings per Share (AP4–7)

P4-8
LO1, 2, 3, 5

St. Denis, Inc., a small service company, keeps its records without the help of an accountant. After much effort, an outside accountant prepared the following unadjusted trial balance as of the end of the annual accounting period, December 31, 2011:

Account Titles	Debit	Credit
Cash	$48,000	
Accounts receivable	10,400	
Supplies	640	
Prepaid insurance	800	
Service trucks	16,000	
Accumulated depreciation		$9,600
Other assets	8,960	
Accounts payable		2,400

(continued)

Account Titles	Debit	Credit
Wages payable		
Income taxes payable		
Note payable (3 years; 10% interest due each December 31)		16,000
Contributed capital (5,000 shares outstanding)		22,560
Retained earnings		6,000
Service revenue		61,600
Remaining expenses (not detailed; excludes income tax)	33,360	
Income tax expense		
Totals	$118,160	$118,160

Data not yet recorded at December 31, 2011:
a. The supplies counted on December 31, 2011, reflected $240 remaining on hand to be used in 2012.
b. Insurance expired during 2011, $400.
c. Depreciation expense for 2011, $3,200.
d. Wages earned by employees not yet paid on December 31, 2011, $720.
e. Income tax expense was $5,880.

Required:
1. Record the 2011 adjusting entries.
2. Prepare an income statement and a classified balance sheet that include the effects of the preceding five transactions.
3. Record the 2011 closing entry.

P4-9
LO1, 2, 3, 4, 5

eXcel

www.mhhe.com/libby6e

Comprehensive Review Problem: From Recording Transactions (including Adjusting and Closing Entries) to Preparing a Complete Set of Financial Statements and Performing Ratio Analysis (see Chapters 2, 3, and 4) (AP4–8)

Brothers Steve and Herman Hargenrater began operations of their tool and die shop (H & H Tool, Inc.) on January 1, 2010. The annual reporting period ends December 31. The trial balance on January 1, 2011, follows:

Account Titles	Debit	Credit
Cash	$ 4,000	
Accounts receivable	7,000	
Supplies	16,000	
Land		
Equipment	78,000	
Accumulated depreciation (on equipment)		$ 8,000
Other assets (not detailed to simplify)	5,000	
Accounts payable		
Wages payable		
Interest payable		
Income taxes payable		
Long-term notes payable		
Contributed capital (85,000 shares)		85,000
Retained earnings		17,000
Service revenue		
Depreciation expense		
Income tax expense		
Interest expense		
Supplies expense		
Wages expense		
Remaining expenses (not detailed to simplify)		
Totals	$110,000	$110,000

Transactions during 2011 follow:

a. Borrowed $12,000 cash on a five-year, 10 percent note payable, dated March 1, 2011.
b. Purchased land for a future building site; paid cash, $12,000.
c. Earned revenues for 2011, $208,000, including $52,000 on credit and the rest in cash.
d. Sold 4,000 additional shares of capital stock for cash at $1 market value per share on January 1, 2011.
e. Incurred $111,000 in Remaining Expenses for 2011, including $20,000 on credit and the rest paid in cash.
f. Collected accounts receivable, $31,000.
g. Purchased other assets, $13,000 cash.
h. Paid accounts payable, $17,000.
i. Purchased supplies on account for future use, $23,000.
j. Signed a three-year $33,000 service contract to start February 1, 2012.
k. Declared and paid cash dividends, $22,000.

Data for adjusting entries:

l. Supplies counted on December 31, 2011, $18,000.
m. Depreciation for the year on the equipment, $8,000.
n. Interest accrued on notes payable (to be computed).
o. Wages earned by employees since the December 24 payroll but are not yet paid, $16,000.
p. Income tax expense was $10,000, payable in 2012.

Required:

1. Set up T-accounts for the accounts on the trial balance and enter beginning balances.
2. Prepare journal entries for transactions (*a*) through (*k*) and post them to the T-accounts.
3. Journalize and post the adjusting entries (*l*) through (*p*).
4. Prepare an income statement (including earnings per share), statement of stockholders' equity, balance sheet, and statement of cash flows.
5. Journalize and post the closing entry.
6. Prepare a post-closing trial balance.
7. Compute the following ratios for 2011 and explain what the results suggest about the company:
    a. Financial leverage
    b. Total asset turnover
    c. Net profit margin

ALTERNATE PROBLEMS

Preparing a Trial Balance (P4–1)

AP4-1
LO2
Starbucks Corporation

Starbucks Corporation purchases and roasts high-quality whole bean coffees and sells them along with fresh-brewed coffees, Italian-style espresso beverages, a variety of pastries and confections, coffee-related accessories and equipment, and a line of premium teas. In addition to sales through its company-operated retail stores, Starbucks also sells coffee and tea products through other channels of distribution. The following is a simplified list of accounts and amounts reported in recent financial statements. The accounts have normal debit or credit balances, and the dollars are rounded to the nearest million. Assume that the year ended on September 30, 2009.

Accounts Payable	$ 56	Inventories	$ 181
Accounts Receivable	48	Long-Term Investments	68
Accrued Liabilities	131	Long-Term Liabilities	40
Accumulated Depreciation	321	Net Revenues	1,680
Cash	66	Other Current Assets	21
Contributed Capital	647	Other Long-Lived Assets	38
Cost of Sales	741	Other Operating Expenses	51
Depreciation Expense	98	Prepaid Expenses	19
General and Administrative		Property, Plant, and Equipment	1,081
Expenses	90	Retained Earnings	?
Income Tax Expense	62	Short-Term Bank Debt	64
Interest Expense	1	Short-Term Investments	51
Interest Income	9	Store Operating Expenses	544

Required:

1. Prepare an adjusted trial balance at September 30, 2009.
2. How did you determine the amount for retained earnings?

AP4-2
LO1

Recording Adjusting Entries (P4-2)

Brandon Company's annual accounting year ends on June 30. It is June 30, 2010, and all of the 2010 entries except the following adjusting entries have been made:

a. On March 30, 2010, Brandon paid a six-month premium for property insurance, $3,200, for coverage starting on that date. Cash was credited and Prepaid Insurance was debited for this amount.
b. At June 30, 2010, wages of $900 were earned by employees but not yet paid. The employees will be paid on the next payroll date, July 15, 2010.
c. On June 1, 2010, Brandon collected two months' maintenance revenue of $450. At that date, Brandon debited Cash and credited Unearned Maintenance Revenue for $450.
d. Depreciation of $3,000 must be recognized on a service truck that cost $15,000 when purchased on July 1, 2009.
e. Cash of $4,200 was collected on May 1, 2010, for services to be rendered evenly over the next year beginning on May 1. Unearned Service Revenue was credited when the cash was received.
f. On February 1, 2010, the company borrowed $16,000 from a local bank and signed a 9 percent note for that amount. The principal and interest are payable on maturity date, January 31, 2011.
g. On June 30, 2010, the company estimated that it owed $500 in property taxes on land it owned in the first half of 2010. The taxes will be paid when billed in August 2010.
h. The company earned service revenue of $2,000 on a special job that was completed June 29, 2010. Collection will be made during July 2010; no entry has been recorded.

Required:

1. Indicate whether each transaction relates to an unearned revenue, prepaid expense, accrued revenue, or accrued expense.
2. Give the adjusting entry required for each transaction at June 30, 2010.

AP4-3
LO1

Recording Adjusting Entries (P4-3)

Wendy's Catering Company is at its accounting year-end, December 31, 2011. The following data that must be considered were developed from the company's records and related documents:

a. During 2011, office supplies amounting to $1,200 were purchased for cash and debited in full to Supplies. At the beginning of 2011, the count of supplies on hand was $350 and, at December 31, 2011, was $400.
b. On December 31, 2011, the company catered an evening gala for a local celebrity. The $7,500 bill was payable by the end of January 2012. No cash has been collected, and no journal entry has been made for this transaction.
c. On December 31, 2011, repairs on one of the company's delivery vans were completed at a cost estimate of $600; the amount is not yet paid or recorded. The repair shop will bill Wendy's Catering at the beginning of January 2012.
d. On October 1, 2011, a one-year insurance premium on equipment in the amount of $1,200 was paid and debited in full to Prepaid Insurance on that date. Coverage began on November 1.
e. In November 2011, Wendy's signed a lease for a new retail location, providing a down payment of $2,100 for the first three months' rent that was debited in full to Prepaid Rent. The lease began on December 1, 2011.
f. On July 1, 2011, the company purchased new refrigerated display counters at a cash cost of $18,000. Depreciation of $1,600 has not been recorded for 2011.
g. On November 1, 2011, the company loaned $4,000 to one of its employees on a one-year, 12 percent note. The principal plus interest is payable by the employee at the end of 12 months.

h. The income before any of the adjustments or income taxes was $22,400. The company's federal income tax rate is 30 percent. Compute adjusted income based on (*a*) through (*g*) to determine income tax expense.

Required:
1. Indicate whether each transaction relates to an unearned revenue, prepaid expense, accrued revenue, or accrued expense.
2. Give the adjusting entry required for each transaction at December 31, 2011.

Determining Financial Statement Effects of Adjusting Entries (P4–4)

Refer to AP4–2.

AP4-4
LO1

Required:
1. Indicate whether each transaction relates to a deferred revenue, deferred expense, accrued revenue, or accrued expense.
2. Using the following headings, indicate the effect of each adjusting entry and the amount of the effect. Use + for increase, − for decrease, and NE for no effect. (**Reminder:** Assets = Liabilities + Stockholders' Equity; Revenues − Expenses = Net Income; and Net Income accounts are closed to Retained Earnings, a part of Stockholders' Equity.)

	BALANCE SHEET			INCOME STATEMENT		
Transaction	Assets	Liabilities	Stockholders' Equity	Revenues	Expenses	Net Income
a.						
b.						
c.						
etc.						

Determining Financial Statement Effects of Adjusting Entries (P4–5)

Refer to AP4–3.

AP4-5
LO1

Required:
1. Indicate whether each transaction relates to an unearned revenue, prepaid expense, accrued revenue, or accrued expense.
2. Using the following headings, indicate the effect of each adjusting entry and the amount of each. Use + for increase, − for decrease, and NE for no effect. (**Reminder:** Assets = Liabilities + Stockholders' Equity; Revenues − Expenses = Net Income; and Net Income accounts are closed to Retained Earnings, a part of Stockholders' Equity.)

	BALANCE SHEET			INCOME STATEMENT		
Transaction	Assets	Liabilities	Stockholders' Equity	Revenues	Expenses	Net Income
a.						
b.						
c.						
etc.						

AP4-6

LO1, 2, 4, 5

Inferring Year-End Adjustments, Computing Earnings per Share and Net Profit Margin, and Recording Closing Entries (P4–7)

Abraham Company is completing the information processing cycle at the end of its fiscal year, December 31, 2009. Following are the correct balances at December 31, 2009, for the accounts both before and after the adjusting entries for 2009.

	Trial Balance, December 31, 2009					
	Before Adjusting Entries		Adjustments		After Adjusting Entries	
Items	Debit	Credit	Debit	Credit	Debit	Credit
a. Cash	$ 18,000				$ 18,000	
b. Accounts receivable					1,500	
c. Prepaid rent	1,200				800	
d. Property, plant, and equipment	210,000				210,000	
e. Accumulated depreciation		$ 52,500				$ 70,000
f. Income taxes payable						6,500
g. Unearned revenue		16,000				8,000
h. Contributed capital		110,000				110,000
i. Retained earnings, January 1, 2009		21,700				21,700
j. Service revenue		83,000				92,500
k. Salary expense	54,000				54,000	
l. Depreciation expense					17,500	
m. Rent expense					400	
n. Income tax expense					6,500	
	$283,200	$283,200			$308,700	$308,700

Required:

1. Compare the amounts in the columns before and after the adjusting entries to reconstruct the adjusting entries made in 2009. Provide an explanation of each.
2. Compute the amount of income, assuming that it is based on the amount (*a*) before adjusting entries and (*b*) after adjusting entries. Which income amount is correct? Explain why.
3. Compute earnings per share, assuming that 5,000 shares of stock are outstanding.
4. Compute the net profit margin. What does this suggest to you about the company?
5. Record the closing entries at December 31, 2009.
6. Prepare a post-closing trial balance at December 31, 2009.

AP4-7

LO1, 2, 3, 5

Recording Adjusting and Closing Entries and Preparing a Balance Sheet and Income Statement Including Earnings per Share (P4–8)

Austin Co., a small service repair company, keeps its records without the help of an accountant. After much effort, an outside accountant prepared the following unadjusted trial balance as of the end of the annual accounting period, December 31, 2010:

Account Titles	Debit	Credit
Cash	$19,600	
Accounts receivable	7,000	
Supplies	1,300	
Prepaid insurance	900	
Equipment	27,000	
Accumulated depreciation		$12,000
Other assets	5,100	
Accounts payable		2,500
Wages payable		
Income taxes payable		
Note payable (2 years; 12% interest due each December 31)		5,000
Contributed capital (4,000 shares outstanding all year)		16,000
Retained earnings		10,300
Service revenue		48,000
Remaining expenses (not detailed; excludes income tax)	32,900	
Income tax expense		
Totals	$93,800	$93,800

Data not yet recorded at December 31, 2010:

a. Depreciation expense for 2010, $3,000.

b. Insurance expired during 2010, $450.

c. Wages earned by employees but not yet paid on December 31, 2010, $1,100.

d. The supplies count on December 31, 2010, reflected $600 remaining on hand to be used in 2011.

e. Income tax expense was $2,950.

Required:

1. Record the 2010 adjusting entries.

2. Prepare an income statement and a classified balance sheet for 2010 to include the effects of the preceding five transactions.

3. Record the 2010 closing entry.

Comprehensive Review Problem: From Recording Transactions (including Adjusting and Closing Entries) to Preparing a Complete Set of Financial Statements and Performing Ratio Analysis (see Chapters 2, 3, and 4) (P4–9)

AP4-8
LO1, 2, 3, 4, 5

Joe Gaskins and Matthew Perry began operations of their furniture repair shop (New Again Furniture, Inc.) on January 1, 2010. The annual reporting period ends December 31. The trial balance on January 1, 2011, was as follows:

Account Titles	Debit	Credit
Cash	$ 5,000	
Accounts receivable	4,000	
Supplies	2,000	
Small tools	6,000	
Equipment		
Accumulated depreciation (equipment)		
Other assets (not detailed to simplify)	9,000	
Accounts payable		$ 7,000
Notes payable		
Wages payable		
Interest payable		
Income taxes payable		
Unearned revenue		
Contributed capital (15,000 shares)		15,000
Retained earnings		4,000
Service revenue		
Depreciation expense		
Wages expense		
Income tax expense		
Interest expense		
Remaining expenses (not detailed to simplify)		
Totals	$26,000	$26,000

Transactions during 2011 follow:
a. Borrowed $20,000 cash on July 1, 2011, signing a one-year, 10 percent note payable.
b. Purchased equipment for $18,000 cash on July 1, 2011.
c. Sold 5,000 additional shares of capital stock for cash at $1 market value per share.
d. Earned revenues for 2011, $65,000, including $9,000 on credit and the rest for cash.
e. Incurred remaining expenses for 2011, $35,000, including $7,000 on credit and the rest paid with cash.
f. Purchased additional small tools, $3,000 cash.
g. Collected accounts receivable, $8,000.
h. Paid accounts payable, $11,000.
i. Purchased $10,000 of supplies on account.
j. Received a $3,000 deposit on work to start January 15, 2012.
k. Declared and paid a cash dividend, $10,000.

Data for adjusting entries:
l. Supplies of $4,000 and small tools of $8,000 were counted on December 31, 2011 (debit Remaining Expenses).
m. Depreciation for 2011, $2,000.
n. Interest accrued on notes payable (to be computed).
o. Wages earned since the December 24 payroll but not yet paid, $3,000.
p. Income tax expense was $4,000, payable in 2012.

Required:
1. Set up T-accounts for the accounts on the trial balance and enter beginning balances.
2. Prepare journal entries for transactions (*a*) through (*k*) and post them to the T-accounts.
3. Journalize and post the adjusting entries (*l*) through (*p*).
4. Prepare an income statement (including earnings per share), statement of stockholders' equity, balance sheet, and the statement of cash flows.
5. Journalize and post the closing entry.
6. Prepare a post-closing trial balance.
7. Compute the following ratios for 2011 and explain what the results suggest about the company:
   a. Financial leverage
   b. Total asset turnover
   c. Net profit margin

CASES **AND PROJECTS**

Annual Report Cases

Finding Financial Information

Refer to the financial statements of American Eagle Outfitters in Appendix B at the end of this book.

Required:
(**Hint:** The notes to the financial statements may be helpful for many of these questions.)
1. How much cash did the company pay for income taxes in its 2006 fiscal year (for the year ended February 3, 2007)?
2. What was the company's best quarter in terms of sales in its 2006 fiscal year? Where did you find this information?
3. Give the closing entry for the Other Income (net) account.
4. What does Accounts and Notes Receivable consist of? Provide the names of the accounts and their balances as of February 3, 2007. Where did you find this information?
5. Compute the company's net profit margin for the three years reported. What does the trend suggest to you about American Eagle Outfitters?

CP4-1
LO1, 3, 4, 5
AMERICAN EAGLE
OUTFITTERS

Finding Financial Information

Refer to the financial statements of Urban Outfitters in Appendix C at the end of this book.

Required:
1. How much is in the prepaid expenses account at the end of the most recent year (for the year ended January 31, 2007)? Where did you find this information?
2. What did the company report for deferred rent at January 31, 2007? Where did you find this information?
3. What is the difference between prepaid rent and deferred rent?
4. Describe in general terms what accrued liabilities are.
5. What would generate the interest income that is reported on the income statement?
6. What company accounts would not have balances on a post-closing trial balance?
7. Give the closing entry, if any, for Prepaid Expenses.
8. What is the company's earnings per share (basic only) for the three years reported?
9. Compute the company's net profit margin for the three years reported. What does the trend suggest to you about Urban Outfitters?

CP4-2
LO1, 3, 4, 5
Urban Outfitters

Comparing Companies within an Industry and Over Time

Refer to the financial statements of American Eagle Outfitters in Appendix B, Urban Outfitters in Appendix C, and the Industry Ratio Report given in Appendix D at the end of this book.

Required:
1. What was Advertising Expense for each company for the most recent year? Where did you find the information?
2. Compute the percentage of Advertising Expense to Net Sales for the most recent year for both companies. Which company incurred the higher percentage? Show computations. Are you

CP4-3
LO2, 4
AMERICAN EAGLE
OUTFITTERS
Urban Outfitters
 e**X**cel
www.mhhe.com/
libby6e

able to perform the same comparison for the previous two years? If so, show the computations. If not, explain why not.

3. Compare the Advertising Expense to Net Sales ratio for the most recent year computed in requirement (2) to the industry average found in the Industry Ratio Report. Were these two companies spending more or less than their average competitor on advertising (on a relative basis)? What does this ratio tell you about the general effectiveness of each company's advertising strategy?

4. Both companies have a note to the financial statements explaining the accounting policy for advertising. How do the policies differ, if at all?

5. Compute each company's net profit margin for the three years reported. What do your results suggest to you about each company over time and in comparison to each other?

6. Compare each company's net profit margin for the most recent year to the industry average net profit margin in the Industry Ratio Report. Were these two companies performing better or worse than the average company in the industry?

Financial Reporting and Analysis Cases

CP4-4   **Interpreting the Financial Press**

A March 8, 2004, article in *The Wall Street Journal* discusses the underlying cause of accounting scandals and offers a suggestion for improved reporting.* You can access the article on the Libby/Libby/Short website at **www.mhhe.com/libby6e**.

*Alfred Rappaport, "Shareholder Scoreboard (A Special Report): The Best & Worst Performers of the WSJ 1000—Beyond Quarterly Earnings: How to Improve Financial Reporting," *The Wall Street Journal*, March 8, 2004.

Required:
Read the brief article and answer the following questions:

1. What did the author suggest as the root cause of accounting scandals?
2. What are the uncertainties referred to in the article and why does the author believe these are problems in current financial reporting?

CP4-5   **Using Financial Reports: Inferring Adjusting Entries and Information Used in Computa-**
LO1, 2, 5   **tions and Recording Closing Entries**

The pre-closing balances in the T-accounts of Hook M Horns Company at the end of the third year of operations, December 31, 2010, follow. The 2010 adjusting entries are identified by letters.

Cash	
Bal. 20,000	

Note Payable (8%)	
	Bal. 10,000

Contributed Capital (8,000 shares)	
	Bal. 56,000

Maintenance Supplies	
Bal. 500	(a) 300

Interest Payable	
	(b) 800

Retained Earnings	
	Bal. 9,000

Service Equipment	
Bal. 90,000	

Income Taxes Payable	
	(f) 13,020

Service Revenue	
(c) 6,000	Bal. 220,000

Accumulated Depreciation, Service Equipment	
	Bal. 18,000
	(d) 9,000

Wages payable	
	(e) 500

Expenses	
Bal. 160,000	
(a) 300	
(b) 800	
(d) 9,000	
(e) 500	
(f) 13,020	

Remaining Assets	
Bal. 42,500	

Unearned Revenue	
	(c) 6,000

Required:

1. Develop three 2010 trial balances for Hook M Horns Company using the following format:

	Unadjusted Trial Balance		Adjusted Trial Balance		Post-Closing Trial Balance	
Account	Debit	Credit	Debit	Credit	Debit	Credit

2. Write an explanation for each adjusting entry for 2010.
3. Record the closing journal entry.
4. What was the average income tax rate for 2010?
5. What was the average issue (sale) price per share of the capital stock?

Using Financial Reports: Analyzing the Effects of Adjustments

CP4-6
LO2

S. Shirley Land Company, a closely held corporation, invests in commercial rental properties. Shirley's annual accounting period ends on December 31. At the end of each year, numerous adjusting entries must be made because many transactions completed during current and prior years have economic effects on the financial statements of the current and future years. Assume that the current year is 2011.

Required:
This case concerns four transactions that have been selected for your analysis. Answer the questions for each.

Transaction (a): On January 1, 2009, the company purchased office equipment costing $14,000 for use in the business. The company estimates that the equipment's cost should be allocated at $1,400 annually.

1. Over how many accounting periods will this transaction directly affect Shirley's financial statements? Explain.
2. How much depreciation expense was reported on the 2009 and 2010 income statements?
3. How should the office equipment be reported on the 2011 balance sheet?
4. Would Shirley make an adjusting entry at the end of each year during the life of the equipment? Explain your answer.

Transaction (b): On September 1, 2011, Shirley collected $24,000 rent on office space. This amount represented the monthly rent in advance for the six-month period, September 1, 2011, through February 29, 2012. Unearned Rent Revenue was increased (credited) and Cash was increased (debited) for $24,000.

1. Over how many accounting periods will this transaction affect Shirley's financial statements? Explain.
2. How much rent revenue on this office space should Shirley report on the 2011 income statement? Explain.
3. Did this transaction create a liability for Shirley as of the end of 2011? Explain. If yes, how much?
4. Should Shirley make an adjusting entry on December 31, 2011? Explain why. If your answer is yes, give the adjusting entry.

Transaction (c): On December 31, 2011, Shirley owed employees unpaid and unrecorded wages of $7,500 because the employees worked the last three days in December 2011. The next payroll date is January 5, 2012.

1. Over how many accounting periods does this transaction affect Shirley's financial statements? Explain.
2. How would this $7,500 affect Shirley's 2011 income statement and balance sheet?
3. Should Shirley make an adjusting entry on December 31, 2011? Explain why. If your answer is yes, give the adjusting entry.

Transaction (*d*): On January 1, 2011, Shirley agreed to supervise the planning and subdivision of a large tract of land for a customer, V. Vulchkov. This service job that Shirley will perform involves four separate phases. By December 31, 2011, three phases had been completed to Vulchkov's satisfaction. The remaining phase will be performed during 2012. The total price for the four phases (agreed on in advance by both parties) was $60,000. Each phase involves about the same amount of services. On December 31, 2011, Shirley had collected no cash for the services already performed.

1. Should Shirley record any service revenue on this job for 2011? Explain why. If yes, how much?
2. If your answer to part (1) is yes, should Shirley make an adjusting entry on December 31, 2011? If yes, give the entry. Explain.
3. What entry will Shirley make when it completes the last phase, assuming that the full contract price is collected on the completion date, February 15, 2012?

CP4-7
L01, 2, 4, 5

Using Financial Reports: Inferring Adjusting and Closing Entries and Answering Analytical Questions

Erickson Company was organized on January 1, 2009. At the end of the first year of operations, December 31, 2009, the bookkeeper prepared the following trial balances (amounts in thousands of dollars):

Account Titles	Unadjusted Trial Balance		Adjustments		Adjusted Trial Balance	
	Debit	Credit	Debit	Credit	Debit	Credit
Cash	40				40	
Accounts Receivable	17				17	
Prepaid Insurance	2				1	
Rent Receivable					2	
Property, Plant, and Equipment	46				46	
Accumulated Depreciation						11
Other Assets	6				6	
Accounts Payable		27				27
Wages Payable						3
Income Taxes Payable						5
Unearned Rent Revenue		7				4
Note Payable (10% interest; dated January 1, 2009)		20				20
Contributed Capital (1,000 shares)		30				30
Retained Earnings	3				3	
Revenues (total)		98				103
Expenses (total including interest)	68				83	
Income Tax Expense					5	
Totals	182	182			203	203

Required:

1. Based on inspection of the two trial balances, give the 2009 adjusting entries developed by the bookkeeper (provide brief explanations).
2. Based on these data, give the 2009 closing entry with a brief explanation.
3. Answer the following questions (show computations):
   a. How many shares of stock were outstanding at year-end?
   b. What was the amount of interest expense included in the total expenses?
   c. What was the balance of Retained Earnings on December 31, 2009 after closing the books?
   d. What was the average income tax rate?
   e. How would the two accounts Rent Receivable and Unearned Rent Revenue be reported on the balance sheet?
   f. Explain why cash increased by $40,000 during the year even though net income was comparatively very low.
   g. What was the amount of earnings per share for 2009?
   h. What was the average selling price of the shares?
   i. When was the insurance premium paid and over what period of time did the coverage extend?
   j. What was the net profit margin for the year?

Using Financial Reports: Analyzing Financial Information in a Sale of a Business: A Challenging Case

CP4-8
LO2, 3

www.mhhe.com/libby6e

Crystal Mullinex owns and operates Crystal's Day Spa and Salon, Inc. She has decided to sell the business and retire. She has had discussions with a representative from a regional chain of day spas. The discussions are at the complex stage of agreeing on a price. Among the important factors have been the financial statements of the business. Crystal's secretary, Tiana, under Crystal's direction, maintained the records. Each year they developed a statement of profits on a cash basis; no balance sheet was prepared. Upon request, Crystal provided the other company with the following statement for 2011 prepared by Tiana:

CRYSTAL'S DAY SPA AND SALON, INC.
Statement of Profits
2011

Spa fees collected		$1,115,000
Expenses paid:		
Rent for office space	$130,000	
Utilities expense	43,600	
Telephone expense	12,200	
Salaries expense	522,000	
Supplies expense	31,900	
Miscellaneous expenses	12,400	
Total expenses		752,100
Profit for the year		$ 362,900

Upon agreement of the parties, you have been asked to examine the financial figures for 2011. The other company's representative said, "I question the figures because, among other things, they appear to be on a 100 percent cash basis." Your investigations revealed the following additional data at December 31, 2011:

a. Of the $1,115,000 in spa fees collected in 2011, $132,000 was for services performed prior to 2011.

b. At the end of 2011, spa fees of $29,000 for services performed during the year were uncollected.

c. Office equipment owned and used by Crystal cost $205,000. Depreciation was estimated at $20,500 annually.

d. A count of supplies at December 31, 2011, reflected $5,200 worth of items purchased during the year that were still on hand. Also, the records for 2010 indicate that the supplies on hand at the end of that year were about $3,125.

e. At the end of 2011, the secretary whose salary is $18,000 per year had not been paid for December because of a long trip that extended to January 15, 2012.

f. The December 2011 telephone bill for $1,400 has not been received or paid. In addition, the $12,200 amount on the statement of profits includes payment of the December 2010 bill of $1,800 in January 2011.

g. The $130,000 office rent paid was for 13 months (it included the rent for January 2012).

Required:

1. On the basis of this information, prepare a corrected income statement for 2011 (ignore income taxes). Show your computations for any amounts changed from those in the statement prepared by Crystal's secretary. (Suggested solution format with four-column headings: Items; Cash Basis per Crystal's Statement, $; Explanation of Changes; and Corrected Basis, $.)

2. Write a memo to support your schedule prepared in requirement (1). The purpose should be to explain the reasons for your changes and to suggest other important items that should be considered in the pricing decision.

Critical Thinking Cases

CP4-9
LO2, 3, 4

Using Financial Reports: Evaluating Financial Information as a Bank Loan Officer

Magliochetti Moving Corporation has been in operation since January 1, 2010. It is now December 31, 2010, the end of the annual accounting period. The company has not done well financially during the first year, although revenue has been fairly good. The three stockholders manage the company, but they have not given much attention to recordkeeping. In view of a serious cash shortage, they have applied to your bank for a $20,000 loan. You requested a complete set of financial statements. The following 2010 annual financial statements were prepared by a clerk and then were given to the bank.

MAGLIOCHETTI MOVING CORP. Income Statement For the Period Ended December 31, 2010	
Transportation revenue	$85,000
Expenses:	
Salaries expense	17,000
Supplies expense	12,000
Other expenses	18,000
Total expenses	47,000
Net income	$38,000

MAGLIOCHETTI MOVING CORP. Balance Sheet At December 31, 2010	
Assets	
Cash	$ 2,000
Receivables	3,000
Supplies	6,000
Equipment	40,000
Prepaid insurance	4,000
Remaining assets	27,000
Total assets	$82,000
Liabilities	
Accounts payable	$ 9,000
Stockholders' Equity	
Contributed capital (10,000 shares outstanding)	35,000
Retained earnings	38,000
Total liabilities and stockholders' equity	$82,000

After briefly reviewing the statements and "looking into the situation," you requested that the statements be redone (with some expert help) to "incorporate depreciation, accruals, inventory counts, income taxes, and so on." As a result of a review of the records and supporting documents, the following additional information was developed:

a. The Supplies of $6,000 shown on the balance sheet has not been adjusted for supplies used during 2010. A count of the supplies on hand on December 31, 2010, showed $1,800.

b. The insurance premium paid in 2010 was for years 2010 and 2011. The total insurance premium was debited in full to Prepaid Insurance when paid in 2010 and no adjustment has been made.

c. The equipment cost $40,000 when purchased January 1, 2010. It had an estimated annual depreciation of $8,000. No depreciation has been recorded for 2010.

d. Unpaid (and unrecorded) salaries at December 31, 2010, amounted to $2,200.

e. At December 31, 2010, transportation revenue collected in advance amounted to $7,000. This amount was credited in full to Transportation Revenue when the cash was collected earlier during 2010.

f. Income tax expense was $3,650 (the tax rate is 25 percent).

Required:

1. Record the six adjusting entries required on December 31, 2010, based on the preceding additional information.

2. Recast the preceding statements after taking into account the adjusting entries. You do not need to use classifications on the statements. Suggested form for the solution:

Items	Amounts Reported	Changes		Corrected Amounts
		Debit	Credit	
(List here each item from the two statements)				

3. Omission of the adjusting entries caused:
   a. Net income to be overstated or understated (select one) by $_____.
   b. Total assets on the balance sheet to be overstated or understated (select one) by $_____.

4. For both of the unadjusted and adjusted balances, calculate these ratios for the company: (a) earnings per share and (b) net profit margin. There were 10,000 shares outstanding all year. Explain the causes of the differences and the impact of the changes on financial analysis.

5. Write a letter to the company explaining the results of the adjustments, your analysis, and your decision regarding the loan.

Evaluating the Effect of Adjusting Unearned Subscriptions on Cash Flows and Performance as a Manager

CP4-10
LO2

You are the regional sales manager for Bruzzese News Company. Bruzzese is making adjusting entries for the year ended March 31, 2011. On September 1, 2010, customers in your region paid $18,000 cash for three-year magazine subscriptions beginning on that date. The magazines are published and mailed to customers monthly. These were the only subscription sales in your region during the year.

Required:

1. What amount should be reported as cash from operations on the statement of cash flows?

2. What amount should be reported on the income statement for subscriptions revenue for the year ended March 31, 2011?

3. What amount should be reported on the March 31, 2011, balance sheet for unearned subscriptions revenue?

4. Give the adjusting entry at March 31, 2011, assuming that the subscriptions received on September 1, 2010, were recorded for the full amount in Unearned Subscriptions Revenue.

5. The company expects your region's annual revenue target to be $4,000.
   a. Evaluate your region's performance, assuming that the revenue target is based on cash sales.
   b. Evaluate your region's performance, assuming that the revenue target is based on accrual accounting.

Financial Reporting and Analysis Team Project

CP4-11
LO2, 3, 4

Team Project: Analysis of Accruals, Earnings per Share, and Net Profit Margin

As a team, select an industry to analyze. Reuters provides lists of industries and their makeup at www.reuters.com/finance/industries. Each team member should acquire the annual report or 10-K for one publicly traded company in the industry, with each member selecting a different company. (Library files, the SEC EDGAR service at www.sec.gov, or the company itself are good sources.)

Required:

On an individual basis, each team member should write a short report answering the following questions about the selected company. Discuss any patterns across the companies that you as a team observe. Then, as a team, write a short report comparing and contrasting your companies.

1. From the income statement, what is the company's basic earnings per share for each of the last three years?
2. Ratio analysis:
    a. What does the Net Profit Margin ratio measure in general?
    b. Compute the Net Profit Margin ratio for the last three years.
    c. What do your results suggest about the company? [You may refer to the Management Discussion and Analysis section of the 10-K or annual report to read what the company says about the reasons for any change over time.]
    d. If available, find the industry ratio for the most recent year, compare it to your results, and discuss why you believe your company differs or is similar to the industry ratio.
3. List the accounts and amounts of accrued expenses payable on the most recent balance sheet. [You may find the detail in the notes to the statements.] What is the ratio of the total accrued expenses payable to total liabilities?

Lectured slideshow–LP5-1
www.mhhe.com/libby6e

LEARNING OBJECTIVES

After studying this chapter, you should be able to:

1. Recognize the people involved in the accounting communication process (regulators, managers, directors, auditors, information intermediaries, and users), their roles in the process, and the guidance they receive from legal and professional standards. p. 233

2. Identify the steps in the accounting communication process, including the issuance of press releases, annual reports, quarterly reports, and SEC filings as well as the role of electronic information services in this process. p. 240

3. Recognize and apply the different financial statement and disclosure formats used by companies in practice. p. 243

4. Analyze a company's performance based on return on equity and its components. p. 252

COMMUNICATING AND INTERPRETING ACCOUNTING INFORMATION

Founded by heralded entrepreneur Ely Callaway, the company that bears his name is the number one manufacturer of premium golf clubs. In just 20 years, Mr. Callaway took a small manufacturer of specialty golf clubs with $500,000 in annual sales and built it into the industry leader with sales of more than $800 million. Callaway Golf's growth was based on its laserlike focus on product innovations that make the game easier to learn and play. Both touring pros like Masters champion Phil Mickelson and average golfers, including former presidents Bill Clinton and George Bush, use Callaway clubs.

Financing this type of growth requires an equal commitment to satisfying the highest standards of integrity in corporate governance and communication with the financial markets. In 1989, Callaway and then chief financial officer (CFO) Carol Kerley applied that commitment to integrity in communication when they persuaded managers of the General Electric Pension Fund to invest $10 million in the company, and during the company's initial public offering (first stock issuance to the public, or IPO) in 1992. The CFO and her accounting staff worked tirelessly with the company's outside auditor, PricewaterhouseCoopers, and its investment bankers at Merrill Lynch to prepare the financial information necessary for the IPO.

As a publicly traded company, Callaway Golf is required to provide detailed information in regular filings with the Securities and Exchange Commission. As the certifying officers of the company, current President and CEO George Fellows and Bradley J. Holiday, Senior Executive Vice President and Chief Financial Officer, are responsible for the accuracy of the filings. The board of directors and auditors monitor the integrity of the system that produces the disclosures. Integrity in communication with investors and other users of financial statements is a key to maintaining relationships with suppliers of capital.

UNDERSTANDING THE BUSINESS

Callaway Golf Company designs, manufactures, and markets high-quality innovative golf clubs that sell at premium prices. Its Fusion Technology and Big Bertha woods and irons account for most of its sales. The company manufactures most of its clubs in its new Carlsbad, California, factories using clubheads, shafts, and grips supplied by independent vendors. The clubs are sold at pro shops and sporting goods stores. Callaway Golf invests considerable sums in research and development and is known for introducing new and innovative products long before the end of existing products' life cycles.

CORPORATE GOVERNANCE is the procedures designed to ensure that the company is managed in the interests of the shareholders.

Callaway Golf also invests in **corporate governance:** the procedures designed to ensure that the company is managed in the interests of the shareholders. Much of its corporate governance system is aimed at ensuring integrity in the financial reporting process. Good corporate governance eases the company's access to capital, lowering both the costs of borrowing (interest rates) and the perceived riskiness of Callaway Golf's stock.

Callaway Golf knows that when investors lose faith in the truthfulness of a firm's accounting numbers, they also normally punish the company's stock. Disclosure of an accounting fraud causes, on average, a 20% drop in the price of a company's stock.[1] The extreme accounting scandals at Enron and WorldCom caused their stock to become worthless. In an attempt to restore investor confidence, Congress passed the Public Accounting Reform and Investor Protection Act (the Sarbanes-Oxley Act), which strengthens financial reporting and corporate governance for public companies. Even with these added safeguards, the wisdom of famed analyst Jack Ciesielski's warning to financial statement users is still evident:

REAL WORLD EXCERPT

ANALYST'S ACCOUNTING OBSERVER

> One usual answer to the question "why does accounting matter?" is that it helps to avoid "blow-ups": the unpleasant outcome when a stock crashes because the firm's management engaged in accounting chicanery that subsequently becomes visible. . . . the analyst who understands accounting matters will know . . . where the "soft spots" are in financial reporting, the ones that can be manipulated in order to meet an expected earnings target or avoid breaking a loan covenant.
>
> Source: Analyst's Accounting Observer, www.accountingobserver.com.

While even the savviest analysts can still be surprised by fraudulent reports in some cases, accounting knowledge and healthy skepticism are the best protection from such surprises.

Chapters 2 through 4 focused on the mechanics of preparing the income statement, balance sheet, statement of stockholders' equity, and cash flow statement. Based on our better understanding of financial statements, we will next take a more detailed look at the people involved and the regulations that govern the process that conveys accounting information to statement users in the Internet age. We will also take a more detailed look at statement formats and additional disclosures provided in financial reports to help you learn how to find relevant information. Finally, we will examine a general framework for assessing a company's performance based on these reports.

---

[1]Z. Palmrose, V. Richardson, and S. Scholz, "Determinants of Market Reactions to Restatement Announcements," *Journal of Accounting and Economics*, 2004, 59–90.

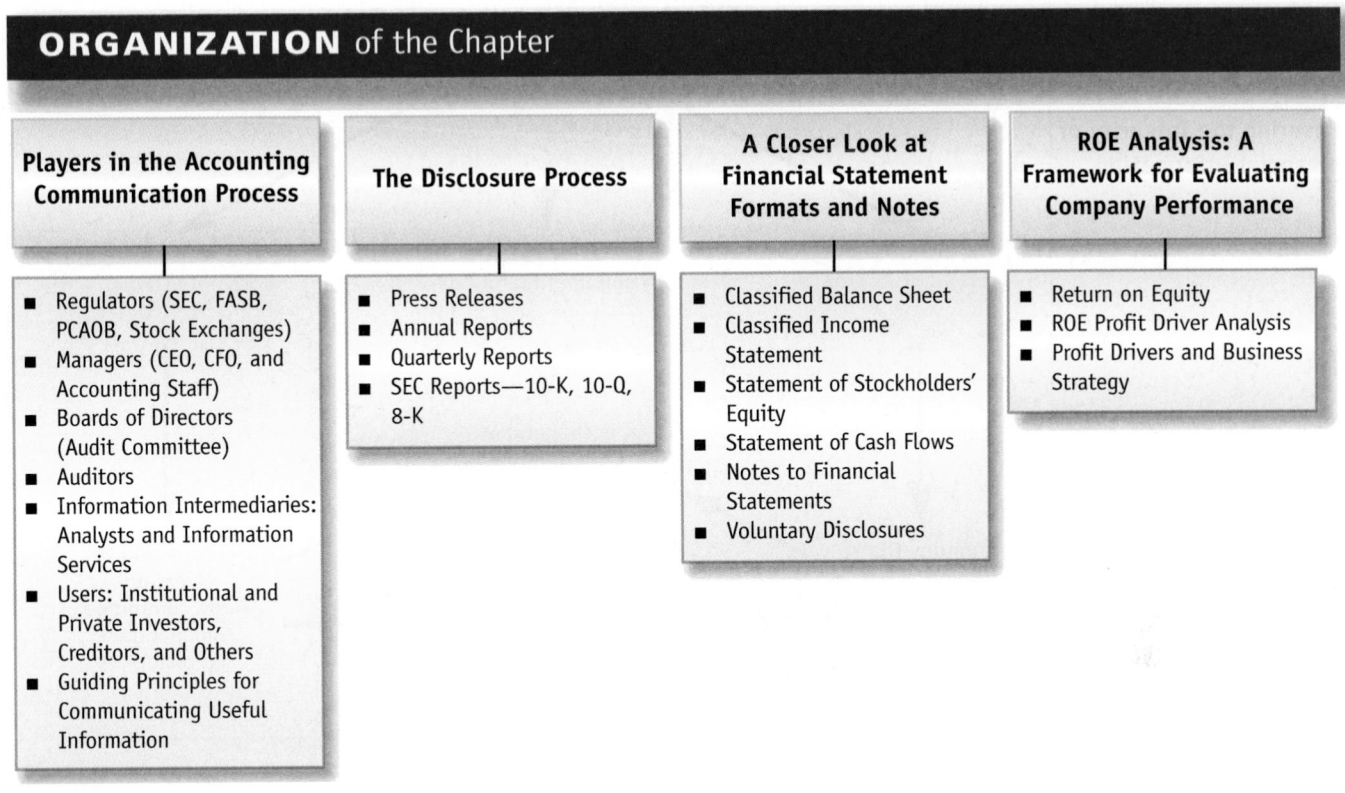

ORGANIZATION of the Chapter

Players in the Accounting Communication Process	The Disclosure Process	A Closer Look at Financial Statement Formats and Notes	ROE Analysis: A Framework for Evaluating Company Performance
■ Regulators (SEC, FASB, PCAOB, Stock Exchanges) ■ Managers (CEO, CFO, and Accounting Staff) ■ Boards of Directors (Audit Committee) ■ Auditors ■ Information Intermediaries: Analysts and Information Services ■ Users: Institutional and Private Investors, Creditors, and Others ■ Guiding Principles for Communicating Useful Information	■ Press Releases ■ Annual Reports ■ Quarterly Reports ■ SEC Reports—10-K, 10-Q, 8-K	■ Classified Balance Sheet ■ Classified Income Statement ■ Statement of Stockholders' Equity ■ Statement of Cash Flows ■ Notes to Financial Statements ■ Voluntary Disclosures	■ Return on Equity ■ ROE Profit Driver Analysis ■ Profit Drivers and Business Strategy

PLAYERS IN THE ACCOUNTING COMMUNICATION PROCESS

Exhibit 5.1 summarizes the major actors involved in ensuring the integrity of the financial reporting process.

Regulators (SEC, FASB, PCAOB, Stock Exchanges)

The mission of the **U.S. Securities and Exchange Commission** (SEC) is to protect investors and maintain the integrity of the securities markets. As part of this mission, the SEC oversees the work of the Financial Accounting Standards Board (FASB) that sets generally accepted accounting principles (GAAP), the Public Company Accounting Oversight Board (PCAOB) that sets auditing standards for independent auditors (CPAs) of public companies, and the Stock Exchanges (e.g., New York Stock Exchange) that, along with state governments, set overall corporate governance standards.

The SEC staff also reviews the reports filed with it for compliance with its standards, investigates irregularities, and punishes violators. During 2002 through 2006, the SEC brought 854 enforcement actions related to financial reporting.[2] As a consequence, a number of high-profile company officers have recently been fined and sentenced to jail. Consequences to the company can include enormous financial penalties as well as bankruptcy as in the cases of Enron and WorldCom. You can read about recent SEC enforcement actions at

www.sec.gov/divisions/enforce/friactions.shtml.

Learning Objective 1
Recognize the people involved in the accounting communication process (regulators, managers, directors, auditors, information intermediaries, and users), their roles in the process, and the guidance they receive from legal and professional standards.

Audio lecture–AP5-1
www.mhhe.com/libby6e

---

[2]Source: CFO.com.

EXHIBIT 5.1

Ensuring the Integrity of Financial Information

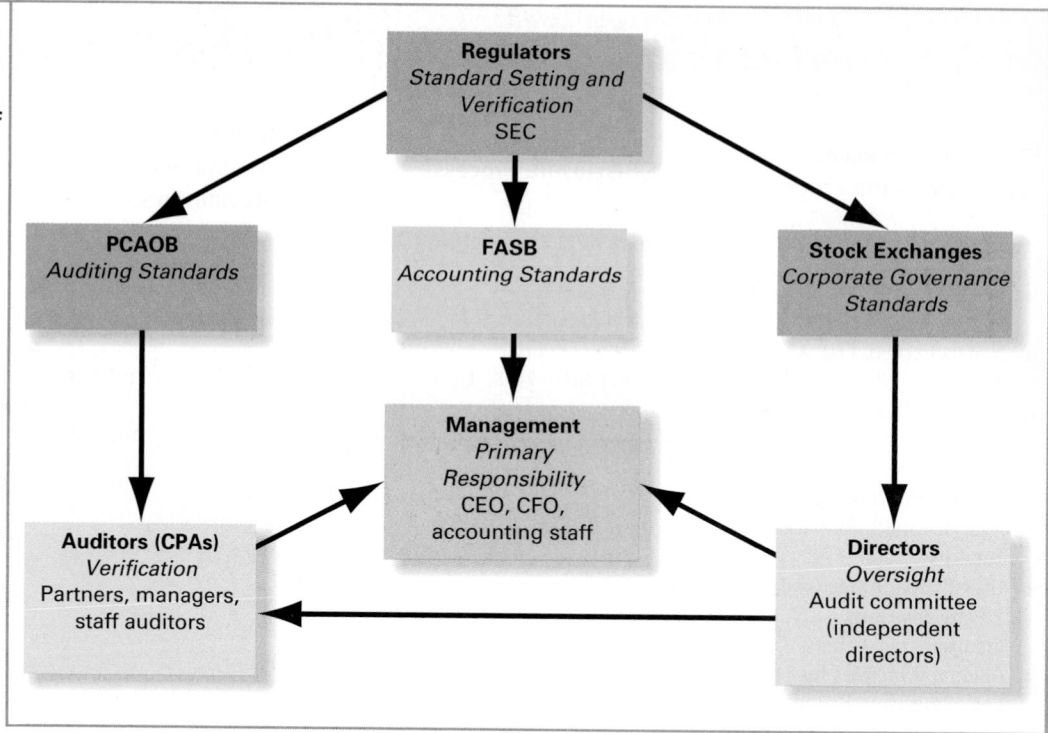

Managers (CEO, CFO, and Accounting Staff)

The primary responsibility for the information in Callaway Golf's financial statements and related disclosures lies with management, specifically the highest officer in the company, often called the **chairman and chief executive officer** (CEO), and the highest officer associated with the financial and accounting side of the business, often called the **chief financial officer** (CFO). At Callaway and all public companies, these two officers must personally certify that:

■ Each report filed with the Securities and Exchange Commission does not contain any untrue material statement or omit a material fact and fairly presents in all material respects the financial condition, results of operations, and cash flows of the company.

■ There are no significant deficiencies and material weaknesses in the internal controls over financial reporting.

■ They have disclosed to the auditors and audit committee of the board any weaknesses in internal controls or any fraud involving management or other employees who have a significant role in financial reporting.

Executives who knowingly certify false financial reports are subject to a fine of $5 million and a 20-year prison term. The members of the **accounting staff,** who actually prepare the details of the reports, also bear professional responsibility for the accuracy of this information, although their legal responsibility is smaller. Their future professional success depends heavily on their reputation for honesty and competence. Accounting managers responsible for financial statements with material errors are routinely fired and often have difficulty finding other employment.[3]

---

[3]H. Desai, C.E. Hogan, and M.S. Wilkins, "The Reputational Penalty for Aggressive Accounting: Earnings Restatements and Management Turnover," *The Accounting Review,* 2006, pp. 83–113.

Board of Directors (Audit Committee)

As Callaway Golf's statement on corporate governance indicates, the **board of directors** (elected by the stockholders) is responsible for ensuring that processes are in place for maintaining the integrity of the company's accounting, financial statement preparation, and financial reporting. The audit committee of the board, which must be composed of non-management (independent) directors with financial knowledge, is responsible for hiring the company's independent auditors. They also meet separately with the auditors to discuss management's compliance with their financial reporting responsibilities.

The **BOARD OF DIRECTORS**, elected by the stockholders to represent their interests, is responsible for maintaining the integrity of the company's financial reports.

Auditors

The SEC requires publicly traded companies to have their statements and their control systems over the financial reporting process audited by an independent registered public accounting firm (independent auditor) following auditing standards established by the PCAOB. Many privately owned companies also have their statements audited. By signing an **unqualified** (or **clean**) **audit opinion,** a CPA firm assumes part of the financial responsibility for the fairness of the financial statements and related presentations. This opinion, which adds credibility to the statements, is also often required by agreements with lenders and private investors. Subjecting the company's statements to independent verification reduces the risk that the company's financial condition is misrepresented in the statements. As a result, rational investors and lenders should lower the rate of return (interest) they charge for providing capital.[4]

UNQUALIFIED (clean) **AUDIT OPINION** is an auditor's statement that the financial statements are fair presentations in all material respects in conformity with GAAP.

Deloitte & Touche is currently Callaway Golf's auditor. This firm, along with KPMG, PricewaterhouseCoopers, and Ernst & Young, make up what are referred to as the "Big 4" CPA firms. Each of these firms employs thousands of CPAs in offices scattered throughout the world. They audit the great majority of publicly traded companies as well as many that are privately held. Some public companies and most private companies are audited by smaller CPA firms. A list of the auditors for selected focus companies follows.

Focus Company	Industry	Auditor
Harrah's	Casinos and hotels	Deloitte & Touche
Deckers' Outdoor	Footwear	KPMG
Papa John's	Fast food	Ernst & Young

Information Intermediaries: Financial Analysts and Information Services

Students often view the communication process between companies and financial statement users as a simple process of mailing the report to individual shareholders who read the report and then make investment decisions based on what they have learned. This simple picture is far from today's reality. Now most investors rely on sophisticated financial analysts and information services to gather and analyze information. Exhibit 5.2 summarizes this process.

Financial analysts receive accounting reports and other information about the company from electronic information services. They also gather information through conversations with company executives and visits to company facilities and competitors.

---

[4]Examples of accounting research that examine this relationship are P. Hribar and N. Jenkins, "The Effect of Accounting Restatements on Earnings Revisions and the Estimated Cost of Capital," *Review of Accounting Studies,* 2004, pp. 337–356 and C.A Botosan and M.A Plumlee, "A Re-examination of Disclosure Level and the Expected Cost of Equity Capital," *Journal of Accounting Research,* March 2002, pp. 21–40.

EXHIBIT 5.2

Using Financial Reports

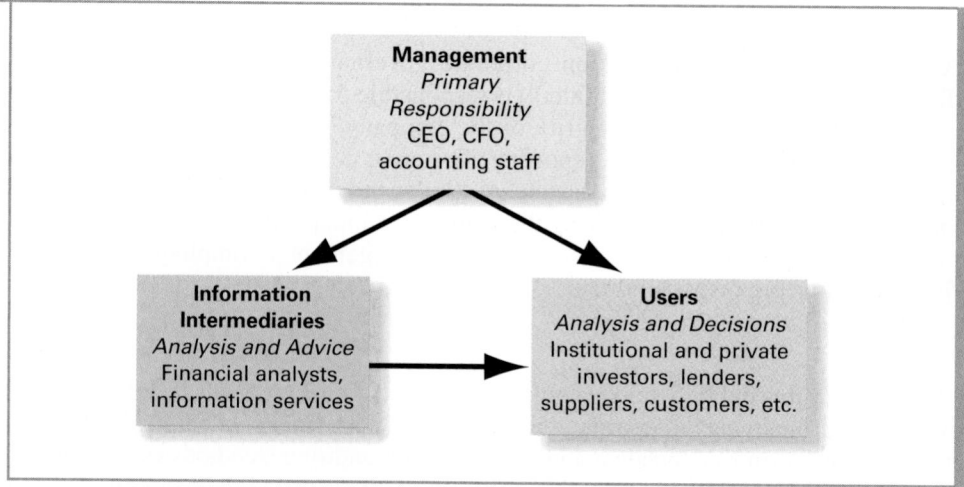

EARNINGS FORECASTS are
predictions of earnings for future
accounting periods.

The results of their analyses are combined into analysts' reports. Analysts' reports normally include forecasts of future quarterly and annual earnings per share and share price; a buy, hold, or sell recommendation for the company's shares; and explanations for these judgments. In making their **earnings forecasts,** the analysts rely heavily on their knowledge of the way the accounting system translates business events into the numbers on a company's financial statements, which is the subject matter of this text. Individual analysts often specialize in particular industries (such as sporting goods or energy companies). Analysts are regularly evaluated based on the accuracy of their forecasts, as well as the profitability of their stock picks.[5] At the time this chapter was written, three major firms provided the following forecasts and recommendations for Callaway Golf:

REAL WORLD EXCERPT

ANALYSTS' REPORTS

Firm	Stock Recommendation	Earnings Forecast for 2007	Earnings Forecast for 2008
Wedbush Morgan	Buy	0.90	1.12
Merriman Curhan Ford	Buy	0.89	1.24
Morgan Joseph & Co.	Buy	0.96	1.15

The relatively small differences among the analysts' forecasts indicate a good deal of agreement about the company's future.

Analysts often work in the research departments of brokerage and investment banking houses such as Merrill Lynch, mutual fund companies such as Fidelity Investments, and investment advisory services such as Value Line that sell their advice to others. Through their reports and recommendations, analysts are transferring their knowledge of accounting, the company, and the industry to their customers who lack this expertise. Many believe that decisions made based on analysts' advice cause stock market prices to react quickly to information in financial statements. A quick, unbiased reaction to information is called **market efficiency** in finance. It is highly unlikely that unsophisticated investors can glean more information from financial statements than the sophisticated analysts have already learned. The **information**

---

[5]See M. B. Mikhail, B. R. Walther, and R. H. Willis, "Does Forecast Accuracy Matter to Security Analysts?" *The Accounting Review,* April 1999, pp. 185–200; and R. A. McEwen and J. E. Hunton, "Is Analyst Forecast Accuracy Associated with Accounting Information Use?" *Accounting Horizons,* March 1999, pp. 1–16.

services discussed next allow investors to gather their own information about the company and monitor the recommendations of a variety of analysts.

Companies actually file their SEC forms electronically through the EDGAR (Electronic Data Gathering and Retrieval) Service, which is sponsored by the SEC. Users can retrieve information from EDGAR within 24 hours of its submission, long before it is available through the mail. EDGAR is a free service available on the Web at

www.sec.gov

Many companies also provide direct access to their financial statements and other information over the web. You can contact Callaway Golf by clicking on "investor relations" at

www.callawaygolf.com

Financial analysts and other sophisticated users obtain much of the information they use from the wide variety of commercial online information services. Services such as Compustat and Thompson Research provide broad access to financial statements and news information. They also allow users to search the database by key words, including various financial statement terms. Their websites describe their services in more detail:

www.compustat.com
www.thomson.com

Readers should be aware that the definitions used to compute key ratios often differ across these sources.

More general information services include Factiva and Bloomberg. Factiva provides access to news stories about companies and company press releases, including the initial announcements of annual and quarterly financial results. The Bloomberg service also provides the ability to combine these sources of information in sophisticated analyses. Their websites describe their services in more detail:

www.factiva.com
www.bloomberg.com

A growing number of other resources offering a mixture of free and fee-based information exist on the Web. These include

www.reuters.com/finance
www.hoovers.com
finance.yahoo.com

Exhibit 5.3 suggests the wide range of information on Callaway Golf available on the Reuters website.

 Information Services and Job Searches

FINANCIAL
ANALYSIS

Information services have become the primary tool for professional analysts who use them to analyze competing firms. Information services are also an important source of information for job seekers. Potential employers expect job applicants to demonstrate knowledge of their companies during an interview, and electronic information services are an excellent source of company information. The best place to begin learning about your potential employers is their website. Be sure to read the material in the employment section and the investor relations section of the site. To learn more about electronic information services, contact the business or reference librarian at your college or university or explore the preceding websites.

Users: Institutional and Private Investors, Creditors, and Others

INSTITUTIONAL INVESTORS are managers of pension, mutual, endowment, and other funds that invest on the behalf of others.

Institutional investors include pension funds (associated with unions and employees of specific companies or government agencies); mutual funds; and endowment, charitable foundation, and trust funds (such as the endowment of your college or university). These institutional stockholders usually employ their own analysts who also rely on the information intermediaries just discussed. Institutional shareholders control the majority of publicly traded shares of U.S. companies. For example, at the end of the current fiscal year, institutional investors owned 99 percent of Callaway Golf stock. Callaway Golf's three largest institutional investors follow:

Institution	Approximate Ownership
Fidelity Management & Research	15.5%
Royce & Associates	5.5%
Barclays Global Investors	4.4%

Most small investors own stock in companies such as Callaway Golf indirectly through mutual and pension funds.

PRIVATE INVESTORS include individuals who purchase shares in companies.

Private investors include large individual investors such as Ely Callaway and his friends who originally invested directly in Callaway Golf, as well as small retail investors who buy shares of publicly traded companies through brokers such as Merrill Lynch. Retail investors normally lack the expertise to understand financial statements and the resources to gather data efficiently. They often rely on the advice of information intermediaries or turn their money over to the management of mutual and pension funds (institutional investors).

LENDERS (CREDITORS) include suppliers and financial institutions that lend money to companies.

Lenders, or **creditors,** include suppliers, banks, commercial credit companies, and other financial institutions that lend money to companies. Lending officers and financial analysts in these organizations use the same public sources of information. They also use additional financial information (e.g., monthly statements) that companies often agree to provide as part of the lending contract. Lenders are the primary external user group for financial statements of private companies. Institutional and private investors also become creditors when they buy a company's publicly traded bonds.

Financial statements also play an important role in the relationships between suppliers and customers. Customers evaluate the financial health of suppliers to determine whether they will be reliable, up-to-date sources of supply. Suppliers evaluate their customers to estimate their future needs and ability to pay debts. Competitors also attempt to learn useful information about a company from its statements. The potential loss of competitive advantage is one of the costs of public financial disclosures. Accounting regulators consider these costs as well as the direct costs of preparation when they consider requiring new disclosures. They apply what is called the **cost-benefit constraint,** which suggests that the benefits of accounting for and reporting information should outweigh the costs.

Guiding Principles for Communicating Useful Information

For accounting information to be useful, it must be relevant and reliable. **Relevant information** is capable of influencing decisions by allowing users to assess past activities and/or predict future activities. **Reliable information** is accurate, unbiased, and verifiable (independent parties can agree on the nature of the transaction and amount). Our discussions of ratio analysis have emphasized the importance of comparing ratios for the same company over time, as well as with those of competitors. Such comparisons are valid only if the information is prepared on a consistent and comparable basis. **Consistent information** means that within a company, similar accounting methods have been applied over time. **Comparable information** means that similar accounting methods have been applied across companies. These characteristics of useful information, along with the full-disclosure principle, guide the FASB in deciding what financial information should be reported.

Accurate interpretation of financial statements requires that the statement reader be aware of important constraints of accounting measurement. First, small amounts do not have to be reported separately or accounted for precisely according to GAAP if they would not influence users' decisions. Accountants usually designate such items and amounts as **immaterial.** Determining **material amounts** is often very subjective.

Second, **conservatism** requires that special care be taken to avoid (1) overstating assets and revenues and (2) understating liabilities and expenses. This guideline attempts to offset managers' natural optimism about their operations, which sometimes creeps into the financial reports they prepare. This constraint produces more conservative income statement and balance sheet amounts. Finally, in certain industries such as public utilities, special industry reporting practices are followed to better reflect the economics of those industries.

The COST-BENEFIT CONSTRAINT suggests that the benefits of accounting for and reporting information should outweigh the costs.

RELEVANT INFORMATION can influence a decision; it is timely and has predictive and/or feedback value.

RELIABLE INFORMATION is accurate, unbiased, and verifiable.

CONSISTENT INFORMATION can be compared over time because similar accounting methods have been applied.

COMPARABLE INFORMATION allows comparisons across businesses because similar accounting methods have been applied.

MATERIAL AMOUNTS are amounts that are large enough to influence a user's decision.

CONSERVATISM suggests that care should be taken not to overstate assets and revenues or understate liabilities and expenses.

International Accounting Standards Board and Global Differences in Accounting Standards

INTERNATIONAL
PERSPECTIVE

IFRS

Financial accounting standards and disclosure requirements are set by national regulatory agencies and standard-setting bodies. Many countries, including the members of the European Union, are committed to adopting international financial reporting standards (IFRS) issued by the International Accounting Standards Board (IASB). IFRS are similar to U.S. GAAP, but there are several important differences. A partial list of the differences at the time

continued

this chapter is being written is presented below, along with the chapter in which these issues will be addressed:

Difference*	U.S. GAAP	IFRS	Chapter
Extraordinary items	Permitted	Prohibited	5
Last-in first-out method for inventory	Permitted	Prohibited	7
Reversal of inventory write-downs	Prohibited	Required	7
Basis for property, plant, and equipment	Historical cost	Fair value or historical cost	8

*Source: *Deloitte IAS Plus*, November 2007.

The FASB and IASB are working together to eliminate these and other differences.

SELF-STUDY QUIZ

Match the key terms in the left column with their definitions in the right column.

1. Relevant information
2. CEO and CFO
3. Financial analyst
4. Auditor
5. Cost-benefit constraint

a. Management primarily responsible for accounting information.

b. An independent party who verifies financial statements.

c. Information that influences users' decisions.

d. Reporting only information that provides benefits in excess of costs.

e. An individual who analyzes financial information and provides advice.

After you have completed your answers, check them with the solutions at the bottom of the page.

Learning Objective 2

Identify the steps in the accounting communication process, including the issuance of press releases, annual reports, quarterly reports, and SEC filings as well as the role of electronic information services in this process.

THE DISCLOSURE PROCESS

As noted in our discussion of information services and information intermediaries, the accounting communication process includes more steps and participants than one would envision in a world in which annual and quarterly reports are simply mailed to shareholders. SEC regulation FD, for "Fair Disclosure," requires that companies provide all investors equal access to all important company news. Managers and other insiders are also prohibited from trading their company's shares based on nonpublic (insider) information so that no party benefits from early access.

Press Releases

A PRESS RELEASE is a written public news announcement normally distributed to major news services.

To provide timely information to external users and to limit the possibility of selective leakage of information, Callaway Golf and other public companies announce quarterly and annual earnings through a **press release** as soon as the verified figures (audited for annual and reviewed for quarterly earnings) are available. Callaway Golf normally issues its earnings press releases within four weeks of the end of the accounting period. The announcements are sent electronically to the major print and electronic

---

Self-Study Quiz Solutions   1. c; 2. a; 3. e; 4. b; 5. d.

CALLAWAY GOLF ANNOUNCES 22% INCREASE IN SALES FOR THE THIRD QUARTER RESULTING IN RECORD SALES FOR THE FIRST NINE MONTHS OF 2007

CARLSBAD, Calif.—(Business Wire)—Nov. 1, 2007—Callaway Golf Company (NYSE:ELY) today announced its financial results for the third quarter ended September 30, 2007. Highlights for the third quarter include: Net sales of $235.5 million, an increase of 22% compared to $193.8 million for the same period in 2006 . . . Fully diluted earnings per share for the period were $0.02 compared with a loss of $0.18 for the prior year. The third quarter 2007 results include a gain of approximately $0.03 per diluted share related to the sale of a building . . .

Gross profit for the third quarter of 2007 increased 39% to $94.0 million (or 40% of net sales) compared to $67.7 million (or 35% of net sales) for the third quarter of 2006. The increase in gross profit as a percent of sales is primarily the result of the Company's gross margin improvement initiatives announced in November 2006 and secondarily a more favorable mix of higher margin Fusion woods and X-series irons products. Operating expenses for the third quarter of 2007 were $93.1 million (or 40% of net sales) compared to $84.6 million (or 44% of net sales) in 2006.

EXHIBIT 5.4

Earnings Press Release Excerpt for Callaway Golf Company

REAL WORLD EXCERPT

PRESS RELEASE

Audio lecture–AP5-2
www.mhhe.com/libby6e

news services including *DowJones, Reuters,* and *Bloomberg,* which make them immediately available to subscribers. Exhibit 5.4 shows an excerpt from a typical earnings press release for Callaway Golf that includes key financial figures. This excerpt is followed by management's discussion of the results and condensed income statements and balance sheets that will be included in the formal report to shareholders, distributed after the press release.

Many companies, including Callaway Golf, follow these press releases with a conference call during which senior managers answer questions about the quarterly results from analysts. These calls are open to the investing public. Listening to these recordings is a good way to learn about a company's business strategy and its expectations for the future, as well as key factors that analysts consider when they evaluate a company.

 How Does the Stock Market React to Earnings Announcements?

FINANCIAL ANALYSIS

For actively traded stocks such as Callaway Golf, most of the stock market reaction (stock price increases and decreases from investor trading) to the news in the press release usually occurs quickly. Recall that a number of analysts follow Callaway Golf and regularly predict the company's earnings. When the actual earnings are published, the market reacts **not** to the amount of earnings but to the difference between expected earnings and actual earnings. This amount is called **unexpected earnings.** In October, analysts expected Callaway Golf to report a **loss** of $.05 per share. Callaway's actual earnings per share for the quarter ended up being a profit of $.02 per share. Unexpected earnings (actual − expected) were thus +$.07 cents per share [2 cents − (−5 cents)], and, as a result, the share price jumped around $1.78, or 11.7 percent, to $17.05.

Companies such as Callaway Golf also issue press releases concerning other important events including new product announcements and new endorsement contracts with professional golfers. Press releases related to annual earnings and quarterly earnings often precede the issuance of the quarterly or annual report by 15 to 45 days. This time is necessary to prepare the additional detail and to print and distribute those reports.

Annual Reports

For privately held companies, **annual reports** are relatively simple documents photo-copied on white bond paper. They normally include only the following:

1. Four basic financial statements: income statement, balance sheet, stockholders' equity or retained earnings statement, and cash flow statement.
2. Related notes (footnotes).
3. Report of Independent Accountants (Auditor's Opinion) if the statements are audited.

The annual reports of public companies are significantly more elaborate, both because of additional SEC reporting requirements and because many companies use their annual reports as public relations tools.

The annual reports of public companies are normally split into two sections. The first, "nonfinancial," section usually includes a letter to stockholders from the Chairman and CEO; descriptions of the company's management philosophy, products, successes (and occasionally failures); and exciting prospects and challenges for the future. Beautiful photographs of products, facilities, and personnel often are included. The second, "financial," section includes the core of the report. The SEC sets minimum disclosure standards for the financial section of the annual reports of public companies. The principal components of the financial section include

1. Summarized financial data for a 5- or 10-year period.
2. Management's Discussion and Analysis of Financial Condition and Results of Operations and Disclosures about Market Risk.
3. The four basic financial statements.
4. Notes (footnotes).
5. Report of Independent Accountants (Auditor's Opinion) and the Management Certification.
6. Recent stock price information.
7. Summaries of the unaudited quarterly financial data (described later).
8. Lists of directors and officers of the company and relevant addresses.

The order of these components varies.

Except for the Management's Discussion and Analysis and Disclosures about Market Risks, most of these elements have been covered in earlier chapters. This element includes an explanation of key figures on the financial statements and the risks the company faces in the future.

Quarterly Reports

Quarterly reports normally begin with a short letter to shareholders. This is followed by a condensed income statement for the quarter, which often shows less detail than the annual income statement, and a condensed balance sheet dated at the end of the quarter (e.g., March 31 for the first quarter). These condensed financial statements are not audited and so are marked **unaudited.** Often the cash flow statement, statement of stockholders' equity (or retained earnings statement), and some notes to the financial statements are omitted. Private companies also normally prepare quarterly reports for their lenders.

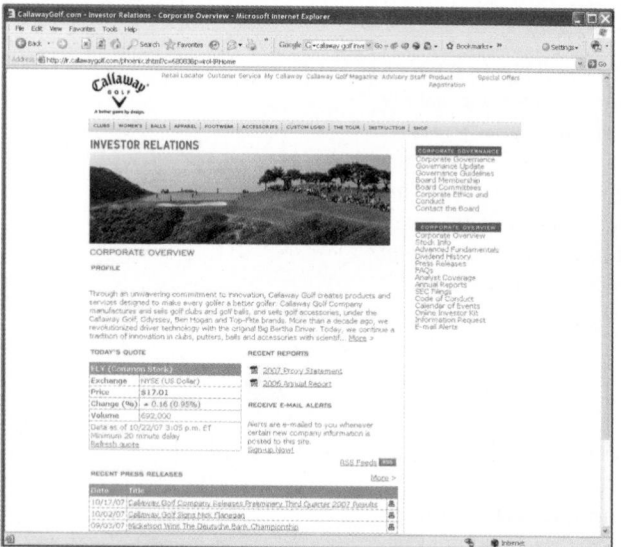

SEC Reports—10-K, 10-Q, 8-K

Public companies must file periodic reports with the SEC. They include the annual report on **Form 10-K,** quarterly reports on **Form 10-Q,** and current event reports on **Form 8-K.** These reports are normally referred to by number (for example, the "10-K"). In general, the 10-K and 10-Q present all information in the annual and quarterly reports, respectively, along with additional management discussion and several required schedules.

For example, the Form 10-K provides a more detailed description of the business including its products, product development, sales and marketing, manufacturing, and competitors. It also lists properties owned or leased, any legal proceedings it is involved in, and significant contracts it has signed. The 10-K also provides more detailed schedules concerning various figures on the income statement and balance sheet including bad debts, warranties, inventories, and advertising. There has been a recent trend to combine the information in the 10-K into the company annual reports. Callaway's current annual report includes eight pages featuring product details and the president's letter to shareholders followed by the complete 10-K for that year.

The FORM 10-K is the annual report that publicly traded companies must file with the SEC.

FORM 10-Q is the quarterly report that publicly traded companies must file with the SEC.

FORM 8-K is used by publicly traded companies to disclose any material event not previously reported that is important to investors (e.g., auditor changes, mergers).

A CLOSER LOOK AT FINANCIAL STATEMENT FORMATS AND NOTES

To make financial statements more useful to investors, creditors, and analysts, specific **classifications** of information are included on the statements. Various classifications are used in practice. You should not be confused when you notice slightly different formats used by different companies. In this section, we will focus on similarities and differences in the classifications and line items presented on Callaway Golf's and Papa John's balance sheet, income statement, and cash flow statement. We also discuss some of Callaway Golf's note disclosures in more detail.

Learning Objective 3
Recognize and apply the different financial statement and disclosure formats used by companies in practice.

Classified Balance Sheet

Exhibit 5.5 shows the December 31, 2006, balance sheet for Callaway Golf. Its balance sheet looks very similar in structure to Papa John's presented in Chapter 4. Its balance sheet is classified as follows:

Assets (by order of liquidity)
   Current assets (short term)
   Noncurrent assets
      Total assets
Liabilities (by order of time to maturity)
   Current liabilities (short-term)
   Long-term liabilities
      Total liabilities
Stockholders' equity (by source)
   Contributed capital (by owners)
   Retained earnings (accumulated earnings minus
      accumulated dividends declared)
         Total stockholders' equity
         Total liabilities and stockholders' equity

These classifications will play a major role in our discussions of ratio analysis in later chapters.

Callaway Golf's balance sheet contains two items, not included in Papa John's, that are worthy of additional discussion. **Intangible assets** have no physical existence and a long life. Examples are patents, trademarks, copyrights, franchises, and goodwill from purchasing other companies. Most intangibles except goodwill, trademarks, and other intangibles with indefinite lives are amortized as they are used, in a manner similar to the depreciation of tangible assets. They are reported net of accumulated amortization on the balance sheet.

Balance Sheet of Callaway Golf

REAL WORLD EXCERPT

ANNUAL REPORT

CALLAWAY GOLF COMPANY Consolidated Balance Sheets* At December 31, 2006 and 2005		
(dollars in thousands, except share and per share data)	December 31,	
	2006	2005
Assets		
Current assets		
Cash and cash equivalents	$ 46,362	$ 49,481
Accounts receivable, net	118,133	98,082
Inventories, net	265,110	241,577
Other current assets	63,595	49,450
Total current assets	$493,200	$438,590
Property, plant and equipment, net	131,224	127,739
Intangible assets, net	175,159	175,191
Other assets	46,364	22,978
	$845,947	$764,498
Liabilities and Shareholders' Equity		
Current liabilities		
Accounts payable and accrued expenses	$143,455	$140,184
Note payable, current portion	80,000	21
Total current liabilities	$223,455	$140,205
Long-term liabilities:		
Other liabilities	43,388	28,245
Minority Interest	1,987	
Commitment and contingencies (Note 13)		
Shareholders' equity		
Common Stock, $.01 par value, 85,096,782 shares and 84,950,694 shares issued at December 31, 2006 and 2005, respectively	851	850
Additional paid-in capital	141,192	164,202
Retained earnings	435,074	430,996
Total shareholders' equity	$577,117	$596,048
	$845,947	$764,498

The accompanying notes are an integral part of these financial statements.

Callaway's statements have been simplified for purposes of our discussion.

PAR VALUE is a legal amount per share established by the board of directors; it establishes the minimum amount a stockholder must contribute and has no relationship to the market price of the stock.

Until this chapter, we have identified the financing by investors as **Contributed Capital**. In practice, however, this account often is shown as two accounts: Common Stock and Additional Paid-in Capital.[6] Each share of common stock usually has a nominal (low) **par value** printed on the face of the certificate. Par value is a legal amount

---

[6]Callaway's actual statement lists an amount as treasury stock that is the shares that have been repurchased by the company from shareholders. Chapter 11 discusses these terms in more detail.

per share established by the board of directors; it has no relationship to the market price of the stock. Its significance is that it establishes the minimum amount that a stockholder must contribute. Callaway Golf's common stock has a par value of $.01 per share, but the 1,000,000 shares were sold in its 1992 initial public offering at a market price of $16 per share.[7] When a corporation issues capital stock, the amount received is recorded in part as Common Stock (Number of Shares × Par Value per Share) and the excess above par as **Additional Paid-In Capital** (also called Paid-In Capital or Contributed Capital in Excess of Par). The journal entry to record Callaway Golf's 1992 initial public offering follows:

ADDITIONAL PAID-IN CAPITAL (Paid-In Capital, Contributed Capital in Excess of Par) is the amount of contributed capital less the par value of the stock.

Cash (+A) ($16 × 1,000,000 shares) 16,000,000
    Common stock (+SE) ($.01 per share × 1,000,000 shares)   10,000
    Additional paid-in capital (+SE) ($16,000,000 − 10,000)   15,990,000

Assets	=	Liabilities	+	Stockholders' Equity	
Cash	+16,000,000			Common Stock	+10,000
				Additional Paid-In Capital	+15,990,000

Classified Income Statement

Callaway Golf's 2006 consolidated income statement is reprinted for you in Exhibit 5.6. Income statements have two major sections. The first presents the income statement as we have in prior chapters. The second presents net income on a per share basis or earnings per share.

Continuing Operations

Callaway Golf's income statements are prepared using the following basic structure.

	Net sales
−	Cost of goods sold
	Gross profit
−	Operating expenses
	Income from operations
+/−	Nonoperating revenues/expenses and gains/losses
	Income before income taxes
−	Income tax expense
	Net income

Callaway Golf is a manufacturing company, whereas Papa John's is a service firm. Consequently, Callaway Golf's income statement includes one subtotal not included in Papa John's. Like most manufacturing and merchandising companies,[8] Callaway Golf reports the subtotal **Gross Profit** (gross margin) which is the difference between net sales and cost of goods sold. Another subtotal—**Income from Operations** (also called operating income)—is computed by subtracting operating expenses from gross profit.

    Nonoperating (other) Items are income, expenses, gains, and losses that do not relate to the company's primary operations. Examples include interest income, interest expense, and gains and losses on the sale of fixed assets and investments. These

GROSS PROFIT (GROSS MARGIN) is net sales less cost of goods sold.

INCOME FROM OPERATIONS (OPERATING INCOME) equals net sales less cost of goods sold and other operating expenses.

---

[7]These numbers are rounded.

[8]A merchandiser buys products from manufacturers for resale, and a manufacturer produces goods for sale to wholesalers or retail merchandisers.

<table>
<tr><td>

EXHIBIT 5.6

Income Statement of Callaway Golf

REAL WORLD EXCERPT

ANNUAL REPORT

</td><td>

CALLAWAY GOLF COMPANY
Consolidated Statement of Operations
For the Years Ended December 31, 2004–2006

(dollars in thousands, except per share data)	Years Ended December 31,					
	2006		**2005**		**2004**	
Net sales	$1,017,907	100%	$998,093	100%	$934,564	100%
Cost of sales	619,832	61%	583,679	58%	575,742	62%
Gross profit	398,075	39%	414,414	42%	358,822	38%
Selling expenses	254,526	25%	290,074	29%	263,089	28%
General and administrative expenses	79,709	8%	80,145	8%	89,878	10%
Research and development expenses	26,785	3%	26,989	3%	30,557	3%
Total operating expenses	361,020	*35%	397,208	40%	383,524	41%
Income from operations	37,055	4%	17,206	2%	(24,702)	(3)%
Interest and other income, net	3,364		(390)		1,934	
Interest expense	(5,421)		(2,279)		(945)	
Income before income taxes	34,998	3%	14,537	1%	(23,713)	(3)%
Provision for income taxes	11,708		1,253		(13,610)	
Net income	$23,290	2%	$13,284	1%	$(10,103)	(1)%
Earnings per common share:	$0.34		$0.19		$(0.15)	
Common equivalent shares:	67,732		68,646		67,721	

The accompanying notes are an integral part of these financial statements.

</td></tr>
</table>

*Does not add up to 25% + 8% + 3% due to rounding

INCOME BEFORE INCOME TAXES (PRETAX EARNINGS) is revenues minus all expenses except income tax expense.

nonoperating items are added to or subtracted from income from operations to obtain **Income before Income Taxes,** also called Pretax Earnings. At this point, Income Tax Provision (Income Tax Expense) is normally subtracted to obtain Net Income. Some companies show fewer subtotals on their income statements. No difference exists in the revenue, expense, gain, and loss items reported using the different formats. Only the categories and subtotals differ.

Nonrecurring Items

Companies may also report one or both of two nonrecurring items on their income statements:

1. Discontinued operations

2. Extraordinary items.

If any one of these items exists, an additional subtotal is presented for Income from Continuing Operations (or Income before Nonrecurring Items), after which the nonrecurring items are presented. These two items are presented separately because they are not useful in predicting the future income of the company given their nonrecurring nature.

When a major component of a business is sold or abandoned, income or loss from that component, as well as any gain or loss on disposal, are included as discontinued operations. Extraordinary Items are gains or losses incurred that are both unusual and infrequent in occurrence. The Chapter Supplement explains and presents an example income statement from La-Z-Boy illustrating these two nonrecurring items.

Earnings per Share

As we discussed in Chapter 4, simple computations for earnings per share (EPS) are as follows:

$$\text{Earnings per Share} = \frac{\text{Net Income*}}{\text{Average Number of Shares of Common Stock Outstanding during the Period}}$$

Common-Size Income Statement

Notice that Callaway Golf also reports income statement line items as a percentage of net sales, which are often called **common-size income statements**. Many analysts compute these common-size statements as a first step in analysis because they ease year-to-year comparisons.

 Interpreting the Common-Size Income Statement

FINANCIAL ANALYSIS

The common-size income statement reports line items as a percentage of net sales (divide each line item by net sales and multiply by 100%). Callaway Golf's common-size statement presented in Exhibit 5.6 dramatically displays the cause of its increasing income. Even though net sales have risen between 2005 and 2006, Cost of sales has risen at a much faster rate, increasing from 58% to 61% of net sales. This resulted from declines in sales of higher gross margin products as well as price pressure from competitors. At the same time, total operating expenses have also dropped from 40% to 35%. Taken together, these factors produced the increase in net profit margin from 1% to 2%.

SELF-STUDY **QUIZ**

1. Prepare a journal entry for the following transaction: Issued 1,000 shares of $1 par value stock for $12 per share.

2. Complete the following tabulation, indicating the direction (+ for increase, − for decrease, and NE for no effect) and amount of the effect of each transaction. Consider each item independently.

   a. Recorded and paid rent expense of $200.

   b. Recorded the sale of goods on account for $400 and cost of goods sold of $300.

Transaction	Current Assets	Gross Profit	Income from Operations
a.			
b.			

After you have completed your answers, check them with the solutions at the bottom of the page.

1. Cash (+A) ($12 × 1,000 shares)   12,000
     Common stock (+SE) ($1 per share × 1,000 shares)   1,000
     Additional paid-in capital (+SE) ($12,000 − 1,000)   11,000
2. a. −200, NE, −200; b. +100, +100, +100

*If there are preferred dividends (discussed in Chapter 11), the amount is subtracted from Net Income in the numerater.

Statement of Stockholders' Equity

The statement of stockholders' (shareholders') equity reports the changes in each of the company's stockholders' equity accounts during the accounting period. We will discuss this statement in more detail in Chapter 11.

Statement of Cash Flows

We introduced the three cash flow statement classifications in prior chapters:

Cash Flows from Operating Activities. This section reports cash flows associated with earning income.

Cash Flows from Investing Activities. Cash flows in this section are associated with purchase and sale of (1) productive assets (other than inventory) and (2) investments in other companies.

Cash Flows from Financing Activities. These cash flows are related to financing the business through debt issuances and repayments, stock (equity) issuances and repurchases, and dividend payments.

Exhibit 5.7 presents Callaway Golf's 2006 consolidated statement of cash flows. The first section (Cash Flows from Operating Activities) can be reported using either the **direct** or **indirect** method. For Callaway Golf, this first section is reported using the indirect method, which presents a reconciliation of net income on an accrual basis to cash flows from operations. This more common format differs from the format in the statement prepared for **Papa John's** in Chapter 3, which was constructed using the direct method.

**FOCUS ON
CASH FLOWS**

Operating Activities (Indirect Method)

The Operating Activities section prepared using the indirect method helps the analyst understand the **causes of differences** between a company's net income and its cash flows. Net income and cash flows from operating activities can be quite different. Remember that the income statement is prepared under the accrual concept. Revenues are recorded when earned without regard to when the related cash flows occur. Likewise, expenses are matched with revenues and recorded in the same period without regard to when the related cash flows occur.

In the indirect method, the operating activities section starts with net income computed under the accrual concept and then eliminates noncash items leaving cash flow from operating activities:

$$\begin{array}{r} \text{Net income} \\ +/- \text{ Adjustments for noncash items} \\ \hline \text{Cash provided by operating activities} \end{array}$$

The items listed between these two amounts explain the reasons they differ. For example, since no cash is paid during the current period for Callaway Golf's depreciation expense reported on the income statement, this amount is added back in the conversion process. Similarly, increases and decreases in certain current assets and liabilities also account for some of the difference between net income and cash flow from operations. For example, sales on account increase net income as well as the current asset accounts receivable, but do not increase cash. As we cover different portions of the income statement and balance sheet in more detail in Chapters 6 through 12, we will also discuss the relevant sections of the cash flow statement. Then we discuss the complete cash flow statement in detail in Chapter 13.

Notes to Financial Statements

While the numbers reported on the various financial statements provide important information, users require additional details to facilitate their analysis. All financial

CALLAWAY GOLF COMPANY Consolidated Statement of Cash Flows For the Years Ended December 31			
(dollars in thousands)	2006	2005	2004
Cash flows from operating activities:			
Net income	$ 23,290	$ 13,284	$ (10,103)
Adjustments to reconcile net income to net cash provided by operating activities:			
Depreciation and amortization	32,274	38,260	51,154
Other noncash items	14,035	9,060	21,089
Changes in assets and liabilities, net of effects from acquisitions:			
Accounts receivable, net	(12,128)	2,296	(1,048)
Inventories, net	(16,842)	(65,595)	10,299
Other assets	(4,475)	7,583	1,554
Accounts payable and accrued expenses	(10,803)	38,768	(23,601)
Income taxes payable	(6,936)	26,676	(40,711)
Other liabilities	(1,128)	(351)	(273)
Net cash provided by operating activities	$ 17,287	$69,981	$8,360
Cash flows from investing activities:			
Capital expenditures	(32,453)	(33,942)	(25,809)
Acquisitions, net of cash acquired	374	—	(9,204)
Investment in marketable securities	(10,008)	—	—
Proceeds from sale of capital assets	469	1,363	431
Net cash used in investing activities	$ (41,618)	$(32,579)	$ (34,582)
Cash flows from financing activities:			
Issuance of common stock	9,606	14,812	20,311
Acquisition of treasury stock	(52,872)	(39)	(6,298)
Dividends paid, net	(19,212)	(19,557)	(19,069)
Proceeds from (payments on) line of credit, net	80,000	(13,000)	13,000
Other financing activities	2,549	(44)	
Net cash used in financing activities	$ 20,071	$(17,828)	$ 7,944
Effect of exchange rate changes on cash and cash equivalents	1,141	(1,750)	2,595
Net increase (decrease) in cash and cash equivalents	(3,119)	17,824	(15,683)
Cash and cash equivalents at beginning of year	49,481	31,657	47,340
Cash and cash equivalents at end of year	$ 46,362	$49,481	$ 31,657

The accompanying notes are an integral part of these financial statements.

EXHIBIT 5.7

Cash Flow Statement
of Callaway Golf

**REAL WORLD
EXCERPT**

ANNUAL REPORT

reports include additional information in notes that follow the statements. Callaway Golf's 2006 notes include three types of information:

1. Descriptions of the key accounting rules applied to the company's statements.

2. Additional detail supporting reported numbers.

3. Relevant financial information not disclosed on the statements.

Accounting Rules Applied in the Company's Statements

One of the first notes is typically a summary of significant accounting policies. As you will see in your study of subsequent chapters, generally accepted accounting principles (GAAP) permit companies to select from alternative methods for measuring the effects of transactions. The summary of significant accounting policies tells the user which accounting methods the company has adopted. Callaway Golf's accounting policy for property, plant, and equipment is as follows:

REAL WORLD EXCERPT

ANNUAL REPORT

NOTE 2: SIGNIFICANT ACCOUNTING POLICIES

Property, Plant, and Equipment

Property, plant and equipment are stated at cost less accumulated depreciation. Depreciation is computed using the straight-line method over estimated useful lives as follows:

Buildings and improvements	10–30 years
Machinery and equipment	5–15 years
Furniture, computers, and equipment	3–5 years
Production molds	2 years

Without an understanding of the various accounting methods used, it is impossible to analyze a company's financial results effectively.

FINANCIAL ANALYSIS

Alternative Accounting Methods and GAAP

Many people mistakenly believe that GAAP permits only one accounting method to be used to compute each value on the financial statements (e.g., inventory). Actually, GAAP often allows a selection of an accounting method from a menu of acceptable methods. This permits a company to choose the methods that most closely reflect its particular economic circumstances. This flexibility complicates the financial statement users' task, however. Users must understand how the company's choice of accounting methods affects its financial statement presentations. As renowned financial analysts Gabrielle Napolitano, Michael Moran, and Abby Joseph Cohen of the investment banking firm of Goldman, Sachs & Co. note in their recent research report,

REAL WORLD EXCERPT

Goldman, Sachs & Co.

ANALYSTS' REPORTS

Discretionary choices in financial reporting that can ultimately lead to or create future earnings shocks that drive stock prices must be identified; analysts must make adjustments to minimize or eliminate the impact of these drivers on corporate performance. As a result, financial statement users must (1) develop a keen understanding of the fundamentals underlying each firm's business operations and (2) familiarize themselves with the corporate reporting practices of the companies they are analyzing.*

*Gabrielle Napolitano, Michael A. Moran, and Abby Joseph Cohen, "Demand for Forensic Accounting Intensifies," *Global Strategy Research* (New York: Goldman, Sachs & Co).

For example, before analyzing two companies' statements prepared using different accounting methods, one company's statements must be converted to the other's methods to make them comparable. Otherwise, the reader is in a situation analogous to comparing distances in kilometers and miles without converting to a common scale. In later chapters, we will focus on developing the ability to make these conversions.

Additional Detail Supporting Reported Numbers

The second category of notes provides supplemental information concerning the data shown on the financial statements. Among other information, these notes may show revenues broken out by geographic region or business segment, describe unusual transactions, and/or offer expanded detail on a specific classification. For example, in Note 6, Callaway Golf indicates the makeup of accounts receivable; inventory; property, plant, and equipment; and other items presented on the balance sheet. Note 16, which follows, shows sales reported on the income statement and long-lived assets from the balance sheet divided by geographic region:

NOTE 16: SEGMENT INFORMATION

	Sales	Long-Lived Assets
	(dollars in thousands)	
2006		
United States	$ 566,600	$ 279,879
Europe	159,886	9,406
Japan	105,705	1,871
Rest of Asia	75,569	4,518
Other foreign countries	110,147	10,709
	$1,017,907	$ 306,383

Relevant Financial Information Not Disclosed on the Statements

The final category includes information that impacts the company financially but is not shown on the statements. Examples include information on legal matters and any material event that occurred subsequent to year-end but before the financial statements are published. In Note 15, Callaway Golf disclosed the details of its lease commitments:

NOTE 15: LEASE COMMITMENTS

The Company leases certain warehouse, distribution and office facilities, vehicles as well as office equipment under operating leases and certain computer and telecommunication equipment under capital leases. Lease terms range from one to ten years expiring at various dates through December 2011, with options to renew at varying terms. Commitments for minimum lease payments under noncancelable operating leases as of December 31, 2006 are as follows:

	(dollars in thousands)
2007	$ 6,031
2008	3,611
2009	2,318
2010	1,975
2011	1,852
Thereafter	6,864
	$22,651

Voluntary Disclosures

GAAP and SEC regulations set only the minimum level of required financial disclosures. Many companies provide important disclosures beyond those required. For example, in its annual report, 10-K, and recent earnings press release, Callaway Golf discloses sales by major product category, which helps investors track the success of new products.

A QUESTION OF ETHICS

Accounting and Sustainable Development

A growing area of voluntary disclosure in the United States is sustainability reporting, as described by *CFO* magazine:

REAL WORLD EXCERPT

CFO MAGAZINE

The idea that a company should conduct its business in ways that benefit not just shareholders but the environment and society, too, is called sustainability, or sustainable development. It's an idea championed by a small but growing number of companies around the globe. One business group, the World Business Council for Sustainable Development, lists some 170 international members, including more than 30 Fortune 500 companies. According to the council's website, these companies share the belief that "the pursuit of sustainable development is good for business and business is good for sustainable development."

To tell their stakeholders about that pursuit, companies are issuing sustainability reports. Many, like Suncor, are doing so following the strict guidelines of the Global Reporting Initiative (GRI), an independent institution founded in 1997, to develop a common framework for sustainability reporting. Enter the words "sustainability reporting" into your favorite search engine and you'll find such well-known company names as Alcoa, Alcan, Bristol-Myers Squibb, General Motors, Baxter International, and FedEx Kinko's. In all, some 500 organizations publish sustainability reports according to GRI guidelines. Some countries, such as France, South Africa, and the Netherlands, now mandate environmental or social sustainability reporting as a condition to being listed on their stock exchanges.

Source: *CFO* magazine, November 2004, pp. 97–100.

Such reports are voluntary disclosures in the United States. However, many believe that managing a company in the interests of a wider group of stakeholders and reporting on these efforts is an ethical imperative.

RETURN ON EQUITY ANALYSIS: A FRAMEWORK FOR EVALUATING COMPANY PERFORMANCE

Learning Objective 4

Analyze a company's performance based on return on equity and its components.

Evaluating company performance is the primary goal of financial statement analysis. Company managers, as well as competitors, use financial statements to better understand and evaluate a company's business strategy. Analysts, investors, and creditors use these same statements to judge company performance when they estimate the value of the company's stock and its creditworthiness. Our discussion of the financial data contained in accounting reports has now reached the point where we can develop an overall framework for using that data to evaluate company performance. The most comprehensive framework of this type is called **return on equity or ROE analysis (also called return on stockholders' equity or return on investment).**

Return on Equity

? ANALYTICAL QUESTION:

How well has management used the stockholders' investment during the period?

% RATIO AND COMPARISONS:

$$\text{Return on Equity} = \frac{\text{Net Income}}{\text{Average Stockholders' Equity}^*}$$

The 2006 ratio for Callaway Golf:

$$\frac{\$23,290}{(596,048 + \$577,117) \div 2} = 0.040 \ (4.0\%)$$

COMPARISONS OVER TIME		
Callaway Golf		
2004	**2005**	**2006**
−1.7%	2.3%	4.0%

COMPARISONS WITH COMPETITORS	
Adams Golf	**Recreational Products Industry**
2006	**2006**
0.24%	23.6%

💡 INTERPRETATIONS:

In General   ROE measures how much the firm earned for each dollar of stockholders' investment. In the long run, firms with higher ROE are expected to have higher stock prices than firms with lower ROE, all other things equal. Managers, analysts, and creditors use this ratio to assess the effectiveness of the company's overall business strategy (its operating, investing, and financing strategies).

Focus Company Analysis   Callaway Golf's ROEs from 1995 to 1997 were 47.5 percent, 41.7 percent, and 31.5 percent. Such high levels of ROE tend to be driven down over time by additional competition from new and existing competitors. Financial analysts sometimes call this **economic gravity.** Callaway Golf is facing just such a situation as large companies such as Adidas-owned Taylor-Made invest millions in marketing to unseat Callaway Golf from the top of its market. At the same time, new entrants such as Adams Golf chip away at Callaway Golf from below. Callaway Golf's ROE was 16% in 2000 and its stock price was $28 level. Its stock price fell to the $10 level in response to the slide in ROE during 2003 and 2004, but returned to $15 in response to the increase reported in 2006. The relationship between ROE and share price is well established in the stock valuation literature.

A Few Cautions   An increasing ROE can also indicate that a company is failing to invest in research and development or modernization of plant and equipment. While such a strategy will decrease expenses and thus increase ROE in the short run, it normally results in future declines in ROE as the company's products or plant and equipment reach the end of their life cycles. As a consequence, experienced decision makers evaluate ROE in the context of a company's business strategy.

*Average Stockholders' Equity = (Beginning Stockholders' Equity + Ending Stockholders' Equity) ÷ 2

ROE Profit Driver Analysis

Effective analysis of Callaway Golf's performance also requires understanding **why** its ROE differs both from prior levels and from those of its competitors. ROE profit driver analysis (also called ROE **decomposition** or **DuPont analysis**) breaks down ROE into the three factors shown in Exhibit 5.8. These factors are often called **profit drivers** or

EXHIBIT 5.8

ROE Profit Driver Analysis

$$\text{ROE} = \text{Net Profit Margin} \times \text{Asset Turnover} \times \text{Financial Leverage}$$

$$\frac{\text{Net Income}}{\text{Average Stockholders' Equity}} = \frac{\text{Net Income}}{\text{Net Sales}} \times \frac{\text{Net Sales}}{\text{Average Total Assets}} \times \frac{\text{Average Total Assets}}{\text{Average Stockholders' Equity}}$$

profit levers because they describe the three ways that management can improve ROE. They are measured by the key ratios you learned in Chapters 2 through 4.

1. **Net profit margin.** Net profit margin is Net Income/Net Sales. It measures how much of every sales dollar is profit. It can be increased by
   a. Increasing sales volume.
   b. Increasing sales price.
   c. Decreasing expenses.

2. **Asset turnover (efficiency).** Asset turnover is Net Sales/Average Total Assets. It measures how many sales dollars the company generates with each dollar of assets. It can be increased by
   a. Increasing sales volume.
   b. Disposing of (decreasing) less productive assets.

3. **Financial leverage.** Financial leverage is Average Total Assets/Average Stockholders' Equity. It measures how many dollars of assets are employed for each dollar of stockholder investment. It can be increased by
   a. Increased borrowing.
   b. Repurchasing (decreasing) outstanding stock.

These three ratios report on the effectiveness of the company's operating, investing, and financing activities, respectively.

Profit Drivers and Business Strategy

Successful manufacturers often follow one of two business strategies. The first is a **high-value** or **product-differentiation** strategy. Companies following this strategy rely on research and development and product promotion to convince customers of the superiority or distinctiveness of their products. This allows the company to charge higher prices and earn a higher net profit margin. The second is a **low-cost strategy,** which relies on efficient management of accounts receivable, inventory, and productive assets to produce high asset turnover.

Callaway Golf follows a classic high-value strategy. The ROE profit driver analysis presented in Exhibit 5.9 indicates the sources of its ROE, as well as reasons for its recent increase. The analysis shows continuing improvement in net profit margin

EXHIBIT 5.9

Callaway Golf ROE Profit Driver Analysis

Fiscal Year Ending	12/31/2004	12/31/2005	12/31/2006
Net Income / Net Sales	−0.011	0.013	0.023
× Net Sales / Avg. Total Assets	1.259	1.331	1.264
× Avg. Total Assets / Avg. Stockholders' Equity	1.262	1.269	1.373
= Net Income / Avg. Stockholders' Equity	−0.017	0.022	0.040

during 2006, as well as a decline in asset turnover. This indicates that Callaway Golf is generating fewer sales dollars for each dollar of assets, but higher profits on each dollar of sales. Callaway Golf's increase in financial leverage multiplies the effects of recent improvements in profit margin, but increases risk to shareholders if it should face another bad year in the future.

Companies often consider a variety of changes to increase ROE. These include

- Increasing sales and reducing operating expenses to increase profit margin.
- Collecting accounts receivable more quickly, centralizing distribution to reduce inventory kept on hand, and consolidating production facilities in fewer factories to reduce the amount of assets necessary to generate each dollar of sales.
- Using more borrowed funds (financial leverage) so that more assets can be employed per dollar of stockholder investment.

If Callaway Golf follows the same strategy it has in the past, the secret to increasing ROE must be improved product development to support premium selling prices. In 2006, Callaway Golf made major strides in new product development and expense reduction, and the success of new product introductions bodes well for further improvements in ROE.

Companies that follow a low-cost strategy, such as HP and Dell Inc., usually produce high ROE with higher asset turnover and higher leverage to make up for their lower net profit margin. This strategy is illustrated in the self-study quiz that follows this section.

As the preceding discussion indicates, a company can take many different actions to try to affect its profit drivers. To understand the impact of these actions, financial analysts disaggregate each of the profit drivers into more detailed ratios. For example, the asset turnover ratio is further disaggregated into turnover ratios for specific assets such as accounts receivable, inventory, and fixed assets. We will develop our understanding of these more specific ratios in the next eight chapters of the book. Then, in Chapter 14, we will combine the ratios in a comprehensive review.

SELF-STUDY QUIZ

We used ROE analysis in Exhibit 5.9 to understand how Callaway Golf's ROE had changed over the last three years. This type of analysis is often called **time-series analysis.** ROE analysis can also be used to explain why a company has an ROE different from its competitors at a single point in time. This type of analysis is called **cross-sectional analysis.** The following is the recent year's ROE analysis for Apple Inc. and HP. Apple uses a product differentiation strategy, developing a reputation for the most innovative products in its markets. HP primarily follows a low-cost strategy by offering good products and service at competitive prices. Apple has produced a higher ROE than HP and its stock price has responded accordingly. Using ROE analysis, explain how Apple has produced its higher ROE.

ROE PROFIT DRIVERS	APPLE	HP
Net Income / Net Sales	.103	.068
× Net Sales / Average Total Assets	1.35	1.15
× Avg. Total Assets / Average Stockholders' Equity	1.65	2.11
= Net Income / Average Stockholders' Equity	0.23	0.17

After you have completed your answers, check them with the solutions at the bottom of the page.

Both Apple and HP have high net profit margins, but Apple's unique products result in a significantly higher net profit margin. They both are also well known for the efficiency of their operations, which is reflected in their high asset turnover ratios, but Apple has the edge in asset efficiency. HP makes up for some of the deficit in both ratios through its higher financial leverage ratio, which reflects the company's greater use of debt.

Self-Study Quiz
Solutions

Epilogue

In the third quarter of 2007, citing improved sales of Fusion drivers and X-series irons, and a successful launch of the Top-Flite D2 golf ball, Callaway Golf declared that earnings would likely be higher than previously estimated for the third quarter and year. In response to that earnings announcement and continuing good news, investors drove its stock price up to about $17 per share. You can evaluate Callaway Golf's progress by going to the Web at **www.callawaygolf.com** to check its latest annual and quarterly reports.

DEMONSTRATION **CASE**

MICROSOFT CORPORATION

Complete the following requirements before proceeding to the suggested solution. Microsoft Corporation, developer of a broad line of computer software including the Windows operating systems, Word (word processing), and Excel (spreadsheet) programs, is now the largest computer-related company in the world. Following is a list of the financial statement items and amounts adapted from a recent Microsoft income statement and balance sheet. These items have normal debit and credit balances and are reported in millions of dollars. For that year, 10,062 million (weighted average) shares of stock were outstanding. The company closes its books on June 30, 2006.

Accounts payable	$ 2,909	Other current assets	$ 5,533
Accounts receivable	9,316	Other current liabilities	6,900
Accrued compensation	1,938	Other investments	9,232
Cash and short-term		Other noncurrent assets	8,311
investments	34,161	Property, plant, and	
Common stock and		equipment (net)	3,044
paid-in capital	59,005	Provision for income taxes	5,663
Cost of goods sold	7,650	Research and development	6,584
General and administrative	3,758	Retained earnings	(18,901)
Income taxes payable	1,557	Sales and marketing	9,818
Investment income (loss) and		Unearned revenue	9,138
other revenues (expenses)	1,790	Long-term liabilities	7,051
Net revenues	44,282		

Required:

1. Prepare in good form a multiple-step income statement (showing gross profit, operating income, and income before income taxes) and a classified balance sheet for the year.

2. Prepare an ROE profit driver analysis. Briefly explain its meaning. (Microsoft's total assets and total shareholders' equity at the beginning of the year were $70,815 million and $48,115 million, respectively.)

SUGGESTED SOLUTION

1.

MICROSOFT CORPORATION
Income Statement
For the Year Ended June 30, 2006
(dollars in millions)

Net revenues	$44,282
Cost of goods sold	7,650
Gross profit	36,632
Operating expenses:	
Research and development	6,584
Sales and marketing	9,818
General and administrative	3,758
Total operating expenses	20,160
Operating income	16,472
Nonoperating income and expenses:	
Investment income (loss)	
and other revenues (expenses)	1,790
Income before income taxes	18,262
Provision for income taxes	5,663
Net income	$ 12,599
Earnings per share	$ 1.25

MICROSOFT CORPORATION
Balance Sheet
June 30, 2006
(dollars in millions)

Assets	
Current assets	
Cash and short-term investments	$34,161
Accounts receivable	9,316
Other current assets	5,533
Total current assets	49,010
Noncurrent assets	
Property, plant, and equipment (net)	3,044
Other investments	9,232
Other noncurrent assets	8,311
Total assets	$69,597
Liabilities	
Current liabilities	
Accounts payable	$ 2,909
Accrued compensation	1,938
Income taxes payable	1,557
Unearned revenue	9,138
Other current liabilities	6,900
Total current liabilities	22,442
Long-term liabilities	7,051
Stockholders' equity	
Common stock and paid-in capital	59,005
Retained earnings	(18,901)
Total stockholders' equity	40,104
Total liabilities and stockholders' equity	$69,597

2.

Fiscal Year Ending	June 30, 2006
Net Income/Net Sales	0.28
× Net Sales/Average Total Assets	0.63
× Avg. Total Assets/Average Stockholders' Equity	1.59
= Net Income/Average Stockholders' Equity	0.28

For the year ended June 30, Microsoft's shareholders earned an ROE of 28 percent. Microsoft maintains high profit margins, earning $0.28 of net income for every $1 of net sales but a lower asset efficiency with only $0.63 in sales generated for each $1 of assets. The analysis also indicates Microsoft's dominance of the computer software business, which allows the company to charge premium prices for its products. However, the financial leverage ratio indicates that Microsoft's capital is primarily equity (not debt) based. With $1.59 in assets for each $1.00 of shareholders' equity, Microsoft has chosen not to leverage (or borrow) as much, for example, as HP or Apple.

Chapter Supplement

Nonrecurring Items

As noted in the chapter, companies may report any of two nonrecurring items: discontinued operations and extraordinary items. The income statement of La-Z-Boy Incorporated., the largest reclining-chair manufacturer in the world, contains both of these items, and is presented in Exhibit 5.10.

Discontinued Operations

DISCONTINUED OPERATIONS result from the disposal of a major component of the business and are reported net of income tax effects.

Discontinued operations result from abandoning or selling a major business component. Operating income generated by the discontinued component and any gain or loss on the disposal (the difference between the book value of the net assets being disposed of and the sale price or the abandonment costs) are included. These amounts may be separately disclosed in a note or on the face of the income statement. Each amount is reported net of the income tax effects. Separate reporting of discontinued operations informs users that these results are not predictive of the company's future.

La-Z-Boy sold its contract (business) furniture unit. The results of the operations of that business and the loss on sale of the business are listed as discontinued operations, net of tax, on the income statement shown in Exhibit 5.10.

Extraordinary Items

EXTRAORDINARY ITEMS are gains and losses that are both unusual in nature and infrequent in occurrence; they are reported net of tax on the income statement.

Extraordinary items are gains or losses that are considered both unusual in nature and infrequent in occurrence. Examples include losses suffered from natural disasters such as floods and hurricanes in geographic areas where such disasters are rare. These items must be reported separately on the income statement net of income tax effects. Separate reporting again informs decision makers that these items are not likely to recur, and so are not predictive of the company's future. Note disclosure is needed to explain the nature of the extraordinary item. **Companies report such items very rarely.**[9] Only five of the 600 companies followed by *Accounting Trends and Techniques* reported extraordinary items.

LA-Z-BOY INCORPORATED
Consolidated Statement of Operations
Fiscal Year Ended April 30, 2005

Sales	$1,815,202
Cost of sales	1,374,174
Gross profit	441,028
Selling, general, and administrative	362,967
Operating income	78,061
Interest expense	(10,442)
Interest income	3,616
Other income (expense), net	(3,443)
Income from continuing operations before income taxes	67,792
Income tax expense	(25,363)
Income (loss) from continuing operations	42,429
Income (loss) from discontinued operations (net of tax of $(3,856) in 2005)	(7,338)
Extraordinary gain (net of tax of $1,283 in fiscal 2005)	2,094
Net income (loss)	$37,185

See notes to consolidated financial statements.

---

[9]Most extraordinary gains result from mergers and acquisitions. Gains and losses on early retirement of debt are separately disclosed (if material) as part of income from continuing operations. They are no longer extraordinary items.

CHAPTER **TAKE-AWAYS**

1. **Recognize the people involved in the accounting communication process (regulators, managers, directors, auditors, information intermediaries, and users), their roles in the process, and the guidance they receive from legal and professional standards.   p. 233**

   Management of the reporting company must decide on the appropriate format (categories) and level of detail to present in its financial reports. Independent audits increase the credibility of the information. Directors monitor managers' compliance with reporting standards and hire the auditor. Financial statement announcements from public companies usually are first transmitted to users through electronic information services. The SEC staff reviews public financial reports for compliance with legal and professional standards, investigates irregularities, and punishes violators. Analysts play a major role in making financial statement and other information available to average investors through their stock recommendations and earnings forecasts.

2. **Identify the steps in the accounting communication process, including the issuance of press releases, annual reports, quarterly reports, and SEC filings as well as the role of electronic information services in this process.   p. 240**

   Earnings are first made public in press releases. Companies follow these announcements with annual and quarterly reports containing statements, notes, and additional information. Public companies must file additional reports with the SEC, including the 10-K, 10-Q, and 8-K, which contain more details about the company. Electronic information services are the key source of dissemination of this information to sophisticated users.

3. **Recognize and apply the different financial statement and disclosure formats used by companies in practice.   p. 243**

   Most statements are classified and include subtotals that are relevant to analysis. On the balance sheet, the most important distinctions are between current and noncurrent assets and liabilities. On the income and cash flow statements, the distinction between operating and nonoperating items are most important. The notes to the statements provide descriptions of the accounting rules applied, add more information about items disclosed on the statements, and present information about economic events not included in the statements.

4. **Analyze a company's performance based on return on equity and its components.   p. 252**

   ROE measures how well management used the stockholders' investment during the period. Its three determinants, net profit margin, asset turnover, and financial leverage, indicate why ROE differs from prior levels or the ROEs of competitors. They also suggest strategies to improve ROE in future periods.

   In Chapter 6, we will begin our in-depth discussion of individual items presented in financial statements. We will start with two of the most liquid assets, cash and accounts receivable, and transactions that involve revenues and certain selling expenses. Accuracy in revenue recognition and the related recognition of cost of goods sold (discussed in Chapter 7) are the most important determinants of the accuracy—and, thus, the usefulness—of financial statements. We will also introduce concepts related to the management and control of cash and receivables, a critical business function. A detailed understanding of these topics is crucial to future managers, accountants, and financial analysts.

KEY **RATIO**

Return on equity (ROE) measures how much the firm earned for each dollar of stockholders' investment. It is computed as follows (p. 253):

$$\text{Return on Equity} = \frac{\text{Net Income}}{\text{Average Stockholders' Equity}}$$

FINDING FINANCIAL INFORMATION

Balance Sheet
Key Classifications
Current and noncurrent assets and liabilities
Contributed capital and retained earnings

Income Statement
Key Subtotals
Gross profit
Income from operations
Income before income taxes
Net income
Earnings per share

Statement of Cash Flows
Under Operating Activities
(indirect method)
Net income
± Adjustments for noncash items
_____
Cash provided by operating activities

Notes
Key Classifications
Descriptions of accounting rules applied in
   the statements
Additional detail supporting reported numbers
Relevant financial information not disclosed
   on the statements

KEY TERMS

Additional Paid-In Capital
   p. 245
Board of Directors p. 235
Comparable Information p. 239
Conservatism p. 239
Consistent Information p. 239
Corporate Governance p. 232
Cost-Benefit Constraint p. 239
Discontinued Operations p. 258
Earnings Forecasts p. 236

Extraordinary Items p. 258
Form 8-K p. 243
Form 10-K p. 243
Form 10-Q p. 243
Gross Profit (Gross Margin)
   p. 245
Income before Income Taxes
   (Pretax Earnings) p. 246
Income from Operations
   (Operating Income) p. 245

Institutional Investors p. 238
Lenders (Creditors) p. 238
Material Amounts p. 239
Par Value p. 244
Press Release p. 240
Private Investors p. 238
Relevant Information p. 239
Reliable Information p. 239
Unqualified (Clean) Audit Opinion
   p. 235

QUESTIONS

1. Describe the roles and responsibilities of management and independent auditors in the financial reporting process.
2. Define the following three users of financial accounting disclosures and the relationships among them: financial analysts, private investors, and institutional investors.
3. Briefly describe the role of information services in the communication of financial information.
4. Explain why information must be relevant and reliable to be useful.
5. What basis of accounting does GAAP require on the (a) income statement, (b) balance sheet, and (c) statement of cash flows?
6. Briefly explain the normal sequence and form of financial reports produced by private companies in a typical year.
7. Briefly explain the normal sequence and form of financial reports produced by public companies in a typical year.
8. What are the four major subtotals or totals on the income statement?
9. Define extraordinary items. Why should they be reported separately on the income statement?
10. List the six major classifications reported on a balance sheet.

11. For property, plant, and equipment, as reported on the balance sheet, explain (a) cost, (b) accumulated depreciation, and (c) net book value.
12. Briefly explain the major classifications of stockholders' equity for a corporation.
13. What are the three major classifications on a statement of cash flows?
14. What are the three major categories of notes or footnotes presented in annual reports? Cite an example of each.
15. Briefly define return on equity and what it measures.

MULTIPLE-CHOICE QUESTIONS

1. If average total assets increase, but net income, net sales, and average stockholders' equity remain the same, what is the impact on the return on equity ratio?
   a. Increases.
   b. Decreases.
   c. Remains the same.
   d. Cannot be determined without additional information.

2. If a company plans to differentiate its products by offering low prices and discounts for items packaged in bulk (like a discount retailer that requires memberships for its customers), which component in the ROE profit driver analysis is the company attempting to boost?
   a. Net profit margin.
   b. Asset turnover.
   c. Financial leverage.
   d. All of the above.

3. If a company reported the following items on its income statement (cost of goods sold $5,000, income tax expense $2,000, interest expense $500, operating expenses $3,500, sales revenue $14,000), what amount would be reported for the subtotal "income from operations"?
   a. $9,000
   b. $3,000
   c. $5,000
   d. $5,500

4. Which of the following is not one of the possible nonrecurring items that must be shown in a separate line item **below** the Income from Continuing Operations subtotal in the income statement?
   a. Gains and losses from the sale of fixed assets.
   b. Discontinued operations.
   c. Extraordinary items.
   d. Both a and b.

5. Which of the following reports is filed annually with the SEC?
   a. Form 10-Q
   b. Form 10-K
   c. Form 8-K
   d. Press release

6. Common-size income statements are used for which of the following?
   a. Comparing the performance of different companies in the same industry.
   b. Comparing the performance of a single company over time.
   c. Both a and b.
   d. None of the above.

7. Which of the following is *not* a normal function of a financial analyst?
   a. Issue earnings forecasts.
   b. Examine the records underlying the financial statements to certify their conformance with GAAP.
   c. Make buy, hold, and sell recommendations on companies' stock.
   d. Advise institutional investors on their securities holdings.

8. The classified balance sheet format allows one to ascertain quickly which of the following?
   a. The most valuable asset of the company.
   b. The specific due date for all liabilities of the company.
   c. What liabilities must be paid within the upcoming year.
   d. None of the above.

9. When companies issue par value stock for cash, which accounts are normally affected?
   a. Common Stock; Additional Paid-In Capital; and Property, Plant, and Equipment, Net.
   b. Cash and Property, Plant, and Equipment, Net.
   c. Common Stock, Additional Paid-In Capital, and Retained Earnings.
   d. Common Stock, Additional Paid-In Capital, and Cash.

10. Net income was $900,000. Beginning and ending stockholders' equity was $8,000,000 and $9,600,000, respectively. What was the return on equity (ROE)?

a. 9.4%   c. 11.25%
b. 10.23%   d. 10.41%

For more practice on more multiple-choice questions, go to the text website at www.mhhe.com/libby6e.

MINI-**EXERCISES**

Available with McGraw-Hill's Homework Manager

M5-1
LO1

Matching Players in the Accounting Communication Process with Their Definitions

Match each player with the related definition by entering the appropriate letter in the space provided.

Players	Definitions
___ (1) CEO and CFO	A. Adviser who analyzes financial and other economic information to form forecasts and stock recommendations.
___ (2) Independent auditor	B. Institutional and private investors and creditors (among others).
___ (3) Users	C. Chief executive officer and chief financial officer who have primary responsibility for the information presented in financial statements.
___ (4) Financial analyst	D. Independent CPA who examines financial statements and attests to their fairness.

M5-2
LO2

Identifying the Disclosure Sequence

Indicate the order in which the following disclosures or reports are normally issued by public companies.

No.	Title
___	Annual report
___	Form 10-K
___	Earnings press release

M5-3
LO3

Finding Financial Information: Matching Financial Statements with the Elements of Financial Statements

Match each financial statement with the items presented on it by entering the appropriate letter in the space provided.

Elements of Financial Statements	Financial Statements
___ (1) Liabilities	A. Income statement
___ (2) Cash from operating activities	B. Balance sheet
___ (3) Losses	C. Cash flow statement
___ (4) Assets	D. None of the above
___ (5) Revenues	
___ (6) Cash from financing activities	
___ (7) Gains	
___ (8) Owners' equity	
___ (9) Expenses	
___ (10) Assets personally owned by a stockholder	

M5-4
LO3

Determining the Effects of Transactions on Balance Sheet and Income Statement Categories

Complete the following tabulation, indicating the sign of the effect (+ for increase, − for decrease, and NE for no effect) of each transaction. Consider each item independently.

a. Recorded sales on account of $80 and related cost of goods sold of $50.

b. Recorded advertising expense of $10 incurred but not paid for.

Transaction	Current Assets	Gross Profit	Current Liabilities
(*a*)			
(*b*)			

Determining Financial Statement Effects of Sales and Cost of Goods Sold and Issuance of Par Value Stock

M5-5
LO3

Using the following categories, indicate the effects of the following transactions. Use + for increase and − for decrease and indicate the accounts affected and the amounts.

a. Sales on account were $500 and related cost of goods sold was $200.

b. Issued 5,000 shares of $1 par value stock for $80,000 cash.

Event	Assets	=	Liabilities	+	Stockholders' Equity

Recording Sales and Cost of Goods Sold and Issuance of Par Value Stock

M5-6
LO3

Prepare journal entries for each transaction listed in M5–5.

Computing and Interpreting Return on Equity

M5-7
LO4

Chen, Inc., recently reported the following December 31 amounts in its financial statements (dollars in thousands):

	Current Year	Prior Year
Gross profit	$ 150	$110
Net income	80	40
Total assets	1,000	900
Total shareholders' equity	800	600

Compute return on equity for the current year. What does this ratio measure?

Available with McGraw-Hill's Homework Manager

EXERCISES

Matching Players in the Accounting Communication Process with Their Definitions

E5-1
LO1

Match each player with the related definition by entering the appropriate letter in the space provided.

Players	Definitions
___ (1) Financial analyst	A. Financial institution or supplier that lends money to the company.
___ (2) Creditor	
___ (3) Independent auditor	B. Chief executive officer and chief financial officer who have primary responsibility for the information presented in financial statements.
___ (4) Private investor	
___ (5) SEC	
___ (6) Institutional investor	C. Manager of pension, mutual, and endowment funds that invest on the behalf of others.
___ (7) Information service	
___ (8) CEO and CFO	D. Securities and Exchange Commission, which regulates financial disclosure requirements.
	E. A company that gathers, combines, and transmits (paper and electronic) financial and related information from various sources.

(*continued on next page*)

F. Adviser who analyzes financial and other economic information to form forecasts and stock recommendations.

G. Individual who purchases shares in companies.

H. Independent CPA who examines financial statements and attests to their fairness.

E5-2
LO2
Matching Definitions with Information Releases Made by Public Companies

Following are the titles of various information releases. Match each definition with the related release by entering the appropriate letter in the space provided.

Information Release	Definitions
___ (1) Form 10-K	A. Report of special events (e.g., auditor changes, mergers) filed by public companies with the SEC.
___ (2) Quarterly report	B. Brief unaudited report for quarter normally containing summary income statement and balance sheet (unaudited).
___ (3) Press release	C. Quarterly report filed by public companies with the SEC that contains additional unaudited financial information.
___ (4) Form 10-Q	D. Written public news announcement that is normally distributed to major news services.
___ (5) Annual report	E. Annual report filed by public companies with the SEC that contains additional detailed financial information.
___ (6) Form 8-K	F. Report containing the four basic financial statements for the year, related notes, and often statements by management and auditors.

E5-3
LO2
Finding Financial Information: Matching Information Items to Financial Reports

Following are information items included in various financial reports. Match each information item with the report(s) where it would most likely be found by entering the appropriate letter(s) in the space provided.

Information Item	Report
___ (1) Summarized financial data for 5- or 10-year period.	A. Form 10-Q
___ (2) Notes to financial statements.	B. Annual report
___ (3) The four basic financial statements for the year.	C. Form 10-K
___ (4) Summarized income statement information for the quarter.	D. Press release
___ (5) Detailed discussion of the company's competition.	E. Quarterly report
___ (6) Initial announcement of hiring of new vice president for sales.	F. Form 8-K
___ (7) Initial announcement of quarterly earnings.	G. None of the above
___ (8) Description of those responsible for the financial statements.	
___ (9) Complete quarterly income statement, balance sheet, and cash flow statement.	
___ (10) Announcement of a change in auditors.	

E5-4
LO3
Ordering the Classifications on a Typical Balance Sheet

Following is a list of classifications on the balance sheet. Number them in the order in which they normally appear on a balance sheet.

No.	Title
_____	Current liabilities
_____	Long-term liabilities
_____	Long-term investments
_____	Intangible assets
_____	Property, plant, and equipment
_____	Current assets
_____	Retained earnings
_____	Contributed capital
_____	Other noncurrent assets

Preparing a Classified Balance Sheet

Campbell Soup Company is the world's leading maker and marketer of soup, and sells other well-known brands of food in 120 countries. Presented here are the items listed on its recent balance sheet (dollars in millions) presented in alphabetical order:

Accounts payable	$ 694	Other assets	338
Accounts receivable	581	Other current assets	151
Accrued expenses	622	Other current debt	714
Cash and cash equivalents	71	Other noncurrent liabilities	3,120
Common stock, $0.0375 par value	351	Property, plant, and equipment, net	2,042
Intangible assets	2,487	Retained earnings	944
Inventories	663	Short-term investments	112

E5-5
LO3
Campbell Soup Co.

Required:
Prepare a classified consolidated balance sheet for Campbell's for the current year (ended July 29) using the categories presented in the chapter.

Preparing and Interpreting a Classified Balance Sheet with Discussion of Terminology (Challenging)

Lance, Inc., manufactures, markets, and distributes a variety of snack foods. Product categories include sandwich crackers, cookies, restaurant crackers and bread basket items, candy, chips, meat snacks, nuts, and cake items. These items are sold under trade names including Lance, Toastchee, Toasty, Choc-O-Lunch, Captain's Wafers, and Cape Cod. Presented here are the items listed on its recent balance sheet (dollars in millions) in alphabetical order:

E5-6
LO3

Accounts payable	$14,718	Inventories	23,205
Accounts receivable, net	47,188	Long-term debt	63,536
Accrued compensation	8,844	Other assets (noncurrent)	3,216
Accrued postretirement health		Other current assets	4,161
care costs	11,317	Other intangible assets, net	10,177
Additional paid-in capital	1,229	Other long-term liabilities	28,231
Cash and cash equivalents	1,224	Other payables and accrued	
Common stock, 28,947,222 shares		liabilities	15,439
outstanding	24,123	Prepaid expenses and other	6,550
Current portion of long-term debt	395	Property, plant, and equipment, net	179,283
Goodwill, net	42,069	Retained earnings	149,241

Required:
1. Prepare a classified consolidated balance sheet for Lance, Inc., for the current year (ended December 31) using the categories presented in the chapter.
2. Four of the items end in the term **net.** Explain what this term means in each case.

Recording Stock Issuances with Par Value

In a recent year, Coach, Inc., a designer and marketer of handbags and other accessories, issued 10,200 shares of its $0.01 par value stock for $43,000 (these numbers are rounded). These additional shares were issued under an employee stock option plan. Prepare the journal entry required to record the stock issuance.

E5-7
LO3
Coach, Inc.

Inferring Stock Issuances and Cash Dividends from Changes in Stockholders' Equity

Oakley, designer and manufacturer of high-performance eyewear, reported the following December 31 balances in its stockholders' equity accounts (dollars in thousands):

E5-8
LO3
Oakley

	Current Year	Prior Year
Common stock	$ 688	$ 686
Paid-in capital	40,805	36,484
Retained earnings	227,648	177,277

During the current year, Oakley reported net income of $50,371.

Required:

1. How much did Oakley pay in dividends for the year?
2. Assume that the only other transaction that affected stockholders' equity during the current year was a single stock issuance. Recreate the journal entry reflecting the stock issuance.

E5-9
LO3

Matching Definitions with Income Statement Related Terms

Following are terms related to the income statement. Match each definition with its related term by entering the appropriate letter in the space provided.

Terms	Definitions
___ (1) Net income	A. Revenues + Gains − Expenses − Losses including effects of discontinued operations and extraordinary items (if any).
___ (2) Pretax income from operations	B. Income Tax on Revenues − Operating Expenses.
___ (3) Income before extraordinary items	C. Sales of services for cash or on credit.
___ (4) Cost of goods sold	D. Sales revenue minus cost of goods sold.
___ (5) Operating expenses	E. Amount of resources used to purchase or produce the goods that were sold during the reporting period.
___ (6) Gross margin on sales	F. Total expenses directly related to operations.
___ (7) EPS	G. Income before all income tax and before discontinued operations and extraordinary items (if any).
___ (8) Interest expense	H. Cost of money (borrowing) over time.
___ (9) Service revenue	I. Item that is both unusual and infrequent.
___ (10) Income tax expense on operations	J. Net income divided by average shares outstanding.
___ (11) Extraordinary item	K. Income before unusual and infrequent items and the related income tax.
	L. None of the above.

E5-10
LO3

Inferring Income Statement Values

Supply the missing dollar amounts for the 2010 income statement of Ultimate Style Company for each of the following independent cases (**Hint:** Organize each case in the format of the classified or multiple-step income statement discussed in the chapter. Rely on the amounts given to infer the missing values.):

	Case A	Case B	Case C	Case D	Case E
Sales revenue	$900	$700	$420	$?	$?
Selling expense	?	100	80	390	240
Cost of goods sold	?	300	?	500	320
Income tax expense	?	30	20	50	20
Gross margin	400	?	?	?	430
Pretax income	200	200	?	190	?
Administrative expense	150	?	70	120	90
Net income	120	?	60	?	80

E5-11
LO3

Preparing a Multiple-Step Income Statement

The following data were taken from the records of Village Corporation at December 31, 2011:

Sales revenue	$79,000
Gross profit	28,000
Selling (distribution) expense	7,000
Administrative expense	?
Pretax income	13,000
Income tax rate	30%
Shares of stock outstanding	3,500

Required:

Prepare a complete multiple-step income statement for the company (showing both gross profit and income from operations). Show all computations. (**Hint:** Set up the side captions or rows starting with sales revenue and ending with earnings per share; rely on the amounts and percentages given to infer missing values.)

Preparing a Multiple-Step Income Statement

E5-12
LO3

The following data were taken from the records of Thayer Appliances, Incorporated, at December 31, 2010:

Sales revenue	$130,000
Administrative expense	16,000
Selling (distribution) expense	18,000
Income tax rate	25%
Gross profit	60,000
Shares of stock outstanding	2,500

Required:
Prepare a complete multiple-step income statement for the company (showing both gross profit and income from operations). Show all computations. (**Hint:** Set up the side captions or rows starting with sales revenue and ending with earnings per share; rely on the amounts and percentages given to infer missing values.)

Determining the Effects of Transactions on Balance Sheet and Income Statement Categories

E5-13
LO3
Hasbro

Hasbro is one of the world's leading toy manufacturers, and maker of such popular board games as Monopoly, Scrabble, and Clue, among others. Listed here are selected aggregate transactions from the first quarter of a recent year (dollars in millions). Complete the following tabulation, indicating the sign (+ for increase, − for decrease, and NE for no effect) and amount of the effect of each transaction. Consider each item independently.

a. Recorded sales on account of $325.4 and related cost of goods sold of $198.6.
b. Borrowed $346.5 on line of credit with a bank with principal payable within one year.
c. Incurred research and development expense of $90, which was paid in cash.

Transaction	Current Assets	Gross Profit	Current Liabilities
a.			
b.			
c.			

Determining the Effects of Transactions on Balance Sheet, Income Statement, and Statement of Cash Flows Categories

E5-14
LO3

Listed here are selected aggregate transactions for Restful Furniture Company from the first quarter of a recent year (dollars in millions). Complete the following tabulation, indicating the sign (+ for increase, − for decrease, and NE for no effect) and amount of the effect of each additional transaction. Consider each item independently.

a. Recorded collections of cash from customers owed on open account of $32.2.
b. Repaid $2.1 in principal on line of credit with a bank with principal payable within one year.

Transaction	Current Assets	Gross Profit	Current Liabilities	Cash Flow from Operating Activities
a.				
b.				

Preparing a Simple Statement of Cash Flows Using the Indirect Method

E5-15
LO3

Blackwell Corporation is preparing its annual financial statements at December 31, 2009. Listed here are the items on its statement of cash flows presented in alphabetical order. Parentheses indicate that a listed amount should be subtracted on the cash flow statement. The beginning balance in cash was $30,000 and the ending balance was $50,000.

Cash borrowed on three-year note	$30,000
Decrease in accounts payable	(3,000)
Decrease in inventory	1,000
Increase in accounts receivable	(9,000)
Land purchased	(36,000)
Net income	20,000
New delivery truck purchased for cash	(7,000)
Stock issued for cash	24,000

Required:

Prepare the 2009 statement of cash flows for Blackwell Corporation. The section reporting cash flows from operating activities should be prepared using the indirect method discussed in the chapter.

E5-16
LO4
Tiffany & Co.

Analyzing and Interpreting Return on Equity

Tiffany & Co. is one of the world's premier jewelers and designer of other fine gifts and housewares. Presented here are selected income statement and balance sheet amounts (dollars in thousands).

	Current Year	Prior Year
Net sales	$2,648,321	$2,395,153
Net income	253,927	234,655
Average shareholders' equity	1,817,904	1,796,037
Average total assets	2,811,391	2,721,695

Required:

1. Compute ROE for the current and prior years and explain the meaning of the change.
2. Explain the major cause(s) of the change in ROE using ROE profit driver analysis.

E5-17
LO4

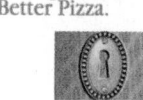

PIZZA
PAPA JOHNS
Better Ingredients.
Better Pizza.

Analyzing and Evaluating Return on Equity from a Security Analyst's Perspective

Papa John's is one of the fastest-growing pizza delivery and carry-out restaurant chains in the country. Presented here are selected income statement and balance sheet amounts (dollars in thousands).

	Current Year	Prior Year
Net sales	$917,378	$946,219
Net income	33,563	46,797
Average shareholders' equity	140,610	148,790
Average total assets	357,023	377,136

Required:

1. Compute ROE for the current and prior years and explain the meaning of the change.
2. Explain the major cause(s) of the change in ROE using ROE profit driver analysis.
3. Would security analysts more likely increase or decrease their estimates of share value on the basis of this change? Explain.

PROBLEMS

 ™ **Available with McGraw-Hill's Homework Manager**

P5-1
LO1, 2

Matching Transactions with Concepts

Following are the concepts of accounting covered in Chapters 2 through 5. Match each transaction with its related concept by entering the appropriate letter in the space provided. Use one letter for each blank.

Concepts	Transactions

Concepts

____ (1) Users of financial statements

____ (2) Objective of financial statements

Qualitative Characteristics

____ (3) Relevance

____ (4) Reliability

Assumptions

____ (5) Separate entity

____ (6) Continuity

____ (7) Unit of measure

____ (8) Time period

Elements of Financial Statements

____ (9) Revenues

____ (10) Expenses

____ (11) Gains

____ (12) Losses

____ (13) Assets

____ (14) Liabilities

____ (15) Stockholders' equity

Principles

____ (16) Cost

____ (17) Revenue

____ (18) Matching

____ (19) Full disclosure

Constraints of Accounting

____ (20) Materiality threshold

____ (21) Cost-benefit constraint

____ (22) Conservatism constraint

____ (23) Special industry practices

Transactions

A. Recorded a $1,000 sale of merchandise on credit.

B. Counted (inventoried) the unsold items at the end of the period and valued them in dollars.

C. Acquired a vehicle for use in operating the business.

D. Reported the amount of depreciation expense because it likely will affect important decisions of statement users.

E. Identified as the investors, creditors, and others interested in the business.

F. Used special accounting approaches because of the uniqueness of the industry.

G. Sold and issued bonds payable of $1 million.

H. Paid a contractor for an addition to the building with $10,000 cash and $20,000 market value of the stock of the company ($30,000 was deemed to be the cash-equivalent price).

I. Engaged an outside independent CPA to audit the financial statements.

J. Sold merchandise and services for cash and on credit during the year; then determined the cost of those goods sold and the cost of rendering those services.

K. Established an accounting policy that sales revenue shall be recognized only when ownership to the goods sold passes to the customer.

L. To design and prepare the financial statements to assist the users in making decisions.

M. Established a policy not to include in the financial statements the personal financial affairs of the owners of the business.

N. Sold an asset at a loss that was a peripheral or incidental transaction.

O. The user value of a special financial report exceeds the cost of preparing it.

P. Valued an asset, such as inventory, at less than its purchase cost because the replacement cost is less.

Q. Dated the income statement "For the Year Ended December 31, 2011."

R. Used services from outsiders—paid cash for some and put the remainder on credit.

S. Acquired an asset (a pencil sharpener that will have a useful life of five years) and recorded it as an expense when purchased for $1.99.

T. Disclosed in the financial statements all relevant financial information about the business; necessitated the use of notes to the financial statements.

U. Sold an asset at a gain that was a peripheral or incidental transaction.

V. Assets of $500,000 − Liabilities of $300,000 = Stockholders' Equity of $200,000.

W. Accounting and reporting assume a "going concern."

P5-2
LO3

Matching Definitions with Balance Sheet–Related Terms

Following are terms related to the balance sheet, which were discussed in Chapters 2 through 5. Match each definition with its related term by entering the appropriate letter in the space provided.

Terms	Definitions
___ (1) Capital in excess of par	A. Nearness of assets to cash (in time).
___ (2) Assets	B. Liabilities expected to be paid out of current assets normally within the next year.
___ (3) Shareholders' equity	C. All liabilities not classified as current liabilities.
___ (4) Book value	D. Total assets minus total liabilities.
___ (5) Other assets	E. Probable future economic benefits owned by the entity from past transactions.
___ (6) Shares outstanding	F. Debts or obligations from past transactions to be paid with assets or services.
___ (7) Retained earnings	G. Assets expected to be collected in cash within one year or operating cycle, if longer.
___ (8) Liquidity	H. Asset offset account (subtracted from asset).
___ (9) Normal operating cycle	I. Balance of the Common Stock account divided by the par value per share.
___ (10) Current assets	J. A miscellaneous category of assets.
___ (11) Current liabilities	K. Sum of the annual depreciation expense on an asset from its acquisition to the current date.
___ (12) Long-term liabilities	L. Assets that do not have physical substance.
___ (13) Fixed assets	M. Accumulated earnings minus accumulated dividends.
___ (14) Liabilities	N. Property, plant, and equipment.
___ (15) Contra-asset account	O. Same as carrying value; cost less accumulated depreciation to date.
___ (16) Accumulated depreciation	P. Amount of contributed capital less the par value of the stock.
___ (17) Intangible assets	Q. The average cash-to-cash time involved in the operations of the business.
	R. None of the above.

P5-3
LO3

eXcel
www.mhhe.com/libby6e

Preparing a Balance Sheet and Analyzing Some of Its Parts (AP5–1)

Gold Jewelers is developing its annual financial statements for 2011. The following amounts were correct at December 31, 2011: cash, $58,000; accounts receivable, $71,000; merchandise inventory, $154,000; prepaid insurance, $1,000; investment in stock of Z corporation (long-term), $36,000; store equipment, $67,000; used store equipment held for disposal, $9,000; accumulated depreciation, store equipment, $13,000; accounts payable, $58,000; long-term note payable, $42,000; income taxes payable, $9,000; retained earnings, $164,000; and common stock, 100,000 shares outstanding, par $1.00 per share (originally sold and issued at $1.10 per share).

Required:
1. Based on these data, prepare a December 31, 2011 balance sheet. Use the following major captions (list the individual items under these captions):
   a. Assets: Current Assets, Long-Term Investments, Fixed Assets, and Other Assets.
   b. Liabilities: Current Liabilities and Long-Term Liabilities.
   c. Stockholders' Equity: Contributed Capital and Retained Earnings.
2. What is the net book value of the store equipment? Explain what this value means.

Reporting Stockholders' Equity on a Balance Sheet and Recording the Issuance of Stock
(AP5–2)

P5-4
LO3
eXcel
www.mhhe.com/libby6e

At the end of the 2009 annual reporting period, El Paso Corporation's balance sheet showed the following:

EL PASO CORPORATION Balance Sheet At December 31, 2009	
Stockholders' Equity	
Contributed capital	
Common stock (par $15; 6,000 shares)	$ 90,000
Paid-in capital	13,000
Total contributed capital	103,000
Retained earnings	
Ending balance	44,000
Total stockholders' equity	$147,000

During 2010, the following selected transactions (summarized) were completed:
a. Sold and issued 1,000 shares of common stock at $25 cash per share (at year-end).
b. Determined net income, $43,000.
c. Declared and paid a cash dividend of $2 per share on the beginning shares outstanding.

Required:
 1. Prepare the stockholders' equity section of the balance sheet at December 31, 2010.
 2. Give the journal entry to record the sale and issuance of the 1,000 shares of common stock.

Preparing a Multiple-Step Income Statement

P5-5
LO3
Tommy Hilfiger
eXcel
www.mhhe.com/libby6e

Tommy Hilfiger Corporation designs, sources, and markets men's and women's sportswear, jeanswear, and childrenswear under the Tommy Hilfiger trademarks. The company prides itself in producing distinctive designs that recognize tradition while adding a fresh, youthful perspective. The items reported on its income statement for a recent year (ended March 31) are presented here (dollars in thousands) in alphabetical order:

Cost of goods sold	$1,012,156
Depreciation and amortization	76,307
Interest expense	31,756
Interest income	3,577
Net revenue	1,875,797
Other selling, general, and administrative expenses	583,502
Provision for income taxes	37,445
Weighted average shares outstanding	90,692

Required:
Prepare a multiple-step consolidated income statement (showing gross profit, operating income, and income before income taxes). Include a presentation of basic earnings per share.

Preparing Both an Income Statement and Balance Sheet from a Trial Balance (AP5–3)

P5-6
LO3
eXcel
www.mhhe.com/libby6e

Thomas Sales Company (organized as a corporation on April 1, 2009) has completed the accounting cycle for the second year, ended March 31, 2011. Thomas also has completed a correct trial balance as follows:

THOMAS SALES COMPANY
Trial Balance
At March 31, 2011

Account Titles	Debit	Credit
Cash	$ 58,000	
Accounts receivable	49,000	
Office supplies inventory	1,000	
Automobiles (company cars)	33,000	
Accumulated depreciation, automobiles		$ 11,000
Office equipment	3,000	
Accumulated depreciation, office equipment		1,000
Accounts payable		22,000
Income taxes payable		0
Salaries and commissions payable		2,000
Note payable, long term		33,000
Capital stock (par $1; 33,000 shares)		33,000
Paid-in capital		5,000
Retained earnings (on April 1, 2010)		7,500
Dividends declared and paid during the current year	8,500	
Sales revenue		99,000
Cost of goods sold	33,000	
Operating expenses (detail omitted to conserve your time)	19,000	
Depreciation expense (on autos and including $500 on office equipment)	6,000	
Interest expense	3,000	
Income tax expense (not yet computed)		
Totals	$213,500	$213,500

Required:

Complete the financial statements, as follows:

a. Classified (multiple-step) income statement for the reporting year ended March 31, 2011. Include income tax expense, assuming a 25 percent tax rate. Use the following subtotals: Gross Profit, Total Operating Expenses, Income from Operations, Income before Income Taxes, and Net Income, and show EPS.

b. Classified balance sheet at the end of the reporting year, March 31, 2011. Include (1) income taxes for the current year in Income Taxes Payable and (2) dividends in Retained Earnings. Use the following captions (list each item under these captions).

Assets	**Stockholders' Equity**
Current assets	Contributed capital
Noncurrent assets	Retained earnings
Liabilities	
Current liabilities	
Long-term liabilities	

P5-7
LO3, 4
Creative Technology

Determining and Interpreting the Effects of Transactions on Income Statement Categories and Return on Equity (AP5–4)

Creative Technology, a computer hardware company based in Singapore, developed the modern standard for computer sound cards in the early 1990s. Recently, Creative has released a line of portable audio products to directly compete with Apple's popular I-Pod mp3 player. Presented here is a recent income statement (dollars in millions).

Net sales	$815
Costs and expenses	
Cost of sales	534
Research and development	70
Selling, general, and administrative	168
Operating income (loss)	43
Interest and other income (expenses), net	82
Income (loss) before provision (benefit) for income taxes	125
Provision (benefit) for income taxes	(9)
Net income (loss)	$134

Its beginning and ending stockholders' equity was $429 and $691, respectively.

Required:

1. Listed here are hypothetical **additional** transactions. Assuming that they had **also** occurred during the fiscal year, complete the following tabulation, indicating the sign of the effect of each **additional** transaction (+ for increase, − for decrease, and NE for no effect). Consider each item independently and ignore taxes.
   a. Recorded sales on account of $500 and related cost of goods sold of $475.
   b. Incurred additional research and development expense of $100, which was paid in cash.
   c. Issued additional shares of common stock for $200 cash.
   d. Declared and paid dividends of $90.

Transaction	Gross Profit	Operating Income (Loss)	Return on Equity
a.			
b.			
c.			
d.			

2. Assume that next period Creative does not pay any dividends, does not issue or retire stock, and earns the same income as during the current period. Will Creative's ROE next period be higher, lower, or the same as the current period? Why?

(Supplement) Preparing a Multiple-Step Income Statement with Discontinued Operations and Cumulative Effects of Accounting Changes

P5-8
Newell Rubbermaid

Newell Rubbermaid Inc. manufactures and markets a broad array of office products, tools and hardware, and home products under a variety of brand names including Sharpie, Paper Mate, Rolodex, Rubbermaid, Levolor, and others. The items reported on its income statement for the year ended December 31, 2006 are presented here (dollars in thousands) in alphabetical order:

Cost of Products Sold	$ 4,131.0
Income Tax Expense	44.2
Interest Expense	141.7
Loss on Sale of Discontinued Operations, Net of Income Taxes	(85.7)
Net Sales	6,201.0
Other Expenses	66.4
Selling, General, and, Administrative Expenses	1,347.0

Required:
Using appropriate headings and subtotals, prepare a multiple-step consolidated income statement (showing gross profit, operating income, and any other subheadings you deem appropriate).

ALTERNATE PROBLEMS

AP5-1
LO3

Preparing a Balance Sheet and Analyzing Some of Its Parts (P5–3)

The Java House is developing its annual financial statements for 2012. The following amounts were correct at December 31, 2012: cash, $58,800; investment in stock of PIZ corporation (long term), $36,400; store equipment, $67,200; accounts receivable, $71,820; inventory, $154,000; prepaid rent, $1,120; used store equipment held for disposal, $9,800; accumulated depreciation, store equipment, $13,440; income taxes payable, $9,800; long-term note payable, $42,000; accounts payable, $58,800; retained earnings, $165,100; and common stock, 100,000 shares outstanding, par $1 per share (originally sold and issued at $1.10 per share).

Required:

1. Based on these data, prepare a 2012 balance sheet. Use the following major captions (list the individual items under these captions):
   a. Assets: Current Assets, Long-Term Investments, Fixed Assets, and Other Assets.
   b. Liabilities: Current Liabilities and Long-Term Liabilities.
   c. Stockholders' Equity: Contributed Capital and Retained Earnings.
2. What is the net book value of the store equipment? Explain what this value means.

AP5-2
LO3

Reporting Stockholders' Equity on a Balance Sheet and Recording the Issuance of Stock (P5–4)

At the end of the 2010 annual reporting period, Zephyr Industries' balance sheet showed the following:

ZEPHYR INDUSTRIES Balance Sheet At December 31, 2010	
Stockholders' Equity	
Common stock (par $15; 7,000 shares)	$105,000
Additional paid-in capital	9,000
Retained earnings—Ending balance	48,000
Total stockholders' equity	$162,000

During 2011, the following selected transactions (summarized) were completed:
a. Sold and issued 1,500 shares of common stock at $24 cash per share (at year-end).
b. Determined net income, $46,000.
c. Declared and paid a cash dividend of $1 per share on the beginning shares outstanding.

Required:

1. Prepare the stockholders' equity section of the balance sheet at December 31, 2011.
2. Give the journal entry to record the sale and issuance of the 1,500 shares of common stock.

AP5-3
LO3

Preparing Both an Income Statement and Balance Sheet from a Trial Balance (P5–6)

Atomic Sales (organized as a corporation on September 1, 2008) has completed the accounting cycle for the second year, ended August 31, 2010. Atomic also has completed a correct trial balance as follows:

ATOMIC SALES Trial Balance At August 31, 2010		
Account Titles	**Debit**	**Credit**
Cash	$ 47,700	
Accounts receivable	40,320	
Office supplies	270	
Company vehicles (delivery vans)	27,000	
Accumulated depreciation, company vehicles		$ 9,000
Equipment	2,700	
Accumulated depreciation, equipment		900
Accounts payable		18,225
Income taxes payable		0
Salaries payable		1,350
Long-term debt		25,000
Capital stock (par $1; 29,000 shares)		29,000
Paid-in capital		4,500
Retained earnings (on September 1, 2009)		6,615
Dividends declared and paid during the current year	7,200	
Sales revenue		81,000
Cost of goods sold	27,000	
Operating expenses (detail omitted to conserve your time)	16,200	
Depreciation expense (on vehicles and including $3,450 on equipment)	4,950	
Interest expense	2,250	
Income tax expense (not yet computed)		
Totals	$175,590	$175,590

Required:

Complete the financial statements, as follows:

a. Classified (multiple-step) income statement for the reporting year ended August 31, 2010. Include income tax expense, assuming a 30 percent tax rate. Use the following subtotals: Gross Profit, Total Operating Expenses, Income from Operations, Income before Income Taxes, and Net Income, and show EPS.

b. Classified balance sheet at the end of the reporting year, August 31, 2010. Include (1) income taxes for the current year in Income Taxes Payable and (2) dividends in Retained Earnings. Use the following captions (list each item under these captions).

Assets

Current assets

Noncurrent assets

Liabilities

Current liabilities

Long-term liabilities

Stockholders' Equity

Contributed capital

Retained earnings

Determining and Interpreting the Effects of Transactions on Income Statement Categories and Return on Equity (P5–7)

AP5-4

LO3, 4

Avon

Avon Products, Inc. is a leading manufacturer and marketer of beauty products and related merchandise. The company sells its products in 143 countries through a combination of direct selling and use of individual sales representatives. Presented here is a recent income statement (dollars in millions).

Net sales	$8,763
Costs and expenses	
Cost of sales	3,435
Selling, general and administrative	4,368
Depreciation and amortization	200
Operating income (loss)	760
Interest and other income (expenses), net	(58)
Income (loss) before provision (benefit) for income taxes	702
Provision (benefit) for income taxes	223
Net income (loss)	$ 479

Its beginning and ending stockholders' equity was $794 and $760, respectively.

Required:

1. Listed here are hypothetical **additional** transactions. Assuming that they had **also** occurred during the fiscal year, complete the following tabulation, indicating the sign of the effect of each **additional** transaction (+ for increase, − for decrease, and NE for no effect). Consider each item independently and ignore taxes.
   a. Recorded and received additional interest income of $7.
   b. Purchased $80 of additional inventory on open account.
   c. Recorded and paid additional advertising expense of $16.
   d. Additional shares of common stock are issued for $40 cash.

Transaction	Operating Income (Loss)	Net Income	Return on Equity
a.			
b.			
c.			
d.			

2. Assume that next period, Avon does not pay any dividends, does not issue or retire stock, and earns 20 percent more than during the current period. Will Avon's ROE next period be higher, lower, or the same as in the current period? Why?

CASES **AND PROJECTS**

ANNUAL REPORT CASES

CP5-1   **Finding Financial Information**

LO2, 3, 4

AMERICAN EAGLE OUTFITTERS

Refer to the financial statements of American Eagle Outfitters given in Appendix B at the end of this book. At the bottom of each statement, the company warns readers to "see accompanying notes." The following questions illustrate the types of information that you can find in the financial statements and accompanying notes. (**Hint:** Use the notes.)

Required:

1. What items were included as noncurrent assets on the balance sheet?
2. How much land did the company own at the end of the most recent reporting year?
3. What portion of current liabilities were "Unredeemed stored value cards and gift certificates" during the current year?
4. At what point were website sales recognized as revenue?

5. The company reported cash flows from operating activities of $749,268,000. However, its cash and cash equivalents decreased for the year. Explain how that happened.

6. What was the highest stock price for the company during fiscal 2006? (**Note:** Some companies will label a year that has a January year-end as having a fiscal year-end dated one year earlier. For example, a January 2007 year-end may be labeled as Fiscal 2006 since the year actually has more months that fall in the 2006 calendar year than in the 2007 calendar year.)

7. Calculate the company's ROE for fiscal 2006 and 2005. Did it increase or decrease? (American Eagle Outfitters' shareholders' equity balance was $963,486,000 at the end of the 2004 fiscal year.) How would you expect the change in ROE to be reflected in the company's share price?

Finding Financial Information

CP5-2
LO2, 3
Urban Outfitters

Refer to the financial statements of Urban Outfitters given in Appendix C at the end of this book. At the bottom of each statement, the company warns readers to "See notes to consolidated financial statements." The following questions illustrate the types of information that you can find in the financial statements and accompanying notes. (**Hint:** Use the notes.)

Required:
1. What subtotals does it report on its income statement?
2. The company spent $212,029,000 on capital expenditures (property, plant, and equipment) and $182,653,000 purchasing investments during the most recent year. Were operating activities or financing activities the major source of cash for these expenditures?
3. What was the company's largest asset (net) at the end of the most recent year?
4. How does the company account for costs associated with developing its websites?
5. Over what useful lives are buildings depreciated?
6. What portion of gross "Property and Equipment" is composed of "Buildings"?

Comparing Companies within an Industry

CP5-3
LO4

AMERICAN EAGLE
OUTFITTERS
Urban Outfitters

www.mhhe.com/libby6e

Refer to the financial statements of American Eagle Outfitters given in Appendix B, Urban Outfitters given in Appendix C, and Industry Ratio Report given in Appendix D at the end of this book.

Required:
1. Compute return on equity for the most recent year. Which company provided the highest return to shareholders during the current year?
2. Use ROE profit driver analysis to determine the cause(s) of any differences. How might the ownership versus the rental of property, plant, and equipment affect the total asset turnover ratio?
3. Compare the ROE profit driver analysis for American Eagle Outfitters and Urban Outfitters to the ROE profit driver analysis for their industry. Where does American Eagle Outfitters outperform or underperform the industry? Where does Urban Outfitters outperform or underperform the industry?

FINANCIAL REPORTING AND ANALYSIS CASES

Interpreting the Financial Press

CP5-4
LO4
The Auditor's Report

The Committee of Sponsoring Organizations (COSO) published a research study that examined financial statement fraud occurrences between 1987 and 1997. A summary of the findings by M. S. Beasley, J. V. Carcello, and D. R. Hermanson, "Fraudulent Financial Reporting: 1987–1997: An Analysis of U.S. Public Companies," *The Auditor's Report,* Summer 1999, pp. 15–17, is available on the Libby/Libby/Short website at www.mhhe.com/libby6e.* You should read the article and then write a short memo outlining the following:

1. The size of the companies involved.
2. The extent of top management involvement.
3. The specific accounting fraud techniques involved.
4. What might lead managers to introduce misstatements into the income statement near the end of the accounting period.

*Copyright © 1999 by American Accounting Association. Reprinted with permission.

CP5-5   **Using Financial Reports: Financial Statement Inferences**

L03

The following amounts were selected from the annual financial statements for Genesis Corporation at December 31, 2012 (end of the third year of operations):

From the 2012 income statement:	
Sales revenue	$275,000
Cost of goods sold	(170,000)
All other expenses (including income tax)	(95,000)
Net income	$10,000
From the December 31, 2012, balance sheet:	
Current assets	$ 90,000
All other assets	212,000
Total assets	$302,000
Current liabilities	40,000
Long-term liabilities	66,000
Capital stock (par $10)	100,000
Paid-in capital	16,000
Retained earnings	80,000
Total liabilities and stockholders' equity	$302,000

Required:

Analyze the data on the 2012 financial statements of Genesis by answering the questions that follow. Show computations.

1. What was the gross margin on sales?
2. What was the amount of EPS?
3. If the income tax rate was 25%, what was the amount of pretax income?
4. What was the average sales price per share of the capital stock?
5. Assuming that no dividends were declared or paid during 2012, what was the beginning balance (January 1, 2012) of retained earnings?

CRITICAL THINKING CASES

CP5-6   **Making Decisions as a Manager: Evaluating the Effects of Business Strategy on Return on**

L04   **Equity**

Sony

Sony is a world leader in the manufacture of consumer and commercial electronics as well as the entertainment and insurance industries. Its ROE has increased from 9% to 14% over the last three years.

Required:

1. Indicate the most likely effect of each of the changes in business strategy on Sony's ROE for the next period and future periods (+ for increase, − for decrease, and NE for no effect), assuming all other things are unchanged. Explain your answer for each. Treat each item independently.
   a. Sony decreases its investment in research and development aimed at products to be brought to market in more than one year.
   b. Sony begins a new advertising campaign for a movie to be released during the next year.
   c. Sony issues additional stock for cash, the proceeds to be used to acquire other high-technology companies in future periods.

Strategy Change	Current Period ROE	Future Periods' ROE
a.		
b.		
c.		

Making a Decision as an Auditor: Effects of Errors on Income, Assets, and Liabilities

CP5-7
LO1, 3

Megan Company (not a corporation) was careless about its financial records during its first year of operations, 2010. It is December 31, 2010, the end of the annual accounting period. An outside CPA examined the records and discovered numerous errors, all of which are described here. Assume that each error is independent of the others.

Required:

Analyze each error and indicate its effect on 2010 and 2011 income, assets, and liabilities if not corrected. Do not assume any other errors. Use these codes to indicate the effect of each dollar amount: O = overstated, U = understated, and NE = no effect. Write an explanation of your analysis of each transaction to support your response.

	Effect On					
	Net Income		Assets		Liabilities	
Independent Errors	2010	2011	2010	2011	2010	2011
1. Depreciation expense for 2010, not recorded in 2010, $950.	O $950	NE	O $950	O $950	NE	NE
2. Wages earned by employees during 2010 not recorded or paid in 2010 but recorded and paid in 2011, $500.						
3. Revenue earned during 2010 but not collected or recorded until 2011, $600.						
4. Amount paid in 2010 and recorded as expense in 2010 but not an expense until 2011, $200.						
5. Revenue collected in 2010 and recorded as revenue in 2010 but not earned until 2011, $900.						
6. Sale of services and cash collected in 2010. Recorded as a debit to Cash and as a credit to Accounts Receivable, $300.						
7. On December 31, 2010, bought land on credit for $8,000, not recorded until payment was made on February 1, 2011.						

Following is a sample explanation of analysis of errors if not corrected, using the first error as an example:

1. Failure to record depreciation in 2010 caused depreciation expense to be too low; therefore, income was overstated by $950. Accumulated depreciation also is too low by $950, which causes assets to be overstated by $950 until the error is corrected.

Evaluating an Ethical Dilemma: Management Incentives and Fraudulent Financial Statements

CP5-8
LO1, 3

Netherlands-based Royal Ahold ranks among the world's three largest food retailers. In the United States it operates the Stop & Shop and Giant supermarket chains. Dutch and U.S regulators and prosecutors have brought criminal and civil charges against the company and its executives for overstating earnings by more than $1 billion. The nature of the fraud is described in the following excerpt:

Two Former Execs of Ahold Subsidiary Plead Not Guilty to Fraud

28 July 2004 Associated Press Newswires (c) 2004. The Associated Press.

NEW YORK (AP)—Two former executives pleaded not guilty Wednesday to devising a scheme to inflate the earnings of U.S. Foodservice Inc., a subsidiary of Dutch supermarket giant Royal Ahold NV.

Former chief financial officer Michael Resnick and former chief marketing officer Mark Kaiser entered their pleas in a Manhattan federal court, a day after prosecutors announced fraud and conspiracy charges against them.

The government contends they worked together to boost the company's earnings by $800 million from 2000 to 2003 by reporting fake rebates from suppliers—and sweetened their own bonuses in the process. Two other defendants have already pleaded guilty in the alleged scheme: Timothy Lee, a former executive vice president, and William Carter, a former vice president. Both are set for sentencing in January. Netherlands-based Ahold's U.S. properties include the Stop & Shop and Giant supermarket chains. U.S. Foodservice is one of the largest distributors of food products in the country, providing to restaurants and cafeterias.

Ahold said last year it had overstated its earnings by more than $1 billion, mostly because of the fraud at U.S. Foodservice. Its stock lost 60 percent of its value, and about $6 billion in market value evaporated.

Required:

Using more recent new reports (*Wall Street Journal Index, Factiva,* and *Bloomberg Business News* are good sources), answer the following questions.

1. Whom did the courts and regulatory authorities hold responsible for the misstated financial statements?
2. Did the company cooperate with investigations into the fraud? How did this affect the penalties imposed against the company?
3. How might executive compensation plans that tied bonuses to accounting earnings motivate unethical conduct in this case?

FINANCIAL REPORTING AND ANALYSIS TEAM PROJECT

CP5-9
LO2, 3

Analyzing the Accounting Communication Process

As a team, select an industry to analyze. *Reuters* provides lists of industries and their makeup at www.reuters.com/finance/industries. Each team member should acquire the annual report or 10-K for one publicly traded company in the industry, with each member selecting a different company. (Library files, the SEC EDGAR service at www.sec.gov or the company itself are good sources.)

Required:

On an individual basis, each team member should write a short report answering the following questions about the selected company. Discuss any patterns across the companies that you as a team observe. Then, as a team, write a short report comparing and contrasting your companies.

1. What formats are used to present the
   a. Balance Sheets?
   b. Income Statements?
   c. Operating Activities section of the Statement of Cash Flows?
2. Find one footnote for each of the following and describe its contents in brief:
   a. An accounting rule applied in the company's statements.
   b. Additional detail about a reported financial statement number.
   c. Relevant financial information but with no number reported in the financial statements.
3. Using electronic sources, find one article reporting the company's annual earnings announcement. When is it dated and how does that date compare to the balance sheet date?

4. Using electronic sources, find two analysts' reports for your company.
   a. Give the date, name of the analyst, and his or her recommendation from each report.
   b. Discuss why the recommendations are similar or different. Look at the analysts' reasoning for their respective recommendation.
5. Using the SEC EDGAR website (www.sec.gov), what is the most recent document filed by your company with the SEC (e.g., 8K, S1) and what did it say in brief?
6. Ratio analysis:
   a. What does the return on equity ratio measure in general?
   b. Compute the ratio for the last three years.
   c. What do your results suggest about the company?
   d. If available, find the industry ratio for the most recent year, compare it to your results, and discuss why you believe your company differs from or is similar to the industry ratio.
7. Use the ROE profit driver analysis to determine the cause(s) of any differences in the ROE ratio over the last three years. [Remember that you computed the three profit driver ratios in the last three chapters.]

LEARNING OBJECTIVES

After studying this chapter, you should be able to:

1. Apply the revenue principle to determine the accepted time to record sales revenue for typical retailers, wholesalers, manufacturers, and service companies. p. 284

2. Analyze the impact of credit card sales, sales discounts, and sales returns on the amounts reported as net sales. p. 285

3. Analyze and interpret the gross profit percentage. p. 288

4. Estimate, report, and evaluate the effects of uncollectible accounts receivable (bad debts) on financial statements. p. 290

5. Analyze and interpret the accounts receivable turnover ratio and the effects of accounts receivable on cash flows. p. 297

6. Report, control, and safeguard cash. p. 299

Lectured slideshow–LP6-1
www.mhhe.com/libby6e

REPORTING AND INTERPRETING SALES REVENUE, RECEIVABLES, AND CASH

6

FOCUS COMPANY:

Deckers Outdoor Corporation

BUILDING BRANDS TO BUILD GROSS PROFIT:

MANAGING PRODUCT DEVELOPMENT,

PRODUCTION, AND WORKING CAPITAL

www.deckers.com

Founded by current Chairman (then UCSB student), Doug Otto, Deckers Outdoor is best known for its Teva sports sandals and UGG sheepskin boots. Deckers has become a major player in the casual, outdoor, and athletic footwear market by building on its commitment to the needs of hikers, trail runners, kayakers, surfers, and whitewater rafters for comfort, function, and performance. Its growth strategy requires building brand recognition by developing and introducing additional innovative footwear that satisfies the company's high standards of comfort, performance, and quality. "Building the brands" allows Deckers to maintain a loyal consumer following and penetrate new markets.

There is a second key component to Deckers' successful growth strategy. Success in the ultracompetitive footwear market requires careful matching of production schedules to customers' needs and careful management of customer receivables. Deckers' successful focus on brand development, product innovation, and working capital management has allowed the company to report the highest gross profit and net income in its history.

UNDERSTANDING THE BUSINESS

The success of each element of Deckers' strategy can be seen in the information presented in the income statement in Exhibit 6.1. Net Sales (Revenue) is reported first, and Cost of Sales (Cost of Goods Sold Expense, Cost of Products Sold) is set out separately from the remaining expenses. Next, the income statement shows **gross profit (gross margin, gross profit margin)**, which is net sales revenue minus cost of sales.

Planning Deckers' growth strategy requires careful coordination of sales and production activities, as well as cash collections from customers. Much of this coordination revolves around the use of credit card and sales discounts, and managing sales returns and bad debts. These activities affect **net sales revenue** on the income statement

EXHIBIT 6.1

Net Sales and Gross
Profit on the
Statement of Income

REAL WORLD EXCERPT

DECKERS
outdoor corporation
ANNUAL REPORT

DECKERS OUTDOOR CORPORATION AND SUBSIDIARIES
Consolidated Statements of Operations
Three Years Ended December 31, 2004, 2005, and 2006
(amounts in thousands of dollars except share data)

	2004	2005	2006
Net sales	$214,787	$264,760	$304,423
Cost of sales	124,354	153,238	163,224
Gross profit	90,433	111,522	141,199

and **cash** and **accounts receivable** on the balance sheet, which are the focus of this chapter. We will also introduce the gross profit percentage ratio as a basis for evaluating changes in gross profit, as well as the receivables turnover ratio as a measure of the efficiency of credit-granting and collection activities. Finally, since the cash collected from customers is also a tempting target for fraud and embezzlement, we will discuss how accounting systems commonly include controls to prevent and detect such misdeeds.

ORGANIZATION of the Chapter

Accounting for Sales Revenue	Measuring and Reporting Receivables	Reporting and Safeguarding Cash
■ Credit Card Sales to Consumers ■ Sales Discounts to Businesses ■ Sales Returns and Allowances ■ Reporting Net Sales ■ Gross Profit Percentage	■ Classifying Receivables ■ Accounting for Bad Debts ■ Reporting Accounts Receivable and Bad Debts ■ Estimating Bad Debts ■ Control over Accounts Receivable ■ Receivables Turnover Ratio	■ Cash and Cash Equivalents Defined ■ Cash Management ■ Internal Control of Cash ■ Reconciliation of Cash Accounts and the Bank Statements

ACCOUNTING FOR SALES REVENUE

Learning Objective 1

Apply the revenue principle to determine the accepted time to record sales revenue for typical retailers, wholesalers, manufacturers, and service companies.

As indicated in Chapter 3, the **revenue principle** requires that revenues be recorded when they are earned (delivery has occurred or services have been rendered, there is persuasive evidence of an arrangement for customer payment, the price is fixed or determinable, and collection is reasonably assured). For sellers of goods, these criteria are most often met and sales revenue is recorded when title and risks of ownership transfer to the buyer.[1] The point at which title (ownership) changes hands is determined by the shipping terms in the sales contract. When goods are shipped **FOB (free on board) shipping point,** title changes hands at shipment, and the buyer normally pays for shipping. When they are shipped **FOB destination,** title changes hands on delivery, and the seller normally pays for shipping. Revenues from goods shipped FOB shipping point are normally recognized at shipment. Revenues from goods shipped FOB delivery are normally recognized at delivery.

---

[1]See SEC Staff Accounting Bulletin 101, *Revenue Recognition in Financial Statements,* 2000.

Service companies most often record sales revenue when they have provided services to the buyer. Companies disclose the revenue recognition rule they follow in the footnote to the financial statements entitled Summary of Significant Accounting Policies. In that note, Deckers reports the following:

REAL WORLD EXCERPT
DECKERS
outdoor corporation
ANNUAL REPORT

NOTES TO CONSOLIDATED FINANCIAL STATEMENTS

1. Summary of Significant Accounting Policies

Recognition of Revenue

The Company recognizes revenue when products are shipped and the customer takes title and assumes risk of loss, collection of relevant receivable is probable, persuasive evidence of an arrangement exists, and the sales price is fixed or determinable.

Like Deckers, many manufacturers, wholesalers, and retailers recognize revenue at shipment. This is when title and risks of ownership pass for Deckers' sales. Auditors expend a great deal of effort ensuring that revenues are recognized in the proper period.

The appropriate **amount** of revenue to record is the **cash equivalent sales price.** Some sales practices differ depending on whether sales are made to businesses or consumers. Deckers sells footwear and apparel to other **businesses** (retailers), including Athlete's Foot and Eastern Mountain Sports, which then sell the goods to consumers. It also operates its own Internet and catalog retailing business that sells footwear directly to **consumers.**

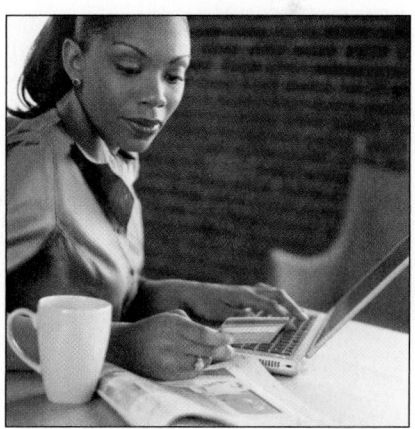

Deckers uses a variety of methods to motivate both groups of customers to buy its products and make payment for their purchases. The principal methods include (1) allowing consumers to use credit cards to pay for purchases, (2) providing business customers direct credit and discounts for early payment, and (3) allowing returns from all customers under certain circumstances. These methods, in turn, affect the way we compute **net sales revenue.**

Credit Card Sales to Consumers

Deckers accepts cash or credit card payment for its catalogue and Internet sales. Deckers' managers decided to accept credit cards (mainly Visa, Mastercard, and American Express) for a variety of reasons:

Learning Objective 2
Analyze the impact of credit card sales, sales discounts, and sales returns on the amounts reported as net sales.

1. Increasing customer traffic.
2. Avoiding the costs of providing credit directly to consumers, including recordkeeping and bad debts (discussed later).
3. Lowering losses due to bad checks.
4. Avoiding losses from fraudulent credit card sales. (As long as Deckers follows the credit card company's verification procedure, the credit card company [e.g., Visa] absorbs any losses.)
5. Receiving money faster. (Since credit card receipts can be directly deposited in its bank account, Deckers receives its money faster than it would if it provided credit directly to consumers.)

Audio lecture–AP6-1
www.mhhe.com/libby6e

The credit card company charges a fee for the service it provides. When Deckers deposits its credit card receipts in the bank, it might receive credit for only 97 percent of the sales price. The credit card company is charging a 3 percent fee (the **credit card discount**) for its service. If daily credit card sales were $3,000, Deckers would report the following:

A CREDIT CARD DISCOUNT is the fee charged by the credit card company for services.

Sales revenue	$3,000
Less: Credit card discounts (0.03 × 3,000)	90
Net sales (reported on the income statement)	$2,910

Video 6-1
www.mhhe.com/libby6e

Sales Discounts to Businesses

Most of Deckers' sales to businesses are credit sales on open account; that is, there is no formal written promissory note or credit card. When Deckers sells footwear to retailers on credit, credit terms are printed on the sales document and invoice (bill) sent to the customer. Often credit terms are abbreviated using symbols. For example, if the full price is due within 30 days of the invoice date, the credit terms would be noted as **n/30**. Here, the **n** means the sales amount **net** of, or less, any sales returns.

Early Payment Incentive

A SALES DISCOUNT (cash discount) is a cash discount offered to encourage prompt payment of an account receivable.

In some cases, a **sales discount** (often called a cash discount) is granted to the purchaser to encourage early payment.[2] For example, Deckers may offer standard credit terms of 2/10, n/30, which means that the customer may deduct 2 percent from the invoice price if cash payment is made within 10 days from the date of sale. If cash payment is not made within the 10-day discount period, the full sales price (less any returns) is due within a maximum of 30 days.

Deckers offers this sales discount to encourage customers to pay more quickly. This provides two benefits to Deckers.

1. Prompt receipt of cash from customers reduces the necessity to borrow money to meet operating needs.

2. Since customers tend to pay bills providing discounts first, a sales discount also decreases the chances that the customer will run out of funds before Deckers' bill is paid.

Companies commonly record sales discounts taken by subtracting the discount from sales if payment is made **within** the discount period (the usual case).[3] For example, if credit sales of $1,000 are recorded with terms 2/10, n/30 and payment of $980 ($1,000 × 0.98 = $980) is made within the discount period, net sales of the following amount would be reported:

Sales revenue	$1,000
Less: Sales discounts (0.02 × $1,000)	20
Net sales (reported on the income statement)	$ 980

If payment is made after the discount period, the full $1,000 would be reported as net sales.

---

[2] It is important not to confuse a cash discount with a trade discount. Vendors sometimes use a **trade discount** for quoting sales prices; the sales price is the list or printed catalog price **less** the trade discount. For example, an item may be quoted at $10 per unit subject to a 20 percent trade discount on orders of 100 units or more; thus, the price for the large order is $8 per unit. Sales revenue should always be recorded net of trade discounts. Deckers also offers discounts for early order and shipment to help manage production flows.

[3] We use the gross method in all examples in this text. Some companies use the alternative net method, which records sales revenue after deducting the amount of the cash discount. Since the choice of method has little effect on the financial statements, discussion of this method is left for an advanced course.

Note that both the purpose of and accounting for sales discounts are very similar to the purpose of and the accounting for credit card discounts. Both sales discounts and credit card discounts provide an attractive service to customers while promoting faster receipt of cash, reducing recordkeeping costs, and minimizing bad debts. Accounting for sales discounts is discussed in more detail in Supplement A.

To Take or Not to Take the Discount, That Is the Question	FINANCIAL ANALYSIS

Customers usually pay within the discount period because the savings are substantial. With terms 2/10, n/30, customers save 2 percent by paying 20 days early (on the 10th day instead of the 30th). This translates into a 37 percent annual interest rate. To calculate the annual interest rate, first compute the interest rate for the discount period. When the 2 percent discount is taken, the customer pays only 98 percent of the gross sales price. For example, on a $100 sale with terms 2/10, n/30, $2 would be saved and $98 would be paid 20 days early.

The interest rate for the 20-day discount period is computed as follows:

$$\frac{\text{Amount Saved}}{\text{Amount Paid}} = \text{Interest Rate for 20 Days}$$

$$\frac{\$2}{\$98} = 2.04\% \text{ for 20 Days}$$

The annual interest rate is:

$$\text{Interest Rate for 20 Days} \times \frac{365 \text{ Days}}{20 \text{ Days}} = \text{Annual Interest Rate}$$

$$2.04\% \times \frac{365 \text{ Days}}{20 \text{ Days}} = 37.23\% \text{ Annual Interest Rate}$$

As long as the bank's interest rate is less than the interest rate associated with failing to take cash discounts, the customer will save by taking the cash discount. For example, even if credit customers had to borrow from that bank at a high rate such as 15 percent, they would save a great deal.

Sales Returns and Allowances

Retailers and consumers have a right to return unsatisfactory or damaged merchandise and receive a refund or an adjustment to their bill. Such returns are often accumulated in a separate account called Sales Returns and Allowances and must be deducted from gross sales revenue in determining net sales. This account informs Deckers' managers of the volume of returns and allowances providing an important measure of the quality of customer service. Assume that Fontana Shoes of Ithaca, New York, buys 40 pairs of sandals from Deckers for $2,000 on account. Before paying for the sandals, Fontana discovers that 10 pairs of sandals are not the color ordered and returns them to Deckers.[4] Deckers computes net sales as follows:

SALES RETURNS AND ALLOWANCES is a reduction of sales revenues for return of or allowances for unsatisfactory goods.

Sales revenue	$2,000
Less: Sales returns and allowances (0.25 × $2,000)	500
Net sales (reported on the income statement)	$1,500

Cost of goods sold related to the 10 pairs of sandals would also be reduced.

---

[4] Alternatively, Deckers might offer Fontana a $200 allowance to keep the wrong-color sandals. If Fontana accepts the offer, Deckers reports $200 as sales returns and allowances.

Reporting Net Sales

On the company's books, credit card discounts, sales discounts, and sales returns and allowances are accounted for separately to allow managers to monitor the costs of credit card use, sales discounts, and returns. Using the numbers in the preceding examples, the amount of net sales reported on the income statement is computed in the following manner:

Sales revenue	$6,000
Less: Credit card discounts (a contra-revenue)	90
Sales discounts (a contra-revenue)	20
Sales returns and allowances (a contra-revenue)	500
Net sales (reported on the income statement)	$5,390

Deckers indicates in its revenue recognition footnote that the appropriate subtractions are made.

REAL WORLD EXCERPT

DECKERS
outdoor corporation

ANNUAL REPORT

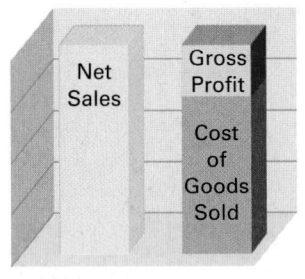

NOTES TO CONSOLIDATED FINANCIAL STATEMENTS

1. The Company and Summary of Significant Accounting Policies

Revenue Recognition

. . . Allowances for estimated returns, discounts . . . are provided for when related revenue is recorded.

In 2006, Deckers disclosed that it provided its customers with $2,430,000 in sales discounts based on meeting certain order, shipment, and payment timelines.

As we noted earlier, net sales less cost of goods sold equals the subtotal **gross profit** or **gross margin.** Analysts often examine gross profit as a percentage of sales (the gross profit or gross margin percentage).

KEY RATIO
ANALYSIS

Gross Profit Percentage

Learning Objective 3

Analyze and interpret the gross profit percentage.

ANALYTICAL QUESTION:

How effective is management in selling goods and services for more than the costs to purchase or product them?

% RATIO AND COMPARISONS:

The gross profit percentage ratio is computed as follows:

$$\text{Gross Profit Percentage} = \frac{\text{Gross Profit}}{\text{Net Sales}}$$

The 2006 ratio for Deckers (see Exhibit 6.1):

$$\frac{\$141,199}{\$304,423} = 0.464 \ (46.4\%)$$

Selected Focus Company Comparisons

Papa John's	41.2%
Harley-Davidson	44.8%
General Mills	43.8%

COMPARISONS OVER TIME		
Deckers		
2004	**2005**	**2006**
42.1%	42.1%	46.4%

COMPARISONS WITH COMPETITORS	
Skechers U.S.A.	**Timberland**
2006	**2006**
43.4%	47.3%

💡 INTERPRETATIONS:

In General   The gross profit percentage measures a company's ability to charge premium prices and produce goods and services at low cost. All other things equal, a higher gross profit results in higher net income.

Business strategy, as well as competition, affects the gross profit percentage. Companies pursuing a product-differentiation strategy use research and development and product promotion activities to convince customers of the superiority or distinctiveness of the company's products. This allows them to charge premium prices, producing a higher gross profit percentage. Companies following a low-cost strategy rely on more efficient management of production to reduce costs and increase the gross profit percentage. Managers, analysts, and creditors use this ratio to assess the effectiveness of the company's product development, marketing, and production strategy.

Focus Company Analysis   Deckers' gross profit percentage has grown over the past three years to above the industry average of 45 percent, and between its competitors Skechers and Timberland.* At the beginning of the chapter, we discussed key elements of Deckers' business strategy that focused on introducing new technologies, product lines, and styles, as well as managing production and inventory costs. Each of these elements can have a large effect on gross margin.

A Few Cautions   To assess the company's ability to sustain its gross margins, you must understand the sources of any change in the gross profit percentage. For example, an increase in margin resulting from increased sales of high-margin boots during a hard winter would be less sustainable than an increase resulting from introducing new products. Also, higher prices must often be sustained with higher R&D and advertising costs, which can eat up any increase in gross margin. Finally, be aware that a small change in the gross profit percentage can lead to a large change in net income.

*www.reuters.com

SELF-STUDY QUIZ

1. Assume that Deckers sold $30,000 worth of footwear to various retailers with terms 1/10, n/30 and half of that amount was paid within the discount period. Gross catalogue and Internet sales were $5,000 for the same period, 80 percent being paid with credit cards with a 3 percent discount and the rest in cash. Compute net sales for the period.

    _____

    _____

2. During the first quarter of 2006, Deckers' net sales totaled $44,272, and cost of sales was $23,866. Verify that its gross profit percentage was 46.09 percent.

    _____

    _____

After you have completed your answers, check them with the solutions at the bottom of the page.

Solutions section

1. | Gross sales | | $35,000 |
    |---|---|---|
    | Less: Sales discounts (0.01 × 1/2 × $30,000) | | 150 |
    | Credit card discounts (0.03 × 0.80 × $5,000) | | 120 |
    | Net Sales | | $34,730 |

2. | Net sales | $44,272 |
    |---|---|
    | Cost of Sales | 23,866 |
    | Gross Profit | $20,406 |

    $20,406/44,272 = 46.09% Gross profit percentage

Self-Study Quiz
Solutions

MEASURING AND REPORTING RECEIVABLES

Classifying Receivables

ACCOUNTS RECEIVABLE (trade receivables, receivables) are open accounts owed to the business by trade customers.

NOTES RECEIVABLE are written promises that require another party to pay the business under specified conditions (amount, time, interest).

Receivables may be classified in three common ways. First, they may be classified as either an account receivable or a note receivable. An **account receivable** is created by a credit sale on an open account. For example, an account receivable is created when Deckers sells shoes on open account to Fontana Shoes in Ithaca, New York. A **note receivable** is a promise in writing (a formal document) to pay (1) a specified amount of money, called the **principal,** at a definite future date known as the maturity date and (2) a specified amount of **interest** at one or more future dates. The interest is the amount charged for use of the principal. We discuss the computation of interest when we discuss notes payable in a later chapter.

Second, receivables may be classified as trade or nontrade receivables. A **trade receivable** is created in the normal course of business when a sale of merchandise or services on credit occurs. A **nontrade receivable** arises from transactions other than the normal sale of merchandise or services. For example, if Deckers loaned money to a new vice president to help finance a home at the new job location, the loan would be classified as a nontrade receivable. Third, in a classified balance sheet, receivables also are classified as either **current** or **noncurrent** (short term or long term), depending on when the cash is expected to be collected. Like many companies, Deckers reports only one type of receivable account, Trade Accounts Receivable, from customers and classifies the asset as a current asset because the accounts receivable are all due to be paid within one year.

Foreign Currency Receivables

Selected Foreign Currency Exchange Rates (in US$)	
Mexican Peso	$0.09
Singapore Dollar	$0.66
Euro	$1.38

Export (international) sales are a growing part of the U.S. economy. For example, international sales amounted to 12.6 percent of Deckers' revenues in 2006. As is the case with domestic sales to other businesses, most export sales to businesses are on credit. When the buyer has agreed to pay in its local currency instead of U.S. dollars, Deckers cannot add the resulting accounts receivable, which are denominated in foreign currency, directly to its U.S. dollar accounts receivable. Deckers' accountants must first convert them to U.S. dollars using the end-of-period exchange rate between the two currencies. For example, if a French department store owed Deckers €20,000 (euros, the common currency of the European Monetary Union) on December 31, 2006, and each euro was worth US$1.38 on that date, it would add US$27,600 to its accounts receivable on the balance sheet.

Accounting for Bad Debts

Learning Objective 4
Estimate, report, and evaluate the effects of uncollectible accounts receivable (bad debts) on financial statements.

For billing and collection purposes, Deckers keeps a separate accounts receivable account for each of the retail stores that resell its footwear and apparel (called a **subsidiary account**). The accounts receivable amount on the balance sheet represents the total of these individual customer accounts.

When Deckers extends credit to its commercial customers, it knows that some of these customers will not pay their debts. The matching principle requires recording of bad debt expense in the **same** accounting period in which the related sales are made.

This presents an important accounting problem. Deckers may not learn which particular customers will not pay until the **next** accounting period. So, at the end of the period of sale, it normally does not know which customers' accounts receivable are bad debts.

Deckers resolves this problem and satisfies the matching principle by using the **allowance method** to measure bad debt expense. The allowance method is based on **estimates** of the expected amount of bad debts. Two primary steps in employing the allowance method are:

1. Making the end-of-period adjusting entry to record estimated bad debt expense.

2. Writing off specific accounts determined to be uncollectible during the period.

The ALLOWANCE METHOD bases bad debt expense on an estimate of uncollectible accounts.

Recording Bad Debt Expense Estimates

Bad debt expense (also called doubtful accounts expense, uncollectible accounts expense, and provision for uncollectible accounts) is the expense associated with estimated uncollectible accounts receivable. An **adjusting journal entry at the end of the accounting period** records the bad debt estimate. For the year ended December 31, 2006, Deckers estimated bad debt expense to be $4,685 (all numbers in thousands of dollars) and made the following adjusting entry:

BAD DEBT EXPENSE (doubtful accounts expense, uncollectible accounts expense, provision for uncollectible accounts) is the expense associated with estimated uncollectible accounts receivable.

| Bad debt expense (+E, −SE)..................................... | 4,685 | |
| Allowance for doubtful accounts (+XA, −A).................... | | 4,685 |

Assets	=	Liabilities	+	Stockholders' Equity
Allowance for doubtful accounts −4,685				Bad debt expense −4,685

Audio lecture–AP6-2
www.mhhe.com/libby6e

The Bad Debt Expense is included in the category "Selling" expenses on the income statement. It decreases net income and stockholders' equity. Accounts Receivable could not be credited in the journal entry because there is no way to know which customers' accounts receivable are involved. So the credit is made, instead, to a contra-asset account called **Allowance for Doubtful Accounts** (Allowance for Bad Debts or Allowance for Uncollectible Accounts). As a contra-asset, the balance in Allowance for Doubtful Accounts is always subtracted from the balance of the asset Accounts Receivable. Thus, the entry decreases the net book value of Accounts Receivable and total assets.

ALLOWANCE FOR DOUBTFUL ACCOUNTS (allowance for bad debts, allowance for uncollectible accounts) is a contra-asset account containing the estimated uncollectible accounts receivable.

Writing Off Specific Uncollectible Accounts

Throughout the year, when it is determined that a customer will not pay its debts (e.g., due to bankruptcy), the write-off of that individual bad debt is recorded through a journal entry. Now that the specific uncollectible customer account receivable has been identified, it can be removed with a credit. At the same time, we no longer need the related estimate in the contra-asset Allowance for Doubtful Accounts, which is removed by a debit. The journal entry summarizing Deckers' total write-offs of $6,969 during 2006 follows:

| Allowance for doubtful accounts (−XA, +A).................... | 6,969 | |
| Accounts Receivable (−A)................................... | | 6,969 |

Assets	=	Liabilities	+	Stockholders' Equity
Allowance for doubtful accounts +6,969				
Accounts receivable −6,969				

Notice that this journal entry did **not affect any income statement accounts.** It did not record a bad debt expense because the estimated expense was recorded with an adjusting entry in the period of sale. Also, the entry did **not change the net book**

value of accounts receivable, since the decrease in the asset account (Accounts Receivable) was offset by the decrease in the contra-asset account (Allowance for Doubtful Accounts). Thus, it also did not affect total assets.

When a customer makes a payment on an account that has already been written off, the journal entry to write off the account is reversed to put the receivable back on the books, and the collection of cash is recorded.

Summary of the Accounting Process

It is important to remember that accounting for bad debts is a two-step process:

Step	Timing	Accounts Affected	Financial Statement Effects
1. Record estimated bad debts adjustment	End of period in which sales are made	Bad Debt Expense (E) ↑ Allowance for Doubtful Accounts (XA) ↑	Net Income ↓ Assets (Accounts Receivable, Net) ↓
2. Identify and write off actual bad debts	Throughout period as bad debts become known	Accounts Receivable (A) ↓ Allowance for Doubtful Accounts (XA) ↓	Net Income Assets (Accounts Receivable, Net) — No effect

Deckers' complete 2006 accounting process for bad debts can now be summarized in terms of the changes in Accounts Receivable (Gross) and the Allowance for Doubtful Accounts:[5]

Accounts Receivable Dec. 31, 2006

Accounts Receivable (Gross) (A)	$55,671
− Allowance for Doubtful Accounts (XA)	6,100
Accounts Receivable (Net) (A)	$49,571

Accounts Receivable (Gross) (A)

Beginning balance	48,067	Collections on account	289,850
Sales on account	304,423	Write-offs	6,969
Ending balance	55,671		

Allowance for Doubtful Accounts (XA)

		Beginning balance	8,384
Write-offs	6,969	Bad debt expense adjustment	4,685
		Ending balance	6,100

Accounts Receivable (Gross) includes the total accounts receivable, both collectible and uncollectible. The balance in the Allowance for Doubtful Accounts is the portion of the accounts receivable balance the company estimates to be uncollectible. Accounts Receivable (Net) reported on the balance sheet is the portion of the accounts the company expects to collect (or its estimated net realizable value).

Reporting Accounts Receivable and Bad Debts

Analysts who want information on Deckers' receivables will find Accounts Receivable, net of allowance for doubtful accounts (the **net book value**), of $39,683 and $49,571 for 2005 and 2006, respectively; reported on the balance sheet (Exhibit 6.2). The balance in the Allowance for Doubtful Accounts ($8,384 in 2005 and $6,100 in

---

[5]This assumes that all sales are on account.

DECKERS OUTDOOR CORPORATION AND SUBSIDIARIES
Consolidated Balance Sheets
December 31, 2005 and 2006
(amounts in thousands of dollars except share data)

	2005	2006
Assets		
Current assets:		
Cash and cash equivalents	$ 50,749	$ 34,255
Short-term investments	2,500	64,637
Trade accounts receivable, less allowance for doubtful accounts of $8,384 and $6,100 as of December 31, 2005 and 2006, respectively	39,683	49,571
Inventories	33,374	32,375
Prepaid expenses and other current assets	1,364	2,199
Deferred tax assets	5,949	4,386
Total current assets	$133,619	$187,423

EXHIBIT 6.2

Accounts Receivable on the Partial Balance Sheet

REAL WORLD EXCERPT
DECKERS outdoor corporation
ANNUAL REPORT

2006) is also reported. Accounts Receivable (Gross), the total accounts receivable, can be computed by adding the two amounts together.

The amounts of bad debt expense and accounts receivable written off for the period normally are not disclosed in the annual report. If they are material, these amounts are reported on a schedule that publicly traded companies include in their Annual Report Form 10-K filed with the SEC. Exhibit 6.3 presents this schedule from Deckers' 2006 filing.[6]

DECKERS OUTDOOR CORPORATION AND SUBSIDIARIES
Valuation and Qualifying Accounts
Three Years Ended December 31, 2004, 2005, and 2006

Description	Balance at Beginning of Year	Additions	Deductions	Balance at End of Year
Allowance for doubtful account year ended				
December 31, 2004	$ 3,573	$10,063	$7,799	$5,837
December 31, 2005	5,837	10,101	7,554	8,384
December 31, 2006:	8,384	4,685	6,969	6,100

EXHIBIT 6.3

Accounts Receivable Valuation Schedule (Form 10-K)

REAL WORLD EXCERPT
DECKERS outdoor corporation
FORM 10-K

[6]Deckers' balance sheet and accompanying note also disclose the reserve for sales discounts, which is also subtracted in computing accounts receivable (net).

SELF-STUDY QUIZ

In a recent year, Timberland, a major Deckers competitor, had a beginning credit balance in the Allowance for Doubtful Accounts of $4,910 (all numbers in thousands of dollars). It wrote off accounts receivable totaling $1,480 during the year and made a bad debt expense adjustment for the year of $2,395.

1. What adjusting journal entry did Timberland make for bad debts at the end of the year?
2. Make the journal entry summarizing Timberland's total write-offs of bad debts during the year.
3. Compute the balance in the Allowance for doubtful accounts at the end of the year.

After you have completed your answers, check them with the solutions at the bottom of the page.

Estimating Bad Debts

The bad debt expense amount recorded in the end-of-period adjusting entry often is estimated based on either (1) a percentage of total credit sales for the period or (2) an aging of accounts receivable. Both methods are acceptable under GAAP and are widely used in practice. The percentage of credit sales method is simpler to apply, but the aging method is generally more accurate. Many companies use the simpler method on a weekly or monthly basis and use the more accurate method on a monthly or quarterly basis to check the accuracy of the earlier estimates. In our example, both methods produce exactly the same estimate, which rarely occurs in practice.

Percentage of Credit Sales Method

PERCENTAGE OF CREDIT SALES METHOD bases bad debt expense on the historical percentage of credit sales that result in bad debts.

Many companies make their estimates using the **percentage of credit sales method,** which bases bad debt expense on the historical percentage of credit sales that result in bad debts. The average percentage of credit sales that result in bad debts can be computed by dividing total bad debt losses by total **credit** sales. A company that has been operating for some years has sufficient experience to project probable future bad debt losses. For example, if we assume that, during the year 2007, Deckers expected bad debt losses of 0.5 percent of credit sales, and its credit sales were $300,000, it would estimate current year's bad debts as:

Credit sales	$300,000
× Bad debt loss rate (.5%)	× .005
Bad debt expense	$ 1,500

This amount would be directly recorded as Bad Debt Expense (and an increase in Allowance for Doubtful Accounts) in the current year. Our beginning balance in the Allowance for Doubtful Accounts for 2007 would be the ending balance for 2006. Assuming write-offs during 2007 of $1,600, the ending balance is computed as follows:

1. Bad debt expense (+E, −SE)	2,395	
Allowance for doubtful accounts (+XA, −A)		2,395
2. Allowance for doubtful accounts (−XA, +A)	1,480	
Accounts receivable (−A)		1,480
3. Beginning Balance + Bad Debt Expense Estimate − Write-Offs = Ending Balance,		
$4,910 + 2,395 − 1,480 = $5,825		

Allowance for Doubtful Accounts (XA)			
2007 Write-offs	1,600	2007 Beginning balance	6,100
		2007 Bad debt expense adjustment	1,500
		2007 Ending balance	?

percent of credit sales estimate = 6,000 ◄───

Beginning balance	$6,100
+ Bad debt expense	1,500
− Write-offs	1,600
Ending balance	$6,000

Aging of Accounts Receivable

As an alternative to the percentage of credit sales method, many companies use the **aging of accounts receivable method.** This method relies on the fact that, as accounts receivable become older and more overdue, it is less likely that they will prove to be collectible. For example, a receivable that was due in 30 days but has not been paid after 45 days is more likely to be collected, on average, than a similar receivable that remains unpaid after 120 days. Based on prior experience, the company can estimate what portion of receivables of different ages will not be paid.

AGING OF ACCOUNTS RECEIVABLE METHOD estimates uncollectible accounts based on the age of each account receivable.

Suppose that Deckers split its 2007 ending balance in accounts receivable (gross) of $60,000 into three age categories. Management would first examine the individual customer accounts receivable and sort them into the three age categories. Management would then **estimate** the probable bad debt loss rates for each category: for example, not yet due, 2 percent; 1 to 90 days past due, 10 percent; over 90 days, 30 percent.

As illustrated in the aging schedule below, this would result in an estimate of total uncollectible amounts of $6,000. This amount computed using the aging method is the ending balance that **should be** in the Allowance for Doubtful Accounts. This is called the **estimated ending balance.** From this, the adjustment to record Bad Debt Expense (and an increase in Allowance for Doubtful Accounts) for 2007 would be computed:

Aging Schedule 2007

Aged Accounts Receivable			Estimated Percentage Uncollectible		Estimated Amount Uncollectible
Not yet due	$30,000	×	2%	=	$600
Up to 90 days past due	18,000	×	10%	=	1,800
Over 90 days past due	12,000	×	30%	=	3,600
Estimated ending balance in Allowance for Doubtful Accounts					$6,000
Less: Balance in Allowance for Doubtful Accounts before adjustment ($6,100 − 1,600)					4,500
Bad Debt Expense for the year					$1,500

Allowance for Doubtful Accounts (XA)			
2007 Write-offs	1,600	2007 Beginning balance	6,100
		2007 Bad debt expense adjustment	?
		2007 Ending balance	6,000

= 1,500 ◄

total estimated ◄─┘
uncollectible acconts

Comparison of the Two Methods

Students often fail to recognize that the approach to recording bad debt expense using the percentage of credit sales method is different from that for the aging method:

■ **Percentage of credit sales.** Directly compute the amount to be recorded as **Bad Debt Expense** on the **income statement** for the period in the adjusting journal entry.

■ **Aging.** Compute the **final ending balance** we would like to have in the **Allowance for Doubtful Accounts** on the **balance sheet** after we make the necessary adjusting entry. The **difference** between the current balance in the account and the estimated balance is recorded as the adjusting entry for Bad Debt Expense for the period.

In either case, the balance sheet presentation for 2007 would show Accounts Receivable, less Allowance for Doubtful Accounts, of $54,000 ($60,000 − $6,000).

Actual Write-Offs Compared with Estimates

Deckers' Form 10-K provides particularly clear information on its approach to estimating uncollectible accounts and the potential effect of any errors in those estimates:

CRITICAL ACCOUNTING POLICIES

Allowance for Doubtful Accounts. We provide a reserve against trade accounts receivable for estimated losses that may result from customers' inability to pay. We determine the amount of the reserve by analyzing known uncollectible accounts, aged trade accounts receivables, economic conditions, historical experience and the customers' credit-worthiness. . . . Our use of different estimates and assumptions could produce different financial results. For example, a 1.0% change in the rate used to estimate the reserve for the accounts not specifically identified as uncollectible would change the allowance for doubtful accounts by $349.

If uncollectible accounts actually written off differ from the estimated amount previously recorded, a higher or lower amount is recorded in the next period to make up for the previous period's error in estimate. **When estimates are found to be incorrect, financial statement values for prior annual accounting periods are not corrected.**

Control Over Accounts Receivable

Many managers forget that extending credit will increase sales volume, but unless the related receivables are collected, they do not add to the bottom line. These companies that emphasize sales without monitoring the collection of credit sales will soon find much of their current assets tied up in accounts receivable. The following practices can help minimize bad debts:

1. Require approval of customers' credit history by a person independent of the sales and collections functions.

2. Age accounts receivable periodically and contact customers with overdue payments.

3. Reward both sales and collections personnel for speedy collections so that they work as a team.

To assess the effectiveness of overall credit-granting and collection activities, managers and analysts often compute the receivables turnover ratio.

Receivables Turnover

? ANALYTICAL QUESTION:
How effective are credit-granting and collection activities?

% RATIO AND COMPARISONS:
The receivables turnover ratio is computed as follows (see Exhibits 6.1 and 6.2):

$$\text{Receivables Turnover} = \frac{\text{Net Sales*}}{\text{Average Net Trade Accounts Receivable}^\dagger}$$

> **Learning Objective 5**
> Analyze and interpret the accounts receivable turnover ratio and the effects of accounts receivable on cash flows.

The 2006 receivables turnover ratio for Deckers:

$$\frac{\$304,423}{(\$39,683 + 49,571) \div 2} = 6.8$$

COMPARISONS OVER TIME			COMPARISONS WITH COMPETITORS	
Deckers			Skechers U.S.A.	Timberland
2004	2005	2006	2006	2006
8.1	6.9	6.8	7.7	8.4

💡 INTERPRETATIONS:

In General   The receivables turnover ratio reflects how many times average trade receivables are recorded and collected during the period. The higher the ratio, the faster the collection of receivables. A higher ratio benefits the company because it can invest the money collected to earn interest income or reduce borrowings to reduce interest expense. Overly generous payment schedules and ineffective collection methods keep the receivables turnover ratio low. Analysts and creditors watch this ratio because a sudden decline may mean that a company is extending payment deadlines in an attempt to prop up lagging sales or is even recording sales that will later be returned by customers. Many managers and analysts compute the related number *average collection period* or *average days sales in receivables,* which is equal to 365 ÷ Receivables Turnover Ratio. It indicates the average time it takes a customer to pay its accounts. For Deckers, the amount would be computed as follows for 2006:

$$\text{Average Collection Period} = \frac{365}{\text{Receivables Turnover}} = \frac{365}{6.8} = 53.7 \text{ days}$$

Selected Industry Comparisons: Receivables Turnover Ratio

Department stores   46.1

Malt beverages   21.4

Forest & wood products   14.7

Focus Company Analysis   Deckers' receivables turnover decreased significantly from a 2004 high of 8.1 to 6.8 in 2006. This indicates that the company is taking longer to convert its receivables into cash. Moreover, the ratio is also below the industry average of 7.8,‡ and its competitors Skechers and Timberland.

A Few Cautions   Since differences across industries and between firms in the manner in which customer purchases are financed can cause dramatic differences in the ratio, a particular firm's ratio should be compared only with its prior years' figures or with other firms in the same industry following the same financing practices.

*Since the amount of net credit sales is normally not reported separately, most analysts use net sales in this equation.
†Average Net Trade Accounts Receivable = (Beginning Net Trade Accounts Receivable + Ending Net Trade Accounts Receivable) ÷ 2.
‡Dun and Bradstreet Industry Norms and Key Business Ratios (2002).

FOCUS ON
CASH FLOWS   **Accounts Receivable**

The change in accounts receivable can be a major determinant of a company's cash flow from operations. While the income statement reflects the revenues of the period, the cash flow from operating activities reflects cash collections from customers. Since sales on account increase the balance in accounts receivable and cash collections from customers decrease the balance in accounts receivable, the change in accounts receivable from the beginning to the end of the period is the difference between sales and collections.

EFFECT ON STATEMENT OF CASH FLOWS

In General   When there is a net **decrease in accounts receivable** for the period, cash collected from customers is more than revenue; thus, the decrease must be **added** in computing cash flows from operations. When a net **increase in accounts receivable** occurs, cash collected from customers is less than revenue; thus, the increase must be **subtracted** in computing cash flows from operations.*

	Effect on Cash Flows
Operating activities (indirect method)	
Net income	$ xxx
Adjusted for	
Add accounts receivable decrease	+
or	
Subtract accounts receivable increase	−

Focus Company Analysis   Exhibit 6.4 shows the Operating Activities section of Deckers' statement of cash flows. Sales growth during 2006 has resulted in an increase in Deckers' balance in receivables. This increase is subtracted in reconciling net income to cash flow from operating activities because revenues are higher than cash collected from customers for 2006. When receivables decrease, the amount of the reduction in receivables is added in reconciling net income to cash flow from operating activities because cash collected from customers is higher than revenues.

For companies with receivables in foreign currency or business acquisitions/dispositions, the change reported on the cash flow statement will not equal the change in the accounts receivable reported on the balance sheet.

SELF-STUDY QUIZ

1. In an earlier year, Deckers' competitor Timberland reported a beginning balance in the Allowance for Doubtful Accounts of $723. It also wrote off bad debts amounting to $648 during the year. At the end of the year, it computed total estimated uncollectible accounts using the aging method to be $904 (all numbers in thousands of dollars). What amount did Timberland record as bad debt expense for the period? (**Solution approach:** Use the Allowance for Doubtful Accounts T-account to solve for the missing value.)

Allowance for Doubtful Accounts (XA)

2. Indicate whether **granting later payment deadlines** (e.g., 60 days instead of 30 days) will most likely **increase** or **decrease** the accounts receivable turnover ratio. Explain.

After you have completed your answer, check them with the solutions at the bottom of the next page.

	2004	2005	2006
DECKERS OUTDOOR CORPORATION AND SUBSIDIARIES			
Consolidated Statements of Cash Flows			
Three Years Ended December 31, 2004, 2005, and 2006			
Cash flows from operating activities:			
Net income (loss)	$25,539	$31,845	$31,522
Adjustments to reconcile net income (loss) to net cash provided by operating activities:			
....	...	...	...
Changes in assets and liabilities:			
(Increase) decrease in:			
Trade accounts receivable, net of provision for doubtful accounts	(22,683)	(2,022)	(9,888)
Inventories	(14,154)	(7,950)	999
	...	...	...
	...	...	...
Net cash provided by operating activities	$12,416	$29,607	$48,498

EXHIBIT 6.4

Accounts Receivable on the Partial Cash Flow Statement

REAL WORLD EXCERPT

DECKERS outdoor corporation
ANNUAL REPORT

REPORTING AND SAFEGUARDING CASH

Cash and Cash Equivalents Defined

Cash is defined as money or any instrument that banks will accept for deposit and immediate credit to a company's account, such as a check, money order, or bank draft. **Cash equivalents** are investments with original maturities of three months or less that are readily convertible to cash and whose value is unlikely to change (that is, are not sensitive to interest rate changes). Typical instruments included as cash equivalents are bank certificates of deposit and treasury bills that the U.S. government issues to finance its activities.

Even though a company may have several bank accounts and several types of cash equivalents, all cash accounts and cash equivalents are usually combined in one amount for financial reporting purposes. Deckers reports a single account, Cash and Equivalents. It also reports that the book values of cash equivalents on the balance sheet equal their fair market values—which we should expect given the nature of the instruments (investments whose value is unlikely to change).

Learning Objective 6
Report, control, and safeguard cash.

CASH is money or any instrument that banks will accept for deposit and immediate credit to a company's account, such as a check, money order, or bank draft.

CASH EQUIVALENTS are short-term investments with original maturities of three months or less that are readily convertible to cash and whose value is unlikely to change.

Self-Study Quiz Solutions

1.

Allowance for Doubtful Accounts (XA)		
	Beginning balance	723
Write-offs 648	Bad debt expense (solve)	829
	Ending balance	904

Estimated ending balance in Allowance for Doubtful Accounts	$904
Less: Current balance in Allowance for Doubtful Accounts ($723 − $648)	75
Bad Debt Expense for the year	$829

2. Granting later payment deadlines will most likely **decrease** the accounts receivable turnover ratio because later collections from customers will increase the average accounts receivable balance (the denominator of the ratio), decreasing the ratio.

Cash Management

Many businesses receive a large amount of cash, checks, and credit card receipts from their customers each day. Anyone can spend cash, so management must develop procedures to safeguard the cash it uses in the business. Effective cash management involves more than protecting cash from theft, fraud, or loss through carelessness. Other cash management responsibilities include:

1. Accurate accounting so that reports of cash flows and balances may be prepared.

2. Controls to ensure that enough cash is available to meet (a) current operating needs, (b) maturing liabilities, and (c) unexpected emergencies.

3. Prevention of the accumulation of excess amounts of idle cash. Idle cash earns no revenue. Therefore, it is often invested in securities to earn a return until it is needed for operations.

Internal Control of Cash

INTERNAL CONTROLS are the processes by which a company safeguards its assets and provides reasonable assurance regarding the reliability of the company's financial reporting, the effectiveness and efficiency of its operations, and its compliance with applicable laws and regulations.

The term **internal controls** refers to the process by which a company safeguards its assets and provides reasonable assurance regarding the reliability of the company's financial reporting, the effectiveness and efficiency of its operations, and its compliance with applicable laws and regulations. Internal control procedures should extend to all assets: cash, receivables, investments, plant and equipment, and so on. Controls that ensure the accuracy of the financial records are designed to prevent inadvertent errors and outright fraud such as occurred in the Maxidrive case discussed in Chapter 1. Because internal control increases the reliability of the financial statements, it is reviewed by the outside independent auditor.

Because cash is the asset most vulnerable to theft and fraud, a significant number of internal control procedures should focus on cash. You have already observed internal control procedures for cash, although you may not have known it at the time. At most movie theaters, one employee sells tickets and another employee collects them. Having one employee do both jobs would be less expensive, but that single employee could easily steal cash and admit a patron without issuing a ticket. If different employees perform the tasks, a successful theft requires participation of both.

Effective internal control of cash should include the following:

1. Separation of duties.

   a. Complete separation of the jobs of receiving cash and disbursing cash.

   b. Complete separation of the procedures of accounting for cash receipts and cash disbursements.

   c. Complete separation of the physical handling of cash and all phases of the accounting function.

2. Prescribed policies and procedures.

   a. Require that all cash receipts be deposited in a bank daily. Keep any cash on hand under strict control.

   b. Require separate approval of the purchases and the actual cash payments. Prenumbered checks should be used. Special care must be taken with payments by electronic funds transfers since they involve no controlled documents (checks).

   c. Assign the responsibilities for cash payment approval and check-signing or electronic funds transfer transmittal to different individuals.

d. Require monthly reconciliation of bank accounts with the cash accounts on the company's books (discussed in detail in the next section).

The separation of duties and the use of prescribed policies and procedures are important elements of the control of cash. Separation of duties deters theft because it requires the collusion of two or more persons to steal cash and then conceal the theft in the accounting records. Prescribed procedures are designed so that work done by one individual is checked against the results reported by other individuals. For example, the amount of cash collected at the cash register by the sales clerk can be compared with the amount of cash deposited at the bank by another employee. Reconciliation of the cash accounts to the bank statements provides a further control on deposits.

Ethics and the Need for Internal Control

Some people are bothered by the recommendation that all well-run companies should have strong internal control procedures. These people believe that control procedures suggest that management does not trust the company's employees. Although the vast majority of employees are trustworthy, employee theft does cost businesses billions of dollars each year. Interviews with convicted felons indicate that in many cases they stole from their employers because they thought that it was easy and that no one cared (there were no internal control procedures).

Many companies have a formal code of ethics that requires high standards of behavior in dealing with customers, suppliers, fellow employees, and the company's assets. Although each employee is ultimately responsible for his or her own ethical behavior, internal control procedures can be thought of as important value statements from management.

Reconciliation of the Cash Accounts and the Bank Statements

Content of a Bank Statement

Proper use of the bank accounts can be an important internal cash control procedure. Each month, the bank provides the company (the depositor) with a **bank statement** that lists (1) each paper or electronic deposit recorded by the bank during the period, (2) each paper or electronic check cleared by the bank during the period, and (3) the balance in the company's account. The bank statement also shows the bank charges or deductions (such as service charges) made directly to the company's account by the bank. A typical bank statement for ROW.COM, Inc., is shown in Exhibit 6.5.

Exhibit 6.5 lists four items that need explanation. Notice the $500 and $100 items listed under Checks and Debits and coded **EFT.**[7] This is the code for **electronic funds transfers.** ROW.COM pays its electricity and insurance bills using electronic checking. When it orders the electronic payments, it records these items on the company's books in the same manner as a paper check. So no additional entry is needed.

Notice that listed under Checks and Debits, there is a deduction for $18 coded **NSF.** This entry refers to a check for $18 received from a customer and deposited by ROW.COM with its bank. The bank processed the check through banking channels to the customer's bank, but the account did not have sufficient funds to cover the check. The customer's bank therefore returned it to ROW.COM's bank, which then charged it back to ROW.COM's account. This type of check often is called an **NSF check** (not sufficient funds). The NSF check is now a receivable; consequently, ROW.COM must make an entry to debit Receivables and credit Cash for the $18.

Notice the $6 listed on June 30 under Checks and Debits and coded **SC.** This is the code for bank service charges. The bank statement included a memo by the bank explaining this service charge (which was not documented by a check). ROW.COM

A BANK STATEMENT is a monthly report from a bank that shows deposits recorded, checks cleared, other debits and credits, and a running bank balance.

---

[7]These codes vary among banks.

EXHIBIT 6.5

Example of a Bank Statement

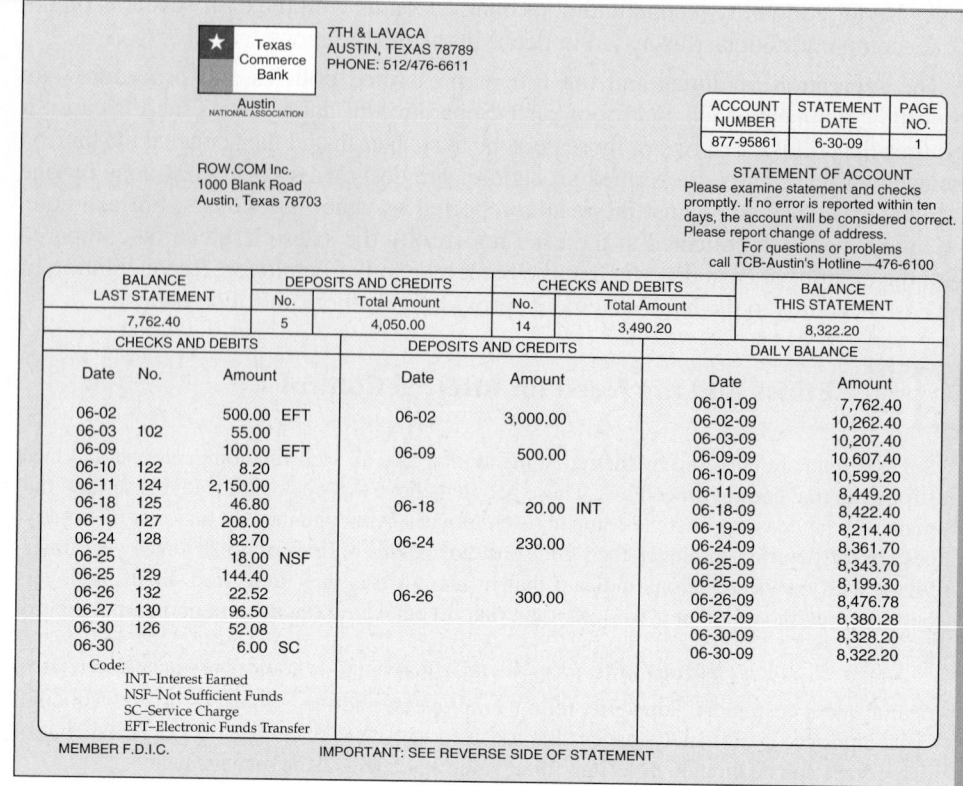

must make an entry to reflect this $6 decrease in the bank balance as a debit to a relevant expense account, such as Bank Service Expense, and a credit to Cash.

Notice the $20 listed on June 18 under Deposits and Credits and the code **INT** for interest earned. The bank pays interest on checking account balances, and increased ROW.COM's account for interest earned during the period. ROW.COM must record the interest by making an entry to debit Cash and credit Interest Income for the $20.

Need for Reconciliation

A BANK RECONCILIATION is the process of verifying the accuracy of both the bank statement and the cash accounts of a business.

A **bank reconciliation** is the process of comparing (reconciling) the ending cash balance in the company's records and the ending cash balance reported by the bank on the monthly bank statement. A bank reconciliation should be completed at the end of each month. Usually, the ending cash balance as shown on the bank statement does not agree with the ending cash balance shown by the related Cash ledger account on the books of the company. For example, the Cash ledger account of ROW.COM showed the following at the end of June (ROW.COM has only one checking account):

Cash (A)			
June 1 balance	7,090.00	June checks written	3,800.00
June deposits	5,750.00		
Ending balance	9,040.00		

The $8,322.20 ending cash balance shown on the bank statement (Exhibit 6.6) differs from the $9,040.00 ending balance of cash shown on the books of ROW.COM. Most of this difference exists because of timing differences in the recording of transactions:

1. Some transactions affecting cash were recorded in the books of ROW.COM but were not shown on the bank statement.

2. Some transactions were shown on the bank statement but had not been recorded in the books of ROW.COM.

Some of the difference may also be caused by errors in recording transactions.

The most common causes of differences between the ending bank balance and the ending book balance of cash are as follows:

1. **Outstanding checks.** These are checks written by the company and recorded in the company's ledger as credits to the Cash account that have not cleared the bank (they are not shown on the bank statement as a deduction from the bank balance). The outstanding checks are identified by comparing the list of canceled checks on the bank statement with the record of checks (such as check stubs or a journal) maintained by the company.

2. **Deposits in transit.** These are deposits sent to the bank by the company and recorded in the company's ledger as debits to the Cash account. The bank has not recorded these deposits (they are not shown on the bank statement as an increase in the bank balance). Deposits in transit usually happen when deposits are made one or two days before the close of the period covered by the bank statement. Deposits in transit are determined by comparing the deposits listed on the bank statement with the company deposit records.

3. **Bank service charges.** An expense for bank services that is listed on the bank statement but is not recorded on the company's books.

4. **NSF checks.** A "bad check" or "bounced check" that was deposited but must be deducted from the company's cash account and rerecorded as an account receivable.

5. **Interest.** The interest paid by the bank to the company on its bank balance.

6. **Errors.** Both the bank and the company may make errors, especially when the volume of cash transactions is large.

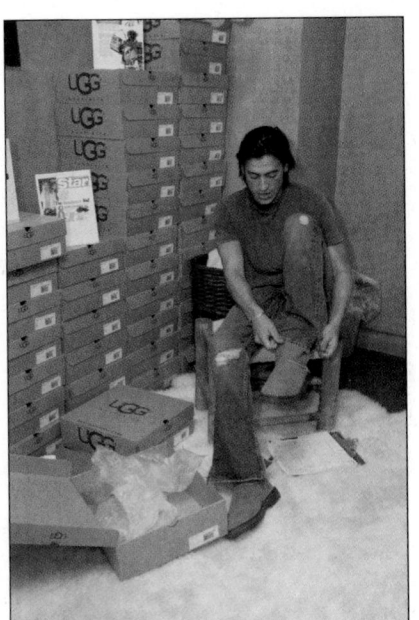

Bank Reconciliation Illustrated

The company should make a bank reconciliation immediately after receiving each bank statement. The general format for the bank reconciliation follows:

Ending cash balance per books	$xxx	Ending cash balance per bank statement	$xxx
+ Interest paid by bank	xx	+ Deposits in transit	xx
− NSF checks/Service charges	xx	− Outstanding checks	xx
± Company errors	xx	± Bank errors	xx
Ending correct cash balance	$xxx	Ending correct cash balance	$xxx

Exhibit 6.6 shows the bank reconciliation prepared by ROW.COM for the month of June to reconcile the ending bank balance ($8,322.20) with the ending book balance ($9,040.00). On the completed reconciliation, the correct cash balance is $9,045.00. This correct balance is the amount that should be shown in the Cash account after the reconciliation. Since ROW.COM has only one checking account and no cash on hand, it is also the correct amount of cash that should be reported on the balance sheet.

ROW.COM followed these steps in preparing the bank reconciliation:

1. **Identify the outstanding checks.** A comparison of the checks and electronic payments listed on the bank statement with the company's record of all checks drawn and electronic payments made showed the following checks were still outstanding (had not cleared the bank) at the end of June:

Check No.	Amount
101	$ 145.00
123	815.00
131	117.20
Total	$1,077.20

This total was entered on the reconciliation as a deduction from the bank account. These checks will be deducted by the bank when they clear the bank.

EXHIBIT 6.6

Bank Reconciliation Illustrated

ROW.COM INC.
Bank Reconciliation
For the Month Ending June 30, 2006

Company's Books		Bank Statement	
Ending cash balance per books	$9,040.00	Ending cash balance per bank statement	$ 8,322.20
Additions		Additions	
Interest paid by the bank	20.00	Deposit in transit	1,800.00
Error in recording check No. 99	9.00		
	9,069.00		10,122.20
Deductions		Deductions	
NSF check of R. Smith	18.00	Outstanding checks	1,077.20
Bank service charges	6.00		
Ending correct cash balance	$9,045.00	Ending correct cash balance	$ 9,045.00

2. **Identify the deposits in transit.** A comparison of the deposit slips on hand with those listed on the bank statement revealed that a deposit of $1,800 made on June 30 was not listed on the bank statement. This amount was entered on the reconciliation as an addition to the bank account. It will be added by the bank when it records the deposit.

3. **Record bank charges and credits:**

   a. Interest received from the bank, $20—entered on the bank reconciliation as an addition to the book balance; it already has been included in the bank balance.

   b. NSF check of R. Smith, $18—entered on the bank reconciliation as a deduction from the book balance; it has been deducted from the bank statement balance.

   c. Bank service charges, $6—entered on the bank reconciliation as a deduction from the book balance; it has been deducted from the bank balance.

4. **Determine the impact of errors.** At this point, ROW.COM found that the reconciliation did not balance by $9. Upon checking the journal entries made during the month, check No. 99 written for $100 to pay an account payable was found. The check was recorded in the company's accounts as $109. Therefore, $9 (i.e., $109 − $100) must be added to the book cash balance on the reconciliation; the bank cleared the check for the correct amount, $100.

Note that in Exhibit 6.6 the two sections of the bank reconciliation now agree at a correct cash balance of $9,045.00.

A bank reconciliation as shown in Exhibit 6.6 accomplishes two major objectives:

1. Checks the accuracy of the bank balance and the company cash records, which involves developing the correct cash balance. The correct cash balance (plus cash on hand, if any) is the amount of cash that is reported on the balance sheet.

2. Identifies any previously unrecorded transactions or changes that are necessary to cause the company's Cash account(s) to show the correct cash balance. Any transactions or changes on the **company's books side** of the bank reconciliation need journal entries. Therefore, the following journal entries based on the company's books side of the bank reconciliation (Exhibit 6.6) must be entered into the company's records.

Accounts of ROW.COM

(*a*) Cash (+A)	20	
Interest income (+R, +SE)		20
To record interest by bank.		
(*b*) Accounts receivable (+A)	18	
Cash (−A)		18
To record NSF check.		
(*c*) Bank service expense (+E, −SE)	6	
Cash (−A)		6
To record service fees charged by bank.		
(*d*) Cash (+A)	9	
Accounts payable (+L)		9
To correct error made in recording a check payable to a creditor.		

Assets	=	Liabilities	+	Stockholders' Equity	
Cash (+20, −18, −6, +9) +5		Accounts payable +9		Interest income	+20
Accounts receivable +18				Bank service expense	−6

Notice again that all of the additions and deductions on the company's books side of the reconciliation need journal entries to update the Cash account. The additions and deductions on the bank statement side do not need journal entries because they will work out automatically when they clear the bank.

SELF-STUDY QUIZ

Indicate which of the following items discovered while preparing a company's bank reconciliation will result in adjustment of the cash balance on the balance sheet.

1. Outstanding checks.

2. Deposits in transit.

3. Bank service charges.

4. NSF checks that were deposited.

After you have completed your answer, check it with the solution at the bottom of the page.

EPILOGUE

As we noted at the beginning of the chapter, Deckers recognized that to turn growth into profits, it had to (1) continually refresh its product lines by introducing new technologies, new styles, and new product categories; (2) become a leaner and more nimble manufacturer, taking advantage of lower-cost, more flexible production locations; and (3) focus attention on inventory management and collections of accounts receivable since an uncollected account is of no value to the company. Each of these efforts is aimed at increasing net sales and/or decreasing cost of goods sold, thereby increasing gross profit. The three quarters of 2007 have sent positive signals about

---

3. Bank service charges are deducted from the company's account; thus, cash must be reduced and an expense must be recorded. 4. NSF checks that were deposited were recorded on the books as increases in the cash account; thus, cash must be decreased and the related accounts receivable increased if payment is still expected.

Self-Study Quiz
Solutions

the continued success of Deckers' strategy. Both net sales and gross profit have increased 41 percent over 2006. You can evaluate the further success of Deckers' strategy by going to the Web at **www.deckers.com** to check Deckers' latest annual and quarterly reports.

DEMONSTRATION **CASE A**

(Complete the requirements before proceeding to the suggested solutions.) Wholesale Warehouse Stores sold $950,000 in merchandise during 2008, $400,000 of which was on credit with terms 2/10, n/30 (75 percent of these amounts were paid within the discount period), $500,000 was paid with credit cards (there was a 3 percent credit card discount), and the rest was paid in cash. On December 31, 2008, the Accounts Receivable balance was $80,000. The beginning balance in the Allowance for Doubtful Accounts was $9,000 and $6,000 of bad debts was written off during the year.

Required:

1. Compute net sales for 2008, assuming that sales and credit card discounts are treated as contra-revenues.

2. Assume that Wholesale uses the percentage of sales method for estimating bad debt expense and that it estimates that 2 percent of credit sales will produce bad debts. Record bad debt expense for 2008.

3. Assume instead that Wholesale uses the aging of accounts receivable method and that it estimates that $10,000 worth of current accounts is uncollectible. Record bad debt expense for 2008.

SUGGESTED SOLUTION

1. Both sales discounts and credit card discounts should be subtracted from sales revenues in the computation of net sales.

Sales revenue	$950,000
Less: Sales discounts (0.02 × 0.75 × $400,000)	6,000
Credit card discounts (0.03 × $500,000)	15,000
Net sales	$929,000

2. The percentage estimate of bad debts should be applied to credit sales. Cash sales never produce bad debts.

Bad debt expense (+E, −SE) (0.02 × $400,000)	8,000	
Allowance for doubtful accounts (+XA, −A)		8,000

Assets	=	Liabilities	+	Stockholders' Equity
Allowance for doubtful accounts −8,000				Bad debt expense −8,000

3. The entry made when using the aging of accounts receivable method is the estimated balance minus the current balance.

Estimated ending balance in Allowance for Doubtful Accounts	$10,000
Less: Current balance in Allowance for Doubtful Accounts ($9,000 − $6,000)	3,000
Bad Debt Expense for the year	$ 7,000

| Bad debt expense (+E, −SE) .... | 7,000 | |
| Allowance for doubtful accounts (+XA, −A) .... | | 7,000 |

Assets	=	Liabilities	+	Stockholders' Equity
Allowance for doubtful accounts −7,000				Bad debt expense −7,000

DEMONSTRATION **CASE B**

(Complete the requirements before proceeding to the suggested solution that follows.) Heather Ann Long, a freshman at a large state university, has just received her first checking account statement. This was her first chance to attempt a bank reconciliation. She had the following information to work with:

Bank balance, September 1	$1,150
Deposits during September	650
Checks cleared during September	900
Bank service charge	25
Bank balance, October 1	875

Heather was surprised that the deposit of $50 she made on September 29 had not been posted to her account and was pleased that her rent check of $200 had not cleared her account. Her checkbook balance was $750.

Required:

1. Complete Heather's bank reconciliation.

2. Why is it important for individuals such as Heather and businesses to do a bank reconciliation each month?

SUGGESTED SOLUTION

1. Heather's bank reconciliation:

Heather's Books		Bank Statement	
October 1 cash balance	$750	October 1 cash balance	$875
Additions		Additions	
None		Deposit in transit	50
Deductions		Deductions	
Bank service charge	(25)	Outstanding check	(200)
Correct cash balance	$725	Correct cash balance	$725

2. Bank statements, whether personal or business, should be reconciled each month. This process helps ensure that a correct balance is reflected in the customer's books. Failure to reconcile a bank statement increases the chance that an error will not be discovered and may result in bad checks being written. Businesses must reconcile their bank statements for an additional reason: The correct balance that is calculated during reconciliation is recorded on the balance sheet.

Chapter Supplement A

Recording Discounts and Returns

In this chapter, both **credit card discounts** and **cash discounts** have been recorded as contra-revenues. For example, if the credit card company is charging a 3 percent fee for its service and Internet credit card sales were $3,000 for January 2, Deckers records the following:

Cash (+A)	2,910	
Credit card discount (+XR, −R, −SE)	90	
Sales revenue (+R, +SE)		3,000

Assets		=	Liabilities	+	Stockholders' Equity	
Cash	+2,910				Sales revenue	+3,000
					Credit card discount	−90

Similarly, if credit sales of $1,000 are recorded with terms 2/10, n/30 ($1,000 × 0.98 = $980), and payment is made within the discount period, Deckers would record the following:

Accounts receivable (+A)	1,000	
Sales revenue (+R, +SE)		1,000

Assets		=	Liabilities	+	Stockholders' Equity	
Accounts receivable	+1,000				Sales revenue	+1,000

Cash (+A)	980	
Sales discount (+XR, −R, −SE)	20	
Accounts receivable (−A)		1,000

Assets		=	Liabilities	+	Stockholders' Equity	
Cash	+980				Sales discount	−20
Accounts receivable	−1,000					

Sales returns and allowances should always be treated as a contra-revenue. Assume that Fontana Shoes of Ithaca, New York, bought 40 pairs of sandals from Deckers for $2,000 on account. On the date of sale, Deckers makes the following journal entry:

Accounts receivable (+A)	2,000	
Sales revenue (+R, +SE)		2,000

Assets		=	Liabilities	+	Stockholders' Equity	
Accounts receivable	+2,000				Sales revenue	+2,000

Before paying for the sandals, Fontana discovered that 10 pairs of sandals were not the color ordered and returned them to Deckers. On that date Deckers records:

Sales returns and allowances (+XR, −R, −SE)	500	
Accounts receivable (−A)		500

Assets		=	Liabilities	+	Stockholders' Equity	
Accounts receivable	−500				Sales returns and allowances	−500

In addition, the related cost of goods sold entry for the 10 pairs of sandals would be reversed.

1. **Apply the revenue principle to determine the accepted time to record sales revenue for typical retailers, wholesalers, manufacturers, and service companies.   p. 284**

   Revenue recognition policies are widely recognized as one of the most important determinants of the fair presentation of financial statements. For most merchandisers and manufacturers, the required revenue recognition point is the time that title changes to the buyer (shipment or delivery of goods). For service companies, it is the time that services are provided.

2. **Analyze the impact of credit card sales, sales discounts, and sales returns on the amounts reported as net sales.   p. 285**

   Both **credit card discounts** and sales or **cash discounts** can be recorded either as contra-revenues or as expenses. When recorded as contra-revenues, they reduce net sales. **Sales returns and allowances,** which should always be treated as a contra-revenue, also reduce net sales.

3. **Analyze and interpret the gross profit percentage.   p. 288**

   Gross profit percentage measures the ability to charge premium prices and produce goods and services at lower cost. Managers, analysts, and creditors use this ratio to assess the effectiveness of the company's product development, marketing, and production strategy.

4. **Estimate, report, and evaluate the effects of uncollectible accounts receivable (bad debts) on financial statements.   p. 290**

   When receivables are material, companies must employ the allowance method to account for uncollectibles. These are the steps in the process:

   a. The end-of-period adjusting entry to record bad debt expense estimates.

   b. Writing off specific accounts determined to be uncollectible during the period.

   The adjusting entry reduces net income as well as net accounts receivable. The write-off affects neither.

5. **Analyze and interpret the accounts receivable turnover ratio and the effects of accounts receivable on cash flows.   p. 297**

   a. **Accounts receivable turnover ratio**—Measures the effectiveness of credit-granting and collection activities. It reflects how many times average trade receivables were recorded and collected during the period. Analysts and creditors watch this ratio because a sudden decline in it may mean that a company is extending payment deadlines in an attempt to prop up lagging sales or even is recording sales that later will be returned by customers.

   b. **Effects on cash flows**—When a net decrease in accounts receivable for the period occurs, cash collected from customers is always more than revenue, and cash flows from operations increases. When a net increase in accounts receivable occurs, cash collected from customers is always less than revenue. Thus, cash flows from operations declines.

6. **Report, control, and safeguard cash.   p. 299**

   Cash is the most liquid of all assets, flowing continually into and out of a business. As a result, a number of critical control procedures, including the reconciliation of bank accounts, should be applied. Also, management of cash may be critically important to decision makers who must have cash available to meet current needs yet must avoid excess amounts of idle cash that produce no revenue.

   Closely related to recording revenue is recording the cost of what was sold. Chapter 7 will focus on transactions related to inventory and cost of goods sold. This topic is important because cost of goods sold has a major impact on a company's gross profit and net income, which are watched closely by investors, analysts, and other users of financial statements. Increasing emphasis on quality, productivity, and costs have further focused production managers' attention on cost of goods sold and inventory. Since inventory cost figures play a major role in product introduction and pricing decisions, they also are important to marketing and general managers. Finally, since inventory accounting has a major effect on many companies' tax liabilities, this is an important place to introduce the effect of taxation on management decision making and financial reporting.

KEY **RATIOS**

Gross profit percentage measures the excess of sales prices over the costs to purchase or produce the goods or services sold as a percentage. It is computed as follows (p. 288):

$$\text{Gross Profit Percentage} = \frac{\text{Gross Profit}}{\text{Net Sales}}$$

Receivables turnover ratio measures the effectiveness of credit-granting and collection activities. It is computed as follows (p. 297):

$$\text{Receivables Turnover} = \frac{\text{Net Sales}}{\text{Average Net Trade Accounts Receivable}}$$

FINDING **FINANCIAL INFORMATION**

Balance Sheet
Under Current Assets
Accounts receivable (net of allowance for
  doubtful accounts)

Income Statement
Revenues
Net sales (sales revenue less discounts
  and sales returns and allowances)
Expenses
Selling expenses (including bad debt
  expense)

Statement of Cash Flows
Under Operating Activities (indirect method)
Net income
 + decreases in accounts receivable (net)
 − increases in accounts receivable (net)

Notes
*Under Summary of Significant Accounting
Policies*
Revenue recognition policy

Under a Separate Note on Form 10-K
Bad debt expense and write-offs of bad debts

KEY **TERMS**

Accounts Receivable
  (trade receivables or
  receivables) p. 290
**Aging of Accounts Receivable
  Method**   p. 295

Allowance for Doubtful Accounts
  (allowance for bad debts or
  allowance for uncollectible
  accounts)   p. 291
Allowance Method   p. 291

Bad Debt Expense (doubtful
  accounts expense, uncollectible
  accounts expense, or provision
  for uncollectible accounts)
  p. 291

Bank Reconciliation   p. 302
Bank Statement   p. 301
Cash   p. 299
Cash Equivalents   p. 299
Credit Card Discount   p. 285

Internal Controls   p. 300
Notes Receivable   p. 290
Percentage of Credit Sales
  Method   p. 294

Sales (or Cash) Discount   p. 286
Sales Returns and Allowances
  p. 287

QUESTIONS

1. Explain the difference between sales revenue and net sales.
2. What is gross profit or gross margin on sales? How is the gross profit ratio computed? In your explanation, assume that net sales revenue was $100,000 and cost of goods sold was $60,000.
3. What is a credit card discount? How does it affect amounts reported on the income statement?
4. What is a sales discount? Use 1/10, n/30 in your explanation.
5. What is the distinction between sales allowances and sales discounts?
6. Differentiate accounts receivable from notes receivable.
7. Which basic accounting principle is the allowance method of accounting for bad debts designed to satisfy?
8. Using the allowance method, is bad debt expense recognized in (a) the period in which sales related to the uncollectible account were made or (b) the period in which the seller learns that the customer is unable to pay?
9. What is the effect of the write-off of bad debts (using the allowance method) on (a) net income and (b) accounts receivable, net?
10. Does an increase in the receivables turnover ratio generally indicate faster or slower collection of receivables? Explain.
11. Define cash and cash equivalents in the context of accounting. Indicate the types of items that should be included and excluded.
12. Summarize the primary characteristics of an effective internal control system for cash.
13. Why should cash-handling and cash-recording activities be separated? How is this separation accomplished?
14. What are the purposes of a bank reconciliation? What balances are reconciled?
15. Briefly explain how the total amount of cash reported on the balance sheet is computed.
16. (Chapter Supplement A) Under the gross method of recording sales discounts discussed in this chapter, is the amount of sales discount taken recorded (a) at the time the sale is recorded or (b) at the time the collection of the account is recorded?

MULTIPLE-CHOICE QUESTIONS

1. Sales discounts with terms 2/10, n/30 mean:
   a. 10 percent discount for payment within 30 days.
   b. 2 percent discount for payment within 10 days or the full amount (less returns) is due within 30 days.
   c. Two-tenths of a percent discount for payment within 30 days.
   d. None of the above.
2. Gross sales total $250,000, one-half of which were credit sales. Sales returns and allowances of $15,000 apply to the credit sales, sales discounts of 2% were taken on all of the net credit sales, and credit card sales of $100,000 were subject to a credit card discount of 3%. What is the dollar amount of net sales?
   a. $227,000   c. $250,000
   b. $229,800   d. $240,000
3. A company has been successful in reducing the costs of its manufacturing process by relocating the factory to another locale. What effect will this factor have on the company's gross profit percentage ratio, all other things equal?
   a. The ratio will not change.   c. The ratio will decrease.
   b. The ratio will increase.   d. Either (b) or (c).

4. When a company using the allowance method writes off a specific customer's $100,000 account receivable from the accounting system, which of the following statements are true?
   1. Total stockholders' equity remains the same.
   2. Total assets remain the same.
   3. Total expenses remain the same.
   a. 2
   b. 1 and 3
   c. 1 and 2
   d. 1, 2, and 3

5. You have determined that Company X estimates bad debt expense with an aging of accounts receivable schedule. Company X's estimate of uncollectible receivables resulting from the aging analysis equals $250. The beginning balance in the allowance for doubtful accounts was $220. Write-offs of bad debts during the period were $180. What amount would be recorded as bad debt expense for the current period?
   a. $180
   b. $250
   c. $210
   d. $220

6. Upon review of the most recent bank statement, you discover that you recently received an "insufficient funds check" from a customer. Which of the following describes the actions to be taken when preparing your bank reconciliation?

	Balance per Books	Balance per Bank
a.	No change	Decrease
b.	Decrease	Increase
c.	Decrease	No change
d.	Increase	Decrease

7. Which of the following is **not** a step toward effective internal control over cash?
   a. Require signatures from a manager and one financial officer on all checks.
   b. Require that cash be deposited daily at the bank.
   c. Require that the person responsible for removing the cash from the register have no access to the accounting records.
   d. All of the above are steps toward effective internal control.

8. When using the allowance method, as bad debt expense is recorded,
   a. Total assets remain the same and stockholders' equity remains the same.
   b. Total assets decrease and stockholders' equity decreases.
   c. Total assets increase and stockholders' equity decreases.
   d. Total liabilities increase and stockholders' equity decreases.

9. Which of the following best describes the proper presentation of accounts receivable in the financial statements?
   a. Gross accounts receivable plus the allowance for doubtful accounts in the asset section of the balance sheet.
   b. Gross accounts receivable in the asset section of the balance sheet and the allowance for doubtful accounts in the expense section of the income statement.
   c. Gross accounts receivable less bad debt expense in the asset section of the balance sheet.
   d. Gross accounts receivable less the allowance for doubtful accounts in the asset section of the balance sheet.

10. Which of the following is not a component of net sales?
    a. Sales returns and allowances
    b. Sales discounts
    c. Cost of goods sold
    d. Credit card discounts

For more practice on more multiple-choice questions, go to the text website www.mhhe.com/libby6e.

MINI-EXERCISES

 Available with McGraw-Hill's Homework Manager

M6-1
L01

Interpreting the Revenue Principle

Indicate the most likely time you expect sales revenue to be recorded for each of the listed transactions.

Transaction	Point A	Point B
a. Airline tickets sold by an airline on a credit card	_____ Point of sale	_____ Completion of flight
b. Computer sold by mail order company on a credit card	_____ Shipment	_____ Delivery
c. Sale of inventory to a business customer on open account	_____ Shipment	_____ Collection of account

Reporting Net Sales with Sales Discounts

Merchandise invoiced at $9,500 is sold on terms 1/10, n/30. If the buyer pays within the discount period, what amount will be reported on the income statement as net sales?

M6-2
LO2

Reporting Net Sales with Sales Discounts, Credit Card Discounts, and Sales Returns

Total gross sales for the period include the following:

Credit card sales (discount 3%)	$8,400
Sales on account (1/15, n/60)	$10,500

Sales returns related to sales on account were $500. All returns were made before payment. One-half of the remaining sales on account was paid within the discount period. The company treats all discounts and returns as contra-revenues. What amount will be reported on the income statement as net sales?

M6-3
LO2

Computing and Interpreting the Gross Profit Percentage

Net sales for the period was $49,000 and cost of sales was $28,000. Compute gross profit percentage for the current year. What does this ratio measure?

M6-4
LO3

Recording Bad Debts

Prepare journal entries for each transaction listed.

a. During the period, bad debts are written off in the amount of $22,000.
b. At the end of the period, bad debt expense is estimated to be $13,000.

M6-5
LO4

Determining Financial Statement Effects of Bad Debts

Using the following categories, indicate the effects of the following transactions. Use + for increase and − for decrease and indicate the accounts affected and the amounts.

a. At the end of the period, bad debt expense is estimated to be $17,000.
b. During the period, bad debts are written off in the amount of $7,000.

M6-6
LO4

Assets	=	Liabilities	+	Stockholders' Equity

Determining the Effects of Credit Policy Changes on Receivables Turnover Ratio

Indicate the most likely effect of the following changes in credit policy on the receivables turnover ratio (+ for increase, − for decrease, and NE for no effect).

a. Granted credit with shorter payment deadlines.
b. Increased effectiveness of collection methods.
c. Granted credit to less creditworthy customers.

M6-7
LO5

Matching Reconciling Items to the Bank Reconciliation

Indicate whether the following items would be added (+) or subtracted (−) from the company's books or the bank statement during the construction of a bank reconciliation.

M6-8
LO6

Reconciling Item	Company's Books	Bank Statement
a. Outstanding checks		
b. Bank service charge		
c. Deposit in transit		

M6-9   **(Supplement A) Recording Sales Discounts**

A sale is made for $8,000; terms are 1/10, n/30. At what amount should the sale be recorded under the gross method of recording sales discounts? Give the required entry. Also give the collection entry, assuming that it is during the discount period.

EXERCISES

 Available with McGraw-Hill's Homework Manager

E6-1   **Reporting Net Sales with Credit Sales and Sales Discounts**

LO2

During the months of January and February, Gold Corporation sold goods to three customers. The sequence of events was as follows:

Jan.	6	Sold goods for $950 to S. Green and billed that amount subject to terms 2/10, n/30.
	6	Sold goods to M. Munoz for $600 and billed that amount subject to terms 2/10, n/30.
	14	Collected cash due from S. Green.
Feb.	2	Collected cash due from M. Munoz.
	28	Sold goods for $450 to R. Reynolds and billed that amount subject to terms 2/10, n/45.

Required:

Assuming that Sales Discounts is treated as a contra-revenue, compute net sales for the two months ended February 28.

E6-2   **Reporting Net Sales with Credit Sales, Sales Discounts, and Credit Card Sales**

LO2

The following transactions were selected from the records of Evergreen Company:

July	12	Sold merchandise to Customer R, who charged the $2,000 purchase on his Visa credit card. Visa charges Evergreen a 2 percent credit card fee.
	15	Sold merchandise to Customer S at an invoice price of $7,000; terms 3/10, n/30.
	20	Sold merchandise to Customer T at an invoice price of $5,000; terms 3/10, n/30.
	23	Collected payment from Customer S from July 15 sale.
Aug.	25	Collected payment from Customer T from July 20 sale.

Required:

Assuming that Sales Discounts and Credit Card Discounts are treated as contra-revenues, compute net sales for the two months ended August 31.

E6-3   **Reporting Net Sales with Credit Sales, Sales Discounts, Sales Returns, and Credit Card**
LO2   **Sales**

The following transactions were selected from among those completed by Clem Retailers in 2011:

Nov. 20   Sold two items of merchandise to Customer B, who charged the $350 sales price on her Visa credit card. Visa charges Clem Wholesalers a 2 percent credit card fee.

25   Sold 20 items of merchandise to Customer C at an invoice price of $4,500 (total); terms 3/10, n/30.

28   Sold 10 identical items of merchandise to Customer D at an invoice price of $9,000 (total); terms 3/10, n/30.

29   Customer D returned one of the items purchased on the 28th; the item was defective, and credit was given to the customer.

Dec. 6   Customer D paid the account balance in full.

30   Customer C paid in full for the invoice of November 25, 2011.

Required:

Assume that Sales Returns and Allowances, Sales Discounts, and Credit Card Discounts are treated as contra-revenues; compute net sales for the two months ended December 31, 2011.

Determining the Effects of Credit Sales, Sales Discounts, Credit Card Sales, and Sales Returns and Allowances on Income Statement Categories

E6-4
LO2

Rockland Shoe Company records Sales Returns and Allowances, Sales Discounts, and Credit Card Discounts as contra-revenues. Complete the following tabulation, indicating the effect (+ for increase, − for decrease, and NE for no effect) and amount of the effects of each transaction, including related cost of goods sold.

July 12   Sold merchandise to customer at factory store who charged the $400 purchase on her American Express card. American Express charges a 1 percent credit card fee. Cost of goods sold was $250.

July 15   Sold merchandise to Customer T at an invoice price of $4,000; terms 3/10, n/30. Cost of goods sold was $2,000.

July 20   Collected cash due from Customer T.

July 21   Before paying for the order, a customer returned shoes with an invoice price of $1,000, and cost of goods sold was $600.

Transaction	Net Sales	Cost of Goods Sold	Gross Profit
July 12			
July 15			
July 20			
July 21			

Evaluating the Annual Interest Rate Implicit in a Sales Discount with Discussion of Management Choice of Financing Strategy

E6-5
LO2

Laura's Landscaping bills customers subject to terms 4/10, n/60.

Required:

1. Compute the annual interest rate implicit in the sales discount. (Round to two decimal places.)
2. If his bank charges 15 percent interest, should the customer borrow from the bank so that he can take advantage of the discount? Explain your recommendation.

E6-6
LO3

Analyzing Gross Profit Percentage on the Basis of an Income Statement and Within-Industry Comparison

Wolverine World Wide Inc. prides itself as being the "world's leading marketer of U.S. branded non-athletic footwear." It competes in many markets with Deckers, often offering products at a lower price point. Its brands include Wolverine, Bates, Sebago, and Hush Puppies. The following data were taken from its recent annual report (dollars in thousands):

Sales of merchandise	$1,141,887
Income taxes	38,645
Cash dividends declared on common stock	16,504
Selling and administrative expense	318,243
Cost of products sold	700,349
Interest expense	2,973
Other income	1,970
Items not included in above amounts:	
Number of shares of common stock outstanding 55,030	

Required:

1. Based on these data, prepare an income statement (showing both gross profit and income from operations). There were no extraordinary items. Include a "percentage" column (see Chapter 5 for a discussion of common-size income statements and percentage analysis).
2. How much was the gross profit margin? What was the gross profit percentage ratio? Explain what these two amounts mean. Compare the gross profit percentage with that of Deckers. What do you believe accounts for the difference?

E6-7
LO2, 3, 4

Analyzing Gross Profit Percentage on the Basis of an Income Statement

The following summarized data were provided by the records of Slate, Incorporated, for the year ended December 31, 2010:

Sales of merchandise for cash	$223,000
Sales of merchandise on credit	40,000
Cost of goods sold	143,000
Selling expense	45,200
Administrative expense	20,000
Sales returns and allowances	8,000
Items not included in above amounts:	
Estimated bad debt loss, 3% of credit sales	
Average income tax rate, 30%	
Number of shares of common stock outstanding 4,000	

Required:

1. Based on these data, prepare an income statement (showing both gross profit and income from operations). Include a percentage analysis column. (See Chapter 5 for a discussion of common-size income statements and percentage analysis.)
2. What was the amount of gross profit margin? What was the gross profit percentage ratio? Explain what these two amounts mean.

E6-8
LO4

Recording Bad Debt Expense Estimates and Write-Offs Using the Percentage of Credit Sales Method

During 2009, Chun Productions, Inc., recorded credit sales of $700,000. Based on prior experience, it estimates a 1 percent bad debt rate on credit sales.

Required:
Prepare journal entries for each transaction:
a. The appropriate bad debt expense adjustment was recorded for the year 2009.
b. On December 31, 2009, an account receivable for $2,000 from March of the current year was determined to be uncollectible and was written off.

Recording Bad Debt Expense Estimates and Write-Offs Using the Percentage of Credit Sales Method

During 2011, Gonzales Electronics, Incorporated, recorded credit sales of $790,000. Based on prior experience, it estimates a 3 percent bad debt rate on credit sales.

Required:
Prepare journal entries for each transaction:
a. The appropriate bad debt expense adjustment was recorded for the year 2011.
b. On December 31, 2011, an account receivable for $240 from a prior year was determined to be uncollectible and was written off.

Determining Financial Statement Effects of Bad Debts Using the Percentage of Credit Sales Method

Using the following categories, indicate the effects of the transactions listed in E6–9. Use + for increase and − for decrease and indicate the accounts affected and the amounts.

Assets	=	Liabilities	+	Stockholders' Equity

Recording and Determining the Effects of Bad Debt Transactions on Income Statement Categories Using the Percentage of Credit Sales Method

During 2012, Kim and Silverman Electronics recorded credit sales of $640,000. Based on prior experience, it estimates a 3.5 percent bad debt rate on credit sales.

Required:
1. Prepare journal entries for each of the following transactions.
   a. The appropriate bad debt expense adjustment was recorded for the year 2012.
   b. On December 31, 2012, an account receivable for $1,800 from a prior year was determined to be uncollectible and was written off.
2. Complete the following tabulation, indicating the amount and effect (+ for increase, − for decrease, and NE for no effect) of each transaction.

Transaction	Net Sales	Gross Profit	Income from Operations
a.			
b.			

Computing Bad Debt Expense Using Aging Analysis

Brown Cow Dairy uses the aging approach to estimate bad debt expense. The balance of each account receivable is aged on the basis of three time periods as follows: (1) not yet due $14,000, (2) up to 120 days past due $4,500, and (3) more than 120 days past due $2,500. Experience has shown that for each age group, the average loss rate on the amount of the receivables at year-end due to uncollectability is (1) 2 percent, (2) 12 percent, and (3) 30 percent, respectively. At December 31, 2011 (end of the current year), the Allowance for Doubtful Accounts balance was $800 (credit) before the end-of-period adjusting entry is made.

Required:
What amount should be recorded as Bad Debt Expense for the current year?

Recording and Reporting a Bad Debt Estimate Using Aging Analysis

Arias Company uses the aging approach to estimate bad debt expense. The balance of each account receivable is aged on the basis of three time periods as follows: (1) not yet due $60,000, (2) up to 180 days past due $12,000, and (3) more than 180 days past due $4,000. Experience has shown that for each age group, the average loss rate on the amount of the receivables at year-end due to uncollectability is (1) 3 percent, (2) 15 percent, and (3) 35 percent, respectively. At December 31, 2011 (end of the current year), the Allowance for Doubtful Accounts balance was $200 (credit) before the end-of-period adjusting entry is made.

Required:
1. Prepare the appropriate bad debt expense adjusting entry for the year 2011.
2. Show how the various accounts related to accounts receivable should be shown on the December 31, 2011 balance sheet.

E6-14
LO4

Recording and Reporting a Bad Debt Estimate Using Aging Analysis

Bhojraj Company uses the aging approach to estimate bad debt expense. The balance of each account receivable is aged on the basis of three time periods as follows: (1) not yet due $250,000, (2) up to 120 days past due $50,000, and (3) more than 120 days past due $30,000. Experience has shown that for each age group, the average loss rate on the amount of the receivables at year-end due to uncollectability is (1) 3.5 percent, (2) 10 percent, and (3) 30 percent, respectively. At December 31, 2010 (end of the current year), the Allowance for Doubtful Accounts balance was $400 (credit) before the end-of-period adjusting entry is made.

Required:
1. Prepare the appropriate bad debt expense adjusting entry for the year 2010.
2. Show how the various accounts related to accounts receivable should be shown on the December 31, 2010 balance sheet.

E6-15
LO4
Siemens AG

Interpreting Bad Debt Disclosures

Siemens is one of the world's largest electrical engineering and electronics companies. Headquartered in Germany, the company has been in business for over 160 years and operates in 190 countries. In a recent filing pursuant to its listing on the New York Stock Exchange, it disclosed the following information concerning its allowance for doubtful accounts (Euros in millions denoted as €):

Balance at Beginning of Period	Charged to Costs and Expenses	Amounts Written Off	Balance at End of Period
1,199	207	(450)	956

Required:
1. Record summary journal entries related to the allowance for doubtful accounts for the current year.
2. If Siemens had written off an additional €10 million of accounts receivable during the period, how would receivables, net, and net income have been affected? Explain why.

E6-16
LO4
Microsoft

Inferring Bad Debt Write-Offs and Cash Collections from Customers

Microsoft develops, produces, and markets a wide range of computer software including the Windows operating system. On its recent financial statements, Microsoft reported the following information about net sales revenue and accounts receivable.

	Current Year	Prior Year
Accounts receivable, net of allowances of $117 and $142	$11,338	$ 9,316
Net revenues	51,122	44,282

According to its Form 10-K, Microsoft recorded bad debt expense of $64 and did not reinstate any previously written-off accounts during the current year. (**Hint:** Refer to the summary of the effects of accounting for bad debts on the Accounts Receivable (Gross) and the Allowance for Doubtful Accounts t-accounts. Use the t-accounts to solve for the missing values.)

Required:
1. What amount of bad debts was written off during the current year?
2. Based on your answer to requirement (1), solve for cash collected from customers for the current year assuming that all of Microsoft's sales during the period were on open account.

Inferring Bad Debt Expense and Determining the Impact of Uncollectible Accounts on Income and Working Capital

A recent annual report for Target contained the following information (dollars in thousands) at the end of its fiscal year:

	Year 1	Year 2
Accounts receivable	$5,992,000	$5,964,000
Allowance for doubtful accounts	(399,000)	(419,000)
	$5,593,000	$5,545,000

E6-17
LO4
Target

A footnote to the financial statements disclosed that uncollectible accounts amounting to $322,000 were written off as bad debts during year 1 and $512,000 during year 2. Assume that the tax rate for Target was 30 percent.

Required:
1. Determine the bad debt expense for year 2 based on the preceding facts. (**Hint:** Use the allowance for doubtful accounts T-account to solve for the missing value.)
2. **Working capital** is defined as current assets minus current liabilities. How was Target's working capital affected by the write-off of $512,000 in uncollectible accounts during year 2? What impact did the recording of bad debt expense have on working capital in year 2?
3. How was net income affected by the $512,000 write-off during year 2? What impact did recording bad debt expense have on net income for year 2?

Recording, Reporting, and Evaluating a Bad Debt Estimate

During 2011, Martin's Camera Shop had sales revenue of $150,000, of which $75,000 was on credit. At the start of 2011, Accounts Receivable showed a $13,000 debit balance, and the Allowance for Doubtful Accounts showed an $800 credit balance. Collections of accounts receivable during 2011 amounted to $60,000.
   Data during 2011 follows:
a. On December 31, 2011, an Account Receivable (J. Doe) of $1,700 from a prior year was determined to be uncollectible; therefore, it was written off immediately as a bad debt.
b. On December 31, 2011, on the basis of experience, a decision was made to continue the accounting policy of basing estimated bad debt losses on 1.5 percent of credit sales for the year.

E6-18
LO4

Required:
1. Give the required journal entries for the two items on December 31, 2011 (end of the accounting period).
2. Show how the amounts related to Accounts Receivable and Bad Debt Expense would be reported on the income statement and balance sheet for 2011. Disregard income tax considerations.
3. On the basis of the data available, does the 1.5 percent rate appear to be reasonable? Explain.

Computing and Interpreting the Receivables Turnover Ratio

A recent annual report for FedEx contained the following data:

E6-19
LO5
FedEx

	(dollars in thousands)	
	Current Year	Previous Year
Accounts receivable	$ 3,178,000	$2,776,000
Less: Allowance for doubtful accounts	151,000	149,000
Net accounts receivable	$ 3,027,000	$2,627,000
Net sales (assume all on credit)	$24,710,000	

Required:
1. Determine the accounts receivable turnover ratio and average days sales in receivables for the current year.
2. Explain the meaning of each number.

E6-20
LO5

Computing and Interpreting the Receivables Turnover Ratio

A recent annual report for Dell, Inc., contained the following data:

	(dollars in thousands)	
	Current Year	Previous Year
Accounts receivable	$ 4,748,000	$4,179,000
Less: Allowance for doubtful accounts	126,000	97,000
Net accounts receivable	$ 4,622,000	$4,082,000
Net sales (assume all on credit)	$57,420,000	

Required:
1. Determine the accounts receivable turnover ratio and average days sales in receivables for the current year.
2. Explain the meaning of each number.

E6-21
LO5
Stride Rite

Interpreting the Effects of Sales Declines and Changes in Receivables on Cash Flow from Operations

Stride Rite Corporation manufactures and markets shoes under the brand names Stride Rite®, Keds®, and Sperry Top-Sider®. Three recent years produced a combination of declining sales revenue and net income culminating in a net loss of $8,430,000. Each year, however, Stride Rite was able to report positive cash flows from operations. Contributing to that positive cash flow was the change in accounts receivable. The current and prior year balance sheets reported the following:

	(dollars in thousands)	
	Current Year	Previous Year
Accounts and notes receivable, less allowances	$48,066	$63,403

Required:
1. On the current year's cash flow statement (indirect method), how would the change in accounts receivable affect cash flow from operations? Explain why it would have this effect.
2. Explain how declining sales revenue often leads to (a) declining accounts receivable and (b) cash collections from customers being higher than sales revenue.

E6-22
LO5
Apple

Interpreting the Effects of Sales Growth and Changes in Receivables on Cash Flow from Operations

Apple, Inc., is best known for its Mac and iPod product lines. Three recent years produced a pattern of strong increases in sales revenue and net income. Cash flows from operations declined in the middle of the period, however. Contributing to that declining cash flow was the change in accounts receivable. The current and prior year balance sheets reported the following:

	(dollars in thousands)	
	Current Year	Previous Year
Accounts receivable, less allowances for doubtful accounts	$707,000	$534,000

Required:
1. On the current year's cash flow statement (indirect method), how would the change in accounts receivable affect cash flow from operations? Explain why it would have this effect.
2. Explain how increasing sales revenue often leads to (a) increasing accounts receivable and thus (b) cash collections from customers being lower than sales revenue.

Preparing Bank Reconciliation, Entries, and Reporting Cash

Jones Company has the June 30, 2010, bank statement and the June ledger accounts for cash, which are summarized here:

BANK STATEMENT			
	Checks	Deposits	Balance
Balance, June 1, 2010			$ 6,900
Deposits during June		$16,200	23,100
Checks cleared during June	$17,000		6,100
Bank service charges	40		6,060
Balance, June 30, 2010			6,060

Cash (A)					
June 1	Balance	6,900	June	Checks written	18,000
June	Deposits	19,100			

Required:
1. Reconcile the bank account. A comparison of the checks written with the checks that have cleared the bank shows outstanding checks of $1,000. A deposit of $2,900 is in transit at the end of June.
2. Give any journal entries that should be made as a result of the bank reconciliation.
3. What is the balance in the Cash account after the reconciliation entries?
4. What is the total amount of cash that should be reported on the balance sheet at June 30?

Preparing Bank Reconciliation, Entries, and Reporting Cash

The September 30, 2011, bank statement for Russell Company and the September ledger accounts for cash are summarized here:

BANK STATEMENT			
	Checks	Deposits	Balance
Balance, September 1, 2011			$ 6,000
Deposits recorded during September		$27,400	33,400
Checks cleared during September	$28,400		5,000
NSF checks—Betty Brown	170		4,830
Bank service charges	60		4,770
Balance, September 30, 2011			4,770

Cash (A)					
Sept. 1	Balance	6,000	Sept.	Checks written	28,900
Sept.	Deposits	28,600			

No outstanding checks and no deposits in transit were carried over from August; however, there are deposits in transit and checks outstanding at the end of September.

Required:
1. Reconcile the bank account.
2. Give any journal entries that should be made as the result of the bank reconciliation.
3. What should the balance in the Cash account be after the reconciliation entries?
4. What total amount of cash should the company report on the September 30 balance sheet?

E6-25   **(Supplement A) Recording Credit Sales, Sales Discounts, Sales Returns, and Credit Card Sales**

The following transactions were selected from among those completed by Hailey Retailers in 2010:

> Nov. 20   Sold two items of merchandise to Customer B, who charged the $450 sales price on her Visa credit card. Visa charges Hailey a 2 percent credit card fee.
>
> 25   Sold 14 items of merchandise to Customer C at an invoice price of $2,800 (total); terms 2/10, n/30.
>
> 28   Sold 12 identical items of merchandise to Customer D at an invoice price of $7,200 (total); terms 2/10, n/30.
>
> 30   Customer D returned one of the items purchased on the 28th; the item was defective, and credit was given to the customer.
>
> Dec. 6   Customer D paid the account balance in full.
>
> 30   Customer C paid in full for the invoice of November 25, 2010.

Required:
Give the appropriate journal entry for each of these transactions, assuming the company records sales revenue under the gross method. Do not record cost of goods sold.

PROBLEMS

 Available with McGraw-Hill's Homework Manager

P6-1
LO1

Applying the Revenue Principle

At what point should revenue be recognized in each of the following independent cases?

Case A. For Christmas presents, a McDonald's restaurant sells coupon books for $10. Each of the $1 coupons may be used in the restaurant any time during the following 12 months. The customer must pay cash when purchasing the coupon book.

Case B. Howard Land Development Corporation sold a lot to Quality Builders to construct a new home. The price of the lot was $50,000. Quality made a down payment of $100 and agreed to pay the balance in six months. After making the sale, Howard learned that Quality Builders often entered into these agreements but refused to pay the balance if it did not find a customer who wanted a house built on the lot.

Case C. Driscoll Corporation has always recorded revenue at the point of sale of its refrigerators. Recently, it has extended its warranties to cover all repairs for a period of seven years. One young accountant with the company now questions whether Driscoll has completed its earning process when it sells the refrigerators. She suggests that the warranty obligation for seven years means that a significant amount of additional work must be performed in the future.

P6-2
LO2, 4

Reporting Net Sales and Expenses with Discounts, Returns, and Bad Debts (AP6–1)

The following data were selected from the records of Larker Company for the year ended December 31, 2010.

> Balances January 1, 2010
> | | |
> |---|---|
> | Accounts receivable (various customers) | $115,000 |
> | Allowance for doubtful accounts | 7,000 |

In the following order, except for cash sales, the company sold merchandise and made collections on credit terms 2/10, n/30 (assume a unit sales price of $500 in all transactions and use the gross method to record sales revenue).

Transactions during 2010

a. Sold merchandise for cash, $234,000.
b. Sold merchandise to R. Jones; invoice price, $13,000.

c. Sold merchandise to K. Black; invoice price, $25,000.

d. Two days after purchase date, R. Jones returned one of the units purchased in (b) and received account credit.

e. Sold merchandise to B. Sears; invoice price, $24,500.

f. R. Jones paid his account in full within the discount period.

g. Collected $98,000 cash from customer sales on credit in prior year, all within the discount periods.

h. K. Black paid the invoice in (c) within the discount period.

i. Sold merchandise to R. Roy; invoice price, $17,500.

j. Three days after paying the account in full, K. Black returned seven defective units and received a cash refund.

k. After the discount period, collected $6,000 cash on an account receivable on sales in a prior year.

l. Wrote off a 2009 account of $3,000 after deciding that the amount would never be collected.

m. The estimated bad debt rate used by the company was 1.5 percent of credit sales net of returns.

Required:

1. Using the following categories, indicate the effect of each listed transaction, including the write-off of the uncollectible account and the adjusting entry for estimated bad debts (ignore cost of goods sold). Indicate the sign and amount of the effect or "NE" for "no effect".

	Sales Revenue	Sales Discounts (taken)	Sales Returns and Allowances	Bad Debt Expense
(a)	$234,000	NE	NE	NE

2. Show how the accounts related to the preceding sale and collection activities should be reported on the 2010 income statement. (Treat sales discounts as a contra-revenue.)

Understanding the Income Statement Based on the Gross Profit Percentage

P6-3
LO3

The following data presented in income statement order were taken from the year-end records of Nomura Export Company. You are to fill in all of the missing amounts. Show computations. (**Hint:** In Case B, start from the bottom.)

eXcel
www.mhhe.com/libby6e

Income Statement Items	Independent Cases	
	Case A	Case B
Gross sales revenue	$239,000	$165,000
Sales returns and allowances	20,000	?
Net sales revenue	?	?
Cost of goods sold	?	(70%)?
Gross profit	(30%)?	?
Operating expenses	?	18,600
Pretax income	22,000	?
Income tax expense (20%)	?	?
Income before extraordinary items	?	?
Extraordinary gain (loss)	(2,000)	10,000
Less: Income tax (20% of extraordinary item)	?	?
Net income	?	?
EPS (10,000 shares)	?	$2.30

Recording Bad Debts and Interpreting Disclosure of Allowance for Doubtful Accounts
(AP6–2)

P6-4
LO4
Peet's Coffee & Tea

Peet's Coffee & Tea, Inc. is a specialty coffee roaster and marketer of branded fresh roasted whole bean coffee. It recently disclosed the following information concerning the Allowance for Doubtful Accounts on its Form 10-K Annual Report submitted to the Securities and Exchange Commission.

A summary of the Allowance for Doubtful Accounts is as follows (dollars in thousands)

Allowance for Doubtful Accounts:	Balance at Beginning of Period	Additions (Charges) to Expense	Write-offs	Balance at End of Period
Year 1	$61	$?	$ 15	$69
Year 2	69	30	?	58
Year 3	58	162	145	75

Required:
1. Record summary journal entries related to bad debts for year 3.
2. Supply the missing dollar amounts noted by (?) for year 1 and year 2.

P6-5
LO4

Determining Bad Debt Expense Based on Aging Analysis (AP6–3)

Blue Skies Equipment Company uses the aging approach to estimate bad debt expense at the end of each accounting year. Credit sales occur frequently on terms n/60. The balance of each account receivable is aged on the basis of three time periods as follows: (1) not yet due, (2) up to one year past due, and (3) more than one year past due. Experience has shown that for each age group, the average loss rate on the amount of the receivable at year-end due to uncollectability is (a) 2 percent, (b) 7 percent, and (c) 30 percent, respectively.

At December 31, 2011 (end of the current accounting year), the Accounts Receivable balance was $46,700, and the Allowance for Doubtful Accounts balance was $920 (credit). In determining which accounts have been paid, the company applies collections to the oldest sales first. To simplify, only five customer accounts are used; the details of each on December 31, 2011, follow:

B. Brown—Account Receivable				
Date	Explanation	Debit	Credit	Balance
3/11/2010	Sale	13,000		13,000
6/30/2010	Collection		4,000	9,000
1/31/2011	Collection		3,800	5,200

D. Donalds—Account Receivable				
2/28/2011	Sale	21,000		21,000
4/15/2011	Collection		8,000	13,000
11/30/2011	Collection		5,000	8,000

N. Napier—Account Receivable				
11/30/2011	Sale	8,000		8,000
12/15/2011	Collection		1,000	7,000

S. Strothers—Account Receivable				
3/2/2009	Sale	4,000		4,000
4/15/2009	Collection		4,000	–0–
9/1/2010	Sale	9,000		9,000
10/15/2010	Collection		4,500	4,500
2/1/2011	Sale	21,000		25,500
3/1/2011	Collection		5,000	20,500
12/31/2011	Sale	2,000		22,500

T. Thomas—Account Receivable				
12/30/2011	Sale	4,000		4,000

Required:
1. Compute the total accounts receivable in each age category.
2. Compute the estimated uncollectible amount for each age category and in total.
3. Give the adjusting entry for bad debt expense at December 31, 2011.
4. Show how the amounts related to accounts receivable should be presented on the 2011 income statement and balance sheet.

Preparing an Income Statement and Computing the Gross Profit Percentage and Receivables Turnover Ratio with Discounts, Returns, and Bad Debts (AP6–4)

P6-6
LO2, 3, 4, 5
eXcel
www.mhhe.com/libby6e

Builders Company, Inc., sells heavy construction equipment. There are 10,000 shares of capital stock outstanding. The annual fiscal period ends on December 31. The following condensed trial balance was taken from the general ledger on December 31, 2009:

Account Titles	Debit	Credit
Cash	$ 33,600	
Accounts receivable (net)	14,400	
Inventory, ending	52,000	
Operational assets	40,000	
Accumulated depreciation		$ 16,800
Liabilities		24,000
Capital stock		72,000
Retained earnings, January 1, 2009		9,280
Sales revenue		145,600
Sales returns and allowances	5,600	
Cost of goods sold	78,400	
Selling expense	13,600	
Administrative expense	14,400	
Bad debt expense	1,600	
Sales discounts	6,400	
Income tax expense	7,680	
Totals	$267,680	$267,680

Required:

1. Beginning with the amount for net sales, prepare an income statement (showing both gross profit and income from operations). Treat sales discounts and sales returns and allowances as a contra-revenue.
2. The beginning balance in Accounts Receivable (net) was $16,000. Compute the gross profit percentage and receivables turnover ratio and explain their meaning.

Preparing a Bank Reconciliation and Related Journal Entries

P6-7
LO6
eXcel
www.mhhe.com/libby6e

The bookkeeper at Hopkins Company has not reconciled the bank statement with the Cash account, saying, "I don't have time." You have been asked to prepare a reconciliation and review the procedures with the bookkeeper.

The April 30, 2010, bank statement and the April ledger accounts for cash showed the following (summarized):

BANK STATEMENT			
	Checks	Deposits	Balance
Balance, April 1, 2010			$31,000
Deposits during April		$36,100	67,100
Interest collected		1,180	68,280
Checks cleared during April	$44,500		23,780
NSF check—A. B. Wright	160		23,620
Bank service charges	70		23,550
Balance, April 30, 2010			23,550

Cash (A)					
Apr. 1	Balance	23,500	Apr.	Checks written	41,100
Apr.	Deposits	41,500			

A comparison of checks written before and during April with the checks cleared through the bank showed outstanding checks at the end of April of $4,100. No deposits in transit were carried over from March, but a deposit was in transit at the end of April.

Required:
1. Prepare a detailed bank reconciliation for April.
2. Give any required journal entries as a result of the reconciliation. Why are they necessary?
3. What was the balance in the cash account in the ledger on May 1, 2010?
4. What total amount of cash should be reported on the balance sheet at the end of April?

P6-8
L06

Computing Outstanding Checks and Deposits in Transit and Preparing a Bank Reconciliation and Journal Entries (AP6-5)

www.mhhe.com/libby6e

The August 2011 bank statement for Hirst Company and the August 2011 ledger account for cash follow:

BANK STATEMENT			
Date	Checks	Deposits	Balance
Aug. 1			$17,510
2	$320		17,190
3		$11,700	28,890
4	430		28,460
5	270		28,190
9	880		27,310
10	250		27,060
15		4,000	31,060
21	350		30,710
24	20,400		10,310
25		6,500	16,810
30	850		15,960
30		2,150*	18,110
31	120†		17,990

*$2,150 interest collected.
†Bank service charge.

Cash (A)				
Aug. 1 Balance	16,490	Checks written		
Deposits		Aug. 2		250
Aug. 2	11,700	4		880
12	4,000	15		280
24	6,500	17		510
31	5,200	18		850
		20		350
		23		20,400

Outstanding checks at the end of July were for $270, $430, and $320. No deposits were in transit at the end of July.

Required:
1. Compute the deposits in transit at the end of August by comparing the deposits on the bank statement to the deposits listed on the cash ledger account.
2. Compute the outstanding checks at the end of August by comparing the checks listed on the bank statement with those on the cash ledger account and list of outstanding checks at the end of July.
3. Prepare a bank reconciliation for August.
4. Give any journal entries that the company should make as a result of the bank reconciliation. Why are they necessary?
5. What total amount of cash should be reported on the August 31, 2011, balance sheet?

(Supplement A) Recording Sales, Returns, and Bad Debts   **P6-9**

Use the data presented in P6–2, which was selected from the records of Larker Company for the year ended December 31, 2010.

Required:
1. Give the journal entries for these transactions, including the write-off of the uncollectible account and the adjusting entry for estimated bad debts. Do not record cost of goods sold. Show computations for each entry.
2. Show how the accounts related to the preceding sale and collection activities should be reported on the 2010 income statement. (Treat sales discounts as a contra-revenue.)

ALTERNATE PROBLEMS

Reporting Net Sales and Expenses with Discounts, Returns, and Bad Debts (P6-2)   **AP6-1**
                                                                                        LO2, 4
The following data were selected from the records of Sharkim Company for the year ended December 31, 2012.

Balances January 1, 2012:	
Accounts receivable (various customers)	$116,000
Allowance for doubtful accounts	5,200

In the following order, except for cash sales, the company sold merchandise and made collections on credit terms 2/10, n/30 (assume a unit sales price of $500 in all transactions and use the gross method to record sales revenue).

Transactions during 2012
a. Sold merchandise for cash, $227,000.
b. Sold merchandise to Abbey Corp; invoice price, $12,000.
c. Sold merchandise to Brown Company; invoice price, $23,500.
d. Abbey paid the invoice in (b) within the discount period.
e. Sold merchandise to Cavendish Inc; invoice price, $26,000.
f. Two days after paying the account in full, Abbey returned one defective unit and received a cash refund.
g. Collected $78,400 cash from customer sales on credit in prior year, all within the discount periods.
h. Three days after purchase date, Brown returned seven of the units purchased in (c) and received account credit.
i. Brown paid its account in full within the discount period.
j. Sold merchandise to Decca Corporation; invoice price, $18,500.
k. Cavendish paid its account in full after the discount period.
l. Wrote off a 2008 account of $2,400 after deciding that the amount would never be collected.
m. The estimated bad debt rate used by the company was 3 percent of credit sales net of returns.

Required:
1. Using the following categories, indicate the effect of each listed transaction, including the write-off of the uncollectible account and the adjusting entry for estimated bad debts (ignore cost of goods sold). Indicate the sign and amount of the effect or "NE" for "no effect."

	Sales Revenue	Sales Discounts (taken)	Sales Returns and Allowances	Bad Debt Expense
(a)	+227,000	NE	NE	NE

2. Show how the accounts related to the preceding sale and collection activities should be reported on the 2012 income statement. (Treat sales discounts as a contra-revenue.)

AP6-2
L04
Saucony, Inc.

Recording Bad Debts and Interpreting Disclosure of Allowance for Doubtful Accounts (P6-4)

Under various registered brand names, Saucony, Inc., and its subsidiaries develop, manufacture, and market bicycles and component parts, athletic apparel, and athletic shoes. It recently disclosed the following information concerning the allowance for doubtful accounts on its Form 10-K Annual Report submitted to the Securities and Exchange Commission.

Schedule II				
Valuation and Qualifying Accounts (dollars in thousands)				
Allowances for Doubtful Accounts	Balance at Beginning of Year	Additions Charged to Costs and Expenses	Deductions from Reserve	Balance at End of Year
Year 3	$2,032	$4,908	$5,060	(?)
Year 2	1,234	(?)	4,677	$2,032
Year 1	940	5,269	(?)	1,234

Required:
1. Record summary journal entries related to bad debts for year 3.
2. Supply the missing dollar amounts noted by (?) for year 1, year 2, and year 3.

AP6-3
L04

Determining Bad Debt Expense Based on Aging Analysis (P6-5)

Briggs & Stratton Engines Inc. uses the aging approach to estimate bad debt expense at the end of each accounting year. Credit sales occur frequently on terms n/45. The balance of each account receivable is aged on the basis of four time periods as follows: (1) not yet due, (2) up to 6 months past due, (3) 6 to 12 months past due, and (4) more than one year past due. Experience has shown that for each age group, the average loss rate on the amount of the receivable at year-end due to uncollectability is (a) 1 percent, (b) 5 percent, (c) 20 percent, and (d) 50 percent, respectively.

At December 31, 2011 (end of the current accounting year), the Accounts Receivable balance was $39,500, and the Allowance for Doubtful Accounts balance was $1,550 (credit). In determining which accounts have been paid, the company applies collections to the oldest sales first. To simplify, only five customer accounts are used; the details of each on December 31, 2011, follow:

Date	Explanation	Debit	Credit	Balance
	R. Devens—Account Receivable			
3/13/2011	Sale	19,000		19,000
5/12/2011	Collection		10,000	9,000
9/30/2011	Collection		7,000	2,000
	C. Howard—Account Receivable			
11/01/2010	Sale	31,000		31,000
06/01/2011	Collection		20,000	11,000
12/01/2011	Collection		5,000	6,000
	D. Mclain—Account Receivable			
10/31/2011	Sale	12,000		12,000
12/10/2011	Collection		8,000	4,000

T. Skibinski—Account Receivable				
05/02/2011	Sale	15,000		15,000
06/01/2011	Sale	10,000		25,000
06/15/2011	Collection		15,000	10,000
07/15/2011	Collection		10,000	0
10/01/2011	Sale	26,000		26,000
11/15/2011	Collection		16,000	10,000
12/15/2011	Sale	4,500		14,500
H. Wu—Account Receivable				
12/30/2011	Sale	13,000		13,000

Required:
1. Compute the total accounts receivable in each age category.
2. Compute the estimated uncollectible amount for each age category and in total.
3. Give the adjusting entry for bad debt expense at December 31, 2011.
4. Show how the amounts related to accounts receivable should be presented on the 2011 income statement and balance sheet.

Preparing an Income Statement and Computing the Gross Profit Percentage and Receivables Turnover Ratio with Discounts, Returns, and Bad Debts (P6-6)   **AP6-4**   **LO2, 3, 4, 5**

Rang Corporation is a local grocery store organized seven years ago as a corporation. At that time, a total of 10,000 shares of common stock were issued to the three organizers. The store is in an excellent location, and sales have increased each year. At the end of 2012, the bookkeeper prepared the following statement (assume that all amounts are correct; note the incorrect terminology and format):

RANG CORPORATION
Profit and Loss
December 31, 2012

	Debit	Credit
Sales		$182,000
Cost of goods sold	$ 98,000	
Sales returns and allowances	7,000	
Selling expense	17,000	
Administrative and general expense	18,000	
Bad debt expense	2,000	
Sales discounts	8,000	
Income tax expense	9,600	
Net profit	22,400	
Totals	$182,000	$182,000

Required:
1. Beginning with the amount of net sales, prepare an income statement (showing both gross profit and income from operations). Treat sales discounts as an expense.
2. The beginning and ending balances in accounts receivable were $16,000 and $18,000, respectively. Compute the gross profit percentage and receivables turnover ratio and explain their meaning.

AP6-5
L06

Computing Outstanding Checks and Deposits in Transit and Preparing a Bank Reconciliation and Journal Entries (P6-8)

The December 31, 2011, bank statement for Packer Company and the December 2011 ledger accounts for cash follow.

BANK STATEMENT			
Date	Checks	Deposits	Balance
Dec. 1			$48,000
2	$400; 300	$17,000	64,300
4	7,000; 90		57,210
6	120; 180; 1,600		55,310
11	500; 1,200; 70	28,000	81,540
13	480; 700; 1,900		78,460
17	12,000; 8,000		58,460
23	60; 23,500	36,000	70,900
26	900; 2,650		67,350
28	2,200; 5,200		59,950
30	17,000; 1,890; 300*	19,000	59,760
31	1,650; 1,350; 150†	5,250‡	61,860

*NSF check, J. Left, a customer.
†Bank service charge.
‡Interest collected.

Cash (A)					
Dec. 1 Balance	64,100	Checks written during December:			
Deposits		60	5,000	2,650	
Dec. 11	28,000	17,000	5,200	1,650	
23	36,000	700	1,890	2,200	
30	19,000	3,300	1,600	7,000	
31	13,000	1,350	120	300	
		180	90	480	
		12,000	23,500	8,000	
		70	500	1,900	
		900	1,200		

The November 2011 bank reconciliation showed the following: correct cash balance at November 30, $64,100; deposits in transit on November 30, $17,000; and outstanding checks on November 30, $400 + $500 = $900.

Required:
1. Compute the deposits in transit December 31, 2011, by comparing the deposits on the bank statement to the deposits listed on the cash ledger account and the list of deposits in transit at the end of November.
2. Compute the outstanding checks at December 31, 2011, by comparing the checks listed on the bank statement with those on the cash ledger account and list of outstanding checks at the end of November.

3. Prepare a bank reconciliation at December 31, 2011.
4. Give any journal entries that should be made as a result of the bank reconciliation made by the company. Why are they necessary?
5. What total amount of cash should be reported on the December 31, 2011, balance sheet?

CASES **AND PROJECTS**

Annual Report Cases

Finding Financial Information

Refer to the financial statements of American Eagle Outfitters given in Appendix B at the end of this book.

Required:

1. What does the company include in its category of cash and cash equivalents? How close do you think the disclosed amount is to actual fair market value? (**Hint:** The notes may be helpful in answering this question.)
2. What expenses does American Eagle Outfitters subtract from net sales in the computation of gross profit? How does this differ from Deckers' practice and how might it affect the manner in which you interpret the gross profit percentage?
3. Compute American Eagle Outfitters' receivables turnover ratio for the year ended February 3, 2007. What characteristics of its business might cause it to be so high?
4. Does the company report an allowance for doubtful accounts on the balance sheet or in the notes? Explain why it does or does not. (**Hint:** Consider the makeup of its receivables.)

CP6-1
LO3, 5, 6

AMERICAN EAGLE
OUTFITTERS

Finding Financial Information

Refer to the financial statements of Urban Outfitters given in Appendix C at the end of this book.

Required:

1. How much cash and cash equivalents does the company report at the end of the current year?
2. What was the change in accounts receivable and how did it affect net cash provided by operating activities for the current year?
3. Compute the company's gross profit percentage for the most recent two years. Has it risen or fallen? Explain the meaning of the change.
4. Where does the company disclose its revenue recognition policy? When does the company record revenues for the "sale" of gift cards?

CP6-2
LO1, 3, 4, 6
Urban Outfitters

Comparing Companies within an Industry

Refer to the financial statements of American Eagle Outfitters given in Appendix B, Urban Outfitters given in Appendix C, and the Industry Ratio Report given in Appendix D at the end of this book.

Required:

1. Compute gross profit percentage for both companies for the current and previous years. What do these changes suggest?
2. Knowing that these two companies are specialty, or niche, retailers compared to some others in their industry (see the list of companies used in the Industry Ratio Report), do you expect their gross profit percentage to be higher or lower than the industry average? Why?
3. Compare the gross profit percentage for each company for the most recent reporting year to the industry average. Are these two companies doing better or worse than the industry average? Does this match your expectations from requirement (2)?

CP6-3
LO3, 5

AMERICAN EAGLE
OUTFITTERS

Urban Outfitters

www.mhhe.com/libby6e

Financial Reporting and Analysis Cases

CP6-4
LO1
UPS, Federal Express, and Airborne

Making a Decision as a Manager: Choosing among Alternative Recognition Points

UPS, Federal Express, and Airborne are three of the major players in the highly competitive package delivery industry. Comparability is a key qualitative characteristic of accounting numbers that allows analysts to compare similar companies. A number of years ago, the revenue recognition footnotes of the three competitors revealed three different revenue recognition points for package delivery revenue: package delivery, percentage of service completed, and package pickup. These points correspond to the end, continuous recognition, and the beginning of the earnings process.

UNITED PARCEL SERVICE OF AMERICA, INC.

Revenue is recognized upon delivery of a package.

FEDERAL EXPRESS CORPORATION

Revenue is generally recognized upon delivery of shipments. For shipments in transit, revenue is recorded based on the percentage of service completed.

AIRBORNE FREIGHT CORP.

Domestic revenues and most domestic operating expenses are recognized when shipments are picked up from the customer. . . .

The Airborne footnote goes on to say, however: "The net revenue resulting from existing recognition policies does not materially differ from that which would be recognized on a delivery date basis."

Required:
1. Do you believe that the difference between Airborne's and UPS's revenue recognition policies materially affects their reported earnings? Why or why not?
2. Assume that all three companies pick up packages from customers and receive payment of $1 million for services each day of the year and that each package is delivered the next day. What would each company's service revenue for a year be given its stated revenue recognition policy?
3. Given your answers to requirement (2), under what conditions would that answer change?
4. Which revenue recognition rule would you prefer as a manager? Why?

Critical Thinking Cases

CP6-5
LO1
Symbol Technologies

Evaluating an Ethical Dilemma: Management Incentives, Revenue Recognition, and Sales with the Right of Return

Symbol Technologies, Inc., was a fast-growing maker of bar-code scanners. According to the federal charges, Tomo Razmilovic, the CEO at Symbol, was obsessed with meeting the stock market's expectation for continued growth. His executive team responded by improperly recording revenue and allowances for returns, as well as a variety of other tricks, to overstate revenues by $230 million and pretax earnings by $530 million. What makes this fraud nearly unique is that virtually the whole senior management team is charged with participating in the six-year fraud. At the time this case is being written, five have pleaded guilty, another eight are under indictment, and the former CEO has fled the country to avoid prosecution. The exact nature of the fraud is described in the following excerpt dealing with the guilty plea by the former vice president for finance:

Ex-Official at Symbol Pleads Guilty

By Kara Scannell
26 March 2003
The Wall Street Journal
(Copyright © 2003, Dow Jones & Company, Inc.)

A former finance executive at Symbol Technologies Inc. pleaded guilty to participating in a vast accounting fraud that inflated revenue at the maker of bar-code scanners by roughly 10%, or $100 million a year, from 1999 through 2001.

. . .

The criminal information and civil complaint filed yesterday accused Mr. Asti and other high-level executives of stuffing the firm's distribution channel with phony orders at the end of each quarter to meet revenue and earnings targets. Under generally accepted accounting practices, revenue can be booked only when the products are shipped to a customer. Symbol's customers include delivery services and grocery stores.

Investigators alleged that Mr. Asti and others engaged in "candy" deals, where Symbol bribed resellers with a 1% fee to "buy" products from a distributor at the end of a quarter, which Symbol would later buy back. Symbol then allegedly would convince the distributor to order more products from the company to satisfy the newly created inventory void.

The SEC said the inflated revenue figures helped boost Symbol's stock price, as well as enriching Mr. Asti. He allegedly sold thousands of shares of Symbol stock, which he received from exercising stock options, when the stock was trading at inflated levels.

Required:
1. What facts, if any, presented in the article suggest that Symbol violated the revenue principle?
2. Assuming that Symbol did recognize revenue when goods were shipped, how could it have properly accounted for the fact that customers had a right to cancel the contracts (make an analogy with accounting for bad debts)?
3. What do you think may have motivated management to falsify the statements? Why was management concerned with reporting continued growth in net income?
4. Explain who was hurt by management's unethical conduct.
5. Assume that you are the auditor for other firms. After reading about the fraud, what types of transactions would you pay special attention to in the audit of your clients in this industry? What ratio might provide warnings about possible channel stuffing?

Evaluating Internal Control

CP6-6
LO6

Cripple Creek Company has one trusted employee who, as the owner said, "handles all of the bookkeeping and paperwork for the company." This employee is responsible for counting, verifying, and recording cash receipts and payments, making the weekly bank deposit, preparing checks for major expenditures (signed by the owner), making small expenditures from the cash register for daily expenses, and collecting accounts receivable. The owners asked the local bank for a $20,000 loan. The bank asked that an audit be performed covering the year just ended. The independent auditor (a local CPA), in a private conference with the owner, presented some evidence of the following activities of the trusted employee during the past year.

a. Cash sales sometimes were not entered in the cash register, and the trusted employee pocketed approximately $50 per month.
b. Cash taken from the cash register (and pocketed by the trusted employee) was replaced with expense memos with fictitious signatures (approximately $12 per day).
c. A $300 collection on an account receivable of a valued out-of-town customer was pocketed by the trusted employee and was covered by making a $300 entry as a debit to Sales Returns and a credit to Accounts Receivable.

    d. An $800 collection on an account receivable from a local customer was pocketed by the trusted employee and was covered by making an $800 entry as a debit to Allowance for Doubtful Accounts and a credit to Accounts Receivable.

Required:
1. What was the approximate amount stolen during the past year?
2. What would be your recommendations to the owner?

Financial Reporting and Analysis Team Project

CP6-7
LO4, 5

Team Project: Analyzing Revenues and Receivables

As a team, select an industry to analyze. *Reuters* provides lists of industries and their makeup at **www.reuters.com/finance/industries**. Each team member should acquire the annual report or 10-K for one publicly traded company in the industry, with each member selecting a different company. (Library files, the SEC EDGAR service at **www.sec.gov**, or the company itself are good sources.)

Required:

On an individual basis, each team member should write a short report answering the following questions about the selected company. Discuss any patterns across the companies that you as a team observe. Then, as a team, write a short report comparing and contrasting your companies.

1. If your company lists receivables in its balance sheet, what percentage is it of total assets for each of the last three years? If your company does not list receivables, discuss why this is so.
2. Ratio analysis
   a. What does the accounts receivable turnover ratio measure in general?
   b. If your company lists receivables, compute the ratio for the last three years.
   c. What do your results suggest about the company?
   d. If available, find the industry ratio for the most recent year, compare it to your results, and discuss why you believe your company differs or is similar to the industry ratio.
3. If your company lists receivables, use the 10-K to determine what additional disclosure is available concerning the allowance for doubtful accounts. (Usually the information is in a separate schedule, Item 15.)
   a. What is bad debt expense as a percentage of sales for the last three years?
4. What is the effect of the change in receivables on cash flows from operating activities for the most recent year (that is, did the change increase or decrease operating cash flows)? Explain your answer.

Lectured slideshow–LP7-1
www.mhhe.com/libby6e

LEARNING OBJECTIVES

After studying this chapter, you should be able to:

1. Apply the cost principle to identify the amounts that should be included in inventory and the matching principle to determine cost of goods sold for typical retailers, wholesalers, and manufacturers. p. 340

2. Report inventory and cost of goods sold using the four inventory costing methods. p. 345

3. Decide when the use of different inventory costing methods is beneficial to a company. p. 350

4. Report inventory at the lower of cost or market (LCM). p. 353

5. Evaluate inventory management using the inventory turnover ratio and the effects of inventory on cash flows. p. 354

6. Compare companies that use different inventory costing methods. p. 358

7. Understand methods for controlling and keeping track of inventory and analyze the effects of inventory errors on financial statements. p. 361

REPORTING AND INTERPRETING COST OF GOODS SOLD AND INVENTORY

FOCUS COMPANY:

Harley-Davidson, Inc.

BUILDING A LEGEND INTO A WORLD-CLASS

MANUFACTURER

www.harley-davidson.com

The Harley-Davidson eagle trademark was once known best as a popular request in tattoo parlors. Now, following 21 consecutive years of growth in sales and profits, Harley-Davidson still faces a problem that most other companies envy. Though the Milwaukee-based company increased annual motorcycle production from 37,000 to 349,000 in that period, meeting customer demand is still difficult. They dominate the heavy-weight motorcycle market in North America with a 48.6% market share. To close the gap between supply and demand for its products, Harley-Davidson spent $1.2 billion over the last five years to expand and improve its production facilities in Wisconsin, Missouri, and Pennsylvania.

However, increasing production numbers is only part of Harley's strategy. It is introducing new and improved products to stay ahead of major competitors Honda, Yamaha, and BMW. It also focuses on controlling inventory quality and cost to maintain gross profit margin. Empowering, educating, and training both salaried and unionized employees; establishing long-term, mutually beneficial relationships with its suppliers; and developing accounting information systems that provide real-time inventory and order information are keys to many of these efforts. Furthermore, selection of appropriate accounting methods for inventory can have a dramatic effect on the amount Harley-Davidson pays in income taxes. Continuous improvement in product development, manufacturing, inventory management, and information system design will be necessary for the Harley-Davidson eagle to continue its rise.

UNDERSTANDING THE BUSINESS

Concerns about the cost and quality of inventory face all modern manufacturers and merchandisers and turn our attention to **cost of goods sold** (cost of sales, cost of products sold) on the income statement and **inventory** on the balance sheet. Exhibit 7.1 presents the relevant excerpts from Harley-Davidson's financial statements that include these accounts. Note that Cost of Goods Sold is subtracted from Net Sales to produce Gross Profit on its income statement. On the balance sheet, Inventory is a current asset; it is reported below Cash, Marketable Securities, and Accounts and Finance Receivables because it is less liquid than those assets.

The primary goals of inventory management are to have sufficient quantities of high-quality inventory available to serve customers' needs while minimizing the costs of carrying inventory (production, storage, obsolescence, and financing). Low quality leads to customer dissatisfaction, returns, and a decline in future sales. Also, purchasing or producing too few units of a hot-selling item causes stock-outs that mean lost sales revenue and decreases in customer satisfaction. Conversely, purchasing too many units of a slow-selling item increases storage costs as well as interest costs on short-term borrowings that finance the purchases. It may even lead to losses if the merchandise cannot be sold at normal prices.

The accounting system plays three roles in the inventory management process. First, the system must provide accurate information for preparation of periodic

---

EXHIBIT 7.1

Income Statement and Balance Sheet Excerpts

REAL WORLD EXCERPT

HARLEY-DAVIDSON, INC.

ANNUAL REPORT

HARLEY-DAVIDSON, INC.
Consolidated Statements of Income
(dollars in thousands, except per share amounts)

Years Ended December 31,	2006	2005	2004
Net sales	$5,800,686	$5,342,214	$5,015,190
Cost of goods sold	3,567,839	3,301,715	3,115,655
Gross profit	2,232,847	2,040,499	1,899,535

HARLEY-DAVIDSON, INC.
Consolidated Balance Sheets
(dollars in thousands, except share amounts)

December 31,	2006	2005
Assets		
Current Assets		
Cash and cash equivalents	$ 238,397	$ 140,975
Marketable securities	658,133	905,197
Accounts receivable, net	143,049	122,087
Finance receivables, net	2,101,366	1,641,766
Inventories	287,798	221,418
Deferred income taxes	73,389	61,285
Prepaid expenses	48,501	52,509
Total current assets	3,550,633	3,145,237

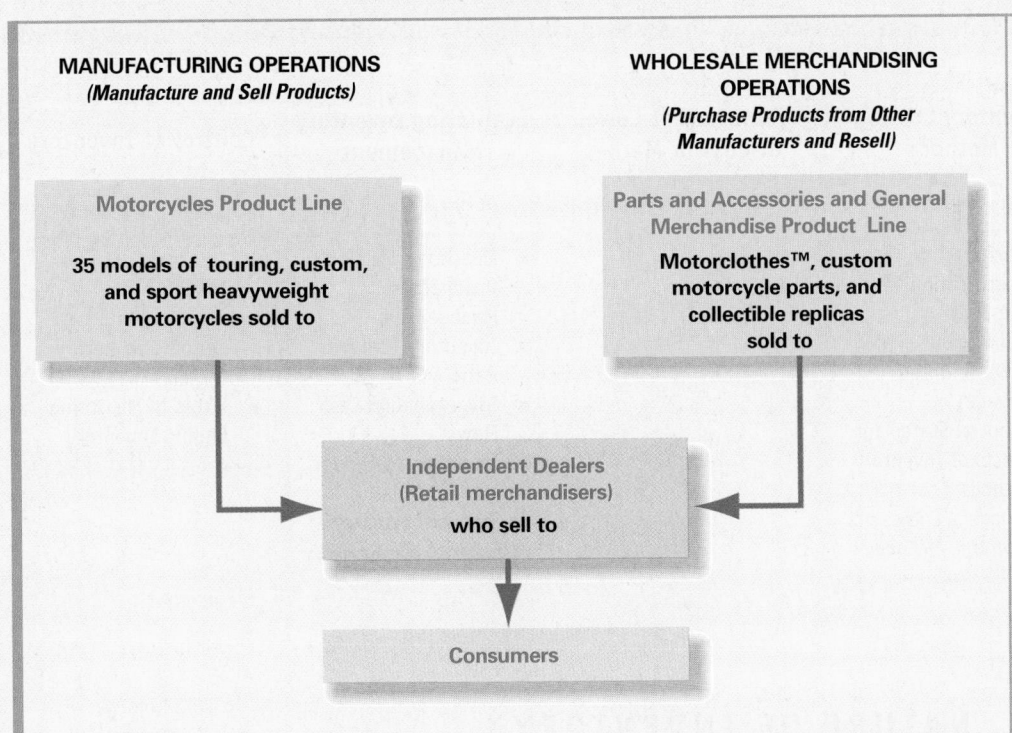

EXHIBIT 7.2

Harley-Davidson Motorcycle Division Product Lines

financial statements and tax returns. Second, it must provide up-to-date information on inventory quantities and costs to facilitate ordering and manufacturing decisions. Third, since inventories are subject to theft and other forms of misuse, the system must also provide the information needed to help protect these important assets.

Harley's successful production and inventory management strategy and its mix of product lines (see Exhibit 7.2) make it a particularly good example for this chapter. Although best known as a **manufacturer** of motorcycles, Harley also purchases and resells completed products such as its popular line of Motorclothes™ apparel. In the second case, it acts as a **wholesaler.** Both the motorcycle and Motorclothes™ product lines are sold to their network of independent dealers. From an accounting standpoint, these independent dealers are Harley-Davidson's customers. The independent dealers are the **retailers** who sell the products to the public.

First we discuss the makeup of inventory, the important choices management must make in the financial and tax reporting process, and how these choices affect the financial statements and taxes paid. Then we will discuss how managers and analysts evaluate the efficiency of inventory management. Finally, we will briefly discuss how accounting systems are organized to keep track of inventory quantities and costs for decision making and control. This topic will be the principal subject matter of your managerial accounting course.

ORGANIZATION of the Chapter

Nature of Inventory and Cost of Goods Sold	Inventory Costing Methods	Valuation at Lower of Cost or Market	Evaluating Inventory Management	Control of Inventory
■ Items Included in Inventory ■ Costs Included in Inventory Purchases ■ Flow of Inventory Costs ■ Nature of Costs of Goods Sold	■ Specific Identification Method ■ Cost Flow Assumptions (FIFO, LIFO, Weighted Average) ■ Financial Statement Effects of Inventory Methods ■ Managers' Choice of Inventory Methods		■ Measuring Efficiency in Inventory Management ■ Inventory Turnover Ratio ■ Inventory and Cash Flows ■ Inventory Methods and Financial Statement Analysis	■ Internal Control of Inventory ■ Perpetual and Periodic Inventory Systems ■ Errors in Measuring Ending Inventory

NATURE OF INVENTORY AND COST OF GOODS SOLD

Items Included in Inventory

Learning Objective 1

Apply the cost principle to identify the amounts that should be included in inventory and the matching principle to determine cost of goods sold for typical retailers, wholesalers, and manufacturers.

INVENTORY is tangible property held for sale in the normal course of business or used in producing goods or services for sale.

MERCHANDISE INVENTORY includes goods held for resale in the ordinary course of business.

RAW MATERIALS INVENTORY includes items acquired for the purpose of processing into finished goods.

WORK IN PROCESS INVENTORY includes goods in the process of being manufactured.

FINISHED GOODS INVENTORY includes manufactured goods that are complete and ready for sale.

Inventory is tangible property that is (1) held for sale in the normal course of business or (2) used to produce goods or services for sale. Inventory is reported on the balance sheet as a current asset, because it normally is used or converted into cash within one year or the next operating cycle. The types of inventory normally held depend on the characteristics of the business.

Merchandisers (wholesale or retail businesses) hold the following:

Merchandise inventory   Goods (or merchandise) held for resale in the normal course of business. The goods usually are acquired in a finished condition and are ready for sale without further processing.

For Harley-Davidson, merchandise inventory includes the Motorclothes™ line and the parts and accessories it purchases for sale to its independent dealers.

Manufacturing businesses hold three types of inventory:

Raw materials inventory   Items acquired for processing into finished goods. These items are included in raw materials inventory until they are used, at which point they become part of work in process inventory.

Work in process inventory   Goods in the process of being manufactured but not yet complete. When completed, work in process inventory becomes finished goods inventory.

Finished goods inventory   Manufactured goods that are complete and ready for sale.

Inventories related to Harley-Davidson's motorcycle manufacturing operations are recorded in these accounts.

Harley-Davidson's recent inventory note reports the following:

HARLEY-DAVIDSON, INC. **Notes to Consolidated Financial Statements**		
2. ADDITIONAL BALANCE SHEET AND CASH FLOWS INFORMATION (dollars in thousands)		
	December 31,	
	2006	**2005**
Inventories:		
Components at the lower of FIFO cost or market:		
Raw materials and work in process	$123,376	$90,955
Motorcycle finished goods	94,399	73,736
Parts and accessories and general merchandise	98,749	80,017

Note that Harley-Davidson combines the raw materials and work in process into one number. Other companies separate the two components. The parts and accessories and general merchandise category includes purchased parts and Motorclothes™ and other accessories that make up merchandise inventory.[1]

Costs Included in Inventory Purchases

Goods in inventory are initially recorded at cost. Inventory cost includes the sum of the costs incurred in bringing an article to usable or salable condition and location. When Harley-Davidson purchases raw materials and merchandise inventory, the amount recorded should include the invoice price to be paid plus other expenditures related to the purchase, such as freight charges to deliver the items to its warehouses (freight-in) and inspection and preparation costs. In general, the company should cease accumulating purchase costs when the raw materials are **ready for use** or when the merchandise inventory is **ready for shipment.** Any additional costs related to selling the inventory to the dealers, such as marketing department salaries and dealer training sessions, are incurred after the inventory is ready for use. So they should be included in selling, general, and administrative expenses in the period they are incurred.

Applying the Materiality Constraint in Practice

FINANCIAL
ANALYSIS

Incidental costs such as inspection and preparation costs often are not material in amount (see the discussion of the materiality constraint in Chapter 5) and do not have to be assigned to the inventory cost. Thus, for practical reasons, many companies use the invoice price, less returns and discounts, to assign a unit cost to raw materials or merchandise and record other indirect expenditures as a separate cost that is reported as an expense.

Flow of Inventory Costs

The flow of inventory costs for merchandisers (wholesalers and retailers) is relatively simple, as Exhibit 7.3A shows. When merchandise is purchased, the merchandise inventory account is increased. When the goods are sold, cost of goods sold is increased and merchandise inventory is decreased.

---

[1]These do not add up to the balance reported in Exhibit 7.1 because they do not include the LIFO adjustment discussed later.

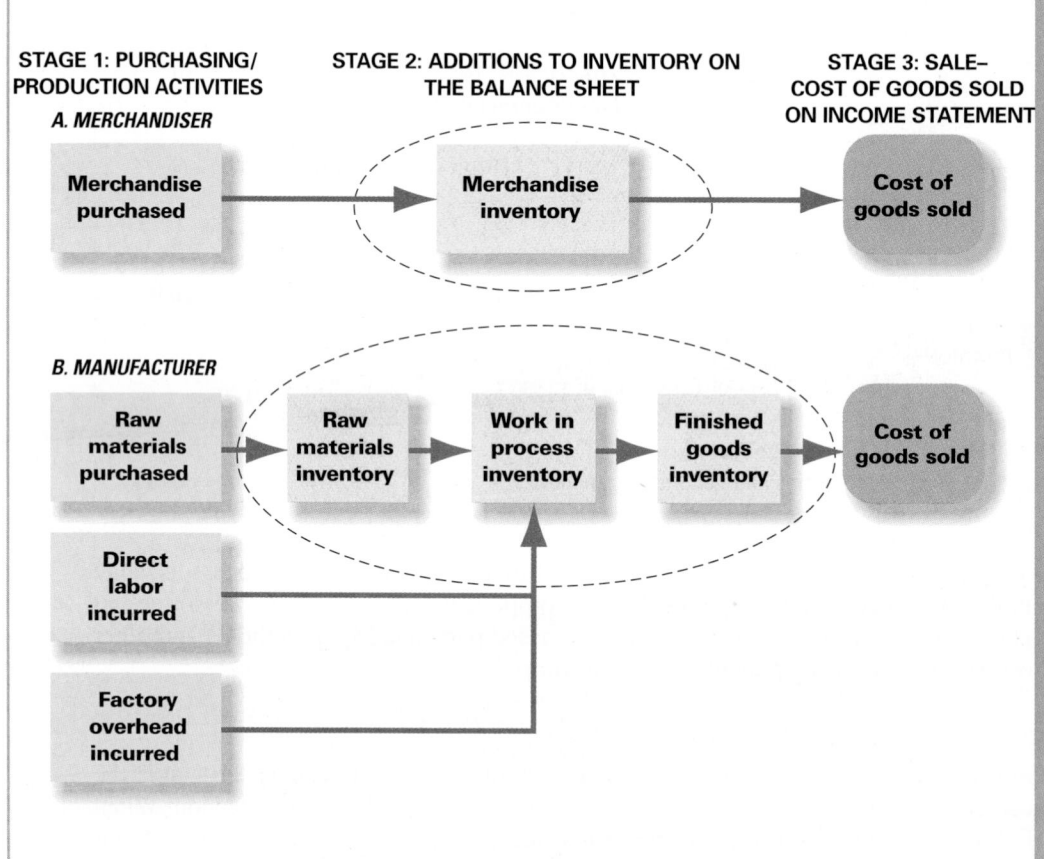

EXHIBIT 7.3
Flow of Inventory Costs

STAGE 1: PURCHASING/PRODUCTION ACTIVITIES

STAGE 2: ADDITIONS TO INVENTORY ON THE BALANCE SHEET

STAGE 3: SALE–COST OF GOODS SOLD ON INCOME STATEMENT

A. MERCHANDISER

Merchandise purchased → Merchandise inventory → Cost of goods sold

B. MANUFACTURER

Raw materials purchased → Raw materials inventory → Work in process inventory → Finished goods inventory → Cost of goods sold

Direct labor incurred →

Factory overhead incurred →

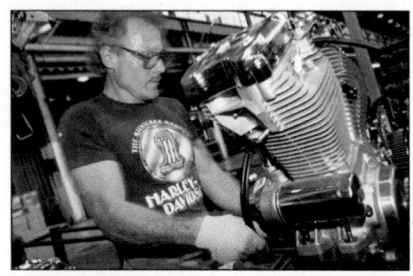

DIRECT LABOR refers to the earnings of employees who work directly on the products being manufactured.

FACTORY OVERHEAD are manufacturing costs that are not raw material or direct labor costs.

The flow of inventory costs in a manufacturing environment is more complex, as diagrammed in Exhibit 7.3B. First, **raw materials** (also called **direct materials**) must be purchased. For Harley-Davidson, these raw materials include steel and aluminum castings, forgings, sheet, and bars, as well as certain motorcycle component parts produced by its small network of suppliers, including carburetors, batteries, and tires. When they are used, the cost of these materials is removed from the raw materials inventory and added to the work in process inventory.

Two other components of manufacturing cost, direct labor and factory overhead, are also added to the work in process inventory when they are used. **Direct labor** cost represents the earnings of employees who work directly on the products being manufactured. **Factory overhead** costs include all other manufacturing costs. For example, the factory supervisor's salary and the cost of heat, light, and power to operate the factory are included in factory overhead. When the motorcycles are completed and ready for sale, the related amounts in work in process inventory are transferred to finished goods inventory. When the finished goods are sold, cost of goods sold increases, and finished goods inventory decreases.

As Exhibit 7.3 indicates, there are three stages to inventory cost flows for both merchandisers and manufacturers. The first involves purchasing and/or production activities. In the second, these activities result in additions to inventory accounts on the balance sheet. In the third stage, the inventory items are sold and the amounts become cost of goods sold expense on the income statement. Since the flow of inventory costs from merchandise inventory and finished goods to cost of goods sold are very similar, we will focus the rest of our discussion on merchandise inventory.

| **FINANCIAL** |
| ANALYSIS |

Modern Manufacturing Techniques and Inventory Costs

The flows of inventory costs diagrammed in Exhibit 7.3B represent the keys to manufacturing cost and quality control. Since the company must pay to finance and store raw materials and purchased parts, minimizing the size of these inventories in keeping with projected manufacturing demand is the first key to the process. To do so, Harley-Davidson must work closely with suppliers in design, production, and delivery of manufactured parts and the delivery of raw materials. (This approach to inventory management is called **just in time.**) Review and redesign of manufacturing operations and worker training and involvement programs are the keys to minimizing direct labor and factory overhead costs. New products are often designed to be simpler to manufacture, which improves product quality and reduces scrap and rework costs.

Harley-Davidson's management accounting system is designed to monitor the success of these changes and promote continuous improvements in manufacturing. The design of such systems is the subject matter of management accounting and cost accounting courses.

Nature of Cost of Goods Sold

Cost of goods sold (CGS) expense is directly related to sales revenue. Sales revenue during an accounting period is the number of units sold multiplied by the sales price. Cost of goods sold is the same number of units multiplied by their unit costs.

Let's examine the relationship between cost of goods sold on the income statement and inventory on the balance sheet. Harley-Davidson starts each accounting period with a stock of inventory called **beginning inventory** (BI). During the accounting period, new **purchases** (P) are added to inventory. The sum of the two amounts is the goods available for sale during that period. What remains unsold at the end of the period becomes **ending inventory** (EI) on the balance sheet. The portion of goods available for sale that is sold becomes **cost of goods sold** on the income statement. The ending inventory for one accounting period then becomes the beginning inventory for the next period. The relationships between these various inventory amounts are brought together in the cost of goods sold equation.

GOODS AVAILABLE FOR SALE refers to the sum of beginning inventory and purchases (or transfers to finished goods) for the period.

COST OF GOODS SOLD EQUATION: BI + P − EI = CGS

To illustrate, assume that Harley-Davidson began the period with $40,000 worth of Motorclothes™ in beginning inventory, purchased additional merchandise during the period for $55,000, and had $35,000 left in inventory at the end of the period. These amounts are combined as follows to compute cost of goods sold of $60,000:

Beginning inventory	$40,000
+ Purchases of merchandise during the year	55,000
Goods available for sale	95,000
− Ending inventory	35,000
Cost of goods sold	$60,000

These same relationships are illustrated in Exhibit 7.4 and can be represented in the merchandise inventory T-account as follows:

Merchandise Inventory (A)			
Beginning inventory	40,000		
Add: Purchases of inventory	55,000	Deduct: Cost of goods sold	60,000
Ending inventory	35,000		

If three of these four values are known, either the cost of goods sold equation or the inventory T-account can be used to solve for the fourth value.

EXHIBIT 7.4

Cost of Goods Sold for Merchandise Inventory

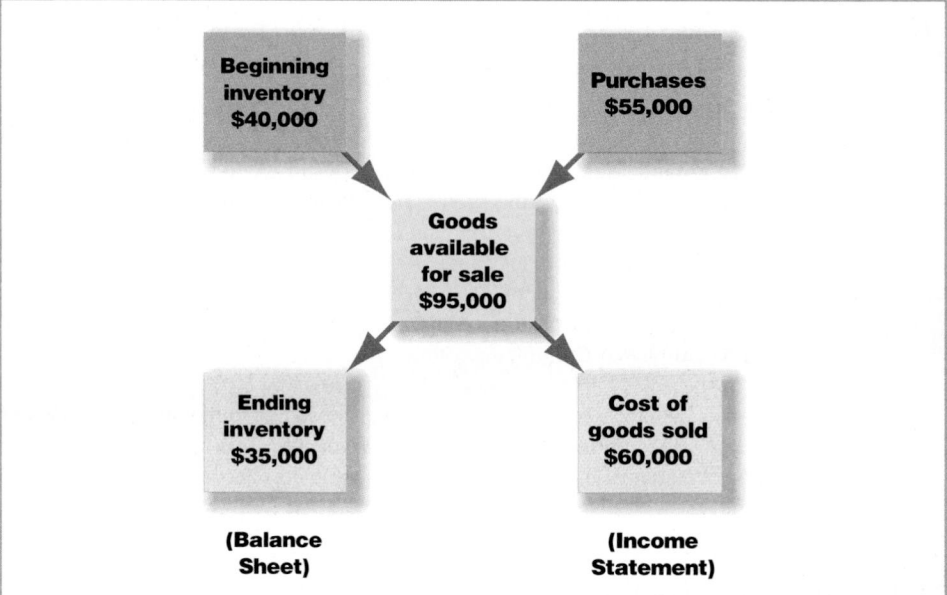

SELF-STUDY QUIZ

1. Assume the following facts for Harley-Davidson's Motorclothes™ leather baseball jacket product line for the year 2007:

   Beginning inventory 400 units at unit cost of $75.

   Purchases 600 units at unit cost of $75.

   Sales 700 units at a sales price of $100 (cost per unit $75).

   Using the cost of goods sold equation, compute the dollar amount of **goods available for sale, ending inventory,** and **cost of goods sold** of leather baseball jackets for the period.

   | Beginning inventory |
+ Purchases of merchandise during the year
Goods available for sale
− Ending inventory
Cost of goods sold

2. Assume the following facts for Harley-Davidson's Motorclothes™ leather baseball jacket product line for the year 2008:

   Beginning inventory 300 units at unit cost of $75.

   Ending inventory 600 units at unit cost of $75.

   Sales 1,100 units at a sales price of $100 (cost per unit $75).

   Using the cost of goods sold equation, compute the dollar amount of **purchases** of leather baseball jackets for the period. Remember that if three of these four values are known, the cost of goods sold equation can be used to solve for the fourth value.

   | Beginning inventory |
   | + Purchases of merchandise during the year |
− Ending inventory
Cost of goods sold

   After you have completed your answers, check them with the solutions at the bottom of the next page.

INVENTORY COSTING METHODS

In the Motorclothes™ example presented in the Self-Study Quiz, the cost of all units of the leather baseball jackets was the same—$75. If inventory costs normally did not change, this would be the end of our discussion. As we are all aware, the prices of most goods do change. In recent years, the costs of many manufactured items such as automobiles and motorcycles have risen gradually. In some industries such as computers, costs of production have dropped dramatically along with retail prices.

When inventory costs have changed, which inventory items are treated as sold or remaining in inventory can turn profits into losses and cause companies to pay or save millions in taxes. A simple example will illustrate these dramatic effects. Do not let the simplicity of our example mislead you. It applies broadly to actual company practices.

Assume that a Harley-Davidson dealer made the following purchases:

Jan.   1   Had beginning inventory of two units of a Model A leather jacket at $70 each.

March 12   Purchased four units of Model A leather jacket at $80 each.

June   9   Purchased one unit of Model A leather jacket at $100 each.

Nov.   5   Sold four units for $120 each.

Note that **cost of the leather jackets rose** rapidly between January and June! On November 5, four units are sold for $120 each and revenues of $480 are recorded. What amount is recorded as cost of goods sold? The answer depends on which specific goods we assume are sold. Four generally accepted inventory costing methods are available for doing so:

1. Specific identification.

2. First-in, first-out (FIFO).

3. Last-in, first-out (LIFO).

4. Average cost.

The four inventory costing methods are alternative ways to assign the total dollar amount of goods available for sale between (1) ending inventory and (2) cost of goods sold. The first method identifies individual items that remain in inventory or are sold. The remaining three methods assume that the inventory costs follow a certain flow.

Specific Identification Method

When the **specific identification method** is used, the cost of each item sold is individually identified and recorded as cost of goods sold. This method requires keeping track of the purchase cost of each item. This is done by either (1) coding the purchase cost on each unit before placing it in stock or (2) keeping a separate record of the unit and identifying it with a serial number. In the leather jacket example, any four of the items could have been sold. If we assume that one of the $70 items, two of the $80 items, and the one $100 item have been sold, the cost of those items ($70 + $80 + $80 + $100) would become cost of goods sold ($330). The cost of the remaining items would be ending inventory.

> **Learning Objective 2**
> Report inventory and cost of goods sold using the four inventory costing methods.

Audio lecture–AP7-1
Video 7-1
www.mhhe.com/libby6e

> The SPECIFIC IDENTIFICATION METHOD identifies the cost of the specific item that was sold.

> Self-Study Quiz
> Solutions

1. | Beginning inventory (400 × $75) | $30,000 |
    |---|---|
    | + Purchases of merchandise during the year (600 × $75) | 45,000 |
    | Goods available for sale (1,000 × $75) | 75,000 |
    | − Ending inventory (300 × $75) | 22,500 |
    | Cost of goods sold (700 × $75) | $52,500 |

2. BI = 300 × $75 = $22,500   BI + P − EI = CGS
    EI = 600 × $75 = $45,000   22,500 + P − 45,000 = 82,500
    CGS = 1,100 × $75 = $82,500   P = 105,000

The specific identification method is impractical when large quantities of similar items are stocked. On the other hand, when dealing with expensive unique items such as houses or fine jewelry, this method is appropriate. This method may also be manipulated when the units are identical because one can affect the cost of goods sold and the ending inventory accounts by picking and choosing from among the several available unit costs. As a consequence, most inventory items are accounted for using one of three cost flow assumptions.

Cost Flow Assumptions

The **choice of an inventory costing method is NOT based on the physical flow of goods** on and off the shelves. That is why they are called **cost flow assumptions.** A useful tool for representing inventory cost flow assumptions is a bin, or container. Try visualizing these inventory costing methods as flows of inventory in and out of the bin. **Following practice, we will apply the methods as if all purchases during the period take place before any sales and cost of goods sold are recorded.**

First-In, First-Out Method

The FIRST-IN, FIRST-OUT (FIFO) METHOD assumes that the first goods purchased (the first in) are the first goods sold.

The **first-in, first-out method,** frequently called **FIFO,** assumes that the earliest goods purchased (the first ones in) are the first goods sold, and the last goods purchased are left in ending inventory. Under FIFO, cost of goods sold and ending inventory are computed as if the flows in and out of the FIFO inventory bin in Exhibit 7.5 had taken place. First, each purchase is treated as if it were deposited in the bin from the top in sequence (two units of beginning inventory at $70 followed by purchases of four units at $80 and one unit at $100) producing goods available for sale of $560. Each good sold is then removed from the *bottom* in sequence (two units at $70 and two at $80); **first in is first out.** These goods totaling $300 become cost of goods sold (CGS). The remaining units (two units at $80 and one at $100 = $260) become ending inventory. FIFO allocates the **oldest** unit costs **to cost of goods sold** and the newest unit costs **to ending inventory.**

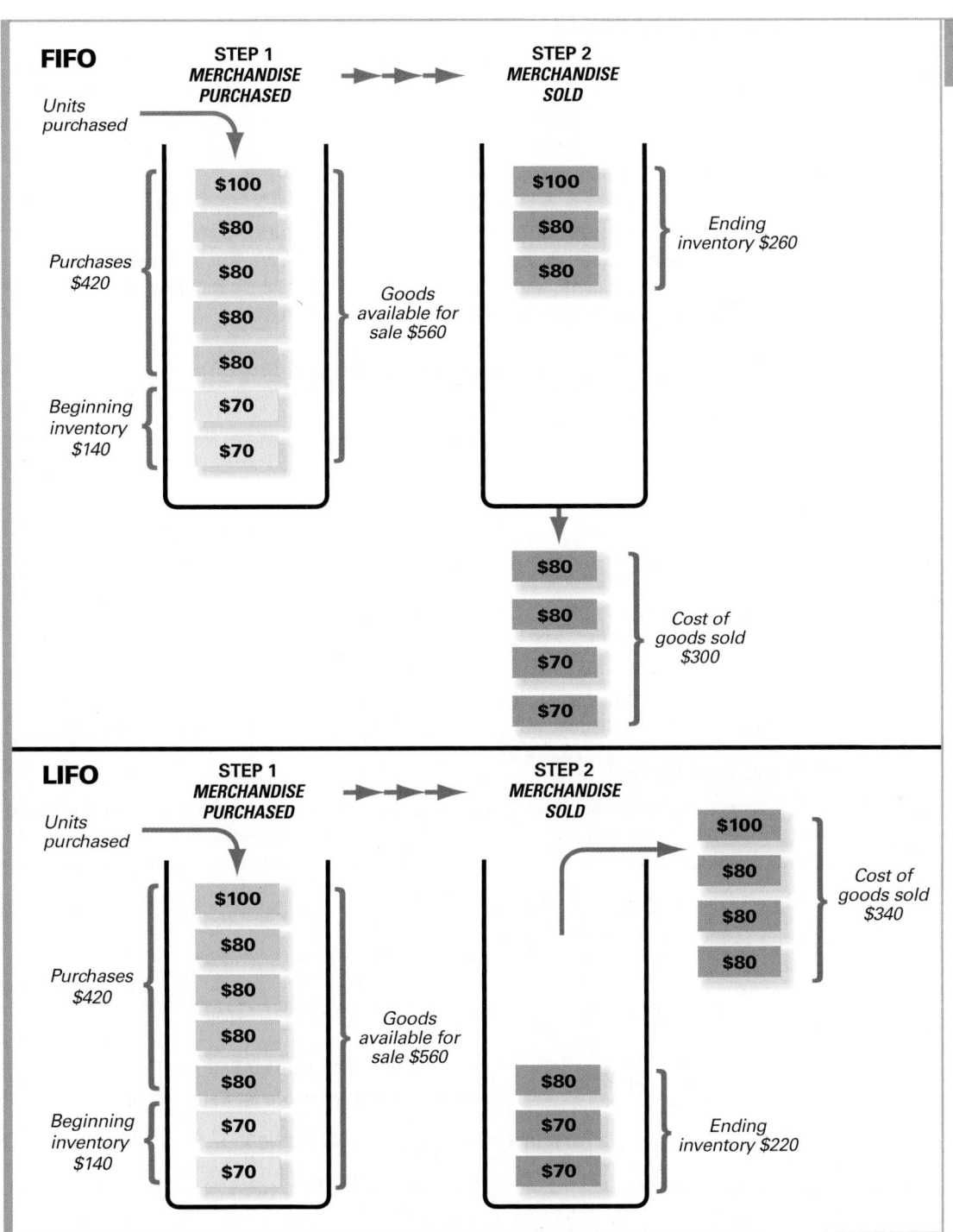

EXHIBIT 7.5

FIFO and LIFO
Inventory Flows

Cost of Goods Sold Calculation (FIFO)		
Beginning inventory	(2 units at $70 each)	$140
+ Purchases	(4 units at $80 each)	320
	(1 unit at $100 each)	100
Goods available for sale		560
− Ending inventory	(2 units at $80 each and 1 unit at $100 each)	260
Cost of goods sold	(2 units at $70 and 2 units at $80 each)	$300

The LAST-IN, FIRST-OUT (LIFO) METHOD assumes that the most recently purchased units (the last in) are sold first.

Last-In, First-Out Method

The **last-in, first-out method,** often called **LIFO,** assumes that the most recently purchased goods (the last ones in) are sold first and the oldest units are left in ending inventory. It is illustrated by the LIFO inventory bin in Exhibit 7.5. As in FIFO, each purchase is treated as if it were deposited in the bin from the top (two units of beginning inventory at $70 followed by purchases of four units at $80 and one unit at $100) resulting in the goods available for sale of $560. Unlike FIFO, however, each good sold is treated as if it were removed from the top in sequence (one unit at $100 followed by three units at $80). These goods totaling $340 become cost of goods sold (CGS). The remaining units (one at $80 and two at $70) become ending inventory. LIFO allocates the **newest** unit costs **to cost of goods sold** and the **oldest** unit costs **to ending inventory.**

Cost of Goods Sold Calculation (LIFO)		
Beginning inventory	(2 units at $70 each)	$140
+ Purchases	(4 units at $80 each)	320
	(1 unit at $100 each)	100
Goods available for sale		560
− Ending inventory	(2 units at $70 each and 1 unit at $80 each)	220
Cost of goods sold	(3 units at $80 and 1 unit at $100 each)	$340

The LIFO flow assumption is the exact opposite of the FIFO flow assumption:

	FIFO	LIFO
Cost of goods sold on income statement	Oldest unit costs	Newest unit costs
Inventory on balance sheet	Newest unit costs	Oldest unit costs

Average Cost Method

The AVERAGE COST METHOD uses the weighted average unit cost of the goods available for sale for both cost of goods sold and ending inventory.

The **average cost method** (weighted average cost method) uses the weighted average unit cost of the goods available for sale for both cost of goods sold and ending inventory. The weighted average unit cost of the goods available for sale is computed as follows.

Number of Units	×	Unit Cost	=	Total Cost
2	×	$70	=	$140
4	×	$80	=	320
1	×	$100	=	100
7				$560

$$\text{Average Cost} = \frac{\text{Cost of Goods Available for Sale}}{\text{Number of Units Available for Sale}}$$

$$\text{Average Cost} = \frac{\$560}{7 \text{ Units}} = \$80 \text{ per Unit}$$

Cost of goods sold and ending inventory are assigned the same weighted average cost per unit of $80.

Cost of Goods Sold Calculation (Average Cost)		
Beginning inventory	(2 units at $70 each)	$140
+ Purchases	(4 units at $80 each)	320
	(1 unit at $100 each)	100
Goods available for sale	(7 units at $80 average cost each)	560
− Ending inventory	(3 units at $80 average cost each)	240
Cost of goods sold	(4 units at $80 average cost each)	$320

These flows are illustrated in Exhibit 7.6.

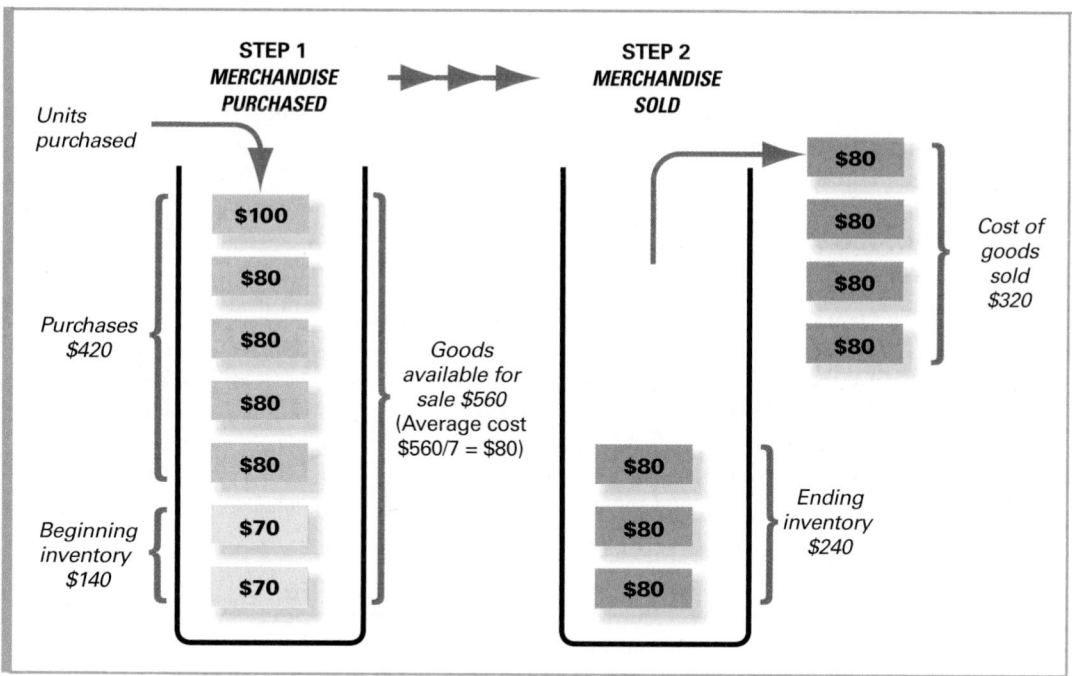

EXHIBIT 7.6

**Average Cost
Inventory Flows**

Financial Statement Effects of Inventory Methods

Each of the four alternative inventory costing methods is in conformity with GAAP and the tax law. To understand why managers choose different methods in different circumstances, we must first understand their effects on the income statement and balance sheet. Exhibit 7.7 summarizes the financial statement effects of FIFO, LIFO, and weighted average methods in our example. Remember that the methods differ only in the portion of goods available for sale allocated to cost of goods sold versus ending inventory. For that reason, the method that gives the highest ending inventory amount also

		FIFO	LIFO	Weighted Average
Effect on the Income Statement				
Sales		$480	$480	$480
Cost of Goods Sold:				
Beginning inventory	$140		$140	$140
Add: Purchases	420		420	420
Goods available for sale	560		560	560
Subtract: Ending inventory (to balance sheet)	260		220	240
Cost of goods sold		300	340	320
Gross profit		180	140	160
Other expenses		80	80	80
Income before income taxes		100	60	80
Income tax expense (25%)		25	15	20
Net income		$ 75	$ 45	$ 60
Effect on the Balance Sheet				
Inventory		$260	$220	$240

EXHIBIT 7.7

**Financial Statement
Effects of Inventory
Costing Methods**

gives the lowest cost of goods sold and the highest gross profit, income tax expense, and income amounts, and vice versa. The weighted average cost method generally gives income and inventory amounts that are between the FIFO and LIFO extremes.

In the comparison in Exhibit 7.7, unit costs were increasing. **When unit costs are rising, LIFO produces lower income and a lower inventory valuation than FIFO.** Even in inflationary times, some companies' costs decline. **When unit costs are declining, LIFO produces higher income and higher inventory valuation than FIFO.** These effects, which hold as long as inventory quantities are constant or rising,[2] are summarized in the following table:

Increasing Costs: Normal Financial Statement Effects

	FIFO	LIFO
Cost of goods sold on income statement	Lower	Higher
Net income	Higher	Lower
Income taxes	Higher	Lower
Inventory on balance sheet	Higher	Lower

Decreasing Costs: Normal Financial Statement Effects

	FIFO	LIFO
Cost of goods sold on income statement	Higher	Lower
Net income	Lower	Higher
Income taxes	Lower	Higher
Inventory on balance sheet	Lower	Higher

Managers' Choice of Inventory Methods

What motivates companies to choose different inventory costing methods? Most managers choose accounting methods based on two factors:

1. Net income effects (managers prefer to report higher earnings for their companies).

2. Income tax effects (managers prefer to pay the least amount of taxes allowed by law as late as possible—the **least–latest rule**).

Any conflict between the two motives is normally resolved by choosing one accounting method for external financial statements and a different method for preparing its tax return. The choice of inventory costing methods is a special case, however, because of what is called the **LIFO conformity rule:** If LIFO is used on the income tax return, it must also be used to calculate inventory and cost of goods sold for the financial statements.

Increasing Cost Inventories

■ **For inventory with increasing costs, LIFO is used on the tax return because it normally results in lower income taxes.**

This is illustrated in Exhibit 7.7, where income before income taxes was lowered from $100 under FIFO to $60 under LIFO. On the income tax expense line, this lowers income taxes from $25 under FIFO to $15 under LIFO, generating cash tax savings of $10 under LIFO.[3] The LIFO conformity rule leads companies to adopt LIFO for **both** tax and financial reporting purposes for increasing cost inventories located in the

---

[2]The impact of a decline in inventory **quantity** on LIFO amounts is discussed in Supplement A to this chapter.

[3]In theory, LIFO cannot provide permanent tax savings because (1) when inventory levels drop or (2) costs drop, the income effect reverses and the income taxes deferred must be paid. The economic advantage of deferring income taxes in such situations is due to the fact that interest can be earned on the money that otherwise would be paid as taxes for the current year.

United States. Harley-Davidson is a fairly typical company facing increasing costs. It has saved approximately $10 million in taxes from the date it adopted the LIFO method through 2006.

For inventory located in countries that do not allow LIFO for tax purposes or that do not have a LIFO conformity rule, companies with increasing costs most often use FIFO or weighted average to report higher income on the income statement.

Decreasing Cost Inventories

 For inventory with decreasing costs, FIFO is most often used for both the tax return and financial statements.

Using this method (along with lower of cost or market valuation, discussed later) produces the lowest tax payments for companies with decreasing cost inventories. Many high-technology companies are facing declining costs. In such circumstances, the FIFO method, in which the oldest, most expensive goods become cost of goods sold, produces the highest cost of goods sold, the lowest pretax earnings, and thus the lowest income tax liability. For example, Apple Inc. and Dell Inc. account for inventories at FIFO.

Since most companies in the same industry face similar cost structures, clusters of companies in the same industries often choose the same accounting method.

Consistency in Use of Inventory Methods

It is important to remember that regardless of the physical flow of goods, a company can use any of the inventory costing methods. Also, a company is not required to use the same inventory costing method for all inventory items, and no particular justification is needed for the selection of one or more of the acceptable methods. Harley-Davidson, and most large companies, use different inventory methods for different inventory items.[4] However, accounting rules require companies to apply their accounting methods on a consistent basis over time. A company is not permitted to use LIFO one period, FIFO the next, and then go back to LIFO. A change in method is allowed only if the change will improve the measurement of financial results and financial position.

	FIFO		LIFO	
Income statement: Costs of goods sold	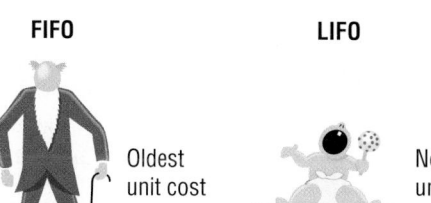	Oldest unit cost		Newest unit cost
Balance sheet: Inventory		Newest unit cost		Oldest unit cost

LIFO and Conflicts between Managers' and Owners' Interests

We have seen that the selection of an inventory method can have significant effects on the financial statements. Company managers may have an incentive to select a method that is not consistent with the owners' objectives. For example, during a period of rising prices, using LIFO may be in the best interests of the owners, because LIFO often reduces a company's tax liability. If managers' compensation is tied to reported profits, they may prefer FIFO, which typically results in higher profits.

While a well-designed compensation plan should reward managers for acting in the best interests of the owners, that is not always the case. Clearly, a manager who selects an accounting method that is not optimal for the company solely to increase his or her compensation is engaging in questionable ethical behavior.

---

[4]*Accounting Trends & Techniques* (New York: AICPA, 2006) reported that, although 229 (38.2 percent) of the 600 companies surveyed reported using LIFO for some portion of inventories, only 16 (2.7 percent) use LIFO for all inventories.

SELF-STUDY QUIZ

1. Compute cost of goods sold and pretax income for **2007** under the FIFO and LIFO accounting methods. Assume that a company's beginning inventory and purchases for 2007 included:

Beginning inventory	10 units @ $ 6 each
Purchases January	5 units @ $10 each
Purchases May	5 units @ $12 each

During 2007, 15 units were sold for $20 each, and other operating expenses totaled $100.

2. Compute cost of goods sold and pretax income for **2008** under the FIFO and LIFO accounting methods. (**Hint:** The 2007 ending inventory amount from Part 1 becomes the 2008 beginning inventory amount.) Assume that the company's purchases for 2008 included:

Purchases March	6 units @ $13 each
Purchases November	5 units @ $14 each

During 2008, 10 units were sold for $24 each, and other operating expenses totaled $70.

3. Which method would you recommend that the company adopt? Why?

After you have completed your answers, check them with the solutions at the bottom of the page.

Self-Study Quiz
Solutions

1.

2007	FIFO	LIFO		FIFO	LIFO
Beginning inventory	$ 60	$ 60	Sales revenue (15 × $20)	$300	$300
Purchases (5 × $10) + (5 × $12)	110	110	Cost of goods sold	110	140
Goods available for sale	170	170	Gross profit	190	160
Ending inventory*	60	30	Other expenses	100	100
Cost of goods sold	$110	$140	Pretax income	$ 90	$ 60

*FIFO ending inventory = (5 × $12) = $60
   Cost of goods sold = (10 × $6) + (5 × $10) = $110
LIFO ending inventory = (5 × $6) = $30
   Cost of goods sold = (5 × $12) + (5 × $10) + (5 × $6) = $140

2.

2008	FIFO	LIFO		FIFO	LIFO
Beginning inventory	$ 60	$ 30	Sales revenue (10 × $24)	$240	$240
Purchases (6 × $13) + (5 × $14)	148	148	Cost of goods sold	125	135
Goods available for sale	208	178	Gross profit	115	105
Ending inventory*	83	43	Other expenses	70	70
Cost of goods sold	$125	$135	Pretax income	$ 45	$ 35

*FIFO ending inventory = (5 × $14) + (1 × $13) = $83
   Cost of goods sold = (5 × $12) + (5 × $13) = $125
LIFO ending inventory = (5 × $6) + (1 × $13) = $43
   Cost of goods sold = (5 × $14) + (5 × $13) = $135

3. LIFO would be recommended because it produces lower pretax income and lower taxes when inventory costs are rising.

VALUATION AT LOWER OF COST OR MARKET

Inventories should be measured initially at their purchase cost in conformity with the cost principle. When the goods remaining in ending inventory can be replaced with identical goods at a lower cost, however, the lower cost should be used as the inventory valuation. Damaged, obsolete, and deteriorated items in inventory should also be assigned a unit cost that represents their current estimated net realizable value (sales price less costs to sell) if that is below cost. This rule is known as measuring inventories at the lower of cost or market (LCM).

This departure from the cost principle is based on the **conservatism** constraint, which requires special care to avoid overstating assets and income. It is particularly important for two types of companies: (1) high-technology companies such as Dell Inc. that manufacture goods for which costs of production and selling price are declining and (2) companies such as American Eagle Outfitters that sell seasonal goods such as clothing, the value of which drops dramatically at the end of each selling season (fall or spring).

Under LCM, companies recognize a "holding" loss in the period in which the replacement cost of an item drops, rather than the period in which the item is sold. The holding loss is the difference between the purchase cost and the lower replacement cost. It is added to the cost of goods sold for the period. To illustrate, assume that Dell Inc. had the following in the current period ending inventory:

Learning Objective 4
Report inventory at the lower of cost or market (LCM).

LOWER OF COST OR MARKET (LCM) is a valuation method departing from the cost principle; it serves to recognize a loss when replacement cost or net realizable value drops below cost.

REPLACEMENT COST is the current purchase price for identical goods.

Item	Quantity	Cost per Item	Replacement Cost (Market) per Item	Lower of Cost or Market per Item	Total Lower of Cost or Market
Intel chips	1,000	$250	$200	$200	1,000 × $200 = $200,000
Disk drives	400	100	110	100	400 × $100 = 40,000

The 1,000 Intel chips should be recorded in the ending inventory at the current market value ($200) because it is **lower** than the cost ($250). Dell makes the following journal entry to record the write-down:

Cost of goods sold (+E, −SE) (1,000 × $50)	50,000	
Inventory (−A)		50,000

Assets	=	Liabilities	+	Stockholders' Equity
Inventory −50,000				Cost of Goods Sold −50,000

Since the market price of the disk drives ($110) is higher than the original cost ($100), no write-down is necessary. The drives remain on the books at their cost of $100 per unit ($40,000 in total). Recognition of holding gains on inventory is not permitted by GAAP.

The write-down of the Pentium chips to market produces the following effects on the income statement and balance sheet:

Effects of LCM Write-Down	Current Period	Next Period (if sold)
Cost of goods sold	Increase $50,000	Decrease $50,000
Pretax income	Decrease $50,000	Increase $50,000
Ending inventory on balance sheet	Decrease $50,000	Unaffected

Note that the effects in the period of sale are the opposite of those in the period of the write-down. Lower of cost or market changes only the timing of cost of goods sold. It transfers cost of goods sold from the period of sale to the period of write-down.

NET REALIZABLE VALUE is the expected sales price less selling costs (e.g., repair and disposal costs).

In the case of seasonal goods such as clothing, obsolete goods, or damaged goods, if the sales price less selling costs (or net realizable value) drops below cost, this difference is subtracted from ending inventory and added to cost of goods sold for the period. This has the same effect on current and future periods' financial statements as the write-down to replacement cost.

Note that in the two examples that follow, both Harley-Davidson, which is a mixed LIFO company, and Dell Inc., which is a FIFO company, report the use of lower of cost or market for financial statement purposes.[5]

REAL WORLD EXCERPT

ANNUAL REPORT

> **HARLEY-DAVIDSON, INC.**
> **Notes to Consolidated Financial Statements**
> **1. SUMMARY OF SIGNIFICANT ACCOUNTING POLICIES**
>
> INVENTORIES—Inventories are valued at the lower of cost or market. Substantially all inventories located in the United States are valued using the last-in, first-out (LIFO) method. Other inventories totaling $103.5 million in 2006 and $77.4 million in 2005 are valued at the lower of cost or market using the first-in, first-out (FIFO) method.

REAL WORLD EXCERPT

ANNUAL REPORT

> **DELL INC.**
> **Notes to Consolidated Financial Statements**
> **NOTE 1—Description of Business and Summary**
> **of Significant Accounting Policies**
>
> Inventories—Inventories are stated at the lower of cost or market with cost being determined on a first-in, first-out basis.

EVALUATING INVENTORY MANAGEMENT

Learning Objective 5

Evaluate inventory management using the inventory turnover ratio and the effects of inventory on cash flows.

Measuring Efficiency in Inventory Management

As noted at the beginning of the chapter, the primary goals of inventory management are to have sufficient quantities of high-quality inventory available to serve customers' needs while minimizing the costs of carrying inventory (production, storage, obsolescence, and financing). The inventory turnover ratio is an important measure of the company's success in balancing these conflicting goals:

KEY RATIO
ANALYSIS   **Inventory Turnover**

? ANALYTICAL QUESTION:
How efficient are inventory management activities?

% RATIO AND COMPARISONS:

$$\text{Inventory Turnover} = \frac{\text{Cost of Goods Sold}}{\text{Average Inventory}}$$

---

[5]For tax purposes, lower of cost or market may be applied with all inventory costing methods except LIFO.

The 2006 ratio for Harley-Davidson (see Exhibit 7.1 for the inputs to the equation):

$$\frac{\$3,567,839}{(\$287,798 + 221,418)/2} = 14.0$$

COMPARISONS OVER TIME			COMPARISONS WITH COMPETITORS	
Harley-Davidson			Ducati Motor	Honda Motor
2004	2005	2006	2006	2006
14.3	14.7	14.0	4.4	7.4

💡 **INTERPRETATIONS:**

In General   The inventory turnover ratio reflects how many times average inventory was produced and sold during the period. A higher ratio indicates that inventory moves more quickly through the production process to the ultimate customer, reducing storage and obsolescence costs. Because less money is tied up in inventory, the excess can be invested to earn interest income or reduce borrowing, which reduces interest expense. More efficient purchasing and production techniques such as just-in-time inventory, as well as high product demand cause this ratio to be high. Analysts and creditors also watch the inventory turnover ratio because a sudden decline may mean that a company is facing an unexpected drop in demand for its products or is becoming sloppy in its production management. Many managers and analysts compute the related number average days to sell inventory, which, for Harley-Davidson, is equal to:

$$\text{Average Days to Sell Inventory} = \frac{365}{\text{Inventory Turnover}} = \frac{365}{14.0} = 26.1 \text{ days.}$$

It indicates the average time it takes the company to produce and deliver inventory to customers.

Focus Company Analysis   Harley-Davidson's inventory turnover has decreased from 14.3 in 2004 to 14.0 in 2006. Harley's ratio is much higher than its smaller European rival, Ducati, whose operations are much less efficient. Harley-Davidson benefits from what economists call *economies of scale.* Harley's turnover is even higher than the ratio for the giant Japanese auto and motorcycle manufacturer Honda.

A Few Cautions: Differences across industries in purchasing, production, and sales processes cause dramatic differences in this ratio. For example, restaurants such as Papa John's, which must turn over their perishable inventory very quickly, tend to have much higher inventory turnover. A particular firm's ratio should be compared only with its figures from prior years' or with figures for other firms in the same industry.

Selected Focus Company Inventory Turnover

Papa John's	22.3
General Mills	6.25
Boston Beer	7.57
HomeDepot	5.03

Inventory and Cash Flows

When companies expand production to meet increases in demand, this increases the amount of inventory reported on the balance sheet. However, when companies overestimate demand for a product, they usually produce too many units of the slow-selling item. This increases storage costs as well as the interest costs on short-term borrowings that finance the inventory. It may even lead to losses if the excess inventory cannot be sold at normal prices. The cash flow statement often provides the first sign of such problems.

FOCUS ON
CASH FLOWS

Inventory

As with a change in accounts receivable, a change in inventories can have a major effect on a company's cash flow from operations. Cost of goods sold on the income statement may be more or less than the amount of cash paid to suppliers during the period. Since most inventory is purchased on open credit (borrowing from suppliers is normally called accounts payable), reconciling cost of goods sold with cash paid to suppliers requires consideration of the changes in both the Inventory and Accounts Payable accounts.

The simplest way to think about the effects of changes in inventory is that buying (increasing) inventory eventually decreases cash, while selling (decreasing) inventory eventually increases cash. Similarly, borrowing from suppliers, which increases accounts payable, increases cash. Paying suppliers, which decreases accounts payable, decreases cash.

EFFECT ON STATEMENT OF CASH FLOWS

In General   When a net **decrease in inventory** for the period occurs, sales are greater than purchases; thus, the decrease must be **added** in computing cash flows from operations.

When a net **increase in inventory** for the period occurs, sales are less than purchases; thus, the increase must be **subtracted** in computing cash flows from operations.

When a net **decrease in accounts payable** for the period occurs, payments to suppliers are greater than new purchases; thus, the decrease must be **subtracted** in computing cash flows from operations.

When a net **increase in accounts payable** for the period occurs, payments to suppliers are less than new purchases; thus, the increase must be **added** in computing cash flows from operations.

Selected Focus Company Comparisons: 3-Year Change in Cash Flows Related to Inventory (Changes in millions)

Wal-Mart   −5,444

Callaway Golf   −10

Effect on Cash Flows

Operating activities (indirect method)	
Net income	$xxx
Adjusted for	
Add inventory **decrease**	+
or	
Subtract inventory **increase**	−
Add accounts payable **increase**	+
or	
Subtract accounts payable **decrease**	−

Focus Company Analysis   Exhibit 7.8 is the Operating Activities section of Harley-Davidson's statement of cash flows. When the inventory balance increases during the period, as was the case at Harley-Davidson in 2006, the company has purchased or produced more inventory than it has sold. Thus, the increase is subtracted in the computation of cash flow from operations. Conversely, when the inventory balance decreases during the period, the company has sold more inventory than it purchased or produced. Thus, the decrease is added in the computation of cash flow from operations. When the accounts payable balance increases during the period, the company has borrowed more from suppliers than it has paid them (or postponed payments). Thus, the increase is added in the computation of cash flow from operations.*

For companies with foreign currency or business acquisitions/dispositions, the amount of the change reported on the cash flow statement will not equal the change in the accounts reported on the balance sheet.

EXHIBIT 7.8

Inventories on the Cash Flow Statement

REAL WORLD EXCERPT
Harley-Davidson, Inc.
ANNUAL REPORT

HARLEY-DAVIDSON, INC.
CONSOLIDATED STATEMENTS OF CASH FLOWS
Years Ended December 31, 2006 and 2005
(dollars in thousands)

	2006	2005
Cash flows from operating activities:		
Net Income	$1,043,153	$ 959,604
Adjustments to reconcile net income to net cash provided by operating activities:		
Depreciation and amortization	213,769	205,705
Provision for long-term employee benefits	80,179	71,461
Stock compensation expense	21,446	22,974
Current year gain on securitizations	(32,316)	(46,581)
Change in wholesale financial receivables	(516,926)	(33,280)
Contributions to pension plan	(13,512)	(296,859)
Deferred income taxes	(39,768)	48,165
Other	24,560	50,684
Net changes in current assets and current liabilities:		
Accounts receivable	(16,361)	(11,556)
Inventories	(54,352)	(6,366)
Prepaid expenses & other current assets	(708)	(9,895)
Finance receivables—accrued interest and other	(23,442)	(16,252)
Accounts payable and accrued liabilities	76,058	24,810
Total adjustments	(281,373)	3,010
Net cash provided by operating activities	$ 761,780	$ 962,614

SELF-STUDY QUIZ

1. Refer to the Key Ratio Analysis for Harley-Davidson's inventory turnover. Based on the computations for 2006, answer the following question. If Harley-Davidson had been able to manage its inventory more efficiently and decrease purchases and ending inventory by $10,000 for 2006, would its inventory turnover ratio have increased or decreased? Explain.

2. Based on the Focus on Cash Flows section, answer the following question. If Harley-Davidson had decreased its accounts payable, would its cash flow from operations have increased or decreased?

After you have completed your answers, check them with the solutions at the bottom of the page.

Self-Study Quiz Solutions

1. Inventory turnover would have increased because the denominator of the ratio (average inventory) would have decreased by $5,000.

$$\frac{\$3,567,839}{(\$277,798 + \$221,418)/2} = 14.3$$

2. A decrease in accounts payable would have decreased cash flow from operations because they would have paid their vendors more than they had borrowed during the period.

Inventory Methods and Financial Statement Analysis

What would analysts do if they wanted to compare two companies that prepared their statements using different inventory accounting methods? Before meaningful comparisons could be made, one company's statements would have to be converted to a comparable basis. Making such a conversion is eased by the requirement that U.S. public companies using LIFO also report beginning and ending inventory on a FIFO basis in the notes if the FIFO values are materially different. We can use this information along with the cost of goods sold equation to convert the balance sheet and income statement to the FIFO basis.

Converting the Income Statement to FIFO

Recall that the choice of a cost flow assumption affects how goods available for sale are allocated to ending inventory and cost of goods sold. It does not affect the recording of purchases. Ending inventory will be different under the alternative methods, and, since last year's ending inventory is this year's beginning inventory, beginning inventory will also be different:

Beginning inventory	**Different**
+ Purchases of merchandise during the year	**Same**
− Ending inventory	**Different**
Cost of goods sold	**Different**

This equation suggests that if we know the differences between a company's inventory valued at LIFO and FIFO for both beginning and ending inventory, we can compute the difference in cost of goods sold. Exhibit 7.9 shows Harley-Davidson's 2006 disclosure of the differences between LIFO and FIFO values for beginning and ending inventory. These amounts, referred to as the **LIFO reserve** or "Excess of FIFO over LIFO," are disclosed by LIFO users in their inventory footnotes.

LIFO RESERVE is a contra-asset for the excess of FIFO over LIFO inventory.

Using Harley-Davidson's LIFO reserve values reported in the footnote in Exhibit 7.9, we see that cost of goods sold would have been $5,436 **lower** had it used FIFO.

Beginning LIFO Reserve (Excess of FIFO over LIFO)	$ 23,290
− Less: Ending LIFO Reserve (Excess of FIFO over LIFO)	− 28,726
Difference in Cost of Goods Sold under FIFO	($ 5,436)

Since FIFO cost of goods sold expense is **lower,** income before income taxes would have been $5,436 **higher.** As a result, income taxes would be that amount times its tax rate of 35 percent **higher** had it used FIFO.

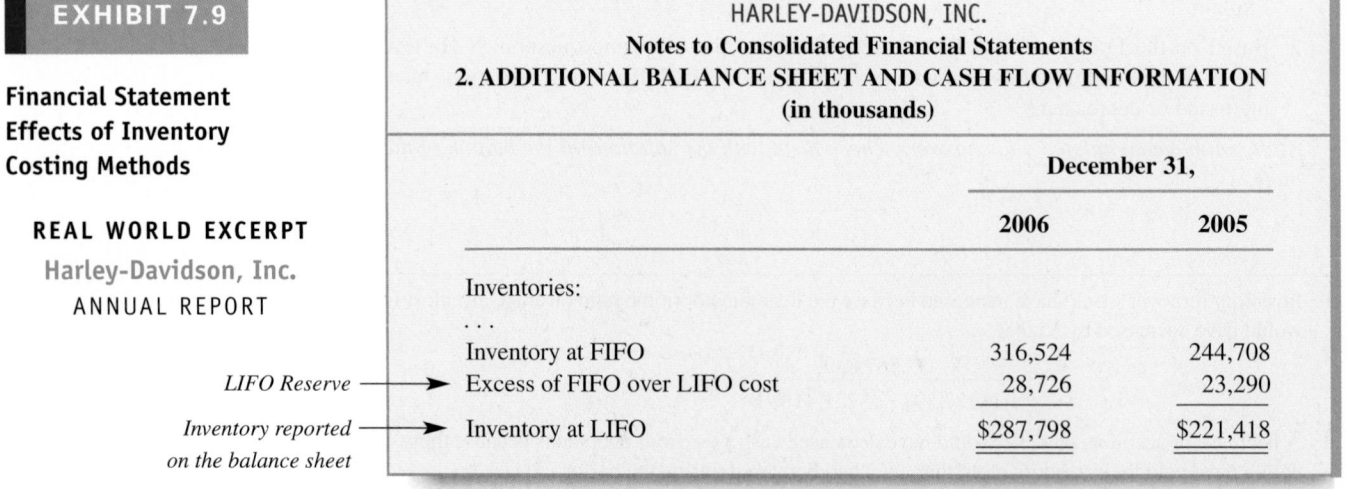

EXHIBIT 7.9

Financial Statement Effects of Inventory Costing Methods

REAL WORLD EXCERPT

Harley-Davidson, Inc.
ANNUAL REPORT

LIFO Reserve →

Inventory reported →
on the balance sheet

HARLEY-DAVIDSON, INC.
Notes to Consolidated Financial Statements
2. ADDITIONAL BALANCE SHEET AND CASH FLOW INFORMATION
(in thousands)

	December 31,	
	2006	**2005**
Inventories:		
. . .		
Inventory at FIFO	316,524	244,708
Excess of FIFO over LIFO cost	28,726	23,290
Inventory at LIFO	$287,798	$221,418

Difference in pretax income under FIFO	$ 5,436
Tax rate	× .35
Difference in taxes under FIFO	$ 1,903

Combining the two effects, net income would be increased by the change in cost of goods sold of $5,436 and decreased by the change in income tax expense of $1,903, resulting in an overall increase in net income of $3,533.

Decrease in Cost of Goods Sold Expense (*Income increases*)	$ 5,436
Increase in Income Tax Expense (*Income decreases*)	(1,903)
Increase in Net Income	$ 3,533

These Harley-Davidson computations are for 2006. It is important to note that even companies that usually face increasing costs occasionally face decreasing costs. For example, during 2000, Harley-Davidson's costs of new inventory declined due to manufacturing efficiencies. Consequently, when we convert from LIFO to FIFO, cost of goods sold for 2000 actually **increases** by $1,851, and the conversion's effect on pretax income is the opposite—a **decrease** of $1,851. As a result, even though LIFO usually **saves** it taxes, Harley paid **extra** taxes in 2000.

Converting Inventory on the Balance Sheet to FIFO

You can adjust the inventory amounts on the balance sheet to FIFO by substituting the FIFO values in the note ($316,524 and $244,708 for 2006 and 2005, respectively) for the LIFO values (see Exhibit 7.9). Alternatively, you can add the LIFO reserve to the LIFO value on the balance sheet to arrive at the same numbers.

LIFO and Inventory Turnover Ratio

For many LIFO companies, the inventory turnover ratio can be deceptive. Remember that, for these companies, the beginning and ending inventory numbers that make up the denominator of the ratio will be artificially small because they reflect old lower costs. Consider Deere & Co., manufacturer of John Deere farm, lawn, and construction equipment. Its inventory note lists the following values:

DEERE & COMPANY		
Notes to Consolidated Financial Statements		
Inventories		
(dollars in millions)		
	2006	**2005**
Total FIFO value	$ 3,097	$3,267
Adjustment to LIFO basis	1,140	1,132
Inventories	$ 1,957	$2,135

REAL WORLD EXCERPT

Deere & Company
ANNUAL REPORT

John Deere's cost of goods sold for 2006 was $15,362 million. If the ratio is computed using the reported LIFO inventory values for the ratio, it would be

$$\text{Inventory Turnover Ratio} = \frac{\$15,362}{(\$1,957 + 2,135)/2} = 7.5$$

Converting cost of goods sold (the numerator) to a FIFO basis and using the more current FIFO inventory values in the denominator, it would be

$$\text{Inventory Turnover Ratio} = \frac{\$15,362 - 8}{(\$3,097 + \$3,267)/2} = 4.8$$

Note that the major difference between the two ratios is in the denominator. FIFO inventory values are nearly two times the LIFO values. So the FIFO ratio is just over half the LIFO amount. The LIFO beginning and ending inventory numbers are artificially small because they reflect older lower costs. Thus, the numerator in the first calculation does not relate in a meaningful way to the denominator.[6]

INTERNATIONAL PERSPECTIVE

LIFO and International Comparisons

The methods of accounting for inventories discussed in this chapter are used in most major industrialized countries. In several countries, however, the LIFO method is not generally used. In England and Canada, for example, LIFO is not acceptable for tax purposes. LIFO is not used in Australia and Singapore, but it may be used in China for both financial reporting and tax purposes. International Financial Reporting Standards (IFRS) prohibit the use of LIFO. These differences can create comparability problems when one attempts to compare companies across international borders. For example, General Motors and Ford use LIFO to value U.S. inventories and average cost or FIFO for non-U.S. inventories, while Honda (of Japan) uses FIFO for all inventories.

SELF-STUDY QUIZ

In a recent year, Caterpillar Inc., a major manufacturer of farm and construction equipment, reported pretax earnings of $1,615 million. Its inventory note indicated "if the FIFO (first-in, first-out) method had been in use, inventories would have been $2,103 and $2,035 higher than reported at the end of the current and prior year, respectively." (The amounts noted are for the LIFO reserve.) Convert pretax earnings for the current year from a LIFO to a FIFO basis.

CATERPILLAR®

Beginning LIFO Reserve (Excess of FIFO over LIFO)   _____
Less: Ending LIFO Reserve (Excess of FIFO over LIFO)   _____
Difference in cost of goods sold under FIFO   _____
Pretax income (LIFO)   _____
Difference in pretax income under FIFO   _____
Pretax income (FIFO)   _____

After you have completed your answers, check them with the solutions at the bottom of the page.

Self-Study Quiz
Solutions

Beginning LIFO Reserve	$2,035		Pretax income (LIFO)	$1,615
Less: Ending LIFO Reserve	2,103		Difference in pretax income	68
Difference in cost of goods sold	($ 68)		Pretax income (FIFO)	$1,683

---

[6]Since the LIFO values for cost of goods sold on the income statement and the FIFO inventory numbers on the balance sheet are closer to current prices, they are often thought to be the most appropriate numerator and denominator, respectively, for use in this ratio.

CONTROL OF INVENTORY

Internal Control of Inventory

After cash, inventory is the asset second most vulnerable to theft. Efficient management of inventory to avoid cost of stock-outs and overstock situations is also crucial to the profitability of most companies. As a consequence, a number of control features focus on safeguarding inventories and providing up-to-date information for management decisions. Key among these are:

Learning Objective 7
Understand methods for controlling and keeping track of inventory and analyze the effects of inventory errors on financial statements.

1. Separation of responsibilities for inventory accounting and physical handling of inventory.
2. Storage of inventory in a manner that protects it from theft and damage.
3. Limiting access to inventory to authorized employees.
4. Maintaining perpetual inventory records (described below).
5. Comparing perpetual records to periodic physical counts of inventory.

Perpetual and Periodic Inventory Systems

The amount of purchases for the period is always accumulated in the accounting system. The amount of cost of goods sold and ending inventory can be determined by using one of two different inventory systems: perpetual or periodic.

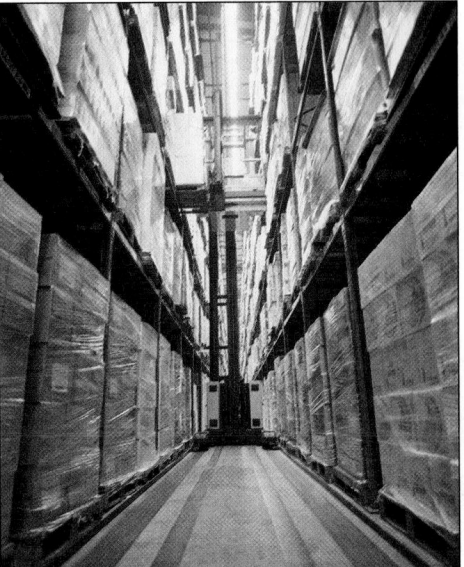

Perpetual Inventory System

In a **perpetual inventory system,** a detailed record is maintained for each type of merchandise stocked, showing (1) units and cost of the beginning inventory, (2) units and cost of each purchase, (3) units and cost of the goods for each sale, and (4) units and cost of the goods on hand at any point in time. This up-to-date record is maintained on a transaction-by-transaction basis. In a complete perpetual inventory system, the inventory record gives the amount of both ending inventory and cost of goods sold at any point in time. Under this system, a physical count should also be performed from time to time to ensure that records are accurate in case of errors or theft.

In a PERPETUAL INVENTORY SYSTEM, a detailed inventory record is maintained, recording each purchase and sale during the accounting period.

To this point in the text, all journal entries for purchase and sale transactions have been recorded using a perpetual inventory system. In a perpetual inventory system, purchase transactions are recorded directly in an inventory account. When each sale is recorded, a companion cost of goods sold entry is made, decreasing inventory and recording cost of goods sold. As a result, information on cost of goods sold and ending inventory is available on a continuous (perpetual) basis.

Periodic Inventory System

Under the **periodic inventory system,** no up-to-date record of inventory is maintained during the year. An actual physical count of the goods remaining on hand is required at the **end of each period.** The number of units of each type of merchandise on hand is multiplied by their unit cost to compute the dollar amount of the ending inventory. Cost of goods sold is calculated using the cost of goods sold equation.

In a PERIODIC INVENTORY SYSTEM, ending inventory and cost of goods sold are determined at the end of the accounting period based on a physical count.

Because the amount of inventory is not known until the end of the period when the inventory count is taken, the amount of cost of goods sold cannot be reliably determined until the inventory count is complete. Inventory purchases are debited to an account called **Purchases,** which is part of the asset inventory. Revenues are recorded at the time of each sale. However, cost of goods sold is not recorded until after the inventory count is completed. At other times, companies using a periodic system must estimate the amount of inventory on hand. Estimation methods are discussed in intermediate accounting courses.

Audio lecture–AP7-2
www.mhhe.com/libby6e

Before affordable computers and bar code readers were available, the primary reason for using a periodic inventory system was its low cost. The primary disadvantage of a periodic inventory system is the lack of inventory information. Managers are not informed about low stock or overstocked situations. Most modern companies could not survive without this information. As noted at the beginning of the chapter, cost and quality pressures brought on by increasing competition, combined with dramatic declines in the cost of computers, have made sophisticated perpetual inventory systems a requirement at all but the smallest companies. The entries made when using both systems are compared in Supplement C at the end of this chapter.

Perpetual Inventory Records and Cost Flow Assumptions in Practice

Systems that do keep track of the costs of individual items or lots normally do so on a FIFO or estimated average (or standard) cost basis. For distinguishable high-value items, specific identification may be used. Perpetual records are rarely kept on a LIFO basis for two reasons: (1) doing so is more complex and costly and (2) it can increase tax payments. LIFO companies convert the outputs of their perpetual inventory system to LIFO with an adjusting entry.

Errors in Measuring Ending Inventory

As the cost of goods sold equation indicates, a direct relationship exists between ending inventory and cost of goods sold because items not in the ending inventory are assumed to have been sold. Thus, the measurement of ending inventory quantities and costs affects both the balance sheet (assets) and the income statement (cost of goods sold, gross profit, and net income). The measurement of ending inventory affects not only the net income for that period but also the net income for the next accounting period. This two-period effect occurs because the ending inventory for one period is the beginning inventory for the next accounting period.

Greeting card maker Gibson Greetings had overstated its net income by 20 percent because one division had overstated ending inventory for the year. You can compute the effects of the error on both the current year's and the next year's income before taxes using the cost of goods sold equation. Assume that ending inventory was overstated by $10,000 due to a clerical error that was not discovered. This would have the following effects in the current year and next year:

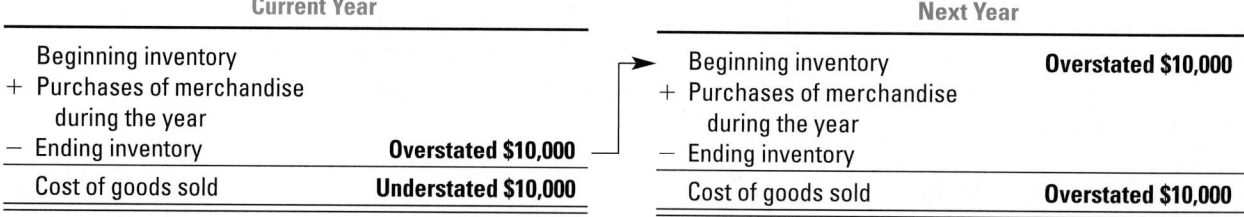

Current Year		Next Year	
Beginning inventory		Beginning inventory	**Overstated $10,000**
+ Purchases of merchandise during the year		+ Purchases of merchandise during the year	
− Ending inventory	**Overstated $10,000**	− Ending inventory	
Cost of goods sold	**Understated $10,000**	Cost of goods sold	**Overstated $10,000**

Because cost of goods sold was understated, **income before taxes would be overstated** by $10,000 in the **current year.** And, since the current year's ending inventory becomes next year's beginning inventory, it would have the following effects: Because cost of goods sold was overstated, **income before taxes would be understated** by $10,000 in the **next year.**

Each of these errors would flow into retained earnings so that at the end of the current year, retained earnings would be overstated by $10,000 (less the related income tax expense). This error would be offset in the next year, and retained earnings and inventory at the end of next year would be correct.

In this example, we assumed that the overstatement of ending inventory was inadvertent, the result of a clerical error. However, inventory fraud is a common form of financial statement fraud. It occurred in the Maxidrive case discussed in Chapter 1 as well as in the real MiniScribe fraud.

Assume that it is now the end of 2008, and for the first time, the company will undergo an audit by an independent CPA. The annual income statement prepared by the company is presented here. Assume further that the independent CPA discovered that the ending inventory for 2008 was understated by $15,000. Correct and reconstruct the income statement in the space provided.

For the Year Ended December 31

	2008 Uncorrected		2008 Corrected
Sales revenue		$750,000	
Cost of goods sold			
Beginning inventory	$ 45,000		
Add purchases	460,000		_____
Goods available for sale	505,000		
Less ending inventory	40,000		_____
Cost of goods sold		465,000	_____
Gross margin on sales		285,000	
Operating expenses		275,000	_____
Pretax income		10,000	
Income tax expense (20%)		2,000	_____
Net income		$ 8,000	_____

After you have completed your answer, check it with the solutions at the bottom of the page.

Sales revenue		$750,000	Self-Study Quiz
Cost of goods sold			Solution
Beginning inventory	$ 45,000		
Add purchases	460,000		
Goods available for sale	505,000		
Less ending inventory	55,000		
Cost of goods sold		450,000	
Gross margin on sales		300,000	
Operating expenses		275,000	
Pretax income		25,000	
Income tax expense (20%)		5,000	
Net income		$ 20,000	

Note: An ending inventory error in one year affects pretax income by the amount of the error and in the next year affects pretax income again by the same amount, but in the opposite direction.

DEMONSTRATION CASE

(Complete the requirements before proceeding to the suggested solution that follows.) This case reviews the application of the FIFO and LIFO inventory costing methods and the inventory turnover ratio.

Balent Appliances distributes a number of household appliances. One product, microwave ovens, has been selected for case purposes. Assume that the following summarized transactions were completed during the year ended December 31, 2008, in the order given (assume that all transactions are cash):

	Units	Unit Cost
a. Beginning inventory	11	$200
b. New inventory purchases	9	220
c. Sales (selling price, $420)	8	?

Required:

1. Compute the following amounts, assuming the application of the FIFO and LIFO inventory costing methods:

	Ending Inventory		Cost of Goods Sold	
	Units	Dollars	Units	Dollars
FIFO				
LIFO				

2. Assuming that inventory cost was expected to follow current trends, which method would you suggest that Balent select to account for these inventory items? Explain your answer.

3. Assuming that other operating expenses were $500 and the income tax rate is 25 percent, prepare the income statement for the period using your selected method.

4. Compute the inventory turnover ratio for the current period using your selected method. What does it indicate?

SUGGESTED SOLUTION

1.

	Ending Inventory		Cost of Goods Sold	
	Units	Dollars	Units	Dollars
FIFO	12	$2,580	8	$1,600
LIFO	12	$2,420	8	$1,760

Computations

Beginning inventory (11 units × $200)	$2,200
+ Purchases (9 units × $220)	1,980
Goods available for sale	$4,180

FIFO inventory (costed at end of period)

Goods available for sale (from above)	$4,180
− Ending inventory (9 units × $220) + (3 units × $200)	2,580
Cost of goods sold (8 units × $200)	$1,600

LIFO inventory (costed at end of period)

Goods available for sale (from above)	$4,180
− Ending inventory (11 units × $200) + (1 unit × $220)	2,420
Cost of goods sold (8 units × $220)	$1,760

2. LIFO should be selected. Because costs are rising, LIFO produces higher cost of goods sold, lower pretax income, and lower income tax payments. It is used on the tax return and income statement because of the LIFO conformity rule.

3.

BALENT APPLIANCES
Statement of Income
Year Ended December 31, 2008

Sales	$3,360
Cost of goods sold	1,760
Gross profit	1,600
Other expenses	500
Income before income taxes	1,100
Income tax expense (25%)	275
Net income	$ 825

Computations
Sales = 8 × $420 = $3,360.

4. Inventory turnover ratio = Cost of Goods Sold ÷   Average Inventory

   = $1,760   ÷ [($2,200 + $2,420) ÷ 2 = $2,310]

   = 0.76

The inventory turnover ratio reflects how many times average inventory was produced or purchased and sold during the period. Thus, Balent Appliances purchased and sold its average inventory less than one time during the year.

Chapter Supplement A

LIFO Liquidations

When a LIFO company sells more inventory than it purchases or manufactures, items from beginning inventory become part of cost of goods sold. This is called a **LIFO liquidation.** When inventory costs are rising, these lower cost items in beginning inventory produce a higher gross profit, higher taxable income, and higher taxes when they are sold. We illustrate this process by continuing our Harley-Davidson store Model A leather jacket example into its second year.

A LIFO LIQUIDATION is a sale of a lower-cost inventory item from beginning LIFO inventory.

Financial Statement Effects of LIFO Liquidations

Recall that, in its first year of operation, the store purchased units for $70, $80, and $100 in sequence. Then, the $100 unit and three of the $80 units were sold under LIFO, leaving one $80 unit and two $70 units in ending inventory. These events were represented using the LIFO inventory bin in Exhibit 7.5. Exhibit 7.10 continues this illustration into a second year. The ending inventory from year 1 becomes the beginning inventory for year 2. In part (a) of Exhibit 7.10, we assume that in year 2, the Harley-Davidson store purchased a total of **three** inventory units at the current $120 price, the sales price has been raised to $140, and three units are sold. Using LIFO, the three recently purchased $120 inventory items become part of cost of goods sold of $360, and the old $80 and $70 items from beginning inventory become ending inventory. Given that revenue is $140 per unit, the gross profit on the three newly purchased units is 3 units × $20 = $60.

Now assume instead, as we do in part (b) of Exhibit 7.10, that the store purchased only *two* additional units at $120 each. Using LIFO, these two new $120 units and the old $80 unit would become cost of goods sold. Given that revenue is $140 per unit, the gross profit on the newly purchased units is 2 units × $20 = $40. Since the cost of the old unit is only $80, the gross profit on this one unit is $60 ($140 − $80) instead of $20, raising total gross profit to $100.

Compared to part (a), cost of goods sold has decreased by $40, and gross profit and income before taxes have increased by $40. This $40 change is the **pretax effect of the LIFO liquidation.** Given the assumed tax rate of 25 percent, taxes paid are $10 (0.25 × $40) higher than in part (a).

In practice, LIFO liquidations and extra tax payments can be avoided even if purchases of additional inventory take place **after** the sale of the item it replaces. Tax law allows LIFO to be applied **as if** all purchases during an accounting period took place before any sales and cost of goods sold were recorded. Thus, temporary LIFO liquidations can be eliminated by purchasing additional inventory before year-end. Most companies apply LIFO in this manner.

LIFO Liquidations and Financial Statement Analysis

During the decade prior to 1993, Deere & Company and other companies in its industry faced declining demand and increasing competition in most major segments of their businesses. These economic changes reduced the inventory quantities necessary to meet customers' needs. Deere had also instituted modern manufacturing techniques that further decreased inventory levels. Deere, a long-time LIFO user, experienced continuing LIFO liquidations over this period. Companies must disclose the effects of LIFO liquidations in the notes when they are material, as Deere did in the note that follows. The second paragraph of the note explains the effect. The last sentence lists the pretax (after-tax) effects of the liquidations.

REAL WORLD EXCERPT

Deere & Company
ANNUAL REPORT

DEERE & COMPANY
Notes to Consolidated Financial Statements

INVENTORIES

Substantially all inventories owned by Deere & Company and its United States equipment subsidiaries are valued at cost on the "last-in, first-out" (LIFO) method. . . .

Under the LIFO inventory method, cost of goods sold ordinarily reflects current production costs thus providing a matching of current costs and current revenues in the income statement. However, when LIFO–valued inventories decline, as they did in 1993 and 1992, lower costs that prevailed in prior years are matched against current year revenues, resulting in higher reported net income. Benefits from the reduction of LIFO inventories totaled $51 million ($33 million or $0.43 per share after income taxes) in 1993, $65 million ($43 million or $0.56 per share after income taxes) in 1992 and $128 million ($84 million or $1.11 per share after income taxes) in 1991.

According to this note, over the prior three years, LIFO liquidations increased Deere's reported income before taxes by a total of $244 million ($51 + $65 + $128). (These numbers are the equivalent of the $40 effect of the liquidation computed in the Harley-Davidson store example.) To compute pretax income as if the liquidations had not taken place (as if current year's production were large enough so that no items from beginning inventory were sold), simply subtract the LIFO liquidation effect from pretax income.

Pretax income on LIFO for 3 years (reported on the income statements)	$290
Less: Pretax effect of LIFO liquidations (from note)	244
Pretax income on LIFO for 3 years as if no liquidations	$ 46

Fully 84 percent ($244 ÷ $290) of Deere's reported pretax profit over the three years resulted from LIFO liquidations. Since the $46 million pretax profit figure reflected Deere's current costs of production, educated analysts used it when comparing Deere's performance to that of other LIFO companies. It is important to emphasize that these numbers still are on a **LIFO** basis but are computed **as if no liquidation had taken place.**

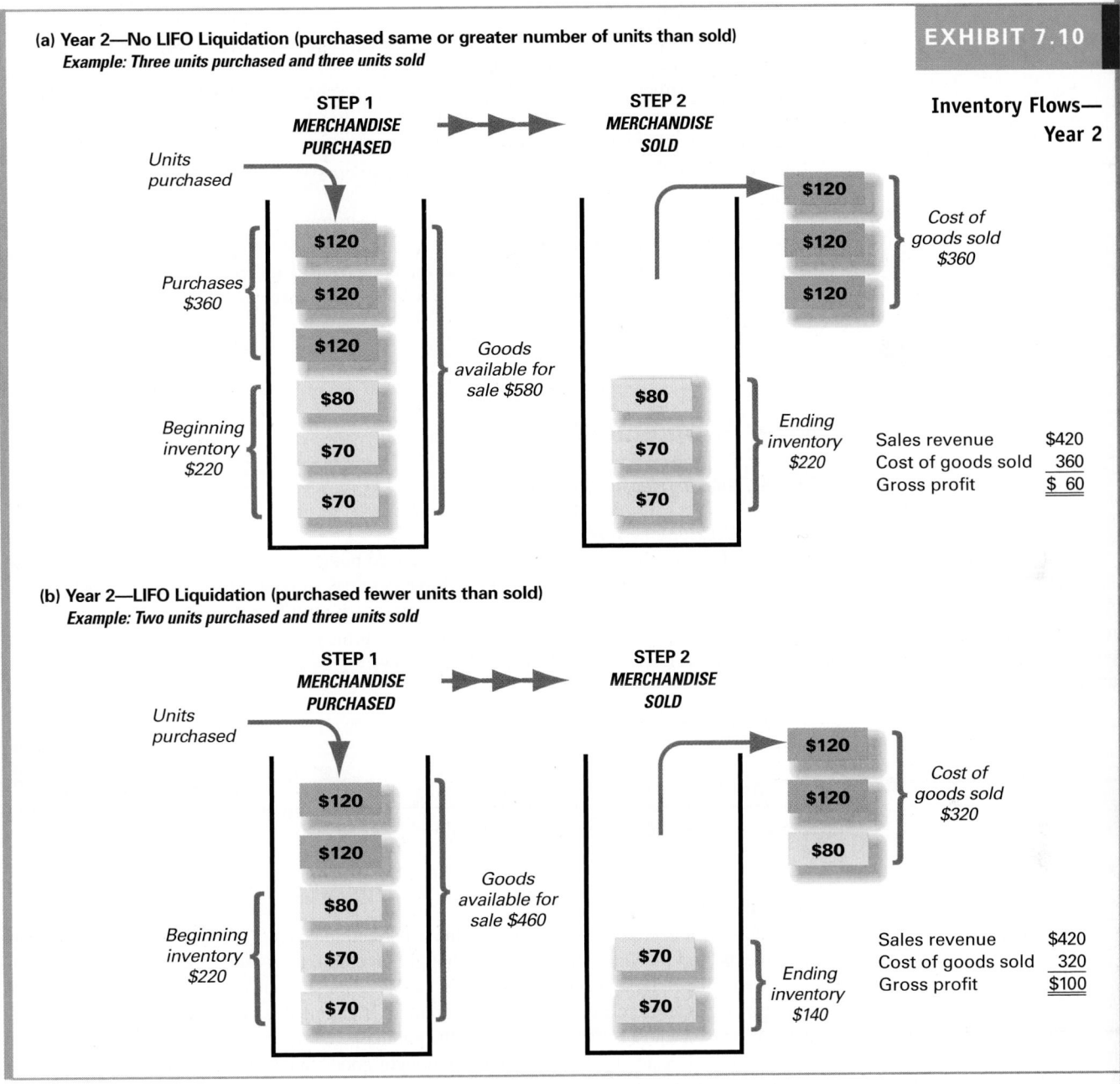

EXHIBIT 7.10

(a) Year 2—No LIFO Liquidation (purchased same or greater number of units than sold)
Example: Three units purchased and three units sold

Inventory Flows—
Year 2

STEP 1
MERCHANDISE PURCHASED

STEP 2
MERCHANDISE SOLD

Units purchased

Purchases $360
- $120
- $120
- $120

Beginning inventory $220
- $80
- $70
- $70

Goods available for sale $580

Cost of goods sold $360
- $120
- $120
- $120

Ending inventory $220
- $80
- $70
- $70

Sales revenue	$420
Cost of goods sold	360
Gross profit	$ 60

(b) Year 2—LIFO Liquidation (purchased fewer units than sold)
Example: Two units purchased and three units sold

STEP 1
MERCHANDISE PURCHASED

STEP 2
MERCHANDISE SOLD

Units purchased

- $120
- $120

Beginning inventory $220
- $80
- $70
- $70

Goods available for sale $460

Cost of goods sold $320
- $120
- $120
- $80

Ending inventory $140
- $70
- $70

Sales revenue	$420
Cost of goods sold	320
Gross profit	$100

Inventory Management and LIFO Liquidations

FINANCIAL
ANALYSIS

Several research studies[7] have documented the year-end inventory purchasing decisions of firms that use LIFO. Many firms avoid LIFO liquidations and the accompanying increase in tax expense by purchasing sufficient quantities of inventory at year-end to ensure that ending inventory quantities are greater than or equal to beginning inventory quantities. While this

---

[7]See, for example, M.R. Kinney and W.F. Wempe. 2004. "JIT Adoption: The Effects of LIFO Reserves and Financial Reporting and Tax Incentives." *Contemporary Accounting Research* 21 (3): 603–638.

practice increases the costs of carrying inventory (storage, financing, etc.), for these firms, the taxes saved exceed these amounts.

As noted earlier in the chapter, Harley-Davidson and many other firms have moved to more efficient just-in-time inventory techniques that greatly reduce the amount of inventory manufacturers keep on hand. When managers compare the savings in carrying costs against the costs of implementing the new system (new computers, training, etc.), they must also consider the added taxes they may pay if they account for the inventory using the LIFO method. When the company switches to the new just-in-time system, ending inventory quantity will normally decline below beginning inventory quantity, causing a LIFO liquidation and a one-time increase in taxes. This cost should be considered when deciding whether to adopt the new system. In this case, the tax law provides an incentive for U.S. companies not to become more efficient.

Chapter Supplement B

Additional Issues in Measuring Purchases

Purchase Returns and Allowances

Purchased goods may be returned to the vendor if they do not meet specifications, arrive in damaged condition, or are otherwise unsatisfactory. **Purchase returns and allowances** require a reduction in the cost of inventory purchases and the recording of a cash refund or a reduction in the liability to the vendor. For example, assume that Harley-Davidson returned to a supplier damaged harness boots that cost $1,000. The return would be recorded as follows:

PURCHASE RETURNS AND ALLOWANCES are a reduction in the cost of purchases associated with unsatisfactory goods.

Accounts payable (−L) (or Cash +A)	1,000
Inventory (−A)	1,000

Assets	=	Liabilities	+	Stockholders' Equity
Inventory −1,000		Accounts Payable −1,000		

Purchase Discounts

Cash discounts must be accounted for by both the seller and the buyer (accounting by the seller was discussed in Chapter 6). When merchandise is bought on credit, terms such as 2/10, n/30 are sometimes specified. That is, if payment is made within 10 days from the date of purchase, a 2 percent cash discount known as the **purchase discount** is granted. If payment is not made within the discount period, the full invoice cost is due 30 days after the purchase.

A **PURCHASE DISCOUNT** is a cash discount received for prompt payment of an account

Assume that on January 17, Harley-Davidson bought goods that had a $1,000 invoice price with terms 2/10, n/30. The purchase should be recorded as follows (using what is called the **gross method**):

Date of Purchase

Jan. 17 Inventory (+A)	1,000
Accounts payable (+L)	1,000

Assets	=	Liabilities	+	Stockholders' Equity
Inventory +1,000		Accounts Payable +1,000		

Date of Payment, within the Discount Period

Jan. 26 Accounts payable (−L)	1,000
Inventory (−A)	20
Cash (−A)	980

Assets	=	Liabilities	+	Stockholders' Equity
Inventory −20		Accounts Payable −1,000		
Cash −980				

If for any reason Harley-Davidson did not pay within the 10-day discount period, the following entry would be needed:

Date of Payment, after the Discount Period

Feb. 1   Accounts payable (−L) 1,000
            Cash (−A) 1,000

Assets	=	Liabilities	+	Stockholders' Equity
Cash −1,000		Accounts Payable −1,000		

Chapter Supplement C

Comparison of Perpetual and Periodic Inventory Systems

To simplify the discussion of how accounting systems keep track of these amounts, we will focus this discussion on the Motorclothes™ line for which Harley-Davidson is a wholesaler. Assume, for this illustration only, that Harley-Davidson stocks and sells only one item, its Eagle Harness Boots, and that only the following events occurred in 2008:

Jan. 1 Had beginning inventory: 800 units, at unit cost of $50.
April 14 Purchased: 1,100 additional units, at unit cost of $50.
Nov. 30 Sold: 1,300 units, at unit sales price of $83.

In the two types of inventory systems, the following sequential steps would take place:

Perpetual Records	Periodic Records
1. Record all purchases in the Inventory account and in a detailed perpetual inventory record.	1. Record all purchases in an account called Purchases.

April 14, 2008
Inventory (+A) (1,100 units at $50)* 55,000
   Accounts payable (+L) (or Cash−A).... 55,000
 	
*Also entered in the detailed perpetual inventory record as 1,100 harness boots at $50 each.
	April 14, 2008
	Purchases (+A) (1,100 units at $50) 55,000
	   Accounts payable (+L) (or Cash−A).... 55,000

2. Record all sales in the Sales Revenue account and record the cost of goods sold.	2. Record all sales in a Sales Revenue account.

November 30, 2008
Accounts receivable (+A) (or Cash+A) ... 107,900
   Sales revenue (+R, +SE)
   (1,300 units at $83) 107,900
Cost of goods sold (+E, −SE)........... 65,000
   Inventory (−A) (1,300 units at $50)*..... 65,000
 	
*Also entered in the perpetual inventory record as a reduction of 1,300 units at $50 each.
	November 30, 2008
	Accounts receivable (+A) (or Cash+A) ... 107,900
	   Sales revenue (+R, +SE)
	   (1,300 units at $83) 107,900

Perpetual Records	Periodic Records
3. Use cost of goods sold and inventory amounts. At the end of the accounting period, the balance in the Cost of Goods Sold account is reported on the income statement. It is not necessary to compute cost of goods sold because the Cost of Goods Sold account is up-to-date. Also, the Inventory account shows the ending inventory amount reported on the balance sheet. A physical inventory count is still necessary to assess the accuracy of the perpetual records and identify theft and other forms of misuse (called **shrinkage**).	3. At end of period: a. Count the number of units on hand. b. Compute the dollar valuation of the ending inventory. c. Compute and record the cost of goods sold.

Periodic Records (continued):

Beginning inventory (last period's ending)	$40,000
Add purchases (balance in the Purchases account)	55,000
Goods available for sale	95,000
Deduct ending inventory (physical count—600 units at $50)	30,000
Cost of goods sold	$65,000

Perpetual: No entry

December 31, 2008

Transfer beginning inventory and purchases to cost of goods sold:

Cost of goods sold (+E, −SE)	95,000	
Inventory (−A) (beginning)		40,000
Purchases (−A)......................		55,000

Subtract the ending inventory amount from the cost of goods sold to complete its computation and establish the ending inventory balance:

Inventory (+A) (ending)	30,000	
Cost of goods sold (−E, +SE)		30,000

Perpetual:

Assets		=	Liabilities		+	Stockholders' Equity	
Inventory	+55,000		Accounts			Sales Revenue	+107,900
Accts. Rec.	+107,900		Payable	+55,000		Cost of Goods	
Inventory	−65,000					Sold	−65,000

Periodic:

Assets		=	Liabilities		+	Stockholders' Equity	
Purchases	+55,000		Accounts			Sales Revenue	+107,900
Accts. Rec.	+107,900		Payable	+55,000		Cost of Goods	
Inventory	−40,000					Sold	−95,000
Purchases	−55,000					Cost of Goods	
Inventory	+30,000					Sold	+30,000

Note that the effects of the entries on the accounting equation are the same under both systems. Only the timing of the recording of amounts changes.

CHAPTER **TAKE-AWAYS**

1. **Apply the cost principle to identify the amounts that should be included in inventory and the matching principle to determine cost of goods sold for typical retailers, wholesalers, and manufacturers.   p. 340**

   Inventory should include all items owned that are held for resale. Costs flow into inventory when goods are purchased or manufactured. They flow out (as an expense) when they are sold or disposed of. In conformity with the matching principle, the total cost of the goods sold during the period must be matched with the sales revenue earned during the period.

2. **Report inventory and cost of goods sold using the four inventory costing methods.   p. 345**

   The chapter discussed four different inventory costing methods used to allocate costs between the units remaining in inventory and the units sold, and their applications in different economic circumstances.

The methods discussed were specific identification, FIFO, LIFO, and average cost. Each of the inventory costing methods conforms to GAAP. Public companies using LIFO must provide note disclosures that allow conversion of inventory and cost of goods sold to FIFO amounts. Remember that the cost flow assumption need not match the physical flow of inventory.

3. **Decide when the use of different inventory costing methods is beneficial to a company.**   p. 350

The selection of an inventory costing method is important because it will affect reported income, income tax expense (and hence cash flow), and the inventory valuation reported on the balance sheet. In a period of rising prices, FIFO normally results in a higher income and higher taxes than LIFO; in a period of falling prices, the opposite occurs. The choice of methods is normally made to minimize taxes.

4. **Report inventory at the lower of cost or market (LCM).**   p. 353

Ending inventory should be measured based on the lower of actual cost or replacement cost (LCM basis). This practice can have a major effect on the statements of companies facing declining costs. Damaged, obsolete, and out-of-season inventory should also be written down to their current estimated net realizable value if below cost. The LCM adjustment increases cost of goods sold, decreases income, and decreases reported inventory in the year of the write-down.

5. **Evaluate inventory management using the inventory turnover ratio and the effects of inventory on cash flows.**   p. 354

The inventory turnover ratio measures the efficiency of inventory management. It reflects how many times average inventory was produced and sold during the period. Analysts and creditors watch this ratio because a sudden decline may mean that a company is facing an unexpected drop in demand for its products or is becoming sloppy in its production management. When a net **decrease in inventory** for the period occurs, sales are more than purchases; thus, the decrease must be **added** in computing cash flows from operations. When a net **increase in inventory** for the period occurs, sales are less than purchases; thus, the increase must be **subtracted** in computing cash flows from operations.

6. **Compare companies that use different inventory costing methods.**   p. 358

These comparisons can be made by converting the LIFO company's statements to FIFO. Public companies using LIFO must disclose the differences between LIFO and FIFO values for beginning and ending inventory. These amounts are often called the LIFO reserve. The beginning LIFO reserve minus the ending LIFO reserve equals the difference in cost of goods sold under FIFO. Pretax income is affected by the same amount in the opposite direction. This amount times the tax rate is the tax effect.

7. **Understand methods for controlling and keeping track of inventory and analyze the effects of inventory errors on financial statements.**   p. 361

Various control procedures can limit inventory theft or mismanagement. A company can keep track of the ending inventory and cost of goods sold for the period using (1) the perpetual inventory system, which is based on the maintenance of detailed and continuous inventory records, and (2) the periodic inventory system, which is based on a physical count of ending inventory and use of the inventory equation to determine cost of goods sold. An error in the measurement of ending inventory affects cost of goods sold on the current period's income statement and ending inventory on the balance sheet. Because this year's ending inventory becomes next year's beginning inventory, it also affects cost of goods sold in the following period by the same amount but in the opposite direction. These relationships can be seen through the cost of goods sold equation (BI + P − EI = CGS).

In this and previous chapters, we discussed the current assets of a business. These assets are critical to operations, but many of them do not directly produce value. In Chapter 8, we will discuss the noncurrent assets property, plant, and equipment; natural resources; and intangibles that are the elements of productive capacity. Many of the noncurrent assets produce value, such as a factory that manufactures cars. These assets present some interesting accounting problems because they benefit a number of accounting periods.

KEY **RATIO**

Inventory turnover ratio measures the efficiency of inventory management. It reflects how many times average inventory was produced and sold during the period (p. 354):

$$\text{Inventory Turnover} = \frac{\text{Cost of Goods Sold}}{\text{Average Inventory}}$$

FINDING **FINANCIAL INFORMATION**

Balance Sheet

Under Current Assets
Inventories

Income Statement

Expenses
Cost of goods sold

Statement of Cash Flows

*Under Operating Activities
(indirect method):*
Net income
  − increases in inventory
  + decreases in inventory
  + increases in accounts payable
  − decreases in accounts payable

Notes

*Under Summary of Significant Accounting
    Policies:*
Description of management's choice of
    inventory accounting policy (FIFO, LIFO,
    LCM, etc.)

In Separate Note
If not listed on balance sheet, components of
    inventory (merchandise, raw materials,
    work in progress, finished goods)
If using LIFO, LIFO reserve (excess of FIFO
    over LIFO)

KEY **TERMS**

Average Cost Method p. 348
**Cost of Goods Sold
    Equation** p. 343
Direct Labor p. 342
Factory Overhead p. 342
Finished Goods Inventory p. 340
**First-In, First-Out (FIFO)
    Method** p. 346
Goods Available for Sale p. 343
Inventory p. 340

**Last-In, First-Out (LIFO)
    Method** p. 348
LIFO Liquidation p. 365
LIFO Reserve p. 358
**Lower of Cost or Market
    (LCM)** p. 353
Merchandise Inventory p. 340
Net Realizable Value p. 354
Periodic Inventory System p. 361
Perpetual Inventory System p. 361

Purchase Discount p. 368
**Purchase Returns and
    Allowances** p. 368
Raw Materials Inventory p. 340
Replacement Cost p. 353
**Specific Identification
    Method** p. 345
Work in Process Inventory p. 340

QUESTIONS

1. Why is inventory an important item to both internal (management) and external users of financial statements?
2. What are the general guidelines for deciding which items should be included in inventory?
3. Explain the application of the cost principle to an item in the ending inventory.

4. Define goods available for sale. How does it differ from cost of goods sold?

5. Define beginning inventory and ending inventory.

6. The chapter discussed four inventory costing methods. List the four methods and briefly explain each.

7. Explain how income can be manipulated when the specific identification inventory costing method is used.

8. Contrast the effects of LIFO versus FIFO on reported assets (i.e., the ending inventory) when (a) prices are rising and (b) prices are falling.

9. Contrast the income statement effect of LIFO versus FIFO (i.e., on pretax income) when (a) prices are rising and (b) prices are falling.

10. Contrast the effects of LIFO versus FIFO on cash outflow and inflow.

11. Explain briefly the application of the LCM concept to the ending inventory and its effect on the income statement and balance sheet when market is lower than cost.

12. When a perpetual inventory system is used, unit costs of the items sold are known at the date of each sale. In contrast, when a periodic inventory system is used, unit costs are known only at the end of the accounting period. Why are these statements correct?

MULTIPLE-CHOICE QUESTIONS

1. Consider the following information: ending inventory $24,000; sales $250,000; beginning inventory $20,000; selling and administrative expenses $70,000; and purchases $90,000. What is cost of goods sold?
   a. $86,000
   b. $94,000
   c. $16,000
   d. $84,000

2. The inventory costing method selected by a company will affect
   a. The balance sheet.
   b. The income statement.
   c. The statement of retained earnings.
   d. All of the above.

3. Which of the following is not a component of the cost of inventory?
   a. Administrative overhead
   b. Direct labor
   c. Raw materials
   d. Factory overhead

4. Consider the following information: beginning inventory 20 units @ $20 per unit; first purchase 35 units @ $22 per unit; second purchase 40 units @ $24 per unit; 50 units were sold. What is cost of goods sold using the **FIFO** method of inventory costing?
   a. $1,000
   b. $1,060
   c. $1,180
   d. $1,200

5. Consider the following information: beginning inventory 20 units @ $20 per unit; first purchase 35 units @ $22 per unit; second purchase 40 units @ $24 per unit; 50 units were sold. What is cost of goods sold using the **LIFO** method of inventory costing?
   a. $1,000
   b. $1,060
   c. $1,180
   d. $1,200

6. An increasing inventory turnover ratio
   a. Indicates a longer time span between the ordering and receiving of inventory.
   b. Indicates a shorter time span between the ordering and receiving of inventory.
   c. Indicates a shorter time span between the purchase and sale of inventory.
   d. Indicates a longer time span between the purchase and sale of inventory.

7. If the ending balance in accounts payable decreases from one period to the next, which of the following is true?
   a. Cash payments to suppliers exceeded current period purchases.
   b. Cash payments to suppliers were less than current period purchases.
   c. Cash receipts from customers exceeded cash payments to suppliers.
   d. Cash receipts from customers exceeded current period purchases.

8. Which of the following regarding the lower of cost or market rule for inventory are true?
   (1) The lower of cost or market rule is an example of the historical cost principle.
   (2) When the replacement cost of inventory drops below the cost shown in the financial records, net income is reduced.

(3) When the replacement cost of inventory drops below the cost shown in the financial records, total assets are reduced.

   a. (1)   c. (2) and (3)

   b. (2)   d. All three

9. Which inventory method provides a better matching of current costs with sales revenue on the income statement and outdated values for inventory on the balance sheet?

   a. FIFO   c. LIFO

   b. Weighted average   d. Specific identification

10. Which of the following is false regarding a perpetual inventory system?

   a. Physical counts are not needed since records are maintained on a transaction-by-transaction basis.

   b. The balance in the inventory account is updated with each inventory purchase and sale transaction.

   c. Cost of goods sold is increased as sales are recorded.

   d. The account Purchases is not used as inventory is acquired.

For more practice on multiple choice questions, go to the text website at www.mhhe.com/libby6e.

MINI-EXERCISES

 Available with McGraw-Hill's Homework Manager

M7-1
LO1

Matching Inventory Items to Type of Business

Match the type of inventory with the type of business in the following matrix:

	TYPE OF BUSINESS	
Type of Inventory	Merchandising	Manufacturing
Merchandise		
Finished goods		
Work in process		
Raw materials		

M7-2
LO1

Recording the Cost of Purchases for a Merchandiser

Elite Apparel purchased 90 new shirts and recorded a total cost of $2,620 determined as follows:

Invoice cost	$2,180
Shipping charges	175
Import taxes and duties	145
Interest (5.5%) on $2,180 borrowed to finance the purchase	120
	$2,620

Required:

Make the needed corrections in this calculation. Give the journal entry(ies) to record this purchase in the correct amount, assuming a perpetual inventory system. Show computations.

M7-3
LO1

Identifying the Cost of Inventories for a Manufacturer

Operating costs incurred by a manufacturing company become either (1) part of the cost of inventory to be expensed as cost of goods sold at the time the finished goods are sold or (2) expenses at the time they are incurred. Indicate whether each of the following costs belongs in category 1 or 2.

_____ a. Wages of factory workers
_____ b. Sales salaries
_____ c. Costs of raw materials purchased
_____ d. Heat, light, and power for the factory building
_____ e. Heat, light, and power for the headquarters office building

Inferring Purchases Using the Cost of Goods Sold Equation

M7-4
LO1
JCPenney

JCPenney Company, Inc., is a major retailer with department stores in all 50 states. The dominant portion of the company's business consists of providing merchandise and services to consumers through department stores that include catalog departments. In a recent annual report, JCPenney reported cost of goods sold of $10,969 million, ending inventory for the current year of $3,062 million, and ending inventory for the previous year of $2,969 million.

Required:
Is it possible to develop a reasonable estimate of the merchandise purchases for the year? If so, prepare the estimate; if not, explain why.

Matching Financial Statement Effects to Inventory Costing Methods

M7-5
LO2

Indicate whether the FIFO or LIFO inventory costing method normally produces each of the following effects under the listed circumstances.

a. Rising costs
    Highest net income _____
    Highest inventory _____
b. Declining costs
    Highest net income _____
    Highest inventory _____

Matching Inventory Costing Method Choices to Company Circumstances

M7-6
LO3

Indicate whether the FIFO or LIFO inventory costing method would normally be selected when inventory costs are rising. Explain why.

Reporting Inventory Under Lower of Cost or Market

M7-7
LO4

Kinney Company had the following inventory items on hand at the end of the year.

	Quantity	Cost per Item	Replacement Cost per Item
Item A	60	$85	$100
Item B	30	60	45

Computing the lower of cost or market on an item-by-item basis, determine what amount would be reported on the balance sheet for inventory.

Determining the Effects of Inventory Management Changes on Inventory Turnover Ratio

M7-8
LO5

Indicate the most likely effect of the following changes in inventory management on the inventory turnover ratio (+ for increase, − for decrease, and NE for no effect).

_____ a. Parts inventory delivered daily by suppliers instead of weekly.
_____ b. Shorten production process from 10 days to 8 days.
_____ c. Extend payments for inventory purchases from 15 days to 30 days.

Determining the Financial Statement Effects of Inventory Errors

M7-9
LO7

Assume the 2009 ending inventory was understated by $100,000. Explain how this error would affect the 2009 and 2010 pretax income amounts. What would be the effects if the 2009 ending inventory were overstated by $100,000 instead of understated?

EXERCISES   **Available with McGraw-Hill's Homework Manager**

E7-1
LO1

Analyzing Items to Be Included in Inventory

Based on its physical count of inventory in its warehouse at year-end, December 31, 2010, Austin Company planned to report inventory of $34,500. During the audit, the independent CPA developed the following additional information:

a. Goods from a supplier costing $700 are in transit with UPS on December 31, 2010. The terms are FOB shipping point (explained in the "Required" section). Because these goods had not arrived, they were excluded from the physical inventory count.

b. Austin delivered samples costing $1,300 to a customer on December 27, 2010, with the understanding that they would be returned to Austin on January 15, 2011. Because these goods were not on hand, they were excluded from the inventory count.

c. On December 31, 2010, goods in transit to customers, with terms FOB shipping point, amounted to $4,000 (expected delivery date January 10, 2011). Because the goods had been shipped, they were excluded from the physical inventory count.

d. On December 31, 2010, goods in transit to customers, with terms FOB destination, amounted to $1,500 (expected delivery date January 10, 2011). Because the goods had been shipped, they were excluded from the physical inventory count.

Required:

Austin's accounting policy requires including in inventory all goods for which it has title. Note that the point where title (ownership) changes hands is determined by the shipping terms in the sales contract. When goods are shipped "F.O.B. shipping point," title changes hands at shipment and the buyer normally pays for shipping. When they are shipped "F.O.B. destination," title changes hands on delivery, and the seller normally pays for shipping. Begin with the $34,500 inventory amount and compute the correct amount for the ending inventory. Explain the basis for your treatment of each of the preceding items. (**Hint:** Set up three columns: Item, Amount, and Explanation.)

E7-2
LO1

Inferring Missing Amounts Based on Income Statement Relationships

Supply the missing dollar amounts for the 2009 income statement of Travis Company for each of the following independent cases (**Hint:** In case B work from the bottom up.):

	Case A		Case B		Case C	
Net sales revenue		$8,000	$?			$6,000
Beginning inventory	$11,200		$ 6,500		$ 4,000	
Purchases	5,000		?		9,500	
Goods available for sale	?		15,050		13,500	
Ending inventory	10,200		11,050		?	
Cost of goods sold		?		?		4,500
Gross profit		?	1,500			?
Expenses		400		?		700
Pretax income		$1,600		$(300)		$ 800

E7-3
LO1

Inferring Missing Amounts Based on Income Statement Relationships

Supply the missing dollar amounts for the 2012 income statement of Lewis Retailers for each of the following independent cases:

Cases	Sales Revenue	Beginning Inventory	Purchases	Total Available	Ending Inventory	Cost of Goods Sold	Gross Profit	Expenses	Pretax Income or (Loss)
A	$ 650	$100	$700	$?	$500	$?	$?	$200	$?
B	900	200	800	?	?	?	?	150	50
C	?	150	?	?	300	200	400	100	?
D	800	?	550	?	300	?	?	200	200
E	1,000	?	900	1,100	?	?	500	?	(50)

Inferring Merchandise Purchases

Abercrombie and Fitch is a leading retailer of casual apparel for men, women, and children. Assume that you are employed as a stock analyst and your boss has just completed a review of the new Abercrombie annual report. She provided you with her notes, but they are missing some information that you need. Her notes show that the ending inventory for Abercrombie in the current year was $427,447,000 and in the previous year was $362,536,000. Net sales for the current year were $3,318,158,000. Cost of goods sold was $1,109,152,000. Net income was $60,000,000. For your analysis, you determine that you need to know the amount of purchases for the year.

Required:
Can you develop the information from her notes? Explain and show calculations. (**Hint:** Use the cost of goods sold equation or the inventory T-account to solve for the needed value.)

E7-4
L01
Abercrombie and Fitch

Calculating Ending Inventory and Cost of Goods Sold Under FIFO, LIFO, and Weighted Average

E7-5
L02

Solar company uses a periodic inventory system. At the end of the annual accounting period, December 31, 2010, the accounting records provided the following information for product 1:

	Units	Unit Cost
Inventory, December 31, 2009	2,000	$4
For the year 2010:		
Purchase, March 21	5,000	7
Purchase, August 1	3,000	8
Inventory, December 31, 2010	4,000	

Required:
Compute ending inventory and cost of goods sold under FIFO, LIFO, and weighted average costing methods. (**Hint:** Set up adjacent columns for each case.)

Calculating Ending Inventory and Cost of Goods Sold Under FIFO, LIFO, and Weighted Average

Clor company uses a periodic inventory system. At the end of the annual accounting period, December 31, 2010, the accounting records provided the following information for product 1:

E7-6
L02

	Units	Unit Cost
Inventory, December 31, 2009	2,000	$5
For the year 2010:		
Purchase, March 21	6,000	3
Purchase, August 1	4,000	2
Inventory, December 31, 2010	3,000	

Required:
Compute ending inventory and cost of goods sold under FIFO, LIFO, and weighted average costing methods. (**Hint:** Set up adjacent columns for each case.)

E7-7

LO2, 3

Analyzing and Interpreting the Financial Statement Effects of LIFO and FIFO

Lunar company uses a periodic inventory system. At the end of the annual accounting period, December 31, 2010, the accounting records provided the following information for product 2:

	Units	Unit Cost
Inventory, December 31, 2009	3,000	$12
For the year 2010:		
Purchase, April 11	9,000	10
Purchase, June 1	8,000	15
Sales ($50 each)	11,000	
Operating expenses (excluding income tax expense), $185,000		

Required:

1. Prepare a separate income statement through pretax income that details cost of goods sold for
   a. Case A: FIFO.
   b. Case B: LIFO.
   For each case, show the computation of the ending inventory. (**Hint:** Set up adjacent columns for each case.)
2. Compare the pretax income and the ending inventory amounts between the two cases. Explain the similarities and differences.
3. Which inventory costing method may be preferred for income tax purposes? Explain.

E7-8

LO2, 3

Analyzing and Interpreting the Financial Statement Effects of LIFO and FIFO

Scoresby Inc. uses a periodic inventory system. At the end of the annual accounting period, December 31, 2012, the accounting records provided the following information for product 2:

	Units	Unit Cost
Inventory, December 31, 2011	7,000	$ 5
For the year 2012:		
Purchase, March 5	19,000	9
Purchase, September 19	10,000	11
Sale ($27 each)	8,000	
Sale ($30 each)	16,000	
Operating expenses (excluding income tax expense), $500,000		

Required:

1. Prepare a separate income statement through pretax income that details cost of goods sold for Cases A and B. For each case, show the computation of the ending inventory. (**Hint:** Set up adjacent columns for each case.)
   a. Case A: FIFO.
   b. Case B: LIFO.
2. Compare the pretax income and the ending inventory amounts between the two cases. Explain the similarities and differences.
3. Which inventory costing method may be preferred for income tax purposes? Explain.

E7-9

LO2, 3

Evaluating the Choice among Three Alternative Inventory Methods Based on Income and Cash Flow Effects

Courtney Company uses a periodic inventory system. Data for 2011: beginning merchandise inventory (December 31, 2010), 2,000 units at $38; purchases, 8,000 units at $40; expenses (excluding income taxes), $144,500; ending inventory per physical count at December 31, 2011, 1,800 units; sales 8,200 units; sales price per unit, $65; and average income tax rate, 30 percent.

Required:

1. Prepare income statements under the FIFO, LIFO, and weighted average costing methods. Use a format similar to the following:

| | | INVENTORY COSTING METHOD | | |
Income Statement	Units	FIFO	LIFO	Weighted Average
Sales revenue	_____	$_____	$_____	$_____
Cost of goods sold				
Beginning inventory	_____	_____	_____	_____
Purchases	_____	_____	_____	_____
Goods available for sale	_____	_____	_____	_____
Ending inventory	_____	_____	_____	_____
Cost of goods sold	_____	_____	_____	_____
Gross profit		_____	_____	_____
Expenses		_____	_____	_____
Pretax income		_____	_____	_____
Income tax expense		_____	_____	_____
Net income		$_____	$_____	$_____

2. Between FIFO and LIFO, which method is preferable in terms of (a) net income and (b) income taxes paid (cash flow)? Explain.
3. What would your answer to requirement 2 be, assuming that prices were falling? Explain.

Evaluating the Choice among Three Alternative Inventory Methods Based on Cash Flow Effects

Following is partial information for the income statement of Timber Company under three different inventory costing methods, assuming the use of a periodic inventory system:

E7-10
LO2, 3

	FIFO	LIFO	Weighted Average
Cost of goods sold			
Beginning inventory (350 units)	$11,200	$11,200	$11,200
Purchases (475 units)	17,100	17,100	17,100
Goods available for sale			
Ending inventory (545 units)	_____	_____	_____
Cost of goods sold	══════	══════	══════
Sales, 280 units; unit sales price, $50			
Expenses, $1,700			

Required:
1. Compute cost of goods sold under the FIFO, LIFO, and weighted average inventory costing methods.
2. Prepare an income statement through pretax income for each method.
3. Rank the three methods in order of income taxes paid (favorable cash flow) and explain the basis for your ranking.

Reporting Inventory at Lower of Cost or Market

E7-11
LO4

Peterson Company is preparing the annual financial statements dated December 31, 2010. Ending inventory information about the five major items stocked for regular sale follows:

| | ENDING INVENTORY, 2010 | | |
Item	Quantity on Hand	Unit Cost When Acquired (FIFO)	Replacement Cost (Market) at Year-End
A	50	$15	$12
B	80	30	40
C	10	45	52
D	30	25	30
E	350	10	5

Required:

Compute the valuation that should be used for the 2010 ending inventory using the LCM rule applied on an item-by-item basis. (**Hint:** Set up columns for Item, Quantity, Total Cost, Total Market, and LCM Valuation.)

E7-12   **Reporting Inventory at Lower of Cost or Market**

LO4

Demski Company was formed on January 1, 2011, and is preparing the annual financial statements dated December 31, 2011. Ending inventory information about the four major items stocked for regular sale follows:

	ENDING INVENTORY, 2011		
Item	Quantity on Hand	Unit Cost When Acquired (FIFO)	Replacement Cost (Market) at Year-End
A	20	$10	$15
B	75	40	36
C	35	57	55
D	10	27	32

Required:

1. Compute the valuation that should be used for the 2011 ending inventory using the LCM rule applied on an item-by-item basis. (**Hint:** Set up columns for Item, Quantity, Total Cost, Total Market, and LCM Valuation.)
2. What will be the effect of the write-down of inventory to lower of cost or market on cost of goods sold for the year ended December 31, 2011?

E7-13   **Analyzing and Interpreting the Inventory Turnover Ratio**

LO5

Dell Inc. is the leading manufacturer of personal computers. In a recent year, it reported the following in dollars in millions:

Net sales revenue	$57,420
Cost of sales	47,904
Beginning inventory	576
Ending inventory	660

Required:

1. Determine the inventory turnover ratio and average days to sell inventory for the current year.
2. Explain the meaning of each number.

E7-14   **Analyzing and Interpreting the Effects of the LIFO/FIFO Choice on Inventory Turnover Ratio**

LO5, 6

The records at the end of January 2012 for All Star Company showed the following for a particular kind of merchandise:

Inventory, December 31, 2011 at FIFO 19 Units @ $16 = $304
Inventory, December 31, 2011 at LIFO 19 Units @ $10 = $190

Transactions	Units	Unit Cost	Total Cost
Purchase, January 9, 2012	25	$14	$350
Purchase, January 20, 2012	50	19	950
Sale, January 21, 2012 (at $38 per unit)	40		
Sale, January 27, 2012 (at $39 per unit)	28		

Required:

Compute the inventory turnover ratio under the FIFO and LIFO inventory costing methods (show computations and round to the nearest dollar). Explain which you believe is the more accurate indicator of the efficiency of inventory management.

Interpreting the Effect of Changes in Inventories and Accounts Payable on Cash Flow from Operations

First Team Sports, Inc., is engaged in the manufacture (through independent contractors) and distribution of in-line roller skates, ice skates, street hockey equipment, and related accessory products. Its recent annual report included the following on its balance sheet:

E7-15
LO5
First Team Sports, Inc.

CONSOLIDATED BALANCE SHEETS		
	Current Year	Previous Year
. . .		
Inventory (Note 3)	22,813,850	20,838,171
. . .		
Trade accounts payable	9,462,883	9,015,376

Required:
Explain the effects of the changes in inventory and trade accounts payable on cash flow from operating activities for the current year.

Analyzing Notes to Adjust Inventory from LIFO to FIFO

The following note was contained in a recent Ford Motor Company annual report:

E7-16
LO6
Ford

NOTE 5. INVENTORIES—AUTOMOTIVE SECTOR		
Inventories at December 31 were as follows (dollars in millions)		
	Current Year	Previous Year
Raw material, work in process, & supplies	$ 3,842	$3,174
Finished products	6,335	4,760
Total inventories at FIFO	10,177	7,934
Less LIFO Adjustment	(996)	(957)
Total	$ 9,181	$6,977
About one-third of inventories were determined under the last-in, first-out method.		

Required:
1. What amount of ending inventory would have been reported in the current year if Ford had used only FIFO?
2. The cost of goods sold reported by Ford for the current year was $129,821 million. Determine the cost of goods sold that would have been reported if Ford had used only FIFO for both years.
3. Explain why Ford management chose to use LIFO for certain of its inventories.

Analyzing the Effects of an Error in Recording Purchases

Garraway Ski Company mistakenly recorded purchases of inventory on account received during the last week of December 2010 as purchases during January of 2011 (this is called a purchases cutoff error). Garraway uses a periodic inventory system, and ending inventory was correctly counted and reported each year.

E7-17
LO7

Required:
Assuming that no correction was made in 2010 or 2011, indicate whether each of the following financial statement amounts will be understated, overstated, or correct.
1. Net Income for 2010.
2. Net Income for 2011.
3. Retained Earnings for December 31, 2010.
4. Retained Earnings for December 31, 2011.

E7-18
LO7

Analyzing the Effect of an Inventory Error Disclosed in an Actual Note to a Financial Statement

Several years ago, the financial statements of Gibson Greeting Cards contained the following note:

> On July 1, the Company announced that it had determined that the inventory . . . had been overstated. . . . The overstatement of inventory . . . was $8,806,000.

Gibson reported an incorrect net income amount of $25,852,000 for the year in which the error occurred and the income tax rate was 39.3 percent.

Required:
1. Compute the amount of net income that Gibson reported after correcting the inventory error. Show computations.
2. Assume that the inventory error was not discovered. Identify the financial statement accounts that would have been incorrect for the year the error occurred and for the subsequent year. State whether each account was understated or overstated.

E7-19
LO7

Analyzing and Interpreting the Impact of an Inventory Error

Dallas Corporation prepared the following two income statements (simplified for illustrative purposes):

	First Quarter 2010		Second Quarter 2010	
Sales revenue		$11,000		$18,000
Cost of goods sold				
Beginning inventory	$ 4,000		$ 3,800	
Purchases	3,000		13,000	
Goods available for sale	7,000		16,800	
Ending inventory	3,800		9,000	
Cost of goods sold		3,200		7,800
Gross profit		7,800		10,200
Expenses		5,000		6,000
Pretax income		$ 2,800		$ 4,200

During the third quarter, it was discovered that the ending inventory for the first quarter should have been $4,200.

Required:
1. What effect did this error have on the combined pretax income of the two quarters? Explain.
2. Did this error affect the EPS amounts for each quarter? (See Chapter 5 discussion of EPS.) Explain.
3. Prepare corrected income statements for each quarter.
4. Set up a schedule with the following headings to reflect the comparative effects of the correct and incorrect amounts on the income statement:

	1st Quarter			2nd Quarter		
Income Statement Item	Incorrect	Correct	Error	Incorrect	Correct	Error

E7-20

(Supplement A) Analyzing the Effects of a Reduction in the Amount of LIFO Inventory

An annual report of Eastman Kodak Company contained the following note:

During this year and last year, inventory usage resulted in liquidations of LIFO inventory quantities. In the aggregate, these inventories were carried at the lower costs prevailing in prior years as compared with the costs of current purchases. The effect of these LIFO liquidations was to reduce cost of goods sold by $53 million in the current year and $31 million in the previous year.

Required:
1. Explain why the reduction in inventory quantity increased net income for Eastman Kodak.
2. If Eastman Kodak had used FIFO, would the reductions in inventory quantity during the two years have increased net income? Explain.

(Supplement B) Recording Sales and Purchases with Cash Discounts   **E7-21**

The Cycle Shop sells merchandise on credit terms of 2.5/15, n/30. A sale invoiced at $900 (cost of sales $600) was made to Missy Clemons on February 1, 2011. The company uses the gross method of recording sales discounts.

Required:
1. Give the journal entry to record the credit sale. Assume use of the perpetual inventory system.
2. Give the journal entry, assuming that the account was collected in full on February 9, 2011.
3. Give the journal entry, assuming, instead, that the account was collected in full on March 2, 2011.

On March 4, 2011, the company purchased bicycles and accessories from a supplier on credit, invoiced at $8,400; the terms were 3.5/10, n/30. The company uses the gross method to record purchases.

Required:
4. Give the journal entry to record the purchase on credit. Assume the use of the perpetual inventory system.
5. Give the journal entry, assuming that the account was paid in full on March 12, 2011.
6. Give the journal entry, assuming, instead, that the account was paid in full on March 28, 2011.

(Supplement C) Recording Purchases and Sales Using a Perpetual and Periodic Inventory   **E7-22**
System

Snowball Company reported beginning inventory of 100 units at a unit cost of $20. It engaged in the following purchase and sale transactions during 2009:

    Jan. 14 Sold 20 units at unit sales price of $45 on open account.
    April 9 Purchased 15 additional units at unit cost of $20 on open account.
    Sept. 2 Sold 45 units at sales price of $50 on open account.

At the end of 2009, a physical count showed that Snowball Company had 50 units of inventory still on hand.

Required:
Record each transaction, assuming that Snowball Company uses (a) a perpetual inventory system and (b) a periodic inventory system (including any necessary entries at the end of the accounting period on December 31).

 Available with McGraw-Hill's Homework Manager   **PROBLEMS**

Analyzing Items to Be Included in Inventory   **P7-1**
LO1

Reggie Company has just completed a physical inventory count at year-end, December 31, 2010. Only the items on the shelves, in storage, and in the receiving area were counted and costed on a FIFO basis. The inventory amounted to $65,000. During the audit, the independent CPA developed the following additional information:

a. Goods costing $750 were being used by a customer on a trial basis and were excluded from the inventory count at December 31, 2010.
b. Goods in transit on December 31, 2010, from a supplier, with terms FOB destination (explained in the "Required" section), cost $900. Because these goods had not arrived, they were excluded from the physical inventory count.
c. On December 31, 2010, goods in transit to customers, with terms FOB shipping point, amounted to $1,300 (expected delivery date January 10, 2011). Because the goods had been shipped, they were excluded from the physical inventory count.
d. On December 28, 2010, a customer purchased goods for cash amounting to $2,650 and left them "for pickup on January 3, 2011." Reggie Company had paid $1,590 for the goods and, because they were on hand, included the latter amount in the physical inventory count.
e. On the date of the inventory count, the company received notice from a supplier that goods ordered earlier at a cost of $2,550 had been delivered to the transportation company on December 27, 2010;

the terms were FOB shipping point. Because the shipment had not arrived by December 31, 2010, it was excluded from the physical inventory.

f. On December 31, 2010, the company shipped $850 worth of goods to a customer, FOB destination. The goods are expected to arrive at their destination no earlier than January 8, 2011. Because the goods were not on hand, they were not included in the physical inventory count.

g. One of the items sold by the company has such a low volume that the management planned to drop it last year. To induce Reggie Company to continue carrying the item, the manufacturer-supplier provided the item on a "consignment basis." This means that the manufacturer-supplier retains ownership of the item, and Reggie Company (the consignee) has no responsibility to pay for the items until they are sold to a customer. Each month, Reggie Company sends a report to the manufacturer on the number sold and remits cash for the cost. At the end of December 2010, Reggie Company had six of these items on hand; therefore, they were included in the physical inventory count at $950 each.

Required:

Assume that Reggie's accounting policy requires including in inventory all goods for which it has title. Note that the point where title (ownership) changes hands is determined by the shipping terms in the sales contract. When goods are shipped "F.O.B. shipping point," title changes hands at shipment and the buyer normally pays for shipping. When they are shipped "F.O.B. destination," title changes hands on delivery, and the seller normally pays for shipping. Begin with the $65,000 inventory amount and compute the correct amount for the ending inventory. Explain the basis for your treatment of each of the preceding items. (**Hint:** Set up three columns: Item, Amount, and Explanation.)

P7-2   **Analyzing the Effects of Four Alternative Inventory Methods** (AP7-1)

LO2

Yalestone Company uses a periodic inventory system. At the end of the annual accounting period, December 31, 2012, the accounting records for the most popular item in inventory showed the following:

Transactions	Units	Unit Cost
Beginning inventory, January 1, 2012	400	$3.00
Transactions during 2012:		
a. Purchase, January 30	600	3.20
b. Purchase, May 1	460	3.50
c. Sale, ($5 each)	(130)	
d. Sale, ($5 each)	(700)	

Required:

Compute the amount of (a) goods available for sale, (b) ending inventory, and (c) cost of goods sold at December 31, 2012, under each of the following inventory costing methods (show computations and round to the nearest dollar):

1. Weighted average cost (Round the average cost per unit to the nearest cent.)
2. First-in, first-out.
3. Last-in, first-out.
4. Specific identification, assuming that the first sale was selected two-fifths from the beginning inventory and three-fifths from the purchase of January 30, 2012. Assume that the second sale was selected from the remainder of the beginning inventory, with the balance from the purchase of May 1, 2012.

P7-3   **Evaluating Four Alternative Inventory Methods Based on Income and Cash Flow** (AP7-2)

LO2, 3

At the end of January 2010, the records of Atlanta Company showed the following for a particular item that sold at $17 per unit:

Transactions	Units	Amount
Inventory, January 1, 2010	500	$2,500
Purchase, January 12	600	3,600
Purchase, January 26	160	1,280
Sale	(370)	
Sale	(250)	

Required:

1. Assuming the use of a periodic inventory system, prepare a summarized income statement through gross profit on sales under each method of inventory: (a) weighted average cost, (b) FIFO, (c) LIFO, and (d) specific identification. For specific identification, assume that the first sale was out of the beginning inventory and the second sale was out of the January 12 purchase. Round the average cost per unit to the nearest cent. Show the inventory computations in detail.

2. Of FIFO and LIFO, which method would result in the higher pretax income? Which would result in the higher EPS?

3. Of FIFO and LIFO, which method would result in the lower income tax expense? Explain, assuming a 30 percent average tax rate.

4. Of FIFO and LIFO, which method would produce the more favorable cash flow? Explain.

Analyzing and Interpreting Income Manipulation under the LIFO Inventory Method (AP7-4)

P7-4
LO2, 3

Pacific Company sells electronic test equipment that it acquires from a foreign source. During the year 2011, the inventory records reflected the following:

	Units	Unit Cost	Total Cost
Beginning inventory	20	$11,500	$230,000
Purchases	42	10,000	420,000
Sales (47 units at $24,500 each)			

Inventory is valued at cost using the LIFO inventory method.

Required:

1. Complete the following income statement summary using the LIFO method and the periodic inventory system (show computations):

Sales revenue	$_____
Cost of goods sold	_____
Gross profit	_____
Expenses	300,000
Pretax income	$_____
Ending inventory	$_____

2. The management, for various reasons, is considering buying 20 additional units before December 31, 2011, at $8,500 each. Restate the income statement (and ending inventory), assuming that this purchase is made on December 31, 2011.

3. How much did pretax income change because of the decision on December 31, 2011? Assuming that the unit cost of test equipment is expected to continue to decline in 2012, is there any evidence of income manipulation? Explain.

Evaluating the LIFO and FIFO Choice When Costs Are Rising and Falling (AP7-5)

P7-5
LO2, 3

Income is to be evaluated under four different situations as follows:

www.mhhe.com/libby6e

a. Prices are rising:
    (1) Situation A: FIFO is used.
    (2) Situation B: LIFO is used.
b. Prices are falling:
    (1) Situation C: FIFO is used.
    (2) Situation D: LIFO is used.

The basic data common to all four situations are sales, 500 units for $12,000; beginning inventory, 300 units; purchases, 400 units; ending inventory, 200 units; and operating expenses, $4,000. The following tabulated income statements for each situation have been set up for analytical purposes:

	PRICES RISING		PRICES FALLING	
	Situation A FIFO	Situation B LIFO	Situation C FIFO	Situation D LIFO
Sales revenue	$12,000	$12,000	$12,000	$12,000
Cost of goods sold:				
Beginning inventory	3,300	?	?	?
Purchases	4,800	?	?	?
Goods available for sale	8,100	?	?	?
Ending inventory	2,400	?	?	?
Cost of goods sold	5,700	?	?	?
Gross profit	6,300	?	?	?
Expenses	4,000	4,000	4,000	4,000
Pretax income	2,300	?	?	?
Income tax expense (30%)	690	?	?	?
Net income	$ 1,610			

Required:

1. Complete the preceding tabulation for each situation. In Situations A and B (prices rising), assume the following: beginning inventory, 300 units at $11 = $3,300; purchases, 400 units at $12 = $4,800. In Situations C and D (prices falling), assume the opposite; that is, beginning inventory, 300 units at $12 = $3,600; purchases, 400 units at $11 = $4,400. Use periodic inventory procedures.
2. Analyze the relative effects on pretax income and on net income as demonstrated by requirement 1 when prices are rising and when prices are falling.
3. Analyze the relative effects on the cash position for each situation.
4. Would you recommend FIFO or LIFO? Explain.

P7-6

LO4

eXcel

www.mhhe.com/libby6e

Evaluating the Income Statement and Cash Flow Effects of Lower of Cost or Market

Smart Company prepared its annual financial statements dated December 31, 2010. The company applies the FIFO inventory costing method; however, the company neglected to apply LCM to the ending inventory. The preliminary 2010 income statement follows:

Sales revenue		$280,000
Cost of goods sold		
Beginning inventory	$ 31,000	
Purchases	184,000	
Goods available for sale	215,000	
Ending inventory (FIFO cost)	46,500	
Cost of goods sold		168,500
Gross profit		111,500
Operating expenses		62,000
Pretax income		49,500
Income tax expense (30%)		14,850
Net income		$ 34,650

Assume that you have been asked to restate the 2010 financial statements to incorporate LCM. You have developed the following data relating to the 2010 ending inventory:

		Acquisition Cost		Current Replacement Unit Cost
Item	Quantity	Unit	Total	(Market)
A	3,050	$3	$ 9,150	$4
B	1,500	5	7,500	3.5
C	7,100	1.5	10,650	3.5
D	3,200	6	19,200	4
			$46,500	

Required:

1. Restate this income statement to reflect LCM valuation of the 2010 ending inventory. Apply LCM on an item-by-item basis and show computations.
2. Compare and explain the LCM effect on each amount that was changed on the income statement in requirement 1.
3. What is the conceptual basis for applying LCM to merchandise inventories?
4. Thought question: What effect did LCM have on the 2010 cash flow? What will be the long-term effect on cash flow?

Evaluating the Effects of Manufacturing Changes on Inventory Turnover Ratio and Cash Flows from Operating Activities

P7-7
LO5

H.–T. Tan and Company has been operating for five years as an electronics component manufacturer specializing in cellular phone components. During this period, it has experienced rapid growth in sales revenue and in inventory. Mr. Tan and his associates have hired you as its first corporate controller. You have put into place new purchasing and manufacturing procedures that are expected to reduce inventories by approximately one-third by year-end. You have gathered the following data related to the changes:

(dollars in thousands)		
	Beginning of Year	End of Year (projected)
Inventory	$495,700	$304,310
		Current Year (projected)
Cost of goods sold		$7,008,984

Required:

1. Compute the inventory turnover ratio based on two different assumptions:
   a. Those presented in the preceding table (a decrease in the balance in inventory).
   b. No change from the beginning of the year in the inventory balance.
2. Compute the effect of the projected change in the balance in inventory on cash flow from operating activities for the year (the sign and amount of effect).
3. On the basis of the preceding analysis, write a brief memo explaining how an increase in inventory turnover can result in an increase in cash flow from operating activities. Also explain how this increase can benefit the company.

Evaluating the Choice between LIFO and FIFO Based on an Inventory Note

P7-8
LO6

An annual report for General Motors Corporation included the following note:

Inventories are stated generally at cost, which is not in excess of market. The cost of substantially all domestic inventories was determined by the last-in, first-out (LIFO) method. If the first-in, first-out (FIFO)

method of inventory valuation had been used by the corporation for U.S. inventories, it is estimated that they would be $2,077.1 million higher at the end of this year, compared with $1,784.5 million higher at the end of last year.

For the year, GM reported net income (after taxes) of $320.5 million. At year-end, the balance of the GM retained earnings account was $15,340 million.

Required:
1. Determine the amount of net income that GM would have reported for the year if it had used the FIFO method (assume a 30 percent tax rate).
2. Determine the amount of retained earnings that GM would have reported at year-end if it always had used the FIFO method (assume a 30 percent tax rate).
3. Use of the LIFO method reduced the amount of taxes that GM had to pay for the year compared with the amount that would have been paid if it had used FIFO. Calculate the amount of this reduction (assume a 30 percent tax rate).

P7-9
L07

www.mhhe.com/libby6e

Analyzing and Interpreting the Effects of Inventory Errors (AP7-3)

The income statement for Sherwood Company summarized for a four-year period shows the following:

	2009	2010	2011	2012
Sales revenue	$2,025,000	$2,450,000	$2,700,000	$2,975,000
Cost of goods sold	1,505,000	1,627,000	1,782,000	2,113,000
Gross profit	520,000	823,000	918,000	862,000
Expenses	490,000	513,000	538,000	542,000
Pretax income	30,000	310,000	380,000	320,000
Income tax expense (30%)	9,000	93,000	114,000	96,000
Net income	$ 21,000	$ 217,000	$ 266,000	$ 224,000

An audit revealed that in determining these amounts, the ending inventory for 2010 was overstated by $22,000. The company uses a periodic inventory system.

Required:
1. Recast the income statements to reflect the correct amounts, taking into consideration the inventory error.
2. Compute the gross profit percentage for each year (a) before the correction and (b) after the correction.
3. What effect would the error have had on the income tax expense assuming a 30 percent average rate?

P7-10
General Electric

(Supplement A) Analyzing LIFO and FIFO When Inventory Quantities Decline Based on an Actual Note

In a recent annual report, General Electric reported the following in its inventory note:

December 31 (dollars in millions)	Current Year	Prior Year
Raw materials and work in progress	$5,603	$5,515
Finished goods	2,863	2,546
Unbilled shipments	246	280
	8,712	8,341
Less revaluation to LIFO	(2,226)	(2,076)
LIFO value of inventories	$6,486	$6,265

It also reported a $23 million change in cost of goods sold due to "lower inventory levels."

Required:
1. Compute the increase or decrease in the pretax operating profit (loss) that would have been reported for the current year had GE employed FIFO accounting for all inventory for both years.
2. Compute the increase or decrease in pretax operating profit that would have been reported had GE employed LIFO but not reduced inventory quantities during the current year.

(Supplement B) Recording Sales and Purchases with Cash Discounts and Returns   P7-11

Campus Stop, Incorporated, is a student co-op. On January 1, 2012, the beginning inventory was $156,000, the Accounts Receivable balance was $4,600, and the Allowance for Doubtful Accounts had a credit balance of $750. Campus Stop uses a perpetual inventory system and records inventory purchases using the gross method.

The following transactions (summarized) have been selected from 2012 for case purposes:

a. Sold merchandise for cash (cost of sales $136,000)	$277,000
b. Received merchandise returned by customers as unsatisfactory,	
for cash refund (cost of sales $1,200)	1,700

Purchased merchandise from vendors on credit; terms 3/10, n/30 as follows:

c. August Supply Company invoice price before deduction of cash discount	5,300
d. Other vendors, invoice price before deduction of cash discount	127,500
e. Purchased equipment for use in store; paid cash	2,100
f. Purchased office supplies for future use in the store; paid cash	650
g. Freight on merchandise purchased; paid cash	350

Paid accounts payable in full during the period as follows:

h. Paid August Supply Company after the discount period	5,300
i. Paid other vendors within the 3 percent discount period	123,675

Required:
Prepare journal entries for each of the preceding transactions.

ALTERNATE **PROBLEMS**

Analyzing the Effects of Four Alternative Inventory Methods (P7-2)   AP7-1
LO2

Smiller Company uses a periodic inventory system. At the end of the annual accounting period, December 31, 2010, the accounting records for the most popular item in inventory showed the following:

Transactions	Units	Unit Cost
Beginning inventory, January 1, 2010	390	$32
Transactions during 2010:		
a. Purchase, February 20	650	34
b. Purchase, June 30	460	37
c. Sale, ($50 each)	(70)	
d. Sale, ($50 each)	(750)	

Required:
Compute the cost of (a) goods available for sale, (b) ending inventory, and (c) goods sold at December 31, 2010, under each of the following inventory costing methods (show computations and round to the nearest dollar):
1. Weighted average cost.
2. First-in, first-out.
3. Last-in, first-out.
4. Specific identification, assuming that the first sale was selected two-fifths from the beginning inventory and three-fifths from the purchase of February 20, 2010. Assume that the second sale was selected from the remainder of the beginning inventory, with the balance from the purchase of June 30, 2010.

AP7-2

LO2, 3

Evaluating Four Alternative Inventory Methods Based on Income and Cash Flow (P7-3)

At the end of January 2012, the records of Southport Company showed the following for a particular item that sold at $15 per unit:

Transactions	Units	Amount
Inventory, January 1, 2012	120	$ 960
Purchase, January 12	380	3,420
Purchase, January 26	200	2,200
Sale	(100)	
Sale	(140)	

Required:
1. Assuming the use of a periodic inventory system, prepare a summarized income statement through gross profit on sales under each method of inventory: (a) weighted average cost, (b) FIFO, (c) LIFO, and (d) specific identification. For specific identification, assume that the first sale was out of the beginning inventory and the second sale was out of the January 12 purchase. Show the inventory computations in detail.
2. Of FIFO and LIFO, which method would result in the higher pretax income? Which would result in the higher EPS?
3. Of FIFO and LIFO, which method would result in the lower income tax expense? Explain, assuming a 30 percent average tax rate.
4. Of FIFO and LIFO, which method would produce the more favorable cash flow? Explain.

AP7-3

LO7

Analyzing and Interpreting the Effects of Inventory Errors (P7–9)

The income statements for four consecutive years for Crown Company reflected the following summarized amounts:

	2009	2010	2011	2012
Sales revenue	$60,000	$63,000	$65,000	$68,000
Cost of goods sold	39,000	43,000	44,000	46,000
Gross profit	21,000	20,000	21,000	22,000
Expenses	15,000	16,000	16,000	18,000
Pretax income	$ 6,000	$ 4,000	$ 5,000	$ 4,000

Subsequent to development of these amounts, it has been determined that the physical inventory taken on December 31, 2010, was understated by $2,000.

Required:
1. Recast the income statements to reflect the correct amounts, taking into consideration the inventory error.
2. Compute the gross profit percentage for each year (a) before the correction and (b) after the correction.
3. What effect would the error have had on the income tax expense assuming a 30 percent average rate?

AP7-4

LO2, 3

Analyzing and Interpreting Income Manipulation under the LIFO Inventory Method (P7-4)

Peterson Products sells specialized mountaineering equipment that it acquires from an outside source. During the year 2011, the inventory records reflected the following:

	Units	Unit Cost	Total Cost
Beginning inventory	16	$12,500	$200,000
Purchases	45	10,100	454,500
Sales (50 units at $24,700 each)			

Inventory is valued at cost using the LIFO inventory method.

Required:

1. Complete the following income statement summary using the LIFO method and the periodic inventory system (show computations):

Sales revenue	$ _____
Cost of goods sold	_____
Gross profit	_____
Expenses	400,000
Pretax income	$ _____
Ending inventory	$ _____

2. The management, for various reasons, is considering buying 20 additional units before December 31, 2011, at $8,600 each. Restate the income statement (and ending inventory), assuming that this purchase is made on December 31, 2011.
3. How much did pretax income change because of the decision on December 31, 2011? Assuming that the unit cost of equipment is expected to continue to decline in 2012, is there any evidence of income manipulation? Explain.

Evaluating the LIFO and FIFO Choice When Costs Are Rising and Falling (P7-5)

AP7-5
LO2, 3

Income is to be evaluated under four different situations as follows:
a. Prices are rising:
   (1) Situation A: FIFO is used.
   (2) Situation B: LIFO is used.
b. Prices are falling:
   (1) Situation C: FIFO is used.
   (2) Situation D: LIFO is used.

The basic data common to all four situations are sales, 510 units for $13,260; beginning inventory, 340 units; purchases, 410 units; ending inventory, 240 units; and operating expenses, $4,000. The following tabulated income statements for each situation have been set up for analytical purposes:

	PRICES RISING		PRICES FALLING	
	Situation A FIFO	Situation B LIFO	Situation C FIFO	Situation D LIFO
Sales revenue	$13,260	$13,260	$13,260	$13,260
Cost of goods sold:				
Beginning inventory	3,060	?	?	?
Purchases	4,100	?	?	?
Goods available for sale	7,160	?	?	?
Ending inventory	2,400	?	?	?
Cost of goods sold	4,760	?	?	?
Gross profit	8,500	?	?	?
Expenses	4,000	4,000	4,000	4,000
Pretax income	4,500	?	?	?
Income tax expense (30%)	1,350	?	?	?
Net income	$ 3,150			

Required:

1. Complete the preceding tabulation for each situation. In Situations A and B (prices rising), assume the following: beginning inventory, 340 units at $9 = $3,060; purchases, 410 units at $10 = $4,100. In Situations C and D (prices falling), assume the opposite; that is, beginning inventory, 340 units at $10 = $3,400; purchases, 410 units at $9 = $3,690. Use periodic inventory procedures.

2. Analyze the relative effects on pretax income and on net income as demonstrated by requirement 1 when prices are rising and when prices are falling.

3. Analyze the relative effects on the cash position for each situation.

4. Would you recommend FIFO or LIFO? Explain.

CASES AND PROJECTS

Annual Report Cases

CP7-1
L04, 5, 7
AMERICAN EAGLE OUTFITTERS

Finding Financial Information

Refer to the financial statements of American Eagle Outfitters given in Appendix B at the end of this book.

Required:
1. How much inventory does the company hold at the end of the most recent year?
2. Estimate the amount of merchandise that the company purchased during the current year. (**Hint:** Use the cost of goods sold equation and ignore "certain buying, occupancy, and warehousing expenses.")
3. What method does the company use to determine the cost of its inventory?
4. Compute the inventory turnover ratio for the current year. What does an inventory turnover ratio tell you?

CP7-2
L01, 2, 5
Urban Outfitters

Finding Financial Information

Refer to the financial statements of Urban Outfitters given in Appendix C at the end of this book.

Required:
1. The company uses lower of cost or market to account for its inventory. At the end of the year, do you expect the company to write its inventory down to replacement cost or net realizable value? Explain your answer.
2. What method does the company use to determine the cost of its inventory?
3. If the company overstated ending inventory by $10 million for the year ended January 31, 2007, what would be the corrected value for Income before Income Taxes?
4. Did inventories increase or decrease over the most recent reporting year? Would net cash provided by operating activities increase or decrease as a result of the change in inventory for the most recent reporting year?

CP7-3
L05
AMERICAN EAGLE OUTFITTERS
Urban Outfitters

e**X**cel
www.mhhe.com/libby6e

Comparing Companies within an Industry

Refer to the financial statements of American Eagle Outfitters given in Appendix B, Urban Outfitters given in Appendix C, and the Industry Ratio Report given in Appendix D at the end of this book.

Required:
1. Compute the inventory turnover ratio for both companies for the current year. What would you infer from the difference?
2. Compare the inventory turnover ratio for both companies to the industry average. Are these two companies doing better or worse than the industry average in turning over their inventory?

Financial Reporting and Analysis Cases

CP7-4
L01
Dana Corporation

Using Financial Reports: Interpreting Effect of a Change in Accounting for Production-Related Costs

Dana Corporation designs and manufactures component parts for the vehicular, industrial, and mobile off-highway original equipment markets. In a recent annual report, Dana's inventory note indicated the following:

Dana changed its method of accounting for inventories effective January 1 . . . to include in inventory certain production-related costs previously charged to expense. This change in accounting principle resulted in a better matching of costs against related revenues. The effect of this change in accounting increased inventories by $23.0 and net income by $12.9.

Required:
   1. Under Dana's previous accounting method, certain production costs were recognized as expenses on the income statement in the period they were incurred. When will they be recognized under the new accounting method?
   2. Explain how including these costs in inventory increased both inventories and net income for the year.

Using Financial Reports: Interpreting Effects of the LIFO/FIFO Choice on Inventory Turnover

CP7-5
LO5, 6

In its annual report, Caterpillar, Inc., a major manufacturer of farm and construction equipment, reported the following information concerning its inventories:

The cost of inventories is determined principally by the LIFO (last-in, first-out) method of inventory valuation. This method was first adopted for the major portion of inventories in 1950. The value of inventories on the LIFO basis represented approximately 90% of total inventories at current cost value on December 31, 1995, 1994, and 1993. If the FIFO (first-in, first-out) method had been in use, inventories would have been $2,103, $2,035, and $1,818 higher than reported at December 31, 1995, 1994, and 1993, respectively.

On its balance sheet, it reported:

	1995	1994	1993
Inventories	$1,921	$1,835	$1,525

On its income statement, it reported:

	1995	1994	1993
Cost of goods sold	$12,000	$10,834	$9,075

Required:
As a recently hired financial analyst, you have been asked to analyze the efficiency with which Caterpillar has been managing its inventory and to write a short report. Specifically, you have been asked to compute inventory turnover for 1995 based on FIFO and on LIFO and compare the two ratios with two standards: (1) Caterpillar for the prior year 1994 and (2) its chief competitor, John Deere. For 1995, John Deere's inventory turnover was 4.2 based on FIFO and 9.8 based on LIFO. In your report, include:
   1. The appropriate ratios computed based on FIFO and LIFO.
   2. An explanation for the differences in the ratios across the FIFO and LIFO methods.
   3. An explanation of whether the FIFO or LIFO ratios provide a more accurate representation of the companies' efficiency in use of inventory.

Critical Thinking Cases

Making a Decision as a Financial Analyst: Analysis of the Effect of a Change to LIFO

CP7-6
LO6
Quaker Oats

A recent annual report for Quaker Oats included the following information:

The company adopted the LIFO cost flow assumption for valuing the majority of remaining U.S. Grocery Products inventories. The company believes that the use of the LIFO method better matches current costs with current revenues. The cumulative effect of this change on retained earnings at the beginning of the year is not determinable, nor are the pro forma effects of retroactive application of LIFO to prior years. The effect of this change on the current year was to decrease net income by $16.0 million, or $0.20 per share.

Required:

As a new financial analyst at a leading Wall Street investment banking firm, you are assigned to write a memo outlining the effects of the accounting change on Quaker's financial statements. Assume a 34 percent tax rate. In your report, be sure to include the following:

1. In addition to the reason that was cited, why did management adopt LIFO?
2. As an analyst, how would you react to the $0.20 per share decrease in income caused by the adoption of LIFO?

CP7-7
LO7
Micro Warehouse

Evaluating an Ethical Dilemma: Earnings, Inventory Purchases, and Management Bonuses

Micro Warehouse was a computer software and hardware online and catalogue sales company*. A *Wall Street Journal* article disclosed the following:

MICRO WAREHOUSE IS REORGANIZING TOP MANAGEMENT

Micro Warehouse Inc. announced a "significant reorganization" of its management, including the resignation of three senior executives. The move comes just a few weeks after the Norwalk, Conn., computer catalogue sales company said it overstated earnings by $28 million since 1992 as a result of accounting irregularities. That previous disclosure prompted a flurry of shareholder lawsuits against the company. In addition, Micro Warehouse said it is cooperating with an "informal inquiry" by the Securities and Exchange Commission.

SOURCE: Stephan E. Frank, *The Wall Street Journal,* November 21, 1996, p. B2.

Its Form 10–Q quarterly report filed with the Securities and Exchange Commission two days before indicated that inaccuracies involving understatement of purchases and accounts payable in current and prior periods amounted to $47.3 million. It also indicated that, as a result, $2.2 million of executive bonuses for 1995 would be rescinded. Micro Warehouse's total tax rate is approximately 40.4 percent. Both cost of goods sold and executive bonuses are fully deductible for tax purposes.

Required:

As a new staff member at Micro Warehouse's auditing firm, you are assigned to write a memo outlining the effects of the understatement of purchases and the rescinding of the bonuses. In your report, be sure to include the following:

1. The total effect on pretax and after-tax earnings of the understatement of purchases.
2. The total effect on pretax and after-tax earnings of the rescinding of the bonuses.
3. An estimate of the percentage of after-tax earnings management is receiving in bonuses.
4. A discussion of why Micro Warehouse's board of directors may have decided to tie managers' compensation to reported earnings and the possible relation between this type of bonus scheme and the accounting errors.

*Micro Warehouse declared bankruptcy in 2003.

Financial Reporting and Analysis Team Project

CP7-8
LO3, 5

Team Project: Analyzing Inventories

As a team, select an industry to analyze. *Reuters* provides lists of industries and their makeup at **www.reuters.com/finance/industries**. Each team member should acquire the annual report or 10-K for one publicly traded company in the industry, with each member selecting a different company. (Library files, the SEC EDGAR service at **www.sec.gov** and the company itself are good sources.)

Required:

On an individual basis, each team member should write a short report answering the following questions about the selected company. Discuss any patterns across the companies that you as a team observe. Then, as a team, write a short report comparing and contrasting your companies.

1. If your company lists inventories in its balance sheet, what percentage is it of total assets for each of the last three years? If your company does not list inventories, discuss why this is so.
2. If your company lists inventories, what inventory costing method is applied to U.S. inventories?
   a. What do you think motivated this choice?
   b. If the company used LIFO, how much higher or lower would net income before taxes be if it had used FIFO or a similar method instead?

3. Ratio Analysis:
   a. What does the inventory turnover ratio measure in general?
   b. If your company reports inventories, compute the ratio for the last three years.
   c. What do your results suggest about the company?
   d. If available, find the industry ratio for the most recent year, compare it to your results, and discuss why you believe your company differs or is similar to the industry ratio.
4. What is the effect of the change in inventories on cash flows from operating activities for the most recent year (that is, did the change increase or decrease operating cash flows)? Explain your answer.

LEARNING OBJECTIVES

After studying this chapter, you should be able to:

1. Define, classify, and explain the nature of long-lived productive assets and interpret the fixed asset turnover ratio. p. 399

2. Apply the cost principle to measure the acquisition and maintenance of property, plant, and equipment. p. 401

3. Apply various cost allocation methods as assets are held and used over time. p. 406

4. Explain the effect of asset impairment on the financial statements. p. 416

5. Analyze the disposal of property, plant, and equipment. p. 417

6. Apply measurement and reporting concepts for natural resources and intangible assets. p. 419

7. Explain the impact on cash flows of acquiring, using, and disposing of long-lived assets. p. 423

Lectured slideshow–LP8-1
www.mhhe.com/libby6e

REPORTING AND INTERPRETING PROPERTY, PLANT, AND EQUIPMENT; NATURAL RESOURCES; AND INTANGIBLES

FOCUS COMPANY:

Southwest Airlines

MANAGING PRODUCTIVE CAPACITY

FOR THE LOW-FARE LEADER

www.southwest.com

As of December 31, 2007, Southwest Airlines operated 520 Boeing 737 aircraft, providing service to 64 domestic cities in 32 states, and was the largest U.S. air carrier in number of originating passengers boarded and number of scheduled domestic departures. Southwest is a capital-intensive company with more than $10.8 billion in property, plant, and equipment reported on its balance sheet. In fiscal year 2007, Southwest spent over $1.3 billion on aircraft and other flight equipment as well as ground equipment. Since the demand for air travel is seasonal, with peak demand occurring during the summer months, planning for optimal productive capacity in the airline industry is very difficult. Southwest's managers must determine how many aircraft are needed in which cities at what points in time to fill all seats demanded. Otherwise, the company loses revenue (not enough seats) or has higher costs (too many seats).

Demand is also highly sensitive to general economic conditions and other events beyond the control of the company. Even the best corporate planners could not have predicted the September 11, 2001, terrorist attacks against the United States that rocked the airline industry. During the first half of 2003, the war in Iraq led to further declines in the demand for air travel. In response to the precipitous drop in demand, many airlines accelerated retirement of various aircraft, temporarily grounded aircraft, and considered delaying the purchase of new aircraft.

UNDERSTANDING THE BUSINESS

One of the major challenges managers of most businesses face is forecasting the company's long-term productive capacity (that is, the amount of plant and equipment) it will need. If managers underestimate the need, the company will not be able to produce enough goods or services to meet demand and will miss an opportunity to earn revenue. On the other hand, if they overestimate the need, the company will incur excessive costs that will reduce its profitability.

The airline industry provides an outstanding example of the difficulty of planning for and analyzing productive capacity. If an airplane takes off from Kansas City, Missouri, en route to New York City with empty seats, the economic value associated with those seats is lost for that flight. There is obviously no way to sell the seat to a customer after the airplane has left the gate. Unlike a manufacturer, an airline cannot "inventory" seats for the future.

Likewise, if an unexpectedly large number of people want to board a flight, the airline must turn away some customers. You might be willing to buy a television set from Sears even if you had to wait one week for delivery, but you probably wouldn't book a flight home on Thanksgiving weekend on an airline that told you no seats were available. You would simply pick another airline or use a different mode of transportation.

Southwest has a number of large competitors with familiar names such as US Airways, American, United, JetBlue, and Delta. Southwest's 10-K report mentions that "We currently compete with other airlines on all of our routes, some of which airlines have larger fleets and some of which airlines have wider name recognition in some markets."

Much of the battle for passengers in the airline industry is fought in terms of property, plant, and equipment. Passengers want convenient schedules (which requires a large number of aircraft), and they want to fly on new, modern airplanes. Because airlines have such a large investment in equipment but no opportunity to inventory unused seats, they work very hard to fill their aircraft to capacity for each flight. Southwest's Annual Report for 2007 describes the keys to its ability to offer low fares and generous frequent flyer benefits.

REAL WORLD EXCERPT

SOUTHWEST

2007 ANNUAL REPORT

> Southwest has a low cost structure, enabling it to charge low fares. Adjusted for stage length, Southwest has lower unit costs, on average, than most major network carriers. Southwest's low cost advantage is facilitated by reliance upon a single aircraft type, an operationally efficient route structure, and highly productive employees.

As you can see from this discussion, issues surrounding property, plant, and equipment have a pervasive impact on a company in terms of strategy, pricing decisions, and profitability. Managers devote considerable time to planning optimal levels of productive capacity, and financial analysts closely review a company's statements to determine the impact of management's decisions.

This chapter is organized according to the life cycle of long-lived assets—acquisition, use, and disposal. First we will discuss the measuring and reporting issues related to land, buildings, and equipment. Then we will discuss the measurement and reporting issues for natural resources and intangible assets. Among the issues we will discuss are maintaining, using, and disposing of property and equipment over time and measuring and reporting assets considered impaired in their ability to generate future cash flows.

ORGANIZATION of the Chapter

Acquisition and Maintenance of Plant and Equipment	**Use, Impairment, and Disposal of Plant and Equipment**	**Natural Resources and Intangible Assets**
■ Classifying Long-Lived Assets ■ Fixed Asset Turnover Ratio ■ Measuring and Recording Acquisition Cost ■ Repairs, Maintenance, and Additions	■ Depreciation Concepts ■ Alternative Depreciation Methods ■ How Managers Choose ■ Measuring Asset Impairment ■ Disposal of Property, Plant, and Equipment	■ Acquisition and Depletion of Natural Resources ■ Acquisition and Amortization of Intangible Assets

Plant and Equipment as a Percent of Total Assets for Selected Focus Companies

Boston Beer   19.9%

Papa John's   52.1%

Harley-Davidson   18.5%

ACQUISITION AND MAINTENANCE OF PLANT AND EQUIPMENT

Exhibit 8.1 shows the asset section of the balance sheet from Southwest's annual report for the fiscal year ended December 31, 2007. Over 65 percent of Southwest's total assets are flight and ground equipment. Southwest also reports other assets with probable long-term benefits. Let's begin by classifying these assets.

Classifying Long-Lived Assets

The resources that determine a company's productive capacity are often called **long-lived assets.** These assets that are listed as noncurrent assets on the balance sheet may be either tangible or intangible, and have the following characteristics:

1. **Tangible assets** have physical substance; that is, they can be touched. This classification is called **property, plant, and equipment** or **fixed assets.** The three kinds of long-lived tangible assets are

   a. **Land** used in operations. As is the case with Southwest, land often is not shown as a separate item on the balance sheet.

   b. **Buildings, fixtures, and equipment** used in operations. For Southwest, this category includes aircraft, ground equipment to service the aircraft, and office space.

   c. **Natural resources** used in operations. Southwest does not report any natural resources on its balance sheet. However, companies in other industries report natural resources such as timber tracts and silver mines.

2. **Intangible assets** are long-lived assets without physical substance that confer specific rights on their owner. Examples are patents, copyrights, franchises, licenses, and trademarks. Southwest does not report any intangibles on its balance sheet.

Learning Objective 1
Define, classify, and explain the nature of long-lived productive assets and interpret the fixed asset turnover ratio.

LONG-LIVED ASSETS are tangible and intangible resources owned by a business and used in its operations over several years.

TANGIBLE ASSETS (or fixed assets) have physical substance.

INTANGIBLE ASSETS have special rights but not physical substance.

EXHIBIT 8.1

Southwest Airlines' Asset
Section of the Balance Sheet

REAL WORLD EXCERPT

SOUTHWEST
ANNUAL REPORT

SOUTHWEST AIRLINES CO.
Consolidated Balance Sheets (partial)
December 31, 2007 and 2006

Assets *(dollars in millions)*	2007	2006
Current assets: *(summarized)*	$ 4,443	$ 2,601
Property and equipment:		
Flight equipment	13,019	11,769
Ground property and equipment	1,515	1,356
Deposits on flight equipment purchase contracts	626	734
	15,160	13,859
Less: Accumulated depreciation	4,286	3,765
Total property and equipment	10,874	10,094
Other assets	1,455	765
Total assets	$16,772	$13,460

**KEY RATIO
ANALYSIS**

Fixed Asset Turnover

**Selected Focus
Companies' Fixed Asset
Turnover Ratios for 2006**

Papa John's   5.32

Timberland   17.71

Callaway Golf   7.86

? ANALYTICAL QUESTION:
How effectively is management utilizing fixed assets to generate revenues?

% RATIO AND COMPARISONS:

$$\text{Fixed Asset Turnover} = \frac{\text{Net Sales (or Operating Revenues)}}{\text{Average Net Fixed Assets*}}$$

[Beginning + Ending Fixed Asset Balance (net of accumulated depreciation)] ÷ 2

The 2007 ratio for Southwest is:

$9,861 operating revenues ÷ [($10,874 + $10,094) ÷ 2] = 0.94 times

COMPARISONS OVER TIME			COMPARISONS WITH COMPETITORS	
Southwest Airlines			Delta	United
2005	2006	2007	2007	2007
0.84	0.94	0.94	1.55	1.77

💡 INTERPRETATIONS:

In General   The fixed asset turnover ratio measures the sales dollars generated by each dollar of fixed assets used. A high rate normally suggests effective management. An increasing rate over time signals more efficient fixed asset use. Creditors and security analysts use this ratio to assess a company's effectiveness in generating sales from its long-lived assets.

Focus Company Analysis   Southwest's fixed asset turnover ratio increased over the past few years indicating more efficient use of equipment. However, it appears at first glance that Southwest is less efficient than perennial money losers Delta and United. This is not the case. Their higher fixed asset turnover is due to the greater age of their fleet (a higher percentage has been depreciated) and the fact that more planes are leased in such a way that they do not appear as fixed assets on the balance sheet.

A Few Cautions   A lower or declining fixed asset turnover rate may indicate that a company is expanding (by acquiring additional productive assets) in anticipation of higher future sales. An increasing ratio could also signal that a firm has cut back on capital expenditures due to a downturn in business. This is not the case at Southwest which continues to expand its fleet. As a consequence, appropriate interpretation of the fixed asset turnover ratio requires an investigation of related activities.

Measuring and Recording Acquisition Cost

Under the **cost principle,** all reasonable and necessary expenditures made in acquiring and preparing an asset for use (or sale as in the case of inventory) should be recorded as the cost of the asset. We say that the expenditures are **capitalized** when they are recorded as part of the cost of an asset instead of as expenses in the current period. Any sales taxes, legal fees, transportation costs, and installation costs are then added to the purchase price of the asset. However, special discounts are subtracted and any interest charges associated with the purchase are expensed as incurred.

In addition to purchasing buildings and equipment, a company may acquire undeveloped land, typically with the intent to build a new factory or office building. When a company purchases land, all of the incidental costs of the purchase, such as title fees, sales commissions, legal fees, title insurance, delinquent taxes, and surveying fees, should be included in its cost.

Sometimes a company purchases an old building or used machinery for the business operations. Renovation and repair costs incurred by the company prior to the asset's use should be included as a part of its cost. Also, when purchasing land, building, and equipment as a group, the total cost is allocated to each asset in proportion to the asset's market value relative to the total market value of the assets as a whole.

For the sake of illustration, let's assume that Southwest purchased a new 737 aircraft from Boeing on January 1, 2010 (the beginning of Southwest's fiscal year), for a list price of $73 million. Let's also assume that Boeing offered Southwest a discount of $4 million for signing the purchase agreement. That means the price of the new plane to Southwest would actually be $69 million. In addition, Southwest paid $200,000 to have the plane delivered and $800,000 to prepare the new plane for use. The amount recorded for the purchase, called the acquisition cost, is the net cash amount paid for the asset or, when noncash assets are used as payment, the fair market value of the asset given or asset received, whichever can be more clearly determined (called the **cash equivalent price**). Southwest would calculate the acquisition cost of the new aircraft as follows:

Learning Objective 2
Apply the cost principle to measure the acquisition and maintenance of property, plant, and equipment.

Audio lecture–AP8-1
Video 8-1
www.mhhe.com/libby6e

The ACQUISITION COST is the net cash equivalent amount paid or to be paid for the asset.

Invoice price	$73,000,000
Less: Discount from Boeing	4,000,000
Net cash invoice price	69,000,000
Add: Transportation charges paid by Southwest	200,000
Preparation costs paid by Southwest	800,000
Cost of the aircraft (added to the asset account)	$70,000,000

For Cash

Assuming that Southwest paid cash for the aircraft and related transportation and preparation costs, the transaction is recorded as follows:

Flight Equipment (+A)   70,000,000

   Cash (−A)   70,000,000

Assets		=	Liabilities	+	Stockholders' Equity
Cash	−70,000,000				
Flight Equipment	+70,000,000				

It might seem unusual for Southwest to pay cash to purchase new assets that cost $70 million, but this is often the case. When it acquires productive assets, a company may pay with cash that was generated from operations or cash recently borrowed. It also is possible for the seller to finance the purchase on credit.

For Debt

Now let's assume that Southwest signed a note payable for the new aircraft and paid cash for the transportation and preparation costs. In that case, Southwest would record the following journal entry:

Flight Equipment (+A)   70,000,000

   Cash (−A)   1,000,000

   Note Payable (+L)   69,000,000

Assets		=	Liabilities		+	Stockholders' Equity
Cash	−1,000,000		Note Payable	+69,000,000		
Flight Equipment	+70,000,000					

For Equity (or Other Noncash Considerations)

Noncash consideration, such as the company's common stock or a right given by the company to the seller to purchase the company's goods or services at a special price, might also be part of the transaction. When noncash consideration is included in the purchase of an asset, the cash-equivalent cost (fair market value of the asset given or received) is determined.

Assume that Southwest gave Boeing 9,000,000 shares of its $1.00 par value common stock with a market value of $5 per share and paid the balance in cash. The journal entry and transaction effects follow:

Flight Equipment (+A)   70,000,000

   Common Stock (+SE) ($1.00 par value × 9,000,000 shares)   9,000,000

   Additional Paid-in Capital (+SE) ($4.00 × 9,000,000 shares)   36,000,000

   Cash (−A)   25,000,000

Assets		=	Liabilities	+	Stockholders' Equity	
Cash	−25,000,000				Common Stock	+9,000,000
Flight Equipment	+70,000,000				Additional Paid-in Capital	+36,000,000

By Construction

In some cases, a company may construct an asset for its own use instead of buying it from a manufacturer. When a company does so, the cost of the asset includes all the necessary costs associated with construction, such as labor, materials, and in most situations, a portion of the interest incurred during the construction period,

CAPITALIZED INTEREST represents interest expenditures included in the cost of a self-constructed asset.

called **capitalized interest.** The amount of interest expense that is capitalized is recorded by debiting the asset and crediting cash when the interest is paid. The amount of interest to be capitalized is a complex computation discussed in detail in other accounting courses.

Capitalizing labor, materials, and a portion of interest expense has the effect of increasing assets, decreasing expenses, and increasing net income. Let's assume Southwest constructed a new hangar, paying $600,000 in labor costs and $1,300,000 in supplies and materials. Southwest also paid $100,000 in interest expense during the year related to the construction project:

| Building (+A) .... | 2,000,000 | |
| Cash (−A) .... | | 2,000,000 |

	Assets	=	Liabilities	+	Stockholders' Equity
Cash	−2,000,000				
Building	+2,000,000				

Capitalized Expenditures:

Wages paid	*600,000*
Supplies used	*1,300,000*
Interest paid	*100,000*

Delta Air Lines includes a note on capitalized interest in a recent annual report:

NOTES TO CONSOLIDATED FINANCIAL STATEMENTS

1. Summary of Significant Accounting Policies:

. . .

Interest Capitalized—We capitalize interest paid on advance payments used to acquire new aircraft and on construction of ground facilities as an additional cost of the related assets.

REAL WORLD EXCERPT

Delta Air Lines
ANNUAL REPORT

SELF-STUDY QUIZ

In a recent year, McDonald's Corporation purchased property, plant, and equipment priced at $1.8 billion. Assume that the company also paid $70 million for sales tax; $8 million for transportation costs; $1.3 million for installation and preparation of the property, plant, and equipment before use; and $100,000 in maintenance contracts to cover repairs to the property, plant, and equipment during use.

1. Compute the acquisition cost for the property, plant, and equipment:

2. How did you account for the sales tax, transportation costs, and installation costs? Explain why.

3. Under the following independent assumptions, indicate the effects of the acquisition on the accounting equation. Use + for increase and − for decrease and indicate the accounts and amounts:

	ASSETS	LIABILITIES	STOCKHOLDERS' EQUITY
a. Paid 30 percent in cash and the rest by signing a note payable.			
b. Issued 10 million shares of common stock ($0.10 per share stated value) at a market price of $45 per share and paid the balance in cash.			

After you have completed your answers, check them with the solutions at the bottom of the page.

Repairs, Maintenance, and Additions

Most assets require substantial expenditures during their lives to maintain or enhance their productive capacity. These expenditures include cash outlays for ordinary repairs and maintenance, major repairs, replacements, and additions.

Self-Study Quiz
Solutions

1. **Property, Plant, and Equipment (PPE)**

Acquisition cost	$1,800,000,000
Sales tax	70,000,000
Transportation	8,000,000
Installation	1,300,000
Total	$1,879,300,000

Because the maintenance contracts are not necessary to readying the assets for use, they are not included in the acquisition cost.

2. Sales tax, transportation, and installation costs were capitalized because they are reasonable and necessary for getting the asset ready for its intended use.

3.

Assets		Liabilities		Stockholders' Equity	
a. PPE	+1,879,300,000	Note Payable	+1,315,510,000		
Cash	−563,790,000				
b. PPE	+1,879,300,000			Common Stock	+1,000,000
Cash	−1,429,300,000			Additional Paid-in Capital	+449,000,000

Expenditures that are made after an asset has been acquired are classified as follows:

1. **Ordinary repairs and maintenance** are expenditures that maintain the productive capacity of the asset during the current accounting period only. These cash outlays are recorded as **expenses** in the current period. Ordinary repairs and maintenance, also called **revenue expenditures,** are expenditures for the normal maintenance and upkeep of long-lived assets. These expenditures are recurring in nature, involve relatively small amounts at each occurrence, and do not directly lengthen the useful life of the asset.

   In the case of Southwest Airlines, examples of ordinary repairs would include changing the oil in the aircraft engines, replacing the lights in the control panels, and fixing torn fabric on passenger seats. Although the cost of individual ordinary repairs is relatively small, in the aggregate these expenditures can be substantial. In 2007, Southwest paid $616 million for aircraft maintenance and repairs. This amount was reported as an expense on its income statement.

2. **Additions and improvements** are expenditures that increase the productive life, operating efficiency, or capacity of the asset. These **capital expenditures** are added to the appropriate asset accounts. They occur infrequently, involve large amounts of money, and increase an asset's economic usefulness in the future through either increased efficiency or longer life. Examples include additions, major overhauls, complete reconditioning, and major replacements and improvements, such as the complete replacement of an engine on an aircraft.

   In many cases, no clear line distinguishes improvements (assets) from ordinary repairs and maintenance (expenses). In these situations, managers must exercise professional judgment and make a subjective decision. Capitalizing expenses will increase assets and net income in the current year, with future years' income lower by the amount of the annual depreciation. On the other hand, for tax purposes, expensing the amount in the current period will lower taxes immediately. Because the decision to capitalize or expense is subjective, auditors review the items reported as capital and revenue expenditures closely.

   To avoid spending too much time classifying additions and improvements (capital expenditures) and repair expenses (revenue expenditures), some companies develop simple policies to govern the accounting for these expenditures. For example, one large computer company expenses all individual items that cost less than $1,000. Such policies are acceptable because immaterial (relatively small dollar) amounts will not affect users' decisions when analyzing financial statements.

ORDINARY REPAIRS AND MAINTENANCE are expenditures for normal operating upkeep of long-lived assets.

REVENUE EXPENDITURES maintain the productive capacity of the asset during the current accounting period only and are recorded as expenses.

ADDITIONS AND IMPROVEMENTS are infrequent expenditures that increase an asset's economic usefulness in the future.

CAPITAL EXPENDITURES increase the productive life, operating efficiency, or capacity of the asset and are recorded as increases in asset accounts, not as expenses.

 WorldCom: Hiding Billions in Expenses through Capitalization

FINANCIAL ANALYSIS

WorldCom

When expenditures that should be recorded as current period expenses are improperly capitalized as part of the cost of an asset, the effects on the financial statements can be enormous. In one of the largest accounting frauds in history, WorldCom (now part of Verizon) inflated its income and cash flows from operations by billions of dollars in just such a scheme. This fraud turned WorldCom's actual losses into large profits.

Over five quarters in 2001 and 2002, the company initially announced that it had capitalized $3.8 billion that should have been recorded as operating expenses. By early 2004, auditors discovered $74.4 billion in necessary restatements (reductions to previously reported pretax income) for 2000 and 2001.

Accounting for expenses as capital expenditures increases current income because it spreads a single period's operating expenses over many future periods as depreciation expense. It increases cash flows from operations by moving cash outflows from the operating section to the investing section of the cash flow statement.

SELF-STUDY **QUIZ**

A building that originally cost $400,000 has been used over the past 10 years and needs continual maintenance and repairs. For each of the following expenditures, indicate whether it should be expensed in the current period or capitalized as part of **the cost of the asset.**

	Expense or Capitalize?
1. Replacing electrical wiring throughout the building.	_____
2. Repairs to the front door of the building.	_____
3. Annual cleaning of the filters on the building's air conditioning system.	_____
4. Significant repairs due to damage from an unusual and infrequent flood.	_____

After you have completed your answers, check them with the solutions at the bottom of the page.

USE, IMPAIRMENT, AND DISPOSAL OF PLANT AND EQUIPMENT

Depreciation Concepts

Learning Objective 3

Apply various cost allocation methods as assets are held and used over time.

Except for land that is considered to have an unlimited life, a long-lived asset with a limited useful life, such as an airplane, represents the prepaid cost of a bundle of future services or benefits. The **matching principle** requires that a portion of an asset's cost be allocated as an expense in the same period that revenues were generated by its use. Southwest Airlines earns revenue when it provides air travel service and incurs an expense when using its aircraft to generate the revenue.

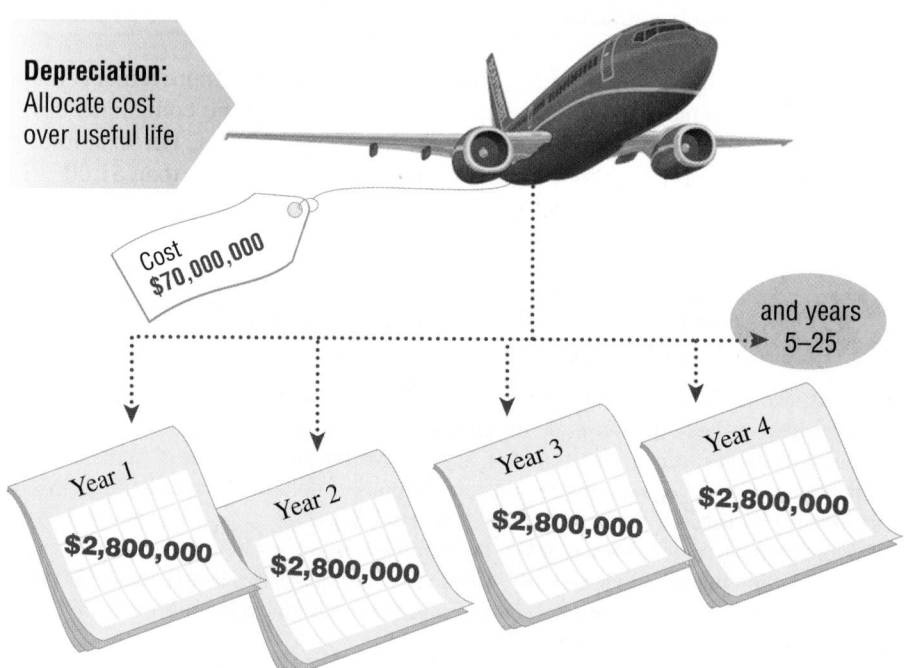

Depreciation: Allocate cost over useful life

Cost $70,000,000

and years 5–25

Year 1 $2,800,000   Year 2 $2,800,000   Year 3 $2,800,000   Year 4 $2,800,000

Using the asset → Depreciation Expense each year

Self-Study Quiz Solutions   1. Capitalize   2. Expense   3. Expense   4. Capitalize

The term used to identify the matching of the cost of using buildings and equipment with the revenues they generated is depreciation. Thus, depreciation is **the process of allocating the cost of buildings and equipment over their productive lives using a systematic and rational method.**

Students often are confused by the concept of depreciation as accountants use it. In accounting, depreciation is a process of **cost allocation,** not a process of determining an asset's current market value or worth. When an asset is depreciated, the remaining balance sheet amount **probably does not represent its current market value.** On balance sheets subsequent to acquisition, the undepreciated cost is not measured on a market or fair value basis.

An adjusting journal entry is needed at the end of each period to reflect the use of buildings and equipment for the period:

DEPRECIATION is the process of allocating the cost of buildings and equipment over their productive lives using a systematic and rational method.

Depreciation Expense (+E, −SE)	xxx	
Accumulated Depreciation (+XA, −A)		xxx

Assets	=	Liabilities	+	Stockholders' Equity
Accumulated				Depreciation
Depreciation (+XA) −xxx				Expense (+E) −xxx

The amount of depreciation recorded during each period is reported on the income statement as **Depreciation Expense.** The amount of depreciation expense accumulated since the acquisition date is reported on the balance sheet as a contra-account, **Accumulated Depreciation,** and deducted from the related asset's cost. The net amount on the balance sheet is called **net book value** or **carrying value.** The net book (or carrying) value of a long-lived asset is its acquisition cost less the accumulated depreciation from acquisition date to the balance sheet date.

NET BOOK (OR CARRYING) VALUE is the acquisition cost of an asset less accumulated depreciation.

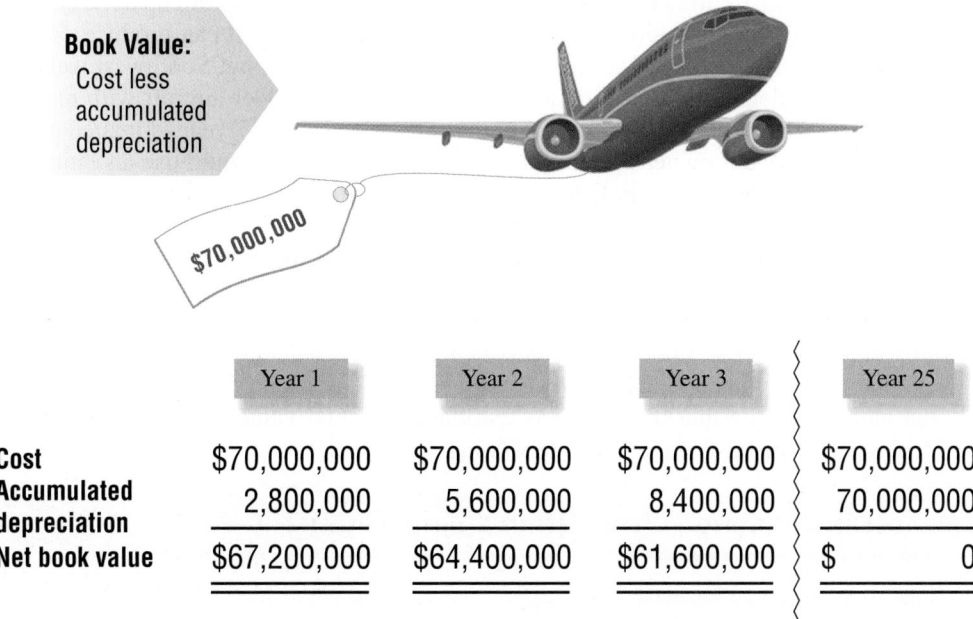

	Year 1	Year 2	Year 3	Year 25
Cost	$70,000,000	$70,000,000	$70,000,000	$70,000,000
Accumulated depreciation	2,800,000	5,600,000	8,400,000	70,000,000
Net book value	$67,200,000	$64,400,000	$61,600,000	$ 0

From Exhibit 8.1 on page 400, we see that Southwest's acquisition cost for property and equipment is $15,160 million at the end of 2007. The accumulated depreciation and amortization on the property and equipment is $4,286 million. Thus, the book value is reported at $10,874 million. Southwest also reported depreciation and amortization expense of $555 million on its income statement for 2007.

Book Value as an Approximation of Remaining Life

**Book Value as a Percentage
of Original Cost**

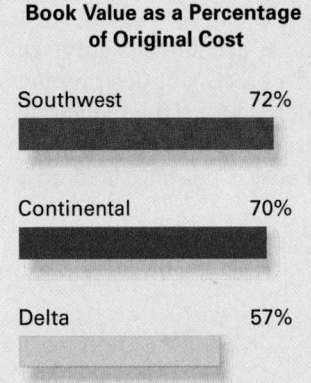

Southwest   72%

Continental   70%

Delta   57%

Some analysts compare the book value of assets to their original cost as an approximation of their remaining life. If the book value of an asset is 100 percent of its cost, it is a new asset; if the book value is 25 percent of its cost, the asset has about 25 percent of its estimated life remaining. In Southwest's case, the book value of its property and equipment is 72 percent of its original cost, compared to 70 percent for Continental Airlines and 57 percent for Delta Airlines. This comparison suggests that Southwest's flight equipment may have more estimated life remaining than that of Continental and Delta. This comparison is only a rough approximation and is influenced by some of the accounting issues discussed in the next section.

To calculate depreciation expense, three amounts are required for each asset:

1. Acquisition cost.

2. Estimated useful life to the company.

3. Estimated residual (or salvage) value at the end of the asset's useful life to the company.

Of these three amounts, two, the asset's useful life and residual value, are estimates. Therefore, **depreciation expense is an estimate.**

ESTIMATED USEFUL LIFE is the expected service life of an asset to the present owner.

Estimated useful life represents management's estimate of the asset's useful **economic life** to the company rather than its total economic life to all potential users. The asset's expected physical life is often longer than the company intends to use the asset. Economic life may be expressed in terms of years or units of capacity, such as the number of hours a machine is expected to operate or units it can produce. Southwest's aircraft fleet is expected to fly for more than 25 years, but Southwest wants to offer its customers a high level of service by replacing its older aircraft with modern equipment. For accounting purposes, Southwest uses a 23- to 25-year estimated useful life. The subsequent owner of the aircraft (a regional airline) would use an estimated useful life based on its own policies.

RESIDUAL (OR SALVAGE) VALUE is the estimated amount to be recovered at the end of the company's estimated useful life of an asset.

Residual (or salvage) value represents management's estimate of the amount the company expects to recover upon disposal of the asset at the end of its estimated useful life. The residual value may be the estimated value of the asset as salvage or scrap or its expected value if sold to another user. In the case of Southwest's aircraft, residual value may be the amount it expects to receive when it sells the asset to a small regional airline that operates older equipment. The notes to Southwest's financial statements indicate that the company estimates residual value to be between 0 and 15 percent of the cost of the asset, depending on the asset.

Differences in Estimated Lives within a Single Industry

Notes to recent actual financial statements of various airline companies reveal the following estimates for the useful lives of flight equipment:

Company	Estimated Life (in years)
Southwest	23 to 25
Continental	25 to 30
US Airways	5 to 25
Singapore Airlines	15
Delta	25

The differences in the estimated lives may be attributed to a number of factors such as the type of aircraft used by each company, equipment replacement plans, operational differences, and the degree of management's conservatism. In addition, given the same type of aircraft, companies that plan to use the equipment over fewer years may estimate higher residual values than companies that plan to use the equipment longer. For example, Singapore Airlines uses a residual value of 10 percent over a relatively short useful life for its passenger aircraft, compared to 5 percent for Delta Air Lines over a 25-year useful life.

Differences in estimated lives and residual values of assets can have a significant impact on a comparison of the profitability of the competing companies. Analysts must be certain to identify the causes of differences in depreciable lives.

Alternative Depreciation Methods

Because of significant differences among companies and the assets they own, accountants have not been able to agree on a single best method of depreciation. As a result, managers may choose from several acceptable depreciation methods that match depreciation expense with the revenues generated in a period. Once selected, the method should be applied consistently over time to enhance comparability of financial information. We will discuss the three most common depreciation methods:

1. Straight-line (the most common, used by more than 95 percent of companies surveyed).
2. Units-of-production.
3. Declining-balance.

To illustrate each method, let's assume that Southwest Airlines acquired a new service vehicle (ground equipment) on January 1, 2010. The relevant information is shown in Exhibit 8.2.

Number of Companies Using Alternative Depreciation Methods*

Straight-line	592
Units-of-production	23
Declining-balance	16
Other	21

* Methods reported by companies sampled in *Accounting Trends & Techniques* (AICPA), 2006.

SOUTHWEST AIRLINES Acquisition of a New Service Vehicle			
Cost, purchased on January 1, 2010	$62,500		
Estimated residual value	$ 2,500		
Estimated useful life		3 years **OR**	100,000 miles
Actual miles driven in:	Year 2010		30,000 miles
	Year 2011		50,000 miles
	Year 2012		20,000 miles

EXHIBIT 8.2

Data for Illustrating the Computation of Depreciation under Alternative Methods

Straight-Line Method

More companies, including Southwest, use **straight-line depreciation** in their financial statements than all other methods combined. Under the straight-line method, an equal portion of an asset's depreciable cost is allocated to each accounting period over its estimated useful life. The formula to estimate annual depreciation expense follows:

STRAIGHT-LINE DEPRECIATION is the method that allocates the cost of an asset in equal periodic amounts over its useful life.

Straight-Line Formula:

$$(\text{Cost} - \text{Residual Value}) \times \frac{1}{\text{Useful Life}} = \text{Depreciation Expense}$$

$$(\$62,500 - \$2,500) \times \frac{1}{3 \text{ years}} = \$20,000$$

In this formula, "Cost minus Residual Value" is the amount to be depreciated, also called the **depreciable cost.** "1 ÷ Useful Life" is the **straight-line rate.** Using the data provided in Exhibit 8.2, the depreciation expense for Southwest's new truck would be $20,000 per year.

Companies often create a **depreciation schedule** that shows the computed amount of depreciation expense each year over the entire useful life of the machine. You can use computerized spreadsheet programs, such as Excel, to create the depreciation schedule. Using the data in Exhibit 8.2 and the straight-line method, Southwest's depreciation schedule follows:

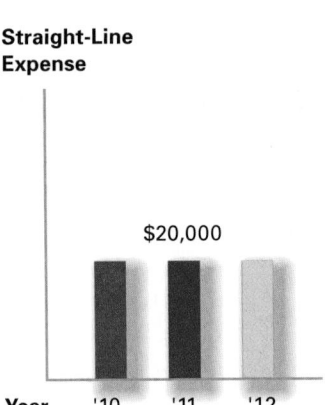

Straight-Line Expense

$20,000

Year   '10   '11   '12

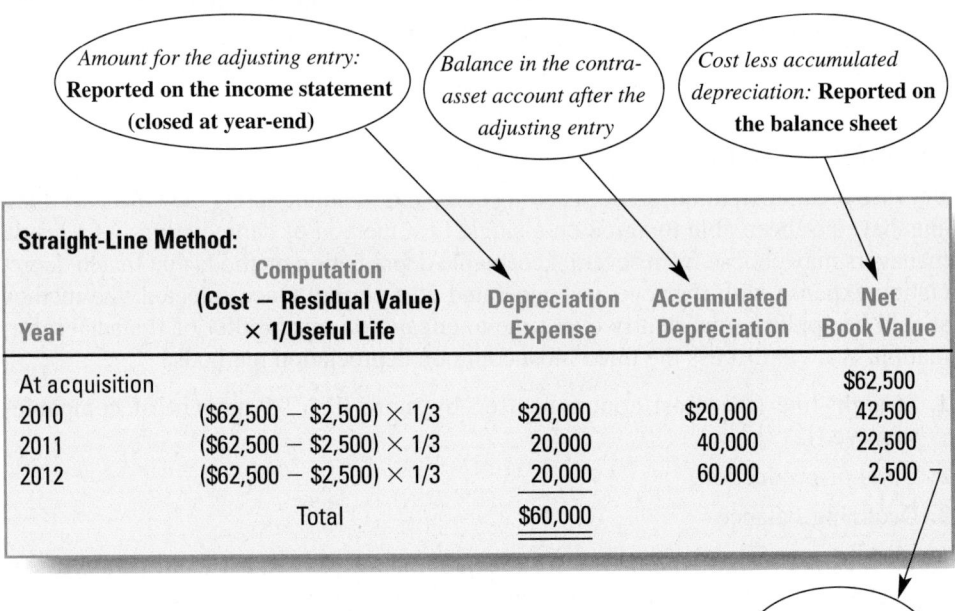

Amount for the adjusting entry: **Reported on the income statement (closed at year-end)**

Balance in the contra-asset account after the adjusting entry

Cost less accumulated depreciation: **Reported on the balance sheet**

Straight-Line Method:

Year	Computation (Cost − Residual Value) × 1/Useful Life	Depreciation Expense	Accumulated Depreciation	Net Book Value
At acquisition				$62,500
2010	($62,500 − $2,500) × 1/3	$20,000	$20,000	42,500
2011	($62,500 − $2,500) × 1/3	20,000	40,000	22,500
2012	($62,500 − $2,500) × 1/3	20,000	60,000	2,500
	Total	$60,000		

Equal to estimated residual value at end of useful life

Notice that

- Depreciation expense is a constant amount each year.
- Accumulated depreciation increases by an equal amount each year.
- Net book value decreases by the same amount each year until it equals the estimated residual value.

This is the reason for the name **straight-line method.** Notice, too, that the adjusting entry can be prepared from this schedule, and the effect on the income statement and balance sheet are known. Southwest Airlines uses the straight-line method for all its assets. The company reported depreciation expense in the amount of $555 million for 2007 equal to almost 6 percent of the airline's revenues for the year. Most companies in the airline industry use the straight-line method.

Units-of-Production Method

UNITS-OF-PRODUCTION DEPRECIATION is a method to allocate the cost of an asset over its useful life based on the relation of its periodic output to its total estimated output.

The **units-of-production depreciation method** relates depreciable cost to total estimated productive output. The formula to estimate annual depreciation expense under this method is as follows:

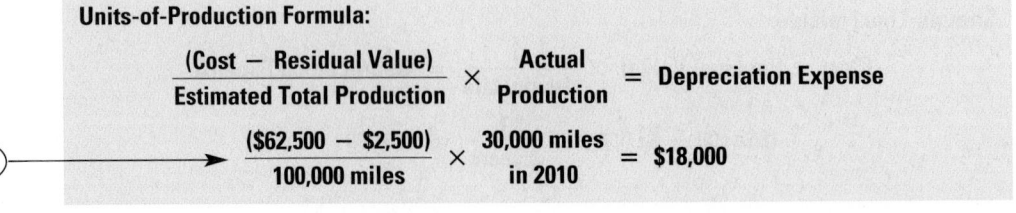

Units-of-Production Formula:

$$\frac{(\text{Cost} - \text{Residual Value})}{\text{Estimated Total Production}} \times \frac{\text{Actual}}{\text{Production}} = \text{Depreciation Expense}$$

$$\frac{(\$62,500 - \$2,500)}{100,000 \text{ miles}} \times \frac{30,000 \text{ miles}}{\text{in 2010}} = \$18,000$$

Depreciation Rate per unit = $.60 per mile

Dividing the depreciable cost by the estimated total production yields the depreciation rate per unit of production, which is then multiplied by the actual production for the period to determine depreciation expense. In our illustration, for every mile that the new vehicle is driven, Southwest would record depreciation expense of $0.60. The depreciation schedule for the truck under the units-of-production method would appear as follows:

Units-of-Production Method:

Year	Computation [(Cost − Residual Value)/ Total Estimated Production] × Actual Production	Depreciation Expense	Accumulated Depreciation	Net Book Value
At acquisition	RATE			$62,500
2010	$.60 per mile × 30,000 miles	$18,000	$18,000	44,500
2011	$.60 per mile × 50,000 miles	30,000	48,000	14,500
2012	$.60 per mile × 20,000 miles	12,000	60,000	2,500
	Total	$60,000		

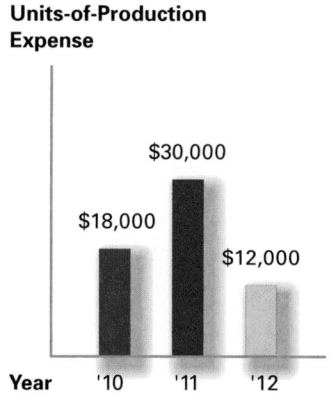

Units-of-Production Expense

Notice that, from period to period, depreciation expense, accumulated depreciation, and book value vary directly with the units produced. In the units-of-production method, depreciation expense is a **variable expense** because it varies directly with production or use.

You might wonder what happens if the total estimated productive output differs from actual total output. Remember that the estimate is management's best guess of total output. If any difference occurs at the end of the asset's life, the final adjusting entry to depreciation expense should be for the amount needed to bring the asset's net book value equal to the asset's estimated residual value. For example, if, in 2012, Southwest's truck ran 25,000 actual miles, the same amount of depreciation expense, $12,000, would be recorded.

Although Southwest does not use the units-of-production method, the Exxon Mobil Corporation, a major energy company that explores, produces, transports, and sells crude oil and natural gas worldwide, does, as notes to the company's annual report explain.

1. Summary of Accounting Policies

Property, Plant, and Equipment

Depreciation, depletion, and amortization, based on cost less estimated salvage value of the asset, are primarily determined under either the unit-of-production method or the straight-line method, which are based on estimated asset service life taking obsolescence into consideration . . . Unit-of-production rates are based on proved developed reserves, which are oil, gas and other mineral reserves that are estimated to be recoverable from existing facilities using current operating methods.

REAL WORLD EXCERPT
Exxon Mobil Corporation
2006 ANNUAL REPORT

The units-of-production method is based on an estimate of an asset's total future productive capacity or output that is difficult to determine. This is another example of the degree of subjectivity inherent in accounting.

Declining-Balance Method

DECLINING-BALANCE DEPRECIATION is the method that allocates the cost of an asset over its useful life based on a multiple of the straight-line rate (often two times).

If an asset is considered to be more efficient or productive when it is newer, managers might choose the declining-balance depreciation method to match a higher depreciation expense with higher revenues in the early years of an asset's life and lower in the later years. We say, then, that this is an **accelerated depreciation** method. Although accelerated methods are seldom used for financial reporting purposes, the method that is used more frequently than others is the declining-balance method

Declining-balance depreciation is based on applying a rate exceeding the straight-line rate to the asset's net book value over time. The rate is often double (two times) the straight-line rate and is termed the **double-declining-balance rate.** For example, if the straight-line rate is 10 percent (1 ÷ 10 years) for a 10-year estimated useful life, then the declining-balance rate is 20 percent (2 × the straight-line rate). Other typical acceleration rates are 1.5 times and 1.75 times. The double-declining-balance rate is adopted most frequently by companies employing an accelerated method, so we will use it in our illustration.

Double-Declining-Balance Formula:

Accumulated Depreciation increases over time

$$(\text{Cost} - \text{Accumulated Depreciation}) \times \frac{2}{\text{Useful Life}} = \text{Depreciation Expense}$$

$$(\$62,500 - \$0 \text{ in } 2010) \times \frac{2}{3 \text{ years}} = \$41,667 \text{ in the first year}$$

There are two important differences between this method and the others described previously:

1. Notice that accumulated depreciation, not residual value, is included in the formula. Since accumulated depreciation increases each year, net book value (cost minus accumulated depreciation) decreases. The double-declining rate is applied to a lower net book value each year, resulting in a decline in depreciation expense over time.

2. An asset's book value cannot be depreciated below residual value. Therefore, if the annual computation reduces net book value below residual value, a lower amount of depreciation expense must be recorded so that net book value equals residual value. No additional depreciation expense is computed in subsequent years.

Computation of double-declining-balance depreciation expense is illustrated in the depreciation schedule:

Double-Declining-Balance Expense

$41,667

$13,889

$4,444

Year   '10   '11   '12

Computed amount is too large.

Year	Computation (Cost − Accumulated Depreciation) × 2/Useful Life		Depreciation Expense	Accumulated Depreciation	Net Book Value
At acquisition					$62,500
2010	($62,500 − $0)	× 2/3	$41,667	$41,667	20,833
2011	($62,500 − $41,667)	× 2/3	13,889	55,556	6,944
2012	($62,500 − $55,556)	× 2/3	~~4,629~~	~~60,185~~	~~2,315~~
			4,444	60,000	2,500
	Total		$60,000		

The calculated depreciation expense for 2012 ($4,629) is not the same as the amount actually reported on the income statement ($4,444). An asset should never be depreciated below the point at which net book value equals its residual value. The asset owned by Southwest has an estimated residual value of $2,500. If depreciation expense were recorded in the amount of $4,629, the book value of the asset would be less than $2,500. The correct depreciation expense for year 2012 is therefore $4,444, the amount that will reduce the book value to exactly $2,500.

Companies in industries that expect fairly rapid obsolescence of their equipment use the declining-balance method. Sony is one of the companies that use this method, as a note to its annual report shows.

2. Summary of significant accounting policies:

Property, Plant, and Equipment and Depreciation

Property, plant and equipment are stated at cost. Depreciation of property, plant and equipment is primarily computed on the declining-balance method for Sony Corporation and its Japanese subsidiaries . . . and on the straight-line method for foreign subsidiaries at rates based on estimated useful lives of the assets, principally, ranging from 15 up to 50 years for buildings and from 2 years up to 10 years for machinery and equipment.

REAL WORLD EXCERPT

Sony Corporation
2006 ANNUAL REPORT

As this note indicates, companies may use different depreciation methods for different classes of assets. Under the consistency principle, they are expected to apply the same methods to those assets over time.

In Summary

The following table summarizes the three depreciation methods, computations, and the differences in depreciation expense over time for each method.

Method	Computation	Depreciation Expense
Straight-line	(Cost − Residual Value) × 1/Useful Life	Equal amounts each year
Units-of-production	[Cost − Residual Value)/Estimated Total Production] × Annual Production	Varying amounts based on production level
Double-declining-balance	(Cost − Accumulated Depreciation) × 2/Useful Life	Declining amounts over time

 Impact of Alternative Depreciation Methods

FINANCIAL ANALYSIS

Assume that you are comparing two companies that are exactly the same, except that one uses accelerated depreciation and the other uses the straight-line method. Which company would you expect to report a higher net income? Actually, this question is a bit tricky. The answer is that you cannot say for certain which company's income would be higher.

The accelerated methods report higher depreciation and therefore lower net income during the early years of an asset's life. As the age of the asset increases, this effect reverses. Therefore, companies that use accelerated depreciation report lower depreciation expense and higher net income during the later years of an asset's life. The graph in the margin shows the pattern of depreciation over the life of an asset for the straight-line and declining-balance methods discussed in this chapter. When the curve for the accelerated method falls below the curve for the straight-line method, the accelerated method produces a higher net income than the straight-line method. However, total depreciation expense by the end of the asset's life is the same for each method.

Users of financial statements must understand the impact of alternative depreciation methods used over time. Differences in depreciation methods rather than real economic differences can cause significant variation in reported net incomes.

Summary Depreciation Expense

SELF-STUDY QUIZ

Assume that Southwest has acquired new computer equipment at a cost of $240,000. The equipment has an estimated life of six years, an estimated operating life of 50,000 hours, and an estimated residual value of $30,000. Determine depreciation expense for the first full year under each of the following methods:

1. Straight-line depreciation

2. Units-of-production method (assume the equipment ran for 8,000 hours in the first year)

3. Double-declining-balance method

After you have completed your answers, check them with the solutions at the bottom of the page.

FINANCIAL ANALYSIS

Increased Profitability Due to an Accounting Adjustment? Reading the Notes

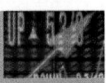

Singapore Airlines

Financial analysts are particularly interested in changes in accounting estimates because they can have a large impact on a company's before-tax operating income. In 2001, Singapore Airlines disclosed in its annual report that it had increased the estimated useful life of its aircraft from 10 to 15 years to reflect a change in its aircraft replacement policy. The change reduced depreciation expenses for the year by $265 million, and would reduce expenses by a similar amount each year over the remaining life of the aircraft. Analysts pay close attention to this number because it represents increased profitability due merely to an accounting adjustment.

How Managers Choose

Financial Reporting

For financial reporting purposes, corporate managers must determine which depreciation method provides the best matching of revenues and expenses for any given asset. If the asset is expected to provide benefits evenly over time, then the straight-line method is preferred. Managers also find this method to be easy to use and to explain. If no other method is more systematic or rational, then the straight-line method is selected. Also, during the early years of an asset's life, the straight-line method reports higher income than the accelerated methods do. For these reasons, the straight-line method is, by far and away, the most common.

On the other hand, certain assets produce more revenue in their early lives because they are more efficient than in later years. In this case, managers select an accelerated method to allocate cost.

Self-Study Quiz
Solutions

1. ($240,000 − $30,000) × 1/6 = $35,000
2. [($240,000 − $30,000) ÷ 50,000] × 8,000 = $33,600
3. ($240,000 − $0) × 2/6 = $80,000

Tax Reporting

Southwest Airlines, like most public companies, maintains two sets of accounting records. Both sets of records reflect the same transactions, but the transactions are accounted for under two sets of measurement rules. One set is prepared under GAAP for reporting to stockholders. The other set is prepared to determine the company's tax obligation under the Internal Revenue Code. The reason that the two sets of rules are different is simple: The objectives of GAAP and the Internal Revenue Code differ.

Financial Reporting (GAAP)	Tax Reporting (IRS)
The objective of financial reporting is to provide economic information about a business that is useful in projecting future cash flows of the business. Financial reporting rules follow generally accepted accounting principles.	The objective of the Internal Revenue Code is to raise sufficient revenues to pay for the expenditures of the federal government. Many of the Code's provisions are designed to encourage certain behaviors that are thought to benefit society (e.g., contributions to charities are made tax deductible to encourage people to support worthy programs).

In some cases, differences between the Internal Revenue Code and GAAP leave the manager no choice but to maintain separate records. In other cases, the differences are the result of management choice. When given a choice among acceptable tax accounting methods, managers apply what is called the **least and the latest rule.** All taxpayers want to pay the lowest amount of tax that is legally permitted and at the latest possible date. If you had the choice of paying $100,000 to the federal government at the end of this year or at the end of next year, you would choose the end of next year. By doing so, you could invest the money for an extra year and earn a significant return on the investment.

Similarly, by maintaining two sets of books, corporations can defer (delay) paying millions and sometimes billions of dollars in taxes. The following companies reported significant gross deferred tax obligations in a recent year. Much of these deferrals were due to differences in asset cost allocation methods:

Company	Deferred Tax Liabilities	Percentage Due to Applying Different Cost Allocation Methods
Southwest Airlines	$2,769 million	87%
PepsiCo	2,304 million	34
Hertz	2,421 million	50
Marriott International	177 million	18

Most corporations use the IRS-approved Modified Accelerated Cost Recovery System (MACRS) to calculate depreciation expense for their tax returns. MACRS is similar to the declining-balance method and is applied over relatively short asset lives to yield high depreciation expense in the early years. The high depreciation expense reported under MACRS reduces a corporation's taxable income and therefore the amount it must pay in taxes. MACRS provides an incentive for corporations to invest in modern property, plant, and equipment in order to be competitive in world markets. **It is not acceptable for financial reporting purposes.**

A QUESTION OF ETHICS   **Two Sets of Books**

When they first learn that companies maintain two sets of books, some people question the ethics or legality of the practice. In reality, **it is both legal and ethical to maintain separate records for tax and financial reporting purposes. However, these records must reflect the same transactions.** Understating revenues or overstating expenses on a tax return can result in financial penalties and/or imprisonment. Accountants who aid tax evaders can also be fined or imprisoned, and lose their professional licenses.

Measuring Asset Impairment

Learning Objective 4
Explain the effect of asset impairment on the financial statements.

Corporations must review long-lived tangible and intangible assets for possible impairment. Two steps are necessary:

1. **Impairment** occurs when events or changed circumstances cause the estimated future cash flows (future benefits) of these assets to fall below their book value.

   If net book value > Estimated future cash flows, then the asset is impaired.

2. For any asset considered to be impaired, companies recognize a loss for the difference between the asset's book value and its fair value (a market concept).

   Impairment Loss = Net Book Value − Fair Value

That is, the asset is **written down** to fair value.

Although Southwest did not report asset impairment losses in its recent annual report, it did report in notes to the financial statements that it follows the practice of reviewing assets for impairment:

REAL WORLD EXCERPT

SOUTHWEST
ANNUAL REPORT

> When appropriate, the Company evaluates its long-lived assets used in operations for impairment. Impairment losses would be recorded when events and circumstances indicate that an asset might be impaired and the undiscounted cash flows to be generated by that asset are less than the carrying amounts of the asset. Factors that would indicate potential impairment include, but are not limited to, significant decreases in the market value of the long-lived asset(s), a significant change in the long-lived asset's physical condition, operating or cash flow losses associated with the use of the long-lived asset, etc. The Company continues to experience positive cash flow and operate all of its aircraft, and there have been no significant impairments of long-lived assets recorded during 2005, 2006, or 2007.

General Motors Corporation, another capital-intensive company, did report large impairment losses in a recent annual report:

REAL WORLD EXCERPT

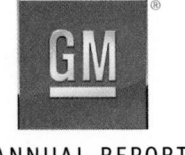

GM
ANNUAL REPORT

> **Note 5.**
>
> *Impairments*
>
> In 2006, GM recorded impairment charges totaling $424 million related to product specific assets based on GM's periodic review of its long-lived assets classified as held and used. . . . In addition, (*the Company*) recorded impairment charges totaling $172 million in 2006 which includes $102 million related to product specific assets and $70 million related to the write-down of various plant assets due to decreased profitability and production associated with the planned cessation of production at the Doraville, Georgia assembly plant in 2008. Additionally, (*the Company*) recorded an asset impairment charge in 2006 of $89 million in connection with the announced closure of GM's Portugal assembly plant, which closed in December 2006.

For illustrative purposes, let's assume that Southwest did a review for asset impairment and identified aircraft with a net book value of $10,000,000 as possibly impaired. If the future cash flows were estimated to be $8,000,000, then the asset was impaired because it was not expected to generate future benefits equal to its net book value. To compute the amount of the impairment loss, **fair value** is determined. For Southwest, that process includes using published sources and third-party bids to obtain the value of the asset. If the asset's fair value was $7,500,000, then the loss is calculated as $2,500,000 ($10,000,000 net book value less $7,500,000 fair value). The following journal entry would be recorded:

> **An asset is impaired if**
> Book value > Future cash flows
>
> **Then the impairment loss is**
> Book value − Fair value

Loss Due to Impairment of Assets (+Loss, −SE)	2,500,000	
Flight Equipment (−A)		2,500,000

Assets	=	Liabilities	+	Stockholders' Equity
Flight Equipment −2,500,000				Loss Due to Impairment −2,500,000

Disposal of Property, Plant, and Equipment

In some cases, a business may **voluntarily** decide not to hold a long-lived asset for its entire life. The company may drop a product from its line and no longer need the equipment that was used to produce its product, or managers may want to replace a machine with a more efficient one. These disposals include sales, trade-ins, or retirements. When Southwest disposes of an old aircraft, the company may sell it to a cargo airline or regional airline. A business may also dispose of an asset **involuntarily,** as the result of a casualty such as a storm, fire, or accident.

Disposals of long-lived assets seldom occur on the last day of the accounting period. Therefore, depreciation must be recorded to the date of disposal. The disposal of a depreciable asset usually requires two journal entries:

> **Learning Objective 5**
> Analyze the disposal of property, plant, and equipment.

1. An adjusting entry to update the depreciation expense and accumulated depreciation accounts.

2. An entry to record the disposal. The cost of the asset **and** any accumulated depreciation at the date of disposal must be removed from the accounts. The difference between any resources received on disposal of an asset and its book value at the date of disposal is treated as a gain or loss on the disposal of the asset. This gain (or loss) is reported on the income statement. It is not an operating revenue (or expense), however, because it arises from peripheral or incidental activities rather than from central operations. Gains and losses from disposals are usually shown as a separate item on the income statement.

Assume that at the end of year 17, Southwest sold an aircraft that was no longer needed because of the elimination of service to a small city. The aircraft was sold for $5 million cash. The original cost of the flight equipment of $20 million was depreciated using the straight-line method over 20 years with no residual value ($1 million depreciation expense per year). The last accounting for depreciation was at the end of year 16; thus, depreciation expense must be recorded for year 17. The computations are:

Cash received		$5,000,000
Original cost of flight equipment	$20,000,000	
Less: Accumulated depreciation ($1,000,000 × 17 years)	17,000,000	
Book value at date of sale		3,000,000
Gain on sale of flight equipment		$2,000,000

The entries and effects of the transaction on the date of the sale are as follows:

(1) Update depreciation expense for year 17:

Depreciation Expense (+E, −SE) 1,000,000

    Accumulated Depreciation (+XA, −A) 1,000,000

(2) Record the sale:

Cash (+A) 5,000,000

Accumulated Depreciation (−XA, +A) 17,000,000

    Flight Equipment (−A) 20,000,000

    Gain on Sale of Flight Equipment (+Gain, +SE) 2,000,000

Assets		=	Liabilities	+	Stockholders' Equity	
(1) Accumulated					Depreciation	
Depreciation	−1,000,000				Expense (+E)	−1,000,000
(2) Flight Equipment	−20,000,000				Gain on Sale	
Accumulated					of Asset	+2,000,000
Depreciation (−XA)	+17,000,000					
Cash	+5,000,000					

SELF-STUDY QUIZ

Now let's assume the same facts as above except that the asset was sold for $2,000,000 cash. Prepare the two entries on the date of the sale.

1. Update depreciation expense for year 17:

2. Record the sale:

Assets	=	Liabilities	+	Stockholders' Equity

After you have completed your answers, check them with the solutions at the bottom of the page.

Self-Study Quiz Solutions

(1) Depreciation Expense (+E, −SE) 1,000,000

    Accumulated Depreciation (+XA, −A) 1,000,000

(2) Cash (+A) 2,000,000

Accumulated Depreciation (−XA, +A) 17,000,000

Loss on Sale of Flight Equipment (+Loss, −SE) 1,000,000

    Flight Equipment (−A) 20,000,000

Assets		=	Liabilities	+	Stockholders' Equity	
(1) Accumulated					Depreciation	
Depreciation	−1,000,000				Expense	−1,000,000
(2) Flight Equipment	−20,000,000				Loss on Sale	
Accumulated					of Asset	−1,000,000
Depreciation	+17,000,000					
Cash	+2,000,000					

INTERNATIONAL
PERSPECTIVE

IFRS

Measurement Basis for Property, Plant, and Equipment

One of the most important differences between U.S. GAAP and International Financial Reporting Standards (IFRS) relates to the measurement basis for property, plant, and equipment. IFRS permit companies to value property, plant, and equipment at historical cost or to revalue them to their fair value as of the balance sheet date. The primary argument in favor of revaluation is that the historical cost of an asset purchased 15 or 20 years ago is not meaningful because of the impact of inflation. For example, most people would not compare the original purchase price of a house acquired in 1978 to the purchase price for the identical house next door acquired in 2008 because the price of houses has changed dramatically between those years. However, revaluation to fair value is prohibited in the United States (under GAAP). A primary argument against revaluation property, plant, and equipment is the lack of objectivity involved in estimating an asset's current cost.

NATURAL RESOURCES AND INTANGIBLE ASSETS

Acquisition and Depletion of Natural Resources

You are probably most familiar with large companies that are involved in manufacturing (Ford, Black & Decker), distribution (Sears, Home Depot), or services (Federal Express, Holiday Inn). A number of large companies, some of which are less well known, develop raw materials and products from **natural resources,** including mineral deposits such as gold or iron ore, oil wells, and timber tracts. These resources are often called **wasting assets** because they are depleted (i.e., physically used up). Companies that develop natural resources are critical to the economy because they produce essential items such as lumber for construction, fuel for heating and transportation, and food for consumption. Because of the significant effect they can have on the environment, these companies attract considerable public attention. Concerned citizens often read the financial statements of companies involved in exploration for oil, coal, and various ores to determine the amount of money they spend to protect the environment.

When natural resources are acquired or developed, they are recorded in conformity with the **cost principle.** As a natural resource is used up, its acquisition cost must be apportioned among the periods in which revenues are earned in conformity with the **matching principle.** The term depletion describes the process of allocating a natural resource's cost over the period of its exploitation.[1] The units-of-production method is often applied to compute depletion.

When a natural resource such as an oil well is depleted, the company obtains inventory (oil). Since depleting the natural resource is necessary to obtain the inventory, the depletion computed during a period is added to the cost of the inventory, not expensed in the period. Consider the following illustration:

A timber tract costing $530,000 is depleted over its estimated cutting period based on a "cutting" rate of approximately 20 percent per year:

> **Learning Objective 6**
> Apply measurement and reporting concepts for natural resources and intangible assets

> NATURAL RESOURCES are assets that occur in nature, such as mineral deposits, timber tracts, oil, and gas.

> DEPLETION is the systematic and rational allocation of the cost of a natural resource over the period of exploitation.

| Timber Inventory (+A) .... | 106,000 | |
| Timber Tract (−A) (or Accumulated Depletion +XA) .... | | 106,000 |

Assets		=	Liabilities	+	Stockholders' Equity
Timber Inventory	+106,000				
Timber Tract	−106,000				

> *Note that the amount of the natural resource that is depleted is capitalized as inventory, not expensed. When the inventory is sold, the cost of goods sold will be included as an expense on the income statement.*

[1]Consistent with the procedure for recording depreciation, an accumulated depletion account may be used. In practice, however, most companies credit the asset account directly for periodic depletion. This procedure is also typically used for intangible assets, which are discussed in the next section.

Audio lecture–AP8-2
www.mhhe.com/libby6e

REAL WORLD EXCERPT

International Paper
2006 ANNUAL REPORT

Following is an excerpt from the asset section of International Paper's 2006 balance sheet along with the related footnote describing the accounting policies for the company's natural resource, forestland:

CONSOLIDATED BALANCE SHEET (DOLLARS IN MILLIONS)

	2006
Assets	
Cash	$1,624
. . .	
Forestlands	259

Note:

Forestlands

At December 31, 2006, International Paper and its subsidiaries owned or managed about 500,000 acres of forestlands in the United States, approximately 370,000 acres in Brazil, and through licenses and forest management agreements, had harvesting rights on approximately 500,000 acres of government-owned forestlands in Russia. Costs attributable to timber are charged against income as trees are cut. The rate charged is determined annually based on the relationship of incurred costs to estimated current merchantable volume.

Acquisition and Amortization of Intangible Assets

Intangible assets are increasingly important resources for organizations. An intangible asset, like any other asset, has value because of certain rights and privileges often conferred by law on its owner. Unlike tangible assets such as land and buildings, however, an intangible asset has no material or physical substance. Examples of intangible assets include patents, trademarks, and licenses. Most intangible assets usually are evidenced by a legal document. Yet the growth in the importance of intangible assets has been the tremendous expansion in computer information systems and Web technologies and the frenzy in companies purchasing other companies at high prices, with the expectation that these intangible resources will provide significant future benefits to the company.

Intangible assets are recorded **at historical cost only if they have been purchased.** If these assets are developed internally by the company, they are expensed when incurred. Upon acquisition of intangible assets, managers determine whether the separate intangibles have definite or indefinite lives:

■ **Definite Life** The cost of an intangible with a definite life is allocated on a straight-line basis each period over its useful life in a process called *amortization* that is similar to depreciation and depletion. Most companies do not estimate a residual value for their intangible assets. Amortization expense is included on the income statement each period and the intangible assets are reported at cost less accumulated amortization on the balance sheet.

AMORTIZATION is the systematic and rational allocation of the acquisition cost of an intangible asset over its useful life.

Let's assume a company purchases a patent for $800,000 and intends to use it for 20 years. The adjusting entry to record $40,000 in patent amortization expense ($800,000 ÷ 20 years) is as follows:

Patent Amortization Expense (+E, −SE)	40,000	
Patents (−A) (or Accumulated Amortization +XA)		40,000

Assets		=	**Liabilities**	+	**Stockholders' Equity**	
Patents	−40,000				Patent Amortization Expense (+E)	−40,000

■ **Indefinite Life** Intangible assets with indefinite lives are **not amortized.** Instead, these assets are to be tested at least annually for possible impairment, and the asset's book value is written down (decreased) to its fair value if impaired. The two-step process is similar to that used for assets discussed previously and summarized in the margin.

The AICPA's 2006 **Accounting Trends & Techniques** summarizes intangible assets most frequently disclosed by the 600 companies surveyed:

	Number of Companies	Percentage of 600
Goodwill recognized in a business combination	542	90%
Trademarks, brand names, copyrights	296	49
Customer lists/relationships	290	48
Patents, patent rights	153	26
Technology	142	24
Licenses, franchises, memberships	111	19
Noncompete covenants	103	17
Contracts, agreements	89	15
Other—described in the annual report	77	13

Goodwill

By far the most frequently reported intangible asset is goodwill (cost in excess of net assets acquired). The term **goodwill,** as used by most businesspeople, means the favorable reputation that a company has with its customers. Goodwill arises from factors such as customer confidence, reputation for good service or quality goods, location, outstanding management team, and financial standing. From its first day of operations, a successful business continually builds goodwill. In this context, the goodwill is said to be **internally generated** and is not reported as an asset (i.e., it was not purchased).

The only way to report goodwill as an asset is to purchase another business. Often the purchase price of the business exceeds the fair market value of all of its net assets (assets minus liabilities). Why would a company pay more for a business as a whole than it would pay if it bought the assets individually? The answer is to obtain its goodwill. You could easily buy modern bottling equipment to produce and sell a new cola drink, but you would not make as much money as you would if you acquired the goodwill associated with Coke or Pepsi brand names.

For accounting purposes, goodwill is defined as the difference between the purchase price of a company as a whole and the fair market value of its net assets:

Purchase price
− Fair market value of identifiable assets and liabilities
Goodwill to be reported

In many acquisitions, the amount recorded as Goodwill can be very large. For example, when Google purchased YouTube in 2006, $1.1 billion of the purchase price was allocated to goodwill. Goodwill is considered to have an indefinite life and must be reviewed at least annually for possible impairment of value. Google reported the following:

In accordance with *SFAS No. 142,* "Goodwill and Other Intangible Assets," we test our goodwill for impairment at least annually or more frequently if events or changes in circumstances indicate that this asset may be impaired. The tests were based on our single operating segment and reporting unit structure. We found no impairment in any of the years presented.

For accounting purposes, GOODWILL (COST IN EXCESS OF NET ASSETS ACQUIRED) is the excess of the purchase price of a business over the fair market value of the business's assets and liabilities.

REAL WORLD EXCERPT
Google Inc.
2006 ANNUAL REPORT

Trademarks

A TRADEMARK is an exclusive legal right to use a special name, image, or slogan.

A **trademark** is a special name, image, or slogan identified with a product or a company; it is protected by law. Trademarks are among the most valuable assets a company can own. For example, most of us cannot imagine the Walt Disney Company without Mickey Mouse. Similarly, you probably enjoy your favorite soft drink more because of the image that has been built up around its name than because of its taste. Many people can identify the shape of a corporate logo as quickly as they can recognize the shape of a stop sign. Although trademarks are valuable assets, they are rarely seen on balance sheets. The reason is simple; intangible assets are not recorded unless they are purchased. Companies often spend millions of dollars developing trademarks, but most of those expenditures are recorded as expenses rather than being capitalized as an intangible asset.

Copyrights

A COPYRIGHT is the exclusive right to publish, use, and sell a literary, musical, or artistic work.

A **copyright** gives the owner the exclusive right to publish, use, and sell a literary, musical, or artistic piece for a period not exceeding 70 years after the author's death.[2] The book you are reading has a copyright to protect the publisher and authors. It is against the law, for example, for an instructor to copy several chapters from this book and hand them out in class. A copyright that is purchased is recorded at cost.

Patents

A PATENT is granted by the federal government for an invention; it is an exclusive right given to the owner to use, manufacture, and sell the subject of the patent.

A **patent** is an exclusive right granted by the federal government for a period of 20 years, typically granted to a person who invents a new product or discovers a new process.[3] The patent enables the owner to use, manufacture, and sell both the subject of the patent and the patent itself. It prevents a competitor from simply copying a new invention or discovery until the inventor has had time to earn an economic return on the new product. Without the protection of a patent, inventors likely would be unwilling to search for new products. Patents are recorded at their purchase price or, if **developed internally,** at only their registration and legal costs because GAAP require the immediate expensing of research and development costs.

Technology

TECHNOLOGY includes costs for computer software and Web development.

The number of companies reporting a **technology** intangible asset continues to rise. Computer software and Web development costs are becoming increasingly significant. In 2006, IBM Corporation reported $1,034 million in software on its balance sheet and disclosed the following in the notes to the financial statements:

REAL WORLD EXCERPT

2006 ANNUAL REPORT

> The company capitalizes certain costs that are incurred to purchase or to create and implement internal use computer software, which includes software coding, installation, testing and certain data conversion. These capitalized costs are amortized on a straight-line basis over two years.

Franchises

A FRANCHISE is a contractual right to sell certain products or services, use certain trademarks, or perform activities in a geographical region.

Franchises may be granted by the government or a business for a specified period and purpose. A city may grant one company a franchise to distribute gas to homes for heating purposes, or a company may sell franchises, such as the right to operate a KFC

---

[2]In general, the limit is 70 years beyond the death of an author. For anonymous authors, the limit is 95 years from the first publication date. For more detail, go to lcweb.loc.gov/copyright.

[3]For more details, go to http://www.uspto.gov/web/offices/pac/doc/general/index.html#patent.

restaurant (owned by Yum Brands!). Franchise agreements are contracts that can have a variety of provisions. They usually require an investment by the franchisee; therefore, they should be accounted for as intangible assets. The life of the franchise agreement depends on the contract. It may be a single year or an indefinite period. Blockbuster, Inc.'s franchise agreement covers a period of 20 years. Blockbuster has more than 1,800 stores in the United States and Internationally under franchise agreements.

Licenses and Operating Rights

Southwest Airline's intangible assets are included on the balance sheet presented in Exhibit 8.1 as other assets. They primarily represent leasehold rights to airport-owned gates. Others include operating rights that are authorized landing slots regulated by the government and are in limited supply at many airports. They are intangible assets that can be bought and sold by the airlines. Other types of **licenses and operating rights** that grant permission to companies include using airwaves for radio and television broadcasts and land for cable and telephone lines.

Research and Development Expense—Not an Intangible Asset under U.S. GAAP

If an intangible asset is developed internally, the cost of development normally is recorded as **research and development expense.** For example, Abbott Laboratories (a manufacturer of pharmaceutical and nutritional products) recently spent more than $2,255 million on research to discover new products. This amount was reported as an expense, not an asset, because research and development expenditures typically do not possess sufficient probability of resulting in measurable future cash flows. If Abbott Labs had spent an equivalent amount to purchase patents for new products from other drug companies, it would have recorded the expenditure as an asset.

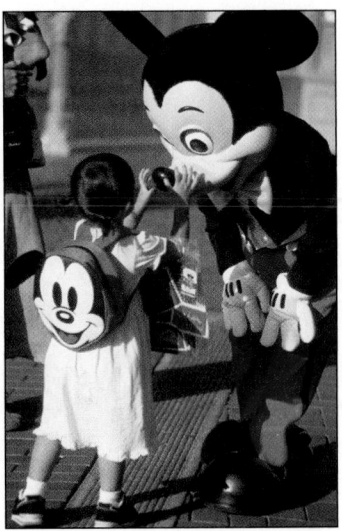

LICENSES AND OPERATING RIGHTS, obtained through agreements with governmental units or agencies, permit owners to use public property in performing their services.

Standards in Process

INTERNATIONAL
PERSPECTIVE

IFRS

While all research and development costs must be reported as an expense under U.S. GAAP, International Financial Reporting Standards (IFRS) require that research expenditures be reported as an expense, but development costs be capitalized as an asset after technical and commercial feasibility of the resulting product or service have been established. The FASB is currently working on a new accounting standard aimed at eliminating this difference.

Productive Assets and Depreciation

FOCUS ON
CASH FLOWS

Effect on Statement of Cash Flows
The indirect method for preparing the operating activities section of the statement of cash flows involves reconciling net income on the accrual basis (reported on the income statement) to cash flows from operations. This means that, among other adjustments, (1) revenues and expenses that do not involve cash and (2) gains and losses that relate to investing or financing activities (not operations) should be eliminated.

When depreciation is recorded, no cash payment is made (i.e., there is no credit to Cash). Since depreciation expense (a noncash expense) is subtracted in calculating net income on the income statement, it must be added back to net income to eliminate its effect. Likewise, since any gain (or loss) on sale of long-lived assets (an investing activity) is added (or subtracted) to determine net income, it must be subtracted (or added) from net income to eliminate its effect.

Learning Objective 7
Explain the impact on cash flows of acquiring, using, and disposing of long-lived assets.

In General   Acquiring, selling, and depreciating long-term assets are reflected on a company's cash flow statement as indicated in the following table:

	Effect on Cash Flows
Operating activities (indirect method)	
Net income	$xxx
Adjusted for: Depreciation and amortization expense	+
Gains on sale of long-lived assets	−
Losses on sale of long-lived assets	+
Losses due to asset impairment write-downs	+
Investing activities	
Purchase of long-lived assets	−
Sale of long-lived assets	+

Focus Company Analysis   The following is a condensed version of Southwest's statement of cash flows for 2007. Buying and selling long-lived assets are investing activities. In 2007, Southwest used $1,331 million in cash to purchase flight equipment and ground property and equipment. Southwest did not sell any flight or ground equipment during the year. Since selling long-lived assets is not an operating activity, any gains (losses) on sales of long-lived assets that were included in net income must be deducted from (added to) net income in the operating activities section to eliminate the effect of the sale. Unless they are large, these gain and loss adjustments normally are not specifically highlighted on the statement of cash flows. Southwest did not list any gains or losses in 2007.

Finally, in capital-intensive industries such as airlines, depreciation is a significant noncash expense. In Southwest's case, depreciation and amortization expense is usually the single largest adjustment to net income in determining cash flows from operations. For example, in 2006, the adjustment for depreciation and amortization expense was nearly 37 percent of operating cash flows. In 2007, the adjustment for depreciation and amortization came in second at $555 million (20 percent of operating cash flows), with increases in Accounts Payable and Accrued Liabilities at $1,609 million of the $1,645 million summarized in Other.

SOUTHWEST AIRLINES CO.
Consolidated Statements of Cash Flows (partial)
For the Years Ended December 31, 2007, 2006, and 2005

(in millions)	2007	2006	2005
Cash Flows from Operating Activities			
Net Income	645	499	484
Adjustment to reconcile net income to cash provided by operating activities:			
Depreciation and amortization	555	515	469
Other (**summarized**)	1,645	392	1,165
Net cash provided by operating activities	2,845	1,406	2,118
Cash Flows from Investing Activities			
Property, flight, and ground equipment additions:			
Purchases of property and equipment, net	(1,331)	(1,399)	(1,146)
Other (**summarized**)	(198)	(96)	0
Net cash used in investing activities	(1,529)	(1,495)	(1,146)

A Misinterpretation

Some analysts misinterpret the meaning of a noncash expense, saying that "cash is provided by depreciation." Although depreciation is added in the operating section of the statement of cash flows, **depreciation is not a source of cash.** Cash from operations can be provided only by selling goods and services. A company with a large amount of depreciation expense does not generate more cash compared with a company that reports a small amount of depreciation expense, assuming that they are exactly the same in every other respect. While depreciation expense reduces the amount of reported net income for a company, it does not reduce the amount of cash generated by the company because it is a noncash expense. Remember that the effects of recording depreciation are a reduction in stockholders' equity and in fixed assets, not in cash. That is why, on the statement of cash flows, depreciation expense is added back to net income on an accrual basis to compute cash flows from operations (on a cash basis).

Although depreciation is a noncash expense, the **depreciation for tax purposes can affect a company's cash flows.** Depreciation is a deductible expense for income tax purposes. The higher the amount of depreciation recorded by a company for tax purposes, the lower the company's taxable income and the taxes it must pay. Because taxes must be paid in cash, a reduction in a company's results reduces the company's cash outflows (that is, lower net income leads to lower tax payments).

DEMONSTRATION **CASE**

(Resolve the requirements before proceeding to the suggested solution that follows.) Diversified Industries started as a residential construction company. In recent years, it has expanded into heavy construction, ready-mix concrete, sand and gravel, construction supplies, and earth-moving services. The company completed the following transactions during 2009. Amounts have been simplified.

2009

Jan. 1   The management decided to buy a 10-year-old building for $175,000 and the land on which it was situated for $130,000. It paid $100,000 in cash and signed a mortgage note payable for the rest.

Jan. 12   Paid $38,000 in renovation costs on the building prior to use.

June 19   Bought a third location for a gravel pit (designated Gravel Pit No. 3) for $50,000 cash. It was estimated that 100,000 cubic yards of gravel could be removed.

July 10   Paid $1,200 for ordinary repairs on the building.

Aug. 1   Paid $10,000 for costs of preparing the new gravel pit for exploitation.

Dec. 31   Year-end adjustments:

a. The building will be depreciated on a straight-line basis over an estimated useful life of 30 years. The estimated residual value is $33,000.

b. During 2009, 12,000 cubic yards of gravel were removed from Gravel Pit No. 3.

c. Diversified purchased another company several years ago at $100,000 over the fair value of the net assets acquired. The goodwill has an indefinite life.

d. At the beginning of the year, the company owned equipment with a cost of $650,000 and accumulated depreciation of $150,000. The equipment is being depreciated using the double-declining-balance method, with a useful life of 20 years and no residual value.

e. At year-end, the company tested its long-lived assets for possible impairment of their value. It identified a piece of old excavation equipment with a cost of $156,000 and remaining book value of $120,000. Due to its smaller size and lack of safety features, the old equipment has limited use. The future cash flows are expected to be $40,000 and the fair value is determined to be $35,000. Goodwill was found not to be impaired.

December 31, 2009, is the end of the annual accounting period.

Required:

1. Indicate the accounts affected and the amount and direction (+ for increase and − for decrease) of the effect of each of the preceding events on the financial statement categories at the end of the year. Use the following headings:

Date	Assets	=	Liabilities	+	Stockholders' Equity

2. Record the adjusting journal entries for December 31(*a*) and (*b*) only.

3. Show the December 31, 2009, balance sheet classification and amount for each of the following items:

   Fixed assets—land, building, equipment, and gravel pit

   Intangible asset—goodwill

4. Assuming that the company had sales of $1,000,000 for the year and a net book value of $500,000 for fixed assets at the beginning of the year, compute the fixed asset turnover ratio. Explain its meaning.

SUGGESTED SOLUTION

1. Effects of events (with computations):

Date	Assets		=	Liabilities		+	Stockholders' Equity	
Jan. 1	Cash	−100,000		Note Payable	+205,000			
	Land	+130,000						
	Building	+175,000						
Jan. 12 (1)	Cash	−38,000						
	Building	+38,000						
June 19 (2)	Cash	−50,000						
	Gravel Pit No. 3	+50,000						
July 10 (3)	Cash	−1,200					Repairs Expense	−1,200
Aug. 1 (4)	Cash	−10,000						
	Gravel Pit No. 3	+10,000						
Dec. 31 *a* (5)	Accumulated Depreciation (+XA)	−6,000					Depreciation Expense	−6,000
Dec. 31 *b* (6)	Gravel Pit No. 3	−7,200						
	Gravel Inventory	+7,200						
Dec. 31 *c* (7)	No entry							
Dec. 31 *d* (8)	Accumulated Depreciation	−50,000					Depreciation Expense	−50,000
Dec. 31 *e* (9)	Equipment	−85,000					Loss Due to Asset Impairment	−85,000

(1) Capitalize the $38,000 expenditure because it is necessary to prepare the asset for use.

(2) This is a natural resource.

(3) This is an ordinary repair (revenue expenditure) and should be expensed.

(4) Capitalize the $10,000 expenditure because it is necessary to prepare the asset for use.

(5)

Cost of Building		Straight-Line Depreciation
Initial purchase price	$175,000	($213,000 cost − $33,000 residual value) ×
Repairs prior to use	38,000	1/30 years = **$6,000** annual depreciation
Acquisition cost	$213,000	

(6)

Cost of Gravel Pit		Units-of-Production Depletion
Initial payment	$50,000	($60,000 cost ÷ 100,000 estimated production) ×
Preparation costs	10,000	12,000 actual cubic yards = **$7,200** annual depletion
Acquisition cost	$60,000	Capitalize the depletion to gravel inventory.

(7) Goodwill has indefinite life and is therefore not amortized. We will test for impairment later.

(8) **Double-declining-balance depreciation**

($650,000 cost − $150,000 accumulated depreciation) × 2/20 years = **$50,000** depreciation for 2009

(9) **Asset impairment**

Impairment Test: The book value of old equipment, $120,000, exceeds expected future cash flows, $40,000. The asset is impaired.

Impairment Loss	
Book value	$120,000
Less: Fair value	− 35,000
Loss due to impairment	$ 85,000

2. Adjusting entries at December 31, 2009:

a. Depreciation Expense (+E, −SE)	6,000	
Accumulated Depreciation (+XA, −A)		6,000
b. Gravel Inventory (+A)	7,200	
Gravel Pit No. 3 (−A)		7,200

3. Partial balance sheet, December 31, 2009:

Assets		
Fixed assets		
Land		$130,000
Building	$213,000	
Less: Accumulated depreciation	6,000	207,000
Equipment ($650,000 − $85,000)	565,000	
Less: Accumulated depreciation		
($150,000 + $50,000)	200,000	365,000
Gravel pit		52,800
Total fixed assets		$754,800
Intangible asset		
Goodwill		$100,000

4. Fixed asset turnover ratio:

$$\frac{\text{Sales}}{(\text{Beginning Net Fixed Asset Balance} + \text{Ending Net Fixed Asset Balance}) \div 2} = \frac{\$1,000,000}{(\$500,000 + \$754,800) \div 2} = 1.59$$

This construction company is capital intensive. The fixed asset turnover ratio measures the company's efficiency at using its investment in property, plant, and equipment to generate sales.

Chapter Supplement A

Changes in Depreciation Estimates

Depreciation is based on two estimates, useful life and residual value. These estimates are made at the time a depreciable asset is acquired. As experience with the asset accumulates, one or both of these initial estimates may need to be revised. In addition, extraordinary repairs and additions may be added to the original acquisition cost at some time during the asset's use. When it is clear that either estimate should be revised to a material degree or that the asset's cost has changed, the undepreciated asset balance (less any residual value at that date) should be apportioned over the remaining estimated life from the current year into the future. This is called a prospective **change in estimate.**

To compute the new depreciation expense due to a change in estimate for any of the depreciation methods described here, substitute the net book value for the original acquisition cost, the new residual value for the original amount, and the estimated remaining life in place of the original estimated life. As an illustration, the formula using the straight-line method follows.

Original Straight-Line Formula Modified for a Change in Estimate:

$$(\text{Cost} - \text{Residual Value}) \times \frac{1}{\text{Useful Life}} = \text{Original Depreciation Expense}$$

$$(\text{Net Book Value} - \text{New Residual Value}) \times \frac{1}{\text{Remaining Life}} = \text{Revised Depreciation Expense}$$

Assume Southwest purchased an aircraft for $60,000,000 with an estimated useful life of 20 years and estimated residual value of $3,000,000. Shortly after the start of year 5, Southwest changed the initial estimated life to 25 years and lowered the estimated residual value to $2,400,000. At the end of year 5, the computation of the new amount for depreciation expense is as follows:

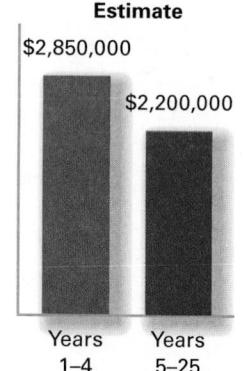

Straight-Line Depreciation Expense with a Change in Estimate

$2,850,000

$2,200,000

Years 1–4   Years 5–25

Original depreciation expense

($60,000,000 − $3,000,000) × 1/20 = $ 2,850,000 per year
                                              × 4 years

Accumulated depreciation at the end of year 4 $11,400,000

Net book value at the end of year 4

Acquisition cost	$60,000,000
Less: Accumulated depreciation	11,400,000
Net book value	$48,600,000

Depreciation in years 5 through 25 based on changes in estimates

(Net book value − New residual value) × 1/remaining years = New depreciation expense

($48,600,000 − $2,400,000) × 1/21 (25 − 4 years) = $2,200,000 per year

Companies may also change depreciation methods (for example, from declining-balance to straight-line). Such a change requires significantly more disclosure since it violates the consistency principle that requires that accounting information reported in the financial statements be comparable across accounting periods. Under GAAP, changes in accounting estimates and depreciation methods should be made only when a new estimate or accounting method "better measures" the periodic income of the business.

SELF-STUDY QUIZ

Assume that Southwest Airlines owned a service truck that originally cost $100,000. When purchased, the truck had an estimated useful life of 10 years with no residual value. After operating the truck for five years, Southwest determined that the remaining life was only two more years. Based on this change in estimate, what amount of depreciation should be recorded over the remaining life of the asset? Southwest uses the straight-line method.

After you have completed your answer, compare it with the solution at the bottom of the page.

CHAPTER TAKE-AWAYS

1. **Define, classify, and explain the nature of long-lived productive assets and interpret the fixed asset turnover ratio.   p. 399**

   a. Noncurrent assets are those that a business retains for long periods of time for use in the course of normal operations rather than for sale. They may be divided into tangible assets (land, buildings, equipment, natural resources) and intangible assets (including goodwill, patents, and franchises).

   b. The cost allocation method utilized affects the amount of net property, plant, and equipment that is used in the computation of the fixed asset turnover ratio. Accelerated methods reduce book value and increase the turnover ratio.

2. **Apply the cost principle to measure the acquisition and maintenance of property, plant, and equipment.   p. 401**

   Acquisition cost of property, plant, and equipment is the cash-equivalent purchase price plus all reasonable and necessary expenditures made to acquire and prepare the asset for its intended use. These assets may be acquired using cash, debt, stock, or through self-construction. Expenditures made after the asset is in use are either additions and improvements (capital expenditures) or ordinary repairs (revenue expenditures):

   a. **Revenue expenditures (ordinary repairs and maintenance)** provide benefits during the current accounting period only. Amounts are debited to appropriate current expense accounts when the expenses are incurred.

   b. **Capital expenditures (additions and improvements)** provide benefits for one or more accounting periods beyond the current period. Amounts are debited to the appropriate asset accounts and depreciated, depleted, or amortized over their useful lives.

3. **Apply various cost allocation methods as assets are held and used over time.   p. 406**

   Cost allocation methods: In conformity with the matching principle, cost (less any estimated residual value) is allocated to periodic expense over the periods benefited. Because of depreciation, the net book value of an asset declines over time and net income is reduced by the amount of

---

($100,000−$0) × 1/10 years = $10,000 original annual depreciation × 5 years = $50,000 accumulated depreciation

$50,000 (book value after 5 years) × 1/2 years (remaining life) = $25,000 depreciation expense per year.

Self-Study Quiz
Solutions

the expense. Common depreciation methods include straight-line (a constant amount over time), units-of-production (a variable amount over time), and double-declining-balance (a decreasing amount over time).

  a. Depreciation—buildings and equipment.

  b. Depletion—natural resources.

  c. Amortization— intangibles.

4. **Explain the effect of asset impairment on the financial statements.** p. 416

When events or changes in circumstances reduce the estimated future cash flows of long-lived assets below their book value, the book values should be written down (by recording a loss) to the fair value of the assets.

5. **Analyze the disposal of property, plant, and equipment.** p. 417

When assets are disposed of through sale or abandonment:

  a. Record additional depreciation since the last adjustment was made.

  b. Remove the cost of the old asset and its related accumulated depreciation, depletion, or amortization.

  c. Recognize the cash proceeds.

  d. Recognize any gain or loss when the asset's net book value is not equal to the cash received.

6. **Apply measurement and reporting concepts for natural resources and intangible assets.** p. 419

The cost principle should be applied in recording the acquisition of natural resources and intangible assets. Natural resources should be depleted (usually by the units-of-production method) usually with the amount of the depletion expense capitalized to an inventory account. Intangibles with definite useful lives are amortized using the straight-line method. Intangibles with indefinite useful lives, including goodwill, are not amortized, but are reviewed at least annually for impairment. Report intangibles at net book value on the balance sheet.

7. **Explain the impact on cash flows of acquiring, using, and disposing of long-lived assets.** p. 423

Depreciation expense is a noncash expense that has no effect on cash. It is added back to net income on the statement of cash flows to determine cash from operations. Acquiring and disposing of long-lived assets are investing activities.

In previous chapters, we discussed business and accounting issues related to the assets a company holds. In Chapters 9, 10, and 11, we shift our focus to the other side of the balance sheet to see how managers finance business operations and the acquisition of productive assets. We discuss various types of liabilities in Chapters 9 and 10 and examine stockholders' equity in Chapter 11.

KEY **RATIO**

The **fixed asset turnover ratio** measures how efficiently a company utilizes its investment in property, plant, and equipment over time. Its ratio can then be compared to competitors' ratios. The fixed asset turnover ratio is computed as follows (p. 400):

$$\text{Fixed Asset Turnover} = \frac{\text{Net Sales (or Operating Revenues)}}{\text{Average Net Fixed Assets}}$$

Balance Sheet

Under Noncurrent Assets

Property, plant, and equipment (net of accumulated depreciation)

Natural resources (net of accumulated depletion)

Intangibles (net of accumulated amortization, if any)

Income Statement

Under Operating Expenses

Depreciation, depletion, and amortization expense **or** included in

Selling, general, and administrative expenses and

Cost of goods sold (with the amount for depreciation expense disclosed in a note)

Statement of Cash Flows

Under Operating Activities (indirect method)

Net income

+ Depreciation and amortization expense

− Gains on sales of assets

+ Losses on sales of assets

Under Investing Activities

+ Sales of assets for cash

− Purchases of assets for cash

Notes

Under Summary of Significant Accounting Policies

Description of management's choice for depreciation and amortization methods, including useful lives, and the amount of annual depreciation expense, if not listed on the income statement.

Under a Separate Footnote

If not specified on the balance sheet, a listing of the major classifications of long-lived assets at cost and the balance in accumulated depreciation, depletion, and amortization.

KEY **TERMS**

Acquisition Cost   p. 401
Additions and Improvements   p. 405
Amortization   p. 420
Capital Expenditures   p. 405
Capitalized Interest   p. 403
Copyright   p. 422
Declining-Balance Depreciation   p. 412
Depletion   p. 419
Depreciation   p. 407

Estimated Useful Life   p. 408
Franchise   p. 422
Goodwill (Cost in Excess of Net Assets Acquired)   p. 421
Intangible Assets   p. 399
Licenses and Operating Rights   p. 423
Long-Lived Assets   p. 399
Natural Resources   p. 419
Net Book (or Carrying) Value   p. 407

Ordinary Repairs and Maintenance   p. 405
Patent   p. 422
Residual (or Salvage) Value   p. 408
Revenue Expenditures   p. 405
Straight-Line Depreciation   p. 409
Tangible Assets   p. 399
Technology   p. 422
Trademark   p. 422
Units-of-Production Depreciation   p. 410

QUESTIONS

1. Define **long-lived assets.** Why are they considered to be a "bundle of future services"?
2. How is the fixed asset turnover ratio computed? Explain its meaning.
3. What are the classifications of long-lived assets? Explain each.
4. Under the cost principle, what amounts should be included in the acquisition cost of a long-lived asset?
5. Describe the relationship between the matching principle and accounting for long-lived assets.
6. Distinguish between
   a. Capital expenditures and revenue expenditures. How is each accounted for?
   b. Ordinary repairs and improvements. How is each accounted for?

7. Distinguish among depreciation, depletion, and amortization.

8. In computing depreciation, three values must be known or estimated; identify and explain the nature of each.

9. The estimated useful life and residual value of a long-lived asset relate to the current owner or user rather than all potential users. Explain this statement.

10. What type of depreciation expense pattern is used under each of the following methods and when is its use appropriate?
   a. The straight-line method.
   b. The units-of-production method.
   c. The double-declining-balance method.

11. Over what period should an addition to an existing long-lived asset be depreciated? Explain.

12. What is **asset impairment?** How is it accounted for?

13. When equipment is sold for more than net book value, how is the transaction recorded? For less than net book value? What is net book value?

14. Define **intangible asset.** What period should be used to amortize an intangible asset with a definite life?

15. Define **goodwill.** When is it appropriate to record goodwill as an intangible asset?

16. Why is depreciation expense added to net income on the statement of cash flows?

MULTIPLE-CHOICE QUESTIONS

1. Simon Company and Allen Company both bought a new delivery truck on January 1, 2008. Both companies paid exactly the same cost, $30,000, for their respective vehicles. As of December 31, 2011, the net book value of Simon's truck was less than Allen Company's net book value for the same vehicle. Which of the following is an acceptable explanation for the difference in net book value?
   a. Both companies elected straight-line depreciation, but Simon Company used a longer estimated life.
   b. Simon Company estimated a lower residual value, but both estimated the same useful life and both elected straight-line depreciation.
   c. Because GAAP specifies rigid guidelines regarding the calculation of depreciation, this situation is not possible.
   d. Simon Company is using the straight-line method of depreciation, and Allen Company is using the double-declining-balance method of depreciation.

2. Barber, Inc., followed the practice of depreciating its building on a straight-line basis. A building was purchased in 2010 and had an estimated useful life of 20 years and a residual value of $20,000. The company's depreciation expense for 2010 was $20,000 on the building. What was the original cost of the building?
   a. $360,000   c. $400,000
   b. $380,000   d. $420,000

3. ACME, Inc., uses straight-line depreciation for all of its depreciable assets. ACME sold a used piece of machinery on December 31, 2011, that it purchased on January 1, 2010, for $10,000. The asset had a five-year life, zero residual value, and $2,000 accumulated depreciation as of December 31, 2010. If the sales price of the used machine was $7,500, the resulting gain or loss upon the sale was which of the following amounts?
   a. Loss of $500   d. Gain of $1,500
   b. Gain of $500   e. No gain or loss upon the sale.
   c. Loss of $1,500

4. Under what method(s) of depreciation is an asset's **net book value** the depreciable base (the amount to be depreciated)?
   a. Straight-line method   c. Declining-balance method
   b. Units-of-production method   d. All of the above

5. What assets should be amortized using the straight-line method?
   a. Natural resources   c. Intangible assets with indefinite lives
   b. Intangible assets with definite lives   d. All of the above

6. A company wishes to report the highest earnings possible for financial reporting purposes. Therefore, when calculating depreciation,
   a. It will follow the MACRS depreciation tables prescribed by the IRS.
   b. It will select the shortest lives possible for its assets.
   c. It will estimate higher residual values for its assets.
   d. It will select the lowest residual values for its assets.

7. How many of the following statements regarding goodwill are true?
   ▦ Goodwill is not reported unless purchased in an exchange.

   ▦ Goodwill must be reviewed annually for possible impairment.

   ▦ Impairment of goodwill results in a decrease in net income.
   a. None   c. Two
   b. One   d. Three

8. Company X is going to retire equipment that is fully depreciated with no residual value. The
   equipment will simply be disposed of, not sold. Which of the following statements is false?
   a. Total assets will not change as a result of this transaction.
   b. Net income will not be impacted as a result of this transaction.
   c. This transaction will not impact cash flow.
   d. All of the above statements are true.

9. When recording depreciation, which of the following statements is true?
   a. Total assets increase and stockholders' equity increases.
   b. Total assets decrease and total liabilities increase.
   c. Total assets decrease and stockholders' equity increases.
   d. None of the above are true.

10. (Supplement) Thornton Industries purchased a machine for $45,000 and is depreciating it with the
    straight-line method over a life of 10 years, using a residual value of $3,000. At the beginning of
    the sixth year, a major overhaul was made costing $5,000, and the total estimated useful life was
    extended to 13 years. Depreciation expense for year 6 is:
    a. $1,885   d. $3,625
    b. $2,000   e. $4,200
    c. $3,250

For more practice on more multiple-choice questions, go to the text website www.mhhe.com/
libby6e.

Available with McGraw-Hill's Homework Manager ▪▾ ™
▪ ▾

MINI-**EXERCISES**

Classifying Long-Lived Assets and Related Cost Allocation Concepts

M8-1
LO1, 3, 6

For each of the following long-lived assets, indicate its nature and related cost allocation concept. Use
the following symbols:

Nature		Cost Allocation Concept	
L	Land	DR	Depreciation
B	Building	DP	Depletion
E	Equipment	A	Amortization
NR	Natural resource	NO	No cost allocation
I	Intangible	O	Other
O	Other		

Asset	Nature	Cost Allocation	Asset	Nature	Cost Allocation
(1) Copyright	___	___	(6) Operating license	___	___
(2) Land held for use	___	___	(7) Land held for sale	___	___
(3) Warehouse	___	___	(8) Delivery vans	___	___
(4) Oil well	___	___	(9) Timber tract	___	___
(5) New engine for old machine	___	___	(10) Production plant	___	___

M8-2
LO1

Computing and Evaluating the Fixed Asset Turnover Ratio

The following information was reported by Cutter's Air Cargo Service for 2007:

Net fixed assets (beginning of year)	$1,500,000
Net fixed assets (end of year)	2,300,000
Net sales for the year	3,300,000
Net income for the year	1,600,000

Compute the company's fixed asset turnover ratio for the year. What can you say about Cutter's ratio when compared to Southwest's 2007 ratio?

M8-3
LO2

Identifying Capital and Revenue Expenditures

For each of the following items, enter the correct letter to the left to show the type of expenditure. Use the following:

Type of Expenditure	Transactions
C Capital expenditure	_____ (1) Paid $400 for ordinary repairs.
R Revenue expenditure	_____ (2) Paid $6,000 for extraordinary repairs.
N Neither	_____ (3) Paid cash, $20,000, for addition to old building.
	_____ (4) Paid for routine maintenance, $200, on credit.
	_____ (5) Purchased a machine, $7,000; gave long-term note.
	_____ (6) Paid three-year insurance premium, $900.
	_____ (7) Purchased a patent, $4,300 cash.
	_____ (8) Paid $10,000 for monthly salaries.
	_____ (9) Paid cash dividends, $20,000.

M8-4
LO3

Computing Book Value (Straight-Line Depreciation)

Calculate the book value of a three-year-old machine that cost $21,000, has an estimated residual value of $1,000, and has an estimated useful life of four years. The company uses straight-line depreciation.

M8-5
LO3

Computing Book Value (Double-Declining-Balance Depreciation)

Calculate the book value of a three-year-old machine that cost $25,000, has an estimated residual value of $5,000, and has an estimated useful life of five years. The company uses double-declining-balance depreciation. Round to the nearest dollar.

M8-6
LO3

Computing Book Value (Units-of-Production Depreciation)

Calculate the book value of a four-year-old machine that cost $21,000, has an estimated residual value of $1,000, and has an estimated useful life of 20,000 machine hours. The company uses units-of-production depreciation and ran the machine 3,200 hours in year 1, 7,050 hours in year 2, and 7,500 hours in year 3.

M8-7
LO4

Identifying Asset Impairment

For each of the following scenarios, indicate whether an asset has been impaired (Y for yes and N for no) and, if so, the amount of loss that should be recorded.

	Book Value	Estimated Future Cash Flows	Fair Value	Is Asset Impaired?	Amount of Loss?
a. Machine	$ 15,500	$ 10,000	$ 8,500		
b. Copyright	31,000	41,000	38,900		
c. Factory building	58,000	29,000	26,000		
d. Building	227,000	227,000	210,000		

Recording the Disposal of a Long-Lived Asset (Straight-Line Depreciation)

M8-8
L05

As part of a major renovation at the beginning of the year, Mullins' Pharmacy, Inc., sold shelving units (store fixtures) that were 10 years old for $3,000 cash. The original cost of the shelves was $6,000 and had been depreciated on a straight-line basis over an estimated useful life of 13 years with an estimated residual value of $800. Record the sale of the shelving units.

Computing Goodwill and Patents

M8-9
L06

Elizabeth Pie Company has been in business for 30 years and has developed a large group of loyal restaurant customers. Bonanza Foods made an offer to buy Elizabeth Pie Company for $5,000,000. The book value of Elizabeth Pie's recorded assets and liabilities on the date of the offer is $4,300,000 with a market value of $4,500,000. Elizabeth Pie also (1) holds a patent for a pie crust fluting machine that the company invented (the patent with a market value of $200,000 was never recorded by Elizabeth Pie because it was developed internally) and (2) estimates goodwill from loyal customers to be $310,000 (also never recorded by the company). Should Elizabeth Pie Company management accept Bonanza Foods' offer of $5,000,000? If so, compute the amount of goodwill that Bonanza Foods should record on the date of the purchase.

Preparing the Statement of Cash Flows

M8-10
L07

Wagner Company had the following activities for the year ended December 31, 2011: Sold land for cash at a cost of $16,000. Purchased $81,000 of equipment, paying $76,000 in cash and the rest on a note payable. Recorded $2,500 in depreciation expense for the year. Net income for the year was $11,000. Prepare the operating and investing sections of a statement of cash flows for the year based on the data provided.

Available with McGraw-Hill's Homework Manager

EXERCISES

Preparing a Classified Balance Sheet

E8-1
L01
Hasbro, Inc.

The following is a list of account titles and amounts (dollars in millions) reported by Hasbro, Inc., a leading manufacturer of games, toys, and interactive entertainment software for children and families:

Buildings and improvements	$206	Goodwill	$ 464
Prepaid expenses and other		Machinery and equipment	304
current assets	212	Accumulated depreciation	358
Allowance for doubtful accounts	39	Inventories	169
Other noncurrent assets	280	Other intangibles	1,146
Accumulated amortization		Land and improvements	18
(other intangibles)	435	Accounts receivable	646
Cash and cash equivalents	521	Tools, dies, and molds	30

Required:
Prepare the asset section of the balance sheet for Hasbro, Inc., classifying the assets into Current Assets, Property, Plant, and Equipment (net), and Other Assets.

Computing and Interpreting the Fixed Asset Turnover Ratio from a Financial Analyst's Perspective

E8-2
L01
Apple Inc.

The following data were included in a recent Apple Inc. annual report ($ in millions):

In millions	2007	2006	2005	2004
Net sales	$24,006	19,315	13,931	8,279
Net property, plant, and equipment	$ 1,832	1,281	817	707

Required:

1. Compute Apple's fixed asset turnover ratio for 2005, 2006, and 2007.
2. How might a financial analyst interpret the results?

E8-3
LO2, 3

Computing and Recording Cost and Depreciation of Assets (Straight-Line Depreciation)

KD Company bought a building for $71,000 cash and the land on which it is located for $107,000 cash. The company paid transfer costs of $3,000 ($1,000 for the building and $2,000 for the land). Renovation costs on the building were $23,000.

Required:

1. Give the journal entry to record the purchase of the property, including all expenditures. Assume that all transactions were for cash and that all purchases occurred at the start of the year.
2. Compute straight-line depreciation at the end of one year, assuming an estimated 10-year useful life and a $15,000 estimated residual value.
3. What would be the net book value of the property (land and building) at the end of year 2?

E8-4
LO2, 3

Determining Financial Statement Effects of an Asset Acquisition and Depreciation (Straight-Line Depreciation)

Kalriess Company ordered a machine on January 1, 2011, at an invoice price of $21,000. On date of delivery, January 2, 2011, the company paid $8,000 on the machine, and the balance was on credit at 10 percent interest. On January 3, 2011, it paid $1,000 for freight on the machine. On January 5, Kalreiss paid installation costs relating to the machine amounting to $1,500. On July 1, 2011, the company paid the balance due on the machine plus the interest. On December 31, 2011 (the end of the accounting period), Kalriess recorded depreciation on the machine using the straight-line method with an estimated useful life of 10 years and an estimated residual value of $3,500.

Required (round all amounts to the nearest dollar):

1. Indicate the effects (accounts, amounts, and + or −) of each transaction (on January 1, 2, 3, 5, and July 1) on the accounting equation. Use the following schedule:

Date	Assets	=	Liabilities	+	Stockholders' Equity

2. Compute the acquisition cost of the machine.
3. Compute the depreciation expense to be reported for 2011.
4. What is the impact on the cost of the machine of the interest paid on the 10 percent note? Under what circumstances can interest expense be included in acquisition cost?
5. What would be the net book value of the machine at the end of 2012?

E8-5
LO2, 3

Recording Depreciation and Repairs (Straight-Line Depreciation)

Stacey Company operates a small manufacturing facility as a supplement to its regular service activities. At the beginning of 2010, an asset account for the company showed the following balances:

Manufacturing equipment	$100,000
Accumulated depreciation through 2009	66,000

During 2010, the following expenditures were incurred for the equipment:

Routine maintenance and repairs on the equipment	$ 1,000
Major overhaul of the equipment that improved efficiency	12,000

The equipment is being depreciated on a straight-line basis over an estimated life of 15 years with a $10,000 estimated residual value. The annual accounting period ends on December 31.

Required:

1. Give the adjusting entry that was made at the end of 2009 for depreciation on the manufacturing equipment.
2. Starting at the beginning of 2010, what is the remaining estimated life?
3. Give the journal entries to record the two expenditures during 2010.

Determining Financial Statement Effects of Depreciation and Repairs (Straight-Line Depreciation)

Refer to the information in E8–5.

Required:
Indicate the effects (accounts, amounts, and + or −) of the following on the accounting equation.

Date	Assets	=	Liabilities	+	Stockholders' Equity

1. The adjustment for depreciation at the end of 2009.
2. The two expenditures during 2010.

Computing Depreciation under Alternative Methods

Rita's Pita Company bought a new dough machine at the beginning of the year at a cost of $6,000. The estimated useful life was four years, and the residual value was $1,000. Assume that the estimated productive life of the machine was 9,000 hours. Actual annual usage was 3,600 hours in year 1; 2,700 hours in year 2; 1,800 hours in year 3; and 900 hours in year 4.

Required:
1. Complete a separate depreciation schedule for each of the alternative methods. Round your answers to the nearest dollar.
   a. Straight-line.
   b. Units-of-production (use four decimal places for the per unit output factor).
   c. Double-declining-balance.

Method: _____				
Year	Computation	Depreciation Expense	Accumulated Depreciation	Net Book Value
At acquisition				
1				
2				
etc.				

2. Assuming that the machine was used directly in the production of one of the products that the company manufactures and sells, what factors might management consider in selecting a preferable depreciation method in conformity with the matching principle?

Computing Depreciation under Alternative Methods

Alexa Plastics Company purchased a new stamping machine at the beginning of the year at a cost of $280,000. The estimated residual value was $30,000. Assume that the estimated useful life was five years, and the estimated productive life of the machine was 250,000 units. Actual annual production was as follows:

Year	Units
1	73,000
2	62,000
3	30,000
4	43,000
5	42,000

Required:
1. Complete a separate depreciation schedule for each of the alternative methods. Round your answers to the nearest dollar.
   a. Straight-line.
   b. Units-of-production.
   c. Double-declining-balance.

Method: _____				
Year	Computation	Depreciation Expense	Accumulated Depreciation	Net Book Value
At acquisition				
1				
2				
etc.				

2. Assuming that the machine was used directly in the production of one of the products that the company manufactures and sells, what factors might management consider in selecting a preferable depreciation method in conformity with the matching principle?

E8-9
LO3
Ford Motor Company

Explaining Depreciation Policy

A recent annual report for Ford Motor Company contained the following note:

Significant Accounting Policies

Depreciation and Amortization of Property, Plant, and Equipment
Property and equipment are stated at cost and depreciated primarily using the straight-line method over the estimated useful life of the asset. Special tools placed in service before January 1, 1999 are amortized using an accelerated method over the estimated life of those tools. Special tools placed in service beginning in 1999 are amortized using the units-of-production method. Maintenance, repairs, and rearrangement costs are expensed as incurred.

Required:
Why do you think the company changed its depreciation method for special tools acquired in 1999 and subsequent years?

E8-10
LO3
FedEx

Interpreting Management's Choice of Different Depreciation Methods for Tax and Financial Reporting

A recent annual report for Federal Express Corporation includes the following information:

For financial reporting purposes, depreciation and amortization of property and equipment is provided on a straight-line basis over the asset's service life. For income tax purposes, depreciation is generally computed using accelerated methods.

Required:
Explain why Federal Express uses different methods of depreciation for financial reporting and tax purposes.

E8-11
LO3, 7

Computing Depreciation and Book Value for Two Years Using Alternative Depreciation Methods and Interpreting the Impact on Cash Flows

Daisey Company bought a machine for $66,000 cash. The estimated useful life was four years, and the estimated residual value was $6,000. Assume that the estimated useful life in productive units is 120,000. Units actually produced were 43,000 in year 1 and 45,000 in year 2.

Required:
1. Determine the appropriate amounts to complete the following schedule. Show computations, and round to the nearest dollar.

Method of Depreciation	Depreciation Expense for		Net Book Value at the End of	
	Year 1	Year 2	Year 1	Year 2
Straight-line				
Units-of-production				
Double-declining-balance				

2. Which method would result in the lowest EPS for year 1? For year 2?

3. Which method would result in the highest amount of cash outflows in year 1? Why?
4. Indicate the effects of (*a*) acquiring the machine and (*b*) recording annual depreciation on the operating and investing activities sections of the statement of cash flows (indirect method) for year 1 (assume the straight-line method).

Inferring Asset Impairment and Recording Disposal of an Asset

E8-12
LO4, 5
United Parcel Service Inc.

United Parcel Service states in a recent 10-K report, "We are the world's largest package delivery company and a leading global provider of specialized transportation and logistics services." The following note and data were reported:

> **Note 1—Summary of Accounting Policies**
>
> ***Impairment of Long-Lived Assets***
> We review long-lived assets for impairment when circumstances indicate the carrying amount of an asset may not be recoverable based on the undiscounted future cash flows of the asset. . . . In December (of a recent year), we permanently removed from service a number of Boeing 727 and DC-8 aircraft. As a result, we conducted an impairment evaluation, which resulted in. . . .

	Dollars in Millions
Cost of property and equipment (beginning of year)	$25,361
Cost of property and equipment (end of year)	26,915
Capital expenditures during the year	1,947
Accumulated depreciation (beginning of year)	11,749
Accumulated depreciation (end of year)	13,007
Depreciation expense during the year	1,549
Cost of property and equipment sold during the year	318
Accumulated depreciation on property sold	291
Cash received on property sold	118

Required:
1. Reconstruct the journal entry for the disposal of property and equipment during the year.
2. Compute the amount of property and equipment that United Parcel wrote off as impaired during the year. (**Hint:** Set up T-accounts.)

Recording the Disposal of an Asset at Three Different Sale Prices

E8-13
LO5
FedEx

Federal Express is the world's leading express-distribution company. In addition to the world's largest fleet of all-cargo aircraft, the company has more than 669 aircraft and 53,000 vehicles and trailers that pick up and deliver packages. Assume that Federal Express sold a small delivery truck that had been used in the business for three years. The records of the company reflected the following:

Delivery truck cost	$28,000
Accumulated depreciation	23,000

Required:
1. Give the journal entry for the disposal of the truck, assuming that the truck sold for
   a. $5,000 cash
   b. $5,600 cash
   c. $4,600 cash
2. Based on the three preceding situations, explain the effects of the disposal of an asset.

Recording the Disposal of an Asset at Three Different Sale Prices

E8-14
LO5
TRUMP
ENTERTAINMENT RESORTS
MARINA   PLAZA   TAJ MAHAL

Trump Entertainment Resorts owns and manages three casino hotel properties, Trump Plaza Hotel and Casino, Trump Taj Mahal Casino Resort, and Trump Marina Hotel Casino, totaling over $1.5 billion in property and equipment. Assume that Trump replaced furniture in one of the hotels that had been used in the business for five years. The records of the company reflected the following regarding the sale of the existing furniture:

Furniture (cost)	$8,000,000
Accumulated depreciation	6,500,000

Required:
1. Give the journal entry for the disposal of the furniture, assuming that it was sold for
    a. $1,500,000 cash.
    b. $2,600,000 cash.
    c. $900,000 cash.
2. Based on the three preceding situations, explain the effects of the disposal of an asset.

E8-15
LO5

Inferring Asset Age and Recording Accidental Loss on a Long-Lived Asset (Straight-Line Depreciation)

On January 1, 2010, the records of Pastuf Corporation showed the following regarding a truck:

Equipment (estimated residual value, $4,000)	$18,000
Accumulated depreciation (straight-line, three years)	6,000

On December 31, 2010, the delivery truck was a total loss as the result of an accident.

Required:
1. Based on the data given, compute the estimated useful life of the truck.
2. Give all journal entries with respect to the truck on December 31, 2010. Show computations.

E8-16
LO6

Freeport-McMoRan
Copper & Gold Inc.

Computing the Acquisition and Depletion of a Natural Resource

Freeport-McMoRan Copper & Gold Inc. is one of the world's largest copper and gold mining and production companies with the majority of its natural resources in Indonesia. Annual revenues exceed $16 billion. Assume that in February 2011, Freeport-McMoRan paid $700,000 for a mineral deposit in Bali. During March, it spent $65,000 in preparing the deposit for exploitation. It was estimated that 900,000 total cubic yards could be extracted economically. During 2011, 60,000 cubic yards were extracted. During January 2012, the company spent another $6,000 for additional developmental work that increased the estimated productive capacity of the mineral deposit.

Required:
1. Compute the acquisition cost of the deposit in 2011.
2. Compute depletion for 2011.
3. Compute the net book value of the deposit after payment of the January 2012 developmental costs.

E8-17
LO6

Computing and Reporting the Acquisition and Amortization of Three Different Intangible Assets

Katie Company had three intangible assets at the end of 2010 (end of the accounting year):
a. A patent purchased from J. Miller on January 1, 2010, for a cash cost of $6,000. Miller had registered the patent with the U.S. Patent Office five years ago.
b. An internally developed trademark registered with the federal government for $12,000 on November 1, 2010. Management decided the trademark has an indefinite life.
c. Computer software and Web development technology purchased on January 1, 2009, for $65,000. The technology is expected to have a four-year useful life to the company.

Required:
1. Compute the acquisition cost of each intangible asset.
2. Compute the amortization of each intangible at December 31, 2010. The company does not use contra-accounts.
3. Show how these assets and any related expenses should be reported on the balance sheet and income statement for 2010.

E8-18
LO6

Computing and Reporting the Acquisition and Amortization of Three Different Intangible Assets

Cambridge Company had three intangible assets at the end of 2012 (end of the accounting year):
a. A copyright purchased on January 1, 2011 for a cash cost of $12,300. The copyright is expected to have a ten-year useful life to Cambridge.
b. Goodwill of $65,000 from the purchase of the Hartford Company on July 1, 2010.

c. A patent purchased on January 1, 2012 for $39,200 from the inventor who had registered the patent with the U.S. Patent Office on January 1, 2006.

Required:
1. Compute the acquisition cost of each intangible asset.
2. Compute the amortization of each intangible at December 31, 2012. The company does not use contra-accounts.
3. Show how these assets and any related expenses should be reported on the balance sheet and income statement for 2012. (Assume there has been no impairment of goodwill.)

Recording Leasehold Improvements and Related Amortization

Starbucks Corporation is a rapidly expanding retailer of specialty coffee with thousands of stores worldwide. Assume that Starbucks planned to open a new store on Commonwealth Avenue near Boston University and obtained a 20-year lease starting January 1, 2011. The company had to renovate the facility by installing an elevator costing $275,000. Amounts spent to enhance leased property are capitalized as intangible assets called Leasehold Improvements. The elevator will be amortized over the useful life of the lease.

E8-19
LO6
Starbucks Corporation

Required:
1. Give the journal entry to record the installation of the new elevator.
2. Give any adjusting entries required at the end of the annual accounting period on December 31, 2011, related to the new elevator. Show computations.

Finding Financial Information as a Potential Investor

You are considering investing the cash gifts you received for graduation in various stocks. You have received several annual reports of major companies.

E8-20
LO1, 2, 3, 4, 5, 6, 7

Required:
For each of the following, indicate where you would locate the information in an annual report. (**Hint:** The information may be in more than one location.)
1. The detail on major classifications of long-lived assets.
2. The accounting method(s) used for financial reporting purposes.
3. Whether the company has had any capital expenditures for the year.
4. Net amount of property, plant, and equipment.
5. Policies on amortizing intangibles.
6. Depreciation expense.
7. Any significant gains or losses on disposals of fixed assets.
8. Prior year's accumulated depreciation.
9. The amount of assets written off as impaired during the year.

(Supplement) Recording a Change in Estimate

Refer to E8-5.

E8-21
LO3

Required:
Give the adjusting entry that should be made at the end of 2010 for depreciation of the manufacturing equipment, assuming no change in the original estimated life or residual value. Show computations.

(Supplement) Recording and Explaining Depreciation, Extraordinary Repairs, and Changes in Estimated Useful Life and Residual Value (Straight-Line Depreciation)

At the end of the annual accounting period, December 31, 2011, Shafer Company's records reflected the following for Machine A:

E8-22
LO2, 3

Cost when acquired	$30,000
Accumulated depreciation	10,200

During January 2012, the machine was renovated at a cost of $14,000. As a result, the estimated life increased from five years to eight years, and the residual value increased from $4,500 to $6,500. The company uses straight-line depreciation.

Required:

1. Give the journal entry to record the renovation.
2. How old was the machine at the end of 2011?
3. Give the adjusting entry at the end of 2012 to record straight-line depreciation for the year.
4. Explain the rationale for your entries in requirements 1 and 3.

E8-23
LO3, 7

(Supplement) Computing the Effect of a Change in Useful Life and Residual Value on Financial Statements and Cash Flows (Straight-Line Depreciation)

Todd Company owns the building occupied by its administrative office. The office building was reflected in the accounts at the end of last year as follows:

Cost when acquired	$330,000
Accumulated depreciation (based on straight-line depreciation, an estimated life of 30 years, and a $30,000 residual value)	130,000

During January of this year, on the basis of a careful study, management decided that the total estimated useful life should be changed to 25 years (instead of 30) and the residual value reduced to $23,000 (from $30,000). The depreciation method will not change.

Required:

1. Compute the annual depreciation expense prior to the change in estimates.
2. Compute the annual depreciation expense after the change in estimates.
3. What will be the net effect of changing estimates on the balance sheet, net income, and cash flows for the year?

PROBLEMS

Available with McGraw-Hill's Homework Manager

P8-1
LO1, 2
Explaining the Nature of a Long-Lived Asset and Determining and Recording the Financial Statement Effects of Its Purchase (AP8–1)

On January 2, 2011, Shallish Company bought a machine for use in operations. The machine has an estimated useful life of eight years and an estimated residual value of $1,800. The company provided the following expenditures:

a. Invoice price of the machine, $84,000.
b. Freight paid by the vendor per sales agreement, $1,000.
c. Installation costs, $2,000 paid in cash.
d. Payment of the $84,000 was made as follows:

On January 2:

■ Shallish Company common stock, par $1; 2,000 shares (market value, $3.50 per share).
■ Note payable, $45,000, 11.5 percent due April 16, 2011 (principal plus interest).
■ Balance of the invoice price to be paid in cash. The invoice allows for a 3 percent discount for cash paid by January 12.

On January 15:

■ Shallish Company paid the balance due.

Required:

1. What are the classifications of long-lived assets? Explain their differences.
2. Record the purchase on January 2 and the subsequent payment on January 15. Show computations.
3. Indicate the accounts, amounts, and effects (+ for increase and − for decrease) of the purchase and subsequent cash payment on the accounting equation. Use the following structure:

Date	Assets	=	Liabilities	+	Stockholders' Equity

4. Explain the basis you used for any questionable items.

Analyzing the Effects of Repairs, an Addition, and Depreciation (AP8–2)

A recent annual report for FedEx included the following note:

P8-2
LO2, 3
FedEx

> **Property and Equipment**
> Expenditures for major additions, improvements, flight equipment modifications and certain equipment overhaul costs are capitalized when such costs are determined to extend the useful life of the asset. Maintenance and repairs are charged to expense as incurred.

Assume that FedEx made extensive repairs on an existing building and added a new wing. The building is a garage and repair facility for delivery trucks that serve the Denver area. The existing building originally cost $720,000, and by the end of 2010 (10 years), it was half depreciated on the basis of a 20-year estimated useful life and no residual value. Assume straight-line depreciation was used. During 2011, the following expenditures related to the building were made:

a. Ordinary repairs and maintenance expenditures for the year, $7,000 cash.
b. Extensive and major repairs to the roof of the building, $122,000 cash. These repairs were completed on December 31, 2011.
c. The new wing was completed on December 31, 2011, at a cash cost of $230,000.

Required:
1. Applying the policies of FedEx, complete the following, indicating the effects for the preceding expenditures. If there is no effect on an account, write NE on the line:

	Building	Accumulated Depreciation	Depreciation Expense	Repairs Expense	Cash
Balance January 1, 2011	$720,000	$360,000			
Depreciation for 2011		_____	_____		_____
Balance prior to expenditures	720,000	_____	_____		
Expenditure (*a*)	_____	_____	_____	_____	_____
Expenditure (*b*)	_____	_____	_____	_____	_____
Expenditure (*c*)	_____	_____	_____	_____	_____
Balance December 31, 2011	_____	_____	_____	_____	

2. What was the book value of the building on December 31, 2011?
3. Explain the effect of depreciation on cash flows.

Computing the Acquisition Cost and Recording Depreciation under Three Alternative Methods (AP8–3)

P8-3
LO2, 3

www.mhhe.com/libby6e

At the beginning of the year, Rattner's Martial Arts Center bought three used fitness machines from Advantage, Inc. The machines immediately were overhauled, installed, and started operating. The machines were different; therefore, each had to be recorded separately in the accounts.

	Machine A	Machine B	Machine C
Amount paid for asset	$8,000	$25,000	$6,000
Installation costs	500	1,000	500
Renovation costs prior to use	2,500	1,000	1,500

By the end of the first year, each machine had been operating 4,800 hours.

Required:
1. Compute the cost of each machine.
2. Give the entry to record depreciation expense at the end of year 1, assuming the following:

	ESTIMATES		
Machine	Life	Residual Value	Depreciation Method
A	5 years	$1,000	Straight-line
B	50,000 hours	2,000	Units-of-production
C	4 years	1,500	Double-declining-balance

P8-4
LO1, 3

REX Stores Corporation

www.mhhe.com/libby6e

Inferring Depreciation Amounts and Determining the Effects of a Depreciation Error on Key Ratios (AP8–4)

REX Stores Corporation, headquartered in Dayton, Ohio, is one of the nation's leading consumer electronics retailers operating more than 190 stores in 35 states. The following is a note from a recent annual report:

(1) SUMMARY OF SIGNIFICANT ACCOUNTING POLICIES—

Property and Equipment—Property and equipment is recorded at cost. Depreciation is computed using the straight-line method. Estimated useful lives are 15 to 40 years for buildings and improvements, and 3 to 12 years for fixtures and equipment. Leasehold improvements are depreciated over 10 to 12 years. The components of cost at January 31 (current year) and (prior year) are as follows (amounts in dollars in thousands):

	Current Year	Prior Year
	(dollars in thousands)	
Land	$ 38,519	$ 38,567
Buildings and improvements	101,448	99,448
Fixtures and equipment	18,567	18,471
Leasehold improvements	9,797	9,882
Construction in progress		1,251
	168,331	167,619
Less: Accumulated depreciation	(36,922)	(33,056)
	$131,409	$134,563

Required:

1. Assuming that REX Stores did not sell any property, plant, and equipment in the current year, what was the amount of depreciation expense recorded during the current year?
2. Assume that REX Stores failed to record depreciation during the current year. Indicate the effect of the error (i.e., overstated or understated) on the following ratios:
   a. Earnings per share.
   b. Fixed asset turnover.
   c. Financial leverage.
   d. Return on equity.

P8-5
LO1, 3

www.mhhe.com/libby6e

Evaluating the Effect of Alternative Depreciation Methods on Key Ratios from an Analyst's Perspective

You are a financial analyst for General Motors Corporation and have been asked to determine the impact of alternative depreciation methods. For your analysis, you have been asked to compare methods based on a machine that cost $93,000. The estimated useful life is 13 years, and the estimated residual value is $2,000. The machine has an estimated useful life in productive output of 182,000 units. Actual output was 20,000 in year 1 and 16,000 in year 2. (Round results to the nearest dollar.)

Required:

1. For years 1 and 2 only, prepare separate depreciation schedules assuming:
   a. Straight-line method.
   b. Units-of-production method.
   c. Double-declining-balance method.

Method: _____				
Year	Computation	Depreciation Expense	Accumulated Depreciation	Net Book Value
At acquisition				
1				
2				

2. Evaluate each method in terms of its effect on cash flow, fixed asset turnover, and EPS. Assuming that General Motors is most interested in reducing taxes and maintaining a high EPS for year 1, what would you recommend to management? Would your recommendation change for year 2? Why or why not?

Recording and Interpreting the Disposal of Three Long-Lived Assets (AP8–5)

P8-6
LO3, 5

eXcel
www.mhhe.com/libby6e

During 2011, Jensen Company disposed of three different assets. On January 1, 2011, prior to their disposal, the accounts reflected the following:

Asset	Original Cost	Residual Value	Estimated Life	Accumulated Depreciation (straight line)
Machine A	$21,000	$3,000	8 years	$13,500 (6 years)
Machine B	41,000	4,000	10 years	29,600 (8 years)
Machine C	73,000	5,000	15 years	54,400 (12 years)

The machines were disposed of in the following ways:
a. Machine A: Sold on January 1, 2011, for $9,200 cash.
b. Machine B: Sold on December 31, 2011, for $7,500; received cash, $3,500, and a $4,000 interest-bearing (12 percent) note receivable due at the end of 12 months.
c. Machine C: On January 1, 2011, this machine suffered irreparable damage from an accident. On January 10, 2011, a salvage company removed the machine at no cost.

Required:
1. Give all journal entries related to the disposal of each machine in 2011.
2. Explain the accounting rationale for the way that you recorded each disposal.

Inferring Activities Affecting Fixed Assets from Notes to the Financial Statements and Analyzing the Impact of Depreciation on Cash Flows

P8-7
LO5, 7
Singapore Airlines

Singapore Airlines reported the following information in the notes to a recent annual report (in Singapore dollars):

SINGAPORE AIRLINES

Notes to the Accounts

13. **Fixed Assets** (dollars in millions)
The Company

	Beginning of Year	Additions	Disposals/ Transfers	End of Year
Cost				
Aircraft	10,293.1	954.4	296.4	10,951.1
Other fixed assets (summarized)	3,580.9	1,499.1	1,156.7	3,923.3
	13,874.0	2,453.5	1,453.1	14,874.4
Accumulated depreciation				
Aircraft	4,024.8	683.7	290.1	4,418.4
Other fixed assets (summarized)	1,433.4	158.5	73.8	1,518.1
	5,458.2	842.2	363.9	5,936.5

Singapore Airlines also reported the following cash flow details:

Cash Flow from Operating Activities (dollars in millions)		
	The Company	
	Current Year	Prior Year
Operating Profit	755.9	816.5
Adjustments for		
Depreciation of fixed assets	842.2	837.5
Loss/(surplus) on sale of fixed assets	(1.3)	(0.3)
Other adjustments (summarized)	82.3	39.4
Net Cash Provided by Operating Activities	1,679.1	1,693.1

Required:

1. Reconstruct the information in Note 13 into T-accounts for Fixed Assets and Accumulated Depreciation:

Fixed Assets		Accumulated Depreciation	
Beg. balance			Beg. balance
Acquisitions	Disposals/transfers	Disposals/transfers	Depreciation expense
End. balance			End. balance

2. Compute the amount of cash the company received for disposals and transfers for the current year. Show computations.
3. Compute the percentage of depreciation expense to cash flows from operations for the current year. What do you interpret from the result?

P8-8   **Determining Financial Statement Effects of Activities Related to Various Long-Lived**
LO2, 3, 6   **Assets** (AP8–6)

During the 2011 annual accounting period, Terwilliger Company completed the following transactions:
a. On January 1, 2011, purchased a patent for $21,000 cash (estimated useful life, seven years).
b. On January 1, 2011, purchased the assets (not detailed) of another business for cash $64,000, including $10,000 for goodwill. The company assumed no liabilities. Goodwill has an indefinite life.
c. On December 31, 2011, constructed a storage shed on land leased from S. Rhoades. The cost was $11,600. The company uses straight-line depreciation. The lease will expire in three years. (Amounts spent to enhance leased property are capitalized as intangible assets called Leasehold Improvements.)
d. Total expenditures during 2011 for ordinary repairs and maintenance were $5,500.
e. On December 31, 2011, sold Machine A for $7,000 cash. Original cost on January 1, 2010, was $25,000; accumulated depreciation (straight line) to December 31, 2010, $16,000 ($5,000 residual value and five-year useful life).
f. On December 31, 2011, paid $5,000 for a complete reconditioning of Machine B acquired on January 1, 2010. Original cost, $31,000; accumulated depreciation (straight line) to December 31, 2010, $9,600 ($7,000 residual value and 10-year useful life).

Required:

1. For each of these transactions, indicate the accounts, amounts, and effects (+ for increase and − for decrease) on the accounting equation. Use the following structure:

Date	Assets	=	Liabilities	+	Stockholders' Equity

2. For each of these assets except the assets not detailed in (*b*), compute depreciation and amortization to be recorded at the end of the year on December 31, 2011.

Computing Goodwill from the Purchase of a Business and Related Depreciation and Amortization

P8-9
LO3, 6

The notes to a recent annual report from Weebok Corporation included the following:

> **Business Acquisitions**
> During the current year, the Company acquired the assets of Sport Shoes, Inc . . .

Assume that Weebok acquired Sport Shoes on January 5, 2010. Weebok acquired the name of the company and all of its assets, except cash, for $472,000 cash. Weebok did not assume the liabilities. The transaction was closed on January 5, 2010, at which time the balance sheet of Sport Shoes reflected the following book values and an independent appraiser estimated the following market values for the assets:

Sport Shoes, Inc.

January 5, 2010	Book Value	Market Value*
Accounts receivable (net)	$ 41,000	$ 41,000
Inventory	215,000	200,000
Fixed assets (net)	33,000	50,000
Other assets	4,000	10,000
Total assets	$293,000	
Liabilities	$ 55,000	
Stockholders' equity	238,000	
Total liabilities and stockholders' equity	$293,000	

*These values for the purchased assets were provided to Weebok by an independent appraiser.

Required:
1. Compute the amount of goodwill resulting from the purchase. (**Hint:** Assets are purchased at market value in conformity with the cost principle.)
2. Compute the adjustments that Weebok would make at the end of the annual accounting period, December 31, 2010, for the following:
   a. Depreciation of the fixed assets (straight line), assuming an estimated remaining useful life of 10 years and no residual value.
   b. Goodwill (an intangible asset with an indefinite life).

Computing Amortization, Book Value, and Asset Impairment Related to Different Intangible Assets (AP8–7)

P8-10
LO4, 6

Fearn Company has five different intangible assets to be accounted for and reported on the financial statements. The management is concerned about the amortization of the cost of each of these intangibles. Facts about each intangible follow:

a. **Patent.** The company purchased a patent at a cash cost of $54,600 on January 1, 2011. The patent has an estimated useful life of 13 years.
b. **Copyright.** On January 1, 2011, the company purchased a copyright for $22,500 cash. It is estimated that the copyrighted item will have no value by the end of 20 years.
c. **Franchise.** The company obtained a franchise from McKenna Company to make and distribute a special item. It obtained the franchise on January 1, 2011, at a cash cost of $14,400 for a 12-year period.
d. **License.** On January 1, 2010, the company secured a license from the city to operate a special service for a period of five years. Total cash expended to obtain the license was $14,000.
e. **Goodwill.** The company started business in January 2008 by purchasing another business for a cash lump sum of $400,000. Included in the purchase price was "Goodwill, $60,000." Company executives stated that "the goodwill is an important long-lived asset to us." It has an indefinite life.

Required:
1. Compute the amount of amortization that should be recorded for each intangible asset at the end of the annual accounting period, December 31, 2011.
2. Give the book value of each intangible asset on December 31, 2012.

3. Assume that on January 2, 2013, the copyrighted item was impaired in its ability to continue to produce strong revenues. The other intangible assets were not affected. Fearn estimated that the copyright will be able to produce future cash flows of $18,000. The fair value of the copyright is determined to be $16,000. Compute the amount, if any, of the impairment loss to be recorded.

P8-11   **(Supplement) Analyzing and Recording Entries Related to a Change in Estimated Life and**
L03   **Residual Value**

Rungano Corporation is a global publisher of magazines, books, and music and video collections, and is a leading direct mail marketer. Many direct mail marketers use high-speed Didde press equipment to print their advertisements. These presses can cost more than $1 million. Assume that Rungano owns a Didde press acquired at an original cost of $400,000. It is being depreciated on a straight-line basis over a 20-year estimated useful life and has a $50,000 estimated residual value. At the end of 2010, the press had been depreciated for a full eight years. In January 2011, a decision was made, on the basis of improved maintenance procedures, that a total estimated useful life of 25 years and a residual value of $73,000 would be more realistic. The accounting period ends December 31.

Required:
1. Compute (*a*) the amount of depreciation expense recorded in 2010 and (*b*) the book value of the printing press at the end of 2010.
2. Compute the amount of depreciation that should be recorded in 2011. Show computations.
3. Give the adjusting entry for depreciation at December 31, 2011.

ALTERNATE PROBLEMS

AP8-1   **Explaining the Nature of a Long-Lived Asset and Determining and Recording the Financial**
L01, 2   **Statement Effects of Its Purchase (P8-1)**

On June 1, 2011, the Wilbur Corp. bought a machine for use in operations. The machine has an estimated useful life of six years and an estimated residual value of $2,000. The company provided the following expenditures:

a. Invoice price of the machine, $60,000.
b. Freight paid by the vendor per sales agreement, $650.
c. Installation costs, $1,500.
d. Payment of the $60,000 was made as follows:

On June 1:

- Wilbur Corp. common stock, par $2; 2,000 shares (market value, $5 per share).
- Balance of the invoice price on a note payable, 12 percent due September 2, 2011 (principal plus interest).

On September 2:

- Wilbur Corp. paid the balance and interest due on the note payable.

Required:
1. What are the classifications of long-lived assets? Explain their differences.
2. Record the purchase on June 1 and the subsequent payment on September 2. Show computations.
3. Indicate the accounts, amounts, and effects (+ for increase and − for decrease) of the purchase and subsequent cash payment on the accounting equation. Use the following structure:

Date	Assets	=	Liabilities	+	Stockholders' Equity

4. Explain the basis you used for any questionable items.

Analyzing the Effects of Repairs, an Addition, and Depreciation (P8–2)

A recent annual report for AMERCO, the holding company for U-Haul International, Inc., included the following note:

AP8-2
LO2, 3
AMERCO

> **Property, Plant and Equipment**
>
> Property, plant and equipment are stated at cost. Interest costs incurred during the initial construction of buildings or rental equipment are considered part of cost. Depreciation is computed for financial reporting purposes principally using the straight-line method over the following estimated useful lives: rental equipment 2-20 years; buildings and non-rental equipment 3-55 years. Major overhauls to rental equipment are capitalized and are amortized over the estimated period benefited. Routine maintenance costs are charged to operating expense as they are incurred.

AMERCO subsidiaries own property, plant, and equipment that are utilized in the manufacture, repair, and rental of U-Haul equipment and that provide offices for U-Haul. Assume that AMERCO made extensive repairs on an existing building and added a new wing. The building is a garage and repair facility for rental trucks that serve the Seattle area. The existing building originally cost $230,000, and by the end of 2011 (its fifth year), the building was one-quarter depreciated on the basis of a 20-year estimated useful life and no residual value. Assume straight-line depreciation. During 2012, the following expenditures related to the building were made:

a. Ordinary repairs and maintenance expenditures for the year, $5,000 cash.
b. Extensive and major repairs to the roof of the building, $17,000 cash. These repairs were completed on December 31, 2012.
c. The new wing was completed on December 31, 2012, at a cash cost of $70,000.

Required:

1. Applying the policies of AMERCO, complete the following, indicating the effects for the preceding expenditures. If there is no effect on an account, write NE on the line:

	Building	Accumulated Depreciation	Depreciation Expense	Repairs Expense	Cash
Balance January 1, 2012	$230,000	$57,500			
Depreciation for 2012		_____	_____		_____
Balance prior to expenditures	230,000	_____	_____		
Expenditure (*a*)	_____	_____	_____	_____	_____
Expenditure (*b*)	_____	_____	_____	_____	_____
Expenditure (*c*)	_____	_____	_____	_____	_____
Balance December 31, 2012	_____	_____	_____	_____	

2. What was the book value of the building on December 31, 2012?
3. Explain the effect of depreciation on cash flows.

Computing the Acquisition Cost and Recording Depreciation under Three Alternative Methods (P8–3)

AP8-3
LO2, 3

At the beginning of the year, Labenski Inc. bought three used machines from Moore Corporation. The machines immediately were overhauled, installed, and started operating. The machines were different; therefore, each had to be recorded separately in the accounts.

	Machine A	Machine B	Machine C
Cost of the asset	$10,800	$32,500	$21,700
Installation costs	800	1,100	1,100
Renovation costs prior to use	600	1,400	1,600

By the end of the first year, each machine had been operating 7,000 hours.

Required:

1. Compute the cost of each machine.
2. Give the entry to record depreciation expense at the end of year 1, assuming the following:

ESTIMATES

Machine	Life	Residual Value	Depreciation Method
A	8 years	$1,000	Straight-line
B	33,000 hours	2,000	Units-of-production
C	5 years	1,400	Double-declining-balance

AP8-4
LO1, 3
The Gap , Inc.

Inferring Depreciation Amounts and Determining the Effects of a Depreciation Error on Key Ratios (P8–4)

The Gap, Inc., is a global specialty retailer of casual wear products for women, men, and children under the Gap, Banana Republic, Old Navy, Forth & Towne, and Piperline brands. As of February 3, 2007, the Company operated 3,131 stores across the globe, as well as online. The following is a note from a recent annual report:

> **(1) Summary of Significant Accounting Policies—**
>
> **Property and Equipment**
> Property and equipment are stated at cost. Depreciation and amortization are computed using the straight-line method over their estimated lives or the related assets, or where applicable, the terms of the respective leases, whichever is shorter.

The components of cost at the end of the current and prior years are as follows (dollars in thousands):

	Current Year	Prior Year
Property and equipment:		
Leasehold improvements	$ 2,926	$ 2,742
Furniture and equipment	2,487	2,532
Land and buildings	1,005	1,008
Construction in progress	123	80
Other	594	596
	7,135	6,958
Less accumulated depreciation and amortization	3,938	3,712
Net property and equipment	$ 3,197	$ 3,246

Required:

1. Assuming that The Gap, Inc., did not have any asset impairment write-offs and did not sell any property, plant, and equipment in the current year, what was the amount of depreciation expense recorded in the current year?
2. Assume that The Gap, Inc., failed to record depreciation in the current year. Indicate the effect of the error (i.e., overstated or understated) on the following ratios:
   a. Earnings per share
   b. Fixed asset turnover
   c. Financial leverage
   d. Return on equity

AP8-5
LO5

Recording and Interpreting the Disposal of Three Long-Lived Assets (P8–6)

During 2010, Kosik Company disposed of three different assets. On January 1, 2010, prior to their disposal, the accounts reflected the following:

Asset	Original Cost	Residual Value	Estimated Life	Accumulated Depreciation (straight line)
Machine A	$24,000	$2,000	5 years	$17,600 (4 years)
Machine B	16,500	5,000	10 years	8,050 (7 years)
Machine C	59,200	3,200	14 years	48,000 (12 years)

The machines were disposed of in the following ways:

a. Machine A: Sold on January 1, 2010, for $5,750 cash.
b. Machine B: Sold on December 31, 2010, for $9,000; received cash, $4,000, and a $5,000 interest-bearing (10 percent) note receivable due at the end of 12 months.
c. Machine C: On January 1, 2010, this machine suffered irreparable damage from an accident and was scrapped.

Required:
  1. Give all journal entries related to the disposal of each machine.
  2. Explain the accounting rationale for the way that you recorded each disposal.

Determining Financial Statement Effects of Activities Related to Various Long-Lived Assets (P8–8)

AP8-6
LO2, 3, 6

During the 2012 annual accounting period, Chu Corporation completed the following transactions:

a. On January 1, 2012, purchased a license for $7,200 cash (estimated useful life, three years).
b. On January 1, 2012, repaved the parking lot of the building leased from I. Kumara. The cost was $7,800; the estimated useful life was five years with no residual value. The company uses straight-line depreciation. The lease will expire in 10 years. (Amounts spent to enhance leased property are capitalized as intangible assets called Leasehold Improvements.)
c. On July 1, 2012, purchased another business for $120,000 cash. The transaction included $115,000 for assets and $24,000 for the liabilities assumed by Chu. The remainder was goodwill with an in-definite life.
d. On December 31, 2012, sold Machine A for $5,000 cash. Original cost, $21,500; accumulated depreciation (straight line) to December 31, 2011, $13,500 ($3,500 residual value and four-year life).
e. Total expenditures during 2012 for ordinary repairs and maintenance were $6,700.
f. On December 31, 2012, paid $8,000 for a complete reconditioning of Machine B acquired on January 1, 2009. Original cost, $18,000; accumulated depreciation (straight line) to December 31, 2011, $12,000 ($2,000 residual value and four-year life).

Required:
  1. For each of these transactions, indicate the accounts, amounts, and effects (+ for increase and − for decrease) on the accounting equation. Use the following structure:

Date	Assets	=	Liabilities	+	Stockholders' Equity

  2. For each of these assets, compute depreciation and amortization to be recorded at the end of the year on December 31, 2012.

Computing Amortization, Book Value, and Asset Impairment Related to Different Intangible Assets (P8–10)

AP8-7
LO3, 4, 6

Evans Corporation has five different intangible assets to be accounted for and reported on the financial statements. The management is concerned about the amortization of the cost of each of these intangibles. Facts about each intangible follow:

a. **Patent.** The company purchased a patent at a cash cost of $18,600 on January 1, 2010. It is amortized over its expected useful life of 15 years.
b. **Copyright.** On January 1, 2010, the company purchased a copyright for $24,750 cash. It is estimated that the copyrighted item will have no value by the end of 30 years.
c. **Franchise.** The company obtained a franchise from Farrell Company to make and distribute a special item. It obtained the franchise on January 1, 2010, at a cash cost of $19,200 for a 12-year period.
d. **License.** On January 1, 2009, the company secured a license from the city to operate a special ser-vice for a period of seven years. Total cash expended to obtain the license was $21,000.
e. **Goodwill.** The company started business in January 2011 by purchasing another business for a cash lump sum of $650,000. Included in the purchase price was "Goodwill, $75,000." Company executives stated that "the goodwill is an important long-lived asset to us." It has an indefinite life.

Required:
  1. Compute the amount of amortization that should be recorded for each intangible asset at the end of the annual accounting period, December 31, 2010.
  2. Give the book value of each intangible asset on January 1, 2013.

3. Assume that on January 2, 2013, the franchise was impaired in its ability to continue to produce strong revenues. The other intangible assets were not affected. Evans estimated that the franchise will be able to produce future cash flows of $14,500, and the fair value is $13,000. Compute the amount, if any, of the impairment loss to be recorded.

CASES **AND PROJECTS**

Annual Report Cases

CP8-1

LO1, 2, 3, 4, 6

AMERICAN EAGLE
OUTFITTERS

Finding Financial Information

Refer to the financial statements of American Eagle Outfitters in Appendix B at the end of this book.

Required:

For each question, answer it and indicate where you located the information to answer the question. (**Hint:** Use the notes to the financial statements for some of these questions.)

1. How much did the company spend on property and equipment (capital expenditures) in fiscal 2006 (the year ended February 3, 2007)?
2. What is the typical estimated useful life of leasehold improvements for amortization purposes?
3. What was the original cost of fixtures and equipment held by the company at the end of the most recent reporting year?
4. What was the amount of depreciation and amortization reported as an expense for the current year? Compare this amount to the change in accumulated amortization and depreciation from fiscal 2005 to fiscal 2006. Why would these numbers be different?
5. What is the company's fixed asset turnover ratio for fiscal 2006?

CP8-2

LO1, 2, 3, 4, 6

Urban Outfitters

Finding Financial Information

Refer to the financial statements of Urban Outfitters given in Appendix C at the end of this book.

Required:

For each question, answer it and indicate where you located the information to answer the question. (**Hint:** Use the notes to the financial statements for many of these questions.)

1. What method of depreciation does the company use?
2. What is the amount of accumulated depreciation and amortization at the end of the most recent reporting year?
3. For depreciation purposes, what is the estimated useful life of furniture and fixtures?
4. What was the original cost of leasehold improvements owned by the company at the end of the most recent reporting year?
5. What amount of depreciation and amortization was reported as expense for the most recent reporting year?
6. What is the company's fixed asset turnover ratio for the most recent year? What does it suggest?

CP8-3

LO1, 3

AMERICAN EAGLE
OUTFITTERS

Urban Outfitters

eXcel

www.mhhe.com/libby6e

Comparing Companies within an Industry

Refer to the financial statements of American Eagle Outfitters in Appendix B, Urban Outfitters in Appendix C, and the Industry Ratio Report in Appendix D at the end of this book.

Required:

1. Compute the percentage of net fixed assets to total assets for both companies for the most recent year. Why do the companies differ?
2. Compute the percentage of gross fixed assets that has been depreciated for both companies for the most recent year. Why do you think the percentages differ?
3. Compute the fixed asset turnover ratio for the most recent year presented for both companies. Which has higher asset efficiency? Why?
4. Compare the fixed asset turnover ratio for both companies to the industry average. Are these companies doing better or worse than the industry average in asset efficiency?

Financial Reporting and Analysis Cases

Broadening Financial Research Skills: Identifying Competitors in an Industry

Reuters provides lists of industries and the competitors in each at **www.reuters.com/finance/industries**. Click on "All Industries," then one of the industries listed below, then "Company Ranks." When you skim down the page, you will find an alphabetical listing of companies in the industry.

Required:
Using your Web browser, contact Reuters and identify three competitors for the following industries:
  1. Airline.
  2. Hotels, motels, and cruise lines.
  3. Footwear.
  4. Computer hardware.

CP8-4

Using Financial Reports: Analyzing the Age of Assets

A note to a recent annual report for Black & Decker contained the following information (dollars in thousands):

	Current Year
Land and improvements	$ 69,091
Buildings	298,450
Machinery and equipment	928,151
	1,295,692
Less accumulated depreciation	468,511
	$ 827,181

Depreciation expense (in thousands of dollars) charged to operations was $99,234 in the current year. Depreciation generally is computed using the straight-line method for financial reporting purposes.

Required:
  1. What is your best estimate of the average expected life for Black & Decker's depreciable assets?
  2. What is your best estimate of the average age of Black & Decker's depreciable assets?

CP8-5
LO3

Using Financial Reports: Analyzing a Note Concerning Depreciation

A recent annual report for the Depp Company contained the following note:

> Property, plant, and equipment is stated at cost, less allowance for depreciation. Depreciation expense is determined principally by the straight-line method. The annual rates of depreciation are 4 percent to 10 percent for buildings and improvements and 10 percent to 40 percent for machinery and equipment.

Required:
  1. What is the range of expected lives for buildings and improvements?
  2. Explain why Depp Company depreciates the cost of its containers instead of including the total in cost of goods sold in the year the product is sold.

CP8-6
LO3

Using Financial Reports: Analyzing Fixed Asset Turnover Ratio and Cash Flows

The Little Company operates in both the beverage and entertainment industries. In June 2001, Little purchased Good Time, Inc., that produces and distributes motion picture, television, and home video products and recorded music; publishes books; and operates theme parks and retail stores. The purchase resulted in $2.7 billion in goodwill. Since 2001, Little has undertaken a number of business acquisitions and divestitures (sales of businesses) as the company expands into the entertainment

CP8-7
LO1, 6, 7

industry. Selected data from a recent annual report are as follows (amounts are in U.S. dollars in millions):

Property, Plant, Equipment, and Intangibles From the Consolidated Balance Sheet	Current Year	Prior Year
Film costs, net of amortization	$1,272	$ 991
Artists' contracts, advances, and other entertainment assets	761	645
Property, plant, and equipment, net	2,733	2,559
Excess of cost over fair value of assets acquired	3,076	3,355
From the Consolidated Statement of Income		
Total revenues	$9,714	$10,644
From the Consolidated Statement of Cash Flows		
Income from continuing operations	$ 880	$ 445
Adjustments:		
Depreciation	289	265
Amortization	208	190
Other adjustments (summarized)	(1,618)	(256)
Net cash provided by continuing operations	(241)	644
From the Notes to the Financial Statements		
Accumulated depreciation on property, plant, and equipment	$1,178	$ 1,023

Required:
1. Compute the cost of the property, plant, and equipment at the end of the current year. Explain your answer.
2. What was the approximate age of the property, plant, and equipment at the end of the current year?
3. Compute the fixed asset turnover ratio for the current year. Explain your results.
4. What is Excess of Cost Over Fair Value of Assets Acquired?
5. On the consolidated statement of cash flows, why are the depreciation and amortization amounts added to income from continuing operations?

CP8-8   Using Financial Reports: Inferring the Sale of Assets

L01, 5, 7

A recent annual report for Eastman Kodak reported that the balance of property, plant, and equipment at the end of the current year was $16,774 million. At the end of the previous year, it had been $15,667 million. During the current year, the company bought $2,118 million worth of new equipment. The balance of accumulated depreciation at the end of the current year was $8,146 million and at the end of the previous year was $7,654 million. Depreciation expense for the current year was $1,181 million. The annual report does not disclose any gain or loss on the disposition of property, plant, and equipment, so you may assume that the amount was zero.

Required:
What amount of proceeds did Eastman Kodak receive when it sold property, plant, and equipment during the current year? (**Hint:** Set up T-accounts.)

Critical Thinking Cases

CP8-9   Making a Decision as a Financial Analyst: Interpreting the Impact of the Capitalization of
L02   Interest on an Accounting Ratio

Hess Corporation

The capitalization of interest associated with self-constructed assets was discussed in this chapter. A recent annual report for Hess Corporation disclosed the following information concerning capitalization of interest:

> Interest costs related to certain long-term construction projects are capitalized to comply with FAS No. 34, "Capitalization of Interest Cost." Capitalized interest in the current year amounted to $34,897,000.

The income statement for that year disclosed that interest expense was $224,200,000. A popular accounting ratio used by some analysts is the interest coverage ratio (Income ÷ Interest Expense).

Required:
1. Explain why an analyst would calculate the interest coverage ratio.
2. Did Hess include the $34,897,000 in the reported interest expense of $224,200,000? If not, should an analyst include it when calculating the interest coverage ratio? Explain.

Evaluating an Ethical Dilemma: Analyzing an Accounting Change

An annual report for Ford Motor Company included the following information:

CP8-10
LO3, 7
Ford Motor Company

> **Note 6. Net Property, Depreciation and Amortization—Automotive**
> Assets placed in service before January 1, 1993, are depreciated using an accelerated method. Assets placed in service beginning in 1993 will be depreciated using the straight-line method of depreciation. This change in accounting principle is being made to reflect improvements in the design and flexibility of manufacturing machinery and equipment and improvements in maintenance practices. These improvements have resulted in more uniform productive capacities and maintenance costs over the useful life of an asset. Straight-line is preferable in these circumstances. The change is expected to improve 1993 after-tax results by $80 to $100 million.

Required:
1. What was the stated reason for the change in method? What other factors do you think management considered when it decided to make this accounting change?
2. Do you think this is an ethical decision?
3. Who were affected by the change and how were they benefited or harmed?
4. What impact did this change have on cash flows for Ford?
5. As an investor, how would you react to the fact that Ford's net income will increase by $80 to $100 million as the result of this change?

Evaluating the Impact of Capitalized Interest on Cash Flows and Fixed Asset Turnover from an Analyst's Perspective

CP8-11
LO1, 2, 7
Marriott International

You are a financial analyst charged with evaluating the asset efficiency of companies in the hotel industry. Recent financial statements for Marriott include the following note:

> **Summary of Significant Accounting Policies**
>
> *Property and Equipment*
> We record property and equipment at cost, including interest, rent and real estate taxes incurred during development and construction. Interest capitalized as a cost of property and equipment totaled $32 million in 2006, $30 million in 2005, and $16 million in 2004. We capitalize the cost of improvements that extend the useful life of property and equipment when incurred.

Required:
1. Assume that Marriott followed this policy for a major construction project this year. How does Marriott's policy affect the following: + for increase, − for decrease, and NE for no effect?
   a. Cash flows.
   b. Fixed asset turnover ratio.
2. Normally, how would your answer to requirement (1b) affect your evaluation of Marriott's effectiveness in utilizing fixed assets?
3. If the fixed asset turnover ratio decreases due to interest capitalization, does this change indicate a real decrease in efficiency? Why or why not?

Financial Reporting and Analysis Team Project

CP8-12

LO1, 2, 3, 4, 6, 7

Team Project: Analysis of Long-Lived Assets

As a team, select an industry to analyze. Reuters provides lists of industries and their makeup at **www.reuters.com/finance/industries.** Each team member should acquire the annual report or 10-K for one publicly traded company in the industry, with each member selecting a different company. (Library files, the SEC EDGAR service at **www.sec.gov,** or the company itself are good sources.)

Required:

1. List the accounts and amounts of the company's long-lived assets (land, buildings, equipment, intangible assets, natural resources, and/or other) for the last three years.
   a. What is the percentage of each to total assets?
   b. What do the results of your analysis suggest about the strategy your company has followed with respect to investing in long-lived assets?

2. What cost allocation method(s) and estimates does the company use for each type of long-lived asset?

3. Compute the approximate average remaining life of property, plant, and equipment overall.

4. What does the company disclose regarding asset impairment? What was its impairment loss, if any, in the most recent year?

5. Ratio analysis:
   a. What does the fixed asset turnover ratio measure in general?
   b. Compute the ratio for the last three years.
   c. What do your results suggest about the company?
   d. If available, find the industry ratio for the most recent year, compare it to your results, and discuss why you believe your company differs or is similar to the industry ratio.

6. What was the effect of depreciation expense on cash flows from operating activities? Compute the percentage of depreciation expense to cash flows from operating activities for each of the past three years.

7. From the statement of cash flows, what were capital expenditures over the last three years? Did the company sell any long-lived assets?

Lectured slideshow–LP9-1
www.mhhe.com/libby6e

LEARNING OBJECTIVES

After studying this chapter, you should be able to:

1. Define, measure, and report current liabilities. p. 461

2. Use the current ratio. p. 462

3. Analyze the accounts payable turnover ratio. p. 464

4. Report notes payable and explain the time value of money. p. 467

5. Report contingent liabilities. p. 469

6. Explain the importance of working capital and its impact on cash flows. p. 471

7. Report long-term liabilities. p. 473

8. Compute present values. p. 475

9. Apply present value concepts to liabilities. p. 479

REPORTING AND INTERPRETING LIABILITIES

Each week, Starbucks serves customers more than 40 million times. The company, founded in 1971, has 12,440 coffeehouses and does business in 37 international markets. The mission statement for the company is "to establish Starbucks as the premier purveyor of the finest coffees in the world." The company's goal is to have approximately 40,000 locations worldwide. It is aggressively pursuing this goal, with plans to open 2,400 stores internationally this year.

To achieve its goals, Starbucks must focus on a number of activities. The annual report identifies several of them:

■ Serve the finest cup of coffee in the world.
■ Grow the company one customer at a time based on exceptional customer service.
■ Make someone's day with a relaxing in-store experience including music, art, and high-speed wireless Internet access.

In addition to these operating activities, management must focus on a number of critical financing activities to ensure that the company remains profitable and is able to generate sufficient resources to eventually open 40,000 coffeehouses. The financing activities for Starbucks serve two important purposes. They generate funds (1) to finance the current operating activities of the business and (2) to acquire long-term assets that permit the company to grow in the future.

UNDERSTANDING THE BUSINESS

Businesses finance the acquisition of their assets from two sources: funds supplied by creditors (debt) and funds provided by owners (equity). The mixture of debt and equity a business uses is called its *capital structure*. In addition to selecting a capital structure, management can select from a variety of sources from which to borrow

STARBUCKS CORPORATION
Consolidated Balance Sheets
In thousands

	October 1, 2006	October 2, 2005
Liabilities and Shareholders' Equity		
Current liabilities:		
Accounts payable	$ 340,937	$ 220,975
Accrued compensation and related costs	288,963	232,354
Accrued occupancy costs	54,868	44,496
Accrued taxes	94,010	78,293
Short-term borrowings	700,000	277,000
Other accrued expenses	224,154	198,082
Deferred revenue	231,926	175,048
Current portion of long-term debt	762	748
Total current liabilities	1,935,620	1,226,996
Long-term debt	1,958	2,870
Other long-term liabilities	262,857	193,565

money, as illustrated by the liability section of the balance sheet from Starbucks shown in Exhibit 9.1.

What factors do managers consider when they borrow money? Two key factors are risk and cost. From the firm's perspective, debt capital is more risky than equity because payments associated with debt are a company's legal obligation. If a company cannot meet a required debt payment (either principal or interest) because of a temporary cash shortage, creditors may force the company into bankruptcy and require the sale of assets to satisfy the debt. As with any business transaction, borrowers and lenders attempt to negotiate the most favorable terms possible. Managers devote considerable effort to analyzing alternative borrowing arrangements.

Companies that include debt in their capital structure must also make strategic decisions concerning the balance between short-term and long-term debt. To evaluate a company's capital structure, financial analysts calculate a number of accounting ratios. In this chapter, we will discuss both short-term and long-term debt, as well as some important accounting ratios. We will also introduce you to present value concepts. In the next chapter, we discuss a special category of long-term debt, bonds payable.

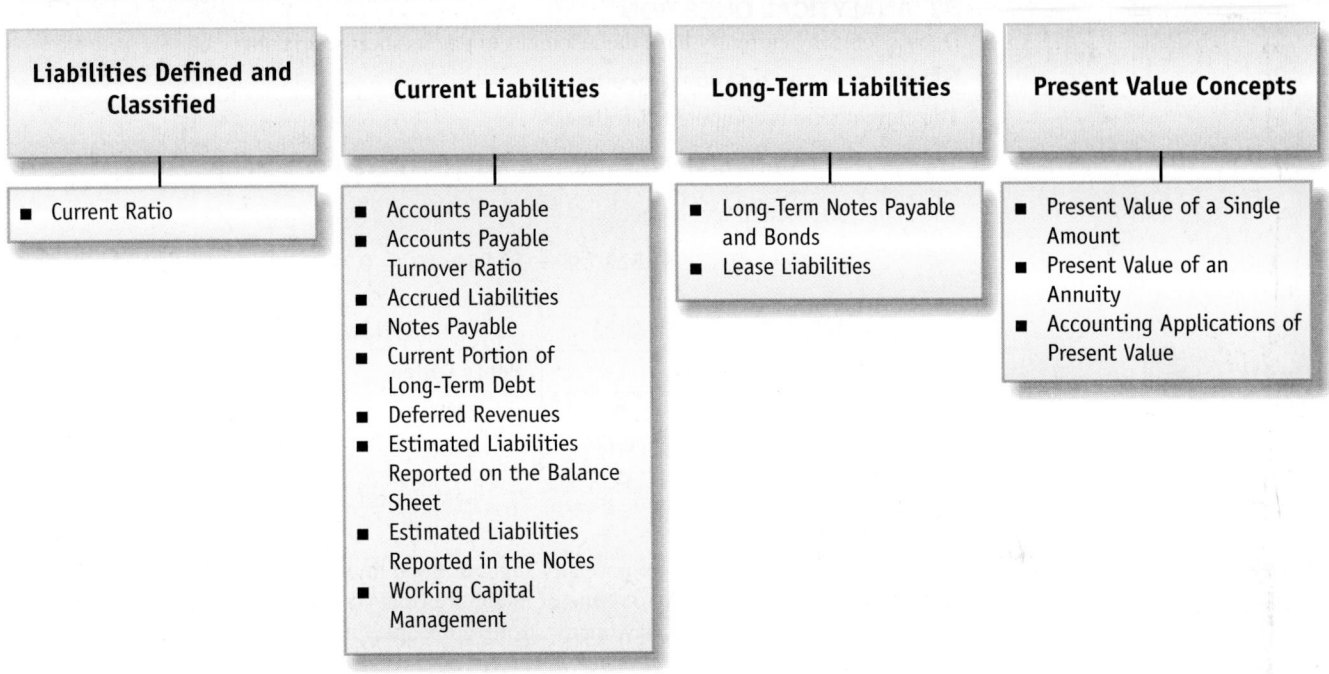

ORGANIZATION of the Chapter

Liabilities Defined and Classified	Current Liabilities	Long-Term Liabilities	Present Value Concepts
■ Current Ratio	■ Accounts Payable ■ Accounts Payable Turnover Ratio ■ Accrued Liabilities ■ Notes Payable ■ Current Portion of Long-Term Debt ■ Deferred Revenues ■ Estimated Liabilities Reported on the Balance Sheet ■ Estimated Liabilities Reported in the Notes ■ Working Capital Management	■ Long-Term Notes Payable and Bonds ■ Lease Liabilities	■ Present Value of a Single Amount ■ Present Value of an Annuity ■ Accounting Applications of Present Value

LIABILITIES DEFINED AND CLASSIFIED

Most people have a reasonable understanding of the definition of the word *liability*. Accountants formally define **liabilities** as probable debts or obligations of the entity that result from past transactions, which will be paid with assets or services. As Exhibit 9.1 shows, as of October 1, 2006, Starbucks had borrowed on a long-term basis $1,958 thousand. The company has a current obligation to pay cash to its creditors at some time in the future based on the borrowing agreements. Because of this obligation, Starbucks must record long-term debt.

When a liability is first recorded, it is measured in terms of its current cash equivalent, which is the cash amount a creditor would accept to settle the liability immediately. Although Starbucks borrowed $1,958 thousand, it will repay much more than that because the company must also pay interest on the debt. Interest that will be paid in the future is not included in the reported amount of the liability because it accrues and becomes a liability with the passage of time.

Like most businesses, Starbucks has several kinds of liabilities as well as a wide range of creditors. The list of liabilities on the balance sheet differs from one company to the next because different operating activities result in different types of liabilities. The liability section of the Starbucks report begins with the caption Current Liabilities. **Current liabilities** are defined as short-term obligations that will be paid within the current operating cycle of the business or within one year of the balance sheet date, whichever is longer. Because most companies have an operating cycle that is shorter than one year, normally, current liabilities can be defined simply as liabilities that are due within one year. Noncurrent liabilities include all other liabilities.

Information about current liabilities is very important to managers and analysts because these obligations must be paid in the near future. Analysts say that a company has **liquidity** if it has the ability to meet its current obligations. A number of financial ratios are useful in evaluating liquidity, including the current ratio.

Learning Objective 1
Define, measure, and report current liabilities.

LIABILITIES are probable debts or obligations that result from past transactions, which will be paid with assets or services.

Video 9-1
www.mhhe.com/libby6e

CURRENT LIABILITIES are short-term obligations that will be paid within the current operating cycle or one year, whichever is longer.

LIQUIDITY is the ability to pay current obligations.

Current Ratio

? ANALYTICAL QUESTION

Does a company currently have the resources to pay its short-term debt?

% RATIO AND COMPARISONS

The current ratio is computed as follows:

$$\text{Current Ratio} = \text{Current Assets} \div \text{Current Liabilities}$$

The 2006 current ratio for Starbucks:

$$\$1,529,788 \div \$1,935,620 = 0.79$$

COMPARISONS OVER TIME			COMPARISONS WITH COMPETITORS	
Starbucks			Peet's Coffee	Caribou Coffee
2004	2005	2006	2006	2006
1.81	0.99	0.79	2.57	0.98

💡 INTERPRETATIONS

In General While a high ratio normally suggests good liquidity, too high a ratio suggests inefficient use of resources. An old rule of thumb was that companies should have a current ratio between 1.0 and 2.0. Today, many strong companies use sophisticated management techniques to minimize funds invested in current assets and, as a result, have current ratios below 1.0.

Focus Company Analysis The current ratio for Starbucks shows a low level of liquidity and the ratio has been decreasing in recent years. The primary cause is a significant increase in short-term borrowing over the previous two years. In some cases, analysts would be concerned about both the level and trend, but the situation is understandable given Starbucks aggressive growth strategy. In addition, the company has over $300 million in cash and was able to generate over $1 billion in cash provided by operating activities. The ratio for Starbucks is lower than both of its competitors. On balance, most analysts would not be concerned about Starbucks' liquidity.

A Few Cautions The current ratio may be a misleading measure of liquidity if significant funds are tied up in assets that cannot easily be converted into cash. A company with a high current ratio might still have liquidity problems if the majority of its current assets is made up of slow-moving inventory. Analysts recognize that managers can manipulate the current ratio by engaging in certain transactions just before the close of the fiscal year. In most cases, for example, the current ratio can be improved by paying creditors immediately prior to preparation of financial statements.

Learning Objective 2
Use the current ratio.

CURRENT LIABILITIES

Many current liabilities have a direct relationship to the operating activities of a business. In other words, specific operating activities are financed, in part, by a related current liability. Some examples from the Starbucks annual report (Exhibit 9.1) are:

Operating Activity	Current Liability
Purchase coffee inventory	Accounts payable
Rent store space for coffeehouse	Accrued occupancy costs
Service performed by employees	Accrued compensation costs
Cash received from customers for future purchases of coffee	Deferred revenue

Early in this chapter, we mentioned that Starbucks is aggressively opening new stores each year. As a result, they must buy more inventory, rent more store space and hire more employees. By understanding the relationship between operating activities and current liabilities, an analyst can easily explain changes in the various current liability accounts.

We will now discuss the current liability accounts that are found on most balance sheets.

Accounts Payable

Most companies do not produce all the goods and services that they use in their basic operating activities. Instead, they purchase some goods and services from other businesses. Typically, these transactions are made on credit with cash payments made after the goods and services have been provided. As a result, these transactions create accounts payable, also called **trade accounts payable.** *Accounting Trends & Techniques* (published by the AICPA) examined the reporting practices of 600 companies and found that most companies use the term **accounts payable.**[1]

For many companies, trade credit is a relatively inexpensive way to finance the purchase of inventory because interest does not normally accrue on accounts payable. As an incentive to encourage more sales, some vendors offer generous credit terms that may allow the buyer to resell merchandise and collect cash before payment must be made to the original vendor.

Some managers may be tempted to delay payment to suppliers as long as possible to conserve cash. This strategy normally is not advisable. Most successful companies develop positive working relationships with suppliers to ensure that they receive quality goods and services. A positive relationship can be destroyed by slow payment of debt. In addition, financial analysts become concerned if a business does not meet its obligations to trade creditors on a timely basis because such slowness often indicates that a company is experiencing financial difficulties. Both managers and analysts use the accounts payable turnover ratio to evaluate effectiveness in managing payables.

Accounts Payable Titles (sample of 600 companies)

0 100 200 300 400 500

- Combined with others
- Trade accounts payable
- Accounts payable

KEY RATIO ANALYSIS

Accounts Payable Turnover

Learning Objective 3
Analyze the accounts payable turnover ratio.

❓ ANALYTICAL QUESTION

How efficient is management in meeting obligations to suppliers?

% RATIO AND COMPARISONS

The accounts payable turnover ratio is computed as follows:

$$\text{Accounts Payable Turnover} = \text{Cost of Goods Sold} \div \text{Average Accounts Payable}$$

The 2006 accounts payable turnover ratio for Starbucks was:

$$\$3,178,791 \div \$280,956^* = 11.3$$
$$^*(\$220,975 + \$340,937) \div 2 = \$280,956$$

COMPARISONS OVER TIME			COMPARISONS WITH COMPETITORS	
Starbucks			Peet's Coffee	Caribou Coffee
2004	2005	2006	2006	2006
9.9	10.2	11.3	8.9	10.2

💡 INTERPRETATIONS

In General   The accounts payable turnover ratio measures how quickly management is paying trade accounts. A high accounts payable ratio normally suggests that a company is paying its suppliers in a timely manner. The ratio can be stated more intuitively by dividing it into the number of days in a year:

$$\text{Average Age of Payables} = 365 \text{ Days} \div \text{Turnover Ratio}$$

The 2006 average age of payables for Starbucks was:

$$365 \text{ Days} \div 11.3 = 32.3 \text{ Days}$$

Focus Company Analysis   The accounts payable turnover for Starbucks is stronger than both of its competitors and is fairly stable over time. Usually, a low ratio would raise questions concerning a company's liquidity. Starbucks, on average, pays its creditors within approximately 30 days, which represent normal credit terms. Analysts would consider this ratio to be strong.

A Few Cautions   The accounts payable turnover ratio is an average based on all accounts payable. The ratio might not reflect reality if a company pays some creditors on time but is late with others. The ratio is also subject to manipulation. Managers could be late in paying creditors during the entire year but catch up at year-end so that the ratio is at an acceptable level. As our focus company analysis indicates, a low ratio can indicate either liquidity problems (i.e., the company is not able to generate sufficient cash to meet its obligations) or aggressive cash management (i.e., the company maintains only the minimum amount of cash necessary to support its operating activities). The first is a problem; the second is a strength. Analysts need to study other factors (such as the current ratio and the amount of cash generated from operating activities) to determine which is the case.

Accrued Liabilities

ACCRUED LIABILITIES are expenses that have been incurred but have not been paid at the end of the accounting period.

In many situations, a business incurs an expense in one accounting period and makes the cash payment in another period. **Accrued liabilities** are expenses that have been incurred before the end of an accounting period but have not been paid. These expenses include items such as property taxes, electricity, and salaries. The balance sheet for Starbucks lists three of these items: accrued compensation and related costs, accrued occupancy costs (rent), and accrued taxes. Accrued liabilities are recorded as adjusting entries at year-end.

Accrued Taxes Payable

Like individuals, corporations must pay taxes on the income they earn. Corporate tax rates are graduated with large corporations paying a top federal tax rate of 35 percent. Corporations may also pay state and local income taxes and, in some cases, foreign income taxes. The notes to the Starbucks annual report include the following information pertaining to taxes:

The provision for income taxes consists of the following (*in thousands*):

Fiscal Year Ended	Oct 1, 2006	Oct 2, 2005	Oct 3, 2004
Current taxes:			
Federal	$332,202	$273,178	$188,647
State	57,759	51,949	36,383
Foreign	12,398	14,106	10,193
Deferred taxes, net	(77,589)	(37,256)	(3,469)
Total	$324,770	$301,977	$231,754

REAL WORLD EXCERPT

STARBUCKS

ANNUAL REPORT

The 2006 federal income tax for Starbucks ($332.2 million) was approximately 59 percent of its U.S. earnings ($564.3 million). For most corporations, federal income taxes represent a major cost.

Accrued Compensation and Related Costs

At the end of each accounting period, employees usually have earned salaries that have not yet been paid. Unpaid salaries may be reported as part of accrued liabilities or as a separate item, as is the case with Starbucks (the amount shown on the balance sheet is $288.9 million). In addition to reporting salaries that have been earned but not paid, companies must report the cost of unpaid benefits, including retirement programs, vacation time, and health insurance.

Let's look at vacation time as an example. Typically, a business grants employees paid vacation time based on the number of months they have worked. Under the matching concept, the cost of vacation time must be recorded in the year employees perform a service rather than the year they actually take vacation. If Starbucks estimates the cost of accrued vacation time to be $125,000, accountants make the following adjusting entry at the end of the fiscal year:

Compensation expense (+E, −SE)	125,000	
Accrued vacation liability (+L)		125,000

Assets	=	Liabilities	+	Stockholders' Equity
		Accrued vacation liability +125,000		Compensation expense −125,000

When the vacations are taken (during the next summer), the accountants record the following:

Accrued vacation liability (−L)	125,000	
Cash (−A)		125,000

Assets	=	Liabilities	+	Stockholders' Equity
Cash −125,000		Accrued vacation liability −125,000		

Starbucks does not separately disclose the amount of accrued vacation liability. Instead, the company reports this liability as part of accrued compensation. Apparently, the amount of accrued vacation liability is not material in management's opinion. Most analysts would probably agree.

Payroll Taxes

All payrolls are subject to a variety of taxes including federal, state, and local income taxes, Social Security taxes, and federal and state unemployment taxes. Employees pay some of these taxes and employers pay others. While we will look at only the two largest deductions for most people, reporting is similar for each type of payroll tax:

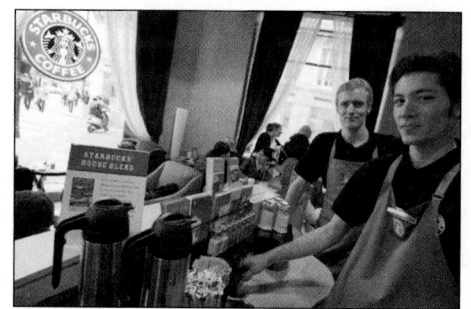

Employee Income Taxes Employers are required to withhold income taxes for each employee. The amount of income tax withheld is recorded by the employer as a current liability between the date of the deduction and the date the amount is remitted to the government. Federal Income Tax Withheld is often referred to as **FITW.**

Employee FICA Taxes The Social Security taxes paid by employees are called **FICA taxes** because they are required by the Federal Insurance Contributions Act. These taxes are imposed in equal amounts on both the employee and the employer. Effective January 1, 2008, the Social Security tax rate was 6.2 percent on the first $102,000 paid to each employee during the year. In addition, a separate 1.45 percent Medicare tax applies to all income. Therefore, the FICA tax rate is 7.65 percent on income up to $102,000 and 1.45 percent on all income above $102,000.

Employee compensation expense includes all funds earned by employees as well as funds paid to others on behalf of employees. As a result, the cost of hiring employees is much more than the amount that those employees actually receive in cash.

To illustrate a payroll, let's assume that Starbucks accumulated the following information in its records for the first two weeks of June 2009:

Salaries and wages earned	$1,800,000
Income taxes withheld	275,000
FICA taxes (employees' share)	105,000

The entry to record the payroll is normally made with two entries. The first entry records amounts paid to employees or withheld from amounts they have earned:

Compensation expense (+E, −SE)	1,800,000	
Liability for income taxes withheld (+L)		275,000
FICA payable (+L)		105,000
Cash (−A)		1,420,000

Assets	=	Liabilities	+	Stockholders' Equity
Cash −1,420,000		FICA payable +105,000		Compensation
		Liability for income		expense −1,800,000
		taxes withheld +275,000		

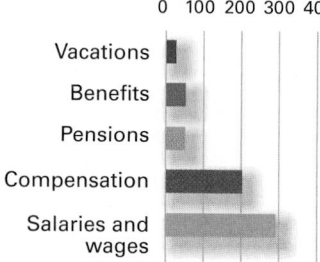

Types of Employee-Related Liabilities (sample of 600 companies)

0 100 200 300 400

- Vacations
- Benefits
- Pensions
- Compensation
- Salaries and wages

The second entry records the FICA tax that employers must pay from their own funds. This additional tax payment is required by federal law. The amount is equal to the amount that is paid by employees:

| Compensation expense (+E, −SE) . . . . | 105,000 | |
| FICA payable (+L) . . . . | | 105,000 |

Assets	=	Liabilities	+	Stockholders' Equity	
		FICA payable +105,000		Compensation expense	−105,000

Accounting Trends & Techniques found that most companies in its sample of 600 companies report employee-related liabilities.[2]

Notes Payable

Learning Objective 4
Report notes payable and explain the time value of money.

When a company borrows money, a formal written contract is usually prepared. Obligations supported by these contracts are called *notes payable*. A note payable specifies the amount borrowed, the date by which it must be repaid, and the interest rate associated with the borrowing.

Creditors are willing to lend cash because they will earn interest in return for giving up the use of their money for a period. This simple concept is called the **time value of money.** The longer borrowed money is held, the larger is the total dollar amount of interest expense. Interest at a given interest rate on a two-year loan is more than interest on a one-year loan. To the borrower, interest is an expense; to the creditor, it is revenue.

The TIME VALUE OF MONEY is interest that is associated with the use of money over time.

To calculate interest, three variables must be considered: (1) the principal (i.e., the cash that was borrowed), (2) the annual interest rate, and (3) the time period for the loan. The interest formula is

Interest = Principal × Interest Rate × Time

To illustrate, assume that on November 1, 2009, Starbucks borrows $100,000 cash on a one-year, 12 percent note payable. The interest is payable on March 31, 2010, and October 31, 2010. The principal is payable at the maturity date, October 31, 2010. The note is recorded in the accounts as follows:

| Cash (+A) . . . . | 100,000 | |
| Notes payable, short-term (+L) . . . . | | 100,000 |

Assets	=	Liabilities	+	Stockholders' Equity
Cash +100,000		Notes payable +100,000		

Interest is an expense of the period in which the money is used. Under the matching concept, interest expense is recorded when it is incurred rather than when the cash actually is paid. Because Starbucks uses the money for two months during 2009, it records interest expense in 2009 for two months, even though cash is not paid until March 31.

The computation of interest expense for 2009 is as follows:

Interest = Principal × Interest Rate × Time
$2,000   = $100,000 ×   12%   × 2/12

---

[2] Reprinted with permission from *Accounting Trends & Techniques*. Copyright © 2006 by the American Institute of Certified Public Accountants, Inc.

The entry to record interest expense on December 31, 2009 is

Interest expense (+E, −SE)	2,000	
Interest payable (+L)		2,000

Assets	=	Liabilities	+	Stockholders' Equity
		Interest payable +2,000		Interest expense −2,000

On March 31, 2010, Starbucks would pay $5,000 in interest, which includes the $2,000 accrued and reported in 2009 plus the $3,000 interest accrued in the first three months of 2010. The following journal entry would be made:

Interest expense (+E, −SE)	3,000	
Interest payable (−L)	2,000	
Cash (−A)		5,000

Assets	=	Liabilities	+	Stockholders' Equity
Cash −5,000		Interest payable −2,000		Interest expense −3,000

Current Portion of Long-Term Debt

The distinction between current and long-term debt is important for both managers and analysts. Because current debt must be paid within the next year, companies must have sufficient cash to repay it. To provide accurate information on its current liabilities, a company must reclassify its long-term debt as a current liability within a year of its maturity date. Assume that Starbucks signed a note payable of $5 million on January 1, 2009. Repayment is required on December 1, 2011. The December 31, 2009 and 2010, balance sheets would report the following:

December 31, 2009

Long-term liabilities:	
Note payable	$5,000,000

December 31, 2010

Current liabilities:	
Current portion of long-term note	$5,000,000

An example of this type of disclosure can be seen in Exhibit 9.1. Notice that in 2006, Starbucks reported $762 thousand as the current portion of long-term debt to be paid in full during the following accounting period. In some cases, companies will refinance debt when it comes due rather than pay out cash currently on hand.

Refinanced Debt: Current or Noncurrent?

Instead of repaying a debt from current cash, a company may refinance it either by negotiating a new loan agreement with a new maturity date or by borrowing money from a new creditor and repaying the original creditor. If a company intends to refinance a currently maturing debt and has the ability to do so, should the debt be classified as a current or a long-term liability? Remember that analysts are interested in a company's current liabilities because those liabilities will generate cash outflows in the next accounting period. If a liability will not generate a cash outflow in the next accounting period, GAAP require that it not be classified as current. This rule is illustrated by a note from the General Mills annual report.

> We have a revolving credit agreement expiring in January 2006 that provides us with the ability to refinance short-term borrowing on a long-term basis. Therefore we have reclassified a portion of our notes payable to long-term debt.

Deferred Revenues

In most business transactions, cash is paid after the product or service has been delivered. In some cases, cash is paid before delivery. You have probably paid for magazines that you will receive at some time in the future. The publisher collects money for your subscription in advance, before the magazine is published. When a company collects cash before the related revenue has been earned, the cash is called **deferred revenues** or unearned revenues. The popular Starbucks card permits customers to pay in advance for their coffee. The advantage for the customer is convenience at the point of sale. The advantage for the company is that Starbucks is able to collect and use cash before customers actually buy the product. The Starbucks report shows that the company has collected $231.926 million from customers prior to providing them with coffee and explains the amount with the following note

> Revenues from stored value cards are recognized upon redemption. Until the redemption of stored value cards, outstanding customer balances on such cards are included in "Deferred revenue."

Under the revenue principle, revenue cannot be recorded until it has been earned. Deferred revenues are reported as a liability because cash has been collected but the related revenue has not been earned by the end of the accounting period. The obligation to provide services or goods in the future still exists. These obligations are classified as current or long term, depending on when they must be satisfied.

Estimated Liabilities Reported on the Balance Sheet

Some recorded liabilities are based on estimates because the exact amount will not be known until a future date. For example, an estimated liability is created when a company offers a warranty with the products it sells. The cost of providing future repair work must be estimated and recorded as a liability (and expense) in the period in which the product is sold.

Starbucks offers a warranty on coffee brewing and espresso equipment sold in its stores but does not record an estimated warranty liability at the time of sale. Rather than repairing brewing machines, the company gives the customer the right to return any defective product for a period of up to 24 months. The estimated amount of product that will be returned is reported as a reduction from sales revenue in the year the sales are recorded.

Estimated Liabilities Reported in the Notes

Each of the liabilities that we have discussed is reported on the balance sheet at a specific dollar amount because they involve the probable future sacrifice of economic benefits. Some transactions or events create only a reasonably possible (but not probable) future sacrifice of economic benefits. These situations create **contingent liabilities,** which are potential liabilities that are created as a result of a past event. A contingent liability may or may not become a recorded liability depending on future events. A situation that produces a contingent liability also causes a contingent loss.

DEFERRED REVENUES (or unearned revenues) are revenues that have been collected but not earned; they are liabilities until the goods or services are provided.

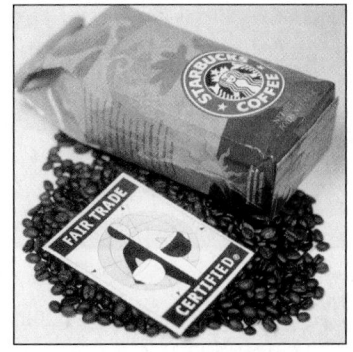

Learning Objective 5
Report contingent liabilities.

A CONTINGENT LIABILITY is a potential liability that has arisen as the result of a past event; not an effective liability until some future event occurs.

Contingent Liability Examples

Lawsuits   Environmental   Product
                          problems   warranties

Whether a situation produces a recorded or a contingent liability depends on two factors: the probability of a future economic sacrifice and the ability of management to estimate the amount of the liability. The following table illustrates the possibilities:

	Probable	**Reasonably Possible**	**Remote**
Subject to estimate	Record as liability	Disclose in note	Disclosure not required
Not subject to estimate	Disclose in note	Disclose in note	Disclosure not required

The probabilities of occurrence are defined in the following manner:

1. Probable—the chance that the future event or events will occur is high.
2. Reasonably possible—the chance that the future event or events will occur is more than remote but less than likely.
3. Remote—the chance that the future event or events will occur is slight.

In summary, (1) a liability that is both probable and capable of being reasonably estimated must be recorded and reported on the balance sheet, (2) a liability that is reasonably possible must be disclosed in a note in the financial statements whether it can be estimated or not, and (3) remote contingencies are not disclosed.

The notes to Starbucks's annual report include the following:

Note 18: Commitments and Contingencies

The Company is party to various legal proceedings arising in the ordinary course of its business, but it is not currently a party to any legal proceeding that management believes would have a material adverse effect on the consolidated financial position or results of operations of the Company.

Starbucks did not need to record a liability on the balance sheet because a loss was not probable. Harley-Davidson disclosed a common contingency in its notes:

Note 7: Commitments and Contingencies

A state court jury in California found the Company liable for compensatory and punitive damages of $7.2 million, including interest, in a lawsuit brought by a supplier of aftermarket exhaust systems. The Company immediately appealed the verdict.

In this case, the existence of a liability was a reasonable possibility. As a result, GAAP required Harley-Davidson to disclose the lawsuit in its notes. The company subsequently reached an out-of-court settlement for $5 million. At that point, the loss was probable, which required recording the loss and the related liability on the balance sheet.

Accounting Trends & Techniques studied the financial statements of 600 companies and found that litigation was the most common type of contingent liability.[3]

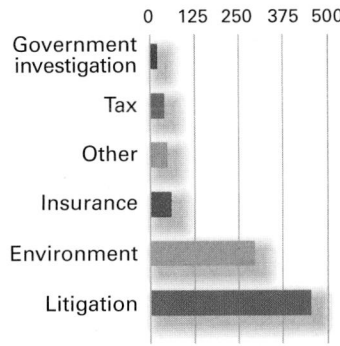

Contingent Liabilities (sample of 600 companies)

Working Capital Management

Working capital is defined as the dollar difference between current assets and current liabilities. Working capital is important to both managers and financial analysts because it has a significant impact on the health and profitability of a company.

The working capital accounts are actively managed to achieve a balance between costs and benefits. If a business has too little working capital, it runs the risk of not being able to meet its obligations to creditors. On the other hand, too much working capital may tie up resources in unproductive assets and incur additional costs. Excess inventory, for example, ties up dollars that could be invested more profitably elsewhere in the business and incurs additional costs associated with storage and deterioration.

Changes in working capital accounts are also important to managers and analysts because they have a direct impact on cash flows from operating activities reported on the statement of cash flows.

Learning Objective 6
Explain the importance of working capital and its impact on cash flows.

WORKING CAPITAL is the dollar difference between total current assets and total current liabilities.

 Working Capital and Cash Flows

FOCUS ON
CASH FLOWS

Many working capital accounts have a direct relationship to income-producing activities. Accounts receivable, for example, are related to sales revenue: Accounts receivable increase when sales are made on credit. Cash is collected when the customer pays the bill. Similarly, accounts payable increase when an expense is incurred without a cash payment. A cash outflow occurs when the account is paid. Changes in working capital accounts that are related to income-producing activities must be considered when computing cash flows from operating activities.

EFFECT ON STATEMENT OF CASH FLOWS

In General On the statement of cash flows, net income is adjusted (under the indirect method) to compute cash flows from operating activities. Changes in working capital accounts have the impact shown in the following table:

	Effect on Cash Flows
Operating activities (indirect method)	
Net income	$xxx
Adjusted for: Decreases in current assets* or increases in current liabilities	+
Adjusted for: Increases in current assets* or decreases in current liabilities	−
*Other than cash	

---

[3]Reprinted with permission form *Accounting Trends & Techniques*. Copyright © 2006 by the American Institute of Certified Public Accountants, Inc.

Focus Company Analysis   A segment of the Starbucks consolidated statements of cash flows, prepared using the indirect method, follows. Notice the steady improvement in cash flows from operations from 2004 to 2006. These substantial cash flows are important for a company with the growth strategy that Starbucks is following.

STARBUCKS CORPORATION Consolidated Statements of Cash Flows In thousands			
Fiscal Year Ended	**Oct 1, 2006**	**Oct 2, 2005**	**Oct 3, 2004**
OPERATING ACTIVITIES			
Net earnings	$ 564,259	$ 494,370	$ 388,880
Adjustments to reconcile net earnings to net cash provided by operating activities:			
Cumulative effect of accounting change for FIN 47, net of taxes	17,214	—	—
Depreciation and amortization	412,625	367,207	314,047
Provision for impairments and asset disposals	19,622	19,464	17,948
Deferred income taxes, net	(84,324)	(31,253)	(3,770)
Equity in income of investees	(60,570)	(49,537)	(31,707)
Distributions of income from equity investees	49,238	30,919	38,328
Stock-based compensation	105,664	—	—
Tax benefit from exercise of stock options	1,318	109,978	63,405
Excess tax benefit from exercise of stock options	(117,368)	—	—
Net amortization of premium on securities	2,013	10,097	11,603
Cash provided/(used) by changes in operating assets and liabilities:			
Inventories	(85,527)	(121,618)	(77,662)
Accounts payable	104,966	9,717	27,948
Accrued compensation and related costs	54,424	22,711	54,929
Accrued taxes	132,725	14,435	7,677
Deferred revenue	56,547	53,276	47,590
Other operating assets and liabilities	(41,193)	(6,851)	3,702
Net cash provided by operating activities	1,131,633	922,915	862,918

Assume that the current ratio for Starbucks is 2.0. For each of the following events, state whether the current ratio and working capital will increase or decrease:

1. Starbucks incurs an account payable of $250,000 with no change in current assets.

2. The company borrows $1,000,000 in long-term debt.

3. The company pays taxes payable in the amount of $750,000.

4. The company finances a new building with long-term debt.

After you have completed your answers, check them with the solutions at the bottom of the page.

LONG-TERM LIABILITIES

Long-term liabilities include all obligations that are not classified as current liabilities, such as long-term notes payable and bonds payable. Typically, a long-term liability will require payment more than one year in the future. These obligations may be created by borrowing money, or they may result from other activities.

Most companies borrow money on a long-term basis in order to purchase operational assets. To reduce risk for creditors, some companies agree to use specific assets as security. If the liability is not satisfied, the creditor may take ownership of the asset. A liability supported by this type of agreement is called a **secured debt.** An unsecured debt is one for which the creditor relies primarily on the borrower's integrity and general earning power.

> **Learning Objective 7**
> Report long-term liabilities.

LONG-TERM LIABILITIES are all of the entity's obligations not classified as current liabilities.

Long-Term Notes Payable and Bonds

Companies can raise long-term debt capital directly from a number of financial service organizations including banks, insurance companies, and pension plans. Raising debt from one of these organizations is known as **private placement.** This type of debt is often called a **note payable,** which is a written promise to pay a stated sum at one or more specified future dates called the **maturity date(s).**

In many cases, a company's need for debt capital exceeds the financial ability of any single creditor. In these situations, the company may issue publicly traded debt called **bonds.** The opportunity to sell a bond in established markets provides bondholders with an important benefit. They can sell their bonds to other investors prior to maturity if they have an immediate need for cash. Because bonds provide liquidity to investors, they are more likely to lend money to a company. Bonds will be discussed in detail in the next chapter.

Accounting for long-term debt is based on the same concepts used in accounting for short-term notes payable. A liability is recorded when the debt is incurred and interest expense is recorded with the passage of time.

*Current ratio	Working capital
1. Decrease	Decrease
2. Increase	Increase
3. Increase	No change
4. No change	No change

Self-Study Quiz
Solutions

Business operations are global in nature. Successful corporations market their products in many countries and locate manufacturing facilities around the world based on cost and productivity. The financing of corporations also has become international, even for companies that do not have international operations. Borrowing money in a foreign currency raises some interesting accounting and management issues.

Borrowing in Foreign Currencies

Many corporations with foreign operations elect to finance those operations with foreign debt to lessen exchange rate risk. This type of risk exists because the relative value of each nation's currency varies on virtually a daily basis. As this book was being written, the British pound was worth approximately $2.00.

A U.S. corporation that conducts business operations in England might decide to borrow pounds to finance its operations there. The profits from the business, which will be in pounds, can be used to pay off the debt, which is in pounds. If this business earned profits in pounds but paid off debt in dollars, it would be exposed to exchange rate risk because the relative value of the dollar and the pound fluctuates.

Foreign corporations face this same problem. A note to a recent annual report from Toyota, a Japanese company that does significant business in the United States, stated:

REAL WORLD EXCERPT

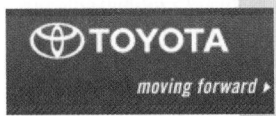

ANNUAL REPORT

> Earnings declined in the current year ended, as the appreciation of the yen aggravated the adverse effects of sluggish demand. . . . The movement in exchange rates reduced operating income of the company. Losses on currency exchange thus offset most of the cost savings we achieved.

Toyota has borrowed a large amount of money in the United States to lessen the exchange rate risk it faces. The company also owns and operates many factories in the United States.

Even if a company does not have international operations, it may elect to borrow in foreign markets. Interest rates often are low in countries experiencing a recession. These situations give corporations the opportunity to borrow at a lower cost.

For reporting purposes, accountants must convert, or translate, foreign debt into U.S. dollars. Conversion rates for all major currencies are published in most newspapers. To illustrate foreign currency translation, assume that Starbucks borrowed 1 million pounds (£). For the Starbucks annual report, the accountant must use the conversion rate as of the balance sheet date, which we assume was £1.00 to $2.00. The dollar equivalent of the debt is $2,000,000 (£1,000,000 × 2.00). The dollar equivalent of foreign debt may change if the conversion rate changes even without any additional borrowings or repayments.

The notes to the balance sheet for Starbucks indicate that the company has borrowed money only in the United States. In contrast, many companies with international operations borrow in the local currency of the countries in which they operate. These companies often repay the foreign currency debt with earnings (in the same currency) from operations with the foreign country.

Lease Liabilities

An OPERATING LEASE does not meet any of the four criteria established by GAAP and does not cause the recording of an asset and liability.

Companies often lease assets rather than purchase them. For example, renting extra delivery trucks during a busy period is more economical than owning them if they are not needed during the rest of the year. When a company leases an asset on a short-term basis, the agreement is called an **operating lease.** No liability is recorded when an operating lease is created. Instead, a company records rent expense as it uses the asset. Assume that on December 15, 2009, Starbucks signed an operating lease contract to rent five large trucks during January 2010. No liability is recorded in 2009. Rent expense is recorded during January 2010 as the trucks are actually used.

For a number of reasons, a company may prefer to lease an asset on a long-term basis rather than purchase it. This type of lease is called a **capital lease.** In essence, a capital lease contract represents the purchase and financing of an asset even though it is legally a lease agreement. Unlike an operating lease, capital leases are accounted for as if an asset had been purchased by recording an asset and a liability. Because of the significant differences between operating and capital leases, GAAP have specified criteria to distinguish between them. If a lease meets any of the following criteria, it is considered a capital lease:

> A CAPITAL LEASE meets at least one of the four criteria established by GAAP and results in the recording of an asset and liability.

- The lease term is 75 percent or more of the asset's expected economic life.
- Ownership of the asset is transferred to the lessee at the end of the lease term.
- The lease contract permits the lessee to purchase the asset at a price that is lower than its fair market value.
- The present value of the lease payments is 90 percent or more of the fair market value of the asset when the lease is signed.

If managers have a choice of recording a lease as operating or capital, most would prefer to record it as an operating lease. By doing so, the company is able to report less debt on its balance sheet. In the notes to their financial statements, Starbucks reports capital lease obligations of $4.1 million which are included on the balance under the category "other long-term liabilities." Many financial analysts are concerned that companies can avoid reporting debt associated with capital leases by structuring the lease agreement in a manner that meets the requirements for recording it as an operating lease.

To record a capital lease, it is necessary to determine the current cash equivalent of the required lease payments. Assume that Starbucks signs a lease for new delivery trucks. The accountant has determined that the lease is a capital lease with a current cash equivalent of $250,000. Once the lease is signed, the transaction would be recorded in a manner similar to the actual purchase of delivery trucks:

Leased equipment (+A)	250,000	
Lease payable (+L)		250,000

Assets	=	Liabilities	+	Stockholders' Equity
Leased equipment +250,000		Lease Payable +250,000		

In this example, we told you the current cash equivalent of the lease. In the next section, on present value concepts, we will show you how this amount is computed.

PRESENT VALUE CONCEPTS

Our discussion of capital leases raised an interesting question about liabilities: Is the recorded amount of the liability the actual amount of cash that will be paid in the future? For example, if I agree to pay you $10,000 five years from now, should I report a liability of $10,000 on my personal balance sheet? To answer such questions, we will now introduce some relatively simple mathematics called **present value concepts.** These concepts will provide a foundation for our discussion of bond liabilities in the next chapter.

> **Learning Objective 8**
> Compute present values.

The concept of **present value** (PV) is based on the time value of money. Quite simply, money received today is worth more than money to be received one year from today (or at any other future date) because it can be used to earn interest. If you invest $1,000 today at 10 percent, you will have $1,100 in one year. In contrast, if you receive $1,000 one year from today, you will lose the opportunity to earn the $100 in interest revenue. The difference between the $1,000 and the $1,100 is the interest that can be earned during the year.

> PRESENT VALUE is the current value of an amount to be received in the future; a future amount discounted for compound interest.

Audio lecture–AP9-1
www.mhhe.com/libby6e

In one of your math classes, you have probably already solved some problems involving the time value of money. In the typical problem, you were told a certain dollar amount had been deposited in a savings account earning a specified rate of interest. You were asked to determine the dollar amount that would be in the savings account after a certain number of years. In this chapter, we will show you how to solve problems that are the opposite of the ones you have worked with. In present value problems, you will be told a dollar amount to be received in the future (such as the balance of a savings account after five years) and will be asked to determine the present value of the amount (which is the amount that must be deposited in the savings account today).

The value of money changes over time because money can earn interest. In a present value problem, you will know the dollar amount of a cash flow that occurs in the future and will need to determine its value now. The opposite situation occurs when you know the dollar amount of a cash flow that occurs today and need to determine its value at some point in the future. These problems are called future value problems. Future value concepts are discussed in a supplement to this chapter.

Present Value of a Single Amount

Present Value of a Single Amount

The present value of a single amount is the worth to you today of receiving that amount some time in the future. For instance, you might be offered an opportunity to invest in a debt instrument that would pay you $10,000 in three years. Before you decided whether to invest, you would want to determine the present value of the instrument. Graphically, the present value of $1 due at the end of the third period with an interest rate of 10 percent can be represented as follows:

To compute the present value of an amount to be received in the future, we will subtract interest that is earned over time from the amount to be received in the future. For example, if you place $100 in a savings account that earns 5%, you will have $105 at the end of a year. In a present value problem, you will be told that you have $105 at the end of the year and must compute the amount to be deposited at the beginning of the year. To solve this type of problem, you must discount the amount to be received in the future at i interest rate for n periods. The formula to compute the present value of a single amount is

$$\text{Present value} = \frac{1}{(1 + i)^n} \times \text{Amount}$$

While the formula is not difficult to use, most analysts use present value tables, calculators, or Excel. We will illustrate how to use present value tables (an explanation of how to use Excel to compute present values is presented in a supplement to this chapter). Assume that today is January 1, 2009, and you have the opportunity to receive $1,000 cash on December 31, 2011. At an interest rate of 10 percent per year, how much is the $1,000 payment worth to you on January 1, 2009? You could discount the amount year by year,[4] but it is easier to use Table A.1, Appendix A, Present Value of $1. For $i = 10\%$, $n = 3$, we find that the present value of $1 is 0.7513. The present value of $1,000 to be received at the end of three years can be computed as follows:

$$\$1,000 \times 0.7513 = \$751.30$$

From Table A.1
Interest rate = 10%
n = 3

Learning how to compute a present value amount is not difficult, but it is more important that you understand what it means. The $751.30 is the amount you would pay now to have the right to receive $1,000 at the end of three years, assuming an interest rate of 10 percent. Conceptually, you should be indifferent between having $751.30 today and receiving $1,000 in three years, because you can use financial institutions to convert dollars from the present to the future and vice versa. If you had $751.30 today but preferred $1,000 in three years, you could simply deposit the money in a savings account and it would grow to $1,000 in three years. Alternatively, if you had a contract that promised you $1,000 in three years, you could sell it to an investor for $751.30 in cash today because it would permit the investor to earn the difference in interest.

To compute the present value using Excel, enter:
= 1000/(1.10)^3

SELF-STUDY **QUIZ**

1. If the interest rate in a present value problem increases from 8 percent to 10 percent, will the present value increase or decrease?

2. What is the present value of $10,000 to be received 10 years from now if the interest rate is 5 percent, compounded annually?

After you have completed your answers, check them with the solutions at the bottom of the page.

Present Values of an Annuity

Instead of a single payment, many business problems involve multiple cash payments over a number of periods. An **annuity** is a series of consecutive payments characterized by

1. An equal dollar amount each interest period.

2. Interest periods of equal length (year, half a year, quarter, or month).

3. An equal interest rate each interest period.

An ANNUITY is a series of periodic cash receipts or payments that are equal in amount each interest period.

Examples of annuities include monthly payments on an automobile or home, yearly contributions to a savings account, and monthly pension benefits.

----

[4]The detailed discounting is as follows:

Periods	Interest for the Year	Present Value*
1	$1,000 − ($1,000 × 1/1.10) = $90.91	$1,000 − $90.91 = $909.09
2	$909.09 − ($909.09 × 1/1.10) = $82.64	$909.09 − $82.64 = $826.45
3	$826.45 − ($826.45 × 1/1.10) = $75.15†	$826.45 − $75.15 = $751.30

*Verifiable in Table A.1.   †Adjusted for rounding.

----

1. The present value will be less.
2. $10,000 × 0.6139 = $6,139

Self-Study Quiz
Solutions

Present Value of an Annuity

The present value of an annuity is the value now of a series of equal amounts to be received (or paid out) for some specified number of periods in the future. It is computed by discounting each of the equal periodic amounts. A good example of this type of problem is a retirement program that offers employees a monthly income after retirement. The present value of an annuity of $1 for three periods at 10 percent may be represented graphically as follows:

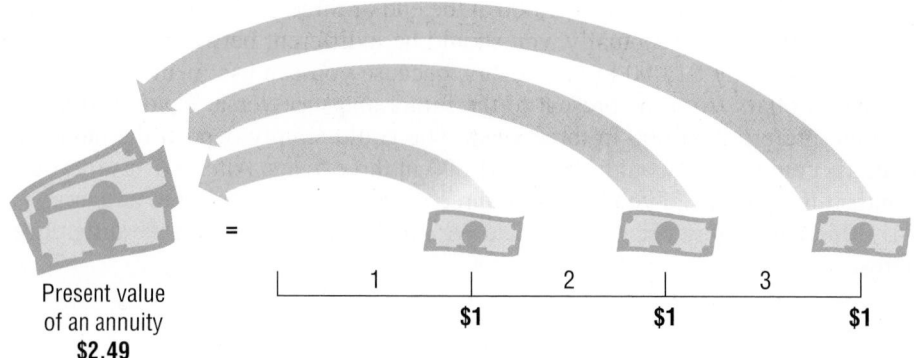

Present value
of an annuity
$2.49

Assume you are to receive $1,000 cash on each December 31, 2009, 2010, and 2011. How much would the sum of these three $1,000 future amounts be worth on January 1, 2009, assuming an interest rate of 10 percent per year? We could use Table A.1, Appendix A to calculate the present value as follows:

Year	Amount		Factor from Table A.1, Appendix A, $i = 10\%$		Present Value
1	$1,000	×	0.9091 ($n = 1$)	=	$ 909.10
2	$1,000	×	0.8264 ($n = 2$)	=	826.40
3	$1,000	×	0.7513 ($n = 3$)	=	751.30
			Total present value	=	$2,486.80

We can compute the present value of this annuity more easily however, by using Table A.2, Appendix A as follows:

From Table A.2, Interest rate = 10% n = 3

$1,000 × 2.4869 = $2,487 (rounded)

Interest Rates and Interest Periods

To compute the present value using Excel, enter:
$f_x = \text{PV}(0.10, 3, -1000)$

The preceding illustrations assumed annual periods for compounding and discounting. Although interest rates are almost always quoted on an annual basis, most compounding periods encountered in business are less than one year. When interest periods are less than a year, the values of n and i must be restated to be consistent with the length of the interest period.

To illustrate, 12 percent interest compounded annually for five years requires the use of $n = 5$ and $i = 12\%$. If compounding is quarterly, however, the interest period is one-quarter of a year (i.e., four periods per year), and the quarterly interest rate is one-quarter of the annual rate (i.e., 3 percent per quarter). Therefore, 12 percent interest compounded quarterly for five years requires use of $n = 20$ and $i = 3\%$.

A QUESTION
OF ETHICS
Truth in Advertising

Newspaper, magazine, and television advertisements are easy to misinterpret if the consumer does not understand present value concepts. For example, most car companies offer seasonal promotions with special financing incentives. A car dealer may advertise 4 percent interest on car loans when banks are charging 10 percent. Typically, the lower interest rate is not really an incentive because the dealer simply charges a higher price for cars the dealership finances. Borrowing from the bank and paying cash at the dealership may help the buyer to negotiate a lower price. Customers should use the present value concepts illustrated in this chapter to compare financing alternatives.

Another misleading advertisement, seen every January, promises magazine subscribers a chance to become an instant millionaire. The fine print discloses that the winner will receive $25,000 for 40 years, which amounts to $1,000,000 (40 × $25,000), but the present value of this annuity at 8 percent is only $298,000. While most winners are happy to get the money, they are not really millionaires.

Some consumer advocates argue that consumers should not have to study present value concepts to understand such advertisements. While some of these criticisms may be valid, the quality of information contained in advertisements that include interest rates has improved over time.

Accounting Applications of Present Values

Many business transactions require the use of future and present value concepts. So that you can enhance your understanding of these concepts, we provide three examples.

Learning Objective 9

Apply present value concepts to liabilities.

Computing the Amount of a Liability with a Single Payment

On January 1, 2009, Starbucks bought some new delivery trucks. The company signed a note and agreed to pay $200,000 on December 31, 2010, an amount representing the cash equivalent price of the trucks plus interest for two years. The market interest rate for this note was 12 percent.

To record this transaction, the accountant must first compute the present value of a single amount paid in the future. In conformity with the cost principle, the cost of the trucks is their current cash equivalent price, which is the present value of the future payment. The problem can be shown graphically as follows:

January 1, 2009	December 31, 2009	December 31, 2010
?		$200,000

The present value of the $200,000 is computed as follows:

$$\textbf{\$200,000} \times \textbf{0.7972} = \textbf{\$159,440}$$

> *From Table A.1,*
> *Interest rate = 12%*
> *n = 2*

Therefore, the journal entry is as follows:

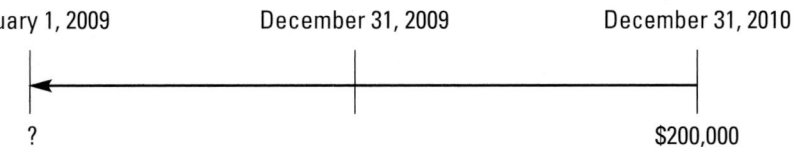

| Delivery trucks (+A) . . . . | 159,440 | |
| Note payable (+L) . . . . | | 159,440 |

Assets	=	Liabilities	+	Stockholders' Equity
Delivery trucks +159,440		Note payable +159,440		

> To compute the present value using Excel, enter:
> = 200000/(1.12)^2

After the initial transaction is recorded, each year's interest expense is recorded in an adjusting entry as follows:

| **December 31, 2009** | Interest expense (+E, −SE) . . . . | 19,133* | |
| | Note payable (+L) . . . . | | 19,133 |

*$159,440 × 12% = $19,133

Assets	=	Liabilities	+	Stockholders' Equity
		Note payable +19,133		Interest expense −19,133

December 31, 2010 Interest expense (+E, −SE) 21,429*

Note payable (+L)   21,429

*($159,440 + $19,133) × 12% = 21,429.

Assets	=	Liabilities		+	Stockholders' Equity	
		Note payable	+21,429		Interest expense	−21,429

At the end of two years, the loan amount must be repaid. The amount owed is the balance of Note Payable, which is the same as the maturity amount on the due date. The journal entry to record full payment of the debt follows:

Note payable (−L)   200,000

Cash (−A)   200,000

Assets		=	Liabilities		+	Stockholders' Equity
Cash	−200,000		Note payable	−200,000		

Computing the Amount of a Liability with an Annuity

On January 1, 2009, Starbucks bought new printing equipment. The company elected to finance the purchase with a note payable to be paid off in three years in annual installments of $163,686. Each installment includes principal plus interest on the unpaid balance at 11 percent per year. The annual installments are due on December 31, 2009, 2010, and 2011. This problem can be shown graphically as follows:

January 1, 2009	December 31, 2009	December 31, 2010	December 31, 2011
?	$163,686	$163,686	$163,686

The amount of the note can be determined by computing the present value of each installment payment, $i = 11\%$ and $n = 3$. This is an annuity because payment is made in three equal installments. The amount of the note is computed as follows:

$163,686 × 2.4437 = $400,000

From Table A.2,
Interest rate = 11%
n = 3

To compute the present value using Excel, enter:
$f_x = \text{PV}(0.11, 3, -163626)$

The acquisition on January 1, 2009 is recorded as follows:

Printing equipment (+A)   400,000

Note payable (+L)   400,000

Assets		=	Liabilities		+	Stockholders' Equity
Printig equipment	+400,000		Note payable	+400,000		

Each year, the accountant must record the payments on this note as follows:

December 31, 2009 Note payable (−L)   119,686

Interest expense (+E, −SE) ($400,000 × 11%). .   44,000

Cash (−A)   163,686

Assets		=	Liabilities		+	Stockholders' Equity	
Cash	−163,686		Note payable	−119,686		Interest expense	−44,000

December 31, 2010   Note payable (−L) 132,851
Interest expense (+E, −SE)
[($400,000 − $119,686 × 11%)] 30,835
Cash (−A) 163,686

Assets		=	Liabilities		+	Stockholders' Equity	
Cash	−163,686		Note payable	−132,851		Interest expense	−30,835

December 31, 2011   Note payable (−L) 147,463
Interest expense (+E, −SE) 16,223*
Cash (−A) 163,686

*Interest: ($400,000 − $119,686 − $132,851) × 11% = $16,223 (rounded to accommodate rounding errors).

Assets		=	Liabilities		+	Stockholders' Equity	
Cash	−163,686		Note payable	−147,463		Interest expense	−16,223

Computing the Amount of a Lease Liability

On January 1, 2009, Starbucks signed a 20-year lease for coffee roasting equipment. The lease is based on an effective interest rate of 8 percent and requires annual payments of $10,000 on December 31 of each year. The term is 100 percent of the expected life of the equipment. As a result, this lease should be recorded as a capital lease. The amount of the liability is the present value of the lease payments, computed as follows:

$10,000 × 9.8181 = $98,181

From Table A.2, Interest rate = 8% n = 20

The signing of the lease on January 1, 2009 is recorded as follows:

Roasting equipment (+A) 98,181
Lease payable (+L) 98,181

Assets		=	Liabilities		+	Stockholders' Equity
Roasting equipment	+98,181		Lease payable	+98,181		

To compute the present value using Excel, enter:
f_x = PV(0.08,20,−10,000)

In the next chapter, we will use the present value techniques you have just learned to understand how to account for bonds.

DEMONSTRATION CASE

(Try to answer the questions before proceeding to the suggested solution that follows.) Muller Construction completed several transactions during the year. In each case, decide if a liability should be recorded and, if so, determine the amount. Assume the current date is December 31, 2009.

1. Employees earned salaries of $100,000 which have not been paid at year-end. The employer share of FICA is $7,000.

2. The Company borrowed $100,000 on June 30th at 7 percent interest. No payments associated with this loan have been made.

3. A customer made a $75,000 down payment on a construction project. Work will begin next month.

4. The company lost a lawsuit for $250,000 but plans to appeal.

5. A new truck was leased for a period equal to 85 percent of the expected life of the truck.

6. On December 31, 2009, a bank lent money to Muller. The company agreed to repay the bank $100,000 on December 31, 2010. The bank charges 5 percent interest.

7. The company signed a loan agreement that requires it to pay $50,000 per year for 20 years. The interest rate is 8 percent.

SUGGESTED SOLUTION

1. A liability of $107,000 should be recorded.

2. The amount borrowed ($100,000) should be recorded as a liability on June 30th. In addition, interest accrued but not paid should be recorded as a liability at year-end. This amount is $100,000 \times 7\% \times 6/12 = \$3,500$.

3. The customer deposit ($75,000) is a liability until work is performed and the related revenue earned.

4. Most likely, the $250,000 should be recorded as a liability, unless the grounds for appeal significantly reduce the probability that the $250,000 will eventually be paid.

5. Because the lease covers more than 75 percent of the estimated life of the truck, a liability should be recorded. The amount is the present value of the lease payments (which were not given in the problem).

6. A liability should be recorded for the present value of the obligation. The amount is determined by using the factor from Table A.1 for $n = 1$, $i = 5\%$: $100,000 \times 0.9524 = \$95,240$.

7. A liability should be recorded for the present value of the obligation. The amount is determined by using the factor from Table A.2 for $n = 20$, $i = 8\%$: $50,000 \times 9.8181 = \$490,905$.

Chapter Supplement A

Income Taxes and Retirement Benefits

Two aspects of business operations, income taxes and employee retirement benefits, may result in the creation of either an asset or a liability. On most financial statements, you will see these items as liabilities, so we will discuss them along with other liabilities.

Deferred Taxes

DEFERRED TAX ITEMS exist because of timing differences caused by reporting revenues and expenses according to GAAP on a company's income statement and according to the Internal Revenue Code on the tax return.

TEMPORARY DIFFERENCES are timing differences that cause deferred income taxes and will reverse, or turn around, in the future.

Because separate rules govern the preparation of financial statements (GAAP) and tax returns (Internal Revenue Code), income tax expense and current taxes payable often differ in amount. To reflect this difference, companies establish a separate account called Deferred Taxes. In practice, deferred taxes can be either assets (such as taxes related to cash collected from a customer, which is taxable before it is reported as a revenue on the income statement) or liabilities (such as taxes related to depreciation, which is reported on the tax return before it is reported on the income statement). Starbucks has deferred tax amounts reported as both assets and liabilities.

Deferred tax items exist because of timing differences in the reporting of revenues and expenses on the income statement and tax return. These temporary differences are caused by differences between GAAP, which govern financial statement preparation, and the Internal Revenue Code, which governs the preparation of tax returns.

Deferred tax amounts always reverse themselves. For example, at some point in the future the accelerated depreciation recorded on the tax return will be less than the straight-line depreciation reported on the income statement (recall from Chapter 8 that accelerated depreciation causes higher depreciation expense compared to straight line in the early years of an asset's life and lower depreciation in the later years). When a deferred tax liability reverses, the deferred tax amount is reduced, and the company pays more taxes to the IRS than the amount of income tax expense reported on the income statement.

Let's consider a simple example. Assume that in 2009, Starbuck's reported $25 million in depreciation expense on its income statement and $33 million in depreciation expense on its tax return. The difference ($33 million − $25 million = $8 million) is a temporary difference that creates a deferred tax liability because it will reverse at sometime in the future and require a payment to the IRS. The amount of the deferred tax liability is found by multiplying the temporary difference by the corporate tax rate. Assuming a tax rate of 35%, the deferred tax amount is $2.8 million ($8 million × 35%). This amount would be recorded as an increase in the deferred tax liability for 2009.

To see a reversal of a deferred tax, assume in 2011, Starbucks reports $40 million in depreciation expense on the income statement and $35 million on the tax return. Because the amount reported on the tax return is less than the amount on the income statement, deferred taxes reverse. The reversal is the difference in depreciation expense multiplied by the corporate tax rate ($40 million − $35 million = $5 million × 35% = $1.75 million. This amount would be reported as a reduction of deferred taxes in 2011.

The computation of deferred taxes involves some complexities that are discussed in advanced accounting courses. At this point, you need to understand only that deferred tax assets and liabilities are caused by temporary differences between the income statement and tax return. Each temporary difference has an impact on the income statement in one accounting period and on the tax return in another.

Accrued Retirement Benefits

Most employers provide retirement programs for their employees. In a defined contribution program, the employer makes cash payments to an investment fund. When employees retire, they are entitled to a portion of the fund. If the investment strategy of the fund is successful, the retirement income for the employees will be larger. If the strategy is not successful, it will be lower. The employer's only obligation is to make the required annual payments to the fund that are recorded as pension expense. Starbucks offers a defined contribution program to its employees and, therefore, does not have any pension liabilities.

Other employers offer defined benefit programs. Under these programs, employees' retirement benefits are based on a percentage of their pay at retirement or a certain number of dollars for each year of employment. In these cases, the pension expense that must be accrued each year is the change in the current cash value of employees' retirement packages. The current cash value changes each year for a variety of reasons. For example, it will change (1) as employees draw closer to receiving benefits, (2) as employees' retirement benefits increase as a result of higher pay or longer service, and (3) if the employees' life expectancies change. The company must report a pension liability based on any portion of the current cash value of the retirement program that has not actually been funded. For example, if the company were to transfer $8 million to the pension fund while the current cash value of the pension obligation was $10 million, the company would report a $2 million pension liability on its balance sheet.

For many corporations, especially those with unionized work forces, the financial obligation associated with defined benefit retirement programs can be huge. A recent financial statement for Ford Motor Company disclosed the following information:

REAL WORLD EXCERPT
Ford Motor Company
ANNUAL REPORT

Note 2

Employee Retirement Benefits (in millions)

Accumulated postretirement benefit obligation	
Retirees	$ 7,035.0
Active employees eligible to retire	2,269.6
Other active employees	5,090.6
Total accumulated obligation	$14,395.2

To put the size of this obligation in perspective, it represents an amount nearly equal to Ford's total stockholders' equity. The retirement benefit expense for the year was $1.3 billion, which exceeded the income Ford earned for the previous three years. This type of information is important to analysts who are interested in forecasting a company's future cash flows. Ford has a very large obligation to transfer cash to its retirement fund.

In recent years, employer-provided health care benefits have been the subject of a great deal of discussion. Many large companies pay for a portion of their employees' health insurance costs. These payments are recorded as an expense in the current accounting period. In addition, some employers continue to pay for health care costs after their employees retire. The cost of these future benefits must be estimated and recorded as an expense for the periods in which the employees perform services. The recording of future health care costs for retired employees is an excellent example of the use of estimates in accounting. Imagine the difficulty of estimating future health care costs when you do not know how long employees will live, how healthy they will be during their retirements, and how much money doctors and hospitals will charge for their services in the future.

Accounting for retirement benefits is a complex topic that is discussed in detail in subsequent accounting courses. We introduce the topic at this point as another example of the application of the matching concept, which requires that expenses be recorded in the year in which benefits are received. This accounting procedure also avoids creating improper incentives for managers. If the future cost of retirement benefits were not included in the period in which work is performed, managers might have the incentive to offer employees increases in their retirement benefits instead of increases in their salaries. In this manner, managers could understate the true cost of employees' services and make their companies appear more profitable.

Chapter Supplement B

Federal Income Tax Concepts

Unlike sole proprietorships and partnerships, corporations are separate legal entities, so they are required to pay income taxes. Corporations must prepare a U.S. Corporate Tax Return (Form 1120), which lists their revenue and expenses for the year. The amount of the tax payable is based on the taxable income reported on their tax return. As was mentioned earlier, taxable income usually differs from the income reported on the income statement because the income statement is prepared in conformity with GAAP, but the tax return is prepared in conformity with the Internal Revenue Code.

Calculation of Taxes Payable

In most cases, a large corporation's tax obligation is determined by multiplying its taxable income by 35 percent. Rates are graduated, however, so that very small corporations pay lower rates than large corporations do.

Exhibit 9.2 illustrates the calculation of taxes payable at various income levels. Notice in Cases B and C that a portion of the income is taxed at a rate that is higher than the maximum of 35 percent. The purpose of the 39 percent rate is to phase out the benefits of the lower rates that were intended to benefit only smaller corporations. The $136,000 total taxes payable on taxable income of $400,000 is an effective tax rate of exactly 34 percent.

A 35 percent tax rate applies to taxable incomes higher than $10 million. A provision phases out the 34 percent tax rate for very large corporations. The tax rate from $15,000,000 to $18,333,333 is 38 percent. At higher incomes, the rate reverts to 35 percent. This provision results in an effective tax rate of 35 percent once a corporation has taxable income greater than $18,333,333.

Revenue and Expense Recognition for Income Tax Purposes

Several differences exist between GAAP and the rules that govern the preparation of the federal income tax return. The following are common examples:

1. Interest revenue on state and municipal bonds is generally excluded from taxable income, although it is included in accounting income.
2. Revenue collected in advance (e.g., rent revenue) is included in taxable income when it is collected and in accounting income when it is earned.

Case A: Taxable Income	$ 90,000
Computation	
0.15 of first $50,000	$ 7,500
0.25 of next $25,000	6,250
0.34 of $15,000 ($90,000 − $75,000)	5,100
Taxes payable	$ 18,850

Case B: Taxable Income	$150,000
Computation	
0.15 of first $50,000	$ 7,500
0.25 of next $25,000	6,250
0.34 of next $25,000	8,500
0.39 of $50,000 ($150,000 − $100,000)	19,500
Taxes payable	$ 41,750

Case C: Taxable Income	$400,000
Computation	
0.15 of first $50,000	$ 7,500
0.25 of next $25,000	6,250
0.34 of next $25,000	8,500
0.39 of next $235,000	91,650
0.34 of $65,000 ($400,000 − $335,000)	22,100
Taxes payable	$136,000

EXHIBIT 9.2

Calculation of Taxes Payable

3. Proceeds from life insurance policies (e.g., key executive insurance) are excluded from taxable income but included in accounting income.
4. Corporations that own less than 20 percent of another corporation's stock may exclude 70 percent of the dividends received from taxable income, although all dividends are included in accounting income. The exclusion is 80 percent if the corporation owns more than 20 percent of the other corporation's stock. A 100 percent exclusion is permitted if 80 percent or more of the stock is owned.
5. For tax purposes, depreciation expense is generally based on the Accelerated Cost Recovery System (ACRS) for assets placed in service after 1980 but before 1987, or on the Modified Accelerated Cost Recovery System (MACRS) for assets placed in service after 1986. These methods were discussed in Chapter 8.

Tax Minimization versus Tax Evasion

Most large corporations spend considerable time and money developing strategies that *minimize* the amount of federal income taxes they must pay. Nothing is wrong with this approach because courts have stated there is no legal obligation to pay more taxes than the law demands. Even if you do not major in accounting, you will probably want to take a course in federal income taxation because knowledge of the Internal Revenue Code is important for most executives. This knowledge offers opportunities to save significant amounts of money.

In contrast, tax evasion involves the use of illegal means to avoid paying taxes. Use of accelerated depreciation is an example of *tax minimization*; failure to report revenue that was collected in cash is an example of *tax evasion*. While efforts at tax minimization represent good business practice, tax evasion is morally and legally wrong. Individuals who evade taxes run the risk of severe financial penalties as well as the possibility of being sent to jail.

Chapter Supplement C

Present Value Computations Using Excel

While the present value tables at the end of this book are useful for educational purposes, most present value problems in business are solved with calculators or Excel spreadsheets. Because of the widespread availability of Excel, we will show you how to solve present value problems using Excel. There are slightly different versions of Excel available, depending on the age of the computer. The illustrations in this text are based on Microsoft Office 2007.

Present Value of a Single Payment

The calculation of a present value amount is based on a fairly simple mathematical formula:

$$PV = \text{Payment}/(1 + i)^n$$

In this formula, *payment* is the cash payment made at some point in the future, i is the interest rate each period, and n is the number of periods in the problem. We could use this formula to solve all problems involving the present value of a single payment. It is, of course, easier to use a present value table (like the one at the end of this book) which is derived by solving the present value formula for various interest rates and numbers of periods. Unfortunately, a table that included all interest rates and numbers of periods actually encountered in business would be too large to work with. As a result, most accountants and analysts use Excel to compute a present value.

To compute the present value of a single payment in Excel, you enter the present value formula in a cell, using the format required by Excel. You should select a cell and enter the following formula:

$$= \text{Payment}/(1 + i)^\wedge n$$

To illustrate, if you want to solve for the present value of a $100,000 payment to be made in five years with an interest rate of 10%, you would enter the following in the function field:

$$= 100000/(1.10)^\wedge 5$$

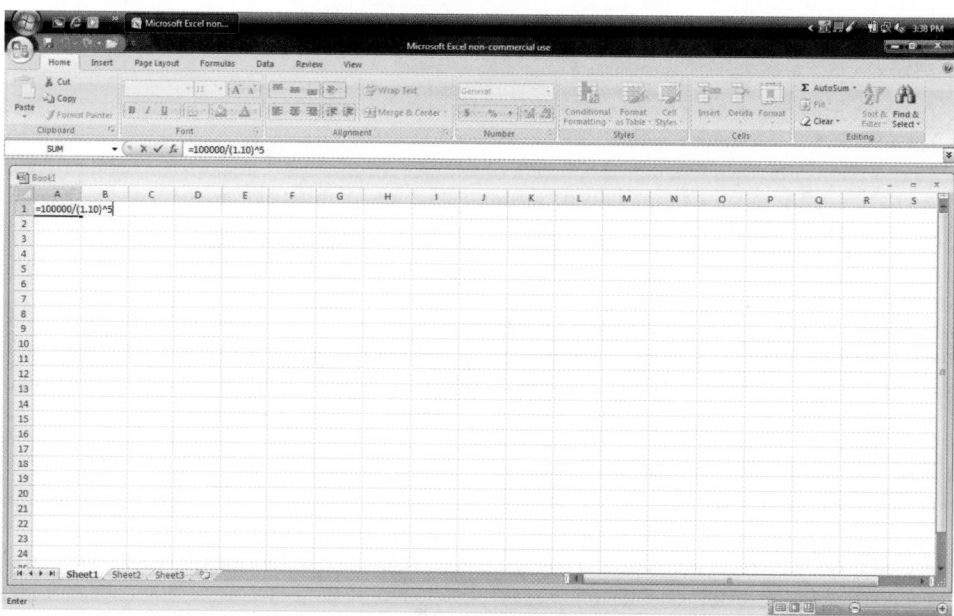

Based on this entry, Excel would compute the present value of $62,092.13. This answer is slightly different than the answer you would have if you used the present value tables at the end of the book. The tables in the book are rounded based on four digits. Excel does not round and, therefore, provides a more accurate computation.

Present Value of an Annuity

The formula for computing the present value of an annuity is a little more complicated than the present value of a single payment. As a result, Excel has been programmed to include the formula so that you do not have to enter it yourself.

To compute the present value of an annuity in Excel, select a cell and click on the insert function button (f_x). The following dropdown box will appear:

Under the Select Category heading, you should pick "Financial," scroll down under "Select a Function," and click on PV. Then, click on "OK" and a new dropdown box will appear:

In this box, you should enter the interest rate, 10% in this example, under Rate. Notice that the rate must be entered as a decimal (i.e., 0.10) Enter the number of periods (20) under Nper. Excel has an unusual convention associated with the payment. It must be entered as a negative amount (−15000) under Pmt. Notice also that a comma should not be included in the amount you enter. When you click on OK, Excel will enter the present value in the cell you selected. In this example, the value determined by Excel is $127,703.46.

Chapter Supplement D

Future Value Concepts

Future value problems are similar to present value problems in the sense that they are both based on the time value of money. As we saw earlier, a present value problem determines the current cash equivalent of

FUTURE VALUE is the sum to which an amount will increase as the result of compound interest.

an amount to be received in the future. In comparison, a **future value** is the sum to which an amount will increase as the result of compound interest. The following table illustrates the basic difference between present value and future value problems:

	Now	Future
Present value	?	$1,000
Future value	$1,000	?

Future Value of a Single Amount

In future value of a single amount problems, you will be asked to calculate how much money you will have in the future as the result of investing a certain amount in the present. If you were to receive a gift of $10,000, for instance, you might decide to put it in a savings account and use the money as a down payment on a house after you graduate. The future value computation would tell you how much money will be available when you graduate.

To solve a future value problem, you need to know three items:

1. Amount to be invested.

2. Interest rate (i) the amount will earn.

3. Number of periods (n) in which the amount will earn interest.

Since the future value concept is based on compound interest, the amount of interest for each period is calculated by multiplying the principal plus any interest not paid out in prior periods. Graphically, the calculation of the future value of $1 for three periods and an interest rate of 10 percent may be represented as follows:

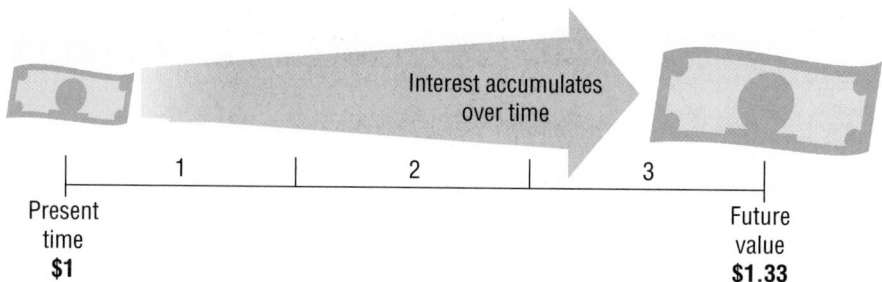

Assume that on January 1, 2009, you deposit $1,000 in a savings account at 10 percent annual interest, compounded annually. At the end of three years, the $1,000 will have increased to $1,331 as follows:

Year	Amount at Start of Year	+	Interest During the Year	=	Amount at End of Year
1	$1,000	+	$1,000 × 10% = $100	=	$1,100
2	1,100	+	1,100 × 10% = $110	=	1,210
3	1,210	+	1,210 × 10% = $121	=	1,331

We can avoid the detailed arithmetic by referring to Table A.3, Future Value of $1. For $i = 10\%$, $n = 3$, we find the value 1.331. We then compute the balance at the end of year 3 as follows:

$$\$1,000 \times 1.3310 = \$1,331$$

From Table A.3, Interest rate = 10% n = 3

Note that the increase of $331 is due to the time value of money. It is interest revenue to the owner of the savings account and interest expense to the savings institution.

Future Value of an Annuity

If you are saving money for some purpose, such as a new car or a trip to Europe, you might decide to deposit a fixed amount of money in a savings account each month. The future value of an annuity computation will tell you how much money will be in your savings account at some point in the future.

The future value of an annuity includes compound interest on each payment from the date of payment to the end of the term of the annuity. Each new payment accumulates less interest than prior payments, only because the number of periods remaining in which to accumulate interest decreases. The future value of an annuity of $1 for three periods at 10 percent may be represented graphically as:

1	2	3	Future value
$1	$1	$1	of an annuity
			$3.31

Assume that each year for three years, you deposit $1,000 cash in a savings account at 10 percent interest per year. You make the first $1,000 deposit on December 31, 2009, the second one on December 31, 2010, and the third and last one on December 31, 2011. The first $1,000 deposit earns compound interest for two years (for a total principal and interest of $1,210); the second deposit earns interest for one year (for a total principal and interest of $1,100). The third deposit earns no interest because it was made on the day that the balance is computed. Thus, the total amount in the savings account at the end of three years is $3,310 ($1,210 + $1,100 + $1,000).

To derive the future value of this annuity, we could compute the interest on each deposit. However, we can refer to Table A.4, Appendix A, Future Value of an Annuity of $1 for $i = 10\%$, $n = 3$ to find the value 3.3100. The future value of your three deposits of $1,000 each can be computed as follows:

$$\$1,000 \times 3.3100 = \$3,310$$

From Table A.4,
Interest rate = 10%
n = 3

The Power of Compounding

Compound interest is a remarkably powerful economic force. Indeed, the ability to earn interest on interest is the key to building economic wealth. If you save $1,000 per year for the first 10 years of your career, you will have more money when you retire than you would if you had saved $15,000 per year for the last 10 years of your career. This surprising outcome occurs because the money you save early in your career will earn more interest than the money you save at the end of your career. If you start saving money now, the majority of your wealth will not be the money you saved but the interest your money was able to earn.

The chart in the margin illustrates the power of compounding over a brief 10-year period. If you deposit $1 each year in an account earning 10 percent interest, at the end of just 10 years, only 64 percent of your balance will be made up of money you have saved; the rest will be interest you have earned. After 20 years, only 35 percent of your balance will be from saved money. The lesson associated with compound interest is clear: Even though saving money is difficult, you should start now.

Effects of Compound Interest

— Deposits
— Deposits with interest

CHAPTER TAKE-AWAYS

1. **Define, measure, and report current liabilities.   p. 461**

   Strictly speaking, accountants define liabilities as probable future sacrifices of economic benefits that arise from past transactions. They are classified on the balance sheet as either current or long term. Current liabilities are short-term obligations that will be paid within the current operating cycle of the business or within one year of the balance sheet date, whichever is longer. Long-term liabilities are all obligations not classified as current.

2. **Use the current ratio.**   p. 462

The current ratio is a comparison of current assets and current liabilities. Analysts use this ratio to assess the liquidity of a company.

3. **Analyze the accounts payable turnover ratio.**   p. 464

This ratio is computed by dividing cost of goods sold by average accounts payable. It shows how quickly management is paying its trade creditors and is considered to be a measure of liquidity.

4. **Report notes payable and explain the time value of money.**   p. 467

A note payable specifies the amount borrowed, when it must be repaid, and the interest rate associated with the debt. Accountants must report the debt and the interest as it accrues. The time value of money refers to the fact that interest accrues on borrowed money with the passage of time.

5. **Report contingent liabilities.**   p. 469

A contingent liability is a potential liability that has arisen as the result of a past event. Such liabilities are disclosed in a note if the obligation is reasonably possible.

6. **Explain the importance of working capital and its impact on cash flows.**   p. 471

Working capital is used to fund the operating activities of a business. Changes in working capital accounts affect the statement of cash flows. Cash flows from operating activities are increased by decreases in current assets (other than cash) or increases in current liabilities. Cash flows from operating activities are decreased by increases in current assets (other than cash) or decreases in current liabilities.

7. **Report long-term liabilities.**   p. 473

Usually, long-term liabilities will be paid in more than one year in the future. Accounting for long-term debt is based on the same concepts used in accounting for short-term debt.

8. **Compute present values.**   p. 475

The present value concept is based on the time value of money. Simply stated, a dollar to be received in the future is worth less than a dollar available today (present value). This concept can be applied either to a single payment or multiple payments called *annuities*. Either tables or Excel can be used to determine present values.

9. **Apply present value concepts to liabilities.**   p. 479

Accountants use present value concepts to determine the reported amounts of liabilities. A liability involves the payment of some amount at a future date. The reported liability is not the amount of the future payment. Instead, the liability is reported at the amount of the present value of the future payment.

In this chapter, we focused on current liabilities and introduced you to present value concepts. In the next chapter, we will use present value concepts to measure long-term liabilities. We will also discuss long-term liabilities in the context of the capital structure of the company.

KEY **RATIO**

Current ratio measures the ability of a company to pay its current obligations. It is computed as follows (p. 462):

$$\text{Current Ratio} = \frac{\text{Current Assets}}{\text{Current Liabilities}}$$

Accounts payable turnover is a measure of how quickly a company pays its creditors. It is computed as follows (p. 464):

$$\text{Accounts Payable Turnover} = \frac{\text{Costs of Goods Sold}}{\text{Average Accounts Payable}}$$

FINDING **FINANCIAL INFORMATION**

Balance Sheet

Under Current Liabilities
Liabilities listed by account title, such as
Accounts payable
Accrued liabilities
Notes payable
Current portion of long-term debt

Under Noncurrent Liabilities
Liabilities listed by account title, such as
Long-term debt
Deferred taxes
Bonds

Income Statement

Liabilities are shown only on the balance sheet, never on the income statement. Transactions affecting liabilities often affect an income statement account. For example, accrued salary compensation affects an income statement account (compensation expense) and a balance sheet account (salaries payable).

Statement of Cash Flows

Under Operating Activities (indirect method)
Net income
+ Increases in most current liabilities
− Decreases in most current liabilities

Under Financing Activities
+ Increases in long-term liabilities
− Decreases in long-term liabilities

Notes

Under Summary of Significant Accounting Policies
Description of pertinent information concerning accounting treatment of liabilities. Normally, there is minimal information.

Under a Separate Note
If not listed on the balance sheet, a listing of the major classifications of liabilities with information about maturities and interest rates. Information about contingent liabilities is reported in the notes.

KEY **TERMS**

Accrued Liabilities   p. 464
Annuity   p. 477
Capital Lease   p. 479
Contingent Liability   p. 469
Current Liabilities   p. 461
Deferred Revenues   p. 469

Deferred Tax Items   p. 482
Future Value   p. 488
Liabilities   p. 461
Liquidity   p. 461
**Long-Term
 Liabilities**   p. 473

Operating Lease   p. 474
Present Value   p. 479
**Temporary
 Differences**   p. 482
Time Value of Money   p. 467
Working Capital   p. 471

QUESTIONS

1. Define *liability*. Differentiate between a current liability and a long-term liability.
2. How can external parties be informed about the liabilities of a business?
3. Liabilities are measured and reported at their current cash equivalent amount. Explain.
4. A *liability* is a known obligation of either a definite or an estimated amount. Explain.
5. Define *working capital*. How is it computed?
6. What is the current ratio? How is it related to the classification of liabilities?

7. Define *accrued liability*. What type of entry usually reflects an accrued liability?
8. Define *deferred revenue*. Why is it a liability?
9. Define *note payable*. Differentiate between a secured and an unsecured note.
10. What is a contingent liability? How is a contingent liability reported?
11. Compute 2009 interest expense for the following note: face, $4,000; 12 percent interest; date of note, April 1, 2009.
12. Explain the concept of the time value of money.
13. Explain the basic difference between future value and present value.
14. If you hold a valid contract that will pay you $8,000 cash in 10 years and the going rate of interest is 10 percent, what is its present value? Show your computations.
15. What is an annuity?
16. Complete the following schedule:

Concept	Table Values
	$i = 5\%, n = 4; i = 10\%, n = 7; i = 14\%, n = 10$
PV of $1	
PV of annuity of $1	

17. You purchased an XIT auto for $18,000 by making a $3,000 cash payment and six semiannual installment payments for the balance at 12 percent interest. Determine the amount of each payment.

MULTIPLE-CHOICE QUESTIONS

1. What is the present value factor for an annuity of five periods and an interest rate of 10%?
   a. 1.6105
   b. 6.1051
   c. 3.7908
   d. 7.7217

2. The university spirit organization needs to buy a car to travel to football games. A dealership in Lockhart has agreed to the following terms: $4,000 down plus 20 monthly payments of $750. A dealership in Leander will agree to a $1,000 down payment plus 20 monthly payments of $850. The local bank is currently charging an annual interest rate of 12% for car loans. Which is the better deal, *and why?*
   a. The Leander offer is better because the total payments of $18,000 are less than the total payments of $19,000 to be made to the Lockhart dealership.
   b. The Lockhart offer is better because the cost in terms of present value is less than the present value cost of the Leander offer.
   c. The Lockhart offer is better because the monthly payments are less.
   d. The Leander offer is better because the cash down payment is less.
   e. The Leander offer is better because the cost in terms of present value is less than the present value cost of the Lockhart offer.

3. Which of the following best describes *accrued liabilities*?
   a. Long-term liabilities.
   b. Current amounts owed to suppliers of inventory.
   c. Current liabilities to be recognized as revenue in a future period.
   d. Current amounts owed to various parties excluding suppliers of inventory.

4. Company X has borrowed $100,000 from the bank to be repaid over the next five years, with payments beginning next month. Which of the following best describes the presentation of this debt in the balance sheet as of today (the date of borrowing)?
   a. $100,000 in the long-term liability section.
   b. $100,000 plus the interest to be paid over the five-year period in the long-term liability section.
   c. A portion of the $100,000 in the current liability section and the remainder of the principal in the long-term liability section.
   d. A portion of the $100,000 plus interest in the current liability section and the remainder of the principal plus interest in the long-term liability section.

5. A company is facing a class-action lawsuit in the upcoming year. It is possible, but not probable, that the company will have to pay a settlement of approximately $2,000,000. How would this fact be reported in the financial statements to be issued at the end of the current month?
   a. $ 2,000,000 in the current liability section.
   b. $ 2,000,000 in the long-term liability section.
   c. In a descriptive narrative in the footnote section.
   d. None because disclosure is not required.
6. Which of the following transactions would usually cause accounts payable turnover to increase?
   a. Payment of cash to a supplier for merchandise previously purchased on credit.
   b. Collection of cash from a customer.
   c. Purchase of merchandise on credit.
   d. None of the above.
7. How is working capital calculated?
   a. Current assets multiplied by current liabilities.
   b. Current assets plus current liabilities.
   c. Current assets minus current liabilities.
   d. Current assets divided by current liabilities.
8. The present value of annuity of $10,000 per year for 10 years discounted at 8% is what amount?
   a. $5,002   c. $53,349
   b. $67,101   d. $80,000
9. Jacobs Company borrowed 100,000 at 8 percent interest for three months. How much interest does the company owe at the end of three months?
   a. $8,000   c. $800
   b. $2,000   d. $200
10. Fred wants to save enough money each year so that he can purchase a sports car in January 2011. Fred receives a large bonus from his employer every December 31. He anticipates that the car will cost $54,000 on January 1, 2011. Which of the following will Fred need to calculate how much he must save each December 31?
   a. The anticipated interest rate and the present value of $1 table.
   b. The anticipated interest rate and the future value of $1 table.
   c. The anticipated interest rate and the present value table for annuities.
   d. The anticipated interest rate and the future value table for annuities.

For more practice with multiple choice questions, go to our website at www.mhhe.com/libby6e.

 Available with McGraw-Hill's Homework Manager

MINI-EXERCISES

Computing Interest Expense

M9-1
LO4

Jacobs Company borrowed $600,000 on a 90-day note at 11 percent interest. The money was borrowed for 30 days in 2009 and 60 days in 2010; the note and interest were to be paid upon maturity in 2010. How much interest expense, if any, would be reported in 2009 and in 2010?

Recording a Note Payable

M9-2
LO4

Farmer Corporation borrowed $290,000 on October 1, 2009. The note carried a 10 percent interest rate with the principal and interest payable on May 1, 2010. Prepare the journal entry to record the note on October 1. Prepare the adjusting entry to record accrued interest on December 31.

Finding Financial Information

M9-3
LO1, 3, 6

For each of the following items, specify whether the information would be found in the balance sheet, the income statement, the statement of cash flows, the notes to the statements, or not at all.

1. The amount of working capital.
2. The total amount of current liabilities.

3. Information concerning company pension plans.

4. The accounts payable turnover ratio.

5. Information concerning the impact of changes in working capital on cash flows for the period.

M9-4
LO2

Computing Measures of Liquidity

The balance sheet for Shaver Corporation reported the following: total assets, $360,000; noncurrent assets, $239,000; current liabilities, $46,000; total stockholders' equity, $92,000. Compute Shaver's current ratio and working capital.

M9-5
LO2

Analyzing the Impact of Transactions on Liquidity

BSO, Inc., has a current ratio of 2.0 and working capital in the amount of $1,240,000. For each of the following transactions, determine whether the current ratio and working capital will increase, decrease, or remain the same.

a. Paid accounts payable in the amount of $50,000.

b. Recorded accrued salaries in the amount of $100,000.

c. Borrowed $250,000 from a local bank, to be repaid in 90 days.

d. Purchased $20,000 of new inventory on credit.

M9-6
LO5

Reporting Contingent Liabilities

Buzz Coffee Shops is famous for its large servings of hot coffee. After a famous case involving McDonald's, the lawyer for Buzz warned management (during 2009) that it could be sued if someone were to spill hot coffee and be burned: "With the temperature of your coffee, I can guarantee it's just a matter of time before you're sued for $1,000,000." Unfortunately, in 2010 the prediction came true when a customer filed suit. The case went to trial in 2011, and the jury awarded the customer $400,000 in damages, which the company immediately appealed. During 2012 the customer and the company settled their dispute for $150,000. What is the proper reporting of this liability each year?

M9-7
LO8

Computing the Present Value of a Single Payment

What is the present value of $500,000 to be paid in 10 years with an interest rate of 8 percent?

M9-8
LO8

Computing the Present Value of an Annuity

What is the present value of 10 equal payments of $15,000, with an interest rate of 10 percent?

M9-9
LO8

Computing the Present Value of a Complex Contract

As a result of a slowdown in operations, Mercantile Stores is offering employees who have been terminated a severance package of $118,000 cash, another $129,000 to be paid in one year, and an annuity of $27,500 to be paid each year for six years beginning in one year. What is the present value of the package, assuming an interest rate of 5 percent?

M9-10

Computing the Future Value of an Annuity (Supplement D)

You plan to retire in 10 years. Is it better for you to save $27,500 a year for the last 5 years before retirement or $16,250 for each of the 10 years? You are able to earn 9 percent interest on your investments.

M9-11

Making a Complex Computation of a Future Value (Supplement D)

You want a retirement fund of $125,000 when you retire in six years. You are able to earn 8 percent on your investments. How much should you deposit each year to build the retirement fund that you want?

EXERCISES

Computing Working Capital; Explaining the Current Ratio and Working Capital

E9-1
LO1, 2, 5, 6

Wilemon Corporation is preparing its 2010 balance sheet. The company records show the following selected amounts at the end of the accounting period, December 31, 2010:

Total assets	$530,000
Total noncurrent assets	362,000
Liabilities:	
Notes payable (8%, due in 5 years)	15,000
Accounts payable	56,000
Income taxes payable	14,000
Liability for withholding taxes	3,000
Rent revenue collected in advance	7,000
Bonds payable (due in 15 years)	90,000
Wages payable	7,000
Property taxes payable	3,000
Note payable (10%, due in 6 months)	12,000
Interest payable	400
Common stock	100,000

Required:
1. Compute (a) working capital and (b) the current ratio (show computations). Why is working capital important to management? How do financial analysts use the current ratio?
2. Would your computations be different if the company reported $250,000 worth of contingent liabilities in the notes to the statements? Explain.

Recording Payroll Costs

E9-2
LO1

Warner Company completed the salary and wage payroll for March 2009. The payroll provided the following details:

Salaries and wages earned	$200,000
Employee income taxes withheld	40,000
Insurance premiums withheld	1,000
FICA payroll taxes*	15,000

*$15,000 each for employer and employees

Required:
1. Give the journal entry to record the payroll for March including employee deductions.
2. Give the journal entry to record the employer's payroll taxes.
3. Give a combined journal entry to show the payment of amounts owed to governmental agencies.

Computing Payroll Costs; Discussion of Labor Costs

E9-3
LO1

Colonial Company has completed the payroll for January 2010, reflecting the following data:

Salaries and wages earned	$86,000
Employee income taxes withheld	10,000
FICA payroll taxes*	6,000

*Assessed on both employer and employee (i.e., $6,000 each).

Required:
1. What amount of additional labor expense to the company was due to tax laws? What was the amount of the employees' take-home pay?

2. List the liabilities and their amounts that are reported on the company's January 31, 2010, balance sheet, assuming the employees have been paid.

3. Would employers react differently to a 10 percent increase in the employer's share of FICA than to a 10 percent increase in the basic level of salaries? Would financial analysts react differently?

E9-4

LO1, 4

Recording a Note Payable through Its Time to Maturity with Discussion of Management Strategy

Many businesses borrow money during periods of increased business activity to finance inventory and accounts receivable. Neiman Marcus is one of America's most prestigious retailers. Each Christmas season, Neiman Marcus builds up its inventory to meet the needs of Christmas shoppers. A large portion of these Christmas sales are on credit. As a result, Neiman Marcus often collects cash from the sales several months after Christmas. Assume that on November 1, 2009, Neiman Marcus borrowed $4.8 million cash from Texas Capital Bank for working capital purposes and signed an interest-bearing note due in six months. The interest rate was 8 percent per annum payable at maturity. The accounting period ends December 31.

Required:

1. Give the journal entry to record the note on November 1.
2. Give any adjusting entry required at the end of the annual accounting period.
3. Give the journal entry to record payment of the note and interest on the maturity date, April 30, 2010.
4. If Neiman Marcus needs extra cash during every Christmas season, should management borrow money on a long-term basis to avoid the necessity of negotiating a new short-term loan each year?

E9-5

LO1, 4

Determining Financial Statement Effects of Transactions Involving Notes Payable

Using the data from the previous exercise, complete the following requirements.

Required:

1. Determine the financial statement effects for each of the following: (a) issuance of the note on November 1, (b) impact of the adjusting entry at the end of the accounting period, and (c) payment of the note and interest on April 30, 2010. Indicate the effects (e.g., cash + or −), using the following schedule:

Date	Assets	Liabilities	Stockholders' Equity

2. If Neiman Marcus needs extra cash every Christmas season, should management borrow money on a long-term basis to avoid negotiating a new short-term loan each year?

E9-6

LO1

PepsiCo. Inc.

Reporting Short-Term Borrowings

PepsiCo, Inc., manufactures a number of products that are part of our daily lives. Its businesses include Pepsi-Cola, Slice, Mountain Dew, and Fritos. The company's annual revenues exceed $22 billion. A recent PepsiCo annual report contained the following information:

At the end of the current year, $3.6 billion of short-term borrowings were classified as long-term, reflecting PepsiCo's intent and ability to refinance these borrowings on a long-term basis, through either long-term debt issuances or rollover of existing short-term borrowings. The significant amount of short-term borrowings classified as long-term, as compared to the end of the previous year when no such amounts were reclassified, primarily reflects the large commercial paper issuances in the current year but also resulted from a refined analysis of amounts expected to be refinanced beyond one year.

Required:

As an analyst, comment on the company's classification of short-term borrowings as long-term liabilities. What conditions should exist to permit a company to make this type of classification?

E9-7

LO2

Using the Current Ratio

Beall's Department Store reported a current ratio of 1.5. A review of their balance sheet revealed the following information:

Current assets	$750,000
Noncurrent assets	450,000
Noncurrent liabilities	300,000

Determine the amount of current liabilities reported in the balance sheet.

Determining the Impact of Transactions, Including Analysis of Cash Flows

E9-8
LO1, 2, 4, 6

Bryant Company sells a wide range of goods through two retail stores operated in adjoining cities. Most purchases of goods for resale are on invoices. Occasionally, a short-term note payable is used to obtain cash for current use. The following transactions were selected from those occurring during 2010:

a. Purchased merchandise on credit, $18,000 on January 10, 2010; the company uses a periodic inventory system.

b. Borrowed $45,000 cash on March 1, 2010, from City Bank and gave an interest-bearing note payable: face amount, $45,000, due at the end of six months, with an annual interest rate of 10 percent payable at maturity.

Required:

1. Describe the impact of each transaction on the balance sheet equation. Indicate the effects (e.g., cash + or −), using the following schedule:

Date	Assets	Liabilities	Stockholders' Equity

2. What amount of cash is paid on the maturity date of the note?
3. Discuss the impact of each transaction on Bryant's cash flows.
4. Discuss the impact of each transaction on the current ratio.

Reporting a Liability

E9-9
LO7

i'm lovin' it®

McDonald's is one of the world's most popular fast-food restaurants, offering good food and convenient locations. Effective management of their properties is a key to their success. As the following note in its current annual report indicates, McDonald's both owns and leases property:

The Company owns and leases real estate primarily in connection with its restaurant business. The Company identifies and develops sites that offer convenience to customers and long-term sales and profit potential to the Company. The Company generally owns the land and building or secures long-term leases for restaurant sites, which ensures long-term occupancy rights and helps control related costs.

Required:

Should McDonald's report lease obligation on its balance sheet? Explain. If the obligation should be reported as a liability, how should the amount be measured?

Evaluating Lease Alternatives

E9-10
LO7

As the new vice president for consumer products at Acme Manufacturing, you are attending a meeting to discuss a serious problem associated with delivering merchandise to customers. Bob Smith, director of logistics, summarized the problem: "It's easy to understand, we just don't have enough delivery trucks given our recent growth." Barb Bader from the accounting department responded: "Maybe it's easy to understand but it's impossible to do anything. Because of Wall Street's concern about the amount of debt on our balance sheet, we're under a freeze and can't borrow money to acquire new assets. There's nothing we can do."

On the way back to your office after the meeting, your assistant offers a suggestion: "Why don't we just lease the trucks we need? That way we can get the assets we want without having to record a liability on the balance sheet."

How would you respond to this suggestion?

Reporting a Liability, with Discussion (Supplement A)

E9-11
LO7
American Airlines

The annual report for American Airlines contained the following information:

In addition to pension benefits, other postretirement benefits, including certain health care and life insurance benefits (which provide secondary coverage to Medicare), are provided to retired employees. The amount of health care benefits is limited to lifetime maximums as outlined in the plan. Substantially all regular employees of American and employees of certain other subsidiaries may become eligible for these benefits if they satisfy eligibility requirements during their working lives.

Required:

Should American report a liability for these benefits on its balance sheet? Explain.

E9-12   Computing Deferred Income Tax: One Temporary Difference, with Discussion (Supplement B)

The comparative income statements of Martin Corporation at December 31, 2010, showed the following summarized pretax data:

	Year 2009	Year 2010
Sales revenue	$75,000	$82,000
Expenses (excluding income tax)	54,000	58,000
Pretax income	$21,000	$24,000

Included in the 2010 data is a $3,000 expense that was deductible only in the 2009 income tax return (rather than in 2010). The average income tax rate was 30 percent. Taxable income from the income tax returns was 2009, $18,000, and 2010, $27,000.

Required:

1. For each year, compute (a) income taxes payable and (b) deferred income tax. Is the deferred income tax a liability or an asset? Explain.
2. Show what amounts related to income taxes should be reported each year on the income statement and balance sheet. Assume that income tax is paid on April 15 of the next year.
3. Explain why tax expense is not simply the amount of cash paid during the year.

E9-13   Recording Deferred Income Tax: One Temporary Difference; Discussion of Management Strategy (Supplement B)

The comparative income statement for Chung Corporation at the end of December 31, 2010, provided the following summarized pretax data:

	Year 2009	Year 2010
Revenue	$55,000	$63,000
Expenses (excluding income tax)	39,000	43,000
Pretax income	$16,000	$20,000

Included in the 2010 data is a $4,000 revenue that was taxable only in the 2009 income tax return. The average income tax rate was 32 percent. Taxable income shown in the tax returns was 2009, $20,000, and 2010, $16,000.

Required:

1. For each year, compute (a) income taxes payable and (b) deferred income tax. Is the deferred income tax a liability or an asset? Explain.
2. Give the journal entry for each year to record income taxes payable, deferred income tax, and income tax expense.
3. Show what amounts related to income taxes should be reported each year on the income statement and balance sheet. Assume that income tax is paid on April 15 of the next year.
4. Why would management want to incur the cost of maintaining separate tax and financial accounting records?

E9-14   Reporting Deferred Taxes (Supplement B)

Colgate-Palmolive

The annual report for Colgate-Palmolive contains the following information (in millions):

Income Taxes

Temporary differences between accounting for financial statement purposes and accounting for tax purposes result in taxes currently payable higher (lower) than the total provision for income taxes as follows:

	2005	2004	2003
Depreciation expense	$(60.2)	$(46.9)	$22.1
Other	22.7	(13.4)	39.2
Total	$(37.5)	$(60.3)	$61.3

Required:
1. Determine whether tax expense is higher or lower than taxes payable for each year.
2. Explain the most likely reason for tax depreciation to be higher than book depreciation.
3. Is the deferred tax liability reported on the 2005 balance sheet $37.5 million? Explain.

Computing Four Present Value Problems

E9-15
LO8

On January 1, 2009, Vigeland Company completed the following transactions (assume a 10 percent annual interest rate):
a. Bought a delivery truck and agreed to pay $50,000 at the end of three years.
b. Rented an office building and was given the option of paying $10,000 at the end of each of the next three years or paying $28,000 immediately.
c. Established a savings account by depositing a single amount that will increase to $40,000 at the end of 7 years.
d. Decided to deposit a single sum in the bank that will provide 10 equal annual year-end payments of $15,000 to a retired employee (payments starting December 31, 2009).

Required (show computations and round to the nearest dollar):
1. What is the cost of the truck that should be recorded at the time of purchase?
2. Which option for the office building should the company select?
3. What single amount must be deposited in this account on January 1, 2009?
4. What single sum must be deposited in the bank on January 1, 2009?

Using Present Value Concepts for Decision Making

E9-16
LO8

You have just won the state lottery and have two choices for collecting your winnings. You can collect $50,000 today or receive $10,100 per year for the next seven years. A financial analyst has told you that you can earn 10 percent on your investments. Which alternative should you select?

Calculating a Retirement Fund

E9-17
LO8

You are a financial adviser who is working with a client who wants to retire in eight years. The client has a savings account with a local bank that pays 9 percent and she wants to deposit an amount that will provide her with $900,000 when she retires. Currently, she has $200,000 in the account. How much additional money should she deposit now to provide her with $900,000 when she retires?

Determining an Educational Fund

E9-18
LO8

Judge Drago has decided to set up an educational fund for his favorite granddaughter, Emma, who will start college in one year. The judge plans to deposit an amount in a savings account that pays 9 percent interest. He wants to deposit an amount that is sufficient to permit Emma to withdraw $13,000 starting in one year and continuing each year for a total of four years. How much should he deposit today to provide Emma with a fund to pay for her college tuition?

Computing a Present Value

E9-19
LO8

An investment will pay $11,000 at the end of the first year, $30,000 at the end of the second year, and $50,000 at the end of the third year. Determine the present value of this investment using a 10 percent interest rate.

Computing a Present Value

E9-20
LO8

An investment will pay $15,000 at the end of each year for eight years and a one-time payment of $120,000 at the end of the eighth year. Determine the present value of this investment using a 7 percent interest rate.

Determining the Value of an Asset

E9-21
LO8

Dan Roger Company has purchased a new office building. The company has agreed to pay the developer $55,000 annually for nine years. Using present value techniques, determine the value that should be recorded for the building when it is purchased. Assume a 6 percent annual interest rate.

E9-22 **Computing Value of an Asset Based on Present Value**

LO8 You have the chance to purchase the royalty interest in a gas well in the Barnett Shale. Your best esti-mate is that the net royalty income will average $25,000 per year for seven years. There will be no residual value at that time. Considering the uncertainty in your estimates, you expect to earn 9 percent per year on the investment. What should you be willing to pay for this investment now?

E9-23 **Computing Growth in a Savings Account: A Single Amount (Supplement D)**

On January 1, 2009, you deposited $6,000 in a savings account. The account will earn 10 percent annual compound interest, which will be added to the fund balance at the end of each year.

Required (round to the nearest dollar):
1. What will be the balance in the savings account at the end of 10 years?
2. What is the amount of interest earned during the 10 years?
3. How much interest revenue did the fund earn in 2009? 2010?

E9-24 **Computing Deposit Required and Accounting for a Single-Sum Savings Account (Supplement D)**

On January 1, 2009, Alan King decided to deposit $58,800 in a savings account that will provide funds four years later to send his son to college. The savings account will earn 8 percent, which will be added to the fund each year-end.

Required (show computations and round to the nearest dollar):
1. How much will be available in four years?
2. Give the journal entry that Alan should make on January 1, 2009.
3. What is the interest for the four years?
4. Give the journal entry that Alan should make on (a) December 31, 2009, and (b) December 31, 2010.

E9-25 **Recording Growth in a Savings Account with Equal Periodic Payments (Supplement D)**

On each December 31, you plan to deposit $2,000 in a savings account. The account will earn 9 percent annual interest, which will be added to the fund balance at year-end. The first deposit will be made December 31, 2009 (end of period).

Required (show computations and round to the nearest dollar):
1. Give the required journal entry on December 31, 2009.
2. What will be the balance in the savings account at the end of the 10th year (i.e., after 10 deposits)?
3. What is the interest earned on the 10 deposits?
4. How much interest revenue did the fund earn in 2010? 2011?
5. Give all required journal entries at the end of 2010 and 2011.

E9-26 **Computing Growth for a Savings Fund with Periodic Deposits (Supplement D)**

On January 1, 2009, you plan to take a trip around the world upon graduation four years from now. Your grandmother wants to deposit sufficient funds for this trip in a savings account for you. On the basis of a budget, you estimate that the trip currently would cost $15,000. To be generous, your grandmother decided to deposit $3,500 in the fund at the end of each of the next four years, starting on December 31, 2009. The savings account will earn 6 percent annual interest, which will be added to the savings account at each year-end.

Required (show computations and round to the nearest dollar):
1. How much money will you have for the trip at the end of year 4 (i.e., after four deposits)?
2. What is the interest for the four years?
3. How much interest revenue did the fund earn in 2009, 2010, 2011, and 2012?

Available with McGraw-Hill's Homework Manager

PROBLEMS

Recording and Reporting Current Liabilities

Curb Company completed the following transactions during 2009. The annual accounting period ends December 31, 2009.

Jan.   15   Purchased and paid for merchandise for resale at an invoice cost of $14,200; periodic inventory system.
Apr.   1   Borrowed $700,000 from Summit Bank for general use; executed an 10-month, 8 percent interest-bearing note payable.
June   14   Received a $15,000 customer deposit from Mark Muller for services to be performed in the future.
July   15   Performed $3,750 of the services paid for by Mr. Muller.
Dec.   12   Received electric bill for $27,860. The company will pay it in early January.
       31   Determined wages of $15,000 earned but not yet paid on December 31 (disregard payroll taxes).

Required:
  1. Prepare journal entries for each of these transactions.
  2. Prepare all adjusting entries required on December 31, 2009.

P9-1
L01

Recording and Reporting Current Liabilities with Discussion of Cash Flow Effects

Smith Company completed the following transactions during 2009. The annual accounting period ends December 31, 2009. (AP9–1)

Jan.   8   Purchased merchandise for resale on account at an invoice cost of $14,860; assume a periodic inventory system.
       17   Paid January 8 invoice.
Apr.   1   Borrowed $35,000 from National Bank for general use; executed a 12-month, 12 percent interest-bearing note payable.
June   3   Purchased merchandise for resale on account at an invoice cost of $17,420.
July   5   Paid June 3 invoice.
Aug.   1   Rented a small office in a building owned by the company and collected six months' rent in advance amounting to $6,000. (Record the collection in a way that will not require an adjusting entry at year-end.)
Dec.   20   Received a $100 deposit from a customer as a guarantee to return a large trailer "borrowed" for 30 days.
       31   Determined wages of $9,500 earned but not yet paid on December 31 (disregard payroll taxes).

Required:
  1. Prepare journal entries for each of these transactions.
  2. Prepare all adjusting entries required on December 31, 2009.
  3. Show how all of the liabilities arising from these transactions are reported on the balance sheet at December 31, 2009.
  4. For each transaction, state whether the current ratio is increased, decreased, or remains the same.
  5. For each transaction, state whether cash flow from operating activities is increased, decreased, or there is no effect.

P9-2
L01, 2, 6

Determining Financial Effects of Transactions Affecting Current Liabilities with Discussion of Cash Flow Effects (AP9–2)

Using data from the previous problem, complete the following requirements.

P9-3
L01, 2, 6

Required:

1. For each transaction (including adjusting entries) listed in the previous problem, indicate the effects (e.g., cash + or −), using the following schedule:

Date	Assets	Liabilities	Stockholders' Equity

2. For each transaction, state whether cash flow from operating activities is increased, decreased, or remains the same.
3. For each transaction, state whether the current ratio is increased, decreased, or there is no change.

P9-4
L01

Recording and Reporting Accrued Liabilities and Deferred Revenue with Discussion

During 2010, Riverside Company completed the following two transactions. The annual accounting period ends December 31.

a. Paid and recorded wages of $130,000 during 2010; however, at the end of December 2010, three days' wages are unpaid and unrecorded because the weekly payroll will not be paid until January 6, 2011. Wages for the three days are $4,000.
b. Collected rent revenue on December 10, 2010, of $2,400 for office space that Riverside rented to another party. The rent collected was for 30 days from December 10, 2010, to January 10, 2011, and was credited in full to Rent Revenue.

Required:

1. Give (a) the adjusting entry required on December 31, 2010, and (b) the January 6, 2011, journal entry for payment of any unpaid wages from December 2010.
2. Give (a) the journal entry for the collection of rent on December 10, 2010, and (b) the adjusting entry on December 31, 2010.
3. Show how any liabilities related to these transactions should be reported on the company's balance sheet at December 31, 2010.
4. Explain why the accrual method of accounting provides relevant information to financial analysts.

P9-5
L01

Determining Financial Statement Effects of Transactions Involving Accrued Liabilities and Deferred Revenue

Using the data from the previous exercise, complete the following requirements.

Required:

1. Determine the financial statement effects for each of the following: (a) the adjusting entry required on December 31, 2010, (b) the January 6, 2011, journal entry for payment of any unpaid wages from December 2010, (c) the journal entry for the collection of rent on December 10, 2010, and (d) the adjusting entry on December 31, 2010. Indicate the effects (e.g., cash + or −), using the following schedule:

Date	Assets	Liabilities	Stockholders' Equity

2. Explain why the accrual method of accounting provides relevant information to financial analysts.

P9-6
L01, 5

Determining Financial Statement Effects of Various Liabilities (AP9–3)

Dell Inc. is a leader in the industry with over $56 billion in sales each year. Its annual report contained the following note:

Warranty   We record warranty liabilities at the time of sale for the estimated costs that may be incurred under its limited warranty. Factors that affect our warranty liability include the number of installed units currently under warranty, historical and anticipated rates of warranty claims on those units, and cost per claim to satisfy our warranty obligation.

Required:

1. Assume that estimated warranty costs for 2009 were $500 million and that the warranty work was performed during 2010. Describe the financial statement effects for each year.

Walt Disney is a well-recognized brand in the entertainment industry with products ranging from broadcast media to parks and resorts. The following note is from its annual report:

Walt Disney

Revenue Recognition

For non-expiring, multi-day tickets to our theme parks, we recognize revenue over a three-year period based on estimated usage patterns which are derived from historical usage patterns.

2. Assume that Disney collected $90 million in 2009 multi-day tickets that will be used in future years. For 2010, the company estimates that 60% of the tickets will be used. Describe the financial statement effects for each year.

Brunswick Corporation is a multinational company that manufactures and sells marine and recreational products. Its annual report contained the following information:

BRUNSWICK

Litigation

A jury awarded $44.4 million in damages in a suit brought by Independent Boat Builders, Inc., a buying group of boat manufacturers and its 22 members. Under the antitrust laws, the damage award has been trebled, and the plaintiffs will be entitled to their attorney's fees and interest.

The Company has filed an appeal contending the verdict was erroneous as a matter of law, both as to liability and damages.

3. How should Brunswick account for this litigation?
4. A recent annual report for The Walt Disney Company reported current assets of $9,562,000,000 and current liabilities of $10,210,000,000. Based on the current ratio, do you think that Disney is experiencing financial difficulty?

Walt Disney

Halliburton is a major corporation involved in the entire life cycle of oil and gas reserves, starting with exploration and development, moving through production, operations, maintenance, conversion, and refining to infrastructure and abandonment. The annual report for the company stated the following:

Haliburton

Environmental Expenditures

Our accrued liabilities from environmental matters were $50 million for the current year and $41 million for the previous year.

5. In your own words, explain Halliburton's accounting policy for environmental expenditures. What is the justification for this policy?

Making a Decision as Chief Financial Officer: Contingent Liabilities

P9-7
LO5

For each of the following situations, determine whether the company should (a) report a liability on the balance sheet, (b) disclose a contingent liability, or (c) not report the situation. Justify and explain your conclusions.

1. An automobile company introduces a new car. Past experience demonstrates that lawsuits will be filed as soon as the new model is involved in any accidents. The company can be certain that at least one jury will award damages to people injured in an accident.
2. A research scientist determines that the company's best-selling product may infringe on another company's patent. If the other company discovers the infringement and files suit, your company could lose millions.
3. As part of land development for a new housing project, your company has polluted a natural lake. Under state law, you must clean up the lake once you complete development. The development project will take five to eight years to complete. Current estimates indicate that it will cost $2 to $3 million to clean up the lake.
4. Your company has just been notified that it lost a product liability lawsuit for $1 million that it plans to appeal. Management is confident that the company will win on appeal, but the lawyers believe that it will lose.
5. A key customer is unhappy with the quality of a major construction project. The company believes that the customer is being unreasonable but, to maintain goodwill, has decided to do $250,000 in repairs next year.

P9-8
LO8

Determining Cash Flow Effects (AP9–4)

For each of the following transactions, determine whether cash flows from operating activities will increase, decrease, or remain the same:

a. Purchased merchandise on credit.
b. Paid an account payable in cash.
c. Accrued payroll for the month but did not pay it.
d. Borrowed money from the bank. The term of the note is 90 days.
e. Reclassified a long-term note as a current liability.
f. Paid accrued interest expense.
g. Disclosed a contingent liability based on a pending lawsuit.
h. Paid back the bank for money borrowed in d. Ignore interest.
i. Collected cash from a customer for services that will be performed in the next accounting period (i.e., deferred revenues are recorded).

P9-9
LO7
PepsiCo. Inc.

Analyzing the Reclassification of Debt (AP9-5)

PepsiCo, Inc., is a $25 billion company in the beverage, snack food, and restaurant businesses. PepsiCo's annual report included the following note:

At year-end, $3.5 billion of short-term borrowings were reclassified as long-term, reflecting PepsiCo's intent and ability to refinance these borrowings on a long-term basis, through either long-term debt issuances or rollover of existing short-term borrowings.

As a result of this reclassification, PepsiCo's current ratio improved from 0.51 to 0.79. Do you think the reclassification was appropriate? Why do you think management made the reclassification? As a financial analyst, would you use the current ratio before the reclassification or after the reclassification to evaluate PepsiCo's liquidity?

P9-10

www.mhhe.com/libby6e

Recording and Reporting Deferred Income Tax: Depreciation (Supplement B)

At December 31, 2009, the records of Pearson Corporation provided the following information:

Income statement	
Revenues	$140,000
Depreciation expense (straight line)	(11,000)†
Remaining expenses (excluding income tax)	(90,000)
Pretax income	$ 39,000

†Equipment depreciated—acquired January 1, 2009, cost $44,000; estimated useful life, four years and no residual value. Accelerated depreciation is used on the tax return as follows: 2009, $17,600; 2010, $13,200; 2011, $8,800; and 2012, $4,400.

a. Income tax rate, 30 percent. Assume that 85 percent is paid in the year incurred.
b. Taxable income from the 2009 income tax return, $32,400.

Required:

1. Compute income taxes payable and deferred income tax for 2009. Is the deferred income tax a liability or an asset? Explain.
2. Show what amounts related to 2009 income taxes should be reported on the income statement and balance sheet.

P9-11
LO8, 9

www.mhhe.com/libby6e

Computing Present Values (AP9-6)

On January 1, 2009, Plymouth Company completed the following transactions (use a 7 percent annual interest rate for all transactions):

a. Borrowed $115,000 for seven years. Will pay $8,050 interest at the end of each year and repay the $115,000 at the end of the 7th year.
b. Established a plant addition fund of $490,000 to be available at the end of year 8. A single sum that will grow to $490,000 will be deposited on January 1, 2009.

c. Agreed to pay a severance package to a discharged employee. The company will pay $75,000 at the end of the first year, $112,500 at the end of the second year, and $150,000 at the end of the third year.

d. Purchased a $170,000 machine on January 1, 2009, and paid cash, $40,000. A five-year note payable is signed for the balance. The note will be paid in five equal year-end payments starting on December 31, 2009.

Required (show computations and round to the nearest dollar):
1. In transaction *a,* determine the present value of the debt.
2. In transaction *b,* what single sum amount must the company deposit on January 1, 2009? What is the total amount of interest revenue that will be earned?
3. In transaction *c,* determine the present value of this obligation.
4. In transaction *d,* what is the amount of each of the equal annual payments that will be paid on the note? What is the total amount of interest expense that will be incurred?

Comparing Options Using Present Value Concepts (AP9–7)

P9-12
LO8
e**X**cel
www.mhhe.com/libby6e

After hearing a knock at your front door, you are surprised to see the Prize Patrol from a large, well-known magazine subscription company. It has arrived with the good news that you are the big winner, having won $12.5 million. You discover that you have three options: (1) you can receive $1.25 million per year for the next 10 years, (2) you can have $10 million today, or (3) you can have $2 million today and receive $1 million for each of the next 10 years. Your lawyer tells you that it is reasonable to expect to earn 10 percent on investments. Which option do you prefer? What factors influence your decision?

Computing Future Values (Supplement D) (AP9–8)

P9-13
e**X**cel
www.mhhe.com/libby6e

On December 31, 2009, Post Company created a fund that will be used to pay the principal amount of a $120,000 debt due on December 31, 2012. The company will make four equal annual deposits on each December 31 in 2009, 2010, 2011, and 2012. The fund will earn 7 percent annual interest, which will be added to the balance at each year-end. The fund trustee will pay the loan principal (to the creditor) upon receipt of the last fund deposit. The company's accounting period ends December 31.

Required (show computations and round to the nearest dollar):
1. How much must be deposited each December 31?
2. What amount of interest will be earned?
3. How much interest revenue will the fund earn in 2009, 2010, 2011, and 2012?

Computing Future Values (Supplement D)

P9-14

On January 1, 2009, Plymouth Company completed the following transactions (use an 8 percent annual interest rate for all transactions):

a. Deposited $50,000 in a debt retirement fund. Interest will be computed at six-month intervals and added to the fund at those times (i.e., semiannual compounding). *(Hint:* Think carefully about *n* and i.)

b. Established a pension retirement fund to be available by the end of year 6 by making six annual deposits of $130,000 at year-end, starting on December 31, 2009.

c. Deposited $250,000 in a debt retirement fund. Interest will be computed annually and added to the fund at those times.

Required:
1. In transaction *a,* what will be the balance in the fund at the end of year 3? What is the total amount of interest revenue that will be earned?
2. In transaction *b,* what is the amount of the retirement fund at the end of year 6? What is the total amount of interest revenue that will be earned?
3. In transaction *c,* what will be the balance in the fund at the end of year 6? What is the total amount of interest revenue that will be earned?

ALTERNATE PROBLEMS

AP9-1
L01, 6

Recording and Reporting Current Liabilities with Discussion of Cash Flow Effects (P9–2)

Curb Company completed the following transactions during 2010. The annual accounting period ends December 31, 2010.

Jan. 15   Recorded tax expense for the year in the amount of $125,000. Current taxes payable were $93,000.

31   Paid accrued interest expense in the amount of $52,000.

Apr. 30   Borrowed $550,000 from Commerce Bank; executed a 12-month, 12 percent interest-bearing note payable.

June 3   Purchased merchandise for resale at an invoice cost of $75,820, on account.

July 5   Paid June 3 invoice.

Aug. 31   Signed contract to provide security service to a small apartment complex and collected six months' fees in advance amounting to $12,000. (Record the collection in a way that will not require an adjusting entry at year-end.)

Dec. 31   Reclassified a long-term liability in the amount of $100,000 to a current liability classification.

31   Determined salary and wages of $85,000 earned but not yet paid December 31 (disregard payroll taxes).

Required:
1. Prepare journal entries for each of these transactions.
2. Prepare all adjusting entries required on December 31, 2010.
3. Show how all of the liabilities arising from these transactions are reported on the balance sheet at December 31, 2010.
4. For each transaction, state whether cash flow from operating activities is increased, decreased, or there is no effect.

AP9-2
L01, 6

Determining Financial Effects of Transactions Affecting Current Liabilities with Discussion of Cash Flow Effects (P9–3)

Using data from problem AP9-1, complete the following requirements.

Required:
1. For each transaction (including adjusting entries) listed in the previous problem, indicate the effects (e.g., cash + or −), using the following schedule:

Date	Assets	Liabilities	Stockholders' Equity

2. For each transaction, state whether cash flow from operating activities is increased, decreased, or there is no effect.

AP9-3
L01, 5
Ford

Determining Financial Statement Effects of Various Liabilities (P9–6)

Ford Motor Company is one of the world's largest companies with annual sales of cars and trucks in excess of $170 billion. Its annual report contained the following note:

Warranties

Estimated warranty costs are accrued for at the time the vehicle is sold to a dealer. Estimates for warranty cost are made based primarily on historical warranty claim experience.

Required:
1. This year, Ford reported claims amounting to $4.0 billion and accrued expenses for warranties in the amount of $3.9 billion. Describe the financial statement effects for this year.

Bally   Bally Total Fitness Holding Corporation is the largest publicly traded commercial operator of fitness centers in North America in terms of members, revenues and square footage of its facilities.

The company operates 409 fitness centers primarily under the Bally Total Fitness name. The following note was contained in their annual report.

Revenue Recognition: As a general principle, revenue is recognized when the following criteria are met: (i) persuasive evidence of an arrangement exists, (ii) delivery has occurred and services have been rendered, (iii) the price to the buyer is fixed or determinable and, (iv) collectability is reasonably assured. Membership revenue is earned on a straight-line basis over the longer of the contractual term or the estimated membership term. The weighted average membership life is 39 months

2. In your own words, explain how unearned revenue is reported in the balance sheet for Bally. Assume that the company collected $23 million in December 2009 for "New Year's Resolution" memberships starting January 1, 2010. What is the amount of unearned revenue that should be reported on the 2009 and 2010 balance sheets?

Sunbeam Corporation is a consumer products company that manufactures and markets a number of familiar brands including Mr. Coffee, Osterizer, First Alert, and Coleman. Annual revenues for the company exceed $2 billion. Its annual report contained the following information: **Sunbeam**

Litigation

The Company and its subsidiaries are involved in various lawsuits arising from time to time that the Company considers to be ordinary routine litigation incidental to its business. In the opinion of the Company, the resolution of these routine matters will not have a material adverse effect upon the financial position, results of operations, or cash flows of the Company. At the end of the current year, the Company had established accruals for litigation matters of $31.2 million.

This year, the Company recorded a $12.0 million charge related to a case for which an adverse development arose. In the fourth quarter of this year, the case was favorably resolved and, as a result, $8.1 million of the charge was reversed into income.

3. Explain the meaning of this note in your own words. Describe how litigation has affected the financial statements for Sunbeam.

4. A recent annual report for ExxonMobil reported a current ratio of 0.90. For the previous year, the ratio was 1.08. Based on this information, do you think that Exxon is experiencing financial difficulty? What other information would you want to consider in making this evaluation?   **ExxonMobil**

Brunswick Corporation is a multinational company that manufactures and sells marine and recreational products. Its annual report contained the following information:

Legal and Environmental

The company is involved in numerous environmental remediation and clean-up projects with an aggregate estimated exposure of approximately $21 million to $42 million. The Company accrues for environmental remediation-related activities for which commitments or clean-up plans have been developed and for which costs can be reasonably estimated.

5. In your own words, explain Brunswick's accounting policy for environmental expenditures. What is the justification for this policy?

Determining Cash Flow Effects (P9–8)

AP9–4
LO6

For each of the following transactions, determine whether cash flows from operating activities will increase, decrease, or remain the same:

a. Purchased merchandise for cash.
b. Paid salaries and wages for the last month of the previous accounting period.
c. Paid taxes to the federal government.
d. Borrowed money from the bank. The term of the note is two years.
e. Withheld FICA taxes from employees' paychecks and immediately paid to the government.
f. Recorded accrued interest expense.
g. Paid cash as the result of losing a lawsuit. A contingent liability associated with the liability had been recorded.
h. Paid salaries and wages for the current month in cash.
i. Performed services for a customer who had paid for them in the previous accounting period (i.e., deferred revenue is earned).

AP9-5
L07

GENERAL MILLS

Analyzing the Reclassification of Debt (P9–9)

General Mills is a multibillion-dollar company that makes and sells products used in the kitchens of most American homes. The company's annual report included the following note:

We have a revolving credit agreement expiring in two years that provides for a credit line (which permits us to borrow money when needed). This agreement provides us with the opportunity to refinance short-term borrowings on a long-term basis.

Should General Mills classify the short-term borrowings as current or noncurrent debt based on this ability to borrow money to refinance the debt if needed? If you were a member of the management team, explain what you would want to do and why. If you were a financial analyst, would your answer be different?

AP9-6
L08, 9

Computing Present Values (P9–11)

On January 1, 2009, Neeley Company completed the following transactions (use an 8 percent annual interest rate for all transactions):

a. Borrowed $2,000,000 to be repaid in five years. Agreed to pay $150,000 interest each year for the five years.

b. Established a plant addition fund of $1,000,000 to be available at the end of year 10. A single sum that will grow to $1,000,000 will be deposited on January 1, 2009.

c. Purchased a $750,000 machine on January 1, 2009, and paid cash, $400,000. A four-year note payable is signed for the balance. The note will be paid in four equal year-end payments starting on December 31, 2009.

Required (show computations and round to the nearest dollar):

1. In transaction *a,* determine the present value of the obligation.

2. In transaction *b,* what single amount must the company deposit on January 1, 2009? What is the total amount of interest revenue that will be earned?

3. In transaction *c,* what is the amount of each of the equal annual payments that will be paid on the note? What is the total amount of interest expense that will be incurred?

AP9-7
L08

Comparing Options Using Present Value Concepts (P9–12)

After completing a long and successful career as senior vice president for a large bank, you are preparing for retirement. After visiting the human resources office, you have found that you have several retirement options: (1) you can receive an immediate cash payment of $750,000, (2) you can receive $60,000 per year for life (you have a life expectancy of 20 years), or (3) you can receive $50,000 per year for 10 years and then $80,000 per year for life (this option is intended to give you some protection against inflation). You have determined that you can earn 6 percent on your investments. Which option do you prefer and why?

AP9-8

Computing Future Values (P9–13) (Supplement D)

On January 1, 2009, Jacobs Auto Company decided to accumulate a fund to build an addition to its plant. The company will deposit $320,000 in the fund at each year-end, starting on December 31, 2009. The fund will earn 9 percent interest, which will be added to balance at each year-end. The accounting period ends December 31.

Required:

1. What will be the balance in the fund immediately after the December 31, 2011, deposit?

2. Complete the following fund accumulation schedule:

Date	Cash Payment	Interest Revenue	Fund Increase	Fund Balance
12/31/2009				
12/31/2010				
12/31/2011				
Total				

Annual Report Cases

Finding Financial Information

Refer to the financial statements of American Eagle given in Appendix B at the end of this book.

Required:
1. What is the amount of accrued compensation and benefits at the end the most recent reporting year?
2. By what amount did accounts payable change over the most recent reporting year? How did this change in accounts payable affect cash flows from operating activities during the most recent reporting year?
3. What is the amount of long-term liabilities at the end of the most recent reporting year?
4. Describe the company's policy if gift cards are not redeemed.

CP9-1
LO1, 4, 5, 7
AMERICAN EAGLE
OUTFITTERS

Finding Financial Information

Refer to the financial statements of Urban Outfitters given in Appendix C at the end of this book.

Required:
1. What is the amount of accrued compensation and payroll taxes liability at the end of the most recent reporting year?
2. By what amount did accounts payable change over the most recent reporting year? How did this change in accounts payable affect cash flows from operating activities during the most recent reporting year?
3. What is the amount of long-term liabilities at the end of the most recent reporting year?
4. Does the company have any liabilities associated with gift cards and merchandise credits?

CP9-2
LO1, 5, 7
Urban Outfitters

Comparing Companies within an Industry

Refer to the financial statements of American Eagle given in Appendix B, Urban Outfitters given in Appendix C, and the Standard and Poor's Industry Ratio Report given in Appendix D at the end of this book.

Required:
1. Compute the current ratio for each company for fiscal 2007.
2. Compare the most recent current ratio for each company to the industry average from the Industry Ratio report. Based solely on the current ratio, are these companies more or less liquid than the average company in their industry?
3. Compute the payable turnover ratio for each company for the most recent reporting year.
4. Compare the latest year payable turnover ratio for each company to the industry average from the Industry Ratio report. Are these companies doing better or worse than the average company in their industry at paying trade creditors?
5. Using this information and any other data from the annual report, write a brief assessment of the liquidity for the two companies.

CP9-3
LO2, 3
AMERICAN EAGLE
OUTFITTERS
Urban Outfitters
Standard & Poors

www.mhhe.com/libby6e

Financial Reporting and Analysis Cases

Analyzing Hidden Interest in a Real Estate Deal: Present Value

Many advertisements contain offers that seem too good to be true. A few years ago, an actual newspaper ad offered "a $150,000 house with a zero interest rate mortgage" for sale. If the purchaser made monthly payments of $3,125 for four years ($150,000 ÷ 48 months), no interest would be charged. When the offer was made, mortgage interest rates were 12 percent. Present value for $n = 48$, and $i = 1\%$ is 37.9740.

CP9-4
LO8

Required:

1. Did the builder actually provide a mortgage at zero interest?
2. Estimate the true price of the home that was advertised. Assume that the monthly payment was based on an implicit interest rate of 12 percent.

Critical Thinking Cases

CP9-5
LO1, 2

Making Decisions as a Manager: Liquidity

In some cases, a manager can engage in transactions that improve the appearance of financial reports without affecting the underlying economic reality. In this chapter, we discussed the importance of liquidity as measured by the current ratio and working capital. For each of the following transactions, (a) determine whether reported liquidity is improved and (b) state whether you believe that the fundamental liquidity of the company has been improved. Assume that the company has positive working capital and a current ratio of 2.0.

a. Borrowed $1 million from the bank, payable in 90 days.
b. Borrowed $10 million with a long-term note, payable in five years.
c. Reclassified current portion of long-term debt as long term as the result of a new agreement with the bank that guarantees the company's ability to refinance the debt when it matures.
d. Paid $100,000 of the company's accounts payable.
e. Entered a borrowing agreement that guarantees the ability to borrow up to $10 million when needed.
f. Required all employees to take accrued vacation to reduce its liability for vacation compensation.

CP9-6
LO2

Evaluating an Ethical Dilemma: Managing Reported Results

The president of a regional wholesale distribution company planned to borrow a significant amount of money from a local bank at the beginning of the next fiscal year. He knew that the bank placed a heavy emphasis on the liquidity of potential borrowers. To improve the company's current ratio, the president told his employees to stop shipping new merchandise to customers and to stop accepting merchandise from suppliers for the last three weeks of the fiscal year. Is this behavior ethical? Would your answer be different if the president had been concerned about reported profits and asked all of the employees to work overtime to ship out merchandise that had been ordered at the end of the year?

CP9-7
LO8

Evaluating an Ethical Dilemma: Fair Advertising

The New York State Lottery Commission ran the following advertisement in a number of New York newspapers:

The Lotto jackpot for Wednesday, August 25 will be $3 million including interest earned over a 20-year payment period. Constant payments will be made each year.

Explain the meaning of this advertisement in your own words. Evaluate the "fairness" of this advertisement. Could anyone be misled? Do you agree that the lottery winner has won $3 million? If not, what amount is more accurate? State any assumptions you make.

Financial Reporting and Analysis Team Project

CP9-8
LO1, 2, 3, 4, 6

Team Project: Examining an Annual Report

As a team, select an industry to analyze. *Reuters* provides lists of industries and their makeup at **www.reuters.com/finance/industries**. Each team member should acquire the annual report or 10-K for one publicly traded company in the industry, with each member selecting a different company. (Library files, the SEC EDGAR service at **www.sec.gov**, Compustat CD, or the company itself are good sources.)

Required:

On an individual basis, each team member should write a short report answering the following questions about the selected company. Discuss any patterns across the companies that you as a team observe. Then, as a team, write a short report comparing and contrasting your companies.

1. List the accounts and amounts of the company's liabilities for the last three years.
   a. What is the percentage of each to the respective year's total liabilities?
   b. What do the results of your analysis suggest about the strategy your company has followed with respect to borrowed funds overall and over time?
   c. Does the company disclose any lease liabilities in the footnotes? If so, compute the percentage of lease commitments to total liabilities.
2. What, if any, contingent liabilities are reported by the company for the most recent year and what is your assessment of the risk of each after reading the footnote(s)?
3. Ratio analysis:
   a. What does the current ratio measure in general?
   b. Compute the ratio for the last three years.
   c. What do your results suggest about the company?
   d. If available, find the industry ratio for the most recent year, compare it to your results, and discuss why you believe your company differs or is similar to the industry ratio.
4. Ratio analysis:
   a. What does the accounts payable turnover ratio measure in general?
   b. Compute the ratio for the last three years.
   c. What do your results suggest about the company?
   d. If available, find the industry ratio for the most recent year, compare it to your results, and discuss why you believe your company differs from or is similar to the industry ratio.
5. What is the effect of the change in accounts payable on cash flows from operating activities for the most recent year (that is, did the change increase or decrease operating cash flows)? Explain your answer.

Lectured slideshow–LP10-1
www.mhhe.com/libby6e

LEARNING OBJECTIVES

After studying this chapter, you should be able to:

1. Describe the characteristics of bonds. p. 515

2. Report bonds payable and interest expense for bonds sold at par and analyze the times interest earned ratio. p. 522

3. Report bonds payable and interest expense for bonds sold at a discount p. 523

4. Report bonds payable and interest expense for bonds sold at a premium. p. 528

5. Analyze the debt-to-equity ratio. p. 531

6. Report the early retirement of bonds. p. 532

7. Explain how financing activities are reported on the statement of cash flows. p. 533

REPORTING AND INTERPRETING BONDS

Gaming (gambling) has become big business in this country. Casinos are now just a short drive from most major cities. Many of the most popular ones are owned and operated by major corporations whose stock is traded on the New York Stock Exchange. One of the most successful gaming companies is Harrah's Entertainment, Inc., which operates casinos under the names Harrah's, Horseshoe, Harveys, Showboat, and Rio. Harrah's annual report states the following:

Harrah's Entertainment's strategy is different from that of our competitors. With casinos in more locations, Harrah's Entertainment has more opportunities to develop valuable relationships with more customers than any other company. Harrah's Entertainment's distribution allows us to serve customers both in their home casino markets and as they travel.

As the gaming industry has grown and become more competitive, companies such as Harrah's have had to invest large amounts of money to create unique gaming environments. As Harrah's annual report states, "Nothing else matters if customers aren't dazzled with every encounter at every property." To illustrate the magnitude of the investment that is needed, consider the Harrah's casino in Tunica, Mississippi, 30 miles south of Memphis. The facility includes 35,000 square feet of gaming space, 1,180 slot machines, and 22 table games. To support the casino, Harrah's built a hotel with 182 rooms and 18 suites, three restaurants and a snack bar, a 250-seat showroom, a retail shop, 13,464 square feet of convention space, a golf course, and parking for 2,708 cars.

Because of the company's strategy of investing in large and unique casinos, Harrah's has had to raise large amounts of new capital in addition to retaining much of its income. In this chapter, we will study Harrah's sale of $500 million in new bonds. Harrah's has disclosed information concerning its long-term debt shown in Exhibit 10.1. Much of the terminology in this note is new to you. After studying this chapter, you will understand each of the terms used in the note.

NOTE 8—DEBT

Long-term debt consisted of the following as of December 31:

(In millions)	2006	2005
Credit facilities		
5.825%–7.25% at December 31, 2006, maturities to 2011	$ 4,307.0	$ 2,681.0
Secured Debt		
6.0%, maturity 2010	25.0	25.0
7.1%, maturity 2028	89.3	90.9
LIBOR plus 1%–2.75%, maturity 2011	67.0	—
S. African prime less 1.5%, maturity 2009	11.4	—
4.25%–10.125%, maturities to 2035	6.8	3.2
Unsecured Senior Notes		
8.5%, maturity 2006	—	413.3
7.125%, maturity 2007	497.8	494.4
Floating Rate Notes, maturity 2008	250.0	250.0
7.5%, maturity 2009	136.2	499.3
7.5%, maturity 2009	452.4	461.9
5.5%, maturity 2010	746.0	745.0
8.0%, maturity 2011	71.7	497.0
5.375%, maturity 2013	497.4	497.1
7.0%, maturity 2013	328.4	332.2
5.625%, maturity 2015	995.9	995.5
6.5%, maturity 2016	743.8	—
5.75%, maturity 2017	745.5	745.2
Floating Rate Contingent Convertible		
Senior Notes, maturity 2024	367.8	364.8
Unsecured Senior Subordinated Notes		
9.375%, maturity 2007	499.2	524.5
8.875%, maturity 2008	423.3	436.3
7.875%, maturity 2010	403.4	411.5
8.125%, maturity 2011	388.2	395.7
Other Unsecured Borrowings		
Commercial Paper, maturities to 2007	—	140.9
LIBOR plus 4.5%, maturity 2010	33.9	38.6
Other, various maturities	1.6	2.1
Capitalized Lease Obligations		
5.77%–11.5%, maturities to 2011	0.9	0.4
	12,089.9	11,045.8
Current portion of long-term debt	(451.2)	(7.0)
	$11,638.7	$11,038.8

UNDERSTANDING THE BUSINESS

Capital structure is the mixture of debt and equity a company uses to finance its operations. Almost all companies employ some debt in their capital structure. Indeed, large corporations need to borrow billions of dollars, which makes borrowing from individual creditors impractical. Instead, these corporations issue bonds to raise debt capital.

Bonds are securities that corporations and governmental units issue when they borrow large amounts of money. After bonds have been issued, they can be traded on established exchanges such as the New York Bond Exchange. The ability to sell a bond on the bond exchange is a significant advantage for creditors because it provides them with liquidity, or the ability to convert their investments into cash. If you lend money directly to a corporation for 20 years, you must wait that long before your cash investment is repaid. If you lend money by purchasing a bond, you can always sell it to another creditor if you need cash before it matures.

The liquidity of publicly traded bonds offers an important advantage to corporations. Because most creditors are reluctant to lend money for long periods with no opportunity to receive cash prior to maturity, they demand a higher interest rate for long-term loans. By issuing more liquid debt, corporations can reduce the cost of long-term borrowing.

This chapter provides a basic understanding of the management, accounting, and financial issues associated with bonds. We begin with a description of bonds payable. Then we see how bond transactions are analyzed and recorded. The chapter closes with a discussion of the early retirement of debt.

ORGANIZATION of the Chapter

Characteristics of Bonds Payable	Reporting Bond Transactions	Early Retirement of Debt
■ Bonds Issued at Par ■ Times Interest Earned Ratio	■ Bonds Issued at a Discount ■ Straight-Line Amortization ■ Effective-Interest Amortization	■ Bonds Issued at a Premium ■ Straight-Line Amortization ■ Effective-Interest Amortization ■ Debt-to-Equity Ratio

CHARACTERISTICS OF BONDS PAYABLE

Both stock and bonds are issued by corporations to raise money for long-term purposes. Several reasons why a corporation would want to issue bonds instead of stock are:

1. **Stockholders maintain control.** Bondholders do not vote or share in the company's earnings.

> **Learning Objective 1**
> Describe the characteristics of bonds.

Video 10-1
www.mhhe.com/libby6e

2. **Interest expense is tax deductible.** The tax deductibility of interest expense reduces the net cost of borrowing. This is an advantage compared to dividends paid on stock which are not tax deductible.

3. **The impact on earnings is positive.** Money can often be borrowed at a low interest rate and invested at a higher rate. Assume that Home Video, Inc., owns a video rental store. The company has stockholders' equity of $100,000 invested in the store and earns net income of $20,000 per year. Management plans to open a new store that will also cost $100,000 and earn $20,000 per year. Should management issue new stock or borrow the money at an interest rate of 8 percent? The following analysis shows that the use of debt will increase the return to the owners:

	Option 1 Stock	Option 2 Debt
Income before interest and taxes	$ 40,000	$ 40,000
Interest (8% × $100,000)		8,000
Income before taxes	40,000	32,000
Income taxes (35%)	14,000	11,200
Net income	26,000	20,800
Stockholders' equity	200,000	100,000
Return on equity	13%	20.8%

Unfortunately, bonds carry higher risk than equity. The following are the major disadvantages associated with issuing bonds:

1. **Risk of bankruptcy.** Interest payments to bondholders are fixed charges that must be paid each period whether the corporation earns income or incurs a loss.

2. **Negative impact on cash flows.** Debt must be repaid at a specified time in the future. Management must be able to generate sufficient cash to repay the debt or have the ability to refinance it.

The BOND PRINCIPAL is the amount (a) payable at the maturity of the bond and (b) on which the periodic cash interest payments are computed.

PAR VALUE is another name for bond principal, or the maturity amount of a bond.

FACE AMOUNT is another name for principal, or the maturity amount of the bond.

The STATED RATE is the rate of cash interest per period stated in the bond contract.

A bond usually requires the payment of interest over its life with repayment of principal on the maturity date. The **bond principal** is the amount (1) that is payable at the maturity date and (2) on which the periodic cash interest payments are computed. The principal is also called the **par value, face amount,** and maturity value. All bonds have a par value, which is the amount that will be paid when the bond matures. For most individual bonds, the par value is $1,000, but it can be any amount.

A bond always specifies a **stated rate** of interest and the timing of periodic cash interest payments, usually annually or semiannually. Each periodic interest payment is computed as principal times the stated interest rate. The selling price of a bond does not affect the periodic cash payment of interest. For example, a $1,000, 8 percent bond always pays cash interest of (1) $80 on an annual basis or (2) $40 on a semiannual basis.

Different types of bonds have different characteristics for good economic reasons. Individual creditors have different risk and return preferences. A retired person may be willing to receive a lower interest rate in return for greater security. This type of creditor might want a mortgage bond that pledges a specific asset as security in case the company cannot repay the bond. Another type of creditor might be willing to accept a low interest rate and an unsecured status in return for the opportunity to convert the bond into common stock at some point in the future. Companies try to design bond features that are attractive to different groups of creditors just as automobile manufacturers try to design cars that appeal to different groups of consumers. Some key types of bonds are shown here:

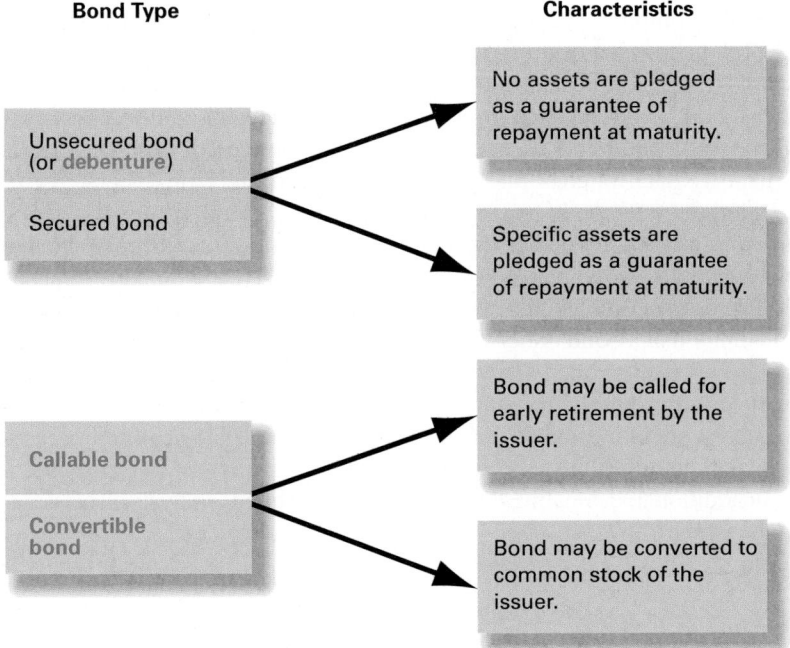

Bond Type

Unsecured bond (or debenture)

Secured bond

Callable bond

Convertible bond

Characteristics

No assets are pledged as a guarantee of repayment at maturity.

Specific assets are pledged as a guarantee of repayment at maturity.

Bond may be called for early retirement by the issuer.

Bond may be converted to common stock of the issuer.

A DEBENTURE is an unsecured bond; no assets are specifically pledged to guarantee repayment.

CALLABLE BONDS may be called for early retirement at the option of the issuer.

CONVERTIBLE BONDS may be converted to other securities of the issuer (usually common stock).

An INDENTURE is a bond contract that specifies the legal provisions of a bond issue.

When Harrah's decided to issue new bonds, it prepared a bond **indenture** (bond contract) that specified the legal provisions of the bonds. These provisions include the maturity date, rate of interest to be paid, date of each interest payment, and any conversion privileges. The indenture also contains covenants designed to protect the creditors. Harrah's indenture included limitations on new debt that the company might issue in the future. Other typical covenants include limitations on the payment of dividends and required minimums of certain accounting ratios, such as the current ratio. Because covenants may limit the company's future actions, management prefers those that are least restrictive. Creditors, however, prefer more restrictive covenants, which lessen the risk of the investment. As with any business transaction, the final result is achieved through negotiation.

Bond covenants are typically reported in the notes to the financial statements. *Accounting Trends & Techniques* (published by the AICPA) reviewed the reporting practices of 600 companies.[1] The graph in the margin shows the percentage of companies that disclosed debt covenants. Harrah's reported the following information about its debt covenants.

Disclosure of Debt Covenants (sample of 600 Companies)

■ Disclosed covenants
■ Did not disclose covenants

Long-Term Debt

Our debt agreements contain financial covenants requiring us to maintain a specific tangible net worth and to meet other financial ratios. Covenants limit our ability to pay dividends and to repurchase our outstanding shares.

REAL WORLD EXCERPT

Harrah's
ENTERTAINMENT, INC.
ANNUAL REPORT

[1]Reprinted with permission from *Accounting Trends & Techniques.* Copyright © 2006 by the American Institute of Certified Public Accounts, Inc.

A BOND CERTIFICATE is the bond document that each bondholder receives.

A TRUSTEE is an independent party appointed to represent the bondholders.

The bond issuer also prepares a prospectus, which is a legal document that is given to potential bond investors. The prospectus describes the company, the bonds, and how the proceeds of the bonds will be used. In the prospectus for the Harrah's bonds, we learn that the company plans to use the proceeds to repay some of its outstanding debt. This debt reduction was required as part of an agreement to purchase another company (Showboat) a few months earlier.

When a bond is issued to an investor, the person receives a **bond certificate.** All bond certificates for a single bond issue are identical. The face of each certificate shows the same maturity date, interest rate, interest dates, and other provisions. An independent party, called the **trustee,** is usually appointed to represent the bondholders. A trustee's duties are to ascertain whether the issuing company fulfills all provisions of the bond indenture. Harrah's appointed IBJ Whitehall Bank & Trust Company to act as trustee.

Because of the complexities associated with bonds, several agencies exist to evaluate the probability that a bond issuer will not be able to meet the requirements specified in the indenture. This risk is called *default risk.* Moody's and Standard and Poor's use letter ratings to specify the quality of a bond. Bonds with ratings above Baa/BBB are investment grade; bonds with ratings below that level are speculative and are often called *junk bonds.* Many banks, mutual funds, and trusts are permitted to invest only in investment-grade bonds. In addition to evaluating the risk of a specific bond, analysts also assess the overall risk of the issuer.

FINANCIAL ANALYSIS

Bond Information from the Business Press

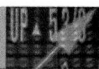

Bond prices are reported each day in the business press based on transactions that occurred on the bond exchange. The following is typical of the information you will find:

Bond	Yield	Volume	Close	Change
Safeway 6.0 13	6.8	58	97.2	−1/4
Sears 7.0 07	6.77	25	101.4	−3/8
Harrah's 7.5 09	6.9	580	104.1	−7/8

This listing states that the Harrah's bond has a coupon interest rate of 7.5 percent and will mature in the year 2009. The bond currently provides an effective interest yield of 6.9 percent and has a selling price of 104.1 percent of par, or $1,041.00. On this date, 580 bonds were sold, and the price fell 7/8 point from the closing price on the previous trading day (a point is 1 percent).

It is important to remember that these changes do not affect the company's financial statements. For financial reporting purposes, the company uses the interest rates that existed when the bonds were first sold to the public.

REPORTING BOND TRANSACTIONS

When Harrah's issued its bonds, it specified two types of cash payment in the bond contract:

1. **Principal.** This amount is usually a single payment that is made when the bond matures. It is also called the **par,** or **face, value.**

2. **Cash interest payments.** These payments, which represent an annuity, are computed by multiplying the principal amount times the interest rate stated in the bond

contract. This interest is called the **contract, stated,** or **coupon rate** of interest. The bond contract specifies whether the interest payments are made quarterly, semiannually, or annually. When you are asked to work problems in which interest payments are made more frequently than once a year, you must adjust both the periodic interest rate and the number of periods. For example, a $1,000 (face value) bond with an annual interest rate of 6 percent and a life of 10 years would pay interest of $30 ($1,000 × 6% × 1/2) for 20 periods (each six months for 10 years, or 10 × 2).

The COUPON RATE is the stated rate of interest on bonds.

Neither the issuing company nor the underwriter determines the price at which the bonds sell. Instead, the market determines the price using the present value concepts introduced in the last chapter. To determine the present value of the bond, you compute the present value of the principal (a single payment) and the present value of the interest payments (an annuity) and add the two amounts.

Creditors demand a certain rate of interest to compensate them for the risks related to bonds, called the **market interest rate** (also known as the **yield** or **effective-interest rate**). Because the market rate is the interest rate on a debt when it is incurred, it is the rate that should be used in computing the present value of a bond.

MARKET INTEREST RATE is the current rate of interest on a debt when incurred; also called the YIELD or EFFECTIVE-INTEREST RATE.

The present value of a bond may be the same as par, above par (**bond premium**), or below par (**bond discount**). If the stated and the market interest rates are the same, a bond sells at par; if the market rate is higher than the stated rate, a bond sells at a discount; and if the market rate is lower than the stated rate, the bond sells at a premium. This relationship can be shown graphically as follows:

BOND PREMIUM is the difference between the selling price and par when the bond is sold for more than par.

BOND DISCOUNT is the difference between the selling price and par when the bond is sold for less than par.

In commonsense terms, when a bond pays an interest rate that is less than the rate creditors demand, they will not buy it unless its price is reduced (i.e., a discount must be provided). When a bond pays more than creditors demand, they will be willing to pay a premium to buy it.

When a bond is issued at par, the issuer receives cash equal to its par value. When a bond is issued at a discount, the issuer receives less cash than the par value. When a bond is issued at a premium, the issuer receives more cash than the par value. Corporations and creditors do not care whether a bond is issued at par, at a discount, or at a premium because bonds are always priced to provide the market rate of interest. To illustrate, consider a corporation that issues three separate bonds on the same day. The bonds are the same except that one has a stated interest rate of 8 percent, another a rate of 10 percent, and a third a rate of 12 percent. If the market rate of interest were 10 percent, the first would be issued at a discount, the second at par, and the third at a premium. As a result, a creditor who bought any one of the bonds would earn the market interest rate of 10 percent.

During the life of the bond, its market price will change as market interest rates change. While this information is reported in the financial press, it does not affect the company's financial statements and the way its interest payments are accounted for from one period to the next.

In the next section of this chapter, we will see how to account for bonds issued at par, bonds issued at a discount, and bonds issued at a premium.

Your study of bonds will be easier if you understand the new terminology that has been introduced in this chapter. Let's review some of those terms. Define the following:

1. Market interest rate.
2. Coupon interest rate.
3. Synonyms for coupon interest rate.
4. Bond discount.
5. Bond premium.
6. Synonyms for market interest rate.

After you have completed your answers, check them with the solutions at the bottom of the page.

Bonds Issued at Par

Learning Objective 2
Report bonds payable and interest expense for bonds sold at par and analyze the times interest earned ratio.

Bonds sell at their par value when buyers are willing to invest in them at the interest rate stated in the bond contract. To illustrate, let's assume that on January 1, 2009, Harrah's issued 10 percent bonds with a par value of $100,000 and received $100,000 in cash (which means that the bonds sold at par). The bonds were dated to start earning interest on January 1, 2009, and will pay interest each June 30 and December 31. The bonds mature in two years on December 31, 2010.

The amount of money a corporation receives when it sells bonds is the present value of the future cash flows associated with them. When Harrah's issued its bonds, it agreed to make two types of payments in the future: a single payment of $100,000

Self-Study Quiz
Solutions

1. The market rate is the interest rate demanded by creditors. It is the rate used in the present value computations to discount future cash flows.
2. Coupon interest rate is the stated rate on the bonds.
3. Coupon rate is also called stated rate and contract rate.
4. A bond that sells for less than par is sold at a discount. This occurs when the coupon rate is lower than the market rate.
5. A bond that sells for more than par is sold at a premium. This occurs when the coupon rate is higher than the market rate.
6. Market interest rate is also called yield or effective-interest rate.

when the bond matures in two years, and an annuity of $5,000 payable twice a year for two years. The bond payments can be shown graphically as follows:

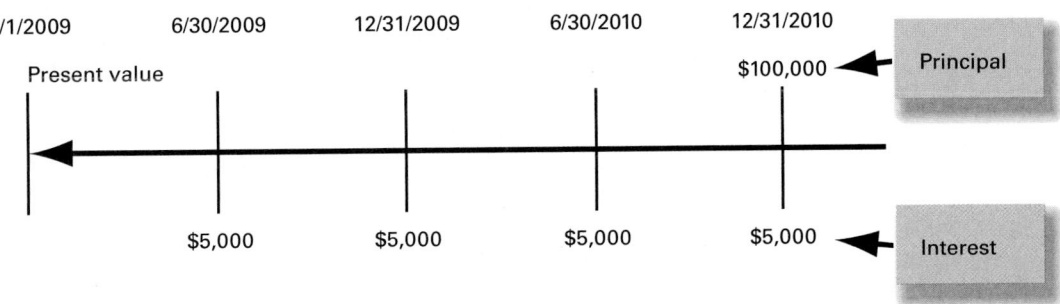

The present value of the bond payments can be computed with the tables contained in Appendix A using the factor for four periods and an interest rate of 5 percent per period:

To compute the present value using Excel, enter:
a. $= 100000/(1.05)^4$
b. $f_x = \text{PV}(0.05,4,-5000)$

	Present Value
a. Single payment: $100,000 × 0.8227	$ 82,270
b. Annuity: $5,000 × 3.5460	17,730
Issue price of Harrah's bonds	$100,000

When the effective rate of interest equals the stated rate of interest, the present value of the future cash flows associated with a bond always equals the bond's par amount. Remember a bond's selling price is determined by the present value of its future cash flows, not the par value. On date of issue, bond liabilities are recorded at the present value of future cash flows on date of issue, not the par value, as follows:

Cash (+A) 100,000
   Bonds payable (+L) 100,000

Assets	=	Liabilities	+	Stockholders' Equity
Cash +100,000		Bonds payable +100,000		

Bonds may pay interest each month, each quarter, each half-year, or each year. In all cases, the present value of the bond is determined using the interest rate factor for the number of interest periods and the interest rate for each period.

SELF-STUDY QUIZ

Assume that Harrah's issued $500,000 bonds that will mature in five years. The bonds pay interest at the end of each year at an annual rate of 8 percent. They were sold when the market rate was 8 percent. Compute the selling price of the bonds.

After you have completed your answer, check it with the solution at the bottom of the page.

1. $500,000 × 0.6806 = $340,300
($500,000 × 8%) × 3.9927 = 159,708
       $500,000 (rounded)

Self-Study Quiz
Solutions

Reporting Interest Expense on Bonds Issued at Par

The creditors who bought the bonds did so with the expectation that they would earn interest over the life of the bond. Harrah's will pay interest at 10 percent per year on the par value of the bonds each June 30 and December 31 until the bond's maturity date. The amount of interest each period will be $5,000 (10% $\times$ $100,000 $\times$ 1/2). The entry to record the interest payments is as follows:

| Interest expense (+E, −SE) | 5,000 | |
| Cash (−A) | | 5,000 |

Assets	=	Liabilities	+	Stockholders' Equity	
Cash −5,000				Interest expense	−5,000

Interest expense is reported on the income statement. Because interest is related to financing activities rather than operating activities, it is normally not included in operating expenses on the income statement. Instead, interest expense is reported as a deduction from "income from operations." The income statement for Harrah's shows how interest expense is usually reported.

HARRAH'S ENTERTAINMENT, INC.	
Consolidated Statement of Income	
(in thousands)	
	2006
Income from operations	1,556.6
Interest expense, net of interest capitalized (Note 12)	(670.5)
Losses on early extinguishments of debt (Note 8)	(62.0)
Other income, including interest income	10.7
Income from continuing operations before income taxes and minority interests	834.8

Bond interest payment dates rarely coincide with the last day of a company's fiscal year. Under the matching concept, interest expense that has been incurred but not paid must be accrued with an adjusting entry. If Harrah's fiscal year ended on May 31, the company would accrue interest for five months and record interest expense and interest payable.

Because interest payments are a legal obligation for the borrower, financial analysts want to be certain that a business is generating sufficient resources to meet its obligations. The times interest earned ratio is useful when making this assessment.

KEY RATIO ANALYSIS

Times Interest Earned

? ANALYTICAL QUESTION

Is the company generating sufficient resources from its profit-making activities to meet its current interest obligations?

% RATIO AND COMPARISONS

The times interest earned ratio is computed as follows:

$$\text{Times Interest Earned} = \frac{\text{Net Income} + \text{Interest Expense} + \text{Income Tax Expense}}{\text{Interest Expense}}$$

The 2006 ratio for Harrah's:

$$(\$535.8 + \$670.5 + \$295.6) \div 670.5 = 2.24$$

COMPARISONS OVER TIME			COMPARISONS WITH COMPETITORS	
Harrah's			**Mirage Resorts**	**Trump Casinos**
2004	**2005**	**2006**	**2006**	**2006**
3.05	1.96	2.24	3.71	0.74

💡 INTERPRETATIONS

In General   A high times interest earned ratio is viewed more favorably than a low one. The ratio shows the amount of resources generated for each dollar of interest expense. A high ratio indicates an extra margin of protection in case profitability deteriorates. Analysts are particularly interested in a company's ability to meet its required interest payments because failure to do so could result in bankruptcy.

Focus Company Analysis   In 2006, profit-making activities for Harrah's generated $2.24 for each dollar of interest, a very comfortable safety margin. Harrah's is able to generate significant cash flows from its operating activities. As a result, required interest payments are not at risk. Notice the ratio for Trump Casinos. It is extremely low and represents an early warning of serious danger.

A Few Cautions   The times interest earned ratio is often misleading for new or rapidly growing companies, which tend to invest considerable resources to build their capacity for future operations. In such cases, the times interest earned ratio will reflect significant amounts of interest expense associated with the new capacity but not the income that will be earned with the new capacity. Analysts should consider the company's long-term strategy when using this ratio. Some analysts prefer to compare interest expense to the amount of cash a company can generate. Because creditors cannot be paid with "income" that is generated, they must be paid with cash.

Bonds Issued at a Discount

Bonds sell at a discount when the market rate of interest is higher than the stated interest rate on them. Let's assume that the market rate of interest was 12 percent when Harrah's sold its bonds (which have a par value of $100,000). The bonds have a stated rate of 10 percent, payable twice a year on June 30 and December 31. Because the stated rate of interest is less than the market rate on the date of issue, the bonds sold at a discount.

To compute the cash issue price of the bonds, we can use the tables in Appendix A. As in the previous example, the number of periods is four and we use an interest rate of 6 percent per period, which is the market rate of interest. The cash issue price of the Harrah's bonds is computed as follows:

> **Learning Objective 3**
> Report bonds payable and interest expense for bonds sold at a discount.

	Present Value
a. Single payment: $100,000 × 0.7921	$79,210
b. Annuity: $5,000 × 3.4651	17,326
Issue (sale) price of Harrah's bonds	$96,536*

The amount of the discount: $100,000 − $96,536 = $3,464.

> To compute the present value using Excel, enter:
> *a.* = 100000/(1.06)^4
> *b.* f_x = PV(0.06,4,−5000)

The cash price of the bonds issued by Harrah's is $96,536. Some people refer to this price as 96.5, which means that the bonds were sold at 96.5 percent of their par value ($96,536 ÷ $100,000).

When a bond is sold at a discount, the Bonds Payable account is credited for the par amount, and the discount is recorded as a debit to Discount on Bonds Payable. The issuance of the Harrah's bonds at a discount is recorded as follows:

Cash (+A)	96,536	
Discount on bonds payable (+XL, −L)	3,464	
Bonds payable (+L)		100,000

Assets		=	Liabilities		+	Stockholders' Equity
Cash	+96,536		Bonds payable	+100,000		
			Discount on bonds	− 3,464		

Note that the discount is recorded in a separate contra-liability account (Discount on Bonds Payable) as a debit. The balance sheet reports the bonds payable at their book value, which is their maturity amount less any unamortized discount. Harrah's, like most companies, does not separately disclose the amount of unamortized discount or premium when the amount is small relative to other balance sheet amounts.

While Harrah's received only $96,536 when it sold the bonds, it must repay $100,000 when the bonds mature. The extra cash that must be paid is an adjustment of interest expense to ensure that creditors earn the market rate of interest. To adjust interest expense, the borrower apportions or amortizes the bond discount to each interest period as an increase in interest expense. Therefore, the amortization of bond discount results in an increase in interest expense. Two amortization methods are often used by companies: (1) straight line and (2) effective interest. Many companies use straight-line amortization because it is easy to compute the required numbers. However, the effective-interest method is the method required by GAAP. You may wonder why companies are permitted to use a method that is not the one required by accounting rules. The answer is materiality. Companies are permitted to use the straight-line method because the results are normally not materially different than the effective-interest method. We will first discuss the straight-line method and then the effective-interest method.

Part A: Reporting Interest Expense on Bonds Issued at a Discount Using Straight-line Amortization

STRAIGHT-LINE AMORTIZATION is a simplified method of amortizing a bond discount or premium that allocates an equal dollar amount to each interest period.

To amortize the $3,464 bond discount over the life of Harrah's bonds using **straight-line amortization,** we allocate an equal dollar amount to each interest period. Harrah's bonds have four interest periods. The amortization of discount each period is: $3,464 ÷ 4 periods = $866. We add this amount to the cash payment of interest ($5,000) to compute interest expense for the period ($5,866). The interest payments on Harrah's bonds each period are as follows:

Interest expense (+E, −SE)	5,866	
Discount on bonds payable (−XL, +L)		866
Cash (−A)		5,000

Assets		=	Liabilities		+	Stockholders' Equity	
Cash	−5,000		Discount on bonds	+866		Interest expense	−5,866

Bonds payable are reported on the balance sheet at their book value. At the end of the first interest period (June 30, 2009), the book value of Harrah's bonds is more than the original issue price. The book value increases to $97,402 ($96,536 + $866) because of the amortization of the discount. In each interest period, the book value of the bonds increases by $866 because the unamortized discount decreases by $866. At the maturity date of the bonds, the unamortized discount (i.e., the balance in the Discount on Bonds Payable account) is zero. At that time, the maturity amount of the bonds and the book value are the same (i.e., $100,000). This process can be seen in the following amortization schedule:

	AMORTIZATION SCHEDULE: BOND DISCOUNT (STRAIGHT-LINE)			
Date	(a) Interest to Be Paid (10% × $100,000 × 1/2)	(b) Interest Expense (a + c)	(c) Amortization ($3,464 ÷ 4 periods)	(d) Book Value Beginning Book Value + (c)
1/1/2009				$96,536
6/30/2009	$5,000	$5,866	$866	97,402
12/31/2009	5,000	5,866	866	98,268
6/30/2010	5,000	5,866	866	99,134
12/31/2010	5,000	5,866	866	100,000

SELF-STUDY QUIZ

Assume that Harrah's issued $100,000 bonds that will mature in 10 years. The bonds pay interest at the end of each year at an annual rate of 5 percent. They were sold when the market rate was 6 percent. The bonds were sold at a price of $92,641. What amount of interest was paid at the end of the first year? What amount of interest expense would be reported at the end of the first year using straight-line amortization?

After you have completed your answers, check them with the solution at the bottom of the page.

Part B: Reporting Interest Expense on Bonds Issued at a Discount Using Effective-Interest Amortization

Under the **effective-interest method,** interest expense for a bond is computed by multiplying the current unpaid balance times the market rate of interest that existed on the date the bonds were sold. The periodic amortization of a bond premium or discount is then calculated as the difference between interest expense and the amount of cash paid or accrued. This process can be summarized as follows:

The EFFECTIVE–INTEREST METHOD amortizes a bond discount or premium on the basis of the effective-interest rate; it is the theoretically preferred method.

Step 1:   Compute interest expense

Unpaid Balance × Effective Interest Rate × $n/12$

n = Number of Months in Each Interest Period

Step 2:   Compute amortization amount

Interest Expense − Cash Interest

The first interest payment on Harrah's bonds is made on June 30, 2009. Interest expense at the end of the first interest period (June 30, 2009) is calculated by multiplying the unpaid balance of the debt by the market rate of interest ($96,536 × 12% × 1/2 = $5,792). The amount of cash paid is calculated by multiplying the principal by the stated

---

1. $5,000 (5% × $100,000)
2. $5,736 [$5,000 + ($7,359 ÷ 10)]

Self-Study Quiz
Solutions

rate of interest ($100,000 × 10% × 1/2 = $5,000). The difference between the interest expense and the cash paid (or accrued) is the amount of discount that has been amortized ($5,792 − $5,000 = $792).

Effective-interest amortization causes these amounts to change each period.

Interest expense (+E, −SE)	5,792	
Discount on bonds payable (−XL, +L)		792
Cash (−A)		5,000

Assets		=	Liabilities		+	Stockholders' Equity	
Cash	−5,000		Discount on bonds	+792		Interest expense	−5,792

Each period, the amortization of the bond discount increases the bond's book value (or unpaid balance). The amortization of bond discount can be thought of as interest earned by the bondholders but not paid to them. During the first interest period, the bondholders earned interest of $5,792 but received only $5,000 in cash. The additional $792 was added to the principal of the bond and will be paid to bondholders when the bond matures.

Interest expense for the next interest period must reflect the change in the unpaid balance of bonds payable that occurred with amortization of the bond discount. The interest expense for the second half of 2009 is calculated by multiplying the unpaid balance ($96,536 + $792 = $97,328) on June 30, 2009, by the market rate of interest ($97,328 × 12% × 1/2 = $5,840). Thus amortization of the bond discount on December 31, 2009 is $840.

Interest expense (+E, −SE)	5,840	
Discount on bonds payable (−XL, +L)		840
Cash (−A)		5,000

Assets		=	Liabilities		+	Stockholders' Equity	
Cash	−5,000		Discount on bonds	+840		Interest expense	−5,840

Notice that interest expense for December 31, 2009, is more than interest expense for June 30, 2009. Harrah's effectively borrowed more money during the second half of the year because of the unpaid interest. Because of the amortization of the bond discount, interest expense increases each year during the life of the bond. This process can be illustrated with the amortization schedule shown below:

	AMORTIZATION SCHEDULE: BOND DISCOUNT(EFFECTIVE-INTEREST)			
Date	(a) Interest to Be Paid (10% × $100,000 × 1/2)	(b) Interest Expense (12% × Begining of Period Book Value × 1/2)	(c) Amortization (b) − (a)	(d) Book Value Beginning Book Value + (c)
1/1/2009				$96,536
6/30/2009	$5,000	$5,792	$792	97,328
12/31/2009	5,000	5,840	840	98,168
6/31/2010	5,000	5,890	890	99,058
12/31/2010	5,000	5,943	943	100,001*

This amount should be exactly $100,000. The $1 error is due to rounding.

Interest expense (column b) is computed by multiplying the market rate of interest by the book value of the bonds at the beginning of the period (column d). Amortization is computed by subtracting cash interest (column a) from interest expense (column b). The book value of the bonds (column d) is computed by adding amortization (column c) to the book value at the beginning of the period. In summary, under the effective-interest method, interest expense changes each accounting period as the effective amount of the liability changes. Under the straight-line method, interest expense remains constant over the life of the bond. The chart in the margin illustrates these differences.

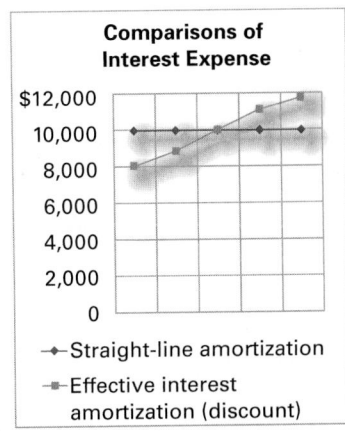

Comparisons of Interest Expense

→ Straight-line amortization

→ Effective interest amortization (discount)

SELF-STUDY QUIZ

Assume that Harrah's issued $100,000 bonds that will mature in 10 years. The bonds pay interest at the end of each year at an annual rate of 5 percent. They were sold when the market rate was 6 percent. The bonds were sold at a price of $92,641. What amount of interest was paid at the end of the first year? What amount of interest expense would be reported at the end of the first year using effective-interest amortization?

After you have completed your answers, check them with the solution at the bottom of the page.

FINANCIAL ANALYSIS

Zero Coupon Bonds

So far, we have discussed common bonds that are issued by many corporations. For a number of reasons, corporations may issue bonds with unusual features. The concepts you have learned will help you understand these bonds. For example, a corporation might issue a bond that does not pay periodic cash interest. These bonds are often called *zero coupon bonds*. Why would an investor buy a bond that did not pay interest? Our discussion of bond discounts has probably given you a good idea of the answer. The coupon interest rate on a bond can be virtually any amount and the price of the bond will be adjusted so that investors earn the market rate of interest. A bond with a zero coupon interest rate is simply a deeply discounted bond that will sell for substantially less than its maturity value.

Let's use the $100,000 Harrah's bond to illustrate a zero coupon rate. Assume that market rate is 10 percent and the bond pays no cash interest. The bond matures in five years. The selling price of the bond is the present value of the maturity amount because no other cash payments will be made over the life of the bond. We can compute the present value with the tables contained in Appendix A, using the factor for five periods and an interest rate of 10%:

To compute the present value using Excel, enter:
= 100000/(1.10)^5

	Present Value
Single payment: $100,000 × 0.6209	$62,090

1. $5,000 (5% × $100,000)
2. $5,558 (6% × $92,641)

Accounting for a zero coupon bond is no different from accounting for other bonds sold at a discount. However, the amount of the discount is much larger. The annual report for General Mills contained the following information concerning the company's zero coupon bonds:

Note 9. Long-Term Debt

(in millions)	2003	2002
Zero Coupon notes, yield 11.1% $261 due 2013	$87	$78

While these bonds do not pay cash interest, they have been priced to provide the investor with an effective interest rate of 11.1 percent. Notice that the amount of the obligation increases from 2002 to 2003. This increase is the result of the amortization of the bond discount.

Learning Objective 4
Report bonds payable and interest expense for bonds sold at a premium.

Bonds Issued at a Premium

Bonds sell at a premium when the market rate of interest is lower than their stated interest rate. Let's assume that the market rate of interest is 8 percent while the Harrah's bonds pay cash interest of 10 percent. The bonds pay interest semiannually and mature in two years. The bonds are issued on January 1, 2009.

The present value of Harrah's 10 percent bonds can be computed from the tables contained in Appendix A using the factor for four periods and an interest rate of 4% per period:

To compute the present value using Excel, enter:
$a. = 100000/(1.04)^4$
$b. f_x = PV(0.04,4,-5000)$

	Present Value
a. Single payment: $100,000 × 0.8548	$ 85,480
b. Annuity: $5,000 × 3.6299	18,150
Issue (sale) price of Harrah's bonds	$103,630

When a bond is sold at a premium, the Bonds Payable account is credited for the par amount, and the premium is recorded as a credit to Premium on Bonds Payable. The January 1, 2009, issuance of Harrah's bonds at a premium would be recorded as follows:

Audio lecture–AP10-1
www.mhhe.com/libby6e

Cash (+A)	103,630	
Premium on bonds payable (+L)		3,630
Bonds payable (+L)		100,000

Assets	=	Liabilities	+	Stockholders' Equity
Cash +103,630		Premium on bonds +3,630 Bonds payable +100,000		

The book value of the bond is the sum of the two accounts, Premium on Bonds Payable and Bonds Payable, or $103,630.

Part A: Reporting Interest Expense on Bonds Issued at a Premium Using Straight-line Amortization

As with a discount, the recorded premium of $3,630 must be apportioned to each interest period. Using the straight-line method, the amortization of premium each annual interest period is $908 ($3,630 ÷ 4 periods). This amount is subtracted from the cash interest payment ($5,000) to calculate interest expense ($4,092). Thus, amortization of a bond premium decreases interest expense.

The payment of interest on the bonds is recorded as follows:

Interest expense (+E, −SE)	4,092	
Premium on bonds payable (−L)	908	
Cash (−A)		5,000

Assets	=	Liabilities	+	Stockholders' Equity
Cash −5,000		Premium on bonds −908		Interest expense −4,092

Notice that the $5,000 cash paid each period includes $4,092 interest expense and $908 premium amortization. Thus, the cash payment to investors includes the current interest they have earned plus a return of part of the premium they paid when they bought the bonds.

The book value of the bonds is the amount in the Bonds Payable account plus any unamortized premium. On June 30, 2009, the book value of the bonds is $102,722 ($100,000 + $3,630 − $908). A complete amortization schedule follows:

	AMORTIZATION SCHEDULE: BOND PREMIUM (STRAIGHT-LINE)			
Date	(a) Interest to Be Paid (10% × $100,000 × 1/2)	(b) Interest Expense (a − c)	(c) Amortization ($3,630 ÷ 4 periods)	(d) Book Value Beginning Book Value − (c)
1/1/2009				$103,630
6/30/2009	$5,000	$4,092	$908	102,722
12/31/2009	5,000	$4,092	908	101,814
6/31/2010	5,000	$4,092	908	100,906
12/31/2010	5,000	$4,092	908	99,998*

This amount should be exactly $100,000. The $2 error is due to rounding.

At maturity, after the last interest payment, the bond premium is fully amortized, and the maturity amount equals the book value of the bonds. When the bonds are paid off in full, the same entry will be made whether the bond was originally sold at par, at a discount, or at a premium. Exhibit 10.2 compares the effects of the amortization of bond discount and bond premium on a $1,000 bond.

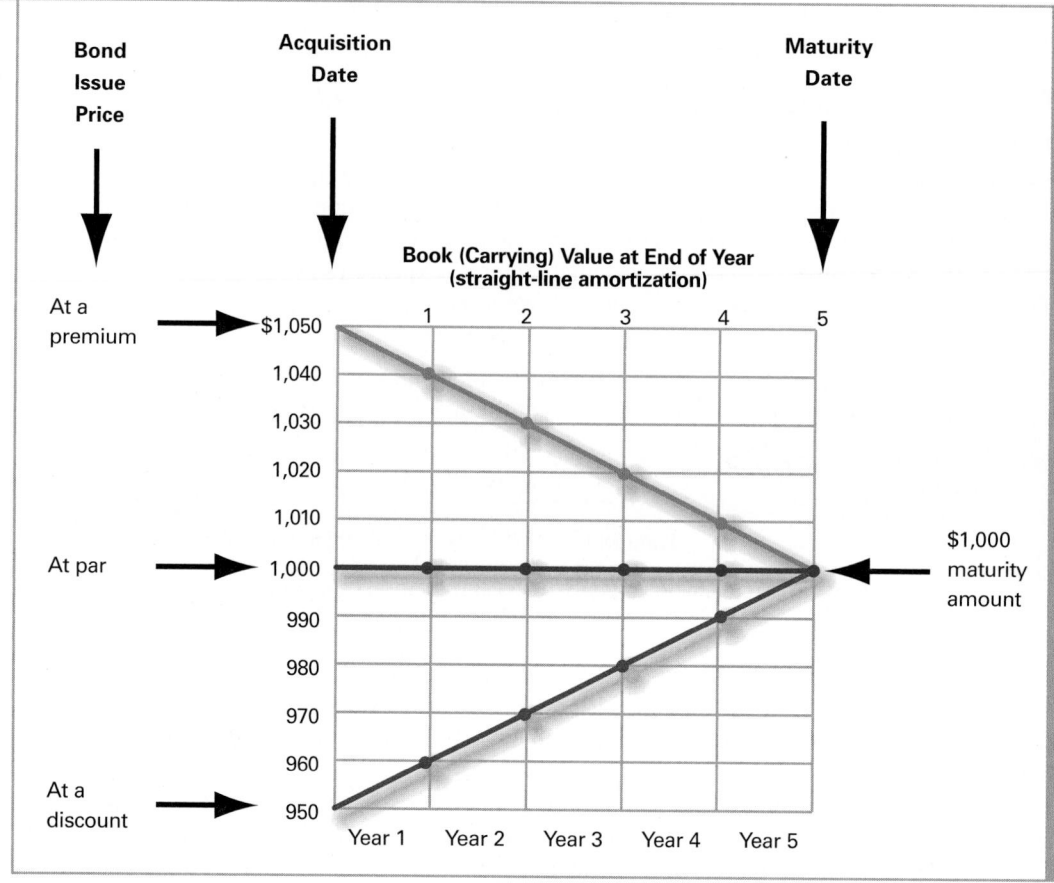

EXHIBIT 10.2

Amortization of Bond Discount and Premium Compared

Bond Issue Price

Acquisition Date

Maturity Date

Book (Carrying) Value at End of Year
(straight-line amortization)

At a premium → $1,050

At par → 1,000

$1,000 maturity amount

At a discount → 950

Year 1 Year 2 Year 3 Year 4 Year 5

SELF-STUDY QUIZ

Assume that Harrah's issued $100,000 bonds that will mature in 10 years. The bonds pay interest at the end of each year at an annual rate of 9 percent. They were sold when the market rate was 8 percent. The bonds were sold at a price of $106,711. What amount of interest was paid at the end of the first year? What amount of interest expense would be reported at the end of the first year using straight-line amortization?

After you have completed your answers, check them with the solution at the bottom of the page.

Part B: Reporting Interest Expense on Bonds Issued at a Premium Using Effective-interest Amortization

The effective-interest method is basically the same for a discount or a premium. In either case, interest expense for a bond is computed by multiplying the current unpaid balance by the market rate of interest on the date the bonds were sold. The periodic amortization of a bond premium or discount is then calculated as the difference between interest expense and the amount of cash paid or accrued.

The first interest payment on Harrah's bonds is made on June 30, 2009. The interest expense on that date is calculated by multiplying the unpaid balance of the debt by the market rate of interest ($103,630 × 8% × 1/2 = $4,145). The amount of cash paid is

Self-Study Quiz
Solutions

1. $9,000 (9% × $100,000)
2. $8,329 [$9,000 − ($6,711 ÷ 10)]

calculated by multiplying the principal by the stated rate of interest ($100,000 × 10% × 1/2 = $5,000). The difference between the interest expense and the cash paid (or accrued) is the amount of premium that has been amortized ($5,000 − $4,145 = $855).

Interest expense (+E, −SE) 4,145
Bond premium (−L) 855
   Cash (−A) 5,000

Assets	=	Liabilities	+	Stockholders' Equity	
Cash	−5,000	Bond premium	−855	Interest expense	−4,145

The basic difference between effective-interest amortization of a bond discount and a bond premium is that the amortization of a discount increases the book value of the liability and the amortization of a premium reduces it. The following schedule illustrates the amortization of a premium over the life of a bond.

	AMORTIZATION SCHEDULE: BOND PREMIUM (EFFECTIVE-INTEREST)			
Date	(a) Interest to Be Paid (10% × $100,000 × 1/2)	(b) Interest Expense (8% × Begining of Book Value × 1/2)	(c) Amortization (b) − (a)	(d) Book Value Beginning Book Value − (c)
1/1/2009				$103,630
6/30/2009	$5,000	$4,145	$855	102,775
12/31/2009	5,000	4,111	889	101,886
6/30/2010	5,000	4,075	925	100,961
12/31/2010	5,000	4,039*	961	100,000

*Rounded.

Assume that Harrah's issued $100,000 bonds that will mature in 10 years. The bonds pay interest at the end of each year at an annual rate of 9 percent. They were sold when the market rate was 8 percent. The bonds were sold at a price of $106,711. What amount of interest was paid at the end of the first year? What amount of interest expense would be reported at the end of the first year using effective-interest amortization?

After you have completed your answers, check them with the solution at the bottom of the page.

KEY RATIO
ANALYSIS

 Debt-to-Equity

? ANALYTICAL QUESTION
What is the relationship between the amount of capital provided by owners and the amount provided by creditors?

Learning Objective 5
Analyze the debt-to-equity ratio

% RATIO AND COMPARISONS
The debt-to-equity ratio is computed as follows:

Debt-to-Equity = Total Liabilities ÷ Stockholders' Equity

1. $9,000 (9% × $100,000)
2. $8,537 (8% × $106,711)

Self-Study Quiz
Solutions

The 2006 ratio for Harrah's is:

$$\$16,161.4 \div \$6,071.1 = 2.66$$

COMPARISONS OVER TIME			COMPARISONS WITH COMPETITORS	
Harrah's			Mirage Resorts	Trump Casinos
2004	2005	2006	2006	2003
2.75	2.62	2.66	3.08	5.12

💡 INTERPRETATIONS

In General   A high ratio suggests that a company relies heavily on funds provided by creditors. Heavy reliance on creditors increases the risk that a company may not be able to meet its contractual financial obligations during a business downturn.

Focus Company Analysis   The debt-to-equity ratio for Harrah's has decreased over the past few years. While the company has invested heavily in the acquisition of other companies and the expansion of facilities, it has been able to do so with cash generated by its operating activities. The company's strong operating results have permitted it to expand and reduce debt in comparison to equity. Most analysts would see this as a very positive situation. As was the case with the times interest earned ratio, the Trump debt-to-equity ratio is more of a cause for concern. The ratio is higher than similar companies and warrants further investigation.

A Few Cautions   The debt-to-equity ratio tells only part of the story with respect to the risks associated with debt. It does not help the analyst understand whether the company's operations can support its debt. Remember that debt carries an obligation to make cash payments for interest and principal. As a result, most analysts would evaluate the debt-to-equity ratio within the context of the amount of cash the company can generate from operating activities.

Learning Objective 6

Report the early retirement of bonds.

EARLY RETIREMENT OF DEBT

Bonds are normally issued for long periods, such as 20 or 30 years. As mentioned earlier, bondholders who need cash prior to the maturity date can simply sell the bonds to another investor. This transaction does not affect the books of the company that issued the bonds. In several situations, a corporation may decide to retire bonds before their maturity date. A bond with a call feature may be called in for early retirement at the issuer's option. Typically, the bond indenture includes a call premium for bonds retired before the maturity date, which often is stated as a percentage of par value. The prospectus for Harrah's bonds included the following:

REAL WORLD EXCERPT

The Notes are redeemable, in whole or in part, at any time, at our option at a redemption price equal to the greater of (a) 100% of the principal amount of the Notes then outstanding or (b) the sum of the present values of the remaining scheduled payments of principal and interest thereon discounted at the Treasury Rate, plus .30% interest.

Assume that several years ago, Harrah's issued bonds in the amount of $1 million and that the bonds sold at par. If Harrah's called the bonds in 2009 at 102% of par, the company's accountants would make the following journal entry:

Bonds payable (−L)	1,000,000	
Loss on bond call (+Loss, −SE)	20,000	
Cash (−A)		1,020,000

Assets	=	Liabilities	+	Stockholders' Equity
Cash −1,020,000		Bonds payable −1,000,000		Loss −20,000

The loss on the bond call is the amount over par that must be paid according to the bond indenture. This loss on the bond call would be reported on the income statement. The notes to Harrah's statements include the following:

> **EXTINGUISHMENTS OF DEBT.**   Funds from new debt, as well as proceeds from our Credit Agreement, were used to retire certain of our outstanding debt, to reduce our effective interest rate and/or lengthen maturities.

In some cases, a company may elect to retire debt early by purchasing it on the open market, just as an investor would. This approach is necessary when the bonds do not have a call feature. It might also be an attractive approach if the price of the bonds fell after the date of issue. What could cause the price of a bond to fall? The most common cause is a rise in interest rates. As you may have noticed during our discussion of present value concepts, bond prices move in the opposite direction of interest rates. If interest rates go up, bond prices fall, and vice versa. When interest rates have gone up, a company that wants to retire a bond before maturity may find buying the bond on the open market is less expensive than paying a call premium.

SELF-STUDY QUIZ

Which company has a higher level of risk, a company with a high debt-to-equity ratio and a high interest coverage ratio or a company with a low debt-to-equity ratio and a low interest coverage ratio?

After you have completed your answer, check it with the solution at the bottom of the page.

 Bonds Payable

FOCUS ON
CASH FLOWS

The issuance of a bond payable is reported as a cash inflow from financing activities on the statement of cash flows. The repayment of principal is reported as a cash outflow from financing activities. Many students are surprised to learn that the payment of interest is not reported in the financing activities section of the statement of cash flows. Interest expense is reported on the income statement and is related directly to the computation net income. As a result, GAAP requires that interest payments be reported in the cash flows from operating activities section of the statement. Companies are also required to report the amount of cash paid for interest expense each accounting period. *Accounting Trends & Techniques* reports that companies disclose this information in a variety of locations.

Learning Objective 7
Explain how financing activities are reported on the statement of cash flows.

EFFECT ON STATEMENT OF CASH FLOWS

In General   As we saw in Chapter 9, transactions involving short-term creditors (e.g., accounts payable) affect working capital and are therefore reported in the operating activities section of the statement of cash flows. Cash received from long-term creditors is reported as

---

A company can be forced into bankruptcy if it does not meet its interest obligations to creditors. Many successful companies borrow very large amounts of money without creating unreasonable risk because they generate sufficient funds from normal operations to meet their obligations. Even a small amount of debt can be a problem if a company does not generate funds to meet current interest obligations. Usually, the company with a high debt-to-equity ratio and a high interest coverage ratio is viewed as being less risky.

Self-Study Quiz
Solutions

Disclosure of Cash Interest Payments (sample of 600 Companies)

	0	175	350
Not disclosed			
Within SCF			
Bottom of SCF			
Notes to SCF			

Selected Focus Company Comparisons: Cash Flows from Financing Activities (in millions)

General Mills	($102.3)
Outback	(54.7)
Home Depot	737.0

an inflow from financing activities. Cash payments made to long-term creditors (with the exception of interest expense) are reported as outflows from financing activities. Examples are shown in the following table:

	Effect on Cash Flows
Financing activities	
Issuance of bonds	+
Debt retirement	−
Repayment of bond principal upon maturity	−

Focus Company Analysis   A segment of Harrah's statement of cash flows follows. Several items pertain to issues discussed in this chapter. The remaining items will be discussed in other chapters. Notice that Harrah's reports both the early extinguishments (retirement) of debt and new borrowings. Although businesses normally borrow money to finance the acquisition of long-lived assets, they also borrow to rearrange their capital structure. In the case of Harrah's, the company had outstanding debt with an interest rate of 9.25 percent. The company was able to retire this debt by borrowing at an interest rate of 7.875 percent, saving the company nearly $8 million in annual interest cost.

Analysts are particularly interested in the financing activities section of the statement of cash flows because it provides important insights about the future capital structure for a company. Rapidly growing companies typically report significant amounts of funds in this section of the statement.

HARRAH'S ENTERTAINMENT, INC Consolidated Statements of Cash Flows (in thousands)			
Cash flows from financing activities	2006	2005	2004
Proceeds from issuance of senior notes, net of discount and issue costs of $10.9, $20.7, and $12.0	739.1	2,004.3	738.0
Borrowings under lending agreements, net of financing costs of $4.4, $7.6, and $6.2	6,946.5	11,599.4	4,157.9
Repayments under lending agreements	(5,465.8)	(10,522.9)	(3,424.1)
Losses on derivative instruments	(2.6)	(7.9)	(0.8)
Early extinguishments of debt	(1,195.0)	(690.5)	—
Premiums paid on early extinguishments of debt	(56.7)	(4.9)	—
Scheduled debt retirements	(5.0)	(307.5)	(1.6)
Dividends paid	(282.7)	(208.2)	(141.3)
Proceeds from exercises of stock options	66.3	106.7	90.0
Excess tax benefit from stock equity plans	21.3	—	—
Purchases of treasury stock	—	—	(53.4)
Minority interests' distributions, net of contributions	(1.9)	(12.2)	(8.9)
Other	1.3	(0.2)	0.7
Cash flows provided by financing activities	764.8	1,956.1	1,356.5

(Try to answer the questions before proceeding to the suggested solution that follows.) To raise funds to build a new plant, Reed Company's management issued bonds. The bond indenture specified the following:

> Par value of the bonds: $100,000.
>
> Date of issue: January 1, 2009; due in 10 years.
>
> Interest rate: 12 percent per annum, payable semi-annually on June 30 and December 31.

All the bonds were sold on January 1, 2009, at 106. The market rate of interest on the date of issue was 11%.

Required:

1. How much cash did Reed Company receive from the sale of the bonds payable? Show computations.
2. What was the amount of premium on the bonds payable?
3. Give the journal entry to record the sale and issuance of the bonds payable.
4. Give the journal entry for payment of interest and amortization of premium for the first interest payment.

SUGGESTED SOLUTION

1. Sale price of the bonds: $100,000 × 106\% = \$106,000$.

2. Premium on the bonds payable: $\$106,000 - \$100,000 = \$6,000$.

3. January 1, 2009 (issuance date):

Cash (+A)	106,000	
Premium on bonds payable (+L)		6,000
Bonds payable (+L)		100,000
To record sale of bonds payable at 106.		

4. **Part A: straight-line amortization**

June 30, 2009		
Interest expense (+E, −SE) ($6,000 − $300)	5,700	
Premium on bonds payable* (−L)	300	
Cash (−A) ($100,000 × 12% × 1/2)		6,000
To record payment of interest.		

  *$6,000 ÷ 20 periods = $300

  Part B: effective-interest amortization

June 30, 2009		
Interest expense* (+E, −SE)	5,830	
Premium on bonds payable (−L)	170	
Cash (−A) ($100,000 × 12% × 1/2)		6,000
To record payment of interest.		

  *$106,000 × 11% × 1/2 = 5,830

Chapter Supplement A

Bond Calculations Using Excel

Instead of using the present value tables in Appendix A, most accountants and analysts use Excel to do the financial computations that are necessary when working with bonds. We can illustrate the Excel process by using the bond example from this chapter. Assume that Harrah's issued a $100,000 bond that matured in five years and paid $10,000 interest per year. When the bond was issued, the market rate of interest was 12%. The present value of this bond can be computed with the following steps:

1. **Determine the present value of the maturity payment** In cell A1, enter the formula for calculating the present value of a single payment. In the format used by Excel, the formula is = *100000/(1.12)^5* where 100000 is the maturity value, 1.12 is 1 plus the market rate of interest per period, and ^5 is the number of periods. Excel will compute this value as $56,742.69. An Excel screen follows:

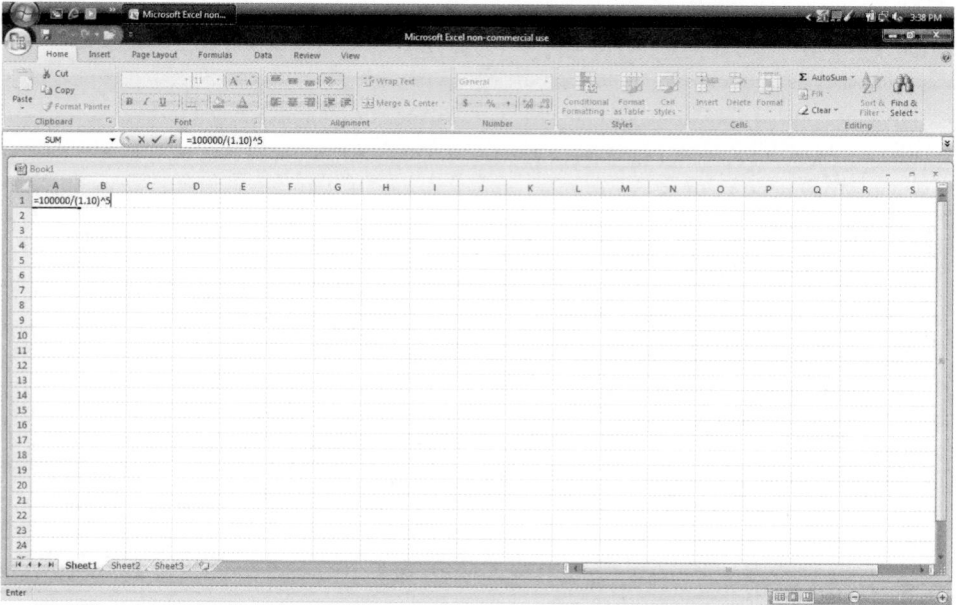

2. **Determine the present value of the interest payments** The present value of an annuity can be computed using an Excel function (you don't have to enter the formula yourself). On the toolbar, click on the insert function button (f_x). A dropdown box will appear. Under select a category, pick "Financial" and under select a function, pick "PV" which is the abbreviation for present value function. Click on "OK" at the bottom and a second dropdown box will appear. You should enter the amounts from the problem in this box: "Rate" is the market rate of interest per period. For this problem, you should enter 0.12. "NPER" is the number of periods. You should enter 5. "PMT" is the cash interest payment per period which is −10000 for this problem. Notice that when using Excel, this amount must be entered as a negative number because it represents a payment and you should not enter a comma between the numbers. Excel will compute this value as $36,047.76. An Excel screen with the data entered follows:

3. **Add the two present value amounts** In cell A3, add the values from cells A1 and A2 using the AutoSum function (**Σ**) from the tool bar. Excel will compute this amount as $92,790.45. Earlier in the chapter, we computed the present value of this bond as $92,788. The small difference is the result of rounding errors that occur when using the values from the tables. The answer provided by the Excel spreadsheet is more precise, which is why spreadsheets and calculators are used in business instead of the present value tables that are used for educational purposes. The final Excel screen, with the present value of the bond, follows:

CHAPTER **TAKE-AWAYS**

1. **Describe the characteristics of bonds.**　p. 515

   Bonds have a number of characteristics designed to meet the needs of both the issuing corporation and the creditor. A complete listing of bond characteristics is discussed in the chapter.

   Corporations use bonds to raise long-term capital. Bonds offer a number of advantages compared to stock, including the ability to earn a higher return for stockholders, the tax deductibility of interest, and the fact that control of the company is not diluted. Bonds do carry additional risk, however, because interest and principal payments are not discretionary.

2. **Report bonds payable and interest expense for bonds sold at par and analyze the times interest earned ratio.**　p. 522

   Three types of events must be recorded over the life of a typical bond: (1) the receipt of cash when the bond is first sold, (2) the periodic payment of cash interest, and (3) the repayment of principal at the maturity of the bond. Bonds are reported at the present value of the future cash flows specified in the bond contract. When the market interest rate and the coupon interest rate are the same, the bond will sell at par, which is the same as the maturity value of the bond.

   The times interest earned ratio measures a company's ability to meet its interest obligations with resources from its profit-making activities. It is computed by comparing interest expense to earnings (including net income, interest expense, and income tax expense).

3. **Report bonds payable and interest expense for bonds sold at a discount.**　p. 523

   Bonds are sold at a discount whenever the coupon interest rate is less than the market rate of interest. A discount is the dollar amount of the difference between the par value of the bond and its selling price. The discount is recorded as a contra-liability when the bond is sold and is amortized over the life of the bond as an adjustment to interest expense.

4. **Report bonds payable and interest expense for bonds sold at a premium.** p. 528

   Bonds are sold at a premium whenever the coupon interest rate is more than the market rate of interest. A premium is the dollar amount of the difference between the selling price of the bond and its par value. The premium is recorded as a liability when the bond is sold and is amortized over the life of the bond as an adjustment to interest expense.

5. **Analyze the debt-to-equity ratio.**　p. 531

   The debt-to-equity ratio compares the amount of capital supplied by creditors to the amount supplied by owners. It is a measure of a company's debt capacity. It is an important ratio because of the high risk associated with debt capital that requires interest and principal payments.

6. **Report the early retirement of bonds.**　p. 532

   A corporation may retire bonds before their maturity date. The difference between the book value and the amount paid to retire the bonds is reported as a gain or loss, depending on the circumstances.

7. **Explain how financing activities are reported on the statement of cash flows.**　p. 533

   Cash flows associated with transactions involving long-term creditors are reported in the Financing Activities section of the statement of cash flows. Interest expense is reported in the Operating Activities section.

KEY **RATIOS**

Times interest earned ratio measures a company's ability to generate resources from current operations to meet its interest obligations. The ratio is computed as follows (p. 522):

$$\text{Times Interest Earned} = \frac{\text{Net Income} + \text{Interest Expense} + \text{Income Tax Expense}}{\text{Interest Expense}}$$

Debt-to-equity ratio measures the balance between debt and equity. Debt funds are viewed as being riskier than equity funds. The ratio is computed as follows (p. 531):

$$\text{Debt-to-Equity} = \frac{\text{Total Liabilities}}{\text{Stockholders' Equity}}$$

FINDING **FINANCIAL INFORMATION**

Balance Sheet

Under Current Liabilities

Bonds are normally listed as long-term liabilities. An exception occurs when the bonds are within one year of maturity. Such bonds are reported as current liabilities with the following title: Current Portion of Long-term Debt

Under Noncurrent Liabilities

Bonds are listed under a variety of titles, depending on the characteristics of the bond. Titles include

Bonds Payable

Debentures

Convertible Bonds

Income Statement

Bonds are shown only on the balance sheet, never on the income statement. Interest expense associated with bonds is reported on the income statement. Most companies report interest expense in a separate category on the income statement.

Statement of Cash Flows

Under Financing Activities

+ Cash inflows from long-term creditors
− Cash outflows to long-term creditors

Under Operating Activities

The cash outflow associated with interest expense is reported as an operating activity.

Notes

Under Summary of Significant Accounting Policies

Description of pertinent information concerning accounting treatment of liabilities. Normally, there is minimal information. Some companies report the method used to amortize bond discounts and premiums.

Under a Separate Note

Most companies include a separate note called "Long-Term Debt" that reports information about each major debt issue, including amount and interest rate. The note also provides detail concerning debt covenants.

KEY **TERMS**

Bond Certificate p. 518
Bond Discount p. 519
Bond Premium p. 519
Bond Principal p. 516
Callable Bonds p. 517
Convertible Bonds p. 517
Coupon Rate p. 519

Debenture p. 517
Effective-Interest Method p. 525
Effective-Interest Rate p. 519
Face Amount p. 516
Indenture p. 517
Market Interest Rate p. 519
Par Value p. 516

Stated Rate p. 516
Straight-Line Amortization p. 524
Trustee p. 518
Yield p. 519

QUESTIONS

1. What are the primary characteristics of a bond? For what purposes are bonds usually issued?
2. What is the difference between a bond indenture and a bond certificate?
3. Differentiate secured bonds from unsecured bonds.
4. Differentiate between callable and convertible bonds.
5. From the perspective of the issuer, what are some advantages of issuing bonds instead of capital stock?
6. As the tax rate increases, the net cost of borrowing money decreases. Explain.
7. At the date of issuance, bonds are recorded at their current cash equivalent amount. Explain.
8. Explain the nature of the discount and premium on bonds payable.
9. What is the difference between the stated interest rate and the effective-interest rate on a bond?
10. Differentiate among the stated and effective rates of interest on a bond (a) sold at par, (b) sold at a discount, and (c) sold at a premium.
11. What is the book value of a bond payable?
12. Explain the basic difference between the straight-line and effective-interest methods of amortizing bond discount or premium. Explain when each method should or may be used.

MULTIPLE-CHOICE QUESTIONS

1. Annual interest expense for a single bond issue continues to increase over the life of the bonds. Which of the following explains this?
   a. The market rate of interest has increased since the bonds were sold.
   b. The coupon rate of interest has increased since the bonds were sold.
   c. The bonds were sold at a discount.
   d. The bonds were sold at a premium.
2. Which of the following is not an advantage of issuing bonds when compared to issuing additional shares of stock in order to obtain additional capital?
   a. Stockholders maintain proportionate ownership percentages.
   b. Interest expense reduces taxable income.
   c. Timing flexibility associated with the payment of interest.
   d. All of the above are advantages associated with bonds.
3. A bond with a maturity value of $100,000 has a stated interest rate of 8 percent. The bond matures in 10 years. When the bond is issued, the market rate of interest is 10 percent. What amount should be reported when the bond is issued?
   a. $100,000   c. $49,157
   b. $87,707   d. $113,421
4. Which account would not be included in the debt-to-equity ratio calculation?
   a. Unearned Revenue.   c. Income Taxes Payable.
   b. Retained Earnings.   d. All of the above are included.
5. Which of the following is false when a bond is issued at a premium?
   a. The bond will issue for an amount above its par value.
   b. Bonds payable will be credited for the par value of the bond.
   c. Interest expense will exceed the cash interest payments.
   d. All of the above are false.
6. A bond with a face value of $100,000 was issued for $113,500 on January 1, 2009. The stated rate of interest is 8 percent and the market rate of interest was 10 percent when the bond was sold. Interest is paid annually. How much interest will be paid on December 31, 2009?
   a. $10,000   c. $11,350
   b. $8,000   d. $9,080
7. To determine whether a bond will be sold at a premium, discount, or face value, one must know which of the following pairs of information?
   a. The par value and the coupon rate on the date the bonds were issued.
   b. The par value and the market rate on the date the bonds were issued.

c. The coupon rate and the market rate on the date the bonds were issued.

d. The coupon rate and the stated rate on the date the bonds were issued.

8. When using the effective-interest method of amortization, interest expense reported in the income statement is impacted by the

a. Par value of the bonds.

b. Coupon rate of interest stated in the bond certificate.

c. Market rate of interest on the date the bonds were issued.

d. Both (a) and (b).

9. A bond with a face value of $100,000 is sold on January 1. The bond has a stated interest rate of 10 percent and matures in 10 years. When the bond was issued the market rate on interest was 10 percent. On December 31, the market interest increased to 11 percent. What amount should be reported on December 31 as the bond liability?

a. $100,000   c. $94,460

b. $94,112   d. $87,562

10. When using the effective-interest method of amortization, the book value of the bonds changes by what amount on each interest payment date?

a. Interest expense   c. Amortization

b. Cash interest payment   d. None of the above

For more practice with multiple choice questions, go to our website at www.mhhe.com/libby6e.

Available with McGraw-Hill's Homework Manager

MINI-EXERCISES

Finding Financial Information

M10-1
L01,2

For each of the following items, specify whether the information would be found in the balance sheet, the income statement, the statement of cash flows, the notes to the statements, or not at all.

1. The amount of a bond liability.

2. Interest expense for the period.

3. Cash interest paid for the period.

4. Interest rates for specific bond issues.

5. The names of major holders of bonds.

6. The maturity date of specific bond issues.

Computing Bond Issuance Price

M10-2
L02

Price Company plans to issue $600,000, 10-year bonds that pay 8 percent payable semiannually on June 30 and December 31. All of the bonds will be sold on January 1, 2009. Determine the issuance price of the bonds assuming a market yield of 8 percent.

Computing Bond Issuance Price

M10-3
L03

Waterhouse Company plans to issue $900,000, 10-year, 6 percent bonds. Interest is payable semiannually on June 30 and December 31. All of the bonds will be sold on January 1, 2009. Determine the issuance price of the bonds assuming a market yield of 8.5 percent.

Recording the Issuance of a New Bond and the Payment of Interest (Effective-Interest Amortization)

M10-4
L03

Hopkins Company issued $1,000,000, 10-year, 10 percent bonds on January 1, 2009. The bonds sold for $940,000. Interest is payable semiannually each June 30 and December 31. Record the sale of the bonds on January 1, 2009, and the payment of interest on June 30, 2009, using effective-interest amortization. The yield on the bonds is 11 percent.

Recording the Issuance of a New Bond and the Payment of Interest (Straight-Line Amortization)

M10-5
L03

Garland Company issued $600,000, 10-year, 10 percent bonds on January 1, 2009. The bonds sold for $580,000. Interest is payable semiannually each June 30 and December 31. Record the sale of the bonds on January 1, 2009, and the payment of interest on June 30, 2009, using straight-line amortization.

M10-6
L04
Computing Bond Issuance Price

Coopers Company plans to issue $500,000, 10-year, 10 percent bonds. Interest is paid semiannually on June 30 and December 31. All of the bonds will be sold on January 1, 2009. Determine the issuance price of the bonds, assuming a market yield of 8 percent.

M10-7
L04
Recording the Issuance of a New Bond and the Payment of Interest (Straight-Line Amortization)

Price Company issued $600,000, 10-year, 9 percent bonds on January 1, 2009. The bonds sold for $620,000. Interest is payable annually each December 31. Record the sale of the bonds on January 1, 2009, and the payment of interest on December 31, 2009, using straight-line amortization.

M10-8
L04
Recording the Issuance of a New Bond and the Payment of Interest (Effective-Interest Amortization)

IDS Company issued $850,000, 10-year, 8 percent bonds on January 1, 2009. The bonds sold for $900,000. Interest is payable annually each December 31. Record the sale of the bonds on January 1, 2009, and the payment of interest on December 31, 2009, using the effective-interest method of amortization. The yield on the bonds is 7 percent.

M10-9
L05
Understanding Financial Ratios

The debt-to-equity and times interest earned ratios were discussed in this chapter. Which is a better indicator of a company's ability to meet its required interest payment? Explain.

M10-10
L06
Determining Financial Statement Effects of an Early Retirement of Debt

If interest rates fell after the issuance of a bond and the company decided to retire the debt, would you expect the company to report a gain or loss on debt retirement? Describe the financial statement effects of a debt retirement under these circumstances.

M10-11
L07
Determining Cash Flow Effects

If a company issues a bond at a discount, will interest expense each period be more or less than the cash payment for interest? If another company issues a bond at a premium, will interest expense be more or less than the cash payment for interest? Is your answer to either question affected by the method used to amortize the discount or premium?

M10-12
L07
Reporting Cash Flow Effects

In what section of the statement of cash flow would you find cash paid to retire bonds? In what section would you find cash paid for interest?

EXERCISES
 Available with McGraw-Hill's Homework Manager

E10-1
L01
Bond Terminology: Fill in the Missing Blanks

1. The _____ is the amount (a) payable at the maturity of the bond and (b) on which the periodic cash interest payments are computed.
2. _____ is another name for bond principal, or the maturity amount of a bond.
3. _____ is another name for principal, or the principal amount of the bond.
4. The _____ is the rate of cash interest per period stated in the bond contract.
5. A _____ is an unsecured bond; no assets are specifically pledged to guarantee repayment.
6. _____ bonds may be called for early retirement at the option of the issuer.
7. _____ bonds may be converted to other securities of the issuer (usually common stock).

Interpreting Information Reported in the Business Press

As this book was being written, the business press reported the following information concerning bonds issued by AT&T:

E10-2
LO1
AT&T

Bonds	Yield	Close
AT&T 6.5	7.3	89.5

Explain the meaning of the reported information. If you bought AT&T bonds with $10,000 face value, how much would you pay (based on the preceding information reported)? Assume that the bonds were originally sold at par. What impact would the decline in value have on the financial statements for AT&T?

Analyzing a Conversion Feature

Wynn Resorts owns a variety of popular gaming resorts. Their annual report contained the following information:

E10-3
LO2

Wynn Resorts

Debenture Conversions

Our convertible debentures are currently convertible at each holder's option into shares of the Company's common stock at a conversion price of $23.00 per share (equivalent to 43.4782 shares per $1,000 principal amount). During the fourth quarter of 2006, we issued 1,434 shares of common stock upon the conversion of $33,000 of convertible debentures.

The current selling price for Wynn stock is $90. Explain why some bondholders have not converted the bonds to common stock, given that they can do so at $23 per share.

Computing Issue Prices of Bonds for Three Cases

Thompson Corporation is planning to issue $100,000, seven-year, 8 percent bonds. Interest is payable each December 31. All of the bonds will be sold on January 1, 2009.

E10-4
LO2,3,4

Required:
Compute the issue (sale) price on January 1, 2009, for each of the following independent cases (show computations):
a. **Case A:** Market (yield) rate, 8 percent.
b. **Case B:** Market (yield) rate, 6 percent.
c. **Case C:** Market (yield) rate, 10 percent.

Computing Issue Prices of Bonds for Three Cases

Oxxford Corporation is planning to issue $500,000 worth of bonds that mature in 10 years and pay 6 percent interest each June 30 and December 31. All of the bonds will be sold on January 1, 2009.

E10-5
LO2,3,4

Required:
Compute the issue (sale) price on January 1, 2009, for each of the following independent cases (show computations):
a. **Case A:** Market (yield) rate, 4 percent.
b. **Case B:** Market (yield) rate, 6 percent.
c. **Case C:** Market (yield) rate, 8 percent.

Analyzing Financial Ratios

You have just started your first job as a financial analyst for a large stock brokerage company. Your boss, a senior analyst, has finished a detailed report evaluating bonds issued by two different companies. She stopped by your desk and asked for help: "I have compared two ratios for the companies and found something interesting." She went on to explain that the debt-to-equity ratio for Applied Technologies, Inc., is much lower than the industry average and that the one for Innovative Solutions, Inc., is much higher. On the other hand, the times interest earned ratio for Applied Technologies is much higher than the industry average, and the ratio for Innovative Solutions is much lower. Your boss then asked you to think about what the ratios indicate about the two companies so that she could include the explanation in her report. How would you respond to your boss?

E10-6
LO2,5

E10-7   **Computing the Issue Price of a Bond**

LO3   Wilson Corporation issued a $100,000 bond that matures in five years. The bond has a stated interest rate of 6 percent. On January 1, 2009, when the bond was issued, the market rate was 8 percent. The bond pays interest twice per year, on June 30 and December 31. At what price was the bond issued?

E10-8   **Recording Bond Issue and First Interest Payment with Discount (Straight-Line Amortization)**

On January 1, 2009, Seton Corporation sold a $750,000, 8 percent bond issue (9 percent market rate). The bonds were dated January 1, 2009, pay interest each December 31, and mature in 10 years.

Required:
1. Give the journal entry to record the issuance of the bonds.
2. Give the journal entry to record the interest payment on December 31, 2009. Use straight-line amortization.
3. Show how the interest expense and the bonds payable should be reported on the December 31, 2009, annual financial statements.

E10-9   **Recording Bond Issue and First Interest Payment with Discount (Effective-Interest**
LO3   **Amortization)**

On January 1, 2009, Hyde Corporation sold a $600,000, 7.5 percent bond issue (8.5 percent market rate). The bonds were dated January 1, 2009, pay interest each June 30 and December 31, and mature in four years.

Required:
1. Give the journal entry to record the issuance of the bonds.
2. Give the journal entry to record the interest payment on December 31, 2009. Use effective-interest amortization.
3. Show how the bond interest expense and the bonds payable should be reported on the June 30, 2009, income statement and balance sheet.

E10-10   **Recording Bond Issue: Entries for Issuance and Interest (Straight-Line Amortization)**
LO3
Northland Corporation had $300,000, 10-year bonds outstanding on December 31, 2009 (end of the accounting period). Interest is payable each December 31. The bonds were issued on January 1, 2009. The company uses the straight-line method to amortize any premium or discount. The December 31, 2009 annual financial statements showed the following:

Income statement	
Bond interest expense	$ 23,100
Balance sheet	
Bonds payable (net liability)	281,100

Required (show computations):
1. What was the issue price of the bonds? Give the journal entry to record the issuance of the bonds.
2. Give the entry to record 2009 interest.

E10-11   **Analyzing a Bond Amortization Schedule: Reporting Bonds Payable**
LO3
Stein Corporation sold a $1,000 bond on January 1, 2009. The bond specified an interest rate of 6 percent payable at the end of each year. The bond matures at the end of 2011. It was sold at a market rate of 8 percent per year. The following spreadsheet was completed:

	Cash Paid	Interest Expense	Amortization	Balance
January 1, 2009				$ 948
End of year 2009	$60	$76	$16	964
End of year 2010	60	77	17	981
End of year 2011	60	79	19	1,000

Required:
1. What was the bond's issue price?
2. Did the bond sell at a discount or a premium? How much was the premium or discount?
3. What amount of cash was paid each year for bond interest?
4. What amount of interest expense should be shown each year on the income statement?
5. What amount(s) should be shown on the balance sheet for bonds payable at each year-end? (For year 2011, show the balance just before retirement of the bond.)
6. What method of amortization was used?
7. Show how the following amounts were computed for year 2010: (a) $60, (b) $77, (c) $17, and (d) $981.
8. Is the method of amortization that was used preferable? Explain why.

Explaining Why Debt Is Sold at a Discount

E10-12
LO3
American Airlines

The annual report of American Airlines contained the following note:

The Company recorded the issuance of $775 million in bonds (net of $25 million discount) as long-term debt on the consolidated balance sheet. The bonds bear interest at fixed rates, with an average effective rate of 8.06 percent, and mature over various periods of time, with a final maturity in 2031.

After reading this note, an investor asked her financial advisor why the company didn't simply sell the notes for an effective yield of more than 8.06 percent and avoid having to account for a small discount over the next 20 years. Prepare a written response to this question.

Explaining Bond Features

E10-13
LO3
Disney

The annual report for Disney Company contained the following note:

The Company has outstanding $1.3 billion of convertible senior notes due on April 15, 2023. The notes bear interest at a fixed annual rate of 2.13 percent. The notes are convertible into common stock, under certain circumstances, at a conversion rate of 33.9443 shares of common stock per $1,000 principal amount of notes. This is equivalent to a conversion price of $29.46.

When the notes were issued, interest rates were much higher than the 2.13 percent offered by Disney. Why would an investor accept such a low interest rate?

Evaluating Bond Features

E10-14
LO3

You are a personal financial planner working with a married couple in their early 40s who have decided to invest $100,000 in corporate bonds. You have found two bonds that you think will interest your clients. One is a zero coupon bond issued by PepsiCo with an effective interest rate of 9 percent and a maturity date of 2018. It is callable at par. The other is a Walt Disney bond that matures in 2093. It has an effective interest rate of 9.5 percent and is callable at 105 percent of par. Which bond would you recommend and why? Would your answer be different if you expected interest rates to fall significantly over the next few years? Would you prefer a different bond if the couple were in their late 60s and retired?

Recording Bond Issue and First Interest Payment with Premium (Straight-Line Amortization)

E10-15
LO4

On January 1, 2009, Bochini Corporation sold a $1,400,000, 8 percent bond issue (6 percent market rate). The bonds were dated January 1, 2009, pay interest each June 30 and December 31, and mature in four years.

Required:
1. Give the journal entry to record the issuance of the bonds.
2. Give the journal entry to record the interest payment on June 30, 2009. Use straight-line amortization.
3. Show how the bond interest expense and the bonds payable should be reported on the June 30, 2009 balance sheet and income statement.

E10-16
LO4
Recording Bond Issue and First Interest Payment with Premium (Effective-Interest Amortization)

On January 1, 2009, Frog Corporation sold a $2,000,000, 10 percent bond issue (8.5 percent market rate). The bonds were dated January 1, 2009, pay interest each June 30 and December 31, and mature in 10 years.

Required:
1. Give the journal entry to record the issuance of the bonds.
2. Give the journal entry to record the interest payment on June 30, 2009. Use effective-interest amortization.
3. Show how the bond interest expense and the bonds payable should be reported on the June 30, 2009, financial statements.

E10-17
LO4
Preparing a Debt Payment Schedule with Effective-Interest Method of Amortization and Determining Reported Amounts

Shuttle Company issued a $10,000, three-year, 5 percent bond on January 1, 2009. The bond interest is paid each December 31. The bond was sold to yield 4 percent.

Required:
1. Complete a bond payment schedule. Use the effective-interest method.
2. What amounts will be reported on the income statement and balance sheet at the end of 2009, 2010, and 2011?

E10-18
LO4
Determining Financial Statement Effects for Bond Issue and First Interest Payment with Premium (Straight-Line Amortization)

Grocery Corporation sold a $300,000, 6 percent bond issue on January 1, 2009, at a market rate of 3 percent. The bonds were dated January 1, 2009, with interest to be paid each December 31; they mature in 10 years. The company uses the straight-line method to amortize any discount or premium).

Required:
1. How are the financial statements affected by the issuance of the bonds? Describe the impact on the debt-to-equity and times interest earned ratios, if any.
2. How are the financial statements affected by the payment of interest on December 31? Describe the impact on the debt-to-equity and times interest earned ratios, if any.
3. Show how the bond interest expense and the bonds payable should be reported on the December 31, 2009, annual financial statements.

E10-19
LO4,7
Computing the Issue Price of a Bond with Analysis of Income and Cash Flow Effects

Imai Company issued a $1 million bond that matures in 10 years. The bond has a 10 percent stated rate of interest. When the bond was issued, the market rate was 8 percent. The bond pays interest each six months. Record the issuance of the bond on June 30. Notice that the company received more than $1 million when it issued the bond. How will this premium affect future income and future cash flows?

E10-20
LO6
Reporting the Early Retirement of a Bond

Several years ago, Walters Company issued a $600,000 bond at par value. As a result of declining interest rates, the company has decided to call the bond at a call premium of 8 percent. Record the retirement of the bonds.

E10-21
LO6
Reporting the Early Retirement of a Bond with a Discount

The Nair Company issued $500,000 in bonds at a discount five years ago. The current book value of the bonds is $475,000. The company now has excess cash on hand and plans to retire the bonds. The company must pay a 7 percent (of par) call premium to retire the bonds. Record the retirement of the bonds.

Determining Effects on the Statement of Cash Flows

E10-22
LO7

A number of events over the life of a bond have effects that are reported on the statement of cash flows. For each of the following events, determine whether the event affects the statement of cash flows. If so, describe the impact and specify where on the statement the effect is reported.

Required:
1. A $1,000,000 bond is issued at a discount. The reported amount of the bond on the balance sheet is $960,000.
2. At year-end, $45,000 accrued interest is reported and $1,000 of the bond discount is amortized using the straight-line method.
3. Early in the second year, accrued interest is paid. At the same time, $9,000 interest that accrued in the second year is paid.
4. The company elects to retire the debt in the fifth year. At that time, the reported carrying value of the bonds is $960,000 and the company reports a $20,000 gain on the early retirement of debt.

HM™ **Available with McGraw-Hill's Homework Manager**

PROBLEMS

Analyzing the Use of Debt

P10-1
LO1

Cricket Corporation's financial statements for 2009 showed the following:

Income Statement

Revenues	$300,000
Expenses	(196,000)
Interest expense	(4,000)
Pretax income	100,000
Income tax (40%)	(40,000)
Net income	$ 60,000

Balance Sheet

Assets	$360,000
Liabilities (average interest rate, 10%)	$ 40,000
Common stock, par $10	230,000
Retained earnings	90,000
	$360,000

Notice in these data that the company had a debt of only $40,000 compared with common stock outstanding of $230,000. A consultant recommended the following: debt, $90,000 (at 10 percent) and common stock outstanding of $180,000 (18,000 shares). That is, the company should finance the business with more debt and less owner contribution.

Required (round to nearest percent):
1. You have been asked to develop a comparison between (a) the actual results and (b) the results had the consultant's recommendation been followed. To do this, you decided to develop the following schedule:

Item	Actual Results for 2009	Results with an Increase in Debt and Reduction in Equity
a. Total debt		
b. Total assets		
c. Total stockholders' equity		
d. Interest expense (total at 10 percent)		

e. Net income
f. Return on total assets
g. Earnings available to stockholders:
    (1) Amount
    (2) Per share
    (3) Return on stockholders' equity

2. Based on the completed schedule in requirement (1), provide a comparative analysis and interpretation of the actual results and the recommendation.

P10-2 **Reporting Bonds Issued at Par** (AP10-1)

LO2

On January 1, 2009, Donovan Company issued $300,000 in bonds that mature in five years. The bonds have a stated interest rate of 8 percent and pay interest on June 30 and December 31 each year. When the bonds were sold, the market rate of interest was 8 percent.

Required:

1. What was the issue price on January 1, 2009?
2. What amount of interest should be recorded on June 30, 2009? How much on December 31, 2009?
3. What amount of cash interest should be paid on June 30, 2009? How much on December 31, 2009?
4. What is the book value of the bonds on December 31, 2009? What is the amount on December 31, 2010?

P10-3 **Completing Schedule Comparing Bonds Issued at Par, Discount, and Premium (Straight-**
LO2,3,4 **Line Amortization)** (AP10-2)

Quartz Corporation sold a $500,000, 7 percent bond issue on January 1, 2009. The bonds pay interest each June 30 and December 31 and mature 10 years from January 1, 2009. For comparative study and analysis, assume three separate cases. Use straight-line amortization and disregard income tax unless specifically required. Assume three independent selling scenarios:

Required:

Complete the following schedule as of December 31, 2009, to analyze the differences among the three cases.

	Case A (Par)	Case B (at 95)	Case C (at 103)
a. Cash received at issue			
b. Bond interest expense, pretax for 2009			
c. Bonds payable, 7 percent			
d. Unamortized discount			
e. Unamortized premium			
f. Net liability			
g. Stated interest rate			

P10-4 **Comparing Bonds Issued at Par, Discount, and Premium (Straight-Line Amortization)**
LO2,3,4

Sikes Corporation, whose annual accounting period ends on December 31, issued the following bonds:

Date of bonds: January 1, 2009
Maturity amount and date: $100,000 due in 10 years
Interest: 10 percent per annum payable each June 30 and December 31
Date sold: January 1, 2009
Straight-line amortization is used

Required:

1. Provide the following amounts to be reported on the December 31, 2009 financial statements:

	Issued at Par Case A	at 99 Case B	at 104 Case C
a. Interest expense	$	$	$
b. Bonds payable			
c. Unamortized premium or discount			
d. Net liability			
e. Stated rate of interest			
f. Cash interest paid			

2. Explain why items *a* and *f* in requirement (1) are different.
3. Assume that you are an investment adviser and a retired person has written to you asking, "Why should I buy a bond at a premium when I can find one at a discount? Isn't that stupid? It's like paying list price for a car instead of negotiating a discount." Write a brief letter in response to the question.

Determining Reported Amounts with Discussion of Management Strategy (Effective-Interest Amortization)

P10-5
LO3,5

On January 1, 2009, Carter Corporation issued $200,000 in bonds that mature in 10 years. The bonds have a stated interest rate of 6 percent and pay interest on December 31. When the bonds were sold, the market rate of interest was 8 percent. Carter uses the effective-interest method. By December 31, 2009, the market rate of interest had increased to 10 percent.

Required:
1. What amount of bond liability is recorded on January 1, 2009?
2. What amount of interest is recorded on December 31, 2009?
3. As a manager of a company, would you prefer the straight-line or effective-interest method?
4. Determine the impact of these transactions at year-end on the debt-to-equity ratio and times interest earned ratio.

Reporting Bonds Issued at a Discount (Straight-Line Amortization) (AP10-3)

P10-6
LO3

On January 1, 2009, Neeley Company issued $700,000 in bonds that mature in 10 years. The bonds have a stated interest rate of 8 percent and pay interest on June 30 and December 31 each year. When the bonds were sold, the market rate of interest was 10 percent. Neeley uses the straight-line amortization method.

Required:
1. What was the issue price on January 1, 2009?
2. What amount of interest should be recorded on June 30, 2009? How much on December 31, 2009?
3. What amount of cash interest should be paid on June 30, 2009? How much on December 31, 2009?
4. What is the book value of the bonds on June 30, 2009? What is the amount on December 31, 2009?

Reporting Bonds Issued at a Discount (Effective-Interest Amortization) (AP10-4)

P10-7
LO3

On January 1, 2009, TCU Utilities issued $1,000,000 in bonds that mature in 10 years. The bonds have a stated interest rate of 10 percent and pay interest on June 30 and December 31 each year. When the bonds were sold, the market rate of interest was 12 percent. TCU uses the effective-interest amortization method.

Required:
1. What was the issue price on January 1, 2009?
2. What amount of interest should be recorded on June 30, 2009? How much on December 31, 2009?
3. What amount of cash interest should be paid on June 30, 2009? How much on December 31, 2009?
4. What is the book value of the bonds on June 30, 2009? What is the amount on December 31, 2009?

P10-8

LO3

e**X**cel

www.mhhe.com/libby6e

Computing Amounts for Bond Issue and Comparing Amortization Methods

Dektronik Corporation manufactures electrical test equipment. The company's board of directors authorized a bond issue on January 1, 2009, with the following terms:

Maturity (par) value: $800,000
Interest: 8 percent per annum payable each December 31.
Maturity date: December 31, 2013.
Effective-interest rate when sold: 12 percent.

Required:
1. Compute the bond issue price. Explain why both the stated and effective-interest rates are used in this computation.
2. Assume that the company used the straight-line method to amortize the discount on the bond issue. Compute the following amounts for each year (2009–2013):
   a. Cash payment for bond interest.
   b. Amortization of bond discount or premium.
   c. Bond interest expense.
   d. Effective-interest rate (Item *c* ÷ $800,000).
   e. The straight-line rate is theoretically deficient when interest expense, *d,* is related to the net liability (i.e., book value of the debt). Explain.
3. Assume instead that the company used the effective-interest method to amortize the discount. Prepare an effective-interest bond amortization schedule similar to the one in the text. The effective-interest method provides a constant interest rate when interest expense is related to the net liability. Explain by referring to the bond amortization schedule.
4. Which method should the company use to amortize the bond discount? As a financial analyst, would you prefer one method over the other? If so, why?

P10-9

LO4

e**X**cel

www.mhhe.com/libby6e

Reporting Bonds Issued at a Premium (Straight Line) (AP10-5)

On January 1, 2009, Vigeland Corporation issued $2,000,000 in bonds that mature in 10 years. The bonds have a stated interest rate of 10 percent and pay interest on June 30 December 31 each year. When the bonds were sold, the market rate of interest was 8 percent. Vigeland uses the straight-line amortization method.

Required:
1. What was the issue price on January 1, 2009?
2. What amount of interest should be recorded on June 30, 2009? How much on December 31, 2009?
3. What amount of cash interest should be paid on June 30, 2009? How much on December 31, 2009?
4. What is the book value of the bonds on June 30, 2009? What is the amount on December 31, 2009?

P10-10

LO4

Reporting Bonds Issued at a Premium (Effective-Interest Amortization) (AP10-6)

On January 1, 2009, Moncrief Corporation issued $700,000 in bonds that mature in five years. The bonds have a stated interest rate of 13 percent and pay interest on June 30 and December 31 each year. When the bonds were sold, the market rate of interest was 12 percent. Moncrief uses the effective-interest amortization method.

Required:
1. What was the issue price on January 1, 2009?
2. What amount of interest should be recorded on June 30, 2009? How much on December 31, 2009?
3. What amount of cash interest should be paid on June 30, 2009? How much on December 31, 2009?
4. What is the book value of the bonds on June 30, 2009? What is the amount on December 31, 2009?

P10-11

LO4

Recording Bond Issuance and Interest Payments (Straight-Line Amortization)

West Company issued bonds with the following provisions:

Maturity value: $300,000
Interest: 11 percent per annum payable annually each December 31
Terms: Bonds dated January 1, 2009, due five years from that date

The annual accounting period ends December 31. The bonds were sold on January 1, 2009, at a 10 percent market rate.

Required:
1. Compute the issue (sale) price of the bonds (show computations).
2. Give the journal entry to record the issuance of the bonds.
3. Give the journal entries at the following date (use straight-line amortization): December 31, 2009.
4. How much interest expense would be reported on the income statement for 2009? Show how the liability related to the bonds should be reported on the December 31, 2009, balance sheet.

Completing an Amortization Schedule (Effective-Interest Amortization)

Berkley Corporation issued bonds and received cash in full for the issue price. The bonds were dated and issued on January 1, 2009. The stated interest rate was payable at the end of each year. The bonds mature at the end of four years. The following schedule has been completed (amounts in thousands):

P10-12
LO4

www.mhhe.com/libby6e

Date	Cash	Interest	Amortization	Balance
January 1, 2009				$48,808
End of year 2009	$3,600	$3,417	$183	48,625
End of year 2010	3,600	?	?	48,429
End of year 2011	3,600	?	?	?
End of year 2012	3,600	?	?	48,000

Required:
1. Complete the amortization schedule.
2. What was the maturity amount of the bonds?
3. How much cash was received at the date of issuance (sale) of the bonds?
4. Was there a premium or a discount? If so, which and how much?
5. How much cash will be disbursed for interest each period and in total for the full life of the bond issue?
6. What method of amortization is being used? Explain.
7. What is the stated rate of interest?
8. What is the effective rate of interest?
9. What amount of interest expense should be reported on the income statement each year?
10. Show how the bonds should be reported on the balance sheet at the end of each year (show the last year immediately before retirement of the bonds).

Comparing Carrying Value and Market Value

DirectTV is the largest provider of direct-to-home digital television services and the second largest provider in the multichannel video programming distribution industry in the United States. They provide over 16 million subscribers with access to hundreds of channels of digital-quality video pictures and CD-quality audio programming that they transmit directly to subscribers' homes via high-powered geosynchronous satellites. The company's annual report contained the following note:

P10-13
LO6
DirectTV

Long-Term Debt
The unamortized bond premium included in total debt for the current year was $2.8 million and $3.1 million for the prior year.

Required:
Explain why the unamortized premium is included in total debt and why the premium decreased in amount from one year to the next.

Explaining Note to a Financial Statement (AP10–7)

McDermott International is an engineering and construction company with significant oil and gas operations. The annual report for McDermott contains the following note:

P10-14
LO6
McDermott

The company used cash on hand to purchase the entire $200 million in aggregate principal amount of its Secured Notes outstanding for approximately $249.0 million, including accrued interest of approximately $10.9 million. As a result of this early retirement of debt, we recognized $49.0 million of expense during the year ended December 31.

Required:
1. In your own words, explain the meaning of this note.
2. Why did management incur an expense on the early retirement of this debt?

P10-15
LO7

Reporting Bond Transaction on the SCF

Determine whether each of the following would be reported in the financing activities section of the statement of cash flows and, if so, specify whether it is a cash inflow or outflow.
1. Sale of bonds at a discount.
2. Payment of interest on a bond.
3. Early retirement of a bond with a 5 percent call premium.
4. Amortization of a bond discount.
5. Payment of bond principal upon maturity.
6. Sale of bond from one investor to another. Transaction was in cash.

ALTERNATE PROBLEMS

AP10-1
LO2

Reporting Bonds Issued at Par (P10-2)

On January 1, 2009, Trucks R Us Corporation issued $2,000,000 in bonds that mature in five years. The bonds have a stated interest rate of 10 percent and pay interest on June 30 and December 31 each year. When the bonds were sold, the market rate of interest was 10 percent.

Required:
1. What was the issue price on January 1, 2009?
2. What amount of interest should be recorded on June 30, 2009? How much on December 31, 2009?
3. What amount of cash interest should be paid on June 30, 2009? How much on December 31, 2009?
4. What is the book value of the bonds on December 31, 2009? What is the amount on December 31, 2010?

AP10-2
LO2, 3, 4

Completing a Schedule That Involves a Comprehensive Review of the Issuance of Bonds at Par, Discount, and Premium (Straight-Line Amortization) (P10-3)

On January 1, 2009, Delaware Corporation sold and issued $100,000, five-year, 10 percent bonds. The bond interest is payable each June 30 and December 31. Assume three separate and independent selling scenarios: Case A, at par; Case B, at 95; and Case C, at 110.

Required:
Complete a schedule similar to the following for each separate case assuming straight-line amortization of discount and premium. Disregard income tax. Give all dollar amounts in thousands.

	At End of 2009	At End of 2010	At End of 2011	At End of 2012
Case A: sold at par (100)	$	$	$	$
Interest expense on income statement				
Net liability on balance sheet				
Case B: sold at a discount (95)				
Interest expense on income statement				
Net liability on balance sheet				
Case C: sold at a premium (110)				
Interest expense on income statement				
Net liability on balance sheet				

AP10-3
LO3

Reporting Bonds Issued at a Discount (Straight Line) (P10-6)

On January 1, 2009, Williams Corporation issued $1,000,000 in bonds that mature in five years. The bonds have a stated interest rate of 7 percent and pay interest on December 31 each year. When the bonds were sold, the market rate of interest was 9 percent. The company uses the straight-line amortization method.

Required:
1. What was the issue price on January 1, 2009?
2. What amount of interest should be recorded on December 31, 2009? How much on December 31, 2010?
3. What amount of cash interest should be paid on December 31, 2009? How much on December 31, 2010?
4. What is the book value of the bonds on December 31, 2009? What is the amount on December 31, 2010?

Reporting Bonds Issued at a Discount (Effective Interest) (P10-7)

AP10-4
LO3

On January 1, 2009, Colonial Life Corporation issued $2,000,000 in bonds that mature in five years. The bonds have a stated interest rate of 6 percent and pay interest on December 31 each year. When the bonds were sold, the market rate of interest was 7 percent. Colonial uses the effective-interest amortization method.

Required:
1. What was the issue price on January 1, 2009?
2. What amount of interest should be recorded on December 31, 2009? How much on December 31, 2010?
3. What amount of cash interest should be paid on December 31, 2009? How much on December 31, 2010?
4. What is the book value of the bonds on December 31, 2009? What is the amount on December 31, 2010?

Reporting Bonds Issued at a Premium (Straight Line) (P10-9)

AP10-5
LO4

On January 1, 2009, Wellington Corporation issued $900,000 in bonds that mature in five years. The bonds have a stated interest rate of 10 percent and pay interest on December 31 each year. When the bonds were sold, the market rate of interest was 9 percent. Wellington uses the straight-line amortization method.

Required:
1. What was the issue price on January 1, 2009?
2. What amount of interest should be recorded on December 31, 2009? How much on December 31, 2010?
3. What amount of cash interest should be paid on December 31, 2009? How much on December 31, 2010?
4. What is the book value of the bonds on December 31, 2009? What is the amount on December 31, 2010?

Reporting Bonds Issued at a Premium (Effective Interest) (P10-10)

AP10-6
LO4

On January 1, 2009, Fey Insurance Corporation issued $4,000,000 in bonds that mature in five years. The bonds have a stated interest rate of 9 percent and pay interest on December 31 each year. When the bonds were sold, the market rate of interest was 6 percent. Fey uses the effective-interest amortization method.

Required:
1. What was the issue price on January 1, 2009?
2. What amount of interest should be recorded on December 31, 2009? How much on December 31, 2010?
3. What amount of cash interest should be paid on December 31, 2009? How much on December 31, 2010?
4. What is the book value of the bonds on December 31, 2009? What is the amount on December 31, 2010?

Understanding the Early Retirement of Debt (P10-14)

AP10-7
LO4
AMC Entertainment

AMC Entertainment, Inc., owns and operates 243 movie theaters with 1,617 screens in 22 states. The company sold 11 7/8 percent bonds in the amount of $52,720,000 and used the cash proceeds to retire bonds with a coupon rate of 13.6 percent. At that time, the 13.6 percent bonds had a book value of $50,000,000.

Required:

1. Prepare the journal entry to record the early retirement of the 13.6 percent bonds.
2. How should AMC report any gain or loss on this transaction?
3. Why did the company issue new bonds in order to retire the old bonds?

CASES **AND PROJECTS**

Annual Report Cases

CP10-1
LO1, 2

AMERICAN EAGLE
OUTFITTERS

Finding Financial Information

Refer to the financial statements of American Eagle given in Appendix B at the end of this book.

Required:

1. How much interest was paid in cash during the most recent reporting year?
2. Explain why the company does not report bonds payable on its balance sheet.
3. Describe the company's established arrangements, if any, that permit it to borrow money if needed.

CP10-2
LO1, 2
Urban Outfitters

Finding Financial Information

Refer to the financial statements of Urban Outfitters given in Appendix C at the end of this book.

Required:

1. How much interest was paid in cash during the most recent reporting year?
2. Explain why the company does not report bonds payable on its balance sheet.
3. Describe the company's established arrangements, if any that permit it to borrow money if needed.

CP10-3
LO2, 5, 7

AMERICAN EAGLE
OUTFITTERS

Urban Outfitters

www.mhhe.com/libby6e

Comparing Companies within an Industry

Refer to the financial statements of American Eagle given in Appendix B, Urban Outfitters given in Appendix C, and the Industry Ratio Report given in Appendix D at the end of this book. Most companies report some amounts of bonds payable on their balance sheets. It is somewhat surprising, therefore, that neither company reports any bond liabilities.

Required:

1. Examine the statements of cash flow for both companies. What is the primary source for cash flow for both companies?
2. Two financial ratios (the debt-to-equity ratio and times interest earned) are discussed in this chapter. Are they relevant for these companies? Explain.

CP10-4
LO3
JCPenney

Analyzing Zero Coupon Bonds from an Actual Company

JCPenney Company was one of the first companies to issue zero coupon bonds. It issued bonds with a face (maturity) value of $400 million due eight years after issuance. When the bonds were sold to the public, similar bonds paid 15 percent effective interest. An article in *Forbes* magazine discussed the JCPenney bonds and stated: "It's easy to see why corporations like to sell bonds that don't pay interest. But why would anybody want to buy that kind of paper [bond]?"

Required:

1. Explain why an investor would buy a JCPenney bond with a zero interest rate.
2. If investors could earn 15 percent on similar investments, how much did JCPenney receive when it issued the bonds with a face value of $400 million?

Critical Thinking Cases

Evaluating an Ethical Dilemma

CP10-5
LO1

You work for a small company considering investing in a new Internet business. Financial projections suggest that the company will be able to earn in excess of $40 million per year on an investment of $100 million. The company president suggests borrowing the money by issuing bonds that will carry a 7 percent interest rate. He says, "This is better than printing money! We won't have to invest a penny of our own money, and we get to keep $33 million per year after we pay interest to the bondholders." As you think about the proposed transaction, you feel a little uncomfortable about taking advantage of the creditors in this fashion. You feel that it must be wrong to earn such a high return by using money that belongs to other people. Is this an ethical business transaction?

Evaluating an Ethical Dilemma

CP10-6
LO1

Assume that you are a portfolio manager for a large insurance company. The majority of the money you manage is from retired school teachers who depend on the income you earn on their investments. You have invested a significant amount of money in the bonds of a large corporation and have just received a call from the company's president explaining that it is unable to meet its current interest obligations because of deteriorating business operations related to increased international competition. The president has a recovery plan that will take at least two years. During that time, the company will not be able to pay interest on the bonds and, she admits, if the plan does not work, bondholders will probably lose more than half of their money. As a creditor, you can force the company into immediate bankruptcy and probably get back at least 90 percent of the bondholders' money. You also know that your decision will cause at least 10,000 people to lose their jobs if the company ceases operations. Given only these two options, what should you do?

Financial Reporting and Analysis Team Project

Team Project: Examining an Annual Report

CP10-7
LO1, 2, 3, 4, 5, 7

As a team, select an industry to analyze. *Reuters* provides lists of industries and their makeup at www.reuters.com/finance/industries. Each team member should acquire the annual report or 10-K for one publicly traded company in the industry, with each member selecting a different company. (Library files, the SEC EDGAR service at www.sec.gov, Compustat CD, or the company itself are good sources.)

Required:
On an individual basis, each team member should write a short report answering the following questions about the selected company. Discuss any patterns across the companies that you as a team observe. Then, as a team, write a short report comparing and contrasting your companies.

1. Has your company issued any long-term bonds or notes? If so, read the footnote and list any unusual features (e.g., callable, convertible, secured by specific collateral).
2. If your company issued any bonds, were they issued at either a premium or a discount? If so, does the company use the straight-line or effective-interest amortization method?
3. Ratio analysis:
   a. What does the debt-to-equity ratio measure in general?
   b. Compute the ratio for the last three years.
   c. What do your results suggest about the company?
   d. If available, find the industry ratio for the most recent year, compare it to your results, and discuss why you believe your company differs from or is similar to the industry ratio.
4. Ratio analysis:
   a. What does the times interest earned ratio measure in general?
   b. Compute the ratio for the last three years. If interest expense is not separately disclosed, you will not be able to compute the ratio. If so, state why you think it is not separately disclosed.
   c. What do your results suggest about the company?
   d. If available, find the industry ratio for the most recent year, compare it to your results, and discuss why you believe your company differs from or is similar to the industry ratio.
5. During the recent year, how much cash did the company receive on issuing debt? How much did it pay on debt principal? What does management suggest were the reasons for issuing and/or repaying debt during the year?

LEARNING OBJECTIVES

After studying this chapter, you should be able to:

1. Explain the role of stock in the capital structure of a corporation. p. 559
2. Analyze the earnings per share ratio. p. 562
3. Describe the characteristics of common stock and analyze transactions affecting common stock. p. 563
4. Discuss dividends and analyze transactions. p. 566
5. Analyze the dividend yield ratio. p. 566
6. Discuss the purpose of stock dividends and stock splits, and report transactions. p. 569
7. Describe the characteristics of preferred stock and analyze transactions affecting preferred stock. p. 571
8. Discuss the impact of capital stock transactions on cash flows. p. 573

Lectured slideshow–LP11-1
www.mhhe.com/libby6e

REPORTING AND INTERPRETING OWNERS' EQUITY

In 1953, an entrepreneur named Troy Smith opened a drive-in restaurant in Shawnee, Oklahoma. Today, the company is known as Sonic Drive-In restaurants with nearly 3,200 units from coast to coast and in northern Mexico. To finance that type of growth, management recognized the need to raise large amounts of new capital. In order to do so, Sonic would have to "go public," allowing the company's stock to be traded on a major stock exchange. Currently, Sonic has nearly 57,000 stockholders with its stock listed on the NASDAQ.

As part of a publicly traded company, managers of Sonic must focus on a number of priorities including the development of

- A business strategy to ensure the long-term profitable growth of Sonic.

- A financial plan to ensure that capital is available to support planned growth.

- A strategy to maximize stockholders' wealth.

In this chapter, we study the role that stockholders' equity plays in building a successful business and strategies that managers use to maximize stockholders' wealth.

UNDERSTANDING THE BUSINESS

To some people, the words *corporation* and *business* are almost synonymous. You've probably heard friends refer to a career in business as "the corporate world." Equating business with corporations is understandable because corporations are the dominant form of business organization in terms of volume of operations. If you were to write the names of 50 familiar businesses on a piece of paper, probably all of them would be corporations.

The popularity of the corporate form can be attributed to a critical advantage that corporations have over sole proprietorships and partnerships: They can raise large amounts of capital because both large and small investors can easily participate in their ownership. This ease of participation is related to several factors.

- Shares of stock can be purchased in small amounts. You could buy a single share of Sonic stock for about $20 and become one of the owners of this successful company.

- Ownership interests can easily be transferred through the sale of shares on established markets such as the New York Stock Exchange.

- Stock ownership provides investors with limited liability because in bankruptcy, creditors have claims against only the corporation's assets, not the assets of the individual owners.

Many Americans own stock either directly or indirectly through a mutual fund or pension program. Stock ownership offers them the opportunity to earn higher returns than they could on deposits to bank accounts or investments in corporate bonds. Unfortunately, stock ownership also involves higher risk. The proper balance between risk and the expected return on an investment depends on individual preferences.

Exhibit 11.1 presents financial information from Sonic's annual report. Notice that the stockholders' equity section of the balance sheet lists two primary sources of stockholders' equity:

1. Contributed capital from the sale of stock. This is the amount of money stockholders invested through the purchase of shares.

2. Retained earnings generated by the company's profit-making activities. This is the cumulative amount of net income the corporation has earned since its organization less the cumulative amount of dividends paid since organization.

Most companies generate a significant portion of their stockholders' equity from retained earnings. In the case of Sonic, retained earnings represents about 73 percent of the company's total stockholders' equity.

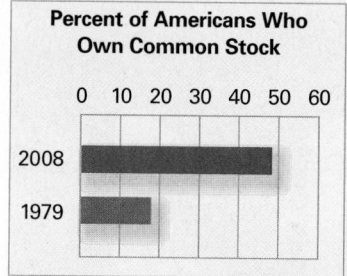

Percent of Americans Who Own Common Stock

	0	10	20	30	40	50	60
2008							
1979							

EXHIBIT 11.1

Excerpt from Consolidated Balance Sheet for Sonic

REAL WORLD EXCERPT

SONIC DRIVE-IN

ANNUAL REPORT

	2006	2005
Stockholders' equity:		
Preferred stock, par value $.01; 1,000,000 shares authorized; none outstanding	—	—
Common stock, par value $.01; 245,000,000 shares authorized; shares issued 114,988,369 in 2006 and 113,649,009 in 2005	1,150	1,136
Paid-in capital	173,802	153,776
Retained earnings	476,694	397,989
Accumulated other comprehensive income	(484)	—
	651,162	552,901
Treasury stock, at cost; 29,506,003 shares in 2006 and 24,676,380 shares in 2005	(259,469)	(164,984)
Total stockholders' equity	391,693	387,917
Total liabilities and stockholders' equity	$ 638,018	$ 563,316

ORGANIZATION of the Chapter

Ownership of a Corporation	Common Stock Transactions	Dividends on Common Stock
■ Benefits of Stock Ownership ■ Authorized, Issued, and Outstanding Shares ■ Earnings per Share (EPS)	■ Initial Sale of Stock ■ Sale of Stock in Secondary Markets ■ Stock Issued for Employee Compensation ■ Repurchase of Stock	■ Dividend Yield Ratio

Preferred Stock	Stock Dividends and Stock Splits
■ Dividends on Preferred Stock	■ Stock Dividends ■ Stock Splits

OWNERSHIP OF A CORPORATION

The corporation is the only business form the law recognizes as a separate entity. As a distinct entity, the corporation enjoys a continuous existence separate and apart from its owners. It may own assets, incur liabilities, expand and contract in size, sue others, be sued, and enter into contracts independently of its stockholder owners.

To protect everyone's rights, the creation and governance of corporations are tightly regulated by law. Corporations are created by application to a state government (not the federal government). On approval of the application, the state issues a charter, sometimes called the articles of incorporation. Corporations are governed by a board of directors elected by the stockholders.

Each state has different laws governing the organization of corporations created within its boundaries. Although Sonic has its headquarters in Oklahoma, it elected to incorporate in the state of Delaware. You will find that an unusually large number of corporations are incorporated in Delaware because the state has some of the most favorable laws for establishing corporations.

Video 11-1
Audio lecture–AP11-1
www.mhhe.com/libby6e

Benefits of Stock Ownership

When you invest in a corporation, you are known as a stockholder or shareholder. As a stockholder, you receive shares of stock that you subsequently can sell on established stock exchanges. Owners of common stock receive a number of benefits:

■ **A voice in management** You may vote in the stockholders' meeting on major issues concerning management of the corporation.

■ **Dividends** You receive a proportional share of the distribution of profits.

■ **Residual claim** You will receive a proportional share of the distribution of remaining assets upon the liquidation of the company.

Learning Objective 1
Explain the role of stock in the capital structure of a corporation.

Owners, unlike creditors, are able to vote at the annual stockholders' meeting, with a number of votes equal to the number of shares owned. The following Notice of Annual Meeting of Shareholders was recently sent to all owners of Sonic stock:

REAL WORLD EXCERPT

SONIC DRIVE-IN

NOTICE OF STOCKHOLDERS' MEETING

Dear Stockholder:

It is my pleasure to invite you to the annual meeting of the stockholders of Sonic Corp. (the "Company"). We will hold the meeting on Wednesday, January 31, 2007, at 1:30 p.m. on the Fourth Floor of the Sonic Headquarters Building, located at 300 Johnny Bench Drive, Oklahoma City, Oklahoma, for the following purposes:

1. *To elect four directors;*

2. *To ratify the selection of Ernst & Young LLP as our independent registered public accounting firm; and*

3. *To act upon any such other matters as may properly come before the meeting or any adjournments or postponements thereof.*

The foregoing items of business are more fully described in the Proxy Statement accompanying this Notice. The Board of Directors has chosen the close of business on December 4, 2006, as the date used to determine the stockholders who will be able to attend and vote at the Annual Meeting. If you own stock in Sonic Corp. at the close of business on that date, you are cordially invited to attend the meeting.

EXHIBIT 11.2

Typical Organizational Structure of a Corporation

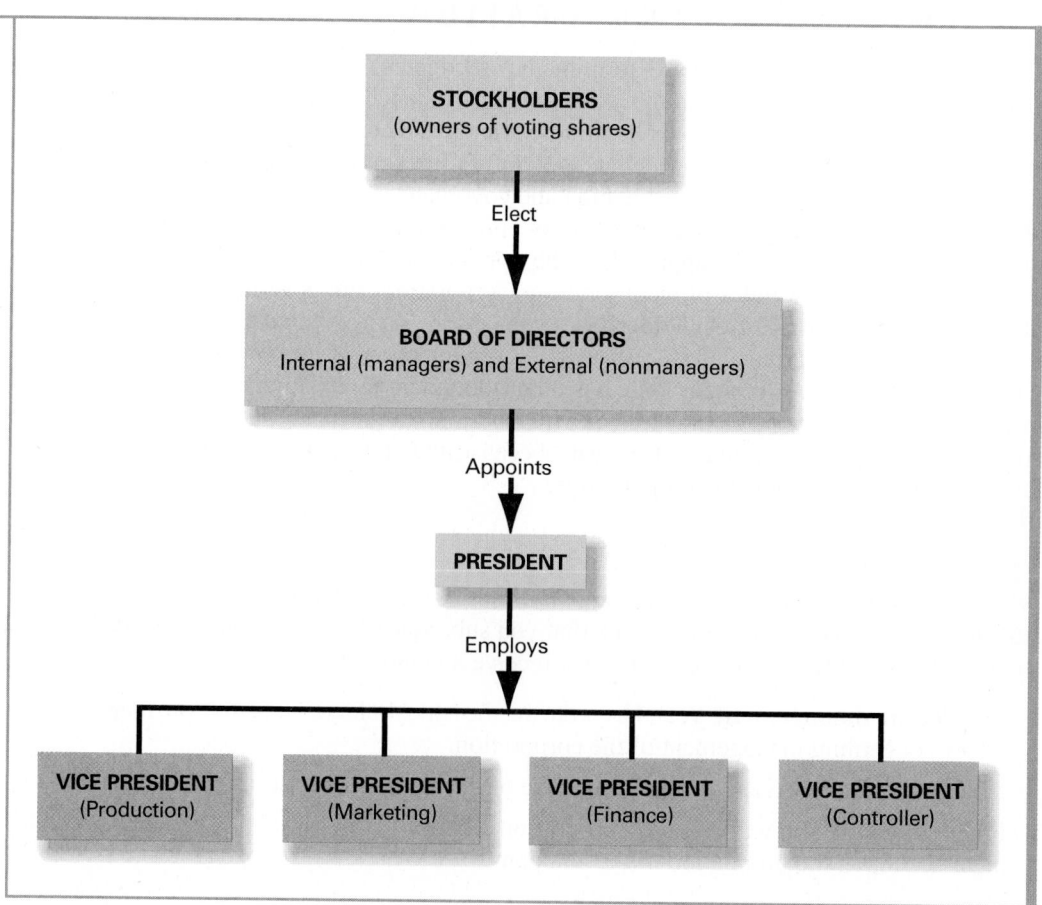

This notice also contained several pages of information concerning the people who were nominated to be members of the board of directors as well as a variety of financial information. Since most owners do not actually attend the annual meeting, the notice included a proxy card, similar to an absentee ballot. Owners may complete the proxy and mail it to the company, which will include it in the votes at the annual meeting.

As shown in Exhibit 11.2, stockholders have ultimate authority in a corporation. The board of directors and, indirectly, all employees are accountable to the stockholders. The organizational structure shown is typical of most corporations, but the specific structure depends on the nature of the company's business.

Authorized, Issued, and Outstanding Shares

The corporate charter specifies the maximum number of shares that can be sold to the public. The financial statements must report information concerning the number of shares that have been sold to date. Let's look at the share information reported by Sonic as of August 31, 2006, shown in Exhibit 11.1 on page 558. For Sonic, the maximum number of common shares that can be sold, called the **authorized number of shares,** is 245,000,000. As of August 31, 2006, the company had sold 114,988,369 shares. Stock that has been sold to the public is called **issued shares.**

For a number of reasons, a company might want to buy back stock that has already been sold to the public. Stock that has been bought back is called *treasury stock.* When a company buys back its stock, a difference is created between the number of issued shares and the number of **outstanding shares,** or shares currently held by individual stockholders. We can compute outstanding shares for Sonic using data from the August 31, 2006, balance sheet shown in Exhibit 11.1:

Issued shares	114,988,369
Less: Treasury stock	(29,506,003)
Outstanding shares	85,482,366

The AUTHORIZED NUMBER OF SHARES is the maximum number of shares of a corporation's capital stock that can be issued as specified in the charter.

ISSUED SHARES represent the total number of shares of stock that have been sold.

OUTSTANDING SHARES refer to the total number of shares of stock that are owned by stockholders on any particular date.

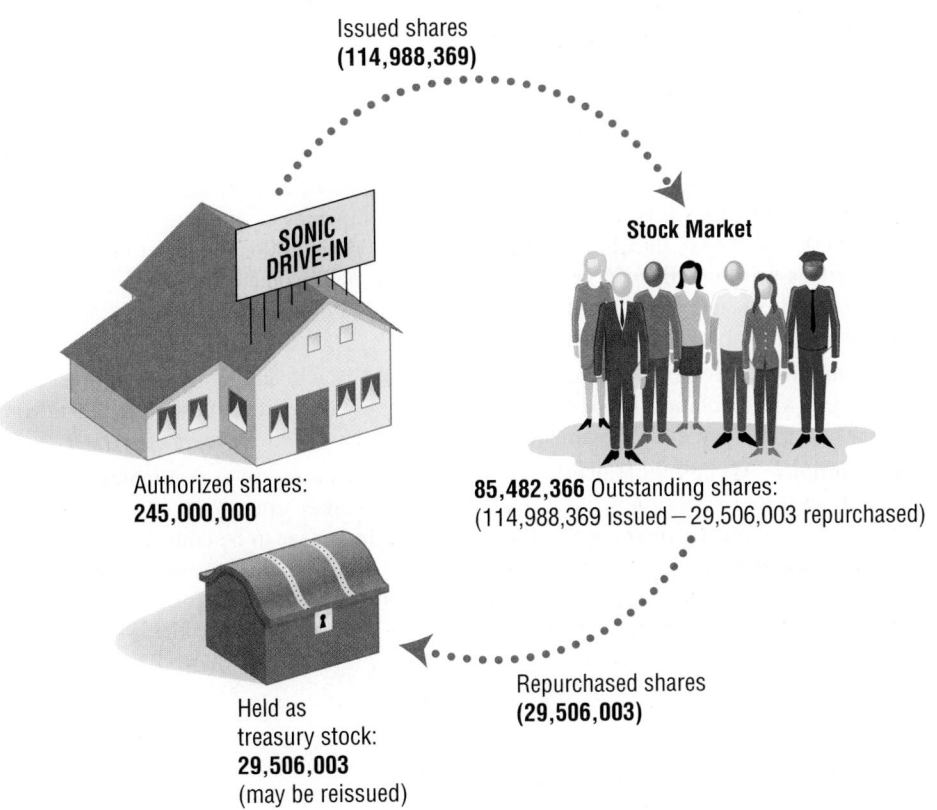

Issued shares
(114,988,369)

SONIC DRIVE-IN

Stock Market

Authorized shares:
245,000,000

85,482,366 Outstanding shares:
(114,988,369 issued − 29,506,003 repurchased)

Held as
treasury stock:
29,506,003
(may be reissued)

Repurchased shares
(29,506,003)

The number of outstanding shares is also reported on the balance sheet shown in Exhibit 11.1 on page 558. Notice that when treasury stock is held, the number of shares issued and the number of shares outstanding differ by the number of shares of treasury stock held (treasury stock is included in "issued" but not in "outstanding"). The number of shares outstanding is important to financial analysts who need to express certain dollar amounts on a per share basis. One example is the earnings per share ratio.

KEY RATIO ANALYSIS

Earnings per Share (EPS)

Learning Objective 2
Analyze the earnings per share ratio.

? ANALYTICAL QUESTION:
How well is a company performing?

% RATIO AND COMPARISONS:
Earnings per share is computed as follows:

Earnings per Share = Net Income* ÷ Average Number of Common Shares Outstanding

*If there are preferred dividends, the amount is subtracted from net income in the numerator.

The 2006 ratio for Sonic:

$$\$78,705,000 \div 86,260,000 \text{ shares*} = \$0.91$$

*As reported in the notes to the financial statements

COMPARISONS OVER TIME			COMPARISONS WITH COMPETITORS	
Sonic			**Jack in the Box**	**Wendy's**
2004	**2005**	**2006**	**2006**	**2006**
$0.65	$0.78	$0.91	$3.84	$1.10

💡 INTERPRETATIONS

In General   All analysts and investors are interested in a company's earnings. You have probably seen newspaper headlines announcing a company's earnings. Notice that those news stories normally report earnings on an earnings per share (EPS) basis. EPS is a popular measure because income numbers are much easier to compare on a per share basis. For example, in 2006, Sonic earned income of $78,705,000 compared to $70,443,000 in the previous year. If we make that comparison on a per share basis, we can say that EPS increased from $0.78 to $0.91. EPS is also useful in comparing companies of different sizes. Jack in the Box, a larger company than Sonic, earned $108,030,000 in 2006. While net income for Jack in the Box was more than 50 percent larger than the net income earned by Sonic, EPS for Jack in the Box is more than four times larger than the EPS for Sonic because Jack in the Box has a fewer number of shares outstanding.

Focus Company Analysis   Sonic has a strategy of rapid growth and reinvestment of earnings. Analysts are watching EPS to be sure the company will achieve its strategy. Sonic's EPS increased by 40 percent between 2004 and 2006, which is a strong level of growth.

A Few Cautions   While EPS is an effective and widely used measure of profitability, it can be misleading if there are significant differences in the market values of the shares being compared. Two companies earning $1.50 per share might appear to be comparable, but if shares in one company cost $10 while shares of the other cost $175, they are not comparable. The stock price for Jack in the Box is over $60 per share while the price for Sonic stock is just over $20. Obviously, investors expect a large EPS number for companies with higher stock prices.

COMMON STOCK TRANSACTIONS

Learning Objective 3
Describe the characteristics of common stock and analyze transactions affecting common stock.

Most corporations issue two types of stock, common stock and preferred stock. All corporations must issue common stock, but only some issue preferred stock. In this section, we discuss common stock and in a subsequent section, we discuss preferred stock.

COMMON STOCK is the basic voting stock issued by a corporation.

Common stock is held by individuals who are often thought of as the "owners" of the corporation because they have the right to vote and share in the profitability of the business through dividends. Periodically, the board of directors declare dividends based on the company's profitability.

The fact that common stock dividends may increase with increases in the company's profitability helps to explain why investors can make money in the stock market. Basically, you can think of the price of a share of stock as the present value of all its future dividends. If a company's profitability improves so that it can pay higher dividends, the present value of its common stock will increase.

Common stock normally has a par value, a nominal value per share established in the corporate charter. Par value has no relationship to the market value of a stock. The annual report for Sonic states that the common stock has a par value of $0.01 while its market value is more than $20 per share.

PAR VALUE is the nominal value per share of capital stock specified in the charter; serves as the basis for legal capital.

Most states require stock to have a par value. The original purpose of this requirement was to protect creditors by specifying a permanent amount of capital that owners could not withdraw before a bankruptcy, which would leave creditors with an empty corporate shell. This permanent amount of capital is called legal capital. Today, this requirement has little importance because of other contractual protections for creditors.

LEGAL CAPITAL is the permanent amount of capital defined by state law that must remain invested in the business; serves as a cushion for creditors.

Some states require the issuance of no-par value stock, which does not have a specified amount per share. When a corporation issues no-par stock, legal capital is as defined by the state law.

NO-PAR VALUE STOCK is capital stock that has no par value specified in the corporate charter.

Initial Sale of Stock

Two names are applied to transactions involving the initial sale of a company's stock to the public. An **initial public offering,** or IPO, involves the very first sale of a company's stock to the public (i.e., when the company first "goes public"). You have probably heard stories of Internet stocks that have increased dramatically in value the day of the IPO. While investors sometimes earn significant returns on IPOs, they also take significant risks. Once a company's stock has been traded on established markets, additional sales of new stock to the public are called **seasoned new issues.**

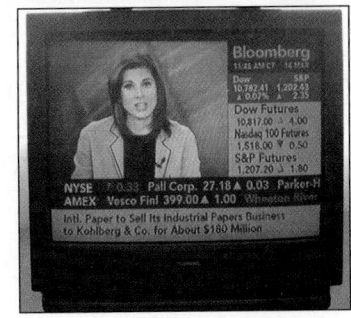

Most sales of stock to the public are cash transactions. To illustrate the accounting for an initial sale of stock, assume that Sonic sold 100,000 shares of its $0.01 par value stock for $20 per share. The company would record the following journal entry:

Cash (+A) (100,000 × $20).....................................	2,000,000	
Common stock (+SE) (100,000 × $0.01)		1,000
Capital in excess of par value (+SE).........................		1,999,000

Assets	=	Liabilities	+	Stockholders' Equity	
Cash +2,000,000				Common stock	+1,000
				Capital in excess of par	+1,999,000

Notice that the common stock account is credited for the number of shares sold times the par value per share, and the capital in excess of par value account is credited for the remainder. If the corporate charter does not specify a par value for the stock, the stated value is used in the same manner that par value is used. If there is no par or stated value, the entire proceeds from the sale will be entered in the common stock account.

Sale of Stock in Secondary Markets

When a company sells stock to the public, the transaction is between the issuing corporation and the buyer. Subsequent to the initial sale, investors can sell shares to other investors without directly affecting the corporation. For example, if investor Jon Drago sold 1,000 shares of Sonic stock to Jennifer Lea, Sonic would not record a journal entry on its books. Mr. Drago received cash for the shares he sold, and Ms. Lea received stock for the cash she paid. Sonic did not receive or pay anything.

Each business day, *The Wall Street Journal* reports the results of thousands of transactions between investors in secondary markets, such as the New York Stock Exchange

(NYSE), the American Stock Exchange (AMEX), and the NAS-DAQ market. Managers of corporations closely follow the price movements of their company's stock. Stockholders expect to earn money on their investments through both dividends and increases in the stock price. In many instances, senior management has been replaced because of a stock's poor performance in the stock market. While managers watch the stock price on a daily basis, transactions between investors do not directly affect the company's financial statements.

Stock Issued for Employee Compensation

One of the advantages of the corporate form is the ability to separate the management of a business from its ownership. Separation can also be a disadvantage because some managers may not act in the owners' best interests. This problem can be overcome in a number of ways. Compensation packages can be developed to reward managers for meeting goals that are important to stockholders. Another strategy is to offer managers stock options, which permit them to buy stock at a fixed price.

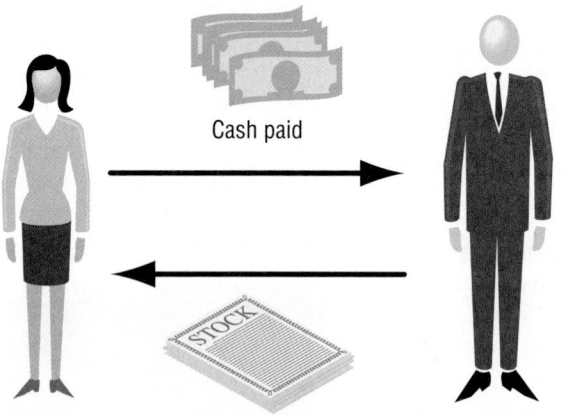

Ms. Lea   Sonic drive-in stock   Mr. Drago

The holder of a stock option has an interest in a company's performance just as an owner does. Stock option plans have become an increasingly common form of compensation over the past few years. Indeed, 98 percent of the companies surveyed by *Accounting Trends & Techniques* now offer stock option plans to their employees.

Sonic offers employees stock options as part of their compensation. The options specify that shares could be bought at the then current market price. Granting a stock option is a form of compensation, even if the grant price and the current stock price are the same. You can think of a stock option as a risk-free investment. If you hold a stock option and the stock price declines, you have lost nothing. If the stock price increases, you can exercise your option at the low grant price and sell the stock at the higher price for a profit.

Companies must estimate and report compensation expense associated with stock options. The specific procedures will be discussed in the intermediate accounting course.

Repurchase of Stock

A corporation may want to repurchase its stock from existing stockholders for a number of reasons. One common reason is the existence of an employee bonus plan that provides workers with shares of the company's stock as part of their compensation. Because of Securities and Exchange Commission regulations concerning newly issued shares, most companies find it less costly to give employees repurchased shares than to issue new ones. Stock that has been reacquired and held by the issuing corporation is called **treasury stock.** These shares have no voting, dividend, or other stockholder rights while held as treasury stock.

Most companies record the purchase of treasury stock based on the cost of the shares that were purchased. Assume that Sonic bought 100,000 shares of its stock in the open market when it was selling for $20 per share. Using the cost method, the company would record the following journal entry:

| Treasury stock (+XSE, −SE) (100,000 × $20) .... | 2,000,000 | |
| Cash (−A) .... | | 2,000,000 |

Assets	=	Liabilities	+	Stockholders' Equity	
Cash −2,000,000				Treasury stock −2,000,000	

Intuitively, many students expect the Treasury Stock account to be reported as an asset. Such is not the case because a company cannot create an asset by investing in itself. The Treasury Stock account is actually a contra-equity account, which means that it is subtracted from total stockholders' equity. This practice makes sense because treasury stock is stock that is no longer outstanding and therefore should not be included in stockholders' equity.

As the information in Exhibit 11.1 indicates, Sonic reported treasury stock in the amount of $259,469 (thousand) on its balance sheet as of August 31, 2006. The statement of stockholders' equity reports the same amount plus additional information.

When a company sells its treasury stock, it does not report an accounting profit or loss on the transaction, even if it sells the stock for more or less than it paid. GAAP do not permit a corporation to report income or losses from investments in its own stock because transactions with the owners are not considered normal profit-making activities. Based on the previous example, assume that Sonic resold 10,000 shares of treasury stock for $30 per share. Remember that the company had purchased the stock for $20 per share. Sonic would record the following journal entry:

Cash (+A) (10,000 × $30)	300,000	
Treasury stock (−XSE, +SE) (10,000 × $20)		200,000
Capital in excess of par (+SE)		100,000

Assets	=	Liabilities	+	Stockholders' Equity	
Cash +300,000				Treasury stock +200,000	
				Capital in excess of par +100,000	

If treasury stock were sold at a price below its purchase price (i.e., at an economic loss), stockholders' equity would be reduced by the amount of the difference between purchase price and the sale price. Assume that Sonic had sold the stock in the previous illustration for only $15 per share:

Cash (+A) (10,000 × $15)	150,000	
Capital in excess of par (−SE) (10,000 × $5)	50,000	
Treasury stock (−XSE, +SE) (10,000 × $20)		200,000

Assets	=	Liabilities	+	Stockholders' Equity	
Cash +150,000				Treasury stock +200,000	
				Capital in excess of par −50,000	

TREASURY STOCK is a corporation's own stock that had been issued but was subsequently reacquired and is still being held by that corporation.

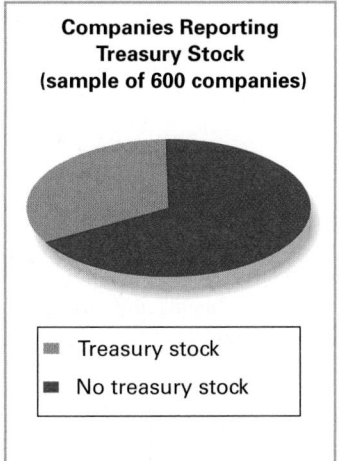

Companies Reporting Treasury Stock (sample of 600 companies)

- Treasury stock
- No treasury stock

SELF-STUDY QUIZ

1. Assume that Applied Technology Corporation issued 10,000 shares of its common stock, par value $2, for $150,000 cash. Prepare the journal entry to record this transaction.

2. Assume that Applied Technology repurchased 5,000 shares of its stock in the open market when the stock was selling for $12 per share. Record this transaction.

After you have completed your answers, check them with the solutions at the bottom of the page.

DIVIDENDS ON COMMON STOCK

Learning Objective 4

Discuss dividends and analyze transactions.

Audio lecture–AP11-2
www.mhhe.com/libby6e

Investors buy common stock because they expect a return on their investment. This return can come in two forms: stock price appreciation and dividends. Some investors prefer to buy stocks that pay little or no dividends because companies that reinvest the majority of their earnings tend to increase their future earnings potential, along with their stock price. Wealthy investors in high tax brackets prefer to receive their return in the form of higher stock prices because capital gains may be taxed at a lower rate than dividend income. Other investors, such as retired people who need a steady income, prefer to receive their return in the form of dividends. These people often seek stocks that will pay very high dividends, such as utility stocks. Because of the importance of dividends to many investors, analysts often compute the dividend yield ratio to evaluate a corporation's dividend policy.

KEY RATIO
ANALYSIS

Dividend Yield

Learning Objective 5

Analyze the dividend yield ratio.

❓ ANALYTICAL QUESTION

What is return on investment based on dividends?

% RATIO AND COMPARISONS

Sonic does not pay dividends. The dividend yield ratio is computed as follows:

Dividend Yield Ratio = Dividends per Share ÷ Market Price per Share

COMPARISONS OVER TIME			COMPARISONS WITH COMPETITORS	
Sonic			Jack in the Box	Wendy's
2004	2005	2006	2006	2006
0%	0%	0%	0%	1.5%

💡 INTERPRETATIONS

In General Investors in common stock earn a return from both dividends and capital appreciation (increases in the market price of the stock). Growth-oriented companies often rely mainly on increases in their market price to provide a return to investors. Others pay large dividends but have more stable market prices. Each type of stock appeals to different types of investors with different risk and return preferences.

Self-Study Quiz
Solutions

1.	Cash (+A)		150,000	
	Common stock (+SE)			20,000
	Capital in excess of par (+SE)			130,000
2.	Treasury stock (+XSE, −SE)		60,000	
	Cash (−A)			60,000

Focus Company Analysis   As a growth-oriented company, Sonic established a policy not to pay dividends. Instead, the company is using its cash flows from operating activities to expand the business and repurchase shares from current stockholders. Notice that Jack in the Box also does not pay dividends and the dividend yield for Wendy's is small. None of these stocks would appeal to investors who need a steady income from dividends.

A Few Cautions   Remember that the dividend yield ratio tells only part of the return on investment story. Often potential capital appreciation is a much more important consideration. Sonic is currently reinvesting a large portion of its earnings. As a result, the company is growing rapidly, and its stock price has increased significantly. Investors in Sonic have bought the stock with the expectation of earning a return from increases in its market value, not from dividends. During the period 2004 to 2006, investors in Sonic stock earned a 60% return on their investment because of stock price increases.

Because Sonic does not pay dividends, let's look at the dividend policy for another familiar name in the fast food industry. The *International Herald Tribune* contained the following article concerning a dividend announcement from McDonald's:

On September 27, 2006, McDonald's, the world's largest restaurant company, raised its annual dividend almost 50 percent Wednesday, the biggest gain in three years, as sales climbed.

The increase to $1 from 67 cents follows more than three years of higher sales at restaurants open at least a year.

The dividend is payable Dec. 1 to shareholders of record Nov. 15, said the company based in Oak Brook, Illinois.

REAL WORLD EXCERPT

i'm lovin' it®

INTERNATIONAL HERALD
TRIBUNE

This article contains three important dates:

1. **Declaration date—September 27, 2006.** The declaration date is the date on which the board of directors officially approves the dividend. As soon as it makes the declaration, it creates a dividend liability.
2. **Date of record—November 15, 2006.** The record date follows the declaration; it is the date on which the corporation prepares the list of current stockholders based on its records. The dividend is payable only to those names listed on the record date. No journal entry is made on this date.
3. **Date of payment—December 1, 2006.** The payment date is the date on which the cash is disbursed to pay the dividend liability. It follows the date of record, as specified in the dividend announcement.

The DECLARATION DATE is the date on which the board of directors officially approves a dividend.

The RECORD DATE is the date on which the corporation prepares the list of current stockholders as shown on its records; dividends can be paid only to the stockholders who own stock on that date.

The PAYMENT DATE is the date on which a cash dividend is paid to the stockholders of record.

These three dates apply for all cash dividends and can be shown graphically as follows:

Declaration Date   Date of Record   Date of Payment

On the declaration date, a company records a liability related to the dividend. To illustrate, on September 27, McDonald's records the following journal entry. Assuming 75 million shares are outstanding, the dividend amounts to $75,000,000 ($1.00 × 75,000,000):

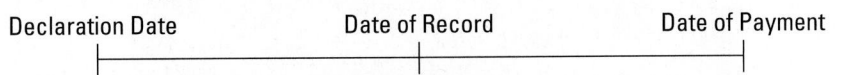

Retained earnings (−SE)   75,000,000
   Dividends payable (+L)   75,000,000

Assets	=	Liabilities	+	Stockholders' Equity
		Dividends payable +75,000,000		Retained earnings −75,000,000

The payment of the liability on December 1 is recorded as follows:

Dividends payable (−L)   75,000,000
    Cash (−A)   75,000,000

Assets	=	Liabilities	+	Stockholders' Equity
Cash −75,000,000		Dividends payable −75,000,000		

Notice that the declaration and payment of a cash dividend reduce assets (cash) and stockholders' equity (retained earnings) by the same amount. This observation explains the two fundamental requirements for payment of a cash dividend:

1. **Sufficient retained earnings.** The corporation must have accumulated a sufficient amount of retained earnings to cover the amount of the dividend. State incorporation laws often limit cash dividends to the balance in the Retained Earnings account.

2. **Sufficient cash.** The corporation must have sufficient cash to pay the dividend and meet the operating needs of the business. The mere fact that the Retained Earnings account has a large credit balance does not mean that the board of directors can declare and pay a cash dividend. The cash generated in the past by earnings represented in the Retained Earnings account may have been expended to acquire inventory, buy operational assets, and pay liabilities. Consequently, no necessary relationship exists between the balance of retained earnings and the balance of cash on any particular date. Quite simply, retained earnings is not cash.

**FINANCIAL
ANALYSIS**   **Impact of Dividends on Stock Price**

Another date that is important in understanding dividends has no accounting implications. The date two business days before the date of record is known as the *ex-dividend date*. This date is established by the stock exchanges to make certain that dividend checks are sent to the right people. If you buy stock before the ex-dividend date, you will receive the dividend. If you buy stock on the ex-dividend date or later, the previous owner will receive the dividend.

If you follow stock prices, you will notice that they often fall on the ex-dividend date because the stock is worth less on the date that it no longer includes the right to receive the next dividend.

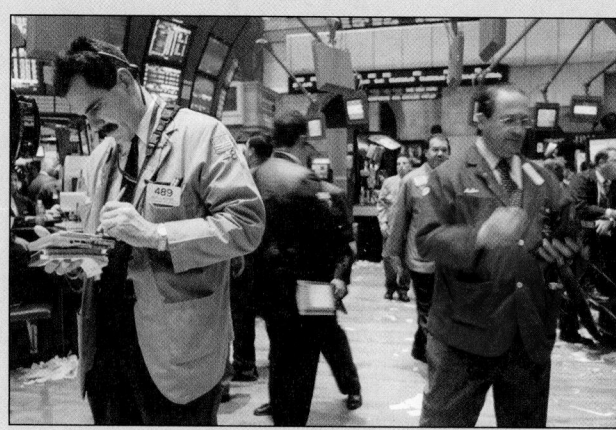

Answer the following questions concerning dividends:

1. On which dividend date is a liability created?

2. A cash outflow occurs on which dividend date?

3. What are the two fundamental requirements for the payment of a dividend?

After you have completed your answers, check them with the solutions at the bottom of the page.

STOCK DIVIDENDS AND STOCK SPLITS

Stock Dividends

Without a qualifier, the term *dividend* means a cash dividend, but dividends can also be paid with additional shares of stock. A **stock dividend** is a distribution of additional shares of a corporation's stock to its stockholders on a pro rata basis at no cost to the stockholder. The phrase *pro rata basis* means that each stockholder receives additional shares equal to the percentage of shares held. A stockholder with 10 percent of the outstanding shares would receive 10 percent of any additional shares issued as a stock dividend.

The term *stock dividend* is sometimes misused in annual reports and news articles. A recent *Wall Street Journal* headline announced that a particular company had just declared a "stock dividend." A close reading of the article revealed that the company had actually declared a cash dividend on the stock.

The value of a stock dividend is the subject of much debate. In reality, a stock dividend by itself has no economic value. All stockholders receive a pro rata distribution of shares, which means that each stockholder owns exactly the same portion of the company as before. The value of an investment is determined by the percentage of the company that is owned, not the number of shares held. If you get change for a dollar, you do not have more wealth because you hold four quarters instead of only one dollar. Similarly, if you own 10 percent of a company, you are not wealthier simply because the company declares a stock dividend and gives you (and all other stockholders) more shares of stock.

The stock market reacts immediately when a stock dividend is issued, and the stock price falls proportionally. Theoretically, if the stock price was $60 before a stock dividend and the number of shares is doubled, in the absence of events affecting the company, the price would fall to $30. Thus, an investor would own 100 shares worth $6,000 before the stock dividend (100 × $60) and 200 shares worth $6,000 after the stock dividend (200 × $30).

In reality, the fall in price is not exactly proportional to the number of new shares issued. In some cases, the stock dividend makes the stock more attractive to new investors. Many investors prefer to buy stock in

Learning Objective 6
Discuss the purpose of stock dividends and stock splits, and report transactions.

A STOCK DIVIDEND is a distribution of additional shares of a corporation's own stock.

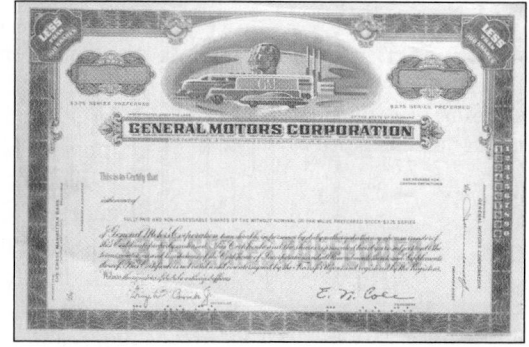

---

1. Declaration date.
2. Date of payment.
3. Dividends can be paid only if sufficient retained earnings and sufficient cash are both available.

Self-Study Quiz
Solutions

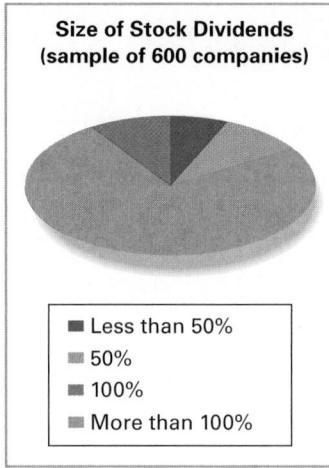

**Size of Stock Dividends
(sample of 600 companies)**

- Less than 50%
- 50%
- 100%
- More than 100%

round lots, which are multiples of 100 shares. An investor with $10,000 might not buy a stock selling for $150, for instance, because she cannot afford to buy 100 shares. She might buy the stock if the price were less than $100 as the result of a stock dividend. In other cases, stock dividends are associated with increases in cash dividends, which are attractive to some investors.

When a stock dividend occurs, the company must transfer an additional amount from either Retained Earnings or Capital in Excess of Par into the Common Stock account to reflect the additional shares issued. The amount transferred depends on whether the stock dividend is classified as large or small. Most stock dividends are classified as large. A large stock dividend involves the distribution of additional shares that amount to more than 20–25 percent of currently outstanding shares. A small stock dividend involves the distribution of shares that amounts to less than 20–25 percent of the outstanding shares. If the stock dividend is classified as large, the amount transferred to the Common Stock account is based on the par value of the additional shares issued. If the stock dividend is small (i.e., less than 20–25 percent), the amount transferred should be the total market value of the shares issued, with the par value of the stock transferred to the Common Stock account and the excess transferred to the Capital in Excess of Par Value account.

Sonic Drive-In issued a 50% stock dividend in 2006. The company declared and issued 38,219,000 shares as a large stock dividend, and made the following journal entry:

Retained earnings (−SE) ($0.01 × 38,219,000)	382,190	
Common stock (+SE)		382,190

Assets	=	Liabilities	+	Stockholders' Equity	
				Retained earnings	−382,190
				Common stock	+382,190

This journal entry moves an amount from Retained Earnings to the company's Common Stock account. Notice that the stock dividend did not change total stockholders' equity. It changed only the balances of some of the accounts that constitute stockholders' equity.

Stock Splits

A STOCK SPLIT is an increase in the total number of authorized shares by a specified ratio; does not decrease retained earnings.

Stock splits are not dividends. While they are similar to a stock dividend, they are quite different in terms of their impact on the stockholders' equity accounts. In a **stock split,** the total number of authorized shares is increased by a specified amount, such as 2-for-1. In this instance, each share held is called in and two new shares are issued in its place. Typically, a stock split is accomplished by reducing the par or stated value per share of all authorized shares, so that their total par value is unchanged. For instance, if Sonic executes a 2-for-1 stock split, it reduces the par value of its stock from $0.01 to $0.005 and doubles the number of shares outstanding. In contrast to a stock dividend, a stock split does not result in the transfer of a dollar amount to the Common Stock account. The reduction in the par value per share compensates for the increase in the number of shares, so that no transfer is needed.

In both a stock dividend and a stock split, the stockholder receives more shares of stock without having to invest additional resources to acquire the shares. A stock dividend requires a journal entry; a stock split does not but is disclosed in the notes to the financial statements. The comparative effects of a large stock dividend versus a stock split may be summarized as follows:

STOCKHOLDERS' EQUITY

	Before	After a 100% Stock Dividend	After a Two-for-One Stock Split
Number of shares outstanding	30,000	60,000	60,000
Par value per share	$ 10	$ 10	$ 5
Total par value outstanding	300,000	600,000	300,000
Retained earnings	650,000	350,000	650,000
Total stockholders' equity	950,000	950,000	950,000

SELF-STUDY QUIZ

Barton Corporation issued 100,000 new shares of common stock (par value $10) in a stock dividend when the market value was $30 per share.

1. Record this transaction, assuming that it was a small stock dividend.

2. Record this transaction, assuming that it was a large stock dividend.

3. What journal entry would be required if the transaction were a stock split?

After you have completed your answers, check them with the solutions at the bottom of the page.

PREFERRED STOCK

In addition to common stock, some corporations issue **preferred stock.** Notice in Exhibit 11.1 that Sonic is authorized to issue 1 million shares of preferred stock but has not done so. Sonic included this amount in its corporate charter so that it could raise additional funds, if needed, without having to amend its charter.

Preferred stock differs from common stock based on a number of rights granted to the stockholders. The most significant differences are:

- **Preferred stock does not grant voting rights.** As a result, preferred stock does not appeal to investors who want some control over the operations of a corporation. Indeed, this is one of the main reasons some corporations issue preferred stock to raise their equity capital: preferred stock permits them to raise funds without diluting common stockholders' control. The chart in the margin shows the percentage of companies surveyed by *Accounting Trends & Techniques* that include preferred stock in their capital structure.

- **Lower risk for preferred stock.** Generally, preferred stock is less risky than common stock because holders receive priority payment of dividends and distribution of assets if the corporation goes out of business. Usually a specified amount per share must be paid to preferred stockholders upon dissolution, before any remaining assets can be distributed to the common stockholders.

Learning Objective 7
Describe the characteristics of preferred stock and analyze transactions affecting preferred stock.

PREFERRED STOCK is stock that has specified rights over common stock.

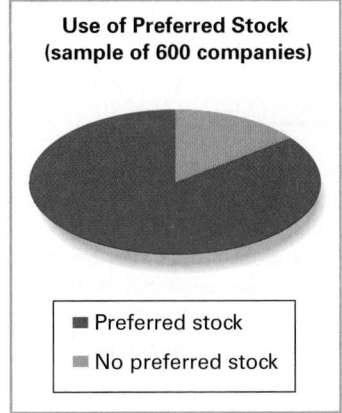

Use of Preferred Stock (sample of 600 companies)

■ Preferred stock
■ No preferred stock

Self-Study Quiz Solutions

1. Retained earnings	3,000,000	
Common stock		1,000,000
Capital in excess of par		2,000,000
2. Retained earnings	1,000,000	
Common stock		1,000,000

3. No journal entry is required in the case of a stock split.

■ **Preferred stock typically has a fixed dividend rate.** For example, "6 percent preferred stock, par value $10 per share" pays an annual dividend of 6 percent of par, or $0.60 per share. If preferred stock has no par value, the preferred dividend would be specified as $0.60 per share. The fixed dividend is attractive to certain investors who want a stable income from their investments.

Dividends on Preferred Stock

Because investors who purchase preferred stock give up certain advantages that are available to investors in common stock, preferred stock offers a dividend preference. The two most common dividend preferences are current and cumulative.

Current Dividend Preference

CURRENT DIVIDEND PREFERENCE is the feature of preferred stock that grants priority on preferred dividends over common dividends.

The **current dividend preference** requires the current preferred dividend to be paid before any dividends are paid on the common stock. This preference is always a feature of preferred stock. After the current dividend preference has been met and if no other preference is operative, dividends can be paid to the common stockholders.

Declared dividends must be allocated between preferred stock and common stock. First, the preferred stock preference must be met; then the remainder of the total dividend can be allocated to the common stock. To illustrate, assume the Sophia company has the following stock outstanding:

SOPHIA COMPANY
Preferred stock outstanding, 6%, par $20; 2,000 shares = $40,000 par
Common stock outstanding, par $10; 5,000 shares = $50,000 par

Assuming a current dividend preference only, dividends would be allocated as follows:

Example	Total Dividends	6% Preferred Stock*	Common Stock
No. 1	$ 3,000	$2,400	$ 600
No. 2	18,000	2,400	15,600

*Preferred dividend preference, $40,000 × 6% = $2,400.

Cumulative Dividend Preference

CUMULATIVE DIVIDEND PREFERENCE is the preferred stock feature that requires specified current dividends not paid in full to accumulate for every year in which they are not paid. These cumulative preferred dividends must be paid before any common dividends can be paid.

DIVIDENDS IN ARREARS are dividends on cumulative preferred stock that have not been declared in prior years.

The **cumulative dividend preference** states that if all or a part of the current dividend is not paid in full, the cumulative unpaid amount, known as **dividends in arrears,** must be paid before any common dividends can be paid. Of course, if the preferred stock is noncumulative, dividends can never be in arrears; any preferred dividends that are not declared are permanently lost. Because preferred stockholders are unwilling to accept this unfavorable feature, preferred stock is usually cumulative.

To illustrate the cumulative preference, assume that Sophia Company has the same amount of stock outstanding as in the last example. In this case, dividends have been in arrears for two years.

Example	Total Dividends	6% Preferred Stock*	Common Stock
No. 1	$ 8,000	$7,200	$ 800
No. 2	30,000	7,200	22,800

*Current dividend preference, $40,000 × 6% = $2,400; dividends in arrears preference, $2,400 × 2 years = $4,800; current dividend preference plus dividends in arrears = $7,200.

Restrictions on the Payment of Dividends

FINANCIAL
ANALYSIS

Two common constraints on the ability of a corporation to pay dividends are the existence of loan covenants and preferred stock dividends in arrears. For additional security, some creditors include a loan covenant that limits the amount of dividends a corporation can pay. These debt covenants often also include a limit on borrowing and require a minimum balance of cash or working capital. If debt covenants are violated, the creditor can demand immediate repayment of the debt. The full-disclosure principle requires the disclosure of loan covenants, typically in a separate note to the financial statements.

The existence of dividends in arrears on preferred stock can also limit a company's ability to pay dividends to common stockholders and can affect a company's future cash flows. Because dividends are never an actual liability until the board of directors declares them, dividends in arrears are not reported on the balance sheet. Instead, they are disclosed in the notes to the statements. The following note from Lone Star Industries is typical:

REAL WORLD EXCERPT

Lone Star Industries
ANNUAL REPORT

> The total of dividends in arrears on the $13.50 preferred stock at the end of the year was $11,670,000. The aggregate amount of such dividend must be paid before any dividends are paid on common stock.

Analysts are particularly interested in information concerning these restrictions because of the impact they have on the company's dividend policy and future cash flows.

Financing Activities

FOCUS ON
CASH FLOWS

Transactions involving capital stock have a direct impact on the capital structure of a business. Because of the importance of these transactions, they are reported in the section of the statement called Cash Flows from Financing Activities. Examples of cash flows associated with capital stock are included in the statement of cash flows for Sonic Drive-In, shown in Exhibit 11.3.

EFFECT ON STATEMENT OF CASH FLOWS

In General   Cash received from owners is reported as an inflow; cash payments made to owners are reported as outflows. See the following example:

	Effect on Cash Flows
Financing activities	
Issuance of capital stock	+
Purchase of treasury stock	−
Sale of treasury stock	+
Payment of cash dividends	−

Focus Company Analysis   Notice that for each of the last three years, Sonic has paid out an increasing amount of cash for purchases of treasury stock but does not pay any dividends (Exhibit 11.3). Clearly, Sonic is generating sufficient cash to pay dividends but management has elected to distribute cash to owners by buying back stock instead of paying dividends. This dividend policy is not rare but it is not typical as indicated in the focus company comparison.

Learning Objective 8
Discuss the impact of capital stock transactions on cash flows.

**Selected Focus Company Comparisons
Comparisons:
Dividends Paid (in millions)**

Lowe's	$260
Starbucks	$871
Home Depot	$595

SONIC DRIVE-IN
Consolidated Statements of Cash Flows

| | Year ended August 31, | | |
	2006	2005	2004
	(In Thousands)		
Cash flows from financing activities			
Proceeds from borrowings	$ 274,763	$ 127,415	$ 76,421
Payments on long-term debt	(206,806)	(149,390)	(141,978)
Purchases of treasury stock	(93,689)	(42,324)	(3,067)
Payments on capital lease obligations	(2,444)	(2,139)	(1,839)
Exercises of stock options	7,194	10,546	5,310
Excess tax benefit from exercise of employee stock options	4,645	4,595	3,398
Net cash used in financing activities	(16,337)	(51,297)	(61,755)

DEMONSTRATION CASE

(Try to resolve the requirements before proceeding to the suggested solution that follows.)

This case focuses on the organization and operations for the first year of Shelly Corporation, which was organized by 10 local entrepreneurs on January 1, 2009, for the purpose of operating a business to sell various supplies to hotels. The charter authorized the following capital stock:

Common stock, no-par value, 20,000 shares

Preferred stock, 5 percent, $100 par value, 5,000 shares

The laws of the state specify that the legal capital for no-par stock is the full sale amount.

The following summarized transactions, selected from 2009, were completed on the dates indicated:

a. Jan. Sold a total of 8,000 shares of common stock to the 10 entrepreneurs for cash at $50 per share. Credit the Common Stock account for the total issue amount.

b. Feb. Sold 2,000 shares of preferred stock at $102 per share; cash collected in full.

c. Mar. Declared cash dividend of $1 on common stock.

d. July Purchased 100 shares of preferred stock that had been sold and issued earlier. Shelly Corporation paid the stockholder $104 per share.

e. Aug. Sold 20 shares of the preferred treasury stock at $105 per share.

Required:

1. Give the appropriate journal entries with a brief explanation for each transaction.

2. Prepare the Stockholders' Equity section of the balance sheet for Shelly Corporation at December 31, 2009. Assume retained earnings is $23,000.

SUGGESTED SOLUTION

1. Journal entries:

a. Jan. 2009	Cash (+A)	400,000	
	Common stock (+SE)		400,000
	Sale of no-par common stock ($50 × 8,000 shares = $400,000).		
b. Feb. 2009	Cash (+A)	204,000	
	Preferred stock (+SE)		200,000
	Capital in excess of par, preferred stock (+SE). .		4,000
	Sale of preferred stock ($102 × 2,000 shares = $204,000).		
c. March 2009	Retained earnings (−SE)	8,000	
	Dividend payable (+L)		8,000
	Declared cash dividend.		
d. July 2009	Treasury stock (+XSE, −SE)	10,400	
	Cash (−A)		10,400
	Purchased 100 shares of preferred stock ($104 × 100 shares = $10,400).		
e. Aug. 2009	Cash (+A)	2,100	
	Treasury stock (−XSE, +SE)		2,080
	Capital in excess of par, preferred stock (+SE). .		20
	Sold 20 shares of the preferred treasury stock at $105.		

2. Stockholders' equity section of the balance sheet:

SHELLY CORPORATION
Partial Balance Sheet
At December 31, 2009

Stockholders' Equity

Contributed capital

Preferred stock, 5% (par value $100; authorized 5,000 shares, issued 2,000 shares of which 80 shares are held as treasury stock)	$200,000
Capital in excess of par, preferred stock	4,020
Common stock (no-par value; authorized 20,000 shares, issued and outstanding 8,000 shares)	400,000
Total contributed capital	$604,020
Retained earnings	23,000
Total contributed capital and retained earnings	$627,020
Less cost of preferred treasury stock held (80 shares)	(8,320)
Total stockholders' equity	$618,700

Chapter Supplement A

Accounting for Owners' Equity for Sole Proprietorships and Partnerships

Owner's Equity for a Sole Proprietorship

A *sole proprietorship* is an unincorporated business owned by one person. Only two owner's equity accounts are needed: (1) a capital account for the proprietor (J. Doe, Capital) and (2) a drawing (or withdrawal) account for the proprietor (J. Doe, Drawings).

The capital account of a sole proprietorship serves two purposes: (1) to record investments by the owner and (2) to accumulate periodic income or loss. The drawing account is used to record the owner's withdrawals of cash or other assets from the business. The drawing account is closed to the capital account at the end of each accounting period. Thus, the capital account reflects the cumulative total of all investments by the owner and all earnings of the entity less all withdrawals from the entity by the owner.

In most respects, the accounting for a sole proprietorship is the same as for a corporation. Exhibit 11.4 presents the recording of selected transactions of Doe Retail Store and the statement of owner's equity.

EXHIBIT 11.4
Accounting for Owner's Equity for a Sole Proprietorship

Selected Entries during 2009

January 1, 2009

J. Doe started a retail store by investing $150,000 of personal savings. The journal entry follows:

Cash (+A) 150,000

 J. Doe, capital (+OE) 150,000

Assets	=	Liabilities	+	Owners' Equity	
Cash	+150,000			J. Doe, capital	+150,000

During 2009

Each month during the year, Doe withdrew $1,000 cash from the business for personal living costs. Accordingly, each month the following journal entry was made:

J. Doe, drawings (−OE) 1,000

 Cash (−A) 1,000

Assets	=	Liabilities	+	Owners' Equity	
Cash	−1,000			J. Doe, drawing	−1,000

Note: At December 31, 2009, after the last withdrawal, the drawings account reflected a debit balance of $12,000.

December 31, 2009

The usual journal entries for the year, including adjusting and closing entries for the revenue and expense accounts, resulted in an $18,000 net income, which were closed to the capital account as follows:

Individual revenue and expense accounts (−R&E) 18,000

 J. Doe, capital (+OE) 18,000

Assets	=	Liabilities	+	Owners' Equity	
				Revenues and expenses	−18,000
				J. Doe, capital	+18,000

EXHIBIT 11.4

concluded

December 31, 2009
The drawings account was closed as follows:

J. Doe, capital (−OE)	12,000	
J. Doe, drawings (+OE)		12,000

Assets	=	Liabilities	+	Owners' Equity	
				J. Doe, capital	−12,000
				J. Doe, drawings	+12,000

Balance Sheet December 31, 2009 (partial)

Owner's equity	
J. Doe, capital, January 1, 2009	$150,000
Add: Net income for 2009	18,000
Total	168,000
Less: Withdrawals for 2009	(12,000)
J. Doe, capital, December 31, 2009	$156,000

Because a sole proprietorship does not pay income taxes, its financial statements do not reflect income tax expense or income taxes payable. Instead, the net income of a sole proprietorship is taxed when it is included on the owner's personal income tax return. Likewise, the owner's salary is not recognized as an expense in a sole proprietorship because an employer/employee contractual relationship cannot exist with only one party involved. The owner's salary is therefore accounted for as a distribution of profits (i.e., a withdrawal).

Owners' Equity for a Partnership

The Uniform Partnership Act, which most states have adopted, defines partnership as "an association of two or more persons to carry on as co-owners of a business for profit." Small businesses and professionals such as accountants, doctors, and lawyers often use the partnership form of business.

A partnership is formed by two or more persons reaching mutual agreement about the terms of the relationship. The law does not require an application for a charter as in the case of a corporation. Instead, the agreement between the partners constitutes a partnership contract. This agreement should specify matters such as division of periodic income, management responsibilities, transfer or sale of partnership interests, disposition of assets upon liquidation, and procedures to be followed in case of the death of a partner. If the partnership agreement does not specify these matters, the laws of the resident state are binding.

The primary advantages of a partnership are (1) ease of formation, (2) complete control by the partners, and (3) lack of income taxes on the business itself. The primary disadvantage is the unlimited liability of each partner for the partnership's debts. If the partnership does not have sufficient assets to satisfy outstanding debt, creditors of the partnership can seize the partners' personal assets.

As with a sole proprietorship, accounting for a partnership follows the same underlying principles as any other form of business organization, except for those entries that directly affect owners' equity. Accounting for partners' equity follows the same pattern as for a sole proprietorship, except that separate capital and drawings accounts must be established for each partner. Investments by each partner are credited to that partner's capital account; withdrawals are debited to the respective drawings account. The net income of a partnership is divided among the partners in accordance with the partnership agreement and credited to each account. The respective drawings accounts are closed to the partner capital accounts. After the closing process, each partner's capital account reflects the cumulative total of all of that partner's investments plus that partner's share of the partnership earnings less all that partner's withdrawals.

Exhibit 11.5 presents selected journal entries and partial financial statements for AB Partnership to illustrate the accounting for the distribution of income and partners' equity.

EXHIBIT 11.5

Accounting for Partners' Equity

Selected Entries during 2009
January 1, 2009
A. Able and B. Baker organized AB Partnership on this date. Able contributed $60,000 and Baker $40,000 cash to the partnership and agreed to divide net income (and net loss) 60% and 40%, respectively. The journal entry for the business to record the investment was as follows:

Cash (+A) 100,000
  A. Able, capital (+OE) 60,000
  B. Baker, capital (+OE) 40,000

Assets	=	Liabilities	+	Owners' Equity	
Cash +100,000				A. Able, capital	+ 60,000
				B. Baker, capital	+ 40,000

During 2009
The partners agreed that Able would withdraw $1,000 and Baker $650 per month in cash. Accordingly, each month the following journal entry was made:

A. Able, drawings (−OE) 1,000
B. Baker, drawings (−OE) 650
  Cash (−A) 1,650

Assets	=	Liabilities	+	Owners' Equity	
Cash −1,650				A. Able, drawings	− 1,000
				B. Baker, drawings	− 650

December 31, 2009
Assume that the normal closing entries for the revenue and expense accounts resulted in a net income of $30,000. The partnership agreement specified Able would receive 60% of earnings and Baker would get 40%. The closing entry was as follows:

Individual revenue and expense accounts (−R&E) 30,000
  A. Able, capital (+OE) 18,000
  B. Baker, capital (+OE) 12,000

Assets	=	Liabilities	+	Owners' Equity	
				Revenues and expenses	− 30,000
				A. Able, capital	+ 18,000
				B. Baker, capital	+ 12,000

December 31, 2006
The journal entry required to close the drawings accounts follows:

A. Able, capital (−OE) 12,000
B. Baker, capital (−OE) 7,800
  A. Able, drawings (+OE) 12,000
  B. Baker, drawings (+OE) 7,800

Assets	=	Liabilities	+	Owners' Equity	
				A. Able, capital	−12,000
				B. Baker, capital	− 7,800
				A. Able, drawings	+12,000
				B. Baker, drawings	+ 7,800

EXHIBIT 11.5

concluded

A separate statement of partners' capital, similar to the following, is customarily prepared to supplement the balance sheet:

AB PARTNERSHIP
Statement of Partners' Capital
For the Year Ended December 31, 2009

	A. Able	B. Baker	Total
Investment, January 1, 2009	$60,000	$40,000	$100,000
Add: Additional investments during the year	0	0	0
Net income for the year	18,000	12,000	30,000
Totals	78,000	52,000	130,000
Less: Drawings during the year	(12,000)	(7,800)	(19,800)
Partners' equity, December 31, 2009	$66,000	$44,200	$110,200

The financial statements of a partnership follow the same format as those for a corporation except that (1) the income statement includes an additional section entitled Distribution of Net Income, (2) the partners' equity section of the balance sheet is detailed for each partner, (3) the partnership has no income tax expense because partnerships do not pay income tax (partners must report their share of the partnership profits on their individual tax returns), and (4) salaries paid to the partners are not recorded as expenses but are treated as distributions of earnings.

CHAPTER TAKE-AWAYS

1. **Explain the role of stock in the capital structure of a corporation. p. 559**

   The law recognizes corporations as separate legal entities. Owners invest in a corporation and receive capital stock that can be traded on established stock exchanges. Stock provides a number of rights, including the right to receive dividends.

2. **Analyze the earnings per share ratio. p. 562**

   The earnings per share ratio facilitates the comparison of a company's earnings over time or with other companies' at a single point in time. By expressing earnings on a per share basis, differences in the size of companies becomes less important.

3. **Describe the characteristics of common stock and analyze transactions affecting common stock. p. 563**

   Common stock is the basic voting stock issued by a corporation. Usually it has a par value, but no-par stock can be issued. Common stock offers some special rights that appeal to certain investors.

   A number of key transactions involve capital stock: (1) initial sale of stock, (2) treasury stock transactions, (3) cash dividends, and (4) stock dividends and stock splits. Each is illustrated in this chapter.

4. **Discuss dividends and analyze transactions.** p. 566

The return associated with an investment in capital stock comes from two sources: appreciation and dividends. Dividends are recorded as a liability when they are declared by the board of directors (i.e., on the date of declaration). The liability is satisfied when the dividends are paid (i.e., on the date of payment).

5. **Analyze the dividend yield ratio.** p. 566

The dividend yield ratio measures the percentage of return on an investment from dividends. For most companies, the return associated with dividends is very small.

6. **Discuss the purpose of stock dividends and stock splits, and report transactions.** p. 569

Stock dividends are pro rata distributions of a company's stock to existing owners. The transaction involves transferring an additional amount into the common stock account. A stock split also involves the distribution of additional shares to owners but no additional amount is transferred into the common stock account. Instead, the par value of the stock is reduced.

7. **Describe the characteristics of preferred stock and analyze transactions affecting preferred stock.** p. 571

Preferred stock provides investors certain advantages including dividend preferences and a preference on asset distributions in the event the corporation is liquidated.

8. **Discuss the impact of capital stock transactions on cash flows.** p. 573

Both inflows (e.g., the issuance of capital stock) and outflows (e.g., the purchase of treasury stock) are reported in the Financing Activities section of the statement of cash flows. The payment of dividends is reported as an outflow in this section.

This chapter concludes a major section of the book. In the previous several chapters, we have discussed individual sections of the balance sheet. We will now shift our focus to a common business transaction that affects many accounts on each of the financial statements. For a number of strategic reasons, businesses often invest in other businesses. In the next chapter, you will see why companies invest in other companies and how those investments affect their financial statements.

KEY **RATIOS**

The **earnings per share** ratio states the net income of a corporation on a per share of common stock basis. The ratio is computed as follows (p. 562):

$$\text{Earnings per Share} = \frac{\text{Net Income*}}{\text{Average Number of Shares of Common Stock Outstanding}}$$

The **dividend yield ratio** measures the dividend return on the current price of the stock. The ratio is computed as follows (p. 566):

$$\text{Dividend Yield Ratio} = \frac{\text{Dividends per Share}}{\text{Market Price per Share}}$$

*If there are preferred dividends, the amount is subtracted from net income in the numerator.

FINDING **FINANCIAL INFORMATION**

Balance Sheet

Under Current Liabilities
Dividends, once declared by the board of directors, are reported as a liability (usually current).

Under Noncurrent Liabilities
Transactions involving capital stock do not generate noncurrent liabilities.

Under Stockholders' Equity
Typical accounts include
Preferred stock
Common stock
Capital in excess of par
Retained earnings
Treasury stock

Statement of Stockholders' Equity

This statement reports detailed information concerning stockholders' equity, including
(1) amounts in each equity account,
(2) number of shares outstanding,
(3) impact of transactions such as earning income, payment of dividends, and purchase of treasury stock.

Income Statement

Capital stock is never shown on the income statement. Dividends paid are not an expense. They are a distribution of income and are, therefore, not reported on the income statement.

Statement of Cash Flows

Under Financing Activities
+ Cash inflows from initial sale of stock
+ Cash inflows from sale of treasury stock
− Cash outflows for dividends
− Cash outflows for purchase of treasury stock

Notes

Under Summary of Significant Accounting Policies
Usually, very little information concerning capital stock is provided in this summary.

Under a Separate Note
Most companies report information about their stock option plans and information about major transactions such as stock dividends or significant treasury stock transactions. A historical summary of dividends paid per share is typically provided. Also, dividends in arrears on preferred stock, if any, would be reported as a note.

KEY **TERMS**

Authorized Number of Shares p. 560
Common Stock p. 563
Cumulative Dividend Preference p. 572
Current Dividend Preference p. 572
Declaration Date p. 567
Dividends in Arrears p. 572
Issued Shares p. 560
Legal Capital p. 563
No-Par Value Stock p. 563
Outstanding Shares p. 560
Par Value p. 563
Payment Date p. 567
Preferred Stock p. 571
Record Date p. 567
Stock Dividend p. 569
Stock Split p. 570
Treasury Stock p. 565

QUESTIONS

1. Define the term *corporation* and identify the primary advantages of this form of business organization.
2. What is the charter of a corporation?
3. Explain each of the following terms: (a) authorized capital stock, (b) issued capital stock, and (c) outstanding capital stock.

4. Differentiate between common stock and preferred stock.
5. Explain the distinction between par value and no-par value capital stock.
6. What are the usual characteristics of preferred stock?
7. What are the two basic sources of stockholders' equity? Explain each.
8. Stockholders' equity is accounted for by source. What does source mean?
9. Define treasury stock. Why do corporations acquire treasury stock?
10. How is treasury stock reported on the balance sheet? How is the "gain or loss" on treasury stock that has been sold reported on the financial statements?
11. What are the two basic requirements to support the declaration of a cash dividend? What are the effects of a cash dividend on assets and stockholders' equity?
12. Differentiate between cumulative and noncumulative preferred stock.
13. Define *stock dividend.* How does a stock dividend differ from a cash dividend?
14. What are the primary reasons for issuing a stock dividend?
15. Identify and explain the three important dates with respect to dividends.
16. Define *retained earnings.* What are the primary components of retained earnings at the end of each period?

MULTIPLE-CHOICE QUESTIONS

1. Katz Corporation has issued 400,000 shares of common stock and holds 20,000 shares in treasury. The charter authorized the issuance of 500,000 shares. The company has declared and paid a dividend of $1 per share. What is the total amount of the dividend?
   a. $400,000
   b. $20,000
   c. $380,000
   d. $500,000
2. Which statement regarding treasury stock is false?
   a. Treasury stock is considered to be issued but not outstanding.
   b. Treasury stock has no voting, dividend, or liquidation rights.
   c. Treasury stock reduces total equity on the balance sheet.
   d. None of the above are false.
3. Which of the following statements about stock dividends is true?
   a. Stock dividends are reported on the statement of cash flow.
   b. Stock dividends are reported on the statement of retained earnings.
   c. Stock dividends increase total equity.
   d. Stock dividends decrease total equity.
4. Which order best describes the largest number of shares to the smallest number of shares?
   a. shares authorized, shares issued, shares outstanding
   b. shares issued, shares outstanding, shares authorized
   c. shares outstanding, shares issued, shares authorized
   d. shares in the treasury, shares outstanding, shares issued
5. A company issues 100,000 shares of common stock with a par value of $1 per share. The stock sold for $20 per share. By what amount does stockholders' equity increase?
   a. $100,000
   b. $1,900,000
   c. $2,000,000
   d. No change in stockholder's equity
6. A journal entry is not recorded on what date?
   a. date of declaration
   b. date of record
   c. date of payment
   d. A journal entry is recorded on all of these dates.
7. A company has net income $225,000 and declares and pays dividends in the amount of $75,000. What is the net impact on retained earnings?
   a. Increase of $225,000
   b. Decrease of $75,000
   c. Increase of $150,000
   d. Decrease of $150,000
8. Which statement regarding dividends is false?
   a. Dividends represent a sharing of corporate profits with owners.
   b. Both stock and cash dividends reduce retained earnings.
   c. Cash dividends paid to stockholders reduce net income.
   d. None of the above statements are false.

9. When treasury stock is purchased with cash, what is the impact on the balance sheet equation?
   a. No change: the reduction of the asset cash is offset with the addition of the asset treasury stock.
   b. Assets decrease and stockholders' equity increases.
   c. Assets increase and stockholders' equity decreases.
   d. Assets decrease and stockholders' equity decreases.
10. Does a stock dividend increase an investor's personal wealth immediately?
   a. No, because the stock price falls when a stock dividend is issued.
   b. Yes, because the investor has more shares.
   c. Yes, because the investor acquired additional shares without paying a brokerage fee.
   d. Yes, because the investor will receive more in cash dividends by owning more shares.

For more practice with multiple choice questions, go to our website at www.mhhe.com/libby6e.

HM™ **Available with McGraw-Hill's Homework Manager**   MINI-**EXERCISES**

Evaluating Stockholders' Right

Name three rights of common stockholders. Which of these is most important in your opinion? Why?

M11-1
LO1

Computing the Number of Unissued Shares

The balance sheet for Crutcher Corporation reported 168,000 shares outstanding, 268,000 shares authorized, and 10,000 shares in treasury stock. Compute the maximum number of new shares that Crutcher could issue.

M11-2
LO1

Recording the Sale of Common Stock

To expand operations, Aragon Consulting issued 170,000 shares of previously unissued stock with a par value of $1. The selling price for the stock was $21 per share. Record the sale of this stock. Would your answer be different if the par value was $2 per share? If so, record the sale of stock with a par value of $2.

M11-3
LO3

Comparing Common Stock and Preferred Stock

Your parents have just retired and have asked you for some financial advice. They have decided to invest $100,000 in a company very similar to Sonic. The company has issued both common and preferred stock. What factors would you consider in giving them advice? Which type of stock would you recommend?

M11-4
LO3, 7

Determining the Effects of Treasury Stock Transactions

Trans Union Corporation purchased 20,000 shares of its own stock for $45 per share. The next year, the company sold 5,000 shares for $50 per share and the following year, it sold 10,000 shares for $37 per share. Determine the impact (increase, decrease, or no change) of each of these transactions on the following classifications:
   1. Total assets.
   2. Total liabilities.
   3. Total stockholders' equity.
   4. Net income.

M11-5
LO3

Determining the Amount of a Dividend

Jacobs Company has 288,000 shares of common stock authorized, 260,000 shares issued, and 60,000 shares of treasury stock. The company's board of directors declares a dividend of 65 cents per share. What is the total amount of the dividend that will be paid?

M11-6
LO4

Recording Dividends

On April 15, 2009, the board of directors for Auction.com declared a cash dividend of 65 cents per share payable to stockholders of record on May 20. The dividends will be paid on June 14. The company has 100,000 shares of stock outstanding. Prepare any necessary journal entries for each date.

M11-7
LO4

M11-8
LO7

Determining the Amount of a Preferred Dividend

Colliers, Inc., has 200,000 shares of cumulative preferred stock outstanding. The preferred stock pays dividends in the amount of $2 per share but because of cash flow problems, the company did not pay any dividends last year. The board of directors plans to pay dividends in the amount of $1.4 million this year. What amount will go to preferred stockholders?

M11-9
LO6

Determining the Impact of Stock Dividends and Stock Splits

Armstrong Tools, Inc., announced a 100 percent stock dividend. Determine the impact (increase, decrease, no change) of this dividend on the following:
1. Total assets.
2. Total liabilities.
3. Common stock.
4. Total stockholders' equity.
5. Market value per share of common stock.

Assume that the company announced a 2-for-1 stock split. Determine the impact of the stock split.

M11-10
LO6

Recording a Stock Dividend

Shriver Food Systems, Inc., has issued a 40 percent stock dividend. The company has 752,000 shares authorized and 200,000 shares outstanding. The par value of the stock is $10 per share, and the market value is $130 per share. Record the payment of this stock dividend.

EXERCISES

 Available with McGraw-Hill's Homework Manager

E11-1
LO1
Philip Morris

Computing Shares Outstanding

The annual report for Philip Morris Companies, Inc., disclosed that 4 billion shares of common stock have been authorized. At the end of last year, 2,805,961,317 shares had been issued and the number of shares in treasury stock was 380,474,028. During the current year, no additional shares were issued, but additional shares were purchased for treasury stock and shares were sold from treasury stock. The net change was a decrease of 5,047,286 shares of treasury stock. Determine the number of shares outstanding at the end of the current year.

E11-2
LO1

Computing Number of Shares

The charter of Mansfield Corporation specifies that it may issue 200,000 shares of common stock. Since the company was incorporated, it has sold a total of 160,000 shares to the public but bought back a total of 20,000. The par value of the stock is $3 and the stock was sold at an average price of $16. When the stock was bought back from the public, the market price was $20.

Required:
1. Determine the authorized shares.
2. Determine the issued shares.
3. Determine the outstanding shares.

E11-3
LO1, 3, 7

Determining the Effects of the Issuance of Common and Preferred Stock

Kelly, Incorporated, was issued a charter on January 15, 2009, that authorized the following capital stock:

Common stock, no-par, 103,000 shares.

Preferred stock, 9 percent, par value $8 per share, 4,000 shares.

The board of directors established a stated value on the no-par common stock of $10 per share. During 2009, the following selected transactions were completed in the order given:

a. Sold and issued 20,000 shares of the no-par common stock at $16 cash per share.
b. Sold and issued 3,000 shares of preferred stock at $20 cash per share.
c. At the end of 2009, the accounts showed net income of $40,000.

Required:
1. Prepare the stockholders' equity section of the balance sheet at December 31, 2009.
2. Assume that you are a common stockholder. If Kelly needed additional capital, would you prefer to have it issue additional common stock or additional preferred stock? Explain.

Reporting Stockholders Equity

E11-4
LO1, 3

The financial statements for Texas Media Corporation included the following selected information:

Common Stock	$1,600,000
Retained earnings	$900,000
Net income	$1,000,000
Shares issued	90,000
Shares outstanding	80,000
Dividends declared and paid	$800,000

The common stock was sold at a price of $20 per share.

Required:
1. What is the amount of capital in excess of par?
2. What was the amount of retained earnings at the beginning of the year?
3. How many shares are in treasury stock?
4. Compute earnings per share.

Reporting Stockholders' Equity and Determining Dividend Policy

E11-5
LO1, 3, 4

Butler Corporation was organized in 2009 to operate a financial consulting business. The charter authorized the following capital stock: common stock, par value $10 per share, 11,500 shares. During the first year, the following selected transactions were completed:

a. Sold and issued 5,600 shares of common stock for cash at $20 per share.
b. Sold and issued 1,000 shares of common stock for cash at $25 per share.
c. At year-end, the accounts reflected a $6,000 loss. Because a loss was incurred, no income tax expense was recorded.

Required:
1. Give the journal entry required for each of these transactions.
2. Prepare the stockholders' equity section as it should be reported on the year-end balance sheet.
3. Can the company pay dividends at this time? Explain.

Finding Amounts Missing from the Stockholders' Equity Section

E11-6
LO1, 3
Dillard's

The stockholders' equity section on the balance sheet of Dillard's, a popular department store, is shown below. The company earned net income of $122,726,000 and declared and paid dividends of $12,987,000 in 2006.

Stockholders' equity (in thousands):	2006	2005
Common stock, Class A—115,237,382 and 114,581,524 shares issued; ? and ? shares outstanding	?	1,146
Common stock, Class B (convertible)—4,010,929 shares issued and outstanding	40	40
Additional paid-in capital	749,068	739,620
Retained earnings	2,429,065	?
Less treasury stock, at cost, Class A—39,953,949 and 35,386,849 shares	(809,637)	(708,769)

Required:
Complete the following statements and show your computations.
1. Common stock, class A at par value for 2006 was _____ .
2. The number of shares of common stock outstanding was _____ in 2005 and in 2006 _____ .

3. Retained earnings for 2005 was _____ .
4. Have the treasury stock transactions in 2006 (a) increased corporate resources or (b) decreased resources ? _____ By how much? _____ .
5. For 2006, the treasury stock transactions increased (decreased) stockholders' equity by _____ .
6. For 2006, how much did the treasury stock held cost per share? $ _____ .
7. For 2006, total stockholders' equity is $ _____ .

E11-7
L01, 3

Reporting Stockholders' Equity

Travis Corporation was organized in 2009 to operate a tax preparation business. The charter authorized the following capital stock: common stock, par value $2 per share, 80,000 shares. During the first year, the following selected transactions were completed:

a. Sold and issued 50,000 shares of common stock for cash at $50 per share.
b. Bought 1,000 shares from a stockholder for cash at $52 per share.

Required:
1. Give the journal entry required for each of these transactions.
2. Prepare the stockholders' equity section as it should be reported on the year-end balance sheet.

E11-8
L01, 3, 7

Reporting Stockholders' Equity

Ruth's Chris Steakhouse is the largest upscale steakhouse company in the United States, based on total company- and franchisee-owned restaurants. The company's menu features a broad selection of high-quality USDA Prime grade steaks and other premium offerings. There were 100 Ruth's Chris restaurants, of which 50 were company-owned and 50 were franchisee-owned, including 10 international franchisee-owned restaurants in Mexico, Hong Kong, Taiwan, and Canada. Information from the company's annual report is shown below:

a. Common stock, par value $0.01, 100,000,000 shares authorized, 23,074,496 issued and outstanding at December 31, 2005; 23,237,630 issued and outstanding at December 31, 2006.
b. Additional paid-in capital $162, 567,000 in 2005 and $166,489,000 in 2006.
c. Accumulated deficit $122,533,000 in 2005.
d. Net income in 2006 was $23,790,000. No dividends were paid.

Required:
Prepare the stockholders' equity section of the balance sheet at December 31, 2006.

E11-9
L01, 3, 7

Determining the Effects of Transactions on Stockholders' Equity

Carter Corporation was organized in January 2009 to operate several car repair businesses in a large metropolitan area. The charter issued by the state authorized the following capital stock:

Common stock, $10 par value, 98,000 shares.

Preferred stock, $50 par value, 8 percent, 59,000 shares.

During January and February 2009, the following stock transactions were completed:

a. Sold 78,000 shares of common stock at $20 per share and collected cash.
b. Sold 20,000 shares of preferred stock at $80 per share; collected the cash and immediately issued the stock.
c. Bought 4,000 shares of common stock from a current stockholder for $20 per share.

Required:
Net income for 2009 was $90,000; cash dividends declared and paid at year end were $30,000. Prepare the stockholders' equity section of the balance sheet at December 31, 2009.

E11-10
L03, 7

Recording Stockholders' Equity Transactions

Electronic Teacher Corporation obtained a charter at the start of 2009 that authorized 52,000 shares of no-par common stock and 23,000 shares of preferred stock, par value $10. The corporation was organized by four individuals who purchased a total of 20,000 shares of the common stock. The remaining shares were to be sold to other individuals at $37 per share on a cash basis. During 2009, the following selected transactions occurred:

a. Collected $20 per share cash from the four organizers and issued 5,000 shares of common stock to each of them.

b. Sold and issued 6,000 shares of common stock to an outsider at $40 cash per share.

c. Sold and issued 7,000 shares of preferred stock at $30 cash per share.

Required:
1. Give the journal entries indicated for each of these transactions.
2. Is it ethical to sell stock to outsiders at a higher price than the amount paid by the organizers?

Finding Amounts Missing from the Stockholders' Equity Section

E11-11
LO3, 7

The stockholders' equity section on the December 31, 2009, balance sheet of Chemfast Corporation follows:

Stockholders' Equity	
Contributed capital	
Preferred stock (par $20; authorized 10,000 shares, ? issued, of which 500 shares are held as treasury stock)	$100,000
Common stock (no-par; authorized 20,000 shares, issued and outstanding 8,000 shares)	600,000
Contributed capital (includes $1,500 from treasury stock transactions)	16,500
Retained earnings	34,000
Cost of treasury stock, preferred	(9,500)

Required:
Complete the following statements and show your computations.
1. The number of shares of preferred stock issued was _____ .
2. The number of shares of preferred stock outstanding was _____ .
3. The average sale price of the preferred stock when issued was $_____ per share.
4. Have the treasury stock transactions (a) increased corporate resources or (b) decreased resources ? _____ By how much?_____ .
5. The treasury stock transactions increased (decreased) stockholders' equity by _____ .
6. How much did the treasury stock held cost per share? $_____ .
7. Total stockholders' equity is $_____ .
8. The average issue price of the common stock was $_____ .

Finding Information Missing from an Annual Report

E11-12
LO1, 3, 4

Procter & Gamble is a $38 billion company that sells products that are part of most of our daily lives, including Mr. Clean, Cheer, Crest, Vicks, Scope, Pringles, Folgers, Vidal Sassoon, Zest, and Charmin. The annual report for P&G contained the following information:

a. Retained earnings at the end of 2005 totaled $31,004 million.

b. Net income for 2006 was $8,684 million.

c. Par value of the stock is $1 per share.

d. Cash dividends declared in 2006 were $1.15 per share.

e. The Common Stock, Par Value account totaled $3,976 million at the end of 2006 and $2,977 at the end of 2005.

Required: *(Assume that no other information concerning stockholders' equity is relevant.)*
1. Estimate the number of shares outstanding at the end of 2006.
2. Estimate the amount of retained earnings at the end of 2006.

Analyzing the Repurchase of Stock

E11-13
LO3, 4
Phelps Dodge

The business section of *The New York Times* recently contained the following article:

The Phelps Dodge Corporation, one of the world's largest copper producers, said yesterday that it would repurchase up to five million shares of its common stock in the open market and through private transactions. The company, based in Phoenix, said it recently completed a program announced last September to buy back 2.5 million shares. Phelps Dodge said the purchases were being made to enhance shareholders' value. The company has about 70.7 million shares outstanding. Shares of Phelps Dodge fell 37.5 cents, to $53.50, on the New York Stock Exchange yesterday.

Required:
1. Determine the impact of the stock repurchase on the financial statements.
2. Why do you think the board decided to repurchase the stock?
3. What impact will this purchase have on the company's future dividend obligations?

E11-14
LO1, 3, 4, 5

Preparing a Statement of Stockholders' Equity and Evaluating Dividend Policy

The following account balances were selected from the records of Blake Corporation at December 31, 2009, after all adjusting entries were completed:

Common stock (par $20; authorized 100,000 shares, issued 34,000 shares, of which 2,000 shares are held as treasury stock)	$680,000
Capital in excess of par	163,000
Dividends declared and paid in 2009	16,000
Retained earnings, January 1, 2009	75,000
Treasury stock at cost (2,000 shares)	25,000

Net income for the year was $30,000. Restriction on retained earnings equal to the cost of treasury stock held is required by law in this state. The stock price is currently $22.29 per share.

Required:
1. Prepare the stockholders' equity section of the balance sheet at December 31, 2009.
2. Compute and evaluate the dividend yield ratio. Determine the number of shares of stock that received dividends.

E11-15
LO3

Recording Treasury Stock Transactions and Analyzing Their Impact

During 2009 the following selected transactions affecting stockholders' equity occurred for Jacobs Corporation:

a. Apr. 1 Purchased in the market 200 shares of the company's own common stock at $20 per share.
b. Jun. 14 Sold 40 shares of treasury stock for $25 cash per share.
c. Sept. 1 Sold 30 shares of treasury stock for $15 cash per share.

Required:
1. Give journal entries for each of these transactions.
2. Describe the impact, if any, that these transactions have on the income statement.

E11-16
LO3, 4, 8

Recording Treasury Stock Transactions and Analyzing Their Impact

During 2009 the following selected transactions affecting stockholders' equity occurred for Italy Corporation:

a. Feb. 1 Purchased in the open market 160 shares of the company's own common stock at $20 cash per share.
b. Jul. 15 Sold 80 of the shares purchased on February 1 for $21 cash per share.
c. Sept. 1 Sold 50 more of the shares purchased on February 1 for $19 cash per share.

Required:
1. Give the indicated journal entries for each of the transactions.
2. What impact does the purchase of treasury stock have on dividends paid?
3. What impact does the sale of treasury stock for an amount higher than the purchase price have on net income and the statement of cash flows?

E11-17
LO4, 6

Analyzing the Impact of Dividend Policy

McDonald and Associates is a small manufacturer of electronic connections for local area networks. Consider three independent situations.

Case 1: McDonald increases its cash dividends by 50 percent, but no other changes occur in the company's operations.

Case 2: The company's income and cash flows increase by 50 percent, but this does not change its dividends.

Case 3: McDonald issues a 50 percent stock dividend, but no other changes occur.

Required:
1. How do you think each situation would affect the company's stock price?
2. If the company changed its accounting policies and reported higher net income, would the change have an impact on the stock price?

Computing Dividends on Preferred Stock and Analyzing Differences

E11-18
LO4, 7

The records of Hoffman Company reflected the following balances in the stockholders' equity accounts:

Common stock, par $12 per share, 30,000 shares outstanding.

Preferred stock, 10 percent, par $10 per share, 5,000 shares outstanding.

Retained earnings, $216,000.

On September 1, 2009, the board of directors was considering the distribution of a $65,000 cash dividend. No dividends were paid during the previous two years. You have been asked to determine dividend amounts under two independent assumptions (show computations):

a. The preferred stock is noncumulative.
b. The preferred stock is cumulative.

Required:
1. Determine the total and per share amounts that would be paid to the common stockholders and to the preferred stockholders under the two independent assumptions.
2. Write a brief memo to explain why the dividends per share of common stock were less for the second assumption.
3. What factor would cause a more favorable per share result to the common stockholders?

Determining the Impact of Dividends

E11-19
LO4, 7

Average Corporation has the following capital stock outstanding at the end of 2009:

Preferred stock, 6 percent, par $15, outstanding shares, 8,000.

Common stock, par $8, outstanding shares, 30,000.

On October 1, 2009, the board of directors declared dividends as follows:

Preferred stock: Full cash preference amount, payable December 20, 2009.

Common stock: 50 percent common stock dividend issuable December 20, 2009.

On December 20, 2009, the market prices were preferred stock, $40, and common stock, $32.

Required:
Explain the overall effect of each of the dividends on the assets, liabilities, and stockholders' equity of the company.

Recording the Payment of Dividends

E11-20
LO4, 7
Sears

A recent annual report for Sears disclosed that the company paid preferred dividends in the amount of $119.9 million. It declared and paid dividends on common stock in the amount of $2 per share. During the year, Sears had 1,000,000,000 shares of common authorized; 387,514,300 shares had been issued; 41,670,000 shares were in treasury stock. Assume that the transaction occurred on July 15.

Required:
Prepare a journal entry to record the declaration and payment of dividends.

Evaluating the Dividend Yield Ratio

E11-21
LO5
Cinergy

Cinergy is a utility company that provides gas and electric service in Ohio, Kentucky, and Indiana. The company's dividend yield is 6.6 percent. Starbucks, a well-known retailer of coffee products, does not pay dividends, resulting in a dividend yield of 0.0 percent. Both companies are approximately the same size with market values of $5 billion.

Required:

1. Based on this limited information, why do you think the dividend policies of the two companies are so different?
2. Will the two companies attract different types of investors? Explain.

E11-22
LO6

Analyzing Stock Dividends

At the beginning of the year, the stockholders' equity section of the balance sheet of R & B Corporation reflected the following:

Common stock (par $12; authorized 65,000	
shares, outstanding 30,000 shares)	$360,000
Capital in excess of par	120,000
Retained earnings	736,000

On February 1, 2009, the board of directors declared a 60 percent stock dividend to be issued April 30, 2009. The market value of the stock on February 1, 2009, was $15 per share.

Required:

1. For comparative purposes, prepare the Stockholders' Equity section of the balance sheet (a) immediately before the stock dividend and (b) immediately after the stock dividend. (*Hint:* Use two amount columns for this requirement.)
2. Explain the effects of this stock dividend on assets, liabilities, and stockholders' equity.

E11-23
LO3

Recording Dividends

Two billion times a day, Proctor & Gamble (P&G) brands touch the lives of people around the world. The company has one of the largest and strongest portfolios of trusted, quality brands, including Pampers, Tide, Bounty, Pringles, Folgers, Charmin, Downy, Crest, and Clairol Nice 'n Easy. The P&G community consists of nearly 98,000 employees working in almost 80 countries worldwide. The company has 5,000 million shares of common stock authorized and 2,500 million shares issued and outstanding. Par value is $1 per share. The company issued the following press release:

CINCINNATI, January 9, 2007—The Procter & Gamble Company (NYSE: PG) declared a quarterly dividend of thirty-one cents ($ .31) per share on the Common Stock payable on February 15, 2007 to shareholders of record at the close of business on January 19, 2007. P&G has been paying dividends without interruption since incorporation in 1890.

Required:
Prepare journal entries as appropriate for each date mentioned in the press release.

E11-24
LO6

Comparing Stock Dividends and Splits

On July 1, 2009, Jones Corporation had the following capital structure:

Common stock (par $3)	$600,000
Capital in excess of par	900,000
Retained earnings	700,000
Treasury stock, none	

Required:
Complete the following comparative tabulation based on two independent cases:

Case 1: The board of directors declared and issued a 50 percent stock dividend when the stock was selling at $5 per share.

Case 2: The board of directors voted a 6-to-5 stock split (i.e., a 20 percent increase in the number of shares). The market price prior to the split was $5 per share.

Items	Before Dividend and Split	After Stock Dividend	After Stock Split
Common stock account	$	$	$
Par per share	$ 3	$	$
Shares outstanding	#	#	#
Capital in excess of par	$900,000	$	$
Retained earnings	700,000	$	$
Total stockholders' equity	$	$	$

Recording a Stock Dividend

GameStop issued the following press release when the company's stock was selling for $27 per share:

GRAPEVINE, Texas—(BUSINESS WIRE)—Feb. 12, 2007—GameStop Corp. (NYSE: GME), the world's largest video game and entertainment software retailer, today announced that its Board of Directors approved a two-for-one stock split of the Company's common stock to be effected in the form of a stock dividend.

Each shareholder of record at the close of business on February 20, 2007, will receive one additional share of GameStop common stock for every outstanding share held on the record date. The additional shares will be distributed on March 16, 2007.

"As GameStop continues to rapidly grow, we wanted to make our stock more attractive to a broader range of potential investors. This stock split also reinforces the confidence that the Board and I have in the GameStop buy, sell, trade strategy and the future of video game growth worldwide," indicated R. Richard Fontaine, Chairman and Chief Executive Officer.

The stock split is GameStop's first since becoming a publicly traded company in February 2002. GameStop had approximately 76 million common shares outstanding as of February 3, 2007. Upon completion of the split, the outstanding shares of GameStop's common stock (par value $0.01) will increase to approximately 152 million.

Required:
1. Give any journal entries that would be required.
2. Describe the impact that this transaction will have on future cash dividends.

Comparing Stock Dividends and Splits

Sally Corporation has 80,000 shares of common stock (par value $8) outstanding.

Required:
Complete the following comparative tabulation based on two independent cases:

Case 1: The board of directors declared and issued a 40 percent stock dividend when the stock was selling at $15 per share. The dividend will be accounted for as a large stock dividend.

Case 2: The board of directors voted a 5-to-3 stock split (i.e., a 66.67 percent increase in the number of shares). The market price prior to the split was $15 per share.

Items	Before Dividend and Split	After Stock Dividend	After Stock Split
Common stock account	$	$	$
Par per share	$ 8	$	$
Shares outstanding	#	#	#
Capital in excess of par	$280,000	$	$
Retained earnings	$1,300,000	$	$
Total stockholders' equity	$	$	$

Evaluating Dividend Policy

Ford Motor Company is an internationally known manufacturer of automobiles and trucks. The company recently lost over $12 billion in a single year of operations. Despite that staggering loss, the company issued the following press release:

E11-25
LO6
GameStop

E11-26
LO6

E11-27
LO4
Ford Motor Co.

DEARBORN, Mich., July 13 /PRNewswire-FirstCall/—The Board of Directors of Ford Motor Company (NYSE: F) today declared a third quarter dividend of 5 cents per share on the company's common stock. The dividend, which is payable on Sept. 1 to shareholders of record on Aug. 2 is a reduction of 5 cents per share from the dividend paid in the second quarter.

Required:

1. Explain why Ford can pay dividends despite its loss.
2. What factors did the board of directors consider when it declared the dividends?

E11-28
LO7
Archon

Analyzing Dividends in Arrears

Archon Corporation operates the Pioneer Hotel & Gambling Hall in Nevada. In addition, the company owns real estate on Las Vegas Boulevard South (the "Strip") in Las Vegas, Nevada, and investment properties in Dorchester, Massachusetts, and Gaithersburg, Maryland. An investor found the following note contained in the Archon annual report:

The Company has not declared dividends on its preferred stock since fiscal 1996. Dividends of approximately $1.5 million, $1.5 million, $1.6 million, $1.5 million and $1.6 million for fiscal 2006, 2005, 2004, 2003, and 2002, respectively, have not been declared and are in arrears. Total accumulated preferred stock dividends in arrears for the five preceding years ended on September 30, 2006 are $12.3 million, $10.8 million, $9.5 million, $8.2 million and $7.3 million, respectively.

The investor who read the note suggested that the Archon preferred stock would be a good investment because of the large amount of dividend income that would be earned when the company started paying dividends again: "As the owner of the stock, I'll get dividends for the period I hold the stock plus some previous periods when I didn't even own the stock." Do you agree? Explain.

PROBLEMS

 Available with McGraw-Hill's Homework Manager

P11-1
LO1, 2, 3, 4, 6

Finding Missing Amounts (AP11–1)

At December 31, 2009, the records of Nortech Corporation provided the following selected and incomplete data:

Common stock (par $10; no changes during the year)
Shares authorized, 200,000.
Shares issued, _____?_____; issue price $17 per share; cash collected in full, $2,125,000.
Shares held as treasury stock, 3,000 shares, cost $20 per share.
Net income, $118,000.
Dividends declared and paid, $73,200.
Retained earnings balance, January 1, 2009, $555,000.
The treasury stock was acquired after a stock split was issued.

Required:

1. Complete the following tabulation:
   Shares authorized _____ .
   Shares issued _____ .
   Shares outstanding _____ .
2. The balance in the Capital in excess of Par account appears to be $_____ .
3. Earnings Per Share is $_____ .
4. Dividend paid per share of common stock is $_____ .
5. Treasury stock should be reported on the balance sheet under the major caption _____ in the amount of $_____ .
6. Assume that the board of directors voted a 2 for 1 stock split (the number of shares will double). After the stock split, the par value per share will be $_____, and the number of outstanding shares will be _____ .

7. Assuming the stock split mentioned above, give any journal entry that should be made. If none, explain why.

8. Disregard the stock split (assumed above). Assume instead that a 10 percent stock dividend was declared and issued when the market price of the common stock was $21. Give any journal entry that should be made.

Preparing the Stockholders' Equity Section of the Balance Sheet

Skyhawk Corporation received its charter during January 2009. The charter authorized the following capital stock:

> Preferred stock: 10 percent, par $10, authorized 21,000 shares.
> Common stock: par $8, authorized 50,000 shares.

During 2009, the following transactions occurred in the order given:

a. Issued a total of 40,000 shares of the common stock to the four organizers at $12 per share.
b. Sold 5,500 shares of the preferred stock at $16 per share.
c. Sold 3,000 shares of the common stock at $15 per share and 1,000 shares of the preferred stock at $26.
d. Net income for the year was $51,000.

Required:
Prepare the stockholders' equity section of the balance sheet at December 31, 2009.

P11-2
LO1, 3, 7

www.mhhe.com/libby6e

Recording Transactions Affecting Stockholders' Equity (AP11–2)

McGee Corporation began operations in January 2009. The charter authorized the following capital stock:

> Preferred stock: 10 percent, $10 par, authorized 40,000 shares.
> Common stock: $5 par, authorized 85,000 shares.

During 2009, the following transactions occurred in the order given:

a. Issued 22,000 shares of common stock to each of the three organizers and collected $9 cash per share from each of them.
b. Sold 9,000 shares of the preferred stock at $20 per share.
c. Sold 1,000 shares of the preferred stock at $20 and 1,500 shares of common stock at $10 per share.

Required:
Give the journal entries indicated for each of these transactions.

P11-3
LO3, 7

Recording Transactions and Comparing Par and No-Par Stock

The following press release was issued by Haynes International:

NEW YORK, March 19 (Reuters)—Haynes International Inc., a producer of high-performance nickel and cobalt-based alloys, on Monday raised $136.5 million with a U.S. initial public offering that was priced above the forecast range.

The 2.1-million-share offering was sold for $65 per share, compared with a $61 to $64 forecast range.

Required:
1. Record the issuance of stock, assuming the stock was no-par value common stock.
2. Record the issuance of stock, assuming the common stock had a par value of $1 per share.
3. Should a stockholder care whether a company issues par or no-par value stock? Explain.

P11-4
LO1, 3
Haynes

Preparing the Stockholders' Equity Section after Selected Transactions (AP11–3)

Global Marine Company obtained a charter from the state in January 2009, which authorized 200,000 shares of common stock, $1 par value. During the first year, the company earned $475,000 and the following selected transactions occurred in the order given:

a. Sold 100,000 shares of the common stock in an initial public offering at $12 per share.
b. Repurchased 20,000 shares of the previously issued shares at $15 cash per share for treasury stock.
c. Resold 5,000 of the shares of the treasury stock at $18 cash per share.

P11-5
LO1, 3

Required:

Prepare the stockholders' equity section of the balance sheet at December 31, 2009.

P11-6
L01, 3
Tim Hortons

Recording Stockholders' Equity Transactions (AP11–4)

Tim Hortons restaurants operate in a variety of formats. A standard Tim Hortons restaurant is a free-standing building typically ranging in size from 1,400 to 3,090 square feet with a dining room and single or double drive-thru window. The company also has nonstandard restaurants designed to fit anywhere, consisting of kiosks in offices, hospitals, colleges, airports, gas station convenience stores, and drive-thru only units on smaller pieces of property. The company's annual report included the following information:

	2006	2005	2004
Cash flows from financing activities:			
Proceeds from issuance of debt, net of issuance costs	501,263	3,192	2,812
Proceeds from issuance of common stock	903,825	—	—
Financing costs	(61,918)	—	—
Purchase of common stock for settlement of restricted stock units	(5,489)	—	—
Purchase of treasury stock	(64,971)	—	—
Purchase of common stock held in trust	(9,171)	—	—
Dividend payments	(27,046)	—	—
Long-term borrowings from Wendy's	—	—	54,377
Repayment of borrowings from Wendy's	(1,087,968)	(77,448)	(52,552)
Principal payments on other long-term debt obligations	(206,750)	(4,148)	(4,130)
Net cash provided by (used in) financing activities	(58,225)	(78,404)	507

Required:

For 2006, prepare journal entries to record the purchase of treasury stock, the issuance of common stock, and the declaration and payment of dividends. The common stock has a par value of $0.001 and 50,000,000 shares were issued during 2006.

P11-7
L03, 4, 6

Analyzing Stockholders' Equity Transactions, Including Treasury Stock

1. Compare a stock dividend with a cash dividend.
2. Compare a large stock dividend with a small stock dividend.
3. Describe the impact of the sale of treasury stock for more than cost on the income statement and the statement of cash flows.
4. Explain why a company might purchase treasury stock.

P11-8
L03, 4, 6
RadioShack

Analyzing Treasury Stock Transactions

RadioShack Corporation primarily engages in the retail sale of consumer electronics goods and services through 4,467 company-operated stores under the RadioShack brand, located throughout the United States, as well as in Puerto Rico and the U.S. Virgin Islands. These stores are located in major shopping malls and strip centers, as well as individual storefronts. The company's statement of cash flows contained the following information (in million):

	2006	2005	2004
Cash flows from financing activities:			
Purchases of treasury stock	—	(625.8)	(251.1)
Sale of treasury stock	10.5	30.1	35.4

Required:

1. Record the purchase of treasury stock in 2005.
2. Record the sale of treasury stock in 2006. Assume the stock had been purchased at a cost of $9 million.
3. Would RadioShack have reported a loss if the stock sold in 2006 had been purchased originally for $13 million?

Comparing Stock and Cash Dividends (AP11-5)

P11-9
LO4, 6, 7

e**X**cel

www.mhhe.com/libby6e

Water Tower Company had the following stock outstanding and retained earnings at December 31, 2009:

Common stock (par $8; outstanding, 35,000 shares)	$280,000
Preferred stock, 10% (par $15; outstanding, 8,000 shares)	120,000
Retained earnings	281,000

The board of directors is considering the distribution of a cash dividend to the two groups of stockholders. No dividends were declared during the previous two years. Three independent cases are assumed:

Case A: The preferred stock is noncumulative; the total amount of dividends is $31,000.

Case B: The preferred stock is cumulative; the total amount of dividends is $25,000.

Case C: Same as Case B, except the amount is $67,000.

Required:
1. Compute the amount of dividends, in total and per share, that would be payable to each class of stockholders for each case. Show computations.
2. Assume the company issued a 30 percent common stock dividend on the outstanding shares when the market value per share was $24. Complete the following comparative schedule including explanation of the comparative differences.

	Amount of Dollar Increase (Decrease)	
Item	Cash Dividend—Case C	Stock Dividend
Assets	$	$
Liabilities	$	$
Stockholders' equity	$	$

Analyzing Dividend Policy

P11-10
LO4

D❤LL

Heather and Scott, two young financial analysts, were reviewing financial statements for Dell, one of the world's largest manufacturers of personal computers. Scott noted that the company did not report any dividends in the financing activity section of the statement of cash flows and said, "I have heard that Dell is one of the best performing companies. If it's so good, I wonder why it isn't paying any dividends." Heather wasn't convinced that Scott was looking in the right place for dividends but didn't say anything.

Scott continued the discussion by noting, "Sales for Dell are up nearly 35 percent over the previous two years. While net income is up over $500 million compared to last year, cash flow from operating activities declined by nearly $500 million compared to the previous year."

At that point, Heather noted that the statement of cash flows reported that Dell had repurchased nearly $3 billion in common stock. She also was surprised to see that inventory and accounts receivable had decreased by nearly $2 billion in the previous year. "No wonder it can't pay dividends. With cash flows declining by $500 million, the Board is probably reluctant to obligate itself to dividends."

Required:
1. Correct any misstatements that either Heather or Scott made. Explain.
2. Which of the factors presented in the case help you understand Dell's dividend policy?

Determining the Financial Statement Effects of Dividends

P11-11
LO4, 6, 7

Lynn Company has outstanding 52,000 shares of $10 par value common stock and 25,000 shares of $20 par value preferred stock (8 percent). On December 1, 2009, the board of directors voted an 8 percent cash dividend on the preferred stock and a 30 percent stock dividend on the common stock. At the date of declaration, the common stock was selling at $35 and the preferred at $20 per share. The dividends are to be paid, or issued, on February 15, 2010. The annual accounting period ends December 31.

Required:
Explain the comparative effects of the two dividends on the assets, liabilities, and stockholders' equity (a) through December 31, 2009, (b) on February 15, 2010, and (c) the overall effects from December 1, 2009, through February 15, 2010. A schedule similar to the following might be helpful:

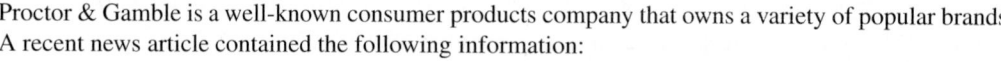

| | Comparative Effects Explained | |
	Cash Dividend on Preferred	Stock Dividend on Common
Item		
1. Through December 31, 2009: Assets, etc.		

P11-12
LO4, 6

Recording Dividends

Proctor & Gamble is a well-known consumer products company that owns a variety of popular brands. A recent news article contained the following information:

CINCINNATI, March 9 /PRNewswire-FirstCall/—The Procter & Gamble Company (NYSE: PG) today said that earnings per share for the January through March quarter as well as the fiscal year is expected to exceed current consensus estimates by $0.01 to $0.02. The increased earnings are being driven by continued strong organic volume growth.

Stock Dividend

The company also announced today that its board of directors approved a 10% stock dividend to shareholders of record on May 21. This move does not change the proportionate interest a shareholder maintains in the company. The additional shares will be distributed on June 18. In a separate action, the board declared an increase in the annual rate of its common stock dividend from $1.82 to $2.00 per share.

Required:
1. Prepare any journal entries that P&G should make as the result of information in the preceding report. Assume that the company has 2,500 million shares outstanding, the par value is $1.00 per share, and the market value is $50 per share.
2. What do you think happened to the company's stock price after the announcement?
3. What factors did the board of directors consider in making this decision?

P11-13
LO1

(Chapter Supplement A) Comparing Stockholders' Equity Sections for Alternative Forms of Organization

www.mhhe.com/libby6e

Assume for each of the following independent cases that the annual accounting period ends on December 31, 2009, and that the Income Summary account at that date reflected a debit balance (loss) of $20,000.

Case A: Assume that the company is a *sole proprietorship* owned by Proprietor A. Prior to the closing entries, the capital account reflected a credit balance of $52,000 and the drawings account a balance of $9,000.

Case B: Assume that the company is a *partnership* owned by Partner A and Partner B. Prior to the closing entries, the owners' equity accounts reflected the following balances: A, Capital, $43,000; B, Capital, $43,000; A, Drawings, $5,000; and B, Drawings, $7,000. Profits and losses are divided equally.

Case C: Assume that the company is a *corporation*. Prior to the closing entries, the stockholders' equity accounts showed the following: Common Stock, par $10, authorized 30,000 shares, outstanding 14,000 shares; Capital in excess of Par, $9,000; Retained Earnings, $62,000.

Required:
1. Give all the closing entries indicated at December 31, 2009, for each of the separate cases.
2. Show how the owners' equity section of the balance sheet would appear at December 31, 2009, for each case.

Finding Missing Amounts (P11–1)

AP11-1
LO1, 2, 3, 4, 6

At December 31, 2009, the records of Kozmetsky Corporation provided the following selected and incomplete data:

Common stock (par $1; no changes during the year)
Shares authorized, 5,000,000.
Shares issued, _____?_____; issue price $80 per share.
Shares held as treasury stock, 100,000 shares, cost $60 per share.
Net income, $4,800,000.
Common stock account, $1,500,000.
Dividends declared and paid, $2 per share.
Retained earnings balance, January 1, 2009, $82,900,000.
The treasury stock was acquired after a stock split was issued.

Required:
1. Complete the following tabulation:
   Shares issued _____.
   Shares outstanding _____.
2. The balance in the Capital in Excess of Par account appears to be $_____.
3. EPS on net income is $_____.
4. Total dividends paid on common stock during 2009 is $_____.
5. Treasury stock should be reported on the balance sheet under the major caption _____ in the amount of $_____.
6. Assume that the board of directors voted a 100 percent stock split (the number of shares will double). After the stock split, the par value per share will be $_____, and the number of outstanding shares will be _____.

Recording Transactions Affecting Stockholders' Equity (P11–3)

AP11-2
LO3, 7

Gerald Company was granted a charter that authorized the following capital stock:

Common stock: 100,000 shares, par value per share is $40.
Preferred stock: 8 percent, par $5, 20,000 shares.

During the first year, 2009, the following selected transactions occurred in the order given:

a. Sold 30,000 shares of the common stock at $40 cash per share and 5,000 shares of the preferred stock at $26 cash per share.
b. Issued 2,000 shares of preferred stock when the stock was selling at $32.
c. Repurchased 3,000 shares of the common stock sold earlier; paid cash, $38 per share.

Required:
Give journal entries for each of these transactions.

Preparing the Stockholders' Equity Section After Selected Transactions (P11–5)

AP11-3
LO1, 3

Global Marine obtained a charter from the state in January 2009, which authorized 1,000,000 shares of common stock, $5 par value. During the first year, the company earned $429,000, and the following selected transactions occurred in the order given:

a. Sold 700,000 shares of the common stock at $54 per share. Collected the cash and issued the stock.
b. Purchased 25,000 shares at $50 cash per share to use as stock incentives for senior management.

Required:
Prepare the stockholders' equity section of the balance sheet at December 31, 2009.

AP11-4

LO4

Recording Stockholders' Equity Transactions (P11-6)

Whole Foods Market, Inc. is the world's leading natural and organic foods supermarket. The company is based in Austin, Texas, and conducts business through various wholly-owned subsidiaries. The following information was contained in the company's balance sheet:

	2006	2005
Shareholders' equity:		
Common stock, no par value, 300,000 shares authorized; 142,198 and 136,017 shares issued, 139,607 and 135,908 shares outstanding in 2006 and 2005, respectively	1,147,872	874,972
Common stock in treasury, at cost	(99,964)	—
Retained earnings	349,260	486,299

Required:

Prepare journal entries to record the issuance of common stock and the purchase of treasury stock in 2006. The company earned net income of $203,828 in 2006. Record the declaration and payment of dividends, if any, in 2006.

AP11-5

LO4, 6, 7

Comparing Stock and Cash Dividends (P11-9)

Ritz Company had the following stock outstanding and retained earnings at December 31, 2009:

Common stock (par $1; outstanding, 500,000 shares)	$500,000
Preferred stock, 8% (par $10; outstanding, 21,000 shares)	210,000
Retained earnings	900,000

The board of directors is considering the distribution of a cash dividend to the two groups of stockholders. No dividends were declared during the previous two years. Three independent cases are assumed:

Case A: The preferred stock is noncumulative; the total amount of dividends is $25,000.

Case B: The preferred stock is cumulative; the total amount of dividends is $25,000.

Case C: Same as Case B, except the amount is $75,000.

Required:

1. Compute the amount of dividends, in total and per share, payable to each class of stockholders for each case. Show computations.
2. Assume that the company issued a 40 percent common stock dividend on the outstanding shares when the market value per share was $50. Complete the following comparative schedule, including explanation of the comparative differences.

	Amount of Dollar Increase (Decrease)	
Item	Cash Dividend—Case C	Stock Dividend
Assets	$	$
Liabilities	$	$
Stockholders' equity	$	$

CASES **AND PROJECTS**

Annual Report Cases

CP11-1

LO1, 3, 4, 6

AMERICAN EAGLE
OUTFITTERS

Finding Financial Information

Refer to the financial statements of American Eagle given in Appendix B at the end of this book.

Required:

1. Does the company have any treasury stock as of February 3, 2007? If so, how much?
2. Does the company pay dividends? If so, how much per share?

3. Over the most recent three years, was there a stock dividend or a stock split? If so, describe.
4. What is the par value of the common stock?

Finding Financial Information

Refer to the financial statements of Urban Outfitters given in Appendix C at the end of this book.

Required:
1. How many shares of common stock are authorized as of January 31, 2007? How many shares are issued and outstanding as of January 31, 2007?
2. Did the company pay dividends during the most recent reporting year? If so, what was the total amount of dividends paid and how much were they per share?
3. Does the company have any treasury stock as of January 31, 2007? If so, how much?
4. Has the company issued a stock dividend or a stock split over the past three reporting years? If so, describe.
5. Does the company's common stock have a par value? If it does, what is the par value?

CP11-2
LO1, 3, 4, 6
Urban Outfitters

Comparing Companies within an Industry

Refer to the financial statements of American Eagle given in Appendix B and Urban Outfitters given in Appendix C.

Required:
1. American Eagle Outfitters has recently split its stock. Describe the impact that the split would have on the market value of the stock compared to a company that did not split its stock. Why do some companies elect to split their stock?
2. Calculate the dividend yield ratios for Urban Outfitters (assume the market price of the stock is $25) and American Eagle (assume the market price of the stock is $21) for the most recent reporting year.
3. Why would an investor choose to invest in a stock that does not pay dividends?
4. Using the information from the following table, compare the dividend-related industry average ratios for the retail apparel industry to the pharmaceutical industry and the electric utility industry. What type of investor would be interested in buying stock in a utility instead of a retail store? Why?

CP11-3
LO3, 4
AMERICAN EAGLE
OUTFITTERS
Urban Outfitters
eXcel
www.mhhe.com/libby6e

Dividend Ratios for Various Industries

	Retail Apparel	Pharmaceuticals	Electric Utilities
Dividend yield	1.1%	2.6%	3.8%
Example company	The GAP	Eli Lilly	American Electric Power

Financial Reporting and Analysis Cases

Computing Dividends for an Actual Company

A recent annual report for Halliburton Company contained the following information (in millions of dollars):

CP11-4
LO4
Halliburton

Stockholders' Equity	Current Year	Previous Year
Common stock, par value $2.50, authorized 2,000 shares	$ 298.3	$ 298.4
Paid-in capital in excess of par	130.5	129.9
Retained earnings	2,080.8	2,052.3
Less 12.8 and 13.0 treasury stock, at cost	382.2	384.7

In the current year, Halliburton declared and paid cash dividends of $1 per share. What would be the total amount of dividends declared and paid if they had been based on the amount of stock outstanding at the end of the year?

Critical Thinking Cases

CP11-5
LO4, 6

Evaluating an Ethical Dilemma

You are a member of the board of directors of a large company that has been in business for more than 100 years. The company is proud of the fact that it has paid dividends every year it has been in business. Because of this stability, many retired people have invested large portions of their savings in your common stock. Unfortunately, the company has struggled for the past few years as it tries to introduce new products and is considering not paying a dividend this year. The president wants to skip the dividend in order to have more cash to invest in product development: "If we don't invest this money now, we won't get these products to market in time to save the company. I don't want to risk thousands of jobs." One of the most senior board members speaks next: "If we don't pay the dividend, thousands of retirees will be thrown into financial distress. Even if you don't care about them, you have to recognize our stock price will crash when they all sell." The company treasurer proposes an alternative: "Let's skip the cash dividend and pay a stock dividend. We can still say we've had a dividend every year." The entire board now turns to you for your opinion. What should the company do?

CP11-6
LO4

Evaluating an Ethical Dilemma

You are the president of a very successful Internet company that has had a remarkably profitable year. You have determined that the company has more than $10 million in cash generated by operating activities not needed in the business. You are thinking about paying it out to stockholders as a special dividend. You discuss the idea with your vice president, who reacts angrily to your suggestion:

"Our stock price has gone up by 200 percent in the last year alone. What more do we have to do for the owners? The people who really earned that money are the employees who have been working 12 hours a day, six or seven days a week to make the company successful. Most of them didn't even take vacations last year. I say we have to pay out bonuses and nothing extra for the stockholders." As president, you know that you are hired by the board of directors, which is elected by the stockholders. What is your responsibility to both groups? To which group would you give the $10 million?

Financial Reporting and Analysis Team Project

CP11-7
LO1, 3, 4, 7

Team Project: Examining an Annual Report

As a team, select an industry to analyze. *Reuters* provides lists of industries and their makeup at **www.reuters.com/finance/industries**. Each team member should acquire the annual report or 10-K for one publicly traded company in the industry, with each member selecting a different company. (Library files, the SEC EDGAR service at **www.sec.gov**, Compustat CD, or the company itself are good sources.)

Required:
On an individual basis, each team member should write a short report answering the following questions about the selected company. Discuss any patterns across the companies that you as a team observe. Then, as a team, write a short report comparing and contrasting your companies.
1. *a.* List the accounts and amounts of the company's stockholders' equity.
    b. From the footnotes, identify any unusual features in its contributed capital accounts (e.g., convertible preferred, nonvoting common, no par value), if any.
2. What amount of stock was issued in the most recent year? [You will need to refer to the statement of cash flows for the cash proceeds and the statement of stockholders' equity for the amounts in the capital accounts.]
    a. What was the average market value per share of the issuance?
    b. Recreate the journal entry for the issuance.
3. What amount of treasury stock, if any, did the company purchase during the year?
4. What types of dividends, if any, did the company declare during the year? How much was paid in cash?

LEARNING OBJECTIVES

After studying this chapter, you should be able to:

1. Analyze and report bond investments held to maturity. p. 606

2. Analyze and report passive investments in securities using the market value method. p. 607

3. Analyze and report investments involving significant influence using the equity method. p. 615

4. Analyze and report investments in controlling interests. p. 621

5. Analyze and interpret the return on assets ratio. p. 625

Lectured slideshow–LP12-1
www.mhhe.com/libby6e

REPORTING AND INTERPRETING INVESTMENTS IN OTHER CORPORATIONS

12

FOCUS COMPANY:

The Washington Post Company

INVESTMENT STRATEGIES

IN THE MEDIA INDUSTRY

www.washpostco.com

The Washington Post Company is best known for publishing the most important newspaper in our nation's capital. However, the company does much more. It owns television stations, *Newsweek* magazine, Cable One (a TV cable company), and a variety of community newspapers. Many users of this text have already been Post Company customers and not known it. The company also owns Kaplan, Inc., the king of admissions test preparation services that will even help you prepare for the Certified Public Accounting or Chartered Financial Analyst exam. The Post Company also recognizes that new technologies bring increased efficiency to its operations while expanding business opportunities. For example, it publishes electronic versions of *The Washington Post* and *Newsweek*, and shares news resources with NBC News and MSNBC.

The company has achieved its diversity in part by investing in the stock of other companies. For example, it spent $350 million over the last three years to purchase other companies including the online magazine *Slate* and a variety of private education companies around the world. It jointly owns (with another publisher) the company that produces the Europe, Middle East, and Africa editions of *Newsweek*. It also jointly owns one of the major providers of the paper *The Washington Post* is printed on. In addition, the company's investment portfolio consists of over $350 million worth of stock of other companies.

UNDERSTANDING THE BUSINESS

Many strategic factors motivate managers to invest in securities. A company that has extra cash and simply wants to earn a return on the idle funds can invest those funds in the stocks and bonds of other companies, either long or short term. We say these investments are passive because the managers are not interested in influencing or controlling the other companies. Washington Post's 2006 balance sheet, shown in Exhibit 12.1, reflects both short-term and long-term "Investments in Marketable Equity Securities" accounts.

EXHIBIT 12.1	WASHINGTON POST COMPANY Consolidated Balance Sheet	

Washington Post Company Consolidated Balance Sheet (Condensed)

(In millions)	December 2006
Assets	
Current assets	
Cash and cash equivalents	$ 348
Investments in marketable equity securities	29
Other current assets	558
	935
Property, plant, and equipment, net	1,218
Investments in marketable equity securities	326
Investments in affiliates	54
Goodwill and other intangible assets, net	1,790
Other noncurrent assets	1,059
	$5,382
Liabilities and Shareholders' Equity	
Current liabilities	$ 803
Long-term debt	402
Other noncurrent liabilities	1,005
	2,210
Stockholders' Equity	
Preferred stock	12
Common stock	20
Capital in excess of par	206
Retained earnings	4,120
Accumulated other comprehensive income, net of	
Cumulative foreign currency translation adjustment	23
Unrealized gain on available-for-sale securities	85
Unrealized gain on pensions	270
Treasury stock	(1,564)
	3,172
	$5,382

Sometimes a company decides to invest in another company with the purpose of influencing that company's policies and activities. Washington Post's balance sheet reports these types of investments as "Investments in Affiliates." Finally, managers may determine that controlling another company, either by purchasing it directly or becoming the majority shareholder, is desirable. In this case, the two companies' financial reports are combined into consolidated financial statements, as Washington Post has done (see the title to its **consolidated** balance sheet). In the notes to the annual report, we find that Washington Post's recent acquisitions include PMBR, a bar exam test preparation company, and *Slate* magazine.

In this chapter, we discuss the accounting for four types of investments. First, we discuss using the amortized cost method to account for passive investments in bonds. Second, we examine the market value method of accounting for passive investments in stocks. Third, we present the equity method used to account for stock held to exert significant influence. The chapter closes with a discussion of accounting for mergers and consolidated statements.

ORGANIZATION of the Chapter

Types of Investments and Accounting Methods	Debt Held to Maturity: Amortized Cost Method	Passive Stock Investments: Market Value Method	Investments for Significant Influence: Equity Method	Controlling Interests: Mergers and Acquisitions
■ Passive Investments in Debt and Equity Securities ■ Investments in Stock for Significant Influence ■ Investments in Stock for Control	■ Bond Purchases ■ Interest Earned ■ Principal at Maturity	■ Classifying Passive Stock Investments ■ Securities Available for Sale ■ Comparing Trading and Available-for-Sale Securities	■ Recording Investments under the Equity Method ■ Reporting Investments under the Equity Method	■ What Are Consolidated Statements? ■ Recording a Merger ■ Reporting a Merger ■ Return on Assets

TYPES OF INVESTMENTS AND ACCOUNTING METHODS

The accounting methods used to record investments are directly related to how much is owned and how long management intends to hold the investments.

Passive Investments in Debt and Equity Securities

Passive investments are made to earn a high rate of return on funds that may be needed for future short-term or long-term purposes. This category includes both investments in debt (bonds and notes) and equity securities (stock). Debt securities are always considered passive investments. If the company intends to hold the securities until they reach maturity date, the investments are measured and reported at amortized cost. If they are to be sold before maturity, they are reported using the market value method.

For investments in equity securities, the investment is presumed passive if the investing company owns less than 20 percent of the outstanding voting shares of the other company. The market value method is used to measure and report the investments.

Investments in Stock for Significant Influence

Significant influence is the ability to have an important impact on the operating and financing policies of another company in which it owns voting stock. Significant influence is presumed if the investing company owns from 20 to 50 percent of the outstanding voting shares of the other company. However, other factors may also indicate that significant influence exists, such as membership on the board of directors of the other company, participation in the policy-making processes, evidence of material transactions between the two companies, an interchange of management personnel, or technological dependency. The equity method is used to measure and report this category of investments.

Investments in Stock for Control

Control is the ability to determine the operating and financing policies of another company through ownership of voting stock. For all practical purposes, control is

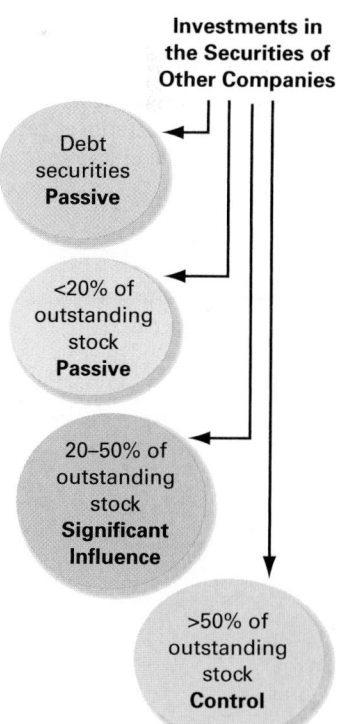

Investments in the Securities of Other Companies

Debt securities **Passive**

<20% of outstanding stock **Passive**

20–50% of outstanding stock **Significant Influence**

>50% of outstanding stock **Control**

presumed when the investing company owns more than 50 percent of the outstanding voting stock of the other company. Rules for consolidation are applied to combine the companies.

These categories and the appropriate measuring and reporting methods can be summarized as follows:

	Investment in Debt Securities of Another Entity		Investment in the Voting Common Stock of Another Entity		
Investment Category	Passive		Passive	Significant Influence	Control
Level of Ownership	Held to maturity	Not held to maturity	< 20% of outstanding shares	20–50% of outstanding shares	> 50% of outstanding shares
Measuring and Reporting Method	Amortized cost method	Market value method		Equity method	Consolidation method

DEBT HELD TO MATURITY: AMORTIZED COST METHOD

Learning Objective 1

Analyze and report bond investments held to maturity.

HELD-TO-MATURITY INVESTMENTS are investments in bonds that management has the intent and ability to hold until maturity.

AMORTIZED COST METHOD reports investments in debt securities held to maturity at cost minus any premium or plus any discount.

When management plans to hold a bond (or note) until its maturity date (when the principal is due), it is reported in an account appropriately called **held-to-maturity investments.** Bonds should be classified as held-to-maturity investments if management has the intent and the ability to hold them until maturity. These investments in debt instruments are listed at cost adjusted for the amortization of any bond discount or premium (**amortized cost method**), not at their fair market value.

Bond Purchases

On the date of purchase, a bond may be acquired at the maturity amount (at **par**), for less than the maturity amount (at a **discount**), or for more than the maturity amount (at a **premium**).[1] The total cost of the bond, including all incidental acquisition costs such as transfer fees and broker commissions, is debited to the Held-to-Maturity Investments account.

To illustrate accounting for bond investments, assume that on July 1, 2008, Washington Post paid the par value of $100,000 for 8 percent bonds that mature on June 30, 2013.[2] Interest at 8 percent is paid each June 30 and December 31. Management plans to hold the bonds for five years, until maturity.

The journal entry to record the purchase of the bonds follows:

Held-to-Maturity Investments (+A)	100,000	
Cash (−A)		100,000

Assets		=	Liabilities	+	Stockholders' Equity
Cash	−100,000				
Held-to-Maturity Investments	+100,000				

---

[1]The determination of the price of the bond is based on the present value techniques discussed in Chapter 9. Many analysts refer to a bond price as a **percentage of par.** For example, *The Wall Street Journal* might report that an ExxonMobil bond with a par value of $1,000 is selling at 82.97. This means it would cost $829.70 (82.97 percent of $1,000) to buy the bond.

[2]When bond investors accept a rate of interest on a bond investment that is the same as the stated rate of interest on the bonds, the bonds will sell at par (i.e., at 100 or 100% of face value).

Interest Earned

The bonds in this illustration were purchased at par, or face value. Since no premium or discount needs to be amortized, the book value remains constant over the life of the investment. In this situation, revenue earned from the investment each period is measured as the amount of interest collected in cash or accrued at year-end. The following journal entry records the receipt of interest on December 31:

Cash (+A) ($100,000 × 8% × 6/12)   4,000
    Interest Revenue (+R, +SE)   4,000

Assets	=	Liabilities	+	Stockholders' Equity	
Cash +4,000				Interest Revenue	+4,000

The same entry is made on succeeding interest payment dates.

Principal at Maturity

When the bonds mature on June 30, 2013, the journal entry to record receipt of the principal payment would be:

Cash (+A)   100,000
    Held-to-Maturity Investments (−A)   100,000

Assets	=	Liabilities	+	Stockholders' Equity
Cash +100,000				
Held-to-Maturity				
Investments −100,000				

If the bond investment must be sold before maturity, any difference between market value (the proceeds from the sale) and net book value would be reported as a gain or loss on sale. If management **intends** to sell the bonds before the maturity date, they are treated in the same manner as investments in stock classified as available-for-sale securities discussed in the next section.

PASSIVE STOCK INVESTMENTS: THE MARKET VALUE METHOD

When the investing company owns less than 20 percent of the outstanding voting stock of another company, the investment is considered passive. Among the assets and liabilities on the balance sheet, only passive investments in marketable securities are required to be reported using the **market value method** on the date of the balance sheet.[3] This violates the historical cost principal. Before we discuss the specific accounting for these investments, we should consider the implications of using market value:

1. **Why are passive investments reported at fair market value on the balance sheet?** Two primary factors determine the answer to this question:

   ■ **Relevance.** Analysts who study financial statements often attempt to forecast a company's future cash flows. They want to know how a company can generate cash for purposes such as expansion of the business, payment of dividends, or survival during a prolonged economic downturn. One source of cash is the sale of stock from its passive investments portfolio. The best estimate of the cash that could be generated by the sale of these securities is their current market value.

Learning Objective 2
Analyze and report passive investments in securities using the market value method

MARKET VALUE METHOD is used to report securities at their current market value.

Audio lecture–AP12-1
www.mhhe.com/libby6e

---

[3]All **nonvoting** stock is accounted for under the market value method without regard to the level of ownership.

■ **Measurability.** Accountants record only items that can be measured in dollar terms with a high degree of reliability (an unbiased and verifiable measurement). Determining the fair market value of most assets is very difficult because they are not actively traded. For example, the John Hancock building is an important part of the Boston skyline. John Hancock's balance sheet reports the building in terms of its original cost less accumulated depreciation in part because of the difficulty in determining an objective market value for it. Contrast the difficulty of determining the value of a building with the ease of determining the value of securities that John Hancock may own. A quick look at *The Wall Street Journal* or an Internet financial service is all that is necessary to determine the current price of IBM or ExxonMobil stock because these securities are traded each day on established stock exchanges.

2. **When the investment account is adjusted to reflect changes in fair market value, what other account is affected when the asset account is increased or decreased?** Under the double-entry method of accounting, every journal entry affects at least two accounts. To report market value, one account is a valuation allowance that is added to or subtracted from the investment account maintained at cost. The other account affected is for **unrealized holding gains or losses** that are recorded whenever the fair market value of investments changes. These are unrealized because no actual sale has taken place; simply by holding the security, the value has changed. If the value of the investments increased by $100,000 during the year, an adjusting journal entry records the increase in the allowance account and an unrealized holding gain for $100,000. If the value of the investments decreased by $75,000 during the year, an adjusting journal entry records the decrease in the allowance and an unrealized holding loss of $75,000. Recording an unrealized holding gain is a departure from the revenue principle that states that revenues and gains should be recorded when the company has completed the earnings process that generated them. The financial statement treatment of the unrealized holding gains or losses depends on the classification of the passive stock investments.

UNREALIZED HOLDING GAINS OR LOSSES are amounts associated with price changes of securities that are currently held.

Classifying Passive Stock Investments

Depending on management's intent, passive investments may be classified as trading securities or securities available for sale.

Trading Securities

TRADING SECURITIES are all investments in stocks or bonds held primarily for the purpose of active trading (buying and selling) in the near future (classified as short term).

Trading securities are actively traded with the objective of generating profits on short-term changes in the price of the securities. This approach is similar to the one taken by many mutual funds. The portfolio manager actively seeks opportunities to buy and sell securities. Trading securities are classified as **current assets** on the balance sheet.

Securities Available for Sale

SECURITIES AVAILABLE FOR SALE are all passive investments other than trading securities (classified as short or long term).

Most companies do not actively trade the securities of other companies. Instead, they invest to earn a return on funds they may need for future operating purposes. These investments are called **securities available for sale.** They are classified as current or noncurrent assets on the balance sheet depending on whether management intends to sell the securities during the next year.

Trading securities (TS for short) are most commonly reported by financial institutions that actively buy and sell short-term investments to maximize returns. Most corporations, however, invest in short- and long-term securities available for sale (SAS for short). We will focus on this category in the next section by analyzing Washington Post's investing activities.

Securities Available for Sale

Washington Post's Investments in Marketable Equity Securities accounts are reported for the year 2006 at $29 million for the current asset and $326 million for the noncurrent asset. The notes to Washington Post's annual report contain the following information concerning this investment portfolio:

Notes to Consolidated Financial Statements

A. Summary of Significant Accounting Policies

Investments in Marketable Equity Securities. The Company's investments in marketable equity securities are classified as available-for-sale and therefore are recorded at fair value in the Consolidated Balance Sheets, with the change in fair value during the period excluded from earnings and recorded net of tax as a separate component of comprehensive income. Marketable equity securities the Company expects to hold long term are classified as non-current assets. If the fair value of a marketable equity security declines below its cost basis, and the decline is considered other than temporary, the Company will record a write-down, which is included in earnings.

For simplification, let's assume that Washington Post had no passive investments at the end of 2007. In the following illustration, we will apply the accounting policy used by Washington Post.

Purchase of Stock

At the beginning of 2008, Washington Post purchases 10,000 shares of Internet News[4] (INews for short) common stock for $60 per share. There were 100,000 outstanding shares, so Washington Post owns 10 percent of INews (10,000 ÷ 100,000), which is treated as a passive investment. Such investments are recorded initially at cost:

Investment in SAS (+A) 600,000
    Cash (−A) 600,000

Assets	=	Liabilities	+	Stockholders' Equity
Investments in SAS +600,000				
Cash −600,000				

This entry and those that follow are illustrated in T-accounts in Exhibit 12.2.

Dividends Earned

Investments in equity securities earn a return from two sources: (1) price increases and (2) dividend income. Price increases (or decreases) are analyzed both at year-end and when a security is sold. Dividends earned are reported as investment income on the income statement and are included in the computation of net income for the period. Washington Post received a $1 per share cash dividend from INews, which totals $10,000 ($1 × 10,000 shares).

Cash (+A) 10,000
    Investment Income (+R, +SE) 10,000

Assets	=	Liabilities	+	Stockholders' Equity
Cash +10,000				Investment Income (+R) +10,000

This entry is the same for both the trading securities and available-for-sale securities.

---

[4] Internet News is a fictitious company.

Year-End Valuation

At the end of the accounting period, passive investments are reported on the balance sheet at fair market value. Assume that INews had a $58 per share market value at the end of the year. That is, the investment had lost value ($60 − $58 = $2 per share) for the year. However, since the investment has not been sold, there is only a holding loss, not a realized loss.

Reporting the SAS investment at market value requires adjusting it to market value at the end of each period using the account Allowance to Value at Market— SAS with an offset to Net Unrealized Gains and Losses in SAS. If the Allowance to Value at Market—SAS account has a **debit balance,** it is **added** to the Investment in SAS account. If it has a **credit balance,** it is **subtracted.** The Net Unrealized Gains and Losses in SAS account is reported in the stockholders' equity section of the balance sheet under other comprehensive income. Thus, the balance sheet remains in balance. Since the SAS investment is expected to be held into the future, the unrealized holding gain or loss is not reported as part of net income. Only when the security is sold are any realized gains or losses included in net income.

The following chart is used to compute any unrealized gain or loss in the SAS portfolio:

Year	Market Value	−	Cost	=	Balance Needed in Valuation Allowance	−	Unadjusted Balance in Valuation Allowance	=	Amount for Adjusting Entry
2008	$580,000 ($58 × 10,000)	−	$600,000 ($60 × 10,000)	=	($20,000)	−	$0 (We assume there were no passive investments at the end of the prior year.)	=	($20,000) An unrealized loss for the period

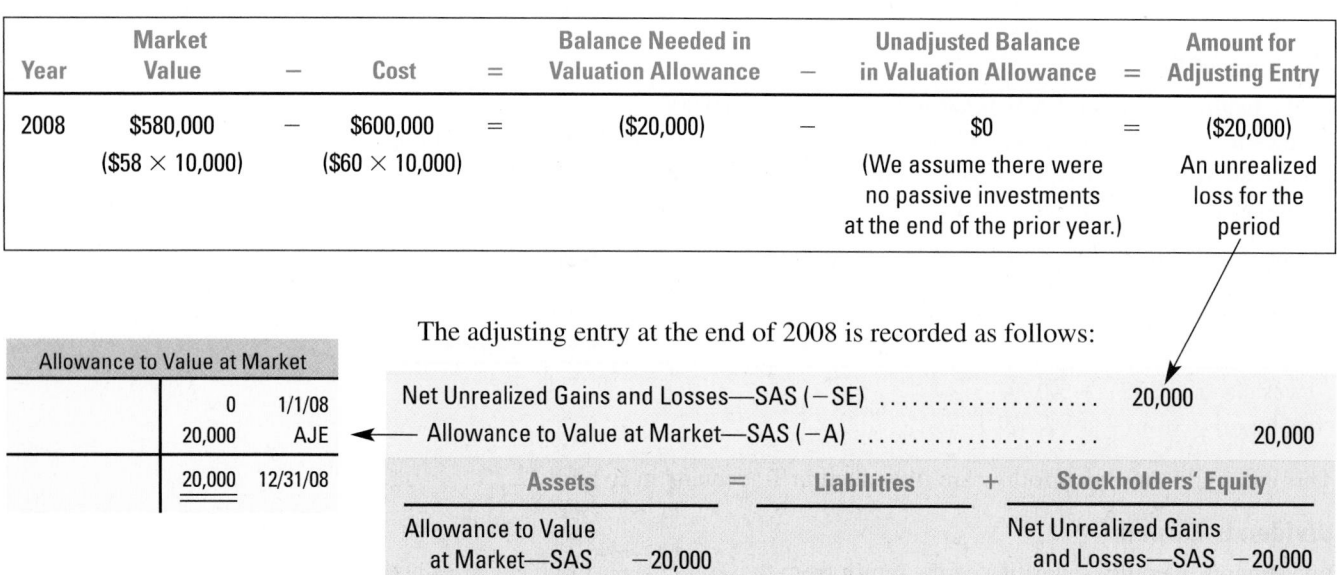

The adjusting entry at the end of 2008 is recorded as follows:

Net Unrealized Gains and Losses—SAS (−SE) 20,000
Allowance to Value at Market—SAS (−A) 20,000

Assets	=	Liabilities	+	Stockholders' Equity
Allowance to Value at Market—SAS −20,000				Net Unrealized Gains and Losses—SAS −20,000

Allowance to Value at Market

	0	1/1/08
	20,000	AJE
	20,000	12/31/08

On the Balance Sheet:

Assets
Investment in SAS $600,000
Allowance to value
    at market—SAS   (20,000)
Net investment $580,000
Stockholders' Equity
Other Comprehensive
    Income:
    Net unrealized loss
        in SAS $(20,000)

On the 2008 balance sheet under other investments, Washington Post would report an investment in securities available for sale of $580,000 ($600,000 cost less the $20,000 credit balance in the valuation allowance). It would also report under other comprehensive income its net unrealized loss on securities available for sale of $20,000. The only item reported on the income statement for 2008 would be investment income of $10,000 from the dividends earned, classified under other nonoperating items.

Now let's assume that the INews securities were held through the year 2009. At the end of 2009, the stock had a $61 per share market value. The adjustment for 2009 would be computed as follows:

Year	Market Value	−	Cost	=	Balance Needed in Valuation Allowance	−	Unadjusted Balance in Valuation Allowance	=	Amount for Adjusting Entry
2009	$610,000 ($61 × 10,000)	−	$600,000 ($60 × 10,000)	=	$10,000	−	($20,000)	=	$30,000 An unrealized gain for the period

The adjusting entry at the end of 2009 would be:

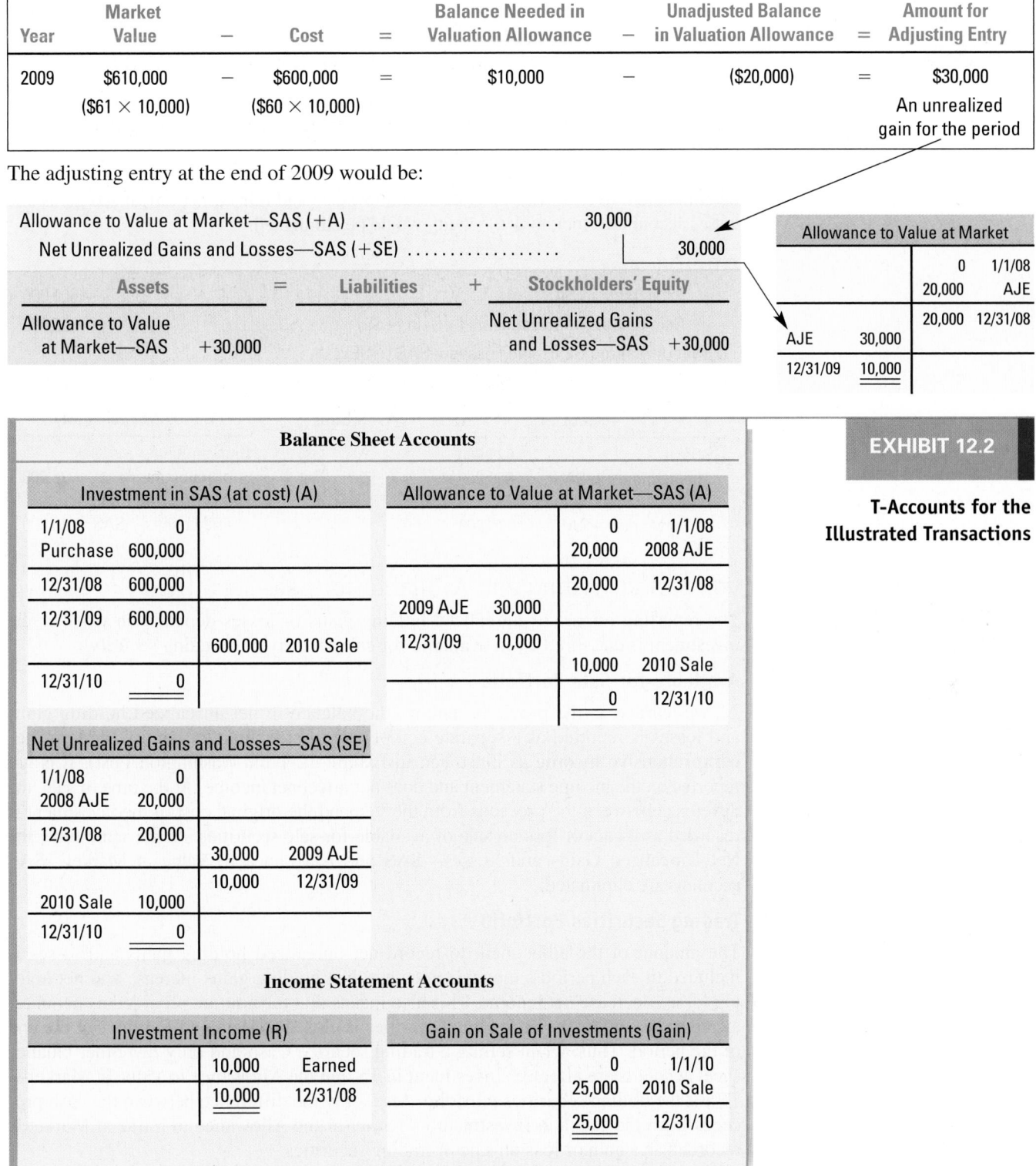

Allowance to Value at Market—SAS (+A) 30,000
    Net Unrealized Gains and Losses—SAS (+SE) 30,000

Assets	=	Liabilities	+	Stockholders' Equity
Allowance to Value at Market—SAS +30,000				Net Unrealized Gains and Losses—SAS +30,000

Allowance to Value at Market

		0	1/1/08
		20,000	AJE
		20,000	12/31/08
AJE	30,000		
12/31/09	10,000		

Balance Sheet Accounts

EXHIBIT 12.2

T-Accounts for the Illustrated Transactions

Investment in SAS (at cost) (A)

1/1/08	0		
Purchase	600,000		
12/31/08	600,000		
12/31/09	600,000		
		600,000	2010 Sale
12/31/10	0		

Allowance to Value at Market—SAS (A)

		0	1/1/08
		20,000	2008 AJE
		20,000	12/31/08
2009 AJE	30,000		
12/31/09	10,000		
		10,000	2010 Sale
		0	12/31/10

Net Unrealized Gains and Losses—SAS (SE)

1/1/08	0		
2008 AJE	20,000		
12/31/08	20,000		
		30,000	2009 AJE
		10,000	12/31/09
2010 Sale	10,000		
12/31/10	0		

Income Statement Accounts

Investment Income (R)

| | | 10,000 | Earned |
| | | 10,000 | 12/31/08 |

Gain on Sale of Investments (Gain)

		0	1/1/10
		25,000	2010 Sale
		25,000	12/31/10

Sale of Stock

When securities available for sale are sold, **three** accounts on the balance sheet (in addition to Cash) are affected:

- Investment in SAS (A)
- Allowance to Value at Market (XA)
- Net Unrealized Gains and Losses (equal to the valuation allowance) (SE).

Let's assume that in 2010 Washington Post sold all of its SAS investment in INews for $62.50 per share. The company would receive $625,000 in cash ($62.50 × 10,000 shares) for stock it paid $600,000 for in 2008 ($60 × 10,000 shares). In entry (1), a gain on sale of $25,000 ($625,000 − $600,000) would be recorded and the Investment in SAS would be eliminated. In entry (2), the valuation allowance and related net unrealized gains and losses account in stockholders' equity would be eliminated.

(1) Cash (+A)	625,000	
Investment in SAS (−A)		600,000
Gain on Sale of Investments (+Gain, +SE)		25,000
(2) Net Unrealized Gains and Losses—SAS (−SE)	10,000	
Allowance to Value at Market—SAS (−A)		10,000

Assets		=	Liabilities	+	Stockholders' Equity	
(1) Cash	+625,000				Gain on Sale	
Investments in SAS	−600,000				of Investments	+25,000
(2) Alllowance to Value					Net Unrealized Gains	
at Market—SAS	−10,000				and Losses—SAS	−10,000

Comparing Trading and Available-for-Sale Securities

The reporting impact of unrealized holding gains or losses depends on whether the investment is classified as an available-for-sale security or a trading security.

Available-for-Sale Portfolio

As we learned in the previous section, the balance in net unrealized holding gains and losses is reported as a separate component of stockholders' equity (under **other comprehensive income** as illustrated in Exhibit 12-1 for Washington Post). It is not reported on the income statement and does not affect net income. At the time of sale, the difference between the proceeds from the sale and the original cost of the investment is recorded as a gain or loss on sale of available-for-sale securities. At the same time, the Net Unrealized Gains and Losses—SAS and Allowance to Value at Market—SAS accounts are eliminated.

Trading Securities Portfolio

The amount of the adjustment to record net unrealized holding gains and losses is included in each period's income statement. Net holding gains increase and net holding losses decrease net income. This also means that the amount recorded as net unrealized gains and losses on trading securities is closed to Retained Earnings at the end of the period. Thus, when selling a trading security, Cash and only *two* other balance sheet accounts are affected: Investment in TS and the Allowance to Value at Market—TS for the trading securities portfolio. Also, only the difference between the cash proceeds from the sale and Investment in TS *net* of the Allowance to Value at Market is recorded as a gain or loss on sale of trading securities.

Exhibit 12.3 provides comparative journal entries and financial statement balances for the transactions illustrated for Washington Post from 2008 to 2010. **Note that total income reported for the three years is the same $35,000 for both trading securities and securities available for sale. Only the allocation across the three periods differs.**

Income in	Trading Securities	Securities Available for Sale
2008	$ 10,000 dividends	$10,000 dividends
	(20,000) unrealized loss	---
2009	30,000 unrealized gain	---
2010	15,000 realized gain	25,000 realized gain
Total	$ 35,000	$35,000

Comparison of Accounting for Available-for-Sale and Trading Securities Portfolios

EXHIBIT 12.3

PART A: ENTRIES	TRADING SECURITIES		SECURITIES AVAILABLE FOR SALE	
2008:				
• Purchase	Investment in TS (+A) 600,000		Investment in SAS (+A) 600,000	
(for $600,000 cash)	Cash (−A)	600,000	Cash (−A)	600,000
• Receipt of dividends	Cash (+A) 10,000		Cash (+A) 10,000	
($10,000 cash)	Investment income (+R,+SE) . . .	10,000	Investment income (+R,+SE) . . .	10,000
• Year-end adjustment	Net unrealized gains/losses—TS		Net unrealized gains/losses—SAS	
to market	(+Loss, −SE) 20,000		(−SE) 20,000	
(market = $580,000)	Allowance to value		Allowance to value	
	at market—TS (−A)	20,000	at market—SAS (−A)	20,000
2009:				
• Year-end adjustment	Allowance to value at market—		Allowance to value	
to market	TS (+A) 30,000		at market—SAS (+A) 30,000	
(market = $610,000)	Net unrealized gains/losses—		Net unrealized gains/losses—SAS	
	TS (+Gain,+SE)	30,000	(+SE)	30,000
2010:				
• Sale (for $625,000)	*Two balance sheet accounts are eliminated:*		*Three balance sheet accounts are eliminated:*	
	Cash (+A) 625,000		Cash (+A) 625,000	
	Investment in TS (−A)	600,000	**Investment in SAS (−A)**	600,000
	Allowance to value		Gain on sale of investment	
	at market—TS (−A)	10,000	(+Gain,+SE)	25,000
	Gain on sale of investment		**Net unrealized gains/**	
	(+Gain, +SE)	15,000	**losses—SAS (−SE)**	10,000
			Allowance to value	
			at market—SAS (−A)	10,000

PART B: FINANCIAL REPORTING	TRADING SECURITIES				SECURITIES-AVAILABLE-FOR-SALE			
• **Balance Sheet reporting:**	**Assets**	**2010**	**2009**	**2008**	**Assets**	**2010**	**2009**	**2008**
	Investment in TS	—	600,000	600,000	Investment in SAS	—	600,000	600,000
	Allow. to market-TS	—	10,000	(20,000)	Allow. to market-SAS	—	10,000	(20,000)
	Net Investment in TS	—	610,000	580,000	Net Investment in SAS	—	610,000	580,000
					Stockholders' Equity			
					Other comprehensive income:			
					Net unreal. gains/losses-SAS	10,000		(20,000)
• **Income Statement reporting:**		**2010**	**2009**	**2008**		**2010**	**2009**	**2008**
	Investment income	—	—	10,000	Investment income	—	—	10,000
	Gain on sale	15,000	—	—	Gain on sale	25,000	—	—
	Net unreal. gains/							
	losses-TS	—	30,000	(20,000)				

FINANCIAL ANALYSIS

Passive Investments and the Fair Value Option

Fair Value

Both U.S. GAAP and IFRS allow the option to account for bonds held to maturity and securities available for sale at fair value. Fair value is the price that would be received if the assets were sold. The election is made when each security is purchased. Once the accounting for a particular security has been selected, it cannot be changed. If a company decides to account for a held-to-maturity or available-for-sale security at fair value, it is transferred to the trading securities portfolio, and is accounted for in the same manner as other trading securities.

SELF-STUDY QUIZ

Answer the following questions using the T-accounts to help you infer the amounts. The dollars are in thousands.

Balance Sheet Accounts

(In Other Investments)

Investment in SAS					Allowance to Value at Market—SAS			
1/1	4,022				1/1	1,565		
Purchase	19,000	?	Sale		AJE	?	1,092	Sale
12/31	8,875				12/31	5,683		

(In Accumulated Other → Comprehensive Income)

Net Unrealized Gains and Losses—SAS			
		1,565	1/1
Sale	?	?	AJE
		5,683	12/31

Income Statement Accounts

Investment Income				Gain on Sale of Investments		
	?	Earned			2,384	Sale
	7,771	12/31			2,384	12/31

a. Purchased securities available for sale for cash. Prepare the journal entry.	
b. Received cash dividends on the investments. Prepare the journal entry.	
c. Sold SAS investments at a gain. Prepare the journal entries.	
d. At year-end, the SAS portfolio had a market value of $14,558. Prepare the adjusting entry.	
e. What would be reported on the balance sheet related to the SAS investments on December 31? On the income statement for the year?	
f. How would year-end reporting change if the investments were categorized as trading securities instead of securities available for sale?	

After you have completed your answers, check them with the solutions at the bottom of the next page.

INVESTMENTS FOR SIGNIFICANT INFLUENCE: EQUITY METHOD

When Washington Post invests cash in securities that are reported on its balance sheet as Investments in Marketable Equity Securities, it is a passive investor. However, when the company reports Investments in Affiliates on its balance sheet, it is taking a more active role as an investor. For a variety of reasons, an investor may want to exert influence (presumed by owning 20 to 50 percent of the outstanding voting stock) without becoming the controlling shareholder (presumed when owning more than 50 percent of the voting stock). Examples follow:

■ A retailer may want to influence a manufacturer to be sure that it can obtain certain products designed to its specifications.

■ A manufacturer may want to influence a computer consulting firm to ensure that it can incorporate the consulting firm's cutting-edge technology in its manufacturing processes.

■ A manufacturer may recognize that a parts supplier lacks experienced management and could prosper with additional managerial support.

The **equity method** must be used when an investor can exert significant influence over an investee. On the balance sheet these long-term investments are classified as

EQUITY METHOD is used when an investor can exert significant influence over an investee; the method permits recording the investor's share of the investee's income.

Self-Study Quiz
Solutions

a. Investment in SAS (+A)	19,000	
Cash (−A)		19,000
b. Cash (+A)	7,771	
Investment income (+R,+SE)		7,771
c. (1) Cash (+A)	16,531	
Gain on sale of investments (+Gain,+SE)		2,384
Investment in SAS (−A)		14,147
(2) Net unrealized gains/losses—SAS (−SE)	1,092	
Allowance to value at market—SAS (−A)		1,092
d. Allowance to value at market—SAS (+A)	5,210	
Net unrealized gains/losses—SAS (+SE)		5,210

Market Value − Cost =	Balance Needed in Valuation Allowance −	Unadjusted Balance in Valuation Allowance =	Adjustment to Valuation Allowance
$14,558 − $8,875 =	+$5,683 −	$473 = ($1,565 beg. bal. − $1,092 sale)	+$5,210

e. **Balance Sheet**

Assets
Other investments $14,558

Stockholders' Equity
Net unrealized gains/losses   5,683
(in Accumulated Other Comprehensive Income)

Income Statement

Nonoperating Items
Gain on sale of investments $ 2,384
Investment income   7,771

f. If the securities were categorized as trading securities, no net unrealized gain would appear on the balance sheet. Therefore, when the securities were sold in (*c*), no debit would be made to the Net Unrealized Gains/Losses account. Rather, there would be a gain on the sale of $1,292 [$16,531 cash − ($14,147 cost + $1,092 allowance)] reported on the income statement. Then at year-end, the net unrealized gain of $5,210 would be reported on the income statement (not in stockholders' equity).

INVESTMENTS IN AFFILIATES or ASSOCIATED COMPANIES are investments in stock held for the purpose of influencing the operating and financing strategies of the entity for the long term.

REAL WORLD EXCERPT

ANNUAL REPORT

investments in affiliates (or **associated companies**). Washington Post reported one investment in affiliates in its 2006 annual report. It sold its other affiliate during 2006.

Notes to Financial Statements

A. Summary of Significant Accounting Policies

Investments in Affiliates. The Company uses the equity method of accounting for its investments in and earnings or losses of affiliates that it does not control, but over which it does exert significant influence.

. . . .

C. Investments in Affiliates

The Company's investments in affiliates at December 31, 2006 and January 1, 2006 include the following (in thousands):

	2006	2005
Bowater Mersey Paper Company	$49,230	$54,407.

Recording Investments under the Equity Method

With a passive investment (less than 20 percent stock ownership), an investor usually cannot influence the investee's operating and financing activities—for example, by compelling the investee to pay dividends. So any dividends the investor receives from the investee are reported as dividend revenue.

Under the equity method, however, the investor's 20 to 50 percent ownership in a company presumes significant influence over the investee's operating and financing policies. Often, the investee's board of directors may include a representative of the investor who influences the investee's board to declare dividends, among other decisions. Because of this influence, the investment is accounted for as if the two companies were one. That is, the net income earned by the investee increases the investee's net assets (assets minus liabilities). Likewise, the investor should report a portion of the investee's net income as its income and an increase in the investment account. Dividends paid by the investee decrease the investee's net assets. Similarly, the receipt of dividends by the investor is treated as a reduction of the investment account, not revenue. A summary follows:

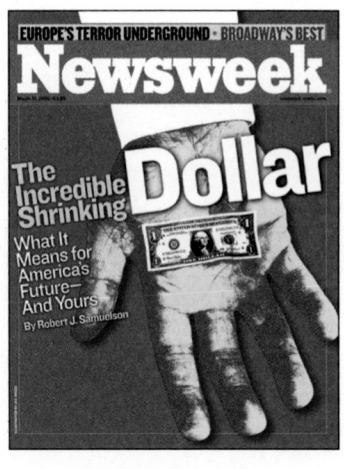

- *Net income of investee:* If the investee reports positive results of operations for the year, the investor then records investment income equal to its percentage share of the investee's net income and increases its asset account Investments in Affiliated (or Associated) Companies. If the investee reports a net loss, the investor records the opposite effect.

- *Dividends paid by investee:* If the investee declares and pays dividends during the year (a financing decision), the investor reduces its investment account and increases cash when it receives its share of the dividends.

Investments in Affiliated Companies (A)

Beginning balance Purchases	Sales
Company's % share of investee's net income (credit Equity in Investee's Earnings)	Company's % share of investee's net loss (debit Equity in Investee's Earnings)
	Company's % share of investee's dividends declared for the period (debit Cash)
Ending balance	

Purchase of Stock

For simplification, let's assume that, at the beginning of 2008, Washington Post had no long-term investments in companies over which it exerted significant influence. In 2008, Washington Post purchased 40,000 shares of the outstanding voting common stock of Internet News (INews) for $400,000 in cash. Since INews had 100,000 shares of common stock outstanding, Washington Post acquired 40 percent and was presumed to have significant influence over the investee. Therefore, Washington Post must use the equity method to account for this investment. The purchase of the asset would be recorded at cost.

Investments in Affiliated Companies (+A) 400,000
   Cash (−A) 400,000

Assets	=	Liabilities	+	Stockholders' Equity
Investments in Affiliated Companies +400,000				
Cash −400,000				

Investee Earnings

Because the investor can influence the process of earning income for the investee, the investor company bases its investment income on the investee's earnings rather than the dividends it pays. During 2008, INews reported a net income of $500,000 for the year. Washington Post's percentage share of INews's income was $200,000 (40% × $500,000) and is recorded as follows:

Investments in Affiliated Companies (+A) 200,000
   Equity in Investee Earnings (+R, +SE) 200,000

Assets	=	Liabilities	+	Stockholders' Equity
Investments in Affiliated Companies +200,000				Equity in Investee Earnings +200,000

If the investee reports a net loss for the period, the investor records its percentage share of the loss by decreasing the investment account and recording Equity in Investee Loss. The Equity in Investee Earnings (or Loss) is reported in the Other Items section of the income statement, with interest revenue, interest expense, and gains and losses on sales of assets.

Dividends Received

Because Washington Post can influence the dividend policies of its equity-method investments, any dividends it receives should **not** be recorded as investment income. Instead, dividends received reduce its investment account. During 2008, INews declared and paid a cash dividend of $2 per share to stockholders. Washington Post received $80,000 in cash ($2 × 40,000 shares) from INews.

Cash (+A) 80,000
   Investments in Affiliated Companies (−A) 80,000

Assets	=	Liabilities	+	Stockholders' Equity
Cash + 80,000				
Investments in Affiliated Companies − 80,000				

In summary, the effects for 2008 are reflected in the following T-accounts:

Investments in Affiliated Companies		
1/1/08 0		
Purchase 400,000		
	80,000	Share of
Share of		investee
investee net		dividends
earnings 200,000		
12/31/08 520,000		

Equity in Investee Earnings		
	0	1/1/08
	200,000	Share of
		investee
		net earnings
	200,000	12/31/08

Reporting Investments under the Equity Method

The Investments in Affiliated Companies account is reported on the balance sheet as a long-term asset. However, as these last two entries show, the investment account does not reflect either cost or market value. Instead, the following occurs:

- The investment account is increased by the cost of shares that were purchased and the proportional share of the investee company income.

- The account is reduced by the amount of dividends received from the investee company and the proportional share of any investee company losses.

At the end of the accounting period, accountants **do not adjust the investment account to reflect changes in the fair market value** of the securities that are held.[4] When the securities are sold, the difference between the cash received and the book value of the investment is recorded as a gain or loss on the sale of the asset and is reported on the income statement in the Other Items section.

A QUESTION
OF ETHICS   **Improper Influence**

A key assumption underlying accounting is that all transactions occur at "arm's length." That is, each party to the transaction is acting in his or her own self-interest. But when one corporation exerts significant influence over another (i.e., it owns 20 to 50 percent of the common stock), it is unreasonable to assume that transactions between the corporations are made at arm's length.

Consider what might happen if an investor corporation could affect the investee's dividend policy. If the investor reported dividends paid by the investee as dividend income, the investor could manipulate its income by influencing the other company's dividend policy. In a bad year, the investor might request large dividend payments to bolster its income. In a good year, it might try to cut dividend payments to build up the investee company's retained earnings to support large dividends in the future.

The equity method prevents this type of manipulation. Instead of recognizing dividends as income, income from the investment is based on a percentage of the affiliated company's reported net income.

---

[4]FAS 159 does allow companies to elect fair value treatment for equity method investments, but few companies are expected to take the election.

Answer the following questions, using the T-accounts to help you infer the amounts. The dollars are in thousands.

Investments in Affiliated Companies			
1/1/2009	83,619		
Purchase	12,844		
Share of investee net income	?	10,102	Share of investee dividends
12/31/2009	89,230		

Equity in Investee Earnings		
1/1/2009		0
	2,869	Share of investee net income
	2,869	12/31/2009

a. Purchased additional investments in affiliated companies for cash. Prepare the journal entry.	
b. Received cash dividends on the investments. Prepare the journal entry.	
c. At year-end, the investments in affiliated companies had a market value of $62,000; the companies also reported $5,800 in net income for the year. Prepare the adjusting entry.	
d. What would be reported on the December 31, 2009, balance sheet related to the investments in affiliated companies? What would be reported on the income statement for 2009?	

After you have completed your answers, check them with the solutions at the bottom of the page.

a. Investments in affiliated companies (+A)	12,844	
Cash (−A)		12,844
b. Cash (+A)	10,102	
Investments in affiliated companies (−A)		10,102
c. Investments in affiliated companies (+A)	2,869	
Equity in investee earnings (+R, +SE)		2,869

d. **Balance Sheet**
   Assets
     Investments in affiliated
      companies $89,230

   Income Statement
   Other Items
     Equity in investee
      earnings $2,869

Transaction Structuring: Selecting Accounting Methods for Minority Investments

Managers can choose freely between LIFO and FIFO or accelerated depreciation and straight-line depreciation. In the case of minority ($\leq$ 50% owned) investments, they may **not** simply choose between the market value and equity methods. Investments of less than 20 percent of a company's outstanding stock are usually accounted for under the market value method and investments of 20 percent to 50 percent under the equity method.

However, managers may be able to structure the acquisition of stock in a manner that permits them to use the accounting method that they prefer. For example, a company that wants to use the market value method could purchase only 19.9 percent of the outstanding stock of another company and achieve the same investment goals as they would with a 20 percent investment. Why might managers want to avoid using the equity method? Most managers prefer to minimize variations in reported earnings. If a company were planning to buy stock in a firm that reported large earnings in some years and large losses in others, it might want to use the market value method to avoid reporting its share of the investee's earnings and losses.

Analysts who compare several companies must understand management's reporting choices and the way in which differences between the market value and equity methods can affect earnings.

Investments

Many of the effects from applying the market value method to passive investments and the equity method to investments held for significant influence affect net income but not cash flow. These items require adjustments under the indirect method when converting net income to cash flows from operating activities.

In General **Sales of securities** require a number of adjustments:

1. Any gain on the sale is subtracted from net income in the Operating Activities section.
2. Any loss on the sale is added back in the Operating Activities section.
3. The cash resulting from the sale or purchase is reflected in the Investing Activities section.

Income under the equity method also requires adjustments. Recall that cash dividends received from investees are not recorded as income. In addition, investors record as income their share of investees' earnings even though no cash is involved, resulting in the following:

1. Dividends received are added to net income in the Operating Activities section.
2. Any equity in investee earnings needs to be subtracted in the Operating Activities section.
3. Any equity in investee losses needs to be added in the Operating Activities section.

EFFECT ON STATEMENT OF CASH FLOWS

	Effect on Cash Flows
Operating Activities	
Net income	$xxx
Adjusted for	
Gains/losses on sale of investments	−/+
Equity in net earnings/losses of affiliated companies	−/+
Dividends received from affiliated companies	+
Net unrealized holding gains/losses on trading securities	−/+
Investing Activities	
Purchase of investments	−
Sale of investments	+

Focus Company Analysis   A partial statement of cash flows for Washington Post for 2006 follows. Washington Post subtracted the equity in earnings of affiliated companies and added in dividends received from affiliated companies, showing the net effect on the cash flow statement. Washington Post sold securities during the year and the gain was subtracted in the operating section for both investment portfolios (SAS and affiliated companies). A loss would have been added. The investing section would show the actual cash paid or received for purchases and sales of investments during the period.

WASHINGTON POST COMPANY
Consolidated Statement of Cash Flows (partial)
For the year ended December, 31, 2006
(dollars in millions)

Cash flows from operating activities:		
Net income	$ 324,459	
Adjustments to reconcile net income to net cash		
provided by operating activities:		
Gain on sale of marketable equity securities	(33,805)	Equity in earnings −790
Equity in (earnings) losses of affiliates, net of distributions	110	Dividends received 900
(Other adjustments—not detailed here)	303,986	110
Net cash provided by operating activities	**594,750**	
Cash flows from investing activities:		
Proceeds from sale of investments	82,910	
Purchases of investments	(205,006)	
Investments in affiliates	(3,349)	
(Other investing activies—not detailed here)	(195,825)	
Net cash used in investing activities	**$(321,270)**	

CONTROLLING INTERESTS: MERGERS AND ACQUISITIONS

Before we discuss financial reporting issues for situations in which a company owns more than 50 percent of the outstanding common stock of another corporation, we should consider management's reasons for acquiring this level of ownership. The following are some of the reasons for acquiring control of another corporation:

Learning Objective 4
Analyze and report investments in controlling interests.

1. **Vertical integration.** In this type of acquisition, a company acquires another at a different level in the channels of distribution. For example, Washington Post owns a newsprint company that provides raw materials.

2. **Horizontal growth.** These acquisitions involve companies at the same level in the channels of distribution. For example, Washington Post has expanded internationally by creating or acquiring companies in major international markets.

3. **Synergy.** The operations of two companies together may be more profitable than the combined profitability of the companies as separate entities. Washington Post has created or purchased a number of broadcast and Internet services. Merging these companies and sharing news content may create more profits than operating separate entities could.

Understanding why one company has acquired control over other companies is a key factor in understanding the company's overall business strategy.

The PARENT COMPANY is the entity that gains control over another company.

The SUBSIDIARY COMPANY is the entity that is acquired by the parent.

CONSOLIDATED FINANCIAL STATEMENTS combine the operations of two or more companies into a single set of statements.

REAL WORLD EXCERPT

WASHINGTON POST

ANNUAL REPORT

What Are Consolidated Statements?

Any corporate acquisition involves two companies. The **parent company** is the company that gains control over the other company. The **subsidiary company** is the company that the parent acquires. When a company acquires another, **consolidated financial statements** must be presented. These statements combine the operations of two or more companies into a single set of statements. Basically, **consolidated statements can be thought of as the adding together of the separate financial statements for two or more companies to make it appear as if a single company exists.** Thus, the cash accounts for each company are added as are the inventory accounts, land accounts, and others.

The notes to Washington Post's 2006 annual report provide the following information:

Notes to Financial Statements

A. Summary of Significant Accounting Policies

Principles of Consolidation. The accompanying financial statements include the accounts of the Company and its subsidiaries; significant intercompany transactions have been eliminated.

. . .

As the note indicates, eliminating any intercompany items is necessary when consolidated statements are prepared. **Remember that consolidated statements make it appear as though a single company exists when in fact there are two or more separate legal entities.** Intercompany items do not exist for a single corporation. For example, a debt owed by Washington Post (the parent) to its newsprint subsidiary is not reported on a consolidated statement because a company cannot owe itself money. We discuss the preparation of consolidated statements in more detail in Supplement A at the end of this chapter.

Recording a Merger

A MERGER occurs when one company purchases all of the net assets of another and the target company goes out of existence.

We learned that consolidated statements are presented in such a way that two companies appear to have merged into one. In fact, the simplest way to understand the statements that result from the consolidation process is to consider the case of a simple **merger** where one company purchases all of the net assets of another and the target company goes out of existence. In such a situation, the purchasing company records the net assets of the target according to the cost principle, at the cash equivalent purchase price.

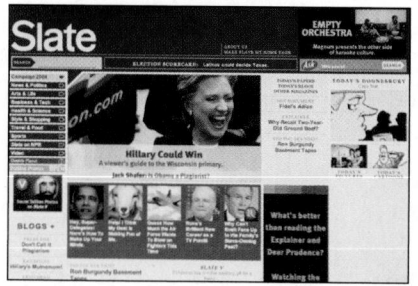

To illustrate, we will use simplified data for Washington Post (the purchaser) and INews (the hypothetical target). Let's assume that, on January 1, 2008, Washington Post paid $100 (all numbers in millions) in cash to buy all of INews's stock.[5] It then merges INews into its operations and INews goes out of existence as a separate legal entity. Exhibit 12.4 presents Washington Post and INews's balance sheets, and market value data for INews's assets and liabilities, immediately **before** the merger.

Note that Washington Post paid $100 for 100 percent of INews even though the total book value of INews's net assets was only $80 ($90 assets − $10 liabilities). This is not surprising because **the book value of a company's net assets is not the same as the fair market value.** We will assume that an analysis of INews's assets and liabilities on the date of acquisition revealed the following facts:

■ INews's Plant and Equipment had a current market value of $35 (net book value of $30).

■ The book values of Other Assets ($60) and Current Liabilities ($10) on INews's balance sheet were equal to market values.

---

[5]Purchasing 100 percent of the outstanding stock results in a wholly owned subsidiary. Purchasing less than 100 percent of the stock results in **minority interest** in the subsidiary, which represents the shares owned by other than the parent.

(dollars in millions)	Washington Post	INews Book Value	INews Market Value
Assets			
Cash and other current assets	$ 935		
Plant and equipment (net)	1,218	$30	$35
Other assets	3,229	60	60
Total assets	$5,382	$90	
Liabilities and Stockholders' Equity			
Current liabilities	$ 803	$10	$10
Noncurrent liabilities	1,407		
Stockholders' equity	3,172	80	
Total liabilities and stockholders' equity	$5,382	$90	

EXHIBIT 12.4

Balance Sheets Immediately before the Merger

■ INews had developed a good reputation with an important group of online readers, which increased INews's overall value. For these reasons, Washington Post was willing to pay an additional $15 to acquire INews. The $15 difference between the purchase price of the company and the fair market value of its net assets (assets minus liabilities) creates an account called **Goodwill** (or **Cost in Excess of Net Assets Acquired**). It may be computed as follows:

For accounting purposes, GOODWILL (COST IN EXCESS OF NET ASSETS ACQUIRED) is the excess of the purchase price of a business over the fair market value of the business's assets and liabilities.

Purchase price for INews	$100
Less: Net assets purchased, at market ($35 + $60 − $10)	85
Goodwill purchased	$ 15

As noted, the cost principle requires that the assets and liabilities of INews be recorded by Washington Post on its books at the purchase price (fair market value) on the date of the merger. This method of recording mergers and acquisitions, called the **purchase method,** is the only method allowed by U.S. GAAP. Washington Post would record the merger as follows:

The PURCHASE METHOD records assets and liabilities acquired in a merger or acquisition at their fair market value.

Plant and Equipment (net) (+A)	35	
Other Assets (+A)	60	
Goodwill (+A)	15	
Current Liabilities (+L)		10
Cash (−A)		100

Assets		=	Liabilities	+	Stockholders' Equity
Plant and Equipment (net)	+35		Current Liabilities +10		
Other Assets	+60				
Goodwill	+15				
Cash	−100				

It is important to remember that goodwill can be reported on the balance sheet **only if it is acquired in a purchase transaction.**

Reporting a Merger

Postmerger Balance Sheet

The postmerger balance sheet shown in Exhibit 12.5 was prepared by combining the preceding journal entry with Washington Post's balance sheet shown in Exhibit 12.4.

EXHIBIT 12.5	(dollars in millions)	Washington Post
Washington Post's Balance Sheet Immediately After the Merger	**Assets**	
	Cash and other current assets ($935 − $100)	$ 835
	Plant and equipment (net) ($1218 + $35)	1,253
	Other assets ($3,229 + $60)	3,289
	Goodwill ($100 − $85)	15
	Total assets	$5,392
	Liabilities and Stockholders' Equity	
	Current liabilities ($803 + $10)	$ 813
	Noncurrent liabilities	1,407
	Stockholders' equity	3,172
	Total liabilities and stockholders' equity	$5,392

Remember the following:

1. INews's assets and liabilities are added at their fair market values, not their original book values.

2. Goodwill = Purchase Price − Net Assets Purchased (at their market prices).

3. The cash payment made for the acquisition is subtracted from cash on the balance sheet. If the company is purchased through issuance of additional stock, contributed capital is increased (credited) instead.

4. The balance sheet would be the same if Washington Post and INews continued as separate legal entities after the purchase, and consolidated statements were prepared.

Postmerger Income Statements

After the merger, Washington Post's accounting system will capture all of the revenues and expenses of the combined company. The resulting income statement is presented in Exhibit 12.6. The combined amounts include the following:

1. Revenues that would have been recorded in the separate accounting systems had the combination not taken place (Washington Post $3,989 + INews's $120 = $4,109).

2. Expenses that would have been recorded in the separate accounting systems had the combination not taken place (Washington Post $3,665 + INews's $106 = $3,771).

3. Additional expenses related to the recording of INews's assets and liabilities at market value; $1 additional depreciation assuming a five-year useful life ($5 additional plant and equipment over book value ÷ 5 years= $1 per year).[6]

Again, it is important to remember that the income statement would be the same if Washington Post and INews continued as separate legal entities after the purchase and consolidated statements were prepared. These circumstances are illustrated in Chapter Supplement A.

EXHIBIT 12.6	(dollars in millions)	Washington Post
Washington Post's Partial Income Statement for the Year Following the Acquisition	Revenues ($3,989 + $120)	$4,109
	Expenses ($3,665 + $106 + $1)	3,772
	Net Income	$ 337

---

[6]Ignoring taxes.

As we noted in Chapter 8, goodwill is considered to have an indefinite life. As a consequence, it is not amortized, but, like all long-lived assets, goodwill is reviewed for possible impairment of value. Recording an impairment loss would increase expenses for the period and reduce the amount of goodwill on the balance sheet. Washington Post described GAAP for goodwill in its recent note.

REAL WORLD EXCERPT

ANNUAL REPORT

A. Summary of Significant Accounting Policies

The Company reviews goodwill and indefinite-lived intangibles at least annually for impairment. All other intangible assets are amortized over their useful lives. The Company reviews the carrying value of goodwill and indefinite-lived intangible assets generally utilizing a discounted cash flow model. . . . The Company must make assumptions regarding estimated future cash flows and market values to determine a reporting unit's estimated fair value. If these estimates or related assumptions change in the future, the Company may be required to record an impairment charge.

KEY RATIO
ANALYSIS

Return on Assets (ROA)

? ANALYTICAL QUESTION:

During the period, how well has management used the company's total invested capital provided by both debt holders and stockholders?

% RATIO AND COMPARISONS:

$$\text{Return on Assets} = \frac{\text{Net Income*}}{\text{Average Total Assets}^\dagger}$$

The 2006 ratio for Washington Post:

$$\frac{\$324,469}{(\$5,381,372 + \$4,584,773) \div 2} = .065\ (6.5\%)$$

COMPARISONS OVER TIME			COMPARISONS WITH COMPETITORS	
Washington Post			**News Corporation**	**Gannett**
2004	**2005**	**2006**	**2006**	**2006**
8.1%	7.1%	6.5%	5.7%	6.6%

Learning Objective 5
Analyze and interpret the return on assets ratio.

**Selected Focus Companies'
Return on Assets
Ratio for 2006**

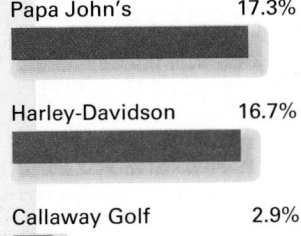

Papa John's — 17.3%

Harley-Davidson — 16.7%

Callaway Golf — 2.9%

💡 INTERPRETATIONS:

In General   ROA measures how much the firm earned for each dollar of investment. It is the broadest measure of profitability and management effectiveness, independent of financing strategy. ROA allows investors to compare management's investment performance against alternative investment options. Firms with higher ROA are doing a better job of selecting new investments, all other things equal. Company managers often compute the measure on a division-by-division basis and use it to evaluate division managers' relative performance.

Focus Company Analysis   Like many companies in the printing and publishing industry, Washington Post remains profitable, but faces a declining ROA. ROA has declined because its steady net income has not increased at the same rate as its growth in assets. Its current ROA is in line with competitor Gannett and above that of giant international publisher and broadcaster News Corporation.

A Few Cautions Like ROE, ROA can be decomposed into its components:

$$\text{ROA} = \text{Net Profit Margin} \times \text{Asset Turnover}$$

$$\frac{\text{Net Income}}{\text{Average Total Assets}} = \frac{\text{Net Income}}{\text{Net Sales}} \times \frac{\text{Net Sales}}{\text{Average Total Assets}}$$

Like ROE, effective analysis of ROA requires understanding why ROA differs from prior levels and that of its competitors. The preceding decomposition, as well as more detailed analyses of components of net profit margin and asset turnover, provides that understanding. In the case of Washington Post, it reveals that the decline in ROA is due mainly to a decline in net profit margin.

*In more complex return on total asset analyses, interest expense (net of tax) and minority interest are added back to net income in the numerator of the ratio, since the measure assesses return on capital independent of its source.

†Average Total Assets = (Beginning Total Assets + Ending Total Assets) ÷ 2

Available from www.investor.reuters.com.

SELF-STUDY QUIZ

Lexis Corporation purchased 100 percent of Nexis Company for $10 million and merged Nexis into Lexis. On the date of the merger, the market value of Nexis's other assets was $11 and the book value of Nexis's liabilities was equal to market value. The two companies' summary balance sheets appeared as follows immediately *before* the merger:

	Lexis (parent)	Nexis (subsidiary)
Cash	$10	
Other Assets	90	$10
Liabilities	30	4
Stockholders' Equity	70	6

On the balance sheet after the merger was recorded, what would be the following balances?

1. Goodwill

2. Stockholders' Equity

3. Other Assets (excluding Goodwill)

After you have completed your answers, check them with the solutions at the bottom of the page.

Self-Study Quiz
Solutions

1. Purchase Price ($10) − Market Value of Net Assets ($11 − $4) = Goodwill $10 − ($11 − $4) = $3.
2. Lexis's stockholders' equity is unchanged, leaving $70.
3. Lexis's other assets + Nexis's other assets (at market) = $90 + $11 = $101.

DEMONSTRATION CASE A

(Try to resolve the requirements before proceeding to the suggested solution that follows.)
Howell Equipment Corporation sells and services a major line of farm equipment. Both sales
and service operations have been profitable. The following transactions affected the company
during 2008:

a. Jan. 1 Purchased 2,000 shares of common stock of Dear Company at $40 per share.
This purchase represented one percent of the shares outstanding. Management
intends to trade these shares actively.

b. Dec. 28 Received $4,000 cash dividend on the Dear Company stock.

c. Dec. 31 Determined that the current market price of the Dear stock was $39.

Required:

1. Prepare the journal entry for each of these transactions.

2. What accounts and amounts will be reported on the balance sheet at the end of 2008? On
the income statement for 2008?

SUGGESTED SOLUTION FOR CASE A

1. a. Jan. 1 Investment in TS (+A) 80,000
                 Cash (−A) (2,000 shares × $40) 80,000
  b. Dec. 28 Cash (+A) 4,000
                 Investment income (+R, +SE) 4,000
  c. Dec. 31 Net unrealized gains/losses—TS (+Loss, −SE) 2,000
                 Allowance to value at market—TS (−A) 2,000

Year	Market Value	−	Cost	=	Balance Needed in Valuation Allowance	−	Unadjusted Balance in Valuation Allowance	=	Adjustment to Valuation Allowance
2008	$78,000 ($39 × 2000 shares)	−	$80,000	=	($2,000)	−	$0	=	($2,000) an unrealized loss for the period

2. On the Balance Sheet:

Current Assets
Investment in TS $78,000
  ($80,000 cost − $2,000 allowance)

On the Income Statement:

Other Items
Investment income $4,000
Net unrealized loss on trading securities   2,000

DEMONSTRATION CASE B

Assume the same facts as in Case A except that the securities were purchased as securities
available for sale rather than as trading securities.

Required:

1. Prepare the journal entry for each of these transactions.

2. What accounts and amounts will be reported on the balance sheet at the end of 2008? On
the income statement for 2008?

SUGGESTED SOLUTION FOR CASE B

1. *a.* Jan. 1   Investment in SAS (+A)   80,000

   Cash (−A) (2,000 shares × $40 per share)   80,000

   b. Dec. 28   Cash (+A)   4,000

   Investment income (+R,+SE)   4,000

   c. Dec. 31   Net unrealized gains/losses—SAS (−SE)   2,000

   Allowance to value at market—SAS (−A)   2,000

Year	Market Value	−	Cost	=	Balance Needed in Valuation Allowance	−	Unadjusted Balance in Valuation Allowance	=	Adjustment to Valuation Allowance
2008	$78,000 ($39 × 2000 shares)	−	$80,000	=	($2,000)	−	$0	=	($2,000) an unrealized loss for the period

2. On the Balance Sheet:

Current or Noncurrent Assets
Investment in SAS $78,000
   ($80,000 cost − $2,000 allowance)

Stockholders' Equity
Accumulated other comprehensive income:
   Net unrealized gain/loss on SAS   (2,000)

On the Income Statement:

Other Items
Investment income $4,000

DEMONSTRATION CASE C

On January 1, 2007, Connaught Company purchased 40 percent of the outstanding voting shares of London Company on the open market for $85,000 cash. London declared and paid $10,000 in cash dividends on December 1 and reported net income of $60,000 for the year.

Required:

1. Prepare the journal entries for 2007.

2. What accounts and amounts were reported on Connaught's balance sheet at the end of 2007? On Connaught's income statement for 2007?

SUGGESTED SOLUTION FOR CASE C

1. Jan. 1   Investments in affiliated companies (+A)   85,000

   Cash (−A)   85,000

   Dec. 1   Cash (+A) (40% × $10,000)   4,000

   Investments in affiliated companies (−A)   4,000

   Dec. 31   Investments in affiliated companies (+A) (40% × $60,000) ...   24,000

   Equity in investee earnings (+R, +SE)   24,000

2. On the Balance Sheet:

Noncurrent Assets
Investments in affiliated companies $105,000
   ($85,000 − $4,000 + $24,000)

On the Income Statement:

Other Items
Equity in investee earnings $24,000

On January 1, 2009, Hilton Company purchased 100 percent of the outstanding voting shares of Paris Company in the open market for $85,000 cash and Paris was merged into Hilton. On the date of acquisition, the market value of Paris Company's plant and equipment was $79,000 (net book value, $70,000). Hilton had no liabilities or other assets.

Required:

1. Analyze the merger to determine the amount of goodwill purchased.

2. Give the journal entry that Hilton Company should make on the date of the acquisition. If none is required, explain why.

3. Should Paris Company's assets be included on Hilton's balance sheet at book value or market value? Explain.

SUGGESTED SOLUTION FOR CASE D

1. Purchase price for Paris Company $85,000
   Less: Market value of net assets purchased   79,000

   Goodwill $ 6,000

2. Jan. 1, 2009 Plant and Equipment (+A) 79,000
                        Goodwill (+A) 6,000
                             Cash (−A)   85,000

3. Paris Company's assets should be included on the postmerger balance sheet at their market values as of the date of acquisition. The cost principle applies as it does with all asset acquisitions.

Chapter Supplement A

Preparing Consolidated Statements

As noted in the chapter, when one company acquires another and **both companies continue their separate legal existence, consolidated financial statements** must be presented. These statements combine the statements of two or more companies into a single set of statements prepared as if they were one company.

Recording Acquisition of a Controlling Interest

By offering cash or shares of its stock or a combination of the two to a target company's shareholders, one company can acquire control of another. When the target company's shareholders accept the offer and the exchange is made, the parent company records the investment in its accounts at the acquisition cost using the purchase method. When both companies maintain their separate legal identities after the acquisition, we say that a **parent-subsidiary relationship** exists. Since both companies continue to exist, both companies' accounting systems continue to record their respective transactions.

Using the same data we used when we discussed the merger of Washington Post (the parent) and INews (the hypothetical subsidiary), let's assume that, on January 1, 2008, Washington Post paid $100 (dollars in millions) cash to buy all of INews's stock.[7] Washington Post would record the acquisition as follows:

Investment in INews (+A) 100
    Cash (−A)   100

Assets	=	Liabilities	+	Stockholders' Equity
Investment in INews +100				
Cash −100				

---

[7]Purchasing 100 percent of the outstanding stock results in a wholly owned subsidiary. Purchasing less than 100 percent of the stock results in **minority interest** in the subsidiary.

EXHIBIT 12.7

Spreadsheet for Consolidated Balance Sheet on the Date of Acquisition

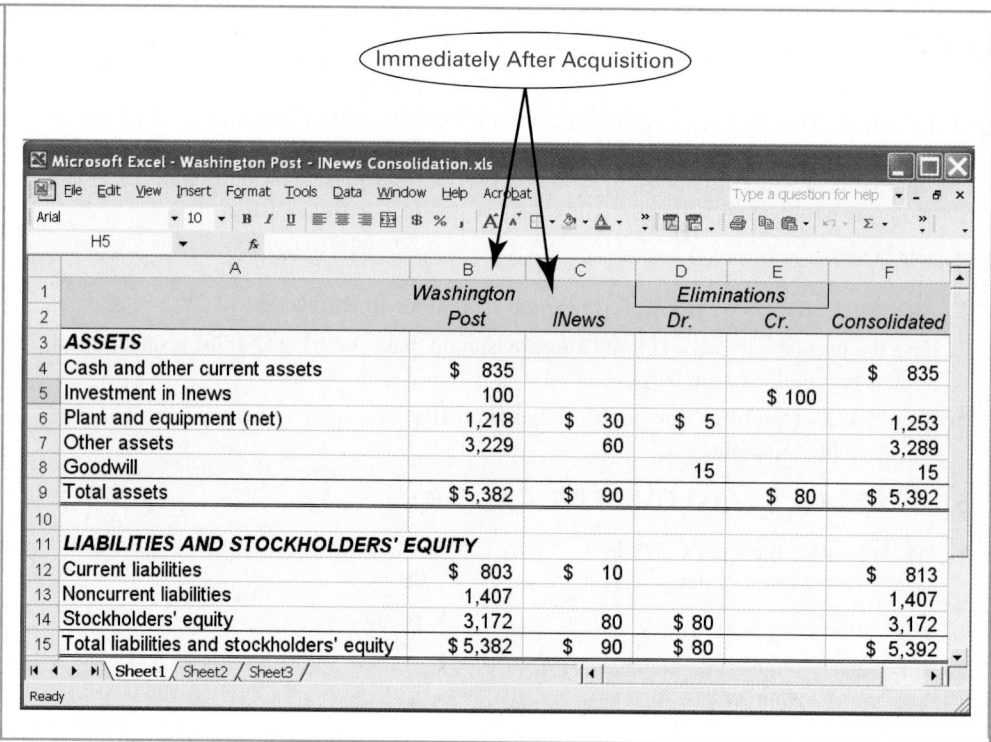

Immediately After Acquisition

	Washington Post	INews	Eliminations Dr.	Eliminations Cr.	Consolidated
ASSETS					
Cash and other current assets	$ 835				$ 835
Investment in Inews	100			$ 100	
Plant and equipment (net)	1,218	$ 30	$ 5		1,253
Other assets	3,229	60			3,289
Goodwill			15		15
Total assets	$ 5,382	$ 90		$ 80	$ 5,392
LIABILITIES AND STOCKHOLDERS' EQUITY					
Current liabilities	$ 803	$ 10			$ 813
Noncurrent liabilities	1,407				1,407
Stockholders' equity	3,172	80	$ 80		3,172
Total liabilities and stockholders' equity	$ 5,382	$ 90	$ 80		$ 5,392

Because the acquisition of INews is simply an exchange of shares among owners, no entry is made on INews's books. The spreadsheet in Exhibit 12.7 presents Washington Post's and INews's balance sheets immediately **after** the acquisition is recorded by Washington Post. The Investment in INews account is included in Washington Post's balance sheet.

Preparing Consolidated Financial Statements after Acquisition

The Balance Sheet

In consolidation, the separate financial statements of the parent (Washington Post) and the subsidiary (INews) are combined into a single consolidated statement. The investment account must be eliminated to avoid double counting the subsidiary's assets and liabilities and the parent company's investment in those assets. Washington Post paid $100 for all of INews's stock even though the total **book value** of INews's stockholders' equity was only $80. Thus, the investment account balance of $100 on Washington Post's books represents the market value of INews's net assets (assets minus liabilities) on the date of acquisition. Washington Post paid $20 in excess of book value for the following reasons:

- INews's plant and equipment had a current market value of $35 and a net book value of $30. (The book values of all other assets and liabilities already on INews's balance sheet were equal to their market values.)

- INews had developed a good reputation with an important group of online investors, which increased INews's overall value. For these reasons, Washington Post was willing to pay $15 more than book value to acquire INews's stock. The $15 difference between the purchase price of the company and the fair market value of its net assets (assets minus liabilities) is called goodwill. It may be analyzed as follows:

Purchase price for 100% interest in INews	$100
Less: Net assets purchased, at market ($80 + $5)	85
Goodwill purchased	$ 15

To complete the process of consolidating Washington Post and INews, we must **eliminate** Washington Post's investment account and replace it with the assets and liabilities of INews along with the acquired goodwill. In this process, the goodwill is reported separately, and INews's assets and

---

WASHINGTON POST AND SUBSIDIARIES
Consolidated Balance Sheet
January 1, 2008

Assets

Cash and other current assets	$ 835
Plant and equipment (net)	1,253
Other assets	3,289
Goodwill	15
Total assets	$5,392

Liabilities and Stockholders' Equity

Current liabilities	$ 813
Noncurrent liabilities	1,407
Stockholders' equity	3,172
Total liabilities and stockholders' equity	$5,392

EXHIBIT 12.8

Consolidated Balance Sheet on the Date of Acquisition (dollars in millions)

---

liabilities must be adjusted to market value for items where market value is different than book value, such as the plant and equipment in this illustration. We can accomplish this in the following five steps:

1. Subtract the investment account balance of $100.

2. Add the $15 goodwill purchased as an asset.

3. Add $5 to plant and equipment to adjust the balance to market value.

4. Subtract the INews stockholders' equity.

5. Add together what remains of the Washington Post and INews balance sheets.

When these procedures are accomplished, the balance sheet shown in Exhibit 12.8 is produced. Note that this is the same balance sheet presented in Exhibit 12.5 that resulted from the merger of Washington Post and INews into one company. This should not be surprising because consolidated statements present a single set of statements as if the parent and subsidiary companies were one.

The Income Statement
When we prepared the consolidated balance sheet, we combined the separate balance sheets to make it appear as if a single company exists. Consolidating the income statements requires a similar process. The revenues and expenses generated by the parent company's own operations, excluding any investment income from the subsidiary, must now be combined with the subsidiary's revenues and expenses. The revaluation of assets to market value, if any, also has implications for the consolidated income statement. The increase in the assets must be depreciated or amortized in the consolidation process.

In this example, preparing the consolidated income statement requires three steps (ignoring taxes):

1. Add Washington Post's revenues from its own operations of $3,989 and INews's revenues of $120.

2. Add Washington Post's expenses related to its own operations of $3,665 and INews's expenses of $106.

3. Add to the expenses the $1 additional depreciation expense, assuming a five-year useful life ($5 additional plant and equipment over book value ÷ 5 years= $1 per year).

Due to the simplicity of this example, you can directly prepare the simplified consolidated income statement in Exhibit 12.9. Complex adjustments and eliminations would normally be entered into a spreadsheet program.

EXHIBIT 12.9

Consolidated Income Statement

WASHINGTON POST AND SUBSIDIARIES
Consolidated Income Statement
Year Ended December 31, 2007
(dollars in millions)

Revenues ($3,989 + $120)	$4,109
Expenses ($3,665 + $106 + $1)	3,772
Net income	$ 337

DEMONSTRATION CASE E

On January 1, 2007, Connaught Company purchased 100 percent of the outstanding voting shares of London Company on the open market for $85,000 cash. On the date of acquisition, the market value of London Company's operational assets was $79,000.

Required:

1. Give the journal entry that Connaught Company should make on the date of acquisition. If none is required, explain why.

2. Give the journal entry that London Company should make on the date of acquisition. If none is required, explain why.

3. Analyze the acquisition to determine the amount of goodwill that was purchased.

4. Should London Company's assets be included on the consolidated balance sheet at book value or market value? Explain.

SUGGESTED SOLUTION FOR CASE E

1. Jan. 1, 2007   Investment in Subsidiary (+A) 85,000
                             Cash (−A) 85,000

2. London Company does not record a journal entry related to the purchase of its stock by Connaught Company. The transaction was between Connaught and the stockholders of London Company; it did not directly involve London Company.

3.

Purchase price for London Company	$85,000
Market value of net assets purchased	79,000
Goodwill	$ 6,000

4. London Company's assets should be included on the consolidated balance sheet at their market values **as of the date of acquisition.** The cost principle applies as it does with all asset acquisitions.

1. **Analyze and report bond investments held to maturity.**   p. 606

When management intends to hold a bond investment until it matures, the held-to-maturity bond is recorded at cost when acquired and reported at amortized cost on the balance sheet. Any interest earned during the period is reported on the income statement.

2. **Analyze and report passive investments in securities using the market value method.**   p. 607
   - Acquiring less than 20 percent of the outstanding voting shares of an investee's common stock is presumed to be a passive stock investment. Passive investments may be classified as
     - Trading securities (actively traded to maximize return) **or**
     - Securities available for sale (earn a return but are not as actively traded), depending on management's intent.
   - The investments are recorded at cost and adjusted to **market value** at year-end. A valuation allowance is increased or decreased to arrive at market value with the resulting unrealized holding gain or loss recorded.
     - For trading securities, the net unrealized gains and losses are reported in net income.
     - For securities available for sale, the net unrealized gains and losses are reported as a component of stockholders' equity in other comprehensive income.
   - Any dividends earned are reported as revenue, and any gains or losses on sales of passive investments are reported on the income statement.

3. **Analyze and report investments involving significant influence using the equity method.**   p. 615

If between 20 and 50 percent of the outstanding voting shares are owned, significant influence over the investee firm's operating and financing policies is presumed, and the equity method is applied. Under the **equity method,** the investor records the investment at cost on the acquisition date. Each period thereafter, the investment amount is increased (or decreased) by the proportionate interest in the income (or loss) reported by the investee corporation and decreased by the proportionate share of the dividends declared by the investee corporation.

The investing section of the statement of cash flows discloses purchases and sales of investments. In the operating section, net income is adjusted for any gains or losses on sales of investments and equity in the earnings of associated companies (net of dividends received).

4. **Analyze and report investments in controlling interests.**   p. 621

Mergers occur when one company purchases all of the net assets of another and the target company ceases to exist as a separate legal entity. Mergers and ownership of a controlling interest of another corporation (more than 50 percent of the outstanding voting shares) must be accounted for using the purchase method. In conformity with the cost principle, the investee's assets and liabilities are measured at their market values. Any amount paid above the market value of the net assets is reported as goodwill by the investor. The concept of consolidation is based on the view that a parent company and its subsidiaries constitute one economic entity. Therefore, the separate income statements, balance sheets, and statements of cash flows should be combined each period on an item-by-item basis as a single set of consolidated financial statements. Consolidated statements are the same as those that result from a merger when all of the assets and liabilities are acquired and the target company ceases to exist.

5. **Analyze and interpret the return on assets ratio.**   p. 625

The return on assets ratio measures how much the company earned for each dollar of assets. It provides information on profitability and management's effectiveness with an increasing ratio over time suggesting increased efficiency. ROA is computed as net income divided by average total assets.

Each year, many companies report healthy profits but file for bankruptcy. Some investors consider this situation to be a paradox, but sophisticated analysts understand how this situation can occur. These analysts recognize that the income statement is prepared under the accrual concept (revenue is reported when earned and the related expense is matched with the revenue). The income statement does not report cash collections and cash payments. Troubled companies usually file for bankruptcy because they cannot meet their cash obligations (for example, they cannot pay their suppliers or meet their required interest payments). The income statement does not help analysts assess the cash flows of a company. The statement of cash flows discussed in Chapter 13 is designed to help statement users evaluate a company's cash inflows and outflows.

KEY **RATIO**

Return on assets measures how much the company earned on every dollar of assets during the period. A high or rising ratio suggests that the company is managing its assets efficiently. It is computed as follows (p. 625):

$$\text{Return on Assets (ROA)} = \frac{\text{Net Income}}{\text{Average Total Assets}^*}$$

*(Beginning Total Assets + Ending Total Assets) ÷ 2

FINDING **FINANCIAL INFORMATION**

Balance Sheet

Current Assets
  Investment in trading securities
    (net of valuation allowance)
  Investment in securities available for sale
    (net of valuation allowance)

Noncurrent Assets
  Investment in securities available
    for sale (net of valuation allowance)
  Investment in associated companies
  Investments held to maturity

Stockholders' Equity
  Accumulated other comprehensive
    income:
    Net unrealized gains and losses on
      securities available for sale

Income Statement

Under "Other Items"
  Investment income
  Loss or gain on sale of investments
  Net unrealized gains and losses on
    trading securities
  Equity in investee earnings or losses

Notes

In Various Notes
  Accounting policies for investments
  Details on securities held as trading and
    available-for-sale securities and
    investments in affiliates

Statement of Cash Flows

Operating Activities
  Net income adjusted for:
  Gains/losses on sale of investments
  Equity in earnings/losses of associated
    companies
  Dividends received from associated
    companies
  Net unrealized gains/losses on trading
    securities

KEY TERMS

Amortized Cost Method   p. 606
Consolidated Financial
   Statements   p. 622
Equity Method   p. 615
Goodwill (Cost in
   Excess of Net Assets
   Acquired)   p. 623

Held-to-Maturity
   Investments   p. 606
Investments in Affiliates
   or Associated Companies   p. 616
Market Value Method   p. 607
Merger   p. 622
Parent Company   p. 622

Purchase Method   p. 623
Securities Available
   for Sale   p. 608
Subsidiary Company   p. 622
Trading Securities   p. 608
Unrealized Holding
   Gains or Losses   p. 608

QUESTIONS

1. Explain the difference between a short-term investment and a long-term investment.
2. Explain the difference in accounting methods used for passive investments, investments in which the investor can exert significant influence, and investments in which the investor has control over another entity.
3. Explain how bonds held to maturity are reported on the balance sheet.
4. Explain the application of the cost principle to the purchase of capital stock in another company.
5. Under the market value method, when and how does the investor company measure revenue?
6. Under the equity method, why does the investor company measure revenue on a proportionate basis when income is reported by the investee company rather than when dividends are declared?
7. Under the equity method, dividends received from the investee company are not recorded as revenue. To record dividends as revenue involves double counting. Explain.
8. What is a business combination by purchase?
9. What is goodwill?
10. What is a parent–subsidiary relationship?
11. Explain the basic concept underlying consolidated statements.
12. What is the basic element that must be present before consolidated statements are appropriate?
13. (Supplement A) What are intercompany eliminations?

MULTIPLE-CHOICE QUESTIONS

1. Company A owns 40 percent of Company B and exercises significant influence over the management of Company B. Therefore, Company A uses what method of accounting for reporting its ownership of stock in Company B?
   a. The amortized cost method.
   b. The market-value method.
   c. The equity method.
   d. Consolidation of the financial statements of companies A and B.
2. Company A purchases 10 percent of Company X and Company A intends to hold the stock for at least five years. At the end of the current year, how would Company A's investment in Company X be reported on Company A's December 31 (year-end) balance sheet?
   a. At original cost in the current assets section.
   b. At the December 31 market value in the current assets section.
   c. At original cost in the long-term assets section.
   d. At the December 31 market value in the long-term assets section.
3. Dividends received from a stock that is reported as a security available for sale in the long-term assets section of the balance sheet are reported as which of the following?
   a. An increase to cash and a decrease to the investment in stock account.
   b. An increase to cash and an unrealized gain on the balance sheet.
   c. An increase to cash and an increase to revenue.
   d. An increase to cash and an unrealized gain on the income statement.

4. Realized gains and losses are recorded on the income statement for which of the following transactions in trading securities and available-for-sale securities?
   a. When adjusting a trading security to its market value.
   b. When adjusting an available-for-sale security to its market value.
   c. Only when recording the sale of a trading security.
   d. When recording the sale of either a trading security or an available-for-sale security.

5. When recording dividends received from a stock investment accounted for using the equity method, which of the following statements is true?
   a. Total assets are increased and net income is increased.
   b. Total assets are increased and total shareholders' equity is increased.
   c. Total assets are decreased and total shareholders' equity is decreased.
   d. Total assets and total owners' equity do not change.

6. When using the equity method of accounting, when is revenue recorded on the books of the investor company?
   a. When the market value of the investee stock increases.
   b. When a dividend is received from the investee.
   c. When the investee company reports net income.
   d. Both (b) and (c).

7. Kelly Company acquired 500 shares of stock of Drucker Company at $60 per share as a long-term investment. This represents 10 percent of the outstanding voting shares of Drucker. During the year, Drucker paid stockholders $2 per share in dividends. At year-end, Drucker reported net income of $40,000. Drucker's stock price at the end of the year was $63 per share. The amount of investments reported on the balance sheet at year-end and the amount reported on the income statement for the year are:

	Balance Sheet	Income Statement
a.	$31,500	$1,000
b.	$30,000	$1,000
c.	$33,000	$4,000
d.	$31,500	$4,000

8. Kelly Company acquired 500 shares of stock of Drucker Company at $60 per share as a long-term investment. This represents 40 percent of the outstanding voting shares of Drucker. During the year, Drucker paid stockholders $2 per share in dividends. At year-end, Drucker reported net income of $40,000. Drucker's stock price at the end of the year was $63 per share. The amount of investments reported on the balance sheet at year-end and the amount reported on the income statement for the year are:

	Balance Sheet	Income Statement
a.	$31,500	$ 1,000
b.	$45,000	$16,000
c.	$31,000	$ 0
d.	$31,500	$16,000

9. Which of the following is true regarding the return on assets ratio?
   a. This ratio is used to evaluate the efficiency of a company given the capital contributed by owners.
   b. This ratio is used to evaluate the financing strategy of a company.
   c. Return on assets can be separated into two components, net profit margin and inventory turnover.
   d. This ratio is used to evaluate how efficiently a company manages its total assets.

10. Consolidated financial statements are required in which of the following situations?
   a. Only when a company can exert significant influence over another company.
   b. Only when a company acquires goodwill in the purchase of another company.
   c. Only when a parent company can exercise control over its subsidiary.
   d. Only when a company acquires another company for vertical integration.

For more practice on more multiple-choice questions, go to the text website www.mhhe.com/libby6e.

MINI-**EXERCISES**

Matching Measurement and Reporting Methods

Match the following. Answers may be used more than once:

M12-1
LO1, 2, 3, 4

Measurement Method

A. Market value method
B. Equity method
C. Consolidation
D. Amortized cost

____ 1. More than 50 percent ownership
____ 2. Bonds held to maturity
____ 3. Less than 20 percent ownership
____ 4. At least 20 percent but not more than 50 percent ownership
____ 5. Current market value
____ 6. Original cost less any amortization of premium or discount associated with the purchase
____ 7. Original cost plus proportionate part of the income of the investee less proportionate part of the dividends declared by the investee

Recording a Bond Investment

Wall Company purchased $1,200,000, 7 percent bonds issued by Janice Company on January 1, 2010. The purchase price of the bonds was $1,250,000. Interest is payable semiannually each June 30 and December 31. Record the purchase of the bonds on January 1, 2010.

M12-2
LO1

Recording Trading Securities Transactions

During 2011, Princeton Company acquired some of the 50,000 outstanding shares of the common stock, par $12, of Cox Corporation as trading securities. The accounting period for both companies ends December 31. Give the journal entries for each of the following transactions that occurred during 2011:

M12-3
LO2

Dec. 2   Purchased 7,500 shares of Cox common stock at $28 per share.

Dec. 15   Cox Corporation declared and paid a cash dividend of $3 per share.

Dec. 31   Determined the current market price of Cox stock to be $23 per share.

Recording Available-for-Sale Securities Transactions

Using the data in M12–3, assume that Princeton Company purchased the voting stock of Cox Corporation for the available-for-sale portfolio instead of the trading securities portfolio. Give the journal entries for each of the transactions listed.

M12-4
LO2

Determining Financial Statement Effects of Trading Securities Transactions

Using the following categories, indicate the effects of the transactions listed in M12–3 assuming trading securities. Use + for increase and − for decrease and indicate the amounts.

M12-5
LO2

	Balance Sheet			Income Statement		
Transaction	Assets	Liabilities	Stockholders' Equity	Revenues	Expenses	Net Income

Determining Financial Statement Effects of Available-for-Sale Securities Transactions

Using the following categories, indicate the effects of the transactions listed in M12–3 assuming securities available for sale. Use + for increase and − for decrease and indicate the amounts.

M12-6
LO2

	Balance Sheet			Income Statement		
Transaction	Assets	Liabilities	Stockholders' Equity	Revenues	Expenses	Net Income

M12-7
LO3

Recording Equity Method Securities Transactions

On January 1, 2011, Ubuy.com acquired 30 percent (1,200,000 shares) of the common stock of E-Net Corporation. The accounting period for both companies ends December 31. Give the journal entries for each of the following transactions that occurred during 2011:

July 2   E-Net declared and paid a cash dividend of $5 per share.

Dec. 31   E-Net reported net income of $200,000

M12-8
LO3

Determining Financial Statement Effects of Equity Method Securities

Using the following categories, indicate the effects of the transactions listed in M12–7. Use + for increase and − for decrease and indicate the accounts affected and the amounts.

	Balance Sheet			Income Statement		
Transaction	Assets	Liabilities	Stockholders' Equity	Revenues	Expenses	Net Income

M12-9
LO4

Recording a Merger

Philadelphia Textile Company acquired Boston Fabric Company for $590,000 cash when Boston's only assets, property and equipment, had a book value of $590,000 and a market value of $650,000. Philadelphia also assumed Boston's bonds payable of $125,000. After the acquisition, Boston would cease to exist as a separate legal entity after merging with Philadelphia. Record the acquisition.

M12-10
LO5

Computing and Interpreting Return on Assets Ratio

M.A.D. Company reported the following information at the end of each year:

Year	Net Income	Total Assets
2009	$150,500	$ 54,000
2010	196,000	70,000
2011	200,000	130,000
2012	211,500	143,000

Compute return on assets for 2010, 2011, and 2012. What do the results suggest about M.A.D. Company?

M12-11
The Walt Disney
Company

(Supplement A) Interpreting Goodwill Disclosures

Disney owns theme parks, movie studios, television and radio stations, newspapers, and television networks, including ABC and ESPN. Its balance sheet recently reported goodwill in the amount of $22 billion, which is more than 33 percent of the company's total assets. This percentage is very large compared to that of most companies. Explain why you think Disney has such a large amount of goodwill reported on its balance sheet.

EXERCISES   **Available with McGraw-Hill's Homework Manager**

E12-1
LO1
Macy's

Recording Bonds Held to Maturity

Macy's, Inc., operates over 850 Macy's and Bloomingdale's department stores nationwide. The company does more than $26 billion in sales each year.

Assume that as part of its cash management strategy, Macy's purchased $10 million in bonds at par for cash on July 1, 2010. The bonds pay 10 percent interest annually with payments each June 30 and December 31 and mature in 10 years. Macy's plans to hold the bonds until maturity.

Required:
1. Record the purchase of the bonds on July 1, 2010.
2. Record the receipt of interest on December 31, 2010.

Comparing Market Value and Equity Methods

E12-2
LO2, 3

Company A purchased a certain number of Company B's outstanding voting shares at $20 per share as a long-term investment. Company B had outstanding 20,000 shares of $10 par value stock. Complete the following table relating to the measurement and reporting by Company A after acquisition of the shares of Company B stock.

Questions	Market Value Method	Equity Method
a. What is the applicable level of ownership by Company A of Company B to apply the method?	_____ %	_____ %

For *b*, *e*, *f*, and *g*, assume the following:

Number of shares acquired of Company B stock	1,500	5,000
Net income reported by Company B in the first year	$59,000	$59,000
Dividends declared by Company B in the first year	$12,000	$12,000
Market price at end of first year, Company B stock	$ 17	$ 17

	Market Value Method	Equity Method
b. At acquisition, the investment account on the books of Company A should be debited at what amount?	$_____	$_____
c. When should Company A recognize revenue earned on the stock of Company B? Explanation required.	_____	_____
d. After the acquisition date, how should Company A change the balance of the investment account net of the allowance with respect to the stock owned in Company B (other than for disposal of the investment)? Explanation required.	_____	_____
e. What is the net balance in the investment account on the balance sheet of Company A at the end of the first year?	$_____	$_____
f. What amount of revenue from the investment in Company B should Company A report at the end of the first year?	$_____	$_____
g. What amount of unrealized loss should Company A report at the end of the first year?	$_____	$_____

Recording Transactions in the Trading Securities Portfolio

E12-3
LO2

On June 30, 2010, MetroMedia, Inc., purchased 7,000 shares of Mitek stock for $20 per share. Management purchased the stock for speculative purposes and recorded the stock in the trading securities portfolio. The following information pertains to the price per share of Mitek stock:

	Price
12/31/2010	$24
12/31/2011	31
12/31/2012	25

MetroMedia sold all of the Mitek stock on February 14, 2013, at a price of $23 per share. Prepare any journal entries that are required by the facts presented in this case.

Recording Transactions in the Available-for-Sale Portfolio

E12-4
LO2

Using the data in E12–3, assume that MetroMedia management purchased the Mitek stock for the available-for-sale portfolio instead of the trading securities portfolio. Prepare any journal entries that are required by the facts presented in the case.

Reporting Gains and Losses in the Trading Securities Portfolio

E12-5
LO2

On March 10, 2009, General Solutions, Inc., purchased 10,000 shares of MicroTech stock for $45 per share. Management purchased the stock for speculative purposes and recorded it in the trading securities portfolio. The following information pertains to the price per share of MicroTech stock:

	Price
12/31/2009	$50
12/31/2010	35
12/31/2011	37

General Solutions sold all of the MicroTech stock on September 12, 2012, at a price of $34 per share. Prepare any journal entries that are required by the facts presented in this case.

E12-6

LO2

Reporting Gains and Losses in the Available-for-Sale Portfolio

Using the data in E12–5, assume that General Solutions management purchased the MicroTech stock for the available-for-sale portfolio instead of the trading securities portfolio. Prepare any journal entries that are required by the facts presented in the case.

E12-7

LO3

Recording and Reporting an Equity Method Security

Felicia Company acquired some of the 65,000 shares of outstanding common stock (no-par) of Nueces Corporation during 2011 as a long-term investment. The annual accounting period for both companies ends December 31. The following transactions occurred during 2011:

Jan.   10   Purchased 22,750 shares of Nueces common stock at $11 per share.

Dec. 31   a. Received the 2011 financial statements of Nueces Corporation that reported net income of $80,000.

b. Nueces Corporation declared and paid a cash dividend of $0.60 per share.

c. Determined the market price of Nueces stock to be $10 per share.

Required:
1. What accounting method should the company use? Why?
2. Give the journal entries for each of these transactions. If no entry is required, explain why.
3. Show how the long-term investment and the related revenue should be reported on the 2011 financial statements (balance sheet and income statement) of the company.

E12-8

LO3

Interpreting the Effects of Equity Method Investments on Cash Flow from Operations

Using the data in E12–7, answer the following questions.

Required:
1. On the current year cash flow statement, how would the investing section of the statement be affected by the preceding transactions?
2. On the current year cash flow statement (indirect method), how would the equity in the earnings of the affiliated company and the dividends from the affiliated company affect the operating section? Explain the reasons for the effects.

E12-9

LO4

Determining the Appropriate Accounting Treatment for an Acquisition

The notes to recent financial statements of Colgate-Palmolive contained the following information:

The Colgate-Palmolive Company

2. Acquisitions

On December 18, the Company agreed to acquire GABA Holding AG (GABA), a privately owned European oral care company headquartered in Switzerland. The transaction is structured as an all-cash acquisition of between 80% and 100% of the outstanding shares of GABA for an aggregate price ranging from 800 million Swiss francs to 1,050 million Swiss francs (approximately $645.0 to $846.5 based on December 31, exchange rates). . . .

Assume that Colgate-Palmolive acquired 100 percent of the fair value of the net assets of GABA in the recent year for $700 million in cash. GABA's assets at the time of the acquisition had a book value of $510 million and a market value of $550 million. Colgate-Palmolive also assumed GABA's liabilities of $170 million (book value and market value are the same). Prepare the entry on the date of the acquisition assuming it is a merger.

Analyzing and Interpreting the Return on Assets Ratio

Timberland is a leading designer of shoes and clothing. In a recent year, it reported the following:

	Current Year	Prior Year
Revenue	$1,342,123	$1,190,896
Net income	117,879	95,113
Total assets	641,716	538,671
Total stockholders' equity	428,463	372,785

Required:
1. Determine the return on assets ratio for the current year.
2. Explain the meaning of the ratio.

E12-10
LO5
Timberland

(Supplement A) Interpreting Consolidation Policy

Toyota Motor Corporation produces passenger car brands Lexus, Toyota, and Scion. A recent annual report includes the statement that "The consolidated financial statements include the accounts of the parent company and those of its majority-owned subsidiary companies." It then suggests that "All significant intercompany transactions and accounts have been eliminated." In your own words, explain the meaning of this last statement. Why is it necessary to eliminate all intercompany accounts and transactions in consolidation?

E12-11

(Supplement A) Analyzing Goodwill and Reporting the Consolidated Balance Sheet

E12-12

On January 1, 2010, Company P purchased 100 percent of the outstanding voting shares of Company S in the open market for $80,000 cash. On that date, the separate balance sheets (summarized) of the two companies reported the following book values:

	IMMEDIATELY AFTER THE ACQUISITION JANUARY 1, 2010	
	Company P	Company S
Cash	$ 11,500	$17,500
Investment in Co. S (at cost)	80,000	
Property and equipment (net)	31,000	41,500
Total assets	$122,500	$59,000
Liabilities	$ 41,000	$10,000
Common stock:		
Company P (no-par)	77,000	
Company S (par $10)		40,500
Retained earnings	4,500	8,500
Total liabilities and stockholders' equity	$122,500	$59,000

It was determined on the date of acquisition that the market value of the assets and liabilities of Company S were equal to their book values.

Required:
1. Give the journal entry that Company P made at date of acquisition to record the investment. If none is required, explain why.
2. Analyze the acquisition to determine the amount of goodwill purchased.
3. Prepare a consolidated balance sheet immediately after acquisition.

(Supplement A) Determining Consolidated Net Income

E12-13

Assume that P Company acquired S Company on January 1, 2011, for $110,000 cash. At the time, the net book value of S Company was $86,000. The market value was $95,000 with property and equipment having a market value of $9,000 over book value. The property and equipment has a three-year remaining life and is depreciated straight-line with no residual value. During 2011, the companies reported the following operating results:

	P Company	S Company
Revenues related to their own operations	$460,000	$80,000
Expenses related to their own operations	340,000	60,000

Compute consolidated net income for the year ended December 31, 2011.

PROBLEMS

 Available with McGraw-Hill's Homework Manager

P12-1
LO1
Starbucks Corporation

Determining Financial Statement Effects for Bonds Held to Maturity (AP12-1)

Starbucks is a rapidly expanding company that provides high-quality coffee products. Assume that as part of its expansion strategy, Starbucks plans to open numerous new stores in Mexico in five years. The company has $5 million to support the expansion and has decided to invest the funds in corporate bonds until the money is needed. Assume that Starbucks purchased bonds with $5 million face value at par for cash on July 1, 2011. The bonds pay 8 percent interest each June 30 and December 31 and mature in five years. Starbucks plans to hold the bonds until maturity.

Required:
1. What accounts are affected when the bonds are purchased on July 1, 2011?
2. What accounts are affected when interest is received on December 31, 2011?
3. Should Starbucks prepare a journal entry if the market value of the bonds decreased to $4,000,000 on December 31, 2011? Explain.

P12-2
LO2

www.mhhe.com/libby6e

Recording Passive Investments (AP12–2)

On March 1, 2009, HiTech Industries purchased 10,000 shares of Integrated Services Company for $17 per share. The following information applies to the stock price of Integrated Services:

	Price
12/31/2009	$15
12/31/2010	21
12/31/2011	27

Required:
1. Prepare journal entries to record the facts in the case, assuming that HiTech purchased the shares for the trading portfolio.
2. Prepare journal entries to record the facts in the case, assuming that HiTech purchased the shares for the available-for-sale portfolio.

P12-3
LO2

Reporting Passive Investments (AP12–3)

During January 2011, Nash Glass Company purchased the following shares as a long-term investment:

Stock	Number of Shares Outstanding	Shares Purchased	Cost per Share
Q Corporation Common (no-par)	95,000	11,000	$ 9
R Corporation Preferred, nonvoting (par $10)	25,000	11,300	26

Subsequent to acquisition, the following data were available:

	2011	2012
Net income reported at December 31		
Q Corporation	$31,000	$41,000
R Corporation	36,000	55,000
Dividends declared and paid per share during the year		
Q Corporation common stock	$ 0.70	$ 0.75
R Corporation preferred stock	0.75	0.75
Market value per share at December 31		
Q Corporation common stock	$ 8.00	$ 8.00
R Corporation preferred stock	25.00	26.00

Required:

1. What accounting method should be used for the investment in Q common stock? R preferred stock? Why?
2. Give the journal entries for the company for each year in parallel columns (if none, explain why) for each of the following:
   a. Purchase of the investments.
   b. Income reported by Q and R Corporations.
   c. Dividends received from Q and R Corporations.
   d. Market value effects at year-end.
3. For each year, show how the following amounts should be reported on the financial statements:
   a. Long-term investment.
   b. Stockholders' equity—net unrealized gains and losses.
   c. Revenues.

Recording Passive Investments and Investments for Significant Influence

On August 4, 2010, Coffman Corporation purchased 3,000 shares of Dittman Company for $150,000. The following information applies to the stock price of Dittman Company:

P12-4
LO2, 3
eXcel
www.mhhe.com/libby6e

	Price
12/31/2010	$57
12/31/2011	52
12/31/2012	43

Dittman Company declares and pays cash dividends of $1 per share on June 1 of each year.

Required:

1. Prepare journal entries to record the facts in the case, assuming that Coffman purchased the shares for the trading portfolio.
2. Prepare journal entries to record the facts in the case, assuming that Coffman purchased the shares for the available-for-sale portfolio.
3. Prepare journal entries to record the facts in the case, assuming that Coffman used the equity method to account for the investment. Coffman owns 30 percent of Dittman and Dittman reported $45,000 in income each year.

Comparing Methods to Account for Various Levels of Ownership of Voting Stock

Company C had outstanding 25,000 shares of common stock, par value $10 per share. On January 1, 2010, Company D purchased some of these shares as a long-term investment at $25 per share. At the end of 2010, Company C reported the following: income, $45,000, and cash dividends declared and paid during the year, $21,250. The market value of Company C stock at the end of 2010 was $22 per share.

P12-5
LO2, 3
eXcel
www.mhhe.com/libby6e

Required:

1. For each of the following cases (in the tabulation), identify the method of accounting that Company D should use. Explain why.
2. Give the journal entries for Company D at the dates indicated for each of the two independent cases, assuming that the investments will be held long term. If no entry is required, explain why. Use the following format:

Tabulation of Items	Case A: 3,000 Shares Purchased	Case B: 8,750 Shares Purchased

1. Accounting method?
2. Journal entries:
   a. To record the acquisition at January 1, 2010.
   b. To recognize the income reported by Company C for 2010.
   c. To recognize the dividends declared and paid by Company C.
   d. Entry to recognize market value effect at end of 2010.
3. Complete the following schedule to show the separate amounts that should be reported on the 2010 financial statements of Company D:

	DOLLAR AMOUNTS	
	Case A	Case B
Balance sheet		
Investments		
Stockholders' equity		
Income statement		
Investment income		
Equity in earnings of investee		

4. Explain why assets, stockholders' equity, and revenues for the two cases are different.

P12-6
LO2, 3

www.mhhe.com/libby6e

Comparing the Market Value and Equity Methods (AP12-4)

Ship Corporation had outstanding 100,000 shares of no-par common stock. On January 10, 2011, Shore Company purchased a block of these shares in the open market at $20 per share for long-term investment purposes. At the end of 2011, Ship reported net income of $320,000 and cash dividends of $0.60 per share. At December 31, 2011, Ship stock was selling at $18 per share. This problem involves two separate cases:

Case A Purchase of 10,000 shares of Ship common stock.

Case B Purchase of 40,000 shares of Ship common stock.

Required:

1. For each case, identify the accounting method that the company should use. Explain why.
2. For each case, in parallel columns, give the journal entries for each of the following (if no entry is required, explain why):
   a. Acquisition.
   b. Revenue recognition.
   c. Dividends received.
   d. Market value effects.
3. For each case, show how the following should be reported on the 2011 financial statements:
   a. Long-term investments.
   b. Shareholders' equity.
   c. Revenues.
4. Explain why the amounts reported in requirement (3) are different for the two cases.

Determining Cash Flow Statement Effects of Investments for Significant Influence
(AP12-5)

P12-7
LO3

During 2011, Oscar Company purchased some of the 90,000 shares of common stock, par $6, of Selma, Inc., as a long-term investment. The annual accounting period for each company ends December 31. The following transactions occurred during 2011:

Jan. 7   Purchased 40,500 shares of Selma stock at $35 per share.
Dec. 31   a. Received the 2011 financial statement of Selma, which reported net income of
          $205,000.
      b. Selma declared and paid a cash dividend of $2.50 per share.
      c. Determined that the current market price of Selma stock was $39 per share.

Required:
Indicate how the Operating Activities and Investing Activities sections of the cash flow statement (indirect method) will be affected by each transaction.

Analyzing Goodwill and Reporting a Merger (AP12-6)

P12-8
LO4

On January 4, 2010, Pronti Company acquired all of the net assets of Scott Company for $124,000 cash. The two companies merged with Pronti Company surviving. The balance sheets for each company prior to the merger follow.

Balance Sheets at January 4, 2011	Pronti Company	Scott Company
Cash	$118,000	$23,000
Property and equipment (net)	132,000	65,000*
Total assets	$250,000	$88,000
Liabilities	$ 27,000	$12,000
Common stock (par $5)	120,000	40,000
Retained earnings	103,000	36,000
Total liabilities and stockholders' equity	$250,000	$88,000

Determined by Pronti Company to have a market value of $72,000 at date of acquisition.

Required:
1. How much goodwill was involved in this merger? Show computations.
2. Record the merger by Pronti Company on January 4, 2010.
3. Prepare a consolidated balance sheet immediately after the acquisition.

Interpreting the Return on Assets Ratio (AP12-7)

P12-9
LO5
Verizon
Communications, Inc.

Verizon Communications Inc. was formed by the merger of Bell Atlantic Corporation and GTE Corporation in 2000. It is the largest provider of wireline and wireless communication services in the United States with presence in over 150 other countries. The following information was reported in the company's 2006 annual report:

	(DOLLARS IN MILLIONS)			
	2006	2005	2004	2003
Net income	$ 6,197	$ 7,397	$ 7,831	$ 3,077
Total assets	188,804	168,130	165,958	165,968

Required:
1. Compute the return on assets ratio for 2006, 2005, and 2004.
2. What do the results in requirement (1) suggest about Verizon?

P12-10 **(Supplement A) Analyzing Goodwill and Reporting the Consolidated Balance Sheet**

On January 4, 2011, Penn Company acquired all 8,000 outstanding shares of Syracuse Company for $12 cash per share. Immediately after the acquisition, the balance sheets reflected the following:

Balance Sheets at January 4, 2011	Penn Company	Syracuse Company
Cash	$ 22,000	$23,000
Investment in Syracuse Company	96,000	
Property and equipment (net)	132,000	65,000*
Total assets	$250,000	$88,000
Liabilities	$ 27,000	$12,000
Common stock (par $5)	120,000	40,000
Retained earnings	103,000	36,000
Total liabilities and stockholders' equity	$250,000	$88,000

* Determined by Penn Company to have a market value of $72,000 at date of acquisition.

Required:
1. Give the journal entry that Penn Company made to record the acquisition.
2. Analyze the acquisition to determine the amount of goodwill purchased.
3. Should Syracuse Company's assets be included on the consolidated balance sheet at book value or market value? Explain.
4. Prepare a consolidated balance sheet immediately after acquisition. (**Hint:** Consider your answer to requirement 3.)

ALTERNATE PROBLEMS

AP12-1
L01
Sonic Corp.

Determining Financial Statement Effects for Bonds Held to Maturity (P12-1)

Sonic Corp. operates and franchises a chain of quick-service drive-in restaurants in most of the United States and in Mexico. Customers drive up to a canopied parking space and order food through an intercom speaker system. A carhop then delivers the food to the customer. Assume that Sonic has $10 million in cash to support future expansion and has decided to invest the funds in corporate bonds until the money is needed. Sonic purchases bonds with $10 million face value for $10.3 million cash on January 1, 2011. The bonds pay 8 percent interest annually with payments each June 30 and December 31 and mature in four years. Sonic plans to hold the bonds until maturity.

Required:
1. What accounts were affected when the bonds were purchased on January 1, 2011?
2. What accounts were affected when interest was received on June 30, 2011?
3. Should Sonic prepare a journal entry if the market value of the bonds decreased to $9,700,000 on December 31, 2011? Explain.

AP12-2
L02

Recording Passive Investments (P12–2)

On September 15, 2010, James Media Corporation purchased 5,000 shares of Community Broadcasting Company for $32 per share. The following information applies to the stock price of Community Broadcasting:

	Price
12/31/2010	$34
12/31/2011	25
12/31/2012	21

Required:
1. Prepare journal entries to record the facts in the case, assuming that James Media purchased the shares for the trading portfolio.

2. Prepare journal entries to record the facts in the case, assuming that James Media purchased the shares for the available-for-sale portfolio.

Reporting Passive Investments (P12–3)

AP12-3
LO2

During January 2011, Hexagon Company purchased 12,000 shares of the 200,000 outstanding common shares (no-par value) of Seven Corporation at $30 per share. This block of stock was purchased as a long-term investment. Assume that the accounting period for each company ends December 31. Subsequent to acquisition, the following data were available:

	2011	2012
Income reported by Seven Corporation at December 31	$40,000	$60,000
Cash dividends declared and paid by Seven Corporation during the year	60,000	80,000
Market price per share of Seven common stock on December 31	28	29

Required:
1. What accounting method should the company use? Why?
2. Give the journal entries for the company for each year (use parallel columns) for the following (if none, explain why):
   a. Acquisition of Seven Corporation stock.
   b. Net income reported by Seven Corporation.
   c. Dividends received from Seven Corporation.
   d. Market value effects at year-end.
3. Show how the following amounts should be reported on the financial statements for each year:
   a. Long-term investment.
   b. Stockholders' equity—net unrealized gain/loss.
   c. Revenues.

Comparing the Market Value and Equity Methods (P12–6)

AP12-4
LO2, 3

Packer Company purchased, as a long-term investment, some of the 200,000 shares of the outstanding common stock of Boston Corporation. The annual accounting period for each company ends December 31. The following transactions occurred during 2012:

Jan. 10   Purchased shares of common stock of Boston at $15 per share as follows:
          Case A—30,000 shares.
          Case B—80,000 shares.
Dec. 31   a. Received the 2012 financial statements of Boston Corporation; the reported net income was $90,000.
          b. Received a cash dividend of $0.60 per share from Boston Corporation
          c. Determined that the current market price of Boston stock was $9 per share.

Required:
1. For each case, identify the accounting method that the company should use. Explain why.
2. Give the journal entries for each case for these transactions. If no entry is required, explain why.
   (**Hint:** Use parallel columns for Case A and Case B.)
3. Give the amounts for each case that should be reported on the 2012 financial statements. Use the following format:

	Case A	Case B
Balance sheet (partial)		
Investments		
Investments in common stock, Boston Corporation		
Stockholders' equity		
Net unrealized gain or loss		
Income statement (partial)		
Investment income		
Equity in earnings of investee		

AP12-5
LO2, 3
Determining Cash Flow Statement Effects of Passive Investments and Investments for Significant Influence (P12-7)

For each of the transactions in AP12-4, indicate how the operating activities and investing activities sections of the cash flow statement (indirect method) will be affected.

AP12-6
LO4
Analyzing Goodwill and Reporting a Merger (P12-8)

On June 1, 2011, Kappa Company acquired all of the net assets of Delta Company for $120,000 cash. The two companies merged with Kappa Company surviving. The balance sheets for each company prior to the merger follow.

Balance Sheets at June 1, 2011	Kappa Company	Delta Company
Cash	$176,000	$ 13,000
Property and equipment (net)	352,000	165,000*
Total assets	$528,000	$178,000
Liabilities	$ 93,000	$ 82,000
Common stock (par $1)	250,000	65,000
Retained earnings	185,000	31,000
Total liabilities and stockholders' equity	$528,000	$178,000

* *Determined by Kappa Company to have a market value of $180,000 at date of acquisition.*

Required:
1. How much goodwill was involved in this merger? Show computations.
2. Record the merger by Kappa Company on June 1, 2011.
3. Prepare a consolidated balance sheet immediately after the acquisition.

AP12-7
LO5
Marriott International

Interpreting the Return on Assets Ratio (P12-9)

Marriott International, Inc., is a global leader in the hospitality industry operating or franchising more than 2,800 lodging units and over 2,000 furnished corporate housing units in 68 countries. The following information was reported in the company's 2006 annual report:

	(IN MILLIONS)			
	2006	2005	2004	2003
Net income	$ 608	$ 669	$ 596	$ 502
Total assets	8,588	8,530	8,668	8,177

Required:
1. Compute the return on assets ratio for 2006, 2005, and 2004.
2. What do the results in requirement (1) suggest about Marriott?

CASES **AND PROJECTS**

Annual Report Cases

CP12-1
LO1, 2, 5
AMERICAN EAGLE
OUTFITTERS
Finding Financial Information

Refer to the financial statements of American Eagle Outfitters in Appendix B at the end of this book.

Required:
1. What types of securities were included in the short-term investments reported on the company's balance sheet as of the end of fiscal 2006 (statement dated February 3, 2007)? (**Hint:** The notes to the financial statements may be helpful for this question.)

2. Has the firm increased or decreased its performance as measured by return on assets from fiscal 2005 to 2006? Note that the company's total assets as of January 29, 2005 (the beginning of fiscal 2005) were $1,328,926,000.

3. What was the balance of goodwill reported by the company at February 3, 2007? What does the change in goodwill from January 28, 2006, imply about corporate acquisition activities in the 2006 fiscal year? Do the notes to the financial statements indicate any acquisition or disposition activity in either fiscal 2005 or 2006? If so, what were the activities?

Finding Financial Information

CP12-2
LO1, 2, 5
Urban Outfitters

Refer to the financial statements of Urban Outfitters in Appendix C at the end of this book.

Required:
1. What was the balance in short-term marketable securities reported by the company on January 31, 2007? What types of securities were included in this account? (**Hint:** The notes to the financial statements may be helpful for this question.)
2. How much cash did the company use to purchase marketable securities during the year ended January 31, 2007?
3. Has the firm increased or decreased its performance as measured by return on assets from the prior year to the current year? Note that the company's total assets as of January 31, 2005 (the beginning of the prior year) were $556,684,000.

Comparing Companies within an Industry

CP12-3
LO5

AMERICAN EAGLE
OUTFITTERS
Urban Outfitters

www.mhhe.com/libby6e

Refer to the financial statements of American Eagle Outfitters in Appendix B, Urban Outfitters in Appendix C, and the Industry Ratio Report in Appendix D at the end of this book.

Required:
1. Compute the profit margin, asset turnover, and return on assets ratios for both companies for the most recent reporting year. Which company provided the higher return on its total assets during the current year?
2. Was the difference in ROA due primarily to profitability or efficiency differences? How did you know?
3. Was the return on assets for American Eagle Outfitters and Urban Outfitters higher or lower than the industry average?

Financial Reporting and Analysis Cases

Using Financial Reports: Analyzing the Financial Effects of the Market Value and Equity Methods

CP12-4
LO2, 3

On January 1, 2011, Woodrow Company purchased 30 percent of the outstanding common stock of Trevor Corporation at a total cost of $560,000. Management intends to hold the stock for the long term. On the December 31, 2011, balance sheet, the investment in Trevor Corporation was $720,000, but no additional Trevor stock was purchased. The company received $80,000 in cash dividends from Trevor. The dividends were declared and paid during 2011. The company used the equity method to account for its investment in Trevor. The market price of Trevor stock increased during 2011 to a total value of $600,000.

Required:
1. Explain why the investment account balance increased from $560,000 to $720,000 during 2011.
2. What amount of revenue from the investment was reported during 2011?
3. If Woodrow did not have significant influence over Trevor and used the market value method, what amount of revenue from the investment should have been reported in 2011?
4. If Woodrow did not have significant influence over Trevor and used the market value method, what amount should be reported as the investment in Trevor Corporation on the December 31, 2011, balance sheet?

CP12-5
LO4
Diageo

Using Financial Reports: Interpreting International Goodwill Disclosures

Diageo is a major international company located in London, best known for its Smirnoff, Johnnie Walker, and Bailey's brands of spirits. Its financial statements are accounted for under IFRS. A recent annual report contained the following information concerning its accounting policies.

> Acquired brands and other intangible assets are recognised when they are controlled through contractual or other legal rights, or are separable from the rest of the business, and the fair value can be reliably measured.
>
> Goodwill and intangible assets that are regarded as having indefinite useful economic lives are not amortised. Intangible assets that are regarded as having limited useful economic lives are amortised on a straight-line basis over those lives. Assets with indefinite lives are reviewed for impairment annually and other assets are reviewed for impairment whenever events or circumstances indicate that the carrying amount may not be recoverable. To ensure that goodwill and intangible assets are not carried at above their recoverable amounts, impairment reviews are carried out . . . Amortisation and any impairment write downs are charged in the income statement.

Required:
Discuss how this accounting treatment compares with procedures used in this country.

Critical Thinking Cases

CP12-6
LO4

Evaluating an Ethical Dilemma: Using Inside Information

Assume that you are on the board of directors of a company that has decided to buy 80 percent of the outstanding stock of another company within the next three or four months. The discussions have convinced you that this company is an excellent investment opportunity, so you decide to buy $10,000 worth of the company's stock for your personal portfolio. Is there an ethical problem with your decision? Would your answer be different if you planned to invest $500,000? Are there different ethical considerations if you don't buy the stock but recommend that your brother do so?

CP12-7
LO5

Evaluating an Acquisition from the Standpoint of a Financial Analyst

Assume that you are a financial analyst for a large investment banking firm. You are responsible for analyzing companies in the retail sales industry. You have just learned that a large West Coast retailer has acquired a large East Coast retail chain for a price more than the net book value of the acquired company. You have reviewed the separate financial statements for the two companies before the announcement of the acquisition. You have been asked to write a brief report explaining what will happen when the financial results of the companies are consolidated under the purchase method, including the impact on the return on assets ratio.

Financial Reporting and Analysis Team Project

CP12-8
LO2, 3, 4, 5

Team Project: Examining an Annual Report

As a team, select an industry to analyze. Reuters provides lists of industries and their makeup at **www.reuters.com/finance/industries**. Each team member should acquire the annual report or 10-K for one publicly traded company in the industry, with each member selecting a different company. (Library files, the SEC EDGAR service at **www.sec.gov**, or the company itself are good sources.)

Required:
On an individual basis, each team member should write a short report answering the following questions about the selected company. Discuss any patterns across the companies that you as a team observe. Then, as a team, write a short report comparing and contrasting your companies.

On an individual basis, each team member should write a short report that answers the following questions:

a.   Determine whether the company prepared consolidated financial statements. If so, did it use the purchase method? How do you know?
b.   Does the company use the equity method for any of its investments?
c.   Does the company hold any investments in securities? If so, what is their market value? Does the company have any unrealized gains or losses?
d.   Identify the company's lines of business. Why does management want to engage in these business activities?
e.   Compute the return on assets ratio for the two most recent years reported. What do the results suggest about your company?

LEARNING OBJECTIVES

After studying this chapter, you should be able to:

1. Classify cash flow statement items as part of net cash flows from operating, investing, and financing activities. p. 655

2. Report and interpret cash flows from operating activities using the indirect method. p. 661

3. Analyze and interpret the quality of income ratio. p. 667

4. Report and interpret cash flows from investing activities. p. 668

5. Analyze and interpret the capital acquisitions ratio. p. 670

6. Report and interpret cash flows from financing activities. p. 671

7. Understand the format of the cash flow statement and additional cash flow disclosures. p. 674

Lectured slideshow–LP13-1
www.mhhe.com/libby6e

STATEMENT OF CASH FLOWS

It was no accident when Jim Koch, founder of Boston Beer Company, named his products for Samuel Adams, the American revolutionary who led the Boston Tea Party. When Koch delivered the first 25 cases of Samuel Adams Boston Lager to a Boston bar in 1985, he fired the first shot in a revolution that stunned the brewing industry. At that point, megabrewers such as Anheuser-Busch and Miller dominated beer brewing; annual sales by all small "craft" brewers totaled just over 100,000 barrels. By the year 2006, Boston Beer alone sold more than 1.6 million barrels and reported net income of nearly $18.2 million.

Although it may seem puzzling, growing profitable operations does not always ensure positive cash flow. Also, seasonal fluctuations in sales, purchases of inventory, and advertising expenditures may bring **high profits** and **net cash outflows** in some quarters and **losses** and **net cash inflows** in others. As we have seen in earlier chapters, this occurs because the timing of revenues and expenses does not always match cash inflows and outflows. As a consequence, Boston Beer must carefully manage cash flows as well as profits. For the same reasons, financial analysts must consider the information provided in Boston Beer's cash flow statement in addition to its income statement and balance sheet.

FOCUS COMPANY:

Boston Beer Company

MANAGING PRODUCTION AND CASH FLOWS

IN A SEASONAL BUSINESS

www.bostonbeer.com

UNDERSTANDING THE BUSINESS

Clearly, net income is important, but cash flow is also critical to a company's success. Cash flow permits a company to expand operations, replace worn assets, take advantage of new investment opportunities, and pay dividends to its owners. Some Wall Street analysts go so far as to say "cash flow is king." Both managers and analysts need to understand the various sources and uses of cash that are associated with business activity.

The cash flow statement focuses attention on a firm's ability to generate cash internally, its management of current assets and current liabilities, and the details of its investments and its external financing. It is designed to help both managers and analysts answer important cash-related questions such as these:

- Will the company have enough cash to pay its short-term debts to suppliers and other creditors without additional borrowing?
- Is the company adequately managing its accounts receivable and inventory?
- Has the company made necessary investments in new productive capacity?
- Did the company generate enough cash flow internally to finance necessary investments, or did it rely on external financing?
- Is the company changing the makeup of its external financing?

Boston Beer is a particularly good example to illustrate the importance of the cash flow statement for two reasons. First, like all companies in its industry, Boston Beer's inventory purchases and sales vary with the seasons. This seasonal variation has surprising effects on cash flows and net income. Second, an important element of Boston Beer's business strategy is the outsourcing of much of its product manufacturing. The decision to outsource dramatically affects investments in plant and equipment and the need for external financing.

We begin our discussion with an overview of the statement of cash flows. Then we examine the information reported in each section of the statement in depth. The chapter ends with a discussion of additional cash flow disclosures.

ORGANIZATION of the Chapter

Classifications of the Statement of Cash Flows	Reporting and Interpreting Cash Flows from Operating Activities	Reporting and Interpreting Cash Flows from Investing Activities	Reporting and Interpreting Cash Flows from Financing Activities	Additional Cash Flow Disclosures
■ Cash Flows from Operating Activities ■ Cash Flows from Investing Activities ■ Cash Flows from Financing Activities ■ Net Increase (Decrease) in Cash ■ Relationships to the Balance Sheet and Income Statement	■ Reporting Cash Flows from Operating Activities—Indirect Method ■ Interpreting Cash Flows from Operating Activities ■ Quality of Income Ratio	■ Reporting Cash Flows from Investing Activities ■ Interpreting Cash Flows from Investing Activities ■ Capital Acquisitions Ratio	■ Reporting Cash Flows from Financing Activities ■ Interpreting Cash Flows from Financing Activities	■ Statement Structure ■ Noncash Investing and Financing Activities ■ Supplemental Cash Flow Information ■ Epilogue

CLASSIFICATIONS OF THE STATEMENT OF CASH FLOWS

Basically, the statement of cash flows explains how the amount of cash on the balance sheet at the beginning of the period became the amount of cash reported at the end of the period. For purposes of this statement, the definition of cash includes cash and cash equivalents. **Cash equivalents** are short-term, highly liquid investments that are both

1. Readily convertible to known amounts of cash.
2. So near to maturity there is little risk that their value will change if interest rates change.

Generally, only investments with original maturities of three months or less qualify as a cash equivalent under this definition.[1] Examples of cash equivalents are Treasury bills (a form of short-term U.S. government debt), money market funds, and commercial paper (short-term notes payable issued by large corporations).

As you can see in Exhibit 13.1, the statement of cash flows reports cash inflows and outflows in three broad categories: (1) operating activities, (2) investing activities, and (3) financing activities. Together, these three cash flow categories explain the change from the beginning balance to the ending balance in cash on the balance sheet.

Cash Flows from Operating Activities

Cash flows from operating activities (cash flows from operations) are the cash inflows and outflows that relate directly to revenues and expenses reported on the income statement. There are two alternative approaches for presenting the operating activities section of the statement:

1. The **direct method** reports the components of cash flows from operating activities as gross receipts and gross payments.

Inflows	Outflows
Cash received from	**Cash paid for**
Customers	Purchase of goods for resale and
Dividends and interest on investments	services (electricity, etc.)
	Salaries and wages
	Income taxes
	Interest on liabilities

The difference between the inflows and outflows is called the **net cash inflow (outflow) from operating activities.** Boston Beer experienced a net cash outflow of $2,131 (dollars in thousands) from its operations for the first quarter of 2007. Though the FASB recommends the direct method, it is rarely used in the United States. The direct method is the required format in a number of countries. Many financial executives have reported that they do not use it because it is more expensive to implement than the indirect method.

2. The **indirect method** starts with net income from the income statement and then eliminates noncash items to arrive at net cash inflow (outflow) from operating activities.

Net income
+/− Adjustments for noncash items

Net cash inflow (outflow) from operating activities

Learning Objective 1
Classify cash flow statement items as part of net cash flows from operating, investing, and financing activities.

A CASH EQUIVALENT is a short-term, highly liquid investment with an original maturity of less than three months.

Video 13-1
Audio lecture–AP13-1
www.mhhe.com/libby6e

CASH FLOWS FROM OPERATING ACTIVITIES (cash flows from operations) are cash inflows and outflows directly related to earnings from normal operations.

The DIRECT METHOD of presenting the operating activities section of the cash flow statement reports components of cash flows from operating activities as gross receipts and gross payments.

The INDIRECT METHOD of presenting the operating activities section of the cash flow statement adjusts net income to compute cash flows from operating activities.

---

[1] **Original maturity** means original maturity to the entity holding the investment. For example, both a three-month Treasury bill and a three-year Treasury note purchased three months from maturity qualify as cash equivalents. A Treasury note purchased three years ago, however, does not become a cash equivalent when its remaining maturity is three months.

EXHIBIT 13.1

Consolidated Statement
of Cash Flows

REAL WORLD EXCERPT

The Boston Beer
Company, Inc.

SAMUEL
ADAMS

QUARTERLY REPORT

THE BOSTON BEER COMPANY, INC.
Consolidated Statement of Cash Flows
Three months ended March 31, 2007

(unaudited)
Dollars in Thousands*

Cash flows from operating activities	
Net income	$ 5,768
Adjustments to reconcile net income to net cash	
provided by operating activities:	
Depreciation and amortization	1,726
Changes in assets and liabilities:	
Accounts receivable	(1,967)
Inventory	(1,917)
Prepaid expenses	(1,677)
Accounts payable	(3,320)
Accrued expenses	(744)
Net cash used in operating activities	(2,131)
Cash flows from investing activities	
Purchases of property, plant, and equipment	(1,736)
Proceeds from disposal of property, plant, and equipment	2
Purchase of short-term investments	(802)
Net cash used in investing activities	(2,536)
Cash flows from financing activities	
Purchase of treasury stock	(2,729)
Proceeds from issuance of stock	5,698
Net cash provided by financing activities	2,969
Net decrease in cash and cash equivalents	(1,698)
Cash and cash equivalents at beginning of period	63,147
Cash and cash equivalents at end of period	$ 61,449

Certain amounts have been adjusted to simplify the presentation.

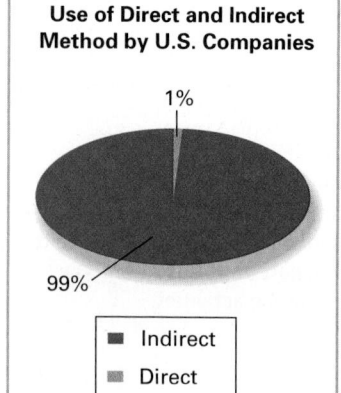

Use of Direct and Indirect Method by U.S. Companies

1%

99%

■ Indirect
■ Direct

Almost 99 percent of large U.S. companies, including Boston Beer, use this method.[2] Notice in Exhibit 13.1 that in the first quarter of 2007, Boston Beer reported positive net income of $5,768 but generated negative cash flows from operating activities of $2,131. Why should income and cash flows from operating activities differ? Remember that on the income statement, revenues are recorded when they are earned, without regard to when the related cash inflows occur. Similarly, expenses are matched with revenues and recorded without regard to when the related cash outflows occur.

For now, the most important thing to remember about the two methods is that they are simply alternative ways to arrive at the same number. The total amount of **cash flows from operating activities is always the same** (an outflow of $2,131 in Boston Beer's case), **regardless of whether it is computed using the direct or indirect method.**

[2]*Accounting Trends & Techniques* (New York: American Institute of CPAs, 2007).

Cash Flows from Investing Activities

Cash flows from investing activities are cash inflows and outflows related to the purchase and disposal of long-lived productive assets and investments in the securities of other companies. Typical cash flows from investing activities include:

Inflows	Outflows
Cash received from	**Cash paid for**
Sale or disposal of property, plant, and equipment	Purchase of property, plant, and equipment
Sale or maturity of investments in securities	Purchase of investments in securities

The difference between these cash inflows and outflows is called **net cash inflow (outflow) from investing activities.**

For Boston Beer, this amount was an outflow of $2,536 for the first quarter of 2007. Most of the activity related to the purchase of property, plant, and equipment and short-term securities. Since purchases exceeded sales (sales were zero), there was a net cash outflow.

CASH FLOWS FROM INVESTING ACTIVITIES are cash inflows and outflows related to the acquisition or sale of productive facilities and investments in the securities of other companies.

Cash Flows from Financing Activities

Cash flows from financing activities include exchanges of cash with creditors (debtholders) and owners (stockholders). Usual cash flows from financing activities include the following:

Inflows	Outflows
Cash received from	**Cash paid for**
Borrowing on notes, mortgages, bonds, etc. from creditors	Repayment of principal to creditors (excluding interest, which is an operating activity)
Issuing stock to owners	Repurchasing stock from owners
	Dividends to owners

The difference between these cash inflows and outflows is called **net cash inflow (outflow) from financing activities.**

Boston Beer experienced a net cash inflow from financing activities of $2,969 for the first quarter of 2007. The Financing Activities section of its statement shows that Boston Beer paid $2,729 to repurchase its stock from owners and received $5,698 for new stock issuances. No dividends were paid and no cash was borrowed or repaid.

CASH FLOWS FROM FINANCING ACTIVITIES are cash inflows and outflows related to external sources of financing (owners and creditors) for the enterprise.

Net Increase (Decrease) in Cash

The combination of **the net cash flows from operating activities, investing activities, and financing activities must equal the net increase (decrease) in cash** for the reporting period. For the first quarter of 2007, Boston Beer reported a net decrease in cash of $1,698, which explains the change in cash on the balance sheet from the beginning balance of $63,147 to the ending balance of $61,449.

Net cash used in operating activities	$ (2,131)
Net cash used in investing activities	(2,536)
Net cash provided by financing activities	2,969
Net decrease in cash and cash equivalents	(1,698)
Cash and cash equivalents at beginning of period	63,147
Cash and cash equivalents at end of period	$ 61,449

To give you a better understanding of the statement of cash flows, we now discuss Boston Beer's statement in more detail including the way that it relates to the balance sheet and income statement. Then we will examine the way each section of the statement describes a set of important decisions that Boston Beer management made and the way financial analysts use each section to evaluate the company's performance.

SELF-STUDY QUIZ

Big Rock Brewery Ltd. is one of the larger craft brewers in Canada. A listing of some of its cash flows follows. Indicate whether each item is disclosed in the Operating Activities (O), Investing Activities (I), or Financing Activities (F) section of the statement of cash flows.

___ 1. Shares repurchased from stockholders

___ 2. Collections from customers

___ 3. Payment of interest on debt

___ 4. Purchase of plant and equipment

___ 5. Acquisition of investment securities

After you have completed your answers, check them with the solutions at the bottom of the page.

Relationships to the Balance Sheet and Income Statement

Preparing and interpreting the cash flow statement requires an analysis of the balance sheet and income statement accounts that relate to the three sections of the cash flow statement. In previous chapters, we emphasized that companies record transactions as journal entries that are posted to T-accounts, which are used to prepare the income statement and the balance sheet. But companies cannot prepare the statement of cash flows using the amounts recorded in the T-accounts because those amounts are based on accrual accounting. Instead, they must analyze the numbers recorded under the accrual method and adjust them to a cash basis. To prepare the statement of cash flows, they need the following data:

1. **Comparative balance sheets** used in calculating the cash flows from all activities (operating, investing, and financing).

2. A **complete income statement** used primarily in calculating cash flows from operating activities.

3. **Additional details** concerning selected accounts where the total change amount in an account balance during the year does not reveal the underlying nature of the cash flows.

Our approach to preparing and understanding the cash flow statement focuses on the changes in the balance sheet accounts. It relies on a simple manipulation of the balance sheet equation:

$$\text{Assets} = \text{Liabilities} + \text{Stockholders' Equity}$$

First, assets can be split into cash and noncash assets:

$$\text{Cash} + \text{Noncash Assets} = \text{Liabilities} + \text{Stockholders' Equity}$$

If we move the noncash assets to the right side of the equation, then:

$$\text{Cash} = \text{Liabilities} + \text{Stockholders' Equity} - \text{Noncash Assets}$$

Self-Study Quiz Solutions   1. F, 2. O, 3. O, 4. I, 5. I

Category	Transaction	Cash Effect	Other Account Affected
Operating	Collect accounts receivable	+Cash	−Accounts Receivable (A)
	Pay accounts payable	−Cash	−Accounts Payable (L)
	Prepay rent	−Cash	+Prepaid Rent (A)
	Pay interest	−Cash	−Retained Earnings (SE)
	Sale for cash	+Cash	+Retained Earnings (SE)
Investing	Purchase equipment for cash	−Cash	+Equipment (A)
	Sell investment securities for cash	+Cash	−Investments (A)
Financing	Pay back debt to bank	−Cash	−Notes Payable—Bank (L)
	Issue stock for cash	+Cash	+Common Stock and Paid-in-Capital (SE)

EXHIBIT 13.2

Selected Cash Transactions and Their Effects on Other Balance Sheet Accounts

Given this relationship, the changes (Δ) in cash between the beginning and the end of the period must equal the changes (Δ) in the amounts on the right side of the equation between the beginning and the end of the period:

$$\Delta \text{ Cash } = \Delta \text{ Liabilities } + \Delta \text{ Stockholders' Equity } - \Delta \text{ Noncash Assets}$$

Thus, **any transaction that changes cash must be accompanied by a change in liabilities, stockholders' equity, or noncash assets.** Exhibit 13.2 illustrates this concept for selected cash transactions.

Next, we will compute the change in each balance sheet account (ending balance – beginning balance) and classify each change as relating to operating (O), investing (I), or financing (F) activities by marking them with the corresponding letter. **The balance sheet accounts related to earning income (operating items) should be marked with an O.** These accounts include the following:

- Most current assets (other than short-term investments, which relate to investing activities, and cash).[3]

- Most current liabilities (other than amounts owed to investors and financial institutions,[4] all of which relate to financing activities).

- Retained earnings because it increases by the amount of net income, which is the starting point for the operating section. (Retained earnings also decreases by dividends declared and paid, which is a financing outflow noted by an F.)

In Exhibit 13.3, all of the relevant current assets and liabilities have been marked with an O. These items include:

- Accounts Receivable
- Inventories
- Prepaid Expenses
- Accounts Payable
- Accrued Expenses

As we have noted, retained earnings is also relevant to operations.

---

[3]Certain noncurrent assets such as long-term receivables from customers and noncurrent liabilities such as postretirement obligations to employees are considered to be operating items. These items are covered in more advanced accounting classes.

[4]Examples of the accounts excluded are Dividends Payable, Short-Term Debt to Financial Institutions, and Current Maturities of Long-Term Debt. Current maturities of long-term debt are amounts of debt with an original term of more than one year that are due within one year of the statement date.

EXHIBIT 13.3				

The Boston Beer Company: Comparative Balance Sheet and Current Income Statement

THE BOSTON BEER COMPANY, INC.
Consolidated Balance Sheet

	(unaudited) Dollars in Thousands*	March 31, 2007	December 31, 2006	Change
Related Cash Flow Section	Assets			
	Current assets:			
Change in Cash	Cash and cash equivalents	$ 61,449	$ 63,147	−1,698
I	Short-term investments	20,025	19,223	+802
O	Accounts receivable	19,737	17,770	+1,967
O	Inventories	18,951	17,034	+1,917
O	Prepaid expenses	4,398	2,721	+1,677
	Total current assets	124,560	119,895	
I†	Equipment, net	31,887	31,879	+8
	Total assets	$156,447	$151,774	
	Liabilities and Stockholders' Equity			
	Current liabilities:			
O	Accounts payable	$ 14,622	$ 17,942	−3,320
O	Accrued expenses	22,184	22,928	−744
	Total current liabilities	36,806	40,870	
	Stockholders' equity:			
F	Contributed capital	84,206	81,237	+2,969
O and F	Retained earnings	35,435	29,667	+5,768
	Total stockholders' equity	119,641	110,904	
	Total liabilities and stockholders' equity	$156,447	$151,774	

THE BOSTON BEER COMPANY, INC.
Consolidated Statements of Operations
Three Months Ended March 31, 2007

(unaudited)
Dollars in Thousands

Net sales	$72,448
Cost of sales	32,126
Gross profit	40,322
Operating expenses:	
Selling, general, and administrative expense	30,078
Depreciation and amortization expense	1,726
Total operating expenses	31,804
Operating income	8,518
Interest income	1,132
Income before provision for income taxes	9,650
Provision for income taxes	3,882
Net income	$ 5,768

*Certain balances have been adjusted to simplify the presentation.
†The Accumulated Depreciation account is also related to operations because it relates to depreciation.

The balance sheet accounts related to investing activities should be marked with an I. These include all of the remaining assets on the balance sheet. In Exhibit 13.3:

■ Short-term Investments
■ Equipment, net

The balance sheet accounts related to financing activities should be marked with an F. These include all of the remaining liability and stockholders' equity accounts on the balance sheet. In Exhibit 13.3:

■ Contributed Capital
■ Retained Earnings (for decreases resulting from dividends declared and paid)

Next, we use this information to prepare each section of the statement.

REPORTING AND INTERPRETING CASH FLOWS FROM OPERATING ACTIVITIES

As noted above, the operating section can be prepared in two formats, and virtually all U.S. companies choose the indirect method. As a result, we discuss the indirect method here and the direct method in Supplement A at the end of the chapter.
    Remember that

1. Cash flow from operating activities is always the same regardless of whether it is computed using the direct or indirect method.

2. The investing and financing sections are always presented in the same manner regardless of the format of the operating section.

Reporting Cash Flows from Operating Activities—Indirect Method

Exhibit 13.3 shows Boston Beer's comparative balance sheet and income statement. Remember that the indirect method starts with net income and converts it to cash flows from operating activities. This involves adjusting net income for the differences in the timing of accrual basis net income and cash flows. The general structure of the operating activities section is:

> **Operating Activities**
> Net income
>   Add/Subtract to convert to cash basis:
>   +Depreciation and amortization expense
>   −Gain on sale of long-term asset
>   +Loss on sale of long-term asset
>   +Decreases in current assets
>   +Increases in current liabilities
>   −Increases in current assets
>   −Decreases in current liabilities
> **Net Cash Flow from Operating Activities**

Learning Objective 2
Report and interpret cash flows from operating activities using the indirect method.

Audio lecture–AP13-2
www.mhhe.com/libby6e

To keep track of all the additions and subtractions made to convert net income to cash flows from operating activities, it is helpful to set up a schedule to record the computations. We will construct a schedule for Boston Beer in Exhibit 13.4.

We begin our schedule presented in Exhibit 13.4 with net income of $5,768 taken from Boston Beer's income statement (Exhibit 13.3). Completing the operating section using the indirect method involves two steps:

Step 1. Adjust net income for depreciation and amortization expense and gains and losses on sale of long-term assets. Recording depreciation and amortization expense does not affect the cash account (or any other current asset or liability). It affects a noncurrent asset (such as Equipment, net). **Since depreciation and amortization expense are subtracted in computing net income but do not affect cash, we always add each back** to convert net income to cash flow from operating activities. In the case of Boston Beer, we need to remove the effect of depreciation and amortization expense by adding back $1,726 to net income (see Exhibit 13.4).

If Boston Beer had sold property, plant, and equipment at a gain or loss, the amount of cash received would be classified as an investing cash inflow. Since all of the cash received is an investing cash flow, an adjustment must also be made in the operating activities section to avoid double counting the gain or loss. **Gains on sales of property, plant, and equipment are subtracted and losses on such sales are added** to convert net income to cash flow from operating activities.[5]

Step 2. Adjust net income for changes in current assets and current liabilities marked as operating (O). Each **change** in current assets (other than cash and short-term investments) and current liabilities (other than amounts owed to owners and financial institutions) causes a difference between net income and cash flow from operating activities.[6] When converting net income to cash flow from operating activities, apply the following general rules:

- Add the change when a current asset decreases or current liability increases.
- Subtract the change when a current asset increases or current liability decreases.

Understanding what makes these current assets and current liabilities increase and decrease is the key to understanding the logic of these additions and subtractions.

Change in Accounts Receivable

We illustrate this logic with the first operating item (O) listed on Boston Beer's balance sheet (Exhibit 13.3), accounts receivable. Remember that the income statement reflects sales revenue, but the cash flow statement must reflect cash collections from customers. As the following accounts receivable T-account illustrates, when sales revenues are recorded, accounts receivable increases, and when cash is collected from customers, accounts receivable decreases.

	Accounts Receivable (A)			
Beginning balance	17,770			
Sales revenue (on account)	72,448	Collections from customers	70,481
Ending balance	19,737			

Change $1,967 brackets the Beginning balance, Sales revenue (on account), and Ending balance rows.

In the Boston Beer example, sales revenue reported on the income statement is greater than cash collections from customers by $72,448 − $70,481 = $1,967. Since less money was collected from customers, this amount must be subtracted from net income to convert to cash flows from operating activities. Note that this amount is also the same as the **change** in the accounts receivable account:

Ending balance	$19,737
− Beginning balance	17,770
Change	$ 1,967

This same underlying logic is used to determine adjustments for the other current assets and liabilities.

---

[5]Other similar additions and subtractions are discussed in more advanced accounting courses.

[6]As noted earlier, certain noncurrent assets such as long-term receivables from customers and noncurrent liabilities such as postretirement obligations to employees are considered to be operating items. These items are covered in more advanced accounting classes.

To summarize, the income statement reflects revenues of the period, but cash flow from operating activities must reflect cash collections from customers. Sales on account increase the balance in accounts receivable, and collections from customers decrease the balance.

Accounts Receivable (A)	
Beg. 17,770	
Increase 1,967	
End. 19,737	

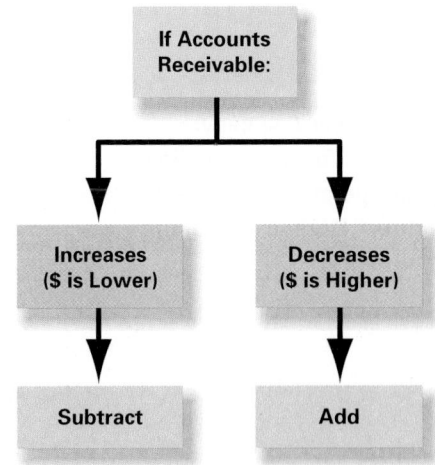

The balance sheet for Boston Beer Company (Exhibit 13.3) indicates an **increase** in accounts receivable of $1,967 for the period, which means that cash collected from customers is lower than revenue. To convert to cash flows from operating activities, the amount of the increase (the reduced collections) must be **subtracted** in Exhibit 13.4. (A decrease is added.)

Change in Inventory

The income statement reflects merchandise sold for the period, whereas cash flow from operating activities must reflect cash purchases. As shown in the T-account on the left, purchases of goods increase the balance in inventory, and recording merchandise sold decreases the balance in inventory.

Inventories (A)		Inventories (A)	
Beg. bal.	Cost of goods sold	Beg. 17,034	
Purchases		Increase 1,917	
End. Bal.		End. 18,951	

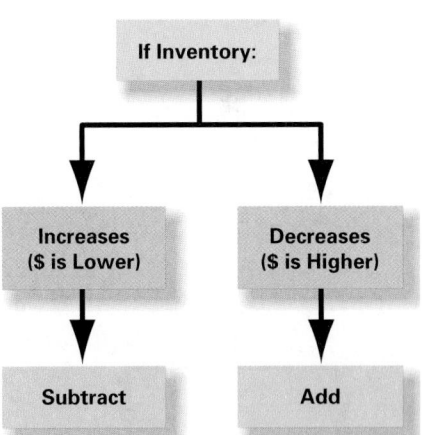

Boston Beer's balance sheet (Exhibit 13.3) indicates that inventory **increased** by $1,917, which means that the amount of purchases is more than the amount of merchandise sold. The increase (the extra purchases) must be **subtracted** from net income to convert to cash flow from operating activities in Exhibit 13.4. (A decrease is added.)

Change in Prepaid Expenses

The income statement reflects expenses of the period, but cash flow from operating activities must reflect the cash payments. Cash prepayments increase the balance in prepaid expenses, and recording of expenses decreases the balance in prepaid expenses.

Prepaid Expenses (A)		Prepaid Expenses (A)	
Beg. bal.	Services used	Beg. 2,721	
Cash prepayments	(expense)	Increase 1,677	
End. Bal.		End. 4,398	

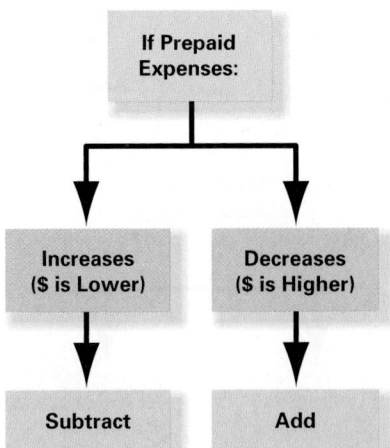

The Boston Beer balance sheet (Exhibit 13.3) indicates a $1,677 **increase** in prepaid expenses, which means that new cash prepayments are more than the amount of expenses. The increase (the extra prepayments) must be **subtracted** from net income in Exhibit 13.4. (A decrease is added.)

Change in Accounts Payable

Cash flow from operations must reflect cash purchases, but not all purchases are for cash. Purchases on account increase accounts payable and cash paid to suppliers decreases accounts payable.

EXHIBIT 13.4	CONVERSION OF NET INCOME TO NET CASH FLOW FROM OPERATING ACTIVITIES		
	Items	**Amount**	**Explanation**
Boston Beer Company: Schedule for Net Cash Flow from Operating Activities, Indirect Method (dollars in thousands)	Net income, accrual basis	$ 5,768	From income statement.
	Add (subtract) to convert to cash basis:		
	Depreciation and amortization	+ 1,726	Add back because depreciation and amortization expense does not affect cash.
	Accounts receivable increase	− 1,967	Subtract because cash collected from customers is less than accrual basis revenues.
	Inventory increase	− 1,917	Subtract because purchases are more than cost of goods sold expense.
	Prepaid expense increase	− 1,677	Subtract because cash prepayments for expenses are more than accrual basis expenses.
	Accounts payable decrease	− 3,320	Subtract because cash payments to suppliers are more than amounts purchased on account (borrowed from suppliers).
	Accrued expenses decrease	− 744	Subtract because cash payments for expenses are more than accrual basis expenses.
	Net cash used in operating activities	$(2,131)	Reported on the statement of cash flows.

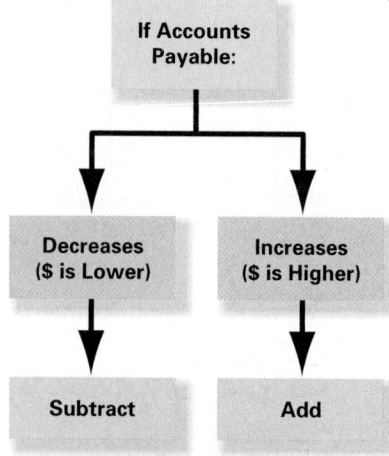

Accounts Payable (L)			Accounts Payable (L)	
Cash payments	Beg. bal. Purchases on account	Decrease 3,320	Beg.	17,942
	End. bal.		End.	14,622

Boston Beer's accounts payable **decreased** by $3,320, which means that cash payments were more than purchases on account, and this decrease (the extra payments) must be **subtracted** in Exhibit 13.4. (An increase is added.)

Change in Accrued Expenses

The income statement reflects all accrued expenses, but the cash flow statement must reflect actual payments for those expenses. Recording accrued expenses increases the balance in the liability accrued expenses and cash payments for the expenses decrease accrued expenses.

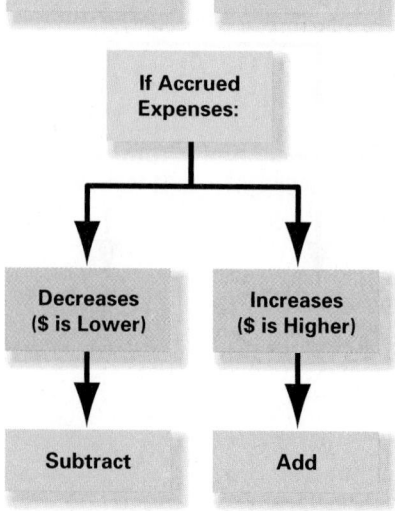

Accrued Expenses (L)			Accrued Expenses (L)	
Pay off accruals	Beg. bal. Accrued expenses	Decrease 744	Beg.	22,928
	End. bal.		End.	22,184

Boston Beer's accrued expenses (Exhibit 13.3) **decreased** by $744, which indicates that cash paid for the expenses is more than accrual basis expenses. The decrease (the extra cash paid) must be **subtracted** in Exhibit 13.4. (An increase is added.)

Summary

We can summarize the typical additions and subtractions that are required to reconcile net income with cash flow from operating activities as follows:

**ADDITIONS AND SUBTRACTIONS
TO RECONCILE NET INCOME TO CASH FLOW
FROM OPERATING ACTIVITIES**

Item	When Item Increases	When Item Decreases
Depreciation and amortization	+	NA
Accounts receivable	−	+
Inventory	−	+
Prepaid expenses	−	+
Accounts payable	+	−
Accrued expense liabilities	+	−

Notice again in this table that to reconcile net income to cash flows from operating activities, you must:

■ **Add the change when a current asset decreases or current liability increases.**

■ **Subtract the change when a current asset increases or current liability decreases.**

The cash flow statement for Boston Beer (Exhibit 13.1) shows the same additions and subtractions to reconcile net income to cash flows from operating activities described in Exhibit 13.4.

Foreign Currency and the Cash Flow Statement		**INTERNATIONAL** PERSPECTIVE

Consolidated statements may include one or more subsidiaries located in other countries whose statements report in a currency other than the U.S. dollar (for example, the euro or Mexican peso). The process of translating those statements into dollars may cause the changes in the current assets and liabilities on the balance sheet not to match the changes reported on the cash flow statement. Acquisitions and sales of subsidiaries during the period can have a similar effect.[7]

---

[7]For further discussion, see Wilkins, M. S., & Loudder, M. L. (2000). Articulation in cash flow statements: a resource for financial accounting courses. *Journal of Accounting Education* 18(2), 115–126.

Indicate which of the following items taken from Big Rock Brewery's cash flow statement would be added (+), subtracted (−), or not included (0) in the reconciliation of net income to cash flow from operations.

_____ 1. Increase in inventories.   _____ 4. Decrease in accounts receivable.

_____ 2. Increase in bank indebtedness.   _____ 5. Increase in accounts payable.

_____ 3. Amortization expense.   _____ 6. Increase in prepaid expenses.

After you have completed your answers, check them with the solutions at the bottom of the page.

Interpreting Cash Flows from Operating Activities

The operating activities section of the cash flow statement focuses attention on the firm's ability to generate cash internally through operations and its management of current assets and current liabilities (also called **working capital**). Most analysts believe that this is the most important section of the statement because, in the long run, operations are the only source of cash. That is, investors will not invest in a company if they do not believe that cash generated from operations will be available to pay them dividends or expand the company. Similarly, creditors will not lend money if they do not believe that cash generated from operations will be available to pay back the loan. For example, many dot.com companies crashed when investors lost faith in their ability to turn business ideas into cash flows from operations.

A common rule of thumb followed by financial and credit analysts is to avoid firms with rising net income but falling cash flow from operations. Rapidly rising inventories or receivables often predict a slump in profits and the need for external financing. A true understanding of the meaning of the difference requires a detailed understanding of its causes.

In the first quarter of 2007, Boston Beer reported that net income was higher than cash flow from operations. What caused this relationship? To answer these questions, we must carefully analyze how Boston Beer's operating activities are reported in its cash flow statement. To properly interpret this information, we also must learn more about the brewing industry.

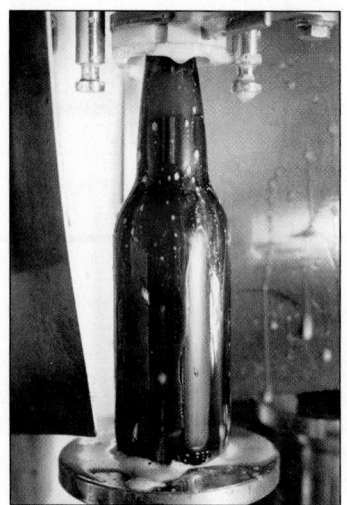

Analyzing Accounts Receivable Changes

Managers sometimes attempt to boost declining sales by extending credit terms (for example, from 30 to 60 days) or by lowering credit standards (that is, lending to riskier customers). The resulting increase in accounts receivable can cause net income to outpace cash flow from operations. As a consequence, many analysts view this pattern as a warning sign.

However, analysts who cover the beverage industry know that Boston Beer normally sees an increase in receivables from normal seasonal fluctuations in beer sales to distributors. Beer sales to distributors are low in the last month of the fourth quarter (December) because of the onset of winter. As a result, the beginning balance in Accounts Receivable in January is low. However, sales are high at the end of the first quarter (March) in anticipation of spring. The higher March sales cause accounts receivable to increase, but the cash is not collected until April. This normal seasonal fluctuation in sales is clearly not a sign of problems for Boston Beer.

Self-Study Quiz Solutions   1. −, 2. 0, 3. +, 4. +, 5. +, 6. −.

Analyzing Inventory Changes

An unexpected increase in inventory can also cause net income to outpace cash flow from operations. Such inventory growth can be a sign that planned sales growth did not materialize. Alternatively, a decline in inventory can be a sign that the company is anticipating lower sales in the next quarter. In the case of Boston Beer, an increase in inventory at the end of the first quarter results from the normal inventory buildup in anticipation of higher spring sales. Again, this normal seasonal fluctuation is clearly not a sign of problems for Boston Beer. Many analysts compute the quality of income ratio as a general warning sign of these and similar problems.

 Quality of Income Ratio

❓ ANALYTICAL QUESTION:

How much cash does each dollar of net income generate?

% RATIO AND COMPARISONS:

$$\text{Quality of Income Ratio} = \frac{\text{Cash Flow from Operating Activities}}{\text{Net Income}}$$

Boston Beer ratio for the *year** 2006 was:

$$\frac{\$28,977}{\$18,192} = 1.59\ (159\%)$$

COMPARISONS OVER TIME		
Boston Beer (Annual)		
2004	**2005**	**2006**
1.54	1.85	1.59

COMPARISONS WITH COMPETITORS	
Anheuser-Busch	**Coors**
2006	**2006**
1.38	2.31

Learning Objective 3

Analyze and interpret the quality of income ratio.

Selected Focus Company Comparisons

General Mills	1.62
Deckers Outdoor	1.54
Papa John's	1.35

💡 INTERPRETATIONS:

In General   The quality of income ratio measures the portion of income that was generated in cash. All other things equal, a higher quality of income ratio indicates greater ability to finance operating and other cash needs from operating cash inflows. A higher ratio also indicates that it is less likely that the company is using aggressive revenue recognition policies to increase net income, and therefore is less likely to experience a decline in earnings in the future.[†] When this ratio does not equal 1.0, analysts must establish the sources of the difference to determine the significance of the findings. There are four potential causes of any difference:

1. **The corporate life cycle (growth or decline in sales).** When sales are increasing, receivables and inventory normally increase faster than accounts payable. This often reduces operating cash flows below income, which, in turn, reduces the ratio. When sales are declining, the opposite occurs, and the ratio increases.

2. **Seasonality.** As is the case for Boston Beer, seasonal variations in sales and purchases of inventory can cause the ratio to deviate from 1.0.

3. **Changes in revenue and expense recognition.** Aggressive revenue recognition or failure to accrue appropriate expenses will inflate net income and reduce the ratio.

(continued)

---

*To eliminate the effects of seasonality, we look at the ratio for the annual period.
[†]See S. Richardson, "Earnings Quality and Short Sellers," *Accounting Horizons,* Supplement 2003, pp. 49–61 for a discussion of related research.

4. **Changes in management of operating assets and liabilities.** Inefficient management will increase operating assets and decrease liabilities, reducing operating cash flows and the quality of income ratio. More efficient management, such as shortening of payment terms, will have the opposite effect.

Focus Company Analysis   During the past three years, Boston Beer's quality of income ratio has ranged from 1.54 to 1.85. During the last three years, its ratio has remained between those for Anheuser-Busch and Coors. The variation in Boston Beer's ratio would prompt analysts to read the management's discussion and analysis section of the annual report to determine its causes.

A Few Cautions   The quality of income ratio can be interpreted based only on an understanding of the company's business operations and strategy. For example, a low ratio can be due simply to normal seasonal changes. However, it also can indicate obsolete inventory, slowing sales, or failed expansion plans. To test for these possibilities, analysts often analyze this ratio in tandem with the accounts receivable turnover and inventory turnover ratios.

Fraud and Cash Flows from Operations

The cash flow statement often gives outsiders the first hint that financial statements may contain errors and irregularities. The importance of this indicator as a predictor is receiving more attention in the United States and internationally. *Investors Chronicle* recently reported on an accounting fraud at a commercial credit company, suggesting that

REAL WORLD EXCERPT

Investors Chronicle

> . . . a look at Versailles's cash flow statement—an invaluable tool in spotting creative accounting—should have triggered misgivings. In the company's last filed accounts . . . Versailles reported operating profits of . . . $25 million but a cash outflow from operating activities of $24 million . . . . such figures should . . . have served as a warning. After all, what use is a company to anyone if it reports only accounting profits which are never translated into cash?

As noted in earlier chapters, unethical managers sometimes attempt to reach earnings targets by manipulating accruals and deferrals of revenues and expenses to inflate income. Since these adjusting entries do not affect the cash account, they have no effect on the cash flow statement. A growing difference between net income and cash flow from operations can be a sign of such manipulations. This early warning sign has signaled some famous bankruptcies, such as that of W. T. Grant in 1975. The company had inflated income by failing to make adequate accruals of expenses for uncollectible accounts receivable and obsolete inventory. The more astute analysts noted the growing difference between net income and cash flow from operations and recommended selling the stock long before the bankruptcy.

Source: James Chapman, "Creative Accounting: Exposed!" *Investors Chronicle,* February 3, 2001.

REPORTING AND INTERPRETING CASH FLOWS FROM INVESTING ACTIVITIES

Reporting Cash Flows from Investing Activities

Preparing this section of the cash flow statement requires an analysis of the accounts related to property, plant, and equipment; intangible assets; and investments in the securities of other companies. Normally, the relevant balance sheet accounts include Short-Term Investments and long-term asset accounts such as Long-Term Investments and Property, Plant, and Equipment. The following relationships are the ones that you will encounter most frequently:

Related Balance Sheet Account(s)	Investing Activity	Cash Flow Effect
Property, plant, and equipment and intangible assets (patents, etc.)	Purchase of property, plant, and equipment or intangible assets for cash	Outflow
	Sale of property, plant, and equipment or intangible assets for cash	Inflow
Short- or long-term investments (stocks and bonds of other companies)	Purchase of investment securities for cash	Outflow
	Sale (maturity) of investment securities for cash	Inflow

Remember this:

- **Only purchases paid for with cash or cash equivalents are included.**
- **The amount of cash that is received from the sale of assets is included, regardless of whether the assets are sold at a gain or loss.**

In Boston Beer's case, the balance sheet (Exhibit 13.3) shows two investing assets (noted with an I) that have changed during the period: Equipment, net and Short-term investments. To determine the causes of these changes, accountants need to search the related company records.

Cash Flows from Investing Activities

Equipment, Net

They would discover that the company purchased new equipment for $1,736 cash, which is a cash outflow. The company also sold old equipment for $2, an amount equal to its net book value. This is a cash inflow. These investing items are listed in the schedule of investing activities in Exhibit 13.5. These items, less the amount of depreciation expense added back in the Operations section ($1,726), explain the increase in Equipment, net of $8.

Equipment, Net (A)			
Beg.	31,879	Sold	2
Purch.	1,736	Depr.	1,726
End.	31,887		

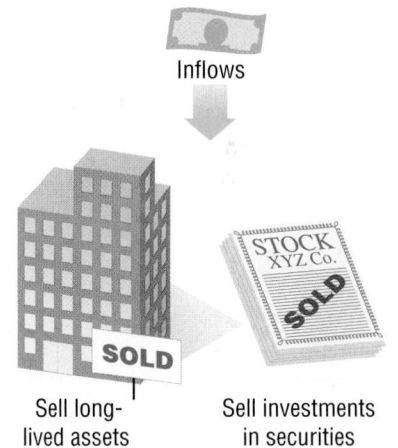

Sell long-lived assets Sell investments in securities

Investments

Boston Beer's records also indicate that it purchased $802 in short-term investments during the quarter for cash, which is an investing cash outflow. This investing item is listed in the schedule of investing activities in Exhibit 13.5. It explains the $802 increase ($20,025 − $19,223 = $802) in short-term investments reported on the balance sheet.

Short-Term Investments (A)			
Beg.	19,223		
Purch.	802	Sold	0
End.	20,025		

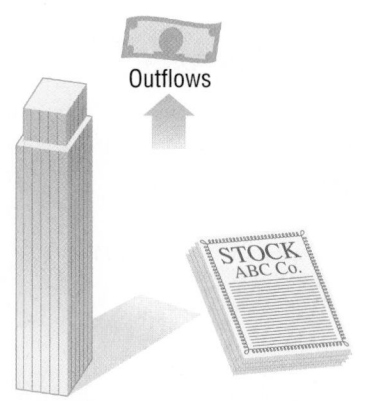

Purchase long-lived assets Purchase investments in securities

The net cash flow from investing activities resulting from these three items is a $2,536 outflow (see Exhibit 13.5).

EXHIBIT 13.5

Boston Beer Company: Schedule for Net Cash Flow from Investing Activities (dollars in thousands)

Items	Cash Inflows (Outflows)	Explanation
Purchase of equipment	$ (1,736)	Payment in cash for equipment
Proceeds from disposal of equipment	2	Receipt of cash from sale of equipment
Purchase of short-term investments	(802)	Payment in cash for new investments
Net cash inflow (outflow) from investing activities	$ (2,536)	Reported on the statement of cash flows

Interpreting Cash Flows from Investing Activities

Two common ways to assess a company's ability to internally finance its expansion needs are the capital acquisitions ratio and free cash flow.

KEY RATIO ANALYSIS

Capital Acquisitions Ratio

Learning Objective 5
Analyze and interpret the capital acquisitions ratio.

❓ ANALYTICAL QUESTION:

To what degree was the company able to finance purchases of property, plant, and equipment with cash provided by operating activities?

% RATIO AND COMPARISONS:

$$\text{Capital Acquisitions Ratio} = \frac{\text{Cash Flow from Operating Activities}}{\text{Cash Paid for Property, Plant, and Equipment}}$$

Boston Beer's ratio for 2004 through 2006* was

$$\frac{\$77,091}{\$27,588} = 2.79$$

Examine the ratio using two techniques:

COMPARISONS OVER TIME		COMPARISONS WITH COMPETITORS	
Boston Beer		Anheuser-Busch	Redhook Ale
2001–2003	2004–2006	2004–2006	2004–2006
7.49	2.79	2.74	3.90

💡 INTERPRETATIONS:

In General   The capital acquisitions ratio reflects the portion of purchases of property, plant, and equipment financed from operating activities (without the need for outside debt or equity financing or the sale of other investments or fixed assets). A high ratio indicates less need for outside financing for current and future expansion. It benefits the company because it provides the company opportunities for strategic acquisitions, avoids the cost of additional debt, and reduces the risk of bankruptcy that comes with additional leverage (see Chapter 10).

Focus Company Analysis   Boston Beer's capital acquisitions ratio has decreased from 7.49 to 2.79 in recent years. The high ratio for the 2001–2003 period may be attributable to general slow growth in beer sales and its dampening effects on new investment. When

Selected Focus Company Comparisons

Harley-Davidson   4.05

Outback Steakhouse   1.16

General Mills   3.41

*Since capital expenditures for plant and equipment often vary greatly from year to year, this ratio is often computed over longer periods of time than one year, such as three years used here.

companies in an industry acquire more productive capacity than is necessary to meet customer demand, the costs of maintaining and financing an idle plant can drive a company to ruin. Boston Beer minimizes the risks of overcapacity by outsourcing a significant portion of its production to other brewers. This practice lowers Boston Beer's borrowing, depreciation, and transportation costs compared to those of companies with a single large brewery. Redhook's moderate ratio for the 2004–2006 period indicates that it has decreased capital investments in recent years compared to 2001–2003 when its ratio was 2.04. Anheuser-Busch falls just below Boston Beer with respect to capital acquisitions.

A Few Cautions   Since the needs for investment in plant and equipment differ dramatically across industries (for example, airlines versus pizza delivery restaurants), a particular firm's ratio should be compared only with its prior years' figures or with other firms in the same industry. Also, a high ratio may indicate a failure to update plant and equipment, which can limit a company's ability to compete in the future.

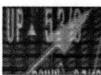 **Free Cash Flow**

FINANCIAL
ANALYSIS

Managers and analysts often calculate free cash flow[8] as a measure of a firm's ability to pursue long-term investment opportunities. Free cash flow is normally calculated as follows:

**Free Cash Flow = Cash Flows from Operating Activities −
Dividends − Capital Expenditures**

Any positive free cash flow is available for additional capital expenditures, investments in other companies, and mergers and acquisitions without the need for external financing or reductions in dividends to shareholders. While free cash flow is considered a positive sign of financial flexibility, it also can represent a hidden cost to shareholders. Sometimes managers use free cash flow to pursue unprofitable investments just for the sake of growth or to obtain perquisites (such as fancy offices and corporate jets) that do not benefit the shareholders. In these cases, the shareholders would be better off if free cash flow were paid as additional dividends or used to repurchase the company's stock on the open market.

FREE CASH FLOW = Cash Flows from Operating Activities − Dividends − Capital Expenditures

REPORTING AND INTERPRETING CASH FLOWS FROM FINANCING ACTIVITIES

Reporting Cash Flows from Financing Activities

Financing activities are associated with generating capital from creditors and owners. This section of the cash flow statement reflects changes in two current liabilities, Notes Payable to Financial Institutions (often called short-term debt) and Current Maturities of Long-Term Debt, as well as changes in long-term liabilities and stockholders' equity accounts. These balance sheet accounts relate to the issuance and

Learning Objective 6
Report and interpret cash flows from financing activities.

---

[8]An alternative definition which does not subtract dividends and interest is often called the **total cash flow of the firm** in finance.

retirement of debt and stock and the payment of dividends. The following relationships are the ones that you will encounter most frequently:

Related Balance Sheet Account(s)	Financing Activity	Cash Flow Effect
Short-term debt (notes payable)	Borrowing cash from bank or other financial institution	Inflow
	Repayment of loan principal	Outflow
Long-term debt	Issuance of bonds for cash	Inflow
	Repayment of bond principal	Outflow
Common stock and additional paid-in capital	Issuance of stock for cash	Inflow
	Repurchase (retirement) of stock with cash	Outflow
Retained earnings	Payment of cash dividends	Outflow

Cash Flows from Financing Activities

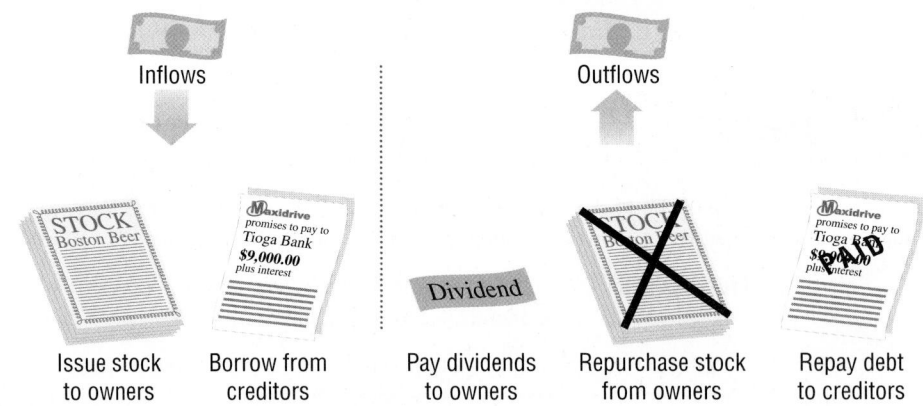

Remember this:

- **Cash repayments of principal are cash flows from financing activities.**
- **Interest payments are cash flows from operating activities.** Since interest expense is reported on the income statement, the related cash flow is shown in the operating section.
- **Dividend payments are cash flows from financing activities.** They are not reported on the income statement because they represent a distribution of income to owners, so they are shown in the financing section.
- **If debt or stock is issued for other than cash, it is not included in this section.**

To compute cash flows from financing activities, you should review changes in debt and stockholders' equity accounts. In the case of Boston Beer Company, the analysis of changes in the balance sheet (Exhibit 13.3) finds that only contributed capital changed during the period (noted with an F).

Contributed Capital

The change in contributed capital resulted from two decisions. First, Boston Beer repurchased outstanding stock for $2,729 cash, which is a cash outflow. The company

Contributed Capital (SE)			
		Beg.	81,237
Repurch.	2,729	Issue	5,698
		End.	84,206

EXHIBIT 13.6

Boston Beer Company: Schedule for Net Cash Flow from Financing Activities (dollars in thousands)

Items	Cash Inflows (Outflows)	Explanation
Repurchase of stock (treasury stock)	($2,729)	Cash payments to repurchase outstanding stock
Net proceeds from stock issuance	5,698	Cash proceeds from issue of common stock
Net cash inflow (outflow) from financing activities	$2,969	Reported on the statement of cash flows

also issued common stock to employees for $5,698 in cash, which is a cash inflow. Together, these two amounts account for the $2,969 increase in contributed capital. They are listed in the schedule of financing activities in Exhibit 13.6, which shows a net cash inflow of $2,969.

Short- and Long-Term Debt

If Boston Beer had borrowed or repaid principal on short- or long-term debt during the period, these also would be listed in this section. The appropriate amounts would be determined by analyzing the short- and long-term debt accounts.

Short- or Long-Term Debt (L)	
Retire (repay)	Beginning Issue (borrow)
	Ending

Retained Earnings

Finally, retained earnings should be analyzed. Retained earnings rise when income is earned and fall when dividends are declared and paid. Boston Beer's retained earnings rose by an amount equal to its net income, so no dividends were declared and paid. Should Boston Beer ever decide to pay dividends, it would also list them as financing cash outflows.

Retained Earnings (SE)			
		Beg.	29,667
Dividends	0	Net Income	5,768
		End.	35,435

Interpreting Cash Flows from Financing Activities

The long-term growth of a company is normally financed from three sources: internally generated funds (cash from operating activities), the issuance of stock, and money borrowed on a long-term basis. As we discussed in Chapter 10, companies can adopt a number of different capital structures (the balance of debt and equity). The financing sources that management uses to fund growth will have an important impact on the firm's risk and return characteristics. The statement of cash flows shows how management has elected to fund its growth. This information is used by analysts who wish to evaluate the capital structure and growth potential of a business.

SELF-STUDY QUIZ

Pyramid Breweries

Indicate which of the following items taken from the cash flow statement of Pyramid Breweries Inc. would be reported in the Investing section (I) or Financing section (F) and whether the amount would be an inflow (+) or an outflow (−).

____ 1. Purchases of short-term investments.

____ 2. Repayment of principal on note payable (to bank).

____ 3. Cash dividends paid.

____ 4. Proceeds from sale of common stock.

____ 5. Proceeds from sale of fixed assets.

After you have completed your answers, check them with the solutions at the bottom of the page.

COMPLETING THE STATEMENT AND ADDITIONAL DISCLOSURES

Statement Structure

Learning Objective 7
Understand the format of the cash flow statement and additional cash flow disclosures.

Refer to the formal statement of cash flows for Boston Beer Company shown in Exhibit 13.1. As you can see, it is a simple matter to construct the statement after the detailed analysis of the accounts and transactions has been completed (shown in Exhibits 13.4, 13.5, and 13.6). Exhibit 13.7 summarizes the general structure of the statement for companies that use the indirect method. As you can see, when the **net increase or decrease in cash and cash equivalents** is added to the cash and cash equivalents taken from the beginning of the period balance sheet, it equals the cash and cash equivalents amount reported on the end of the period balance sheet. Companies also must provide two other disclosures related to the cash flow statement.

Noncash Investing and Financing Activities

NONCASH INVESTING AND FINANCING ACTIVITIES are transactions that do not have direct cash flow effects; they are reported as a supplement to the statement of cash flows in narrative or schedule form.

Certain transactions are important investing and financing activities but have no cash flow effects. These are called **noncash investing and financing activities.** For example, the purchase of a $100,000 building with a $100,000 mortgage given by the former owner does not cause either an inflow or an outflow of cash. As a result, these noncash activities are not listed in the three main sections of the cash flow statement. However, supplemental disclosure of these transactions is required, in either narrative or schedule form. Boston Beer's statement of cash flows does not list any noncash investing and financing activities. However, when Northwest Airlines purchases airplanes from AIRBUS or Boeing, the manufacturer provides some of the financing for those purchases. These amounts are disclosed as follows at the bottom of its cash flow statement:

REAL WORLD EXCERPT

Northwest Airlines
ANNUAL REPORT

Northwest Airlines Corporation

(in millions) Investing and Financing Activities Not Affecting Cash:	Year ended December 31,		
	2006	2005	2004
Manufacturer financing of aircraft and other non-cash transactions	$280	$344	$705

Statement of Cash Flows (Indirect Method)
Operating Activities:
Net income
+Depreciation and amortization expense
−Gain on sale of long-term asset
+Loss on sale of long-term asset
+Decreases in current assets
+Increases in current liabilities
−Increases in current assets
−Decreases in current liabilities
Net Cash Flow from Operating Activities
Investing Activities:
−Purchase of property, plant, and equipment or intangible assets
+Sale of property, plant, and equipment or intangible assets
−Purchase of investment securities
+Sale (maturity) of investment securities
Net Cash Flow from Investing Activities
Financing Activities:
+Borrowing from bank or other financial institution
−Repayment of loan principal
+Issuance of bonds for cash
−Repayment of bond principal
+Issuance of stock
−Repurchase (retirement) of stock
−Payment of (cash) dividends
Net Cash Flow from Financing Activities
Net increase or decrease in cash and cash equivalents
Cash and cash equivalents at beginning of period
Cash and cash equivalents at end of period

EXHIBIT 13.7

Structure of the Statement of Cash Flows (Indirect Method)

Supplemental Cash Flow Information

Companies that use the indirect method of presenting cash flows from operations also must provide two other figures: cash paid for interest and cash paid for income taxes. These are normally listed at the bottom of the statement or in the notes.

Epilogue

Our more detailed analysis of Boston Beer's first-quarter cash flow indicates the causes of the difference between net income and cash flows in the first quarter. In fact, it was a normal consequence of seasonal variations in sales and purchases of raw materials. Our further analysis of Boston Beer's investing and financing indicates that the cash needed to continue its investment strategy should be more than met by operations.

DEMONSTRATION **CASE**

Redhook Ale Brewery

Complete the following requirements before proceeding to the suggested solution. During a recent year (ended December 31), Redhook Ale Brewery, a Seattle-based craft brewer, reported net income of $3,182 (all numbers in thousands of dollars) and cash and cash equivalents at the beginning of the year of $472. It also engaged in the following activities:

a. Paid $18,752 in principal on debt.

b. Received $46,202 in cash from initial public offering of common stock.

c. Incurred other noncurrent accrued operating expenses of $857.

d. Paid $18,193 in cash for purchase of fixed assets.

e. Accounts receivable increased by $881.

f. Borrowed $16,789 from various lenders.

g. Refundable deposits payable increased by $457.

h. Inventories increased by $574.

i. Made cash deposits on equipment of $5,830.

j. Income tax refund receivable decreased by $326.

k. Sold (issued) stock to employees for $13 in cash.

l. Accounts payable decreased by $391.

m. Received $4 from other investing activities.

n. Accrued expenses increased by $241.

o. Prepaid expenses increased by $565.

p. Recorded depreciation of $1,324.

q. Paid $5 cash in other financing activities.

Required:

Based on this information, prepare the cash flow statement using the indirect method.

SUGGESTED SOLUTION

REDHOOK ALE BREWERY
Statement of Cash Flows
For the Year Ended December 31
(dollars in thousands)

Operating activities	
Net income	$ 3,182
Adjustments:	
Depreciation	1,324
Other noncurrent accrued expenses	857
Change in accounts receivable	(881)
Change in inventories	(574)
Change in income taxes receivable	326
Change in prepaid expenses	(565)
Change in accounts payable	(391)
Change in accrued expenses	241
Change in refundable deposits payable	457
Net cash flow from operating activities	3,976
Investing activities	
Expenditures for fixed assets	(18,193)
Deposits on equipment	(5,830)
Other	4
Net cash flow from investing activities	(24,019)
Financing activities	
Proceeds from debt	16,789
Repayment of debt	(18,752)
Proceeds from sale of stock (IPO)	46,202
Proceeds from sale of stock (options)	13
Other	(5)
Net cash flow from financing activities	44,247
Increase in cash and cash equivalents	24,204
Cash and cash equivalents:	
Beginning of year	472
End of year	$24,676

Chapter Supplement A

Reporting Cash Flows From Operating Activities—Direct Method

The direct method presents a summary of all operating transactions that result in either a debit or a credit to cash. It is prepared by adjusting each item on the income statement from an accrual basis to a cash basis. We will complete this process for all of the revenues and expenses reported in Boston Beer's income statement in Exhibit 13.3 and accumulate them in a new schedule in Exhibit 13.8.

Cash Flows from Operating Activities

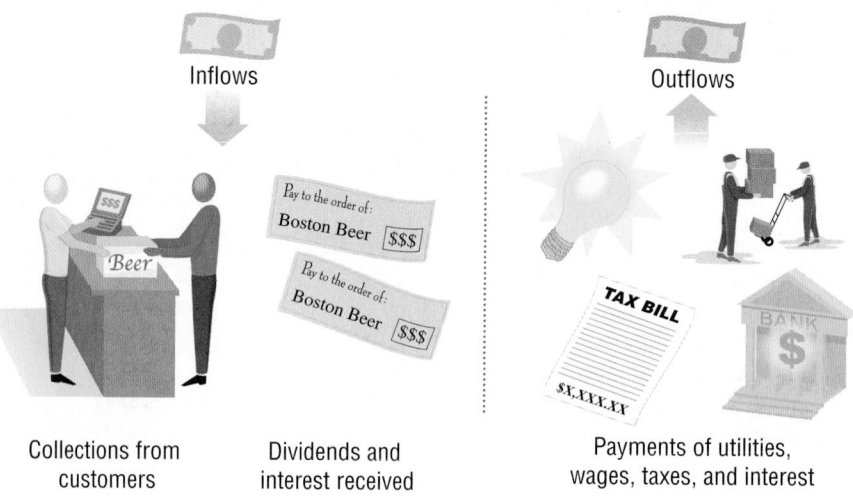

Inflows		Outflows
Collections from customers	Dividends and interest received	Payments of utilities, wages, taxes, and interest

Converting Revenues to Cash Inflows

When sales are recorded, accounts receivable increases, and when cash is collected, accounts receivable decreases. Thus, the following formula will convert sales revenue amounts from the accrual basis to the cash basis:

Using information from Boston Beer's income statement and balance sheet presented in Exhibit 13.3, we can compute cash collected from customers as follows:

		Accounts Receivable (A)	
Net sales	$72,448	Beg.	17,770
− Increase in accounts receivable	1,967 ◄	Increase	1,967
Cash collected from customers	$70,481	End.	19,737

Boston Beer's second revenue is interest income. Since there is no interest receivable balance, using the same logic, we can see that interest income must be equal to cash collected for interest.

Interest income	$1,132
No change in interest receivable	0
Cash collected for interest	$1,132

Converting Cost of Goods Sold to Cash Paid to Suppliers

Cost of goods sold represents the cost of merchandise sold during the accounting period. It may be more or less than the amount of cash paid to suppliers during the period. In Boston Beer's case, inventory increased during the quarter because the company bought more merchandise from suppliers than it sold to customers. If the company paid cash to suppliers of inventory, it must have paid more cash to suppliers than the amount of cost of goods sold, so the increase in inventory must be added to compute cash paid to suppliers.

Typically, companies owe their suppliers money (an accounts payable balance will appear on the balance sheet). To convert cost of goods sold to cash paid to suppliers, the borrowing and repayments represented by the accounts payable must also be considered. Borrowing increases cash and accounts payable and repayment decreases cash and accounts payable, so Boston Beer's decrease in accounts payable must also be added in the computation. Cost of goods sold can therefore be converted to a cash basis in the following manner:

Using information from Exhibit 13.3, we can compute cash paid to suppliers as follows:

Inventories (A)		
Beg.	17,034	
Increase	1,917	
End.	18,951	

Cost of goods sold $32,126
+ Increase in inventory 1,917
+ Decrease in accounts payable 3,320
Cash payments to suppliers $37,363

Accounts Payable (L)		
	Beg.	17,942
Decrease 3,320		
	End.	14,622

Converting Operating Expenses to a Cash Outflow

The total amount of an expense on the income statement may differ from the cash outflow associated with that activity. Some expenses are paid before they are recognized as expenses (e.g., prepaid rent). When prepayments are made, the balance in the asset prepaid expenses increases; when expenses are recorded, prepaid expenses decreases. When Boston Beer's prepaid expenses increased by $1,677 during the period, it paid more cash than it recorded as operating expenses. The increase must be added in computing cash paid for expenses.

Some other expenses are paid for after they are recognized (e.g., accrued expenses). In this case, when expenses are recorded, the balance in the liability accrued expenses increases; when payments are made, accrued expenses decreases. When Boston Beer's accrued expenses decreased by $744, it paid more cash than it recorded as operating expenses. The decrease must also be added in computing cash paid for expenses.

Generally, other expenses can be converted from the accrual basis to the cash basis in the following manner:

Using information from Exhibit 13.3, we can compute cash paid for expenses as follows:

Prepaid Expenses (A)				
Beg.	2,721			
Increase	1,677			
End.	4,398			

Selling, general, and administrative expense		$30,078
+ Increase in prepaid expenses		1,677
+ Decrease in accrued expenses		744
Cash payments for expenses		$32,499

Accrued Expenses (L)		
	Beg.	22,928
Decrease 744		
	End.	22,184

The same logic can be applied to income taxes. Boston Beer presents income tax expense of $3,882. Since there is no balance in Income Taxes Payable (or change in Deferred Taxes), income taxes paid must be the same as income tax expense.

Income tax expense	$3,882
No change in taxes payable	0
Cash payments for income taxes	$3,882

These amounts of the operating cash inflows and outflows are accumulated in Exhibit 13.8.

To summarize, the following adjustments must commonly be made to convert income statement items to the related operating cash flow amounts:

Income Statement Account	+/− Change in Balance Sheet Account(s)	= Operating Cash Flow
Sales revenue	+Decrease in Accounts Receivable (A) −Increase in Accounts Receivable (A)	= Collections from customers
Interest/Dividend revenue	+Decrease in Interest/Dividends Receivable (A) −Increase in Interest/Dividends Receivable (A)	= Collections of interest/ dividends on investments
Cost of goods sold	+Increase in Inventory (A) −Decrease in Inventory (A) −Increase in Accounts Payable (L) +Decrease in Accounts Payable (L)	= Payments to suppliers of inventory
Other expenses	+Increase in Prepaid Expenses (A) −Decrease in Prepaid Expenses (A) −Increase in Accrued Expenses (L) +Decrease in Accrued Expenses (L)	= Payments to suppliers of services (e.g., rent, utilities, wages, interest)
Income tax expense	+Increase in Prepaid Income Taxes (Deferred Taxes) (A) −Decrease in Prepaid Income Taxes (Deferred Taxes) (A) −Increase in Income Taxes Payable (Deferred Taxes) (L) +Decrease in Income Taxes Payable (Deferred Taxes) (L)	= Payments of income taxes

EXHIBIT 13.8

Boston Beer Company: Schedule for Net Cash Flow from Operating Activities, Direct Method (dollars in thousands)

Cash flows from operating activities	
Cash collected from customers	$70,481
Cash collected for interest	1,132
Cash payments to suppliers	(37,363)
Cash payments for expenses	(32,499)
Cash payments for income taxes	(3,882)
Net cash provided by operating activities	($ 2,131)

It is important to note again that the net cash inflow or outflow is the same regardless of whether the direct or indirect method of presentation is used (in this case, an outflow of $2,131). The two methods differ only in terms of the details reported on the statement.

Indicate which of the following line items taken from the cash flow statement would be added (+), subtracted (−), or not included (0) in the cash flow from operations section when the **direct** method is used.

____ 1. Increase in inventories.

____ 2. Payment of dividends to stockholders.

____ 3. Cash collections from customers.

____ 4. Purchase of plant and equipment for cash.

____ 5. Payments of interest to debtholders.

____ 6. Payment of taxes to the government.

After you have completed your answers, check them with the solutions at the bottom of the page.

Chapter Supplement B

Spreadsheet Approach—Statement of Cash Flows: Indirect Method

As situations become more complex, the analytical approach that we used to prepare the statement of cash flows for Boston Beer Company becomes cumbersome and inefficient. In actual practice, many companies use a spreadsheet approach to prepare the statement of cash flows. The spreadsheet is based on the same logic that we used in our previous illustration. The spreadsheet's primary advantage is that it offers a more systematic way to keep track of data. You may find it useful even in simple situations.

Exhibit 13.9 shows Boston Beer Company's spreadsheet, which is organized as follows:

1. Four columns to record dollar amounts are established. The first column is for the beginning balances for items reported on the balance sheet; the next two columns reflect debit and credit changes to those balances; the final column contains the ending balances for the balance sheet accounts.

2. On the far left of the top half of the spreadsheet, each account name from the balance sheet is entered.

3. On the far left of the bottom half of the spreadsheet, the name of each item that will be reported on the statement of cash flows is entered.

Changes in the various balance sheet accounts are analyzed in terms of debits and credits in the top half of the spreadsheet with the offsetting debits and credits being recorded in the bottom half of the spreadsheet in terms of their impact on cash flows. Each change in the noncash balance sheet accounts explains part of the change in the Cash account. To illustrate, let's examine each of the entries on the spreadsheet for Boston Beer Company shown in Exhibit 13.9. You will note that they follow each of the items presented in the schedules to prepare the cash flow statement shown in Exhibits 13.4, 13.5, and 13.6.

a. This entry is used to start the reconciliation; net income of $5,768 is shown as an inflow in the operating activities section to be adjusted by the noncash reconciling entries. The credit to

1. 0, 2. 0, 3. +, 4. 0, 5. −, 6. −.

Self-Study Quiz Solutions

EXHIBIT 13.9   Spreadsheet to Prepare Statement of Cash Flows, Indirect Method

BOSTON BEER COMPANY
Quarter Ended March 31, 2007
(dollars in thousands)

	Beginning Balances, 12/30/2006	Analysis of Change Debit		Analysis of Change Credit		Ending Balances, 3/31/2007
Items from Balance Sheet						
Cash and cash equivalents	63,147			(n)	1,698	61,449
Short-term investments	19,223	(k)	802	(j)	—	20,025
Accounts receivable	17,770	(d)	1,967			19,737
Inventories	17,034	(e)	1,917			18,951
Prepaid expenses	2,721	(f)	1,677			4,398
Equipment, net	31,879	(i)	1,736	(b)	1,726	31,887
				(c)	2	
Accounts payable	17,942	(g)	3,320			14,622
Accrued expenses	22,928	(h)	744			22,184
Contributed capital	81,237	(l)	2,729	(m)	5,698	84,206
Retained earnings	29,667			(a)	5,768	35,435

		Inflows		Outflows		Subtotals
Statement of Cash Flows						
Cash flows from operating activities:						
Net income		(a)	5,768			
Adjustments to reconcile net income to cash provided by operating activities						
Depreciation and amortization		(b)	1,726			
Changes in assets and liabilities:						
Accounts receivable				(d)	1,967	
Inventories				(e)	1,917	
Prepaid expenses				(f)	1,677	
Accounts payable				(g)	3,320	
Accrued expenses				(h)	744	
						(2,131)
Cash flows from investing activities:						
Proceeds from sale of equipment		(c)	2			
Purchases of equipment				(i)	1,736	
Maturities (sale) of short-term investments		(j)	—			
Purchase of short-term investments				(k)	802	
						(2,536)
Cash flows from financing activities:						
Purchase of treasury stock				(l)	2,729	
Net proceeds from stock issuance		(m)	5,698			
						2,969
Net decrease in cash and cash equivalents		(n)	1,698			
			29,784		29,784	(1,698)

Retained Earnings reflects the effects of the original closing entry. This is the starting point for the reconciliation.

b. Depreciation expense of $1,726 is a noncurrent accrued expense. It is added back to net income because this type of expense does not cause a cash outflow when it is recorded. The credit to Accumulated Depreciation reflects the effects of the original entry to record depreciation.

c. When an asset that was classified as part of fixed assets is sold, the actual cash proceeds of $2 appear in the Investing Section of the statement of cash flows.

d. This entry reconciles the change in accounts receivable during the period with net income. It is subtracted from net income because cash collections from customers totaled $1,967 less than sales revenue.

e. This entry reconciles the purchases of inventory with cost of goods sold. It is subtracted from net income because $1,917 more inventory was purchased than was sold.

f. This entry reconciles the prepayment of expenses with their expiration. It is subtracted from net income because cash payments for new prepayments are $1,677 more than the amounts that expired and were recorded on the income statement during the period.

g. This entry reconciles cash paid to suppliers with purchases on account. It is subtracted because $3,320 more cash was paid than was borrowed during the period.

h. This entry reconciles the accrual of expenses with payments for these expenses. It is subtracted because cash payments for expenses are $744 more than new accruals.

i. This entry records the purchases of new plant and equipment (fixed assets) for $1,736 cash.

j. This entry records the receipt of cash on maturity of some short-term investments. In this case, there was no receipt.

k. This entry records the purchases of short-term investments for $802 cash.

l. This entry records $2,727 cash paid to repurchase some of Boston Beer's own stock from shareholders.

m. This entry records the $5,698 cash received from the issuance of stock.

n. This entry shows that the net increase or decrease reported on the statement of cash flows is the same as the change in the cash balance on the balance sheet during the period.

The preceding entries complete the spreadsheet analysis because all accounts are reconciled. The accuracy of the analysis can be checked by adding the two analysis columns to verify that Debits = Credits. You should also note that the debits and credits to the balance sheet accounts directly match those recorded in the T-accounts presented in the body of the chapter. The formal statement of cash flows can be prepared directly from the spreadsheet.

The analytical technique that you have learned for preparing the statement of cash flows will help you deal with other significant business problems. For example, this type of analysis is useful for developing cash budgets for a business. Many small businesses that experience rapid sales growth get into serious financial difficulties because they did not forecast the cash flow effects associated with credit sales and large increases in inventory.

CHAPTER TAKE-AWAYS

1. **Classify cash flow statement items as part of net cash flows from operating, investing, and financing activities.   p. 655**

The statement has three main sections: Cash Flows from Operating Activities, which are related to earning income from normal operations; Cash Flows from Investing Activities, which are related to the acquisition and sale of productive assets; and Cash Flows from Financing Activities, which are related to external financing of the enterprise. The net cash inflow or outflow for the year is the same amount as the increase or decrease in cash and cash equivalents for the year on the balance sheet. Cash equivalents are highly liquid investments with original maturities of three months or less.

2. **Report and interpret cash flows from operating activities using the indirect method.   p. 661**

The indirect method for reporting cash flows from operating activities reports a conversion of net income to net cash flow from operating activities. The conversion involves additions and subtractions for (1) noncurrent accruals including expenses (such as depreciation expense) and revenues that do not affect current assets or current liabilities and (2) changes in each of the individual current assets (other than cash and short-term investments) and current liabilities (other than short-term debt to financial institutions and current maturities of long-term debt, which relate to financing), which reflect differences in the timing of accrual basis net income and cash flows.

3. **Analyze and interpret the quality of income ratio.   p. 667**

Quality of income ratio (Cash Flow from Operating Activities ÷ Net Income) measures the portion of income that was generated in cash. A higher quality of income ratio indicates greater ability to finance operating and other cash needs from operating cash inflows. A higher ratio also indicates that it is less likely that the company is using aggressive revenue recognition policies to increase net income.

4. **Report and interpret cash flows from investing activities.   p. 668**

Investing activities reported on the cash flow statement include cash payments to acquire fixed assets and short- and long-term investments and cash proceeds from the sale of fixed assets and short- and long-term investments.

5. **Analyze and interpret the capital acquisitions ratio.   p. 670**

The capital acquisitions ratio (Cash Flow from Operating Activities ÷ Cash Paid for Property, Plant, and Equipment) reflects the portion of purchases of property, plant, and equipment financed from operating activities without the need for outside debt or equity financing or the sale of other investments or fixed assets. A high ratio benefits the company because it provides the company with opportunities for strategic acquisitions.

6. **Report and interpret cash flows from financing activities.   p. 671**

Cash inflows from financing activities include cash proceeds from issuance of short- and long-term debt and common stock. Cash outflows include cash principal payments on short- and long-term debt, cash paid for the repurchase of the company's stock, and cash dividend payments. Cash payments associated with interest are a cash flow from operating activities.

7. **Understand the format of the cash flow statement and additional cash flow disclosures. p. 674**

The statement of cash flows splits transactions that affect cash into three categories: Operating, Investing, and Financing Activities. The operating section is most often prepared using the indirect method that begins with Net Income and adjusts the amount to eliminate noncash transactions. Noncash investing and financing activities are investing and financing activities that do not involve cash. They include, for example, purchases of fixed assets with long-term debt or stock, exchanges of fixed assets, and exchanges of debt for stock. These transactions are disclosed only as supplemental disclosures to the cash flow statement along with cash paid for taxes and interest under the indirect method.

Throughout the preceding chapters, we emphasized the conceptual basis of accounting. An understanding of the rationale underlying accounting is important for both preparers and users of financial statements. In Chapter 14, we bring together our discussion of the major users of financial statements and how they analyze and use them. We discuss and illustrate many widely used analytical techniques discussed in earlier chapters, as well as additional techniques. As you study Chapter 14, you will see that an understanding of accounting rules and concepts is essential for effective analysis of financial statements.

Quality of income ratio indicates what portion of income was generated in cash. It is computed as follows (p. 667):

$$\text{Quality of Income Ratio} = \frac{\text{Cash Flow from Operating Activities}}{\text{Net Income}}$$

Capital acquisitions ratio measures the ability to finance purchases of plant and equipment from operations. It is computed as follows (p. 670):

$$\text{Capital Acquisitions Ratio} = \frac{\text{Cash Flow from Operating Activities}}{\text{Cash Paid for Property, Plant, and Equipment}}$$

FINDING **FINANCIAL INFORMATION**

Balance Sheet

Changes in Assets, Liabilities, and Stockholders' Equity

Income Statement

Net Income and Noncurrent Accruals

Statement of Cash Flows

Cash Flows from Operating Activities

Cash Flows from Investing Activities

Cash Flows from Financing Activities

Separate Schedule (or note)
  Noncash investing and financing
    activities
  Interest and taxes paid

Notes

Under Summary of Significant Accounting Policies
  Definition of cash equivalents

Under Separate Note
  If not listed on cash flow statement:
    Noncash investing and financing
      activities
    Interest and taxes paid

KEY **TERMS**

Cash Equivalent   p. 655
Cash Flows from Financing
  Activities   p. 657
Cash Flows from Investing
  Activities   p. 657

Cash Flows from Operating
  Activities (Cash Flows from
  Operations)   p. 655
Direct Method   p. 655
Free Cash Flow   p. 671

Indirect Method   p. 655
Noncash Investing and Financing
  Activities   p. 674

QUESTIONS

1. Compare the purposes of the income statement, the balance sheet, and the statement of cash flows.
2. What information does the statement of cash flows report that is not reported on the other required financial statements? How do investors and creditors use that information?
3. What are cash equivalents? How are purchases and sales of cash equivalents reported on the statement of cash flows?
4. What are the major categories of business activities reported on the statement of cash flows? Define each of these activities.

5. What are the typical cash inflows from operating activities? What are the typical cash outflows from operating activities?

6. Under the indirect method, depreciation expense is added to net income to report cash flows from operating activities. Does depreciation cause an inflow of cash?

7. Explain why cash paid during the period for purchases and for salaries is not specifically reported on the statement of cash flows, indirect method, as cash outflows.

8. Explain why a $50,000 increase in inventory during the year must be included in developing cash flows for operating activities under both the direct and indirect methods.

9. Compare the two methods of reporting cash flows from operating activities in the statement of cash flows.

10. What are the typical cash inflows from investing activities? What are the typical cash outflows from investing activities?

11. What are the typical cash inflows from financing activities? What are the typical cash outflows from financing activities?

12. What are noncash investing and financing activities? Give two examples. How are they reported on the statement of cash flows?

13. How is the sale of equipment reported on the statement of cash flows using the indirect method?

MULTIPLE-CHOICE QUESTIONS

1. In what order do the three sections of the statement of cash flows appear when reading from top to bottom?
   a. Financing, Investing, Operating
   b. Investing, Operating, Financing
   c. Operating, Financing, Investing
   d. Operating, Investing, Financing

2. Total cash inflow in the operating section of the statement of cash flows should include which of the following?
   a. cash received from customers at the point of sale
   b. cash collections from customer accounts receivable
   c. cash received in advance of revenue recognition (unearned revenue)
   d. all of the above

3. If the balance in prepaid expenses increased during the year, what action should be taken on the statement of cash flows when following the indirect method, and why?
   a. The change in the account balance should be subtracted from net income because the net increase in prepaid expenses did not impact net income but did reduce the cash balance.
   b. The change in the account balance should be added to net income because the net increase in prepaid expenses did not impact net income but did increase the cash balance.
   c. The net change in prepaid expenses should be subtracted from net income to reverse the income statement effect that had no impact on cash.
   d. The net change in prepaid expenses should be added to net income to reverse the income statement effect that had no impact on cash.

4. Consider the following: Net income = $10,000, depreciation expense = $2,000, accounts receivable increased by $700, inventory decreased by $400, and accounts payable increased by $300. Based on this information alone, what is cash flow from operating activities?
   a. $12,000
   b. $8,000
   c. $11,700
   d. $10,000

5. Which of the following would not appear in the investing section of the statement of cash flows?
   a. purchase of inventory
   b. sale of obsolete equipment used in the factory
   c. purchase of land for a new office building
   d. All of the above would appear.

6. Which of the following items would not appear in the financing section of the statement of cash flows?
   a. the repurchase of the company's own stock
   b. the receipt of dividends
   c. the repayment of debt
   d. the payment of dividends

7. Which of the following is not added to net income when computing cash flows from operations under the indirect method?
   a. the net increase in accounts payable
   b. the net decrease in accounts receivable
   c. depreciation expense reported on the income statement
   d. All of the above are added.

8. Consider the following: Issued common stock for $25,000, sold office equipment for $1,200, paid cash dividends $6,000, purchased investments for $2,000, paid accounts payable of $4,000. What was the net cash inflow (outflow) from financing activities?
   a. $19,000   c. ($19,000)
   b. $14,000   d. ($14,000)

9. Consider the following: Issued common stock for $25,000, sold office equipment for $1,200, paid cash dividends $6,000, purchased investments for $2,000, purchased new equipment for $4,000. What was the net cash inflow (outflow) from investing activities?
   a. $20,200   c. ($10,800)
   b. ($2,800)   d. ($4,800)

10. The **total** change in cash as shown near the bottom of the statement of cash flows for the year should agree to which of the following?
   a. the difference in retained earnings when reviewing the comparative balance sheet
   b. net income or net loss as found on the income statement
   c. the difference in cash when reviewing the comparative balance sheet
   d. none of the above

For more practice with multiple-choice questions, go to the text website at www.mhhe.com/libby6e.

Available with McGraw-Hill's Homework Manager

MINI-EXERCISES

Matching Items Reported to Cash Flow Statement Categories (Indirect Method)

Coors Brewing Company, founded in 1873, is the third largest U.S. brewer. Its tie to the magical appeal of the Rocky Mountains is one of its most powerful trademarks. Some of the items included in its recent annual consolidated statement of cash flows presented using the **indirect method** are listed here. Indicate whether each item is disclosed in the Operating Activities (O), Investing Activities (I), or Financing Activities (F) section of the statement or (NA) if the item does not appear on the statement. (**Note:** This is the exact wording used on the actual statement.)

_____ 1. Purchase of stock. [This involves repurchase of its own stock.]
_____ 2. Principal payment on long-term debt.
_____ 3. Proceeds from sale of properties.
_____ 4. Inventories (decrease).
_____ 5. Accounts payable (decrease).
_____ 6. Depreciation, depletion, and amortization.

M13-1
L01
Coors

Determining the Effects of Account Changes on Cash Flow from Operating Activities (Indirect Method)

Indicate whether each item would be added (+) or subtracted (−) in the computation of cash flow from operating activities using the indirect method.

_____ 1. Accrued expenses (increase).
_____ 2. Inventories (increase).
_____ 3. Accounts receivable (decrease).
_____ 4. Accounts payable (decrease).
_____ 5. Depreciation, depletion, and amortization.

M13-2
L02

M13-3

LO1

Lion Nathan

Matching Items Reported to Cash Flow Statement Categories (Direct Method)

Lion Nathan, brewer of XXXX, Toohey's, and other well-known Australian brands, has net revenue of nearly $2 billion Australian. Some of the items included in its recent annual consolidated statement of cash flows presented using the **direct method** are listed here. Indicate whether each item is disclosed in the Operating Activities (O), Investing Activities (I), or Financing Activities (F) section of the statement or (NA) if the item does not appear on the statement. (**Note:** This is the exact wording used on the actual statement.)

_____ 1. Receipts from customers.
_____ 2. Dividends paid.
_____ 3. Payment for share buy-back.
_____ 4. Proceeds from sale of property, plant, and equipment.
_____ 5. Repayments of borrowings (bank debt).
_____ 6. Net interest paid.

M13-4

LO3

Analyzing the Quality of Income Ratio

Lisa K. Corporation reported net income of $86,000, depreciation expense of $2,000, and cash flow from operations of $52,500. Compute the quality of income ratio. What does the ratio tell you about the company's ability to finance operating and other cash needs from operating cash inflows?

M13-5

LO3

Computing Cash Flows from Investing Activities

Based on the following information, compute cash flows from investing activities.

Cash collections from customers	$550
Sale of used equipment	250
Depreciation expense	200
Purchase of short-term investments	285

M13-6

LO6

Computing Cash Flows from Financing Activities

Based on the following information, compute cash flows from financing activities.

Purchase of short-term investments	$ 500
Dividends paid	900
Interest paid	300
Additional short-term borrowing from bank	950

M13-7

LO7

Reporting Noncash Investing and Financing Activities

Which of the following transactions qualify as noncash investing and financing activities?
_____ Purchase of building with mortgage payable
_____ Additional short-term borrowing from bank
_____ Dividends paid in cash
_____ Purchase of equipment with short-term investments

EXERCISES

 Available with McGraw-Hill's Homework Manager

E13-1

LO1

Reebok

Matching Items Reported to Cash Flow Statement Categories (Indirect Method)

Reebok International Ltd. is a global company that designs and markets sports and fitness products, including footwear, apparel, and accessories. Some of the items included in its recent annual consolidated statement of cash flows presented using the **indirect method** are listed here.

Indicate whether each item is disclosed in the Operating Activities (O), Investing Activities (I), or Financing Activities (F) section of the statement or (NA) if the item does not appear on the statement. (**Note:** This is the exact wording used on the actual statement.)

_____ 1. Dividends paid
_____ 2. Repayments of long-term debt
_____ 3. Depreciation and amortization
_____ 4. Proceeds from issuance of common stock to employees
_____ 5. [Change in] Accounts payable and accrued expenses
_____ 6. Cash collections from customers
_____ 7. Net repayments of notes payable to banks
_____ 8. Net income
_____ 9. Payments to acquire property and equipment
_____ 10. [Change in] Inventory

Matching Items Reported to Cash Flow Statement Categories (Direct Method)

E13-2
LO1
BHP Billiton

The Australian company BHP Billiton is the world's biggest mining company. Some of the items included in its recent annual consolidated statement of cash flows presented using the **direct method** are listed here.

Indicate whether each item is disclosed in the Operating Activities (O), Investing Activities (I), or Financing Activities (F) section of the statement or (NA) if the item does not appear on the statement. (**Note:** This is the exact wording used on the actual statement.)

_____ 1. Proceeds from sale of property, plant, and equipment
_____ 2. Interest received
_____ 3. Repayments of loans
_____ 4. Income taxes paid
_____ 5. Proceeds from ordinary share [stock] issues
_____ 6. Dividends paid
_____ 7. Payments in the course of operations
_____ 8. Receipts from customers
_____ 9. Payments for property, plant, and equipment
_____ 10. Net income

Determining Cash Flow Statement Effects of Transactions

E13-3
LO1
Stanley Furniture

Stanley Furniture Company is a Virginia-based furniture manufacturer. For each of the following first-quarter transactions, indicate whether **net cash inflows (outflows)** from operating activities (NCFO), investing activities (NCFI), or financing activities (NCFF) are affected and whether the effect is an inflow (+) or outflow (−), or (NE) if the transaction has no effect on cash. (**Hint:** Determine the journal entry recorded for the transaction. The transaction affects net cash flows *if and only if* the account Cash is affected.)

_____ 1. Recorded an adjusting entry to record accrued salaries expense.
_____ 2. Paid cash to purchase new equipment.
_____ 3. Collected payments on account from customers.
_____ 4. Recorded and paid interest on debt to creditors.
_____ 5. Declared and paid cash dividends to shareholders.
_____ 6. Sold used equipment for cash at book value.
_____ 7. Prepaid rent for the following period.
_____ 8. Repaid principal on revolving credit loan from bank.
_____ 9. Purchased raw materials inventory on account.
_____ 10. Made payment to suppliers on account.

Determining Cash Flow Statement Effects of Transactions

E13-4
LO1
Hewlett-Packard

Hewlett-Packard is a leading manufacturer of computer equipment for the business and home markets. For each of the following recent transactions, indicate whether **net cash inflows (outflows)** from operating activities (NCFO), investing activities (NCFI), or financing activities (NCFF) are affected and whether the effect is an inflow (+) or outflow (−), or (NE) if the transaction has no effect on cash. (**Hint:** Determine the journal entry recorded for the transaction. The transaction affects net cash flows *if and only if* the account Cash is affected.)

_____ 1. Purchased raw materials inventory on account.
_____ 2. Prepaid rent for the following period.
_____ 3. Purchased new equipment by signing a three-year note.

_____ 4. Recorded an adjusting entry for expiration of a prepaid expense.
_____ 5. Recorded and paid income taxes to the federal government.
_____ 6. Purchased investment securities for cash.
_____ 7. Issued common stock for cash.
_____ 8. Collected payments on account from customers.
_____ 9. Sold equipment for cash equal to its net book value.
_____ 10. Issued long-term debt for cash.

E13-5
LO1

Comparing the Direct and Indirect Methods

To compare statement of cash flows reporting under the direct and indirect methods, enter check marks to indicate which items are used with each method.

Cash Flows (and Related Changes)	STATEMENT OF CASH FLOWS METHOD	
	Direct	Indirect
1. Accounts payable increase or decrease		
2. Payments to employees		
3. Cash collections from customers		
4. Accounts receivable increase or decrease		
5. Payments to suppliers		
6. Inventory increase or decrease		
7. Wages payable, increase or decrease		
8. Depreciation expense		
9. Net income		
10. Cash flows from operating activities		
11. Cash flows from investing activities		
12. Cash flows from financing activities		
13. Net increase or decrease in cash during the period		

E13-6
LO2

Reporting Cash Flows from Operating Activities (Indirect Method)

The following information pertains to Night Company:

Income Statement		
Sales		$75,000
Expenses		
Cost of goods sold	$46,875	
Depreciation expense	8,500	
Salaries expense	12,000	67,375
Net income		$ 7,625

Partial Balance Sheet	2010	2009
Accounts receivable	$12,500	$10,000
Inventory	8,000	15,000
Salaries payable	1,750	800

Required:

Present the operating activities section of the statement of cash flows for Night Company using the indirect method.

E13-7
LO2

Reporting and Interpreting Cash Flows from Operating Activities from an Analyst's Perspective (Indirect Method)

Able Company completed its income statement and balance sheet for 2010 and provided the following information:

Income Statement		
Service revenue		$51,000
Expenses		
Salaries	$41,000	
Depreciation	5,000	
Amortization of copyrights	200	
Other expenses	8,700	54,900
Net loss		($ 3,900)
Partial Balance Sheet	**2010**	**2009**
Accounts receivable	$ 8,000	$25,000
Salaries payable	14,000	1,000
Other accrued liabilities	1,000	5,100

In addition, Able bought a small service machine for $5,000.

Required:
1. Present the operating activities section of the statement of cash flows for Able Company using the indirect method.
2. What were the major reasons that Able was able to report a net loss but positive cash flow from operations? Why are the reasons for the difference between cash flow from operations and net income important to financial analysts?

Reporting and Interpreting Cash Flows from Operating Activities from an Analyst's Perspective (Indirect Method)

E13-8
LO2
Time Warner Telecom

Time Warner Telecom, Inc., offers network, local, and long-distance voice services, data transmission services, high-speed dedicated Internet access, and intercarrier services to business customers and organizations throughout the United States. The company's recent annual report contained the following information (dollars in thousands):

Net loss	$ (98,819)
Depreciation and amortization	259,380
Increase in receivables	18,161
Decrease in accrued interest	18,207
Increase in accounts payable	571
Decrease in accrued payroll and benefits	3,236
Increase in other liabilities (current)	53,030
Increase in long-term debt	94,248
Additions to equipment	192,269

Required:
1. Based on this information, compute cash flow from operating activities using the indirect method.
2. What were the major reasons that Time Warner was able to report a net loss but positive cash flow from operations? Why are the reasons for the difference between cash flow from operations and net income important to financial analysts?

Inferring Balance Sheet Changes from the Cash Flow Statement (Indirect Method)

E13-9
LO2
Colgate-Palmolive

A recent statement of cash flows for Colgate-Palmolive reported the following information (dollars in millions):

Operating Activities	
Net income	$1,353.4
Depreciation	328.7
Cash effect of changes in	
Receivables	(116.0)
Inventories	(118.5)
Other current assets	8.2
Payables	149.9
Other	215.8
Net cash provided by operations	$1,821.5

Required:

Based on the information reported on the statement of cash flows for Colgate-Palmolive, determine whether the following accounts increased or decreased during the period: Receivables, Inventories, Other Current Assets, and Payables.

E13-10

L02

Apple, Inc.

Inferring Balance Sheet Changes from the Cash Flow Statement (Indirect Method)

A recent statement of cash flows for Apple contained the following information (dollars in thousands):

Operations	
Net income	$ 310,178
Depreciation	167,958
Changes in assets and liabilities	
Accounts receivable	(199,401)
Inventories	418,204
Other current assets	33,616
Accounts payable	139,095
Income taxes payable	50,045
Other current liabilities	39,991
Other adjustments	(222,691)
Cash generated by operations	$ 736,995

Required:

For each of the asset and liability accounts listed on the statement of cash flows, determine whether the account balances increased or decreased during the period.

E13-11

L04

Reporting Cash Flows from the Sale of Plant and Equipment

During two recent years A. Klein, Inc. disposed of the following plant and equipment:

	Year 1	Year 2
Plant and equipment (at cost)	$55,000	$ 8,500
Accumulated depreciation on equipment disposed of	29,677	3,616
Cash received	14,692	11,616
Gain (loss) on sale	(10,631)	6,732

Required:

1. Determine the cash flow from the sale of property for each year that would be reported in the investing activities section of the cash flow statement.
2. Klein uses the indirect method for the operating activities section of the cash flow statement. What amounts related to the sales would be added or subtracted in the computation of Net Cash Flows from Operating Activities for each year?

Reporting Cash Flows from the Sale of Equipment

E13-12
LO4

During the period, English Company sold some excess equipment at a loss. The following information was collected from the company's accounting records:

From the income statement	
Depreciation expense	$ 630
Loss on sale of equipment	2,700
From the balance sheet	
Beginning equipment	13,000
Ending equipment	7,700
Beginning accumulated depreciation	1,800
Ending accumulated depreciation	1,900

No new equipment was bought during the period.

Required:

1. For the equipment that was sold, determine its original cost, its accumulated depreciation, and the cash received from the sale. (Use the equipment and accumulated depreciation T-accounts to infer the book value of the equipment sold.)
2. English Company uses the indirect method for the Operating Activities section of the cash flow statement. What amount related to the sales would be added or subtracted in the computation of Net Cash Flows from Operating Activities?
3. What amount related to the sales would be added or subtracted in the computation of Net Cash Flows from Investing Activities?

Analyzing Cash Flows from Operating Activities; Interpreting the Quality of Income Ratio

E13-13
LO2, 3
PepsiCo

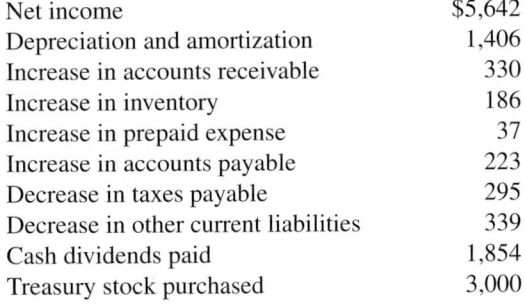

A recent annual report for PepsiCo contained the following information for the period (dollars in millions):

Net income	$5,642
Depreciation and amortization	1,406
Increase in accounts receivable	330
Increase in inventory	186
Increase in prepaid expense	37
Increase in accounts payable	223
Decrease in taxes payable	295
Decrease in other current liabilities	339
Cash dividends paid	1,854
Treasury stock purchased	3,000

Required:

1. Compute cash flows from operating activities for PepsiCo using the indirect method.
2. Compute the quality of income ratio.
3. What were the major reasons that Pepsi's quality of income ratio did not equal 1.0?

Reporting Cash Flows from Investing and Financing Activities

E13-14
LO4, 6

Randall's Furniture Corporation is a Virginia-based manufacturer of furniture. In a recent quarter, it reported the following activities:

Net income	$ 4,135
Purchase of property, plant, and equipment	871
Borrowings under line of credit (bank)	1,417
Proceeds from issuance of stock	11
Cash received from customers	29,164
Payments to reduce long-term debt	46
Sale of marketable securities	134
Proceeds from sale of property and equipment	6,594
Dividends paid	277
Interest paid	90
Purchase of treasury stock (stock repurchase)	1,583

Required:

Based on this information, present the cash flow from investing and financing activities sections of the cash flow statement.

E13-15
LO2, 4, 6

Preparing a Statement of Cash Flows (Indirect Method)

Dive In Company was started several years ago by two diving instructors. The company's comparative balance sheets and income statement are presented below, along with additional information.

	2008	2007
Balance sheet at December 31		
Cash	$ 3,200	$ 4,000
Accounts receivable	700	500
Prepaid expenses	100	50
Equipment	300	0
	$ 4,300	$ 4,550
Wages payable	$ 350	$ 1,100
Contributed capital	1,200	1,000
Retained earnings	2,750	2,450
	$ 4,300	$ 4,550
Income statement for 2008		
Lessons revenue	$33,950	
Wages expense	30,000	
Other expenses	3,650	
Net income	$ 300	

Additional Data:
a. Prepaid expenses relate to rent paid in advance.
b. Other operating expenses were paid in cash.
c. Purchased equipment for $300 cash at the end of 2008 to be used starting in 2009.
d. An owner contributed capital by paying $200 cash in exchange for the company's stock.

Required:

Prepare the statement of cash flows for the year ended December 31, 2008, using the indirect method.

E13-16
LO4, 5, 6

Reporting and Interpreting Cash Flows from Investing and Financing Activities with Discussion of Management Strategy

Gibraltar Industries is a Buffalo, New York-based manufacturer of high-value-added steel products. In a recent year, it reported the following activities:

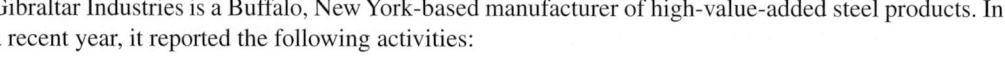

Acquisitions (investments in other companies)	$ (84,243)
Decrease in inventories	11,056
Depreciation and amortization	22,448
Long-term debt reduction	(118,100)
Net cash provided by operating activities	64,663
Net income	26,953
Net proceeds from issuance of common stock	73,558
Net proceeds from sale of property and equipment	436
Payment of dividends	(2,733)
Proceeds from long-term debt	122,144
Purchases of other equity investments	(7,797)
Purchases of property, plant, and equipment	(22,571)

Required:

1. Based on this information, present the cash flow from investing and financing activities sections of the cash flow statement.
2. Compute the capital acquisitions ratio. What does the ratio tell you about Gibraltar's ability to finance purchases of property, plant, and equipment with cash provided by operating activities?
3. What do you think was Gibraltar management's plan for the use of the cash generated by the issuance of common stock?

Reporting Noncash Transactions on the Statement of Cash Flows; Interpreting the Effect on the Capital Acquisitions Ratio

E13-17
LO5, 7

An analysis of Martin Corporation's operational asset accounts provided the following information:

a. Acquired a large machine that cost $26,000, paying for it by giving a $15,000, 12 percent interest-bearing note due at the end of two years and 500 shares of its common stock, with a par value of $10 per share and a market value of $22 per share.
b. Acquired a small machine that cost $8,700. Full payment was made by transferring a tract of land that had a book value of $8,700.

Required:

1. Show how this information should be reported on the statement of cash flows.
2. What would be the effect of these transactions on the capital acquisitions ratio? How might these transactions distort interpretation of the ratio?

Reporting Cash Flows from Operating Activities from an Analyst's Perspective (Direct Method) (Supplement A)

E13-18

Refer to the information for Night Company in Exercise 13.6.

Required:
Present the operating activities section of the statement of cash flows for Night Company using the direct method.

Reporting and Interpreting Cash Flows from Operating Activities from an Analyst's Perspective (Direct Method) (Supplement A)

E13-19

Refer to the information for Able Company in Exercise 13.7.

Required:

1. Present the operating activities section of the statement of cash flows for Able Company using the direct method. Assume that other accrued liabilities relate to other expenses on the income statement.
2. What were the major reasons that Able was able to report a net loss but positive cash flow from operations? Why are the reasons for the difference between cash flow from operations and net income important to financial analysts?

Reporting and Interpreting Cash Flows from Operating Activities from an Analyst's Perspective (Direct Method) (Supplement A)

E13-20

Refer to the following summarized income statement and additional selected information for Sizzler, Inc.:

Income statement		Other information:	
Revenues	$136,500	Increase in receivables	$ 170
Cost of sales	45,500	Decrease in inventories	643
Gross margin	91,000	Increase in prepaid expenses	664
Salary expense	56,835	Decrease in accounts payable	2,282
Depreciation and amortization	33,305	Decrease in accrued liabilities	719
Other expense	7,781	Increase in income taxes payable	1,861
Net loss before tax	(6,921)		
Income tax expense	2,561		
Net loss	$ (9,482)		

Required:

1. Based on this information, compute cash flow from operating activities using the direct method. Assume that prepaid expenses and accrued liabilities relate to other expense.
2. What were the major reasons that Sizzler was able to report a net loss but positive cash flow from operations? Why are the reasons for the difference between cash flow from operations and net income important to financial analysts?

E13-21   Preparing a Statement of Cash Flows, Indirect Method: Complete Spreadsheet (Supplement B)

An analysis of accounts follows:

a.   Purchased equipment, $16,000, and issued capital stock in full payment.
b.   Purchased a long-term investment for cash, $10,000.
c.   Paid cash dividend, $15,000.
d.   Sold operational asset for $6,000 cash (cost, $21,000, accumulated depreciation, $15,000).
e.   Sold capital stock, 300 shares at $12 per share cash.

Items from Financial Statements	Beginning Balances, 12/31/2010	ANALYSIS OF CHANGES		Ending Balances, 12/31/2011
		Debit	Credit	
Income statement items				
Sales			$140,000	
Cost of goods sold		$59,000		
Depreciation		3,000		
Wage expense		28,000		
Income tax expense		9,000		
Interest expense		5,000		
Remaining expenses		15,800		
Net income		20,200		
Balance sheet items				
Cash	$ 20,500			$ 18,800
Accounts receivable	22,000			22,000
Merchandise inventory	68,000			75,000
Investments, long-term				10,000
Equipment	114,500			109,500
Total debits	$225,000			$235,300
Accumulated depreciation	$ 32,000			$ 20,000
Accounts payable	17,000			14,000
Wages payable	2,500			1,500
Income taxes payable	3,000			4,500
Bonds payable	54,000			54,000
Common stock, no par	100,000			119,600
Retained earnings	16,500			21,700
Total credits	$225,000			$235,300
		Inflows	Outflows	
Statement of cash flows				
Cash flows from operating activities:				
Cash flows from investing activities:				
Cash flows from financing activities:				
Net increase (decrease) in cash				
Totals				

Required:

Complete the spreadsheet for the statement of cash flows, indirect method.

Preparing a Statement of Cash Flows (Indirect Method) (AP13-1)

PROBLEMS

Preparing a Statement of Cash Flows (Indirect Method) (AP13-1)

P13-1
LO1, 2, 4, 6
eXcel
www.mhhe.com/libby6e

MetroVideo Inc. is developing its annual financial statements at December 31, 2011. The statements are complete except for the statement of cash flows. The completed comparative balance sheets and income statement are summarized:

	2011	2010
Balance sheet at December 31		
Cash	$ 68,250	$ 65,500
Accounts receivable	15,250	22,250
Merchandise inventory	22,250	18,000
Property and equipment	209,250	150,000
Less: Accumulated depreciation	(59,000)	(45,750)
	$256,000	$210,000
Accounts payable	$ 9,000	$ 19,000
Wages payable	4,000	1,200
Note payable, long-term	59,500	71,000
Contributed capital	98,500	65,900
Retained earnings	85,000	52,900
	$256,000	$210,000
Income statement for 2011		
Sales	$195,000	
Cost of goods sold	92,000	
Depreciation expense	13,250	
Other expenses	43,000	
Net income	$ 46,750	

Additional Data:
a. Bought equipment for cash, $59,250.
b. Paid $11,500 on the long-term note payable.
c. Issued new shares of stock for $32,600 cash.
d. Dividends of $14,650 were declared and paid.
e. Other expenses all relate to wages.
f. Accounts payable includes only inventory purchases made on credit.

Required:
1. Prepare the statement of cash flows using the indirect method for the year ended December 31, 2011.
2. Based on the cash flow statement, write a short paragraph explaining the major sources and uses of cash by MetroVideo during 2011.

Preparing a Statement of Cash Flows (Indirect Method) (AP13-2)

P13-2
LO1, 2, 4, 6

XS Supply Company is developing its annual financial statements at December 31, 2010. The statements are complete except for the statement of cash flows. The completed comparative balance sheets and income statement are summarized:

	2010	2009
Balance sheet at December 31		
Cash	$ 34,000	$ 29,000
Accounts receivable	35,000	28,000
Merchandise inventory	41,000	38,000
Property and equipment	121,000	100,000
Less: Accumulated depreciation	(30,000)	(25,000)
	$201,000	$170,000
Accounts payable	$ 36,000	$ 27,000
Accrued expenses	1,200	1,400
Note payable, long-term	38,000	44,000
Contributed capital	88,600	72,600
Retained earnings	37,200	25,000
	$201,000	$170,000
Income statement for 2009		
Sales	$120,000	
Cost of goods sold	70,000	
Other expenses	37,800	
Net income	$ 12,200	

Additional Data:
a. Bought equipment for cash, $21,000.
b. Paid $6,000 on the long-term note payable.
c. Issued new shares of stock for $16,000 cash.
d. No dividends were declared or paid.
e. Other expenses included depreciation, $5,000; wages, $20,000; taxes, $6,000; other, $6,800.
f. Accounts payable includes only inventory purchases made on credit. Because there are no liability accounts relating to taxes or other expenses, assume that these expenses were fully paid in cash.

Required:
1. Prepare the statement of cash flows for the year ended December 31, 2010, using the indirect method.
2. Based on the cash flow statement, write a short paragraph explaining the major sources and uses of cash during 2010.

P13-3   **(Supplement A) Preparing a Statement of Cash Flows (Direct Method)** (AP13-3)

Use the information concerning MetroVideo Inc. provided in Problem 13-1 to fulfill the following requirements.

Required:
1. Prepare the statement of cash flows using the direct method for the year ended December 31, 2011.
2. Based on the cash flow statement, write a short paragraph explaining the major sources and uses of cash by MetroVideo during 2011.

P13-4   **(Supplement A) Comparing Cash Flows from Operating Activities (Direct and Indirect Methods)**

Beta Company's accountants just completed the income statement and balance sheet for the year and have provided the following information (dollars in thousands):

INCOME STATEMENT

Sales revenue		$19,800
Expenses		
Cost of goods sold	$9,030	
Depreciation expense	2,900	
Salaries expense	5,070	
Rent expense	2,800	
Insurance expense	900	
Utilities expense	720	
Interest expense on bonds	600	
Loss on sale of investments	650	22,670
Net loss		$ (2,870)

SELECTED BALANCE SHEET ACCOUNTS

	2010	2011
Merchandise inventory	$ 65	$ 84
Accounts receivable	530	440
Accounts payable	212	245
Salaries payable	23	31
Rent payable	8	4
Prepaid rent	7	4
Prepaid insurance	7	17

Other Data:

The company issued $20,000, 8 percent bonds payable during the year.

Required:

1. Prepare the cash flows from operating activities section of the statement of cash flows using the direct method.
2. Prepare the cash flows from operating activities section of the statement of cash flows using the indirect method.

(Supplement B) Preparing Statement of Cash Flows Spreadsheet, Statement of Cash Flows, and Schedules Using Indirect Method

P13-5

eXcel

www.mhhe.com/libby6e

Hunter Company is developing its annual financial statements at December 31, 2011. The statements are complete except for the statement of cash flows. The completed comparative balance sheets and income statement are summarized:

	2011	2010
Balance sheet at December 31		
Cash	$ 44,000	$ 18,000
Accounts receivable	27,000	29,000
Merchandise inventory	30,000	36,000
Fixed assets (net)	75,000	72,000
	$176,000	$155,000
Accounts payable	$ 25,000	$ 22,000
Wages payable	800	1,000
Note payable, long-term	38,000	48,000
Common stock, no par	80,000	60,000
Retained earnings	32,200	24,000
	$176,000	$155,000

continued

Income statement for 2011

Sales	$100,000
Cost of goods sold	(61,000)
Expenses	(27,000)
Net income	$ 12,000

Additional Data:

a. Bought fixed assets for cash, $9,000.
b. Paid $10,000 on the long-term note payable.
c. Sold unissued common stock for $20,000 cash.
d. Declared and paid a $3,800 cash dividend.
e. Incurred expenses that included depreciation, $6,000; wages, $10,000; taxes, $3,000; other, $8,000.

Required:

1. Prepare a statement of cash flows spreadsheet using the indirect method to report cash flows from operating activities.
2. Prepare the statement of cash flows.
3. Prepare a schedule of noncash investing and financing activities if necessary.

ALTERNATE PROBLEMS

AP13-1   Preparing a Statement of Cash Flows (Indirect Method) (P13–1)
LO1, 2, 4, 6

McPherson Construction Supply Company is developing its annual financial statements at December 31, 2011. The statements are complete except for the statement of cash flows. The completed comparative balance sheets and income statement are summarized:

	2011	2010
Balance sheet at December 31		
Cash	$ 34,000	$ 29,000
Accounts receivable	45,000	28,000
Merchandise inventory	31,000	38,000
Property and equipment	121,000	100,000
Less: Accumulated depreciation	(30,000)	(25,000)
	$201,000	$170,000
Accounts payable	$ 36,000	$ 27,000
Wages payable	1,200	1,400
Note payable, long-term	38,000	44,000
Contributed capital	88,600	72,600
Retained earnings	37,200	25,000
	$201,000	$170,000
Income statement for 2011		
Sales	$130,000	
Cost of goods sold	70,000	
Other expenses	37,800	
Net income	$ 22,200	

Additional Data:

a. Bought equipment for cash, $21,000.
b. Paid $6,000 on the long-term note payable.
c. Issued new shares of stock for $16,000 cash.

d. Dividends of $10,000 were declared and paid in cash.

e. Other expenses included depreciation, $5,000; wages, $20,000; taxes, $6,000; other, $6,800.

f. Accounts payable includes only inventory purchases made on credit. Because there are no liability accounts relating to taxes or other expenses, assume that these expenses were fully paid in cash.

Required:

1. Prepare the statement of cash flows using the indirect method for the year ended December 31, 2011.
2. Evaluate the statement of cash flows.

Preparing a Statement of Cash Flows (Indirect Method) (P13-2)

AP13-2
LO1, 2, 4, 6

Audio City, Inc., is developing its annual financial statements at December 31, 2010. The statements are complete except for the statement of cash flows. The completed comparative balance sheets and income statement are summarized:

	2010	2009
Balance sheet at December 31		
Cash	$ 63,000	$ 65,000
Accounts receivable	15,000	20,000
Inventory	22,000	20,000
Property and equipment	210,000	150,000
Less: Accumulated depreciation	(60,000)	(45,000)
	$250,000	$210,000
Accounts payable	$ 8,000	$ 19,000
Taxes payable	2,000	1,000
Note payable, long-term	85,000	75,000
Contributed capital	75,000	70,000
Retained earnings	80,000	45,000
	$250,000	$210,000
Income statement for 2010		
Sales	$190,000	
Cost of goods sold	90,000	
Other expenses	60,000	
Net income	$ 40,000	

Additional Data:

a. Bought equipment for cash, $60,000.

b. Borrowed an additional $10,000 and signed an additional long-term note payable.

c. Issued new shares of stock for $5,000 cash.

d. Dividends of $5,000 were declared and paid in cash.

e. Other expenses included depreciation, $15,000; wages, $20,000; taxes, $25,000.

f. Accounts payable includes only inventory purchases made on credit. Because a liability relating to taxes does not exist, assume that they were fully paid in cash.

Required:

1. Prepare the statement of cash flows for the year ended December 31, 2010, using the indirect method.
2. Based on the cash flow statement, write a short paragraph explaining the major sources and uses of cash during 2010.

(Supplement A) Preparing a Statement of Cash Flows (Direct Method) (P13-3)

AP13-3

Use the information concerning McPherson Construction Supply provided in Alternate Problem 13-1 to fulfill the following requirements.

Required:

1. Prepare the statement of cash flows using the direct method for the year ended December 31, 2011.
2. Evaluate the statement of cash flows.

CASES **AND PROJECTS**

Annual Report Cases

CP13-1
LO2, 4, 6

AMERICAN EAGLE
OUTFITTERS

Finding Financial Information

Refer to the financial statements of American Eagle Outfitters given in Appendix B at the end of this book.

Required:
1. Excluding proceeds from the sale of trading securities, what was the largest item (in absolute value) listed under "Adjustments to reconcile net income from continuing operations to net cash provided by operating activities"? What was the largest "Changes in assets and liabilities" in the operating section of the cash flow statement? Explain the direction of the effect of each in the reconciliation.
2. Examine American Eagle Outfitters' investing and financing activities. List the company's three largest uses of cash over the past three years. List two major sources of cash for these activities.
3. What was free cash flow for the year ended February 3, 2007? What does this imply about the company's financial flexibility?

CP13-2
LO2A, 4, 6
Urban Outfitters

Finding Financial Information

Refer to the financial statements of Urban Outfitters given in Appendix C at the end of this book.

Required:
1. Does Urban Outfitters use the direct or indirect method to report cash flows from operating activities?
2. What amount of tax payments did the company make during the most recent reporting year? (**Hint:** The statement of cash flows may be helpful to answer this question.)
3. Explain why the "stock compensation" and "depreciation and amortization" were added in the reconciliation of net income to net cash provided by operating activities.
4. Has the company paid cash dividends during the last three years? How did you know?
5. What was free cash flow for the year ended January 31, 2007?

CP13-3
LO3, 5

AMERICAN EAGLE
OUTFITTERS

Urban Outfitters

www.mhhe.com/libby6e

Comparing Companies within an Industry

Refer to the financial statements of American Eagle Outfitters given in Appendix B, Urban Outfitters given in Appendix C, and the Industry Ratio Report given in Appendix D at the end of this book.

Required:
1. Compute the quality of income ratio for both companies for the most recent reporting year. Which company has a better quality of income ratio?
2. Compare the quality of income ratio for both companies to the industry average. Are these companies producing more or less cash from operating activities relative to net income than the average company in the industry?
3. Compute the capital acquisitions ratio for both companies for the most recent reporting year. Compare their abilities to finance purchases of property, plant, and equipment with cash provided by operating activities.
4. Compare the capital acquisitions ratio for both companies to the industry average. How do these two companies' abilities to finance the purchase of property, plant, and equipment with cash provided by operating activities compare those of the industry?

Financial Reporting and Analysis Cases

CP13-4
LO1, 2, 4, 6

Preparing a Complex Statement of Cash Flows (Indirect Method)

Rocky Mountain Chocolate Factory manufactures an extensive line of premium chocolate candies for sale at its franchised and company-owned stores in malls throughout the United States. Its balance sheet for the first quarter of a recent year is presented along with an analysis of selected accounts and transactions:

ROCKY MOUNTAIN CHOCOLATE FACTORY, INC.
Balance Sheets

Assets	May 31 (Unaudited)	February 29
Current assets		
Cash and cash equivalents	$ 921,505	$ 528,787
Accounts and notes receivable—trade, less allowance for doubtful accounts of $43,196 at May 31 and $28,196 at February 29	1,602,582	1,463,901
Inventories	2,748,788	2,504,908
Deferred tax asset	59,219	59,219
Other	581,508	224,001
Total current assets	5,913,602	4,780,816
Property and equipment—at cost	14,010,796	12,929,675
Less accumulated depreciation and amortization	−2,744,388	−2,468,084
	11,266,408	10,461,591
Other assets		
Notes and accounts receivable due after one year	100,206	111,588
Goodwill and other intangibles, net of accumulated amortization of $259,641 at May 31 and $253,740 at Feb. 29	330,359	336,260
Other	574,130	624,185
	1,004,695	1,072,033
	$18,184,705	$16,314,440

Liabilities and Equity	May 31 (Unaudited)	February 29
Current liabilities		
Short-term debt	$ 0	$ 1,000,000
Current maturities of long-term debt	429,562	134,538
Accounts payable—trade	1,279,455	998,520
Accrued liabilities	714,473	550,386
Income taxes payable	11,198	54,229
Total current liabilities	2,434,688	2,737,673
Long-term debt, less current maturities	4,193,290	2,183,877
Deferred income taxes	275,508	275,508
Stockholders' Equity		
Common stock—authorized 7,250,000 shares, $.03 par value; issued 3,034,302 shares at May 31 and at Feb. 29	91,029	91,029
Additional paid-in capital	9,703,985	9,703,985
Retained earnings	2,502,104	2,338,267
	12,297,118	12,133,281
Less common stock held in treasury, at cost—129,153 shares at May 31 and at February 29	1,015,899	1,015,899
	11,281,219	11,117,382
	$18,184,705	$16,314,440

Analysis of Selected Accounts and Transactions:

a. Net income was $163,837. Notes and accounts receivable due after one year relate to operations.
b. Depreciation and amortization totaled $282,205.
c. No "other" noncurrent assets (which relate to investing activities) were purchased this period.
d. No property, plant, and equipment were sold during the period. No goodwill was acquired or sold.
e. Proceeds from issuance of long-term debt were $4,659,466 and principal payments were $2,355,029. (Combine the current maturities with the long-term debt in your analysis.)
f. No dividends were declared or paid.
g. Ignore the "deferred tax asset" and "deferred income taxes" accounts.

Required:
Prepare a statement of cash flows, indirect method, for the first quarter.

Making a Decision as a Financial Analyst: Analyzing Cash Flow for a New Company

CP13-5
LO2
Carlyle Golf, Inc.

Carlyle Golf, Inc., was formed in September of last year. The company designs, contracts for the manufacture of, and markets a line of men's golf apparel. A portion of the statement of cash flows for Carlyle follows:

CURRENT YEAR	
Cash flows from operating activities	
Net income	$(460,089)
Depreciation	3,554
Noncash compensation (stock)	254,464
Deposits with suppliers	(404,934)
Increase in prepaid assets	(42,260)
Increase in accounts payable	81,765
Increase in accrued liabilities	24,495
Net cash flows	$(543,005)

Management expects a solid increase in sales in the near future. To support the increase in sales, it plans to add $2.2 million to inventory. The company did not disclose a sales forecast. At the end of the current year, Carlyle had less than $1,000 in cash. It is not unusual for a new company to experience a loss and negative cash flows during its start-up phase.

Required:
As a financial analyst recently hired by a major investment bank, you have been asked to write a short memo to your supervisor evaluating the problems facing Carlyle. Emphasize typical sources of financing that may or may not be available to support the expansion.

Critical Thinking Cases

CP13-6   **Ethical Decision-Making: A Real-Life Example**

In a February 19, 2004, press release, the Securities and Exchange Commission described a number of fraudulent transactions that Enron executives concocted in an effort to meet the company's financial targets. One particularly well-known scheme is called the "Nigerian barge" transaction, which took place in the fourth quarter of 1999. According to court documents, Enron arranged to sell three electricity-generating power barges moored off the coast of Nigeria. The "buyer" was the investment banking firm of Merrill Lynch. Although Enron reported this transaction as a sale in its income statement, it turns out this was no ordinary sale. Merrill Lynch didn't really want the barges and had only agreed to buy them because Enron guaranteed, in a secret side deal, that it would arrange for the barges to be bought back from Merrill Lynch within six months of the initial transaction. In addition, Enron promised to pay Merrill Lynch a hefty fee for doing the deal. In an interview on National Public Radio on August 17, 2002, Michigan Senator Carl Levin declared, "(t)he case of the Nigerian barge transaction was, by any definition, a loan."

Required:

1. Discuss whether the Nigerian barge transaction should have been considered a loan rather than a sale. As part of your discussion, consider the following questions. Doesn't the Merrill Lynch payment to Enron at the time of the initial transaction automatically make it a sale, not a loan? What aspects of the transaction are similar to a loan? Which aspects suggest that the four criteria for revenue recognition (summarized near the end of Chapter 3) are not fulfilled?

2. The income statement effect of recording the transaction as a sale rather than a loan is fairly clear: Enron was able to boost its revenues and net income. What is somewhat less obvious, but nearly as important, are the effects on the statement of cash flows. Describe how recording the transaction as a sale rather than as a loan would change the statement of cash flows.

3. How would the two different statements of cash flows (described in your response to requirement 2) affect financial statement users?

Financial Reporting and Analysis Team Project

Team Project: Analyzing Cash Flows

CP13-7
LO1, 2, 3, 4, 5, 6

As a team, select an industry to analyze. *Reuters* provides lists of industries and their makeup at www.reuters.com/finance/industries. Each team member should acquire the annual report or 10-K for one publicly traded company in the industry, with each member selecting a different company. (Library files, the SEC EDGAR service at www.sec.gov, or the company itself are good sources.)

Required:

On an individual basis, each team member should write a short report answering the following questions about the selected company. Discuss any patterns across the companies that you as a team observe. Then, as a team, write a short report comparing and contrasting your companies.

1. Which of the two basic reporting approaches for cash flows from operating activities did the company adopt?

2. What is the quality of earnings ratio for the most current year? What were the major causes of differences between net income and cash flow from operations?

3. What is the capital acquisitions ratio for the three-year period presented in total? How is the company financing its capital acquisitions?

4. What portion of the cash from operations in the current year is being paid to stockholders in the form of dividends?

LEARNING OBJECTIVES

After studying this chapter, you should be able to:

1. Explain how a company's business strategy affects financial analysis. p. 713

2. Discuss how analysts use financial statements. p. 714

3. Compute and interpret component percentages. p. 716

4. Compute and interpret profitability ratios. p. 718

5. Compute and interpret liquidity ratios. p. 723

6. Compute and interpret solvency ratios. p. 727

7. Compute and interpret market test ratios. p. 729

Lectured slideshow–LP14-1
www.mhhe.com/libby6e

ANALYZING FINANCIAL STATEMENTS

The history of Home Depot is an unusual success story. Founded in 1978 in Atlanta, Home Depot has grown to be America's largest home improvement retailer with over 2,100 stores in the United States, Canada, China, and Mexico. According to *Fortune* magazine, Home Depot is one of the nation's 30 largest retailers. Financial statements for Home Depot are presented in Exhibit 14.1. As you can see, Home Depot's rapid growth has continued in recent years. Sales revenue for the year ended January 28, 2007, was nearly 25 percent higher than in 2005, and the company's net earnings increased more than 15 percent.

With this rapid growth, would you want to invest in Home Depot? A number of professional analysts think you should, including those who work for Edward Jones, a large brokerage firm. In a report in which they recommended investors buy stock in Home Depot, they wrote: "We view Home Depot's market dominance, favorable long-term growth outlook, and compelling valuation as reasons to rate its shares a Buy."

Professional analysts consider a large number of factors in developing the type of recommendation contained in the Edward Jones report, including information reported in a company's financial statements. In this chapter, we use accounting information and a variety of analytical tools to study Home Depot and its major competitor, Lowe's.

UNDERSTANDING THE BUSINESS

Companies spend billions of dollars each year preparing, auditing, and publishing their financial statements. These statements are then mailed to current and prospective investors. Most companies also make financial information available to investors on the Internet. Home Depot has a particularly interesting home page (http://www.homedepot.com) that contains current financial statements, recent news articles about the company, and a variety of relevant information.

EXHIBIT 14.1

Home Depot Financial
Statements

THE HOME DEPOT, INC. AND SUBSIDIARIES
Consolidated Statements of Earnings

	Fiscal Year Ended		
amounts in millions, except per share data	January 28, 2007	January 29, 2006	January 30, 2005
NET SALES	$90,837	$81,511	$73,094
Cost of Sales	61,054	54,191	48,664
GROSS PROFIT	29,783	27,320	24,430
Operating Expenses:			
Selling, General and Administrative	18,348	16,485	15,256
Depreciation and Amortization	1,762	1,472	1,248
Total Operating Expenses	20,110	17,957	16,504
OPERATING INCOME	9,673	9,363	7,926
Interest Income (Expense):			
Interest and Investment Income	27	62	56
Interest Expense	(392)	(143)	(70)
Interest, net	(365)	(81)	(14)
EARNINGS BEFORE PROVISION FOR INCOME TAXES	9,308	9,282	7,912
Provision for Income Taxes	3,547	3,444	2,911
NET EARNINGS	$ 5,761	$ 5,838	$ 5,001
Weighted Average Common Shares	2,054	2,138	2,207
BASIC EARNINGS PER SHARE	$ 2.80	$ 2.73	$ 2.27
Diluted Weighted Average Common Shares	2,062	2,147	2,216
DILUTED EARNINGS PER SHARE	$ 2.79	$ 2.72	$ 2.26

THE HOME DEPOT, INC. AND SUBSIDIARIES
Consolidated Balance Sheets

amounts in millions, except per share data	January 28, 2007	January 29, 2006
ASSETS		
Current Assets:		
Cash and Cash Equivalents	$ 600	$ 793
Short-Term Investments	14	14
Receivables, net	3,223	2,396
Merchandise Inventories	12,822	11,401
Other Current Assets	1,341	665
Total Current Assets	18,000	15,269

continued

EXHIBIT 14.1

continued

Property and Equipment, at cost:		
Land	8,355	7,924
Buildings	15,215	14,056
Furniture, Fixtures and Equipment	7,799	7,073
Leasehold Improvements	1,391	1,207
Construction in Progress	1,123	843
Capital Leases	475	427
	34,358	31,530
Less Accumulated Depreciation and Amortization	7,753	6,629
Net Property and Equipment	26,605	24,901
Notes Receivable	343	348
Goodwill	6,314	3,286
Other Assets	1,001	601
Total Assets	**$52,263**	**$44,405**

LIABILITIES AND STOCKHOLDERS' EQUITY

Current Liabilities:

Short-Term Debt	$ —	$ 900
Accounts Payable	7,356	6,032
Accrued Salaries and Related Expenses	1,295	1,068
Sales Taxes Payable	475	488
Deferred Revenue	1,634	1,757
Income Taxes Payable	217	388
Current Installments of Long-Term Debt	18	513
Other Accrued Expenses	1,936	1,560
Total Current Liabilities	12,931	12,706
Long-Term Debt, excluding current installments	11,643	2,672
Other Long-Term Liabilities	1,243	1,172
Deferred Income Taxes	1,416	946

STOCKHOLDERS' EQUITY

Common Stock, par value $0.05; authorized:		
10,000 shares; issued 2,421 shares at January 28, 2007 and		
2,401 shares at January 29, 2006;		
outstanding 1,970 shares at January 28, 2007 and		
2,124 shares at January 29, 2006	121	120
Paid-In Capital	7,930	7,149
Retained Earnings	33,052	28,943
Accumulated Other Comprehensive Income	310	409
Treasury Stock, at cost, 451 shares at January 28, 2007 and		
277 shares at January 29, 2006	(16,383)	(9,712)
Total Stockholders' Equity	25,030	26,909
Total Liabilities and Stockholders' Equity	**$52,263**	**$44,405**

EXHIBIT 14.1

continued

THE HOME DEPOT, INC. AND SUBSIDIARIES
Consolidated Statements of Cash Flows

	Fiscal Year Ended		
amounts in millions	January 28, 2007	January 29, 2006	January 30, 2005
CASH FLOWS FROM			
OPERATING ACTIVITIES:			
Net Earnings	$5,761	$ 5,838	$ 5,001
Reconciliation of Net Earnings to			
Net Cash Provided by Operating Activities:			
Depreciation and Amortization	1,886	1,579	1,319
Impairment Related to Disposition			
of EXPO Real Estate	—	78	—
Stock-Based Compensation Expense	297	175	125
Changes in Assets and Liabilities, net			
of the effects of acquisitions:			
Decrease (Increase) in Receivables, net	96	(358)	(266)
Increase in Merchandise Inventories	(563)	(971)	(849)
(Increase) Decrease in Other Current Assets	(225)	16	29
Increase in Accounts Payable and Accrued			
Liabilities	531	148	645
(Decrease) Increase in Deferred Revenue	(123)	209	263
(Decrease) Increase in Income Taxes Payable	(172)	175	2
Increase (Decrease) in Deferred Income Taxes	46	(609)	319
(Decrease) Increase in Other Long-Term			
Liabilities	(51)	151	119
Other	178	189	(75)
Net Cash Provided by Operating Activities	7,661	6,620	6,632
CASH FLOWS FROM INVESTING			
ACTIVITIES:			
Capital Expenditures, net of $49, $51, and $38			
of noncash capital expenditures in fiscal			
2006, 2005, and 2004, respectively	(3,542)	(3,881)	(3,948)
Payments for Businesses Acquired, net	(4,268)	(2,546)	(727)
Proceeds from Sales of Property and Equipment	138	164	96
Purchases of Investments	(5,409)	(18,230)	(25,890)
Proceeds from Sales and Maturities of Investments	5,434	19,907	25,990
Net Cash Used in Investing Activities	(7,647)	(4,586)	(4,479)
CASH FLOWS FROM FINANCING			
ACTIVITIES:			
(Repayments of) Proceeds from Short-Term			
Borrowings, net	(900)	900	—
Proceeds from Long-Term Borrowings, net			
of discount	8,935	995	995
Repayments of Long-Term Debt	(509)	(24)	(510)

continued

Repurchases of Common Stock	**(6,684)**	(3,040)	(3,106)
Proceeds from Sale of Common Stock	**381**	414	285
Cash Dividends Paid to Stockholders	**(1,395)**	(857)	(719)
Other Financing Activities	**(31)**	(136)	272
Net Cash Used in Financing Activities	**(203)**	(1,748)	(2,783)
(Decrease) Increase in Cash and Cash Equivalents	**(189)**	286	(630)
Effect of Exchange Rate Changes on Cash and Cash Equivalents	**(4)**	1	33
Cash and Cash Equivalents at Beginning of Year	**793**	506	1,103
Cash and Cash Equivalents at End of Year	**$ 600**	$ 793	$ 506
SUPPLEMENTAL DISCLOSURE OF CASH PAYMENTS MADE FOR:			
Interest, net of interest capitalized	**$ 270**	$ 114	$ 78
Income Taxes	**$3,963**	$3,860	$2,793

EXHIBIT 14.1

continued

The reason that Home Depot and other companies spend so much money to provide information to investors is simple: Financial statements help people to make better economic decisions. In fact, published financial statements are designed primarily to meet the needs of external decision makers, including present and potential owners, investment analysts, and creditors.

ORGANIZATION of the Chapter

The Investment Decision	Understanding a Company's Strategy	Financial Statement Analysis	Ratio and Percentage Analysis	Interpreting Ratios and Other Analytical Considerations

	■ Component Percentages
	■ Tests of Profitability
	  1. Return on Equity (ROE)
	  2. Return on Assets (ROA)
	  3. Financial Leverage Percentage
	  4. Earnings per Share (EPS)
	  5. Quality of Income
	  6. Profit Margin
	  7. Fixed Asset Turnover
		■ Tests of Liquidity
		  8. Cash Ratio
		  9. Current Ratio
		  10. Quick Ratio (Acid Test)
		  11. Receivable Turnover
		  12. Inventory Turnover
			■ Tests of Solvency
			  13. Times Interest Earned Ratio
			  14. Cash Coverage Ratio
			  15. Debt-to-Equity Ratio
			■ Market Tests
			  16. Price/Earnings (PE) Ratio
			  17. Dividend Yield Ratio
				■ Other Financial Information
				■ Information in an Efficient Market

THE INVESTMENT DECISION

Of the people who use financial statements, investors are perhaps the single largest group. They often rely on the advice of professional analysts, who develop recommendations on widely held stocks such as Home Depot. Most individual investors use analysts' reports and track their recommendations. As this book was being written, professional analysts issued the following investment recommendations for Home Depot:

	Current	1 Month ago	2 Months ago	3 Months ago
Strong buy	5	4	4	4
Moderate buy	6	6	6	6
Hold	11	9	10	11
Moderate Sell	0	1	1	1
Strong Sell	0	0	0	0

Source: Quicken.com/investments/

Perhaps the most important thing to notice about this summary of investment recommendations is the degree of disagreement. Currently, 11 analysts recommend buying more Home Depot stock, while 11 others recommend holding Home Depot stock only if one already owns it. This level of disagreement shows that financial analysis is part art and part science.

In considering an investment in stock, investors should evaluate the company's future income and growth potential on the basis of three factors:

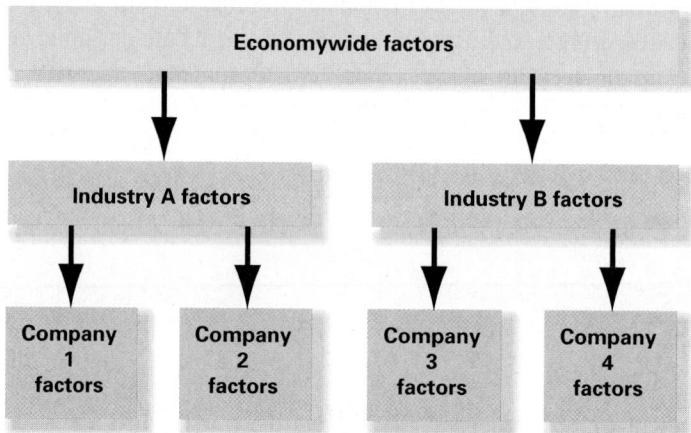

1. **Economywide factors.** Often the overall health of the economy has a direct impact on the performance of an individual business. Investors should consider data such as the unemployment rate, general inflation rate, and changes in interest rates. For example, in a research report issued by Edward Jones, a large brokerage firm, an analyst determined "rising interest rates could negatively impact Home Depot's sales." The reason for a negative impact on sales, according to the analyst, is nearly one-third of the dollars saved on refinancing mortgages are spent on home-improvement projects.

2. **Industry factors.** Certain events have a major impact on each company within an industry, but only a minor impact on other companies outside the industry. For example, the Edward Jones report predicted increased sales at Home Depot because of "a new consumer trend toward 'nestling,' which refers to spending more time and money transforming one's home into a sanctuary."

3. **Individual company factors.** To properly analyze a company, good analysts do not rely only on the information contained in the financial statements. They visit the company, buy its products, and read about it in the business press. If you evaluate McDonald's, it is equally important to assess the quality of its balance sheet and the quality of its Big Mac. An example of company-specific information is contained in the Edward Jones report: New managers have been hired because the management skills "that grew Home Depot to 1,000 stores was probably different from the skill set needed as the company grows beyond 2,000 stores."

Besides considering these factors, investors should understand a company's business strategy when evaluating its financial statements. Before discussing analytical techniques, we will show you how business strategy affects financial statement analysis.

UNDERSTANDING A COMPANY'S STRATEGY

Financial statement analysis involves more than just "crunching numbers." Before you start looking at numbers, you should know what you are looking for. While financial statements report on transactions, each of those transactions is the result of a company's operating decisions as it implements its business strategy.

Video 14-1
www.mhhe.com/libby6e

The DuPont model (introduced in Chapter 5) helps us understand that a number of business strategies affect the profitability of a business. The model follows:

Businesses can earn a high rate of return by following different strategies. These are two fundamental strategies:

1. **Product differentiation.** Under this strategy, companies offer products with unique benefits, such as high quality or unusual style or features. These unique benefits allow a company to charge higher prices. In general, higher prices yield higher profit margins, which lead to higher returns on equity (as shown in the ROE model).

2. **Cost advantage.** Under this strategy, companies attempt to operate more efficiently than their competitors, which permits them to offer lower prices to attract customers. The efficient use of resources is captured in the asset turnover ratio, and as the ROE model illustrates, higher asset turnover ratio leads to higher return on investment.

You can probably think of a number of companies that have followed one of these two basic strategies. Here are some examples:

Differentiation on Quality	Differentiation on Cost
Cars: Cadillac Mercedes Lincoln	**Cars:** Ford Focus Chevrolet Aveo Kia Rio
Retail Stores: Nordstrom Tiffany Saks	**Retail Stores:** Kmart Wal-Mart Dollar General

The best place to start financial analysis is with a solid understanding of a company's business strategy. To evaluate how well a company is doing, you must know what managers are trying to do. You can learn a great deal about a company's business strategy by reading its annual report, especially the letter from the president. It also is useful to read articles about the company in the business press.

Home Depot's business strategy is described in its 10-K report as follows:

REAL WORLD EXCERPT

10-K REPORT

Operating Strategy

Our operating strategy is to offer a broad assortment of high-quality merchandise and services at competitive prices using knowledgeable, service-oriented personnel and strong marketing and credit promotions. We believe that our associates' knowledge of products and home improvement techniques and applications is very important to our marketing approach and our ability to maintain and enhance customer satisfaction.

This strategy has several implications for our analysis of Home Depot:

1. Cost control is critical. Home Depot must be able to purchase merchandise at low prices in order to beat competitors.

2. To cover the cost of operating large stores, Home Depot must be able to generate a high volume of business.

3. To offer a high level of service, Home Depot must incur employee compensation and training costs that are higher than competitors' costs. This puts pressure on Home Depot to control costs in other areas.

With these implications in mind, we can attach more meaning to the information contained in Home Depot's financial statements.

FINANCIAL STATEMENT ANALYSIS

Learning Objective 2
Discuss how analysts use financial statements.

Analyzing financial data without a basis for comparison is impossible. For example, would you be impressed with a company that earned $1 million last year? You are probably thinking, "It depends." A $1 million profit might be very good for a company that lost money the year before but not good for a company that made $500 million the preceding year. It might be good for a small company but not for a very large company. And it might be considered good if all the other companies in the industry lost money the same year but not good if they all earned much larger profits.

As you can see from this simple example, financial results cannot be evaluated in isolation. To properly analyze the information reported in financial statements, you must develop appropriate comparisons. The task of finding appropriate benchmarks requires judgment and is not always easy. Financial analysis is a sophisticated skill, not a mechanical process.

There are two methods for making financial comparisons, times series analysis and comparisons with similar companies.

Audio lecture–AP14-1
www.mhhe.com/libby6e

1. **Time series analysis.** Information on a single company is compared over time. For example, a key measure of performance for most companies is the change in sales volume each year. The following time series chart shows that Home Depot is not growing as rapidly as it did a few years ago. Analysts would want to examine this trend. The notes to the financial statements help us understand this problem:

> Net Sales growth was primarily driven by sales from new stores. Retail comparable store sales decreased 2.8% for fiscal 2006 compared to an increase of 3.1% for fiscal 2005. Our retail comparable store sales results reflect in part the impact of cannibalization. In order to meet our customer service objectives, we strategically open stores near market areas served by existing stores ("cannibalize") to enhance service levels, gain incremental sales and increase market penetration.

REAL WORLD EXCERPT

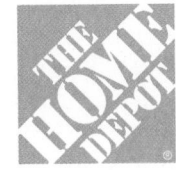

Notice that our understanding of the reported numbers is directly tied to understanding Home Depot's business strategy.

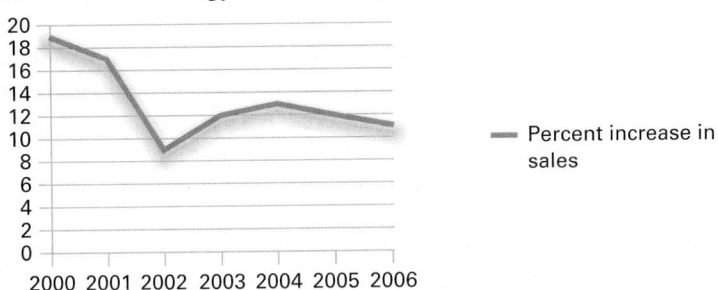

2. **Comparison with similar companies.** We have seen that financial results are often affected by industry and economywide factors. By comparing a company with another one in the same line of business, an analyst can gain better insight into its performance. The comparison of various measures for Home Depot and Lowe's (in the following graph) shows very similar results suggesting that the companies are both affected by industry factors. The gross profit percentage shows that Home Depot is operating a little less efficiently than Lowe's. Sales growth for both companies is similar, which helps analysts understand the decline in sales growth over time for Home Depot discussed in the previous section. The comparison with Lowe's indicates that Home Depot is growing at a rate that is comparable to others in the industry.

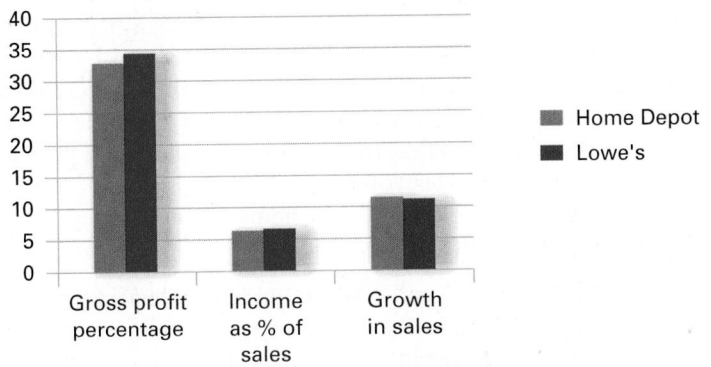

Finding comparable companies is often very difficult. Fortune Brands, for example, is a well-known company that each year sells more than $9 billion worth of distilled spirits, home improvement products, office products, and golf equipment. No other company sells exactly that group of products. Care must be exercised in selecting comparable companies from the same basic industry. Days Inn, La Quinta, Hilton, Four Seasons, Marriott, and Mirage Resorts are all well-known companies in the hotel industry, but not all could be considered comparable companies for purposes of financial analysis. These hotels offer different levels of quality and appeal to different types of customers.

The federal government has developed the North American Industry Classification System for use in reporting economic data. The system assigns a specific industry code to each corporation based on its business operations. Analysts often use these six-digit codes to identify companies that have similar business operations. In addition, financial information services such as Robert Morris Associates provide averages for many common accounting ratios for various industries defined by the industrial classification codes. Because of the diversity of companies included in each industry classification, however, these data should be used with great care. For this reason, some analysts prefer to compare two companies that are very similar instead of using industry-wide comparisons.

RATIO AND PERCENTAGE ANALYSIS

RATIO (PERCENTAGE) ANALYSIS is an analytical tool that measures the proportional relationship between two financial statement amounts

All financial analysts use **ratio analysis** or **percentage analysis** when they review companies. A ratio or percentage expresses the proportionate relationship between two different amounts, allowing for easy comparisons. Assessing a company's profitability is difficult if you know only that it earned a net income of $500,000. Comparing income to other numbers, such as stockholders' equity, provides additional insights. If stockholders' equity is $5 million, for example, then the relationship of earnings to investment is $500,000 ÷ $5,000,000 = 10 percent. This measure indicates a different level of performance than would be the case if stockholders' equity were $250 million. Ratio analysis helps decision makers to identify significant relationships and make meaningful comparisons between companies.

Learning Objective 3
Compute and interpret component percentages.

Ratios may be computed using amounts in one statement, such as the income statement, or in two different statements, such as the income statement and the balance sheet. In addition, amounts on a single statement may be expressed as a percentage of a base amount.

Component Percentages

COMPONENT PERCENTAGES express each item on a particular financial statement as a percentage of a single base amount.

Analysts often compute **component percentages,** which express each item on a financial statement as a percentage of a single base amount (the ratio's denominator). To compute component percentages for the income statement, the base amount is net sales revenue. Each expense is expressed as a percentage of net sales revenue. On the balance sheet, the base amount is total assets; each balance sheet account is divided by total assets.

Exhibit 14.2 shows a component percentage analysis for Home Depot's income statement (shown in Exhibit 14.1). If you simply reviewed the dollar amounts on the income statement, you might be concerned about several significant differences. For example, selling, general, and administrative expense increased by nearly $2 billion between 2006 and 2007. But the component percentage provides an important insight: this expense category decreased slightly as a percentage of sales during that period. In other words, selling, general, and administrative expense increased primarily because of the increase in the company's sales volume.

The component analysis (in Exhibit 14.2) helps to highlight several additional issues for Home Depot, such as these:

1. Earnings decreased between 2007 and 2006, despite more than a $9 billion increase in sales revenue. The primary cause for the decline in earnings was a reduction in the gross profit margin caused by an increase in cost of merchandise as a percentage of sales.

	COMPONENT PERCENTAGES		
Income Statement	**2007**	**2006**	**2005**
Net sales	100.0%	100.0%	100.0%
Cost of merchandise sold	67.2	66.5	66.6
Gross profit	32.8	33.5	33.4
Operating expenses			
Selling, general, and administrative	20.1	20.2	20.9
Depreciation and amortization	2.0	1.8	1.7
Total operating expenses	22.1	22.0	22.6
Operating income	10.7	11.5	10.8
Interest and investment income	0.0	0.1	0.0
Interest expense	(0.4)	(0.2)	(0.0)
Interest, net	(0.4)	(0.1)	(0.0)
Earnings, before taxes	10.3	11.4	10.8
Income taxes	3.9	4.2	4.0
Net earnings	6.4	7.2	6.8

EXHIBIT 14.2

Component Percentages for Home Depot

2. Some of the percentage changes may seem immaterial, but they involve significant amounts of money. The improvement in the ratio of selling, general, and administrative expense as a percentage of sales from 2006 to 2007 is very small but this improvement in efficiency added $90 million to earnings before taxes.

3. Cost of merchandise sold as a percentage of sales increased between 2006 and 2007. As we mentioned earlier, a key part of Home Depot's strategy is selling merchandise at low prices. Companies following this strategy must control the margin between the cost of merchandise and its selling price. The deterioration in the ratio of cost of goods sold to sales revenue is a negative indication of the degree of success the company is having implementing its strategy.

4. Significant stability in all income statement relationships indicates a well-run company. Note that most of the individual income statement items changed less than one percentage point over the three-year period.

Many analysts use graphics software in their study of financial results. Graphic representation is especially useful when communicating findings during meetings or in printed form. The charts in the margin summarize key 2007 data from Exhibit 14.2 along with comparable data from Lowe's, a key competitor.

In addition to component percentages, analysts use ratios to compare related items from the financial statements. Of the many ratios that can be computed from a single set of financial statements, analysts use only those that can be helpful in a given situation. Comparing cost of goods sold to property, plant, and equipment is never useful because these items have no natural relationship. Instead, an analyst will often compute certain widely used ratios and then decide which additional ratios could be relevant to a particular decision. Research and development costs as a percentage of sales is not a commonly used ratio, for example, but it is useful when analyzing companies that depend on new products, such as drug or computer firms.

When you compute ratios, remember a basic fact about financial statements: Balance sheet amounts relate to an instant in time while income statement amounts relate to an entire period. In comparing an income statement amount to a balance sheet amount, you should express the balance sheet as an average of the beginning

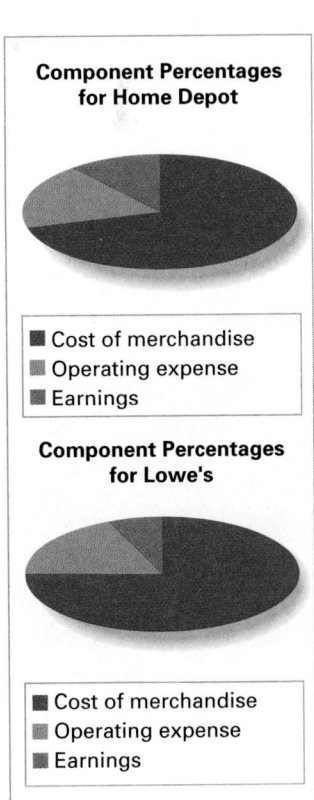

Component Percentages for Home Depot

- ■ Cost of merchandise
- ■ Operating expense
- ■ Earnings

Component Percentages for Lowe's

- ■ Cost of merchandise
- ■ Operating expense
- ■ Earnings

and ending balances. In practice, many analysts simply use the ending balance sheet amount, an approach that is appropriate only if no significant changes have occurred in the balance sheet amounts. For consistency, we always use average amounts.

Financial statement analysis is a judgmental process; not all ratios are helpful in a given situation. We will discuss several ratios that are appropriate to most situations. They can be grouped into the categories shown in Exhibit 14.3.

Tests of Profitability

Profitability is a primary measure of the overall success of a company. Indeed, it is necessary for a company's survival. Several **tests of profitability** focus on measuring the adequacy of income by comparing it to other items reported on the financial statements. Return on equity is a widely used measure of profitability.

TESTS OF PROFITABILITY compare income with one or more primary activities.

1. Return on Equity (ROE)

Return on equity relates income earned to the investment made by the owners. This ratio reflects the simple fact that investors expect to earn more money if they invest more money. Two investments that offer a return of $10,000 are not comparable if one requires a $100,000 investment and the other requires a $250,000 investment. The return on equity ratio is computed as follows:[1]

$$\text{Return on Equity} = \frac{\text{Net Income}}{\text{Average Stockholders' Equity}}$$

$$\text{Home Depot 2007} = \frac{\$5,761}{\$25,970*} = 22.2\%$$

*($25,030 + $26,909) ÷ 2 = $25,970.

Home Depot earned 22.2 percent on the owners' investment. Was that return good or bad? We can answer this question by comparing Home Depot's return on equity with the ratio for a similar company. Return on equity for Lowe's was 20.7 percent in 2007, less than the return earned by Home Depot.

We can gain additional insight by examining Home Depot's ROE over time:

	2007	2006	2005
ROE	22.2%	22.9%	21.5%

This comparison shows that Home Depot's performance in 2007 as measured by its ROE has improved compared to 2005. As mentioned earlier, new management was hired to improve Home Depot's performance. This comparison suggests that they have been effective.

2. Return on Assets (ROA)

Another test of profitability compares income to the total assets (i.e., total investment) used to earn the income. Many analysts consider the return on assets ratio to be a better measure (compared to ROE) of management's ability to utilize assets effectively because it is not affected by the way in which the assets were financed. For example, the return on equity could be very high for a

---

[1]The figures for Home Depot used throughout the following examples are taken from the financial statements in Exhibit 14.1.

Ratio	Basic Computation
Tests of Profitability	
1. Return on equity (ROE)	$\dfrac{\text{Net Income}}{\text{Average Stockholders' Equity}}$
2. Return on assets (ROA)	$\dfrac{\text{Net Income} + \text{Interest Expense (net of tax)}}{\text{Average Total Assets}}$
3. Financial leverage percentage	Return on Equity − Return on Assets
4. Earnings per share (EPS)	$\dfrac{\text{Net Income}}{\text{Average Number of Shares of Common Stock Outstanding}}$
5. Quality of income	$\dfrac{\text{Cash Flows from Operating Activities}}{\text{Net Income}}$
6. Profit margin	$\dfrac{\text{Net Income}}{\text{Net Sales Revenue}}$
7. Fixed asset turnover ratio	$\dfrac{\text{Net Sales Revenue}}{\text{Average Net Fixed Assets}}$
Tests of Liquidity	
8. Cash ratio	$\dfrac{\text{Cash} + \text{Cash Equivalents}}{\text{Current Liabilities}}$
9. Current ratio	$\dfrac{\text{Current Assets}}{\text{Current Liabilities}}$
10. Quick ratio	$\dfrac{\text{Quick Assets}}{\text{Current Liabilities}}$
11. Receivable turnover ratio	$\dfrac{\text{Net Credit Sales}}{\text{Average Net Receivables}}$
12. Inventory turnover ratio	$\dfrac{\text{Cost of Goods Sold}}{\text{Average Inventory}}$
Tests of Solvency	
13. Times interest earned	$\dfrac{\text{Net Income} + \text{Interest Expense} + \text{Income Taxes Expense}}{\text{Interest Expense}}$
14. Cash coverage ratio	$\dfrac{\text{Cash Flows from Operating Activities (before interest and tax paid)}}{\text{Interest Paid}}$
15. Debt-to-equity ratio	$\dfrac{\text{Total Liabilities}}{\text{Stockholders' Equity}}$
Market Tests	
16. Price/earnings ratio	$\dfrac{\text{Current Market Price per Share}}{\text{Earnings per Share}}$
17. Dividend yield ratio	$\dfrac{\text{Dividends per Share}}{\text{Market Price per Share}}$

EXHIBIT 14.3

Widely Used Accounting Ratios

company that has borrowed a large amount of debt compared to a company that earned the same return on the same amount of assets but borrowed less money. Return on assets is computed as follows:

$$\text{Return on Assets} = \frac{\text{Net Income} + \text{Interest Expense (net of tax)}^*}{\text{Average Total Assets}}$$

$$\text{Home Depot 2007} = \frac{\$5,761 + (\$392 \times 66\%)}{\$48,334^\dagger} = 12.5\%$$

*This illustration assumes a corporate tax rate of 34 percent.
†($52,263 + $44,405) ÷ 2 = $48,334.

Note that interest expense has been added to net income in the numerator of the ratio. Because the denominator of the ratio includes resources provided by both owners and creditors, the numerator must include the return that was available to each group. Interest expense is added back because it was previously deducted in the computation of net income. Note, too, that interest expense is measured net of income tax. This amount is used because it represents the net cost to the corporation for the funds provided by creditors.

The return on assets for Lowe's was 11.9 percent, lower than Home Depot's. This comparison indicates that Home Depot utilizes its assets more effectively than Lowe's.

3. Financial Leverage Percentage

Financial leverage percentage measures the advantage or disadvantage that occurs when a company's return on equity differs from its return on assets (i.e., ROE − ROA). In the DuPont model discussed earlier in this chapter, **financial leverage** was defined as the proportion of assets acquired with funds supplied by owners. The ratio **financial leverage percentage** measures a related but different concept. This ratio describes the relationship between the return on equity and the return on assets. Leverage is positive when the rate of return on a company's assets exceeds the average after-tax interest rate on its borrowed funds. Basically, the company borrows at one rate and invests at a higher rate of return. Most companies have positive leverage

Financial leverage percentage can be measured by comparing the two return ratios as follows:

$$\text{Financial Leverage Percentage} = \text{Return on Equity} - \text{Return on Assets}$$

$$\text{Home Depot 2007} = 22.2\% - 12.5\% = 9.7\% \text{ (positive leverage)}$$

When a company borrows funds at an after-tax interest rate and invests those funds to earn a higher after-tax rate of return, the difference accrues to the benefit of the owners. The notes to Home Depot's annual report indicate that the company borrowed money at rates ranging from 3.75 percent to 5.875 percent and invested it in assets earning 12.5 percent. The difference between the income earned on the money it borrows and the interest it paid to creditors is available for the owners of Home Depot. This benefit of financial leverage is the primary reason most companies obtain a significant amount of their resources from creditors rather than from the sale of capital stock. Note that financial leverage can be enhanced either by investing effectively (i.e., earning a high return on investment) or by borrowing effectively (i.e., paying a low rate of interest).

Lowe's financial leverage ratio (8.8 percent) is lower than Home Depot's. Lowe's ratio is lower because it utilizes comparatively less debt in its capital structure.

4. Earnings per Share (EPS)

The earnings per share ratio is a measure of return on investment that is based on the number of shares outstanding instead of the dollar amounts reported on the balance sheet. In simple situations, EPS is computed as follows:[2]

$$\text{Earnings per Share} = \frac{\text{Net Income*}}{\text{Average Number of Shares of Common Stock Outstanding}}$$

$$\text{Home Depot 2007} = \frac{\$5,761}{2,047**} = \$2.81 \text{ per share}$$

$$**(1,970 + 2,124) \div 2 = 2,047$$

Earnings per share is probably the single most widely watched ratio. Its importance is illustrated by a news story published in *The Financial Times* (August 15, 2007):

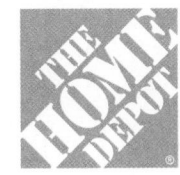

REAL WORLD EXCERPT

THE FINANCIAL TIMES

5. Quality of Income

Most financial analysts are concerned about the quality of a company's earnings because some accounting procedures can be used to report higher income. For example, a company that uses LIFO and short estimated lives for depreciable assets will report lower earnings than a similar company that uses FIFO and longer estimated lives. One method of evaluating the quality of a company's earnings is to compare its reported earnings to its cash flows from operating activities, as follows:

$$\text{Quality of Income} = \frac{\text{Cash Flows from Operating Activities}}{\text{Net Income}}$$

$$\text{Home Depot 2007} = \frac{\$7,661}{\$5,761} = 1.33$$

A quality of income ratio that is higher than 1 is considered to indicate high-quality earnings, because each dollar of income is supported by one dollar or more of cash flow. A ratio that is below 1 represents lower-quality earnings.

A research report from Edward Jones discusses the issue of quality of earnings for Home Depot:

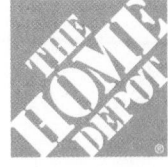

REAL WORLD EXCERPT

EDWARD JONES

6. Profit Margin

The profit margin measures the percentage of each sales dollar, on average, that represents profit. It is computed as follows:

$$\text{Profit Margin} = \frac{\text{Net Income}}{\text{Net Sales Revenue}}$$

$$\text{Home Depot 2007} = \frac{\$5,761}{\$90,837} = 6.3\%$$

---

*If preferred stock dividends are paid, they should be subtracted from net income.

[2]Notice that the EPS number we calculated is slightly different from the one reported by Home Depot on its income statement shown in Exhibit 14.1. The reason is that we estimated the average number of shares outstanding by computing the average based on the number of shares at the beginning and end of the year. Home Depot computed the average based on the actual number of days that the stock was outstanding.

For 2007, each dollar of Home Depot's sales generated 6.3 cents of profit. In comparison, Lowe's earned 6.6 cents for each dollar of sales. Although the difference might seem small, it represents a significant advantage for Lowe's.

While profit margin is a good measure of operating efficiency, care must be used in analyzing it because it does not consider the resources (i.e., total investment) needed to earn income. It is very difficult to compare profit margins for companies in different industries. For example, profit margins are low in the food industry while profit margins in the jewelry business are high. Both types of business can be quite profitable, however, because a high sales volume can compensate for a low profit margin. Grocery stores have low profit margins, but they generate a high sales volume from their relatively inexpensive stores and inventory. Although jewelry stores earn comparatively more profit from each sales dollar, they require a large investment in luxury stores and very expensive inventory.

The trade-off between profit margin and sales volume can be stated in simple terms: Would you prefer to have 5 percent of $1,000,000 or 10 percent of $100,000? As you can see, a larger profit margin is not always better.

7. Fixed Asset Turnover Ratio

Another measure of operating efficiency is the fixed asset turnover ratio, which compares sales volume with a company's investment in fixed assets. The term *fixed assets* is synonymous with property, plant, and equipment. The ratio is computed as follows:

$$\text{Fixed Asset Turnover Ratio} = \frac{\text{Net Sales Revenue}}{\text{Average Net Fixed Assets}}$$

$$\text{Home Depot 2007} = \frac{\$90,837}{\$25,753*} = 3.53$$

*($26,605 + $24,901) ÷ 2 = $25,753

In 2007, Home Depot's fixed asset turnover ratio was better than Lowe's (2.7). In simple terms, this means that Home Depot had a competitive advantage over Lowe's in terms of its ability to effectively utilize its fixed assets to generate revenue. For each dollar Home Depot invested in property, plant, and equipment, the company was able to earn $3.53 in sales revenue while Lowe's could earn only $2.70. This comparison is extremely important because it indicates that management of Home Depot was able to operate more efficiently than its main competitor.

The fixed asset turnover ratio is used widely to analyze capital-intensive companies such as airlines and electric utilities. For companies that hold large amounts of inventory and accounts receivable, analysts often prefer to use the asset turnover ratio, which is based on total assets rather than fixed assets:

$$\text{Asset Turnover Ratio} = \frac{\text{Net Sales Revenue}}{\text{Average Total Assets}}$$

$$\text{Home Depot 2007} = \frac{\$90,837}{\$48,334*} = 1.88$$

*($52,263 + $44,405) ÷ 2 = $48,334.

In 2007, Home Depot was able to generate $1.88 in revenue for each dollar invested in assets. In comparison, Lowe's asset turnover ratio was 1.79. Both turnover ratios show that Home Depot was able to operate more efficiently than Lowe's. This comparison is important because operating efficiency has a significant impact on profitability as shown by the DuPont model (presented earlier in this chapter).

Show how to compute the following ratios:

1. Return on equity =

2. Return on assets =

3. Profit margin =

After you have completed your answers, check them with the solutions at the bottom of the page.

Tests of Liquidity

Liquidity refers to a company's ability to meet its currently maturing debts. **Tests of liquidity** focus on the relationship between current assets and current liabilities. The ability to pay current liabilities is an important factor in evaluating a company's short-term financial strength. A company that does not have cash available to pay for purchases on a timely basis will lose its cash discounts and run the risk of having its credit discontinued by vendors. We discuss three ratios that are used to measure liquidity: the cash ratio, the current ratio, and the quick ratio.

> **Learning Objective 5**
> Compute and interpret liquidity ratios.

> TESTS OF LIQUIDITY are ratios that measure a company's ability to meet its currently maturing obligations.

8. Cash Ratio

Cash is the lifeblood of a business. Without cash, a company cannot pay its employees or meet its obligations to creditors. Even a profitable business will fail without sufficient cash. One measure of the adequacy of available cash, called the *cash ratio*, is computed as follows:

$$\text{Cash Ratio} = \frac{\text{Cash + Cash Equivalents}}{\text{Current Liabilities}}$$

$$\text{Home Depot 2007} = \frac{\$600}{\$12,931} = 0.05 \text{ to } 1$$

In 2007, Lowe's cash ratio was 0.06, indicating that its cash reserve was approximately the same as the ratio for Home Depot. The Home Depot ratio of 0.05 means that the company has on hand 5 cents of cash for each $1 of current liabilities. Would analysts be concerned about this fairly low margin of safety? In this case, the answer is no because there were other factors to consider. For example, Home Depot's statement of cash flows showed that the company generated a large amount of cash from its operating activities. As a result, it did not need to keep a large amount of cash on hand to meet unexpected needs. Indeed, most analysts believe the cash ratio should not be too high because holding excess cash is usually uneconomical. It is far better to invest the cash in productive assets or reduce debt.

Some analysts do not use the cash ratio because it is very sensitive to small events. The collection of a large account receivable, for example, could have a significant

---

1. $\dfrac{\text{Net Income}}{\text{Average Stockholders' Equity}}$

2. $\dfrac{\text{Net Income + Interest Expense (net of tax)}}{\text{Average Total Assets}}$

3. $\dfrac{\text{Net Income}}{\text{Net Sales Revenue}}$

Self-Study Quiz
Solutions

impact on a company's cash ratio. The current ratio and the quick ratio are much less sensitive to the timing of such transactions.

9. Current Ratio

The current ratio measures the relationship between total current assets and total current liabilities on a specific date. It is computed as follows:

$$\text{Current Ratio} = \frac{\text{Current Assets}}{\text{Current Liabilities}}$$

$$\text{Home Depot 2007} = \frac{\$18,000}{\$12,931} = 1.39 \text{ to } 1$$

The current ratio measures the cushion of working capital that companies maintain to allow for the inevitable unevenness in the flow of funds through the working capital accounts. At the end of 2007, Home Depot had $1.39 in current assets for each $1 in current liabilities. Most analysts would judge that ratio to be very strong, given Home Depot's ability to generate cash.

To properly use the current ratio, analysts must understand the nature of a company's business. Many manufacturing companies have developed sophisticated systems to minimize the amount of inventory they must hold. These systems, called *just-in-time inventory,* are designed to have an inventory item arrive just when it is needed. While these systems work well in manufacturing processes, they do not work as well in retailing. Customers expect to find merchandise in the store when they want it, and it has proven difficult to precisely forecast consumer behavior. As a result, most retailers have comparatively high current ratios because they must carry large inventories. Home Depot, for example, maintains an inventory of 50,000 different products in each store.

Analysts consider a current ratio of 2 to be financially conservative. Indeed, most companies have current ratios that are below 2. The optimal level of the current ratio depends on the business environment in which a company operates. If cash flows are predictable and stable (as they are for a utility company), the current ratio can be low, even less than 1. For example, Procter & Gamble, a strong and fiscally conservative company, has a current ratio of 0.78. When cash flows are highly variable, a higher current ratio is desirable.

Analysts become concerned if a company's current ratio is high compared to that of other companies. A firm is operating inefficiently when it ties up too much money in inventory or accounts receivable. There is no reason, for instance, for a Home Depot store to hold 1,000 hammers in stock if it sells only 100 hammers a month.

10. Quick Ratio (Acid Test)

The quick ratio is a more stringent test of short-term liquidity than is the current ratio. The quick ratio compares quick assets, defined as *cash and near-cash assets,* to current liabilities. Quick assets include cash, short-term investments, and accounts receivable (net of the allowance for doubtful accounts). Inventory is omitted from quick assets because of the uncertainty of the timing of cash flows from its sale. Prepaid expenses are also excluded from quick assets. The quick ratio is computed as follows:

$$\text{Quick Ratio} = \frac{\text{Quick Assets}}{\text{Current Liabilities}}$$

$$\text{Home Depot 2007} = \frac{\$3,837}{\$12,931} = 0.30 \text{ to } 1$$

The quick ratio is a measure of the safety margin that is available to meet a company's current liabilities. Home Depot has 30 cents in cash and near-cash assets for every $1 in current liabilities. This margin of safety is typical of the retail industry and would be considered a good margin in light of the large amount of cash Home Depot generates from its operating activities. In comparison, the quick ratio for Lowe's is better than Home Depot (0.40 to 1).

11. Receivable Turnover Ratio

Accounts receivable are closely related to both short-term liquidity and operating efficiency. A company that can quickly collect cash from its customers has good liquidity and does not needlessly tie up funds in unproductive assets. The receivable turnover ratio is computed as follows:

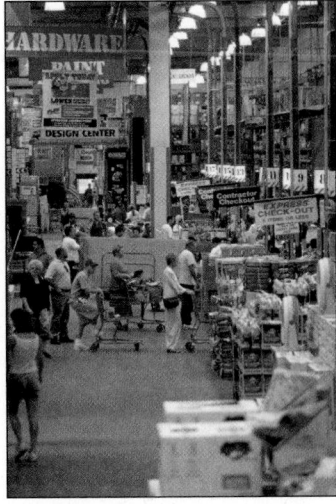

$$\text{Receivable Turnover Ratio} = \frac{\text{Net Credit Sales*}}{\text{Average Net Receivables}}$$

$$\text{Home Depot 2007} = \frac{\$90,837}{\$2,810^{\dagger}} = 32.3 \text{ Times}$$

*When the amount of credit sales is not known, total sales may be used as a rough approximation.
†($3,223 + $2,396) ÷ 2 = $2,810

A high receivable turnover ratio suggests that a company is effective in its credit-granting and collection activities. Granting credit to poor credit risks and making ineffective collection efforts will produce a low receivable turnover ratio. While a very low ratio is obviously a problem, a very high ratio also can be troublesome because it suggests an overly stringent credit policy that could cause lost sales and profits.

The receivable turnover ratio is often converted to a time basis known as the *average age of receivables.* The computation is as follows:

$$\text{Average Age of Receivables} = \frac{\text{Days in a Year}}{\text{Receivable Turnover Ratio}}$$

$$\text{Home Depot 2007} = \frac{365}{32.3} = 11.3 \text{ Average Days to Collect}$$

The effectiveness of credit and collection activities is sometimes judged by the rule of thumb that the average days to collect should not exceed 1.5 times the credit terms. For example, if the credit terms require payment in 30 days, the average days to collect should not exceed 45 days (i.e., not more than 15 days past due). Like all rules of thumb, this one has many exceptions.

Although the receivable turnover ratio normally provides useful insights, the one for Home Depot is not meaningful. It is highly unlikely that Home Depot collects cash from its credit customers in just 11.3 days, on average. Because we did not know the amount of Home Depot's credit sales, we used total sales as an approximation. In this case, the approximation is not reasonable. Think about the last time you watched a customer buying merchandise on credit in a retail store. Most customers use a bank credit card such as MasterCard or Visa. From the seller's perspective, a sales transaction involving a bank credit card is recorded in virtually the same manner as a cash sale. In other words, a sale involving a credit card does not create an account receivable on the seller's books; instead, the account receivable is recorded on the credit card company's books. In practice, the majority of Home Depot's credit sales involve bank credit cards. As a result, Home Depot's accounts receivable turnover ratio is not meaningful.

12. Inventory Turnover Ratio

Like receivable turnover, inventory turnover is a measure of both liquidity and operating efficiency. This ratio reflects the relationship of inventory to the volume of goods sold during the period. It is computed as follows:

$$\text{Inventory Turnover Ratio} = \frac{\text{Cost of Goods Sold}}{\text{Average Inventory}}$$

$$\text{Home Depot 2007} = \frac{\$61,054}{\$12,112*} = 5.0 \text{ Times}$$

*($12,822 + $11,401) ÷ 2 = $12,112.

Because a company normally realizes profit each time inventory is sold, an increase in this ratio is usually favorable. If the ratio is too high, however, it may be an indication that sales were lost because desired items were not in stock. The cost of a lost sale is often much higher than the lost profit. When a business is out of stock on an item desired by a customer, the individual will often go to a competitor to find it. That visit may help the competitor establish a business relationship with the customer. Thus, the cost of being out of stock may be all future profits on sales to a lost customer.

On average, Home Depot's inventory was acquired and sold to customers five times during the year. The inventory turnover ratio is critical for Home Depot because of its business strategy. They want to be able to offer customers the right product when they need it at a price that beats the competition. If Home Depot does not effectively manage its inventory levels, it will incur extra costs that must be passed on to the customer.

Inventory turnover for Lowe's was 4.5. Historically, Home Depot has enjoyed a significant advantage over Lowe's in terms of inventory management. Home Depot's effectiveness in inventory management means that the company is able to tie up less money in carry inventory compared to Lowe's.

Turnover ratios vary significantly from one industry to the next. Companies in the food industry (grocery stores and restaurants) have high inventory turnover ratios because their inventory is subject to rapid deterioration in quality. Companies that sell expensive merchandise (automobiles and high-fashion clothes) have much lower ratios because although sales of those items are infrequent, customers want to have a selection to choose from when they do buy.

The turnover ratio is often converted to a time basis called the *average days' supply in inventory*. The computation is:

$$\text{Average Days' Supply in Inventory} = \frac{\text{Days in Year}}{\text{Inventory Turnover Ratio}}$$

$$\text{Home Depot 2007} = \frac{365}{5.0} = 73 \text{ Average Days' Supply in Inventory}$$

Using Ratios to Analyze the Operating Cycle In Chapter 3, we introduced the concept of the operating cycle, which is the time it takes for a company to pay cash to its suppliers, sell goods to its customers, and collect cash from its customers. Analysts are interested in the operating cycle because it helps them evaluate a company's cash needs and is a good indicator of management efficiency.

The operating cycle for most companies involves three distinct phases: the acquisition of inventory, the sale of the inventory, and the collection of cash from the customer. We have discussed several ratios that are helpful when evaluating a company's operating cycle:

Ratio	Operating Activity
Accounts payable turnover ratio*	Purchase of inventory
Inventory turnover ratio	Sale of inventory
Accounts receivable turnover ratio	Collection of cash from customers
*Discussed in Chapter 9	

Each of the ratios measures the number of days it takes, on average, to complete an operating activity. We have already computed two of the needed ratios for Home Depot, so if we compute the accounts payable turnover ratio, we can analyze the operating cycle:

$$\text{Payable Turnover Ratio} = \frac{\text{Cost of Goods Sold}}{\text{Average Accounts Payable}}$$

$$\text{Home Depot 2007} = \frac{\$61,054}{\$6,694^*} = 9.1 \text{ Times}$$

*($7,356 + $6,032) ÷ 2 = $6,694

$$\text{Average Age of Payables} = \frac{\text{Days in a Year}}{\text{Payable Turnover Ratio}}$$

$$\text{Home Depot 2007} = \frac{365}{9.1} = 40.1 \text{ Average Days to Pay Suppliers}$$

The length of the component parts for Home Depot's operating cycle are:

Ratio	Time
Accounts payable turnover	40.1 days
Inventory turnover	73.0 days
Accounts receivable turnover	11.3 days

The component parts of the operating cycle help us understand the cash needs of the company. Home Depot, on average, pays for its inventory 40.1 days after it receives it. It takes, on average, 84.3 days (73 + 11.3) for it to sell and for the company to collect cash from the customer. Therefore, Home Depot must invest cash in its operating activities for nearly 44 days between the time it pays its vendors and the time it collects from its customers. Companies prefer to minimize the time between paying vendors and collecting cash from customers because it frees up cash for other productive purposes. Home Depot could reduce this time by slowing payments to creditors or by increasing the inventory turnover.

> ## SELF-STUDY **QUIZ**
>
> Show how to compute the following ratios:
>
> 1. Quality of income =
>
> 2. Quick ratio =
>
> 3. Cash ratio =
>
> *After you have completed your answers, check them with the solutions at the bottom of the page.*

Tests of Solvency

Solvency refers to a company's ability to meet its long-term obligations. **Tests of solvency,** which are measures of a company's ability to meet these obligations, include the times interest earned, cash coverage, and debt-to-equity ratios.

Learning Objective 6
Compute and interpret solvency ratios.

13. Times Interest Earned Ratio

Interest payments are a fixed obligation. If a company fails to make required interest payments, creditors may force it into bankruptcy. Because of the importance of

TESTS OF SOLVENCY are ratios that measure a company's ability to meet its long-term obligations

---

1. $\dfrac{\text{Cash Flows from Operating Activities}}{\text{Net Income}}$

2. $\dfrac{\text{Quick Assets}}{\text{Current Liabilities}}$

3. $\dfrac{\text{Cash + Cash Equivalents}}{\text{Current Liabilities}}$

Self-Study Quiz
Solutions

meeting interest payments, analysts often compute a ratio called *times interest earned:*

$$\text{Time Interest Earned} = \frac{\text{Net Income} + \text{Interest Expense} + \text{Income Tax Expense}}{\text{Interest Expense}}$$

$$\text{Home Depot 2007} = \frac{\$5,761 + \$392 + \$3,547}{\$392} = 24.7 \text{ Times}$$

The times interest earned ratio compares the income a company generated in a period to its interest obligation for the same period. It represents a margin of protection for creditors. In 2007, Home Depot generated $24.70 in income for each $1 of interest expense, a high ratio that indicates a secure position for creditors.

Some analysts prefer to calculate the times interest earned ratio based on all contractually required payments, including principal and rent payments. Others believe that the ratio is flawed because interest expense and other obligations are paid in cash, not with net income. These analysts prefer to use the cash coverage ratio.

14. Cash Coverage Ratio

Given the importance of cash flows and required interest payments, it is easy to understand why many analysts use the cash coverage ratio. It is computed as follows:

$$\text{Cash Coverage Ratio} = \frac{\text{Cash Flows from Operating Activities before Interest and Taxes Paid}}{\text{Interest Paid (from statement of cash flows)}}$$

$$\text{Home Depot 2007} = \frac{\$7,661 + \$270 + \$3,963}{\$270} = 44.1$$

The cash coverage ratio compares the cash generated by a company to its cash obligations for the period. Remember that analysts are concerned about a company's ability to make required interest payments. Home Depot's cash coverage ratio shows that the company generated $44 in cash for every $1 of interest paid, which is strong coverage. Note that the denominator of the cash coverage ratio uses **interest paid** from the statement of cash flows instead of **interest expense** from the income statement. Accrued interest and interest payments are normally similar in amount, but are not always the same.

15. Debt-to-Equity Ratio

The debt-to-equity ratio expresses a company's debt as a proportion of its stockholders' equity. It is computed as follows:

$$\text{Debt-to-Equity Ratio} = \frac{\text{Total Liabilities}}{\text{Stockholders' Equity}}$$

$$\text{Home Depot 2007} = \frac{\$27,233}{\$25,030} = 1.09$$

In 2007 for each $1 of stockholders' equity, Home Depot had $1.09 worth of liabilities. By comparison, Lowe's debt-to-equity ratio was 0.77.

Debt is risky for a company because specific interest payments must be made even if the company has not earned sufficient income to pay them. In contrast, dividends are always at the company's discretion and are not legally enforceable until they are declared by the board of directors. Thus, equity capital is usually considered much less risky than debt.

Despite the risk associated with debt, however, most companies obtain significant amounts of resources from creditors because of the advantages of financial leverage discussed earlier. In addition, interest expense is a deductible expense on the corporate income tax return. In selecting a capital structure, a company must balance the higher returns available through leverage against the higher risk associated with debt. Because of the importance of the risk-return relationship, most analysts consider the debt-to-equity ratio a key part of any company evaluation.

Market Tests

Several ratios, often called **market tests,** relate the current price per share of stock to the return that accrues to investors. Many analysts prefer these ratios because they are based on the current value of an owner's investment in a company.

16. Price/Earnings (P/E) Ratio

The price/earnings (P/E) ratio measures the relationship between the current market price of a stock and its earnings per share. Recently, when the price of Home Depot stock was $34 per share, EPS for Home Depot (as reported in Exhibit 14.1) was $2.80. The P/E ratio for Home Depot is computed as follows:

$$\text{Price/Earnings Ratio} = \frac{\text{Current Market Price per Share}}{\text{Earnings per Share}}$$

$$\text{Home Depot 2007} = \frac{\$34}{\$2.80} = 12.1$$

This P/E ratio indicates that Home Depot's stock was selling at a price that was 12.1 times its earnings per share. The P/E ratio reflects the stock market's assessment of a company's future performance. A high ratio indicates that earnings are expected to grow rapidly. Home Depot's P/E ratio is lower compared to previous years and is lower than Lowe's, which reported a P/E ratio of 14.4. The P/E ratio for Home Depot suggests that the market believes that Home Depot does not have the same growth potential that it had in recent years.

In economic terms, the value of a stock is related to the present value of the company's future earnings. Thus, a company that expects to increase its earnings in the future is worth more than one that cannot grow its earnings (assuming other factors are the same). But while a high P/E ratio and good growth prospects are considered favorable, there are risks. When a company with a high P/E ratio does not meet the level of earnings expected by the market, the negative impact on its stock can be dramatic.

17. Dividend Yield Ratio

When investors buy stock, they expect two kinds of return: dividend income and price appreciation. The dividend yield ratio measures the relationship between the dividends per share paid to stockholders and the current market price of a stock. Home Depot paid dividends of 67.5 cents per share when the market price of its stock was $34 per share. Its dividend yield ratio is computed as follows:

$$\text{Dividend Yield Ratio} = \frac{\text{Dividends per Share}}{\text{Market Price per Share}}$$

$$\text{Home Depot 2007} = \frac{\$0.675}{\$34} = 2\%$$

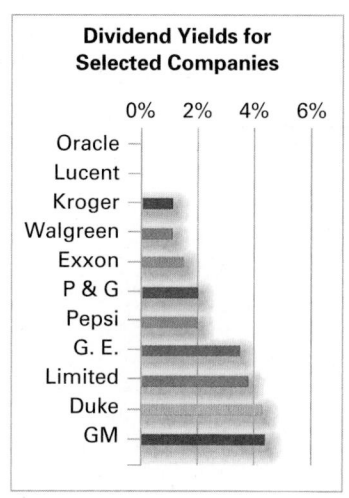

Dividend Yields for Selected Companies

You might be surprised that Home Depot's dividend yield was just 2 percent, when an investor could earn more than 4 percent in a federally insured savings account. In fact, the dividend yield for most stocks is not high compared to alternative investments. Investors are willing to accept low dividend yields if they expect that the price of a stock will increase while they own it. Clearly, investors who bought Home Depot's stock did so with the expectation that its price would increase. In contrast, stocks with low growth potential tend to offer much higher dividend yields than do stocks with high growth potential. These stocks often appeal to retired investors who need current income rather than future growth potential.

The dividend yield for Lowe's is even lower than the one for Home Depot, 0.1 percent in 2007. The chart in the margin on page 729 shows dividend yields for some companies in other industries.

SELF-STUDY QUIZ

Show how to compute the following ratios:

1. Current ratio =

2. Inventory turnover ratio =

3. Price/earnings ratio =

After you have completed your answers, check them with the solutions at the bottom of the page.

INTERPRETING RATIOS AND OTHER ANALYTICAL CONSIDERATIONS

Except for earnings per share, the computation of financial ratios has not been standardized by either the accounting profession or security analysts. Thus, users of financial statements should compute the various ratios in accordance with their decision objectives. Before using ratios computed by others, they should determine the computational approach that was used.

As we have seen, ratios can be interpreted only by comparing them to other ratios or to some optimal value. Some ratios, by their very nature, are unfavorable at either very high or very low values. For example, a very low current ratio may indicate an inability to meet maturing debts, and while a very high current ratio may indicate an unprofitable use of funds. Furthermore, an optimal ratio for one company may not be optimal for another. Comparisons among the ratios for different companies are appropriate only if the companies are comparable in terms of their industry, operations, size, and accounting policies.

Because ratios are based on the aggregation of information, they may obscure underlying factors that are of interest to the analyst. For example, a current ratio that is considered optimal can obscure a short-term liquidity problem in a company with a large amount of inventory but a minimal amount of cash with which to pay debts as they mature. Careful analysis can uncover this type of problem.

In other cases, analysis cannot uncover obscured problems. For example, consolidated statements include financial information about a parent company and its subsidiaries. The parent company could have a high current ratio and the subsidiary a low one, but when their statements are consolidated, their current ratios are in effect averaged and can fall within an acceptable range. The fact that the subsidiary could have a serious liquidity problem is obscured.

Despite limitations, ratio analysis is a useful analytical tool. For instance, financial ratios are effective for predicting bankruptcy. Exhibit 14.4 presents the current and

Self-Study Quiz
Solutions

1. $\dfrac{\text{Current assets}}{\text{Current liabilities}}$

2. $\dfrac{\text{Cost of goods sold}}{\text{Average inventory}}$

3. $\dfrac{\text{Current market price per share}}{\text{Earnings per share}}$

YEARS BEFORE BANKRUPTCY					
	5	**4**	**3**	**2**	**1**
Current ratio	1.8	1.7	1.7	1.2	1.2
Debt-to-equity ratio	1.6	1.8	2.0	5.0	5.6

EXHIBIT 14.4

Selected Financial Ratios for Hechinger

debt-to-equity ratios for Hechinger, a former competitor of Home Depot, for the five years before its recent bankruptcy. Notice the progressive deterioration of these ratios. Analysts who studied these ratios probably were not surprised when Hechinger filed for bankruptcy.

Financial statements provide information to all investors, both sophisticated and unsophisticated. However, users who understand basic accounting principles and terminology are able to more effectively analyze the information contained in financial statements. For example, some unsophisticated users who do not understand the cost principle believe that assets are reported on the balance sheet at their fair market value. Interpreting accounting numbers correctly without an understanding of the concepts that were used to develop them is impossible.

In analyzing different companies, you will find that they rarely use exactly the same accounting policies. Comparisons among companies are appropriate only if the analyst who is making them understands the impact of different accounting alternatives. For example, one company may use conservative accounting alternatives such as accelerated depreciation and LIFO while another may use income-maximizing alternatives such as straight-line depreciation and FIFO. Analysts who do not understand the different effects of these accounting methods could misinterpret financial results. Perhaps the most important first step in analyzing financial statements is a review of the company's accounting policies, which are disclosed in a note to the statements.

Other Financial Information

The ratios we have discussed are useful for most analytical purposes. Because each company is different, however, you must exercise professional judgment when you conduct each financial analysis. To illustrate, let's look at some special factors that could affect our analysis of Home Depot.

1. **Rapid growth.** Growth in total sales volume does not always indicate that a company is successful. Sales volume from new stores may obscure the fact that existing stores are not meeting customer needs and are experiencing declines in sales. The family pizza chain Chuck-E-Cheese appeared to be a success when it reported rapid growth in total sales revenue by opening new restaurants. Unfortunately, the novelty of the new Chuck-E-Cheese restaurants proved to be short-lived fads, and their sales volume fell quickly. Because its older restaurants were unprofitable, Chuck-E-Cheese was forced to reorganize. In contrast, Home Depot's annual report shows that the company's stores posted sales increases ranging from 3 percent to 15 percent in each of the previous 10 years. Clearly, Home Depot can generate sales increases from both new and existing stores.

2. **Uneconomical expansion.** Some growth-oriented companies will open stores in less desirable locations if good locations cannot be found. These poor locations can cause a company's average productivity to decline. One measure of productivity in

the retail industry is sales volume per square foot of selling space. For Home Depot, productivity results are a cause for concern:

Year	Sales per Square Foot
2007	$358
2006	377
2005	375
2004	371
2003	370

Sales per square foot have been in a steady decline for the past several years. In the 1990s, sales per square foot average over $400. Management explains the slowdown in growth is the direct result of its strategy:

REAL WORLD EXCERPT

ANNUAL REPORT

> We strategically open stores near market areas served by existing stores ("cannibalize") to gain incremental sales and increase market penetration. New stores cannibalized approximately 13.5% of our existing stores and reduced sales volume by approximately 1.9%.

As the note indicates, Home Depot is willing to accept lower productivity at certain existing stores in order to achieve high sales levels in a region. An analyst who reviewed only the number reported in the annual report without a careful reading of the notes would probably misinterpret the decline in sales per square foot.

3. **Subjective factors.** Remember that vital information about a company is not contained in the annual report. The best way to evaluate Home Depot's strategy of being a price leader, for instance, is to visit its stores and those of competitors. An analyst who studied Home Depot for Smith Barney did exactly that:

REAL WORLD EXCERPT

SMITH BARNEY
RESEARCH REPORT

> On July 15, we surveyed the Boca Raton, Florida, market. The Home Depot store is about two years old and was particularly impressive with respect to its in-stock position, customer service and total store presentation. We were able to compare Home Depot's pricing on 20 sample items. Our price analysis revealed that Home Depot is the price leader in the market by an average of 11 percent below the average total price of our 20-item market basket. Given the Home Depot's low cost structure, we believe that it will remain the price leader in this important market.

As these examples illustrate, no single approach can be used to analyze all companies. Furthermore, an effective analyst will look beyond the information contained in an annual report.

A QUESTION OF ETHICS   **Insider Information**

Financial statements are an important source of information for investors. Announcement of unexpected information can cause a substantial movement in the price of a company's stock.

A company's accountants often are aware of important financial information before it is made available to the public. This type of data is called *insider information*. Some people might be tempted to buy or sell stock based on insider information, but to do so is a serious criminal offense. The Securities and Exchange Commission has brought a number of cases against individuals who traded on insider information. Their convictions resulted in large fines and time served in jail.

In some cases, determining whether something is insider information is difficult. For example, an individual could overhear a comment made in the company elevator by two executives. A well-respected Wall Street investment banker gave good advice on dealing with such situations: "If you are not sure if something is right or wrong, apply the newspaper headline test. Ask yourself how you would feel to have your family and friends read about what you had done in the newspaper." Interestingly, many people who have spent time in jail and lost small fortunes in fines because of insider trading say that the most difficult part of the process was telling their families.

To uphold the highest ethical standard, many public accounting firms have adopted rules that prevent their staff from investing in companies that the firms audit. Such rules are designed to ensure that a company's auditors cannot be tempted to engage in insider trading.

Information in an Efficient Market

Considerable research has been performed on the way in which stock markets react to new information. Much of this evidence supports the view that the markets react very quickly to new information in an unbiased manner (that is, the market does not systematically overreact or underreact to new information). A market that reacts to information in this manner is called an **efficient market.** In an efficient market, the price of a security fully reflects all available information.

It is not surprising that the stock markets react quickly to new information. Many professional investors manage stock portfolios valued in the hundreds of millions of dollars. These investors have a financial incentive to discover new information about a company and to trade quickly based on it.

The research on efficient markets has important implications for financial analysts. It probably is not beneficial to study old information (say an annual report that was released six months earlier) in an effort to identify an undervalued stock. In an efficient market, the price of a stock reflects all information contained in the annual report shortly after its release. In an efficient market, moreover, a company cannot manipulate the price of its stock by manipulating its accounting policy. The market should be able to differentiate between a company whose earnings are increasing due to improved productivity and one whose earnings have increased simply because of changes in accounting policies.

EFFICIENT MARKETS are securities markets in which prices fully reflect available information.

CHAPTER **TAKE-AWAYS**

1. **Explain how a company's business strategy affects financial analysis.** p. 713

   In simple terms, a business strategy establishes the objectives a business is trying to achieve. Performance is best evaluated by comparing the financial results to the objectives that the business was working to achieve. In other words, an understanding of a company's strategy provides the context for conducting financial statement analysis.

2. **Discuss how analysts use financial statements.** p. 714

   Analysts use financial statements to understand present conditions and past performance as well as to predict future performance. Financial statements provide important information to help users understand and evaluate corporate strategy. The data reported on statements can be used for either time-series analysis (evaluating a single company over time) or in comparison with similar companies at a single point in time. Most analysts compute component percentages and ratios when using statements.

3. **Compute and interpret component percentages.** p. 716

   To compute component percentages for the income statement, the base amount is net sales revenue. Each expense is expressed as a percentage of net sales revenue. On the balance sheet, the base amount is total assets; each balance sheet account is divided by total assets.

Component percentages are evaluated by comparing them over time for a single company or by comparing them with percentages for similar companies.

4. **Compute and interpret profitability ratios.   p. 718**

Several tests of profitability focus on measuring the adequacy of income by comparing it to other items reported on the financial statements. Exhibit 14.3 lists these ratios and shows how to compute them. Profitability ratios are evaluated by comparing them over time for a single company or by comparing them with ratios for similar companies.

5. **Compute and interpret liquidity ratios.   p. 723**

Tests of liquidity measure a company's ability to meet its currently maturing debt. Exhibit 14.3 lists these ratios and shows how to compute them. Liquidity ratios are evaluated by comparing them over time for a single company or by comparing them with ratios for similar companies.

6. **Compute and interpret solvency ratios.   p. 727**

Solvency ratios measure a company's ability to meet its long-term obligations. Exhibit 14.3 lists these ratios and shows how to compute them. Solvency ratios are evaluated by comparing them over time for a single company or by comparing them with ratios for similar companies.

7. **Compute and interpret market test ratios.   p. 729**

Market test ratios relate the current price of a stock to the return that accrues to investors. Exhibit 14.3 lists these ratios and shows how to compute them. Market test ratios are evaluated by comparing them over time for a single company or by comparing them with ratios for similar companies.

FINDING FINANCIAL INFORMATION

Balance Sheet

Ratios are not reported on the balance sheet, but analysts use balance sheet information to compute many ratios. Most analysts use an average of the beginning and ending amounts for balance sheet accounts when comparing the account to an income statement account.

Income Statement

Earnings per share is the only ratio that is required to be reported on the financial statements. It is usually reported at the bottom of the income statement.

Statement of Cash Flows

Ratios are not reported on this statement, but some analysts use amounts from this statement to compute some ratios.

Statement of Stockholders' Equity

Ratios are not reported on this statement, but analysts use amounts from this statement to compute some ratios.

Notes

Under Summary of Significant Accounting Policies
This note has no information pertaining directly to ratios, but it is important to understand accounting differences if you are comparing two companies.

Under a Separate Note
Most companies include a 10-year financial summary as a separate note. These summaries include data for significant accounts, some accounting ratios, and nonaccounting information.

KEY TERMS

Component Percentage p. 716	**Ratio (Percentage)**	**Tests of**
Efficient Markets p. 733	**Analysis** p. 716	**Profitability** p. 718
Market Tests p. 729	**Tests of Liquidity** p. 723	**Tests of Solvency** p. 727

QUESTIONS

1. What are some of the primary items on financial statements about which creditors usually are concerned?
2. Why are the notes to the financial statements important to decision makers?
3. What is the primary purpose of comparative financial statements?
4. Why are statement users interested in financial summaries covering several years? What is the primary limitation of long-term summaries?
5. What is ratio analysis? Why is it useful?
6. What are component percentages? Why are they useful?
7. Explain the two concepts of return on investment.
8. What is financial leverage? How is it measured as a percentage?
9. Is profit margin a useful measure of profitability? Explain.
10. Compare and contrast the current ratio and the quick ratio.
11. What does the debt-to-equity ratio reflect?
12. What are market tests?
13. Identify two factors that limit the effectiveness of ratio analysis.

MULTIPLE-CHOICE QUESTIONS

1. A company has total assets of $500,000 and noncurrent assets of $400,000. Current liabilities are $40,000. What is the current ratio?
   a. 12.5
   b. 10.0
   c. 2.5
   d. Cannot be determined without additional information.
2. Which of the following would *not* change the receivables turnover ratio for a retail company?
   a. Increases in the retail prices of inventory.
   b. A change in credit policy.
   c. Increases in the cost incurred to purchase inventory.
   d. None of the above.
3. Which of the following ratios is used to analyze liquidity?
   a. Earnings per share   c. Current ratio
   b. Debt-to-equity ratio   d. Both (a) and (c)
4. Positive financial leverage indicates
   a. Positive cash flow from financing activities.
   b. A debt-to-equity ratio of higher than 1.
   c. A rate of return on assets exceeding the interest rate on debt.
   d. A profit margin in one year exceeding the previous year's profit margin.
5. If a potential investor is analyzing three companies in the same industry and wishes to invest in only one, which ratio is least likely to affect the investor's decision?
   a. Quick ratio   c. Price to earnings ratio
   b. Earnings per share   d. Dividend yield ratio
6. A company has quick assets of $300,000 and current liabilities of $150,000. The company purchased $50,000 in inventory on credit. After the purchase, the quick ratio would be
   a. 2.0   c. 1.5
   b. 2.3   d. 1.75
7. The average days' supply in inventory for Natural Foods Stores is 14.6 days. The company reported cost of goods sold in the amount of $1,500,000 and total sales of $2,500,000. What is the average amount of inventory for Natural Foods?
   a. $102,740   c. $100,000
   b. $171,233   d. $60,000

8. Given the following ratios for four companies, which company is least likely to experience problems paying its current liabilities promptly?

	Quick Ratio	Receivable Turnover Ratio
a.	1.2	58
b.	1.2	45
c.	1.0	55
d.	.5	60

9. A decrease in selling and administrative expenses would impact what ratio?
   a. Fixed asset turnover ratio.
   b. Times interest earned.
   c. Debt-to-equity ratio.
   d. Current ratio.

10. A creditor is least likely to use what ratio when analyzing a company that has borrowed funds on a long-term basis?
   a. Cash coverage ratio.
   b. Debt-to-equity ratio.
   c. Times interest earned ratio.
   d. Profit margin.

For more practice with multiple-choice questions, go to the text website www.mhhe.com/libby6e.

MINI-**EXERCISES**

Available with McGraw-Hill's Homework Manager

M14-1
LO3

Inferring Financial Information Using Component Percentages

A large retailer reported revenue of $1,665,000. The company's gross profit percentage was 44 percent. What amount of cost of goods sold did the company report?

M14-2
LO3

Inferring Financial Information Using Component Percentages

A consumer products company reported a 5.4 percent increase in sales from 2009 to 2010. Sales in 2009 were $29,600. In 2010, the company reported cost of goods sold in the amount of $9,107. What was the gross profit percentage in 2010?

M14-3
LO4

Computing the Return on Owners' Investment Ratio

Compute the return on equity ratio for 2010 given the following data:

	2010	2009
Net income	$ 183,000	$ 159,000
Stockholders' equity	1,100,000	1,250,000
Total assets	2,460,000	2,630,000
Interest expense	42,000	32,000

M14-4
LO4

Inferring Financial Information

Compute the financial leverage percentage for 2010 given the following data:

	2010	2009
Return on equity	21%	26%
Return on assets	6	8
Profit margin	12	12

M14-5
LO5

Analyzing the Inventory Turnover Ratio

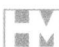

A manufacturer reported an inventory turnover ratio of 8.6 during 2009. During 2010, management introduced a new inventory control system that was expected to reduce average inventory levels by 25 percent without affecting sales volume. Given these circumstances, would you expect the inventory turnover ratio to increase or decrease during 2010? Explain.

Inferring Financial Information Using a Ratio

M14-6
LO5

Scruggs Company reported total assets of $1,400,000 and noncurrent assets of $480,000. The company also reported a current ratio of 3.5. What amount of current liabilities did the company report?

Analyzing Financial Relationships

M14-7
LO4, 5

Doritos Company has prepared draft financial results now being reviewed by the accountants. You notice that the financial leverage percentage is negative. You also note that the current ratio is 2.4 and the quick ratio is 3.7. You recognize that these financial relationships are unusual. Does either imply that a mistake has been made? Explain.

Inferring Financial Information Using a Ratio

M14-8
LO7

In 2009, Drago Company reported earnings per share of $9.50 when its stock was selling for $228. In 2010, its earnings increased by 13 percent. If all other relationships remain constant, what is the price of the stock? Explain.

Inferring Financial Information Using a Ratio

M14-9
LO7

An Internet company earned $6.50 per share and paid dividends of $3.50 per share. The company reported a dividend yield of 5 percent. What was the price of the stock?

Analyzing the Impact of Accounting Alternatives

M14-10
LO3, 4, 5

Lexis Corporation is considering changing its inventory method from FIFO to LIFO and wants to determine the impact on selected accounting ratios. In general, what impact would you expect on the following ratios: profit margin, fixed asset turnover ratio, current ratio, and quick ratio?

Available with McGraw-Hill's Homework Manager

EXERCISES

Using Financial Information to Identify Mystery Companies

E14-1
LO1, 2, 3, 5, 6

The following selected financial data pertain to four unidentified companies:

	COMPANIES			
	1	2	3	4
Balance Sheet Data (component percentage)				
Cash	3.5	4.7	8.2	11.7
Accounts receivable	16.9	28.9	16.8	51.9
Inventory	46.8	35.6	57.3	4.8
Property and equipment	18.3	21.7	7.6	18.7
Income Statement Data (component percentage)				
Gross profit	22.0	22.5	44.8	N/A*
Profit before taxes	2.1	0.7	1.2	3.2
Selected Ratios				
Current ratio	1.3	1.5	1.6	1.2
Inventory turnover ratio	3.6	9.8	1.5	N/A
Debt-to-equity ratio	2.6	2.6	3.2	3.2

*N/A = Not applicable

This financial information pertains to the following companies:
a. Retail fur store
b. Advertising agency
c. Wholesale candy company
d. Car manufacturer

Required:
Match each company with its financial information.

E14-2
LO1, 2, 3, 5, 6

Using Financial Information to Identify Mystery Companies

The following selected financial data pertain to four unidentified companies:

	COMPANIES			
	1	2	3	4
Balance Sheet Data				
(component percentage)				
Cash	7.3	21.6	6.1	11.3
Accounts receivable	28.2	39.7	3.2	22.9
Inventory	21.6	0.6	1.8	27.5
Property and equipment	32.1	18.0	74.6	25.1
Income Statement Data				
(component percentage)				
Gross profit	15.3	N/A*	N/A	43.4
Profit before taxes	1.7	3.2	2.4	6.9
Selected Ratios				
Current ratio	1.5	1.2	0.6	1.9
Inventory turnover ratio	27.4	N/A	N/A	3.3
Debt-to-equity ratio	1.7	2.2	5.7	1.3

*N/A = Not applicable

This financial information pertains to the following companies:
a. Travel agency
b. Hotel
c. Meat packer
d. Drug company

Required:
Match each company with its financial information.

E14-3
LO1, 2, 3, 5, 6

Using Financial Information to Identify Mystery Companies

The following selected financial data pertain to four unidentified companies:

	COMPANIES			
	1	2	3	4
Balance Sheet Data				
(component percentage)				
Cash	5.1	8.8	6.3	10.4
Accounts receivable	13.1	41.5	13.8	4.9
Inventory	4.6	3.6	65.1	35.8
Property and equipment	53.1	23.0	8.8	35.7
Income Statement Data				
(component percentage)				
Gross profit	N/A*	N/A	45.2	22.5
Profit before taxes	0.3	16.0	3.9	1.5
Selected Ratios				
Current ratio	0.7	2.2	1.9	1.4
Inventory turnover ratio	N/A	N/A	1.4	15.5
Debt-to-equity ratio	2.5	0.9	1.7	2.3

*N/A = Not applicable

This financial information pertains to the following companies:
a. Cable TV company
b. Grocery store
c. Accounting firm
d. Retail jewelry store

Required:
Match each company with its financial information.

Using Financial Information to Identify Mystery Companies

The selected financial data on the following page pertain to four unidentified companies:

	COMPANIES			
	1	2	3	4
Balance Sheet Data				
(component percentage)				
Cash	11.6	6.6	5.4	7.1
Accounts receivable	4.6	18.9	8.8	35.6
Inventory	7.0	45.8	65.7	26.0
Property and equipment	56.0	20.3	10.1	21.9
Income Statement Data				
(component percentage)				
Gross profit	56.7	36.4	14.1	15.8
Profit before taxes	2.7	1.4	1.1	0.9
Selected Ratios				
Current ratio	0.7	2.1	1.2	1.3
Inventory turnover ratio	30.0	3.5	5.6	16.7
Debt-to-equity ratio	3.3	1.8	3.8	3.1

E14-4
LO1, 2, 3, 5, 6

This financial information pertains to the following companies:
a. Full-line department store
b. Wholesale fish company
c. Automobile dealer (both new and used cars)
d. Restaurant

Required:
Match each company with its financial information.

Matching Each Ratio with Its Computational Formula

Match each ratio or percentage with its computation.

E14-5
LO3, 4, 5, 6, 7

Ratios or Percentages	Definitions
1. Profit margin	A. Net income ÷ Net Sales
2. Inventory turnover ratio	B. Days in Year ÷ Receivable Turnover ratio
3. Average collection period	C. Income ÷ Average Stockholders' Equity
4. Dividend yield ratio	D. Income ÷ Average Number of Shares of Common Stock Outstanding
5. Return on equity	E. Return on Equity − Return on Assets
6. Current ratio	F. Quick Assets ÷ Current Liabilities
7. Debt-to-equity ratio	G. Current Assets ÷ Current Liabilities
8. Price/earnings ratio	H. Cost of Goods Sold ÷ Average Inventory
9. Financial leverage percentage	I. Net Credit Sales ÷ Average Net Receivables
10. Receivable turnover ratio	J. Days in Year ÷ Inventory Turnover ratio
11. Average days' supply of inventory	K. Total Liabilities ÷ Stockholders' Equity
12. Earnings per share	L. Dividends per Share ÷ Market Price per Share
13. Return on assets	M. Current Market Price per Share ÷ Earnings per Share
14. Quick ratio	

continued

15. Times interest earned
16. Cash coverage ratio
17. Fixed asset turnover ratio

N. [Net income + Interest Expense (net of tax)] ÷ Average Total Assets

O. Cash from Operating Activities (before interest and taxes) ÷ Interest Paid

P. Net Sales Revenue ÷ Average Fixed Assets

Q. (Net Income + Interest Expense + Income Tax Expense) ÷ Interest Expense

E14-6

L03

Lowe's

Preparing a Schedule Using Component Percentages

Lowe's is a leading retailer in the home improvement field. Complete the component percentage analysis on the company's income statement that follows. Discuss any insights provided by this analysis.

(IN MILLIONS, EXCEPT PER SHARE DATA) YEARS ENDED ON	FEBRUARY 2, 2007	% SALES	FEBRUARY 1, 2006	% SALES
Net sales	**$ 46,927**	%	**$ 43,243**	
Cost of sales	30,729		28,453	
Gross profit	**16,198**		**14,790**	
Expenses:				
Selling, general, and administrative	9,738		9,014	
Store opening costs	146		142	
Depreciation	1,162		980	
Interest	154		158	
Total expenses	**11,200**		**10,294**	
Pre-Tax earnings	4,998		4,496	
Income tax provision	1,893		1,731	
Net earnings	**$ 3,105**		**$ 2,765**	

E14-7

L05

Analyzing the Impact of Selected Transactions on the Current Ratio

Current assets totaled $54,000, and the current ratio was 1.5. Assume that the following transactions were completed: (1) purchased merchandise for $7,000 on short-term credit and (2) purchased a delivery truck for $12,000, paid $3,000 cash, and signed a two-year interest-bearing note for the balance.

Required:
Compute the cumulative current ratio after each transaction.

E14-8

L05

Bombay

Analyzing the Impact of Selected Transactions on the Current Ratio

The Bombay Company, Inc. marketed a line of proprietary home furnishings that includes large furniture, occasional furniture, wall decor, and decorative accessories that is timeless, classic, and traditional in its styling through a network of retail locations throughout the United States and Canada, through its direct-to-customer operations, and international licensing arrangements. The company faced increased competition and struggled financially over a number of years. It was forced to file for bankruptcy and was liquidated in 2008.

In its last financial statement prior to bankruptcy, Bombay reported current assets of $161,604,000 and current liabilities of $113,909,000. Determine the impact of the following transactions on the current ratio for Bombay: (1) sold long-term assets that represented excess capacity, (2) accrued severance pay and fringes for employees who will be terminated, (3) wrote down the carrying value of certain inventory items that were deemed to be obsolete, and (4) acquired new inventory; supplier was not willing to provide normal credit terms, so an 18-month interest-bearing note was signed.

E14-9

L05

P&G

Analyzing the Impact of Selected Transactions on Accounts Receivable and Inventory Turnover

Procter & Gamble is a multinational corporation that manufactures and markets many products that are probably in your home. Last year, sales for the company were $76,476 (all amounts in millions).

The annual report did not disclose the amount of credit sales, so we will assume that 90 percent of sales was on credit. The average gross profit rate was 52 percent on sales. Account balances follow:

	Beginning	Ending
Accounts receivable (net)	$6,629	$5,725
Inventory	6,819	6,291

Required:

Compute the turnover for the accounts receivable and inventory, the average age of receivables, and the average days' supply of inventory.

Computing Financial Leverage

Texas Instruments is a global leader in the semiconductor business providing products to the world's most innovative electronics companies. Its financial statements reported the following at year-end (in millions):

Total assets	$13,930
Total debt (average 8% interest)	2,570
Net income (average tax rate 30%)	4,341

Required:

Compute the financial leverage percentage. Was it positive or negative?

E14-10
LO4
Texas Instruments

Analyzing the Impact of Selected Transactions on the Current Ratio

Current assets totaled $100,000, and the current ratio was 1.5. Assume that the following transactions were completed: (1) paid $6,000 for merchandise purchased on short-term credit, (2) purchased a delivery truck for $11,000 cash, (3) wrote off a bad account receivable for $3,000, and (4) paid previously declared dividends in the amount of $28,000.

Required:

Compute the cumulative current ratio after each transaction.

E14-11
LO5

Inferring Financial Information

Dollar General Corporation operates general merchandise stores that feature quality merchandise at low prices to meet the needs of middle-, low-, and fixed-income families. All stores are located in the United States, predominantly in small towns in 24 midwestern and southeastern states. In a recent year, the company reported average inventories of $1,456,414,000 and an inventory turnover of 4.6. Average total fixed assets were $1,218,874,000, and the fixed asset turnover ratio was 7.5. Determine the gross profit for Dollar General.

E14-12
LO3, 5
Dollar General Corporation

Computing Selected Ratios

Sales for the year were $1,000,000, of which half was on credit. The average gross profit rate was 50 percent on sales. Account balances follow:

	Beginning	Ending
Accounts receivable (net)	$45,000	$60,000
Inventory	70,000	25,000

Required:

Compute the turnover for the accounts receivable and inventory, the average age of receivables, and the average days' supply of inventory.

E14-13
LO5

Analyzing the Impact of Selected Transactions on the Current Ratio

Current assets for Bond Corporation totaled $410,000 and the current ratio was 2.0. Assume that the following transactions were completed: (1) sold $11,000 in merchandise on short-term credit, (2) declared but did not pay dividends of $50,000, (3) paid prepaid rent in the amount of $12,000, (4) paid previously

E14-14
LO5

declared dividends in the amount of $50,000, (5) collected an account receivable in the amount of $11,000, and (6) reclassified $30,000 of long-term debt as a short-term liability.

Required:
Compute the cumulative current ratio after each transaction.

E14-15
L05
Cintas

Computing Liquidity Ratios

Cintas designs, manufactures, and implements corporate identity uniform programs that it rents or sells to customers throughout the United States and Canada. The company's stock is traded on the NASDAQ and has provided investors with significant returns over the past few years. Selected information from the company's balance sheet follows. For 2007, the company reported sales revenue of $3,706,900 and cost of goods sold of $1,515,815.

CINTAS		
Balance Sheet		
(Amount in Thousands)		
Cintas	**2007**	**2006**
Cash	$ 35,360	$ 38,914
Marketable securities	120,053	202,539
Accounts receivable, net	408,870	389,905
Inventories	231,741	198,000
Prepaid expense	15,781	11,163
Accounts payable	64,622	71,635
Accrued taxes	70,763	95,363
Accrued liabilities	263,512	239,061
Long-term debt due within one year	4,141	26,653

Required:
Compute the current ratio, inventory turnover ratio, and accounts receivable turnover ratio (assuming that 60 percent of sales was on credit).

PROBLEMS

 Available with McGraw-Hill's Homework Manager

P14-1
L05, 6, 7

Analyzing an Investment by Comparing Selected Ratios (AP14–1)

You have the opportunity to invest $10,000 in one of two companies from a single industry. The only information you have follows. The word *high* refers to the top third of the industry; *average* is the middle third; *low* is the bottom third. Which company would you select? Write a brief paper justifying your recommendation.

Ratio	Company A	Company B
Current	High	Average
Quick	Low	Average
Debt-to-equity ratio	High	Average
Inventory turnover ratio	Low	Average
Price/earnings	Low	Average
Dividend yield ratio	High	Average

Analyzing an Investment by Comparing Selected Ratios (AP14–2)

You have the opportunity to invest $10,000 in one of two companies from a single industry. The only information you have is shown here. The word *high* refers to the top third of the industry; *average* is the middle third; *low* is the bottom third. Which company would you select? Write a brief paper justifying your recommendation.

P14-2
LO5, 6, 7

Ratio	Company A	Company B
Current	Low	Average
Quick	Average	Average
Debt-to-equity ratio	Low	Average
Inventory turnover ratio	High	Average
Price/earnings	High	Average
Dividend yield	Low	Average

Identifying Companies Based on the Price/Earnings Ratio

The price/earnings ratio provides important information concerning the stock market's assessment of the growth potential of a business. The following are price/earnings ratios for selected companies as of the date this book was written. Match the company with its ratio and explain how you made your selections. If you are not familiar with a company, you should contact its website.

P14-3
LO7

Company	Price/Earnings Ratio
1. Commerce Bank	A. 33
2. Duke Energy	B. 12
3. Ford	C. 15
4. Home Depot	D. not applicable (no earnings)
5. Motorola	E. 20
6. Starbucks	F. 13
7. Pepsi	G. 99
8. Continental Airlines	H. 8

Analyzing Ratios (AP14–3)

Sears, Roebuck and JCPenney are two giants of the retail industry. Both offer full lines of moderately priced merchandise. Annual sales for Sears total $53 billion. JCPenney is smaller with $20 billion in revenues. Compare the two companies as a potential investment based on the following ratios:

P14-4
LO1, 2, 3, 4, 5, 6, 7
Sears
JCPenney

Ratio	Sears	JCPenney
P/E	15.0	10.9
Gross profit margin	28.6	39.3
Profit margin	2.8	5.7
Current ratio	1.5	1.9
Debt-to-equity ratio	1.4	2.0
Return on equity	12.0	27.8
Return on assets	5.2	9.3
Dividend yield ratio	0.0%	1.4%
Earnings per share	$ 9.17	$ 5.20

P14-5

LO3, 4, 5, 6, 7

Comparing Alternative Investment Opportunities (AP14–4)

The 2010 financial statements for Armstrong and Hamilton companies are summarized here:

	Armstrong Company	Hamilton Company
Balance Sheet		
Cash	$ 41,000	$ 21,000
Accounts receivable (net)	38,000	31,000
Inventory	99,000	40,000
Operational assets (net)	140,000	401,000
Other assets	84,000	305,00
Total assets	402,000	798,000
Current liabilities	$99,000	$ 49,000
Long-term debt (10%)	65,000	60,000
Capital stock (par $10)	148,000	512,000
Contributed capital in excess of par	29,000	106,000
Retained earnings	61,000	71,000
Total liabilities and stockholders' equity	402,000	798,000
Income Statement		
Sales revenue (1/3 on credit)	447,000	802,000
Cost of goods sold	(241,000)	(398,000)
Expenses (including interest and income tax)	(161,000)	(311,000)
Net income	45,000	93,000
Selected data from the 2009 statements		
Accounts receivable (net)	18,000	38,000
Inventory	94,000	44,000
Long-term debt	60,000	48,000
Other data		
Per share price at end of 2010 (offering price)	17	15
Average income tax rate	30%	30%
Dividends declared and paid in 2010	33,000	148,000

The companies are in the same line of business and are direct competitors in a large metropolitan area. Both have been in business approximately 10 years, and each has had steady growth. The management of each has a different viewpoint in many respects. Hamilton is more conservative, and as its president said, "We avoid what we consider to be undue risk." Neither company is publicly held. Armstrong Company has an annual audit by a CPA but Hamilton Company does not.

Required:
1. Complete a schedule that reflects a ratio analysis of each company. Compute the ratios discussed in the chapter.
2. A client of yours has the opportunity to buy 10 percent of the shares in one or the other company at the per share prices given and has decided to invest in one of the companies. Based on the data given, prepare a comparative written evaluation of the ratio analyses (and any other available information) and give your recommended choice with the supporting explanation.

Analyzing Comparative Financial Statement Using Percentages (AP14–5)

The comparative financial statements prepared at December 31, 2010, for King Company showed the following summarized data:

P14-6
LO3
e**X**cel
www.mhhe.com/libby6e

	2010	2009
Income Statement		
Sales revenue	$190,000[1]	$167,000
Cost of goods sold	112,000	100,000
Gross profit	78,000	67,000
Operating expenses and interest expense	56,000	53,000
Pretax income	22,000	14,000
Income tax	8,000	4,000
Net income	14,000	10,000
Balance Sheet		
Cash	$ 4,000	$ 7,000
Accounts receivable (net)	14,000	18,000
Inventory	40,000	34,000
Operational assets (net)	45,000	38,000
	103,000	97,000
Current liabilities (no interest)	$ 16,000	$ 17,000
Long-term liabilities (10% interest)	45,000	45,000
Common stock (par $5)	30,000	30,000
Retained earnings[2]	12,000	5,000
	103,000	97,000

[1] One-third was credit sales.

[2] During 2010, cash dividends amounting to $3,000 were declared and paid.

Required:
1. Complete the following columns for each item in the preceding comparative financial statements:

INCREASE (DECREASE)
2010 OVER 2009

Amount	Percent

2. By what amount did working capital change? What was the amount of cash inflow from revenues for 2010?

Analyzing Comparative Financial Statements Using Percentages and Selected Ratios (AP14–6)

Use the data given in P14–6 for King Company.

P14-7
LO3, 4, 6

Required:
1. Present component percentages for 2010 only.
2. Respond to the following for 2010:
   a. What was the average percentage markup on sales (i.e, the difference between cost and selling price)?
   b. What was the average income tax rate?

c. Compute the profit margin. Was it a good or poor indicator of performance? Explain.
d. What percentage of total resources was invested in operational assets?
e. Compute the debt-to-equity ratio. Does it look good or bad? Explain.
f. What was the return on equity?
g. What was the return on assets?
h. Compute the financial leverage percentage. Was it positive or negative? Explain.

P14-8
LO3, 4, 5, 6, 7
eXcel
www.mhhe.com/libby6e

Analyzing a Financial Statement Using Ratios

Use the 2010 data in P14–6 for King Company. Assume a stock price of $28 per share. Compute the appropriate ratios.

P14-9
LO3, 4, 5, 6, 7

Analyzing the Impact of Alternative Inventory Methods on Selected Ratios

Company A uses the FIFO method to cost inventory, and Company B uses the LIFO method. The two companies are exactly alike except for the difference in inventory costing methods. Costs of inventory items for both companies have been rising steadily in recent years, and each company has increased its inventory each year. Each company has paid its tax liability in full for the current year (and all previous years), and each company uses the same accounting methods for both financial reporting and income tax reporting.

Required:
Identify which company will report the higher amount for each of the following ratios. If it is not possible, explain why.
1. Current ratio.
2. Quick ratio.
3. Debt-to-equity ratio.
4. Return on equity.
5. Earnings per share.

P14-10
LO3, 4, 5, 6, 7
Hershey's

Analyzing a Financial Statement Using Appropriate Ratios (AP14–7)

Hershey's is a familiar name in snacks. There's a good chance you have recently enjoyed one of their products. The company manufactures confectionery products in a variety of packaged forms and markets them under more than 50 brands. Among the principal confectionery products in the United States are: *HERSHEY'S* chocolates, *HERSHEY'S KISSES* chocolates, *KIT KAT, KRACKEL* chocolate bars, *MR. GOODBAR* chocolate bars, *REESE'S* peanut butter cups, *ALMOND JOY* candy bars, *BUBBLE YUM* bubble gum, *GOOD & PLENTY* candy, *MOUNDS* candy bars, *PAYDAY* candy bars, and *5TH AVENUE* candy bars.

The following information was reported in a recent annual statement. For the year 2006, compute the ratios discussed in this chapter. If there is not sufficient information, describe what is missing and explain what you would do. Assume a 34% tax rate.

THE HERSHEY COMPANY			
Consolidated Statements of Income			
For the years ended December 31,	**2006**	**2005**	**2004**
In thousands of dollars except per share amounts			
Net Sales	**$ 4,944,230**	$ 4,819,827	$ 4,416,389
Costs and Expenses:			
Cost of sales	**3,076,718**	2,956,682	2,672,716
Selling, marketing and administrative	**860,378**	912,986	867,104
Business realignment and asset impairments, net	**14,576**	96,537	—
Total costs and expenses	**3,951,672**	3,966,205	3,539,820
			continued

Income before Interest and Income Taxes	992,558	853,622	876,569
Interest expense, net	116,056	87,985	66,533
Income before Income Taxes	876,502	765,637	810,036
Provision for income taxes	317,441	277,090	235,399
Net Income	$ 559,061	$ 488,547	$ 574,637
Net Income Per Share—Basic—Common Stock	$ 2.44	$ 2.05	$ 2.31
Net Income Per Share—Basic—Class B Common Stock	$ 2.19	$ 1.85	$ 2.11
Net Income Per Share—Diluted	$ 2.34	$ 1.97	$ 2.24
Cash Dividends Paid Per Share:			
Common Stock	$ 1.030	$ .9300	$ .8350
Class B Common Stock	.925	.8400	.7576

THE HERSHEY COMPANY
Consolidated Balance Sheets

December 31,	2006	2005
In thousands of dollars		
ASSETS		
Current Assets:		
Cash and cash equivalents	$ 97,141	$ 67,183
Accounts receivable—trade	522,673	507,119
Inventories	648,820	634,910
Deferred income taxes	61,360	73,203
Prepaid expenses and other	87,818	93,988
Total current assets	1,417,812	1,376,403
Property, Plant and Equipment, Net	1,651,300	1,659,138
Goodwill	501,955	487,338
Other Intangibles	140,314	142,626
Other Assets	446,184	597,194
Total assets	$ 4,157,565	$ 4,262,699
LIABILITIES AND STOCKHOLDERS' EQUITY		
Current Liabilities:		
Accounts payable	$ 155,517	$ 167,812
Accrued liabilities	454,023	486,832
Accrued income taxes	—	16,623
Short-term debt	655,233	819,059
Current portion of long-term debt	188,765	56
Total current liabilities	1,453,538	1,490,382
Long-term Debt	1,248,128	942,755
Other Long-term Liabilities	486,473	412,929
Deferred Income Taxes	286,003	400,253
Total liabilities	3,474,142	3,246,319

continued

Commitments and Contingencies	—	—
Stockholders' Equity:		
Preferred Stock, shares issued: none in 2006 and 2005	—	—
Common Stock, shares issued: 299,085,666 in 2006 and 299,083,266 in 2005	**299,085**	299,083
Class B Common Stock, shares issued: 60,816,078 in 2006 and 60,818,478 in 2005	**60,816**	60,818
Additional paid-in capital	**298,243**	252,374
Unearned ESOP compensation	—	(3,193)
Retained earnings	**3,965,415**	3,641,483
Treasury—Common Stock shares, at cost: 129,638,183 in 2006 and 119,377,690 in 2005	**(3,801,947)**	(3,224,863)
Accumulated other comprehensive loss	**(138,189)**	(9,322)
Total stockholders' equity	**683,423**	1,016,380
Total liabilities and stockholders' equity	**$ 4,157,565**	$ 4,262,699

ALTERNATE **PROBLEMS**

AP14-1
LO4, 5, 6, 7

Analyzing an Investment by Comparing Selected Ratios (P14–1)

You have the opportunity to invest $10,000 in one of two companies from a single industry. The only information you have is shown here. The word *high* refers to the top third of the industry; *average* is the middle third; *low* is the bottom third. Which company would you select? Write a brief paper justifying your recommendation.

Ratio	Company A	Company B
EPS	High	Low
ROA	Low	High
Debt-to-equity ratio	High	Average
Current	Low	Average
Price/earnings	Low	High
Dividend yield ratio	High	Average

AP14-2
LO4, 5, 6, 7

Analyzing an Investment by Comparing Selected Ratios (P14–2)

You have the opportunity to invest $10,000 in one of two companies from a single industry. The only information you have is shown here. The word *high* refers to the top third of the industry; *average* is the middle third; *low* is the bottom third. Which company would you select? Write a brief paper justifying your recommendation.

Ratio	Company A	Company B
ROA	High	Average
Profit margin	High	Low
Financial leverage	High	Low
Current	Low	High
Price/earnings	High	Average
Debt-to-equity ratio	High	Low

Analyzing Ratios (P14–4)

Coke and Pepsi are well-known international brands. Coca-Cola sells more than $13 billion worth of beverages each year while annual sales of Pepsi products exceed $22 billion. Compare the two companies as a potential investment based on the following ratios:

Ratio	Coca-Cola	PepsiCo
P/E	65.0	26.5
Gross profit margin	69.3	58.4
Profit margin	12.2	8.8
Quick ratio	0.4	0.7
Current ratio	0.6	1.1
Debt-to-equity ratio	0.7	0.4
Return on equity	27.4	29.1
Return on assets	28.0	16.6
Dividend yield ratio	1.0%	1.6%
Dividend payout ratio	65.0%	41.0%

AP14-3
LO3, 4, 5, 6, 7
Coca-Cola
PepsiCo

Analyzing a Financial Statement Using Ratios

AP14-4
LO3, 4, 5, 6, 7

Summer Corporation has just completed its comparative statements for the year ended December 31, 2010. At this point, certain analytical and interpretive procedures are to be undertaken. The completed statements (summarized) are as follows:

	2010	2009
Income Statement		
Sales revenue	$453,000[1]	$447,000[1]
Cost of goods sold	250,000	241,000
Gross profit	203,000	206,000
Operating expenses (including interest on bonds)	167,000	168,000
Pretax income	36,000	38,000
Income tax	10,800	11,400
Net income	25,200	26,600
Balance Sheet		
Cash	$ 6,800	$ 3,900
Accounts receivable (net)	42,000	29,000
Merchandise inventory	25,000	18,000
Prepaid expenses	200	100
Operational assets (net)	130,000	120,000
	204,000	171,000
Accounts payable	$ 17,000	$ 18,000
Income taxes payable	1,000	1,000
Bonds payable (10% interest rate)	70,000[2]	50,000
Common stock (par $5)	100,000[3]	100,000
Retained earnings	16,000[4]	2,000
	204,000	171,000

[1] Credit sales totaled 40 percent.

[2] $20,000 of bonds were issued on 1/2/2010. Assume the tax rate is 30%.

[3] The market price of the stock at the end of 2010 was $18 per share.

[4] During 2010, the company declared and paid a cash dividend of $9,000.

Required:

1. Compute appropriate ratios for 2010 and explain the meaning of each.
2. Respond to the following for 2010:
   a. Evaluate the financial leverage. Explain its meaning using the computed amount(s).
   b. Evaluate the profit margin amount and explain how a stockholder might use it.
   c. Explain to a stockholder why the current ratio and the quick ratio are different. Do you observe any liquidity problems? Explain.
   d. Assuming that credit terms are 1/10, n/30, do you perceive an unfavorable situation for the company related to credit sales? Explain.

AP14-5   **Analyzing a Financial Statement Using Ratios and Percentage Changes** (P14–6)
LO3, 4, 5, 6, 7

Taber Company has just prepared the following comparative annual financial statements for 2010:

TABER COMPANY
Comparative Income Statement
For the Years Ended December 31, 2010, and 2009

		2010		2009
Sales revenue (one-half on credit)		$110,000		$99,000
Cost of goods sold		52,000		48,000
Gross profit		$ 58,000		$51,000
Expenses (including $4,000 interest expense each year)		40,000		37,000
Pretax income		$ 18,000		$14,000
Income tax on operations (30%)		5,400		4,200
Income before extraordinary items		$ 12,600		$ 9,800
Extraordinary loss	$2,000			
Less income tax saved	600	1,400		
Extraordinary gain			$3,000	
Applicable income tax			900	2,100
Net income		$ 11,200		$11,900

TABER COMPANY
Comparative Balance Sheet
At December 31, 2010, and 2009

	2010	2009
Assets		
Cash	$ 49,500	$ 18,000
Accounts receivable (net; terms 1/10, n/30)	37,000	32,000
Inventory	25,000	38,000
Operational assets (net)	95,000	105,000
Total assets	$206,500	$193,000
Liabilities		
Accounts payable	$ 42,000	$ 35,000
Income taxes payable	1,000	500
Note payable, long-term	40,000	40,000
Stockholders' equity		
Capital stock (par $10)	90,000	90,000
Retained earnings	33,500	27,500
Total liabilities and stockholders' equity	$206,500	$193,000

Required (round percentage and ratios to two decimal places):

1. For 2010, compute the tests of (a) profitability, (b) liquidity, (c) solvency, and (d) market. Assume that the quoted price of the stock was $23 for 2010. Dividends declared and paid during 2010 were $6,750.

2. Respond to the following for 2010:

   a. Compute the percentage changes in sales, income before extraordinary items, net income, cash, inventory, and debt.

   b. What appears to be the pretax interest rate on the note payable?

3. Identify at least two problems facing the company that are suggested by your responses to requirements 1 and 2.

Using Ratios to Analyze Several Years of Financial Data (P14–7)

AP14-6
LO3, 4, 5

The following information was contained in the annual financial statements of Pine Company, which started business January 1, 2009 (assume account balances only in Cash and Capital Stock on this date; all amounts are in thousands of dollars).

	2009	2010	2011	2012
Accounts receivable (net; terms n/30)	$11	$12	$18	$ 24
Merchandise inventory	12	14	20	30
Net sales (3/4 on credit)	44	66	80	100
Cost of goods sold	28	40	55	62
Net income (loss)	(8)	5	12	11

Required (show computations):

1. Complete the following tabulation

Items	2009	2010	2011	2012

   a. Profit margin percentage
   b. Gross profit ratio
   c. Expenses as percentage of sales, excluding cost of goods sold
   d. Inventory turnover ratio
   e. Days' supply in inventory
   f. Receivable turnover ratio
   g. Average days to collect

2. Evaluate the results of the related ratios *a, b,* and *c* to identify the favorable or unfavorable factors. Give your recommendations to improve the company's operations.

3. Evaluate the results of the last four ratios (*d, e, f,* and *g*) and identify any favorable or unfavorable factors. Give your recommendations to improve the company's operations.

Analyzing a Financial Statement Using Appropriate Ratios (P14–10)

AP14-7
LO4, 5, 6, 7

Dell Computers engages in the design, development, manufacture, marketing, sale, and support of various computer systems and services to customers worldwide. It offers desktop computer systems and workstations; mobility products, such as notebook computers, mobile workstations, MP3 players, and handhelds; software and peripherals, projectors, software titles, notebook accessories, networking and wireless products, digital cameras, power adapters, scanners, servers and networking products; and storage devices.

Compute each of the ratios discussed in this chapter. If there is not sufficient information, state what is needed. If a ratio is not meaningful for this type of company, explain why.

DELL INC. Consolidated Statements of Financial Position (in millions)		
	February 2, 2007	**February 3, 2006**
ASSETS		
Current assets:		
Cash and cash equivalents	$ 9,546	$ 7,054
		continued

Short-term investments	752	2,016
Accounts receivable, net	4,622	4,082
Financing receivables, net	1,530	1,366
Inventories	660	588
Other	2,829	2,688
Total current assets	19,939	17,794
Property, plant, and equipment, net	2,409	1,993
Investments	2,147	2,686
Long-term financing receivables, net	323	325
Other non-current assets	817	454
Total assets	$ 25,635	$ 23,252

LIABILITIES AND STOCKHOLDERS' EQUITY

Current liabilities:

Short-term borrowings	$ 188	$ 65
Accounts payable	10,430	9,868
Accrued and other	7,173	6,240
Total current liabilities	17,791	16,173
Long-term debt	569	625
Other non-current liabilities	2,836	2,407
Total liabilities	21,196	19,205
Commitments and contingencies (Note 9)		
Redeemable common stock and capital in excess of $.01 par value; 5 shares issued and outstanding (Note 5)	111	—
Stockholders' equity:		
Preferred stock and capital in excess of $.01 par value; shares issued and outstanding: none	—	—
Common stock and capital in excess of $.01 par value; shares authorized: 7,000; shares issued: 3,307 and 2,818, respectively; shares outstanding: 2,226 and 2,330, respectively	10,107	9,503
Treasury stock at cost: 606 and 488 shares, respectively	(21,033)	(18,007)
Retained earnings	15,282	12,699
Accumulated other comprehensive loss	(28)	(101)
Other	—	(47)
Total stockholders' equity	4,328	4,047
Total liabilities and equity	$ 25,635	$ 23,252

**Consolidated Statements
of Income (in millions)**

	Fiscal Year Ended		
	February 2, 2007	February 3, 2006	January 28, 2005
Net revenue	$ 57,420	$ 55,788	$ 49,121
Cost of net revenue	47,904	45,897	40,103
Gross profit	9,516	9,891	9,018
Operating expenses:			
Selling, general, and administrative	5,948	5,051	4,352
Research, development, and engineering	498	458	460
Total operating expenses	6,446	5,509	4,812

continued

Operating income	3,070	4,382	4,206
Investment and other income, net	275	226	197
Income before income taxes	3,345	4,608	4,403
Income tax provision	762	1,006	1,385
Net income	$ 2,583	$ 3,602	$ 3,018

CASES AND PROJECTS

Annual Report Cases

Analyzing Financial Statements

Refer to the financial statements of American Eagle given in Appendix B at the end of this book. Compute the following ratios for the most recent reporting year for which you have available information: return on equity, earnings per share, profit margin, current ratio, inventory turnover, debt/equity ratio, price earnings ratio, and dividend yield. Assume the stock price is $21.

CP14-1
LO4, 5, 6, 7
AMERICAN EAGLE
OUTFITTERS

Analyzing Financial Statements

Refer to the financial statements of Urban Outfitters given in Appendix C at the end of this book. Compute the following ratios for the most recent reporting year for which you have available information: return on equity, earnings per share, profit margin, current ratio, inventory turnover, debt/equity ratio, price earnings ratio, and dividend yield. Assume the stock price is $25.

CP14-2
LO4, 5, 6, 7
Urban Outfitters

Comparing Companies within an Industry

Refer to the financial statements of American Eagle given in Appendix B, Urban Outfitters given in Appendix C and the Industry Ratio Report given in Appendix D at the end of this book. Compute the following ratios for the most recent reporting year for which you have available information: return on equity, earnings per share, net profit margin, current ratio, inventory turnover, debt/equity ratio, price earnings ratio, and dividend yield. Assume the stock price is $25 for Urban Outfitters and $21 for American Eagle. Compare the ratios for each company to the industry average ratios.

CP14-3
LO4, 5, 6, 7
AMERICAN EAGLE
OUTFITTERS
Urban Outfitters
eXcel
www.mhhe.com/libby6e

Financial Reporting and Analysis Cases

Inferring Information from the ROE Model

In this chapter, we discussed the ROE profit driver (or DuPont model). Using that framework, find the missing amount in each case that follows:

CP14-4
LO1

Case 1: ROE is 10 percent, net income is $200,000; asset turnover ratio is 5, and net sales are $1,000,000. What is the amount of average stockholders' equity?

Case 2: Net income is $1,500,000; net sales are $8,000,000; average stockholders' equity is $12,000,000; ROE is 22 percent and asset turnover ratio is 8. What is the amount of average total assets?

Case 3: ROE is 15 percent; net profit margin is 10 percent; asset turnover ratio is 5; and average total assets are $1,000,000. What is the amount of average stockholders' equity?

Case 4: Net income is $500,000; ROE is 15 percent; asset turnover ratio is 5; net sales are $1,000,000; and financial leverage is 2. What is the amount of average total assets?

CP14-5
LO1

Interpreting Financial Results Based on Corporate Strategy

In this chapter, we discussed the importance of analyzing financial results based on an understanding of the company's business strategy. Using the ROE model, we illustrated how different strategies could earn high returns for investors. Assume that two companies in the same industry adopt fundamentally different strategies. One manufactures high-quality consumer electronics. Its products employ state-of-the-art technology, and the company offers a high level of customer service both before and after the sale. The other company emphasizes low cost with good performance. Its products utilize well-established technology but are never innovative. Customers buy these products at large, self-service warehouses and are expected to install the products using information contained in printed brochures. Which of the ratios discussed in this chapter would you expect to differ for these companies as a result of their different business strategies?

Critical Thinking Cases

CP14-6
LO5

Evaluating an Ethical Dilemma

Barton Company requested a sizable loan from First Federal Bank to acquire a large tract of land for future expansion. Barton reported current assets of $1,900,000 ($430,000 in cash) and current liabilities of $1,075,000. First Federal denied the loan request for a number of reasons, including the fact that the current ratio was below 2:1. When Barton was informed of the loan denial, the comptroller of the company immediately paid $420,000 that was owed to several trade creditors. The comptroller then asked First Federal to reconsider the loan application. Based on these abbreviated facts, would you recommend that First Federal approve the loan request? Why? Are the comptroller's actions ethical?

Financial Reporting and Analysis Team Project

CP14-7
LO3, 4, 5, 6, 7

Team Project: Examining an Annual Report

As a team, select an industry to analyze. *Reuters* provides lists of industries and their makeup at **www.reuters.com/finance/industries**. Each team member should acquire the annual report or 10-K for one publicly traded company in the industry, with each member selecting a different company. (Library files, the SEC EDGAR service at **www.sec.gov**, Compustat CD, or the company itself are good sources.)

Required:

On an individual basis, each team member should write a short report providing the following information about the selected company. Discuss any patterns across the companies that you as a team observe. Then, as a team, write a short report comparing and contrasting your companies.

Compute and interpret each of the ratios discussed in this chapter. The most frequently used sections will be the financial statements. Also, you may want to review footnotes, summary of financial information (usually for the past five years or longer), and management's discussion and analysis.

TABLE A.1
Present Value of $1

Periods	2%	3%	3.75%	4%	4.25%	5%	6%	7%	8%
1	0.9804	0.9709	0.9639	0.9615	0.9592	0.9524	0.9434	0.9346	0.9259
2	0.9612	0.9426	0.9290	0.9246	0.9201	0.9070	0.8900	0.8734	0.8573
3	0.9423	0.9151	0.8954	0.8890	0.8826	0.8638	0.8396	0.8163	0.7938
4	0.9238	0.8885	0.8631	0.8548	0.8466	0.8227	0.7921	0.7629	0.7350
5	0.9057	0.8626	0.8319	0.8219	0.8121	0.7835	0.7473	0.7130	0.6806
6	0.8880	0.8375	0.8018	0.7903	0.7790	0.7462	0.7050	0.6663	0.6302
7	0.8706	0.8131	0.7728	0.7599	0.7473	0.7107	0.6651	0.6227	0.5835
8	0.8535	0.7894	0.7449	0.7307	0.7168	0.6768	0.6274	0.5820	0.5403
9	0.8368	0.7664	0.7180	0.7026	0.6876	0.6446	0.5919	0.5439	0.5002
10	0.8203	0.7441	0.6920	0.6756	0.6595	0.6139	0.5584	0.5083	0.4632
20	0.6730	0.5537	0.4789	0.4564	0.4350	0.3769	0.3118	0.2584	0.2145

Periods	9%	10%	11%	12%	13%	14%	15%	20%	25%
1	0.9174	0.9091	0.9009	0.8929	0.8850	0.8772	0.8696	0.8333	0.8000
2	0.8417	0.8264	0.8116	0.7972	0.7831	0.7695	0.7561	0.6944	0.6400
3	0.7722	0.7513	0.7312	0.7118	0.6931	0.6750	0.6575	0.5787	0.5120
4	0.7084	0.6830	0.6587	0.6355	0.6133	0.5921	0.5718	0.4823	0.4096
5	0.6499	0.6209	0.5935	0.5674	0.5428	0.5194	0.4972	0.4019	0.3277
6	0.5963	0.5645	0.5346	0.5066	0.4803	0.4556	0.4323	0.3349	0.2621
7	0.5470	0.5132	0.4817	0.4523	0.4251	0.3996	0.3759	0.2791	0.2097
8	0.5019	0.4665	0.4339	0.4039	0.3762	0.3506	0.3269	0.2326	0.1678
9	0.4604	0.4241	0.3909	0.3606	0.3329	0.3075	0.2843	0.1938	0.1342
10	0.4224	0.3855	0.3522	0.3220	0.2946	0.2697	0.2472	0.1615	0.1074
20	0.1784	0.1486	0.1240	0.1037	0.0868	0.0728	0.0611	0.0261	0.0115

TABLE A.2
Present Value of Annuity of $1

Periods*	2%	3%	3.75%	4%	4.25%	5%	6%	7%	8%
1	0.9804	0.9709	0.9639	0.9615	0.9592	0.9524	0.9434	0.9346	0.9259
2	1.9416	1.9135	1.8929	1.8861	1.8794	1.8594	1.8334	1.8080	1.7833
3	2.8839	2.8286	2.7883	2.7751	2.7620	2.7232	2.6730	2.6243	2.5771
4	3.8077	3.7171	3.6514	3.6299	3.6086	3.5460	3.4651	3.3872	3.3121
5	4.7135	4.5797	4.4833	4.4518	4.4207	4.3295	4.2124	4.1002	3.9927
6	5.6014	5.4172	5.2851	5.2421	5.1997	5.0757	4.9173	4.7665	4.6229
7	6.4720	6.2303	6.0579	6.0021	5.9470	5.7864	5.5824	5.3893	5.2064
8	7.3255	7.0197	6.8028	6.7327	6.6638	6.4632	6.2098	5.9713	5.7466
9	8.1622	7.7861	7.5208	7.4353	7.3513	7.1078	6.8017	6.5152	6.2469
10	8.9826	8.5302	8.2128	8.1109	8.0109	7.7217	7.3601	7.0236	6.7101
20	16.3514	14.8775	13.8962	13.5903	13.2944	12.4622	11.4699	10.5940	9.8181

*There is one payment each period.

TABLE A.2 *(continued)*

Present Value of Annuity of $1

Periods*	9%	10%	11%	12%	13%	14%	15%	20%	25%
1	0.9174	0.9091	0.9009	0.8929	0.8550	0.8772	0.8696	0.8333	0.8000
2	1.7591	1.7355	1.7125	1.6901	1.6681	1.6467	1.6257	1.5278	1.4400
3	2.5313	2.4869	2.4437	2.4018	2.3612	2.3216	2.2832	2.1065	1.9520
4	3.2397	3.1699	3.1024	3.0373	2.9745	2.9137	2.8550	2.5887	2.3616
5	3.8897	3.7908	3.6959	3.6048	3.5172	3.4331	3.3522	2.9906	2.6893
6	4.4859	4.3553	4.2305	4.1114	3.9975	3.8887	3.7845	3.3255	2.9514
7	5.0330	4.8684	4.7122	4.5638	4.4226	4.2883	4.1604	3.6046	3.1611
8	5.5348	5.3349	5.1461	4.9676	4.7988	4.6389	4.4873	3.8372	3.3289
9	5.9952	5.7590	5.5370	5.3282	5.1317	4.9464	4.7716	4.0310	3.4631
10	6.4177	6.1446	5.8892	5.6502	5.4262	5.2161	5.0188	4.1925	3.5705
20	9.1285	8.5136	7.9633	7.4694	7.0248	6.6231	6.2593	4.8696	3.9539

There is one payment each period.

TABLE A.3

Future Value of $1

Periods	2%	3%	3.75%	4%	4.25%	5%	6%	7%	8%
0	1.	1.	1.	1.	1.	1.	1.	1.	1.
1	1.02	1.03	1.0375	1.04	1.0425	1.05	1.06	1.07	1.08
2	1.0404	1.0609	1.0764	1.0816	1.0868	1.1025	1.1236	1.1449	1.1664
3	1.0612	1.0927	1.1168	1.1249	1.1330	1.1576	1.1910	1.2250	1.2597
4	1.0824	1.1255	1.1587	1.1699	1.1811	1.2155	1.2625	1.3108	1.3605
5	1.1041	1.1593	1.2021	1.2167	1.2313	1.2763	1.3382	1.4026	1.4693
6	1.1262	1.1941	1.2472	1.2653	1.2837	1.3401	1.4185	1.5007	1.5869
7	1.1487	1.2299	1.2939	1.3159	1.3382	1.4071	1.5036	1.6058	1.7138
8	1.1717	1.2668	1.3425	1.3686	1.3951	1.4775	1.5938	1.7182	1.8509
9	1.1951	1.3048	1.3928	1.4233	1.4544	1.5513	1.6895	1.8385	1.9990
10	1.2190	1.3439	1.4450	1.4802	1.5162	1.6289	1.7908	1.9672	2.1589
20	1.4859	1.8061	2.0882	2.1911	2.2989	2.6533	3.2071	3.8697	4.6610

Periods	9%	10%	11%	12%	13%	14%	15%	20%	25%
0	1.	1.	1.	1.	1.	1.	1.	1.	1.
1	1.09	1.10	1.11	1.12	1.13	1.14	1.15	1.20	1.25
2	1.1881	1.2100	1.2321	1.2544	1.2769	1.2996	1.3225	1.4400	1.5625
3	1.2950	1.3310	1.3676	1.4049	1.4429	1.4815	1.5209	1.7280	1.9531
4	1.4116	1.4641	1.5181	1.5735	1.6305	1.6890	1.7490	2.0736	2.4414
5	1.5386	1.6105	1.6851	1.7623	1.8424	1.9254	2.0114	2.4883	3.0518
6	1.6771	1.7716	1.8704	1.9738	2.0820	2.1950	2.3131	2.9860	3.8147
7	1.8280	1.9487	2.0762	2.2107	2.3526	2.5023	2.6600	3.5832	4.7684
8	1.9926	2.1436	2.3045	2.4760	2.6584	2.8526	3.0590	4.2998	5.9605
9	2.1719	2.3579	2.5580	2.7731	3.0040	3.2519	3.5179	5.1598	7.4506
10	2.3674	2.5937	2.8394	3.1058	3.3946	3.7072	4.0456	6.1917	9.3132
20	5.6044	6.7275	8.0623	9.6463	11.5231	13.7435	16.3665	38.3376	86.7362

TABLE A.4

Future Value of Annuity of $1

Periods*	2%	3%	3.75%	4%	4.25%	5%	6%	7%	8%
1	1.	1.	1.	1.	1.	1.	1.	1.	1.
2	2.02	2.03	2.0375	2.04	2.0425	2.05	2.06	2.07	2.08
3	3.0604	3.0909	3.1139	3.1216	3.1293	3.1525	3.1836	3.2149	3.2464
4	4.1216	4.1836	4.2307	4.2465	4.2623	4.3101	4.3746	4.4399	4.5061
5	5.2040	5.3091	5.3893	5.4163	5.4434	5.5256	5.6371	5.7507	5.8666
6	6.3081	6.4684	6.5914	6.6330	6.6748	6.8019	6.9753	7.1533	7.3359
7	7.4343	7.6625	7.8386	7.8983	7.9585	8.1420	8.3938	8.6540	8.9228
8	8.5830	8.8923	9.1326	9.2142	9.2967	9.5491	9.8975	10.2598	10.6366
9	9.7546	10.1591	10.4750	10.5828	10.6918	11.0266	11.4913	11.9780	12.4876
10	10.9497	11.4639	11.8678	12.0061	12.1462	12.5779	13.1808	13.8164	14.4866
20	24.2974	26.8704	29.0174	29.7781	30.5625	33.0660	36.7856	40.9955	45.7620

Periods*	9%	10%	11%	12%	13%	14%	15%	20%	25%
1	1.	1.	1.	1.	1.	1.	1.	1.	1.
2	2.09	2.10	2.11	2.12	2.13	2.14	2.15	2.20	2.25
3	3.2781	3.3100	3.3421	3.3744	3.4069	3.4396	3.4725	3.6400	3.8125
4	4.5731	4.6410	4.7097	4.7793	4.8498	4.9211	4.9934	5.3680	5.7656
5	5.9847	6.1051	6.2278	6.3528	6.4803	6.6101	6.7424	7.4416	8.2070
6	7.5233	7.7156	7.9129	8.1152	8.3227	8.5355	8.7537	9.9299	11.2588
7	9.2004	9.4872	9.7833	10.0890	10.4047	10.7305	11.0668	12.9159	15.0735
8	11.0285	11.4359	11.8594	12.2997	12.7573	13.2328	13.7268	16.4991	19.8419
9	13.0210	13.5975	14.1640	14.7757	15.4157	16.0853	16.7858	20.7989	25.8023
10	15.1929	15.9374	16.7220	17.5487	18.4197	19.3373	20.3037	25.9587	33.2529
20	51.1601	57.2750	64.2028	72.0524	80.9468	91.0249	102.4436	186.6880	342.9447

*There is one payment each period.

AMERICAN EAGLE OUTFITTERS 2006 ANNUAL REPORT*

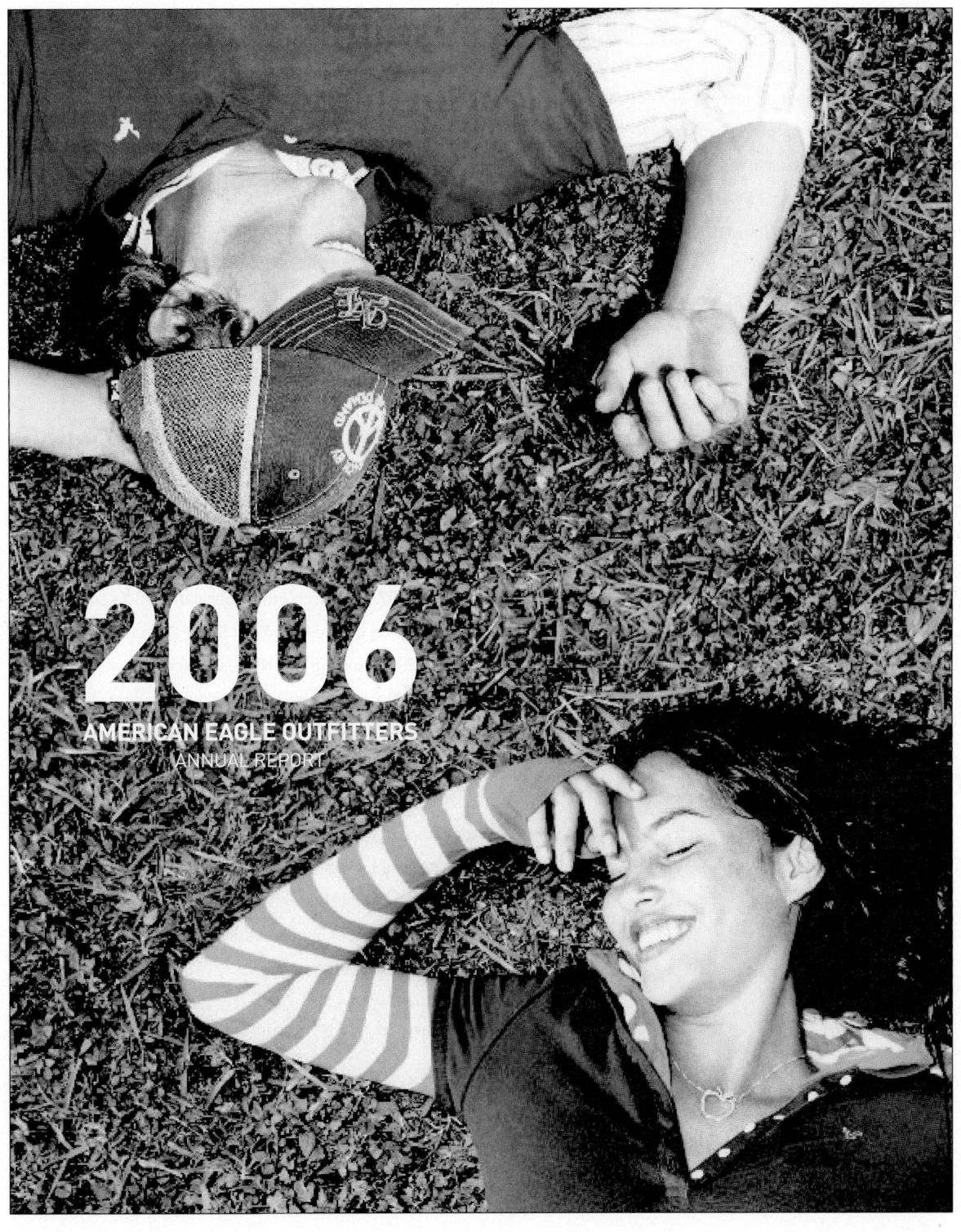

*This appendix contains excerpts. Go to the text website at www.mhhe.com/libby6e for the complete report.

Dear Stockholders:

Fiscal 2006 was a remarkable year for American Eagle Outfitters. It was our third consecutive year of record profitability and industry-leading performance. We delivered strong results, while also investing in future growth within our core brand, as well as with the launch of two new brands, aerie and MARTIN + OSA.

Our performance in 2006 reflects the strength of the American Eagle brand, driven by our relentless customer focus, as well as the depth and diversity of talent within our teams. By making appropriate investments in the areas of research, design, quality assurance and merchandising, we further strengthened the ever-important connection with our customer and our ability to deliver on-trend assortments with a high quality-to-price value ratio.

2006 was our third consecutive year of record profitability and industry-leading performance.

AE is well-positioned to sustain strong performance.

Total sales reached $2.8 billion for 2006, up 20% from the prior year. Contributing to the record sales, comparable store sales rose 12%. Our operating profit margin was 21.0%, an improvement over last year's record 19.8%, reflecting our efforts to deliver a strong merchandise margin and a commitment to operational excellence. Net income for 2006 increased 32% to $387 million, or $1.70 per diluted share. We also strengthened the company's cash position to $1.1 billion at year-end, while continuing to invest in our growth initiatives and a share repurchase program.

I would like to highlight an important milestone that took place early in 2007. On March 8th, American Eagle's common stock began trading on the New York Stock Exchange under the symbol "AEO." Joining the NYSE is a true mark of our progress in building a global brand and delivering world-class financial performance. I thank all of our AE associates whose efforts over the years contributed to this achievement.

As we look ahead, we are confident that American Eagle is well-positioned to sustain strong performance. We are excited about our growth strategies and continue to invest in talent and strengthen our operations with new systems and upgraded facilities.

We are driving growth through selectively opening new stores and upgrading existing locations. In 2006, new AE stores continued to perform extremely well, quickly achieving sales productivity comparable to our mature stores, and a first-year ROI of more than 70%. We also focused on maximizing existing real estate by increasing the size of our smaller AE stores, as well as relocating stores to better sites. This strategy not only benefited sales productivity, but also had a meaningful lift to store profitability. We ended 2006 with sales per foot productivity of $524, an 11% increase from the prior year. Our 2007 plans call for approximately 10% growth in total square footage, including roughly 45-50 new AE stores and 45 remodels, at least 15 new aerie stores, and 12 MARTIN + OSA stores.

Building powerful brand-defining categories that resonate with our customers is at the heart of our "Destination AE" strategy. A perfect example is our AE jeans business. Over the past several years, we have established a dominant position in jeans, which have become a cornerstone for the AE brand, driven by consistent fits, on-trend styles and a strong value and quality offering.

Building powerful brand-defining categories is at the heart of our Destination AE strategy.

Looking ahead, we will continue to build upon our number one market share position by offering innovation and newness in jeans that is on-target for the AE customer. We will also pursue similar growth in categories such as knit tops and accessories, where we see meaningful opportunity to be the brand-of-choice. To build these categories, we are devoting extensive resources in merchandising, design and sourcing to offer our customers on-trend styling combined with unsurpassed quality and value.

Through innovation we're creating the best online experience at ae.com.

An increasingly important part of the American Eagle brand experience is ae.com. Our online business continued to grow rapidly in 2006, with increased traffic and a higher conversion rate, driving a 48% increase in sales. Technology, the Internet in particular, is second-nature to our customers and important to how they live their lives. Our Web site must not only offer world-class shopping, but also become an online destination where our girls and guys come to be informed, inspired and entertained. We continue to improve ae.com by adding new features and functionality, exclusive offers and products, as well as entertaining, interactive content that creates a deeper brand experience.

In 2007 we are accelerating the growth of aerie.

In 2006 we celebrated a major milestone with the launch of "aerie by American Eagle," our new intimates sub-brand. Our collections feature undies, bras and dorm-wear with a comfortable, cozy and sweetly sexy feeling for the 15 to 25 year-old AE girl. Customers have responded enthusiastically to aerie, which is offered in all AE stores and three aerie stand-alone stores. Based on positive results, we are accelerating our real estate strategy for aerie, planning at least 15 stand-alone stores and five new side-by-side locations for 2007. We also have opportunities to build the brand further by expanding the collection and adding accessories, personal care and other complementary categories. We are excited about the growth potential of this business, and believe aerie can eventually be a $500 million to $1 billion brand.

MARTIN + OSA is an important long-term growth opportunity targeting an entirely new customer base.

MARTIN + OSA, our new lifestyle brand launched in 2006, represents an important long-term growth opportunity. Targeted at 25 to 40 year-olds, MARTIN + OSA provides this underserved demographic with sportswear-influenced fashion that can go effortlessly from the workplace to leisure activities. As with any new brand, there are elements that have been well-received and others that we are refining. Based on the response from customers, we are confident that the brand, demographic and store environment are right on-target. We had five MARTIN + OSA stores at the end of last year, and plan to open 12 more in 2007.

American Eagle Outfitters' marketing mission is to be the most relevant, valuable and important lifestyle brand among our targeted customers. The AE brand is the leader among 15 to 25 year-olds, and we will continue to build and further strengthen this leadership position in the years to come. Further, we hope to apply our customer-centric approach to build aerie as a sub-brand, as well as MARTIN + OSA among the 25 to 40 year-old demographic.

We're creating a 360-degree customer relationship to be relevant and important wherever they are.

We will never stop learning about what's important to our customers – investing in focus groups, fit clinics and customer intercepts to sharpen our awareness of their passions, perspectives and preferences. We're working to create a 360-degree customer relationship to be relevant and important wherever they are. That means that our stores, Web site and external marketing all work together cohesively to deliver a consistent message. We know that customers don't segregate the brand by channel, and we want to maximize the customer experience for each. Further, we hope to create a relationship with our customers even beyond the stores and ae.com with innovative, authentic programs that reflect what's important to them.

Underlying everything we do at American Eagle is a strong commitment to operating discipline. This includes investing in systems and solutions that contribute to our growth by enhancing the customer experience, supporting our new brands, and promoting advances in productivity and cost-efficiency.

Our efforts to improve margins and manage inventory levels have benefited from a markdown optimization system which allows us to make more effective pricing decisions. Investments in retail size profiling and demand forecasting for planning and replenishment also should contribute to enhanced inventory management. In the sourcing and supply chain areas, we are adopting various technologies that allow closer coordination with vendors and agents, improve transportation functions, evaluate vendor performance and optimize logistics capacity. And, in 2007, we are implementing a new point-of-sale system to enhance customer service and speed the check-out process. Going forward, our position as an early adopter of advanced retailing technologies will continue to be a key factor in our performance and a source of competitive strength.

American Eagle has a strong commitment to operational excellence.

At American Eagle, we are passionate about providing support to worthy causes and giving back to our communities. Through the AE Foundation, we donated cash and clothing to non-profit organizations across the U.S. and Canada last year. Among the groups we have supported are Big Brothers Big Sisters of America; the JumpStart program, which recruits and trains college students to mentor pre-school children; the Student Conservation Association, which involves students in preserving the environment; and many local charities in our Pittsburgh community that focus on youth development, disaster relief and the environment. We also get involved in issues that matter to our customers and associates by offering small grants of gift cards or cash to support their personal charitable events and volunteer efforts.

We are passionate about giving back to our communities.

As we look toward 2007, we are excited about our plans to grow the AE brand, expand new concepts, and further strengthen our financial performance. I'm confident that our efforts to forge a strong connection with customers, our commitment to operating disciplines, and the talent and energy of our team will deliver profitable growth to our shareholders for years to come.

I thank you for your support of American Eagle and look forward to sharing our achievements with you in the future.

Sincerely,

James V. O'Donnell
Chief Executive Officer

FINANCIAL HIGHLIGHTS

FOR THE YEARS ENDED [1] (In thousands, except per share amounts, ratios and other financial information)	February 3, 2007	January 28, 2006	January 29, 2005	January 31, 2004	February 1, 2003
SUMMARY OF OPERATIONS [2]					
Net sales [3]	$2,794,409	$2,321,962	$1,889,647	$1,441,864	$1,388,758
Comparable store sales increase (decrease) [4]	12%	16%	21%	(7%)	(4%)
Gross profit	$1,340,429	$1,077,749	$881,188	$552,559	$543,104
Gross profit as a percentage of net sales	48.0%	46.4%	46.6%	38.3%	39.1%
Operating income [5]	$586,790	$458,689	$360,968	$131,778	$158,061
Operating income as a percentage of net sales	21.0%	19.8%	19.1%	9.1%	11.4%
Income from continuing operations	$387,359	$293,711	$224,232	$83,108	$99,644
Income from continuing operations as a percentage of net sales	13.9%	12.7%	11.9%	5.8%	7.2%
Income from continuing operations per common share-diluted [6]	$1.70	$1.26	$1.00	$0.38	$0.46
BALANCE SHEET INFORMATION					
Total cash and short-term investments	$827,113	$751,518	$589,607	$337,812	$241,573
Long-term investments	$251,644	$145,774	$84,416	$24,357	$ –
Current ratio [7]	2.60	3.06	3.06	2.44	2.51
Stockholders' equity	$1,417,312	$1,155,552	$963,486	$637,377	$571,590
Average return on stockholders' equity	30.1%	27.8%	26.7%	9.9%	16.5%
OTHER FINANCIAL INFORMATION [8]					
Total stores at year-end	911	869	846	805	753
Net sales per average gross square foot [9]	$524	$471	$412	$343	$374
Total gross square feet at end of period	5,173,065	4,772,487	4,540,095	4,239,497	3,817,442

(1) Except for the fiscal year ended February 3, 2007, which includes 53 weeks, all fiscal years presented include 52 weeks.

(2) All amounts presented are from continuing operations and exclude Bluenotes' results of operations for all periods.

(3) Amount for the year ended February 3, 2007 includes proceeds from merchandise sell-offs.

   Amounts for prior periods were not adjusted to reflect this change as the amounts were determined to be immaterial. All amounts presented include shipping and handling amounts billed to customers.

(4) The comparable store sales increase for the period ended February 3, 2007 is compared to the corresponding 53 week period last year.

(5) All amounts presented exclude gift card service fee income, which was reclassified within other income, net.

(6) Per share results for all periods presented reflect the three-for-two stock split distributed on December 18, 2006.

(7) Calculations for the years ended January 28, 2006 and January 29, 2005 reflect certain assets of NLS as held-for-sale.

(8) All amounts exclude Bluenotes for all periods presented.

(9) Net sales per average square foot is calculated using retail sales for the year divided by the straight average of the beginning and ending square footage for the year.

UNITED STATES
SECURITIES AND EXCHANGE COMMISSION
WASHINGTON, D.C. 20549

FORM 10-K

[X] ANNUAL REPORT PURSUANT TO SECTION 13 OR 15(D) OF THE
SECURITIES EXCHANGE ACT OF 1934

For the Fiscal Year Ended February 3, 2007

OR

[   ] TRANSITION REPORT PURSUANT TO SECTION 13 OR 15(D) OF THE
SECURITIES EXCHANGE ACT OF 1934

Commission File Number: 1-33338

American Eagle Outfitters, Inc.

(Exact name of registrant as specified in its charter)

Delaware	**No. 13-2721761**
(State or other jurisdiction of incorporation or organization)	(I.R.S. Employer Identification No.)
150 Thorn Hill Drive, Warrendale, PA	**15086-7528**
(Address of principal executive offices)	(Zip Code)

Registrant's telephone number, including area code: **(724) 776-4857**

Securities registered pursuant to Section 12(b) of the Act:

Common Shares, $0.01 par value	New York Stock Exchange
(Title of class)	(Name of each exchange on which registered)

Securities registered pursuant to Section 12(g) of the Act: None

Indicate by check mark if the registrant is a well-known seasoned issuer, as defined in Rule 405 of the Securities Act.   YES [X]   NO [   ]

Indicate by check mark if the registrant is not required to file reports pursuant to Section 13 or Sections 15(d) of the Act.   YES [   ]   NO [X]

Indicate by check mark whether the registrant (1) has filed all reports required to be filed by Section 13 or 15(d) of the Securities Exchange Act of 1934 during the preceding 12 months, and (2) has been subject to the filing requirements for at least the past 90 days.   YES [X]   NO [   ]

Indicate by check mark if disclosure of delinquent filers pursuant to Item 405 of Regulation S-K is not contained herein, and will not be contained, to the best of registrant's knowledge, in definitive proxy or information statements incorporated by reference in Part III of this Form 10-K or any amendment to this Form 10-K. [   ]

Indicate by check mark whether the registrant is a large accelerated filer, an accelerated filer, or a non-accelerated filer. See definition of "accelerated filer and large accelerated filer" in Rule 12b-2 of the Exchange Act. (Check one):
[X] Large accelerated filer   [   ] Accelerated filer   [   ] Non-accelerated filer

Indicate by check mark whether the registrant is a shell company (as defined in Rule 12b-2 of the Act).   YES [   ]   NO [X]

The aggregate market value of voting and non-voting common equity held by non-affiliates of the registrant as of July 29, 2006 was $4,125,890,813.

Indicate the number of shares outstanding of each of the registrant's classes of common stock, as of the latest practicable date: 220,145,869 Common Shares were outstanding at March 15, 2007.

DOCUMENTS INCORPORATED BY REFERENCE
Part III—Proxy Statement for 2007 Annual Meeting of Stockholders, in part, as indicated.

PART I

ITEM 1. BUSINESS.

General

American Eagle Outfitters, Inc., a Delaware corporation, is a leading retailer that operates under the American Eagle Outfitters® and MARTIN + OSA™ brands.

American Eagle Outfitters designs, markets and sells its own brand of laidback, current clothing targeting 15 to 25 year-olds, providing high-quality merchandise at affordable prices. We opened our first American Eagle Outfitters store in the United States in 1977 and expanded the brand into Canada in 2001. American Eagle® also distributes merchandise via its e-commerce operation ("ae.com") which offers additional sizes, colors and styles of favorite AE® merchandise and ships to 41 countries around the world. AE's original collection includes standards like jeans and graphic Ts, as well as essentials like accessories, outerwear, footwear, basics and swimwear under our American Eagle Outfitters, American Eagle and AE brand names. During Fiscal 2006, American Eagle launched its new intimates sub-brand, *aerie*™ by American Eagle ("*aerie*"). The *aerie* collection of dormwear and intimates includes bras, undies, camis, hoodies, robes, boxers and sweats for the AE girl.

We also introduced MARTIN + OSA, a new sportswear concept targeting 25 to 40 year-old women and men, in the fall of 2006. MARTIN + OSA carries apparel, accessories and footwear, using denim and sport inspiration to design fun and sport back into sportswear.

As used in this report, all references to "we," "our," and the "Company" refer to American Eagle Outfitters, Inc. and its wholly-owned subsidiaries. "American Eagle Outfitters," "American Eagle," "AE," and the "AE Brand" refer to our U.S. and Canadian American Eagle Outfitters stores, including the *aerie* sub-brand and ae.com. "MARTIN + OSA" refers to our new sportswear concept launched during Fiscal 2006. "Bluenotes" refers to the Bluenotes/Thriftys specialty apparel chain which we operated in Canada prior to its disposition during Fiscal 2004.

As of February 3, 2007, we operated 906 American Eagle Outfitters stores in the United States and Canada (including three *aerie* stand-alone stores) and five MARTIN + OSA stores.

In December 2004, we completed the disposition of Bluenotes to 6295215 Canada Inc. (the "Bluenotes Purchaser"), a privately held Canadian company. As a result, our Consolidated Statements of Operations and Consolidated Statements of Cash Flows reflect Bluenotes' results of operations as discontinued operations for all periods presented. See Note 9 of the Consolidated Financial Statements for additional information regarding this transaction.

In January 2006, we entered into an agreement to sell certain assets of National Logistics Services ("NLS") to 6510965 Canada Inc. (the "NLS Purchaser"), a privately held Canadian company. The sale of these assets was completed in February 2006, at which time we exited our NLS operations. As a result, our Consolidated Balance Sheets reflect the assets subject to the agreement as held-for-sale for all periods presented. See Note 9 of the Consolidated Financial Statements for additional information regarding this transaction.

Our financial year is a 52/53 week year that ends on the Saturday nearest to January 31. As used herein, "Fiscal 2008" and "Fiscal 2007" refer to the 52 week periods ending January 31, 2009 and February 2, 2008, respectively. "Fiscal 2006" refers to the 53 week period ended February 3, 2007. "Fiscal 2005" and "Fiscal 2004" refer to the 52 week periods ended January 28, 2006 and January 29, 2005, respectively.

Information concerning our business segments and certain geographic information is contained in Note 2 of the Consolidated Financial Statements included in this Form 10-K and is incorporated herein by reference.

Growth Strategy

During Fiscal 2006, we made significant progress on our key growth initiatives. As we enter Fiscal 2007, we remain focused on several well-defined strategies that we have in place to grow our business and sustain our financial performance. Our primary growth strategies are focused on the following key areas of opportunity:

Real Estate

We are continuing the expansion of our brands throughout the United States and Canada. At the end of Fiscal 2006, we operated in all 50 states, the District of Columbia, Puerto Rico and Canada. During Fiscal 2006, we opened 50 new stores, consisting of 41 U.S. AE stores, one Canadian AE store, three *aerie* stand-alone stores and five MARTIN + OSA stores. These store openings, offset by eight AE store closings, increased our total store base by approximately 5% to 911 stores. Additionally, our gross square footage increased by approximately 8% during Fiscal 2006, with approximately 5% attributable to new store openings and the remaining 3% attributable to the incremental square footage from 65 store remodels.

During Fiscal 2006, we continued to grow in the western and southeastern U.S. with 66% of our AE store openings in those regions. Approximately 50% of our U.S. AE store base is located in those two regions.

During Fiscal 2006, we increased our total Canadian AE store base to 72 stores. We remain pleased with the results of our American Eagle expansion into Canada and look to a long-term potential of approximately 80 AE stores across the country. In addition to the AE stores, we believe that there are opportunities to open *aerie* stand-alone stores in Canada.

In Fiscal 2007, we plan to open 45 to 50 new AE stores, at least 15 new *aerie* stand-alone stores and approximately 12 new MARTIN + OSA stores. Additionally, we plan to remodel approximately 45 existing AE stores. Our square footage growth is expected to be 10%. We believe that there are attractive retail locations where we can continue to open American Eagle stores in enclosed regional malls, urban areas and lifestyle centers.

The table below shows certain information relating to our historical store growth in the U.S. and Canada:

	Fiscal 2006	Fiscal 2005	Fiscal 2004	Fiscal 2003	Fiscal 2002
Stores at beginning of period	869	846	805	753	678
Stores opened during the period*	50	36	50	59	79
Stores closed during the period *	(8)	(13)	(9)	(7)	(4)
Total stores at end of period **	**911**	**869**	**846**	**805**	**753**

* Stores closed during Fiscal 2005 include one AE store closed due to Hurricane Katrina, as well as one AE store closed due to a fire. The store closed due to fire was reopened during Fiscal 2006 and is included in stores opened during that period.

** Fiscal 2005 ending store count includes one AE store that was temporarily closed due to Hurricane Katrina, which reopened during February 2006.

We continue to remodel our older AE stores into our current store format. In order to maintain a balanced presentation and to accommodate additional product categories, we selectively enlarge our stores during the remodeling process, to approximately 6,000 to 6,500 square feet, either within their existing location or by upgrading the store location within the mall. We believe the larger format can better accommodate our expansion of merchandise categories. We select stores for expansion or relocation based on market demographics and store volume forecasts. During Fiscal 2006, we remodeled 63 stores in the U.S. and two stores in Canada to the current store design. Of the 65 remodeled stores, 32 stores were expanded in place, 32 stores were relocated to a larger space within the mall and one store was refurbished as further discussed below. As of February 3, 2007, approximately 88% of all American Eagle stores in the U.S. are in our current store format.

We maintain a store refurbishment program targeted towards our lower volume stores, typically located in smaller markets. Stores selected as part of this program maintain their current location and size but are updated to include certain aspects of our current store format, including paint and certain new fixtures. This program provides a cost effective update for our lower volume stores.

Destination AE

Under our Destination AE initiative, we believe that we can leverage the success we have had in making American Eagle the denim destination brand and increase market share in other brand-defining key categories. In Fiscal 2007, we expect to build upon this success by continuing to focus on knit tops, including men's and women's polos and graphic Ts and women's tank tops. Additionally, we believe that our customer loyalty program, the AE All-Access Pass, helps us to continue making AE a destination for our customers. This program gives us a direct, one-on-one connection with our best customers and allows us to develop a relationship with these customers while rewarding brand loyalty.

aerie by American Eagle

In the fall of 2006, we launched our new intimates sub-brand, *aerie* by American Eagle, which targets our core AE customers. The *aerie* collection of dormwear and intimates includes bras, undies, camis, hoodies, robes, boxers and sweats for the AE girl. It is intended to drive store productivity by expanding the product categories and building upon our experience. The *aerie* collection is offered in all American Eagle stores, including 18 side-by-side stores, three stand-alone stores and on ae.com. Based on the positive customer response to *aerie*, we are expanding our real estate strategy and plan to open at least 15 stand-alone stores during Fiscal 2007.

ae.com

American Eagle sells merchandise via its e-commerce operation, ae.com, which is an extension of the lifestyle that we convey in our stores. During Fiscal 2006, ae.com expanded its international shipping to 41 countries, providing an opportunity to grow in regions where we do not currently have store locations. We are continuing to focus on the growth of ae.com through various initiatives, including improved site efficiency and faster check-out, expansion of sizes and styles, unique online content and targeted marketing strategies.

MARTIN + OSA

During Fiscal 2006, we opened five MARTIN + OSA stores. MARTIN + OSA, a new sportswear concept targeting 25 to 40 year-old women and men, carries apparel, accessories and footwear, designed using denim and sport inspiration. We expect to open approximately 12 MARTIN + OSA stores in premier shopping centers throughout the United States during Fiscal 2007.

Consolidated Store Locations

Our stores average approximately 5,700 gross square feet and approximately 4,600 on a selling square foot basis. At February 3, 2007, we operated 911 stores in the United States and Canada under the American Eagle Outfitters and MARTIN + OSA brands as shown below:

United States, including the Commonwealth of Puerto Rico – 839 stores

Alabama	18	Illinois	29	Montana	2	Puerto Rico	2
Alaska	3	Indiana	18	Nebraska	6	Rhode Island	3
Arizona	13	Iowa	12	Nevada	5	South Carolina	13
Arkansas	6	Kansas	8	New Hampshire	5	South Dakota	2
California	79	Kentucky	11	New Jersey	22	Tennessee	20
Colorado	14	Louisiana	13	New Mexico	3	Texas	62
Connecticut	10	Maine	3	New York	41	Utah	10
Delaware	3	Maryland	18	North Carolina	24	Vermont	3
District of Columbia	1	Massachusetts	27	North Dakota	4	Virginia	28
Florida	46	Michigan	30	Ohio	37	Washington	18
Georgia	26	Minnesota	16	Oklahoma	12	West Virginia	7
Hawaii	4	Mississippi	7	Oregon	9	Wisconsin	15
Idaho	3	Missouri	17	Pennsylvania	49	Wyoming	2

Canada – 72 stores

Alberta	8	New Brunswick	3	Ontario	37
British Columbia	12	Newfoundland	2	Quebec	4
Manitoba	2	Nova Scotia	2	Saskatchewan	2

Purchasing

We purchase merchandise from suppliers who either manufacture their own merchandise, supply merchandise manufactured by others, or both. During Fiscal 2006, we purchased a majority of our merchandise from non-North American suppliers.

All of our merchandise suppliers receive a vendor compliance manual that describes our quality standards and shipping instructions. We maintain a quality control department at our distribution centers to inspect incoming merchandise shipments for uniformity of sizes and colors, and for overall quality of manufacturing. Periodic inspections are also made by our employees and agents at manufacturing facilities to identify quality problems prior to shipment of merchandise.

Global Labor Compliance

We are firmly committed to the goal of using only the most highly regarded and efficient suppliers throughout the world. We require our suppliers to provide a workplace environment that not only meets basic human rights standards, but also one that complies with all local legal requirements and encourages opportunity for all, with dignity and respect.

For many years, we have had a policy for the inspection of factories throughout the world where goods are produced to our order. This inspection process is an important component of our comprehensive vendor compliance program that was developed with the assistance of an internationally recognized consulting firm. This program contractually requires all suppliers to meet our global workplace standards, including human rights standards, as set forth in our Vendor Code of Conduct. The Vendor Code of Conduct is required to be posted in all factories in the local language. The program utilizes third party inspectors to audit compliance by vendor factories with our workplace standards and Vendor Code of Conduct. Additionally, a copy of the Vendor Code of Conduct is posted on our website, www.ae.com.

Security Compliance

During recent years, there has been an increasing focus within the international trade community on concerns related to global terrorist activity. The security issues posed by 9/11 and other terrorist threats have brought increased demands from the Bureau of Customs and Border Protection ("CBP") and other agencies within the Department of Homeland Security that importers take responsible action to secure their supply chains. In response, we became a certified member of the Customs – Trade Partnership Against Terrorism program ("C-TPAT") during 2004. C-TPAT is a voluntary program offered by CBP in which an importer agrees to work with CBP to strengthen overall supply chain security. Our internal security procedures were reviewed by CBP during February 2005 and a validation of processes with respect to our external partners was completed in June 2005. We received a formal written validation of our security procedures from CBP during the first quarter of Fiscal 2006 indicating the highest level of benefits afforded to C-TPAT members. Additionally, we took significant steps to expand the scope of our security procedures during 2004, including, but not limited to: a significant increase in the number of factory audits performed; a revision of the factory audit format to include a review of all critical security issues as defined by CBP; a review of security procedures of our other international trading partners, including forwarders, consolidators, shippers and brokers; and a requirement that all of our international trading partners be members of C-TPAT.

Trade Compliance

We act as the importer of record for substantially all of the merchandise we purchase overseas from foreign suppliers. Accordingly, we have an affirmative obligation to comply with the rules and regulations established for importers by the CBP regarding issues such as merchandise classification, valuation and country of origin. We have developed and implemented a comprehensive series of trade compliance procedures to assure that we adhere to all CBP requirements. In its most recent review and audit of our import operations and procedures, CBP found no unacceptable risks of non-compliance.

Merchandise Inventory, Replenishment and Distribution

Purchase orders are entered into the merchandise system at the time of order. Merchandise is normally shipped directly from vendors and routed to our two US distribution centers, one in Warrendale, Pennsylvania and the other in Ottawa, Kansas, or to our third-party distribution provider in Canada. Historically, our stores in Canada received merchandise from NLS. Beginning in Fiscal 2006, our stores in Canada receive merchandise through logistics services provided under a transitional services agreement with the NLS Purchaser. Upon receipt, merchandise is entered into the merchandise system, then processed and prepared for shipment to the stores or forwarded to a warehouse holding area to be used as store replenishment goods. The allocation of merchandise among stores varies based upon a number of factors, including geographic location, customer demographics and store size. Merchandise is shipped to our stores two to five times per week depending upon the season and store requirements. Currently, ae.com uses a third-party vendor for its fulfillment services.

During Fiscal 2006, we began construction of an expansion to our Ottawa, Kansas distribution center, which will be completed during Fiscal 2007. Upon completion of the expansion, the fulfillment services for ae.com will be performed by the Company at the Ottawa distribution center. The expansion will also enhance our operating efficiency and is central to our plan for supporting future growth, especially in areas such as ae.com, *aerie* and MARTIN + OSA.

Customer Credit and Returns

We offer our AE customers in the U.S. an American Eagle private label credit card, issued by a third-party bank. We have no liability to the card issuer for bad debt expense, provided that purchases are made in accordance with the issuing bank's procedures. We believe that providing in-store credit through use of our proprietary credit card promotes incremental sales and encourages customer loyalty. Our credit card holders receive special promotional offers and advance notice of all American Eagle in-store sales events. Our customers in the U.S. and Canada may also pay for their purchases with American Express®, Discover®, MasterCard®, Visa®, bank debit cards, cash or check.

AE gift cards can be purchased in our American Eagle stores in the U.S. and Canada, as well as through ae.com. MARTIN + OSA gift cards are available in our MARTIN + OSA stores. When the recipient uses the gift card, the value of the purchase is electronically deducted from the card and any remaining value can be used for future purchases. If a gift card remains inactive for greater than twenty-four months, the Company assesses the recipient a one dollar per month service fee, where allowed by law, which is automatically deducted from the remaining value of the card. This service fee is recorded within other income, net on our Consolidated Statements of Operations.

We offer our customers a hassle-free return policy. We believe that certain of our competitors offer similar credit card and customer service policies.

Competition

The retail apparel industry, including retail stores and e-commerce, is highly competitive. We compete with various individual and chain specialty stores, as well as the casual apparel and footwear departments of department stores and discount retailers, primarily on the basis of quality, fashion, service, selection and price.

Trademarks and Service Marks

We have registered American Eagle Outfitters® in the U.S. Patent and Trademark Office as a trademark for clothing and for a variety of non-clothing products, including jewelry, perfume, and personal care products, and as a service mark for retail clothing stores and credit card services. We have also registered AE® as a trademark for clothing and footwear products and as a service mark for a variety of retail clothing store and related services and an application is pending to register AE® for a variety of non-clothing items. Additionally, American Eagle® is registered for a variety of clothing items.

We have registered American Eagle Outfitters® in the Canadian Trademark Office for a wide variety of clothing products, as well as for retail clothing store services. In addition, we are exclusively licensed in Canada to use AE® and AEO® in connection with the sale of a wide range of clothing products.

We have pending applications for MARTIN + OSA™ in the U.S. Patent and Trademark Office and Canadian Trademark Office as a trademark for clothing and for a variety of non-clothing products and as a service mark for retail clothing store services.

We have pending applications for *aerie*™ in the U.S. Patent and Trademark Office and Canadian Trademark Office as a trademark for clothing and for a variety of non-clothing products and as a service mark for retail clothing store services.

We have also registered a number of other marks used in our business.

Employees

As of February 3, 2007, we had approximately 27,600 employees in the United States and Canada, of whom approximately 22,100 were part-time and seasonal hourly employees. We consider our relationship with our employees to be satisfactory.

Seasonality

Historically, our operations have been seasonal, with a large portion of net sales and net income occurring in the fourth fiscal quarter, reflecting increased demand during the year-end holiday selling season and, to a lesser extent, the third quarter, reflecting increased demand during the back-to-school selling season. During Fiscal 2006, the third and fourth fiscal quarters accounted for approximately 60% of our sales and approximately 65% of our income from continuing operations. As a result of this seasonality, any factors negatively affecting us during the third and fourth fiscal quarters of any year, including adverse weather or unfavorable economic conditions, could have a material adverse effect on our financial condition and results of operations for the entire year. Our quarterly results of operations also may fluctuate based upon such factors as the timing of certain holiday seasons, the number and timing of new store openings, the acceptability of seasonal merchandise offerings, the timing and level of markdowns, store closings and remodels, competitive factors, weather and general economic conditions.

Available Information

Our Annual Reports on Form 10-K, Quarterly Reports on Form 10-Q, Current Reports on Form 8-K and amendments to those reports are available, free of charge, under the "About AE" section of our website at www.ae.com. These reports are available as soon as reasonably practicable after such material is electronically filed with the Securities and Exchange Commission (the "SEC").

Our corporate governance materials, including our corporate governance guidelines, the charters of our audit, compensation, and nominating and corporate governance committees, and our code of ethics may also be found under the "About AE" section of our website at www.ae.com. Any amendments or waivers to our code of ethics will also be available on our website. A copy of the corporate governance materials is also available upon written request.

Additionally, our investor presentations are available under the "About AE" section of our website at www.ae.com. These presentations are available as soon as reasonably practicable after they are presented at investor conferences.

PART II

ITEM 5. MARKET FOR THE REGISTRANT'S COMMON EQUITY, RELATED STOCKHOLDER MATTERS AND ISSUER PURCHASES OF EQUITY SECURITIES.

Effective March 8, 2007, our common stock is traded on the NYSE under the symbol "AEO." Prior to that time, our stock was traded on the NASDAQ Stock Market LLC under the symbol "AEOS." The following table sets forth the range of high and low sales prices of the common stock as reported on the NASDAQ Stock Market during the periods indicated. As of March 15, 2007, there were 808 stockholders of record. However, when including associates who own shares through our employee stock purchase plan, and others holding shares in broker accounts under street name, we estimate the stockholder base at approximately 70,000. The following information reflects the December 2006 three-for-two stock split.

For the Quarters Ended	Market Price High	Low	Cash Dividends per Common Share
February 3, 2007	$34.80	$29.43	$0.075
October 28, 2006	$31.50	$20.61	$0.075
July 29, 2006	$24.10	$20.07	$0.075
April 29, 2006	$21.85	$16.57	$0.050
January 28, 2006	$17.96	$12.97	$0.050
October 29, 2005	$22.40	$13.55	$0.050
July 30, 2005	$22.69	$17.04	$0.050
April 30, 2005	$20.30	$16.52	$0.033

During Fiscal 2005 and Fiscal 2006, we paid quarterly dividends as shown in the table above. The payment of future dividends is at the discretion of our Board of Directors (the "Board") and is based on future earnings, cash flow, financial condition, capital requirements, changes in U.S. taxation and other relevant factors. It is anticipated that any future dividends paid will be declared on a quarterly basis.

ITEM 6. SELECTED CONSOLIDATED FINANCIAL DATA.

The following Selected Consolidated Financial Data should be read in conjunction with "Management's Discussion and Analysis of Financial Condition and Results of Operations," included under Item 7 below and the Consolidated Financial Statements and Notes thereto, included in Item 8 below. Most of the selected data presented below is derived from our Consolidated Financial Statements, which are filed in response to Item 8 below. The selected Consolidated Statement of Operations data for the years ended January 31, 2004 and February 1, 2003 and the selected Consolidated Balance Sheet data as of January 29, 2005, January 31, 2004 and February 1, 2003 are derived from audited Consolidated Financial Statements not included herein.

(In thousands, except per share amounts, ratios and other financial information)	For the Years Ended (1)				
	February 3, 2007	January 28, 2006	January 29, 2005	January 31, 2004	February 1, 2003
Summary of Operations (2)					
Net sales (3)	$2,794,409	$2,321,962	$1,889,647	$1,441,864	$1,388,758
Comparable store sales increase (decrease) (4)	12%	16%	21%	(7)%	(4)%
Gross profit	$1,340,429	$1,077,749	$ 881,188	$ 552,559	$ 543,104
Gross profit as a percentage of net sales	48.0%	46.4%	46.6%	38.3%	39.1%
Operating income (5)	$ 586,790	$ 458,689	$ 360,968	$ 131,778	$ 158,061
Operating income as a percentage of net sales	21.0%	19.8%	19.1%	9.1%	11.4%
Income from continuing operations	$ 387,359	$ 293,711	$ 224,232	$ 83,108	$ 99,644
Income from continuing operations as a percentage of net sales	13.9%	12.7%	11.9%	5.8%	7.2%
Per Share Results (6)					
Income from continuing operations per common share - basic	$ 1.74	$ 1.29	$ 1.03	$ 0.39	$ 0.46
Income from continuing operations per common share - diluted	$ 1.70	$ 1.26	$ 1.00	$ 0.38	$ 0.46
Weighted average common shares outstanding - basic	222,662	227,406	217,725	213,339	215,127
Weighted average common shares outstanding - diluted	228,384	233,031	225,366	216,621	218,349
Cash dividends per common share (7)	$ 0.28	$ 0.18	$ 0.04	$ -	$ -
Balance Sheet Information					
Total cash and short-term investments	$ 827,113	$ 751,518	$ 589,607	$ 337,812	$ 241,573
Total assets (8)	$1,987,484	$1,605,649	$1,328,926	$ 946,229	$ 824,510
Long-term investments	$ 251,644	$ 145,774	$ 84,416	$ 24,357	$ -
Long-term debt	$ -	$ -	$ -	$ 13,874	$ 16,356
Stockholders' equity	$1,417,312	$1,155,552	$ 963,486	$ 637,377	$ 571,590
Working capital (8)	$ 737,790	$ 725,294	$ 582,739	$ 321,721	$ 272,288
Current ratio (8)	2.60	3.06	3.06	2.44	2.51
Average return on stockholders' equity	30.1%	27.8%	26.7%	9.9%	16.5%
Other Financial Information (9)					
Total stores at year-end	911	869	846	805	753
Capital expenditures (000's)	$ 225,939	$ 81,545	$ 97,288	$ 77,544	$ 78,787
Net sales per average selling square foot (10)	$ 642	$ 577	$ 504	$ 420	$ 460
Total selling square feet at end of period	4,220,929	3,896,441	3,709,012	3,466,368	3,108,556
Net sales per average gross square foot (10)	$ 524	$ 471	$ 412	$ 343	$ 374
Total gross square feet at end of period	5,173,065	4,772,487	4,540,095	4,239,497	3,817,442
Number of employees at end of period	27,600	23,000	20,600	15,800	14,100

(See footnotes on page 16)

(1) Except for the fiscal year ended February 3, 2007, which includes 53 weeks, all fiscal years presented include 52 weeks.

(2) All amounts presented are from continuing operations and exclude Bluenotes' results of operations for all periods. See Note 9 of the accompanying Consolidated Financial Statements for additional information regarding discontinued operations and the disposition of Bluenotes.

(3) Amount for the fiscal year ended February 3, 2007 includes proceeds from merchandise sell-offs. Amounts for prior periods were not adjusted to reflect this change as the amounts were determined to be immaterial. All amounts presented include shipping and handling amounts billed to customers. See Note 2 of the accompanying Consolidated Financial Statements for additional information regarding the components of net sales.

(4) The comparable store sales increase for the period ended February 3, 2007 is compared to the corresponding 53 week period last year.

(5) All amounts presented exclude gift card service fee income, which was reclassified to other income, net. See Note 2 of the accompanying Consolidated Financial Statements for additional information regarding gift cards.

(6) Per share results for all periods presented reflect the three-for-two stock split distributed on December 18, 2006. See Note 2 of the accompanying Consolidated Financial Statements for additional information regarding the stock split.

(7) Amount for the fiscal year ended January 29, 2005 represents cash dividends paid for two quarters only. Note that the Company initiated quarterly dividend payments during the third quarter of Fiscal 2004.

(8) Calculations for the years ended January 28, 2006 and January 29, 2005 reflect certain assets of NLS as held-for-sale. See Note 9 of the accompanying Consolidated Financial Statements for additional information regarding assets held-for-sale.

(9) All amounts exclude Bluenotes for all periods presented. See Note 9 of the accompanying Consolidated Financial Statements for additional information regarding the disposition of Bluenotes.

(10) Net sales per average square foot is calculated using retail sales for the year divided by the straight average of the beginning and ending square footage for the year.

ITEM 8. FINANCIAL STATEMENTS AND SUPPLEMENTARY DATA.

Index to Consolidated Financial Statements

Report of Independent Registered Public Accounting Firm 30

Consolidated Balance Sheets 31

Consolidated Statements of Operations 32

Consolidated Statements of Comprehensive Income 33

Consolidated Statements of Stockholders' Equity 34

Consolidated Statements of Cash Flows 35

Notes to Consolidated Financial Statements 36

Report of Independent Registered Public Accounting Firm

The Board of Directors and Stockholders of
American Eagle Outfitters, Inc.

We have audited the accompanying consolidated balance sheets of American Eagle Outfitters, Inc. (the Company) as of February 3, 2007 and January 28, 2006, and the related consolidated statements of operations, comprehensive income, stockholders' equity, and cash flows for each of the three fiscal years in the period ended February 3, 2007. These financial statements are the responsibility of the Company's management. Our responsibility is to express an opinion on these financial statements based on our audits.

We conducted our audits in accordance with the standards of the Public Company Accounting Oversight Board (United States). Those standards require that we plan and perform the audit to obtain reasonable assurance about whether the financial statements are free of material misstatement. An audit includes examining, on a test basis, evidence supporting the amounts and disclosures in the financial statements. An audit also includes assessing the accounting principles used and significant estimates made by management, as well as evaluating the overall financial statement presentation. We believe that our audits provide a reasonable basis for our opinion.

In our opinion, the financial statements referred to above present fairly, in all material respects, the consolidated financial position of American Eagle Outfitters, Inc. at February 3, 2007 and January 28, 2006, and the consolidated results of their operations and their cash flows for each of the three fiscal years in the period ended February 3, 2007, in conformity with U.S. generally accepted accounting principles.

As discussed in Note 3 to the consolidated financial statements, the Company adopted Statement of Financial Accounting Standards No. 123(R), "Share-Based Payment," effective January 29, 2006.

We also have audited, in accordance with the standards of the Public Company Accounting Oversight Board (United States), the effectiveness of the Company's internal control over financial reporting as of February 3, 2007, based on criteria established in Internal Control-Integrated Framework issued by the Committee of Sponsoring Organizations of the Treadway Commission and our report dated April 2, 2007 expressed an unqualified opinion thereon.

/s/ Ernst & Young LLP

Pittsburgh, Pennsylvania
April 2, 2007

AMERICAN EAGLE OUTFITTERS, INC.
CONSOLIDATED BALANCE SHEETS

(In thousands, except per share amounts)	February 3, 2007	January 28, 2006
Assets		
Current assets:		
Cash and cash equivalents	$ 59,737	$ 130,529
Short-term investments	767,376	620,989
Merchandise inventory	263,644	210,739
Accounts and note receivable	26,045	29,146
Prepaid expenses and other	33,720	30,110
Deferred income taxes	47,732	43,085
Assets held-for-sale	-	12,183
Total current assets	1,198,254	1,076,781
Property and equipment, at cost, net of accumulated depreciation and amortization	481,645	345,518
Goodwill	9,950	9,950
Long-term investments	251,644	145,774
Other assets, net	45,991	27,626
Total assets	$1,987,484	$1,605,649
Liabilities and Stockholders' Equity		
Current liabilities:		
Accounts payable	$ 171,150	$ 139,197
Accrued compensation and payroll taxes	58,371	48,050
Accrued rent	57,543	52,506
Accrued income and other taxes	87,780	43,273
Unredeemed stored value cards and gift certificates	54,554	43,045
Current portion of deferred lease credits	12,803	10,406
Other liabilities and accrued expenses	18,263	15,010
Total current liabilities	460,464	351,487
Non-current liabilities:		
Deferred lease credits	65,114	60,087
Other non-current liabilities	44,594	38,523
Total non-current liabilities	109,708	98,610
Commitments and contingencies	-	-
Stockholders' equity:		
Preferred stock, $0.01 par value; 5,000 shares authorized; none issued and outstanding	-	-
Common stock, $0.01 par value; 250,000 shares authorized; 248,155 and 243,571 shares issued; 221,284 and 221,897 shares outstanding, respectively	2,461	2,416
Contributed capital	453,418	369,807
Accumulated other comprehensive income	21,714	22,028
Retained earnings	1,302,345	978,855
Deferred compensation	-	(1,041)
Treasury stock, 25,699 and 20,534 shares, respectively	(362,626)	(216,513)
Total stockholders' equity	1,417,312	1,155,552
Total liabilities and stockholders' equity	$1,987,484	$1,605,649

See Notes to Consolidated Financial Statements

AMERICAN EAGLE OUTFITTERS, INC.
CONSOLIDATED STATEMENTS OF OPERATIONS

	For the Years Ended		
(In thousands, except per share amounts)	February 3, 2007	January 28, 2006	January 29, 2005
Net sales	$2,794,409	$2,321,962	$1,889,647
Cost of sales, including certain buying, occupancy and warehousing expenses (exclusive of depreciation shown separately below)	1,453,980	1,244,213	1,008,459
Gross profit	1,340,429	1,077,749	881,188
Selling, general and administrative expenses	665,606	540,332	450,777
Depreciation and amortization expense	88,033	78,728	69,443
Operating income	586,790	458,689	360,968
Other income, net	42,277	18,278	5,867
Income before income taxes	629,067	476,967	366,835
Provision for income taxes	241,708	183,256	142,603
Income from continuing operations	387,359	293,711	224,232
Income (loss) from discontinued operations, net of tax	-	442	(10,889)
Net income	$ 387,359	$ 294,153	$ 213,343
Basic income per common share:			
Income from continuing operations	$ 1.74	$ 1.29	$ 1.03
Loss from discontinued operations	-	-	(0.05)
Net income per basic share	$ 1.74	$ 1.29	$ 0.98
Diluted income per common share:			
Income from continuing operations	$ 1.70	$ 1.26	$ 1.00
Loss from discontinued operations	-	-	(0.05)
Net income per diluted share	$ 1.70	$ 1.26	$ 0.95
Weighted average common shares outstanding—basic	222,662	227,406	217,725
Weighted average common shares outstanding—diluted	228,384	233,031	225,366

See Notes to Consolidated Financial Statements

AMERICAN EAGLE OUTFITTERS, INC.
CONSOLIDATED STATEMENTS OF COMPREHENSIVE INCOME

	For the Years Ended		
(In thousands)	February 3, 2007	January 28, 2006	January 29, 2005
Net income	$387,359	$294,153	$213,343
Other comprehensive income:			
Unrealized loss on investments, net of tax	(191)	(642)	(227)
Reclassification adjustment for losses (gain) realized in net income due to the sale of available-for-sale securities, net of tax	356	99	(4)
Reclassification adjustment for gain realized in net income related to the transfer of investment securities from available-for-sale classification to trading classification, net of tax	(177)	-	-
Foreign currency translation adjustment	(1,180)	8,823	7,315
Reclassification adjustment for loss realized in net income related to the disposition of National Logistics Services	878	-	-
Reclassification adjustment for loss realized in net income related to the sale of Bluenotes	-	-	2,467
Unrealized derivative gains on cash flow hedge, net of tax	-	-	71
Reclassification adjustment for losses realized in net income related to termination of the cash flow hedge, net of tax	-	-	437
Other comprehensive income	(314)	8,280	10,059
Comprehensive income	$387,045	$302,433	$223,402

See Notes to Consolidated Financial Statements

AMERICAN EAGLE OUTFITTERS, INC.
CONSOLIDATED STATEMENTS OF STOCKHOLDERS' EQUITY

(In thousands, except per share amounts)	Shares Outstanding (1)	Common Stock	Contributed Capital	Retained Earnings	Treasury Stock (2)	Deferred Compensation Expense	Accumulated Other Comprehensive Income	Stockholders' Equity
Balance at January 31, 2004	**213,573**	**$2,174**	**$155,335**	**$ 522,258**	**$ (45,018)**	**$(1,061)**	**$ 3,689**	**$ 637,377**
Stock awards	10,659	105	112,189	-	-	(746)	-	111,548
Net income	-	-	-	213,343	-	-	-	213,343
Other comprehensive income, net of tax	-	-	-	-	-	-	10,059	10,059
Cash dividends ($0.04 per share) (3)	-	-	-	(8,841)	-	-	-	(8,841)
Balance at January 29, 2005	**224,232**	**2,279**	**267,524**	**726,760**	**(45,018)**	**(1,807)**	**13,748**	**963,486**
Stock awards	8,706	137	102,283	-	-	766	-	103,186
Repurchase of common stock as part of publicly announced programs	(10,500)	-	-	-	(161,008)	-	-	(161,008)
Repurchase of common stock from employees	(541)	-	-	-	(10,487)	-	-	(10,487)
Net income	-	-	-	294,153	-	-	-	294,153
Other comprehensive income, net of tax	-	-	-	-	-	-	8,280	8,280
Cash dividends ($0.18 per share)	-	-	-	(42,058)	-	-	-	(42,058)
Balance at January 28, 2006	**221,897**	**2,416**	**369,807**	**978,855**	**(216,513)**	**(1,041)**	**22,028**	**1,155,552**
Stock awards	4,556	45	83,615	-	-	1,041	-	84,701
Repurchase of common stock as part of publicly announced programs	(5,250)	-	-	-	(146,485)	-	-	(146,485)
Repurchase of common stock from employees	(443)	-	-	-	(7,635)	-	-	(7,635)
Cash paid for fractional shares in three-for-two stock split	(4)	-	(113)	-	-	-	-	(113)
Reissuance of treasury stock	528	-	109	(2,348)	8,007	-	-	5,768
Net income	-	-	-	387,359	-	-	-	387,359
Other comprehensive loss, net of tax	-	-	-	-	-	-	(314)	(314)
Cash dividends ($0.28 per share)	-	-	-	(61,521)	-	-	-	(61,521)
Balance at February 3, 2007	**221,284**	**$2,461**	**$453,418**	**$1,302,345**	**$(362,626)**	**$ -**	**$21,714**	**$1,417,312**

All amounts presented have been restated to reflect the December 18, 2006 three-for-two stock split and the March 7, 2005 two-for-one stock split.

(1) 250,000 authorized, 248,155 issued and 221,284 outstanding (excluding 1,172 shares of non-vested restricted stock), $0.01 par value common stock at February 3, 2007; 250,000 authorized, 243,571 issued and 221,897 outstanding (excluding 1,140 shares of non-vested restricted stock) at January 28, 2006; and 250,000 authorized, 235,154 issued and 224,232 outstanding (excluding 1,430 shares of non-vested restricted stock) at January 29, 2005. The Company has 5,000 authorized, with none issued or outstanding, $0.01 par value preferred stock at February 3, 2007, January 28, 2006 and January 29, 2005.

(2) 25,699 shares, 20,534 shares and 9,492 shares at February 3, 2007, January 28, 2006 and January 29, 2005, respectively. During Fiscal 2006, 528 shares were reissued from treasury stock for the issuance of share-based payments.

(3) Amount represents cash dividends paid for two quarters only. Note that the Company initiated quarterly dividend payments during the third quarter of Fiscal 2004.

See Notes to Consolidated Financial Statements

AMERICAN EAGLE OUTFITTERS, INC.
CONSOLIDATED STATEMENTS OF CASH FLOWS

	For the Years Ended		
(In thousands)	February 3, 2007	January 28, 2006	January 29, 2005
Operating activities:			
Net income	$ 387,359	$ 294,153	$ 213,343
(Income) loss from discontinued operations	-	(442)	10,889
Income from continuing operations	387,359	293,711	224,232
Adjustments to reconcile income from continuing operations to net cash provided by operating activities:			
Depreciation and amortization	88,033	78,728	69,443
Stock-based compensation	36,556	19,620	25,166
Deferred income taxes	(27,615)	4,752	(17,087)
Tax benefit from share-based payments	25,465	35,371	28,800
Excess tax benefit from share-based payments	(19,541)	-	-
Loss on impairment of assets	-	1,185	1,399
Proceeds from sale of trading securities	183,968	-	-
Changes in assets and liabilities:			
Merchandise inventory	(53,527)	(39,137)	(44,540)
Accounts and note receivable, including related party	2,778	4,638	3,878
Prepaid expenses and other	(4,204)	(3,642)	1,918
Accounts payable	32,345	29,366	23,166
Unredeemed stored value cards and gift certificates	11,623	10,137	7,373
Deferred lease credits	7,791	2,784	3,359
Accrued liabilities	78,237	42,906	41,576
Total adjustments	361,909	186,708	144,451
Net cash provided by operating activities from continuing operations	**749,268**	**480,419**	**368,683**
Investing activities:			
Capital expenditures	(225,939)	(81,545)	(97,288)
Proceeds from sale of assets	12,345	-	-
Purchase of investments	(1,353,339)	(1,187,556)	(508,768)
Sale of investments	915,952	876,111	330,390
Other investing activities	(140)	(74)	(14)
Net cash used for investing activities from continuing operations	**(651,121)**	**(393,064)**	**(275,680)**
Financing activities:			
Payments on note payable and capital leases	(3,020)	(745)	(2,655)
Proceeds from issuance of note payable	2,025	-	-
Retirement of note payable and termination of swap agreement	-	-	(16,915)
Repurchase of common stock as part of publicly announced programs	(146,485)	(161,008)	-
Repurchase of common stock from employees	(7,635)	(10,487)	-
Cash paid for fractional shares in connection with three-for-two stock split	(113)	-	-
Net proceeds from stock options exercised	28,447	48,198	57,533
Excess tax benefit from share-based payments	19,541	-	-
Cash dividends paid	(61,521)	(42,058)	(8,841)
Net cash (used for) provided by financing activities from continuing operations	**(168,761)**	**(166,100)**	**29,122**
Effect of exchange rates on cash	(178)	4,680	1,903
Cash flows of discontinued operations			
Net cash (used for) provided by operating activities	-	(15,214)	3,315
Net cash provided by investing activities	-	-	5,371
Net cash provided by financing activities	-	-	-
Effect of exchange rates on cash	-	436	762
Net cash (used for) provided by discontinued operations	**-**	**(14,778)**	**9,448**
Net (decrease) increase in cash and cash equivalents	**(70,792)**	**(88,843)**	**133,476**
Cash and cash equivalents - beginning of period	130,529	219,372	85,896
Cash and cash equivalents - end of period	$ 59,737	$ 130,529	$ 219,372

See Notes to Consolidated Financial Statements

AMERICAN EAGLE OUTFITTERS, INC.
NOTES TO CONSOLIDATED FINANCIAL STATEMENTS
FOR THE YEAR ENDED FEBRUARY 3, 2007

1. Business Operations

American Eagle Outfitters, Inc. is a leading retailer that operates under the American Eagle Outfitters and MARTIN + OSA brands.

American Eagle Outfitters designs, markets and sells its own brand of laidback, current clothing targeting 15 to 25 year-olds, providing high-quality merchandise at affordable prices. The Company opened its first American Eagle Outfitters store in the United States in 1977 and expanded the brand into Canada in 2001. American Eagle also distributes merchandise via its e-commerce operation, ae.com, which offers additional sizes, colors and styles of favorite AE merchandise and ships to 41 countries around the world. AE's original collection includes standards like jeans and graphic Ts as well as essentials like accessories, outerwear, footwear, basics and swimwear under our American Eagle Outfitters, American Eagle and AE brand names. During Fiscal 2006, American Eagle launched its new intimates sub-brand, *aerie* by American Eagle. The *aerie* collection of dormwear and intimates includes bras, undies, camis, hoodies, robes, boxers and sweats for the AE girl.

The Company also introduced MARTIN + OSA, a new sportswear concept targeting 25 to 40 year-old women and men, in the fall of 2006. MARTIN + OSA carries apparel, accessories and footwear, using denim and sport inspiration to design fun and sport back into sportswear.

The following table sets forth the approximate consolidated percentage of net sales attributable to each merchandise group for each of the periods indicated:

	For the Years Ended		
	February 3, 2007	January 28, 2006	January 29, 2005
Men's apparel and accessories	35%	35%	34%
Women's apparel, accessories and intimates	60%	60%	61%
Footwear – men's and women's	5%	5%	5%
Total	100%	100%	100%

2. Summary of Significant Accounting Policies

Principles of Consolidation

The Consolidated Financial Statements include the accounts of the Company and its wholly-owned subsidiaries. All intercompany transactions and balances have been eliminated in consolidation. At February 3, 2007, the Company operated in one reportable segment, American Eagle. MARTIN + OSA was determined to be immaterial for classification as a separate reportable segment and therefore is included within the American Eagle segment.

In December 2004, the Company completed the disposition of Bluenotes, which refers to the Bluenotes/Thriftys specialty apparel chain that we operated in Canada. As a result, the Company's Consolidated Statements of Operations and Consolidated Statements of Cash Flows reflect Bluenotes' results of operations as discontinued operations for all periods presented. Prior to the disposition, Bluenotes was presented as a separate reportable segment. Additional information regarding the disposition is contained in Note 9 of the Consolidated Financial Statements.

Fiscal Year

Our financial year is a 52/53 week year that ends on the Saturday nearest to January 31. As used herein, "Fiscal 2008" and "Fiscal 2007" refer to the 52 week periods ending January 31, 2009 and February 2, 2008, respectively. "Fiscal 2006" refers to the 53 week period ended February 3, 2007. "Fiscal 2005" and "Fiscal 2004" refer to the 52 week periods ended January 28, 2006 and January 29, 2005, respectively.

Estimates

The preparation of financial statements in conformity with accounting principles generally accepted in the United States of America requires our management to make estimates and assumptions that affect the reported amounts of assets and liabilities and disclosure of contingent assets and liabilities at the date of the financial statements and the reported amounts of revenues and expenses during the reporting period. Actual results could differ from those estimates. On an ongoing basis, our management reviews its estimates based on currently available information. Changes in facts and circumstances may result in revised estimates.

Recent Accounting Pronouncements

In February 2007, the FASB issued SFAS No. 159, *The Fair Value Option for Financial Assets and Financial Liabilities* ("SFAS No. 159"). SFAS No. 159 provides companies with an option to report selected financial assets and liabilities at fair value. The statement also establishes presentation and disclosure requirements to facilitate comparisons between companies that choose different measurement attributes for similar assets and liabilities. SFAS No. 159 is effective for fiscal years beginning after November 15, 2007 and the Company will adopt SFAS No. 159 in connection with the adoption of SFAS No. 157, *Fair Value Measurements* ("SFAS No. 157"), in the first quarter of Fiscal 2008. The Company is currently assessing the impact of SFAS No. 159 on its Consolidated Financial Statements.

In September 2006, the SEC issued SAB No. 108, *Considering the Effects of Prior Year Misstatements when Quantifying Misstatements in Current Year Financial Statements* ("SAB No. 108"). SAB No. 108 provides guidance on how prior year misstatements should be taken into consideration when quantifying misstatements in current year financial statements for purposes of determining whether the current year's financial statements are materially misstated. SAB No. 108 is effective for annual financial statements covering the first fiscal year ending after November 15, 2006 and was adopted by the Company for Fiscal 2006. The adoption of SAB No. 108 did not have a material impact on the Company's Consolidated Financial Statements.

In September 2006, the FASB issued SFAS No. 157. SFAS No. 157 addresses how companies should measure fair value when they are required to use fair value as a measure for recognition or disclosure purposes under generally accepted accounting principles. SFAS No. 157 is effective for fiscal years beginning after November 15, 2007 and the Company will adopt SFAS No. 157 beginning in the first quarter of Fiscal 2008. The Company is currently assessing the impact of SFAS No. 157 on its Consolidated Financial Statements.

In July 2006, the FASB issued FASB Interpretation No. 48, *Accounting for Uncertainty in Income Taxes—an interpretation of FASB Statement 109* ("FIN No. 48"). FIN No. 48 prescribes a comprehensive model for recognizing, measuring, presenting and disclosing in the financial statements tax positions taken or expected to be taken on a tax return, including a decision whether to file or not to file in a particular jurisdiction. Under FIN No. 48, a tax benefit from an uncertain position may be recognized only if it is "more likely than not" that the position is sustainable based on its technical merits. FIN No. 48 is effective for fiscal years beginning after December 15, 2006, and the Company will adopt FIN No. 48 beginning in the first quarter of Fiscal 2007. Upon adoption, the cumulative effect of applying the provisions of FIN No. 48 will be accounted for as an adjustment to the beginning balance of retained earnings for the first quarter of Fiscal 2007. The Company is currently assessing the impact of FIN No. 48 on its Consolidated Financial Statements.

In June 2006, the FASB ratified the consensus reached by the Emerging Issues Task Force on Issue No. 06-3, *How Sales Taxes Collected from Customers and Remitted to Governmental Authorities Should Be Presented in the Income Statement (That Is, Gross Versus Net Presentation)* ("EITF No. 06-3"). EITF No. 06-3 indicates that a company may adopt a policy of presenting taxes within the scope of EITF No. 06-3 either gross within revenue or net. If taxes subject to EITF No. 06-3 are significant, a company is required to disclose its accounting policy for presenting taxes and the amounts of the taxes that are recognized on a gross basis. EITF No. 06-3 is effective for the first interim period beginning after December 15, 2006, and the Company will adopt EITF No. 06-3 beginning in the first quarter of Fiscal 2007. The Company presents sales taxes collected from customers on a net basis within accrued income and other taxes on its Consolidated Balance Sheets, and will include disclosure of this accounting policy in its Consolidated Financial Statements upon adoption of EITF No. 06-3.

Foreign Currency Translation

The Canadian dollar is the functional currency for the Canadian businesses. In accordance with SFAS No. 52, *Foreign Currency Translation*, assets and liabilities denominated in foreign currencies were translated into U.S. dollars (the reporting currency) at the exchange rate prevailing at the balance sheet date. Revenues and expenses denominated in foreign currencies were translated into U.S. dollars at the monthly average exchange rate for the period. Gains or losses resulting from foreign currency transactions are included in the results of operations, whereas, related translation adjustments are reported as an element of other comprehensive income in accordance with SFAS No. 130, *Reporting Comprehensive Income* (see Note 7 of the Consolidated Financial Statements).

Fair Value of Financial Instruments

SFAS No. 107, *Disclosures about Fair Value of Financial Instruments* ("SFAS No. 107"), requires management to disclose the estimated fair value of certain assets and liabilities defined by SFAS No. 107 as financial instruments. At February 3, 2007, management believes that the carrying amounts of cash and cash equivalents, receivables and payables approximate fair value because of the short maturity of these financial instruments. Short-term and long-term investments consist of available-for-sale securities and are recorded on the Consolidated Balance Sheets at fair value, which is estimated based on quoted market prices for the investments. Any difference between the original cost and the fair value of these investments is recorded in other comprehensive income.

Cash and Cash Equivalents, Short-term Investments and Long-term Investments

Cash includes cash equivalents. The Company considers all highly liquid investments purchased with a maturity of three months or less to be cash equivalents.

As of February 3, 2007, short-term investments generally included investments with remaining maturities of less than 12 months (averaging approximately three months), consisting primarily of tax-exempt municipal bonds, taxable agency bonds and corporate notes classified as available-for-sale. Additionally, short-term investments include variable rate demand notes ("VRDNs") and auction rate securities classified as available-for-sale, which have long-term contractual maturities but feature variable interest rates that reset at short-term intervals.

As of February 3, 2007, long-term investments included investments with remaining maturities of greater than 12 months, but not exceeding five years (averaging approximately 27 months) and consisted primarily of agency bonds classified as available-for-sale.

Unrealized gains and losses on the Company's available-for-sale securities are excluded from earnings and are reported as a separate component of stockholders' equity, within accumulated other comprehensive income, until realized. When available-for-sale securities are sold, the cost of the securities is specifically identified and is used to determine any realized gain or loss. Proceeds from the sale of available-for-sale securities were $916.0 million, $876.1 million and $330.4 million for Fiscal 2006, Fiscal 2005 and Fiscal 2004, respectively. These proceeds are offset against purchases of $1.353 billion, $1.188 billion and $508.8 million for Fiscal 2006, Fiscal

2005 and Fiscal 2004, respectively. For Fiscal 2006 and Fiscal 2005, realized losses related to available-for-sale securities of $0.6 million and $0.2 million, respectively, were included in other income, net. For Fiscal 2004, a nominal amount of realized gain related to the sale of available-for-sale securities was included in other income, net.

During Fiscal 2006, the Company transferred certain investment securities from available-for-sale classification to trading classification (the "trading securities"). As a result of this transfer, during Fiscal 2006 a reclassification adjustment of $(0.3) million was recorded in other comprehensive income related to the gain realized in net income at the time of transfer. As a result of trading classification, the Company realized $3.5 million of capital gains, which were recorded in other income, net during Fiscal 2006. The trading securities were sold during Fiscal 2006, at which time the Company received proceeds of $184.0 million. As of February 3, 2007, the Company had no investments classified as trading securities.

The following table summarizes the fair market value of our cash and marketable securities, which are recorded as cash and cash equivalents on the Consolidated Balance Sheets, our short-term investments and our long-term investments:

(In thousands)	February 3, 2007		
	Balance	Unrealized Holding Gains	Unrealized Holding Losses
Cash and cash equivalents:			
Cash and money market investments	$ 59,079	$ -	$ -
Taxable investments	658	-	-
Total cash and cash equivalents	$ 59,737	$ -	$ -
Short-term investments:			
Tax exempt and advantaged investments	$ 659,906	$ -	$ 28
Taxable investments	107,470	-	130
Total short-term investments	$ 767,376	$ -	$158
Long-term investments			
Tax exempt and advantaged investments	$ 7,477	$4	$ 23
Taxable investments	244,167	1	366
Total long-term investments	$ 251,644	$5	$389
Total	$1,078,757	$5	$547

(In thousands)	January 28, 2006		
	Balance	Unrealized Holding Gains	Unrealized Holding Losses
Cash and cash equivalents:			
Cash and money market investments	$ 69,641	$-	$ -
Taxable investments	60,888	-	-
Total cash and cash equivalents	$ 130,529	$-	$ -
Short-term investments:			
Tax exempt and advantaged investments	$ 517,199	$-	$ 57
Taxable investments	103,790	-	61
Total short-term investments	$ 620,989	$-	$118
Long-term investments			
Taxable investments	$ 145,774	$-	$636
Total long-term investments	$ 145,774	$-	$636
Total	$ 897,292	$-	$754

Merchandise Inventory

Merchandise inventory is valued at the lower of average cost or market, utilizing the retail method. Average cost includes merchandise design and sourcing costs and related expenses. The Company records merchandise receipts at the time merchandise is delivered to the foreign shipping port by the manufacturer (FOB port). This is the point at which title and risk of loss transfer to the Company.

The Company reviews its inventory levels in order to identify slow-moving merchandise and generally uses markdowns to clear merchandise. Additionally, the Company estimates a markdown reserve for future planned markdowns related to current inventory. Markdowns may occur when inventory exceeds customer demand for reasons of style, seasonal adaptation, changes in customer preference, lack of consumer acceptance of fashion items, competition, or if it is determined that the inventory in stock will not sell at its currently ticketed price. Such markdowns may have a material adverse impact on earnings, depending on the extent and amount of inventory affected. The Company also estimates a shrinkage reserve for the period between the last physical count and the balance sheet date. The estimate for the shrinkage reserve can be affected by changes in merchandise mix and changes in actual shrinkage trends.

The Company and its subsidiaries sell end-of-season, overstock and irregular merchandise to third party vendors. Historically, the proceeds and cost of sell-offs, which are without recourse, were presented on a net basis within cost of sales. During the three months ended October 28, 2006, the Company began classifying its merchandise sell-offs on a gross basis, with proceeds and cost of sell-offs recorded in net sales and cost of sales, respectively. Amounts for prior periods were not adjusted to reflect this change as the amounts were determined to be immaterial. Below is a summary of merchandise sell-offs for Fiscal 2006, Fiscal 2005 and Fiscal 2004.

	For the Years Ended		
(in thousands)	February 3, 2007	January 28, 2006	January 29, 2005
Proceeds from sell-offs	$16,061	$14,472	$15,421
Marked-down cost of merchandise disposed of via sell-offs	$22,656	$18,832	$15,780

Property and Equipment

Property and equipment is recorded on the basis of cost with depreciation computed utilizing the straight-line method over the estimated useful lives as follows:

Buildings	25 years
Leasehold improvement	Lesser of 5 to 10 years or the term of the lease
Fixtures and equipment	3 to 5 years

In accordance with SFAS No. 144, management evaluates the ongoing value of the Company's property and equipment, including but not limited to leasehold improvements and store fixtures associated with retail stores which have been open longer than one year. Impairment losses are recorded on long-lived assets used in operations when events and circumstances indicate that the assets might be impaired and the undiscounted cash flows estimated to be generated by those assets are less than the carrying amounts of those assets. When events such as these occur, the impaired assets are adjusted to estimated fair value and an impairment loss is recorded in selling, general and administrative expenses. The Company did not recognize any impairment losses during Fiscal 2006 and recognized $1.2 million and $1.4 million in impairment losses during Fiscal 2005 and Fiscal 2004, respectively.

Goodwill

As of February 3, 2007, the Company had approximately $10.0 million of goodwill, which is primarily related to the acquisition of our importing operations on January 31, 2000. In accordance with SFAS No. 142, *Goodwill and Other Intangible Assets*, management evaluates goodwill for possible impairment on at least an annual basis.

Other Assets

Other assets consist primarily of deferred taxes, assets related to our deferred compensation plans and trademark costs. Trademark costs are amortized over five to fifteen years. These assets, net of amortization, are presented as other assets (long-term) on the Consolidated Balance Sheets.

Deferred Lease Credits

Deferred lease credits represent the unamortized portion of construction allowances received from landlords related to the Company's retail stores. Construction allowances are generally comprised of cash amounts received by the Company from its landlords as part of the negotiated lease terms. The Company records a receivable and a deferred lease credit liability at the lease commencement date (date of initial possession of the store). The deferred lease credit is amortized on a straight-line basis as a reduction of rent expense over the term of the lease (including the pre-opening build-out period) and the receivable is reduced as amounts are received from the landlord.

Self-Insurance Reserve

The Company is self-insured for certain losses related to employee medical benefits. Costs for self-insurance claims filed and claims incurred but not reported are accrued based on known claims and historical experience. Management believes that it has adequately reserved for its self-insurance liability, which is capped through the use of stop loss contracts with insurance companies. However, any significant variation of future claims from historical trends could cause actual results to differ from the accrued liability.

Customer Loyalty Program

During Fiscal 2005, the Company introduce the AE All-Access Pass (the "Pass"), a customer loyalty program. Using the Pass, customers accumulate points based on purchase activity and earn rewards by reaching certain point thersholds during three month earning periods. Rewards earned during these periods are valid through the stated expiration date, which is approximately one month from the mailing date. These rewards can be redeemed for a discount on a purchase of merchandise. Rewards no redeemed during the one month redemption period are forfeited. A current liability is recorded for the estimated cost of anticipated redemptions and the impact of adjustments to the liability is recorded in cost of sales.

Gift Cards

The value of a gift card is recorded as a current liability upon purchase and revenue is recognized when the gift card is redeemed for merchandise. If a gift card remains inactive for greater than 24 months, the Company assesses the recipient a one dollar per month service fee, where allowed by law, which is automatically deducted from the remaining value of the card. For those jurisdictions where assessing a service fee is not allowable by law, the estimated breakage is recorded in a manner consistent with that described above, starting after 24 months of inactivity. Both gift card service fees and breakage estimates are recorded within other income, net.

Derivative Instruments and Hedging Activities

On November 30, 2000, the Company entered into an interest rate swap agreement totaling $29.2 million in connection with a $29.1 million non-revolving term loan facility (the "term facility"). The swap amount decreased on a monthly basis beginning January 1, 2001 until the early termination of the agreement during Fiscal 2004. The Company also retired its term facility for $16.2 million at that time.

In accordance with SFAS No. 133, *Accounting for Derivative Instruments and Hedging Activities*, the Company recognized its derivative on the balance sheet at fair value at the end of each period. Changes in the fair value of the derivative, which was designated and met all the required criteria for a cash flow hedge, were recorded in accumulated other comprehensive income. During Fiscal 2004, the interest rate swap was terminated at its fair value, which represented a net loss of $0.7 million, in conjunction with the payoff of the term facility. As a result, the Company reclassified approximately $0.4 million, net of tax, of unrealized net losses from other comprehensive income into earnings during Fiscal 2004. As of January 28, 2006, the Company did not have any remaining derivative instruments. The Company had no derivative activity during Fiscal 2006.

Stock Repurchases

The Company did not repurchase any shares of its common stock on the open market during Fiscal 2004. During Fiscal 2005, the Company repurchased 10.5 million shares of its common stock under various repurchase authorizations made by the Board. During Fiscal 2006, the Company repurchased the remaining 5.3 million shares of its common stock under the November 15, 2005 authorization for approximately $146.5 million, at a weighted average share price of $27.89. As of February 3, 2007, the Company had no shares remaining authorized for repurchase. See Note 15 of the Consolidated Financial Statements for information on subsequent events related to our stock repurchase program.

Additionally, during Fiscal 2006 and Fiscal 2005, the Company purchased 0.4 million and 0.5 million shares, respectively, from certain employees at market prices totaling $7.6 million and $10.5 million, respectively, for the payment of taxes in connection with the vesting of share-based payments as permitted under the 2005 Stock Award and Incentive Plan and the 1999 Stock Incentive Plan. No shares were repurchased during Fiscal 2004.

The aforementioned share repurchases have been recorded as treasury stock.

Stock Split

On November 13, 2006, the Company's Board approved a three-for-two stock split. This stock split was distributed on December 18, 2006, to stockholders of record on November 24, 2006. All share amounts and per share data presented herein have been restated to reflect this stock split.

Income Taxes

The Company calculates income taxes in accordance with SFAS No. 109, which requires the use of the asset and liability method. Under this method, deferred tax assets and liabilities are recognized based on the difference between the consolidated financial statement carrying amounts of existing assets and liabilities and their respective tax bases. Deferred tax assets and liabilities are measured using the tax rates, based on certain judgments regarding enacted tax laws and published guidance, in effect in the years when those temporary differences are expected to reverse. A valuation allowance is established against the deferred tax assets when it is more likely than not that some portion or all of the deferred taxes may not be realized.

Revenue Recognition

Revenue is recorded for store sales upon the purchase of merchandise by customers. The Company's e-commerce operation records revenue upon the estimated customer receipt date of the merchandise. Prior to Fiscal 2006, these amounts were recorded at the time the goods were shipped. Amounts for prior periods were not adjusted to reflect this change as the amounts were determined to be immaterial.

Revenue is recorded net of estimated and actual sales returns and deductions for coupon redemptions and other promotions. The Company records the impact of adjustments to its sales return reserve quarterly within net sales and cost of sales. The sales return reserve reflects an estimate of sales returns based on projected merchandise returns determined through the use of historical average return percentages. A summary of activity in the sales return reserve account follows:

	For the Years Ended	
(In thousands)	February 3, 2007	January 28, 2006
Beginning balance	$ 3,755	$ 3,369
Returns	(78,290)	(67,668)
Provisions	80,533	68,054
Ending balance	$ 5,998	$ 3,755

Revenue is not recorded on the purchase of gift cards. A current liability is recorded upon purchase and revenue is recognized when the gift card is redeemed for merchandise.

During the three months ended October 28, 2006, the Company began classifying sell-offs of end-of-season, overstock and irregular merchandise on a gross basis, with proceeds and cost of sell-offs recorded in net sales and cost of sales, respectively. Historically, the Company has presented the proceeds and cost of sell-offs on a net basis within cost of sales. For Fiscal 2006, the Company recorded $5.3 million of proceeds and $6.5 million of cost of sell-offs within net sales and cost of sales, respectively. Amounts for prior periods were not adjusted to reflect this change as the amounts were determined to be immaterial.

During Fiscal 2006, the Company reviewed its accounting policies related to revenue recognition. As a result of this review, the Company determined that shipping and handling amounts billed to customers, which were historically recorded as a reduction to cost of sales, should be recorded as revenue. Accordingly, beginning in Fiscal 2006, these amounts are recorded within net sales. As a result of this change, the Company recorded $17.7 million in net sales for Fiscal 2006 and reclassified $12.6 million and $8.4 million for Fiscal 2005 and Fiscal 2004, respectively, from cost of sales to net sales.

Cost of Sales, Including Certain Buying, Occupancy and Warehousing Expenses

Cost of sales consists of merchandise costs, including design, sourcing, importing and inbound freight costs, as well as markdowns, shrinkage and certain promotional costs. Buying, occupancy and warehousing costs consist of compensation, employee benefit expenses and travel for our buyers and certain senior merchandising executives; rent and utilities related to our stores, corporate headquarters, distribution centers and other office space; freight from our distribution centers to the stores; compensation and supplies for our distribution centers, including purchasing, receiving and inspection costs; and shipping and handling costs related to our e-commerce operation.

Selling, General and Administrative Expenses

Selling, general and administrative expenses consist of compensation and employee benefit expenses, including salaries, incentives and related benefits associated with our stores and corporate headquarters. Selling, general and administrative expenses also include advertising costs, supplies for our stores and home office, communication costs, travel and entertainment, leasing costs and services purchased. Selling, general and administrative expenses do not include compensation, employee benefit expenses and travel for our design, sourcing and importing teams, our buyers and our distribution centers as these amounts are recorded in cost of sales.

When the Company closes, remodels or relocates a store prior to the end of its lease term, the remaining net book value of the assets related to the store is recorded as a write-off of assets. Prior to February 3, 2007, the Company recorded this write-off of assets within selling, general and administrative expenses. However, the Company has now determined that classification within depreciation and amortization expense is more appropriate. As a result of this change, the Company recorded $6.1 million related to asset write-offs within depreciation and amortization expense for Fiscal 2006. Prior year amounts of $4.1 million and $1.2 million for Fiscal 2005 and Fiscal 2004, respectively, have been reclassified for comparative purposes.

Advertising Costs

Certain advertising costs, including direct mail, in-store photographs and other promotional costs are expensed when the marketing campaign commences. Costs associated with the production of television advertising are expensed over the life of the campaign. All other advertising costs are expensed as incurred. The Company recognized $64.3 million, $53.3 million and $41.4 million in advertising expense during Fiscal 2006, Fiscal 2005 and Fiscal 2004, respectively.

Design Costs

The Company has certain design costs, including compensation, rent, travel, supplies and samples, which are included in cost of sales as the respective inventory is sold.

Store Pre-Opening Costs

Store pre-opening costs consist primarily of rent, advertising, supplies and payroll expenses. These costs are expensed as incurred.

Other Income, Net

Other income, net consists primarily of interest income, as well as interest expense and foreign currency transaction gain/loss. Beginning in Fiscal 2006, the Company records gift card service fee income in other income, net. These amounts were previously recorded as a reduction to selling, general and administrative expenses. The Company recorded gift card service fee income of $2.3 million in Fiscal 2006. Prior year amounts of $2.4 million and $1.7 million for Fiscal 2005 and Fiscal 2004, respectively, have been reclassified for comparative purposes.

Legal Proceedings and Claims

The Company is subject to certain legal proceedings and claims arising out of the conduct of its business. In accordance with SFAS No. 5, *Accounting for Contingencies* ("SFAS No. 5"), management records a reserve for estimated losses when the loss is probable and the amount can be reasonably estimated. If a range of possible loss exists, the Company records the accrual at the low end of the range, in accordance with FASB Interpretation No. 14, *Reasonable Estimation of the Amount of a Loss – an interpretation of FASB Statement No. 5*. As the Company believes that it has provided adequate reserves, it anticipates that the ultimate outcome of any matter currently pending against the Company will not materially affect the financial position or results of operations of the Company.

Supplemental Disclosures of Cash Flow Information

The table below shows supplemental cash flow information for cash amounts paid during the respective periods:

	For the Years Ended		
(In thousands)	February 3, 2007	January 28, 2006	January 29, 2005
Cash paid during the periods for:			
Income taxes	$204,179	$133,461	$121,138
Interest	$ 19	$ —	$ 1,188

Earnings Per Share

The following table shows the amounts used in computing earnings per share from continuing operations and the effect on income from continuing operations and the weighted average number of shares of potential dilutive common stock (stock options and restricted stock).

	For the Years Ended		
(In thousands)	February 3, 2007	January 28, 2006	January 29, 2005
Income from continuing operations	$387,359	$293,711	$224,232
Weighted average common shares outstanding:			
Basic shares	222,662	227,406	217,725
Dilutive effect of stock options and non-vested restricted stock	5,722	5,625	7,641
Diluted shares	228,384	233,031	225,366

Equity awards to purchase 1,074,004 and 172,500 shares of common stock during Fiscal 2006 and Fiscal 2005, respectively, were outstanding, but were not included in the computation of weighted average diluted common share amounts as the effect of doing so would have been anti-dilutive. Additionally, for Fiscal 2006, 1,034,075 shares of performance based restricted stock were not included in the computation of weighted average diluted common share amounts because the number of shares ultimately issued is contingent on the Company's performance compared to pre-established annual EPS performance goals. For Fiscal 2005, 1,050,036 shares of performance based restricted stock were not included in the computation of weighted average diluted common share amounts due to this contingent issuance.

Segment Information

In accordance with SFAS No. 131, *Disclosures about Segments of an Enterprise and Related Information* ("SFAS No. 131"), the Company has identified four operating segments (American Eagle U.S. retail stores, American Eagle Canadian retail stores, ae.com and MARTIN + OSA) that reflect the basis used internally to review performance and allocate resources. Three of the operating segments (American Eagle U.S. retail stores, American Eagle Canadian retail stores and ae.com, collectively the "AE brand") have been aggregated and are presented as one reportable segment, as permitted by SFAS No. 131, based on their similar economic characteristics, products, production processes, target customers and distribution methods. Our new intimates sub-brand, *aerie* by American Eagle, was not identified as a separate operating segment under SFAS No. 131 as it is reviewed and operated as a component of the operating segments comprising the AE brand. MARTIN + OSA was determined to be immaterial for segment reporting purposes. Therefore, the Company will combine MARTIN + OSA with the AE Brand operating segment as one reportable segment. The Company will continue to monitor the materiality of MARTIN + OSA and will present it as a separate reportable segment at the time it becomes material to the Consolidated Financial Statements. Prior to its disposition, Bluenotes was presented as a separate reportable segment (see Note 9 of the Consolidated Financial Statements).

The following tables present summarized geographical information:

	For the Years Ended		
(In thousands)	February 3, 2007	January 28, 2006	January 29, 2005
Net sales (1):			
United States	$2,562,831	$2,144,429	$1,760,111
Foreign (2)	231,578	177,533	129,536
Total net sales	$2,794,409	$2,321,962	$1,889,647

(1) Bluenotes' net sales amounts have been excluded from all periods as they are being presented in discontinued operations. See Note 9 of the Consolidated Financial Statements for additional information regarding Bluenotes.

(2) Amounts represent sales from American Eagle's Canadian retail stores, as well as ae.com sales, that are billed to and/or shipped to foreign countries.

(In thousands)	February 3, 2007	January 28, 2006
Long-lived assets, net:		
United States	$470,494	$329,050
Foreign (1)	21,101	26,418
Total long-lived assets, net (1)	$491,595	$355,468

(1) Long-lived assets as of January 28, 2006 do not include the assets of NLS subject to the sales agreement entered into during the fourth quarter of Fiscal 2005, as they have been classified as held-for-sale. As of February 3, 2007, there were no remaining assets related to NLS. See Note 9 of the Consolidated Financial Statements for additional information regarding NLS.

Reclassification

Certain reclassifications have been made to the Consolidated Financial Statements for prior periods in order to conform to the Fiscal 2006 presentation, including unaudited quarterly financial information. See Note 14 of the Consolidated Financial Statements.

3. Share-Based Payments

At February 3, 2007, the Company had three share-based compensation plans, which are described below. Prior to January 29, 2006, the Company accounted for these plans under the recognition and measurement provisions of APB No. 25, and related interpretations, as permitted by SFAS No. 123. No share-based employee compensation cost related to stock options was recognized in the Consolidated Statements of Operations prior to January 29, 2006, as all options granted under those plans had an exercise price equal to the market value of the underlying common stock on the date of grant.

Effective January 29, 2006, the Company adopted the fair value recognition provisions of SFAS No. 123(R), using the modified prospective transition method. Under this transition method, share-based compensation cost recognized in Fiscal 2006 includes: (a) compensation cost for all share-based payments granted prior to, but not yet vested as of January 29, 2006, based on the grant date fair value estimated in accordance with the original provisions of SFAS No. 123 and (b) compensation cost for all share-based payments granted subsequent to January 29, 2006, based on the grant date fair value estimated using the Black-Scholes option pricing model. The Company recognizes compensation expense for stock option awards and time-based restricted stock awards on a straight-line basis over the requisite service period of the award (or to an employee's eligible retirement date, if earlier). Performance-based restricted stock awards are recognized as compensation expense based on the fair value of the Company's common stock on the date of grant, the number of shares ultimately expected to vest and the vesting period. Total share-based compensation expense included in the Consolidated Statements of Operations for Fiscal 2006, Fiscal 2005 and Fiscal 2004 was $36.6 million ($22.6 million, net of tax), $19.6 million ($12.1 million, net of tax) and $25.2 million ($15.4 million, net of tax), respectively. In accordance with the modified prospective transition method of SFAS No. 123(R), financial results for prior periods have not been restated.

Historically, for pro forma reporting purposes, the Company had followed the nominal vesting period approach for stock-based compensation awards with retirement eligibility provisions. Under this approach, the Company recognized compensation expense over the vesting period of the award. If an employee retired before the end of the vesting period, any remaining unrecognized compensation cost was recognized at the date of retirement. SFAS No. 123(R) requires recognition of compensation cost under a non-substantive vesting period approach. This approach requires recognition of compensation expense over the period from the grant date to the date retirement eligibility is achieved, if that is expected to occur during the nominal vesting period. Additionally, for awards granted to retirement eligible employees, the full compensation cost of an award must be recognized immediately upon grant. Had the Company applied the non-substantive vesting period approach for retirement eligible employees, there would not have been an impact to our reported pro forma income per common share for Fiscal 2005 or Fiscal 2004. In accordance with SFAS No. 123(R), beginning in Fiscal 2006, the Company applies the non-substantive vesting period approach to new stock award grants that have retirement eligibility provisions.

As a result of adopting SFAS No. 123(R) on January 29, 2006, the Company's income before income taxes and net income were lower by $3.9 million and $2.4 million, respectively, for Fiscal 2006, than if the Company had continued to account for share-based compensation under APB No. 25. Net income per basic and diluted common share are each lower by $0.01 for Fiscal 2006 than if the Company had not adopted SFAS No. 123(R).

Prior to the adoption of SFAS No. 123(R), the Company presented all tax benefits from share-based payments as operating cash flows in the Consolidated Statements of Cash Flows. SFAS No. 123(R) requires that cash flows resulting from the benefits of tax deductions in excess of recognized compensation cost be classified as financing cash flows. Accordingly, for Fiscal 2006, the $19.5 million excess tax benefit from share-based payments classified as a financing cash flow would have been classified as an operating cash flow if the company had not adopted SFAS No. 123(R).

The following table illustrates the effect on net income and income per common share as if the Company had applied the fair value recognition provisions of SFAS No. 123 to employee stock options granted in all periods presented. For purposes of this pro forma disclosure, the fair value for these options was estimated at the date of grant using a Black-Scholes option pricing model and amortized to expense over the options' vesting period.

| | For the Years Ended | |
	January 28, 2006	January 29, 2005
(In thousands, except per share amounts)		
Net Income, as reported	$294,153	$213,343
Add: stock option compensation expense included in reported net income, net of tax	304	1,301
Less: total stock option compensation expense determined under fair value method, net of tax	(9,283)	(10,948)
Pro forma net income	$285,174	$203,696
Basic income per common share:		
As reported	$ 1.29	$ 0.98
Pro forma	$ 1.25	$ 0.94
Diluted income per common share:		
As reported	$ 1.26	$ 0.95
Pro forma	$ 1.22	$ 0.90

Share-based compensation plans

1994 Stock Option Plan

On February 10, 1994, the Company's Board adopted the American Eagle Outfitters, Inc. 1994 Stock Option Plan (the "1994 Plan"). The 1994 Plan provided for the grant of 12,150,000 incentive or non-qualified options to purchase common stock. The 1994 Plan was subsequently amended to increase the shares available for grant to 24,300,000 shares. Additionally, the amendment provided that the maximum number of options that may be granted to any individual may not exceed 8,100,000 shares. The options granted under the 1994 Plan were approved by the Compensation Committee of the Board, primarily vest over five years, and expire ten years from the date of grant. The 1994 Plan terminated on January 2, 2004 with all rights of the optionees and all unexpired options continuing in force and operation after the termination.

1999 Stock Incentive Plan

The 1999 Stock Option Plan (the "1999 Plan") was approved by the stockholders on June 8, 1999. The 1999 Plan authorized 18,000,000 shares for issuance in the form of stock options, stock appreciation rights, restricted stock awards, performance units or performance shares. The 1999 Plan was subsequently amended to increase the shares available for grant to 33,000,000. Additionally, the 1999 Plan provided that the maximum number of shares awarded to any individual may not exceed 9,000,000 shares. The 1999 Plan allowed the Compensation Committee to determine which employees and consultants received awards and the terms and conditions of these awards. The 1999 Plan provided for a grant of 1,875 stock options quarterly (not to be adjusted for stock splits) to each director who is not an officer or employee of the Company starting in August 2003. The Company ceased making these quarterly stock option grants in June 2005. Through February 3, 2007, 33,159,233 non-qualified stock options and 6,708,369 shares of restricted stock were granted under the 1999 Plan to employees and certain non-employees (without considering cancellations to date of awards for 7,758,782 shares). Approximately 33% of the options granted were to vest over eight years after the date of grant but were accelerated as the Company met annual performance goals. Approximately 34% of the options granted under the 1999 Plan vest over three years, 23% vest over five years and the remaining grants vest over one year. All options expire after ten years. Performance-based restricted stock was earned if the Company met established performance goals. The 1999 Plan terminated on June 15, 2005 with all rights of the awardees and all unexpired awards continuing in force and operation after the termination.

2005 Stock Award and Incentive Plan

The 2005 Stock Award and Incentive Plan (the "2005 Plan") was approved by the stockholders on June 15, 2005. The 2005 Plan authorized 18,375,000 shares for issuance, of which 6,375,000 shares are available for full value awards in the form of restricted stock awards, restricted stock units or other full value stock awards and 12,000,000 shares are available for stock options, stock appreciation rights, dividend equivalents, performance awards or other non-full value stock awards. The 2005 Plan provides that the maximum number of shares awarded to any individual may not exceed 6,000,000 shares per year plus the amount of the unused annual limit of the previous year. The 2005 Plan allows the Compensation Committee to determine which employees receive awards and the terms and conditions of these awards. The 2005 Plan provides for grants to directors who are not officers or employees of the Company, which are not to exceed 20,000 shares per year (not to be adjusted for stock splits). Through February 3, 2007, 3,235,231 non-qualified stock options, 1,382,679 shares of restricted stock and 60,582 shares of common stock had been granted under the 2005 Plan to employees and directors (without considering cancellations to date of awards for 287,702 shares). Approximately 98% of the options granted under the 2005 Plan vest over three years and 2% vest over five years. Options were granted for ten and seven-year terms. Approximately 93% of the restricted stock awards are performance-based and are earned if the Company meets established performance goals. The remaining 7% of the restricted stock awards are time-based and vest over three years.

Stock Option Grants

A summary of the Company's stock option activity under all plans for Fiscal 2006 follows:

| | For the Year Ended February 3, 2007 (1) | | | |
	Options	Weighted-Average Exercise Price	Weighted-Average Remaining Contractual Life (In Years)	Average Intrinsic Value (In Thousands)
Outstanding - beginning of year	13,507,365	$ 8.15		
Granted (Exercise price equal to fair value)	3,082,231	$20.24		
Exercised (2)	(3,971,272)	$ 7.29		
Cancelled	(408,982)	$15.36		
Outstanding - end of year	12,209,342	$11.24	5.7	$256,656
Exercisable - end of year	7,666,687	$ 7.76	5.2	$187,950

(1)   As of February 3, 2007, the Company had 9,495,536 shares available for stock option grants.
(2)   Options exercised during Fiscal 2006 ranged in price from $0.85 to $18.03.

The weighted-average grant date fair value of stock options granted during Fiscal 2006, Fiscal 2005 and Fiscal 2004 was $20.24, $17.71 and $10.42, respectively. The aggregate intrinsic value of options exercised during Fiscal 2006, Fiscal 2005 and Fiscal 2004 was $73.4 million, $90.8 million and $76.9 million, respectively. Cash received from the exercise of stock options and the actual tax benefit realized from stock option exercises were $28.4 million and $25.5 million, respectively, for Fiscal 2006.

The fair value of stock options was estimated at the date of grant using a Black-Scholes option pricing model with the following weighted-average assumptions:

| | For the Years Ended | |
Black-Scholes Option Valuation Assumptions	February 3, 2007	January 28, 2006
Risk-free interest rates (1)	4.9%	3.8%
Dividend yield	1.0%	1.1%
Volatility factors of the expected market price of the Company's common stock (2)	41.3%	38.0%
Weighted-average expected term (3)	4 years	5 years
Expected forfeiture rate (4)	8.0%	13.9%

(1)   Based on the U.S. Treasury yield curve in effect at the time of grant with a term consistent with the expected life of our stock options.
(2)   For Fiscal 2006, expected stock price volatility is based on a combination of historical volatility of the Company's common stock and implied volatility. Prior to the adoption of SFAS No. 123(R), expected stock price volatility was estimated using only historical volatility.
(3)   Represents the period of time options are expected to be outstanding. The weighted average expected option term was determined using a combination of the "simplified method" for plain vanilla options, as permitted by SAB No. 107, and past exercise behavior. The "simplified method" calculates the expected term as the average of the vesting term and original contractual term of the options. The weighted average expected option term for Fiscal 2005 is based upon historical experience.
(4)   Based upon historical experience.

As of February 3, 2007, there was $16.5 million of unrecognized compensation expense related to nonvested stock option awards that is expected to be recognized over a weighted average period of 1.9 years.

Restricted Stock Grants

Under the 2005 Plan, the fair value of restricted stock awards is based on the closing market price of the Company's common stock on the date of grant. A summary of the activity of the Company's restricted stock is presented in the following tables.

Time-Based Restricted Stock	For the Year Ended February 3, 2007	
	Shares	Weighted-Average Grant Date Fair Value
Nonvested - January 29, 2006 (1)	90,000	$ 9.63
Granted	93,000	$20.02
Vested	(45,000)	$ 9.63
Cancelled	-	-
Nonvested - February 3, 2007	138,000	$16.63

(1) Nonvested time-based restricted stock at January 29, 2006 is related to an award that was issued under the 1999 Plan. Under this plan, time-based awards were valued using the average of the high and low market price of the Company's common stock on the date of grant.

Performance-Based Restricted Stock	For the Year Ended February 3, 2007	
	Shares	Weighted-Average Grant Date Fair Value
Nonvested - January 29, 2006 (1)	1,050,036	$17.36
Granted	1,089,429	$17.88
Vested	(1,050,036)	$17.36
Cancelled	(55,354)	$16.98
Nonvested - February 3, 2007	1,034,075	$17.93

(1) Nonvested performance-based restricted stock at January 29, 2006 includes awards issued under the 1999 Plan and the 2005 Plan. Under the 1999 Plan, awards were valued using the average of the high and low market price of the Company's common stock at the end of the performance period. Under the 2005 Plan, awards were valued using the closing price of the Company's common stock at the end of the performance period.

As of February 3, 2007, there was $3.1 million of unrecognized compensation expense related to nonvested restricted stock awards that is expected to be recognized over a weighted average period of 10 months. The total fair value of restricted stock awards vested during Fiscal 2006 and Fiscal 2005 was $18.9 million and $25.9 million, respectively. No restricted stock awards vested during Fiscal 2004.

4. Accounts and Note Receivable

Accounts and note receivable are comprised of the following:

(In thousands)	February 3, 2007	January 28, 2006
Construction allowances	$ 9,345	$ 8,212
Merchandise sell-offs	2,488	6,904
Taxes	1,012	1,860
Distribution services	-	1,618
Interest income	7,251	2,982
Property insurance claims	2,530	4,081
Other	3,419	3,489
Total	$26,045	$29,146

5. Property and Equipment

Property and equipment consists of the following:

(In thousands)	February 3, 2007	January 28, 2006
Land	$ 6,869	$ 4,284
Buildings	34,093	30,682
Leasehold improvements	434,881	391,820
Fixtures and equipment	289,828	239,139
Construction in progress	92,019	1,098
	$ 857,690	$ 667,023
Less: Accumulated depreciation and amortization	(376,045)	(321,505)
Net property and equipment	$ 481,645	$ 345,518

Amounts as of January 28, 2006 reflect certain assets of NLS as held-for-sale. As of February 3, 2007, there were no remaining assets related to NLS. See Note 9 of the Consolidated Financial Statements for additional information regarding assets held-for-sale.

Depreciation expense is summarized as follows:

	For the Years Ended		
(In thousands)	February 3, 2007	January 28, 2006	January 29, 2005
Depreciation expense	$87,869	$77,372	$67,495

6. Note Payable and Other Credit Arrangements

Pennsylvania Industrial Development Authority Loan

During Fiscal 2006, the Company entered into an agreement with the Pennsylvania Industrial Development Authority ("PIDA") to borrow approximately $2.2 million with a fixed interest rate of 3.25% and a maturity date of October 1, 2021. The proceeds from the PIDA loan were restricted for construction costs related to the Company's new home office building in Pittsburgh, Pennsylvania. During the three months ended October 28, 2006, the Company received approximately $2.0 million of the proceeds. During the fourth quarter, prior to the receipt of the remaining $0.2 million, the Company repaid the outstanding principal balance of the loan in full and terminated the loan agreement. A nominal amount of interest was paid under the PIDA loan during Fiscal 2006.

Unsecured Demand Lending Arrangement

During Fiscal 2006, the Company received a temporary increase in the amount available for letters of credit under its unsecured demand lending agreement. This increase will be used to support commitments for merchandise inventory purchases and will remain in place until terminated by the Company. As a result of the increase, the Company has a $130.0 million unsecured letter of credit facility for letters of credit and a $40.0 million unsecured demand line of credit that can be used for letters of credit and/or direct borrowing, totaling $170.0 million. The interest rate is at the lender's prime lending rate (8.25% at February 3, 2007) or at LIBOR plus a negotiated margin rate. Because there were no direct borrowings during any of the past three years, there were no amounts paid for interest on this facility. At February 3, 2007, letters of credit in the amount of $70.5 million were outstanding on this facility, leaving a remaining available balance on the line of $99.5 million.

Uncommitted Letter of Credit Facility

During Fiscal 2006, the Company also received a temporary increase in the amount available for letters of credit under its uncommitted letter of credit facility with a separate financial institution. This increase will be used to support commitments for merchandise inventory purchases and will remain in place until terminated by the Company. As a result of the increase, the Company has an uncommitted letter of credit facility for $100.0 million. At February 3, 2007, letters of credit in the amount of $48.3 million were outstanding on this facility, leaving a remaining available balance on the line of $51.7 million.

Non-revolving Term Facility

During Fiscal 2004, the Company retired its $29.1 million non-revolving term facility (the "term facility") for $16.2 million. The term facility required annual payments of $4.8 million, with interest at the one-month Bankers' Acceptance Rate plus 140 basis points, and was originally scheduled to mature in December 2007. Interest paid under the term facility was $1.2 million for Fiscal 2004.

7. Other Comprehensive Income

The accumulated balances of other comprehensive income included as part of the Consolidated Statements of Stockholders' Equity follow:

(In thousands)	Before Tax Amount	Tax (Expense) Benefit	Other Comprehensive Income
Balance at January 31, 2004	**$ 6,078**	**$(2,389)**	**$ 3,689**
Unrealized loss on investments	(372)	145	(227)
Reclassification adjustment for gain realized in net income related to sale of available-for-sale securities	(6)	2	(4)
Foreign currency translation adjustment (1)	4,581	2,734	7,315
Reclassification adjustment for loss realized in net income related to the disposition of Bluenotes	2,467	-	2,467
Unrealized derivative gains on cash flow hedge	116	(45)	71
Reclassification adjustment for losses realized in net income related to termination of the cash flow hedge	714	(277)	437
Balance at January 29, 2005	**13,578**	**170**	**13,748**
Unrealized loss on investments	(1,072)	430	(642)
Reclassification adjustment for losses realized in net income related to sale of available-for-sale securities	159	(60)	99
Foreign currency translation adjustment	8,823	-	8,823
Balance at January 28, 2006	**21,488**	**540**	**22,028**
Unrealized loss on investments	(276)	85	(191)
Reclassification adjustment for losses realized in net income related to sale of available-for-sale securities	578	(222)	356
Reclassification adjustment for gain realized in net income related to the transfer of investment securities from available-for-sale classification to trading classification	(287)	110	(177)
Foreign currency translation adjustment	(1,180)	-	(1,180)
Reclassification adjustment for loss realized in net income related to the disposition of National Logistics Services	878	-	878
Balance at February 3, 2007	**$21,201**	**$ 513**	**$21,714**

(1) During Fiscal 2004, the Company reclassified the income tax provision related to its foreign currency translation gains, as it is the Company's intention to utilize the earnings of its foreign subsidiaries in the foreign operations for an indefinite period of time. See Note 10 of the Consolidated Financial Statements for additional information.

The components of accumulated other comprehensive income were as follows:

(In thousands)	For the Years Ended	
	February 3, 2007	January 28, 2006
Net unrealized losses on available-for-sale securities, net of tax	$ (811)	$ (799)
Foreign currency translation adjustment	22,525	22,827
Accumulated other comprehensive income	$21,714	$22,028

8. Leases

The Company leases all store premises, some of its office space and certain information technology and office equipment. The store leases generally have initial terms of ten years. Most of these store leases provide for base rentals and the payment of a percentage of sales as additional rent when sales exceed specified levels. Additionally, most leases contain construction allowances and/or rent holidays. In recognizing landlord incentives and minimum rent expense, the Company amortizes the charges on a straight line basis over the lease term (including the pre-opening build-out period). These leases are classified as operating leases.

A summary of fixed minimum and contingent rent expense for all operating leases follows:

| | For the Years Ended | | |
| | February 3, 2007 | January 28, 2006 | January 29, 2005 |
(In thousands)			
Store rent:			
Fixed minimum	$145,519	$136,876	$124,507
Contingent	19,138	13,248	6,788
Total store rent, excluding common area maintenance charges, real estate taxes and certain other expenses	164,657	150,124	131,295
Offices, distribution facilities, equipment and other	12,540	10,752	11,265
Total rent expense	$177,197	$160,876	$142,560

In addition, the Company is typically responsible under its store, office and distribution center leases for common area maintenance charges, real estate taxes and certain other expenses.

The table below summarizes future minimum lease obligations, consisting of fixed minimum rent, under operating leases in effect at February 3, 2007:

Fiscal years: (In thousands)	Future Minimum Lease Obligations
2007	$ 166,582
2008	168,450
2009	163,394
2010	151,500
2011	132,763
Thereafter	398,477
Total	$1,181,166

9. Assets Held-for-Sale and Discontinued Operations

On January 27, 2006, the Company entered into an asset purchase agreement (the "Agreement") with the NLS Purchaser, a privately held Canadian company, for the sale of certain assets of NLS. During February 2006, the Company completed this transaction with an effective date of February 28, 2006. In accordance with SFAS No. 144, the accompanying Consolidated Balance Sheet as of January 28, 2006 reflects the assets subject to the Agreement as held-for-sale. As of February 3, 2007, there were no remaining assets related to NLS. An impairment loss of $0.6 million was recorded in selling, general and administrative expenses on the Company's Consolidated Statement of Operations during Fiscal 2005 to record these assets at their fair value less costs to sell. Additionally, a $0.3 million loss was recorded in cost of sales during Fiscal 2006 to record the obligation related to the remaining lease term at a former NLS distribution sub-center location. These losses were partially offset by a $0.1 million adjustment to the fair value of the assets upon final disposition, which was recorded in selling, general and administrative expenses during Fiscal 2006.

During December 2004, the Company completed its disposition of Bluenotes to the Bluenotes Purchaser. The transaction had an effective date of December 5, 2004. The accompanying Consolidated Statements of Operations and Consolidated Statements of Cash Flows reflect Bluenotes' results of operations as discontinued operations for all periods presented. As of January 28, 2006, there were no remaining amounts recorded in the Company's Consolidated Balance Sheets related to Bluenotes.

The Company received approximately $23 million as consideration for the sale of certain of its Bluenotes assets, including inventory and property and equipment. The transaction resulted in an after-tax loss of $4.8 million, or $0.02 per diluted share, during Fiscal 2004 and was partially offset by net income from the disposition of $0.4 million during Fiscal 2005. Additionally, during Fiscal 2005, the Company recorded a $6.0 million income tax benefit related to the completion of the Bluenotes' disposition. At this time, the realization of the aforementioned income tax benefit is uncertain. As a result, the Company has recorded a reserve for the full amount.

The operating results of Bluenotes, which are being presented as discontinued operations, were as follows:

(In thousands)	January 28, 2006	January 29, 2005
Net sales	$ -	$ 69,825
Loss from operations, net of tax	$ -	$ (6,070)
Income (loss) on disposition, net of tax	442	(4,819)
Income (loss) from discontinued operations, net of tax (1)	$442	$(10,889)

(1) Amounts are net of tax (expense) benefit of $(0.3) million and $3.9 million, respectively.

10. Income Taxes

The components of income from continuing operations before taxes on income were:

(In thousands)	February 3, 2007	January 28, 2006	January 29, 2005
U.S.	$561,178	$448,442	$339,328
Foreign	67,889	28,525	27,507
Total	$629,067	$476,967	$366,835

The significant components of the Company's deferred tax assets and liabilities were as follows:

(In thousands)	February 3, 2007	January 28, 2006
Deferred tax assets:		
Current:		
Inventories	$ 8,668	$ 7,018
Rent	16,963	16,393
Deferred compensation	13,224	12,315
Capital loss	-	1,173
Valuation allowance	-	(477)
Other	8,877	6,663
Total current deferred tax assets	47,732	43,085
Long-term:		
Deferred compensation	25,167	13,435
Property and equipment	953	2,194
Other	4,220	1,783
Total long-term deferred tax assets	30,340	17,412
Total deferred tax assets	$78,072	$60,497
Deferred tax liabilities:		
Property and equipment	$12,080	$22,077
Total deferred tax liabilities	$12,080	$22,077

The net change in the deferred tax assets and liabilities increased by $27.6 million primarily due to an increase in share-based payments and incentives, as well as a reduction of property and equipment deferred tax liabilities.

Significant components of the provision for income taxes are as follows:

	For the Years Ended		
(In thousands)	February 3, 2007	January 28, 2006	January 29, 2005
Current:			
Federal	$235,666	$152,416	$130,988
State	33,614	26,722	24,338
Total current	269,280	179,138	155,326
Deferred:			
Federal	(26,141)	(3,387)	(18,860)
Foreign taxes	2,694	8,109	9,572
State	(4,125)	(604)	(3,435)
Total deferred	(27,572)	4,118	(12,723)
Provision for income taxes	$241,708	$183,256	$142,603

As a result of additional tax deductions related to share-based payments, tax benefits have been recognized as contributed capital for the years ended February 3, 2007, January 28, 2006 and January 29, 2005 in the amounts of $25.5 million, $35.4 million and $28.8 million, respectively.

In December 2004, the FASB issued Staff Position No. FAS 109-2, *Accounting and Disclosure Guidance for the Foreign Earnings Repatriation Provision within the American Jobs Creation Act of 2004* ("FSP No. 109-2"). FSP No. 109-2 provides guidance to companies to determine how the American Jobs Creation Act of 2004 (the

"Act") affects a company's accounting for the deferred tax liabilities on un-remitted foreign earnings. The Act provides for a special one-time deduction of 85% of certain foreign earnings that are repatriated and that meet certain requirements. During Fiscal 2006, the Company repatriated $83.4 million as extraordinary dividends from its Canadian subsidiaries. As a result of the repatriation, the Company recognized total income tax expense of $4.4 million, of which $3.8 million was recorded during Fiscal 2005 and $0.6 million was recorded during Fiscal 2006.

The decision to take advantage of the special one-time deduction under the Act is a discrete event, and it has not changed the Company's intention to indefinitely reinvest accumulated earnings from its Canadian operations to the extent not repatriated under the Act. Accordingly, no provision will be made for income taxes that would be payable upon the distributions of such earnings.

Income tax accruals of $57.9 million and $19.8 million were recorded at February 3, 2007 and January 28, 2006, respectively. As of February 3, 2007, contingent tax reserves of approximately $16.9 million were recorded, of which $8.5 million related to potential state and local income tax liabilities.

As of February 3, 2007, the Company had a deferred tax asset of $1.4 million relating to certain state tax credits that can be used to offset state income tax. The credits will expire over a period from July 2012 to July 2014. No valuation allowance has been provided against this deferred tax asset as the Company believes that it is more likely than not that the benefit of this asset will be realized prior to the expiration dates of the tax credits.

A reconciliation between the statutory federal income tax rate and the effective tax rate from continuing operations follows:

	For the Years Ended		
	February 3, 2007	January 28, 2006	January 29, 2005
Federal income tax rate	35%	35%	35%
State income taxes, net of federal income tax effect	4	4	4
Accrued tax on unremitted Canadian earnings	-	1	-
State tax credits, net of federal income tax effect	-	(1)	-
Tax impact of tax exempt interest	(1)	(1)	-
	38%	38%	39%

11. Retirement Plan and Employee Stock Purchase Plan

The Company maintains a profit sharing and 401(k) plan (the "Retirement Plan"). Under the provisions of the Retirement Plan, full-time employees and part-time employees are automatically enrolled to contribute 3% of their salary if they have attained 21 years of age, have completed 60 days of service and work at least 20 hours per week. Individuals can decline enrollment or can contribute up to 30% of their salary to the 401(k) plan on a pretax basis, subject to IRS limitations. After one year of service, the Company will match up to 4.5% of participants' eligible compensation. Contributions to the profit sharing plan, as determined by the Board, are discretionary. The Company recognized $6.9 million in expense during Fiscal 2006 and $4.8 million in expense during both Fiscal 2005 and Fiscal 2004 in connection with the Retirement Plan.

The Employee Stock Purchase Plan is a non-qualified plan that covers all full-time employees and part-time employees who are at least 18 years old, have completed 60 days of service and work at least 20 hours per week. Contributions are determined by the employee, with the Company matching 15% of the investment up to a maximum investment of $100 per pay period. These contributions are used to purchase shares of Company stock in the open market.

12. Related Party Transactions

The Company and its wholly-owned subsidiaries historically had various transactions with related parties. The nature of the Company's relationship with the related parties and a description of the respective transactions is stated below.

As of February 3, 2007, the Schottenstein-Deshe-Diamond families (the "families") owned approximately 13% of the outstanding shares of Common Stock of the Company. The families also own a private company, Schottenstein Stores Corporation ("SSC"), which includes a publicly-traded subsidiary, Retail Ventures, Inc. ("RVI"), formerly Value City Department Stores, Inc., and also owned 99% of Linmar Realty Company II ("Linmar Realty") until June 4, 2004. During Fiscal 2004, the Company implemented a strategic plan to eliminate related party transactions with the families. As a result, we did not have any material transactions remaining with the families subsequent to January 28, 2006. We believe that the terms of the prior transactions were as favorable to the Company as those that could have been obtained from unrelated third parties.

During Fiscal 2004, the Company, through a subsidiary, Linmar Realty Company II LLC, acquired for $20.0 million Linmar Realty Company II, a general partnership that owned the Company's corporate headquarters and distribution center. The acquisition price, less a straight-line rent accrual adjustment of $2.0 million, was recorded as land and building on the consolidated balance sheet during Fiscal 2004 and is being depreciated over its anticipated useful life of twenty-five years. Prior to the acquisition, the Company had an operating lease with Linmar Realty for these properties. Rent expense under the lease was $0.8 million during Fiscal 2004.

The Company and its subsidiaries sell end-of-season, overstock and irregular merchandise to various parties, which have historically included RVI. During April 2004, the Company entered into an agreement with an independent third-party vendor for the sale of merchandise sell-offs, thus reducing sell-offs to related parties. As a result, there have been no sell-offs of merchandise to related parties since the date of the agreement. Prior to the agreement, during Fiscal 2004, $0.1 million of merchandise, at cost, was sold to RVI. See Note 2 of the Consolidated Financial Statements for additional information regarding merchandise sell-offs.

Prior to the implementation of the Company's plan to eliminate related party transactions, SSC and its affiliates charged the Company for various professional services provided, including certain legal, real estate and insurance services. For Fiscal 2004, the Company paid approximately $0.2 million for these services.

During Fiscal 2004, the Company discontinued its cost sharing arrangement with SSC for the acquisition of an interest in several corporate aircraft. The Company paid $0.1 million during Fiscal 2004 to cover its share of operating costs based on usage of the corporate aircraft under the cost sharing arrangement. No payments were made during Fiscal 2005 or 2006, as a result of the discontinuation of this arrangement.

See Part III, Item 13 of this Form 10-K for additional information regarding related party transactions.

13. Contingencies

Guarantees

In connection with the disposition of Bluenotes, the Company has provided guarantees related to two store leases that were assigned to the Bluenotes Purchaser. These guarantees were provided to the applicable landlords and will remain in effect until the leases expire in 2007 and 2015, respectively. The lease guarantees require the Company to make all required payments under the lease agreements in the event of default by the Bluenotes Purchaser. The maximum potential amount of future payments (undiscounted) that the Company could be required to make under the guarantees is approximately $1.1 million as of February 3, 2007. In the event that the Company would be required to make any such payments, it would pursue full reimbursement from YM, Inc., a related party of the Bluenotes Purchaser, in accordance with the Bluenotes Asset Purchase Agreement.

In accordance with FIN No. 45, as the Company issued the guarantees at the time it became secondarily liable under a new lease, no amounts have been accrued in the Company's Consolidated Financial Statements related to these guarantees. Management believes that it is unlikely that the Company will be required to perform under the guarantees.

14. Quarterly Financial Information - Unaudited

The sum of the quarterly EPS amounts may not equal the full year amount as the computations of the weighted average shares outstanding for each quarter and the full year are calculated independently.

	Quarters Ended (1)			
(In thousands, except per share amounts)	April 30, 2005	July 30, 2005	October 29, 2005	January 28, 2006
Net sales	$456,477	$515,868	$580,547	$769,070
Gross profit	222,723	228,476	270,096	356,454
Income from continuing operations, net of tax	55,184	58,034	73,357	107,136
Income (loss) from discontinued operations, net of tax	89	(15)	(37)	405
Net income	55,273	58,019	73,320	107,541
Basic per common share amounts:				
Income from continuing operations	0.24	0.25	0.32	0.48
Loss from discontinued operations	-	-	-	-
Net income per basic share	0.24	0.25	0.32	0.48
Diluted per common share amounts:				
Income from continuing operations	0.24	0.25	0.31	0.47
Loss from discontinued operations	-	-	-	-
Net income per diluted share	0.24	0.25	0.31	0.47

	Quarters Ended (1)			
(In thousands, except per share amounts)	April 29, 2006	July 29, 2006	October 28, 2006	February 3, 2007
Net sales	$522,428	$602,326	$696,290	$973,365
Gross profit	254,369	275,261	344,324	466,475
Net income	64,156	72,099	100,945	150,159
Basic income per common share	0.29	0.32	0.45	0.68
Diluted income per common share	0.28	0.31	0.44	0.66

(1)   Quarters are presented in 13 week periods consistent with the Company's fiscal year discussed in Note 2 of the Consolidated Financial Statements, except for the fourth quarter ended February 3, 2007, which is presented as a 14 week period.

15. Subsequent Event

On March 6, 2007, the Company's Board authorized an additional 7.0 million shares of its common stock to be repurchased under the Company's share repurchase program. Subsequent to this authorization, the Company repurchased 2.8 million shares of its common stock. The shares were repurchased for approximately $85.2 million, at a weighted average share price of $30.42. As of March 30, 2007, the Company had 4.2 million shares remaining authorized for repurchase. These shares will be repurchased at the Company's discretion. See Note 2 of the Consolidated Financial Statements for additional information regarding our repurchase program.

On March 8, 2007, shares of the Company's common stock began trading on the New York Stock Exchange under the symbol "AEO." Prior to March 8, 2007, shares of the Company's common stock traded on the NASDAQ Stock Market.

ITEM 9. CHANGES IN AND DISAGREEMENTS WITH ACCOUNTANTS ON ACCOUNTING AND FINANCIAL DISCLOSURE.

None.

ITEM 9A. CONTROLS AND PROCEDURES.

Disclosure Controls and Procedures

We maintain disclosure controls and procedures that are designed to provide reasonable assurance that information required to be disclosed in our reports under the Securities Exchange Act of 1934, as amended (the "Exchange Act"), is recorded, processed, summarized and reported within the time periods specified in the SEC's rules and forms, and that such information is accumulated and communicated to the management of American Eagle Outfitters, Inc. (the "Management"), including our Principal Executive Officer and our Principal Financial Officer, as appropriate, to allow timely decisions regarding required disclosure. In designing and evaluating the disclosure controls and procedures, Management recognized that any controls and procedures, no matter how well designed and operated, can provide only reasonable assurance of achieving the desired control objectives.

In connection with the preparation of this Annual Report on Form 10-K as of February 3, 2007, an evaluation was performed under the supervision and with the participation of our Management, including the Principal Executive Officer and Principal Financial Officer, of the effectiveness of the design and operation of the Company's disclosure controls and procedures (as defined in Rule 13a-15(e) under the Exchange Act). Based upon that evaluation, our Principal Executive Officer and our Principal Financial Officer have concluded that our disclosure controls and procedures were effective at the reasonable assurance level as of the end of the period covered by this Annual Report on Form 10-K.

Management's Annual Report on Internal Control Over Financial Reporting

Our Management is responsible for establishing and maintaining adequate internal control over financial reporting (as defined in Rule 13a-15(f) under the Exchange Act). Our internal control over financial reporting is designed to provide a reasonable assurance to our Management and our Board regarding the preparation and fair presentation of published financial statements.

All internal control systems, no matter how well designed have inherent limitations. Therefore, even those systems determined to be effective can provide only reasonable assurance with respect to financial statement preparation and presentation.

Our Management assessed the effectiveness of our internal control over financial reporting as of February 3, 2007. In making this assessment, our Management used the criteria set forth by the Committee of Sponsoring Organizations of the Treadway Commission (COSO) in Internal Control – Integrated Framework. Based on this assessment, our Management concluded that we maintained effective internal control over financial reporting as of February 3, 2007.

Our Management's assessment of the effectiveness of internal control over financial reporting as of February 3, 2007, has been audited by Ernst & Young LLP, the independent registered public accounting firm who also audited our Consolidated Financial Statements. Ernst & Young's attestation report on Management's assessment of our internal control over financial reporting is located below.

Changes in Internal Control Over Financial Reporting

There were no changes in our internal control over financial reporting during the three months ended February 3, 2007 that have materially affected, or are reasonably likely to materially affect, our internal control over financial reporting.

Report of Independent Registered Public Accounting Firm

The Board of Directors and Stockholders of
American Eagle Outfitters, Inc.

We have audited management's assessment, included in the accompanying Management's Annual Report on Internal Control over Financial Reporting, that American Eagle Outfitters, Inc. (the "Company") maintained effective internal control over financial reporting as of February 3, 2007, based on criteria established in Internal Control – Integrated Framework issued by the Committee of Sponsoring Organizations of the Treadway Commission (the COSO criteria). American Eagle Outfitters, Inc.'s management is responsible for maintaining effective internal control over financial reporting and for its assessment of the effectiveness of internal control over financial reporting. Our responsibility is to express an opinion on management's assessment and an opinion on the effectiveness of the Company's internal control over financial reporting based on our audit.

We conducted our audit in accordance with the standards of the Public Company Accounting Oversight Board (United States). Those standards require that we plan and perform the audit to obtain reasonable assurance about whether effective internal control over financial reporting was maintained in all material respects. Our audit included obtaining an understanding of internal control over financial reporting, evaluating management's assessment, testing and evaluating the design and operating effectiveness of internal control, and performing such other procedures as we considered necessary in the circumstances. We believe that our audit provides a reasonable basis for our opinion.

A company's internal control over financial reporting is a process designed to provide reasonable assurance regarding the reliability of financial reporting and the preparation of financial statements for external purposes in accordance with generally accepted accounting principles. A company's internal control over financial reporting includes those policies and procedures that (1) pertain to the maintenance of records that, in reasonable detail, accurately and fairly reflect the transactions and dispositions of the assets of the company; (2) provide reasonable assurance that transactions are recorded as necessary to permit preparation of financial statements in accordance with generally accepted accounting principles, and that receipts and expenditures of the company are being made only in accordance with authorizations of management and directors of the company; and (3) provide reasonable assurance regarding prevention or timely detection of unauthorized acquisition, use, or disposition of the company's assets that could have a material effect on the financial statements.

Because of its inherent limitations, internal control over financial reporting may not prevent or detect misstatements. Also, projections of any evaluation of effectiveness to future periods are subject to the risk that controls may become inadequate because of changes in conditions, or that the degree of compliance with the policies or procedures may deteriorate.

In our opinion, management's assessment that American Eagle Outfitters, Inc. maintained effective internal control over financial reporting as of February 3, 2007, is fairly stated, in all material respects, based on the COSO criteria. Also, in our opinion, American Eagle Outfitters, Inc. maintained, in all material respects, effective internal control over financial reporting as of February 3, 2007, based on the COSO criteria.

We also have audited, in accordance with the standards of the Public Company Accounting Oversight Board (United States), the consolidated balance sheets of American Eagle Outfitters, Inc. as of February 3, 2007 and January 28, 2006, and the related consolidated statements of operations, comprehensive income, stockholders' equity, and cash flows for each of the three fiscal years in the period ended February 3, 2007 and our report dated April 2, 2007 expressed an unqualified opinion thereon.

/s/ Ernst & Young LLP

Pittsburgh, Pennsylvania
April 2, 2007

SIGNATURES

Pursuant to the requirements of Section 13 or 15(d) of the Securities Exchange Act of 1934, the Registrant has duly caused this report to be signed on its behalf by the undersigned, thereunto duly authorized.

Dated April 4, 2007

AMERICAN EAGLE OUTFITTERS, INC.
By: /s/ James V. O'Donnell
James V. O'Donnell
Chief Executive Officer

Pursuant to the requirements of the Securities Exchange Act of 1934, this report has been signed by the following persons in the capacities indicated on April 4, 2007.

Signature	Title
/s/ James V. O'Donnell James V. O'Donnell	Chief Executive Officer and Director (Principal Executive Officer)
/s/ Joan Holstein Hilson Joan Holstein Hilson	Executive Vice President and Chief Financial Officer, AE Brand (Principal Financial Officer and Principal Accounting Officer)
* Jay L. Schottenstein	Chairman of the Board and Director
* Jon P. Diamond	Director
* Michael G. Jesselson	Director
* Alan Kane	Director
* Roger S. Markfield	Director
* Janice E. Page	Director
* J. Thomas Presby	Director
* Gerald E. Wedren	Director
* Larry M. Wolf	Director

*By: /s/ Joan Holstein Hilson
       Joan Holstein Hilson, Attorney-in-Fact

Exhibit 31.1

CERTIFICATIONS

I, James V. O'Donnell, certify that:

1.   I have reviewed this Annual Report on Form 10-K of American Eagle Outfitters, Inc.;

2.   Based on my knowledge, this report does not contain any untrue statement of a material fact or omit to state a material fact necessary to make the statements made, in light of the circumstances under which such statements were made, not misleading with respect to the period covered by this report;

3.   Based on my knowledge, the financial statements, and other financial information included in this report, fairly present in all material respects the financial condition, results of operations and cash flows of the registrant as of, and for, the periods presented in this report;

4.   The registrant's other certifying officer(s) and I are responsible for establishing and maintaining disclosure controls and procedures (as defined in Exchange Act Rules 13a-15(e) and 15d-15(e)) and internal control over financial reporting (as defined in Exchange Act Rules 13a-15(f) and 15d-15(f)) for the registrant and have:

   a) Designed such disclosure controls and procedures, or caused such disclosure controls and procedures to be designed under our supervision, to ensure that material information relating to the registrant, including its consolidated subsidiaries, is made known to us by others within those entities, particularly during the period in which this report is being prepared;

   b) Designed such internal control over financial reporting, or caused such internal control over financial reporting to be designed under our supervision, to provide reasonable assurance regarding the reliability of financial reporting and the preparation of financial statements for external purposes in accordance with generally accepted accounting principles;

   c) Evaluated the effectiveness of the registrant's disclosure controls and procedures and presented in this report our conclusions about the effectiveness of the disclosure controls and procedures, as of the end of the period covered by this report based on such evaluation; and

   d) Disclosed in this report any change in the registrant's internal control over financial reporting that occurred during the registrant's most recent fiscal quarter (the registrant's fourth fiscal quarter in the case of an annual report) that has materially affected, or is reasonably likely to materially affect, the registrant's internal control over financial reporting; and

5.   The registrant's other certifying officer(s) and I have disclosed, based on our most recent evaluation of internal control over financial reporting, to the registrant's auditors and the audit committee of the registrant's board of directors (or persons performing the equivalent functions):

   a) All significant deficiencies and material weaknesses in the design or operation of internal control over financial reporting which are reasonably likely to adversely affect the registrant's ability to record, process, summarize and report financial information; and

   b) Any fraud, whether or not material, that involves management or other employees who have a significant role in the registrant's internal control over financial reporting.

April 4, 2007
/s/ James V. O'Donnell
James V. O'Donnell
Chief Executive Officer
(Principal Executive Officer)

Exhibit 31.2

CERTIFICATIONS

I, Joan Holstein Hilson, certify that:

1. I have reviewed this Annual Report on Form 10-K of American Eagle Outfitters, Inc.;

2. Based on my knowledge, this report does not contain any untrue statement of a material fact or omit to state a material fact necessary to make the statements made, in light of the circumstances under which such statements were made, not misleading with respect to the period covered by this report;

3. Based on my knowledge, the financial statements, and other financial information included in this report, fairly present in all material respects the financial condition, results of operations and cash flows of the registrant as of, and for, the periods presented in this report;

4. The registrant's other certifying officer(s) and I are responsible for establishing and maintaining disclosure controls and procedures (as defined in Exchange Act Rules 13a-15(e) and 15d-15(e)) and internal control over financial reporting (as defined in Exchange Act Rules 13a-15(f) and 15d-15(f)) for the registrant and have:

    a) Designed such disclosure controls and procedures, or caused such disclosure controls and procedures to be designed under our supervision, to ensure that material information relating to the registrant, including its consolidated subsidiaries, is made known to us by others within those entities, particularly during the period in which this report is being prepared;

    b) Designed such internal control over financial reporting, or caused such internal control over financial reporting to be designed under our supervision, to provide reasonable assurance regarding the reliability of financial reporting and the preparation of financial statements for external purposes in accordance with generally accepted accounting principles;

    c) Evaluated the effectiveness of the registrant's disclosure controls and procedures and presented in this report our conclusions about the effectiveness of the disclosure controls and procedures, as of the end of the period covered by this report based on such evaluation; and

    d) Disclosed in this report any change in the registrant's internal control over financial reporting that occurred during the registrant's most recent fiscal quarter (the registrant's fourth fiscal quarter in the case of an annual report) that has materially affected, or is reasonably likely to materially affect, the registrant's internal control over financial reporting; and

5. The registrant's other certifying officer(s) and I have disclosed, based on our most recent evaluation of internal control over financial reporting, to the registrant's auditors and the audit committee of the registrant's board of directors (or persons performing the equivalent functions):

    a) All significant deficiencies and material weaknesses in the design or operation of internal control over financial reporting which are reasonably likely to adversely affect the registrant's ability to record, process, summarize and report financial information; and

    b) Any fraud, whether or not material, that involves management or other employees who have a significant role in the registrant's internal control over financial reporting.

April 4, 2007
/s/ Joan Holstein Hilson
Joan Holstein Hilson
Executive Vice President and Chief Financial Officer, AE Brand
(Principal Financial Officer and Principal Accounting Officer)

DIRECTORS, OFFICERS AND STOCKHOLDER INFORMATION

BOARD OF DIRECTORS	EXECUTIVE OFFICERS	CORPORATE OFFICERS
JAY L. SCHOTTENSTEIN Chairman of the Board	**JAY L. SCHOTTENSTEIN** Chairman of the Board	**JOHN BEZEK** Vice President, Construction
JAMES V. O'DONNELL Chief Executive Officer	**JAMES V. O'DONNELL** Chief Executive Officer	**GUY BRADFORD** Executive Vice President, Blue Star Imports; Customs Compliance Officer
ROGER S. MARKFIELD Former President and Vice Chairman of the Board	**SUSAN P. MCGALLA** President and Chief Merchandising Officer	**NEIL BULMAN, JR.** Vice President, General Counsel and Secretary
JON P. DIAMOND President and Chief Operating Officer of Safe Auto Insurance Company	**THOMAS A. DIDONATO** Executive Vice President, Human Resources	**MICHAEL J. FOSTYK** Senior Vice President, Logistics
MICHAEL G. JESSELSON President of Jesselson Capital Corporation	**JOAN HOLSTEIN HILSON** Executive Vice President and Chief Financial Officer - AE Brand	**SCOTT GRIFFITH** Vice President, Tax
ALAN KANE Dean of the School of Business and Technology, Fashion Institute of Technology	**JOSEPH E. KERIN** Executive Vice President and Director of Store Operations, Real Estate and Construction	**STEVE LYMAN** Vice President, Retail Distribution - East
JANICE E. PAGE Retired Executive of Sears Roebuck & Company	**LEANN NEALZ** Executive Vice President and Chief Design Officer	**DAVID MCNULTY** Vice President, Recruiting
J. THOMAS PRESBY Retired Partner of Deloitte Touche Tohmatsu	**DENNIS R. PARODI** Executive Vice President and Chief Operating Officer, NY Design Center	**RICK MILAZZO** Chief Information Officer Vice President, Information Technology
GERALD E. WEDREN President of Craig Capital Co.	**KATHERINE J. SAVITT** Executive Vice President and Chief Marketing Officer	**CHRIS PUMA** Senior Vice President, Finance
LARRY M. WOLF Retired Senior Vice President of The Rouse Company		**MICHAEL REMPELL** Senior Vice President and Chief Supply Chain Officer
		JAMES ROBERSON Vice President, Controller
		HANK SHECHTMAN Executive Vice President, Blue Star Imports
		JANI STRAND Vice President, Public Relations & Corporate Communications
		KEN WATTS Vice President, Technical Infrastructure

AE BRAND OFFICERS	MARTIN + OSA OFFICERS	STOCKHOLDER INFORMATION
KATE BALL-YOUNG Vice President, Sourcing & Production **CARMEN BLANCO** Vice President, Zone Director of Stores (East) **ROBERTO L. CROCE** Vice President, General Merchandising Manager - Women's Wovens, Accessories and Outdoors **ADAM S. DIAMOND** Vice President, Brand Marketing **CHRISTOPHER FIORE** Senior Vice President, New Concept Development **JAMES M. FORD** Vice President, Planning and Allocation **HENRY GASKINS** Vice President, Integrated Marketing **AMIE C. GOELLER** Vice President, Women's Design **FREDRICK W. GROVER** Executive Vice President, E-Commerce and AE International **CINDY HALL** Vice President, Design - aerie **JANET HAYES-DANIEL** Vice President, General Merchandising Manager - Destination Knits **SWATI KELKAR** Vice President, Pre-Production & Quality Assurance **ROKHEE KIM** Vice President, Women's Design **MONICA KOHL** Vice President, Production **KASEY MAZZONE** Senior Vice President, Sourcing & Production **FRANK SCAVETTA** Vice President, Technical Design **BETSY SCHUMACHER** Senior Vice President, Chief Merchandising Officer - aerie **HENRY STAFFORD** Senior Vice President, Chief Merchandising Officer - AE Brand **RENEE SUAREZ** Vice President, Zone Director of Stores (West) **CHARLES L. TETI** Vice President, Men's Design **BARBARA WATKOFF** Vice President, Production	**LAURA DUBIN WANDER** President **CHUCK CHUPEIN** Vice President, Chief Operating Officer **ARNIE COHEN** Chief Marketing Officer **MICHELE DONNAN-MARTIN** Chief of Design, General Merchandising Manager - Women's **HOWARD LANDON** Executive Vice President, Production and Sourcing **IRENE MAK** Vice President, Technical Design **CHARLES MARTIN** Chief of Design, General Merchandising Manager - Men's **JAMES OLSSON** Vice President, General Merchandising Manager - Men's	**HEADQUARTERS OF THE COMPANY** 150 Thorn Hill Drive Warrendale, PA 15086-7528 (724) 776-4857 **FORM 10-K** A copy of our Annual Report on Form 10-K for the period ended February 3, 2007 is included herein and has been filed with the Securities and Exchange Commission. Additional copies are available to any stockholder without charge by visiting our Web site at ae.com or by making a written request to Judy Meehan at our address. **STOCK EXCHANGE LISTING** New York Stock Exchange (Trading Symbol: AEO) **INVESTOR CONTACT** Judy Meehan Senior Director of Investor Relations (724) 776-4857 **INDEPENDENT AUDITORS** Ernst & Young LLP 2100 One PPG Place Pittsburgh, PA 15222 **STOCK TRANSFER AGENT, REGISTRAR & DIVIDEND AGENT** National City Bank Shareholder Services LOC 01-5352 P.O. Box 92301 Cleveland, OH 44101-4301 Toll-free telephone: 1-800-622-6757 Shareholder Services website: www.nationalcity.com/shareholderservices

APPENDIX C

URBAN OUTFITTERS, INC.
Form 10-K Annual Report*

*This appendix contains excerpts. Go to the text website at www.mhhe.com/libby6e for the complete report.

UNITED STATES
SECURITIES AND EXCHANGE COMMISSION
Washington, DC 20549

FORM 10-K

FOR ANNUAL AND TRANSITION REPORTS PURSUANT TO SECTIONS 13 OR 15(d) OF THE SECURITIES EXCHANGE ACT OF 1934

☒ **ANNUAL REPORT PURSUANT TO SECTION 13 OR 15(d) OF THE SECURITIES EXCHANGE ACT OF 1934**

For the fiscal year ended January 31, 2007

☐ **TRANSITION REPORT PURSUANT TO SECTION 13 OR 15(d) OF THE SECURITIES EXCHANGE ACT OF 1934**

For the transition period from   to

Commission File No. 000-22754

URBAN OUTFITTERS, INC.
(Exact Name of Registrant as Specified in Its Charter)

Pennsylvania	**23-2003332**
(State or Other Jurisdiction of Incorporation or Organization)	(I.R.S. Employer Identification No.)
5000 South Broad Street, Philadelphia, PA	**19112-1495**
(Address of Principal Executive Offices)	(Zip Code)

Registrant's telephone number, including area code: (215) 454-5500

Securities registered pursuant to Section 12(b) of the Act:

Title of Each Class	Name of Exchange on Which Registered
Common Shares, $.0001 par value	The NASDAQ Stock Market LLC

Securities registered pursuant to Section 12(g) of the Act: None

Indicate by checkmark if the registrant is a well-known seasoned issuer, as defined in Rule 405 of the Securities Act.   Yes ☒   No ☐

Indicate by checkmark if the registrant is not required to file reports pursuant to Section 13 or Section 15(d) of the Act.   Yes ☐   No ☒

Indicate by checkmark whether the registrant (1) has filed all reports required to be filed by Section 13 or 15(d) of the Securities Exchange Act of 1934 during the preceding 12 months (or for such shorter period that the registrant was required to file such reports), and (2) has been subject to such filing requirements for the past 90 days.   Yes ☒   No ☐

Indicate by checkmark if disclosure of delinquent filers pursuant to Item 405 of Regulation S-K is not contained herein, and will not be contained, to the best of Registrant's knowledge, in definitive proxy or information statements incorporated by reference in Part III of this Form 10-K or any amendment to this Form 10-K. ☒

Indicate by checkmark whether the registrant is a large accelerated filer, an accelerated filer, or a non-accelerated filer. See definition of "accelerated filer" and "large accelerated filer" in Rule 12b-2 of the Exchange Act.

Large accelerated filer ☒   Accelerated filer ☐   Non-accelerated filer ☐

Indicate by a checkmark whether the registrant is a shell company (as defined in Rule 12b-2 of the Act).   Yes ☐   No ☒

The aggregate market value of the voting and non-voting common equity held by non-affiliates computed by reference to the price at which the common equity was last sold, or the average bid and asked price of such common equity, as of the last business day of the registrant's most recently completed second fiscal quarter, was $1,640,624,909.

The number of shares outstanding of the registrant's common stock on March 23, 2007 was 165,084,463.

DOCUMENTS INCORPORATED BY REFERENCE

Certain information required by Items 10, 11, 12, 13 and 14 is incorporated by reference into Part III hereof from portions of the Proxy Statement for the registrant's 2007 Annual Meeting of Shareholders.

URBAN OUTFITTERS, INC.

Index to Consolidated Financial Statements

	Page
Report of Independent Registered Public Accounting Firm—Deloitte & Touche LLP	F-2
Report of Independent Registered Public Accounting Firm—KPMG LLP	F-3
Consolidated Balance Sheets as of January 31, 2007 and January 31, 2006	F-4
Consolidated Statements of Income for the fiscal years ended January 31, 2007, 2006 and 2005	F-5
Consolidated Statements of Shareholders' Equity for the fiscal years ended January 31, 2007, 2006 and 2005	F-6
Consolidated Statements of Cash Flows for the fiscal years ended January 31, 2007, 2006 and 2005	F-7
Notes to Consolidated Financial Statements	F-8

REPORT OF INDEPENDENT REGISTERED PUBLIC ACCOUNTING FIRM

To the Board of Directors and Stockholders of
Urban Outfitters, Inc.
Philadelphia, Pennsylvania

We have audited the accompanying consolidated balance sheets of Urban Outfitters, Inc. and subsidiaries (the "Company") as of January 31, 2007 and 2006, and the related consolidated statements of income, shareholders' equity, and cash flows for each of the years then ended. These financial statements are the responsibility of the Company's management. Our responsibility is to express an opinion on these financial statements based on our audits.

We conducted our audits in accordance with the standards of the Public Company Accounting Oversight Board (United States). Those standards require that we plan and perform the audit to obtain reasonable assurance about whether the financial statements are free of material misstatement. An audit includes examining, on a test basis, evidence supporting the amounts and disclosures in the financial statements. An audit also includes assessing the accounting principles used and significant estimates made by management, as well as evaluating the overall financial statement presentation. We believe that our audits provide a reasonable basis for our opinion.

In our opinion, such consolidated financial statements present fairly, in all material respects, the financial position of the Company as of January 31, 2007 and 2006, and the results of its operations and its cash flows for each of the years then ended, in conformity with accounting principles generally accepted in the United States of America.

We have also audited, in accordance with the standards of the Public Company Accounting Oversight Board (United States), the effectiveness of the Company's internal control over financial reporting as of January 31, 2007, based on the criteria established in *Internal Control—Integrated Framework* issued by the Committee of Sponsoring Organizations of the Treadway Commission and our report dated March 30, 2007, expressed an unqualified opinion on management's assessment of the effectiveness of the Company's internal control over financial reporting and an unqualified opinion on the effectiveness of the Company's internal control over financial reporting.

/s/ DELOITTE & TOUCHE LLP

Philadelphia, Pennsylvania
March 30, 2007

REPORT OF INDEPENDENT REGISTERED PUBLIC ACCOUNTING FIRM

The Board of Directors and Shareholders
Urban Outfitters, Inc.:

We have audited the accompanying consolidated statements of income, shareholders' equity, and cash flows of Urban Outfitters, Inc. and subsidiaries for the year ended January 31, 2005. These consolidated financial statements are the responsibility of the Company's management. Our responsibility is to express an opinion on these consolidated financial statements based on our audit.

We conducted our audit in accordance with the standards of the Public Company Accounting Oversight Board (United States). Those standards require that we plan and perform the audit to obtain reasonable assurance about whether the financial statements are free of material misstatement. An audit includes examining, on a test basis, evidence supporting the amounts and disclosures in the financial statements. An audit also includes assessing the accounting principles used and significant estimates made by management, as well as evaluating the overall financial statement presentation. We believe that our audit provides a reasonable basis for our opinion.

In our opinion, the consolidated financial statements referred to above present fairly, in all material respects, the results of operations and cash flows of Urban Outfitters, Inc. and subsidiaries for the year ended January 31, 2005, in conformity with U.S. generally accepted accounting principles.

/s/ KPMG LLP
Philadelphia, Pennsylvania
April 18, 2005, except as to the
fourth paragraph of Note 2,
which is as of March 31, 2006

URBAN OUTFITTERS, INC.
Consolidated Balance Sheets
(in thousands, except share and per share data)

	January 31,	
	2007	**2006**
Assets		
Current assets:		
Cash and cash equivalents	$ 27,267	$ 49,912
Marketable securities	132,011	141,883
Accounts receivable, net of allowance for doubtful accounts of $849 and $445, respectively	20,871	14,324
Inventories	154,387	140,377
Prepaid expenses and other current assets	27,286	33,993
Deferred taxes	4,583	4,694
Total current assets	366,405	385,183
Property and equipment, net	445,698	299,291
Marketable securities	62,322	64,748
Deferred income taxes and other assets	24,826	19,983
	$899,251	$769,205
Liabilities and Shareholders' Equity		
Current liabilities:		
Accounts payable	$ 57,934	$ 41,291
Accrued compensation	5,092	12,673
Accrued expenses and other current liabilities	72,292	79,544
Total current liabilities	135,318	133,508
Deferred rent	88,650	74,817
Total liabilities	223,968	208,325
Commitments and contingencies (see Note 10)		
Shareholders' equity:		
Preferred shares; $.0001 par value, 10,000,000 shares authorized, none issued	—	—
Common shares; $.0001 par value, 200,000,000 shares authorized, 164,987,463 and 164,831,477 issued and outstanding, respectively	17	16
Additional paid-in capital	128,586	134,146
Retained earnings	542,396	426,190
Accumulated other comprehensive income	4,284	528
Total shareholders' equity	675,283	560,880
	$ 899,251	$ 769,205

The accompanying notes are an integral part of these consolidated financial statements.

URBAN OUTFITTERS, INC.
Consolidated Statements of Income
(in thousands, except share and per share data)

	Fiscal Year Ended January 31,		
	2007	2006	2005
Net sales	$ 1,224,717	$ 1,092,107	$ 827,750
Cost of sales, including certain buying, distribution and occupancy costs	772,796	643,501	489,000
Gross profit	451,921	448,606	338,750
Selling, general and administrative expenses	287,932	240,907	190,384
Income from operations	163,989	207,699	148,366
Interest income	6,531	5,486	2,577
Other income	353	775	435
Other expenses	(715)	(1,563)	(1,186)
Income before income taxes	170,158	212,397	150,192
Income tax expense	53,952	81,601	59,703
Net income	$ 116,206	$ 130,796	$ 90,489
Net income per common share:			
Basic	$ 0.71	$ 0.80	$ 0.56
Diluted	$ 0.69	$ 0.77	$ 0.54
Weighted average common shares outstanding:			
Basic	164,679,786	163,717,726	161,419,898
Diluted	168,652,005	169,936,041	167,303,450

The accompanying notes are an integral part of these consolidated financial statements.

URBAN OUTFITTERS, INC.
Consolidated Statements of Shareholders' Equity
(in thousands, except share data)

| | Compre-hensive Income | Common Shares | | Additional Paid-in Capital | Unearned Compen-sation | Retained Earnings | Accumulated Other Compre-hensive Income | Total |
		Number of Shares	Par Value					
Balances as of February 1, 2004		159,553,084	$ 16	$ 83,271	$ —	$ 204,905	$ 1,938	$290,130
Net income	$ 90,489	—	—	—	—	90,489	—	90,489
Foreign currency translation	1,002	—	—	—	—	—	1,002	1,002
Unrealized losses on marketable securities, net of tax	(470)	—	—	—	—	—	(470)	(470)
Comprehensive income	$ 91,021							
Restricted stock issued		400,000	—	5,766	(5,766)	—	—	—
Amortization of unearned compensation		—	—	—	708	—	—	708
Exercise of stock options		2,941,804	—	6,917	—	—	—	6,917
Tax effect of exercises		—	—	13,468	—	—	—	13,468
Balances as of January 31, 2005		162,894,888	16	109,422	(5,058)	295,394	2,470	402,244
Net income	$ 130,796	—	—	—	—	130,796	—	130,796
Foreign currency translation	(1,909)	—	—	—	—	—	(1,909)	(1,909)
Unrealized losses on marketable securities, net of tax	(33)	—	—	—	—	—	(33)	(33)
Comprehensive income	$ 128,854							
Amortization of unearned compensation		—	—	—	1,153	—	—	1,153
Exercise of stock options		1,936,589	—	15,230	—	—	—	15,230
Tax effect of exercises		—	—	13,399	—	—	—	13,399
Balances as of January 31, 2006		164,831,477	16	138,050	(3,905)	426,190	528	560,880
Net income	$ 116,206	—	—	—	—	116,206	—	116,206
Foreign currency translation	3,614	—	—	—	—	—	3,614	3,614
Unrealized losses on marketable securities, net of tax	142	—	—	—	—	—	142	142
Comprehensive income	$ 119,962							
Share-based compensation		—	—	3,497	—	—	—	3,497
Unearned compensation reclass		—	—	(3,905)	3,905	—	—	
Exercise of stock options		1,375,986	1	6,350	—	—	—	6,351
Tax effect of exercises		—	—	5,394	—	—	—	5,394
Share repurchase		(1,220,000)	—	(20,801)	—	—	—	(20,801)
Balances as of January 31, 2007		164,987,463	$ 17	$ 128,586	$ —	$ 542,396	$ 4,284	$ 675,283

The accompanying notes are an integral part of these consolidated financial statements.

URBAN OUTFITTERS, INC.
Consolidated Statements of Cash Flows
(in thousands)

	Fiscal Year Ended January 31,		
	2007	**2006**	**2005**
Cash flows from operating activities:			
Net income	$ 116,206	$ 130,796	$ 90,489
Adjustments to reconcile net income to net cash provided by operating activities:			
Depreciation and amortization	55,713	39,340	31,858
Provision for deferred income taxes	(4,959)	(6,870)	(2,884)
Tax benefit of stock option exercises	(5,394)	13,399	13,468
Stock-based compensation expense	3,497	1,153	708
Loss (gain) on disposition of property and equipment, net	1,393	(631)	—
Changes in assets and liabilities:			
Increase in receivables	(6,371)	(6,002)	(1,635)
Increase in inventories	(13,416)	(41,597)	(35,651)
Decrease (increase) in prepaid expenses and other assets	6,848	(14,201)	(6,231)
Increase in accounts payable, accrued expenses and other liabilities	33,600	33,804	59,873
Net cash provided by operating activities	187,117	149,191	149,995
Cash flows from investing activities:			
Cash paid for property and equipment	(212,029)	(127,730)	(75,141)
Proceeds on disposition of property and equipment	—	3,769	—
Purchases of marketable securities	(182,653)	(416,018)	(586,093)
Sales and maturities of marketable securities	193,274	396,304	530,301
Net cash used in investing activities	(201,408)	(143,675)	(130,933)
Cash flows from financing activities:			
Exercise of stock options	6,351	15,230	6,917
Excess tax benefit of stock option exercises	5,394	—	—
Share Repurchases	(20,801)	—	—
Net cash (used in) provided by financing activities	(9,056)	15,230	6,917
Effect of exchange rate changes on cash and cash equivalents	702	(565)	433
(Decrease) increase in cash and cash equivalents	(22,645)	20,181	26,412
Cash and cash equivalents at beginning of period	49,912	29,731	3,319
Cash and cash equivalents at end of period	$ 27,267	$ 49,912	$ 29,731
Supplemental cash flow information:			
Cash paid during the year for:			
Interest	$ 153	$ 18	$ 126
Income taxes	$ 52,535	$ 79,182	$ 44,970
Non-cash investing activities—Accrued capital expenditures	$ 14,618	$ 27,986	$ 4,296

The accompanying notes are an integral part of these consolidated financial statements.

URBAN OUTFITTERS, INC.
Notes to Consolidated Financial Statements
(in thousands, except share and per share data)

1. Nature of Business

Urban Outfitters, Inc. (the "Company" or "Urban Outfitters"), which was founded in 1970 and originally operated by a predecessor partnership, was incorporated in the Commonwealth of Pennsylvania in 1976. The principal business activity of the Company is the operation of a general consumer product retail business through retail stores, three catalogs and four web sites. As of January 31, 2007 and 2006, the Company operated 207 and 175 stores, respectively. Stores located in the United States totaled 195 as of January 31, 2007 and 165 as of January 31, 2006, while operations in Europe and Canada included nine stores and three stores as of January 31, 2007, respectively and seven stores and three stores as of January 31, 2006, respectively. In addition, the Company engages in the wholesale distribution of apparel to approximately 1,500 better specialty retailers worldwide.

2. Summary of Significant Accounting Policies

Fiscal Year-End

The Company operates on a fiscal year ending January 31 of each year. All references to fiscal years of the Company refer to the fiscal years ended on January 31 in those years. For example, the Company's fiscal 2007 ended on January 31, 2007.

Principles of Consolidation

The consolidated financial statements include the accounts of Urban Outfitters, Inc. and its wholly owned subsidiaries. All inter-company transactions and accounts have been eliminated in consolidation.

Use of Estimates

The preparation of financial statements in conformity with accounting principles generally accepted in the United States requires management to make estimates and assumptions that affect the reported amounts of assets and liabilities and disclosure of contingent assets and liabilities at the date oft he financial statements and the reported amounts of net sales and expenses during the reporting period. Actual results could differ from those estimates.

Stock Split

On August 17, 2005, the Company's Board of Directors authorized a two-for-one split of the Company's common shares in the form of a 100% stock dividend. The additional shares issued as a result of the stock split were distributed on September 23, 2005 to shareholders of record as of September 6, 2005. All relevant amounts included in the consolidated financial statements and the notes thereto have been restated to reflect the stock split for all periods presented.

Cash and Cash Equivalents

Cash and cash equivalents are defined as cash and highly liquid investments with maturities of less than three months at the time of purchase. As of January 31, 2007 and 2006, cash and cash equivalents included cash on hand, cash in banks and money market accounts.

Marketable Securities

The Company's marketable securities may be classified as either held-to-maturity or available-for-sale. Held-to-maturity securities represent those securities that the Company has both the intent and ability to hold to maturity and are carried at amortized cost. Interest on these securities, as well as amortization of discounts and premiums, is included in interest income. Available-for-sale securities represent debt securities that do not meet the classification of held-to-maturity, are not actively traded and are carried at fair value, which approximates amortized cost. Unrealized gains and losses on these securities are excluded from earnings and are reported as a separate component of shareholders' equity until realized. When available-for-sale securities are sold, the cost of the securities is specifically identified and is used to determine the realized gain or loss. Securities classified as current have maturity dates of less than one year from the balance sheet date. Securities classified as long-term have maturity dates greater than one year from the balance sheet date. Marketable securities as of January 31, 2007 and 2006 were classified as available-for-sale.

The Company also includes disclosure about its investments that are in an unrealized loss position for which other-than-temporary impairments have not been recognized in accordance with the Emerging Issues Task Force ("EITF") Issue No. 03-01, "The Meaning of Other-Than-Temporary Impairment and its Applications to Certain Investments".

Accounts Receivable

Accounts receivable primarily consists of amounts due from our wholesale customers as well as credit card receivables. The activity of the allowance for doubtful accounts for the years ended January 31, 2007, 2006 and 2005 is as follows:

	Balance at beginning of year	Additions	Deductions	Balance at end of year
Year ended January 31, 2007	$445	$2,192	$(1,788)	$849
Year ended January 31, 2006	586	1,156	(1,297)	445
Year ended January 31, 2005	651	922	(987)	586

Inventories

Inventories, which consist primarily of general consumer merchandise held for sale, are valued at the lower of cost or market. Cost is determined on the first-in, first-out method and includes the cost of merchandise and import related costs, including freight, import taxes and agent commissions. A periodic review of inventory quantities on hand is performed in order to determine if inventory is properly stated at the lower of cost or market. Factors related to current inventories such as future consumer demand and fashion trends, current aging,current and anticipated retail markdowns or wholesale discounts, and class or type of inventory are analyzed to determine estimated net realizable value. Criteria utilized by the Company to quantify aging trends includes factors such as average selling cycle and seasonality of merchandise, the historical rate at which merchandise has sold below cost during the average selling cycle, and merchandise currently priced below original cost. A provision is recorded to reduce the cost of inventories to the estimated net realizable values, if required. The majority of inventory at January 31, 2007 and 2006 consisted of finished goods. Unfinished goods and work-in-process were not material to the overall net inventory value.

Property and Equipment

Property and equipment are stated at cost and primarily consist of store related leasehold improvements, buildings and furniture and fixtures. Depreciation and amortization are typically computed using the straight-line method over five years for furniture and fixtures, the lesser of the lease term or useful life for leasehold improvements, three to ten years for other operating equipment and 39 years for buildings. Major renovations or improvements that extend the service lives of our assets are capitalized over the extension period or life of the improvement, whichever is less.

The Company reviews long-lived assets for possible impairment whenever events or changes in circumstances indicate the carrying amount may not be recoverable. This determination includes evaluation of factors such as future asset utilization and future net undiscounted cash flows expected to result from the use of the assets. Management believes there has been no impairment of the Company's long-lived assets as of January 31, 2007.

Deferred Rent

Rent expense on leases is recorded on a straight-line basis over the lease period. The excess of rent expense over the actual cash paid is recorded as deferred rent. In addition, certain store leases provide for contingent rentals when sales exceed specified break-point levels that are weighted based upon historical cyclically. For leases where achievement of these levels is considered probable based on cumulative lease year revenue versus the established breakpoint at any given point in time, contingent rent is accrued. This may be expensed concurrently with minimum rent which is recorded on a straight-line basis over the lease period.

Operating Leases

The Company leases its retail stores under operating leases. Many of the lease agreements contain rent holidays, rent escalation clauses and contingent rent provisions or some combination of these items. The Company recognizes rent expense on a straight-line basis over the accounting lease term.

The Company records rent expense on a straight-line basis over the lease period commencing on the date that the premises is turned over from the landlord. The lease period includes the construction period to make the leased space suitable for operating during which time the Company is not permitted to occupy the space. For purposes of calculating straight-line rent expense, the commencement date of the lease term reflects the date the Company takes possession of the building for initial construction and setup.

The Company classifies tenant improvement allowances on its consolidated financial statements within deferred rent that will be amortized as a reduction of rent expense over the straight-line period. Tenant improvement allowance activity is presented as part of cash flows from operating activities in the accompanying consolidated statements of cash flows.

Revenue Recognition

Revenue is recognized at the point-of-sale for retail store sales or when merchandise is shipped to customers for wholesale and direct-to-consumer sales, net of estimated customer returns. Payment for merchandise at the Company's stores and direct-to-consumer business is by cash, check,credit card, debit card or gift card. Therefore, the Company's need to collect outstanding accounts receivable for its retail and direct-to-consumer business is negligible and mainly results from returned checks or unauthorized credit card charges. The Company maintains an allowance for doubtful accounts for its wholesale business accounts receivable which management reviews on a monthly basis and believes is sufficient to cover potential credit losses and billing adjustments. Deposits for custom orders are recorded as a liability and recognized as a sale upon delivery of the merchandise to the customer. These custom orders, typically for upholstered furniture, have not been material. Gift card sales to customers are initially recorded as liabilities and recognized as sales upon redemption.

Sales Return Reserve

We record a reserve for estimated product returns where the sale has occurred during the period reported, but the return is likely to occur subsequent to the period reported and may otherwise be considered in-transit. The reserve for estimated in-transit product returns is based on our most recent historical return trends. If the actual return rate or experience is materially higher than our estimate, additional sales returns would be recorded in the future. The activity of the sales returns reserve for the years ended January 31, 2007, 2006 and 2005 is as follows:

	Balance at beginning of year	Additions	Deductions	Balance at end of year
Year ended January 31, 2007	$6,390	$29,376	$(26,850)	$8,916
Year ended January 31, 2006	4,527	21,959	(20,096)	6,390
Year ended January 31, 2005	2,312	14,898	(12,683)	4,527

Cost of Sales, Including Certain Buying, Distribution and Occupancy Costs

Cost of sales, including certain buying, distribution and occupancy costs includes the following: the cost of merchandise; merchandise markdowns; obsolescence and shrink; store occupancy costs including rent and depreciation; customer shipping expense for direct-to-consumer orders; in-bound and outbound freight; U.S. Customs related taxes and duties; inventory acquisition and purchasing costs; warehousing and handling costs and other inventory acquisition related costs.

Selling, General and Administrative Expenses

Selling, general and administrative expenses includes expenses such as (i) direct selling and selling supervisory expenses; (ii) various corporate expenses such as information systems, finance, loss prevention, human resources, and executive management expenses; and (iii) other associated general expenses.

Shipping and Handling Fees and Costs

The Company includes shipping and handling revenues in net sales and shipping and handling costs in cost of sales. The Company's shipping and handling revenues consist of amounts billed to customers for shipping and handling merchandise. Shipping and handling costs include shipping supplies, related labor costs and third-party shipping costs.

Advertising

The Company expenses the costs of advertising when the advertising occurs, except for direct-to-consumer advertising, which is capitalized and amortized over its expected period of future benefit. Advertising costs primarily relate to our direct-to-consumer marketing which are composed of catalog printing, paper, postage and other costs related to production of photographic images used in our catalogs and on our web sites. These costs are amortized over the period in which the customer responds to the marketing material and is determined based on historical response trends to a similar season's advertisement. Amortization rates are reviewed on a regular basis during the fiscal year and may be adjusted if the predicted customer response appears materially different than the historical response rate. The Company has the ability to measure the response rate to direct marketing early in the course of the advertisement based on its customers' reference to a specific catalog or by product placed and sold. The average amortization period for a catalog or web promotion is typically three months. If there is no expected future benefit, the cost of advertising is expensed when incurred. Advertising costs reported as prepaid expenses were $2,155 and $2,747 as of January 31, 2007 and 2006, respectively. Advertising expenses were $35,882, $30,033 and $22,455 for fiscal 2007, 2006 and 2005, respectively.

Start-up Costs

The Company expenses as incurred all start-up and organization costs, including travel, training, recruiting, salaries and other operating costs.

Web Site Development Costs

The Company capitalizes applicable costs incurred during the application and infrastructure development stage and expenses costs incurred during the planning and operating stage. During fiscal 2007, 2006 and 2005, the Company did not capitalize any internal-use software development costs because substantially all costs were incurred during the planning stage, and costs incurred during the application and infrastructure development stage were not material.

Income Taxes

The Company applies Statement of Financial Accounting Standards ("SFAS") No. 109, "Accounting for Income Taxes,"which principally utilizes a balance sheet approach to provide for income taxes. Under this method, deferred tax assets and liabilities are recognized for the expected future tax consequences of net operating loss carry forwards and temporary differences between the carrying amounts and the tax bases of assets and liabilities. The Company files a consolidated United States federal income tax return (see Note 7).

Net Income Per Common Share

Basic net income per common share is computed by dividing net income available to common shareholders by the weighted average number of common shares outstanding. Diluted net income per common share is computed by dividing net income available to common shareholders by the weighted average number of common shares outstanding, after giving effect to the potential dilution from the exercise of securities, such as stock options and non-vested shares, into shares of common stock as if those securities were exercised (see Note 9).

Accounting for Stock-Based Compensation

In December 2004, the Financial Accounting Standards Board ("FASB") issued SFAS No. 123 (revised 2004),*"Share-Based payment"*, ("SFAS No. 123R"), which replaces SFAS No. 123, "Accounting for Stock-Based Compensation" and supersedes Accounting Principles Board ("APB") Opinion No. 25, "Accounting for Stock Issued to Employees" ("APB No. 25"). SFAS No. 123R requires all share-based payments, including grants of employee stock options and non-vested shares, to be recognized in the financial statements based on their fair values at date of grant. Under SFAS No. 123R, companies are required to measure the cost of services received in exchange for stock options and similar awards based on the grant-date fair value of the award and to recognize this cost in the income statement over the period during which an award recipient is required to provide service in exchange for the award. The pro forma disclosures previously permitted under SFAS No. 123 are no longer an alternative to financial statement recognition.

Effective February 1, 2006, the Company adopted SFAS No. 123R using the modified prospective method and as such, results for prior periods have not been restated. Under this transition method, the measurement and the method of amortization of costs for share-based payments granted prior to, but not vested as of January 31, 2006, are based on the same estimate of the grant-date fair value and the same amortization method that was previously used in the SFAS No. 123 pro forma disclosure. The Company has used the Black-Scholes-Merton ("Black Scholes") model to determine the grant date fair value of its share-based awards and FASB Interpretation No. 28 ("FIN 28") to amortize its stock-based compensation expense over the vesting term and has continued using these two methods under SFAS No. 123R. Compensation expense is recognized based on grant date fair value only for share-based payments expected to vest. The Company estimates forfeitures at the date of grant based on historical experience and future expectations. Prior to the adoption of SFAS No. 123R, the Company utilized the intrinsic-value based method of accounting under APB No. 25, and related interpretations, and adopted the pro forma disclosure requirements of SFAS No. 123 and SFAS No. 148, "Accounting for Stock-Based Compensation—Transition and Disclosure." The effect of forfeitures on the pro forma expense amounts were recognized based on actual historical forfeitures. No compensation expense was historically recognized for the Company's stock option plans because the quoted market price of the Company's common shares at the date of grant was not in excess of the amount an employee must pay to acquire the common shares (see Note 8).

Accumulated Other Comprehensive Income

Comprehensive income is comprised of two subsets—net income and other comprehensive income. Amounts in accumulated other comprehensive income relate to foreign currency translation adjustments and unrealized gains (losses) on marketable securities. The foreign currency translation adjustments are not adjusted for income taxes because these adjustments relate to indefinite investments in non-U.S. subsidiaries. As of January 31, 2007, 2006 and 2005, accumulated other comprehensive income consists of foreign currency translation adjustments of $4,667, $1,053 and $2,962, respectively and unrealized losses on marketable securities, net of tax of $383, $525 and $490, respectively. In addition, reclassification adjustments for realized losses of $8 for fiscal 2007, and realized gains of $32 and $123 for fiscal 2006 and 2005, respectively, are included in net income.

Foreign Currency Translation

The financial statements of the Company's foreign operations are translated into U.S. dollars. Assets and liabilities are translated at current exchange rates while income and expense accounts are translated at the average rates in effect during the year. Translation adjustments are not included in determining net income, but are included in accumulated other comprehensive income within shareholders' equity. Transaction gains and losses are included in operating results and were not material in fiscal 2007, 2006 and 2005.

Fair Value of Financial Instruments

The Company's financial instruments consist primarily of cash and cash equivalents, marketable securities, accounts receivable and accounts payable. Management believes that the carrying value of these assets and liabilities are representative of their respective fair values.

Concentration of Credit Risk

Financial instruments that potentially subject the Company to concentrations of credit risk consist principally of cash, cash equivalents, marketable securities and accounts receivable. The Company manages the credit risk associated with cash, cash equivalents and marketable securities by investing with high-quality institutions and, by policy, limiting the amount of credit exposure to any one institution. Receivables from third-party credit cards are processed by financial institutions, which are monitored for financial stability. The Company periodically evaluates the financial condition of its wholesale segment customers. The Company's allowance for doubtful accounts reflects current market conditions and management's assessment regarding the likelihood of collecting its accounts receivable. The Company maintains cash accounts that, at times, may exceed federally insured limits. The Company has not experienced any losses from maintaining cash accounts in excess of such limits. Management believes that it is not exposed to any significant risks related to its cash accounts.

Recently Issued Accounting Pronouncements

In February 2007, the Financial Accounting Standards Board ("FASB") issued SFAS No. 159, "The Fair Value Option for Financial Assets and Financial Liabilities: Including an Amendment of FASB Statement No. 115." SFAS No. 159 provides companies with an option to report selected financial assets and liabilities at fair value and requires entities to display the fair value of those assets and liabilities for which the Company has chosen to use fair value on the face of the balance sheet. SFAS No. 159 is effective for financial statements issued for fiscal years beginning after November 15, 2007. The Company is currently evaluating what impact, if any, the adoption of SFAS No. 159 could have on its consolidated financial statements.

In September 2006, the FASB issued SFAS No. 157, "Fair Value Measurements." SFAS No. 157 defines fair value, establishes a framework for measuring fair value in U.S. generally accepted accounting principles, and expands disclosures about fair value measurements. SFAS No. 157 is effective for financial statements issued for fiscal years beginning after November 15, 2007, and interim periods within those fiscal years. The Company is currently evaluating what impact, if any, the adoption of SFAS No. 157 could have on its consolidated financial statements.

In September 2006, the SEC staff published Staff Accounting Bulletin No. 108, "Considering the Effects of Prior Year Misstatements when Quantifying Misstatements in Current Year Financial Statements" ("SAB 108"). SAB 108 addresses quantifying the financial statement effects of misstatements, specifically, how the effects of prior year uncorrected errors must be considered in quantifying misstatements in the current year financial statements. This statement is effective for fiscal years ending after November 15, 2006. SAB 108 did not have an effect on the Company's consolidated financial statements.

In June 2006, the EITF ratified its consensus on Issue No. 06-03, "How Taxes Collected from Customers and Remitted to Governmental Authorities Should Be Presented in the Income Statement". EITF 06-3 addresses what type of government assessments should be included within the scope of EITF 06-3, and how such government assessments should be presented in the income statement. The EITF concluded that the scope of EITF06-3 includes any tax assessed by a governmental authority that is directly imposed on a revenue-producing transaction between a seller and a customer and may include, but is not limited to, sales, use, value added and some excise taxes. In addition the EITF also concluded that the presentation of taxes, within the scope of EITF 06-3, on either a gross or net basis, is an accounting policy decision that should be disclosed pursuant to APB Opinion No. 22, "Disclosure of Accounting Policies". In addition, for any such taxes that are reported on a gross basis, a company should disclose the amounts of those taxes in interim and annual financial statements for each period for which an income statement is presented if those amounts are significant. The EITF observed that because EITF 06-3 requires only the presentation of additional disclosures, an entity would not be required to re-evaluate its existing policies related to taxes assessed by a governmental authority that are directly imposed on a revenue-producing transaction between a seller and a customer. EITF 06-3 is effective for reporting periods beginning after December 15, 2006. The Company will adopt the disclosure requirements of EITF 06-3 effective February 1, 2007; however, since the Company presents its revenue on a net basis, no further disclosure under EITF 06-3 will be required.

In July 2006, the FASB issued FASB Interpretation No. 48, "Accounting for Uncertainty in Income Taxes" ("FIN 48").This interpretation was issued to clarify the accounting for uncertainty in income taxes recognized in the financial statements by pre-scribing a recognition threshold and measurement attribute for the financial statement recognition and measurement of a tax position taken or expected to be taken in a tax return. The new standard also provides guidance on derecognition, classifica-tion, interest and penalties, accounting in interim periods, disclosure, and transition. The interpretation is effective for fiscal years beginning after December 15, 2006. The adoption of FIN 48 is expected to result in adjustments to our tax contingency reserves and deferred income taxes which could be material, with an offsetting adjustment to retained earnings in the first quarter of fiscal year 2008. We have not completed our evaluation of FIN 48 nor measured its impact on our consolidated financial statements.

3. Marketable Securities

The amortized cost, gross unrealized gains (losses) and fair value of available-for-sale securities by major security type and class of security as of January 31, 2007 and 2006 are as follows:

	Amortized Cost	Unrealized Gains	Unrealized (Losses)	Fair Value
As of January 31, 2007				
Municipal bonds:				
Maturing in less than one year	$33,287	$—	$(126)	$33,161
Maturing after one year through four years	62,784	9	(471)	62,322
	96,071	9	(597)	95,483
Auction rate instruments:				
Maturing in less than one year	98,850	—	—	98,850
	$194,921	$9	$(597)	$194,333
As of January 31, 2006				
Municipal bonds:				
Maturing in less than one year	$ 30,891	$12	$ (95)	$ 30,808
Maturing after one year through four years	65,472	1	(725)	64,748
	96,363	13	(820)	95,556
Auction rate instruments:				
Maturing in less than one year	111,075	—	—	111,075
	$207,438	$13	$(820)	$206,631

Proceeds from the sale and maturities of available-for-sale securities were $193,274, $396,304 and $530,301 in fiscal 2007, 2006 and 2005, respectively. The Company included in other income, gross realized losses of $8 in fiscal 2007, and gross realized gains in fiscal 2006 and 2005 of $32 and $123 respectively.

The following tables show the gross unrealized losses and fair value of the Company's marketable securities with unrealized losses that are not deemed to be other-than-temporarily impaired aggregated by the length of time that individual securities have been in a continuous unrealized loss position, at January 31, 2007 and January 31, 2006, respectively.

	JANUARY 31, 2007					
	LESS THAN 12 MONTHS		12 MONTHS OR GREATER		TOTAL	
	Fair Value	Unrealized Loss	Fair Value	Unrealized Loss	Fair Value	Unrealized Loss
Total municipal bonds	$35,802	$(110)	$54,670	$(487)	$90,472	$(597)

	JANUARY 31, 2006					
	LESS THAN 12 MONTHS		12 MONTHS OR GREATER		TOTAL	
	Fair Value	Unrealized Loss	Fair Value	Unrealized Loss	Fair Value	Unrealized Loss
Total municipal bonds	$32,996	$(236)	$48,489	$(584)	$81,485	$(820)

The unrealized losses presented above are primarily due to changes in market interest rates. At January 31, 2007 and 2006, there were a total of 53 and 50 issued securities, respectively, with an unrealized loss position within the Company's portfolio. The Company has the intent and the ability to hold these securities for a reasonable period of time sufficient for a forecasted recovery of fair value up to (or beyond) the initial cost of the investment. The Company has the ability to realize the full value of all of these investments upon maturity.

4. Property and Equipment

Property and equipment is summarized as follows:

	JANUARY 31,	
	2007	2006
Land	$ 543	$ 543
Buildings	92,376	4,331
Furniture and fixtures	153,594	115,946
Leasehold improvements	370,435	280,640
Other operating equipment	27,175	26,961
Construction-in-progress	15,903	39,200
	660,026	467,621
Accumulated depreciation and amortization	(214,328)	(168,330)
Total	$445,698	$299,291

Depreciation and amortization expense for property and equipment for fiscal 2007, 2006 and 2005 was $53,895, $37,080 and $29,777, respectively.

5. Accrued Expenses and Other Current Liabilities

Accrued expenses and other current liabilities consist of the following:

	JANUARY 31,	
	2007	2006
Accrued rents and estimated property taxes	$ 6,966	$ 5,968
Gift certificates and merchandise credits	17,268	14,348
Accrued construction	10,704	23,982
Accrued income taxes	10,592	12,075
Other current liabilities	26,762	23,171
Total	$72,292	$79,544

6. Line of Credit Facility

On September 30, 2004, we renewed and amended our line of credit facility (the "Line"). The Line is a three-year revolving credit facility with an accordion feature allowing an increase in available credit to $50,000 at our discretion, subject to a seven day request period. As of January 31, 2007, the credit limit under the Line is $42,500. The Line contains a sub-limit for borrowings by our European subsidiaries that are guaranteed by us. Cash advances bear interest at LIBOR plus 0.50% to 1.60% based on our achievement of prescribed adjusted debt ratios. The Line subjects us to various restrictive covenants, including maintenance of certain financial ratios and covenants such as fixed charge coverage and adjusted debt. The covenants also include limitations on our capital expenditures, ability to repurchase shares and the payment of cash dividends. On November 30, 2006 we amended our line to increase our capital expenditure limit and add additional subsidiaries that are permitted to borrow. As of January 31, 2007,we were in compliance with all covenants under the Line. As of and during the fiscal year ended January 31, 2007, there were no borrowings under the Line. Outstanding letters of credit and stand-by letters of credit under the Line totaled approximately $32,341 as of January 31, 2007. The available borrowing, including the accordion feature, under the Line was $17,659 as of January 31, 2007. We plan to renew the Line during fiscal 2008 and expect the renewal will include the expansion of the available credit limit under the Line to an amount that will satisfy our letter of credit needs through fiscal 2010.

7. Income Taxes

The components of income before income taxes are as follows:

	FISCAL YEAR ENDED JANUARY 31,		
	2007	2006	2005
Domestic	$161,985	$206,902	$145,844
Foreign	8,173	5,495	4,348
	$170,158	$212,397	$150,192

The components of the provision for income tax expense are as follows:

	FISCAL YEAR ENDED JANUARY 31,		
	2007	2006	2005
Current:			
Federal	$48,893	$68,865	$54,700
State	8,442	17,588	6,546
Foreign	1,576	2,018	1,341
	58,911	88,471	62,587
Deferred:			
Federal	6	(2,388)	(2,133)
State	(2,333)	(3,628)	(665)
Foreign	284	(2,049)	107
	(2,043)	(8,065)	(2,691)
Change in valuation allowances	(2,916)	1,195	(193)
	$53,952	$81,601	$59,703

The Company's effective tax rate was different than the statutory U.S. federal income tax rate for the following reasons:

	FISCAL YEAR ENDED JANUARY 31,		
	2007	2006	2005
Expected provision at statutory U.S. federal tax rate	35.0%	35.0%	35.0%
State and local income taxes, net of federal tax benefit	2.3	4.2	4.4
Foreign taxes	(2.3)	(0.1)	(0.2)
Federal rehabilitation tax credits	(2.8)	—	—
Other	(0.5)	(0.7)	0.6
Effective tax rate	31.7%	38.4%	39.8%

The significant components of deferred tax assets and liabilities as of January 31, 2007 and 2006 are as follows:

	JANUARY 31,	
	2007	2006
Deferred tax liabilities:		
Prepaid expenses	$(1,911)	$(1,504)
Depreciation	(14,718)	(11,892)
Gross deferred tax liabilities	(16,629)	(13,396)
Deferred tax assets:		
Deferred rent	34,681	29,819
Inventories	3,721	3,460
Accounts receivable	648	572
Net operating loss carryforwards	2,692	3,361
Accrued salaries and benefits, and other	3,602	3,181
Gross deferred tax assets, before valuation allowances	45,344	40,393
Valuation allowances	(231)	(3,147)
Net deferred tax assets	$28,484	$23,850

Net deferred tax assets are attributed to the jurisdictions in which the Company operates. As of January 31, 2007 and 2006, respectively, $17,335 and $16,696 were attributable to U.S. federal, $8,204 and $6,778 were attributed to state jurisdictions and $2,945 and $376 were attributed to foreign jurisdictions.

As of January 31, 2007, certain non-U.S. subsidiaries of the Company had net operating loss carry forwards for tax purposes of approximately $2,692 that do not expire. At January 31, 2006, The Company had a full valuation allowance for certain foreign net operating loss carry forwards where it was uncertain the carryforwards would be utilized. In fiscal 2007, the Company determined that it was more likely than not, that these carryforwards would be utilized; therefore, valuation allowances were reversed. The Company had no valuation allowance for certain other foreign net operating loss carryforwards where management believes it is more likely than not the tax benefit of these carryforwards will be realized. As of January 31, 2007 and 2006, the non-current portion of net deferred tax assets aggregated $23,901 and $19,156, respectively.

The cumulative amount of the Company's share of undistributed earnings of non-U.S. subsidiaries for which no deferred taxes have been provided was $17,007 as of January 31, 2007. These earnings are deemed to be permanently re-invested to finance growth programs.

As of January 31, 2007, the Company has tax contingency reserves of approximately $5,945 included in accrued expenses and other current liabilities. The Company recorded interest, net of any applicable related tax benefit, on potential tax contingencies as a component of its tax expense.

8. Share-Based Compensation

The Company's 2004 Stock Incentive Plan and 2000 Stock Incentive Plan both authorize up to 10,000,000 common shares, which can be granted as restricted shares, incentive stock options or nonqualified stock options. Grants under these plans generally expire ten years from the date of grant, thirty days after termination, or six months after the date of death or termination due to disability. Stock options generally vest over a period of three or five years, with options becoming exercisable in equal installments over the vesting period. However, options granted to non-employee directors generally vest over a period of one year and certain grants issued during fiscal 2006 and 2005 fully vested within six months of the date of grant. The Company's 1997 Stock Option Plan (the "1997 Plan"), which replaced the previous 1987, 1992 and 1993 Stock Option Plans (the "Superseded Plans"), expired during the year ended January 31, 2004. Individual grants outstanding under the 1997 Plan and certain of the Superseded Plans have expiration dates, which extend into the year 2010. Grants under the 1997 Plan and the Superseded Plans generally expire ten years from the date of grant, thirty days after termination, or six months after the date of death or termination due to disability. Stock options generally vest over a five year period, with options becoming exercisable in equal installments of twenty percent per year. As of January 31, 2007, 940,750 and 701,600 common shares were available for grant under the 2004 Stock Incentive Plan and 2000 Stock Incentive Plan, respectively.

Under the provisions of SFAS No. 123R, the Company recorded $2,344 of stock compensation related to stock option awards as well as related tax benefits of $499 in the Company's Consolidated Statements of Income for the fiscal year ended January 31, 2007, or less than $0.01 for both basic and diluted earnings per share. During fiscal 2007, the Company granted 125,000 stock options. The estimated fair value of options granted was calculated using a Black Scholes option pricing model. The Black Scholes model incorporates assumptions to value stock-based awards. The Company uses historical data on exercise timing to determine the expected life assumption. The risk-free rate of interest for periods within the contractual life of the option is based on U.S. Government Securities Treasury Constant Maturities over the expected term of the equity instrument. Expected volatility is based on the historical volatility of the Company's stock. The table below outlines the weighted average assumptions for these grants:

	Fiscal 2007	Fiscal 2006	Fiscal 2005
Expected life, in years	6.8	6.5	5.3
Risk-free interest rate	4.8%	4.4%	4.3%
Volatility	54.4%	55.5%	51.0%
Dividend rate	—	—	—

Based on the Company's historical experience, the Company has assumed an annualized forfeiture rate of 2% for its unvested options. Under the true-up provisions of SFAS No. 123R, the Company will record additional expense if the actual forfeiture rate is lower than it estimated, and will record a recovery of prior expense if the actual forfeiture is higher than estimated.

No compensation expense related to stock option grants has been recorded in the Consolidated Statements of Income for fiscal 2006 and 2005, as all of the options granted had an exercise price equal to the market value of the underlying stock on the date of grant. Results for prior periods have not been restated.

SFAS No. 123R requires the Company to present pro forma information for the comparative period prior to the adoption as if it had accounted for all its employee stock options under the fair value method of the original SFAS No. 123. The following table illustrates the effect on net income and net income per common share if the Company had applied the fair value recognition provisions of SFAS No. 123 to stock-based employee compensation for the years ended January 31, 2006 and 2005.

	FISCAL YEAR ENDED JANUARY 31,	
	2006	2005
Net income—as reported	$130,796	$90,489
Add: Stock-based employee compensation expense included in the determination of net income as reported, net of related tax effect	710	427
Deduct: Total stock-based employee compensation expense determined under fair value based method for all awards, net of related tax effect	(60,462)	(24,912)
Net income—pro forma	$ 71,044	$66,004
Net income per common share—basic—as reported	$ 0.80	$ 0.56
Net income per common share—basic—pro forma	$ 0.43	$ 0.41
Net income per common share—diluted—as reported	$ 0.77	$ 0.54
Net income per common share—diluted—pro forma	$ 0.42	$ 0.40

Total compensation cost of stock options granted but not yet vested, as of January 31, 2007, was $1,677, which is expected to be recognized over the weighted average period of 1.57 years.

The following tables summarize activity under all stock option plans for the respective periods:

	FISCAL YEAR ENDED JANUARY 31,		
	2007	2006	2005
	(In thousands, except per share data)		
Weighted-average fair value of options granted per share	$ 11.62	$ 13.62	$ 7.14
Intrinsic value of options exercised	20,822	33,080	35,103
Cash received from option exercises	6,351	15,230	6,917
Actual tax benefit realized for tax deductions from option exercises	5,394	13,399	13,468

Information regarding options under these plans is as follows:

	FISCAL 2007			
	Shares	Weighted Average Exercise Price	Weighted Average Remaining Contractual Term (years)	Aggregate Intrinsic Value (1)
Options outstanding at beginning of year	15,022,161	$14.76		
Options granted	125,000	19.93		
Options exercised	(1,375,986)	4.63		
Options forfeited	(140,000)	4.00		
Options expired	(275,500)	22.58		
Options outstanding at end of year	13,355,675	15.61	7.0	$ 117,396
Options outstanding expected to vest at end of year	13,091,600	15.61	7.0	$ 115,075
Options exercisable at end of year	11,474,894	17.27	7.1	$ 81,816
Weighted average fair value of options granted per share	$ 11.62			

(1) The aggregate intrinsic value in this table was calculated based upon the closing price of the Company's common shares on January 31,2007, which was $24.40, and the exercise price of the underlying options, provided the closing price exceeded the exercise price.

The following table summarizes information concerning currently outstanding and exercisable options as of January 31, 2007:

	OPTIONS OUTSTANDING			OPTIONS EXERCISABLE	
Range of Exercise Prices	Amount Outstanding	Wtd. Avg. Remaining Contractual Life	Wtd. Avg. Exercise Price	Amount Exercisable	Wtd. Avg. Exercise Price
$ 0.00 − $ 3.11	2,690,115	4.5	$ 1.84	2,040,034	$ 1.64
$ 3.12 − $ 6.22	2,367,750	6.0	4.34	1,458,950	4.32
$ 6.23 − $ 9.33	256,000	5.0	9.10	144,000	9.12
$12.44 − $15.56	3,255,660	7.4	14.33	3,167,660	14.32
$18.67 − $21.78	110,000	9.4	19.59	—	—
$21.79 − $24.89	280,000	8.0	23.57	265,000	23.63
$24.90 − $28.00	202,000	8.4	27.45	202,000	27.45
$28.01 − $31.11	4,194,150	8.8	30.98	4,197,250	30.98
	13,355,675	7.0	15.61	11,474,894	17.27

Nonvested Shares

The Company may make non-vested share awards to employees, non-employee directors and consultants. A non-vested shares award is an award of common shares that is subject to certain restrictions during a specified period, such as an employee's continued employment combined with the Company achieving certain financial goals. The Company holds the common shares during the restriction period, and the grantee cannot transfer the shares before the termination of that period. The grantee is, however, generally entitled to vote the common shares and receive any dividends declared and paid on the Company's common shares during the restriction period. Unearned compensation was recorded as a component of shareholders'equity and amortized over the vesting period of the award as stock compensation expense in the Company's results of operations. During the year ended January 31, 2005, the Company granted 400,000 shares of restricted common stock with a grant date fair value of $5,766 and a weighted average grant date fair value of $14.42 per share. Share-based compensation resulting from this grant of $1,153 is included in the accompanying Consolidated Statements of Income for each fiscal year ended January 31, 2007, 2006 and $708 for the fiscal year ended January 31, 2005, as well as, related tax benefits of $484, $763 and $0, respectively. As of January 31, 2007, this is the only grant of non-vested shares and none of these shares have vested as of January 31, 2007. Total unrecognized compensation cost of non-vested shares granted, as of January 31, 2007 was $ 2,752, which is expected to be recognized over the period of 2.4 years.

9. Net Income Per Common Share

The following is a reconciliation of the weighted average shares outstanding used for the computation of basic and diluted net income per common share:

	FISCAL YEAR ENDED JANUARY 31,		
	2007	2006	2005
Basic weighted average shares outstanding	164,679,786	163,717,726	161,419,898
Effect of dilutive options and restricted stock	3,972,219	6,218,315	5,883,552
Diluted weighted average shares outstanding	168,652,005	169,936,041	167,303,450

For the fiscal years ended January 31, 2007, 2006 and 2005, options to purchase 4,763,375 shares ranging in price from $15.48 to $31.11, options to purchase 1,256,688 shares ranging in price from $23.55 to $31.11 and options to purchase 1,114,000 shares ranging in price from $13.72 to $23.76, were excluded from the calculation of diluted net income per common share for the respective fiscal years because the effect was anti-dilutive.

10. Commitments and Contingencies

Leases

The Company leases its stores under non-cancelable operating leases. The following is a schedule by year of the future minimum lease payments for operating leases with original terms in excess of one year:

Fiscal Year	
2008	$ 92,280
2009	95,008
2010	89,598
2011	77,963
2012	74,234
Thereafter	290,702
Total minimum lease payments	$719,785

Amounts noted above include commitments for 27 executed leases for stores not opened as of January 31, 2007. The majority of our leases allow for renewal options between five and ten years upon expiration of the initial lease term. The store leases generally provide for payment of direct operating costs including real estate taxes. Certain store leases provide for contingent rentals when sales exceed specified levels. Additionally, the Company has entered into store leases that require a percentage of total sales to be paid to landlords in lieu of minimum rent.

Rent expense consisted of the following:

	FISCAL YEAR ENDED JANUARY 31,		
	2007	2006	2005
Minimum and percentage rentals	$73,058	$61,603	$54,992
Contingent rentals	1,991	3,309	2,329
Total	$75,049	$64,912	$57,321

The Company also has commitments for un-fulfilled purchase orders for merchandise ordered from our vendors in the normal course of business,which are liquidated within 12 months, of $26,769 and contracts with store construction contractors, fully liquidated upon the completion of construction, which is typically within 12 months, of $4,922.

Benefit Plan

Full and part-time U.S. based employees who are at least 18 years of age are eligible after six months of employment to participate in the Urban outfitters 401(k) Savings Plan (the "Plan"). Under the Plan, employees can defer 1% to 25% of compensation as defined. The Company makes matching contributions in cash of $0.25 per employee contribution dollar on the first 6% of the employee contribution. The employees' contribution is 100% vested while the Company's matching contribution vests at 20% per year of employee service. The Company's contributions were $812, $691 and $527 for fiscal years 2007, 2006 and 2005, respectively.

Contingencies

The Company is party to various legal proceedings arising from normal business activities. Management believes that the ultimate resolution of these matters will not have a material adverse effect on the Company's financial position, results of operations or cash flows.

11. Related Party Transactions

Harry S. Cherken, Jr., a director of the Company, is a partner in the law firm of Drinker Biddle & Reath LLP ("DBR"), which provides real estate, regulatory and general legal services to the Company. Fees paid to DBR during fiscal 2007, 2006 and 2005 were $1,493, $1,458 and $1,162, respectively. Fees due to DBR as of January 31, 2007 for services rendered were approximately $572.

The McDevitt Company, a real estate company, acted as a broker in substantially all of the Company's new real estate transactions during fiscal 2007, 2006 and 2005. The Company has not paid any compensation to The McDevitt Company, but the Company has been advised that The McDevitt Company has received commissions from other parties to such transactions. Wade L. McDevitt is the brother-in-law of Scott Belair, one of the Company's directors and is president and the sole shareholder of The McDevitt Company. There were no amounts due to The McDevitt Company as of January 31, 2007.

12. Segment Reporting

The Company is a national retailer of lifestyle-oriented general merchandise with two reporting segments—"Retail" and "Wholesale". The Company's Retail segment consists of the aggregation of its three brands operating through 207 stores under the retail names "Urban Outfitters," "Anthropologie" and "Free People" and includes their direct marketing campaigns which consist of three catalogs and four web sites as of January 31, 2007. Our retail stores and their direct marketing campaigns are considered operating segments. Net sales from the retail segment accounted for more than 93% of total consolidated net sales for the years ended January 31, 2007, 2006 and 2005. The remainder is derived from the Company's Wholesale segment that manufactures and distributes apparel to the retail segment and to approximately 1,500 better specialty retailers worldwide.

The Company has aggregated its retail stores and associated direct marketing campaigns into a Retail segment based upon their unique management, customer base and economic characteristics. Reporting in this format provides management with the financial information necessary to evaluate the success of the segments and the overall business. The Company evaluates the performance of the segments based on the net sales and pre-tax income from operations (excluding inter-company charges) of the segment. Corporate expenses include expenses incurred and directed by the corporate office that are not allocated to segments. The principal identifiable assets for each operating segment are inventories and property and equipment. Other assets are comprised primarily of general corporate assets, which principally consist of cash and cash equivalents, marketable securities, and other assets, and which are typically not allocated to the Company's segments. The Company accounts for inter-segment sales and transfers as if the sales and transfers were made to third parties making similar volume purchases.

The accounting policies of the operating segments are the same as the policies described in Note 2, "Summary of Significant Accounting Policies." Both the retail and wholesale segment are highly diversified. No customer comprises more than 10% of sales.

A summary of the information about the Company's operations by segment is as follows:

	FISCAL YEAR		
	2007	2006	2005
Net sales			
Retail operations	$1,150,511	$1,038,842	$800,361
Wholesale operations	79,687	57,363	29,389
Intersegment elimination	(5,481)	(4,098)	(2,000)
Total net sales	$1,224,717	$1,092,107	$827,750
Income from operations			
Retail operations	$ 159,338	$ 202,790	$153,217
Wholesale operations	18,319	13,888	4,091
Intersegment elimination	(1,504)	(891)	(300)
Total segment operating income	176,153	215,787	157,008
General corporate expenses	(12,164)	(8,088)	(8,642)
Total income from operations	$ 163,989	$ 207,699	$148,366
Depreciation and amortization expense for property and equipment			
Retail operations	$ 53,458	$ 36,924	$ 29,623
Wholesale operations	437	156	154
Total depreciation and amortization expense for property and equipment	$ 53,895	$ 37,080	$ 29,777
Inventories			
Retail operations	$ 141,850	$ 131,704	$ 94,914
Wholesale operations	12,537	8,673	4,082
Total inventories	$ 154,387	$ 140,377	$ 98,996
Property and equipment, net			
Retail operations	$ 443,879	$ 297,509	$191,695
Wholesale operations	1,819	1,782	1,097
Total property and equipment, net	$ 445,698	$ 299,291	$192,792
Cash paid for property and equipment			
Retail operations	$ 211,533	$ 126,790	$ 74,954
Wholesale operations	496	940	187
Total cash paid for property and equipment	$ 212,029	$ 127,730	$ 75,141

The Company has foreign operations in Europe and Canada. Revenues and long-lived assets, based upon our domestic and foreign operations, are as follows:

Net sales			
Domestic operations	$1,132,053	$1,026,589	$781,894
Foreign operations	92,664	65,518	45,856
Total net sales	$1,224,717	$1,092,107	$827,750
Property and equipment, net			
Domestic operations	$ 405,345	$ 260,398	$174,778
Foreign operations	40,353	38,893	18,014
Total property and equipment, net	$ 445,698	$ 299,291	$192,792

INDUSTRY RATIO REPORT
Retail Family Clothing Stores

Liquidity

Current Ratio	2.70
Quick Ratio	1.48

Activity

Inventory Turnover	5.13
Days to Sell Inventory	78.27 days
Receivables Turnover	86.28
Average Collection Period	9.61 days
Fixed Asset Turnover	6.76
Total Asset Turnover	1.85
Accounts Payable Turnover	7.93

Profitability

Gross Profit Margin	40.23%
Operating Profit Margin	11.74%
Net Profit Margin	7.69%
Return on Equity	20.68%
Return on Assets	14.16%
Quality of Income	1.62

Leverage

Times Interest Earned	41.28
Interest Coverage Ratio	41.42
Total Debt/Total Equity	0.77
Total Assets/Total Equity	1.77

Dividends

Dividend Payout	11.82%
Dividend Yield	0.64%

Other

Advertising-to-Sales	2.39%
Sales Growth	10.94%
Capital Acquisitions Ratio	2.42
Price/Earnings	22.47

Companies Used in Industry Analysis

Company Name	Ticker Symbol
Abercrombie & Fitch	ANF
Aeropostale Inc	ARO
American Eagle Outfitters	AEO
Ann Taylor Stores	ANN
bebe stores Inc	BEBE
Carter's Inc	CRI
Chico's FAS Inc	CHS
Collective Brands Inc	PSS
Foot Locker, Inc	FL
Gap Inc	GPS
Guess? Inc	GES
J. Crew Group Inc	JCG
Limited Brands Inc	LTD
Nordstrom, Inc.	JWN
Pacific Sunwear of California Inc	PSUN
Ross Stores Inc	ROST
The Buckle Inc	BKE
The Men's Wearhouse Inc	MW
TJX Companies Inc	TJX
Urban Outfitters Inc	URBN

A

Account A standardized format that organizations use to accumulate the dollar effects of transactions on each financial statement item. (54)

Accounting A system that collects and processes (analyzes, measures, and records) financial information about an organization and reports that information to decision makers. (4)

Accounting Cycle The process used by entities to analyze and record transactions, adjust the records at the end of the period, prepare financial statements, and prepare the records for the next cycle. (165)

Accounting Entity The organization for which financial data are to be collected. (7)

Accounting Period The time period covered by the financial statements. (11)

Accounts Receivable (Trade Receivables, Receivables) Open accounts owed to the business by trade customers. (290)

Accrual Basis Accounting Records revenues when earned and expenses when incurred, regardless of the timing of cash receipts or payments. (110)

Accrued Expenses Previously unrecorded expenses that need to be adjusted at the end of the accounting period to reflect the amount incurred and its related payable account. (172)

Accrued Liabilities Expenses that have been incurred but have not been paid at the end of the accounting period. (464)

Accrued Revenues Previously unrecorded revenues that need to be adjusted at the end of the accounting period to reflect the amount earned and its related receivable account. (170)

Acquisition Cost Net cash equivalent amount paid or to be paid for the asset. (401)

Additional Paid-In Capital (Paid-In Capital, Contributed Capital in Excess of Par) The amount of contributed capital less the par value of the stock. (245)

Additions and Improvements Infrequent expenditures that increase an asset's economic usefulness in the future. (405)

Adjusting Entries Entries necessary at the end of the accounting period to measure all revenues and expenses of that period. (165)

Aging of Accounts Receivable Method Estimates uncollectible accounts based on the age of each account receivable. (295)

Allowance for Doubtful Accounts (Allowance for Bad Debts, Allowance for Uncollectible Accounts) Contra-asset account containing the estimated uncollectible accounts receivable. (291)

Allowance Method Bases bad debt expense on an estimate of uncollectible accounts. (291)

Amortization Systematic and rational allocation of the acquisition cost of an intangible asset over its useful life. (420)

Amortized Cost Method Reports investments in debt securities held to maturity at cost minus any premium or plus any discount. (606)

Annuity A series of periodic cash receipts or payments that are equal in amount each interest period. (477)

Assets Probable future economic benefits owned by the entity as a result of past transactions. (50)

Audit An examination of the financial reports to ensure that they represent what they claim and conform with generally accepted accounting principles. (21)

Authorized Number of Shares Maximum number of shares of a corporation's capital stock that can be issued as specified in the charter. (560)

Average Cost Method Uses the weighted average unit cost of the goods available for sale for both cost of goods sold and ending inventory. (348)

B

Bad Debt Expense (Doubtful Accounts Expense, Uncollectible Accounts Expense, Provision for Uncollectible Accounts) Expense associated with estimated uncollectible accounts receivable. (291)

Balance Sheet (Statement of Financial Position) Reports the amount of assets, liabilities, and stockholders' equity of an accounting entity at a point in time. (7)

Bank Reconciliation Process of verifying the accuracy of both the bank statement and the cash accounts of a business. (302)

Bank Statement Monthly report from a bank that shows deposits recorded, checks cleared, other debits and credits, and a running bank balance. (301)

Basic Accounting Equation (Balance Sheet Equation) Assets = Liabilities + Stockholders' Equity. (8)

Board of Directors Elected by the shareholders to represent their interests; is responsible for maintaining the integrity of the company's financial reports. (235)

Bond Certificate The bond document that each bondholder receives. (518)

Bond Discount The difference between selling price and par when a bond is sold for less than par. (519)

Bond Premium The difference between selling price and par when a bond is sold for more than par. (519)

Bond Principal The amount (1) payable at the maturity of the bond and (2) on which the periodic cash interest payments are computed. (516)

C

Callable Bonds Bonds that may be called for early retirement at the option of the issuer. (517)

Capital Expenditures Expenditures that increase the productive life, operating efficiency, or capacity of the asset and are recorded as increases in asset accounts, not as expenses. (405)

Capital Lease meets at least one of the four criteria established by GAAP and results in the recording of an asset and liability. (479)

Capitalized Interest Interest expenditures included in the cost of a self-constructed asset. (403)

Cash Money or any instrument that banks will accept for deposit and immediate credit to the company's account, such as a check, money order, or bank draft. (299)

Cash Basis Accounting Records revenues when cash is received and expenses when cash is paid. (110)

Cash Equivalents Short-term investments with original maturities of three months or less that are readily convertible to cash and whose value is unlikely to change. (299, 655)

Cash Flows from Financing Activities Cash inflows and outflows related to external sources of financing (owners and creditors) for the enterprise. (657)

Cash Flows from Investing Activities Cash inflows and outflows related to the acquisition or sale of productive facilities and investments in the securities of other companies. (657)

Cash Flows from Operating Activities (Cash Flows from Operations) Cash inflows and outflows directly related to earnings from normal operations. (655)

Closing Entries Made at the end of the accounting period to transfer balances in temporary accounts to Retained Earnings and to establish a zero balance in each of the temporary accounts. (182)

Common Stock The basic voting stock issued by a corporation. (563)

Comparable Information Information that can be compared across businesses because similar accounting methods have been applied. (239)

Component Percentage Expresses each item on a particular financial statement as a percentage of a single base amount. (716)

Conservatism Suggests that care should be taken not to overstate assets

and revenues or understate liabilities and expenses. (239)

Consistent Information Information that can be compared over time because similar accounting methods have been applied. (239)

Consolidated Financial Statements The financial statements of two or more companies that have been combined into a single set of financial statements as if the companies were one. (622)

Contingent Liability Potential liability that has arisen as the result of a past event; not an effective liability until some future event occurs. (469)

Continuity (Going-Concern) Assumption States that businesses are assumed to continue to operate into the foreseeable future. (50)

Contra-Account An account that is an offset to, or reduction of, the primary account. (168)

Contributed Capital Results from owners providing cash (and sometimes other assets) to business. (53)

Convertible Bonds Bonds that may be converted to other securities of the issuer (usually common stock). (517)

Copyright Exclusive right to publish, use, and sell a literary, musical, or artistic work. (422)

Corporate Governance The procedures designed to ensure that the company is managed in the interests of the shareholders. (232)

Cost-Benefit Constraint Suggests that the benefits of accounting for and reporting of information should outweigh the costs. (239)

Cost of Goods Sold Equation $BI + P - EI = CGS$. (343)

Cost Principle See *historical cost principle*.

Coupon Rate The stated rate of interest on bonds. (519)

Credit The right side of an account. (61)

Credit Card Discount Fee charged by the credit card company for its services. (285)

Cumulative Dividend Preference Preferred stock feature that requires specified current dividends not paid in full to accumulate for every year in

which they are not paid. These cumulative preferred dividends must be paid before any common dividends can be paid. (572)

Cumulative Effects of Changes in Accounting Methods Amounts reflected on the income statement for adjustments made to balance sheet accounts when applying different accounting principles.

Current Assets Assets that will be used or turned into cash within one year. Inventory is always considered a current asset regardless of the time needed to produce and sell it. (51)

Current Dividend Preference The feature of preferred stock that grants priority on preferred dividends over common dividends. (572)

Current Liabilities Short-term obligations that will be paid in cash (or other current assets) within the current operating cycle or one year, whichever is longer. (52, 461)

D

Debenture An unsecured bond; no assets are specifically pledged to guarantee repayment. (517)

Debit The left side of an account. (61)

Declaration Date The date on which the board of directors officially approves a dividend. (567)

Declining-Balance Depreciation The method that allocates the cost of an asset over its useful life based on a multiple of (often two times) the straight-line rate. (412)

Deferred Expenses Previously acquired assets that need to be adjusted at the end of the accounting period to reflect the amount of expense incurred in using the asset to generate revenue. (469)

Deferred Tax Items Timing differences caused by reporting revenues and expenses according to GAAP on a company's income statement and according to the Internal Revenue Code on the tax return. (482)

Depletion Systematic and rational allocation of the cost of a natural resource over the period of exploitation. (419)

Depreciation Process of allocating the cost of buildings and equipment over their productive lives using a systematic and rational allocation of the cost of property, plant, and equipment (but not land) over their useful lives. (407)

Direct Labor The earnings of employees who work directly on the products being manufactured. (342)

Direct Method The method of presenting the operating activities section of the statement of cash flows reporting components of cash flows from operating activities as gross receipts and gross payments. (655)

Discontinued Operations Financial results from the disposal of a major component of the business, reported net of income tax effects. (258)

Dividends in Arrears Dividends on cumulative preferred stock that have not been declared in prior years. (572)

E

Earnings Forecasts Predictions of earnings for future accounting periods. (236)

Effective-Interest Method Amortizes a bond discount or premium on the basis of the effective-interest rate; it is the theoretically preferred method. (525)

Effective-Interest Rate Another name for the market rate of interest on a bond. (519)

Efficient Markets Securities markets in which prices fully reflect available information. (733)

Equity Method Used when an investor can exert significant influence over an investee. It permits recording the investor's share of the investee's income. (615)

Estimated Useful Life Expected service life of an asset to the present owner. (408)

Expenses Decreases in assets or increases in liabilities from ongoing operations incurred to generate revenues during the period. (108)

Extraordinary Items Gains and losses that are both unusual in nature and infrequent in occurrence; they are reported net of tax on the income statement. (258)

F

Face Amount Another name for principal or the principal amount of a bond. (516)

Factory Overhead Manufacturing costs that are not raw material or direct labor costs. (342)

Financial Accounting Standards Board (FASB) The private sector body given the primary responsibility to work out the detailed rules that become generally accepted accounting principles. (20)

Finished Goods Inventory Manufactured goods that are completed and ready for sale. (340)

First-In, First-Out (FIFO) Method Assumes that the first goods purchased (the first in) are the first goods sold. (346)

Form 8-K The report used by publicly traded companies to disclose any material event not previously reported that is important to investors. (243)

Form 10-K The annual report that publicly traded companies must file with the SEC. (243)

Form 10-Q The quarterly report that publicly traded companies must file with the SEC. (243)

Franchise A contractual right to sell certain products or services, use certain trademarks, or perform activities in a geographical region. (422)

Free Cash Flow Cash Flows from Operating Activities — Dividends — Capital Expenditures. (671)

Future Value The sum to which an amount will increase as the result of compound interest. (488)

G

Gains Increases in assets or decreases in liabilities from peripheral transactions. (109)

Generally Accepted Accounting Principles (GAAP) The measurement rules used to develop the information in financial statements. (19)

Goods Available for Sale The sum of beginning inventory and purchases (or transfers to finished goods) for the period. (343)

Goodwill (Cost in Excess of Net Assets Acquired) For accounting purposes, the excess of the purchase price of a business over the market value of the business's assets and liabilities. (421, 623)

Gross Profit (Gross Margin) Net sales less cost of goods sold. (245)

H

Held-to-Maturity Investments A long-term investment in bonds that management has the ability and intent to hold until maturity. (606)

Historical Cost Principle Requires assets to be recorded at the historical cash-equivalent cost, which on the date of the transaction is cash paid plus the current dollar value of all noncash considerations also given in the exchange. (50)

I

Income before Income Taxes (Pretax Earnings) Revenues minus all expenses except income tax expense. (246)

Income from Operations (Operating Income) Equals net sales less cost of goods sold and other operating expenses. (245)

Income Statement (Statement of Income, Statement of Earnings, Statement of Operations) Reports the revenues less the expenses of the accounting period. (10)

Indenture A bond contract that specifies the legal provisions of a bond issue. (517)

Indirect Method The method of presenting the operating activities section of the statement of cash flows that adjusts net income to compute cash flows from operating activities. (655)

Institutional Investors Managers of pension, mutual, endowment, and other funds that invest on the behalf of others. (238)

Intangible Assets Assets that have special rights but not physical substance. (399)

Internal Controls Processes by which a company provides reasonable assurance regarding the reliability of the company's financial reporting, the effectiveness and efficiency of its operations, and its compliance with applicable laws and regulations. (300)

Inventory Tangible property held for sale in the normal course of business or used in producing goods or services for sale. (340)

Investments in Associated (or Affiliated) Companies are investments in stock held for the purpose of influencing the operating and financing strategies for the long term. (616)

Issued Shares Total number of shares of stock that have been sold; shares outstanding plus treasury shares held. (560)

J

Journal Entry An accounting method for expressing the effects of a transaction on accounts in a debits-equal-credits format. (62)

L

Last-In, First-Out (LIFO) Method Assumes that the most recently purchased units (the last in) are sold first. (348)

Legal Capital The permanent amount of capital defined by state law that must remain invested in the business; serves as a cushion for creditors. (563)

Lenders (Creditors) Suppliers and financial institutions that lend money to companies. (238)

Liabilities Probable debts or obligations of the entity that result from past transactions, which will be paid with assets or services. (52, 461)

Licenses and **Operating Rights** Obtained through agreements with governmental units or agencies; permit owners to use public property in performing its services. (423)

LIFO Liquidation A sale of a lower-cost inventory item from beginning LIFO inventory. (365)

LIFO Reserve A contra-asset for the excess of FIFO over LIFO inventory. (358)

Liquidity The ability to pay current obligations. (461)

Long-Lived Assets Tangible and intangible resources owned by a business and used in its operations over several years. (399)

Long-Term Liabilities All of the entity's obligations that are not classified as current liabilities. (473)

Losses Decreases in assets or increases in liabilities from peripheral transactions. (109)

Lower of Cost or Market (LCM) Valuation method departing from the cost principle; it serves to recognize a loss when replacement cost or net realizable value drops below cost. (353)

M

Market Interest Rate Current rate of interest on a debt when incurred; also called *yield* or *effective-interest rate.* (519)

Market Tests Ratios that tend to measure the market worth of a share of stock. (729)

Market Value Method Reports securities at their current market value. (607)

Matching Principle Requires that expenses be recorded when incurred in earning revenue. (113)

Material Amounts Amounts that are large enough to influence a user's decision. (239)

Merchandise Inventory Goods held for resale in the ordinary course of business. (340)

Merger Occurs when one company purchases all of the net assets of another and the target company goes out of existence. (622)

N

Natural Resources Assets occurring in nature, such as mineral deposits, timber tracts, oil, and gas. (419)

Net Book Value (Book Value, Carrying Value) The acquisition cost of an asset less accumulated depreciation, depletion, or amortization. (168, 407)

Net Realizable Value The expected sales price less selling costs (e.g., repair and disposal costs). (354)

Noncash Investing and Financing Activities Transactions that do not have direct cash flow effects; reported as a supplement to the statement of cash flows in narrative or schedule form. (674)

No-Par Value Stock Capital stock that has no par value specified in the corporate charter. (563)

Notes (Footnotes) Provide supplemental information about the financial condition of a company, without which the financial statements cannot be fully understood. (17)

Notes Receivable Written promises that require another party to pay the business under specified conditions (amount, time, interest). (290)

O

Operating Cycle (Cash-to-Cash Cycle) The time it takes for a company to pay cash to suppliers, sell those goods and services to customers, and collect cash from customers. (105)

Operating Lease Does not meet any of the four criteria established by GAAP and does not cause the recording of an asset and liability. (474)

Ordinary Repairs and Maintenance Expenditures for the normal operating upkeep of long-lived assets. (405)

Outstanding Shares Total number of shares of stock that are owned by stockholders on any particular date. (560)

P

Paid-In Capital (Additional Paid-in Capital, Contributed Capital in Excess of Par) The amount of contributed capital less the par value of the stock. (245)

Par Value (1) A legal amount per share of stock established by the board of directors; it establishes the minimum amount a stockholder must contribute and has no relationship to the market price of the stock. (2) Also, another name for bond principal or the maturity amount of a bond. (244, 516, 563)

Parent Company The entity that gains a controlling influence over another company (the subsidiary). (622)

Patent Granted by the federal government for an invention; gives the owner the exclusive right to use, manufacture, and sell the subject of the patent. (422)

Payment Date The date on which a cash dividend is paid to the stockholders of record. (567)

Percentage of Credit Sales Method Bases bad debt expense on the historical percentage of credit sales that result in bad debts. (294)

Periodic Inventory System Ending inventory and cost of goods sold determined at the end of the accounting period based on a physical inventory count. (361)

Permanent (Real) Accounts The balance sheet accounts that carry their ending balances into the next accounting period. (182)

Perpetual Inventory System A detailed inventory record that is maintained to record each purchase and sale during the accounting period. (361)

Post-Closing Trial Balance Should be prepared as the last step in the accounting cycle to check that debits equal credits and all temporary accounts have been closed. (184)

Preferred Stock Stock that has specified rights over common stock. (571)

Prepaid Expenses Previously acquired assets that need to be adjusted at the end of the accounting period to reflect the amount of expense incurred in using the asset to generate revenue. (171)

Present Value The current value of an amount to be received in the future; a future amount discounted for compound interest. (479)

Press Release A written public news announcement normally distributed to major news services. (240)

Primary Objective of External Financial Reporting Provides useful economic information about a business to help external parties make sound financial decisions. (49)

Private Investors Individuals who purchase shares in companies. (238)

Public Company Accounting Oversight Board (PCAOB) The private sector body given the primary responsibility to work out detailed auditing standards. (22)

Purchase Discount Cash discount received for prompt payment of an account. (368)

Purchase Method Records assets and liabilities acquired in a merger or acquisition at their fair market value. (623)

Purchase Returns and Allowances A reduction in the cost of purchases associated with unsatisfactory goods. (368)

R

Ratio (Percentage) Analysis An analytical tool that measures the proportional relationship between two financial statement amounts. (716)

Raw Materials Inventory Items acquired for the purpose of processing into finished goods. (340)

Record Date The date on which the corporation prepares the list of current stockholders as shown on its records; dividends can be paid only to the stockholders who own stock on that date. (567)

Relevant Information Information that can influence a decision; it is timely and has predictive and/or feedback value. (239)

Reliable Information Information that is accurate, unbiased, and verifiable. (239)

Replacement Cost The current purchase price for identical goods. (353)

Residual (or Salvage) Value Estimated amount to be recovered, less disposal costs, at the end of the company's estimated useful life of an asset. (408)

Retained Earnings Cumulative earnings of a company that are not distributed to the owners and are reinvested in the business. (53)

Revenue Expenditures Expenditures that maintain the productive capacity of an asset during the current accounting period only and are recorded as expenses. (405)

Revenue Principle Revenues are recognized when goods or services are delivered, there is evidence of an arrangement for customer payment, the price is fixed or determinable, and collection is reasonably assured. (106)

Revenues Increases in assets or settlements of liabilities from ongoing operations. (106)

S

Sales (or Cash) Discount Cash discount offered to encourage prompt payment of an account receivable. (286)

Sales Returns and Allowances Reduction of sales revenues for return of or allowances for unsatisfactory goods. (287)

Securities and Exchange Commission (SEC) The U.S. government agency that determines the financial statements that public companies must provide to stockholders and the measurement rules that they must use in producing those statements. (19)

Securities Available for Sale All passive investments other than trading securities (classified as either short-term or long-term). (608)

Separate-Entity Assumption States that business transactions are separate from the transactions of the owners. (50)

Specific Identification Method Identifies the cost of the specific item that was sold. (345)

Stated Rate The rate of cash interest per period specified in the bond contract. (516)

Statement of Cash Flows Reports inflows and outflows of cash during the accounting period in the categories of operating, investing, and financing. (14)

Statement of Retained Earnings Reports the way that net income and the distribution of dividends affected the financial position of the company during the accounting period. (13)

Stock Dividend Distribution of additional shares of a corporation's own stock. (569)

Stock Split An increase in the total number of authorized shares by a specified ratio; does not decrease retained earnings. (570)

Stockholders' Equity (Owners' Equity or Shareholders' Equity) The financing provided by the owners and the operations of the business. (53)

Straight-Line Amortization Simplified method of amortizing a bond discount or premium that allocates an equal dollar amount to each interest period. (524)

Straight-Line Depreciation Method that allocates the cost of an asset in equal periodic amounts over its useful life. (409)

Subsidiary Company The entity that is acquired by the parent company. (622)

T

T-account A tool for summarizing transaction effects for each account, determining balances, and drawing inferences about a company's activities. (63)

Tangible Assets (or fixed assets) Assets that have physical substance. (399)

Technology Includes costs for computer software and Web development. (422)

Temporary (Nominal) Accounts Income statement (and sometimes dividends declared) accounts that are closed to Retained Earnings at the end of the accounting period. (182)

Temporary Differences Timing differences that cause deferred income taxes and will reverse, or turn around, in the future. (482)

Tests of Liquidity Ratios that measure a company's ability to meet its currently maturing obligations. (723)

Tests of Profitability Compare income with one or more primary activities. (718)

Tests of Solvency Ratios that measure a company's ability to meet its long-term obligations. (727)

Time Period Assumption The long life of a company can be reported in shorter time periods. (106)

Time Value of Money Interest that is associated with the use of money over time. (467)

Trademark An exclusive legal right to use a special name, image, or slogan. (422)

Trading Securities All investments in stocks or bonds that are held primarily for the purpose of active trading (buying and selling) in the near future (classified as short-term). (608)

Transaction (1) An exchange between a business and one or more external parties to a business or (2) a measurable internal event such as the use of assets in operations. (53)

Transaction Analysis The process of studying a transaction to determine its economic effect on the business in terms of the accounting equation. (55)

Treasury Stock A corporation's own stock that has been issued but was subsequently reacquired and is still being held by that corporation. (565)

Trial Balance A list of all accounts with their balances to provide a check on the equality of the debits and credits. (167)

Trustee An independent party appointed to represent the bondholders. (518)

U

Unearned (Deferred) Revenues Previously recorded liabilities that need to be adjusted at the end of the period to reflect the amount of revenue earned. (168)

Unit-of-Measure Assumption States that accounting information should be measured and reported in the national monetary unit. (50)

Units-of-Production Depreciation Method that allocates the cost of an asset over its useful life based on its periodic output related to its total estimated output. (410)

Unqualified (Clean) Audit Opinion Auditors' statement that the financial statements are fair presentations in all material respects in conformity with GAAP. (235)

Unrealized Holding Gains and Losses Amounts associated with price changes of securities that are currently held. (608)

W

Work in Process Inventory Goods in the process of being manufactured. (340)

Working Capital The dollar difference between total current assets and total current liabilities. (471)

Y

Yield (Effective Interest Rate) The current rate of interest on a debt when incurred. (519)

Page numbers followed by n indicate
material found in notes.

A

Abbott Labs, 423
Abercrombie and Fitch, 377
Adelphia, 24
Adolph Coors, 687
AIG, 24
Airborne, 332
Alcan, 252
Alcoa, 252
AMERCO, 449
American Airlines, 398, 497, 545
American Eagle Outfitters, 41–42, 96–97,
    156–157, 221–222, 276–277, 331,
    353, 392, 452, 509, 554, 598–599,
    648–649, 702, 753
  annual report, B–1—B–56
  balance sheet, B–21
  business description, B–9—B–15
  Form 10-K report, B–8—B–56
  income statement, B–22, B–23
  notes to financial statements, B–26—B–49
  statement of cash flows, B–25
  statement of stockholders' equity, B–24
Anheuser-Busch, 653
Applebee's, 48
Apple Computer, 15, 22, 320
Apple Inc., 4, 11, 24–25, 255, 255n, 351,
    435, 692
Archon, 592
Arthur Andersen, 24
Athlete's Foot, 285
Aurora Foods, 24
Avon, 275–276
A&W, 182n

B

Bally, 506–507
Barclays Global Investors, 238
Baxter International, 252
BHP Billiton, 689
Big Dog Holdings, Inc., 154
Bi-Lo, 101
Black & Decker, 419, 453
Blockbuster, 423
Bloomberg, 237
Bloomberg, 240–241
BMW Group, 88, 109, 337
Boeing, 401
Bombay, 740
Boston Beer Company, 127, 355, 399
  balance sheet, 660
  business description, 653–654
  cash flows from financing activities,
    657, 673
  cash flows from investing activities, 657,
    668–671
  cash flows from operations, 655–656,
    661–668, 677–683
  income statement, 660
  statement of cash flows, 656, 674, 675

Bristol-Myers Squibb, 252
Brunswick Corporation, 503, 507
BusinessWeek, 98, 158

C

Cable One, 603
California Pizza Kitchen, Inc., 70, 71
Callaway Golf, 356, 400, 625
  auditor, 235
  balance sheet, 243–245
  board of directors, 235
  business description, 231–232
  disclosure process, 240–252
  financial analysts, 236, 238
  income statement, 245–247
  institutional investors, 238–239
  investor relations, 237
  managers, 234
  notes to the financial statements,
    248–251
  return on equity analysis, 252–256
  statement of cash flows, 248, 249
Campbell Soup Co., 265
Cardinal Health, 24
Carlyle Golf, Inc., 704
Caterpillar Inc., 360, 393
Cedar Fair, L.P., 152
CFO Magazine, 252
Chili's, 48
Chuck-E-Cheese, 731
Cinergy, 589
Cintas, 742
Coach, Inc., 265
Coca-Cola Company, 52, 749
Colgate-Palmolive Company, 498, 640, 691
CompUSA, 4
Compustat, 237, 394
Computer Associates, 24, 113
Continental, 408
Creative Technology, 272–273

D

Dana Corporation, 392–393
Days Inn, 716
Deckers Outdoor Corporation, 235, 667
  balance sheet, 283–284, 293
  business description, 283–284
  cash and cash equivalent accounting,
    298, 299–305
  gross profit percentage, 288–289
  income statement, 284
  notes to financial statements, 285, 288,
    296
  receivables accounting, 290–299
  receivables turnover, 297
  sales revenue accounting, 284–289
  statement of cash flows, 298, 299
Deere & Company, 206, 359–360, 366
Dell, Inc., 4, 11, 15, 93, 94, 210, 255, 320,
    351, 353, 354, 380, 502, 595,
    751–753
  balance sheet, 751–752

  income statement, 752–753
Deloitte IAS Plus, 20, 240n
Deloitte & Touche, 27, 235
Delta Air Lines, 398, 400, 403, 408–409
Diageo, 650
DirecTV, 551
Disney, 422, 503, 545, 638
Dollar General Corporation, 741
Domino's, 47, 182
DowJones, 240–241
Dynegy, 24

E

Eastern Mountain Sports, 285
Eastman Kodak, 382, 454
Edward Jones, 721
Enron, 23–24, 113, 232, 233, 704–705
Ernst & Young LLP, 27, 163, 235
Ethan Allen Interiors, Inc., 95, 96
Exxon Mobil Corporation, 91, 156, 411, 507

F

Factiva, 237
Fannie Mae, 24
FedEx, 151–152, 319, 332, 419, 438, 439,
    443
FedEx Kinko's, 252
Fidelity Management & Research, 238
First Team Sports, Inc., 381
FMR Corporation, 53
Fontana Shoes, 290
Foot Locker, Inc., 90
Ford Motor Company, 360, 419, 438, 455,
    483–484, 506, 591–592
Fortune Brands, 716
Four Seasons, 716
Freddie Mac, 24
Freeport-McMoRan Copper & Gold Inc., 440

G

GameStop, 591
The Gap, Inc., 450
Gateway, Inc., 98–99, 100
General Electric, 52, 388
General Mills, 288, 355, 508, 534, 667, 670
  refinanced debt, 468–469
  zero coupon bonds, 528
General Motors Corporation, 55, 252, 360,
    387–388, 416
Gerber Scientific, 24
Giant food stores, 101
Gibraltar Industries, 694
Gibson Greeting Cards, 362, 382
GlaxoSmithKline, 55, 109
Global Crossing, 24
Goldman, Sachs & Co., 250
Goodyear, 24
Google Inc., 421

H

Halliburton, 24, 503, 599
Harley-Davidson, 71, 127, 182, 288, 399,
    625, 670
    balance sheet, 338, 358
    business description, 337–339
    commitments and contingencies, 470–471
    cost of goods sold, 343–344
    income statement, 338
    inventory, 340–343
    inventory costing methods, 345–351
    inventory management, 356, 366–370
    inventory methods and cost of goods sold,
        358–360
    inventory purchases, 368–369
    inventory turnover, 354–355
    inventory valuation, 354
    LIFO liquidations, 366–368
    notes to financial statements, 341, 358
    statement of cash flows, 357, 358
Harrah's Entertainment, Inc., 71, 235
    bonds payable, 514, 517–532, 533–534
    business description, 513–515
    debt-to-equity ratio, 531–532
    early retirement of debt, 532–533
    income statement, 522
    notes to financial statements, 514
    statement of cash flows, 534
Hasbro, Inc., 267, 435
Haynes, 593
HealthSouth, 24
Hechinger, 730–731
Hershey Company
    balance sheet, 747–748
    income statement, 746–747
Hess Corporation, 454–455
Hewlett-Packard Company, 201, 255,
    255n, 689
Hilton Hotels, 90, 716
Holiday Inn, 419
Home Depot, 71, 355, 419, 534, 573
    balance sheet, 708–709
    business description, 707–711
    business strategy of, 713–714
    financial statement analysis, 714–716
    income statement, 708
    investment decisions for, 712–713
    ratio and percentage analysis, 716–730
    statement of cash flows, 710–711
Homestore.com, 24
Honda, 337, 355
Hoovers, 237

I

IBJ Whitehall Bank & Trust Company, 518
IBM Corporation, 422
International Paper, 420
Investors Chronicle, 668

J

Jack in the Box, 566
JCPenney, 375, 743
JetBlue, 398
John Hancock, 608

K

Kaplan, Inc., 603
KFC, 127, 182n, 422–423
KPMG, 27, 235

L

Lance, Inc., 265
La Quinta, 716
La-Z-Boy Incorporated, 258
Lion Nathan, 688
Little Caesar's, 47
Lone Star Industries, 573
Long John Silver's, 182n
Lowe's, 573, 715, 717, 718, 720, 722, 723,
    726, 729–730, 740

M

Macy's, 638
Marriott International, Inc., 455, 648, 716
Mattel, Inc., 94
McDermott, 551
McDonald's Corporation, 11, 99–100, 404,
    497, 567–568
McKesson, 24
Merrill Lynch, 236, 238, 704–705
Merriman Curhan Ford, 236
Microsoft Corporation, 256–257, 318
Micro Warehouse Inc., 394
Miller, 653
MINI, 88
MiniScribe, 23–24, 362–363
Mirage Resorts, 716
Morgan Joseph & Co., 236

N

Newell Rubbermaid, 273
News Corp., 626
Newsweek magazine, 603
New York Times Company, The, 148
Nike, Inc., 86
Nortel, 24
Northwest Airlines, 674

O

Oakley, 265
Outback Steakhouse, 534, 670

P

Papa John's International, 97, 268, 288,
    355, 399, 400, 625, 667
    accounting cycle, 165, 182–185
    adjusting entries, 166–174
    annual report, 111, 123–124
    balance sheet, 51–53, 63–71, 121,
        124–125, 179–180, 243
    business description, 47–48, 103–104,
        163–164
    changes in financial statement amounts,
        53–55
    closing entries, 182–185
    estimating revenues and expenses at year
        end, 163

    financial leverage ratio, 70–71
    financial statement preparation, 122–126,
        175–182
    income statement, 106–121, 121,
        123–124, 177–178, 245
    net profit margin, 181–182
    notes to financial statements, 123–124
    operating activities, 110–116
    operating cycle, 105–106
    statement of cash flows, 72–73,
        125–127
    statement of retained earnings, 124
    statement of stockholders' equity, 179
    stock market reactions to announcements,
        115–116
    total asset turnover ratio, 126–127
    transaction analysis, 55–60, 63–68,
        117–121
    trial balance, 167–168, 169, 176,
        184–185
Parmalat, 24
Peet's Coffee & Tea, 323–324
PepsiCo, Inc., 496, 504, 693, 749
Phelps Dodge, 587–588
Philip Morris, 584
Pizza Hut, Inc., 47, 103, 127, 182n
Pizza Inn, Inc., 70
Polaroid Corporation, 85
PricewaterhouseCoopers, 27, 235
Procter & Gamble, 32, 587, 590, 596,
    724, 740

Q

Quaker Oats, 381, 393–394
Qwest Communication, 24

R

RadioShack, 594
Redhook Ale Brewery, 676
Reebok, 688
Reuters, 44, 101, 160, 228, 240–241, 280,
    334, 394, 650, 705, 754
Reuters.com, 237, 238
REX Stores Corporation, 444
Rite-Aid Corporation, 24, 113
Rocky Mountain Chocolate Factory, Inc.,
    702–703
Rolls-Royce, 88
Royal Ahold, 279–280
Royce & Associates, 238
Ruth's Chris Steakhouse, 586

S

Safeway, 518
SAS, 621
Saucony, Inc., 328
Sears, Roebuck, 419, 518, 589, 743
Siemens AG, 318
Singapore Airlines, 414, 445–446
Sizzler International, Inc., 695
Skechers, 297
Smith Barney, 732
Sonic Corp., 646

Sonic Drive-In
  authorized, issued, and outstanding
    shares, 560–562
  balance sheet, 558
  business description, 557–558, 559
  common stock transactions, 563–567, 570
  dividends, 566–568, 572–573
  dividend yield, 566–567
  earnings per share (EPS), 562
  notice of shareholders' meeting, 560
  preferred stock, 571–572
  statement of cash flows, 573–574
  stock dividends, 570
Sony Corporation, 278, 413
Southwest Airlines, 127
  acquisition cost, 401–403
  asset impairment, 416–417
  balance sheet, 400
  business description, 397–398
  depreciation, 406–415, 423–424, 428–429
  disposal of plant and equipment, 417–418
  fixed asset turnover, 400–401
  intangible assets, 423
  plant and equipment, 399–418
  repairs and maintenance, 404–405
  statements of cash flows, 424
Standard & Poor's, 509
Stanley Furniture, 689
Stanley Works, 24
Starbucks Corporation, 215, 441, 573, 642
  accounts payable turnover, 464
  balance sheet, 460, 469
  business description, 459–460
  current liabilities, 462–472
  current ratio, 462
  deferred taxes, 483
  long-term liabilities, 461, 473–475,
    479–481
  notes to financial statements, 469–471
  present value of liabilities, 479–481
  statement of cash flows, 471–472
  working capital management, 471–472
Stride Rite, 320
Sunbeam, 507

Symbol Technologies, 332–333
Sysco, 143–144

T

Taco Bell, 127, 182n
Target, 319
Texas Instruments, 741
Thompson Research, 237
Tiffany & Co., 268
Timberland, 297, 400, 641
Time Warner Telecom, 691
Tim Hortons, 594
Tommy Hilfiger, 271
Tootsie Roll, 32–33
Toyota Motor Corporation, 33, 474, 641
Toys R Us, 105
Trump Casinos, 523
Trump Entertainment Resorts, 439
Tyco, 24

U

Unilever, 109
United Airlines, 398, 400
United Parcel Service, 332, 439
U.S. Foodservice Inc., 101
UPS, 332, 439
Urban Outfitters, Inc., 42, 97, 157,
  221–222, 277, 331, 392, 452, 509,
  554, 599, 649, 702, 753
  balance sheet, C-17—C-18
  business description, C-3—C-10
  Form 10-K report, C-2—C-37
  income statement, C-18
  statement of cash flows, C-20
  statement of shareholders' equity, C-19
US Airways, 398

V

Vail Resorts, Inc., 144
Value Line, 236
Verizon Communications, Inc., 645

W

W. T. Grant, 668
Walgreen Co., 34
Wall Street Journal, 222
Wal-Mart Stores, 11, 182, 356
Walt Disney Company, 422, 503,
  545, 638
Washington Post Company, 182
  balance sheet, 604, 623, 630–631
  business description, 603–604
  consolidated financial statements, 604,
    622–625, 629–632
  income statement, 624, 631–632
  investments for significant influence,
    615–621
  mergers and acquisitions, 621–626,
    629–632
  return on assets (ROA), 625–626
  securities available for sale, 609–614
  statement of cash flows, 621–626
  trading securities, 612–614
Wedbush Morgan, 236
Wendy's International, Inc., 53, 72, 150,
  566, 567
Whole Foods Market, 180, 598
Wolverine World Wide, Inc., 143
WorldCom, 23–24, 113, 232, 233, 405

X

Xerox, 24

Y

Yahoo!, 237
Yamaha, 337
YouTube, 421
Yum! Brands, 182, 182n, 422–423

Z

ZZZZ Best, 113

Page numbers followed by n indicate
material found in notes.

A

Accelerated depreciation, 412–413
Account(s)
 chart of, 54–55
 defined, 54
 in foreign financial statements, 109
 impact of transactions on, 55–60
 nature of, 54–55
Accounting
 accrual basis, 110–114
 assumptions of, 50
 careers in, 26–27
 cash basis, 110
 defined, 4
 nature of business transactions, 53–54
Accounting communication, 18–23,
   233–240
 auditing in, 21–22
 disclosure process, 240–243
 ethics and, 23
 financial statements in, 239. See also
  Financial statement(s)
 generally accepted accounting principles
  (GAAP), 19–20, 52, 233, 250,
  414–417
 legal liability and, 23
 players in, 233–240
 reputation and, 23
 return on equity analysis, 252–256
Accounting cycle
 during-period steps in, 60, 165
 end-of-period steps in, 60, 165, 166,
  182–185, 291
 steps in, 60, 165
Accounting entity, 7–8
Accounting equation. See Balance sheet
  equation
Accounting period, 10–11
Accounting staff, 234
Accounting standards. See also Generally
  accepted accounting principles (GAAP)
 Financial Accounting Standards (FAS),
  20, 233
 global differences in, 239–240
 International Financial Reporting
  Standards (IFRS), 20, 55, 109,
  419, 423
Accounts payable, 463–464
 change in, 663–664
 defined, 56, 463
Accounts payable turnover, 464, 490
Accounts receivable
 accrued revenues, 170
 aging of, 295–296
 bad debts and, 290–296
 on the balance sheet, 283–284
 cash flows and, 298, 299
 change in, 662–663, 666
 control over, 296–299
 defined, 290
 receivables turnover, 297, 310, 719, 725
Accrual accounting, 110–114

Accrued expenses
 defined, 166, 172, 664
 types of, 172–174
Accrued liabilities, 464–467
 accrued compensation and related costs,
  465–466
 accrued taxes payable, 465
 deferred taxes, 482–483
 payroll taxes, 466–467
 retirement benefits, 483–484
Accrued revenues
 defined, 166, 170
 types of, 170–171
Accumulated depreciation, 168, 407, 412
Acid test, 719, 724–725
Acquisition cost, 401–403
 for cash, 402
 by construction, 403
 for debt, 402
 defined, 401
 for equity, 402
 of intangible assets, 420–423
 of natural resources, 419–420
Adams, Samuel, 653
Additional details, 658
Additional Paid-In Capital (Paid-In
  Capital), 245
Additions, to property, plant, and
  equipment, 405
Adjusted trial balance, 175, 176
Adjusting entries, 164
 accrued expenses, 166, 172–174, 664
 accrued revenues, 166, 170–171
 adjustment process, 167–174
 for bad debt expense estimates, 291
 defined, 165
 end of the accounting period, 60, 165,
  166, 182–185, 291
 for expenses, 165–175
 prepaid expenses, 166, 171–172
 purpose of, 165–166
 for revenues, 165–175
 securities available for sale, 610–611
 types of, 166
 unearned revenues, 166, 168–170
Affiliates, investments in, 616
Aging of accounts receivable, 295–296
Allowance for doubtful accounts, 291,
  292, 296
Alternative accounting methods, 250
American Institute of Certified Public
  Accountants (AICPA), 23
Amortization
 of bonds issued at a discount, 519,
  523–528, 530
 of bonds issued at a premium, 529–531
 defined, 420
 effective-interest methods, 525–527,
  530–531
 of intangible assets, 420–423
 straight-line methods, 524–525, 529–530
Amortized cost method, for held-to-maturity
  investments, 606
Announcements, stock market reactions to,
  115–116, 241
Annual reports, 7, 242, 243

Annuity
 defined, 477
 future value of, 488–489, A–3
 present value of, 477–479, 480–481,
  486–487, A–1—A–2
Asset(s). See also specific assets
 adjusting entries for, 166
 on balance sheet, 9–10, 50–52
 defined, 50
 depreciation of. See Depreciation
 disposal of, 417–418
 historical cost principle and, 50–51,
  167–168, 420
 impairment of, 416–418
 intangible, 52, 243, 399, 420–423
 interpreting, 9–10
 tangible, 399
 total asset turnover ratio, 126–127, 134
 typical account titles, 54
Asset turnover, 126–127, 134, 254
Associated companies, investments in, 616
Assurance services, 27
Audit(s)
 defined, 21
 nature of, 21–22
Audit committee, 235
Auditing
 audit or assurance services, 27
 management responsibility for, 21–22
Auditors, 235
Audit reports, 21
Authorized number of shares, 560, 561
Average cost inventory method, 348–349
Average days' supply in inventory, 726

B

Bad debt expense, 291
Bad debts, 290–296
 accounting process for, 292
 allowance method, 291
 estimating, 291, 293–296
 recording, 291, 292–293
 reporting, 292–293
 summary of accounting process, 292
 writing off specific uncollectible accounts,
  291–292
Balance sheet, 6, 7–10. See also Financial
  statement(s)
 account balances on, 60–68
 accounts receivable on, 283–284
 basic accounting equation and, 8–9,
  57, 122
 chart of accounts, 54–55
 classified, 68–71, 124–125, 243–245
 comparative, 658, 660
 consolidated, 604, 623–624, 630–631
 converting to FIFO inventory method, 359
 defined, 7
 elements of, 9, 19, 50–53
 estimated liabilities reported on, 469
 formula for, 8–9, 57, 122
 passive investments on, 607–608, 611
 permanent (real) accounts, 177, 182
 preparing, 68–71, 124–125, 177, 179–180
 purpose of, 7, 19

relationships with other financial
    statements, 17, 658–661
Statement of Stockholders' Equity, 177,
    179, 248
structure of, 7–9, 19
temporary (nominal) accounts, 177,
    182–183
transaction analysis, 55–60, 121
Balance sheet equation
    balancing, 57
    described, 8–9, 122
Bank reconciliation, 302–305
    defined, 302
    illustration of, 303–305
    need for, 302–303
Bankruptcy, bonds payable and, 516,
    523, 533n
Bank service charges, 303, 304, 305n
Bank statements
    contents of, 301–302
    defined, 301
    example of, 302
    reconciliation of, 302–305
Basic accounting equation. See Balance
    sheet equation
Beginning inventory (BI), in cost of goods
    sold, 343–344
Board of directors, 235
Bond(s), 473–474, 513–537
    cash flows from financing activities,
        672, 673
    held-to-maturity, 606–607
    as investments, 605–607
    notes to financial statements, 514
    types of, 516–517
    zero coupon, 527–528
Bond certificate, 518
Bond discounts, 519, 523–528, 530
Bond premium, 519, 528–531
Bond principal, 516, 518
Bonds payable
    bankruptcy risk and, 516, 523, 533n
    cash flows and, 516, 533–534
    characteristics of, 515–518
    debt-to-equity ratio, 531–532, 539, 719,
        728–729, 730–731
    early retirement of, 532–533
    issued at a discount, 519, 523–528, 530
    issued at a premium, 529, 531
    issued at par, 520–522
    par value of, 516, 518
    present value of interest payment,
        536, 537
    present value of maturity payment,
        536, 537
    reporting transactions in, 518–532
    times interest earned, 522–523, 538, 719,
        727–728
    types of, 516–517
Bonuses, 18, 175
Book value, 412, 630. See also Net book
    value
    as approximation of remaining life, 408
Botosan, C. A., 235n
Buildings, defined, 399
Bush, George, 231
Business entities
    accounting for owners' equity, 576–579
    types of, 26

Business strategy, 254–255, 713–714

C

Callable bonds, 517
Callaway, Ely, 231, 238
Capital, contributed, 53, 244–245, 672–673
Capital acquisitions ratio, 670–671, 685
Capital expenditures, defined, 405
Capital gains, 53
Capitalization, 401, 405
Capitalized interest, 403
Capital leases, 475
Capital structure, 459–460, 515
Carrying value, 407. See Net book value
Cash, 299–305
    acquisition cost based on, 402
    on the balance sheet, 283–284
    bank reconciliations, 302–305
    for cash dividends, 568
    cash management, 300
    converting operating expenses to inflow
        of, 679–680
    converting revenues to, 678
    defined, 299
    internal control of, 300–301
    net increase (decrease) in, 657–658
Cash basis accounting, 110
Cash coverage ratio, 719, 728
Cash discounts, 308
Cash dividends
    on common stock, 566–568
    impact on stock price, 568
Cash equivalent price, 401
Cash equivalents, 299–305
    bank reconciliations, 302–305
    in cash management, 300
    defined, 299, 655
    internal control of, 300–301
    on statement of cash flows, 655
Cash equivalent sales price, 285
Cash flows. See also Statement of cash flows
    accounts receivable and, 298, 299
    bonds payable and, 516, 533–534
    depreciation of productive assets,
        423–424
    disclosures and, 179
    from financing activities. See Cash flows
        from financing activities
    impact of dividend payments on, 573–574
    inventory management and, 355–356
    from investing activities. See Cash flows
        from investing activities
    from operating activities. See Cash flows
        from operating activities
    working capital and, 471–472, 666
Cash flows from financing activities, 72,
    248, 573–574, 671–673
    defined, 16, 657
    interpreting, 673
    reporting, 671–673
Cash flows from investing activities, 15–16,
    72, 248, 609, 617–618, 620–621,
    668–671
    defined, 15, 657
    interpreting, 670–671
    reporting, 668–670
Cash flows from operating activities,
    125–127, 181, 655–656

conversion of net income to, 664
    defined, 15
    direct method, 248, 655, 677–681
    fraud and, 668
    indirect method, 248, 655–656, 661–665
    interpreting, 666–668
    reporting, 661–665, 677–681
Cash management, 300
Cash ratio, 719, 723–724
Cash-to-cash (operating) cycle, 105–106,
    726–727
Certified internal auditors (CIAs), 26–27
Certified management accountants (CMAs),
    26–27
Certified public accountants (CPAs), 21,
    26–27
Chairman and chief executive officer
    (CEO), 234
Chapman, James, 668n
Chart of accounts, 54–55
Chief financial officer (CFO), 234
Classified balance sheet, 68–71, 124–125,
    243–245
Classified income statement, 123–124,
    245–247
Clinton, Bill, 231
Closing entries, 182–183
Cohen, Abby Joseph, 250
Common-size income statement, 247
Common stock, 563–571. See also Stock
    market
    authorized shares, 560, 561
    cash dividends on, 566–568
    cash flows from financing activities, 672
    characteristics of ownership, 559–560
    controlling interests in, 605–606,
        621–626
    defined, 563
    dividends payable, 566–568, 569–570
    earnings per share (EPS), 109, 178, 247,
        562, 580, 719, 721
    initial sale of, 563
    issued for employee compensation, 564
    issued shares, 560, 561
    outstanding shares, 560, 561
    passive investment in, 605, 607–614
    repurchase of, 564–565
    sale in secondary markets, 564
    securities available for sale, 608–615
    stock dividends on, 569–570
    stock splits on, 570–571
    trading securities, 608, 612–613
Company strategy, 254–255, 713–714
Comparable information, in accounting
    communication process, 239
Comparative balance sheets, 658, 660
Comparison with similar companies,
    715–716
Compensation
    accrued compensation and related costs,
        465–466
    accrued retirement benefits, 483–484
    bonuses in, 18, 175
    payroll taxes, 466–467
    salaries expense in, 108, 172–173
    stock issued for, 564
Complete income statement, 658
Component percentages, 716–718
Compound entries, 63

Compounding, power of, 489
Comprehensive income, 612
Conservatism principle, 164, 186, 239, 353
Consistent information, in accounting
    communication process, 239
Consolidated financial statements
    after acquisition, 630–632
    balance sheet, 604, 623–624, 630–631
    for a controlling interest, 604, 622,
        629–630
    income statement, 624–625, 631–632
    nature of, 622
    preparing, 629–632
    statement of cash flows, 656
Construction, acquisition cost based
    on, 403
Consumers, 285
Contingent liabilities, 469–471
Continuing operations, income statement
    and, 245–246
Continuity assumption, 50, 245–246
Contra-accounts, 167–168, 358, 565
Contra-asset accounts, 358
Contract rate of interest, 519
Contra-equity accounts, 565
Contributed capital, 53, 244–245, 672–673
Contributed Capital in Excess of Par, 245
Controlling interests, 605–606, 621–626
    consolidated financial statements for,
        604, 622, 629–630
    nature of, 605–606
Convertible bonds, 517
Copyrights
    amortization of, 422
    defined, 422
    as intangible assets, 52
Corporate governance, 232
Corporations, 26
    ownership of, 559–562. See also
        Stockholders' equity
Cost advantage strategy, 713
Cost-benefit constraint, 239
Cost in excess of net assets acquired, 623
Cost of goods sold
    converting to cash paid to suppliers,
        678–679
    defined, 337–338
    equation for, 343, 346–347
    nature of, 343–344
Cost of sales, 108
Cost principle, 401, 419
Coupon rate, 519
Credit balances, 116, 610
Credit card discounts, 285, 308
Credit card sales, 285
Credit managers, 18
Creditors, 3–4
    in accounting communication process,
        238–239
    liabilities and, 52–53
Credits, in T accounts, 61, 64
Credit sales
    bad debts, 290–296
    terms for, 286–287
Credit terms, 286–287
Cross-sectional analysis, 255
Cumulative dividend preference, 572
Current assets
    nature of, 51–52

trading securities as, 608, 612–613
    working capital management,
        471–472, 666
Current dividend preference, 572
Current liabilities, 462–472
    accounts payable, 56, 463–464, 663–664
    accrued liabilities, 464–467, 482–484
    current portion of long-term debt, 468
    deferred revenues, 166, 168–170, 469
    defined, 52, 461
    notes payable, 467–468, 472–474
    refinanced debt, 468–469
    reported in the notes, 469–471
    reported on the balance sheet, 469
    working capital management, 471–472
Current market value, 407
Current portion of long-term debt, 468
Current ratio, 462, 490, 719, 724
Current receivables, 290
Customers, 4
Cut-off errors, 163–164

D

Debentures, 517
Debit balances, 116, 610
Debits, in T accounts, 61, 64
Debt. See also Bad debts; Bond(s); Bonds
        payable; Notes payable
    acquisition cost based on, 402
    in capital structure, 459–460
    cash flows from financing activities, 672
    current portion of long-term, 468
    held to maturity, 606–607
    notes receivable, 290–296
    passive investments in, 605
    refinanced, 468–469
Debt covenants, restrictive, 573
Debt-to-equity ratio, 531–532, 539, 719,
        728–729, 730–731
Declaration date, of dividends, 567–568
Declining-balance depreciation method,
        409, 412–413
Decomposition analysis, 253–254
Decreasing cost inventories, 351
Default risk, 518
Deferred (unearned) revenues
    defined, 166, 168, 469
    examples of, 168–170
Deferred tax items, 482–483
Definite life, of intangible assets, 420
Depletion
    defined, 419
    of natural resources, 419–420
Deposits in transit, 303, 304
Depreciable cost, 410
Depreciation, 406–416
    accelerated, 412–413
    accumulated, 168, 407, 412
    changes in estimates, 428–429
    concepts concerning, 406–408
    declining-balance method, 409, 412–413
    defined, 167, 407
    effect on statement of cash flows,
        423–424
    manager choice of method, 414–416
    straight-line method, 409–410, 413,
        428–429
    in tax reporting, 415, 416

units-of-production method, 409,
        410–411, 413
Depreciation expense, 407–408
Depreciation schedule, 410
Desai, H., 234n
Direct labor cost, 342
Direct materials. See Raw materials
    inventory
Direct method
    for cash flows from operating activities,
        248, 655, 677–681
    for statement of cash flows, 677–681
Disclosure, 240–243. See also Financial
        statement(s)
    annual reports in, 7, 242, 243
    cash flows and, 179
    press releases in, 240–242
    quarterly reports in, 7, 242, 243
    SEC reports in, 243
    stock market reactions to earnings
        announcements, 115–116, 241
Disclosures about Market Risks, 242
Discontinued operations, 258
Discount(s)
    amortization of bonds issued at,
        523–528, 530
    bond, 519, 523–528, 530
    bonds purchased at, 606
    cash, 308
    credit card, 285, 308
    deciding to take, 287
    purchase, 368–369
    recording, 308
    sales, 286–287
    trade, 286n
Disposal of assets, 417–418
Dividend income
    under equity method, 617–618
    on securities available for sale, 609
Dividends in arrears, 572, 573
Dividends payable, 4, 53
    cash, 566–568
    common stock, 566–568, 569–570
    impact on cash flows, 573–574
    preferred stock, 572, 573
    restrictions on payment of, 573
    on statement of retained earnings, 13–14
    stock, 569–570
Dividend yield, 566–567, 580, 719,
        729–730
Double-declining-balance rate, 412–413
Doubtful accounts, allowance for, 291,
        292, 296
DuPont analysis, 253–254, 713–714
During-period steps, in accounting cycle,
        60, 165

E

Earnings
    quality of, 181, 186
    unexpected, 115–116, 241
Earnings forecasts, 236
Earnings per share (EPS), 109, 178, 247,
        562, 580, 719, 721
Ebbers, Bernie, 113
Economic life, 408–409
Economywide factors, in investment
        decision, 712

Effective-interest rate, 519, 521
  amortization of bonds issued at a
    discount, 525–527
Effective-interest rates, amortization of
  bonds issued at a premium, 530–531
Efficient markets, 733
Electronic funds transfer (EFT), 301
Elements
  of balance sheet, 9, 19, 50–53
  defined, 5
  of income statement, 11–12, 19, 106–109
  of statement of cash flows, 15–16, 19,
    248, 249
  of statement of retained earnings,
    13–14, 19
Elliott, J., 175n
Employee bonuses, 18
Employee compensation. See Compensation
Employee FICA taxes, 466–467
Employee income taxes, 466
Employees' union, 18
Ending inventory
  in cost of goods sold, 343–344, 346–347
  errors in measuring, 362–363
  income before income taxes, 362–363
End of the accounting period
  adjusting entries, 165, 166, 182–185
  inventory in, 343–344, 346–347, 361, 362
  steps in accounting cycle, 60, 165, 166,
    182–185, 291
End-of-the-year retained earnings, 14
Equipment. See also Property, plant, and
  equipment
  cash flows from investing activities, 669
  defined, 399
Equity. See Common stock; Preferred stock;
  Stockholders' equity
Equity method
  defined, 615
  investment income under, 620
  for investments of significant influence,
    605, 615–618
  recording investments under, 616–618
  reporting investments under, 618
Errors
  in bank reconciliation process, 303, 304
  in measuring ending inventory, 362
Estimated liabilities
  reported in the notes, 469–471
  reported on the balance sheet, 469
Estimated useful life, 408–409
Estimates
  bad debt expense, 291, 293–296
  change in, 428–429
  of expenses at year-end, 163–164
Ethics
  accounting communication and, 23
  fraud and cash flow from operations, 668
  "greening of GAAP" and, 52
  improper influence and, 618
  insider information, 732–733
  internal control of cash, 300–301
  inventory costing methods and, 351
  management incentives to violate
    accounting rules, 112–113, 175
  separate records for tax and financial
    reporting, 416
  sustainable development and, 252
  truth in advertising, 478–479

Exchanges
  nature of, 53–54
  in transaction analysis, 56–57
Expenses
  accrued, 166, 172–174, 664
  adjusting entries for, 166, 167–174
  bad debt, 291
  converting operating expenses to cash
    outflow, 679–680
  defined, 12, 108
  depreciation, 407–408
  estimating at year end, 163–164
  income tax, 109
  interest. See Interest expense
  operating, 108, 679–680
  prepaid, 166, 171–172, 663
  recognition for income tax purposes,
    484–485
  repair and maintenance, 405
  typical account titles, 54
  variable, 411
External decision makers, 4, 5
  generally accepted accounting principles
    and, 20–21
  primary objective of external financial
    reporting and, 49–50
External events, 53–54
Extraordinary items, 258

F

Face amount, bond, 516, 518
Factory overhead, 342
Fair value option, 614
Federal Income Tax Withheld (FITW), 466
Fellows, George, 231
FICA taxes, 466–467
Financial accounting
  external decision makers and, 49–50
  nature of, 4, 5
  separate records for tax accounting
    and, 416
Financial Accounting Standards (FAS), 20
Financial Accounting Standards Board
  (FASB), 20, 233
Financial analysts, in accounting
  communication process, 235–237
Financial leverage, 720
Financial leverage percentage, 79, 254,
  719, 720
Financial leverage ratio, 70–71, 79, 254,
  719, 720
Financial position, 9
Financial ratios. See Ratio analysis
Financial reporting. See also Financial
  statement(s)
  annual reports, 7, 242, 243
  cash flows from financing activities,
    671–673
  cash flows from investing activities,
    668–670
  cash flows from operating activities,
    661–665
  interim reports, 106n
  manager choice of depreciation method,
    414–416
  primary objective of external, 49–50
  quarterly reports, 7, 242, 243
  separate records for tax reporting and, 416

Financial statement(s). See also Balance
  sheet; Generally accepted accounting
  principles (GAAP); Income statement;
  Statement of cash flows; Statement of
  retained earnings
  in accounting communication
    process, 239
  accounts on, 54–55
  analysis of. See Financial statement
    analysis
  business activities causing changes in,
    53–55
  consolidated, 604, 622, 623–625,
    629–632
  to determine value of company, 22
  foreign, 109. See also International
    perspective
  formats of, 243–248
  inventory costing methods and, 349–350
  management use of, 18
  notes to. See Notes to financial
    statements
  overview of, 6–18
  preparation and analysis of, 122–126,
    175–182
  relationships among, 17
  summary of, 18, 19
  voluntary disclosures, 252
Financial statement analysis, 48, 707–733.
  See also Balance sheet; Income
  statement; Ratio analysis; Statement
  of cash flows; Statement of retained
  earnings
  alternative accounting methods and, 250
  bond information from business press, 518
  book value as approximation of remaining
    life, 408
  business strategy and, 713–714
  capitalization and, 405
  common-size income statement, 247
  comparison with other companies in,
    715–716
  component percentages in, 716–718
  depreciation in, 423–425
  differences in estimated lives within
    single industry, 408–409
  of discounts, 287
  efficient markets and, 733
  financial statements to determine
    value, 22
  flows of inventory costs, 343
  free cash flow, 671
  impact of alternative depreciation
    methods, 413, 414
  impact of change on accounting
    adjustments, 414
  impact of dividends on stock price, 568
  insider information and, 732–733
  intangible assets, 52
  interpreting assets, liabilities, and
    stockholders' equity, 9–10
  interpreting cash flow statement, 16
  interpreting retained earnings, 14
  inventory methods and, 358–360,
    365–366
  investment decision and, 712–713
  job searches and, 237
  LIFO and inventory turnover ratio, 354–355,
    359–360, 372, 719, 725–726

Financial statement analysis—*Cont.*
  LIFO liquidations and inventory
      management, 367–368
  market tests, 719, 729–730
  nature of, 714–716
  net income, 181
  notes to financial statements, 123–124
  quality of earnings, 181, 186
  ratio and percentage analysis in, 716–733
  refinanced debt, 468
  restriction on payment of dividends, 573
  stock market reactions to accounting
      announcements, 115–116, 241
  T-accounts in, 68
  tests of liquidity, 719, 723–727
  tests of profitability, 718–722
  tests of solvency, 719, 727–729
  time series analysis in, 255, 715
  transaction structuring for minority
      investments, 620, 629n
  zero coupon bonds, 527–528
Financing activities, 573–574
  cash flows from. *See* Cash flows from
      financing activities
  events in, 58
  nature of, 4, 48
Finished goods inventory, 340
First-in, first-out (FIFO) inventory method
  converting balance sheet to, 359
  converting income statement to, 358–359
  described, 346–347, 349
  financial statement effects of, 349–350
Fixed assets, defined, 399
Fixed asset turnover, 400–401, 430, 719, 722
Fixtures, defined, 399
FOB (free on board) destination, 284
FOB (free on board) shipping point, 284
Footnotes. *See* Notes to financial
      statements
Forecasts, earnings, 236
Foreign currency
  borrowing in, 474
  cash flow statement and, 665
  receivables in, 290
Form 8-K, 243
Form 10-K, 243
Form 10-Q, 243
Franchises, 48n, 107
  amortization of, 422–423
  defined, 422
  unearned franchise fees, 168–170
Fraud, and cash flow from operations, 668
Free cash flow, 671
Full-disclosure principle, in accounting
      communication process, 239
Fundamental accounting model, 55–56
Future value concepts, 487–489
  future value, defined, 488
  future value of annuity, 488–489, A–3
  future value of single amount, 488, A–2
  power of compounding, 489

G

GAAP. *See* Generally accepted accounting
      principles (GAAP)
Gains
  on sale of assets, 109
  unrealized, 608

General journal, 61, 62–63
General ledger, 61, 63
Generally accepted accounting principles
      (GAAP), 19–20, 233
  alternative accounting methods and, 250
  application to company's statements, 250
  depreciation method and, 414–416
  determination of, 19–20
  "greening of GAAP" and, 52
  importance to managers and external
      users, 20–21
Going-concern assumption, 50
Goods available for sale, 343
Goodwill, 623, 625
  amortization of, 421
  defined, 421
Government Accounting Office (GAO), 27
Grass, Martin, 113
Gross method, 368–369
Gross profit (gross margin), 245, 283,
      288, 310
Gross profit percentage, 288–289, 310
Growth
  horizontal, 621
  rapid, 731
  sustainable, 252
Gulmi, Y., 116n

H

Halsey, R., 181, 181n
Held-to-maturity investments, 606–607
High quality information, 164
High-value strategy, 254–255
Historical cost principle, 50–51, 167–168, 420
Hogan, C. E., 234n
Holiday, Bradley, 231
Horizontal growth, 621
Hribar, P., 235n
Human resource managers, 18
Hunton, J. E., 236n

I

Immaterial amounts, in accounting
      communication process, 239
Impairment
  defined, 416
  measuring, 416–418
Improper influence, 618
Improvements, to property, plant, and
      equipment, 405
Income before income taxes, 106, 246
  ending inventory and, 362–363
Income from Operations, 245
Income statement, 6, 10–13, 103–132
  accrual accounting, 110–114
  analyzing, 13
  chart of accounts, 54–55
  classified, 123–124, 245–247
  common-size, 247
  consolidated, 624–625, 631–632
  continuing operations, 245–246
  converting to FIFO inventory method,
      358–359
  defined, 10
  elements of, 11–12, 19, 106–109
  formula for, 122
  interest expense reported on, 522

operating cycle, 105–106, 726–727
  preparing, 123–124, 175, 177–178
  purpose of, 10, 19
  recognizing and measuring operating
      activities, 110–116
  relationships with other financial
      statements, 17, 658–661
  structure of, 10–11, 19
  transaction analysis, 118–121
Income Summary, 182n
Income taxes. *See also* Tax reporting
  deferred tax items, 482–483
  income before, 106, 246, 362–363
  income taxes payable. *See* Income taxes
      payable
  revenue and expense recognition for
      income tax purposes, 484–485
  tax minimization versus tax evasion, 485
Income taxes payable, 484
  accrued, 465
  as accrued expense, 173–174
  employee, 466
Income tax expense, 109
Increasing cost inventories, 350–351
Indefinite life, of intangible assets, 421
Indenture, bond, 517
Independent accountants, 21
Indirect method
  for cash flows from operating activities,
      248, 655–656, 661–665
  for statement of cash flows, 674, 675,
      681–683
Individual company factors, in investment
      decision, 713
Industry factors, in investment
      decision, 712
Information services, in accounting
      communication process, 236–237
Initial public offering (IPO), 563
Insider information, 732–733
Institutional investors, in accounting
      communication process, 238–239
Insurance, as prepaid expense, 171–172
Intangible assets, 52, 243, 420–423
  amortization of, 420–423
  defined, 399
  types of, 421–423
Interest earned, 607
Interest expense, 108, 516, 728
  on bonds issued at par value, 522
  capitalized, 403
  effective-interest amortization of,
      525–527, 530–531
  straight-line amortization of, 524–525,
      529–530
  times interest earned, 522–523, 538, 719,
      727–728
Interest income, on bank statements, 303
Interest paid, 728
Interest payable
  as accrued expense, 172–173
  bond, 518–519
Interest periods, in calculating present
      value, 478
Interest rates
  in calculating present value, 478
  effective, 519, 521, 525–527, 530–531
  market, 519
  stated, 516, 519

Interest receivable, 170–171, 290
Interim reports, 106n
Internal control
of cash, 300–301
defined, 300
of inventory, 361–363
Internal control of cash, 300–301
Internal decision makers, 4, 5
Internal events, 54
International Accounting Standards Board
(IASB), 20
International Financial Reporting Standards
(IFRS), 20, 55, 109, 419, 423
International perspective
borrowing in foreign currencies, 474
differences in accounting standards, 20,
239–240
differences in accounts, 109
foreign currency and the statement of
cash flows, 665
foreign currency receivable, 290
International Financial Reporting
Standards (IFRS), 55, 109, 419, 423
LIFO and international comparisons, 360
measurement basis for property, plant,
and equipment, 419
notes concerning multinationals, 123–124
understanding foreign financial
statements, 55
Inventory
beginning, 343–344
change in, 663, 667
costs included in purchases, 341–343
defined, 340
ending, 343–344, 346–347, 362
financial statement analysis and,
358–360, 365–366
items included in, 340–343
types of, 340
Inventory control, 361–363
errors in measuring ending inventory,
362–363
periodic inventory system, 361–362,
369–370
perpetual inventory system, 361, 362,
369–370
Inventory costing methods, 345–351
average cost method, 348–349
cost flow assumptions in, 346–349
financial statement effects of, 349–350
first-in, first-out (FIFO) method, 346–347,
349–350, 358–359
last-in, first-out (LIFO) method, 347–351
managers' choice of, 350–351
specific identification, 345–346
Inventory management, 354–357
cash flows and, 355–356
LIFO liquidations and, 367–368
measuring efficiency in, 354
statement of cash flows and, 356–357
Inventory turnover, 354–355, 359–360,
372, 719, 725–726
Inventory valuation, 353–354
Investee earnings, under equity
method, 617
Investing activities
events in, 58
nature of, 4, 48
Investment decision, factors in, 712–713

Investment income, 108
under equity method, 620
Investments, 603–632
in affiliates or associated companies, 616
cash flows from. See Cash flows from
investing activities
for control, 605–606, 621–626
held-to-maturity, 606–607
improper influence and, 618
minority interest, 620, 629n
passive, 605, 607–614
return on assets (ROA), 625–626, 634,
718–720
for significant influence, 605, 615–618
Investors. See also Stockholders
(shareholders)
as external decision makers, 4, 5, 49–50
Involuntary disposal of assets, 417–418
Issued shares, 560, 561

J

Jenkins, N., 235n
Journal entries
balance sheet, 55–60
defined, 62
income statement, 118–121
nature of, 62–63
in transaction analysis, 64–68, 117–121
Just-in-time inventory, 343

K

Kerley, Carol, 231
Kinney, M. R., 367n
Koch, Jim, 653
Kumar, Sanjay, 113

L

Land, defined, 399
Last-in, first-out (LIFO) inventory
method, 347
defined, 348
financial statement effects of,
349–350
international comparisons and, 360
inventory turnover ratio and, 359–360
managers' choice of, 350–351
Lease commitments, 251
Lease liabilities, 474–475, 481
Least-latest rule, 350, 415
Legal capital, 563
Legal liability, 23
Lenders, in accounting communication
process, 238–239
Leverage, financial leverage ratio, 70–71,
79, 254, 719, 720
Liabilities, 459–490
accrued, 464–467, 482–484
adjusting entries for, 166
on balance sheet, 9–10, 52, 469
contingent, 469–471
current, 52, 461, 462–472
defined, 52, 461
interpreting, 9–10
present values in calculating, 479–481
typical account titles, 54
Liability
ethics and, 23

limited, 26
unlimited, 26
Licenses and operating rights, defined, 423
LIFO conformity rule, for inventory, 350
LIFO liquidations, 365–368
defined, 365
financial statement effects of, 365–367
inventory management and, 367–368
pretax effects of, 366
LIFO reserve, defined, 358
Limited liability, 26
Liquidity
of bonds, 515
defined, 461, 723
Liquidity order, of assets, 51–52
Liquidity tests, 723–727
cash ratio, 719, 723–724
current ratio, 462, 490, 719, 724
inventory turnover ratio, 354–355,
359–360, 372, 719, 725–726
quick ratio, 719, 724–725
receivables turnover ratio, 297, 310,
719, 725
Long-lived assets, 399–400. See also
Property, plant, and equipment
classifying, 399–400
defined, 399
Long-term liabilities, 473–475
bonds payable, 473–474
borrowing in foreign currencies, 474
cash flows from financing activities,
672, 673
current portion of long-term debt, 468
defined, 473
lease liabilities, 474–475, 481
notes payable, 473–474
refinanced debt, 468–469
Losses
on sale of assets, 109
unrealized, 608
Loudder, M. L., 665n
Low-cost strategy, 254–255
Lower of cost or market (LCM) inventory
valuation, 353–354

M

Maintenance expenses, 404–405
Management accounting. See Managerial
accounting
Management certification, 21–22
Management consulting services, 27
Management's Discussion and
Analysis, 242
Managerial accounting, nature of, 4, 5
Managers. See also Ethics
in accounting communication process, 234
choice of depreciation method, 414–416
choice of inventory costing method,
350–351
generally accepted accounting principles
and, 20–21
incentives to violate accounting rules,
112–113, 175
as internal decision makers, 4, 5
owner-managers, 3–4
responsibility for auditing, 21–22
types of, 18
use of financial statements, 18

Manufacturers
    direct labor cost, 342
    factory overhead, 342
    flow of inventory costs, 342, 343
    inventory types, 340
Marketable securities. See Securities
        available for sale
Market efficiency, 236
Marketing managers, 18
Market interest rate, 519
Market tests, 729–730
    dividend yield ratio, 566–567, 580, 719,
        729–730
    price/earnings (P/E) ratio, 22, 719, 729
Market value method, 607–614
Matching principle, 113–115, 165, 406, 419
Material amounts, in accounting
        communication process, 239
Maturity order, of liabilities, 52
McEwen, R. A., 236n
Measurability, of passive investments, 608
Measurement rules, 18–19
Merchandise inventory, 340
Mergers and acquisitions, 605–606,
        621–626
    consolidated financial statements for,
        604, 622
    mergers, defined, 622
    recording, 622–623
    reporting, 623–625
    types of, 621
Mickelson, Phil, 231
Mikhail, M. B., 236n
Minkow, Barry, 113
Minority interest, 620, 629n
Modified Accelerated Cost Recovery System
        (MACRS), 415
Moran, Michael, 250
Multinationals, 123–124
Multiple-step income statement, 106

N

n/30, 286, 287
Napolitano, Gabrielle, 250
Natural resources
    acquisition of, 419–420
    defined, 399, 419
    depletion of, 419–420
Nelson, M., 175n
Net book value, 168, 292–293
    defined, 407
    depreciation and, 428
Net income, 181
    conversion to net cash flow from
        operating activities, 664
    defined, 10, 12
    on statement of retained earnings, 13–14
Net increase (decrease) in cash, 657–658
Net profit margin, 181–182, 194, 254, 719,
        721–722
Net realizable value, 354
Net sales revenue, 283–284
    computing, 285
    reporting, 288
New issues, 563
"Nigerian barge" transactions, 704–705
Noncurrent receivables, 290
Nonoperating (other) items, 245–246

Nonrecurring items, 246
    discontinued operations, 258
    extraordinary items, 258
Nontrade receivables, 290
Nonvoting stock, 571, 607n
No-par value stock, 563
Notes payable
    cash flows from financing activities, 672,
        673
    defined, 467
    long-term, 473–474
    time value of money, 467–468
Notes receivable
    bad debts and, 290–296
    defined, 290
Notes to financial statements, 17–18,
        123–124, 248–251
    accounting rules applied to company's
        statements, 250, 288
    additional detail supporting reported
        numbers, 251
    debt and, 514
    defined, 17
    estimated liabilities reported on, 469–471
    profits from accounting adjustment, 414
    relevant financial information not
        disclosed on statements, 251
NSF (not sufficient funds) checks, 301,
        303, 304

O

Ongoing operations, 106–108
Operating activities
    accrual accounting, 110–114
    cash basis accounting, 110
    cash flows from. See Cash flows from
        operating activities
    matching principle, 113–115
    nature of, 4
    recognition and measurement of,
        110–116
    revenue principle, 110–111
Operating (cash-to-cash) cycle, 105–106
    nature of, 105–106
    ratios to analyze, 726–727
Operating expenses, 108, 679–680
Operating income, 106
Operating leases, 474
Operating revenues, 106–107
Ordinary repairs and maintenance, 405
Organizational structure, 561
Original maturity, 655n
Other comprehensive income, 612
Outsourcing, 654
Outstanding checks, 303
Outstanding shares, 560–562
Overhead, factory, 342
Owner-managers, 3–4
    incentives to violate accounting rules,
        112–113, 175
Owners' equity. See Stockholders' equity
    acquisition cost based on, 402
    on balance sheet, 9–10, 53
    in capital structure, 459–460
    defined, 53
    interpreting, 9–10
    last-in, first-out (LIFO) inventory costing
        method and, 351

for partnerships, 577–579
for sole proprietorships, 576–577

P

Pacioli, Luca, 19
Paid-In Capital, 245
Palmrose, Z., 232n
Parent company, 622, 629–630
Parent-subsidiary relationship, 629–630
Partnerships
    accounting for owners' equity, 577–579
    defined, 26
Par value
    bond, 516, 518
    bond purchases and, 606
    bonds issued at, 520–522
    common stock, 563
    Contributed Capital in Excess of Par, 245
    defined, 244
    percentage of, 606n
Passive investments, 607–614
    on the balance sheet, 607–608, 611
    defined, 605
    fair value option, 614
    market value method for, 607–614
    securities available for sale, 608–615
    trading securities, 608, 612–613
Patents, 420
    amortization of, 422
    defined, 422
Payment date, of dividends, 567–568
Payroll taxes, 466–467
Percentage analysis. See Ratio analysis
Percentage of credit sales method,
        294–296
Percentage of par, 606n
Periodic inventory system
    compared with perpetual inventory
        system, 369–370
    defined, 361–362
Permanent (real) accounts, 177, 182
Perpetual inventory system
    compared with periodic inventory system,
        369–370
    cost flow assumptions in, 362
    defined, 361
Plant and equipment. See Property, plant,
        and equipment
Plumlee, M. A., 235n
Post-closing trial balance, 184–185
Postmerger balance sheet, 623–624
Preferred stock
    characteristics of ownership, 571–572
    defined, 571
    dividends on, 572, 573
Premium
    amortization of bonds issued at, 529–531
    bond, 519, 528–531
    bonds purchased at, 606
Prepaid expenses
    change in, 663
    defined, 166, 171
    types of, 171–172
Present value concepts, 475–481
    accounting applications of present value,
        479–481
    bond payments and, 521, 536–537
    present value, defined, 475

present value of an annuity, 477–479,
  480–481, 486–487, A-1—A-2
present value of a single amount,
  476–477, 479–480, 486, A-1
Press releases, 240–242
Pretax earnings, 246
Price/earnings (P/E) ratio, 22, 719, 729
Primary objective of external financial
  reporting, 49–50
Principal, 290
  bond, 516, 518
  at maturity, for held-to-maturity
    investments, 607
Private investors, in accounting
  communication process, 238
Private placements, 473
Product-differentiation strategy,
  254–255, 713
Profitability tests, 718–722
  earnings per share (EPS), 109, 178, 247,
    562, 580, 719, 721
  financial leverage, 70–71, 79, 254,
    719, 720
  fixed asset turnover, 400–401, 430,
    719, 722
  net profit margin, 181–182, 194, 254,
    719, 721–722
  quality of income, 667–668, 685,
    719, 721
  return on assets (ROA), 625–626, 635,
    718–720
  return on equity (ROE), 252–256, 259, 718
Profit drivers
  business strategy and, 254–255
  nature of, 253–254
Profit levers, 253–254
Profit margin, net, 181–182, 194, 254, 719,
  721–722
Property, plant, and equipment, 397–419.
  See also Equipment
  acquisition cost, 401–403
  additions, 405
  asset impairment, 416–417
  on balance sheet, 55
  classifying long-lived assets, 399–400
  depreciation, 406–416
  disposal of, 417–418
  fixed asset turnover, 400–401, 430,
    719, 722
  international variations in measuring, 419
  maintenance, 404–405
  measurement basis for, 419
  as prepaid expense, 172
  repairs, 404–405
  sales of, 109
Public accounting, employment in, 26–27
Public Accounting Reform and Investor
  Protection Act (Sarbanes-Oxley
  Act), 232
Public Company Accounting Oversight Board
  (PCAOB), 22, 23, 233, 235
Purchase discounts, 368–369
Purchase method, 623
Purchase of stock, under equity method, 617
Purchase returns and allowances, 368
Purchases in cost of goods sold, 343–344
  in inventory control, 361, 368–369
  measuring, 368–369
Purchasing managers, 18

Q

Quality of earnings, 181, 186
Quality of income ratio, 667–668, 685,
  719, 721
Quarterly reports, 7, 242, 243
Quick ratio, 719, 724–725

R

Rapid growth, 731
Ratio analysis, 716–733
  accounts payable turnover, 464, 490
  asset turnover, 126–127, 134, 254
  capital acquisitions ratio, 670–671, 685
  cash ratio, 719, 723–724
  current ratio, 462, 490, 719, 724
  debt-to-equity, 531–532, 539, 719,
    728–729, 730–731
  defined, 716
  dividend yield, 566–567, 580, 719,
    729–730
  earnings per share (EPS), 109, 178, 247,
    562, 580, 719, 721
  financial leverage, 70–71, 79, 254,
    719, 720
  fixed asset turnover, 400–401, 430,
    719, 722
  gross profit percentage, 288–289, 310
  interpreting ratios, 730–733
  inventory turnover, 354–355, 359–360,
    372, 719, 725–726
  net profit margin, 181–182, 194, 254,
    719, 721–722
  price/earnings (P/E), 22, 719, 729
  profit margin, 181–182, 194, 254, 719,
    721–722
  quality of income ratio, 667–668, 685,
    719, 721
  quick ratio, 719, 724–725
  receivables turnover, 297, 310, 719, 725
  return on assets (ROA), 625–626, 634,
    718–720
  return on equity (ROE), 252–256,
    259, 718
  tests of profitability, 718–722
  times interest earned, 522–523, 538, 719,
    727–728
  total asset turnover, 126–127, 134
Raw materials inventory, 340, 342
Ready for shipment inventory, 341
Ready for use inventory, 341
Receivables, 290–298
  accounts receivable, 283–284, 290–299,
    662–666
  bad debt, 290–296
  classifying, 290
  foreign currency, 290
  nontrade, 290
  notes receivable, 290–296
  trade, 290
Receivables turnover, 297, 310, 719, 725
Record date, of dividends, 567–568
Refinanced debt, 468–469
Regulators, in accounting communication
  process, 233
Relevant financial information, 251, 607
Reliable information, in accounting
  communication process, 239

Rent, as prepaid expense, 171–172
Repair expenses, 404–405
Replacement cost, 353
Report of management, 21–22
Repurchase, of common stock, 564–565
Research and development expense,
  amortization of, 423
Residual (salvage) value, 408
Restrictive covenants, 573
Retailers
  cost of goods sold, 343
  flow of inventory costs, 341
  inventory types, 340
Retained earnings. *See also* Statement of
  retained earnings
  for cash dividends, 568
  cash flows from financing activities,
    672, 673
  defined, 53
  end-of-the-year, 14
  interpreting, 14
Retirement benefits, accrued, 483–484
Return on assets (ROA), 625–626, 634,
  718–720
Return on equity (ROE), 252–256, 259, 718
Revenue expenditures, defined, 405
Revenue principle, 110–111, 165, 284
Revenues
  in accrual accounting, 110–111
  accrued, 166, 170–171
  adjusting entries for, 166, 167–174
  converting to cash inflows, 678
  deferred, 469
  defined, 11, 106
  estimating at year end, 163–164
  franchise fee, 107
  investment, 108
  operating, 106–107
  recognition for income tax purposes,
    484–485
  sales, 107, 284–289
  typical account titles, 54
  unearned, 166, 168–170
Richardson, S., 667n
Richardson, V., 232n
Risk of bonds payable, 516, 518, 523
  financial leverage ratio and, 71, 79, 254,
    719, 720
ROE profit driver analysis, 253–254

S

Salaries expense, 108
Salaries payable, as accrued expense, 172–173
Sales discounts, 286–287
Sales returns and allowances, 287, 308
Sales revenues, 107, 284–289
  credit sales, 285, 286–287, 290–296
  gross profit percentage, 288–289, 310
  reporting net sales, 288
  sales discounts to businesses, 286–287
  sales returns and allowances, 287
Salvage (residual) value, 408
Sarbanes-Oxley Act, 232
Scholz, S., 232n
Seasoned new issues, 563
SEC. *See* U.S. Securities and Exchange
  Commission (SEC)
Secondary markets, common stock, 564

Secured debt, 473
Securities Act of 1933, 19
Securities available for sale, 608–615
  compared with trading securities, 612–613
  defined, 608
  dividends earned, 609
  portfolio of, 612, 613
  purchase of stock, 609
  sale of stock, 612
  year-end valuation, 610–611
Securities Exchange Act of 1934, 19
Segment information, 251
Separate-entity assumption, 50
Separation of duties, 300–301
Shareholders. See Stockholders (shareholders)
Shareholders' equity. See Stockholders' equity
Significant accounting policies, 250, 288, 296
Significant influence
  defined, 605
  equity method for investments, 615–618
Single amount
  future value of, 488, A–2
  present value of, 476–477, 479–480, 486, A–1
Single-step income statement, 106n
Sole proprietorships
  accounting for owners' equity, 576–577
  defined, 26
Solvency tests
  cash coverage ratio, 719, 728
  debt-to-equity ratio, 531–532, 539, 719, 728–729, 730–731
  times interest earned, 522–523, 538, 719, 727–728
Specific identification method, 345–346
Stated rate of interest, 516, 519
Statement of cash flows, 6, 14–16, 653–683. See also Financial statement(s)accounts receivable and, 298, 299
  cash flows from financing activities. See Cash flows from financing activities
  cash flows from investing activities. See Cash flows from investing activities
  cash flows from operating activities. See Cash flows from operating activities
  consolidated, 656
  defined, 14
  direct method, 677–681
  effect of depreciation on, 423–424
  elements of, 15–16, 19, 248, 249
  foreign currency and, 665
  formula for, 122
  impact of dividend payments on, 573–574
  indirect method, 674, 675, 681–683
  interpreting, 16
  inventory impact on, 356–357
  net increase (decrease) in cash, 657–658
  noncash investing and financing activities, 674
  preparing, 125–127
  purpose of, 14, 19
  relationships with other financial statements, 17, 658–661
  spreadsheet approach to preparing, 681–683

statement structure, 14–15, 19, 674, 675, 677–683
  structure of, 19
  supplemental cash flow information, 675
  working capital and, 471–472, 666
Statement of Earnings. See Income statement
Statement of Financial Position. See Balance sheet
Statement of Income. See Income statement
Statement of Operations. See Income statement
Statement of retained earnings, 6, 13–14. See also Financial statement(s)
  defined, 13
  elements of, 13–14, 19
  formula for, 122
  interpreting, 14
  preparing, 124
  purpose of, 13, 19
  relationships with other financial statements, 17
  structure of, 13, 19
Statement of Stockholders' Equity, 177, 179, 248
Stock. See Common stock; Preferred stock
Stock dividends, 569–570
Stockholders (shareholders), 8n, 26
Stockholders' equity, 557–579. See also Owners' equity; Statement of Stockholders' Equity
  authorized, issued, and outstanding shares, 560–562
  benefits of stock ownership, 559–560
  cash dividends, 566–568, 572–573
  common stock transactions, 563–571
  defined, 53
  dividend yield, 566–567, 580, 719, 729–730
  earnings per share (EPS), 109, 178, 247, 562, 580, 719, 721
  financing activities and, 573–574
  preferred stock transactions, 571–572
  stock dividends, 569–570
  stock splits, 570–571
  typical account titles, 54
Stock market. See also Common stock
  financial analysts in communication process, 235–237
  reactions to announcements, 115–116, 241
Stock splits, 570–571
Stouffer, B., 116n
Straight-line amortization, of bonds issued at a premium, 524–525, 529–530
Straight-line depreciation method, 409–410, 413, 428–429
Subjective factors, 732
Subramanyan, K., 181, 181n
Subsidiary accounts, 290–291
Subsidiary company, 622, 629–630
Suppliers, 4
  converting cost of goods sold to cash paid to, 678–679
Supplies
  on balance sheet, 55
  as prepaid expenses, 171
Sustainable development, 252
Synergy, 621

T

T-accounts
  defined, 63
  inferring business activities from, 68
  structure of, 61–64
  in transaction analysis, 63–68, 118–121
Tangible assets, defined, 399
Tarpley, R., 175n
Tax reporting. See also Income taxes; Income taxes payable
  accrued taxes payable, 465
  depreciation in, 415, 416
  separate records for financial reporting and, 416
Tax services, 27
Technology
  amortization of, 422
  defined, 422
Temporary (nominal) accounts, 177, 182–183
Temporary differences, in deferred taxes, 482–483
Time period assumption, 106
Time-series analysis, 255, 715
Times interest earned, 522–523, 538, 719, 727–728
Time value of money, 467–468. See also Future value concepts; Present value concepts
Total asset turnover ratio, 126–127, 134
Total cash flow of the firm, 671n
Trade accounts payable, 463. See also Accounts payable
Trade discounts, 286n
Trademarks
  amortization of, 422
  defined, 422
  as intangible assets, 52
Trade receivables, 290
Trading securities
  compared with securities available for sale, 612–613
  defined, 608
  portfolio of, 612–613
Transaction(s)
  defined, 53
  impact on accounts, 55–60
  nature of, 53–54
Transaction analysis
  account balances and, 60–68
  analytical tools for, 62–64
  balance sheet, 55–60, 121
  direction of transaction effects, 60–68
  dual effects of, 56–57
  illustration of, 64–68
  income statement, 118–121
  journal entries, 62–68, 117–121
  principles of, 55–57
  rules of, 116–117
  T-accounts in, 61–68, 118–121
Treasury stock, 560–562, 564–565
Trial balance
  adjusted, 175, 176
  defined, 167
  post-closing, 184–185
  pre-closing entries, 183
  unadjusted, 167–168, 169
Trustees, 518
Truth in advertising, 478–479

Turnover
   accounts payable, 464, 490
   fixed asset, 400–401, 430, 719, 722
   inventory, 354–355, 359–360, 372, 719,
      725–726
   receivables, 297, 310, 719, 725
   total asset, 126–127, 134

U

Unadjusted trial balance, 167–168, 169
Unaudited reports, 242
Uncollectible accounts, writing off,
   291–292
Unearned (deferred) revenues
   defined, 166, 168, 469
   examples of, 168–170
Uneconomical expansion, 731–732
Unexpected earnings, 115–116, 241
Uniform Partnership Act, 577–579
U.S. Securities and Exchange Commission
      (SEC), 19–20, 109, 233
   EDGAR database, 237
   incentives to violate accounting rules, 175

regulation FD (Fair Disclosure), 240
regulation of new issues, 564–565
reports of, 243
Unit-of-measure assumption, 50
Units-of-production depreciation method,
   409, 410–411, 413
Unlimited liability, 26
Unqualified (clean) audit opinions, 235
Unrealized holding gains and losses, 608
Utilities payable, as accrued expense,
   172–173

V

Variable expenses, 411
Vertical integration, 621
Voluntary disclosures, 252
Voluntary disposal of assets, 417–418
Voting rights, 559, 571, 607n

W

Walther, B. R., 236n
Wasting assets, 419–420

Wempe, W. F., 367n
Wholesalers
   cost of goods sold, 343
   flow of inventory costs, 341
   inventory types, 340
Wild, J., 181, 181n
Wilkins, M. S., 234n, 665n
Willis, R. H., 236n
Working capital
   cash flows and, 471–472, 666
   defined, 471
Work in process inventory, 340
World Business Council for Sustainable
      Development, 252

Y

Year-end valuation, of securities available
      for sale, 610–611
Yield, dividend, 566–567, 580, 719,
      729–730

Z

Zero coupon bonds, 527–528

Ratios Used for Financial Analyses

Ratio		Basic Computation	Chapter
Financial Leverage	=	$\dfrac{\text{Average Total Assets}}{\text{Average Stockholders' Equity}}$	2
Total Asset Turnover	=	$\dfrac{\text{Sales (or Operating) Revenues}}{\text{Average Total Assets}}$	3
Net Profit Margin	=	$\dfrac{\text{Net Income}}{\text{Net Sales}}$	4
Return on Equity	=	$\dfrac{\text{Net Income}}{\text{Average Stockholders' Equity}}$	5
Gross Profit Percentage	=	$\dfrac{\text{Gross Profit}}{\text{Net Sales}}$	6
Receivables Turnover	=	$\dfrac{\text{Net Sales}}{\text{Average Net Trade Accounts Receivable}}$	6
Inventory Turnover	=	$\dfrac{\text{Cost of Goods Sold}}{\text{Average Inventory}}$	7
Fixed Asset Turnover	=	$\dfrac{\text{Net Sales}}{\text{Average Net Fixed Assets}}$	8
Current Ratio	=	$\dfrac{\text{Current Assets}}{\text{Current Liabilities}}$	9
Accounts Payable Turnover	=	$\dfrac{\text{Cost of Goods Sold}}{\text{Average Accounts Payable}}$	9
Debt-to-Equity	=	$\dfrac{\text{Total Liabilities}}{\text{Stockholders' Equity}}$	10
Times Interest Earned	=	$\dfrac{\text{Net Income + Interest Expense + Income Tax Expense}}{\text{Interest Expense}}$	10
Earnings per Share	=	$\dfrac{\text{Net Income*}}{\text{Average Number of Shares of Common Stock Outstanding During the Period}}$	11
Dividend Yield	=	$\dfrac{\text{Dividend per Share}}{\text{Market Price per Share}}$	11
Return on Assets (ROA)**	=	$\dfrac{\text{Net Income}}{\text{Average Total Assets}}$	12
Quality of Income	=	$\dfrac{\text{Cash Flow from Operating Activities}}{\text{Net Income}}$	13
Capital Acquisitions	=	$\dfrac{\text{Cash Flow from Operating Activities}}{\text{Cash Paid for Property, Plant, and Equipment}}$	13

*If there are preferred dividends, the amount is subtracted from the Net Income in the numerator.

**As shown in Chapter 14, in most complex analytical situations, interest expense net of tax is added back to net income in the numerator of the ratio.

Chapter Title	Focus Company	Managerial Focus	Contrast Companies	Key Ratios
1 Financial Statements and Business Decisions	**Maxidrive Corporation** Manufacturer of computer disks	Valuing an acquisition	Apple, Inc.	
2 Investing and Financing Decisions and the Balance Sheet	PAPA JOHNS Better Ingredients. Better Pizza. Pizza restaurant chain (food service)	Investing and financing decisions	GlaxoSmithKline California Pizza Kitchen, Inc. Pizza Inn Inc. Wendy's International Lance, Inc.	**Financial Leverage**
3 Operating Decisions and the Income Statement	PAPA JOHNS Better Ingredients. Better Pizza. Pizza restaurant chain	Operating decisions	GlaxoSmithKline Unilever BMW Group Domino's Inc. Yum! Brands	**Total Asset Turnover**
4 Adjustments, Financial Statements, and the Quality of Earnings	PAPA JOHNS Better Ingredients. Better Pizza. Pizza restaurant chain	Year-end accounting activities	Whole Foods, Inc. Dominos' Inc. Yum! Brands Toys R Us	**Net Profit Margin**
5 Communicating and Interpreting Accounting Information	Callaway GOLF Manufacturer of golf clubs	Corporate communication	Adams Golf Apple, Inc. Microsoft Corporation	**Return on Equity**
6 Reporting and Interpreting Sales Revenue, Receivables, and Cash	**DECKERS** outdoor corporation Shoe manufacturer and clothing merchandiser	Marketing strategy	Skechers U.S.A. Timberland Co.	**Gross Profit Percentage Receivables Turnover**
7 Reporting and Interpreting Cost of Goods Sold and Inventory	HARLEY-DAVIDSON, INC. Motorcycle manufacturer and clothing merchandiser	Manufacturing management	Dell Computer Deere & Company Ducati Motor Honda Motor	**Inventory Turnover**
8 Reporting and Interpreting Property, Plant, and Equipment; Natural Resources; and Intangibles	**SOUTHWEST** Major air carrier	Planning productive capacity	United Airlines Delta Air Lines Singapore Airlines International Paper ExxonMobil Corporation General Motors Google Inc. IBM Corporation	**Fixed Asset Turnover**